Masterplots

Fourth Edition

Masterplots

Fourth Edition

Volume 6
In Dubious Battle—McTeague

Editor

Laurence W. Mazzeno
Alvernia College

SALEM PRESS

Pasadena, California   Hackensack, New Jersey

Editor in Chief: Dawn P. Dawson

Editorial Director: Christina J. Moose   *Editorial Assistant:* Brett S. Weisberg

Development Editor: Tracy Irons-Georges   *Research Supervisor:* Jeffry Jensen

Project Editor: Desiree Dreeuws   *Research Assistant:* Keli Trousdale

Manuscript Editors: Constance Pollock,   *Production Editor:* Joyce I. Buchea

Judy Selhorst, Andy Perry   *Design and Graphics:* James Hutson

Acquisitions Editor: Mark Rehn   *Layout:* William Zimmerman

Cover photo: Christopher Marlowe (The Granger Collection, New York)

Contents

CONTENTS

Complete List of Titles

Volume 1

Volume 2

Volume 3

Contents xcv

Complete List of Titles xcix

Volume 4

Volume 5

Volume 6

Volume 7

Volume 8

Volume 9

Volume 10

Volume 11

Contents. cccxcix
Complete List of Titles. . . . . cdiii

Volume 12

Contents . . . . cdxxxvii

Complete List of Titles. . . . . cdxxxix

Indexes

Masterplots

Fourth Edition

In Dubious Battle

Author: John Steinbeck (1902-1968)
First published: 1936
Type of work: Novel
Type of plot: Social realism
Time of plot: 1930's
Locale: California

Principal characters:
MAC, a Communist labor organizer
JIM NOLAN, his assistant and friend
LONDON, the leader of the fruit pickers
DOC BURTON, a friend of the strikers
AL TOWNSEND, sympathetic to the strikers

The Story:

Jim Nolan's father is a working man brought to his death by the blows of police clubs and pistol butts. As a youngster, Jim witnesses both his father's courage and his despair. Jim sees his mother lose even her religious faith as poverty and starvation overwhelm the family. Older, but still keenly remembering his youth, with the scars of brutality and starvation deeply embedded in his heart, Jim becomes a member of the Communist Party. He is assigned to work with Mac, an able, experienced organizer. Together, they become fruit pickers, at a time when the fruit growers cut wages lower than the workers think possible. A strike is brewing, and Mac and Jim determine to hurry it along and to direct its course.

Luck is with them. Shortly after their arrival at the camp of the workers, Mac, giving the impression that he is a doctor, helps London's thirteen-year-old daughter-in-law Lisa give birth. Word of Mac's accomplishment spreads throughout the area. After Mac and Jim becomes friendly with London, leader of the camp, and the other workers, they persuade the fruit pickers to organize and to strike for higher wages and for better living conditions. This is not easy to do. As usual, the orchard owners make effective use of communism as a bogey. Furthermore, the vigilantes are a constant menace, not to mention deputies, troops, and strikebreakers, all hirelings of the fruit growers. In addition, the authorities can always close down the camp by maintaining that it violates the sanitation laws and is a menace to public health. There is also the problem of money and food; the poor migrant workers desperately need work to supply their daily necessities.

Despite these difficulties, a strike at last is called. On the night that the strikers are to sneak out to meet the strikebreakers called in by the owners, Mac and Jim are ambushed by vigilantes. They succeed in escaping, but Jim is shot in the arm. Word of their plan for the next morning had leaked out, and they suspect that a stool pigeon is in their midst. Nevertheless, the next day they march out to meet the strikebreakers at the railroad station and to implore them not to fight against their fellow workers. Although the police assemble in force, they seem afraid of the strikers. During the encounter, Joy, an old and crippled comrade, is shot and killed. The strikers carry the body back to the camp, and over the body of their comrade, Mac delivers a fiery and eloquent speech, exhorting the strikers to carry on and to fight to the finish. This action proves to be the best of all possible spurs to bring the workers together, and the strikers are aroused to carry on the struggle even more fiercely.

Luck is with them in other ways. They persuade the father of Al Townsend, who owns a lunch cart and gives handouts to Communist Party members, to allow them to camp on his farm, after they promise him that his crop will be picked and that his property will be protected. Doc Burton, a philosopher and skeptic, takes charge of the sanitation, thus protecting the camp against the health inspectors. Dick, a handsome comrade, uses his charms on women in order to get money and food for the strikers. Meanwhile, the owners try everything to break up the strike. They attempt to intimidate the workers, to divide them, to bribe London, but all their efforts fail. Then another problem arises. The owners have an article published in which it is stated that the county is feeding the strikers. The report is not true, but those who sympathize with the strikers believe it and stop helping them altogether. Dick is getting far fewer results from his endeavors, and the situation becomes desperate.

Mac is often on the point of losing his head, of letting his anger get the better of him, so that the strategy of the strike is sometimes imperiled. By contrast, Jim grows more able, more hardened. He ignores the women of the camp who seek to lure him into their tents and does not allow his feelings for Lisa to become anything more than a casual, friendly relationship. Thus, he provides a sort of balance for his more emotional comrades. Conditions grow worse. The strikers have practically no money and no food. Dick finally manages to get a cow and some beans, but the food suffices for only a few days. Meanwhile, Doc Burton vanishes. Without his help, the sick and the wounded cannot be attended to, and the sanitation of the camp grows progressively worse. One night, someone manages to outwit the guards and set a barn afire. The barn and an adjacent kennel housing some favorite pointers are totally destroyed. The next day the owner calls in the sheriff to evict the strikers.

The strike seems lost. The spirits of the men are at a low ebb, and they give signs of yielding. On the following night, a boy comes and tells Jim and Mac that Doc Burton is lying wounded in a field. They rush out, only to realize, when they are fired upon, that they have fallen into a trap. Mac calls out a word of warning and falls to the ground. When he gets up, after the firing stops, he calls out to Jim. He gets no answer. Jim is dead. By that time, the shots have aroused the others, and they come forward. Over the body of his comrade and friend, Mac makes a strong and rousing speech, urging the workers to stick together, to fight on, and to win the strike.

Critical Evaluation:

Critic Tetsumaro Hayashi considers 1936 to 1939 the great years of John Steinbeck's career. The novel that culminated this period of greatness, *The Grapes of Wrath* (1939), won the American Book Award and the Pulitzer Prize. Years later, in 1962, the work of this period contributed to Steinbeck's winning the Nobel Prize in Literature. Although *In Dubious Battle* is a less important book than *The Grapes of Wrath*, most critics see it as a thematic precursor to the greater work. Steinbeck's first full-length novel, *In Dubious Battle* narrates a fictional part of the epic struggle of poverty against wealth and worker against boss. Borrowing his title from book 1, line 104, of John Milton's *Paradise Lost* (1667, 1674), Steinbeck recalls the epic struggle in Heaven between good and evil.

Two important themes in the novel are the idea of waking "sleepers" to social action and the function of the "group man." Sleepers are people who go through life without trying to improve living and working conditions for themselves or others. Henry David Thoreau used a similar metaphor in his essay "Civil Disobedience" (1849). The story opens with the "sleepwalking" young Jim Nolan joining the Communist Party. Jim has no family of his own (both parents are dead); the party becomes his new family. In this sense, Jim is like many other party members in the novel—Mac, Dick, and Joy—who have no families. Other characters who consider joining also have minimal families: Al Anderson has only his father (who has practically disowned him), and London has only his son Joey, Lisa, and a grandchild. Dakin, on the other hand, is slower to join the strike because he has much to lose: a wife, two children, a light truck, and comfortable portable furnishings (when vigilantes later destroy the truck, Dakin withdraws from the group).

Mac's first objective in organizing the fruit pickers' strike is to awaken the people to their exploitation by the orchard owners. Mac himself seldom sleeps in the novel. Individuals awakened from their "sleep" join the party, submit to the will of the majority, and come together to function as "group man," a concept explained by Doc Burton: "A man in a group isn't himself at all, he's a cell in an organism." The group acts or retreats as a whole, and Mac realizes that some cells (individuals) must be sacrificed for the organism to survive. When an "infection," such as poor wages, threatens the organism, the group must rebel as a whole to save itself. Some individuals must die in the workers' struggle to gain fair profit from their labor, and even party members—first Joy and later Jim—are expendable for the good of the group. The "group man" phenomenon makes the striking fruit workers react in predictable ways. When roused, usually by bloodshed, to fight, they move together as an unstoppable force. However, without an immediate goal, the organism relaxes and weaker members are shed, so the organism must be "fed" repeatedly to prevent the movement's failure. Damage (loss or injury of an individual) can be repaired as long as the remaining cells work together toward a common goal. In pursuit of the goal, members take advantage of every opportunity, from delivering a baby and gaining the workers' trust to using the body of a slain comrade to boost morale with a ritual funeral. In "group man's" moral vision, objects and people can and should be used as a means to an end—the ultimate good of the party. In a larger sense, the striking fruit pickers of *In Dubious Battle* are being sacrificed for the success of future party efforts. Mac never truly believes the strike will get the workers the fair wages they demand, yet he proceeds with his plans, knowing that workers will be blacklisted, go hungry, and perhaps even die because of the strike. The party justifies its often brutal practices by arguing that the fruit pickers will benefit from their current troubles when, in the future, farmers will be less likely to lower wages for fear of another strike.

Steinbeck's realistic fiction suggests that it is factual history. Readers should note, however, that although loosely based on historic people and events, the novel is not always historically accurate. Critics have noted the absence of women and Mexican workers among the fruit pickers. London's thirteen-year-old daughter-in-law Lisa is the only developed female character. Moreover, she is first seen in labor and never thereafter appears without her infant son. Although a minor character, her presence in the book allows the reader to see a human side to Jim, Mac, and other characters through the interest they take in Lisa and her baby. What Steinbeck seems to suggest with her constant breastfeeding and confessed enjoyment of the act is that while a masculine revolution fights for better conditions for "group man," an underlying femininity will nurture the group and replenish its humanity. Lisa's character foreshadows Rose of Sharon in *The Grapes of Wrath*, who after the death of her newborn infant offers her breast milk to a starving man, a stranger.

How groups of people react in struggles against society or nature is a common theme throughout Steinbeck's works. Readers may note, for example, his observation of antisegregation demonstrators outside a New Orleans public school in *Travels with Charley* (1962). *In Dubious Battle* fits well in context with other social protest fiction such as Harriet Beecher Stowe's *Uncle Tom's Cabin* (1851-1852), Upton Sinclair's *The Jungle* (1906), Richard Wright's *Native Son* (1940), and Steinbeck's own *The Grapes of Wrath*.

"Critical Evaluation" by Geralyn Strecker

Further Reading

Benson, Jackson J. *The True Adventures of John Steinbeck, Writer.* New York: Viking Press, 1984. Definitive biography considers *In Dubious Battle* in context with the author's life and works.

Benson, Jackson J., and Anne Loftis. "John Steinbeck and Farm Labor Unionization: The Background of *In Dubious Battle*." *American Literature* 52, no. 2 (May, 1980): 194-223. Situates Steinbeck's novel within the social conditions from which it emerged. Just as intriguing as the similarities between fact and fiction are the instances in which Steinbeck altered facts, notably his omission of women from the labor movement and Mexicans from the migrant community.

French, Warren. *John Steinbeck.* 2d rev. ed. Boston: Twayne, 1975. Illustrates Steinbeck's use of Arthurian legend.

George, Stephen K., and Barbara A. Heavilin, eds. *John Steinbeck and His Contemporaries.* Lanham, Md.: Scarecrow Press, 2007. A collection of papers from a 2006 conference about Steinbeck and the writers who influenced or informed his work. Some of the essays discuss his European forebears, particularly Henry Fielding and Sir Thomas Malory, and his American forebears, such as Walt Whitman and Sarah Orne Jewett, while other essays compare his work to Ernest Hemingway, William Faulkner, and other twentieth century American writers.

Hayashi, Tetsumaro, ed. *John Steinbeck: The Years of Greatness, 1936-1939.* Tuscaloosa: University of Alabama Press, 1993. Collection of essays on Steinbeck's life and literary achievements during the late 1930's. Several articles are pertinent to *In Dubious Battle*.

Meyer, Michael J., ed. *The Betrayal of Brotherhood in the Work of John Steinbeck.* Lewiston, N.Y.: Edwin Mellen Press, 2000. Describes how Steinbeck adapted the biblical story of Cain and Abel in many of his works. One essay, "The Evil Other and the Migrant Movement: Cain Sign in *In Dubious Battle*," examines this novel.

Pressman, Richard S. "Individualists or Collectivists? Steinbeck's *In Dubious Battle* and Hemingway's *To Have and Have Not*." *Steinbeck Quarterly* 25, nos. 3/4 (Summer/Fall, 1992): 119-132. Discusses Steinbeck's representation and occasional misrepresentation of American communism.

Simmonds, Roy S. *A Biographical and Critical Introduction of John Steinbeck.* Lewiston, N.Y.: E. Mellen Press, 2000. Charts Steinbeck's evolution as a writer from 1929 through 1968, discussing the themes of his works and the concepts and philosophies that influenced his depictions of human nature and the psyche. Interweaves details about his writings with accounts of his personal life.

In Memoriam

Author: Alfred, Lord Tennyson (1809-1892)
First published: 1850, as *In Memoriam A. H. H., Obiit. MDCCCXXXIII*
Type of work: Poetry

In Memoriam, unquestionably one of the four greatest elegies of English literature, records the intellectual, emotional, religious, and aesthetic changes Alfred, Lord Tennyson un-

derwent in the sixteen-year period following the early and tragic death of his closest friend, Arthur Henry Hallam, in Vienna, on September 15, 1833. The year *In Memoriam* was first published, 1850, was also the year Tennyson married Emily Sellwood and succeeded William Wordsworth as poet laureate.

In Memoriam, the poem for which Tennyson is most remembered, is organized structurally around the three Christmas lyrics strategically placed within the sequence. It bears resemblances not only to the classical elegies and their English counterparts, most notably John Milton's "Lycidas" (1638) and Percy Bysshe Shelley's *Adonais* (1821), but also to the common thematic pattern used to describe the Victorian crisis of faith so aptly characterized in Thomas Carlyle's *Sartor Resartus* (1833-1834): the movement from despair (Carlyle's "Everlasting No") through a period of questioning and doubt ("The Center of Indifference") to a final affirmation of the sense of human existence ("The Everlasting Yea") reached when one is convinced that there is an ultimate purpose to life, even if that purpose is veiled from humankind.

The similarities of Tennyson's poem to *Sartor Resartus* occur not only in structure but in imagery: the poet repeatedly uses "the veil" to suggest a separation between his own world and his dead friend's and between himself and God. Another common image appearing throughout the poem is the hand of his dead friend, metaphorically reaching toward the despairing narrator to touch him and reassure him that his suffering is not in vain.

The poem is not, however, simply an expression of personal grief. Although the "I" of *In Memoriam* is sometimes clearly associated with the poet, Tennyson himself said that it is frequently intended to represent "the voice of the human race speaking thro' him." The poet's personal grief and doubt become a microcosm for the suffering being endured by nineteenth century men and women who were losing faith in received religion, because the advances in science were leading to the conclusion that there was no divine hand guiding existence. The speaker suffers from his loss, but he eventually accepts the notion that, despite the outward signs of chaos, the world is really evolving into something better; his friend Hallam comes to be seen as a harbinger of a "higher race" that will lead humankind to God.

Thus, *In Memoriam* represents the chief Victorian conflict of science and faith as truly as any work of its era; Tennyson's attempt to reconcile the religious doubts arising from his personal sorrow and the effects of pre-Darwinian theories of evolution was hailed by thinkers of his time as an intellectual landmark. The cyclic change—the turn from private grief and despair to the larger public vision and concern for wider, social issues—that can be found in this poem reflects Tennyson's growing acceptance of and reconciliation with the problems of his age.

It appears that Tennyson did not think of publishing the 131 lyrics of *In Memoriam* until late in the 1840's, when he brought them together as one poem, arranged so the three-year time scheme of the poem would reflect the sixteen-year period of his life that they represent. These lyrics were written over a long time span, and they vary considerably in the tone and mood of reaction to Hallam's death, thus dramatizing lyrically Tennyson's psychological condition. Although many organizational schemes have been offered, the most generally accepted views the poem as illustrating a movement from initial grief (1-27), to philosophic doubt and despair (28-77), to rising hope (78-103), and to affirmation of faith (104-131). The actual growth is more subtle than this and requires close attention to repeated images, such as the two yew-tree poems or the two visits to Hallam's house.

The "Prologue," dated 1849, and addressed to "Strong Son of God, immortal Love," expresses the poet's conviction that faith, not knowledge, leads to a harmonious union of the intellectual and the spiritual. The first section relates the poet's nearly complete self-absorption in grief, but even here a change is evident, for example, in the difference between "I held it truth" (1) to "I hold it true" (27). Although Love provides a "higher life" for man hereafter, few can find immediate comfort for present loss in this promise of future tranquillity. Nevertheless, the poet affirms his belief that "'Tis better to have loved and lost/ Than never to have loved at all." This acceptance of his experience, despite its accompanying sorrow, comes only after intervening poems reveal the true depth of his despair; his identification, for instance, with the yew tree, a symbol of death, shows the poet's marked conviction that he, like the yew tree that is not subject to seasonal changes, is imprisoned in grief and can merely endure in "stubborn hardihood."

This fellowship with "Sorrow" (3) induces an intellectual despair and alienates him from comforting Love.

> "The stars," she whispers, "blindly run;
> A web is woven across the sky;
> From out waste places comes a cry,
> And murmurs from the dying sun."

In one sense, this conception of the universe as a blindly run mechanism is the central intellectual conflict of the poem. In his deep melancholy, Tennyson questions not only the justice of Hallam's tragic death, but also the justice of the entire creation.

Tennyson moves alternately from numbed despair to self-awareness (4) and finds composing poetry an anodyne for pain (5). Poems 9 through 17 constitute a group unified by the poet's meditation upon the return of Hallam's body from Italy by ship. A calmer grief now pervades his heart (11). The pain of grief "slowly forms the firmer mind" (18), but the deeper sorrows that words cannot relieve remain locked in his heart (20). He writes not to parade his emotions publicly but because he must (21).

The second section commences with the first Christmas celebration some three months after Hallam's death. The poet hears the bells' message of peace and goodwill but almost wishes never to hear them again. Even in his despondency, however, the bells recall his happy youth, and, touching pain with joy, ease his misery. In the renewal of "old pastimes in the hall" they make a vain pretense (30), but one can find consolation in the thought of an afterlife for the dead, although what that afterlife may be remains unrevealed (31).

The second yew tree poem illustrates a lightening of his burden, for he now sees the tree with "fruitful cloud," subject to change, as is his grief. The group of poems from 11 to 58 represents Tennyson's attempt to resolve the question of an afterlife and also the possibility of a reunion with Hallam. These speculations are not meant to solve the problems, he tells us (48), but were "Short swallow-flights of song" that soothed his mind.

In 54, Tennyson expresses the vague "trust that somehow good/ Will be the final goal of ill." The two following poems call in doubt this qualified optimism, so that all he can permit himself is to "faintly trust the larger hope" (55). In his agitated state of mind, the poet sees nature as "red in tooth and claw" (56). The rest of this section deals with the poet's former relationship with Hallam.

The third section opens with the second Christmas and finds the poet with the sense of the abiding presence of his friend. His subdued grief allows him to treasure their friendship, "Which masters Time indeed, and is Eternal, separate from fears."

Tennyson contemplates the possibility of a visitation by Hallam and experiences a mystic trance in 95, when "The dead man touch'd" him "from the past." The third section concludes with a four-poem series relating to the Tennyson family's removal from Somersby, with its pleasant and sorrowful associations.

With the fourth and final section, the poet turns from the past and his personal grief to the future of humankind; this change is signaled by the famous lyric "Ring out, wild bells" (106). Tennyson resolves not to allow sorrow to alienate him from society (108). Hallam's qualities emerge clearly for the first time; in a series of poems, Tennyson praises his friend, particularly for his attributes of leadership and dedication to social good.

Tennyson draws an important distinction in poem 114 of the difference between knowledge and wisdom; with wisdom, man does not fear death since wisdom is of the soul, but knowledge must learn to submit to wisdom and know its place. Acknowledging Love as his lord and king, Tennyson proclaims that all is well (127). His optimism is buttressed by his knowledge that Hallam "O'erlook'st the tumult from afar,/ And smilest, knowing all is well."

As the elegy draws to a close, the poet more strongly feels the certainty of cosmic design: "That all, as in some piece of art,/ Is toil cooperant to an end" (128). He feels more confident of Hallam's omnipresence: "Thy voice is on the rolling air;/ I hear thee where the waters run" (130). His love, although founded on their previous earthly relationship, is "vaster passion" now that Hallam's presence is spiritual and diffused through God and nature. The elegy concludes with the poet's self-confident assertion of the permanence of the living will that purifies humanity's deeds and of the faith in truths that will not be proved until after death.

In the epilogue, Tennyson celebrates the marriage of his friend, Edward Lushington, to the poet's sister. The wedding ceremony is an appropriate subject for the epilogue: It symbolizes the continuation of life and an affirmation of human nature.

Although the work ends on an affirmative note, many critics have found the strengths of *In Memoriam* to lie principally in its portrayal of doubt. In that sense, it shares affinities with many modern poems. In addition, its fragmented structure suggests something of the modern condition. In these respects, *In Memoriam* is a precursor to other examinations of contemporary life, such as T. S. Eliot's *The Waste Land* (1922), among others.

Further Reading

Barton, Anna. *Tennyson's Name: Identity and Responsibility in the Poetry of Alfred, Lord Tennyson*. Burlington, Vt.: Ashgate, 2008. Traces the development of Tennyson's poetry, focusing on his reaction to the increasing importance of "brand names" in Victorian culture. Argues that Tennyson had a strong sense of his professional identity and the ethics of literature that led him to establish a "responsible" poetry.

Bradley, A. C. *A Commentary on Tennyson's "In Memoriam."* 3d rev. ed. Hamden, Conn.: Archon Books, 1966. Provides a close study of the poem, showing the relation of each section to others. Confronts difficulties in interpretation; traces origin, composition, and structure of the eulogy, with other discussion, prior to commentary. Includes a chart of changes in the text and an appendix.

Buckley, Jerome Hamilton. *Tennyson: The Growth of a Poet.* Cambridge, Mass.: Harvard University Press, 1960. Chapter 6 is devoted to *In Memoriam* and provides biographical background for, and explication of, the work. Relates critical response to it. Sees Tennyson as a major poet, whose work must be understood by familiarity with the imagination that produced it.

Curr, Matthew. *The Consolation of Otherness: The Male Love Elegy in Milton, Gray, and Tennyson.* Jefferson, N.C.: McFarland, 2002. Analyzes *In Memoriam* in order to examine the relationship between Tennyson and Arthur Hallam. Describes how Tennyson used vernacular language to both express and repress his private thoughts about his love for Hallam.

Hood, James W. *Divining Desire: Tennyson and the Poetics of Transcendence.* Brookfield, Vt.: Ashgate, 2000. An analysis of Tennyson's poetry, focusing on his attempt to depict desire in a divine fashion. Argues that "Tennyson's poems, his characters, and his speakers employ erotic devotion and artistic creation as the means by which to approximate the transcendence that constitutes their ultimate goal." Chapter 4 is devoted to an examination of *In Memoriam.*

Mazzeno, Laurence W. *Alfred Tennyson: The Critical Legacy.* Rochester, N.Y.: Camden House, 2004. Traces the critical reception of Tennyson's work, from the opinions of his contemporaries to the end of the twentieth century. Charts how his work has been both reviled and revived since his death, discusses his reputation among the poststructuralists, and provides a twenty-first century prospectus.

Pinion, F. B. *A Tennyson Companion: Life and Works.* New York: St. Martin's Press, 1984. Provides brief coverage of Tennyson's life and lengthy coverage of his writings, including a chapter about *In Memoriam.* Includes illustrations, index, chronology, notes, and appendixes.

Tennyson, Alfred, Lord. *In Memoriam: Authoritative Text, Criticism.* Edited by Erik Gray. New York: W. W. Norton, 2003. In addition to the text of the poem, this edition contains documents providing biographical and historical contexts for the work, including summaries of the opinions of pre-Darwinian scientists who were a source of the poem's imagery and concepts. A selection of critical essays, including a piece by T. S. Eliot, discuss *In Memoriam* in relation to Victorian science, Tennyson's struggles with religious faith, and the poem's structure, images, symbolism, and language.

In the Heart of the Seas
A Story of a Journey to the Land of Israel

Author: Shmuel Yosef Agnon (1888-1970)
First published: Bi-levav yamim: Sipur agadah, 1935 (English translation, 1947)
Type of work: Novel
Type of plot: Folklore
Time of plot: Eighteenth century
Locale: Buczacz, Austro-Hungarian Empire; the Land of Israel; and places in between

Principal characters:
HANANIAH, a wonder-working stranger
RABBI SHMUEL YOSEF, a teller of pious legends
ZUSHA, a robber chief
HIS ABANDONED WIFE

The Story:

Before a group of men and women start on their journey to settle in the Land of Israel, a stranger named Hananiah enters their town of Buczacz, entreating them to allow him to accompany them. The man, barefoot and in rags, carries all his worldly goods tied up in a kerchief. With some prompting, he recounts his adventures, full of perils and narrow escapes. He stayed for a time with robbers who were forced by their oppressors into a life of crime. Asking why the robber chief puts on phylacteries, Hananiah learned of the death of Zusha, the band's former leader, whom the present one imitates by this action. Ashamed to have to decline the chief's offer to lead him through a certain cave to the Land of Israel, Hananiah left the band to resume his journey.

The travelers are delighted to have Hananiah join them,

for he will complete the quorum of ten men required for communal prayer. Among the men are Rabbi Shmuel Yosef, well versed in legends of the Holy Land, and Rabbi Yosef Meir, who divorced his wife because she refused to go to the Land of Israel. Among the women are Milka, who married a man on condition they would immigrate to Israel, only then to have him insist on staying and divorce her, and the wives of four of the men.

Hananiah rejects the group's offer of boots, swearing that his feet must remain bare because, while in a country that never celebrates the Sabbath or festivals, he loses track of the time and fails to honor the Day of Atonement. He proceeds to polish the lamps and the other implements in the House of Study, to repair torn books, to make trunks for the pilgrims, and to fashion a Holy Ark for the Torah Scroll accompanying them to the Land of Israel.

The townspeople gather to speed them on their journey, except Buczacz's rabbi, who believes that settlement in the Land of Israel must await the coming of the Messiah. The group hires and outfits two large wagons, the men and women to ride separately; the wagoner drives one and Hananiah, though denying he is a wagoner, expertly guides the other. Everywhere they stop, people, even rival townsfolk and Gentiles, show them respect upon learning of their destination.

As they approach Lashkovitz, which boasts a grand fair, Satan stands in their path and begins coaxing them to turn aside and indulge in the splendors of the fair. Coming to himself, one of the group urges the wagoner to direct the horses quickly on the road to the next stop. Passing a horde of cripples carrying waxen models of limbs, the pilgrims realize that they have escaped temptation.

Joining the company along the way is a woman whose husband, Zusha, had disappeared. Rumors arise that he became a robber chief and was hanged. According to Jewish law, the woman cannot remarry because her husband's death remains unproved. Refusing to despair, the woman continues to search for Zusha.

Once the women of the company see the sea, on which their journey must continue, they begin to fear for their lives and cry for divorces. When these are obtained, the women remember the pains those buried outside the Land of Israel must endure to reach it. They then entreat their former husbands to remarry them, which the men do.

On board ship, when the men gather for prayer, they discover they lack a quorum and realize that Hananiah was left behind. Miserable, they blame themselves for this loss. As the dawn brightens, they stare in wonder at a man sitting on his kerchief and floating by them on the sea.

Arriving at Istanbul, a city of splendor and squalor, the comrades await the ship hired annually by Istanbul's congregation for pilgrims to the Land of Israel. Boarding the ship with the Buczacz company are Jews and Gentiles of all nationalities. After three peaceful weeks, a storm threatens to sink the ship. Once the danger is past, the passengers find themselves back at Istanbul. A second departure is successful, and all arrive safely in the Holy Land. All along the way, Rabbi Yosef heartened the company with legends extolling the land.

Immediately, however, the group encounters the reality of the land's fierce heat. Upon reaching Jerusalem, the men go to pray at the Western Wall, or the remains of the Holy Temple, adding a special prayer for Hananiah. At the synagogue, during the Sabbath service, they are reunited with him— grown taller and wearing shoes. It was Hananiah who sailed alongside their boat on his kerchief. He also met the robber chief who imitated the holy actions of his predecessor. Hananiah brought this man to the widow searching for her lost husband, thereby resolving the matter of Zusha's fate.

While all eventually are reduced to living on charity, only Leibush the butcher leaves in bitterness. Two of the women die violently, and Rabbi Meir's divorced wife arrives and they remarry. Hananiah lives past the age of one hundred, accruing strength with each year.

Critical Evaluation:

The image Shmuel Yosef Agnon projected in public as well as in his narrating persona is that of a simple, pious man. Certainly a practicing Jew, immersed from childhood in an Orthodox religious tradition, Agnon was also well read in German, Russian, French, and Scandinavian literature. The writer with whom Agnon is most often compared is Franz Kafka, who also evokes, perhaps more vividly, an unsettling world where ordinary laws of time, space, and logic do not apply. While some critics derive this quality directly from the telescoping of time and place that marks Jewish homiletic literature, others trace it to a resurgence of the Romantic spirit in Europe in the late nineteenth century, which, admittedly, was influenced by folklore and spirituality. In any case, characteristic of Romantic writing is the impression made on the reader of the subjective nature of the narrative.

Nightmare and irony result when a character attempts and, inevitably, fails to internalize and comprehend the outside world. Readers may miss the cosmic and bleak comedy in Agnon and Kafka; catastrophes, especially those of modern history, also are likely to influence readers' understandings of works written before the Holocaust. The choice of Agnon as recipient of the 1966 Nobel Prize in Literature not only recognized his prodigious body of work but also—along with that of cowinner Nelly Sachs, a poet of the Holocaust—acknowledged the shocking fate of European Jewry in the twentieth century. Agnon's saturation of his fiction with Jewish folklore and religious tradition can be argued to have fulfilled a historical role, as it preserves, in the pages of books and the minds of readers, a world that faced annihilation.

In the Heart of the Seas clearly reflects Agnon's creative use of folk styles and motifs. A folk device Agnon employs, for example, is that of the story within a story. When a new character is introduced, the main plot line is abandoned while the character's history is related, so that the new character's story is interwoven with the frame story. An often playful narrative personality presides. Agnon slyly projects himself into the novel in the character of Rabbi Shmuel Yosef the storyteller, whose tales of Zion inspire the pilgrims. The style of the novel is that of a pious folktale, its ostensible purpose articulated in a colophon reminiscent of those found in medieval manuscripts: "There are those who shall read my book like a man reading books of legends, and there are those who shall read and derive some benefit for themselves."

In a period marked by the rise of fascism and mass emigration to Palestine, in which secular Zionism dominated Hebrew writing, Agnon revived a romantic, deeply spiritual yearning for Zion. As is demonstrated by *In the Heart of the Seas*, the typical subject of Agnon's fiction is the dispossessed. While this choice of subject is far from unique, Agnon's treatment is distinguished by how he connects dispossession and homelessness to the complex of symbols expressing the concept of exile in Jewish tradition. Agnon is able to draw upon a storehouse of language and imagery to represent the state of rootlessness. Folklore is also a way to interpret the phenomena, endowing his fiction with a remarkable coherence.

In the Heart of the Seas throws the traditional antithesis of exile and Israel into relief. The movement from Buczacz to Jerusalem forms the plot of the novel. The renewal for which one hopes upon entering the Holy Land is exemplified by Hananiah, who appears to grow younger and stronger with each year spent there. Hananiah is an agent of *tikun*, or reparation of the broken and alienated things of the world in exile. He fixes and restores holy objects and also helps to solve the problem of Zusha's widow. The reuniting of Rabbi Yosef Meir and his wife in Israel signifies this power of *tikun*.

Characteristic of the ambivalence that pervades Agnon's writing, however, violence and poverty prey on the pilgrims in Israel, as violence and poverty preyed on them in exile.

Another area of ambivalence is toward the miraculous and pietistic. The reader does not always know if miracles are intended to be accepted at face value or not.

Agnon's conscious incorporation of Jewish folklore in his novels and stories follows a major trend in Hebrew and Yiddish literature since the 1870's. In this tradition, a playful, ironic tone and structural elements betray works of fiction as something other than the naïve work of simple piety. Instead of answers to how one can resolve contradictions between past and present, between practical nation building and spiritual yearning, between vision and reality, Agnon, imaginative writer that he is, gives only wondrous and perplexing stories.

Amy Spitalnick

Further Reading

Alter, Robert. "S. Y. Agnon: The Alphabet of Holiness." In *After the Tradition: Essays on Modern Jewish Writing*. New York: Dutton, 1969. Insightful evaluation of themes and motifs that have preoccupied Agnon. Traces much of the originality of Agnon's art to his painstaking care with words.

Band, Arnold J. *Nostalgia and Nightmare: A Study in the Fiction of S. Y. Agnon*. Berkeley: University of California Press, 1968. A detailed, chronological study of Agnon that illuminates the context and content of his work. Band's analysis of *In the Heart of the Seas* emphasizes its humor and fantastical qualities.

Ezrahi, Sidra DeKoven. "*In the Heart of the Seas*: S. Y. Agnon and the Epic of Return." In *Booking Passage: Exile and Homecoming in the Modern Jewish Imagination*. Berkeley: University of California Press, 2000. Ezrahi examines what she defines as "the poetics of exile and return" in literature written by Jewish authors. She includes an analysis of Agnon's novel, focusing upon its representation of the Jews returning to Israel.

Fisch, Harold. *S. Y. Agnon*. New York: Frederick Ungar, 1975. A brief introduction to Agnon. Fisch argues that Agnon, an endlessly inventive storyteller, attempts to comprehend Jewish history.

Hochman, Baruch. *The Fiction of S. Y. Agnon*. Ithaca, N.Y.: Cornell University Press, 1970. Positing Agnon's gift as more lyrical than novelistic, Hochman determines yearning to be the dominant mode of Agnon's fiction. Describes the ambivalence in Agnon's work.

Negev, Eilat. *Close Encounters with Twenty Israeli Writers*. London: Vallentine Mitchell, 2003. Negev, a literary correspondent for *Yedioth Achronot*, an Israeli journal, has compiled twenty profiles of prominent contemporary Israeli writers, including Agnon, based upon her interviews with the writers and other research.

Ribalow, Menachem. "Samuel Joseph Agnon, Major Novelist of Yesterday and Today." In *The Flowering of Modern*

Hebrew Literature: A Volume of Literary Evaluation, edited and translated by Judah Nadich. New York: Twayne, 1959. A sympathetic look at Agnon's achievement by a leader of the Hebrew movement in America. Identifies the influences in Agnon's work.

In the Time of the Butterflies

Author: Julia Alvarez (1950-   )
First published: 1994
Type of work: Novel
Type of plot: Historical realism
Time of plot: 1938-1960 and 1994
Locale: Dominican Republic

Principal characters:
PATRIA, the oldest, most traditional of the Mirabel sisters
MINERVA, the rebellious sister, who is drawn to the revolution early
DEDE, the surviving sister
MARIA THERESA ("MATE"), the youngest sister

The Story:

In 1994, Dede speaks to a "gringo writer" about her past. Dede, who is in her sixties, maintains a museum in the Dominican Republic in honor of her murdered sisters, who were nicknamed *Los Mariposas* (the butterflies). Dede acts as a guide for her guest, and when the writer leaves, Dede remembers a "clear moonlit night [in 1943] before the future began." She is with her family and remembers her fun-loving father, her mother, and her sisters.

In 1938, Minerva is twelve years old. When she is sent to school, she learns the truth about the brutal Dominican dictator Rafael Trujillo, and she is drawn into her country's resistance movement. She meets Sinita, a charity student whose brother was killed by Trujillo. Later, she is horrified by the fate of Lina Lovaton, the beautiful seventeen-year-old whose life is ruined by Trujillo's courtship. In 1944, at the end of their school years, Minerva, Sinita, and their friends win a recitation contest and are invited to perform before Trujillo. In the dictator's presence, Sinita moves toward Trujillo with her bow and arrow, but Minerva's quick thinking saves her friend

In 1945, Maria Theresa (nicknamed Mate), the family's youngest sister, is ten years old. She comments from her child's point of view on a variety of experiences, including catechism, first communion, problems at school, and interactions with her family. She has positive feelings toward Trujillo but gradually learns the truth from Minerva, whose participation in secret meetings intrigues Mate. When Minerva finds that Mate has recorded her activities in her diary,

she tells Mate that she must bury the diary to protect Minerva and her friends.

In 1946, Patria, the oldest sister, is twenty-two. She reminisces about her past as a religious young woman at convent school. Her struggle between her hope to be a nun and her growing awareness of physical passion is decided when she meets and marries Pedrito Gonzalez. When her first child is stillborn, she feels guilt for her choice. She remembers going on a pilgrimage with her mother and sisters. She had an epiphany looking at the weary faces of other pilgrims, realizing she had been looking "in the wrong direction" before.

Dede, in 1994, is concerned with the "deification" of her sisters. When the interviewer asks her, "When did all the problems start?" she remembers 1948, when the sisters met their radical friend, Lio. Both Dede and Minerva were attracted to him, but the family was upset when they learned Lio was a communist. Her parents' reaction made Dede realize she was living in a police state. When Lio was forced to go into exile, he left a note for Minerva with Dede—just as her cousin Jaimito was proposing to her. Dede accepted the proposal but burned Minerva's letter from Lio.

In 1949, Minerva has been "cooped" at home for several years, longing to be in the capital with Sinita. She is hurt that Lio left without saying goodbye, until she finds several letters. It is too late, however; Lio has gone. Minerva also discovers that her father has a second family and confronts him.

When her family is invited to one of Trujillo's private parties, Minerva fends off the dictator's advances with a slap.

The family leaves in fear. Minerva and her parents are summoned to see the governor, and her father is arrested in order to punish Minerva. At her father's request, Minerva takes money to his second family and, in a change of heart, proposes enrolling her half-sisters in school.

Minerva and her mother go to the capital to petition for her father's release. Minerva is questioned about Lio and propositioned for Trujillo, an offer she refuses. Her father is released three weeks later, but he is ill and out of touch with reality. Trujillo sees Minerva and her mother and accepts a letter of apology from Minerva. The young woman attempts to gain acceptance to law school. Trujillo releases Minerva and her parents, but Minerva realizes they are still in danger.

In 1953, Mate is eighteen years old. Her father dies, and his second family attends the funeral, making Mate angry. Minerva is accepted into law school, where she meets Manolo. Mate graduates from high school and moves to the capital to continue her education. Minerva and Manolo marry in 1955; Minerva gives birth to a daughter, Minou. In 1957, Minerva earns a law degree and leaves the capital. When Mate goes to help Miranda set up her house, she is drawn into the revolution after meeting Palomino (Leandro), who delivers guns to Minerva's house. Mate's involvement has more to do with love than with politics; she and Palomino marry in 1958.

In 1959, Patria is thirty-five. She has been settled with Pedrito for eighteen years, but she feels restless. She is concerned about her two sisters, who are involved in the resistance, and her son, who is old enough to be attracted to the revolutionaries. Patria, pregnant for the first time in thirteen years, is worried about the health of the baby. She goes on a retreat with her priest and women from her church, where the group witnesses the killing of a large number of campesinos, including a young man who reminds Patria of her own son. The priest and the women join the underground. Pedrito, concerned at first that he will lose his land, relents for the sake of his son, and all three join the resistance.

In 1994, Dede, who has been divorced for ten years, recalls her former husband forbidding her from joining the resistance. She also talks about Minerva with Minerva's daughter Minou, who asks why Dede wasn't with her sisters the day they were murdered in 1960. Dede remembers being torn between her husband and her sisters and reluctantly choosing to stay with her husband because of their children. When members of the resistance were picked up after their plot was discovered, Dede became the caretaker of her sisters' children as well as her own.

In 1960, to Patria's horror, Minerva, Mate, the three husbands, and Patria's son are all imprisoned. Patria lives with her mother, praying in her grief to a picture of Trujillo.

Through her father's second family, whose relative works in the prison, Patria receives a note from Mate with news of her sisters. Patria, Dede, and their mother send packages to the prisoners with the help of their half-sister Margarita Mirabel. Margarita has become a pharmacist thanks to the education underwritten by Dede and Minerva. Patria petitions to see the prisoners, finally securing visitor passes and her son's release. Mate and Minerva form a community with the "nonpoliticals" in their cell. Day-to-day life is discouraging, but the worst experience for Mate is being tortured in front of her husband.

The sisters are released from prison into house arrest in August of 1960. Minerva's stay in prison has left her ill and concerned for the husbands still in prison. Manolo and Leandro are moved to a prison that is closer to the family, but reaching it entails making a dangerous drive over an isolated mountain pass. Minerva describes the sisters' final trip to visit their husbands in detail, including a shopping stop, their visit with Manolo and Leandro, and the stop at a little restaurant before they and their driver head up the mountain.

Dede has pieced together what happened next from accounts of many witnesses who have come to see her in the intervening years. She remembers her "crazy" reaction to the news of the murders and caring for her sisters' bodies. Then she talks about the husbands, who have moved on with their lives with new, young wives and families. She comes to terms with her role as survivor and thinks of going to Canada and of the Canadian man she had been attracted to on an earlier trip to Spain. In the end, she is perhaps able to move on and live her own life.

Critical Evaluation:

Julia Alvarez was born in New York City in 1950, but her family returned to the Dominican Republic when she was an infant. In 1960, when she was ten, her father's involvement in a plot to overthrow dictator Rafael Trujillo was discovered. The family was warned by an American agent and escaped to New York. About four months after the Alvarez family's escape, the three Mirabel sisters, who were members of the same underground, were murdered. In the postscript to *In the Time of the Butterflies*, Alvarez notes that from the time she heard about these murders as a young girl, she "could not get the Mirabels out of my mind." On trips to the Dominican Republic, she tried to find out as much as she could about the sisters. Finally, she began to write *In the Time of the Butterflies*, a novel that she says she felt compelled to write, hoping to answer the question that had haunted her for so long: "What gave them that special courage?"

After their deaths, the "butterflies," as the sisters had been called, became legendary. People prayed to them and came often to the museum that Dede ran. Other books have been written about the sisters, but they are almost hagiographies in their one-dimensional portrayal of stereotypically and unambiguously heroic figures. Alvarez manages to avoid this pitfall by inventing the voices and lives of the sisters as children and adolescents. In doing so, she presents the four sisters, their family, and their husbands as real, fallible human beings. She also demonstrates through them the pressures that living in a police state exerts on ordinary people.

In Alvarez's fictionalized account of the Mirabel sisters' story, the author examines especially how living in Dominican society affects women. The novel is divided into three sections, followed by an epilogue and postscript. Each section has four chapters, one from the point of view of each sister. Although other chapters of the book are written in the first person, Dede's are in the third person, emphasizing her distance from her sisters' story. Through the sisters' experiences, a reader sees the male chauvinism of Latino culture, magnified by the distorted power of dictatorship, as well as the effect of misogyny in both internal and externalized forms. Minerva's rebellion, Patria's development from "good Catholic wife" to revolutionary, and Mate's conflating of rebellion and romance are clear illustrations of these pressures.

A main focus of Alvarez's work is language—its use to define and limit social groups, especially immigrants and the lower classes, and its possibilities for a writer, especially a bilingual one. Alvarez's thoughtful use of language, the product of her childhood experience in an oral culture and her love and practice of poetry, is put to good use in her recreation of the unique voices of the four sisters. In addition to the discussion of her own connection to the Mirabel sisters in the postscript of the novel, Alvarez's essay, "Chasing the Butterflies," included in the autobiographical *Something to Declare* (1998), discusses her 1986 trip to the Dominican Republic and her first interviews of people who knew the sisters or had witnessed their last day. The novel has been made into a film.

Elsie Galbreath Haley

Further Reading

Brown, Isabel Zakrzewski. "Historiographic Metafiction in *In the Time of the Butterflies*." *South Atlantic Review* 64, no. 2 (Spring, 1999): 98-112. Discussion of the novel's construction of the early life of the Mirabels, as well as its relation to feminism and postmodernism.

Ink, Lynn Chun. "Remaking Identity, Unmasking Nation: Historical Recovery and the Reconstruction of Community in *In the Time of the Butterflies* and *The Farming of Bones*." *Callaloo* 27, no. 3 (Summer, 2004): 788-807. Postcolonial analysis of the representation of conflicts resulting from women's struggles with patriarchal nationalism and the role of recovering past communities in responding to those conflicts.

McCallum, Shara. "Reclaiming Julia Alvarez: *In the Time of the Butterflies*." *Women's Studies* 29, no. 1 (February, 2000): 165. Discussion of the relationship between language and identity in the novel.

Sirias, Silvis. *Julia Alvarez: A Critical Companion*. Westport, Conn.: Greenwood Press, 2001. A basic guide to Alvarez with chapters on four of her novels, including *In the Time of the Butterflies*, as well as chapters on Alvarez's life and the Latino novel.

Socolovsky, Maya. "Patriotism, Nationalism, and the Fiction of History in Julia Alvarez's *In the Time of the Butterflies* and *In the Name of Salome*." *Latin American Literary Review* 34, no. 68 (July-December, 2006): 5. Discusses Alvarez's ability to distinguish between remembering historical events and the risk of hagiography, forgetting the events by over-memorializing them.

In the Wilderness

Author: Sigrid Undset (1882-1949)
First published: Olav Audunssøn i Hestviken and *Olav Audunssøn og hans børn*, 1925-1927 (*The Master of Hestviken*, 1928-1930; volume 3, *In the Wilderness*, 1929; the complete tetralogy, *The Master of Hestviken*, published in 1934)
Type of work: Novel
Type of plot: Historical
Time of plot: Early fourteenth century
Locale: Norway

Principal characters:
OLAV AUDUNSSØN, the master of Hestviken
EIRIK, his heir
CECILIA, Olav's daughter
BOTHILD ASGARSDATTER, Olav's foster daughter
LADY MÆRTA, Bothild's grandmother
TORHILD BJÖRNSDATTER, the mother of Olav's son Björn
SIRA HALLBJÖRN, a priest

The Story:

Olav Audunssøn has little desire to stay on at Hestviken through the summer following his wife's death. When the sons of the English armorer in Oslo ask him to be shipmaster of their boat on a trading voyage to London, it is plain that the idea pleases him. Eirik, Ingunn's son by the Icelander, also wants to go on the trip, but Olav tells him nay—he must remain at Hestviken and be companion to little Cecilia, the daughter Ingunn bore in her last years.

In England, two adventures befall Olav. At evensong in the Dominican's church, he sees a woman so much like dead Ingunn that for a moment his breath fails him. She resembles Ingunn completely, and yet she is young enough to be his daughter. With her is a blind man, apparently her husband. Olav sees her again, at mass and evensong, and after a time they begin to exchange glances and smiles. One night, her serving woman stops him after the service and leads him to a great house outside the walls. The strange woman is in the garden, her only dress a thin silk shift. For a moment Olav feels that he is about to clasp Ingunn again. Then he realizes that she is only a wanton wife seeking sport with a stranger. Thrusting her from him, he runs away.

At another time he goes with his shipmates to a famous shrine north of London. Separated from his companions, he wanders in the woods until he encounters some men beside a brook. That night they attack him for his rich dress and jewels. While Olav fights with the robbers in the dark, he feels the battle surge he knew in his outlaw youth. Later it seems to him that he was tempted by pleasures of the flesh and of violence, sent to lead him away from the path of redemption he must follow to atone for the secret slaying of Teit, Eirik's father.

When Olav sails home in late summer, he finds Eirik grown taller and strong for his age and Cecilia fairer than ever, with promise of great beauty. Resolving that Liv, the slatternly serving woman, is unfit to train the daughter of Hestviken, he weds Liv to Arnketil, his housecarl, and sends the pair to live at Rundmyr, the farm he manages for Torhild Björnsdatter, who bore him a son out of wedlock two years before. One day he goes across the fjord to Auken, where Torhild is living, to discuss his arrangement. Seeing his son and Torhild again, he thinks of asking the woman to return and keep his house, but he sadly puts the thought out of his mind.

After Liv and Arnketil move to Rundmyr, the place begins to have a bad reputation because of the dicing, wenching, and worse that goes on there. At last Sira Hallbjörn, the priest, warns Olav to keep Eirik away from that thieves' den. Olav is of two minds about Eirik. He wants to like the boy whom he claimed as his heir, yet he cannot abide Eirik's insolence and boasting. He realizes that he should give more time to his training but shrinks from that duty because of the old clash of wills between them. Urged to marry again, he wants no other wife beside him at table and bed.

His problem is solved in part when Asger Magnusson, an old friend, dies in Tunsberg after asking Olav to foster his daughter Bothild and provide for his mother-in-law, Mærta Birgersdatter. Lady Mærta is grim and gaunt but capable. Never is Hestviken better kept than when it is under her charge. Cecilia and Bothild, close in age, live as sisters. Lady Mærta dresses them well, and people say that in the whole southland there are no fairer maids than those at Hestviken.

Eirik sets himself against Lady Mærta from the first, and Olav is always angry when he is drawn into their rows and is forced to rebuke the boy. In the winter of Eirik's sixteenth year, they quarrel after Olav finds him in rude sport with a serving girl. That night Eirik leaves Hestviken without farewell. There is no report of him at Rundmyr or among Olav's distant kin, but at last word comes that he is in Oslo, among the men-at-arms who serve Sir Ragnvald Torvaldsson. Knowing that Sir Ragnvald is a gentle knight from whom Eirik will learn the skills of weapons and courtly ways, Olav is satisfied. He goes to Oslo and gives the runaway money and a squire's gear. There is much kindness between them when they part, Olav almost in envy for Eirik's youth.

Three years pass more quietly than any Olav knew since boyhood. Cecilia is his great delight, with little in her nature to recall her weak-willed, sickly mother. One night some men from another parish come to Hestviken. After drinking in the hall, one of the men tries to seize Bothild and Cecilia. Bothild is terrified, but Cecilia draws her knife and slashes at the man until the blade is red. Olav believes that she should be the boy of the house.

Olav, beginning to grow restless, is often in the company of Sira Hallbjörn, a priestly lover of falconry and hunting. One night, while they sup at a wedding feast, Olav's ancient Viking ax, Kin-fetch, rings. For a moment they see in each other's eyes old pagan stirrings that neither can speak aloud. Riding home later that night, Olav goes into the graveyard and calls to Ingunn to arise. On another day he goes to Auken, where he finds Torhild married to Ketil, a young man on the farm. Olav asks her to send Björn, their son, to live with him. She refuses.

The snows are deep that December when Duke Eirik crosses the border from Sweden to lead his troops against his father-in-law, King Haakon. Torhild brings word of the invasion to Hestviken one frosty dawn. After sending Cecilia, Bothild, and Lady Mærta to Auken for safety, Olav rides off to warn his neighbors. When the franklins try to ambush the Swedes, they are routed by the mailed horsemen. Olav and Sira Hallbjörn are among the few who make their way to the manor at Sundrheim and spend the Yule there. Meanwhile, the Swedes occupy Oslo and besiege Akershus, the royal fortress. Olav is in that great fight at Aker church and at Frysja bridge, where there is hard fighting to keep Duke Eirik from taking the castle. Sira Hallbjörn is killed at the bridge, and in the press a crossbow bolt shatters Olav's jaw.

Olav lies in fever for days. After Duke Eirik withdraws from the siege, a merchant takes Olav into Oslo and cares for him there. One day he looks at himself in a mirror. His cheek is furrowed and scarred, and his hair is gray. When he goes back to Hestviken in the spring, Olav feels that he is an old man.

Critical Evaluation:

The third volume in the Master of Hestviken tetralogy, *In the Wilderness* is set in the Middle Ages, a period whose significance in the development of Western thought and values had achieved great importance in scholarly circles when

Sigrid Undset began writing her novels. More than other works in the series, *In the Wilderness* depends for its action on the large historical movements of the time; the protagonist's journeys and his service in historical conflicts link the novel more closely to other examples of historical fiction, especially since Olav's viewpoint—that of the rank-and-file soldier—on these events is one not likely to be represented in the actual chronicles of the period. The colorful details of war and trade are in fact merely the background for a concentrated examination of the protagonist's character and spiritual condition.

The central theme of *In the Wilderness* is Olav Audunssøn's confrontation with his selfish pride. With the death of his wife Ingunn, recorded in the final pages of *The Snake Pit* (1929), Olav expects to be able to abandon the lie in which he lived for so long. Instead, he finds himself more closely bound to it than before, for he must continue his silence about his act of murder and about the licentiousness of his wife for the sake of his daughter Cecilia and his wife's son Eirik. The tensions created by his inability to articulate his guilt lead him to behave miserably toward Eirik, whom he accepts intellectually as his son and heir but who still brings up in Olav strong feelings of revulsion when he remembers that Eirik is the product of Ingunn's liaison with Teit, the man Olav murders. Away from Hestviken, he hopes to escape the torments of conscience by immersing himself in travel, trade, and warfare. When the struggles of his conscience come to a head at the church for pilgrims near London, however, he decides to resolve the problem by going on pilgrimage to Jerusalem without returning to Hestviken first. He changes his mind when he realizes that his resolution is prompted as much by his desire to avoid the vexed situation at home as by a wish to humble himself before God and be cleansed of his old sin.

In taking up his old life as a cross to be borne for his children's sake, Olav acts out the Christian precept that sin is its own punishment; his decision not to take Torhild into his house again carries out the penitential theme. Nevertheless, in consciously giving up his soul that his children might thrive, he regresses, in effect, into a pre-Christian state of being. The last part of the novel shows him immersing himself in thoughtless paganism: attempting to call Ingunn from her grave, applauding Cecilia's spirited use of a knife, and glorying in the panoply and comradeship of war. In a way, he comes full circle, experiencing again the emotions of his youth and his early manhood.

This sense of returning to his youth gives only temporary and false hope, however, since Olav is unable to shake free from the feelings of emptiness and despair that continue to plague him. He knows he must do something to atone for his transgressions, but he is not yet ready to engage in the final act of abnegation that will bring forgiveness from God. His journey toward self-knowledge and acceptance of Christianity is not yet complete. At the end of the novel he is forced to recognize that his body has deteriorated, and that he has become old. As a result, the link with his early life as Ingunn's husband dissolves, making way for the renewal of the conflict between Christian and pagan values that characterizes the final novel of the series, *The Son Avenger* (1930).

When Undset was awarded the Nobel Prize in Literature in 1928, that award was made, according to the citation, "principally with regard to her powerful pictures of Northern life in medieval times." No one who has read *Kristin Lavransdatter* (1929) or *The Master of Hestviken* will deny the justice of that statement. Those not familiar with her novels must be prepared to find a writer who, while true to the life and spirit of a past age, pays little attention to great personages and big historical events. Undset's stories of medieval life are so rich in detail that there is little need in her books for a parade of names and dates. *In the Wilderness* is the one exception to her usual practice, however, in that the closing episode of this novel deals with a traceable historical event, the invasion of Norway by Duke Eirik of Sweden in 1308.

"Critical Evaluation" by Laurence W. Mazzeno

Further Reading

Allen, Walter Gore. *Renaissance in the North*. London: Sheed & Ward, 1946. Notes the strong Catholic underpinning of Undset's works. Argues that Undset approaches her medieval material with no preconceptions and portrays her hero as living in a golden age, when religious values guided people's lives.

Bayerschmidt, Carl. *Sigrid Undset*. New York: Twayne, 1970. Introductory overview of Undset's life and major works. The commentary on *In the Wilderness* is included in a chapter discussing Undset's novels of the Middle Ages. Concentrates on the moral development of the hero.

Gustafson, Alrik. *Six Scandinavian Novelists*. Minneapolis: University of Minnesota Press, 1971. Analysis of the four novels that make up *The Master of Hestviken* chronicle. Considers Undset's portrait of the hero of *In the Wilderness* as gloomy. Highlights her concern for the perennial battle between flesh and spirit.

Maman, Marie. *Sigrid Undset in America: An Annotated Bibliography and Research Guide*. Lanham, Md.: Rowman and Littlefield, 2000. A useful resource for English-speaking students. Maman has compiled bibliographies of American publications featuring information about Undset, placing them into four categories: reviews and articles about Undset's novels set in the Middle Ages, materials about Undset's contemporary novels, other articles, and book chapters about the writer. Includes a bibliography of autobiographical material found in Undset's own works.

Mishler, William. "The Epic Novelists: Undset, Duun, Uppdal, Falkberget." In *A History of Norwegian Literature*, edited by Harold S. Naess. Lincoln: University of Nebraska Press, in cooperation with the American-Scandinavian Foundation, 1993. Analyzes Undset's works and places them within the broader context of Norwegian epic fiction.

Whitehouse, J. C. "Sigrid Undset." In *Vertical Man: The Human Being in the Catholic Novels of Graham Greene, Sigrid Undset, and Georges Bernanos*. New York: Garland, 1990. Analysis of Undset's view of human nature as reflected in her novels and short stories. The discussion of *In the Wilderness* is included in a consideration of Undset's vision of humanity. Calls Undset a great moralist whose characters reveal her optimism for the future of the human race.

Winsnes, A. H. *Sigrid Undset: A Study in Christian Realism*. Translated by P. G. Foote. London: Sheed & Ward, 1953. A biography of the novelist that traces the strong strand of Christian belief undergirding all of her fiction. Discusses the characters in the multivolume saga of which *In the Wilderness* is a part.

Incidents in the Life of a Slave Girl

Author: Harriet Jacobs (c. 1813-1897)
First published: 1861
Type of work: Autobiography
Type of plot: Historical
Time of plot: 1820's-1850's
Locale: Edenton, North Carolina; Pennsylvania; New York; Massachusetts; England

Principal personages:
LINDA BRENT, the narrator, pseudonym of Harriet Jacobs
WILLIAM, the narrator's brother
AUNT MARTHY, the narrator's grandmother
BENJAMIN, the narrator's uncle
PHILLIP, the narrator's uncle
DR. FLINT, slavemaster of Linda
MRS. FLINT, slavemistress of Linda
BENJAMIN (BENNY), Linda's son
ELLEN, Linda's daughter
BETTY, Linda's friend, who hides her temporarily
MR. SANDS, father of Linda's two children
FIRST MRS. BRUCE, friend to Linda in New York
SECOND MRS. BRUCE, friend who buys Linda's freedom
LYDIA MARIA CHILD, abolitionist and editor of autobiography

The Story:

Linda Brent does not realize she is enslaved until she is six years old. With her maternal grandmother, Aunt Marthy, near them, Linda lives with her parents and her brother William until her mother dies. From ages six to twelve, she lives with her first mistress, who teaches her to read. Linda then is given as property to the niece of her former slavemistress and lives in the home of Dr. Flint, who harasses her sexually and verbally when she turns fifteen years old. The doctor's wife, Mrs. Flint, is jealous and cruel. The Flints own a town residence, several farms, and fifty slaves.

Linda's brother William says that he does not mind the physical experience of being whipped but hates the idea that he can be whipped by people who say they own him. Linda's uncle Benjamin escapes for the North but is discovered on a ship and, despite further escape attempts, is returned to his owner and jailed. He escapes again and reaches New York. Aunt Marthy, who has gained her own freedom, buys freedom for her son Phillip, and they rejoice that Benjamin also has escaped slavery.

Enduring the harassment of Dr. Flint, Linda verbally stands up for herself on multiple occasions. She refuses to give in to his threats of sexual attack, although Mrs. Flint accuses her of doing so. Dr. Flint gives Linda harassing notes that she pretends she cannot read. Linda falls in love with a free African American man who wants to purchase her freedom so they can marry. Dr. Flint, however, refuses to sell her to him.

Linda enters a relationship with a white man, Mr. Sands,

and has two children, Benny and Ellen. The children become links to life, giving Linda reason to carry on. Dr. Flint tries to convince Linda to be his sexual slave, but she refuses. He wants her voluntary compliance and does not rape her. At the age of twenty-one, Linda goes into hiding above stairs at the home of her friend Betty. Dr. Flint, in an effort to find Linda, has her brother and children jailed for two months. The doctor finally sells them, and Mr. Sands buys them from a slavetrader, saying he will free them.

Linda hides in her grandmother's attic crawlspace for seven years, from 1835 to 1842. She calls this space, which is nine feet by seven feet by five feet, her "loophole of retreat." She can look through holes she creates to watch her children playing outside. They are not supposed to know where she is hiding. She finally escapes on a boat to the North. Linda learns that Ellen is being treated as a slave and not as a daughter by her birth father.

Linda knows she has to win her freedom in order to save her children. Dr. Flint still refuses to sell Linda. Linda sees her brother William and her son Benny, who later goes on a whaling voyage. She tells her northern employer, Mrs. Bruce, that she is a fugitive slave, and Mrs. Bruce decides to help her. Linda goes to England for ten months and renews her Christian faith. The second Mrs. Bruce also helps Linda elude capture and buys Linda's freedom in 1852. Linda gains freedom for her children as well. In 1853, she begins writing the story of her enslavement and freedom.

Critical Evaluation:

Not only is *Incidents in the Life of a Slave Girl* the most famous and most analyzed slave narrative by an African American woman, but Harriet Jacobs is also the only enslaved woman in America who left papers testifying to her life and describing how she came to write her narrative. The book, which uses pseudonyms for historically real persons (with Jacobs writing as Linda Brent), exposes the cruelties and injustices of the chattel slavery system in North America. Jacobs says that she wrote her story to make women of the North realize the sufferings of millions of enslaved women in the South. Other abolitionist literature did not expose the sexual vulnerabilities of enslaved women. Challenging in its time, the narrative's subject matter caused its serial publication to end early. The full book was published in 1861, just before the outbreak of the Civil War.

In order to indict the slavery power system for tyranny and sexual ownership of African American women, Jacobs must reveal her participation in a romantic relationship producing two illegitimate children. As an enslaved woman, she is denied freedom to choose a romantic partner or husband. Jacobs asks for her readers' pity for her violation of Christian laws regarding sexuality on the grounds that, because she is considered property, she is powerless to obey them. Jacobs emphasizes the hypocrisy of slaveowners such as her owner who study the Bible and teach slaves verses about loving one's neighbor as oneself but who do not recognize enslaved persons as their neighbors.

This exciting and completely factual narrative addresses diverse topics, including slavery's psychological rupture of black families, relationships among antebellum white women and enslaved women, laws allowing slavery, resistance to bondage, methods of seizing freedom, revision of racial stereotypes, African American networking, and ideals of womanhood. Jacobs finds that racist and discriminatory practices continue in the northern states, as when African Americans cannot ride in the front of trains. While narrating her life, Jacobs mentions historical events such as the Nat Turner uprising, a major slave revolt in Virginia in 1831, and the Fugitive Slave Law of 1850, which strengthened legal requirements that Americans living in any state, regardless of local laws, must return enslaved persons to their masters.

Amy Cummins

Further Reading

Andrews, William L. "Narrating Slavery." In *Teaching African American Literature: Theory and Practice*, edited by Maryemma Graham, Sharon Pineault-Burke, and Marianna White Davis. New York: Routledge, 1998. Offers an excellent overview of slave narratives helpful for teachers and learners at all levels. Andrews shares insights from a long teaching career to describe the history of African American autobiography and constituent elements of slave narratives. Shows the influence of *Incidents in the Life of a Slave Girl* on later autobiographies such as Maya Angelou's *I Know Why the Caged Bird Sings* (1969).

Foster, Frances Smith. "Harriet Jacobs's *Incidents* and the 'Careless Daughters' (and Sons) Who Read It." In *The (Other) American Traditions: Nineteenth-Century Women Writers*, edited by Joyce Warren. New Brunswick, N.J.: Rutgers University Press, 1993. Foster analyzes the history and reception of Jacobs's narrative, charting its rise to recognition as a major work of American autobiographical literature and discussing mid-nineteenth century ideals for women.

Matterson, Stephen. "Shaped by Readers: The Slave Narratives of Frederick Douglass and Harriet Jacobs." In *Soft Canons: American Women Writers and Masculine Tradition*, edited by Karen Kilcup. Iowa City: University of Iowa Press, 1999. Analyzing the two most famous American slave narratives, Matterson contrasts *Incidents in the Life of a Slave Girl* with *Narrative of the Life of Frederick Douglass*. He considers subject, voice, style, and literary genres influencing each author and argues that each implies different actions against slavery.

Sorisio, Carolyn. "'There Is Might in Each': Conceptions of Self in Harriet Jacobs's *Incidents in the Life of a Slave Girl, Written by Herself*." *Legacy: A Journal of American Women Writers* 13, no. 1 (1996): 1-18. Looks at Jacobs's self-representation as an individual with rights of citizenship. Argues that Jacobs situates her own identity both in relation to and apart from others.

Yellin, Jean Fagin. *Harriet Jacobs: A Life*. New York: Basic Books, 2004. The first full-length biography of Harriet Jacobs by a scholar, this text includes a diagram of her hiding place, discussion of family relationships, and documentation of the activism by Jacobs and her daughter Louisa. Yellin is the scholar who definitively established in 1987 that Jacobs wrote her own narrative.

_____. *The Harriet Jacobs Family Papers*. Chapel Hill: University of North Carolina Press, 2008. Yellin devoted more than thirty years to researching Harriet Jacobs. In this two-volume book of letters and papers, Yellin includes three hundred primary-source documents about the Jacobs family. The paper trail documents how Jacobs wrote her life story.

Independence Day

Author: Richard Ford (1944-   )
First published: 1995
Type of work: Novel
Type of plot: Psychological realism
Time of plot: Fourth of July weekend, 1988
Locale: Haddam, New Jersey; the Jersey seashore;
    Deep River, Connecticut; Springfield,
    Massachusetts; Cooperstown, New York

Principal characters:
FRANK BASCOMBE, a real estate agent
ANN, his former wife
PAUL, their son
CHARLIE O'DELL, Ann's husband
SALLY CALDWELL, Bascombe's girlfriend
JOE and PHYLLIS MARKHAM, potential home buyers
IRV ORNSTEIN, Bascombe's stepbrother

The Story:

Frank Bascombe is a real estate agent, divorced and living away from his children. Over the long holiday weekend, he is trying to sell a house to a difficult couple, as he worries over his personal relationship with his girlfriend, Sally Caldwell. He is also trying to connect with his fifteen-year-old son, Paul, who has gotten into trouble. Bascombe's plan is a trip to the basketball and baseball halls of fame, a father and son weekend together.

Bascombe is trying to collect rent on a pair of houses he owns near his hometown of Haddam, New Jersey, where he lives in his former wife's old house. He had moved here when his former wife Ann, remarried—to Charlie O'Dell—and moved with him to Connecticut. Bascombe bought her house so their children would feel some stability, especially since they no longer live in the same town as their father. He is especially worried about Paul, who has been arrested for shoplifting and for a physical confrontation with a security guard, which Paul blames on surprise rather than malevolence. Ann has sent Paul to a therapist, worried about his behavior, which is oddly distant and full of worrisome behavior, including making dog-barking sounds.

Bascombe has no luck collecting the overdue rent; in fact, he is threatened by his renter. He turns to his next task—taking Joe and Phyllis Markham to look at potential houses to buy. They have already looked at dozens of houses and are nearing a breaking point. They are interested in moving from Vermont, looking for an area to raise their daughter, but they cannot afford the home they dream of and are unhappy with the places they have seen in their price range. Bascombe arrives to pick them up, and Joe is surly and angry, dressed inappropriately for going out in public. Bascombe takes them to see one more house: a beautiful home that has just gone on the market. It has one flaw—forming the property's back boundary is the wall of a minimum-security, country-club-style prison. After arguing with Joe, who essentially fires

Bascombe, Bascombe returns to check on his overdue renter. A neighbor calls the police, believing Bascombe is trying to break into the house.

Bascombe leaves for one final errand. He has to stop by a root beer stand he owns, to check on plans to sell hotdogs on Independence Day. His employee insists that people are planning to rob the stand, and he shows Bascombe the sawed-off shotgun he says he will use to protect himself.

Along the Jersey shore, Bascombe meets up with his girlfriend, Sally, but she is distracted and distant. He worries she is thinking about her former husband, Wally, who had disappeared years ago and was declared dead. Bascombe finally leaves and drives at least part of the way to Connecticut, where he plans on picking up his son, Paul, in the morning. Getting tired, he pulls off the road at a small motel and learns, after getting a room, that someone had been murdered in a room at the other end of the motel.

Now in Connecticut, and after sparring a while with Ann, Bascombe leaves with his son for the Basketball Hall of Fame. He tries to strike up a conversation, but the boy ignores him. Paul is uninterested in the museum, and he finally wanders off in search of a snack bar. Bascombe uses this moment to call his girlfriend. Later, he and Paul meet in a room where people are standing on a conveyor belt that moves them past a series of basketball hoops. Bascombe tries to show Paul how to shoot, but he gets heckled as he misses. Paul finally takes a basketball, but just stands there, never shooting as he rides through the room. At the end of the "tour," he asks if they can leave.

In Cooperstown, home of the Baseball Hall of Fame, Bascombe and his son check into a bed and breakfast. Bascombe takes a short nap, and when he awakes, he finds that Paul has disappeared. He checks his phone calls, finding that Joe and Phyllis have been leaving him messages. He calls his girlfriend again and tries to persuade her to fly in. He spends the evening flirting with the cook instead, and as they talk about going out for a drink on the darkened porch, Bascombe realizes Paul has been listening.

The next morning, Bascombe and his son begin to walk to the Baseball Hall of Fame. Paul again is completely uninterested. They come across a batting cage, and Bascombe takes some swings, showing Paul the batting stances of different batters. Paul enters the cage, without a helmet, and then just stands on home plate. The first pitch hits him square in the face.

An ambulance is soon rushing Paul to a hospital. Bascombe is shocked by what happened. What helps him is the coincidence that his stepbrother (a son of his mother's second marriage) Irv Ornstein, happens to be at the hall, too. He takes charge and drives Bascombe to the hospital. Paul has seriously injured his eye and eye socket. His father calls Ann, whose rich husband, Charlie, charters a helicopter to fly her and Paul to an excellent eye surgeon.

The next morning, Independence Day, Bascombe hears that Paul's eye will be okay, considering what had happened. Bascombe takes Joe and Phyllis Markham to a house he owns, which he will rent to them. Then he walks through the parade. He imagines his son coming to live with him, growing more mature. He imagines even remarrying and entering a new period of life, one more stable and one closer to oblivion.

Critical Evaluation:

Richard Ford's *Independence Day* is the second novel in a trilogy—including *The Sportswriter* (1986) and *The Lay of the Land* (2006)—that describes the life of a real estate agent named Frank Bascombe. *Independence Day* received both the PEN/Faulkner Award and a Pulitzer Prize in fiction. Ford has won the Rhea Award for short fiction, and his short stories are contained in many anthologies of contemporary literature.

Independence Day offers a view of the American Dream, but it is a mixed vision of American life. On the one hand, the novel offers a bucolic view of the United States, full of happy families enjoying a Fourth of July parade with a marching band playing a victory march. Bascombe dreams of connecting with his son by visiting shrines to America's popular sports. He imagines having a heart-to-heart discussion about the books he has brought with him, in hopes of persuading his son, Paul, to read them. His books on, for example, the U.S. Constitution cannot compare with a stolen magazine and Paul's deeper interest in the music he can escape to via ear plugs.

Bascombe has learned, as a real estate agent, that the search for a perfect house, the perfect home, is flawed. Part of his own personal philosophy of life is that people will get what they will get, and that just about everyone will end up settling for what they can afford. He shows Joe and Phyllis Markham what looks like the American Dream home, but the reality is that a prison is hidden behind its backyard trees. Even the prison becomes a sales pitch, as Bascombe claims it makes the house safer. The only escapees, if any, would be former politicians or former businessmen imprisoned for defrauding the public. Too much of the world has hidden worries. Bascombe had recently been mugged by some random teens who rode by him, hit him over the head with a bottle, and left the scene laughing. Worse yet, a female coworker had been murdered, and her killer never caught. Even Bascombe's root beer and hotdog stand had been cased by criminals, though they had met their end when trying to rob a neighboring store.

Independence Day also explores Bascombe's personal philosophy of life. He describes this time of his life as his "existence period," where he tries to mentally ignore whatever aspects of life he dislikes, in the belief that these negatives will go away. He has found that, quite often, problems do indeed just go away. He contrasts himself to client Joe Markham, whom he thinks still believes that life has a purpose and meaning. Bascombe feels that Markham will come to stop believing that his, or anyone's, life is going somewhere in particular.

Life, however, forces Bascombe to realize that he has to care. He senses his relationship with Sally is slipping away, worrying that she is still thinking about her former husband, a man who has literally disappeared from life, falling so far off the face of the earth that he was declared dead, after so many years. Even stronger yet, seeing his son injured has forced him to realize how strongly involved in life his heart really is, as he first worries about his son's emotional problems and quirk, and then worries that Paul will be disfigured or will potentially lose his eyesight. Paul's essentially self-inflicted injury will not go away, no matter how much Bascombe wishes it would.

Bascombe has felt that if he could simply ignore life, everything would turn out all right. However, he sees his former wife, Ann, worrying about their children; he sees his girl-friend, Sally, wondering about their relationship; he sees Sally's sense of doubt for future relationships because of the mysterious disappearance, the void of her first husband's loss; he sees Paul suffer physical injury; and he sees so many troubled people around him. He realizes how much his step-brother, Irv Ornstein, has helped him; not so much by doing anything dramatic, but by helping and staying with him, taking care of the little things. Bascombe realizes he needs to do more than ignore—he needs to act.

Those horrible moments waiting for information about his son at the hospital force Bascombe to reassess his personal philosophy. He recognizes that he is leaving his "existence period," that he can no longer avoid life by superficially attending to it but must do so at a personal distance. He recognizes that he is about to enter what he labels "the Permanent Period," one's final stage of life, the time when people move toward the end, oblivion.

Brian L. Olson

Further Reading

Dobozy, Tamas. "How Not to Be a 'Dickhead': Partisan Politics in Richard Ford's *Independence Day*." *Critical Survey* 18 (June, 2006): 40-59. Discusses the political conflict between liberalism and conservatism in the novel, asserting that Ford endorses a concept of freedom that requires openness to others and to the uncertainties of life.

Flora, Joseph M., Amber Vogel, and Bryan Albin Giemza, eds. *Southern Writers: A New Biographical Dictionary.* Baton Rouge: Louisiana State University Press, 2006. Ford is included in this literary dictionary of authors with a significant connection to the American South. Provides information about Ford's birthplace, his upbringing in the South, and his use of the South as a setting.

Guagliardo, Huey, ed. *Conversations with Richard Ford.* Jackson: University Press of Mississippi, 2001. A collection of personal interviews with Ford.

_____. *Perspectives on Richard Ford*. Jackson: University Press of Mississippi, 2000. A collection of critical essays on Ford's work, with essays specific to *Independence Day.*

Hogan, Phil. "To Be Frank." *The Guardian*, September 24, 2006. A reflective piece on the Bascombe trilogy, written upon the publication of *The Lay of the Land* (2006), the third book in the series that includes *Independence Day* and *The Sportswriter* (1986).

Walker, Elinor Ann. *Richard Ford*. New York: Twayne, 2000. Examines Ford's career, provides readings of individual novels that address his dominant themes, and discusses his connection to trends in American and southern literature.

Independent People

Author: Halldór Laxness (1902-1998)
First published: Sjálfstættfólk, 1934-1935 (English translation, 1946)
Type of work: Novel
Type of plot: Social
Time of plot: Twentieth century
Locale: Iceland

Principal characters:
BJARTUR, a crofter
ROSA, his first wife
FINNA, his second wife
ASTA SOLLILJA, Rosa's daughter
GVENDUR, Bjartur's son
NONNI, Bjartur's younger son
INGOLFUR ARNARSON, Asta's father

The Story:

After working for eighteen years for Bailiff Jon, Bjartur is at last able to buy, with a heavy mortgage, the croft (small farm) called Winterhouses. Proud of his new status as a landowner and fiercely independent, Bjartur promptly renames the place Summerhouses. It is a poor place, fit only for sheep grazing. The house, which Bjartur rebuilds, consists of one room over the stable. The walls are of sod, and the roof is made of a few sheets of corrugated iron covered with turf. Nevertheless, it is his own place, and Bjartur is determined to be a hired workman for no one and to put his trust in sheep.

He chooses for his wife the twenty-six-year-old Rosa, a small, sturdy woman with a cast in one eye, who was also in service to the bailiff. Rosa is disappointed in her house, and Bjartur is disappointed in Rosa. He soon finds that she is already pregnant. He suspects, and is sure much later, that the lover is the bailiff's son, Ingolfur.

After a few months of marriage, Bjartur leaves on a cold winter day to look for his sheep. Seeing a buck reindeer in the woods, he jumps on the animal's back and attempts to subdue it. The reindeer, however, is too strong and takes off in mad flight for the river. With Bjartur still holding on, the animal swims downstream and finally lands on the other shore. Bjartur, nearly frozen to death, stays to recuperate at a nearby croft.

He returns home after several days to find his wife dead from childbirth and a baby daughter still alive. Disregarding the parentage of the girl, he proudly names her Asta Sollilja. The bailiff's wife sends the pauper Finna and her mother to look after Bjartur and the baby. Finna is nearly forty years old but strong and well preserved. To settle the problem of the child's care, Bjartur marries her.

Each year Finna has another child, usually stillborn. After some years, however, there are Helgi, Gvendur, and Nonni, and their half-sister Asta. The croft is crowded, and the beds are all dirty and filled with vermin, but the land is clear of debt.

A southerner comes to the croft one day to ask permission to camp and hunt. The stranger delights Asta, who is awkward and uncouth but bursting with love. The stranger hardly notices her, however, and each night he is gone most of the night. The reason for his visit comes out later, when the bailiff's daughter leaves the country in great haste.

After little Helgi is lost on the moor, the tie between Asta and Bjartur becomes closer. When Finna dies from poor diet and childbearing, the father tries his best to make life easier for the girl. He refuses to let Asta go to school, but he does teach her much of the old Icelandic poetry. Bjartur takes Asta on his yearly trip to town, where, after doing the shopping, they stay overnight in a lodging house for country folk. To save money, father and daughter sleep in the same bed. Asta is unhappy. The townspeople laugh at her homely clothes, and the snores of the drunken farmers in the nearby beds are terrifying. She snuggles closer to her father and kisses him. He puts his arms around her, but to his horror he finds that she is kissing him repeatedly. Bjartur abruptly gets up and goes out for their horse. Father and daughter leave for home in the rainy night.

Then a series of misfortunes, which the Icelanders attribute to a witch buried near Summerhouses, greatly reduces Bjartur's flock of sheep, and he goes to town to work. Trying to meet his obligations to his children, Bjartur sends a schoolmaster to instruct Asta, Gvendur, and Nonni during the winter; but Bjartur's choice of teacher is unfortunate. After getting drunk one night, the schoolmaster takes Asta. When Bjartur comes home in the spring, Asta is pregnant. In his rage Bjartur casts out his daughter, who goes gladly, full of romantic notions of her lover. She walks to his fine town house, which turns out to be a shack. There she learns that he has many children and that his wife is again pregnant.

Just before World War II, Nonni goes to America to join his uncle. Only Gvendur, Bjartur, and the old mother-in-law are left. The war boom raises the price of lambs, and Bjartur prospers. He has two cows and three horses. At the same time, a cooperative movement, with Ingolfur at its head, is organized. In the parish, only Bjartur holds out; he remains loyal to the merchants who were gouging him for years.

Nonni sends two hundred dollars from America to pay for Gvendur's passage. In spite of his father's objections, Gvendur, who is seventeen years old and big and strong for his age, decides to emigrate. He puts on his best clothes and goes to town to take the coastal steamer. There he is admired because he is going to America. During the day and night, as Gvendur waits before his ship sails, he meets the bailiff's granddaughter. She takes him riding on the moor, where they spend the night together. Hoping to win her love, Gvendur renounces his emigration and goes back to Summerhouses.

In spite of the depression following the war, Bjartur resolves to build his new house. He goes deeply into debt to buy great supplies of stone and timber. That year he gets the walls and roof completed, but there are no doors and windows. Before he can finish the house, the mortgage is foreclosed, and Summerhouses passes into the hands of the bank. The only place left for the family is the mother-in-law's old croft, long since abandoned. During the moving, Bjartur meets Asta and reconciles with her. Asta has a second child by another man, and she is carrying a third. The family is complete again, except for Nonni.

Asta, like Bjartur, is independent. Ingolfur, now rich and a member of Parliament, reveals to her that he is her father. His offer of support is soundly rejected. Bjartur falls in with some strikers who strike against the government's low wages. For a while he is sympathetic with the men, who are, in a way, led by the Communist Party. Gvendur is even more sympathetic, but they both reject in principle the idea of collective action. They are independent farmers and herders.

They move to the wretched hovel far to the north, with only Blesi, their twenty-five-year-old horse, to do the hauling. By hard work, they continue their old way of life. They have one room in a turf-covered hut. Their diet is cast-off fish. With luck they will be only a little less comfortable than savages in a jungle.

Critical Evaluation:

Independent People is one of the few novels to give a faithful and artistic picture of some essentially unrewarding lives in bleak, small Iceland. In addition to the background, Halldór Laxness has written in a style and with a scope approaching the epic. The reader gets some of the feeling of the traditions of the Vikings and sees the old give way to the new. Only the hard, barren life of the crofter is unchanging, for the Icelander in the remoter sections of his country lives on about the plane of the primitive savage.

Laxness's work is an excellent example of the naturalistic novel, for it demonstrates the thesis that people have no connection with a religious or spiritual world and that people are subject to the natural forces of heredity and environment. According to the tenets of naturalism, one's life is largely determined by the social and economic forces of one's background, which are usually presented by an author of this school with elaborate and minute documentation. The characters usually show strong animal drives, but they are helpless in their fight against sociological pressures. All of these characteristics fit *Independent People*. In it, Laxness starkly presents all the grim details of the life of Bjartur, the "independent man," who fights to rise above his environment, becomes successful for a period, and then sinks back into the miserable life he worked so hard to escape.

Except for occasional references to automobiles and electricity, one would not know that the novel is set in the twentieth century, for the lifestyle of the crofters is no better than that of peasants in medieval times. The poverty of the crofters is almost unbelievable. They live in small, one-room hovels above the stables and are plagued by the smoke of peat-stoked fires, the dampness of spring, and the bitter cold of winter, when snow may cover the entire house. In an environment where humans live little better than beasts, it is almost unavoidable that they become animalistic and lose compassion and emotion. In *Independent People*, there is no communication or understanding among the characters, and any attempt at communication is viewed with suspicion.

The role of women in such circumstances is particularly hard. This is shown in the grotesque death of Rosa, who is found dead on the croft floor in a pool of blood. Her infant is kept alive by the warmth of the dog that lies upon it until Bjartur returns. The harshness of a woman's life is also seen in the yearly pregnancies of Finna and in the miserable life Asta is forced to live after Bjartur drives her from the house.

Even more interesting, however, is the perverted responses that one is conditioned into making by the hard life one lives. For example, Bjartur mourns for neither of his wives. When looking for a housekeeper to care for the infant Asta, he admits that he talks more about animals than about human beings. He dismisses Rosa's death by telling the minister that she just died from loss of blood. No effort to care for her seems to have entered his mind.

There are several prominent themes running through the novel; politics, economics, social reform, and the clash between religion and ancient superstitions are all dealt with in some detail. For years Laxness searched for a sustaining religious and political ideology, and in *Independent People*, the restless energy generated by that search finds its first powerful outlet in his bitter attack on materialism. He holds the greed and the oppression inherent in the materialistic philosophy responsible for the sordidness and suffering that fills the lives of his countrymen in rural Iceland. In exposing the cruelties of rural conditions with all the merciless determination of the naturalist school, the author enraged many Icelanders—who resented having such a brutal picture of their emerging nation published abroad—and impressed liberals all over Europe and America. For all Laxness's revolutionary vigor, hatred of power of and authority, scorn for bourgeois morality, and anger and grim satire, he still is able to express his artist's love of beauty. Alongside scenes of coarseness and themes marked by their bitterness, Laxness displays throughout *Independent People* a great compassion and sensitivity, a capacity for tenderness and concern, and a burning devotion to the spirit of individualism and idealism.

The center of interest, however, is always the character Bjartur. At times, his seeming indifference is nothing more than an attempt to cope with life's harshness. In the spring following Helgi's disappearance, for example, Bjartur, looking for a lost ewe, finds the decayed body of a young boy, which no longer looks like a human being. Bjartur touches it once or twice with his stick, takes a good pinch of snuff, and leaves. Bjartur reveals, at times, that affection is possible in his life. Although he knows Asta is not his child, she is his favorite. He calls her his "little flower" and is horrified when he finds his fingers undoing the fastenings of her undergarment in the bed they share. He also has a poetic side, for he continually composes complicated verses and teaches the ancient poems of Iceland to Asta. However, poetry is the only fancy he allows himself; all else is harsh reality. To Bjartur, the sheep and the land are the most important things in the world, for after years of debt his only desire is to be considered an independent man. When he brings his bride, Rosa, to Summerhouses, he says that independence is the most important thing in life. He intends to maintain his independence. This is the great irony of the book, for his independence is false; he is completely at the mercy of his environment. His stubbornness and pride lead him to disaster when he refuses to take the advice of wiser men and falls into bankruptcy when he borrows money to build a "real" house, which he hopes will rival the bailiff's mansion. Bjartur defies everything and everyone. He refuses to believe in either the Christian religion or in the ancient superstitions of the country. In a show of bravado, he defies the spirit of Gunnvor, the witch buried upon his land, who is supposed to have killed most of her children and to have drunk the blood of those who survived. Everyone else in the district adds a rock to her grave when they pass, but this Bjartur refuses to do. Instead, he purchases a headstone for her grave marked "To Gunnvor from Bjartur." It is after this act of defiance that his financial troubles begin.

Laxness was reared in the country and is able to give an intimate picture of the starkness of Icelandic life on the frontier. This great attention to detail makes the book approach epic proportions. There are, however, some flaws in the author's style. He often makes authorial intrusions, commenting upon politics, economics, or human nature. The style is also uneven. At times, it is smooth and poetic, but at others it is extremely awkward. On the whole, however, the book is valuable as a social document and as the story of Bjartur, the independent man who, struggling against impossible odds, is never defeated psychologically, even when he loses all he has worked so hard for. Without remorse, he plans to begin again at the wretched, abandoned croft of his mother-in-law.

"Critical Evaluation" by Vina Nickels Oldach

Further Reading

Einarsson, Stefán. *A History of Icelandic Literature.* Baltimore: Johns Hopkins University Press, 1957. Sketches Laxness's career and comments on major publications. Claims that in *Independent People* and other novels, Laxness deals sensitively with contemporary themes. Describes how the poor farmer in *Independent People* emerges as a symbol of his class and a hero of great stature.

Hallberg, Peter. *Halldór Laxness.* Translated by Rory McTurk. New York: Twayne, 1971. The chapter devoted to *Independent People* compares the novel with the work of Knut Hamsun and discusses Laxness's infatuation with socialism. Provides extensive commentary on the protagonist and his children.

Hallmundsson, Hallberg. "Halldór Laxness and the Sagas of Modern Iceland." *Georgia Review* 49, no. 1 (Spring, 1995): 39. Assesses Laxness's fiction and essays, discussing his writing style, depiction of women characters, and the enduring importance of his work.

Leithauser, Brad. "The Book of My Life: Halldór Laxness' *Independent People.*" In *Penchants and Places.* New York: Alfred A. Knopf, 1995. Personal commentary on a book that Leithauser claims has great power to evoke sympathetic responses in readers, especially those whose experiences parallel the novelist and his characters.

Magnusson, Magnus, and Jason Cowley. "Seeing the Truth." *New Statesman* 13, no. 637 (December 25, 2000-January 1, 2001): 91-92. Magnusson and Cowley reflect on the reception in the United States of Laxness and his work, noting his early popularity. While concentrating on Laxness's fiction, they also shed light on the writer's character.

Neijmann, Daisy, ed. *A History of Icelandic Literature.* Lincoln: University of Nebraska Press, in cooperation with the American-Scandinavian Foundation, 2006. There are references to Laxness throughout this survey of Icelandic literature, but the majority of the information is contained in chapters 5 and 6, which focus on the twentieth century. Includes information on Laxness's early works, his influences, and his place in world literature, among other topics.

Rossel, Sven H. *A History of Scandinavian Literature, 1870-1980.* Translated by Anne C. Ulmer. Minneapolis: University of Minnesota Press, 1982. Provides a biographical sketch and a summary of Laxness's literary achievements. Places *Independent People* in the context of the author's canon, examining how the novel shows Laxness's faith in socialism as an antidote to capitalism.

Talmor, Sascha. "Bjartur of Summerhouses: An Icelandic Sisyphus." *European Legacy* 5, no. 1 (February, 2000): 87-100. Analysis of *Independent People*, focusing on the struggle of Bjartur, the novel's protagonist, against the hard life in Iceland. Discusses how hard life and suffering are reflected in Laxness's other novels and describes interest in medieval Icelandic sagas.

Indian Summer

Author: William Dean Howells (1837-1920)
First published: 1886
Type of work: Novel
Type of plot: Domestic realism
Time of plot: Shortly after the American Civil War
Locale: Florence, Italy

Principal characters:
THEODORE COLVILLE, a middle-aged bachelor
MRS. LINA BOWEN, a middle-aged friend of Colville
IMOGENE GRAHAM, a girl chaperoned by Mrs. Bowen
EFFIE BOWEN, Mrs. Bowen's thirteen-year-old daughter
MR. MORTON, an admirer of Imogene Graham

The Story:

Theodore Colville studies architecture as a young man and continues his professional education by spending some months in Italy. While there, he goes about with two young women. He falls in love with one of them, but the woman rejects his suit. Soon afterward, he goes back to the United States at the request of his older brother, who had recently purchased a newspaper. Colville becomes the editor of his brother's paper and eventually purchases it. He enters politics in his fortieth year. After being defeated, he leaves his home in Indiana and returns to Italy.

Colville tries to resume the study of architecture but is diverted after meeting Mrs. Bowen, who was the companion he did not fall in love with in Italy years before. Mrs. Bowen, now a widow, invites Colville to visit at her home. Colville meets Mrs. Bowen's thirteen-year-old daughter, Effie, who quickly becomes fond of him, as well as Imogene Graham, a twenty-year-old American woman Mrs. Bowen is chaperoning.

Colville spends many pleasant days and evenings with Mrs. Bowen, Imogene, and Effie. At first, Imogene regards him as an old man, since he is twice her age, but she soon realizes that she enjoys his company much more than that of many men her own age. In an effort to be companionable with her, Colville dances and goes about socially as he did not do for many years. Mrs. Bowen also enjoys Colville's company.

Mrs. Bowen chooses carefully the places where she and her charges go. During the carnival season, she permits Colville to take them all to a masked ball. At the ball, little Effie becomes ill and has to be taken home unexpectedly. As a result, Imogene and Colville spend much of the evening together unchaperoned. They begin to realize their affection for each other.

Mrs. Bowen is quick to realize that a love affair is developing between them. She tactfully points out to Imogene the differences between her and the much older man. When she says, rather less tactfully, that she thinks Colville is only trying to be amusing, the girl reports the conversation to

Colville. Hurt, he goes to Mrs. Bowen and talks with her, finally agreeing to her suggestion that for propriety's sake he leave Florence. Because it is a weekend and Colville has insufficient funds to settle his hotel bill, he is forced to wait until the following Monday. By that time, Imogene decides that it is unfair to make him leave the city because of her. When she asks him to stay, he agrees to do so.

A few days later, Colville and Imogene meet accidentally in a public park. They decide that they love each other, and they go back to Mrs. Bowen's residence to tell her that they have decided to be married. Mrs. Bowen, as Imogene's chaperone, tells them she will be forced to write immediately to the girl's parents to inform them of this recent development. The lovers agree to her plan and promise to say nothing about an official engagement until they hear from Imogene's parents. Imogene warns her chaperone, however, that she will marry Colville even without her parents' consent.

While they await word from America, a young minister named Morton, who is also in love with Imogene, returns to Florence. Both Colville and Mrs. Bowen wish to tell the young man the state of affairs, but the girl refuses to permit it. Finally, word comes from Imogene's parents. Her mother will sail for Europe to see Colville for herself before giving her decision.

During the intervening days before Mrs. Graham's arrival, the four—Mrs. Bowen, Mr. Morton, Imogene, and Colville—go on an excursion to see the Etruscan ruins in Fiesole. At one point, Colville and the young minister walk a short distance beside the carriage. A peasant driving a band of sheep comes over the brow of a hill, frightening the horses, who begin to back the carriage dangerously close to a precipitous drop at the side of the road. The two men rescue the women from the carriage. While Mr. Morton takes Imogene from the vehicle, Colville runs to the horses' heads to try to hold them. When his hand catches in the curb strap, he is dragged with the team when the carriage plunges over the edge of the road.

For two weeks, Colville lies very ill. When he is finally

able to have visitors, Imogene's mother comes to see him and tells him she is taking her daughter back to America immediately. She feels that Colville acts like a gentleman, but she tells him that her daughter is not really in love with him, although she thinks too much of him to break the engagement. Colville is stricken but perceives that Imogene's departure is the only answer to the situation. After her mother leaves, Imogene comes into the sickroom and bids Colville a hasty good-bye.

Some time later, Mrs. Bowen and Colville talk over the affair. During the conversation, they admit that they love each other, but Mrs. Bowen refuses to marry Colville because of the embarrassing position in which she was placed during his affair with Imogene. She hated herself the whole time she tried to prevent the affair because, although she hoped she could see the situation objectively, she always feared that her actions and thinking had been colored by her feeling for Colville.

Little Effie, having formed a very strong attachment for Colville, refuses to hear of his departure. Within a few months, under the influence of their mutual love and Effie's attitude toward her mother's suitor, Mrs. Bowen reconciles to a marriage. They are married quietly and then move to Rome, where no one who knows them can spread gossip about the affair with Imogene. Not long after their marriage, they hear that Mr. Morton, who was deeply in love with Imogene, was appointed to a church in a community near Buffalo, where the Grahams live. Both Mr. and Mrs. Colville hope that he and Imogene Graham will make a match of their own.

Critical Evaluation:

Indian Summer reflects an American realist's interest in the phenomenon of the surge of Americans who traveled abroad after the Civil War. Both of the other major novelists with whom William Dean Howells is usually bracketed had already explored this theme, Mark Twain hilariously in *The Innocents Abroad* (1869) and Henry James with great sophistication in a series of novels and tales beginning with *The American* (1876-1877).

In many ways, Howells, who was one of the first American critics to recognize the genius of Twain and James, occupies a position between them. *Indian Summer*, like *The Innocents Abroad*, although in a much less satirical and pointed way, registers the humorous aspects of American tourists' and expatriates' experiences in Europe. Howells's naïve young Americans face dangers that they realize only dimly, if at all, but, unlike their Jamesian equivalents, they usually manage to avoid catastrophes. Indeed, Imogene Graham's main danger in Florence is the possibility of her marrying another American—the well-intentioned but plainly inappropriate Colville.

Howells uses the Italian setting to provide a backdrop for his novel, but he is less interested in the cultural collisions between American innocents and European predators than in the uneasy relationship between two Americans—a man in his Indian summer and a woman in the early spring of her adulthood—and a man's slowly developing relationship with a woman near his age. This second relationship is complicated by the conflict between her love for him and her obligations as Imogene Graham's chaperone. Imogene is always referred to, not unjustifiably, as a "girl." She is only slightly more mature than James's Daisy Miller. It is because she is a beauty living in the city where Colville had fallen in love seventeen years earlier that she becomes the object of his romantic yearnings. The reader soon recognizes Colville's folly in pursuing her and not Lina Bowen, a mature and still beautiful woman much better suited to Colville at this stage of his life.

Though Howells's hero is foolish, he is basically a gentleman, courtly in a lighthearted way and eager to please not only Imogene but Mrs. Bowen and her daughter Effie. He is witty, self-effacing, kind, and attentive to them all but, of course, most attentive to Imogene. He has reached the dangerous age of forty-one and looks even older. Never having been a handsome man, he is now bordering on corpulence. Though painfully conscious of his physical defects in the eyes of one as young as Imogene, he dares to hope that she may prefer him to the young men who inevitably flock about her. Thus Howells makes Colville a character study in affable, civilized, well-meaning illusion.

The author guards against the possibility that the reader (and for that matter Colville himself) might take him too seriously. Colville is described as having spent years as editor of a newspaper in a midwestern town called Des Vaches (the cows). The name of the paper, *Democrat Republican*, suggests a comic political irresoluteness. Colville, who trained to be an architect, jokes sarcastically about his limited success in journalism and in life to date.

Colville converses with Mrs. Bowen on such topics as "American girlhood," a subject that Howells lightly implies has by that time become an old literary standby, especially among Americans abroad who have the opportunity to compare it to the more socially constrained European variety of girlhood. At one point, Colville and an acquaintance compare themselves with characters in a novel, "one of Mr. James's," Colville offers; the woman counters by mentioning Howells as more appropriate, though in his novels "nothing happens." In such ways Howells sets a light tone that advises the reader that the plot, built around a sophisticated middle-aged man pursuing an unformed twenty-year-old woman, will, though it is serious, not end tragically like James's *Daisy Miller* (1878), in which an older man tries unavailingly to protect the young female from unsuspected peril abroad.

Imogene naturally considers Colville old, but she is romantic enough to be touched by his attention to her and eventually to persuade herself to accept him as a fiancé. As a dedicated foe of the romantic outlook, which in his opinion spoiled most fiction after the time of Jane Austen, Howells tries to reveal the folly of the planned match. He accomplishes this by contradicting his own insistence that in his fiction "nothing happens," by which he means an avoidance of spectacular and purely adventitious incidents. The sight of the injured Colville after he attempts to perform heroically jolts Imogene into an awareness that not love but pity led her to accept his proposal. She also feels guilty that she has somehow seduced an essentially honorable man and is now ready to value the attentions of Mr. Morton, a suitor much closer to her own age.

Howells's fictional worlds are marked neither by Jamesian tragedy nor by Twain's broad comedy; *Indian Summer* is, rather, an ironic comedy of manners in which the characters embroil themselves in troublesome social situations that require them to perceive and work out morally satisfactory solutions. Colville, Imogene, and Mrs. Bowen must struggle to determine the decent way out of the posited dilemma. Although *Indian Summer* does not possess the larger social significance of Howells's earlier *The Rise of Silas Lapham* (1885) or his later *A Hazard of New Fortunes* (1889), it is one of his most finely wrought studies of moral responsibility in the personal lives of deftly delineated central characters.

"Critical Evaluation" by Robert P. Ellis

Further Reading

Eble, Kenneth. *William Dean Howells*. 2d ed. Boston: Twayne, 1982. A chronological assessment of Howells's fiction. In the chapter focusing on *Indian Summer* and the 1888 novel *April Hopes*, Eble ranks the former among Howells's most successful dramatizations of the folly of a romantic and sentimental outlook.

Goodman, Susan, and Carl Dawson. *William Dean Howells: A Writer's Life*. Berkeley: University of California Press, 2005. Broad and compelling biography providing a comprehensive account of Howells's life and work. Among other topics, the biographers discuss Howells's friendships with and support of contemporary writers and his significance in American letters. Includes illustrations and bibliography.

Howe, Patricia. "William Dean Howells's *Indian Summer* and Theodor Fontane's *Effi Briest*: Forms and Phases of the Realistic Novel." *Modern Language Review* 102, no. 1 (January, 2007): 125-138. Compares the two novels and their authors' different conceptions of realism.

Howells, William Dean. *Indian Summer*. Vol. 11 in *A Selected Edition of William Dean Howells*. Bloomington: Indiana University Press, 1971. This edition of the novel contains an introduction and notes by Scott Bennett, who counters the often expressed view of *Indian Summer* as an exercise in nostalgia and argues that the novel reflects Howells's full artistic maturity.

Stratman, Gregory J. *Speaking for Howells: Charting the Dean's Career Through the Language of His Characters*. Lanham, Md.: University Press of America, 2001. Analyzes Howells's interest in language, focusing on the language of his characters and his use of literary dialect. Stratman argues that Howells's use of and writing about language demonstrate how his career moved in a circular path, from Romanticism to realism and back to Romanticism.

Wagenknecht, Edward. *William Dean Howells: The Friendly Eye*. New York: Oxford University Press, 1969. No sustained discussion of *Indian Summer* but shrewd observations on the novel in many references. Wagenknecht notes, for example, that the novel contradicts Howells's critical disapproval of violence in fiction by resolving the hero's love affair through the medium of a carriage accident.

Woodress, James J., Jr. *Howells and Italy*. New York: Greenwood Press, 1952. Assesses *Indian Summer* as a neatly plotted minor masterpiece, though unrepresentative of Howells's work generally. Woodress emphasizes the correlation between Howells's and his own Italian experiences, as well as his skill at evoking the Italian setting in *Indian Summer*.

Wright, Nathalia. *American Novelists in Italy: The Discoverers—Allston to James*. Philadelphia: University of Pennsylvania Press, 1965. Discusses a succession of nineteenth century novelists and gives considerable attention to Howells's Italian novels. Views *Indian Summer* as reflecting his tendency to emphasize that Europe exerted a more pernicious influence on American men than on American women.

Indiana

Author: George Sand (1804-1876)
First published: 1832 (English translation, 1833)
Type of work: Novel
Type of plot: Sentimental
Time of plot: Early nineteenth century
Locale: France

Principal characters:
INDIANA, a young Creole
MONSIEUR DELMARE, her husband
NOUN, her foster sister and maid
RODOLPHE BROWN or SIR RALPH, Indiana's cousin
RAYMON DE RAMIÈRE, her lover

The Story:

Indiana is married to pompous, quick-tempered Monsieur Delmare, a retired army officer no longer young. Loyal to her suspicious and jealous husband, Indiana lives a discontented, uneventful life. Her cousin, Sir Ralph Brown, himself unhappy and frustrated, is her only companion. Although Delmare keeps a watchful eye over the young couple, there is nothing improper in the relationship between them. As a matter of fact, Sir Ralph secures the good graces of Delmare, and he is accepted as one of the household. If not an intimate friend, he is at least a close companion. Indiana is as reserved in her behavior toward Sir Ralph as she is toward her husband, but to a close observer it is apparent that in a friendly, inarticulate manner, Sir Ralph is fond of Indiana.

The submerged tensions of the household erupt one night when someone is discovered scaling the garden wall and entering the grounds of the estate. Delmare rushes out and fires in the darkness at the intruder. When the wounded prowler is brought into the house, he reveals himself as Raymon de Ramière, a young man who, he maintains, wishes to see Delmare regarding his manufacturing enterprise. De Ramière further explains that his brother has a similar business in another part of the country, and that he will profit from Delmare's information.

Delmare's suspicions dissolve. He did not notice the behavior of Noun, Indiana's friend and maid. Noun became extremely agitated at the entrance of de Ramière, a fact that nobody noticed in the excitement. She knows that de Ramière came to the estate not to see Delmare on business but to keep a rendezvous with her. Noun has been his mistress for some time. Once in the house, however, he is immediately attracted to Indiana, especially because he is already tiring of Noun.

De Ramière systematically begins his suit for Indiana's affections, and to that end, he enlists the aid of both his mother and Indiana's aunt. Before long, Indiana begins to reciprocate his attentions, and the affair becomes the subject of much discussion in Parisian salons. Delmare remains ignorant of the gossip. Despite de Ramière's urgent avowals and protestations, however, Indiana refuses to yield herself to

him because she prefers a pure and spiritual love. Upset by her refusals, de Ramière contracts a fever that keeps him confined to his bed for several days. Indiana is strongly affected as well and experiences several spells of swooning.

One night, impatient to achieve his desire, de Ramière impetuously enters the Delmare house. Indiana is away, but Noun is there awaiting the return of her mistress. The two meet in Indiana's room, and Noun, as passionate as ever, entices the young man to surrender. When Indiana returns, Noun escapes, leaving de Ramière to face her mistress alone. Indiana, disturbed to find her suitor in her room, orders him to leave before his presence is discovered.

A short time later, Noun's body is discovered floating in a nearby stream. Pregnant, she took her life because of de Ramière's refusal to marry her or even continue their relationship. Indiana is brokenhearted at the death of her maid, and de Ramière is greatly perturbed. He is tired of his pursuit of Indiana and determines to forget her. One night, Indiana, having decided at last to become his mistress, goes to his rooms. Learning that he is not at home, she waits until he returns at dawn. Then she offers herself to him. Unfortunately, while they are talking, dawn breaks. Compromised by her presence in de Ramière's rooms at that hour, Indiana returns to her home, where Delmare, agitated by the discovery of her absence, receives her with cold suspicion.

Soon afterward, Delmare suffers business reverses and faces complete ruin. Indiana contritely goes with him to the Isle of Bourbon, where he hopes to make another fortune. Unhappy in her new home, she lives only for the letters de Ramière writes her. At last, she decides to leave Delmare and arranges for her secret passage back to France. On her arrival in Paris, she learns that fickle de Ramière recently married.

Indiana for weeks lives a miserable existence. Penniless and starving, she decides to die. When she and Sir Ralph, who followed her to Paris, are strangely reunited, they agree to commit suicide by drowning. At the last minute, however, they change their minds. Moved by Sir Ralph's devotion, Indiana realizes that he is the man she truly loves. Together they forsake civilization and live as recluses, away from all people and society, but satisfied and happy at last.

Critical Evaluation:

George Sand's *Indiana* presents the story of a woman fighting against the oppressions of her society, a woman challenging, as Sand called it in her 1842 preface to the novel, "the false relationship between the sexes." Through this theme, Sand explores a spectrum of issues touched by this struggle—individualism, duty, honor, love, jealousy, fear, falsehood, and truth.

When the public was first introduced to the novel in 1832, it provoked controversy over Sand's criticism of the strictures of traditional roles of men and women, particularly those of husbands and wives. That controversy earned Sand instant fame. She was praised and condemned for her commentary on society's injustices. Some called the novel treacherous for threatening the stability of traditional institutions; others marveled at its capacity to dramatize the struggle and eventual triumph of a single soul fighting against the arbitrary whims of an oppressive husband and the glaring hypocrisies of an unjust society. Sand herself noted that she, as "a young author—a mere neophyte in the world of social ideas, one whose literary and philosophical equipment consisted of a little imagination, a bit of courage, and a love of truth—was thus endowed with a weighty role."

Sand's own personal rebellions—her decision to flee her husband to live a bohemian life in Paris, her preference for men's clothing, her active participation in renowned literary circles, and her liberated sexual attitudes—became as noted as her novels. She was an active member of the literary community in Paris and a close friend to such influential figures as Honoré de Balzac, Alfred de Musset, Eugene Delacroix, Frédéric Chopin, Franz Liszt, and Gustave Flaubert.

Indiana is a quest for the happiness that is possible only through liberty and equality, an assertion of the primacy of the individual over the demands of society. Contrary to the novel's crusade for equality among the sexes, however, is its presentation of women; Sand's depiction of women as nurturers bound by a duty to love and to serve is inconsistent with the ideal of true independence. Her pleas for equality are irreconcilable with her views on the course a woman's life must necessarily take. Sand asserts that women have a fundamentally different temperament than men and that this feminine temperament predisposes them to certain roles. The capacity for boundless love and devotion are, to Sand, distinguishing aspects of what makes a woman noble. A woman's outlet for such nobility is, of course, as mother,

wife, nurse, companion—roles in which a woman's life is conceptualized primarily in terms of her relationship to men.

At the heart of Indiana's struggle is the search for truth. In order for Indiana to develop the spirit of individualism necessary to cast aside the forces that chain her, she must first confront society's values and identify its failings. Indiana refuses to withstand the continued oppression of her married life and leaves her husband. Believing in the integrity of Raymon de Ramière's professions of love, despite evidence to the contrary, she runs to him. She realizes her error when she is confronted with the indisputable fact that his words of love are but momentary fancies, created as much to flatter his own vanity as to win her favor. In the preface to the 1832 edition of *Indiana*, Sand observed that "[de Ramière] is the false reason, the false morality, by which society is governed; the world considers him an honorable man because the world does not examine things closely enough to see them clearly."

Each of the three main male characters represents a prevailing political force at the time of the novel's publication. Monsieur Delmare clings fiercely to his Napoleonic heritage; Sir Ralph supports a democratic society where all are equal under the law; and de Ramière upholds the supremacy of post-Napoleonic aristocracy. Sand's endorsement of a democratic society is evident throughout the novel. As her career as a writer progressed, the importance of politics in her work increased.

As with many of the novels of the early nineteenth century Romantics, the characters' motivations are grounded in psychology. Indiana's desperate urge to liberate herself from the oppressions of her position, Sir Ralph's self-imposed loneliness, Delmare's excessive violence, and de Ramière's compulsive need for romantic conquest illustrate how the culminating forces of social classes, gender roles, personal experiences, and individual judgments influence each character's fundamental beliefs. The parallels between Indiana and Noun, her maid and foster sister, recount the conflict-ridden evolution of Indiana's own character. Sand's use of double characters enables her to examine a duality common to Western culture; the high-born, chaste, and spiritual Indiana contrasts with the low-born, sensual, and earthly Noun. As Indiana begins her journey toward self-fulfillment, Noun dies, and Indiana begins to integrate the parallel characteristics. Noun's death after being betrayed by de Ramière, the man who teaches Indiana a harsh lesson in love, portends the tumultuous passage that Indiana must make before she gains the independence, sexual confidence, and clarity of judgment that will enable her to achieve the happiness she seeks.

The conclusion of the novel reaffirms the individual's responsibility for his or her life and happiness. Indiana realizes that she must make her own decisions if she is to be truly happy and to liberate herself from her abusive husband to join de Ramière. De Ramière's ambivalence toward her devotion leads her to recognize the cruel facade with which society has replaced honor. Those lessons lead Indiana and Sir Ralph to flee to a remote cottage to live out their days in peaceful happiness. As *Indiana* closes, Sir Ralph concludes that "society has no right to demand anything from the person who demands nothing from it" and advises one to "respect [society's] laws if they protect you, accept its judgments if they seem fair—but if someday society slanders and spurns you, have enough self-respect and pride to do without it."

"Critical Evaluation" by H. C. Aubrey

Further Reading

Crecelius, Kathryn J. *Family Romances: George Sand's Early Novels*. Bloomington: Indiana University Press, 1987. Chronicles the early period of Sand's literary career, when her thematic focus was directed toward rebellion against the oppression of traditional marriage. Offers criticism and interpretation of *Indiana*; considers the work in the context of other novels from this period in Sand's career.

Datlof, Natalie, Jeanne Fuchs, and David A. Powell, eds. *The World of George Sand*. New York: Greenwood Press, 1991. Contains papers presented at the Seventh International George Sand Conference at Hofstra University in 1986. A number of articles will prove useful to *Indiana* scholars, such as Marilyn Yalom's "George Sand's Poetics of Autobiography" and Margaret E. Ward and Karen Storz's "Fanny Lewald and George Sand: *Eine Lebensfrage* and *Indiana*."

Dickenson, Donna. *George Sand: A Brave Man, the Most Womanly Woman*. New York: St. Martin's Press, 1988. Offers insight into Sand's work, her life as an author, and her struggle as a woman attaining literary success in a primarily male field. Examines her open rejection of women's roles and discusses her noted rebellions and successes.

Eisler, Benita. *Naked in the Marketplace: The Lives of George Sand*. New York: Basic Books, 2006. Drawing on Sand's substantial body of correspondence, Eisler explores the complicated personality of the radical nineteenth century feminist. This biography focuses especially on Sand's impressively active and lengthy love life and its impact on her literary output.

Goodwin-Jones, Robert. *Romantic Vision: The Novels of George Sand*. Birmingham, Ala.: Summa, 1995. A thematic analysis of about forty of Sand's novels, including *Indiana*. Includes an introductory discussion of Sand as a novelist.

Harkness, Nigel. *Men of Their Words: The Poetics of Masculinity in George Sand's Fiction*. London: Legenda/Modern Humanities Research Association, 2007. Harkness examines questions of masculinity in Sand's fiction within the context of the nineteenth century French novel, describing how her novels repeatedly depict the connection of masculinity, power, and language.

Massardier-Kenney, Françoise. *Gender in the Fiction of George Sand*. Atlanta: Rodopi, 2000. Argues that Sand's novels express a complex and extremely modern conception of gender, in which she questions prevalent patriarchal modes of discourse and redefines masculinity and femininity.

Naginski, Isabelle Hoog. *George Sand: Writing for Her Life*. New Brunswick, N.J.: Rutgers University Press, 1991. This book avoids the biographical approach common to Sand criticism. It identifies four specific periods of Sand's writing and examines each, focusing on common themes rather than on a detailed analysis of each work.

Sand, George. *Story of My Life: The Autobiography of George Sand—A Group Translation*. Edited and translated by Thelma Jurgrau. Albany: State University of New York Press, 1991. Offers a wealth of insight into the author's life and work. A critical introduction by Thelma Jurgrau and a historical introduction by Walter D. Gray provide insightful commentaries that set the context of Sand's autobiography.

Schor, Naomi. *George Sand and Idealism*. New York: Columbia University Press, 1993. An examination of feminism and idealism in Sand's novels. Explores Sand's Romanticism; considers the influence of society and politics on her work.

The Informer

Author: Liam O'Flaherty (1896-1984)
First published: 1925
Type of work: Novel
Type of plot: Psychological realism
Time of plot: 1920's
Locale: Dublin

Principal characters:
FRANCIS JOSEPH MCPHILLIP, a political murderer
GYPO NOLAN, the informer
DAN GALLAGHER, a revolutionist
KATIE FOX, a prostitute

The Story:

Shabbily dressed, Francis McPhillip comes to the door of the public lodging house. With the caution born of necessity, he waits in the doorway until he is sure he is not being followed, keeping his hand inside his raincoat to feel the reassuring butt of his pistol. For six months, he has been a hunted man, hiding out in the wild mountains.

In October, Francis had killed the secretary of the Farmers' Union. His orders from the revolutionary organization were to use his gun only if necessary; after the killing, the organization disavowed his act and expelled him. A lone fugitive since then, he is back in Dublin to see his family.

Francis searches among the public rooms crowded with Dublin's poor. In the dining room, he finds the man he wants to see: Gypo Nolan. Gypo is eating from a huge plate of cabbage and bacon he stole from a locker. Francis sits down and inquires hoarsely of Gypo if the police are still watching his parents' house. At first, Gypo only grunts in response, then he says he thinks the coast is clear. After eating voraciously from Gypo's plate, Francis slips away.

Gypo thinks stolidly of his former companion in the organization, then he reflects bitterly on his empty pockets and on the fact that he cannot buy a bed that night. He tries to link up the two facts, but Gypo thinks only with great difficulty. He was Francis's companion at the time of the murder, and the organization expelled him, too. Without Francis and his agile brain, Gypo is unable to make plans. Now, finally, an idea comes to him. He goes to the police station and tells the officers where they can find Francis. He receives twenty pounds for his information. Shortly afterward, when police officers surround his father's house, Francis shoots himself.

In a public house, Gypo meets Katie Fox, a prostitute who takes care of him occasionally when he is destitute. He buys her a few glasses of gin and tells her he has no need of her bed that night. She is suspicious because he has money and accuses him of robbing a church. During the quarrel, she accidentally lets drop the word "informer." Gypo is startled. He is glad to leave her and go out in the night.

To keep up appearances, Gypo goes to the McPhillip house. He quarrels with Francis's father, who blames him for the wild life his son led, but Francis's mother and his sister, Mary, praise Gypo for his visit of sympathy. As he leaves, he gives Mrs. McPhillip four silver coins.

Bartly, an organization member sent out to bring Gypo in, follows him. When he makes a taunting reference to the coins Gypo gave Francis's mother, Gypo chokes Bartly, who is saved only by the arrival of a friend who is armed. By dint of threats and persuasion, Gypo is led to the organization headquarters, where he meets Dan Gallagher, the revolutionists' feared and respected leader.

Because of his stupidity and his great strength, Gypo has no fear of men or guns, but Dan is intelligent and soon overcomes Gypo's hostility. If Gypo can give them a lead on the person who informed the police of Francis's return, he will be taken back into the organization. Dan brings out a bottle and gives Gypo several drinks. Under the influence of the liquor, Gypo concocts a story that Rat Mulligan had a grudge against Francis for betraying his sister and that he saw Rat following Francis away from the lodging house. Dan is skeptical but sends for Rat and orders Gypo to appear for the hearing that night at one-thirty.

Followed by Bartly, his shadow, Gypo goes out confidently. In a street fight, he knocks out a policeman from sheer exuberance. Trailed by an admiring rabble, he goes to a lunch stand and buys food for all of his admirers. In the confusion, he slips away from Bartly.

Gypo is elated. He has money, he is safe, and he will be back in the organization. He goes to a superior brothel and spends money recklessly. A well-dressed woman with a scar on her face stays aloof. She refuses Gypo's advances, saying she is the wife of an army officer and wants to get back to London. Gypo gives her what she needs for the fare and accepts the companionship of another girl, Maggie. Bartly finds him with her and reminds him of the inquiry. Gypo gives Maggie a pound to take to Katie and follows Bartly willingly.

Dan goes to the McPhillip house to take the family's statements. He briefly makes love to Mary and induces her to accompany him to the inquiry, a kangaroo court held in the wine cellar of a ruined house. Dan acts as prosecutor, and three of his men are judges.

When Rat Mulligan is questioned, it becomes clear that he could not possibly have been the informer. When Gypo is brought in, Dan makes a convincing case that Gypo knew where Francis was going, left the lodging house at the right time, and was squandering money all night. At last, Gypo breaks down and confesses. Dan orders him imprisoned in a cellar room with armed guards at the door.

Much earlier, Francis had discussed with Gypo how to get out of the cell. In the ceiling is a trapdoor covered with dirt. Exerting his great strength, Gypo seizes the iron ring with his hands and with his legs forces up both the trapdoor and the earth covering it. The alerted guards shoot at him as he scrambles out, but he escapes. Dan is terrified that Gypo will go to the police and that the organization will be broken up. Mary is astonished to see how weak Dan is. When he pulls himself together, however, he sends agents to cover the roads leading out of the area, and Gypo is trapped.

Every time Gypo tries to leave the slum district, he finds waiting guards. His only refuge is Katie's room. She lets him stay, and he thankfully falls into brutish sleep. Somehow, Katie begins to think of her own lost and vicious life, and she identifies her misery with Gypo's. With a notion that she will be canonized, she creeps off to inform the organization of Gypo's hiding place.

As four armed men close in on him, Gypo awakens just in time to fight them off. He cripples two of them in a struggle on the stairs, but he is wounded several times as he runs to escape execution.

Gypo becomes weaker as he flees. Dan sees him but shrugs as he turns away. He knows the informer is done for. In growing confusion, Gypo goes into a church where early mass is being celebrated. With dimming vision, he makes out the figure of Mrs. McPhillip. He falls in front of her seat and confesses his treachery. When she forgives him, Gypo stands up and in a loud voice calls to Francis about the forgiveness from his mother. With a gurgle, he falls forward and shivers as blood gushes from his mouth.

Critical Evaluation:

This novel is set in Ireland during the 1920's in a period when the Irish Republican Army (IRA) was dormant after its civil conflict with the Free State. Several isolated bands of rebels—units of the IRA and communists—still waged a quasi-war. Gypo Nolan belongs to one of these communist

groups, but this is not a story about Irish politics or about the way rebels deal with informers. Liam O'Flaherty keeps Gypo's politics vague partly because Gypo himself understands them so vaguely and partly because the author wishes to focus his attention, and the reader's, on the fact of Gypo's abandonment. The novel focuses on the nature and progress of Gypo's torment.

O'Flaherty is recognized as one of the central figures of the literary movement called the Irish Renaissance. Seán O'Faoláin believed that O'Flaherty shared center stage in this period with James Joyce. One of his claims to this honor is *The Informer*, which some critics consider the most universal and least provincial of O'Flaherty's novels. More than any other of his works, it is a novel about humanity and the human condition.

O'Flaherty focuses on the condition of anxiety. The fact that Gypo is an informer is less important than the fact that he is cut off from human society, which O'Flaherty considers to be the state of all people to a greater or lesser degree. In this novel, he explores the pain of this condition and describes it from the point of view of an observer, one outside the soul. The same existential loneliness is described internally, as it were from inside the soul, in one of O'Flaherty's earlier novels, *The Black Soul* (1924), which is the most autobiographical of all his works. He put a great deal of his own loneliness and suffering into the characterizations of that work, to which *The Informer* can best be understood as a companion piece. The two novels explore the same problem in different ways.

O'Flaherty skillfully describes things to create atmosphere, and he deepens the reader's understanding of loneliness by showing the misery of Gypo's surroundings. With deft strokes, O'Flaherty paints the environment in which Gypo, Dan Gallagher, and the other characters operate. By using vivid words, he is able to make settings, rooms, household objects, trolley tracks, and paper packages speak volumes. Not only does the writer conjure up the scenes in the mind's eye of the reader, but also he uses the same scenes to illuminate the lives, thoughts, and very souls of the characters. It has been said that O'Flaherty writes more for the eye than for the ear, and this may be evident in the success of film versions of the novel. In the motion pictures, as in the book, inanimate objects and scenes of action serve to intensify and illuminate the spiritual lives of the main characters. That Gypo is a miserable man becomes clearer when he is shown moving in his miserable world, a world O'Flaherty brings alive for the reader.

One of the underlying themes in the book, which operates on several levels, is that of parallels with the New Testament.

Gypo can be understood in these terms as a Judas figure. This is explicit in the final scene, when Gypo, dying, asks Francis McPhillip's mother to forgive him. She does so because he did not know what he was doing. Gypo turns in his friend to the authorities for a sum of money, and, like Judas, he learns that this betrayal cuts him off from human society. The betrayal does not bring any sort of happiness: both Gypo and Judas throw the money away and die.

O'Flaherty implies that no one can find happiness when cut off from humanity. This is the tragedy of Gypo, Judas Iscariot, and everyone who by his or her actions severs connections to others. Gypo manages to do some good with the money, but in the end he wastes it all and is left with only loneliness.

Gypo's lack of intelligence is the immediate cause of his downfall, although on a deeper level it is his human nature that causes him to be separated from society. In an amazing example of literary skill, O'Flaherty creates sympathy for the informer in the course of the novel by allowing the reader to understand gradually that Gypo is only a child, making childish and inexperienced choices. Gypo is only incidentally a traitor; he is primarily Everyman. O'Flaherty makes this clear by depicting Gypo in his humanity, a literary achievement that is one of the great strengths of O'Flaherty's art.

"Critical Evaluation" by Glenn M. Edwards

Further Reading

Costello, Peter. "Land and Liam O' Flaherty." In *Famine, Land, and Culture in Ireland*, edited by Carla King. Dublin: University College Dublin Press, 2000. Examines the influence of the land in O'Flaherty's fiction.

Donoghue, Denis. Preface to *The Informer*, by Liam O'Flaherty. New York: Harcourt Brace Jovanovich, 1980. In this scholarly introduction to *The Informer*, the leading Irish literary critic of his generation discusses the historical and cultural conditions from which the novel emerged as well as its place in the O'Flaherty canon. Also refers to O'Flaherty's sense of language and to the novel's genre.

Doyle, Paul A. *Liam O'Flaherty*. New York: Twayne, 1971. An introductory survey of the wide range of O'Flaherty's writings. In the chapter devoted to *The Informer*, Doyle notes the novel's methods of representing the atmosphere of a newly independent Ireland. Critical discussion focuses mainly on the novel's characterization. Contains a bibliography of primary and secondary sources.

Friberg, Hedda. *An Old Order and a New: The Split World of Liam O'Flaherty's Novels*. Uppsala, Sweden: Uppsala University Press, 1996. Analyzes the individual novels, with a chapter devoted to *The Informer*. Includes discussion of the novels' literary contexts and critical responses.

O'Brien, James H. *Liam O'Flaherty*. Lewisburg, Pa.: Bucknell University Press, 1973. A brief introductory survey that concentrates on O'Flaherty's fiction, particularly his novels. Provides a biographical sketch as well as a chronology and a bibliography. Discussion of *The Informer* is included in a chapter devoted to O'Flaherty's war novels and focuses on the work's preoccupation with its protagonist.

Sheeran, Patrick F. *"The Informer."* Cork, Ireland: Cork University Press in association with the Film Institute of Ireland, 2002. Calls *The Informer* a "mythogenic text" that readily lends itself to film adaptations and examines the various film versions of the book. Describes how O'Flaherty wrote the novel with an awareness of the silent films of his day; demonstrates O'Flaherty's familiarity with the visual language of melodrama and silent cinema.

_____. *The Novels of Liam O'Flaherty: A Study in Romantic Realism*. Dublin: Wolfhound Press, 1976. Contains valuable information about O'Flaherty's cultural and personal background and its relevance to his major works. Includes a detailed account of the genesis of *The Informer* and an analysis of its cinematic dimension.

Zneimer, John. *The Literary Vision of Liam O'Flaherty*. Syracuse, N.Y.: Syracuse University Press, 1970. Remains one of the most systematic overviews of O'Flaherty's work. Focuses on the darker side of O'Flaherty's imagination and provides information on the complicated genesis of *The Informer* and the author's attitude to the novel. Critical analysis is largely devoted to the work's psychological and spiritual dimensions.

The Inheritors

Author: William Golding (1911-1993)
First published: 1955
Type of work: Novel
Type of plot: Allegory
Time of plot: Paleolithic period
Locale: A mountainous, wooded countryside not far
   from the sea

Principal characters:
MAL, the old leader
THE OLD WOMAN
HA, the wisest of the younger people
NIL, a young mother
THE NEW ONE, Nil's baby
LOK, the people's clown
FA, a young woman
LIKU, a child
MARLAN, the leader, called "the old man"
TUAMI, his successor
VIVANI, Marlan's woman, called "the fat woman"
TANAKIL, a child
TWAL, Tanakil's mother, a servant

The Story:

Each spring, Mal leads his small tribe, the last of their kind, from their winter quarters by the sea to a terrace and overhang above a waterfall, which is their summer home. The way to their summer homeland leads over a river that divides around a rocky island. The people fear water and never consider going to the island. When they discover that the log by which they always cross the river disappeared, they are confused until Mal imagines, in the form of a picture, a past time when wise members of the group took the original log and used it to bridge the water. These pictures of the imagination are an embryonic thought process: They serve as memories and ideas. The pictures are rarely consecutive and fade as soon as the need for them passes because they are an instinctual and not a rational function. The people can share their pictures without words or express them in simple sentences.

The people retain the strong senses of animals, but they also develop their own human rituals concerned with food, fire, and burial. The old woman always carries the fire from the winter to the summer home. When women arrive and the smell of smoke comes to Lok from the island, he is bemused and, tricked by his senses into following the familiar scent, he almost falls into the river. The rest of the people do not catch the faint scent, so Lok cannot communicate his picture. This second indication that something is changed is forgotten in the people's eager journey to the security of the overhang. Lok almost recaptures his experience while guarding the people that night, but the picture fades before he can fully recapture it.

The people's failure to retain ideas not relevant to day-to-day life makes their survival impossible when faced with the challenge of the others. Their lack of the knowledge of evil also makes them powerless to combat it. This is one of the main themes of the novel. When Ha disappears, although the people can tell by the scent that he encountered another, their emotions are grief at the loss rather than abiding fear. What happens next reveals Golding's grim assertion that the meek do not inherit the earth.

After Mal's death and Ha's disappearance, Lok is the only surviving adult male; it is his task to seek out the others. These others are true *Homo sapiens*, with the power of reason. Their senses are weaker and their artifacts far more sophisticated than the people's. They use animal skins for covering, and they have bows and arrows, canoes, and crude alcohol. They also know sexual jealousy. They are near famine because they cannot eat the bulbs, slugs, and fungi that sustain the people (who never kill for food) and because hunting is poor.

When the others capture Liku and the New One on the people's side of the river, Lok hears Liku's screams and tries to reach her. He thus exposes himself to the others' arrows. These weapons merely interest him, although he senses danger when he smells the poison on the barbed heads. Lok's apprehensions of danger are lulled at various times by the others' obvious hunger and by his sympathy for them.

Finally, only Lok and Fa remain; the old woman is drowned and Nil is slain. Lok rejects Fa's suggestion that they escape and survive. Lok insists on trying to rescue Liku and the New One. The others move their camp from the island to the people's side of the river to hunt for deer. The new camp is made by a hollow tree, where Lok and Fa hide from the others. From this tree, the two Neanderthals witness an incomprehensible day of ritual and night of debauchery that includes, while Lok sleeps, the killing of Liku. The only communication between the people and the others was Liku's growing friendship with Tanakil, a girl of her own age. They were able to exchange names, and Liku fed Tanakil fungus when Tanakil was hungry. This deed, together with the others' need for a sacrifice to make their hunting successful, causes them to kill her.

In an attempt to snatch the New One from the camp, Lok becomes separated from Fa and, believing that she is dead, he mourns for her. Although he believes that he is the last of his people, his hope is still sustained by the presence of the others, and at that moment he reaches his furthest point of comprehension, which he does not have the power to retain. Fa finds Lok again, but during a last effort to recover the New One before the others can take him upstream with them, she is stunned and swept away in the falls. After the final disappearance of Fa and the departure of the others, Lok is alone; his humanity leaves him.

Solitary, Lok reverts to an anthropoid state. In a coda passage before the reversal of viewpoint in the last chapter, the first complete physical description of one of the people partly explains the others' destructive terror. The only human aspect remaining to Lok is the tears on his face as he lies down to die on Mal's grave.

In the final chapter, in a reversal of point of view, the others are named. Tuami is the younger leader. The old man is Marlan; the most important woman, who suckles the New One, is Vivani. As Tuami steers the boat toward the open plains, away from "the devils," he and all the others are overcome by grief and bitterness. Tuami cries out to ask what else they could have done. The people are quite human and understandable; their murderous actions against the Neanderthals are dictated by the twin evils of fear and ignorance. Some grace, however, goes out of their lives forever; their slow-moving boat is a point of darkness between the light of the sky and the water as they flee what they perceive to be devil-infected mountains.

Critical Evaluation:

Like *Lord of the Flies* (1954), *The Two Deaths of Christopher Martin* (1956), and *The Spire* (1964), *The Inheritors* has a setting remote from a reader's own life and civilization. In these isolated settings, William Golding explores humanity's struggle for survival: the struggle with fellow human beings, with the physical environment, and with oneself. Such preoccupations are, in themselves, common to many novels, but one of the distinctive features of Golding's work is that at the

opening of each novel his characters are already at their hour of reckoning. The success of Golding's approach is achieved by an exercise of great imaginative power and the ability to create an environment of great believability, so that what has gone before is apparent through implication in the way the characters react to present circumstance. To the Neanderthal people of *The Inheritors*, the natural, physical world of tree, mountain, river, and rock is the prime reality; when forces alien to their world intrude, Golding begins their story.

In many of his novels, Golding structures the thematic material around specific subtexts, with which his text engages in argument. In this novel, one chief subtext is H. G. Wells's *The Outline of History: Being a Plain History of Life and Mankind* (1920), a book that reflects the social evolution theories of the early twentieth century. Wells's book espouses a fairly uncritical belief in progress and in the inferiority of earlier life-forms and cultures. Golding uses a quotation from the book as an epigraph. In opposition to the sanguine view of progress and of humanity in Wells's book, Golding questions in what way *Homo sapiens* may be considered an improvement on *Homo neanderthalis*. A skeptical reading of the novel might suggest that in no way at all may humanity be considered an improvement on its forebears. The Neanderthals, in Golding's view, appear innocent, with a deep reverence for life, respectful to each other, and unafraid. By contrast, the new people kill, kidnap, indulge in crude drunken rituals, are cannibalistic, and plot assassinations.

There are other subtexts, however, that bring further resonances to the novel. For example, Golding reverses a Wells short story in which Neanderthals kidnap a human baby. The two most significant subtexts after Wells's are John Milton's *Paradise Lost* (1667, 1674) and Joseph Conrad's *Heart of Darkness* (1902). Like Milton, Golding explores the concept of a fall from innocence, and what this fall might be like. In *The Inheritors*, Lok and Fa discover the remains of the new people's mead (fermented honey) and get drunk on it. In *Paradise Lost*, Adam and Eve's fall is marked by a similar drunken state. The new people fall, too, as they experience fear and panic, which destroys their previous confidence in themselves and gives outward reality to the evil that readers, godlike perhaps, have already perceived within them. Conrad's famous novella is echoed in the closing chapter, in which the motif of darkness closing in on the new people, as they sail across a wide expanse of water, appears.

Golding's novels contain theological dimensions. *Free Fall* (1959) in general is one such. More specifically in *The Inheritors*, the gentle and numinous female religion of the Neanderthals is contrasted to the masculine, ritualistic, and brutal religion of the new people. The difference is seen more as an effect than a cause of the two peoples' differences. The cause is never described, but part of it must lie in the new people's technical achievements: They can construct boats, thus losing their fear of water; build huts; and make bows and arrows. The new people have also lost an intimate association with nature, and other living things are seen as hostile, including the Neanderthals. From this hostility springs fear. The new people project their inner fears onto the Neanderthals and in this way construct devil figures out of them. This is a typical Golding theme, that evil lies within, not without, but people have to deal with it by inventing beasts, as in *Lord of the Flies.*

The way in which Fa refuses to let Lok understand that Liku has been cannibalized reflects her horror of the taboo against taking any form of life. Secrecy is thus one response to evil, but a wrong one, since it causes Lok to risk their lives in a continued effort to regain the girl.

Golding also explores primitive psychology, especially the relationship among thought, imagination, and language. Lok is shown discovering the power of similitudes (similes), moving from pictures (mental images) to the beginnings of literary creation (figurative language). Tuami, on the other hand, finds it difficult, in his fear, to keep conscious logical thought and imagination focused: Confusion quickly intrudes. The new people's self-awareness is of a much higher mental order. The Neanderthals' body parts, on the other hand, often move independently of brain control.

Golding's style in *The Inheritors* is marked by self-imposed limitations. He tries to confine himself to the consciousness of his two male protagonists. This is especially noticeable when Lok observes the new people's behavior, most of which is incomprehensible to him. Readers are left to guess what is really happening. The language Golding uses is modern literary language, and a tension is set up between primitive perception and sophisticated vocabulary. Readers see with Lok's eyes and yet read with their own.

Golding sets himself fascinating technical problems. His shifts of perspective are dramatically sudden. One example occurs when Golding moves away from Lok, and readers suddenly see Lok as the new people do, basically an animal. There is a short transition passage in which Golding as narrator keeps his own perspective. Readers have become, however, so deeply sympathetic to the Neanderthals that the final chapter is far too short a space to develop any sympathies for the new people. Indeed, readers are not meant to: They are meant, as in satire, to stay alienated from their own species. Other shifts of perspective stem from the Neanderthals' lack of integration; their disconnections jerk readers back to a consciousness of the continuity of the narrative line.

In the last two chapters, the color symbolism becomes noticeable. The redness of the Neanderthals reflects the setting sun and suggestions of fire as symbol of violent and final destruction. This is contrasted to the color blue, which represents sky, a new day, and therefore hope. Blue also, however, represents the deepening night and the shadows that now surround and threaten the life of the new people. They have truly discovered "the darkness of the world."

"Critical Evaluation" by David Barratt

Further Reading

Dick, Bernard F. *William Golding.* Rev. ed. Boston: Twayne, 1987. The chapter on *The Inheritors* views it primarily in the light of Golding's recurring theme of the Fall. Includes selected bibliography and index.

Gindin, James. *William Golding.* New York: Macmillan, 1988. Contains an excellent introduction and a full yet economic reading of *The Inheritors.* Gindin sees the novel achieving something of myth but ultimately having a unique status of its own. Includes selected bibliography and index.

Kinkead-Weekes, Martin, and Ian Gregor. *William Golding: A Critical Study.* 3d rev. ed. London: Faber, 2002. A new edition of one of the standard critical accounts of Golding that features a biographical sketch by Golding's daughter, Judy Carver. Contains a perceptive essay on *The Inheritors.* Discusses the technical problems facing Golding.

McCarron, Kevin. *William Golding.* 2d rev. ed. Tavistock, England: Northcote House/British Council, 2006. Introductory overview to Golding's life and works. Includes bibliography and index.

Oldsey, Bernard S., and Stanley Weintraub. *The Art of William Golding.* New York: Harcourt, Brace & World, 1965. Early introductory study on Golding, with a chapter on each of the early novels. The chapter on *The Inheritors* focuses on the concept of evolution.

Redpath, Philip. *William Golding: A Structural Reading of His Fiction.* New York: Barnes & Noble, 1986. Takes a structural approach to *The Inheritors,* seeing the novel's structure as circular, moving away from any simplistic good-bad antithesis.

Tiger, Virginia. *William Golding: The Unmoved Target.* New York: Marion Boyars, 2003. An examination of Golding's novels in which Tiger draws upon her conversations and correspondence with the author to describe how these books explore themes of human destiny and vision. Devotes a chapter to an analysis of *The Inheritors.*

The Inspector General

Author: Nikolai Gogol (1809-1852)
First produced: Revizor, 1836 (English translation, 1890)
Type of work: Drama
Type of plot: Satire
Time of plot: Early nineteenth century
Locale: Russia

Principal characters:
ANTON ANTONOVICH SKVOZNIK-DMUKHANOVSKY, mayor of a small provincial town
ANNA, his wife
MARIA, his daughter
IVAN ALEXANDROVICH KHLESTAKOV, a traveler
OSIP, Ivan's servant

The Story:

The mayor of the town, Anton Antonovich, receives a disquieting letter. A friend writes that an inspector is coming to visit the province and particularly his district. The inspector will probably travel incognito. The friend advises the mayor to clean up the town and hide evidence of any bribes that might discredit him. The mayor in haste calls a meeting of the local dignitaries and instructs them how to make a good impression on the official from the capital.

Zemlyanika, the hospital manager, is advised to put clean nightcaps on the patients and take away their strong tobacco for a time. The manager is thoughtful; he always proceeds on the theory that if a patient is going to die, he will die anyway. He decides, however, to clean up both the patients and the hospital and to put up a sign in Latin over each bed to tell the patient's malady.

Lyapkin-Tyapkin, the judge, spends most of his time hunting. He keeps a whip and other sporting equipment in his courtroom, and in the vestibule the porter keeps a flock of geese. His assessor always smells of liquor. Ammos protests that the assessor was injured as a baby and has smelled of brandy ever since. Anton suggests that he eat garlic to cover the smell. Hlopov, the head of the school, is advised to cover up the more obvious foibles of his teachers. The one with a fat face, for instance, always makes horrible grimaces when a visitor comes and pulls his beard under his necktie, and the history teacher jumps on his desk when he describes the Macedonian wars.

Piqued by a recital of their weaknesses, the others turn on the mayor and remind him that he takes monetary bribes and only recently had the wife of a noncommissioned officer flogged. During the wrangle the postmaster comes in to see if they have any news of the inspector's arrival. The mayor advises the postmaster to open all letters in an attempt to discover who the inspector might be and when he will arrive. The advice is superfluous, for the postmaster always reads all the letters anyway.

Two squires of the town, Bobchinsky and Dobchinsky, rush in with exciting news. A mysterious stranger, obviously a high-born gentleman, is at that moment lodging in the local inn, and he has been there a fortnight. His servant let it out that his master is from St. Petersburg. Sure that the stranger is the inspector, the company trembles to think what he might already have learned. They scatter to repair any damage they can.

At the inn Osip lies on his master's bed and ruminates on the peculiarities of gentlefolk. His gentleman is always gambling, always broke, always selling his clothes to get funds. They are stuck in this wretched inn because there is no money to pay their bill. At this point, Ivan Alexandrovich Khlestakov bursts in, loudly calling for supper.

When the waiter is summoned, he insolently refuses to serve Khlestakov until the guest pays his bill. After a long argument, some watery soup and a tough hen are brought, and Khlestakov dines poorly. As the dishes are being removed amid a tussle between Osip and the waiter for the remains of the supper, visitors are announced.

Nervous and apologetic, the mayor stands before Khlestakov's august person. Khlestakov thinks, however, that he is to be put in jail. For a time the conversation is at cross-purposes, but Khlestakov has the nimbler wit and allows the mayor to do most of the talking. When he begins to suspect what the mayor is trying to say, he coolly accepts two hundred rubles to pay his bill, an invitation to stay at the mayor's house, and a nomination as the guest of honor at an official dinner at the hospital.

Anna and Maria are arguing about clothes, as usual, when Dobchinsky rushes in to announce the arrival of the inspector and his fine condescension in coming to stay at their house. Dobchinsky thinks that he is being honest when he assures them their guest is a general. Thrilled at the idea of entertaining a general, the two ladies begin to primp and preen. When the men come in, the mayor tries to impress Khlestakov, thought to be the inspector, by saying that he never plays cards. Khlestakov, playing his role, approves; he especially abhors gambling. Osip snickers at his master's remark, but fortunately he is not noticed. To impress the household

Khlestakov then informs them that he is an author; besides writing for the papers he composes poetry and novels. When he refers casually to his high political connections, his hearers are agog, particularly the ladies. Meanwhile Khlestakov is steadily drinking wine. At last he falls into a drunken sleep in his chair.

With Osip remaining conscious, the mayor tries to pump the servant as to his master's habits and tastes, while the ladies try to find out something about Khlestakov's love life. Since Anton keeps giving him money, Osip obliges by telling many details of his master's place in high society.

Khlestakov is put to bed to sleep off the wine. When he awakens, the dignitaries of the town wait on him one by one. Lyapkin-Tyapkin, the judge, introduces himself and asks for the inspector's orders. Khlestakov carelessly promises to speak well of the judge to his friends and just as carelessly borrows money from his suppliant. The postmaster is impressed with Khlestakov's friendliness and is glad to lend him three hundred rubles. Luka and Artemy are glad to lend the inspector three or four hundred rubles, but Bobchinsky and Dobchinsky together can raise only sixty-five rubles.

When the petitioners leave, Osip begs his master to leave while the pickings are still good. Khlestakov, agreeing that immediate departure might be prudent, sends the servant to make arrangements. Osip wangles the best coach the town can offer. In the meantime several shopkeepers also come in to protest against the mayor, who is making them pay tribute. From them Khlestakov borrows five hundred rubles.

When Maria comes in, Khlestakov is so elated at his successes that he speaks lovingly to her and finally kisses her on the shoulder. The daughter scurries away as her mother comes in, and Khlestakov ogles the older lady, too. The daughter comes back, full of curiosity, and in his confusion Khlestakov proposes marriage to Maria, who accepts him graciously. After writing a letter to a friend, in which he details his humorous adventures, Khlestakov leaves town. He promises, however, to return the next day.

In the morning the mayor and his wife receive the envious congratulations of friends. The ladies, green with envy, assure Maria that she will be a belle in St. Petersburg society. The parents, much taken with the idea, decide that their new son-in-law will insist on taking the whole family to live in the capital. The mayor is sure that he will be made a general at least. At that moment the postmaster arrives with Khlestakov's letter. When he reads the frank description of the pretended inspector's love-making and his franker opinion of the muddle-headed town officials, the fact of the hoax gradually dawns on the company. As the crestfallen crowd counts up the losses, a gendarme comes in with an official an-

nouncement. An inspector from St. Petersburg has just arrived and desires them all to wait upon him immediately. He is staying at the inn.

Critical Evaluation:

This comedy, a high point of Nikolai Gogol's work, represents an effective protest against the fumbling, venal bureaucracy of Russia's small towns. The situation, which is credibly presented, makes this comedy work. *The Inspector General* builds almost entirely on the simple device of the mistaken identity of its hero. Ivan Alexandrovich Khlestakov is not a typical hero. Like many of Gogol's characters, he lacks positive qualities and is instead defined by his absence of intellectual and spiritual traits. He appears a mixture of fool and rogue, hero and villain. Throughout the play, he remains passive, guided primarily by vulgar epicureanism and the imagination of town officials. As a social being, Khlestakov is not exceptional. He is a minor civil servant from a landowning family of modest means. The comedy, however, hinges precisely on his status as a nonentity. As an inert, indeterminate character, rather than a confidence man, he participates in the collective fantasy of the town and shares their fear of being unmasked.

Gogol never tries to convince the town members or the audience that Khlestakov could be the inspector; he instead flaunts the incongruity of Khlestakov's demeanor and the interpretation of the town. The comedy concentrates on the town as a collective persona. The town officials, who originate and confirm the rumor of the inspector's arrival, are terrified of being exposed. The mayor heads the group and establishes relations between Khlestakov and the provincial officials. The impression of solidarity created by the collective of officials and gentry is reinforced by their static function. Gogol originally considered the play as a parody of Judgment Day, with Khlestakov representing the deceiving conscience and the townspeople representing the passions, but the play emerged as a satirical commentary on contemporary society. The play presents a social microcosm, specifically in the sphere of public law, based on a hierarchy of rights that sanctions swindling, tyrannizing, and coercing. Gogol portrays officialdom as a tangled web of misunderstandings caused by self-satisfied philistines occupying positions for which they are ill-suited.

The theme of identity is a key to the play. The civil servants in the town are very conscious of rank—their own and Khlestakov's. The comic treatment of character often relies on identity; in this case, Khlestakov's ambiguous persona elicits the hidden identities of the officials, while his own identity is only partially revealed. The mayor, who invariably praises his own virtues, reveals himself as a petty dictator. Zemlyanika, the manager of charitable institutions, is not at all charitable but rather the comic embodiment of the informer. Lyapkin-Tyapkin, reputedly liberal and whose name means "a bungler," acts with military precision. Bobchinsky and Dobchinsky, a slapstick pair, physically realize the duality of the identity and the external persona found in the other characters.

The common human desires to please, impress, and assert authority are wed to the lunatic fantasy of the townspeople. Khlestakov participates in the delusions of the mayor and his associates mainly out of complaisant idiocy. The extraordinary lies he tells about his position as the czar's right-hand man are misplaced poetic inspiration rather than calculation. For Khlestakov, the boundaries between the real and the imaginary are tenuous; therefore, he plays an unwitting role in the confusion. Social satire is frequently overwhelmed by poetry when characters embrace their own fictions. Life in St. Petersburg, as described by Khlestakov, is pure fantasy. The image of St. Petersburg as a symbol of banal glory competes with the sinister character of the city as the center of hypocrisy. The fantasy world unravels after Khlestakov, laden with gifts and betrothed to the mayor's daughter, gallops off. When the officials of the town finally learn of the arrival of the real inspector, they freeze in terror and leave the audience to contemplate the possible ramifications. This sudden draining of comic animation is a hallmark of Gogol. The whole play is, in a manifestation of absurdity, an accidental usurpation of the real drama anticipated in the opening lines of the play, namely, the arrival of the inspector general.

The structure is concentrated in time and space, the action unified by the initial announcement of the inspector's visit and his arrival in the final moments. Gogol also reaches beyond the confines of the stage: Minor characters are mentioned but never appear, action is heard offstage, and actors address the audience directly. Gogol also eliminates common moralizing features of comedy, such as the virtuous lovers, wise elders, and servant-confidants. His treatment of the love interest veers toward parody, with Khlestakov's crude advances toward mother and daughter and their deflating responses. The contrasting aesthetic categories of satire and light comedy are unified within *The Inspector General*. Slips of the tongue, misspoken clichés, and banalities provide much of the comedy. Typical of Gogol's work, the trivial is endowed with extreme importance, so there is a wealth of bizarre and improbable detail, whether from Khlestakov's fantasy of life in St. Petersburg or the other characters' assessment of provincial life.

The two planes of action allow the audience to perceive the "true" plot while the "false" plot is elaborated. The first act of the play creates the false point of view; the second builds on it; the third and fourth acts consolidate the false plot. The false plot concerns primarily the characterization of Khlestakov, out of which the characters of the officials develop. Although the officials seem to triumph near the end of the play, from the audience's point of view, Khlestakov's engagement and departure are a culmination of the misunderstandings and deflation of the town officials. In the final moment of the play, the true and false plots have these points of unity.

Few contemporary critics saw the play's novelty—namely, its lack of positive characters, love intrigue, and stage resolution—and the audience often mistook it for a crude vaudeville. Despite Gogol's careful direction and animated readings, the play's depiction of the bureaucrats and merchants outraged the audience. As time has passed, the appreciation for *The Inspector General* has grown. The clever structure of the play and the insightful evaluation of the instability of identity remain powerful, while his depiction of bureaucracy still rings true.

"Critical Evaluation" by Pamela Pavliscak

Further Reading

Beresford, Michael. *Gogol's "The Government Inspector."* London: Bristol Classical Press, 1997. Examines the composition, reception, and stage history of the play, which Beresford views as a subtle, satirical comedy exposing many forms of corruption. One in a series of books designed for students.

Bojanowska, Edyta M. *Nikolai Gogol: Between Ukrainian and Russian Nationalism.* Cambridge, Mass.: Harvard University Press, 2007. Bojanowska analyzes Gogol's life and works in terms of his conflicted national identity. Gogol was born in Ukraine when it was a part of the Russian empire; Bojanowska describes how he was engaged with questions of Ukrainian nationalism and how his works presented a bleak and ironic portrayal of Russia and Russian themes.

Brown, Nigel. *Notes on Nikolai Gogol's "The Government Inspector."* Nairobi, Kenya: Heinemann Educational Books, 1974. Provides a broad overview of previous criticism of the play and offers detailed consideration of characters, with particular attention devoted to Khlestakov.

Fanger, Donald. *The Creation of Nikolai Gogol.* Cambridge, Mass.: Harvard University Press, 1979. Considers the relationship between Gogol and his audience. Evaluates

Gogol's comic theory and his efforts at staging and self-interpretation.

Gippius, V. V. *Gogol*. Translated by Robert Maguire. Durham, N.C.: Duke University Press, 1989. Classic treatment of Gogol's life and works. The chapter on *The Inspector General* analyzes the play's structure and presents Gogol's play as the beginning of social comedy with a serious purpose in Russia.

Nabokov, Vladimir. *Nikolai Gogol*. New York: New Directions, 1944. The clever tone of Nabokov's book mirrors that of Gogol's prose. The stylistic analysis is brilliant. Focuses on the theme of banality, with Khlestakov as one of its primary representatives. Points out Gogol's genius in his attention to the absurd in everyday life.

Peace, Richard. *The Enigma of Gogol: An Examination of the Writings of N. V. Gogol and Their Place in the Russian Literary Tradition*. New York: Cambridge University Press, 1981. Evaluates the plot, characters, and structure of the play within the larger framework of the Russian tradition. Develops the theme of individual and social identity.

Spieker, Sven, ed. *Gogol: Exploring Absence: Negativity in Nineteenth Century Russian Literature*. Bloomington, Ind.: Slavica, 1999. A collection of essays on Gogol focusing on the negativity in *Dead Souls* and his other works and in the works of other Russian writers. Bibliography and index.

The Interpretation of Dreams

Author: Sigmund Freud (1856-1939)
First published: Die Traumdeutung, 1900 (English translation, 1913)
Type of work: Psychology

In March, 1931, in a foreword to the third English edition of *The Interpretation of Dreams*, Sigmund Freud expressed the opinion that the volume contained the most valuable of all the discoveries he had been fortunate enough to make. The author's estimation of his work concurs with that of most students and critics. The ideas that dreams are wish fulfillments, that dreams disguise the wishes of the unconscious, that dreams are always important and significant, and that dreams express infantile wishes—particularly for the death of the parent of the same sex as that of the dreamer—appear in this masterpiece of psychological interpretation. In this work, the Oedipus complex is first named and explained, and the method of psychoanalysis is given impetus and credibility by its application to the analysis of dreams.

It is a common criticism of Freud to say that the father of psychoanalysis, although inspired in this and other works, went too far in his generalizations concerning the basic drives of the unconscious. Freud is charged with regarding every latent wish as having a sexual object, and he is criticized for supposing that dreams can be understood as complexes of such universally significant symbols as umbrellas and boxes.

Although Freud argues that repressed wishes that show themselves in disguised form in dreams generally have something to do with the unsatisfied sexual cravings of childhood—for dreams are important and concern themselves only with matters that one cannot resolve by conscious deliberation and action—he allows for the dream satisfaction of other wishes that reality has frustrated. These include the desire for the continued existence of a loved one already dead, the desire for sleep as a continuation of the escape from reality, the desire for a return to childhood, and the desire for revenge when revenge is impossible.

As for the charge that Freud regarded dreams as complexes of symbols having the same significance for all dreamers, this is clearly unwarranted. Freud explicitly states that "only the context can furnish the correct meaning" of a dream symbol. He rejects as wholly inadequate the use of any such simple key as a dream book of symbols. All dreamers utilize the material of their own experience in their own way, and only by a careful analytical study of associations—obscured by the manifest content of the dream—is it possible to get at the particular use of symbols in an individual's dream. It is worth noting, Freud admits, that many symbols recur with much the same intent in many dreams of different persons; this knowledge, however, must be used judiciously. The agreement in the use of symbols is only partly a matter of cultural tendencies; it is largely attributable to limitations of the imagination imposed by the material itself. "To use long, stiff objects and weapons as symbols of the female genitals, or hollow objects (chests, boxes, etc.) as symbols of the male genitals, is certainly not permitted by the imagination."

It is not surprising that most of the symbols discussed by Freud, either as typical symbols or as symbols in individual cases, are sexually significant. Although Freud did not regard all dreams as the wish fulfillments of repressed sexual desires, he did suppose that a greater number of dreams have a sexual connotation: "The more one is occupied with the solution of dreams, the readier one becomes to acknowledge that the majority of the dreams of adults deal with sexual material and give expression to erotic wishes." Freud adds, "In dream-interpretation this importance of the sexual complexes must never be forgotten, though one must not, of course, exaggerate it to the exclusion of all other factors."

The technique of dream interpretation is certainly not exhausted, according to Freud, by the technique of symbol interpretation. Dreams involve the use of the images dreamed, the manifest dream content, as a way of disguising the unconscious "dream-thoughts" or latent dream content. The significance of a dream may be revealed only after one has understood the dramatic use of the symbolism of the dream. To interpret dreams, one needs to understand the condensation of the material, the displacement of the conventional meaning of a symbol or utterance, or even a displacement of the "center" of the dream-thoughts. The manifest dream may center about a matter removed from the central concern of the dream. As Freud explains the problems of dream interpretation, making numerous references to dream examples, it becomes clear that dream interpretation must be at least as ingenious as dreaming—and there is nothing more ingenious.

Freud begins *The Interpretation of Dreams* with a history of the scientific literature of dream problems from ancient times to 1900. He then proceeds to make his basic claim: that dreams are interpretable as wish fulfillments. To illustrate his point, he begins with an involved dream of his own, justifying his procedure by arguing that self-analysis is possible and, even when faulty, illustrative.

A problem arises with the consideration of painful dreams. If dreams are wish fulfillments, why are some dreams nightmares? Who wishes to be terrified? Freud's answer is that the problem arises from a confusion between the manifest and the latent dream. What is painful, considered as manifest, may, because of its disguised significance, be regarded as satisfactory to the unconscious. When one realizes, in addi-

tion, that many suppressed wishes are desires for punishment, the painful dream presents itself as a fulfillment of such wishes. To understand the possibility of painful dreams, it is necessary to consider Freud's amended formula: "The dream is the (disguised) fulfillment of a (suppressed, repressed) wish."

In describing the method most useful in enabling people to recall their dreams both by facilitating memory and by inhibiting the censorship tendency of the person recounting the dream, Freud presents what has become familiar as the psychoanalytic method of free association. He suggests that patients be put into a restful position with the eyes closed, that patients be told not to criticize their thoughts or to withhold the expression of them, and that they continue to be impartial about their ideas. This problem of eliminating censorship while recounting the dream is merely an extension of the problem of dealing with the censorship imposed by the dreamer while dreaming. Dreamers do not want to acknowledge their desires; for one reason or another they have repressed them. The fulfillment of the suppressed desire can be tolerated by dreamers only if they leave out anything that would be understandable to the waking mind. Consequently, only a laborious process of undoing (or understanding) the dream can result in some understanding of the meaning that the censor tries to hide.

Among the interesting corollaries of Freud's theory is the idea that the dream stimulus is always to be found among the experiences of the hours prior to sleeping. Some incident from the day becomes the material of the dream, its provocative image. Although the dream stimulus is from the day preceding sleep, the repressed wish that the dream expresses and fulfills is from childhood, at least in the majority of cases: "The deeper we go into the analysis of dreams, the more often are we put on to the track of childish experiences which play the part of dream-sources in the latent dream content." To explain the difficulty of getting at the experiences in childhood that provide the latent dream-content, Freud argues for a conception of dreams as stratified: In the dream, layers of meaning are involved, and it is only at the lowest stratum that the source in some experience of childhood may be discovered.

Among the typical dreams mentioned by Freud are the embarrassment dream of nakedness, interpreted as an exhibition dream, fulfilling a wish to return to childhood (the time when one ran about naked without upsetting anyone); the death-wish dream in which one dreams of the death of a beloved person, interpreted as a dream showing repressed hostility toward brother or sister, father or mother; and the examination dream in which one dreams of the disgrace of flunking an examination, interpreted as reflecting the ineradicable memories of punishments in childhood.

Of these typical dreams, the death-wish dream directed to the father (by the son) or to the mother (by the daughter) is explained in terms of the drama of the *Oedipus* plays by Sophocles. Oedipus unwittingly murders his own father and marries his mother. When he discovers his deeds, he blinds himself and exiles himself from Thebes. The appeal of the story is explained by Freud as resulting from its role as a wish fulfillment. The drama reveals the inner self, the self that directed its first sexual impulses toward (in the case of a male) the mother and its first jealous hatred toward the father. These feelings have been repressed during the course of developing maturity, but they remain latent, ready to manifest themselves only in dreams somewhat more obscure than the Oedipus drama itself. Freud mentions William Shakespeare's *Hamlet, Prince of Denmark* (pr. c. 1600-1601, pb. 1603) as another play in which the same wish is shown, although in *Hamlet, Prince of Denmark* the fulfillment is not achieved. Freud accounts for Hamlet's reluctance to complete the task of revenge by pointing out that Hamlet cannot bring himself to kill a man who accomplished what he himself wishes he had accomplished: the murder of his father and marriage to his mother.

In his discussion of the psychology of the dream process, Freud calls attention to the fact that dreams are quickly forgotten—a natural consequence, if his theory is correct. This fact creates problems for the analyst who wishes to interpret dreams in order to discover the root of neurotic disturbances. The self that forgets the dream, however, is the same self that dreamed, and it is possible by following the implications of even superficial associations to get back to the substance of the dream.

Realizing that many would be offended by his ideas, Freud attempts to forestall criticism by insisting on the universal application of his theory and by claiming that dreams themselves—since they are not acts—are morally innocent, whatever their content.

There seems little question that Freud's contribution to psychology in *The Interpretation of Dreams* will remain one of the great discoveries of the human mind. Whatever its excesses, particularly in the hands of enthusiastic followers, Freud's central idea gains further confirmation constantly in the experiences of dreamers and analysts alike.

Further Reading

Elliott, Anthony, ed. *Freud 2000*. Cambridge, England: Polity Press, 1998. The essayists examine how Freud's theories apply to current issues in the social sciences and humanities.

Frieden, Ken. *Freud's Dream of Interpretation*. Albany: State University of New York Press, 1990. Frieden asserts that despite Freud's denials, he was influenced by biblical and rabbinical modes of dream interpretation. Convincingly argues that because interpretation is never a neutral act, Freud failed to acknowledge the prophetic aspect of his dream work.

Hyman, Stanley Edgar. "*The Interpretation of Dreams*." In *The Tangled Bank: Darwin, Marx, Frazer, and Freud as Imaginative Writers*. New York: Atheneum, 1962. Hyman contends that the power of Freud's ideas owes a great deal to his ability as an imaginative writer. He examines the tone, imaginative organization, and thematic metaphors of *The Interpretation of Dreams*.

Isbister, J. N. *Freud: An Introduction to His Life and Work*. Cambridge, England: Polity Press, 1985. Evaluates Freud's ideas in a biographical and philosophical context and finds them wanting. Criticizes Freudian psychology as reductive and nihilistic. Calls for a revision of psychoanalytic dream theory in light of later studies on sleep.

Liu, Catherine, et al., eds. *The Dreams of Interpretation: A Century down the Royal Road*. Minneapolis: University of Minnesota Press, 2007. A reevaluation of Freud's book, with essays by psychoanalysts, philosophers, literary critics, and other writers who describe how Freud's work changed the way people think about psychology, politics, and culture.

Marinelli, Lydia, and Andreas Mayer. *Dreaming by the Book: Freud's "The Interpretation of Dreams" and the History of the Psychoanalytic Movement*. Translated by Susan Fairfield. New York: Other Press, 2003. Traces the changes in the eight editions of the book that appeared between 1899 and 1930 in relation to psychoanalytic practice.

Neu, Jerome, ed. *The Cambridge Companion to Freud*. New York: Cambridge University Press, 1991. Collection of essays analyzing various aspects of Freud's philosophy. The references to *The Interpretation of Dreams* are listed in the index.

Soule, George. "Freud and *The Interpretation of Dreams*." In *Books That Changed Our Minds*, edited by Malcolm Cowley and Bernard Smith. New York: Kelmscott, 1939. Traces the widespread influence of Freud's ideas on art, language, culture, and the study of history. Attempts to distinguish psychoanalytic theory from popular misconceptions.

The Interrogation

Author: J. M. G. Le Clézio (1940-   )
First published: Le Procès-Verbal, 1963 (English
    translation, 1964)
Type of work: Novel
Type of plot: Para-realism
Time of plot: Summer in the early 1960's
Locale: Carros, France

Principal characters:
ADAM POLLO, a young man
MICHÈLE, his acquaintance

The Story:

Adam Pollo is almost thirty years old, inordinately tall and thin; he looks disheveled and, like a sick and frightened animal, has found a refuge in a deserted house overlooking the sea. He lies on a deck chair, sunbathing by an open window. He writes in a notebook letters to "dear Michèle." Adam is tormented by innumerable fears, and he struggles to remember whether he just left the army or just left a mental home. Living alone and surviving on beer, cigarettes, and cookies, Adam has rejected society, its values, and the human interaction it requires.

Generally shy, Adam can be assertive with Michèle. The two are in a café. In spite of Michèle's repeated efforts to avoid the subject, Adam inflicts upon her a detailed description of the rape she had suffered at his hands. The rape was, apparently, only "in theory," but Michèle's public humiliation by the story that Adam insistently tells "for other people's benefit" is very real. Adam is asserting his virility. He also is seeking confirmation of the rape, a fragment of certainty in his uncertain past. Michèle refuses that confirmation. His attitude, which borders on cruelty, deprives him of the help she could have provided.

Adam does not work; he borrows francs, here and there, from Michèle, and he kills time by doing things such as visiting the zoo or following a dog on a random stroll through town. He discovers a rat in the house where he is living and becomes so disturbed that he launches an epic and victorious battle against the intruder.

For a brief moment, Adam's interaction with Michèle is beneficial. She visits him, they have a beer, and chat. She calms him down when he anticipates that a war might erupt and shake the world. She sets the record straight and he agrees: "so that's it. The atomic war has not happened yet," he tells himself. He repeats that, as she has said, he was too young to fight in the 1940 war. Adam is relieved. His fears evaporate and he sees the world as peaceful. Soon his demons reappear: He analyzes the sentence "What time is it?" grammatically, logically, and metaphysically, and concludes

that these four words are killing him; he insults Michèle for interrupting his meditations, throws her on the ground, and then takes her away, "with his mind far away" and concentrated on the potential trajectory of a shark swimming along the coast. Finally, he runs off by himself, stands petrified at the culminating point of the road, and contemplates from there "his own intelligence of the world."

Adam's solitude is now complete and his activities, such as asking a salesgirl for a record he knows does not exist, are more futile than ever. He finds entertaining the dragging out to sea of the corpse—like a giant tadpole—of a drowned man. Adam searches for Michèle from bar to bar and nightclub to nightclub. He finds her in a park in the company of an American tourist. Adam is drunk and obnoxious. Michèle soon betrays him; she gives away his hiding place to the police. Adam is chased from his Eden—the house on the hill—the following morning.

Adam has nothing left but his words. He stands with his back to the sea; his voice grows stronger, and passers-by, surprised by his prophetic tone, stop to listen to him. He speaks faster and faster, is more and more exalted, and finally becomes incoherent. "In a second, it was over," declares the next day's newspaper: Adam had exposed himself.

Adam likes his little room in the mental home. It is clean and the window bars form a geometrical design, as do the tiles on the floor. Adam meets a group of seven students and the head psychiatrist. The questions asked are innocuous enough, but Adam, in his striped pajamas, feels uncomfortable. A young woman is the only one to show him some sympathy. When she declares that Adam is not insane, the doctor corrects her forcefully by reading the long diagnostic of mental disorders that was established upon Adam's admittance. Deprived of support, Adam lapses into torpor. He shakes himself up, and out of his mouth comes a bombastic tirade, full of confused and irrelevant scholarly references. Nobody pays attention any longer; Adam feels invisible and becomes even more incoherent; his words sound like rumbling noises. A student writes a conclusion in his exercise book: aphasia. Adam is back in his bed, hoping never to be released.

Critical Evaluation:

The Interrogation was published in 1963, and its author, J. M. G. Le Clézio, was a twenty-three-year-old, unknown to the public. The novel received the Renaudot Prize. Critics saw in it the influence of Albert Camus, Jean-Paul Sartre, James Joyce, Franz Kafka, and others. Le Clézio is acclaimed as an heir to *le nouveau roman*, or the New Novel, and as a brilliant writer. He has since published close to fifty works, and he received the Nobel Prize in Literature in 2008.

The novel's preliminary letter to the reader signed by Le Clézio announces that *The Interrogation* is a "kind of game or jigsaw puzzle." Why? In a traditional story, the events, however extraordinary, are presented with certainty. Here, the protagonist himself does not know whether he has just left the army or just left a mental home. Nothing in the plot will clarify his doubts. His mother, in her letter to him, assures him that he was in the army, but the newspaper notice published after his arrest identifies him as a mental patient. For the reader, the question is left unanswered.

An interrogation that takes place in the psychiatric establishment is also the interrogation present in the reader's mind. The interrogation brings only a partial answer, and it brings even more questions: Does it describe Adam's mental condition, or is it the conclusion of medical authorities who are more anxious to be on time for dinner than to reach the human being hidden behind the name Adam Pollo?

What about the name itself? This story's Adam lives in the 1960's, but he is the first man created by young Le Clézio, and also the man by antonomasia. The novel is about the nature of mental illness; it is also about the human condition in general. Furthermore, as critic Jennifer Waelti-Walters points out, combining the protagonist's last name—Pollo—with his first name's initial—A—spells the word "apollo," or Apollo, the Greek god. Apollo is an apt name for the exceptionally intelligent and educated protagonist, who lives his intellectual adventure in August, under the blazing Mediterranean sun that he often complains about.

A second possibility, supported by the text, must be noted here. Pollo is derived from the name Poll, the name of the parrot of novelist Daniel Defoe's character Robinson Crusoe. This possibility is suggested by the quotation from Defoe that heads Le Clézio's novel. In this humorous quotation, Robinson declares that his parrot is the only "person" allowed to talk to him at his table. It is a reference to the solitude in which both Robinson and Adam live. It also suggests that, when it comes to human interaction, human language is as limited as that of a parrot.

Adam is faced with a dilemma. If he relies on his senses, he captures only fragments of reality. The metaphor of the hide-and-seek game describes this situation. When, as a child, he played hide-and-seek in the garden, Adam would catch sight of an eye, or a hand, or some hair, between the clusters of leaves; he had to discard the appearances and rely on a concept to claim that he had discovered his—entire—playmate. On the other hand, when he replaces reality with concepts, the world loses its lushness; ultimately, its elements die, reduced—like the shark whose trajectory Adam constructs—to an "invisible negative eternity." The apollonian sun dries up Adam's world.

The fragmentary perception of reality causes Adam to panic: His surroundings fill with small happenings that he had scarcely noticed before, which now swell to huge proportions. Everything is in motion "with an intense, intestinal, concentrated life."

Sexuality is the domain of the senses by excellence, but Adam fears sexuality as much as human interaction in general. In the first chapter, a letter to Michèle sketches out a solution. Adam has explained that the contact with Michèle—"my own flesh in yours"—could reassure him. In his fantasy, though, he immediately places Michèle, on the ground, next to him, in a space exactly her size: 5 feet 4 inches by 35.5 inches. He has reduced her to geometry. Later, when nostalgia for the senses overwhelms him, Adam will identify with animals, in particular with a dog who mounts a beautiful "bitch" in the basement of a department store.

To avoid the reality in which one can, for instance, be destroyed by moths, Adam needs to organize the infinity of his thought fragments into a theory. He slowly moves toward abstraction. A simple question about the time of day is answered with a long dissertation. At this stage, Adam's human contacts are limited to the intended recipients of his notebook writings; these letters, however, are never mailed—to his friend Michèle. In the chapters that precede Adam's prophetic speech, Le Clézio has incorporated the notebooks, and the narration changes from a third person to a first. The notebooks are reproduced as they were written, with crossed out paragraphs and blank and missing pages.

Adam's adventure, and therefore the novel itself, has become a word game. Reality has been reduced to lists of words, figures, formulas, and maps; and human beings to specters or, at best, ants. The shocking gesture that follows Adam's speech is a revolt against the rules of society; it is also meant to revive his senses and the part of his body that he has killed with his abstractions.

In the room of the final chapter, the abundant production of a language void of any content other than intellectual exercises has changed into a complete aphasia. However, the incoherence of the outside world has been mastered. The window has turned into geometry, and Adam lies in his bed as if in the protective hole into which, since childhood, he has dreamed of crawling.

The novel's themes described here do not cover the complexity of the novel. *The Interrogation* is an intellectual adventure, common to coming-of-age novels. It is also a revolt, representative of the turbulent 1960's, against the rationality of a Western culture that has stimulated the development of technology but has also led to a second world war and to the threat of an atomic catastrophe.

The virtuosity of the novel's then twenty-three-year-old author had dazzled the critics. According to Le Clézio himself, the novel was written while he was on the beach. Maybe the novel owes to this circumstance the humor that runs through its pages and the impertinence that moderates the display of an impressive scholarship. In any case, having drawn readers into their own interrogation, Le Clézio addresses the book's last paragraph to the public: The story is over, he writes, but you can count on more stories about Adam or "some other among him."

Gisèle C. Feal

Further Reading

Amoia, Alba, and Bettina Knapp, eds. *Multicultural Writers Since 1945*. Westport, Conn.: Greenwood Press, 2004. This collection of essays examining the work of postwar multicultural writers includes a five-page introduction to Le Clézio. Basic but useful.

Moser, Keith A. *"Privileged Moments" in the Novels and Short Stories of J. M. G. Le Clézio: His Contemporary Development of a Traditional French Literary Device*. Lewiston, N.Y.: Edwin Mellen Press, 2008. A book-length study of lyrical experiences in Le Clézio's fiction. Includes the chapter "Adam Pollo's Alienation and Existential Anguish."

Redfern-West, Robert. *Le Clézio: A Literary Topography of New Departures, Poetic Adventure, and Sensual Ecstasy—The Man and His Works*. Palo Alto, Calif.: Academica Press, 2009. A scholarly interpretive study of Le Clézio examining his life—including his global travels—and his works. Develops his main themes and places them in the context of contemporary world literature.

Waelti-Walters, Jennifer R. *J. M. G. Le Clézio*. Boston: Twayne, 1977. This biographical account of Le Clézio's life and works covers the period from 1963 to 1975. Includes a clear and complete chapter on *The Interrogation*.

The Intruder

Author: Maurice Maeterlinck (1862-1949)
First produced: L'Intruse, 1891; first published, 1890 (English translation, 1891)
Type of work: Drama
Type of plot: Tragedy
Time of plot: Early twentieth century
Locale: A dark room in an old château

Principal characters:
THE GRANDFATHER, who is blind
THE FATHER, who is weary
THE UNCLE, who is rationalistic
THE THREE DAUGHTERS, who are obedient
THE SISTER OF CHARITY, a nurse
THE MAIDSERVANT, who is defensive

The Story:

Six characters feel enormous tension one Saturday evening between shortly after nine o'clock and midnight in a somber sitting room of an old château surrounded by gardens and a lake. Together with their father, uncle, and grandfather, three young women hopefully await the visit of the father's and the uncle's eldest sister, a nun who is the mother superior of her convent, and of the doctor who is to check on their sickly mother in the room on the left and the silent baby in the room on the right.

The family enters the sitting room, disagreeing. The father and the daughters want to sit outside while the uncle, because it rained for one week, prefers to remain inside. The grandfather resolves the dispute by saying that it is better to stay in since one never knows what might happen. The father declares that his wife, who was sick for several weeks, is out of danger from her illness. The grandfather disagrees, since he heard her voice. The uncle supports his brother and recommends that they all relax and enjoy the first pleasant evening they have had in a long time.

The uncle remarks that sickness is like a stranger in the family, and the father notes that one can count only on family members, not outsiders, for help. The men ask Ursula, the eldest daughter, if she can see anyone in the avenue. She sees no one yet, but reports that the avenue is moonlit and the weather fine, that the nightingales can be heard, and that the trees stir a little in the wind.

The mood changes when the grandfather announces that he no longer hears the nightingales. Ursula believes that someone has entered the garden, although she sees no one. The men disbelieve her, but she persists, since the nightingales suddenly fell silent and the swans became frightened. The father agrees that "there is a stillness of death," but the mood changes again when the uncle asks disgustedly if they are going to discuss nightingales all night.

The conversation turns to the cold room. Ursula and her sisters try to obey their father by shutting the door, but it will not close entirely. The father promises to have the carpenter fix it the next day. The family is then disturbed by the sound of the sharpening of a scythe outside, although the gardener should not be working on a Saturday evening. Ursula again tries to soothe fears by suggesting that perhaps the gardener is occupied in the shadow of the house.

Everyone's attention turns to the lamp, which did not burn very well that evening, although its oil was filled that same morning. One daughter notes that, after not sleeping for three nights, the grandfather finally has dozed off. While he sleeps, the father and the uncle discuss his blindness and his irrationality. When the clock strikes ten, the grandfather awakens, saying someone is standing by the glass door leading to the terrace. Although Ursula reassures him that she sees no one, he thinks someone is waiting there. When he asks the father and the uncle if their sister has arrived, the uncle peevishly remarks that it is now too late for her to come and that it is not very nice of her.

Everyone hears a noise as if someone is entering the house, and they believe it is finally the long-awaited nun. After the father summons the maidservant, the grandfather notes twice that she is not alone. When the father asks the maidservant who entered the house, she replies that no one came in. The father accuses her of pushing open the door to the sitting room, although she is standing three steps from it.

Although blind, the grandfather announces that suddenly everything seems to be dark in the room. The maidservant's exit is marked by eleven strokes of the old clock.

The grandfather thinks the maidservant entered their room and is now sitting at their table. His anxiety grows, and he begs Ursula to tell him the truth. He urges his children to tell him who is sitting beside him, who entered the room, and what is happening around him. He is amazed that they see no one besides the six of them. He announces that he probably will not live much longer and that he wishes he was at home. The father protests that he already is at home. The grandfather wishes to be with his daughter because he wants to know the truth. He reassures the daughters that he knows they would tell him the truth if they were not deceived by the men.

Finally, the father invites the grandfather to enter his daughter's room, but the old man refuses; the uncle remarks that he is not being reasonable. Suddenly the lamp goes out completely, and the men decide to remain in the dark rather than enter the sick woman's room. Now the clock seems very loud. Ursula is asked to open the window a bit. All notice that there is no sound outside. The silence inside and out is extraordinary. The uncle begins to pace in the darkness, after declaring that he does not like the country. The grandfather asks Ursula to shut the window.

Suddenly an odd ray of moonlight penetrates the room's darkness. The clock strikes midnight; someone unidentified seems to rise from the table, the uncle calls for the lamp to be lit, the baby wails in terror, and heavy steps are heard in the mother's room. Then all fall silent. The door to the sick woman's chamber opens. There stands the sister of charity, dressed in black. Her bow and the sign of the cross announce silently that the mother has died. All enter the bedroom except the grandfather, who is left alone to grope about the table in confusion.

Critical Evaluation:

In *The Intruder*, Maurice Maeterlinck superbly evokes feelings of fearful suspense and anxiety through the simple repetition of phrases, the device of light diminishing into darkness, and invocation of nature's response to the unseen intruder when the birds, swans, and dogs are suddenly hushed for no apparent reason. Maeterlinck admired Edgar Allen Poe's ability to create a haunting atmosphere that leads up to tragic consequences. In *The Intruder*, a similar haunted atmosphere evolves as the family converses banally. While the intruder, death, stalks the premises, the six relatives argue about the weather, sounds they hear, the opening and shutting of doors and windows, and the arrival of the long-awaited nun.

Although the play is set in the twentieth century, it resembles a medieval allegory. None of the characters is given a proper name, and the invisible figure of death is really the star of the show. The intruder hovering about the gardens and the château is sensed only by the blind grandfather who alarms the younger members of his family as he persistently asks who is present or whose footsteps are on the stairs. Like a blind prophet, the grandfather intuitively feels the macabre presence, but he is not understood by his family, who even call him demented. His premonitions are justified at the conclusion of the play when the sister of charity silently, by making the sign of the cross, announces the ill mother's death. The father's and uncle's sister never arrives.

The mother was suffering ever since giving birth to an infant who, since it had not yet made a single sound, resembles a wax effigy. The grandfather fears that it may be deaf and mute because his daughter married her cousin. Maeterlinck thus suggests an underlying theme of incest in this very enclosed family; the newborn baby, the new life remaining after the mother's death, seems to be already cursed.

Influenced by medieval mysticism, Maeterlinck suggestively portrays the realm of the irrational, uncontrollable, and unspeakable through contrasting light and darkness, sound and silence, outside and inside, female and male, youth and age, health and illness, and ultimately, life and death. He does not want his brief drama to be fully understood but merely to be felt by the reader or spectator, who silently enters the family's privacy, participates in its anxiety, and understands that nothing and no one can keep death away when it approaches.

It is significant that the grandfather, who can still see bright light, feels that all light has gone out even when the dim lamp still burns. He is probably intuitively sensing death approaching his daughter in the next room. His anguish about this inner darkness is echoed by the others when their lamp extinguishes itself and they are left talking quietly in total darkness. Rays of moonlight at the conclusion of the play suggest that a strange light from outside the family and their home can still penetrate their personal and physical darkness.

The grandfather is also out of tune with the other family members when he hears the footsteps on the stairs not made by the maidservant and the sounds of someone other than his loved ones by him at the table. The others hear none of this and wish that he would be "reasonable." They do, however, experience with him the strange silences that also occasionally invade the premises.

The grandfather's inner world contrasts with the outer world of the others and with the even broader world that lies beyond their enclosed sitting room in the bedrooms of the sick mother and the mute infant and outside in the gardens. The father and the uncle long for their sister's arrival since they distrust persons outside the family. Just as they are enclosed in their sitting room, so are they, despite their external facade of confidence, immured in their fears and prejudices. The three daughters are torn between trying to please their intuitive grandfather and wishing to accommodate their father and uncle. The trust the grandfather places in Ursula, the eldest daughter, suggests that she, too, is intuitive, sensitive, and truthful, but her efforts are often stifled by the patriarchal heads of her family, her father and uncle. They resent her answering the grandfather's questions sincerely since this seems, from their point of view, only to add to his dementia. Thus the women in this strange household are not only as physically enclosed as the men but also psychologically enclosed by the guardians of reason.

There are equal numbers of females and males in the play, with the three daughters balanced by the grandfather, the father, and the uncle; the ill mother rests in the room on the left while her infant son lies in the room on the right. This balance is upset by the three supporting characters, the maidservant who remains outside on the landing of the steps, the sister of charity who stays in the doorway of the mother's bedroom, and the expected sister of the father and the uncle, who never arrives. Maeterlinck does not suggest, however, that all the women are intuitive and all the men rational. The grandfather is misunderstood by all because of his intuitive feelings and premonitions, and at times the daughters try to reason with him much as do the father and the uncle. The dramatist seems to indicate that it is age and blindness rather than gender that confers prophetic power.

The daughters are strongly shaped by the patriarchs of their family. An extreme of feminine passivity is shown by the silent mother's slow death. All of the characters focus on her but choose not to be with her, since they believe that she needs solitary rest; only the sister of charity accompanies her on her last journey. Although the grandfather senses that she is dying, he refuses to enter her room when given the opportunity. Perhaps he fears the time when he, too, will meet death. Thus age recoils from extinction, but the recently born infant finally, after weeks of silence, howls at the moment of the mother's death.

Three generations are represented in this play. Although age seems to bestow wisdom, youth appears to embody courage. The three daughters are the first to enter their dead mother's chambers, while the grandfather gropes around the table in confusion.

The Intruder, Maeterlinck's second play, breaks with traditional, realistic drama. Fascinated by both death and symbolism, the playwright experiments with arousing emotions of uncertainty, anxiety, and horror. He does not fully develop his characters as did the authors of many naturalistic plays of his era. Rather, the family members are only superficially drawn; the focus is on the way they fall prey to the frightening atmosphere around them, which they cannot understand.

All of the characters wish for the good health of the mother, yet illness invades their domain like an unwelcome stranger who cannot be ignored and, despite the doctors' predictions of renewed health, death claims the mother. Illness and death are not "reasonable," and the strong desires and arguments of the father and the uncle are useless against its irrational force. Maeterlinck seems to be communicating that somehow human beings at their best—those always seeking both intuitive and rational truths—must embrace the paradoxical awareness that life and death occur simultaneously.

Carole J. Lambert

Further Reading

Bass, Ruth. "Backstage at the Guggenheim." Review of *The Intruder*, by Maurice Maeterlinck. *Art News* 85, no. 6 (Summer, 1986): 16, 18. In this review of Hanne Tierney's staging of Maeterlinck's play with puppetlike figures at the Guggenheim Museum in New York in January, 1986, Bass shows how the play lends itself to creative revival and aesthetic innovation. Tierney designed her expressionistic figures, controlled them at a keyboard by invisible fishing lines, and spoke all of their parts in a monotone.

Block, Haskell M. *Mallarmé and the Symbolist Drama*. Detroit, Mich.: Wayne State University Press, 1963. Block provides a broad view of Symbolist drama and discusses in depth the aesthetic theory of its precursor, Stéphane Mallarmé, and its masters, of whom Maeterlinck was the most outstanding. Block includes a discussion of *The Intruder*.

Daniels, May. *The French Drama of the Unspoken*. Edinburgh: University Press, 1953. After discussing the positivistic mind-set of the end of the nineteenth century, Daniels devotes two chapters to Maeterlinck's plays, all of which are a strong reaction to naturalistic theater. Analyzes the nature of spectator response to Maeterlinck's theater of the unexpressed in *The Intruder* and *Pelléas et Mélisande* (1892; *Pelléas and Mélisande*, 1894).

Finney, Gail. "Dramatic Pointillism: The Examples of Holz and Schlaf's *Die Familie Selicke* and Maeterlinck's *L'Intruse*." *Comparative Literature Studies* 30, no. 1 (1993): 1-15. Finney describes George Seurat's pointillistic neo-Impressionistic painting style and shows how "temporal or linguistic pointillism" occurs in Johannes Schlaf's *Die Familie Selicke* (1890) and Maeterlinck's *The Intruder*. She indicates that many of the dramatic techniques found in Maeterlinck's play are used by such later twentieth century playwrights as Tennessee Williams, Arthur Miller, Eugene O'Neill, Samuel Beckett, and Harold Pinter.

Heller, Otto. *Prophets of Dissent: Essays on Maeterlinck, Strindberg, Nietzsche, and Tolstoy*. New York: Alfred A. Knopf, 1918. Reprint. Port Washington, N.Y.: Kennikat Press, 1968. Includes one essay devoted to Maeterlinck. Heller in 1918 already understood that the dramatist's secular mysticism represented a retreat into the "central ego" and an effort to express the unknown internal forces that motivate individuals. Maeterlinck's theater communicates humankind's frustration before the invisible, uncontrollable forces, both internal and external, that no longer fall under the old categories of fate and religion.

Ingelbien, Raphael. "Symbolism at the Periphery: Yeats, Maeterlinck, and Cultural Nationalism." *Comparative Literature Studies* 42, no. 3 (2005): 183-204. Compares the works of Maeterlinck with those of William Butler Yeats, pointing out the similarities in the national, sociological, and linguistic contexts in which their work developed at the end of the nineteenth century.

McGuinness, Patrick. *Maurice Maeterlinck and the Making of Modern Theatre*. New York: Oxford University Press, 2000. Traces the development of Maeterlinck's vision of and theories about the theater, including his Symbolist plays and other dramas.

Maeterlinck, Maurice. "The Tragical in Daily Life." In *Theatre/Theory/Theatre: The Major Critical Texts from Aristotle and Zeami to Soyinka and Havel*, edited by Daniel Gerould. New York: Applause, 2000. This essay, written in 1896, expresses some of Maeterlinck's theories about the theater.

Intruder in the Dust

Author: William Faulkner (1897-1962)
First published: 1948
Type of work: Novel
Type of plot: Detective and mystery
Time of plot: Early 1930's
Locale: Jefferson, Yoknapatawpha County, Mississippi

Principal characters:
CHARLES "CHICK" MALLISON, a sixteen-year-old boy
GAVIN STEVENS, his uncle and a lawyer
LUCAS BEAUCHAMP, an old black man
ALECK SANDER, Chick's young black friend
MISS HABERSHAM, an old woman
HOPE HAMPTON, the sheriff

The Story:

On a cold afternoon in November, Chick Mallison, twelve years old, accompanied by two black boys, goes rabbit hunting on Carothers Edmonds's place. When he falls through the ice into a creek, an old black man, Lucas Beauchamp, appears and watches while the boy clambers awkwardly ashore. Then Lucas takes the white boy and his companions to his home. There, Chick dries out in front of the fire and eats Lucas's food. Later, when Chick tries to pay the old man for his hospitality, Lucas spurns his money. Chick throws it down, but Lucas makes one of the other boys pick it up and return it. Chick broods over the incident, ashamed to be indebted to a black man, especially one as arrogant as Lucas. Again trying to repay the old man, he sends Lucas's wife a mail-order dress bought with money he saved; again refusing to acknowledge payment and thus admit his inferiority, Lucas sends Chick a bucket of sorghum sweetening.

Four years later, when Lucas is accused of shooting Vinson Gowrie in the back, Chick still has not forgotten his unpaid debt to the man. Realizing that Vinson's poor white family and friends are sure to lynch Lucas, Chick wants to leave town. Yet, when Sheriff Hope Hampton brings Lucas to the jail in Jefferson, Chick, unable to suppress his sense of obligation, is standing on the street where the old man can see him. Lucas asks Chick to bring his uncle, Gavin Stevens, to the jail.

At the jail, Lucas refuses to tell Stevens what happened at the shooting, whereupon the lawyer leaves in disgust; but Lucas does tell Chick that Vinson was not shot with his gun—a forty-one Colt—and he asks the boy to verify this fact by digging up the corpse. Although the body is buried nine miles from town and the Gowries will be sure to shoot a grave robber, Chick agrees to the request; he knows that Lucas will undoubtedly be lynched if someone does not help him. Barbershop and poolroom loafers already gather, awaiting the arrival of the pine-hill-country Gowries.

Stevens laughs at the story, so Chick's only help comes from a black boy—Aleck Sander—and Miss Habersham, an old woman of good family who grew up with Lucas's wife, now dead. The task of digging up a white man's grave in order to save a haughty, intractable, but innocent black man is left to two adolescents and a seventy-year-old woman who feels it her obligation to protect those more helpless than she. The three succeed in opening the grave without incident. In the coffin, they find not Vinson but Jake Montgomery, whose skull was bashed in. They fill the grave, return to town, awaken Stevens, and go to the sheriff with their story.

This group, joined by old man Gowrie and two of his sons, reopen the grave. When they lift the lid, the coffin is found to be empty. A search discloses Montgomery's body hastily buried nearby and Vinson's sunk in quicksand. When the sheriff takes Montgomery's body into town, the huge crowd gathered in anticipation of the lynching of Lucas soon scatters.

Questioning of Lucas reveals that Crawford Gowrie had murdered his brother, Vinson. Crawford, according to the old man, was cheating his brother in a lumber deal. Jake, to whom Crawford sold the stolen lumber, knew that Crawford was the murderer and dug up Vinson's grave to prove it. Crawford murdered Montgomery at the grave and put him in Vinson's coffin. When he saw Chick and his friends open the grave, he was forced to remove Vinson's body, too. Sheriff Hampton soon captures Crawford, who kills himself in his cell to avoid a trial.

At last, Chick thinks, he has freed himself from his debt to the old black man. A short time later, however, Lucas appears at Stevens's office and insists on paying for services rendered. Stevens refuses payment for both himself and Chick but accepts two dollars for "expenses." Proud, unhumbled to the end, Lucas demands a receipt.

Critical Evaluation:

Intruder in the Dust is an excellent introduction to William Faulkner's numerous and complex novels of the Deep South. Set in Faulkner's mythical Yoknapatawpha County, his standard fictional location, *Intruder in the Dust* also includes such familiar inhabitants as attorney Gavin Stevens and farmer Carothers Edmonds. This novel, however, includes only a few examples of such famous Faulknerian stylistic devices as elongated, periodic sentences, disconnected narratives, multiple narrative perspectives, psychological time, and stream of consciousness. While the very substance of *The Sound and the Fury* (1929), *Absalom, Absalom!* (1936), *Light in August* (1932), and *As I Lay Dying* (1930) consists of these variations in style or form, *Intruder in the Dust* (except for Chick Mallison's meditations and flashbacks) is a relatively straightforward narration. Faulkner novels typically use parable and folklore as a basis for forming a vision of life as a neurotic and involved psychological process. *Intruder in the Dust*, however, blends folklore and parable with a formula mystery story and strikes a much simpler note than most of Faulkner's work.

Aspects of folklore permeate *Intruder in the Dust*. Faulkner's panorama of rural local color includes a generous sampling of cracker-barrel philosophers, bigoted rednecks, mischievous and shoeless youngsters, and fading ladies of breeding long past their prime. The plot crackles with anecdotes, bits of country wisdom, humor, and superstition. It is thematically enriched by Stevens's philosophical speeches. After Chick, Aleck, and Miss Habersham discover that Vinson Gowrie's grave contains the body of Jake Montgomery, *Intruder in the Dust* becomes a highly suspenseful mystery story, with Sheriff Hampton and Stevens solving the crime in barely enough time to prevent Lucas Beauchamp from being lynched by a mob far more interested in violence than justice.

The novel also contains several parables, one of which is a southern version of the biblical Cain and Abel story. The brothers Vinson and Crawford Gowrie join forces in several business ventures, including timber dealing. Crawford, increasingly greedy for his own profits, steals timber from his brother and sells it to the shady Jake. When Lucas sees Crawford stealing the timber and threatens to expose him, Crawford kills his brother in a way that makes Lucas appear to be the murderer. Crawford relies on the townspeople's readiness to blame a black man for the murder of a white man. Much like Mink Snopes in Faulkner's *The Hamlet* (1940), Crawford learns too late that violence, instead of eradicating problems, creates more violence and eventually one's downfall. Truth simply will not stay buried, Faulkner seems to be saying. In a hair-raising midnight scene combining the best of Edgar Allan Poe and Raymond Chandler, plus his own inimitable sense of place and wry humor, the author has three very frightened individuals uncover the truth that frees Lucas.

Beyond the Cain and Abel story, Stevens's speeches expand *Intruder in the Dust* into a parable about the people's right to govern themselves. Some critics condemn Stevens's rhetoric as the propaganda of an unfeeling and aristocratic bigot. While this interpretation holds some validity, Stevens is not a mouthpiece for Faulkner's views; nor should Stevens's pleadings, however prolix, be discounted. In the filibuster tradition of southern oratory, he articulates a code of noninterference, following Candide's words of "till your own garden." The intruder of the title may refer not only to those who open Vinson's grave but also to "outlanders" who would dictate moral action to these people. With their own sense of justice, the southerners close this incident in their own way. They come to realize that Lucas has little to do with what is fundamentally a family feud. As a result of his cruel victimization, Lucas in the future will be shown, or will suffer, innumerable courtesies by white people. He suffered, and he is wise. Lucas will endure. The true villains here are the poor whites, those who pervert the opportunities of their position.

The elderly spinster Eunice Habersham supports Lucas enough to rob a grave to prove his innocence. Had Miss Habersham been less sentimental and more skeptical, Crawford, guilty and white, would have escaped. On the other hand, Hope Hampton, sheriff of Yoknapatawpha County, is highly skeptical and totally unsentimental. Hampton seeks justice, not conviction; evidence, not the will of the voters, persuades him to act. He is a diametric opposite to the familiar stereotype of the rural southern sheriff, a big-bellied hunter and political animal. The villains of *Intruder in the Dust* behave in predictably stereotyped and evil ways, while the figures in power—Hampton, the prosecutor; Stevens, the defender; and Miss Habersham, the moral sentiment—are humane, rounded characters.

As a story of initiation, the novel is an unqualified success. Young Chick Mallison must unlearn old values as well as learn new ones. In attempting to pay Lucas for his act of kindness, Chick denies the old black man his humanity. What others often interpret as arrogance is really Lucas's unyielding demand that he be treated as a human being, worthy of respect. Gradually, Chick comes to realize the moral rightness in the demand Lucas makes. After the death of Mrs. Beauchamp, Chick sees Lucas and understands that grief can come to a black man as well as to a white. By the time Lucas is accused of committing murder, Chick knows that he must act with the same humanity Lucas showed him. Through Lucas, Chick also learns to accept Aleck as an equal. Thus, through the initiation of Chick, Faulkner makes a powerful, positive statement about race relations as fundamentally an encounter between one human being and another.

Intruder in the Dust, because it includes Stevens's philosophical discourses on the South's ability to handle its own problems after the action has essentially been resolved, is too often dismissed as a distasteful polemic, a lapse in Faulkner's series of brilliant novels. However, *Intruder in the Dust* is not so much inferior to such works as *The Sound and the Fury* or *Absalom, Absalom!* as it is different in its approach. Always the experimenter and innovator, Faulkner here turns with considerable success to establishing his vision in genre—namely, detective—fiction, as he did earlier with *Sanctuary* (1931), an even more gothic murder mystery, and *Pylon* (1935), an adventure story about flying.

"Critical Evaluation" by Patrick Morrow

Further Reading

Bassett, John, ed. *William Faulkner: The Critical Heritage*. London: Routledge & Kegan Paul, 1975. Ninety-four critical reviews and essays on Faulkner, including six on *Intruder in the Dust*. Contains a bibliography.

Brooks, Cleanth. *William Faulkner: The Yoknapatawpha Country*. New Haven, Conn.: Yale University Press, 1963. Contains a chapter on *Intruder in the Dust*. Describes the plot and subtexts of the work and compares the characters. One of the most helpful and accessible books for information on Faulkner.

Gresset, Michel, and Patrick Samway, eds. *A Gathering of Evidence: Essays on William Faulkner's "Intruder in the Dust."* New York: Fordham University Press, 2004. Compilation of classic as well as updated essays that analyze the novel, including discussions of its depiction of community, its cultural context, and the film adaptation.

Howe, Irving. *William Faulkner: A Critical Study*. New York: Vintage Books, 1962. Focuses on the southern myth and memory. Howe finds *Intruder in the Dust* to be the novel in which Faulkner frees himself from the southern tradition of racism and stereotypes that are normally inherent to southern life.

Jehlen, Myra. *Class and Character in Faulkner's South*. New York: Columbia University Press, 1976. Jehlen finds class distinctions to be the central theme in Faulkner's novels, including *Intruder in the Dust*. Considers the treatment of characters relative to their classes.

Powers, Lyall H. *Faulkner's Yoknapatawpha Comedy*. Ann Arbor: University of Michigan Press, 1980. Emphasizes Faulkner's vision of good versus evil and his dark optimism. Draws a comparison between *Go Down, Moses* and *Intruder in the Dust*, using the character of Chick Mallison.

Towner, Theresa M. *The Cambridge Introduction to William Faulkner*. New York: Cambridge University Press, 2008. An accessible book aimed at students and general readers. Focusing on Faulkner's work, the book provides detailed analyses of his nineteen novels, discussion of his other works, and information about the critical reception to his fiction.

Wilson, Edmund. "William Faulkner's Reply to the Civil-Rights Program." In *Classics and Commercials: A Literary Chronicle of the Forties*. New York: Farrar, Straus & Giroux, 1950. Wilson maintains that the white characters in the novel come to the rescue of the African American characters with more zeal than in previous Faulkner novels, which may represent "some new stirring of public conscience" about civil rights.

Inundación castálida

Author: Sor Juana Inés de la Cruz (1648-1695)
First published: 1689
Type of work: Poetry

Sor Juana Inés de la Cruz is the most significant poet and writer of the colonial period in the Americas. Born of a poor family in the village of San Miguel de Nepantla near a town called Amecameca, not far from Mexico City, she learned to read at the age of three, and the pursuit of knowledge subsequently became her true passion. Barred from attending the University in Mexico City because she was a woman, her plan to attend classes dressed as a man failed. Sor Juana's intellectual precocity attracted the interest of Viceroy Marquis de la Laguna, and for a time she served in his palace. During this period she became a very good friend of the viceroy's wife, Vicereine Luisa Gonzaga Manrique de Lara, the countess of Paredes, marchioness de la Laguna.

In 1669, Sor Juana took vows as a nun and entered the

Convent of San Jerónimo in Mexico City; at this point she adopted the name Sor Juana Inés de la Cruz, by which she is conventionally known. While there, Sor Juana wrote plays, poetry, and prose. Her life of intellectual pleasure was ruined, however, with the publication in 1700 of her *Respuesta de la poetisa a la muy ilustre Sor Filotea de la Cruz* ("reply to Sister Philotea"), written in response to the bishop of Puebla's recommendation that she turn her mind to spiritual rather than mundane, literary matters. The authorities silenced her; she sold her library and distributed the profits to the poor. She died while tending the sick in Mexico City. Just before her death, in a bout of deep contrition, she signed her name in blood with the words "I, Sister Juana Inés de la Cruz, the worst in the world."

Inundación castálida ("the Castilian flood of the unique poet"), published in Spain in 1689, was dedicated to Vicereine de la Laguna, who was so impressed by its contents that she brought the manuscript to Madrid to have it printed. Its publication was funded by Don Juan Camacho Gayna, a gentleman of the Order of Santiago and then governor of the city of Puerto de Santa María, as the frontispiece of *Inundación castálida* states. While in the Convent of San Jerónimo, Sor Juana continued to write, her fame spread, and she became known as the Tenth Muse of Mexico. When *Inundación castálida* was published, it was a great success and was reprinted nine times (a very high number for a time when the printing of a book was a major financial enterprise and when books rarely went beyond a first edition). It was intended to be the first of the three volumes of her complete works. After the publication of *Inundación castálida*, Sor Juana's confessor, Father Núñez de Miranda, perhaps through jealousy, put pressure on Sor Juana to give up writing poetry in order to concentrate on her religious duties.

The works collected in *Inundación castálida* are not grouped either thematically or chronologically in the original 1689 edition. This may seem strange to the modern reader who expects more order in the edition of a work of literature. It is important to recall, however, that *Inundación castálida* is a compilation and therefore brings together separate pieces of creative writing. It would not have been unusual for parts of this book to have been copied down by readers and then circulated to others. The poems in *Inundación castálida* can, however, be divided into four groups: *loas*, *villancicos*, the extended poem *Neptuno*, and personal lyrics.

The *loas*, *villancicos*, and *Neptuno* in *Inundación castálida* are all circumstantial poems; that is, they were commissioned by a third party, normally to commemorate an important historical or ritual event. The *loa* is an introit, or miniplay, that acts as a preface to a play about to be performed. One of the best examples of the *loa* in *Inundación castálida* is dedicated to Carlos II and was performed on November 6, 1681 or 1682, in the viceroy's palace before the performance of Pedro Calderón de la Barca's 1679 play *En esta vida todo es verdad y todo es mentira* ("in this life everything is true and everything is lies"). It has five speaking parts: La Vida ("life"), La Majestad ("majesty"), La Plebe ("the people"), La Naturaleza ("nature"), and La Lealtad ("loyalty"), and it is accompanied by two choirs. The *loa* begins by praising the king, Carlos II, passes to a discussion of the meaning of majesty (which is presented in positive terms), and then briefly describes the contents of Calderón's play, which is about to begin.

The second type of work in the *Inundación castálida* is the *villancico*, which, like the *loa*, is circumstantial. The *villancico* is a popular poetic composition with a refrain based on a religious theme and normally sung in church at Christmas or at other religious holidays. One of the best set of *villancicos* in this work was originally sung in 1665 in the Cathedral of Mexico in honor of the Virgin Mary to celebrate her Assumption, and then it was printed in the *Inundación castálida*. It has various prayers to the Virgin Mary asking for her protection, choral parts, a refrain that is repeated, and even different linguistic styles and languages; one section is in Latin, another in black Spanish, and another in Basque.

The third element in the *Inundación castálida*, the *Neptuno*, is an allegorical description of the triumphal arch that was built for the viceroys de la Laguna on their arrival in Mexico City in 1680. This poem mixes description of the arch with references to classical mythology and other sources that delve into the symbolic meaning of the arch. It has three main parts: the dedication to the viceroy; the "Razón de la fábrica," in which the building process is described; and the "Explicación del Arco," in which the allegorical meaning of the building is drawn out for the audience.

The three elements described thus far are all circumstantial poems, written at the behest of a third party, whether it be the church, the king, or the viceroy. For this reason, they are sometimes seen by modern readers as not authentic literature. It is important to recall, however, that in the seventeenth century the writer was often backed by a wealthy patron. Later, and particularly during the nineteenth century, when Romanticism was at its height, readers began to demand and expect creative writing that focused on the private sphere of the emotions. In the process, the more practical view of literature fell out of fashion. It is important, however, to remember that Sor Juana's work was produced in an era in which it was normal for a work of literature to be commissioned by the church or the king or the viceroy.

It is on the fourth group of poems, the personal poems, that Sor Juana's international fame is based. These poems have the most varied types of poetic composition, ranging from sonnets (poems that have fourteen eleven-syllable lines) to *décimas* (poems that have ten eight-syllable lines), from *redondillas* (a metrical combination of four eight-syllable lines) to *liras* (a five-line metrical sequence combining lines of seven and eleven syllables). The most common form in this group of poems is the sonnet, a poetic form that denotes seriousness. Like the other three groups, this group of poems has a circumstantial dimension; thus, some poems were written for special circumstances, such as the vicereine's birthday. What differentiates these poems, however, is that the circumstantial aspect becomes the springboard for something more profound. A poem that begins as the description of a portrait painting becomes a philosophical inquiry into the meaning of life: "Este, que ves, engaño colorido" ("this that you gaze on, colorful deceit"). There are a number of common themes in these poems, such as the conflict between appearance and essence and between the natural and the artificial, the brevity of human life, the delusion of love, and baroque disillusionment. The style of these poems is baroque, that is, characterized by a complex and elaborate form, ambiguous imagery, and dynamic intellectual oppositions and contrasts.

The better of the personal poems deal with philosophy and with love. Her philosophical poem "Rosa divina que en gentil cultura" ("divine rose which in gentle culture"), for example, deliberately chooses one of the most beautiful creations of the natural world (the rose) in order, ironically, to expose its frailty. The last line of the poem stresses the contrast between appearance and essence: "viviendo engañas y muriendo enseñas" ("in living you deceive and in dying you teach"). The most intellectually brilliant poems within this group are the ones dedicated to love. Some of these poems, written, it must be assumed, before she took her vows, expose her as caught in an unbearable love triangle. She loves a man who does not love her, and she is loved by another man whom she does not love. The first stanza of "Al que ingrato me deja, busco amante" is a fine example of baroque conceit. It begins, "To the one who leaves me ungratefully, I seek as a lover;/ to the one who pursues me for love, I ungratefully leave;/ I constantly adore the one who mistreats my love;/ and I mistreat him who constantly desires my love." Sor Juana's most celebrated poem, "Hombres necios," looks at the same dilemma but presents it from a universal rather than a subjective point of view. In this poem there is a clear example

of Sor Juana's feminist ideology. With devastating irony she criticizes men for attempting to find in women something they themselves are lacking. The first stanza encapsulates the argument of the whole poem. It reads, "Misguided men who will chastise/ a woman when no blame is due/ oblivious that it is you/ who prompted what you criticize." The various examples that Sor Juana then uses are all designed to flesh out the abstraction of this argument. The sixth stanza, for example, refers to the irony of the man who breathes on a mirror (takes a woman's virginity) and then complains he cannot see his own reflection (complains she is not chaste).

Stephen M. Hart

Further Reading

Bergmann, Emilie L. "Sor Juana Inés de la Cruz: Dreaming in a Double Voice." In *Women, Culture, and Politics in Latin America/Seminar on Feminism and Culture in Latin America*, edited by Emilie Bergmann et al. Berkeley: University of California Press, 1990. Argues that Sor Juana's imagination is gendered; discusses the love poems as well as the "Hombres necios" poem.

Bergmann, Emilie L., and Stacey Schlau, eds. *Approaches to Teaching the Works of Sor Juana Inés de la Cruz.* New York: Modern Language Association of America, 2007. Contains a wide range of essays that analyze Sor Juana's writing and place her work and life in historical and social context. Some of the essays discuss gender, power, and religion in Spanish colonial society, the lives of religious women of her period, her "baroque poetry," and the relationship of her works to those of twenty-first century writers.

Daniel, Lee A. *The Loa of Sor Juana Inés de la Cruz.* Fredericton, N.B.: York, 1994. Contains a general overview of the *loa* in Sor Juana's work. Looks specifically at the echo effect and the distancing effect that the *loa* creates with respect to the main play.

Franco, Jean. *Plotting Women: Gender and Representation in Mexico.* New York: Columbia University Press, 1989. A suggestive reading of Sor Juana's work, in which the author shows that the Mexican nun was able to create a new space for her identity in a patriarchal world through the written word.

Gonzalez, Michelle A. *Sor Juana: Beauty and Justice in the Americas.* Maryknoll, N.Y.: Orbis Books, 2003. Explores Sor Juana's contributions to contemporary theology. Gonzalez argues that Sor Juana's most notable achievement was to join theology with aesthetics in a search for truth and justice. She analyzes Sor Juana's poetry within this context, pointing out its theological undercurrents and the beauty of its form and content.

Leonard, Irving. "A Baroque Poetess." In *Baroque Times in Old Mexico*. Ann Arbor: University of Michigan Press, 1959. An excellent overview of Sor Juana's work, with discussion of the paradoxes in the love sonnets.

Luciani, Frederick. *Literary Self-Fashioning in Sor Juana Inés de la Cruz*. Lewisburg, Pa.: Bucknell University Presses, 2004. Analyzes selected works of poetry, drama, and prose in order to demonstrate how Sor Juana created a literary self through her writing. Includes illustrations.

Merrim, Stephanie, ed. *Feminist Perspectives on Sor Juana Inés de la Cruz*. Detroit, Mich.: Wayne State University Press, 1991. An indispensable collection of essays that make a convincing case for viewing Sor Juana's work in feminist terms. Separate commentary deals with the essays, plays, and the poetry first published in *Inundación castälida*.

Invisible Man

Author: Ralph Ellison (1914-1994)
First published: 1952
Type of work: Novel
Type of plot: Social realism
Time of plot: Late 1930's and early 1940's
Locale: American South and New York City

Principal characters:
THE NARRATOR, an innocent young man
GRANDFATHER, whose deathbed instruction makes the narrator rethink his relationship with society
MR. NORTON, a white northern philanthropist
DR. A. HERBERT BLEDSOE, the president of an all-black college
BROTHER JACK, the head of the Brotherhood
TOD CLIFTON, an idealist
RINEHART, a person who has many identities
RAS, THE DESTROYER, a radical

The Story:

The narrator and protagonist in the novel is nameless. An innocent teenager, he was born and grew up in the South of the United States. He is used to the social patterns of the region. With maturity, the narrator gradually recognizes the chaotic understructure of "orderly" society. The demarcation line between the "two" societies is blurred in his mind for the first time when he hears his grandfather's deathbed instruction to his father. Although the old man seemed to be "obedient" and "obsequious" all his life, he tells his son and grandchildren that he was "a traitor all his born days, a spy in the enemy's country" and advises them to overcome their enemies "with yeses, undermine 'em with grins, agree 'em to death and destruction, let 'em swoller you till they vomit or bust wide open."

Later the narrator witnesses a formal social function that is attended by all "big shots" of the town. The party degenerates into a nightmare of barbarity, vulgarity, and bestial desire. At the battle royal, black students are asked to fight each other for white people's entertainment. The black students are forced to watch a naked white woman dance; they are also urged by the audience to pick up coins on electrified rugs

(the coins later turn out to be advertisement souvenirs). As a reward for his Booker-T.-Washington kind of valedictory speech, the narrator receives a calfskin briefcase. That night, the narrator dreams of meeting his grandfather, who tells him to read a note in the briefcase. The note says: "To Whom It May Concern: Keep This Nigger-Boy Running."

As part of the prize for his speech, the narrator also receives a scholarship to go to college. What he learns there, however, only further confuses him: A white philanthropist and a black sharecropper share the same kind of incestuous desire for their daughters. A black minister who gives a wonderful speech about the importance of education turns out to be blind. The president of the college confesses that he used both black and white people to advance his own career. It is also from Dr. Bledsoe, the president of the all-black college, that the narrator hears for the first time in his life that he is a "nobody," someone who, in a sense, does not exist at all. The narrator is finally expelled from the college for showing Mr. Norton, the white trustee of the college, the "seamy" side of the campus.

Equipped with Dr. Bledsoe's recommendation letter, which the narrator later learns is full of insulting remarks about him, he moves to the North. The road to the North, in a traditional sense, means freedom to African Americans. What the narrator finds there is alienation and disillusionment. While working in a paint factory, whose slogan is Keep America Pure with Liberty Paints, he is caught in the conflict between a skilled black worker and white unionists. After a boiler room accident, the narrator is sent to the factory hospital, where he receives electric shock treatment. After the doctors make sure he forgets his name and family background, the narrator is declared cured and released from the hospital.

Then one day, as he is helping people who are being evicted from an apartment building in New York City, the narrator's oratorical talent is discovered by the Brotherhood, a group meant to represent the poor and downtrodden. Brother Jack, the leader of the Brotherhood, asks the narrator to join the group. Inside the Brotherhood, the narrator not only is confronted again with the paradox of organization and disorder but also completely loses his personal identity: He is given a new name and place to live, expected to become the next Booker T. Washington, and told he is "hired to talk" but not "to think." The narrator's association with the Brotherhood, nevertheless, introduces him to all kinds of people: the white men who, for their own political gains, unscrupulously use blacks; a young black idealist who is killed for his idealism; Rinehart, the man who has multiple identities; and Ras, the Destroyer, a black radical who lashes out indiscriminately and ends up in utter isolation.

The narrator finally realizes that the Brotherhood is just as chaotic, manipulative, and power-hungry as all the other groups of people he meets in both the South and the North. He leaves the Brotherhood feeling thoroughly disillusioned. Walking away from the Brotherhood, he chances upon a riot, where he is mistaken for another person. Suddenly the narrator sees the truth: When a person is associated with either an ethnic group or a social organization, he becomes a person with no identity and, therefore, invisible. He starts to understand the significance of his grandfather's last words. At the end of the novel, the narrator creeps into a dark empty cellar to indulge in his reflections.

Critical Evaluation:

In modern American letters, the development of African American literature has followed a zigzag course. The literary movement of the Harlem Renaissance in the 1920's saw the flourishing of black writing, but the Great Depression dealt it a serious blow. The popularity and success of Richard Wright's *Native Son* (1940) and *Black Boy: A Record of Childhood and Youth* (1945) resurrected African American literature in the 1940's. The emergence of Ralph Ellison and

James Baldwin in the 1950's helped push the development of African American literature to a new height. *Invisible Man*, the only novel that Ellison published, won the National Book Award for fiction in 1953. In a *Book Week* poll of two hundred critics and writers in 1965, the book was voted the "most distinguished single work" published between 1945 and 1965 in the United States.

Besides drawing inspiration from Wright's works, Ellison was also influenced by T. S. Eliot's insistence upon the importance of tradition. Wright's use of lengthy sentences, rapid flow of consciousness conveyed by a string of participles, and long lists of abstract nouns joined together by overworked conjunctions in *Invisible Man* reminds the reader of William Faulkner's writing style. Ellison's originality, however, lies in his skillful depiction and enthusiastic celebration of African American culture. Ellison believed that black vernacular, black folklore, and black music were highly developed cultural forms that helped shape the mainstream culture in America. African American writers who either looked down upon or ignored their own cultural heritage in their writings were often trapped in using stereotypes to portray African American experience; a conscious study and celebration of African American culture could release them from the bondage of stereotypes.

In *Invisible Man*, Ellison took pains to exploit African American culture to the fullest. His portrayal of Rinehart, for example, follows the trickster tradition in African American literature. Rinehart has several identities: He is a lover, a numbers runner, a preacher, and a con man. Meeting Rinehart helps the narrator understand why his grandfather had two identities: a public one (false) and a private one (real). It also makes him realize that the relationship between having an identity and not having an identity is dialectical: A person's invisibility also gives that person an opportunity to create and adopt whichever identity he or she would like to have.

Ellison's use of black-oriented humor in *Invisible Man* produces an effect similar to that of the blues. According to Ellison, blues is an impulse to keep the painful details and episodes of a brutal experience alive in one's aching consciousness, "to finger its jagged grain, and to transcend it, not by the consolation of philosophy but by squeezing from it a near-tragic, near-comic lyricism." Ellison revealed that several of the book's themes and motifs were inspired by jokes that circulated among African Americans. The theme of invisibility, for instance, was developed from the joke that some blacks were so black they could not be seen in the dark. The paint factory's slogan If It's Optic White, It's the Right White originated from another joke: "If you're black, stay back; if you're brown, stick around; if you're white, you're right."

Invisible Man reverberates with the lyrical, musical, and rhythmic cadence of black English. Ellison borrowed phrases freely from different sources and used them effectively to accentuate his thematic concerns. *Invisible Man* abounds with phrases and sentences such as "I'll verse you but I won't curse you—," "I yam what I am!" and "Stephen's problem, like ours, was not actually one of creating the uncreated conscience of his race, but of creating the uncreated features of his face." The first part of the last sentence is taken from James Joyce's *A Portrait of the Artist as a Young Man* (1914-1915) and the second part is added by the author with a bearing on the theme of the book.

The tone of *Invisible Man* is bitter, ironic, and sometimes pessimistic. The style is vivid and flexible. When commenting on the style of the book, Ellison said: "In the South, where he (the protagonist) was trying to fit into a traditional pattern and where his sense of certainty had not yet been challenged, I felt a more naturalistic treatment was adequate."

As the hero passes from the South to the North, from the relatively stable to the swiftly changing, "his sense of certainty is lost and the style becomes expressionistic." Later on, "during his fall from grace in the Brotherhood it becomes somewhat surrealistic." Surrealism permits itself to develop nonlogically in order to reveal the operation of the subconscious mind. Ellison's use of incongruous images in *Invisible Man* works well with his thematic accentuation of the protagonist's phantasmal state of mind and the chaotic state of society.

Even though *Invisible Man* is about African American experience, the novel illuminates the common plight of people who are in earnest search for their true identity. Ellison's thematic treatment of the conflict between dream and reality, between individual and society, and between innocence and experience appeals to both black and white readers. This thematic concern is highlighted by the fact that the book opens with the narrator's claiming that his invisibility is not "exactly a matter of a biochemical accident to" his "epidermis" and it ends with the narrator's making a foreboding declaration to the reader: "Who knows but that, on the lower frequencies, I speak for you?"

Qun Wang

Further Reading

Bell, Bernard W. "Myth, Legend, and Ritual in the Novel of the Fifties." In *The Afro-American Novel and Its Tradition*. Amherst: University of Massachusetts Press, 1987. Proposes that *Invisible Man* begins in medias res, moves simultaneously in linear, vertical, and circular directions, and offers, in its use of blues, jazz, wry humor, and a mythic death and rebirth motif, a "paradoxical affirmation and rejection of American values."

Byerman, Keith E. "History Against History: A Dialectical Pattern in *Invisible Man*." In *Fingering the Jagged Grain: Tradition and Form in Recent Black Fiction*. Athens: University of Georgia Press, 1985. Sees *Invisible Man* as "a crucial text for contemporary black fictionists." In each of the novel's major phases, the college, the move to Harlem, and the Brotherhood, Ellison carefully undermines all fixed, cause-and-effect versions of history.

Callahan, John F. "The Historical Frequencies of Ralph Waldo Ellison." In *Chant of Saints: A Gathering of Afro-American Literature, Art, and Scholarship*, edited by Michael S. Harper and Robert S. Stepto. Urbana: University of Illinois Press, 1979. Asserts that *Invisible Man*'s narrator learns the essential conditions of American life to be "diversity, fluidity, complexity, chaos, swiftness of change," anything but one-dimensionality—be it racial or otherwise. History in *Invisible Man* thus means metamorphosis, "many idioms and styles," rather than the received writ of any one version.

_____, ed. *Ralph Ellison's "Invisible Man": A Casebook*. New York: Oxford University Press, 2004. A collection of critical essays on *Invisible Man* written by a variety of scholars. Includes an Ellison lecture.

Gottesman, Ronald. *The Merrill Studies in "Invisible Man."* Westerville, Ohio: Charles E. Merrill, 1971. A collection of essays focuses on Ellison's thematic concerns, narrative point of view, style, and use of language in *Invisible Man*.

Hersey, John, ed. *Ralph Ellison: A Collection of Critical Essays*. Englewood Cliffs, N.J.: Prentice-Hall, 1974. A collection of essays on different aspects of Ellison's work. Provides a panoramic view of Ellison as an artist, a musician, and a writer. The book also includes Hersey and James McPherson's interview with Ellison.

Hill, Michael D., and Lena M. Hill, eds. *Ralph Ellison's "Invisible Man": A Reference Guide*. Westport, Conn.: Greenwood Press, 2008. Designed for high school and college students, this book provides a detailed plot summary and discussions of the novel's origins, social, historical, and political contexts, themes and issues, and critical reception.

Morel, Lucas E., ed. *Ralph Ellison and the Raft of Hope: A Political Companion to "Invisible Man."* Lexington: University Press of Kentucky, 2004. Collection of essays that view Ellison as a political novelist, essayist, and commentator, whose works reflect the struggle for racial equality. Many of the essays focus on *Invisible Man*, discussing the "political artistry" of this novel, the novel as a literary analogue to the U.S. Supreme Court decision in *Brown vs. Board of Education*, and *"Documenting Turbulence: The Dialectics of Chaos in Invisible Man."*

O'Meally, Robert G. *The Craft of Ralph Ellison*. Cambridge, Mass.: Harvard University Press, 1980. An excellent study of Ellison's work. Contains biographical information about the author, a bibliography, and key references on Ellison and *Invisible Man*.

Ostendorf, Berndt. "Ralph Waldo Ellison: Anthropology, Modernism, and Jazz." In *New Essays on "Invisible Man,"* edited by Robert O'Meally. New York: Cambridge University Press, 1988. Interprets *Invisible Man* through three frames: as a series of ritual transformations, as a work of modernist tactics, and as a jazz improvisation.

Posnock, Ross, ed. *The Cambridge Companion to Ralph Ellison*. New York: Cambridge University Press, 2005. Collection of essays examining various aspects of Ellison's work, including Ellison and the black church, female iconography in *Invisible Man*, and "Invisible Ellison: The Fight to Be a Political Leader."

Rampersad, Arnold. *Ralph Ellison: A Biography*. New York: Alfred A. Knopf, 2007. Excellent, comprehensive account of Ellison's life and work, describing how he came to write *Invisible Man* and how he failed to write another book after completing his masterpiece.

The Invisible Man
A Grotesque Romance

Author: H. G. Wells (1866-1946)
First published: 1897
Type of work: Novel
Type of plot: Science fiction
Time of plot: Late nineteenth century
Locale: England

Principal characters:
GRIFFIN, the Invisible Man
MR. HALL, the landlord of the Coach and Horses Inn
MRS. HALL, his wife
DR. KEMP, a physician in the town of Burdock
COLONEL ADYE, the chief of the Burdock police
MARVEL, a tramp

The Story:

The stranger arrives at Bramblehurst railway station on a cold, snowy day in February. Carrying a valise, he trudges through driving snow to Iping, where he stumbles into the Coach and Horses Inn and asks Mrs. Hall, the host, for a room and a fire. The stranger's face is hidden by dark blue spectacles and bushy sideburns.

He has dinner in his room. When Mrs. Hall takes a mustard jar up to him, she sees that the stranger's head is completely bandaged. While she is in his room, he covers his mouth and his chin with a napkin.

His baggage arrives the next day, consisting of several trunks and boxes of books and a crate of bottles packed in straw. The drayman's dog attacks the stranger, tearing his glove and ripping his trousers. Mr. Hall, landlord of the inn, runs upstairs to see if the stranger was hurt and enters his room without knocking. He is immediately struck on the chest and pushed from the room. When Mrs. Hall takes up the lodger's supper, she sees that he has unpacked his trunks and boxes and set up some strange apparatus. The lodger is not wearing his glasses; his eyes look sunken and hollow.

In the weeks that follow, the villagers make many conjectures as to the stranger's identity. Some think he suffers from a strange disease that left his skin spotted. Unusual happenings also mystify the village. One night, the vicar and his wife are awakened by a noise in the vicar's study and the clinking of money. Upon investigation, they see no one, although a candle is burning and they hear a sneeze.

In the meantime, Mr. Hall finds clothing and bandages scattered about the lodger's room; the stranger disappears. The landlord goes downstairs to call his wife. They hear the front door open and shut, but no one comes into the inn. While they stand wondering what to do, their lodger comes down the stairs. Where he was and how he returned to his room unnoticed are mysteries that he makes no attempt to explain.

A short time later, the stranger's bill being overdue, Mrs. Hall refuses to serve him. When the stranger becomes abusive, Mr. Hall swears out a warrant against him. The constable, the landlord, and a curious neighbor go upstairs to arrest the lodger. After a struggle, the man agrees to unmask. The men are struck with horror; the stranger is invisible to their view. In the confusion, the Invisible Man, as the newspapers are soon to call him, flees from the inn.

The next person to encounter the Invisible Man is a tramp named Marvel. The Invisible Man frightens Marvel into accompanying him to the Coach and Horses Inn to get his clothing and three books. They arrive at the inn while the vicar and the village doctor are reading the stranger's diary. They beat the two men, snatch up the clothes and books, and leave the inn.

Newspapers continue to print stories of unnatural thefts. Money is taken and carried away; the thief is invisible while the money is in plain view. Marvel always seems to be well supplied with funds.

One day Marvel, carrying three books, comes running into the Jolly Cricketers Inn. He says that the Invisible Man is after him. A barman, a policeman, and a cabman await the Invisible Man's arrival after hiding Marvel; the Invisible Man finds Marvel, however, drags him into the inn kitchen, and tries to force him through the door. The three men struggle with the unseen creature while Marvel crawls into the bar. When the voice of the Invisible Man is heard in the inn yard, a villager fires five shots in the direction of the sound, but searchers find no body in the yard.

Meanwhile, Dr. Kemp works late in his study in Burdock. Preparing to retire, he notices drops of drying blood on the stairs. He finds the doorknob of his room smeared with blood and red stains on his bed. While he stares in amazement at a bandage that is apparently wrapping itself about nothing in midair, a voice calls him by name. The Invisible Man takes refuge in Kemp's rooms. He identifies himself as Griffin, a young scientist whom Kemp met at the university where both studied. Griffin asks for whiskey and food. He says that except for short naps he did not sleep for three days and nights.

That night, Kemp sits up to read all the newspaper accounts of the activities of the Invisible Man. At last, after much thought, he writes a letter to Colonel Adye, chief of the Burdock police.

In the morning, Griffin tells his story to Kemp. He explains that for three years he experimented with refractions of light on the theory that a human body will become invisible if the cells can be made transparent. He needed money for his work and robbed his father of money belonging to someone else; after that, his father shot himself. At last, his experiments were successful. After setting fire to his room in order to destroy the evidence of his research, he began his strange

adventures. He terrorized Oxford Street, where passersby saw only his footprints. He discovered that in his invisible state he was compelled to fast, for all unassimilated food and drink was grotesquely visible. At last, prowling London streets and made desperate by his plight, he went to a shop selling theatrical supplies. There he stole the dark glasses, the sideburns, and the clothes he wore on his arrival in Iping.

Griffin plans to use Kemp's house as a headquarters while terrorizing the neighborhood. Kemp, believing that Griffin is insane, attempts to restrain him, but the Invisible Man escapes. Shortly thereafter, a man called Mr. Wicksteed is found murdered, and a manhunt begins.

The next morning, Kemp receives a note announcing that the reign of terror is begun; one person will be executed daily. Kemp is to be the first victim. He is to die at noon; nothing can protect him. Kemp sends at once for Colonel Adye. While they are discussing possible precautions, stones are hurled through the windows. The colonel leaves to return to the police station for some bloodhounds to set on Griffin's trail, but Griffin snatches a revolver from Colonel Adye's pocket and wounds the police officer. When Griffin smashes Kemp's kitchen door with an ax, the doctor climbs through a window and runs to a neighbor's house. He is refused admittance. He runs to the inn. The door is barred. Suddenly, his invisible assailant seizes him. While they struggle, some men come to the doctor's rescue. Kemp gets hold of Griffin's arms. A constable seizes his legs. Someone strikes through the air with a spade. The writhing unseen figure sags to the ground. Kemp announces that he cannot hear Griffin's heartbeats. While the crowd gathers, Griffin's body slowly materializes, naked, dead. A sheet is brought from the inn, and the body is carried away. The reign of terror ends.

Critical Evaluation:

The Invisible Man has an honored place as one of the first works of modern science fiction. H. G. Wells, a science student and teacher, was keenly interested in how the twentieth century would develop its technical knowledge. He was equally concerned with the morality of the scientific experimenter. Griffin is one type of scientist, aloof, aggressive, and contemptuous of his fellow humans. Ordinary people irritate him. They seem petty compared to his lofty concern with the mechanisms of nature. His knowledge isolates him; he thinks only of his discovery and the power that his special knowledge gives him. Consequently, he becomes a menace to society.

Wells does not reveal the full implications of Griffin's threat to order until the last pages of the novel. At first, Griffin is a mysterious stranger seeking seclusion. His gruff man-

The Invisible Man / WELLS

ner is partly excusable because he is fending off the prying questions of his landlady and other villagers. After his plight as an invisible man is revealed, the narrative shifts to an absorbing, intricate account of how he tries to remain at large. The moral implications of his discovery are not considered while society is still mobilizing to cope with this new phenomenon.

Only when Griffin feels cornered and takes refuge in Dr. Kemp's home does Wells fully reveal Griffin's mind and character. For the first time, Griffin has a scientific colleague to whom he can unburden himself. Griffin believes that Kemp will understand the scientific details and share his commitment to terrorizing and remaking society. Griffin reasons in this faulty manner because he has completely lost contact with his fellow man. He sees society only as material that he can manipulate.

Griffin is so absorbed in his own views that he does not detect the revulsion Kemp feels for his murderous plans. Griffin means to use science as an instrument of terror; the scientist will become a dictator, deciding who shall live and who shall die. In the process, the scientist himself becomes a monster, oblivious of humanity.

In a sense, Wells has rewritten Mary Wollstonecraft Shelley's classic *Frankenstein* (1818). In that novel, Victor Frankenstein tries to improve humanity by using parts of human bodies to create a perfect being. Frankenstein also isolates himself from his community, allows his enthusiasm for scientific discovery to outweigh moral considerations, and consequently produces a monster. Frankenstein, however, reacts to his terrible invention with horror and contrition, realizing that he has separated himself from humanity. Griffin, on the other hand, is the model of the disinterested scientist. He is solely concerned with his experiments. He will destroy anything that impedes his scientific progress. He is the modern professional, cool and self-contained. He has no emotional involvement with anything but his experiments.

That Dr. Kemp should triumph over Griffin suggests that there are natural limitations to the damage a scientist such as Griffin can inflict on society. Griffin fails to gain Dr. Kemp as a collaborator precisely because Griffin does not recognize Dr. Kemp's humanity. Because Griffin is himself the monster, he guarantees his own doom. Society will crush him just as he plans to crush it.

There is something heroic in Griffin's dedication to science, but his quest is perverted. Science offers the possibility of specialized knowledge, of improving the human condition, and of learning more about nature. The scientist, however, must realize that he is a part of what he studies and that he cannot set himself apart from it. Frankenstein cannot

make a perfect human being because he himself is imperfect and the human body parts he uses to make his monster are flawed as well. Similarly, Wells shows that Griffin becomes a criminal as soon as he becomes invisible because of his defective nature. Invisibility merely increases his sense of isolation from society and intensifies his sense of uniqueness and superiority; invisibility does not contribute to Griffin's understanding of nature.

Griffin's cruelty is a striking feature of his characterization. It is painful to witness his torturing of the poor tramp, Marvel. Like the other characters in *The Invisible Man*, Marvel is a vivid, colorful creation. He is given a distinct voice. He may seem pathetic, an easy target for Griffin's jeers, but his individuality and his right to his own life are precious values that Griffin would deny him. In Griffin's hands, science becomes a tool of tyranny, a way of denying all individuality, a way of blending all of humanity into the mad scientist's vision of carefully controlled experiments. People become test subjects.

Because Griffin's explanation of his experiments and of his scornful view of humanity are withheld until nearly the end of the novel, Wells is able to maintain extraordinary tension and suspense. How did Griffin make himself invisible? Why did he do it? How does his invisibility affect him? The answers to these questions are held until the denouement of the novel, until the narrative works through several exciting scenes of pursuit and violence. Not until the unbearability of Griffin's isolation is complete is he given an opportunity to explain himself.

These final scenes constitute Griffin's confession, defense, and defiance of society's conventions. He acts as though his invention entitles him to violate morality, even to murder. At this point, he sounds demented, a man overtaken by intellectual passions, in the grip of ideas that strip him of his humanity.

Although Griffin's cruelty seems to deprive the reader of any sense of sympathy for him, the novel ends with a touching image of him, "naked and pitiful on the ground, the bruised and broken body of a young man about thirty." The scene suggests that Griffin is also a victim, hardly yet mature, deluded, fragile, and misled, a representative of erring humanity, vulnerable and tragic.

"Critical Evaluation" by Carl Rollyson

Further Reading

Costa, Richard Hauer. *H. G. Wells*. Boston: Twayne, 1967. Explains the influence of science on *The Invisible Man*, compares the novel to Wells's earlier science fiction, and explores the struggle of the characters to cope with new scientific attitudes.

Hammond, J. R. *An H. G. Wells Companion: A Guide to the Novels, Romances, and Short Stories.* Totowa, N.J.: Barnes & Noble, 1979. Describes the sense of excitement that greeted the first publication of *The Invisible Man*, its circumstantial and realistic setting, the sharp observation of social details, and the economical and dramatic structure of the narrative.

_____. *A Preface to H. G. Wells.* New York: Longman, 2001. Provides information on Wells's life, cultural background, important people and places in his life, critical commentary on his works, and a discussion of his literary reputation.

McConnell, Frank. *The Science Fiction of H. G. Wells.* New York: Oxford University Press, 1981. Emphasizes the novel's grim realism. Considers nineteenth century works that may have influenced Wells's unique sense of the apocalyptic and his powerful descriptions of society in disorder. Analyzes Griffin's character and his proneness to violence, Wells's depiction of middle-class society and how it organizes itself to capture Griffin, and the role of Marvel as a comic character and victim.

Mackenzie, Norman, and Jeanne Mackenzie. *The Time Trav-eller: The Life of H. G. Wells.* Rev. ed. London: Hogarth Press, 1987. Compares Griffin to Wells's other mad scientists and discusses Wells's ambivalence about science, his choice of characters, and the place of the characters in his thinking about science and nature.

McLean, Steven, ed. *H. G. Wells: Interdisciplinary Essays.* Newcastle, England: Cambridge Scholars, 2008. The ten essays analyze individual novels and discuss general characteristics of Wells's work, including Wells and the discussion novel, dwellings and the natural environment in his futuristic vision, and a comparison of Wells and Henry James.

Wagar, W. Warren. *H. G. Wells: Traversing Time.* Middletown, Conn.: Wesleyan University Press, 2004. Analyzes all of Wells's work, focusing on its preoccupation with the unfolding of public time and the history and future of humankind. Demonstrates how Wells's writings remain relevant in the twenty-first century.

Williamson, Jack. *H. G. Wells: Critic of Progress.* Baltimore: Mirage Press, 1973. Discusses Griffin's inhuman qualities and the role of the intellect as a theme in the novel. Explores the precise evocation of setting, Wells's handling of point of view, and his tendency to overlook inconsistencies in order to build his narrative.

Iolanthe
Or, The Peer and the Peri

Author: W. S. Gilbert (1836-1911)
First produced: 1882; first published, 1882
Type of work: Drama
Type of plot: Operetta
Time of plot: Nineteenth century
Locale: England

Principal characters:
THE LORD CHANCELLOR
STREPHON, an Arcadian shepherd
QUEEN OF THE FAIRIES
IOLANTHE, Strephon's fairy mother
PHYLLIS, a shepherdess and ward in Chancery
THE EARL OF MOUNTARARAT and EARL TOLLOLLER, her suitors
PRIVATE WILLIS, a palace guard

The Story:

The Fairy Queen banishes Iolanthe because Iolanthe marries a mortal. Normally the punishment for such an act is death, but the queen so loves Iolanthe that she is unable to enforce the penalty. Iolanthe is sentenced to penal servitude for life, on the condition that she never see her mortal husband again. The other fairies beg the queen to relent, to set aside this punishment. Iolanthe serves twenty-five years of her sentence standing on her head at the bottom of a stream.

The queen, unable to resist their pleas, summons the penitent Iolanthe and pardons her. Iolanthe explains that she stayed in the stream to be near her son Strephon, an Arcadian shepherd who is a fairy to his waist and a human from the waist down. While they speak, Strephon enters, announcing that he is to be married that day to Phyllis, a ward of Chancery. The Lord Chancellor does not give his permission, but Strephon is determined to marry his Phyllis anyway. He is delighted when he learns that his mother is pardoned, but he begs her and all the fairies not to tell Phyllis that he is half fairy. He fears that she will not understand.

The queen determines to make Strephon a member of Parliament, but Strephon says that he will be no good in that August body, for the top of him is a Tory, the bottom a Radical. The queen solves that problem by making him a Liberal-Unionist and taking his mortal legs under her particular care. Phyllis talks with Strephon and warns him that to marry her without the Lord Chancellor's permission will mean lifelong penal servitude for him. Strephon cannot wait the two years until she is of age. He fears that the Lord Chancellor himself or one of the peers of the House of Lords will marry her before that time passes.

Strephon's fears are well founded; the Lord Chancellor does want to marry his ward. Fearing that he will have to punish himself for marrying her without his permission, however, he decides to give her instead to one of the peers of the House of Lords. Two are at last selected, the Earl of Mountararat and Earl Tolloller, but there is no agreement as to the final choice. Phyllis does not wish to accept either, since she loves only Strephon. Then she sees Strephon talking with Iolanthe, who, being immortal, looks like a young and beautiful woman, although she is Strephon's mother. Phyllis is filled with jealousy, augmented by the laughter of the peers when Strephon, in desperation, confesses that Iolanthe is his mother. Weeping that he has betrayed her, Phyllis leaves Strephon. No one ever heard of a son who looks older than his mother.

The Fairy Queen tells the Lord Chancellor and the peers that they will rue their laughter over Iolanthe and her son. To punish them, Strephon will change all existing laws in the House of Lords. He will abolish the rights of peers and give titles to worthy commoners. Worst of all, from then on peers will be chosen by competitive examinations. Strephon will be a foe they will not soon forget.

The queen's prediction comes true. Strephon completely rules the House of Lords. Every bill he proposes passes, the fairies making the other members vote for Strephon even when they want to vote against him. The peers appeal to the fairies, but although the fairies admire the peers, the fairies cannot be swayed against Strephon. The Earl of Mountararat and Earl Tolloller try to decide who should have Phyllis.

Each wants the other to sacrifice himself by giving up all rights to her. Both have a family tradition that they must fight anyone who takes their sweethearts, and since a fight means that one of them will die and the survivor will be left without his friend, each wants to make the sacrifice of losing his friend. At last the two decide that friendship is more important than love. Both renounce Phyllis.

Strephon and Phyllis meet again, and at last he convinces her that Iolanthe is really his mother. Phyllis still cannot believe that Strephon looks like a fairy, and she cannot quite understand that his grandmother and all his aunts look as young as his mother. She is sensible, however, and promises that whenever she sees Strephon kissing a very young woman she will know the woman is an elderly relative. There is still the Lord Chancellor to contend with. When they go to Iolanthe and beg her to persuade him to consent to their marriage, Iolanthe tells them that the Lord Chancellor is her mortal husband. He believes her dead and himself childless, and if she looks on him the queen will carry out the penalty of instant death.

Iolanthe cannot resist the pleas of the young lovers. As she tells the Lord Chancellor that she is his lost wife, the queen enters and prepares to carry out the sentence of death against Iolanthe. Before she can act, however, the other fairies enter and confess that they, too, married peers in the House of Lords. The queen grieves, but the law is clear. Whoever marries a mortal must die. The Lord Chancellor's great knowledge of the law saves the day. The law will now read that whoever does not marry a mortal must die. Thinking that a wonderful solution, the queen takes one of the palace guards, Private Willis, for her husband. Knowing that from now on the House of Lords will be recruited from persons of intelligence, because of Strephon's law, the current peers can see that they are of little use. Sprouting wings, they all fly away to Fairyland.

Critical Evaluation:

While *Patience* was still enjoying a long run at the Savoy Theatre, W. S. Gilbert prepared for his musical collaborator, Arthur Sullivan, the libretto for a new comic opera. Sullivan, as usual, was not wholly satisfied with the preliminary draft of the book, and at his urging Gilbert rewrote the first act. Gilbert had trouble with the title. His last three successful D'Oyly Carte productions had begun with the letter P—*Pinafore* (1878), *The Pirates of Penzance* (1879), and *Patience* (1881)—Gilbert thrashed about for another title beginning with the "lucky" initial. He considered and then rejected "Perola," "Phyllis," and "Princess Pearl" before he chose *Iolanthe*, with the acceptable subtitle *The Peer and the*

Peri. This last matter settled, Gilbert and Sullivan's "entirely new and original fairy opera" opened at the Savoy on the evening of November 25, 1882, and continued to hold the stage for a year and two months.

No doubt Gilbert wished to emphasize the "fairy" elements of *Iolanthe* in order to soften any possible criticism of his spoof upon the House of Lords. In the course of Parliamentary debates in Victorian England, the House of Lords—a privileged and largely hereditary body lacking any democratic representation—was under constant fire as antiquated, unresponsive to the people, and ultraconservative. Almost every one of the era's reform bills widened the franchise and diminished the powers of the Lords, who eventually lost most of their real authority to the House of Commons. Gilbert, clearly on the side of the liberals, wished to satirize the absurdity of the Peers but not so directly as to excite political controversy. For the framework of his plot, he reworked an old idea from one of his Bab Ballads concerning a hero who is half fairy and half human. Not even a crusty Tory could complain that the adventures of Strephon could possibly insult the dignities of a modern Lord. At the conclusion of *Iolanthe*, all the Peers marry the fairies, and the doughtiest Lord in Parliament would have to acquiesce in pleasure to Gilbert's romantic jest.

Behind the jest, Gilbert's satire applies not only to the House of Lords but also to the notion of a privileged class. The Peers announce their arrival ("Loudly Let the Trumpets Bray") with the contemptuous salutation: "Bow, bow, ye lower middle classes . . . ye tradesmen, bow ye masses!" The powerful Lord Chancellor, who argues that the law is the "true embodiment of everything that's excellent," cynically changes the law to suit himself and ensure that every fairy shall die who does not marry a mortal. In "Spurn Not the Nobly Born," Lord Tolloller insists that high rank "involves no shame," so women should never withhold affection from "Blue Bloods." Finally, Lord Mountararat, in "When Britain Really Ruled the Waves," looks backward to the good old days of Queen Bess, when the House of Peers "made no pretence to intellectual eminence or scholarship sublime." By their own merry words, the Peers indict themselves as a class of drones, bores, and fools. Gilbert, not disposed to press the point, permits the Lords to grow wings to fly off to a fairyland blessedly distant from the responsibilities of office.

Further Reading

Ainger, Michael. *Gilbert and Sullivan: A Dual Biography.* New York: Oxford University Press, 2002. Chronicles the lives and working partnership of Gilbert and his collaborator, describing how their different personalities spurred them to produce their best work.

Bailey, Leslie. *Gilbert and Sullivan and Their World.* New York: Thames and Hudson, 1973. Examines the original production of *Iolanthe* and notes its allusions to Wagnerian opera. Contains photographs and sketches of early productions.

Crowther, Andrew. *Contradiction Contradicted: The Plays of W. S. Gilbert.* Cranbury, N.J.: Associated University Presses, 2000. An examination of all of Gilbert's plays, including his collaborations with Sullivan. Crowther compares previous critiques of the plays with the plays themselves.

Dark, Sidney, and Rowland Grey. *W. S. Gilbert: His Life and Letters.* Ann Arbor, Mich.: Gryphon Books, 1971. Shows *Iolanthe*'s indebtedness to *The Bab Ballads* (1869) and considers the development of the patter song in the Lord Chancellor's songs. Examines the role of the chorus in relation to other Gilbert and Sullivan works.

Dunn, George E. *A Gilbert and Sullivan Directory.* New York: Da Capo Press, 1971. A comprehensive dictionary that includes references to Gilbert's many allusions. Shows correlations among various Gilbert and Sullivan works.

Heylar, James, ed. *Gilbert and Sullivan: Papers Presented at the International Conference Held at the University of Kansas in May, 1970.* Lawrence: University of Kansas Library, 1971. Examines the considerable abridgments made to *Iolanthe* over the years and the reasons for these changes. Connects the operetta to similar works.

Moore, Frank Ledlie. *Handbook of Gilbert and Sullivan.* New York: Schocken Books, 1975. Gives an overview of *Iolanthe*. Places the opera in the pastoral tradition and considers its many allusions to the operas of Richard Wagner.

Wren, Gayden. *A Most Ingenious Paradox: The Art of Gilbert and Sullivan.* New York: Oxford University Press, 2001. An analysis of the operettas, in which Wren explores the reasons for the continued popularity of these works. Chapter 9 is devoted to an examination of *Iolanthe*.

Ion

Author: Euripides (c. 485-406 B.C.E.)

First produced: *Iōn*, c. 411 B.C.E. (English translation, 1781)

Type of work: Drama

Type of plot: Tragicomedy

Time of plot: Antiquity

Locale: The temple of Apollo at Delphi

Principal characters:

HERMES, the speaker of the prologue

ION, the son of Apollo and Creusa

CREUSA, the daughter of Erechtheus, king of Athens

XUTHUS, Creusa's husband

AGED SLAVE TO CREUSA

A PRIESTESS OF APOLLO

PALLAS ATHENA, goddess of wisdom

CHORUS OF CREUSA'S HANDMAIDENS

The Story:

Years before, Phoebus Apollo raped Creusa, daughter of King Erechtheus, who subsequently and in secret gave birth to a son. By Apollo's command she hid the infant in a cave, where Hermes was sent to carry him to the temple of Apollo. There he was reared as a temple ministrant. Meanwhile, Creusa married Xuthus as a reward for his aid in the Athenian war against the Euboeans, but the marriage remained without issue. After years of frustration, Xuthus and Creusa decided to make a pilgrimage to Delphi and ask the god for aid in getting a son.

At dawn Ion emerges from the temple of Apollo to sweep the floors, chase away the birds, set out the laurel boughs, and make the usual morning sacrifice. Creusa's handmaidens come to admire the temple built upon the navel of the world and to announce the imminent arrival of their mistress. At the meeting of Creusa and Ion, Creusa confirms the story that her father was drawn from the earth by Athena and was swallowed up by the earth at the end of his life. The credulous Ion explains that his own birth, too, is shrouded in mystery, for he appeared out of nowhere at the temple and was reared by the priestess of Apollo. The greatest sorrow of his life, he says, is not knowing who his mother is. Creusa sympathizes and cautiously reveals that she has a friend with a similar problem, a woman bore a son to Apollo, only to have the infant disappear and to suffer childlessness for the rest of her life.

Ion, shocked and outraged at the insult to his god, demands that Creusa end her accusation of Apollo in his own temple, but the anguished woman assails the god with fresh charges of injustice, breaking off only at the arrival of her husband. Xuthus eagerly takes his wife into the temple, for he was assured by the prophet Trophonius that they would not return childless to Athens. The perplexed Ion is left alone to meditate on the lawlessness of gods who seem to put pleasure before wisdom.

Xuthus, emerging from the temple, falls upon the startled Ion and attempts to kiss and embrace him. He shouts joyfully that Ion must be his son, for the oracle said that the first person he would see upon leaving the temple would be his son by birth. Stunned and unconvinced, Ion demands to know the identity of his mother, but Xuthus can only conjecture that possibly she is one of the Delphian women he encountered at a bacchanal before his marriage. Ion, reluctantly conceding that Xuthus must be his father if Apollo so decrees, begs to remain an attendant in the temple rather than become the unwelcome and suspicious heir to the throne of Athens—for Creusa will surely resent a son she did not bear. Xuthus understands his anxiety and agrees to hide his identity; however, he insists that Ion accompany him to Athens, even if only in the role of distinguished guest. He then gives orders for a banquet of thanksgiving and commands that the handmaidens to Creusa keep their silence on pain of death. As they depart to prepare the feast, Ion expresses the hopes that his mother might still be found and that she might be an Athenian.

Accompanied by the aged slave of her father, Creusa reappears before the temple and demands from her handmaidens an account of the revelation Xuthus received from Apollo. Only under relentless cross-examination do the fearful servants reveal what passed between Xuthus and Ion. Overcome by a sense of betrayal, Creusa curses Apollo for his cruelty but dares not act upon the old slave's suggestion that she burn the temple or murder the husband who was, after all, kind to her.

Murder of the usurper, Ion, however, is another matter. After some deliberation Creusa decides upon a safe and secret method of eliminating the rival of her lost son. From a phial of the Gorgon's blood that Athena gave to Creusa's grandfather and that was passed down to her, the old slave is to pour a drop into Ion's wineglass at the celebration feast.

Eager to serve his master's daughter, the slave departs, and the chorus chants the hope for success.

Some time later a messenger comes running to warn Creusa that the authorities are about to seize her and submit her to death by stoning, for her plot was discovered. He describes how at the feast a flock of doves dipped down to drink from Ion's cup and died in horrible convulsions and how Ion tortured a confession out of the old slave. The court of Delphi sentences Creusa to death for attempting murder of a consecrated person within the sacred precincts of the temple of Apollo. The chorus urges Creusa to fling herself upon the altar and remain there in sanctuary.

A short time later Ion arrives at the head of an infuriated crowd, and he and Creusa begin to hurl angry charges and counter-charges at each other. Suddenly the priestess of the temple appears, bearing the cradle and the tokens with which the infant Ion was found years before. Slowly and painfully the truth emerges: Ion is the lost son of Creusa and Apollo. Creusa is seized with a frenzy of joy, but the astounded Ion remains incredulous. As he is about to enter the temple to demand an explanation from Apollo himself, the goddess Athena appears in midair and confirms the revelation. She urges that Xuthus not be told the truth so that he might enjoy the delusion that his own son is to be his heir, while Creusa and Ion can share their genuine happiness. Creusa renounces all her curses against Apollo and blesses him for his ultimate wisdom. As she and Ion depart for Athens, the chorus calls upon everyone to reverence the gods and take courage.

Critical Evaluation:

Two issues dominate criticism of *Ion*: what genre it belongs to and who Ion's father is. The answer to the first issue can only be that it is neither comedy nor tragedy; it is simple melodrama. After confusion and misunderstandings, the characters work out their differences and are happily reconciled. In this regard, the play is comic. The anger that the characters feel throughout so much of the play, however, establishes a mood that distracts from a comic, festive finale. For example, how can an audience desire a happy ending for Creusa after she plots to poison Ion? Her intention reveals a cruel nature that alienates an audience.

When the flock of doves dies in convulsions after sipping from the cup meant for Ion, the old slave confesses under duress, and Creusa is sentenced to die. Here again, although Ion has cause to beat the old slave in order to obtain the truth, acts of torture coarsen the tone of the play, and they work against the lighthearted tone expected in comedy.

The deception that the characters engage in also detracts from any sympathy felt for them. When Xuthus thinks that he is Ion's father, he accepts Ion's wish to keep their relationship secret from Creusa, even though Xuthus insists that Ion come with him to Athens. When Xuthus organizes a banquet to celebrate his honored guest—the role that Ion agrees to play—he threatens Creusa's servants with death if they reveal the truth. Creusa does learn the truth and curses Apollo, although she does not dare to burn Apollo's temple or to kill her husband.

The second major deception occurs at the end when the priestess materializes and asserts that Ion is, indeed, the lost son of Creusa and Apollo. To make this public knowledge, however, will rob Xuthus of his conviction that he is the biological father of Ion, and so Athena urges Creusa and Ion to enjoy their knowledge in secret. Creusa then retracts all her blasphemies against Apollo, and she thanks him for his superior wisdom. The play ends with a happiness structured upon falsehoods, and the gods are praised for this solution.

The second question concerns Ion's father, Apollo or Xuthus? Greeks of Euripides' day will answer this question according to how they feel about the gods. The pious answer would be that Apollo is truly the father and that Ion was raised just as Hermes explains in the prologue. This is not a difficult story to accept, given the history and reputation of the gods.

The other answer, rational and obvious to anyone skeptical of religious explanations, says that Xuthus—or some other young man—fathered the boy. For a young woman to have an illegitimate child whom she leaves in a cave to die—the same cave, perhaps, where the child is fathered—must have been possible. Apollo's reasoning in the conclusion, then, can be interpreted this way: Creusa suffered enough for abandoning her child. What will make everyone happy? Convince her that this child is really hers, as he apparently is, and let her believe that Apollo is his father if that rationalization helps her; then, let Xuthus keep on thinking that the child is his.

In this way, youthful folly is repaired, Ion and his mother find each other, and Xuthus has the son that fulfills his aspirations. This interpretation attributes genuine benevolence to the gods; however, all three characters remain deceived: Ion and Creusa believe that Apollo is the father, and Xuthus thinks that he is Ion's father by some nameless Delphian woman he encountered at a bacchic festival. What does this say about the gods? Are they mere cynics about the value of truth, or is it their wisdom about human affairs that makes them truly gods? Whatever answer prevails, this melodrama clearly intends to raise questions about the gods' role, and even their existence, and this becomes one of the important themes of *Ion*.

Another theme that deserves comment centers on Ion's historical destiny. Hermes announces at the beginning of the story that Ion will become the leader of the Ionic communities to the east, and at the end, Athena instructs Creusa to raise Ion as royalty so that he and his four sons will be famous. Ion's grandsons will colonize the Asian side of the strait, and the people there will be called Ionians. The practical effect of all this manipulation is to bestow on Ion a supernatural lineage that will provide grandeur for his historic role. Contemporary readers of *Ion* may not be alert to this patriotic theme, but it was not overlooked by Euripides' contemporaries.

Despite its problems of interpretation, *Ion* benefits from Euripides' craftsmanship. Ion grows and matures as the bewildering reversals and revelations overtake him. It is difficult to accept Creusa when she plots to poison Ion, but the scheme does build dramatic interest as it leads up to the crisis that culminates in the priestess's arrival, when she announces that Ion is the lost son of Apollo and Creusa. The cradle and the tokens are effective stage props, and Athena's late appearance is a well-contrived deus ex machina. Except for the selfish and vengeful behavior of its main characters, *Ion* is effective in its melodramatic effects.

"Critical Evaluation" by Frank Day

Further Reading

Burnett, Anne Pippin. *Catastrophe Survived: Euripides' Plays of Mixed Reversals*. Oxford, England: Clarendon Press, 1971. Distinguishes *Ion* from Euripides' other plays because its multiple actions play out simultaneously. Creusa dominates a revenge plot with "catastrophe interrupted," and Ion illustrates the theme of a return to wealth and power.

Conacher, D. J. *Euripidean Drama: Myth, Theme, and Structure*. Toronto, Ont.: University of Toronto Press, 1967. Classifies *Ion* as "romantic tragedy" and praises its technical virtuosity and characterizations. Identifies irony as the dominant tone and the key to the play's interpretation. Situates Ion and Xuthus in the political context of the day.

Euripides. *"The Bacchae," and Other Plays*. Translated by Philip Vellacott. Rev. ed. New York: Penguin Books, 1973. Paperback edition with Vellacott's excellent introduction. Argues that Ion is "the son of some visitor to the Bacchic mysteries" and defends Euripides against the common charge that he was a misogynist.

Grube, G. M. A. *The Drama of Euripides*. New York: Barnes & Noble, 1941. Judges *Ion* a delightful play that at some points achieves genuine tragic effects. Calls the old retainer more comic than tragic. Finds Xuthus to be "slightly ridiculous" and assumes that the secret of Ion's birth will be kept from Xuthus.

Meltzer, Gary S. *Euripides and the Poetics of Nostalgia*. New York: Cambridge University Press, 2006. Demonstrates how *Ion* and three other plays reflect Euripides' nostalgia for an earlier age in which Athenians respected the gods and traditional codes of conduct.

Morwood, James. *The Plays of Euripides*. Bristol, England: Bristol Classical, 2002. Morwood provides a concise overview of all of Euripides' plays, devoting a separate chapter to each one. He demonstrates how Euripides was constantly reinventing himself in his work.

Mossman, Judith, ed. *Euripides*. New York: Oxford University Press, 2003. Collection of essays, some providing a general overview of Euripidean drama, others focusing on specific plays. Includes "Iconography and Imagery in Euripides' *Ion*" by D. J. Mastronarde.

Zacharia, Katerina. *Converging Truths: Euripides' "Ion" and the Athenian Quest for Self-Definition*. Boston: Brill, 2003. Analyzes the political, psychological, religious, and poetic aspects of the play, discussing how many of the play's concepts are related to the god Apollo.

Iphigenia in Aulis

Author: Euripides (c. 485-406 B.C.E.)
First produced: Iphigeneia ē en Aulidi, 405 B.C.E. (English
    translation, 1782)
Type of work: Drama
Type of plot: Tragedy
Time of plot: Beginning of the Trojan War
Locale: Aulis, on the west coast of Euboea

Principal characters:
AGAMEMNON, king of Mycenae
CLYTEMNESTRA, his wife
IPHIGENIA, their daughter
ACHILLES, a Greek warrior
MENELAUS, king of Sparta

The Story:

At Aulis, on the west coast of Euboea, part of Greece, the Greek host assembles for the invasion of Ilium. The war was declared to rescue Helen, wife of King Menelaus, after her abduction by Paris, a prince of Troy. Lack of wind, however, prevents the sailing of the great fleet.

While the ships lie becalmed, Agamemnon, commander of the Greek forces, consults Calchas, a seer. The oracle prophesies that all will go well if Iphigenia, Agamemnon's oldest daughter, is sacrificed to the goddess Artemis. At first, Agamemnon is reluctant to see his daughter so destroyed, but Menelaus, his brother, persuades him that nothing else will move the weather-bound fleet. Agamemnon writes to Clytemnestra, his queen, and asks her to conduct Iphigenia to Aulis, his pretext being that Achilles, the outstanding warrior among the Greeks, will not embark unless he is given Iphigenia in marriage.

After dispatching the letter, Agamemnon has a change of heart; he believes that his continued popularity as coleader of the Greeks is a poor exchange for the life of his beloved daughter. In haste, he dispatches a second letter countermanding the first, but Menelaus, suspicious of his brother, intercepts the messenger and struggles with him for possession of the letter. When Agamemnon comes upon the scene, he and Menelaus exchange bitter words. Menelaus accuses his brother of being weak and foolish, and Agamemnon accuses Menelaus of supreme selfishness in urging the sacrifice of Iphigenia.

During this exchange of charge and countercharge, a messenger announces the arrival of Clytemnestra and Iphigenia in Aulis. The news plunges Agamemnon into despair; weeping, he regrets his kingship and its responsibilities. Even Menelaus is so affected that he suggests disbanding the army. Agamemnon thanks Menelaus but declares that it is too late to turn back from the course they elected to follow. Actually, Agamemnon is afraid of Calchas and Odysseus, and he believes that widespread disaffection and violence will break out in the Greek army if the sacrifice is not made. Some

Chalcian women who come to see the fleet lament that the love of Paris for Helen brings chaos and misery instead of happiness.

When Clytemnestra arrives, accompanied by her young son, Orestes, and Iphigenia, she expresses pride and joy over the approaching nuptials of her daughter and Achilles. Agamemnon greets his family tenderly; touching irony is displayed in the conversation between Agamemnon, who knows that Iphigenia is doomed to die, and Iphigenia, who thinks her father's ambiguous words have a bearing only on her approaching marriage. Clytemnestra inquires in motherly fashion about Achilles' family and background. She is scandalized when the heartbroken Agamemnon asks her to return to Argos, on the excuse that he can arrange the marriage details. When Clytemnestra refuses to leave the camp, Agamemnon seeks the advice of Calchas. Meanwhile the Chalcian women forecast the sequence of events of the Trojan War and hint in their prophecy that death is certain for Iphigenia.

Achilles and his Myrmidons are impatient with the delay and anxious to get on with the invasion of Ilium. Clytemnestra meets Achilles and mentions the impending marriage. Achilles is mystified and professes to know nothing of his proposed marriage to Iphigenia. The messenger then confesses Agamemnon's plans to the shocked Clytemnestra and Achilles. He also mentions the second letter and casts some part of the guilt upon Menelaus. Clytemnestra, grief-stricken, prevails upon Achilles to help her in saving Iphigenia from death by sacrifice.

Clytemnestra then confronts her husband, who is completely unnerved when he realizes that Clytemnestra at last knows the dreadful truth. She rebukes him fiercely, saying that she never really loved him because he murdered her beloved first husband and her first child. Iphigenia, on her knees, implores her father to save her and asks Orestes, in his childish innocence, to add his pleas to his mother's and her own. Although Agamemnon is not heartless, he knows that the sacrifice must be made. He argues that Iphigenia will die for Greece, a country and a cause greater than them all.

Achilles speaks to the army on behalf of Iphigenia, but he admits his failure when even his own Myrmidons threaten to stone him if he persists in his attempt to stop the sacrifice. At last, he musters enough loyal followers to defend the girl against Odysseus and the entire Greek host. Iphigenia refuses his aid, however, saying that she has decided to offer herself as a sacrifice for Greece. Achilles, in admiration, offers to place his men about the sacrificial altar so that she might be snatched to safety at the last moment.

Iphigenia, resigned to certain death, asks her mother not to mourn for her. Then she marches bravely to her death in the field of Artemis. Clytemnestra is left prostrate in her tent. Iphigenia, at the altar, says farewell to all that she holds dear and submits herself to the sacrifice. The Chalcian women, onlookers at the sacrifice, invoke Artemis to fill the Greek sails now with wind so that the ships might carry the army to Troy to achieve eternal glory for Greece.

Critical Evaluation:

This play is a mass of contradictions, a fact that accounts, in part at least, for its rather lukewarm reception until modern times. It is not a tragedy in the Aristotelian sense in its characters, its plot, or its theme, nor is it easily categorized with respect to any of these criteria.

Iphigenia in Aulis has been described as the tragedy of Agamemnon, who must make the horrible decision of whether to sacrifice his daughter or to abandon the war effort he has made a solemn pledge to advance. Although Agamemnon's grief is certainly authentic, there is no real suspense as to what his ultimate decision will be. For example, he sends a second messenger to Clytemnestra, urging her to ignore his earlier summons, but only after he knows that it is too late to prevent the trip. Menelaus cares little for the fate of his niece; his only interest is in retrieving Helen, and more for the sake of his own honor than for any tender feelings for his wife. Clytemnestra berates Agamemnon, but the principal impetus for her tirade is her own welfare, not that of Iphigenia. Achilles is more concerned with the fact that Agamemnon used his name without his permission than with the slaughter of an innocent. Achilles claims he will fight to the last to protect Iphigenia, but his speech sounds hollow, and the chorus immediately follows with an ode lamenting Iphigenia's imminent sacrifice. Iphigenia is to be killed despite her unquestioned innocence, and the resolve she appears to show at the end of the play ironically underscores the hypocrisy of the Greek cause: She is either more courageous than any of the soldiers or, at the very least, willing to pretend

to be the willing victim of the sacrifice (a good omen) in order that the Greeks might retrieve Helen, who appears to have gone to Troy as a result of promiscuity rather than kidnapping.

Even the terms of the plot can be called into question. Whereas in earlier versions of the myth, the Greek fleet must put up at Aulis because of rough water and unfavorable winds, Euripides makes it clear that it is calm seas that force the layover. Greek warships, however, were powered principally by oars, not by sails, and would hardly have been affected adversely by calm seas. The final moments of the play suggest that Iphigenia is not sacrificed but transported off the island by Artemis, who demanded the sacrifice in the first place. The audience, however, must be aware that even seemingly objective narration carries with it a point of view. The messenger, after all, is a specially selected soldier in Agamemnon's army, sent to tell the news of the sacrifice to Clytemnestra, whose wrath might possibly be at least partially assuaged by the thought that her daughter is indeed still alive. Some critics argue that the ending of the play as it now exists was written by someone other than Euripides, perhaps by his son, several years after the original production. Nothing is necessarily what it seems to be.

Euripides almost certainly wrote *Iphigenia in Aulis* in Macedon, while in self-imposed exile from Athens. The play was presented posthumously, along with *The Bacchae* and the lost *Alcmaeon in Corinth*, at the Dionysian festival in 405 B.C.E. Athens had been fighting the Peloponnesian Wars for more than a generation, and it was becoming increasingly clear not only that Athens would probably lose (as indeed it did the year after the play was produced) but also that imperialist overreaching would be a contributing cause to any loss. Athenian politics had been factionalized for several years, with coups and countercoups of oligarchs and of radical democrats contributing to the ferment. Euripides was a pacifist and a political conservative; it should come as no surprise either that the Trojan War is portrayed in *Iphigenia in Aulis* as senseless carnage precipitated by egocentricity, or that one of the greatest dangers the play describes is the chaos resulting from the inability of Agamemnon, Menelaus, and Achilles to control their respective armies. Democracy, to Euripides, was never far from mob rule. Euripides was also an agnostic if not an atheist; not surprisingly, the most bloodthirsty figure in the play may be the high priest, Calchas, who never appears but whose pronouncements incite the action.

In many senses, *Iphigenia in Aulis* is one of the most modern of ancient plays: The characters are complex, flawed human beings, not merely one-dimensional heroes, and the thematic material intertwines in complex and sometimes topical ways. It is easy, perhaps, to criticize the play for not adhering more rigorously to tragic norms, for taking its iconoclasm too far or for relatively frequently lapsing into melodrama. Still, the play is admirably constructed (and in conformity with the so-called three-actor rule of Greek tragedy). The movement from Agamemnon's first letter to Clytemnestra (well before the beginning of the play) to the sacrifice itself is inexorable, and the forces of reason and compassion consistently, but inevitably, fall short of derailing the killing. All of the major characters, except perhaps Menelaus, are given speeches of exceptional eloquence, and the final messenger's speech may be the most evocative of all. The play is rather static in theatrical terms: Agamemnon, Iphigenia, and, to a lesser extent, Clytemnestra and Achilles all engage in fairly lengthy internal debates, and the principal physical actions of the play take place off-stage.

The ambiguities of *Iphigenia in Aulis* make it particularly receptive to readings employing particular critical methodologies. Accordingly, the play has experienced a resurgence of interest from modern critics who analyze it through the lenses of Freudian psychology, power dynamics, and, especially, gender roles. Ultimately, however, it is probably the ambiguities themselves, not critical responses to them, that will serve as the play's most enduring legacy.

"Critical Evaluation" by Richard Jones

Further Reading

Bloom, Harold, ed. *Euripides: Comprehensive Research and Study Guide.* Philadelphia: Chelsea House, 2003. Includes a biography of Euripides and a plot summary, list of characters, and six critical essays providing various interpretations of *Iphigenia in Aulis.*

Conacher, D. J. *Euripidean Drama: Myth, Theme, and Structure.* Toronto, Ont.: University of Toronto Press, 1967. Excellent introduction to Euripides in general, with a particularly good discussion of *Iphigenia in Aulis.* Especially useful for providing mythological and literary background.

Michelakis, Pantelis. *Euripides: "Iphigenia at Aulis."* London: Gerald Duckworth, 2006. A companion to the play, providing a plot summary, discussion of the characters, themes, and issues and placing the play within its mythological, religious, and political contexts. Examines the play's performance history and its changing critical reception and adaptations over the years.

Morwood, James. *The Plays of Euripides.* Bristol, England: Bristol Classical, 2002. Morwood provides a concise overview of all of Euripides' plays, devoting a separate chapter to each one. He demonstrates how Euripides was constantly reinventing himself in his work.

Rabinowitz, Nancy Sorkin. *Anxiety Veiled: Euripides and the Traffic in Women.* Ithaca, N.Y.: Cornell University Press, 1993. Discusses Iphigenia as a voluntary sacrifice, with particular attention to the gender implications of her action.

Smith, Wesley D. "Iphigenia in Love." In *Arktouros: Hellenic Studies Presented to Bernard M. W. Knox on the Occasion of His Sixty-fifth Birthday,* edited by Glen W. Bowersock, Walter Burkert, and Michael C. J. Putnam. New York: Walter de Gruyter, 1979. Argues that Iphigenia's acceptance of her fate is founded on a desire to protect Achilles. Also claims the extant ending to the play is corrupt.

Snell, Bruno. "From Tragedy to Philosophy: *Iphigenia in Aulis.*" In *Oxford Readings in Greek Tragedy,* edited by Erich Segal. New York: Oxford University Press, 1983. Places the play in historical context, with special emphasis on the concepts of knowing and doing. Claims the play is indicative of Euripides' tendency to begin plays with confusion and end them with heroism, the reverse of Sophocles' technique.

Iphigenia in Tauris

Author: Euripides (c. 485-406 B.C.E.)
First produced: Iphigeneia ē en Taurois, c. 414 B.C.E. (English translation, 1782)
Type of work: Drama
Type of plot: Melodrama
Time of plot: Several years after the Trojan War
Locale: Tauris

Principal characters:
IPHIGENIA, a priest of Artemis
ORESTES, her brother
PYLADES, Orestes' friend
THOAS, the king of Tauris
ATHENA, goddess of the hunt

The Story:

When the Greek invasion force, destined for Ilium, was unable to sail from Aulis because of a lack of wind, Agamemnon, the Greek commander, appealed to Calchas, a Greek seer, for aid. Calchas said that unless Agamemnon gave Iphigenia, his oldest daughter, as a sacrifice to Artemis, the Greek fleet would never sail. By trickery Agamemnon succeeded in bringing Clytemnestra, his queen, and Iphigenia to Aulis, where the maiden was offered up to propitiate the goddess. At the last moment, however, Artemis substituted a calf in Iphigenia's place and spirited the maiden off to the barbaric land of Tauris, where she is now doomed to spend the rest of her life as a priest of Artemis. One of Iphigenia's duties is to prepare Greek captives—any Greek apprehended in Tauris is by law condemned to die—for sacrifice in the temple of the goddess.

Iphigenia has been a priest in Tauris for many years when, one night, she has a dream that she interprets to mean that her brother Orestes had met his death; now there can be no future for her family, for Orestes was the only son.

Orestes, however, is alive; in fact, he is actually in Tauris. After he and his sister Electra murdered their mother to avenge their father's death at her hands, the Furies pursued Orestes relentlessly. Seeking relief, Orestes is told by the Oracle of Delphi that he must procure a statue of Artemis that stands in the temple of the goddess in Tauris and take it to Athens. Orestes will then be free of the Furies.

Orestes and his friend Pylades reach the temple and are appalled at the sight of the earthly remains of the many Greeks who lost their lives in the temple. They resolve, however, to carry out their mission of stealing the statue of Artemis.

Meanwhile Iphigenia, disturbed by her dream, arouses her sister priests and asks their help in mourning the loss of her brother. In her loneliness she remembers Argos and her carefree childhood. A messenger interrupts her reverie with the report that one of two young Greeks on the shore in a frenzy slaughtered Taurian cattle that were led to the sea to bathe. The slayer is Orestes, under the influence of the Furies. In the fight that followed, Orestes and Pylades held off great numbers of Taurian peasants, but at last the peasants succeeded in capturing the two youths. The Greeks were brought to Thoas, the king of Tauris.

Iphigenia, as a priest of Artemis, directs that the strangers be brought before her. Heretofore she was always gentle with the doomed Greeks and never participated in the bloody ritual of sacrifice. Now, depressed by her dream, she is determined to be cruel. Orestes and Pylades, bound, are brought before Iphigenia. Thinking of her own sorrow, she asks them if they have sisters who will be saddened by their deaths.

Orestes refuses to give her any details about himself, but he answers her inquiries about Greece and about the fate of the prominent Greeks in the Trojan War. She learns to her distress that her father is dead by her mother's treachery and that Orestes is still alive, a wanderer.

Deeply moved, Iphigenia offers to spare Orestes if he will deliver a letter for her in Argos. Orestes magnanimously gives the mission to Pylades; he himself will remain to be sacrificed. When he learns that Iphigenia will prepare him for the ritual, he wishes for the presence of his sister to cover his body after he is dead. Iphigenia, out of pity, promises to do this for him. She goes to bring the letter. Orestes and Pylades are convinced that she is a Greek. Pylades then declares that he will stay and die with his friend. Orestes, saying that he is doomed to die anyway for the murder of his mother, advises Pylades to return to Greece, marry Electra, and build a temple in his honor.

Iphigenia, returning with the letter, tells Pylades that it must be delivered to one Orestes, a Greek prince. The letter urges Orestes to come to Tauris to take Iphigenia back to her beloved Argos; it explains how she was saved at Aulis and spirited by Artemis to Tauris. Pylades, saying that he has fulfilled the mission, hands the letter to Orestes. Iphigenia, doubtful, is finally convinced of Orestes' identity when he recalls details of their home in Argos. While she ponders escape for the three of them, Orestes explains that first it is necessary for him to take the statue of Artemis, in order to avoid destruction. He asks Iphigenia's aid.

Receiving a promise of secrecy from the priests who are present, Iphigenia carries out her plan of escape. As Thoas, curious about the progress of the sacrifice, enters the temple, Iphigenia appears with the statue in her arms. She explains to the mystified Thoas that the statue miraculously turned away from the Greek youths because their hands were stained by domestic murder. She declares to Thoas that it is necessary for her secretly to cleanse the statue and the two young men in sea water. She commands the people of Tauris to stay in their houses lest they, too, be tainted.

When Orestes and Pylades are led from the temple in chains, Thoas and his retinue cover their eyes so that they will not be contaminated by evil. Iphigenia joins the procession and marches solemnly to the beach. There she orders the king's guards to turn their backs on the secret cleansing rites. Fearful for Iphigenia's safety, the guards look on. When they see the three Greeks entering a ship, they rush down to the vessel and hold it back. The Greeks beat off the Taurians and set sail. The ship, however, is caught by tidal currents and forced back into the harbor.

Thoas, angry, urges all Taurians to spare no effort in capturing the Greek ship. Then the goddess Athena appears to Thoas and directs him not to go against the will of Apollo, whose Oracle of Delphi sent Orestes to Tauris to get the statue of Artemis. Thoas complies. Iphigenia, Orestes, and Pylades return to Greece, where Orestes, having set up the image of the Taurian Artemis in Attica, is at last freed from the wrath of the Furies. Iphigenia continues, in a new temple, to be a priest of Artemis.

Critical Evaluation:

Iphigenia in Tauris is not, strictly speaking, a tragedy but a melodrama. Iphigenia, after years in a barbaric land, may at first still have hatred for her kin, the Greeks, who were willing to kill her to fight a pointless war, but her sentimental longing to return to Argos, her birthplace and the scene of her happy childhood, is intense. She describes her feelings most touchingly. The play abounds in breathtaking situations of danger and in sentimental passages of reminiscence. The recognition scene is perhaps the most thrilling, if not the most protracted, in the classic Greek drama.

Like William Shakespeare, Euripides turned to the melodrama, or romance, in his later years to convey a more optimistic view of the world. In fact, he invented this new dramatic form. *Iphigenia in Tauris* is one of the few surviving examples. As a play, *Iphigenia in Tauris* is masterly. It is carefully plotted, full of suspense, and genuinely moving. The setting is distant, dangerous, and romantic. A wistful love for Greece illuminates the action, especially in the beautiful choral odes. The characters are realistically drawn, and their reactions at tense moments are both unexpected and credible. The mixture of accurate psychology and miraculous occurrences is typical of Euripides. Further, the long recognition scene between Iphigenia and Orestes is thrilling in its execution. It would be hard to find a better piece of pure theater in the repertoire of classical drama. This play also has the penetrating depth of Euripides' finest works, in addition to being high entertainment.

Euripides seems to have been fascinated by the legend of the House of Atreus. From the final years of his life five plays on the subject have survived. *Iphigenia in Tauris*, *Ēlektra* (413 B.C.E.; *Electra*, 1782), *Helenē* (412 B.C.E.; *Helen*, 1782), *Orēstes* (408 B.C.E.; *Orestes*, 1782), and *Iphigeneia ē en Aulidi* (405 B.C.E.; *Iphigenia in Aulis*, 1782) treat this story in different ways. Sometimes the depiction of a character varies from play to play, particularly in the cases of Orestes and Helen. Of these works *Iphigenia in Tauris* comes closest to *Helen* in mood and plot. Both are romances in which a woman has been supernaturally transported to a remote, bar-

baric land and there held in chaste captivity. Iphigenia and Helen long for one deliverer whom they believe to be dead. Promptly they meet the man and a recognition scene follows. Then they plot a means of escape, trick the king, and return home by divine intervention. The similarities are remarkable and suggest that one of these plays attempts to repeat the success of the other, although Euripides may have written more plays along these lines.

The plot of *Iphigenia in Tauris* has two major climaxes and can be divided into two parts. The first part begins with Iphigenia believing her brother, Orestes, to be dead and ends with her accepting the captive Orestes. The second part begins with the two of them planning the escape and ends as they overcome all obstacles with Athena's aid.

Euripides uses an interesting technique. Often a character will state a principle by which he or she intends to act and then immediately betray the principle. Thus, in lines 350-353, Iphigenia states her intention of being harsh to the Greek captives because of her own misery and melts on hearing news of her homeland, offering to spare Orestes. In this case the technique points up her intense homesickness for Greece and Argos, a passion that animates not only her but also the chorus of Greek maidens, Orestes, and Pylades.

With Orestes, Euripides varies the technique in relation to a major theme. When Orestes appears before Iphigenia as a prisoner, he says he disdains self-pity; a few lines after, when Iphigenia asks his name, he replies sullenly, "Call me unfortunate." The method indicates his misery. It also underscores his nobility of character later when he insists on being sacrificed to free his friend, Pylades. Disinterested love is always a sign of redemption in Euripides.

The barbarian king, Thoas, claims no barbarian would murder his mother, as the Greek, Orestes, did. However, he has no compunction about ordering a massacre of all Greeks, including the temple virgins. Euripides uses Thoas as a gullible, vengeful foil to the clever Greeks.

However, the most important theme of the play has to do with divine injustice and human suffering. Iphigenia is in thrall to the goddess Artemis, a victim who is offered up for sacrifice, transported far away from home, and then set to aid in the sacrifices of all strangers and Greeks, a task she loathes. Artemis is the perpetrator of the whole sequence.

Artemis's twin, Apollo, visits similar suffering on Orestes, causing him to kill his mother, to be pursued and driven mad by Furies, and to be sent to Colchis (not Tauris), where he is captured for sacrifice. At first glance the gods Apollo and Artemis appear to be archvillains ruthlessly dealing out anguish.

There is another perspective, however, that mitigates this view. Orestes is working out his redemption and must face death before he can free himself of the guilt of matricide. He is offered a chance to live, but he chooses to save Pylades. Presumably Apollo sends him to Colchis for that very purpose, to act as a free man rather than as an embittered victim. Once this choice occurs, things begin falling into harmony. Iphigenia accepts him as her brother and contrives an escape. Orestes repays the favor by saving her life as they board the ship. Then in the moment of greatest danger the goddess Athena arrives to rescue the Greeks, showing that the gods give help to those who help others.

Euripides is showing that as long as a people regard themselves as victims they can only suffer. When they act freely and unselfishly, their suffering ceases and the gods come to help. Through disinterested love, divine injustice is transmuted to true justice.

"Critical Evaluation" by James Weigel, Jr.

Further Reading

Burnett, Anne Pippin. *Catastrophe Survival: Euripides' Plays of Mixed Reversal.* Oxford, England: Clarendon Press, 1971. Examines how the surprising and redemptive plot in the play operates to upset expectations inherent in the tragic genre. Also sensitive to the mythic overtones of the play, developing them in contrast and parallel to the play's drama.

Hartigan, Karelisa. *Ambiguity and Self-Deception.* Frankfurt: Peter Lang, 1991. Emphasizes the unsettling effect of the play's recognition scenes. Shows how the characteristic Euripidean device of the deus ex machina stresses the artificiality and aestheticism of the play.

Kyriakou, Poulheria. *A Commentary on Euripides' "Iphi-genia in Tauris."* Berlin: De Gruyer, 2006. In addition to its lengthy commentary on the play's text, this book contains chapters analyzing the play's treatment of myth, characters, key scenes, depiction of Greeks and barbarians, and critical reception.

Morwood, James. *The Plays of Euripides.* Bristol, England: Bristol Classical, 2002. Morwood provides a concise overview of all of Euripides' plays, devoting a separate chapter to each one. He demonstrates how Euripides constantly reinvented himself in his work.

Powell, Anton, ed. *Euripides, Women, and Sexuality.* London: Routledge & Kegan Paul, 1990. This collection of essays influenced by gender studies emphasizes Iphigenia as one of Euripides' major female characters as well as the only one seen in both tragic and romantic contexts. Examines how Iphigenia is at once a victim and a redeemer of her male-dominated society.

Rabinowitz, Nancy Sorkin. *Anxiety Veiled: The Traffic in Women in Euripides.* Ithaca, N.Y.: Cornell University Press, 1993. This major feminist study of Euripidean drama is also one of the best available introductions to *Iphigenia in Tauris.* Although Rabinowitz recognizes the more positive role played by women in Euripides' plays as opposed to previous Greek drama, she demonstrates that Euripides tends to use women as tokens of exchange to underscore men's continuing hold over social and economic relations.

Wright, Matthew. *Euripides' Escape-Tragedies: A Study of "Helen," "Andromeda," and "Iphigenia Among the Taurians."* New York: Oxford University Press, 2005. Focuses on three of Euripides' later plays. Wright argues that these plays form a trilogy and analyzes their common ideas about myth, cultural identity, philosophy, religion, and genre.

Irish Melodies

Author: Thomas Moore (1779-1852)
First published: 1807-1834
Type of work: Poetry

Few men of letters have been able to write on Thomas Moore without disparaging the financial and social success of his life or the great mass of his work, mostly verse, from which so little of any worth is still remembered except *Irish Melo-dies.* The quantity of his work and the ready charm that contributed to his success in London society are largely attributable to the fact that Moore, like many other aspirants from the provinces, had to get on as best he could. Starvation in a garret may be the mark of genius but only posterity can decide between the respective merits of Thomas Chatterton and William Blake. Moore took no chances; he stuck by the Whigs, forswore his early Republicanism, and modulated his Irishness into its most acceptable form in the London drawing room, the real source of political power and hence patronage in Regency England. He also sang Irish songs, thereby gaining practically the only claim he has on the memory and affections of later times. The rest of his work fills up that yawning gulf of trivia that kept the London publishers prosperous, their readers contented, the popular authors wealthy, and the best of contemporary English writers—among them Percy Bysshe Shelley, John Keats, and Blake—out of sight.

However, Moore was in his way a pioneer. He always claimed to have originated modern Irish poetry, enjoying a personal application of the song that takes its title from the opening words:

> Dear Harp of my Country! in darkness I found thee,
> The cold chain of silence hung o'er thee long,
> When proudly, my own Island Harp! I unbound thee,
> And gave all thy chords to light, freedom and song!

In the rest of the lyric Moore sums up his subjects—death, love, mirth, and patriotism—and specifies his technique as being "wild sweetness." The revolutionary effect of this combination in London when he began the composition of *Irish Melodies* in 1806 (seven years after his arrival there from Dublin) was more noticeable because of the stolidity of both the serious and the popular light verse of the time, to both of which Moore had contributed enough to acquire a lucrative government post in the Bermudas. He left London in 1803 to take up the post, but he soon returned and set to work on his *Irish Melodies*, exile from London having apparently sharpened his love for Ireland. This new style of drawing-room entertainment, which Moore, being an accomplished musician, often provided in person, was soon earning him five hundred pounds a year. The lyric was restored to popularity in English literature not by William Wordsworth's and Samuel Coleridge's *Lyrical Ballads* (1798), by Robert Burns, or by Blake, all of whom preceded him, but by Moore's *Irish Melodies*.

Moore gave a sample of his ability to write lyrics to folk tunes in the "Canadian Boat Song" of his feebly satirical *Poems Relating to America* (1806); he heard his "voyageurs" sing the song as they rowed down the St. Lawrence from Kingston to Montreal. Both words and music, of *Irish Melodies*, were published in ten parts between 1807 and 1834,

with editions of the words alone appearing from 1820 on. Time established the concert repertoire selected from the songs: "The Harp That Once Thro' Tara's Halls," "Believe Me if All Those Endearing Young Charms," "She Is Far from the Land," "'Tis the Last Rose of Summer," "The Minstrel Boy," and "Sweet Inishfallen, Fare Thee Well," to which may be added the "Canadian Boat Song" and two later songs, the "Vesper Hymn" and "Oft in the Stilly Night" from *National Airs* (1820), lyrics and arrangements of folk songs from most European countries.

Only one of the lyrics remained in the repertory as a poem apart from its setting. "The Time I've Lost in Wooing" shows Moore's abilities to advantage: The rhymes are feminine in the longer lines and in triples (wooing . . . pursuing . . . undoing); the shorter lines (none is long) end in masculine rhyme; the alternations give a pleasing variation to the run of the poem, and the poem in three stanzas reaches a witty conclusion that echoes the Caroline poets. In the conflict between Wisdom and Beauty the poet's time has been wasted in pursuit of the latter; he knows this but still cannot cease his pursuit: "Poor Wisdom's chance/ Against a glance/ Is now as weak as ever." Of the language of the lyrics, English poet and man of letters Edmund Gosse observed that "words of a commonplace character are so strung together as to form poetry easily grasped and enjoyed by the ear." The secret of Moore's original and continuing popularity lies in his having provided acceptable poetry for the ear, not for the eye. Because the gift so enjoyed by Elizabethans has become lost, it is little wonder that later audiences needed to be assisted by folk tunes.

In the collected editions of Moore's works, the *Irish Melodies* number 125, beginning with "Go Where Glory Waits Thee" and ending with "Silence Is in Our Festal Halls," Moore's elegy for Sir John Stevenson, who wrote the arrangements for the parts. Most of the parts as they were issued contained Moore's dedications to his patrons as well as advertisements from his publisher, Power, to the general public, in which it was insisted that there were plenty more "airs" in the treasury of Irish folk song for future parts. A certain amount of national feeling is evident in both advertisements and dedications, especially in that to the first part, which includes a letter from Moore referring to the Irish reputation for song as "the only talent for which our English neighbors ever deigned to allow us any credit." A more important preface is that to the third part. As well as dealing with the age of Irish songs, their resemblance to Scottish song, and the harmonic peculiarities of Irish music, Moore refers to three aspects that in their way sum up much of the melodies: their national feeling, their peculiar mixture of defiance and despondency, and their being not poems but lyrics to songs.

On the last point, he begs exemption from "the rigors of literary criticism" because he can "answer for their sound with somewhat more confidence than for their sense." This statement is admirable but makes it difficult to discuss the *Irish Melodies* as if they were poems. If Moore's guiding principle was to make them singable, only a singer can argue in their behalf. Moreover, many a trite phrase and conventional rhyme can be excused on this ground. Moore's other two remarks point to two obvious features in the lyrics. They often begin strongly and fade into resignation with a parting, death, the passage of time, or the decay of good customs. Where the poems reach a strong conclusion, they do so generally by appealing to the divine or to Ireland. The endings to two patriotic poems illustrate the difference: "Let Erin Remember the Days of Old" declines into "Thus, sighing, look through the waves of time/ For the long-faded glories they cover." By contrast, "Sublime Was the Warning" challenges Irish national aspirations by appealing to the success of Spanish independence after the Napoleonic Wars and concludes with "The young spirit of Freedom shall shelter their grave/ Beneath shamrocks of Erin and olives of Spain."

The Irish quality of the poems is most apparent in their subjects. Some are taken from Irish history, others contain references to Irish legends and customs, but the thread that runs through the volume is "Erin." Much of the reference to Ireland is a prophecy of longed-for independence, a purely poetic exercise Moore's contemporaries in London must have thought it, but history has realized Moore's longing, and it would be an interesting point to settle how much his songs had to do with maintaining Irish nationalism during the struggles of the nineteenth century—such songs as "Erin, Oh Erin," "Oh the Shamrock," "Where Is the Slave?" and the better-known "Minstrel Boy" and "The Harp That Once Thro' Tara's Halls." The most curious of these is "As Vanquished Erin," which describes how the Fiend of Discord persists in sending "his shafts of desolation . . . through all her maddening nation." When Erin asks the "Powers of Good" when this will end, the Demon answers, "Never." This is possibly the most accurate statement Moore made about Ireland.

The phrase that sums up the quality of the lyrics in the *Irish Melodies* is Moore's "wild sweetness," an unusual and romantic combination of opposites, its Irishness, one may say. However, the sweetness of the verses is obtained by both a technical dexterity (Moore maintains, as he must, the rhythm of the melody in a variety of meters) and a neatness of phrasing that might be called Irish wit were it not that, except in a few light pieces of which "The Time I've Lost in Woo-

ing" is the best, this gift is usually spent on general topics and does not show to advantage: "Love, nursed among pleasures, is faithless as they,/ But the love born of Sorrow, like Sorrow, is true." Much of the wild note comes from the subjects of war, chains, and heroic death, and also from the ecstasy of the love poems, tinged as they generally are with sadness. Oddly enough it is probably the romantic combination Moore achieved that was responsible for the gradual disfavor into which the *Irish Melodies* fell about the turn of the century, though they are still referred to in James Joyce and Sean O'Casey. When the Gaelic Revival and the independence of Eire finally arrived, a more genuine folk song with real Irish lyrics seems to have lessened Moore's popularity and reduced it to the proportions of the man himself, whom Sir Walter Scott once called "a little, very little man."

Further Reading

Davis, Leith. "A 'Truly National' Project: Thomas Moore's *Irish Melodies* and the Gendering of the British Cultural Marketplace." In *Music, Postcolonialism, and Gender: The Construction of Irish National Identity, 1724-1874*. Notre Dame, Ind.: University of Notre Dame Press, 2006. Describes how texts concerning Irish music, including Moore's *Irish Melodies*, created a sense of Irish identity and were a means of examining Ireland's colonial relationship with England.

Deane, Seamus. "Thomas Moore (1779-1852)." In *The Field Day Anthology of Irish Writing*, edited by Seamus Deane. 3 vols. New York: W. W. Norton, 1991. Points out that *Irish Melodies* made the Gaelic tradition acceptable to the dominant taste of readers in nineteenth century England and made Irish rebelliousness aesthetic. Provides a representative selection of the songs, with annotations, and a bibliography.

Jones, Howard Mumford. *The Harp That Once—A Chronicle of the Life of Thomas Moore*. New York: Henry Holt, 1937. Reprint. New York: Russell & Russell, 1970. Despite its date, still the authoritative biography of Moore, which depicts him as the embodiment of Romanticism. Places him in his cultural and historical milieu. Balances criticism and appreciation of his character and work with exemplary judgment and elegance.

Kelly, Linda. *Ireland's Minstrel: A Life of Tom Moore—Poet, Patriot, and Byron's Friend*. New York: I. B. Tauris, 2006. Kelly uses Moore's newly published journals and other materials to provide an up-to-date account of Moore's life and work. Chapter 8 focuses on *Irish Melodies*, and there are many other references to the work that are listed in the index.

McMahon, Sean. *The Minstrel Boy: Thomas Moore and His Melodies*. Cork, Ireland: Mercier Press, 2001. A biography depicting Moore as an Irish patriot whose songs fostered a new sense of Irish nationalism.

Nolan, Emer. *Catholic Emancipations: Irish Fiction from Thomas Moore to James Joyce*. Syracuse, N.Y.: Syracuse University Press, 2007. Chronicles the history of Irish literature from the Catholic political resurgence in the 1820's to the publication of Joyce's *Ulysses* in 1922. Shows how Moore and other nineteenth century writers created new narrative forms that were later adapted by Joyce.

Vail, Jeffery W. *The Literary Relationship of Lord Byron and Thomas Moore*. Baltimore: Johns Hopkins University Press, 2001. Argues that Moore, not Percy Bysshe Shelley, was the dominant influence on Byron's life and work. Describes the two poets' friendship, which resulted in Moore's biography of Byron.

Welch, Robert. *Irish Poetry from Moore to Yeats*. Gerrard Cross, England: Smythe, 1980. Points out that Moore's *Irish Melodies* wove lovely verbal patterns around Irish airs and political sentiments and were the starting point for later Anglo-Irish poetry. Maintains that in their fabricated Hibernicism, they are similar to James Macpherson's Ossianic fragments.

Islands in the Stream

Author: Ernest Hemingway (1899-1961)
First published: 1970
Type of work: Novel
Type of plot: Psychological realism
Time of plot: Early 1940's
Locale: The Bahamas and Cuba

Principal characters:
THOMAS HUDSON, an artist
THOMAS, JR.,
ANDREW, and
DAVID, his sons
BOBBY, proprietor of a Bimini bar
ROGER DAVIS, a writer
HUDSON'S FIRST WIFE
HONEST LIL, a Havana prostitute
WILLIE,
ARA,
HENRY,
GEORGE,
EDDY, and
PETERS, crew of Hudson's submarine-seeking boat

The Story:

On the island of Bimini in the Bahamas, Thomas Hudson works and confronts his regrets and insecurities. Self-disciplined and successful as an artist, he finds time to fish, socialize at Bobby's Bar, meet with his art dealer in New York, and host the periodic visits of his three sons. At the bar, Hudson discusses with Bobby possible subjects for future paintings—including the end of the world. Hudson then joins writer and friend Roger Davis on Johnny Goodner's cruiser at the docks, where fireworks mark the celebration of the queen's birthday. The wealthy and snobbish owner of a cruiser moored nearby confronts Hudson and his noisy and rowdy friends for waking his wife. Davis betters the man in the ensuing fistfight.

Hudson's three sons arrive: Tom, the oldest and son of Hudson's first wife, and Andrew and David, sons of his second wife. They discuss their earlier days in Europe, young Tom recalling notables such as James Joyce and Ezra Pound. While spear fishing, the sons narrowly escape a large hammerhead shark. Deep-sea fishing, David hooks a huge swordfish. For six painful and vividly described hours, David determinedly battles the prize fish, only to have it slip away at the last moment.

Roger Davis becomes reacquainted with a past love, the now-married Audrey Bruce, who happens to be vacationing on Bimini. Roger and Audrey depart shortly before Hudson's sons also leave. News arrives that David, Andrew, and their mother have died in an automobile accident in Europe. Advised to flee his sorrows through travel, Hudson tries to escape into his art but increasingly finds solace in drink.

After twelve days at sea searching for German U-boats, Hudson returns to his cats and his home near Havana, Cuba. His mind wanders to a much earlier love affair with a married woman. A chauffeur drives Hudson into Havana, where the artist consults with military officials at the embassy and with Honest Lil and other patrons of La Floridita Bar. They discuss their lives, the war, and local Cuban politics. Hudson discloses that his oldest son, Tom, has perished while serving as a flight commander in Europe. The elder Thomas continues to reminisce about his loves and losses at La Floridita, where he is known for his record-setting drinking bouts.

Hudson is shocked into the present when his never-forgotten first wife unexpectedly walks into La Floridita. Now remarried and a successful actor, she is working for the United Service Organizations (USO). She and Hudson make love, and afterward they rehearse their relationship; she intuitively realizes that their son Tom has died. Clearly still in love, the couple acknowledges the mistakes that drove them apart. They again must part and get on with their separate lives. Hudson receives word that the Navy lieutenant at Guantánamo Bay urgently needs to see him.

Hudson and his friends pursue Germans and German U-boats. Pretending to be a scientific expedition, Hudson's boat happens upon some huts on an outlying island where all the villagers lie dead, along with one German soldier. The village has been looted and burned. The naval station at Guantánamo advises them to continue searching and pursuing westward. Their boat runs aground on a sandy muddy bottom. From their small dinghy they spot and board a camouflaged turtle boat in a mangrove swamp. In the ensuing melee, the single German sailor aboard kills Hudson's radio operator.

One of Hudson's men searches the key for other combatants, his progress marked by the rising flocks of birds from the mangroves. He finds nothing. Hudson wonders about the location of the Germans and the likelihood of their attacking the boat. Fearing that local civilians could be hurt, he instructs his men to remove the booby traps that have been rigged on the turtle boat. After they dislodge their own boat and navigate the narrow channels toward the open sea, they are ambushed by German sailors. In the exchange of gunfire and hand grenades, Hudson sustains three wounds. One of Hudson's men impulsively shoots a sailor who could have been captured and interrogated. Hudson senses that his own injuries are fatal.

Critical Evaluation:

Ernest Hemingway's tremendous fame rests upon his acclaim as a writer and his status as a world celebrity, a celebrity that itself rests upon his eventful life, which furnished the subjects of his art. Works such as *Islands in the Stream* have an autobiographical basis; for example, Hemingway himself actually engaged in such quixotic and, in his case, fruitless exploits as German U-boat hunting during World War II. His best-known fiction includes highly wrought short stories such as "The Killers" (1927), "A Clean, Well-Lighted Place" (1926), and "Hills Like White Elephants" (1927) and longer stories such as "The Snows of Kilimanjaro" (1936). Widely read and often translated novels include *The Sun Also Rises* (1926), *A Farewell to Arms* (1929), and *For Whom the Bell Tolls* (1940). Hemingway's artistic influence stems from his often violent subjects (war and sport), his terse and disciplined style (concentrated and laconic), and his attitudes and values (including famously celebrating the "grace under pressure" of stoic characters).

By most accounts, Hemingway's greatest literary achievements fall early in his career. Many critics find his later works less original and inspired, more mannered and self-imitative. All of his most admired works were written before the United States entered World War II in 1941, twenty years before the author's death in 1961. After 1941, Hemingway's most universally acclaimed work—specifically mentioned in the citation for his 1954 Nobel Prize in Literature—was *The Old Man and the Sea* (1952). (David's soreness, severe abrasions, and persistence in trying to land the prize swordfish during the fishing scene parallel the experience of Santiago as he battles the great marlin in *The Old Man and the Sea*.) In the mid-1940's Hemingway spoke of a major work encompassing air, land, and sea. He worked on the project on and off well into the 1950's, publishing *The Old Man and the Sea* separately in 1952. Other stories, such as "The Strange Country" (1987) and the narratives that became *Islands in the Stream*, were part of this grand scheme.

As Hemingway worked on the manuscript of his grand narrative, he sometimes called three of the interrelated stories "The Sea When Young," "The Sea When Absent," and "The Sea in Being." The posthumously published *Islands in the Stream* comprises sections titled "Bimini," "Cuba," and "At Sea." The title of the book as a whole—whether or not it was the author's final choice—suggests a haven, but also isolation in a stream of time. (The title therefore contrasts to the more characteristically 1930's title of *For Whom the Bell Tolls*: Hemingway drew the latter phrase from a John Donne sermon that posited that "no man is an island," because all are communal parts of the mainland.) Hemingway's fourth wife,

Mary, and the publisher Charles Scribner, Jr., organized and edited *Islands in the Stream* for its 1970 publication.

Islands in the Stream is a novel about relinquishment. The protagonist, Thomas Hudson, faces losses and confusions as he struggles to find meaning and stability in his life. His loves—the women in his life, his family, his art, his conception of duty—each become a subject of his concern. All that had once been added to his life is now being subtracted. He can only remember his loves, and, when his first wife reappears, he realizes that their relationship cannot succeed in the present. He loses each of his three sons. By the third section of the novel, little mention is made of Hudson's painting. In the final chapters of the book, Hudson acts out his notion of duty, desperate for meaningful action (as opposed to meaningless inaction), despite his often cynical view of the world. His duty done, he has exhausted his options.

Early in *Islands in the Stream*, Hudson understands that drink furnishes only a temporary refuge. The discipline of his art, his painting, creates and preserves true order and meaning. David's swordfish gets away, but Hudson's planned painting of the fish would preserve the experience. Even at the end of the novel, Hudson tells himself "if you paint as well as you can and keep out of all other things and do that, it is the true thing." By contrast, the other artist character, the writer Roger Davis, is portrayed as having "sold out" to commercial interests. Hudson advises him "to write straight and simple and good" even though his actual life may not be straight, simple, or good. These details, along with the references to Pound, Joyce, and others, make the novel very much a work of art about art. Hemingway was writing about writing, despite the book's overt action and violence.

Islands in the Stream joins *The Garden of Eden* (1986) and *A Moveable Feast* (1964) among Hemingway's publications after 1961. The novel has augmented a fascination with both the writer and his works. Faulted as inferior to much of the author's earlier fiction, the novel nevertheless possesses merits as a saga of both Hemingway the man and Hemingway the artist.

Benjamin S. Lawson

Further Reading

Baker, Carlos. *Hemingway: The Writer as Artist.* 4th ed. Princeton, N.J.: Princeton University Press, 1972. The first edition of this standard work by Hemingway biographer Baker to be published following the publication of *Islands in the Stream*; discusses the novel in thirty cogent and convincing pages. Stresses techniques, ideas, and autobiographical elements of the novel.

Donaldson, Scott, ed. *The Cambridge Companion to Hemingway.* New York: Cambridge University Press, 1996. Guide to the range of topics and issues related to the author and his works. Especially relevant and revisionist is Robert E. Fleming's essay "Hemingway's Later Fiction: Breaking New Ground," which argues that the writer's late fiction is challenging and worthy.

Hovey, Richard B. "*Islands in the Stream*: Death and the Artist." *University of Hartford Studies in Literature* 12 (1980): 173-194. Views Thomas Hudson as a conflicted character who cannot be freed from depression by his loves or his art yet, in the end, wonders whether he should have dedicated himself to his painting rather than seeking meaning through life-threatening action.

Justice, Hilary K. *The Bones of the Others: The Hemingway Text from the Lost Manuscripts to the Posthumous Novels.* Kent, Ohio: Kent State University Press, 2006. Analyzes the author's creative process and the relationship between his life and his work. The emphasis on textual matters is significant for *Islands in the Stream*, since Mary Hemingway and Scribner necessarily shaped the manuscript when they prepared it for publication.

Lee, A. Robert, ed. *Ernest Hemingway: New Critical Essays.* Totowa, N.J.: Barnes & Noble, 1983. James H. Justus's contribution, "The Later Fiction: Hemingway and the Aesthetics of Failure," argues that Thomas Hudson increasingly loses his confidence and self-discipline as man and artist. Speculates that Hemingway himself was more focused on the quickly written *The Old Man and the Sea*.

Reynolds, Michael. *Hemingway: The Final Years.* New York: W. W. Norton, 1999. Fifth and final volume of Reynolds's exhaustive biography—biography being particularly germane for understanding the work of a writer whose life and art are so interconnected. Covering the years from 1940 until 1961, the book chronicles Hemingway's creative process, as well as his alternating bouts of exhilaration and gloom.

Wagner-Martin, Linda, ed. *Hemingway: Eight Decades of Criticism.* East Lansing: Michigan State University Press, 2009. Wagner-Martin's fourth collection of Hemingway criticism (comprising twenty-six essays) brings together a variety of modern points of view. These critiques, a diverse mix of fresh research and traditional interpretations, range from gender-related readings to biographical ones.

Israel Potter
His Fifty Years of Exile

Author: Herman Melville (1819-1891)
First published: 1855
Type of work: Novel
Type of plot: Historical
Time of plot: 1774-1826
Locale: Vermont, Massachusetts, England, France, and
the Atlantic Ocean

Principal characters:
ISRAEL POTTER, a wanderer
ISRAEL'S FATHER
KING GEORGE III
BENJAMIN FRANKLIN
JOHN PAUL JONES
ETHAN ALLEN
SQUIRE WOODCOCK, an American agent
THE EARL OF SELKIRK

The Story:

Born among the rugged stones of the New England hills, in the Housatonic Valley, Israel Potter grows up with all the virtues of the hard, principled new land. After an argument with his father over a girl whom his stern parent does not think a suitable match, Israel decides to run away from home while his family is attending church. He wanders about the countryside, hunting deer, farming land, becoming a trapper, and dealing in furs. During his wanderings, he learns that most men are unscrupulous. He also hunts whales from Nantucket to the coast of Africa.

In 1775, Israel joins the American forces and takes part in the Battle of Bunker Hill. He fights bravely, but the battle, as he sees it, is simply disorganized carnage. Wounded, Israel enlists aboard an American ship after his recovery. Once at sea, the ship is captured by the British. Israel is taken prisoner and conveyed to England on a British ship, but on his arrival in London, he manages to escape.

Wandering about London, Israel meets various Englishmen who mock his American accent. Some of the English are kind and helpful to him. Others cuff him about and berate the scurrilous Yankee rebels. He finds various odd jobs, including one as a gardener working for a cruel employer. He escapes from this job and finds one as a gardener on the king's staff at Kew Gardens. One day, Israel meets King George III. The king, completely mad, realizes that Israel is an American and is ineffectually kind to him. Eventually, in a slack season, Israel is discharged. He then works for a farmer, but when other farmers in the area discover that he is an American, Israel is forced to run away.

Israel meets Squire Woodcock, a wealthy and secret friend of America, who sends him on a secret mission to Benjamin Franklin in Paris. Israel carries a message in the false heel of his new boots. On his arrival in Paris, while he is

looking for Franklin, a poor man tries to shine his boots on the Pont Neuf. Israel, in fright, kicks the man and runs off. At last, he finds Franklin, who takes the message and then insists that Israel return and pay damages to the bootblack.

In this fashion, Israel, under the tutelage of Franklin, learns his first lesson in European politeness and consideration. From this incident, Franklin proceeds to instruct Israel in the ways of proper behavior. Israel, still innocent, absorbs the teaching carefully, although none of it ever applies to his later experiences. Franklin promises that Israel will be sent back to America, if he will first return to England with a message. While still in Paris, Israel meets the stormy and ferocious Captain John Paul Jones, who also visits Franklin. John Paul Jones finds Israel a bright young man.

Israel makes his way back across the English Channel and goes to Squire Woodcock. The squire urges him to hide in the dungeon for three days, since their plot is in danger of discovery. When Israel emerges from the cell, he recognizes that the good squire must have been killed for his activities in the American cause.

Appropriating some of the squire's clothes, Israel masquerades as Squire Woodcock's ghost and escapes from a house filled with his enemies. He then trades clothes with a farmer, wanders to Portsmouth, and signs on as a foretopman on a British ship bound for the East Indies. In the Channel, his ship meets another ship whose captain has authority to impress some of the men; Israel is among those taken. That same night, the ship is captured by an American ship under the command of Jones. Revealing himself to his old friend, Israel soon becomes the quartermaster of the *Ranger*. With Jones, Israel engages in piracy, capturing and looting ships.

In Scotland, they call on the earl of Selkirk in order to rob him, but the nobleman is not at home. Jones impresses the earl's wife with his Parisian manners, drinks tea with her, and assures her that he and Israel do not intend to do the lady any harm. The crew, however, insists that plunder is a part of piracy, and so Israel and Jones are forced to allow the men to take the family silver and other valuables. Jones promises to restore all articles of value, and when he receives a large sum of money from another exploit, he buys back all the earl's articles from the men and returns them to the Selkirk family.

Other adventures do not end so cheerfully. The sea fight between the *Bon Homme Richard* and the *Serapis* is a violent and bloody battle, fought along national lines and devoid of all the amenities of piracy. Both ships are lost, and Israel and Jones, still hoping to get to America, sail on the *Ariel*. The *Ariel* engages a British vessel, which pretends to surrender. The Americans get ready to board, but only Israel boards before the vessel sails away. No one on the vessel knows where Israel came from. He pretends to have been on the vessel all along and thus ends up once again in the British navy. By feigning madness to hide his Yankee origins, he gets back to England safely.

In England, Israel meets Ethan Allen, a strong, heroic, Samsonlike figure, held prisoner by the English. Israel tries to help Allen escape but is unsuccessful. Disguised as a beggar, he goes to London, where he remains for more than forty years. During that time, he works as a brick-maker and laborer, always hoping to save enough money to return to America but never finding the economic situation in London stable enough to permit saving. A wanderer in an alien land, he becomes part of the grime and poverty of London. During those years, he marries a shopgirl who bears him a son. Finally, in 1826, he secures some credit and, with the help of the American consul, sails for America with his son.

Israel arrives in Boston on July 4, during a public celebration of the Battle of Bunker Hill. No one recognizes him or acknowledges his right to be there. Instead, people laugh at him and think he is mad. He returns to his father's farm, but the homestead has long since disappeared. Old Israel, his wanderings ended, finds no peace, comfort, or friendship in his old age. Although heroes of the American Revolution are publicly venerated, the aged man cannot even get a small pension.

Critical Evaluation:

Israel Potter is called Herman Melville's one piece of historical fiction. In it, Melville pretends to be writing literal biography. In form, it is close to his *Typee: A Peep at Polynesian Life* (1846), *Omoo: A Narrative of Adventures in the South Seas* (1847), *Redburn, His First Voyage* (1849), and *White-Jacket: Or, The World in a Man-of-War* (1850). *Israel*

Potter is basically an unadorned narrative rather than the kind of highly digressive, philosophical novel associated with Melville's later years.

Melville wrote *Israel Potter*, according to his biographers, to make up for the financial and critical failure of *Pierre: Or, The Ambiguities* (1852), and by far the majority of contemporary reviews were favorable. He received an initial $421.50. At first, the book sold fairly well. It quickly went into a third printing, but Melville's royalties were small, ranging between $190 and $240. The money gave Melville what at the time was a fairly good income but only for a short while.

Melville's main source for *Israel Potter* is *Life and Remarkable Adventures of Israel R. Potter, (A Native of Cranston, Rhode Island.) Who Was a Soldier in the American Revolution* (1824), by Henry Trumbull, a first-person narrative of the life of what Trumbull calls "one of the few survivors who fought and bled for American independence." The narrative is a supposedly true account of the life of the real Israel Potter, who fought at Bunker Hill, served in the navy, and ironically led most of his adult life in exile in England. Melville also used as sources biographies of and narratives by Benjamin Franklin, Ethan Allen, and John Paul Jones.

Toward the end of the novel, Melville writes: "The gloomiest and truthfulest dramatist seldom chooses for his theme the calamities, however extraordinary, of inferior and private persons; least of all, the pauper's," for "few feel enticed to the shanty, where, like a pealed knucklebone, grins the unupholstered corpse of the beggar." Nevertheless, it is precisely such a life that Melville recounts in *Israel Potter*. During the Revolutionary War, Potter worked with Benjamin Franklin and John Paul Jones and saw Ethan Allen while Allen was in captivity in England. As Melville depicts him, Potter is a true patriot, a fierce fighter, and may be the one most responsible for the defeat of the *Serapis* by the *Bon Homme Richard*, one of the most famous naval engagements in American history. It was during this battle that Jones uttered his famous words: "I have not yet begun to fight." However, through various twists of fate, Potter was forgotten even during his own lifetime, while Franklin, Allen, and Jones won the admiration of all their countrymen and lasting fame.

Potter, however, ended his days in poverty working at extremely unpleasant jobs for very little reward. Melville describes Potter's later life, especially his forty years in exile in England, in hellish terms. Before he enters the city of London, he works in a brickyard, a period that Melville refers to as Potter's time in Egypt. Then, he enters London, a city Melville describes using Dantesque terms.

When Israel's son finally manages to get passage for his

father and himself back to America, Israel is in his eighties. When he enters Boston on July 4, he is almost run over by "a patriotic triumphal car" inscribed with the words, "Bunker Hill/1775/Glory to the heroes that fought!" The irony is clear: History forgets the modest man, so it often overlooks true heroes. The irony is extended when the reader learns that Potter cannot even get a pension from the nation to which he gave so much.

One of the main things that distinguishes Melville's Potter from his more famous contemporaries is his modesty. Melville describes Franklin as a confidence man, always promoting his maxims, writings, and way of life. Melville treats John Paul Jones as an accomplished naval officer with tremendous energy but also as an incredible braggart absolutely sure of his extraordinary abilities. Melville's Allen is a magnificent figure in captivity, but he also constantly brags and exaggerates. Jones and Allen exaggerate their accomplishments and abilities in the tall-tale tradition. Melville's Potter, on the other hand, is content to let others take the glory while he does the kind of hard work that ultimately results in America's independence from England. Unlike Melville's Jones, who can be incredibly irresponsible, Melville's Potter constantly tries to act responsibly toward others, so much so that he stays in England for forty years after the Revolution ends not only because of economic conditions but also because of loyalty to his wife and son.

Potter's life as Melville recounts it also illustrates the fickleness of fate. As Jones and Potter sail back to America on the *Ariel*, they engage an English frigate class ship. The ship strikes its colors, and Potter boards it. Immediately, with Potter on board, the frigate sails away so that no one else can board it and with no one but Potter knowing how he got there. As a result, he begins his years in exile.

An additional theme Melville treats is the brutality that lies beneath the surface of civilization. He wonders whether humankind has made any progress, and his descriptions of battles, especially naval battles, indicate that it has not. He also comments that the French Revolution shows that in humankind "primeval savageness . . . slumbers."

Israel Potter has been classified as one of Melville's minor works. Still, critics praise it for its humor, its sympathy for the downtrodden, and its unusual view of some of the heroes of the American Revolution.

"Critical Evaluation" by Richard Tuerk

Further Reading

Bloom, Harold, ed. *Herman Melville*. New ed. New York: Bloom's Literary Criticism, 2008. Collection of critical essays analyzing Melville's work, including Bill Christophersen's piece "*Israel Potter*: Melville's 'Citizen of the Universe.'"

Delbanco, Andrew. *Melville: His World and Work*. New York: Knopf, 2005. Delbanco's critically acclaimed biography places Melville in his time, including information about the debate over slavery and details of life in 1840's New York. Delbanco also discusses the significance of Melville's works at the time they were published and in the twenty-first century.

Dillingham, William B. *Melville's Later Novels*. Athens: University of Georgia Press, 1986. Focuses on poverty and liberty in the novel. Sees Potter as a kind of Christ figure, a "sacrificial victim," with whom Melville identifies.

Hillway, Tyrus. *Herman Melville*. Rev. ed. Boston: Twayne, 1979. Briefly treats the work as an example of Melville's awareness of "man's ingratitude to man," of "tragic inconsistencies" in "human conduct," and of the "emptiness of worldly fame."

Karcher, Carolyn L. *Shadow over the Promised Land: Slavery, Race, and Violence in Melville's America*. Baton Rouge: Louisiana State University Press, 1980. Karcher describes the novel as a reconstruction of the American Revolution as seen by "the forgotten common man." Demonstrates that the book shows Melville's sympathy for the oppressed.

Kelley, Wyn, ed. *A Companion to Herman Melville*. Malden, Mass.: Blackwell, 2006. Collection of thirty-five original essays aimed at twenty-first century readers of Melville's works. Includes discussions of Melville's travels; Melville and religion, slavery, and gender; the Melville revival; and "Fluid Identity in *Israel Potter* and *The Confidence-Man*" by Gale Temple.

Melville, Herman. *Israel Potter: His Fifty Years of Exile*. Edited by Harrison Hayford, Hershel Parker, and G. Thomas Tanselle. Evanston, Ill.: Northwestern University Press, 1982. In addition to containing the authoritative text of the novel, this volume has the full text of Henry Trumbull's book, an excellent introduction, useful notes, and an excellent historical essay about the writing and publication of the book.

Rollyson, Carl E., and Lisa Paddock. *Herman Melville A to Z: The Essential Reference to His Life and Work*. New York: Checkmark Books, 2001. A comprehensive and encyclopedic coverage of Melville's life, works, and times; the 675 detailed entries provide information on the characters, settings, allusions, and references in his fiction, his friends and associates, and the critics and scholars who have studied his work.

Samson, John. *White Lies: Melville's Narratives of Facts.* Ithaca, N.Y.: Cornell University Press, 1989. Treats Melville's novel as an ironic narrative of the American Revolution that "breaks narrative conventions" and "frustrates audience expectations."

Spanos, William V. "Herman Melville's Israel Potter: Reflections on a Damaged Life." In *Herman Melville and the American Calling: Fiction After "Moby-Dick," 1851-1857.* Albany: State University of New York Press, 2008. Analyzes the major works that appeared after the publication of *Moby Dick.* Argues that these works share the metaphor of the orphanage: a place that represents both estrangement from a symbolic fatherland, as well as the myth of American exceptionalism.

The Italian
Or, The Confessional of the Black Penitents

Author: Ann Radcliffe (1764-1823)
First published: 1797
Type of work: Novel
Type of plot: Gothic
Time of plot: 1758
Locale: Italy

Principal characters:
VINCENTIO DI VIVALDI, a young nobleman of Naples
ELLENA DI ROSALBA, Vincentio's beloved
THE MARCHESE and MARCHESA DI VIVALDI, Vincentio's parents
SCHEDONI, the marchesa's confessor and formerly the count di Bruno
SIGNORA BIANCHI, Ellena's aunt
SISTER OLIVIA, formerly the countess di Bruno
PAULO MENDRICO, Vincentio's faithful servant

The Story:

Vincentio di Vivaldi sees Ellena di Rosalba for the first time at the Church of San Lorenzo in Naples. He is so impressed by the sweetness of her voice and the grace of her person that at the end of the service he follows the girl and her elderly companion in the hope of catching a glimpse of her features. When the elderly woman stumbles and falls, Vivaldi seizes the opportunity to offer her his arm, a gallant gesture that gives him the excuse to accompany the two women to the Villa Altieri, their modest home on an eminence overlooking the Bay of Naples.

The next day, he returns to inquire about the health of the older woman, Signora Bianchi, who receives her guest courteously. Ellena does not appear. Despondent at her absence, he inquires of his acquaintances into the girl's family but learns only that she is an orphan, the niece and ward of her aged relative.

That night, resolved to see Ellena again, he leaves a reception his mother is giving and returns to the Villa Altieri. The hour is late, and only one window is lighted. Through a lattice, he sees Ellena playing on her lute and singing a midnight hymn to the Virgin Mary. Entranced, he draws near the lattice and hears her pronounce his name; but when he reveals himself, the girl hastily closes the lattice and leaves the room. Vivaldi lingers in the garden for some time before returning to Naples. Lost in reverie, he is passing under a shattered archway extending over the road when a shadowy figure in a monk's robe glides across his path and in a ghostly whisper warns him to beware of future visits to the villa.

Thinking that the warning was given by a rival, he returns the next night in the company of his friend Bonorma. Again, the dark figure appears and utters a sepulchral warning. Later, as the two young men are passing under the arch, the figure shows itself once more. Vivaldi and Bonorma draw their swords and enter the ancient fortress in search of the mysterious visitor. They find no trace of anyone lurking in the ruins.

Still believing that these visitations are those of a rival, Vivaldi decides to end his suspense by making a declaration for Ellena's hand. Signora Bianchi listens to his proposal and then reminds him that a family as old and illustrious as his own will object to an alliance with a girl of Ellena's humble station. Vivaldi realizes that she speaks wisely, but with all the fervor of a young man in love, he argues his suit so eloquently that at last Signora Bianchi withdraws her refusal.

After Vivaldi makes repeated visits to the villa, a night comes when the aged woman places Ellena's hand in his and gives them her blessing. To Vivaldi's great joy, it is decided that the marriage will be solemnized during the coming week.

The marchese and marchesa di Vivaldi were not ignorant of their son's frequent visits at the Villa Altieri. On several occasions, the marchese, a man of great family pride and strict principles, tells his son that marriage to one so far below him in station is impossible. Vivaldi answers by declaring that his affections and intentions are irrevocable. His mother, a haughty and vindictive woman, is likewise determined to end what she regards as her son's foolish infatuation. Realizing that the young man cannot be moved by persuasion or threats, she summons her confessor and secret adviser, the monk Schedoni, and consults him on measures to separate Ellena and Vivaldi.

Schedoni, a monk at the Convent of the Santo Spirito, is a man of unknown family and origins. His spirit appears haughty and disordered, and his appearance conveys an effect of gloom that corresponds to his severe and solitary disposition. Because of his austere manners, brooding nature, and sinister appearance, he is loved by none, hated by many, and feared by most. Vivaldi dislikes the monk and avoids him, even though he has no presentiment of the fate Schedoni is preparing for him and Ellena.

On the morning after his acceptance as Ellena's suitor, Vivaldi hastens to the villa. In the darkened archway, the ghostly figure again appears and tells him that death is in the house. Vivaldi is deeply disturbed and hurries on. Upon his arrival, he learns that Signora Bianchi died suddenly during the night. When Beatrice, the old servant, confides her suspicions that her mistress was poisoned, Vivaldi grows even more concerned. His own suspicions fall on Schedoni, and he confronts the monk in the marchesa's apartment on his return to Venice, but the confessor cleverly parries all the questions Vivaldi puts to him. Vivaldi, apologizing for his conduct and accusing speech, fails to realize that he made an enemy of Schedoni and that the monk is already planning his revenge.

It is decided that Ellena is to find a sanctuary in the Convent of Santa Maria della Pieta after her aunt's funeral, and Vivaldi is in agreement with her desire to withdraw to that shelter during her period of mourning. Ellena is packing in preparation for her departure the next day, when she hears Beatrice scream in another room. At the same moment, three masked men seize Ellena and carry her from the house. Thrust into a closed carriage, she is driven throughout the night and most of the next day into the mountainous region of Abruzzo. There her captors conduct her to a strange religious establishment where she is turned over to the care of the nuns. Almost distracted, the girl is led to a cell where she gives way to her terror and grief.

Knowing nothing of these events, Vivaldi decides that same night to explore the ruined fortress and to discover, if possible, the secret of the strange visitor he encountered there. Paulo Mendrico, his faithful servant, goes with him. When they are within the archway, the figure of the monk suddenly materializes, this time telling Vivaldi that Ellena departed an hour before. Paulo fires his pistol, but the figure eludes them. Following drops of blood, Vivaldi and Paulo come at last to a chamber into which the figure disappeared. As they enter, the great door shuts behind them. In the chamber, they find only a discarded, bloody robe. During the night they spend as prisoners in the gloomy room, Paulo tells his master of a muffled penitent who appeared at the Church of Santa Maria del Pianto and made a confession apparently so strange and horrible that Ansaldo di Rovalli, the grand penitentiary, was thrown into convulsions. During this recital, they are startled by hearing groans close by, but they see no one. In the morning, the door of the chamber stands open, and Vivaldi and Paulo make their escape.

Alarmed for Ellena's safety, Vivaldi goes at once to the villa. There he finds Beatrice tied to a pillar and learns from her that her mistress was abducted. Convinced that the strange events of the night are part of a plot to prevent his intended marriage, he again confronts Schedoni at the Convent of the Santo Spirito and would have assaulted the monk if others had not seized the distraught young man and restrained him. That night, Vivaldi accidentally hears from a fisherman that early in the day a closed carriage was seen driving through Bracelli. Hoping to trace the carriage and to find Ellena, he sets off in pursuit, accompanied by the faithful Paulo.

On the fourth day of her imprisonment, Ellena is conducted to the parlor of the abbess, who informs her that she must choose between taking the veil or marrying the person whom the marchesa di Vivaldi selects as her husband. When Ellena refuses both offers, she is taken back to her cell. Each evening, she is allowed to attend vespers and there her attention is attracted to Sister Olivia, a nun who tries to reconcile her to the hardships of her confinement. For this reason, perhaps, Sister Olivia is the nun chosen by the abbess to inform Ellena that if she persists in refusing a husband proper to her station, she must take holy orders immediately.

Meanwhile, Vivaldi continues his search for Ellena. On the evening of the seventh day, he and Paulo fall in with a company of pilgrims on their way to worship at the shrine of a convent about a league and a half distant. Traveling with this company, Vivaldi arrives at the convent in time to witness the service at which Ellena is to be made a novitiate.

Hearing her voice raised in protest, he rushes to the altar and catches her as she faints. Unable to secure Ellena's freedom, Vivaldi leaves the convent to try another plan to set her free. Although he does not know it, there is need of haste, because the abbess decides to punish Ellena by confining her in a chamber from which none ever returned alive. Alarmed for the girl's life, Sister Olivia promises to help her escape from the convent that night.

Dressed in the nun's veil, Ellena attends a program of music given in honor of several distinguished strangers who are visiting the convent. There Vivaldi, disguised as a pilgrim, passes her a note in which he tells her to meet him at the gate of the nuns' garden. Guided by Sister Olivia, Ellena goes to the gate where Vivaldi is waiting with Brother Jeronimo, a monk he bribes to lead them from the convent by a secret path. Brother Jeronimo tries to betray them, however, and Ellena would have been recaptured if an aged monk they disturbed at his solitary prayers did not take pity on them and unlock the last door standing between the lovers and freedom.

Once in the open air, Vivaldi and Ellena descend the mountains to the place where Paulo waits with the horses for their escape. Instead of taking the road toward Naples, the fugitives turn westward toward Aquila. They are resting at a shepherd's cabin that day, when Paulo brings word that they are being pursued by two Carmelite friars. Eluding their pursuers, they ride toward Lake Celano, where Ellena takes refuge for the night in the Ursuline convent and Vivaldi stays in an establishment of Benedictines.

While these events are taking place, the marchese, who knows nothing of his wife's scheming with Schedoni, is suffering great anxiety over his son's whereabouts and welfare. The marchesa, on the other hand, is apprehensive only that Ellena will be found and her plans undone. When Schedoni suggests in his sly, indirect fashion that Ellena be put out of the way for good, she is at first horrified by his suggestion. Later, she reconsiders, and eventually she and the sinister monk come to agree that Ellena is to die. Schedoni, who has spies everywhere, is not long in locating the fugitives. As Vivaldi and Ellena are about to be married in the chapel of San Sebastian at Celano, armed men break into the church and arrest the two under a warrant of the Holy Inquisition. Ellena is charged with having broken her nun's vows and Vivaldi with having aided her escape. Vivaldi, though wounded in his struggle to prevent arrest, is carried to Rome and after a short hearing before the Inquisitor is imprisoned to await future trial and possibly torture to extort a confession. Paulo is also confined.

After the agents of the Inquisition take Vivaldi and Paulo away, Ellena's guards put her on a waiting horse and set out on a road that leads toward the Adriatic. After traveling with little interruption for two nights and two days, they come to a lonely house on the seashore. There she is turned over to a villainous-looking man whom the guards call Spalatro and locked in a room in which the only furnishing is a tattered mattress on the floor. Exhausted, she falls asleep. Spalatro comes to her room twice during the next day, looking at her with a gaze of impatience and guilt. On one occasion, he takes her to walk on the beach, where she meets Schedoni, whose face is hidden by his cowl. When he speaks to her, Ellena realizes that this monk is neither a friend nor a protector but an enemy, and she faints. She is revived and returned to her room.

Schedoni is determined that Ellena should die that night. When Spalatro confesses pity for the girl and refuses to be the executioner, Schedoni swears to do the deed himself. He goes to the room where the girl is sleeping and stands over her, dagger in hand. Suddenly, he bends to look closely at a miniature she wears about her neck. Agitated, he awakens Ellena and asks her if she knows whose portrait she wears. When she answers that it is the miniature of her father, Schedoni is even more shaken. He is convinced that he has discovered his lost daughter.

Overcome by remorse for his persecution of Ellena and the accusation that exposed Vivaldi to the tortures of the Inquisition, Schedoni tries to make amends. He and Ellena travel as quickly as possible to Naples. After leaving her at the Villa Altieri, the monk hastens to the Vivaldi palace and in an interview with the marchesa begs, without disclosing his connection with Ellena, that objections to Vivaldi's suit be withdrawn. When the marchesa proves inattentive, he determines to solemnize the nuptials of Vivaldi and Ellena without her consent.

Called a second time before the tribunal of the Inquisition, Vivaldi hears again among those present at the trial the voice that warned him on earlier occasions against his visits to the Villa Altieri. That night, a strange monk visits him in his cell and asks how long he has known Schedoni. The monk instructs Vivaldi to reveal to the Inquisition that Schedoni is actually Count Fernando di Bruno, who lived fifteen years in the disguise of a Dominican monk. He is also to ask that Ansaldo di Rovalli, the grand penitentiary of the Black Penitents, be called to testify to a confession he heard in 1752. When Vivaldi is again brought before the Inquisition, he does as he was told; Schedoni is arrested on his way to Rome to intercede for Vivaldi's freedom.

At Schedoni's trial, the mystery that links the sinister father confessor and the two lovers becomes clear. Years before, Schedoni, then a spendthrift younger son known as the count di Marinella, schemed to possess his brother's title, his unencumbered estate, and his beautiful wife. He arranged to have his brother, the count di Bruno, assassinated by Spalatro and contrived the story that the count perished while returning from a journey to Greece. After a proper season of mourning, he solicited the hand of his brother's widow. When she rejected him, he carried her off by force. Although the lady's honor was secured by marriage, she looked on her new husband with disdain; in his jealousy, he became convinced that she was unfaithful. One day, returning unexpectedly, he found a visitor with his wife. Drawing his stiletto with the intention of attacking the guest, he struck and killed his wife instead. This is the confession that so agitated the grand penitentiary, for he himself was the guest and for him an innocent woman died.

Further proof is Spalatro's dying confession, whose death is caused by a wound inflicted by Schedoni. Condemned to die for plotting his brother's death, Schedoni persists in his declaration that Ellena is his daughter. The mystery is cleared up by Sister Olivia, who had returned to the Convent of Santa Maria della Pieta; she is the unfortunate countess di Bruno, the sister of Signora Bianchi. Her wound was not mortal, but the report of her death was given out to protect her from her vengeful husband. Wishing to withdraw from the world, she entrusted her daughter by the first count di Bruno and an infant daughter by the second to Signora Bianchi. The infant died within a year.

Ellena, who knows nothing of this story, was mistaken in her belief that the miniature is that of her father, and it is on her word that Schedoni claims her as his daughter. It is also revealed that Father Nicola, who collected the evidence against Schedoni, was the mysterious monk whose ghostly warnings Vivaldi heard under the arch of the old fortress. Appalled by the father confessor's villainy, he turned against him after being wounded by Paulo's pistol on the night of the midnight search.

Schedoni has his final revenge. In some manner, he administers a fatal dose of poison to Father Nicola and then dies of the same mysterious drug. In his last moments, he boasts that he is escaping an ignominious death at the hands of the Inquisition.

Because of Schedoni's dying confession, Vivaldi is immediately set free. During his imprisonment, the marchesa dies repentant of the harm she plotted against Ellena. Now the marchese, overjoyed to be reunited with his son, withdraws all objections to Vivaldi's suit. With all doubts of Ellena's birth and goodness removed, he goes in person to the Convent of Santa Maria della Pieta and asks Sister Olivia

for her daughter's hand in the name of his son. Vivaldi and Ellena are married in the convent church in the presence of the marchese and Sister Olivia. As a mark of special favor, Paulo is allowed to be present when his master and Ellena are married. Were it not for the holy precincts and the solemnity of the occasion, the faithful fellow would have thrown his cap into the air and shouted that this is indeed a happy day.

Critical Evaluation:

In *A Journey Made in the Summer of 1794 Through Holland and the Western Frontier of Germany* (1795), an account of a trip through Holland and Germany with her husband in 1794, Ann Radcliffe told of her trip up the Rhine River, where she encountered two Capuchins "as they walked along the shore, beneath the dark cliffs of Boppart, wrapt in the long black drapery of their order, and their heads shrouded in cowls, that half concealed their faces." She saw them as "interesting figures in a picture, always gloomily sublime." This vision is commonly believed to have inspired the character of Schedoni, one of the most sinister villains in the genre of the gothic novel. As in her other books, *The Italian* mingles the wild or idyllic beauty of nature with scenes of nightmare and terror.

The Italian is one of the most skillful and successful examples of the gothic novel, a literary genre whose aim is to astound, to terrify, and to thrill its readers. More controlled and convincing than her earlier *The Mysteries of Udolpho* (1794), Radcliffe's novel is filled with such conventional gothic qualities as a highly melodramatic (and unlikely) plot set in the remote past, a minimal degree of character development, and a painstakingly developed setting and atmosphere.

The plot is a familiar one to readers of the gothic: A mysterious and black-hearted villain, Schedoni, plots against a beautiful damsel, Ellena, who spends most of the novel either imprisoned or in imminent danger of death, while her chivalrous and faithful lover, Vivaldi, struggles against incredible odds to rescue her. The character delineation is crude, and, predictably, the villainous monk Schedoni is much more fascinating than the somewhat vapid hero and heroine. The air of mystery and terror in the monk is strikingly described: "A habitual gloom and severity prevailed over the deep lines of his countenance; and his eyes were so piercing that they seemed to penetrate, at a single glance, into the hearts of men, and to read their most secret thoughts."

Setting is crucial to *The Italian*. Here are gloomy monasteries, the dank dungeons of the Inquisition, and the dizzying precipices and crags of Abruzzo. There are also scenes of quiet but spine-tingling terror, as the one between Ellena and Schedoni on the deserted beach. Just as the evil characters are made even more menacing by their contrast to the good characters, the wild landscapes and brooding interiors are made more threatening by their contrast to the descriptions of Naples's beauty at the beginning and the end of the novel.

The excesses and improbabilities of the lurid plot are tempered in a number of ways. Despite the manifold mysteries and hints of ghostly or demoniac forces pervading the work, nothing supernatural or magical actually occurs; unlike the events in Horace Walpole's *The Castle of Otranto* (1765), for instance, there is ultimately a rational explanation for everything. Further, Radcliffe's handling of suspense, mystery, dramatic pacing, and realistic detail and description is expert and gripping throughout. The author also shows a serious concern for the main gothic theme of man's inhumanity to man, as seen, for instance, in Vivaldi's outburst against the brutalities of the Inquisition: "Can this be in human nature!—Can such horrible perversion of right be permitted! Can man, who calls himself endowed with reason, and immeasurably superior to every other created being, argue himself into the commission of such horrible folly, such inveterate cruelty, as exceeds all the acts of the most irrational and ferocious brute . . . !"

Such novels as *The Italian* were adroitly satirized by Jane Austen in *Northanger Abbey* (1818). Radcliffe's novel, however, is significant not only for its literary qualities but also for the influence it had on such later writers as Sir Walter Scott, Charlotte Brontë, Samuel Taylor Coleridge, John Keats, and Edgar Allan Poe, all of whom drew on mysterious, threatening gothic settings and atmospheres in many of their own works.

Further Reading

Ellis, Kate Ferguson. "'Kidnapped Romance' in Ann Radcliffe." In *The Contested Castle: Gothic Novels and the Subversion of Domestic Ideology*. Urbana: University of Illinois Press, 1989. Discusses the gothic in terms of domestic relations. Sees Schedoni as fulfilling his own wishes to be first in a family circle by insinuating himself into the marchesa's confidence.

Flaxman, Rhoda. "Radcliffe's Dual Modes of Vision." In *Fetter'd or Free? British Women Novelists, 1670-1815*, edited by Mary Anne Schofield and Cecilia Macheski. Athens: Ohio University Press, 1986. Recognizes Radcliffe as developing a "new descriptive mode and technique" that include something akin to cinematography.

Hennelly, Mark M., Jr. "The Slow Torture of Delay: Reading *The Italian*." *Studies in Humanities* 14, no. 1 (June, 1987): 1-17. Explores Radcliffe's technique of suspense in the Inquisition segment of the novel.

Miles, Robert. *Ann Radcliffe: The Great Enchantress*. New York: Manchester University Press, 1995. Explores the historical and aesthetic context of Radcliffe's fiction, with separate chapters on her early works and mature novels; *The Italian* is discussed in chapter 8. Considers Radcliffe's role as a woman writer and her place in society. Includes notes and bibliography.

Murray, E. B. *Ann Radcliffe*. New York: Twayne, 1972. An excellent overview of all Radcliffe's novels; contains long passages from obscure eighteenth century novels. Provides psychological and ethical perspectives on *The Italian*.

Ronald, Ann. "Terror-Gothic: Nightmare and Dream in Ann Radcliffe and Charlotte Brontë." In *The Female Gothic*, edited by Juliann E. Fleenor. Montreal: Eden Press, 1983. Discusses archetypal images in works of Radcliffe and Brontë.

Todd, Janet. "Posture and Imposture: The Gothic Manservant in Ann Radcliffe's *The Italian*." In *Men by Woman*, edited by Todd. New York: Holmes and Meier, 1981. Analyzes the character of Paolo and shows how Radcliffe created him to embody ideal qualities of a manservant.

Tooley, Brenda. "Gothic Utopia: Heretical Sanctuary in Ann Radcliffe's *The Italian*." In *Gender and Utopia in the Eighteenth Century: Essays in English and French Utopian Writing*, edited by Nicole Pohl and Brenda Tooley. Burlington, Vt.: Ashgate, 2007. Tooley's analysis of Radcliffe's novel is included in a study of the representation of women in eighteenth century utopian literature. Includes a list of works cited and an index.

Varma, Devendra P. *The Gothic Flame, Being a History of the Gothic Novel in England*. London: Arthur Barker, 1957. In the section on Radcliffe, Varma observes the structure of Radcliffe's novels, her explanations of the supernatural occurrences, and her ability to create suspense.

The Itching Parrot

Author: José Joaquín Fernández de Lizardi (1776-1827)
First published: El periquillo sarniento, 1816 (English translation, 1942)
Type of work: Novel
Type of plot: Picaresque
Time of plot: 1770's to 1820's
Locale: Mexico

Principal characters:
PEDRO SARMIENTO, the Itching Parrot, or Poll, a young Mexican
DON ANTONIO, Poll's prison mate and benefactor
JANUARIO, Poll's schoolmate
AN ARMY COLONEL, Poll's superior and benefactor

The Story:

Pedro Sarmiento is born to upper-middle-class parents in Mexico City between 1771 and 1773; of the actual date, he is not sure. As a child he is willful, and his mother's excessive devotion only makes him worse. He becomes such a scamp that at last his father sends him off to school. At school, he is nicknamed Parrot. A little later, when he contracts the itch, his schoolmates nickname him the Itching Parrot, or Poll for short, and the name sticks to him through most of his life.

In addition to his nickname, Poll acquires many vicious habits from his school fellows. Poll's father resolves to put Poll out as an apprentice in a trade, but Poll's mother, not wishing her son to disgrace her family by becoming a vulgar tradesman, insists that the boy be sent to college. Against his better judgment, the father agrees, and so Poll is sent off to study for a college degree. After learning some Latin, some Aristotle, some logic, and some physics, Poll is awarded a baccalaureate degree by the College of San Ildefonso. Shortly after receiving his degree, Poll goes into the countryside to visit a hacienda owned by the father of a former schoolmate. At the hacienda, he earns the hatred of his schoolmate, Januario, by making advances to the latter's cousin, with whom Januario is infatuated. Januario takes his revenge by tempting Poll into a bullfight. Poll, who loses both the fight and his trousers, becomes the laughingstock of the hacienda. Still unsatisfied, Januario tricks Poll into trying to sleep with the girl cousin. Through Januario, the girl's mother discovers the attempt, beats Poll with her shoe, and sends him back to Mexico City in disgrace.

Upon his return to the city, Poll is told by his father that he must find some means of earning a livelihood. Poll, searching for the easiest way, decides he will study theology and enter the Church. Theology quickly proves uninteresting, and Poll gives up that idea. Trying to escape his father's insistence that he learn a trade, Poll then decides to enter a Franciscan monastery. There he soon finds that he cannot stand the life of a monk; he is glad when his father's death gives him an excuse to leave the monastery. After a short period of mourning, Poll rapidly exhausts his small inheritance

through his fondness for gambling, parties, and women. The sorrow he causes his mother sends her, also, to an early death. After his mother dies, Poll is left alone. None of his relatives, who know him for a rogue, will have anything to do with him.

In his despair, Poll falls in with another schoolmate, who supports himself by gambling and trickery. Poll takes up a similar career in his schoolmate's company. A man Poll gulls discovers his treachery and beats him severely. After his release from the hospital, Poll goes back to his gambling partner, and they decide to turn thieves. On their first attempt, however, they are unsuccessful. Poll is caught and thrown into prison.

Poll has no family or friends to call upon, so he languishes in jail for several months. He makes one friend in jail who helps him; that friend is Don Antonio, a man of good reputation who was unjustly imprisoned. Don Antonio tries to keep Poll away from bad company but is not entirely successful. When Don Antonio is freed, Poll falls in with a mulatto who gets him into all kinds of scrapes. By chance, Poll is taken up by a scrivener who is in need of an apprentice and is pleased with Poll's handwriting. The scrivener has Poll released from prison to become his apprentice. Poll's career as a scrivener's apprentice is short, for he makes love to the man's mistress, is discovered, and is driven from the house. The next step in Poll's adventures is service as a barber's apprentice. He then leaves that work to become a clerk in a pharmacy. After getting into trouble by carelessly mixing a prescription, Poll leaves the pharmacy for the employ of a doctor.

Having picked up some jargon and a few cures from his doctor-employer, Poll sets out to be a physician. Everything goes well until he causes a number of deaths and is forced to leave the profession.

Trying to recoup his fortunes once more, Poll returns to gambling. In a game, he wins a lottery ticket which, in its turn, wins for him a small fortune. For a time, Poll lives well: He even marries a woman who thinks he has a great deal of money. The life the couple leads soon exhausts the lottery money, however, and they are almost penniless again. After his wife dies in childbirth, Poll sets out once again in search of his fortune. His work as a sacristan ends when he robs a corpse. Poll then joins a group of beggars. Finding that they are fakes, he reports them to the authorities. One of the officials, pleased with Poll, secures him a place in government service. For a time all goes well, but Poll, who is left in charge of the district when his superior is absent, abuses his authority so much that he is arrested and sent in chains to Mexico City. There he is tried, found guilty of many crimes, and sent to the army for eight years.

Through his good conduct and pleasing appearance, Poll is made clerk to the colonel of the regiment. The colonel places a great deal of trust in Poll. When the regiment goes to Manila, the colonel sees to it that Poll is given an opportunity to do some trading and save up a small fortune. Poll completes his sentence and prepares to return to Mexico as a fairly rich man. All his dreams and fortune vanish, however, when the ship sinks and he is cast away upon an island. On the island, he makes friends with a Chinese chieftain, in whose company Poll, pretending all the while to be a nobleman, returns to Mexico. When they reach Mexico, the lie is discovered, but the Chinese man continues to be Poll's friend and patron.

Poll stays with the Chinese man for some time, but he finally leaves in disgrace after having introduced prostitutes into the house. Leaving Mexico City, Poll meets the mulatto who was his companion in jail. Along with the mulatto and some other men, Poll turns highwayman but barely escapes with his life from their first holdup. Frightened, Poll goes into retreat at a church, where he discovers his confessor to be a boy he knew years before in school. The kind confessor finds honest employment for Poll as an agent for a rich man. Poll becomes an honest, hardworking citizen, even being known as Don Pedro rather than Poll. Years pass quickly. Then one day, Don Pedro, befriending some destitute people, finds one to be his old benefactor of prison days, Don Antonio. The others are Don Antonio's wife and daughter. Don Pedro marries the daughter, thus completing his respectability. He lives out the rest of his days in honesty, industry, and respect.

Critical Evaluation:

The Itching Parrot is José Joaquín Fernández de Lizardi's masterpiece and is canonized as the first Spanish American novel. It is a picaresque novel, describing the misadventures of a young man driven by hunger and poverty to make his way in the world, in which he must, he says, cheat to survive. The book also has a liberal amount of slapstick humor (good examples of which occur during Poll's spell as a doctor's assistant and the episode in which he attempts to steal jewelry

from a corpse). Like the protagonist of the early picaresque novel *Lazarillo de Tormes* (1554), Poll experiences a series of apprenticeships (in a ranch, a monastery, a barber's shop, a pharmacy), learning a variety of trades that range from the socially prestigious (doctor's assistant, sacristan's assistant) to the dubious (croupier, cardsman) to the illegal (thief). The important part of these learning experiences is that all the occupations are based on deception. Those elements that *The Itching Parrot* shares with the great Spanish classic are effective. Unlike *Lazarillo de Tormes*, however, Fernández de Lizardi's novel inserts long, moralizing passages that describe the moral meaning of events in the plot and, for the modern reader at least, reduce their impact.

The society that *The Itching Parrot* describes is in flux. In the second half of the eighteenth century, Spain's colonies saw a displacement of power from the hands of the Church, the monarchy, and the landowning elite to a new, professional class of doctors, lawyers, and merchants. *The Itching Parrot* is sensitive to this social change and gives a vivid picture of a society that gradually was becoming more politically independent from Spain. An indication of this change of ambience is evident in the opening pages of the novel. The novel's prologue describes an imaginary conversation between the author and a friend, who advises the author against dedicating his work to a wealthy patron, instead saying that the author should dedicate the book to his readers, since they are "the ones who will pay for the printing." It is not by chance that the first Spanish American novel should refer to a new mode of production (capital-based book production) and, by implication, to the new class from which it sprang.

Most critics agree that the main aim of *The Itching Parrot* is to identify the abuse of power in the professions in colonial New Spain. In Spanish America, as elsewhere, the growth of the new professional classes, including doctors, lawyers, merchants, suppliers, and printers, was accompanied by the growth of a parasitic group of unqualified and dishonest professionals; it is these latter that *The Itching Parrot* sets out to satirize. The protagonist is used not so much as a means whereby the hypocrisy and corruption of others is exposed; rather, he becomes himself the object of scorn and ridicule. In part 1, chapter 1, for example, Poll takes great pains to list the circumstances of his upbringing as a way of explaining his wayward ways. He assigns blame to his parents' lack of education, their lack of concern for his upbringing and, in particular, their frequent recourse to wet nurses. The irony underlying these details becomes clear when the narrator refers to the way in which old wives' tales affected him as a young child, and the narrative begins to creak under its self-imposed burden of moralism. It could be argued that the moralistic intention of this passage (which is typical of many others) is too transparent, and that Pedro's credibility as a narrator is diminished as a result.

The rationale behind the many episodes of Pedro's life emerges at the end of the novel. In book 3, chapter 3, the narrator is shipwrecked on an unidentified island in the Pacific Ocean. He finds himself obliged to justify the laws and customs of his native land to a skeptical Chinese chieftain (who may be Fernández de Lizardi's spokesman). In describing his society's customs (such as the idea that nobles cannot work, work being beneath them), Pedro manages to make the customs sound absurd. Pedro's stupidity is revealed when, in the same chapter, he not only fails to recognize a plant but diagnoses its medicinal function in precisely the wrong way. Events finally run against Pedro, and he is humiliated by the Chinese chieftain. When readers ask to what or to whom is the satire being directed, the answer must surely be Spanish American society.

There are some scenes in the novel that show Fernández de Lizardi's consummate skill in allowing irony to emerge from events rather than from commentary. A good example is the frequently anthologized scene in part 2, chapter 6, in which Poll decides to become a doctor, takes on André as his assistant and, with the luck of the devil, manages to revive a tax collector who is on his deathbed. Poll's use of Latin to hoodwink his audience and hide his ignorance, when faced with medical symptoms, is effectively done. In this vignette Fernández de Lizardi offers a convincing picture of a society in which half-learned Latin tags are used to confound the populace and fleece the poor.

"Critical Evaluation" by Stephen M. Hart

Further Reading

Bell, Steven M. "Mexico." In *Handbook of Latin American Literature*, edited by David William Foster. 2d ed. New York: Garland, 1992. The section on *The Itching Parrot* shows that Fernández de Lizardi did not seek to entertain the colonial nobility in his novel but intended to use the novel to enlighten the masses.

Benitez-Rojo, Antonio. "José Joaquín Fernández de Lizardi and the Emergence of the Spanish American Novel as National Project." In *The Places of History: Regionalism Revisited in Latin America*, edited by Doris Sommer. Durham, N.C.: Duke University Press, 1999. Benitez-Rojo describes why *The Itching Parrot* can be considered the first Spanish American novel. He explains how the novel helped create a sense of Mexican nationalism and a definition of "Mexicanness," and he traces the novel's significant influence on subsequent works of Spanish American fiction. He also places the novel within the context of Fernández de Lizardi's other fiction.

Cros, Edmond. "The Values of Liberalism in *El Periquillo Sarniento*." *Sociocriticism* 2 (December, 1985): 85-109. Studies the relationship between the Spanish colony of New Spain and its metropolis through the relationship between father and son, which the first-person novel relies upon as a guiding theme.

Franco, Jean. *An Introduction to Spanish-American Literature*. New York: Cambridge University Press, 1969. The section on *The Itching Parrot* argues that Fernández de Lizardi represents a new type of Spanish American, one for whom the newspaper served as a weapon, and contends that Poll is too passive a hero to be sympathetic to the modern reader.

González, Aníbal. *Journalism and the Development of Spanish American Narrative*. New York: Cambridge University Press, 1993. The section on *The Itching Parrot* argues that the main character is an allegory of the journalist and of the duplicitous nature of writing.

Peden, Margaret Sayers. *Mexican Writers on Writing*. San Antonio, Tex.: Trinity University Press, 2007. Includes a chapter in which Fernández de Lizardi comments on writing *The Itching Parrot*.

Porter, Katherine Anne. "Katherine Anne Porter on José Joaquín Fernández de Lizardi." In *Mutual Impressions: Writers from the Americas Reading One Another*, edited by Ilan Stavans. Durham, N.C.: Duke University Press, 1999. Porter, an American novelist who translated *The Itching Parrot* and wrote an introduction to the novel for a 1942 English-language edition, provides her comments on the work.

Vogeley, Nancy. "Defining the 'Colonial Reader.'" *PMLA* 102, no. 5 (1987): 784-800. Suggests that Fernández de Lizardi's aim in writing the novel was to challenge readers' expectations that a literary work should follow European standards and have an elevated style. Argues that Fernández de Lizardi created a new genre and a new readership.

_____. *Lizardi and the Birth of the Novel in Spanish America*. Gainesville: University Press of Florida, 2001. Chronicles the birth of the Mexican novel after three hundred years of colonial rule. Vogeley focuses on *The Itching Parrot*, describing how this novel became a symbol of Mexican nationhood when it was published during the war for independence, and she recounts how this novel and Fernández de Lizardi's other works contributed to the revolutionary movement.

Ivanhoe
A Romance

Author: Sir Walter Scott (1771-1832)
First published: 1819
Type of work: Novel
Type of plot: Romance
Time of plot: 1194
Locale: England

Principal characters:
CEDRIC THE SAXON, the owner of Rotherwood Grange
WILFRED OF IVANHOE, his disinherited son
THE LADY ROWENA, his ward and Ivanhoe's beloved
ISAAC OF YORK, a Jewish moneylender
REBECCA, his daughter
SIR BRIAN DE BOIS-GUILBERT, a Norman Knight Templar
KING RICHARD I, a king returned from the Third Crusade
ROBIN HOOD, an outlaw

The Story:

Night is drawing near when Prior Aymer of Jorvaux and the haughty Templar Brian de Bois-Guilbert overtake a swineherd and a fool by the roadside and ask directions to Rotherwood, the dwelling of Cedric the Saxon. The answers of these serfs so confuse the Templar and the prior that they would have gone far afield were it not for a pilgrim from the Holy Land whom they encounter shortly afterward. The pilgrim is also traveling to Rotherwood, and he brings them safely to Cedric's hall, where they claim lodging for the night. It is the custom of those rude days to afford hospitality to all travelers, so Cedric gives a grudging welcome to the Norman lords.

There is a feast at Rotherwood that night. On the dais beside Cedric the Saxon sits his ward, the lovely Lady Rowena, descendant of the ancient Saxon princes. It is the old man's ambition to wed her to Athelstane of Coningsburgh, who comes from the line of King Alfred. Because his son, Wilfred of Ivanhoe, fell in love with Lady Rowena, Cedric banished him, and the young knight went with King Richard to Palestine. None in the banquet hall that night suspects that the pilgrim is Ivanhoe himself.

Another traveler who claims shelter at Rotherwood that night is an aged Jew, Isaac of York. Hearing some orders the Templar mutters to his servants at the feast's end, Ivanhoe warns the Jew that Bois-Guilbert has designs on his moneybag or his person. Without taking leave of their host the next morning, the disguised pilgrim and Isaac of York leave Rotherwood together and continue on to the nearby town of Ashby de la Zouche.

Many other travelers are on their way to the town, for a great tournament is to be held there. Prince John, the regent of England in King Richard's absence, is to preside. The winner of the tournament will be allowed to name the Queen of Love and Beauty and receive the prize of the passage of arms from her hands.

Ivanhoe attends the tournament with the word Disinherited written on his shield. Entering the lists, he strikes the shield of Bois-Guilbert with the point of his lance and challenges the knight to mortal combat. In the first passage, both knights splinter their lances, but neither is unhorsed. At the second passage, Ivanhoe's lance strikes Bois-Guilbert's helmet and upsets him. Then, one by one, Ivanhoe vanquishes five knights who agreed to take on all comers. When the heralds declare the Disinherited Knight victor of the tourney, Ivanhoe names Lady Rowena the Queen of Love and Beauty.

In the tournament on the following day, Ivanhoe is pressed hard by three antagonists, but he receives unexpected help from a knight in black, whom the spectators call the Black Sluggard because of his previous inactivity. Because of his earlier triumphs during the day, Ivanhoe is again named champion of the tournament. To receive the gift from Lady Rowena, Ivanhoe removes his helmet, and when he does, he is recognized. He receives the chaplet, his prize, kisses the hand of Lady Rowena, and then faints from loss of blood. Isaac of York and his daughter, Rebecca, are sitting nearby, and Rebecca suggests to her father that they nurse Ivanhoe until he is well. Isaac and his daughter start for their home with the wounded knight carried in a horse litter. On the way, they join the train of Cedric the Saxon, who is still ignorant of the Disinherited Knight's identity.

Before the travelers go far, however, they are set upon and captured by a party led by three Norman knights, Bois-Guilbert, Maurice de Bracy, and Reginald Front de Boeuf. They are imprisoned in Front de Boeuf's castle of Torquilstone. De Bracy has designs on Lady Rowena because she is an heiress of royal lineage. The Templar desires to possess

Rebecca. Front de Boeuf hopes to extort a large sum of money from the aged Jew. Cedric is held for ransom. The wounded knight is put into the charge of an ancient hag named Ulrica.

Isaac and his daughter are placed in separate rooms. Bois-Guilbert goes to Rebecca in her tower prison and asks her to adopt Christianity so that they might be married. The plot of the Norman nobles against their prisoners is thwarted by an assault on the castle by Richard the Lion-Hearted, the knight known as the Black Sluggard at the Ashby tournament, in company with Robin Hood and his outlaws. Ulrica aids the besiegers by starting a fire within the castle walls. Robin Hood and his men take the prisoners to the forest along with the Norman nobles. In the confusion, however, Bois-Guilbert escapes with Rebecca, and Isaac prepares to ransom her from the Templar. De Bracy is set free, and he hurries to inform Prince John that he saw and talked with Richard. John plots to make Richard his prisoner.

Isaac goes to the establishment of the Knights Templar and begs to see Bois-Guilbert. Lucas de Beaumanoir, the grand master of the Templars, orders Isaac admitted to his presence. Isaac is frightened when the grand master asks him his business with the Templar. When he tells his story, the grand master learns that Bois-Guilbert abducted Rebecca. It is suggested that Rebecca cast a spell on Bois-Guilbert. Condemned as a witch, she is sentenced to be burned at the stake. In desperation, she demands, as is her right, a champion to defend her against the charge. Lucas de Beaumanoir agrees and names Bois-Guilbert to face that champion.

The day arrives for Rebecca's execution. A pile of wood is placed around the stake. Seated in a black chair, Rebecca awaits the arrival of her defender. Three times the heralds call on a champion to appear. At the third call, a strange knight rides into the lists and announces himself as Rebecca's champion. When Bois-Guilbert realizes that the stranger is Ivanhoe, he at first refuses combat because Ivanhoe's wounds are not completely healed. Nevertheless, the grand master gives orders for the contest to begin. As everyone expects, the tired horse of Ivanhoe and its exhausted rider go down at the first blow, so that Ivanhoe's lance merely touches the shield of the Templar. To the astonishment of all, however, Bois-Guilbert reels in his saddle and falls to the ground. Ivanhoe arises and draws his sword. Placing his foot on the breast of the fallen knight, he calls on Bois-Guilbert to yield himself or die on the spot. There is no answer from Bois-Guilbert; he is dead, a victim of the violence of his own passions. The grand master declares that Rebecca is acquitted of the charge against her. At that moment, the Black Knight appears, followed by a band of knights and men-at-arms. It is

King Richard, who comes to arrest Rebecca's accusers on a charge of treason. The grand master sees the flag of the Temple hauled down and the royal standard raised in its place.

King Richard returns in secret to reclaim his throne. Robin Hood becomes his true follower. Athelstane forfeits his claims to Lady Rowena's hand so that she and Ivanhoe can be married. Reconciled at last with his son, Cedric the Saxon gives his consent, and Richard himself graces their wedding. Isaac and Rebecca leave England for Granada, hoping to find in that foreign land greater happiness than could ever be theirs in England.

Critical Evaluation:

Since publication, *Ivanhoe* has retained its charm for readers as the epitome of chivalric novels. It has among its characters two of the most popular of English heroes, Richard the Lion-Hearted and Robin Hood, and it tells a powerful story of romance in addition to offering action and color. Although *Ivanhoe* may not be Sir Walter Scott's greatest novel, it is without doubt his most popular.

Scott wrote that he left the Scottish scenes of his previous novels and turned to the Middle Ages in *Ivanhoe* because he feared the reading public was growing weary of the repetition of Scottish themes in his books. He was fascinated with history all his life, and it was logical that he should turn to the past for subject matter. Many faults have been found with the historical facts of *Ivanhoe*; Robin Hood, if he lived at all, would have lived in a later century than that represented in the novel, for example, and by the time of Richard I, the distinction between Saxons and Normans had faded. Nevertheless, whatever liberties Scott took with history, the thrilling drama continues to grip readers.

Scott's four great chivalric novels possess similar structures. They all focus on a moment of crisis between two great individuals, a moment that determines the survival of one and the destruction of the other. In *Ivanhoe*, the contrast is between Richard the Lion-Hearted and his brother John. The struggle reflects one of the principal themes of the novel: the decadence of chivalry. For generations of juvenile readers, *Ivanhoe* represented the glory of chivalric adventure, but Scott actually entertained serious doubts about the tradition. At several strategic points in Ivanhoe, he unequivocally damns the reckless inhumanity of romantic chivalry.

The novel is designed in three parts, each reaching its climax in a great military spectacle. The first part ends with the Ashby tournament, the second with the liberation from the castle of Front de Boeuf, and the third with the trial by combat for Rebecca. The beginning chapters draw together all of the character groups for the tournament, though Ivanhoe is present only as the mysterious palmer. The problem of seating at the tournament provides a sketch of the cultural animosities that divide the world of the novel.

Richard is the moral and political center of the book and, therefore, the proper object of Ivanhoe's fidelity. The captive king does not appear until he fights as the mysterious Black Knight during the second day of the tournament. He saves Ivanhoe and then disappears until the scene of his midnight feast with Friar Tuck, who regards him as a man of "prudence and of counsel." Richard possesses a native humanity and a love of life, as well as the traditional heroic chivalric qualities, and he is always ready to act as a protector of others.

By contrast, John is an ineffectual ruler whose own followers despise him. His forces quickly disintegrate, and his followers abandon him for their selfish ends. He is a petulant, stupid man, incapable of inspiring loyalty. It is inevitable that the historical climax of the novel should be the confrontation between Richard and John. The chivalric code becomes completely corrupt in the England left to John's care. Both the narrator and the characters make clear that chivalry is no more than a mixture of "heroic folly and dangerous imprudence."

Rebecca speaks against chivalry, asking during the bloody siege of the castle if possession by a "demon of vainglory" brings "sufficient rewards for the sacrifice of every kindly affection, for a life spent miserably that yet may make others miserable." (Rebecca is antichivalric, yet she is the most romantic character in the book, suggesting the traditional chivalric attitude toward women.) The narrator speaks most sharply against the chivalric code at the end of the tournament:

> This ended the memorable field of Ashby-de-la-Zouche, one of the most gallantly contested tournaments of that age; for although only four knights, including one who was smothered by the heat of his armour, had died upon the field, yet upwards of thirty were desperately wounded, four or five of whom never recovered. Several more were disabled for life; and those who escaped best carried the marks of the conflict to the grave with them. Hence it is always mentioned in the old records as the "gentle and joyous passage of arms at Ashby."

An argument has been made that Scott's historical novels, such as *Ivanhoe*, are inferior to his earlier novels based on his direct, personal knowledge of the Scottish customs, characters, and land. Even in the historical novels, however, Scott's characters are colorful, full of vitality, and realized with amazing verisimilitude. Scott's knowledge of the past about which he is writing is so deep that he can draw upon it at will to decorate his fictions. He did not find it necessary to research a novel such as *Ivanhoe* in order to write it; the historical lore was already part of him. Years before, at the time when he was beginning the Waverley series, he wrote a study about chivalry. His prolific writing did not seem to exhaust his resources.

Scott was one of the most prolific writers in the history of British fiction; only Anthony Trollope approached his record. Scott's novels were originally published anonymously, although their authorship came to be an open secret. Scott's friends found it difficult to believe that he was the author of the novels, for he lived the life of a county magistrate and landowner and spent long hours in these occupations as well as entertaining lavishly and writing poetry and nonfiction works. He managed to accomplish so much because he habitually rose early and completed all novel-writing before breakfast. In time, his compulsive working injured his health. While writing *Ivanhoe*, he was tortured by a cramp of the stomach and suffered such pain that he could not hold the pen but was forced to dictate much of the story.

Like many great novels, *Ivanhoe* betrays its author's complex attitude. In tandem with Scott's severe view of the code of chivalry is his attraction to the Romantic traditions of the period. Although Richard's personality is not romantic, it is to this character that Scott gives the chivalric virtues. Scott dramatizes his more ambivalent feelings about chivalry in the characters of Rebecca and Lady Rowena, Ivanhoe and Richard. The tension created through these mixed feelings, the dramatic (if historically inaccurate) story, and the vast accumulation of detail on costume and social customs and historical anecdotes combine to create a novel that has remained popular ever since it was first published.

"Critical Evaluation" by Bruce D. Reeves

Further Reading

Dawson, Terence. *The Effective Protagonist in the Nineteenth-Century British Novel: Scott, Brontë, Eliot, Wilde.* Burlington, Vt.: Ashgate, 2004. Argues that the opening situation in a novel depicts an implicit challenge that confronts a minor character, whom Dawson defines as "the effective protagonist." Describes how Cedric is the effective protagonist whose critical function is to order the events of *Ivanhoe*.

DeGategno, Paul J. *Ivanhoe: The Mask of Chivalry.* New York: Twayne, 1994. Provides a good general introduction to the novel. Places *Ivanhoe* in literary and historical context and then focuses on an analysis of the book, emphasizing the novel's pertinence to its own time and its importance as a reflection of Scott's society. Concludes with a selection of deGategno's students' responses to *Ivanhoe*.

Hayden, John O., ed. *Scott: The Critical Heritage*. New York: Barnes & Noble, 1970. A collection of reviews of many of Scott's novels, including *Ivanhoe*. Includes an extended essay on Scott by Samuel Taylor Coleridge and anonymous letters written to Scott about the novel.

Hillhouse, James T. *The Waverley Novels and Their Critics*. New York: Octagon Books, 1970. A history of Scott's critical reception. The first part offers early reviews from *The Edinburgh*, *The Quarterly*, *Blackwood's*, and other periodicals, and the second part provides critical interpretations from the fifty years following Scott's death.

Johnson, Edgar. *Sir Walter Scott: The Great Unknown*. 2 vols. New York: Macmillan, 1970. An immense two-volume set that includes a synopsis and historical explanation of the characters and setting of *Ivanhoe*. Considers the differing treatments of Jews and Christians, and explains aspects of Scott's views on the Catholic Church, morality, and nobility.

Lauber, John. *Sir Walter Scott*. Rev. ed. Boston: Twayne, 1989. Compares *Ivanhoe* with the other Scott novels and places it in the context of Scott's entire oeuvre. Explains the stereotypes and the concept of chivalry.

Lincoln, Andrew. "The Condition of England: *Ivanhoe* and *Kenilworth*." In *Walter Scott and Modernity*. Edinburgh: Edinburgh University Press, 2007. In his examination of Scott's novels and poems, Lincoln argues that these were not works of nostalgia; instead, Scott used the past as a means of exploring modernist moral, political, and social issues.

Shaw, Harry E., ed. *Critical Essays on Sir Walter Scott: The Waverley Novels*. New York: G. K. Hall, 1996. Collection of essays published between 1858 and 1996 about Scott's series of novels. Includes journalist Walter Bagehot's 1858 article about the Waverly novels and discussions of Scott's rationalism, storytelling and subversion of the literary form in his fiction, and what his work meant to Victorian readers.

J

J. B.
A Play in Verse

Author: Archibald MacLeish (1892-1982)
First produced: 1958; first published, 1958
Type of work: Drama
Type of plot: Symbolism
Time of plot: 1940's-1950's
Locale: A large American city

Principal characters:
MR. ZUSS, a bombastic, rundown actor who represents God
NICKLES, a sardonic clown who acts as Satan
J. B., the Job figure and a businessman
SARAH, J. B.'s wife

The Story:

Two broken-down actors—Zuss is a large, red-faced, and dignified man, and Nickles is sarcastic and gaunt to the point of grotesqueness—are drawn into a drama involving J. B., a character who resembles Job. The book of Job is the Old Testament story of a good man who is punished so that God can prove to Satan, his adversary, that there are good people who love God despite their hardships. Unlike Satan in the book of Job, Nickles seems to sympathize with humanity and denounce God for torturing innocent people. It would be Job's demand for reasons, for justice, that would force him to confront God.

In a bedraggled circus sideshow, Zuss (whose attitude reinforces his self-image of what God would be like) and Nickles (who is disillusioned and bitter because this play had been done over and over throughout the centuries, with the same actions and ending) argue over Heaven and Hell as they watch modern Job (J. B.) and his happy family. Nickles mocks Zuss's sincerity, and Zuss declares that God has reasons for testing Job (who represents humanity). Nickles tends to see himself as Job as he claims that God is jealous because Job has a soul and intellect that allows him to question God's actions. As Nickles chants, "If God is God He is not good, If God is good He is not God."

Zuss recalls World War II and its horrors to reveal that someone is always playing Job, punished "for walking round the world in the wrong skin." Modern Jobs are no longer perfect, as Job is described; rather, they are average people trying to survive in an unfriendly universe. Hell is not only suffering, however. According to Nickles, Hell is Job's con-sciousness of consciousness—knowing that he will continue to love God even though he is destroyed and loses his wealth, his children, and everything else.

J. B. is a complacent, successful New Englander in his thirties, with children appropriately named David (age thirteen), Mary (age twelve), Jonathan (age ten), Ruth (age eight), and Rebecca (age six). His wife, Sarah, warns Job not to trust in their "luck" or success. It is Sarah who is devoted to God and Sarah who insists that they give proper thanks to God. She says that justice demands that God punish as well as reward, but J. B. refuses to listen. He trusts that God's gift, symbolized in the greening of the leaves, will never be removed. Nickles and Zuss plot his destruction.

In succession, two messengers in the roles of soldiers, newspapermen, and police officers meet with Job and Sarah to announce the horrifying deaths of their children: first David, shot by his own men after the war ends; then Mary and Jonathan, slammed into a brick wall in a car wreck; Rebecca, raped and killed by a nineteen-year-old; and finally Ruth, crushed beneath a falling wall in their bombed-out city. In every case, the second messenger declares, like his biblical counterpart, "I only am escaped alone to tell thee." This messenger also suggests that some are doomed to witness the destruction and the losses of other people—witnesses, too, suffer.

After every revelation, Sarah weeps and withdraws, while Job continues to believe in God and his goodness. He also calls out to the silence as he seeks an answer to humanity's eternal question—why does God permit the suffering of innocent people? Meanwhile, as J. B. and Sarah sit in the rubble of their home, Nickles sarcastically mocks Zuss for his bad aim—he destroyed an entire city to "blister one man's skin."

For J. B., the meaninglessness of his children's suffering is worse than the curses inflicted upon them. In their despair at losing all of their children, the couple split up rather than hold on to each other. J. B. tries to pray while Sarah rocks and weeps. Nickles is disgusted at Job's acceptance of "God's will"; it is not decent to still love a God who takes those children. Finally, Sarah leaves Job because he insists that he or their children must have been guilty of something for which they were punished. To her, this is a lie calculated to save God's image of goodness. Sarah says that she will not love Job any more if he buys God's goodness in exchange for their children.

Like biblical Job, J. B. is visited by his three "comforters." In the 1950's world, they are a fat priest, a psychiatrist, and a communist. Eliphaz the psychiatrist argues that guilt is an illusion or disease, and Zophar the priest explodes with the cry that guilt is the only reality. The communist also is not much help.

Finally, Job hears the Distant Voice from the Whirlwind, and he matches his silence with God's earlier refusals to speak with Job. Nickles is angry that Job knuckles under to God's grandeur, but it seems that J. B. actually forgives God, as if Job's suffering is justified by his acceptance of God's will.

As Zuss attempts to restore J. B.'s family and wealth, Nickles tries to convince J. B. to renounce God's creation by committing suicide. What saves J. B. is the return of his wife Sarah. As she wandered through the rubble of their bombed-out city, also contemplating suicide, Sarah found forsythia blooming in the debris of ashes and death. This silent promise of life brings J. B. and Sarah back together as she declares that there is no justice in the world, a concept Job believed throughout their ordeal. The only thing left is love. They trust now in each other's love, not in God's justice.

Critical Evaluation:

Awarded three Pulitzer Prizes (one for *J. B.*) and enjoying an illustrious career as a poet, Librarian of Congress, and playwright, Archibald MacLeish relied upon myth and symbolism, particularly biblical symbols, to focus and inform his work. Like T. S. Eliot, MacLeish allowed past and present to intertwine as he sought to create a recurring image of fertility (as in *The Pot of Earth*, 1925) or a determined rationality (as in *Nobodaddy*, 1926) that reinforced the notion of humanity's domination of nature.

J. B. is MacLeish's response to the wanton slaughter of innocent people in World War II. In this play, modern Job is a typical American businessman who takes his good fortune for granted, as somehow "deserved." This humanistic drama elevates humanity while lessening the importance of God, perhaps explaining the negative critical response the play suffered when presented on Broadway in 1958.

Unlike other versions of the Job story, *J. B.* gives Job's wife Sarah (who has the same name as Abraham's wife, who created the Hebrew "dynasty" in the Old Testament) as much a part in the suffering as Job has. Sarah is the one who recognizes that it is God who is killing their children, and it is Sarah's love, not God's, that brings the couple back together and renews their faith in life.

The broken-down actor who plays God is aptly named Zuss, to reinforce his image—Zeus is the king of the ancient Greek gods. That he is a has-been, a failure, adds dimension to the story. Nickles is not only a nickel-plated clown or a phony but also "Old Nick"—the deceiver, Satan himself. The children all have biblical names to reinforce MacLeish's frame of reference. Zuss represents the traditional, theistic (believing in God) view, and Nickles presents a more humanistic interpretation of innocent suffering.

To MacLeish, it is the poet's duty to use his or her experience of life to bring a "human focus" and understanding. This can be seen clearly in his political writings as well. For him, it is humanity's love of life and the urge to endure that is the miracle of existence. *J. B.* reveals that answers come not from a distant or nonexistent God but from humanity itself. MacLeish believed that the answers to the mystery of life must come not from without but from within each person. To deal with the tragic meaninglessness of World War II, MacLeish needed Job as a symbol for those who died senselessly, needlessly, because they were "in the wrong skin" or because the moonlight shone on the water, making an easy bombing target. Although Job is an appropriate myth for humanity's attempt to confront an unjust universe, this play is also a "supreme affirmation of the love of life." That love, MacLeish says, is where "God exists and triumphs."

Some critics derided J. B. (Job) as shallow and self-righteous, but that is the poet's point—humans are no longer the Promethean heroes of the past. (Prometheus stole fire from the gods to help humanity and was tortured by Zeus for this outrage.) People are ordinary, with faults, doubts, and failings.

Nickles insists on humanity's spiritual independence from God, but Zuss reiterates the Distant Voice from the Whirlwind that silences Job. At times, the actors hear another Voice intoning the words from the Bible's book of Job, and their masks seem to have lives of their own. The audience begins to suspect that there still is a Voice beyond the mask—God may be distant, but He still controls the good and the evil that humanity must confront and defeat.

If Job is complacent at first and bitter after his catastrophes, Sarah is a better wife than he deserves. Like William Blake (the English Romantic poet of the eighteenth and nineteenth centuries) and Robert Frost (the twentieth century American poet and author of *A Masque of Reason*, 1945, a verse play about modern Job), MacLeish insists on Sarah's equal participation in the suffering as well as in the renewal of life following the test. She knows before Job that it is God who is torturing them. It is also Sarah who returns with the greening forsythia to rekindle her love of Job and of life.

The suffering, though, is shared by the second messenger, who witnesses each act of terror and so is doomed as well. His repeated line of "I only am escaped alone to tell thee" is key to his character. People of the twentieth century are witnesses to the most heinous crimes imaginable, however, they seem to share the guilt of the victimizers.

J. B. denies Sarah the right to suffer as much as he in the deaths of their children. He makes the deaths a contest between himself and God and ignores the fact that Sarah is as guilty or as innocent as he. She leaves him because of his seeming lack of emotion and of anger and despair at the horrifying details of their children's deaths.

MacLeish must separate J. B. and Sarah so that they face the final crisis alone. Job thus confronts his false comforters and rejects the cliché that he has been spouting—"The Lord giveth, the Lord taketh away." It is not the pain they have suffered so much as the meaninglessness of it all that grieves him.

According to MacLeish, modern humanity's comforters—psychiatrists and religious and political leaders—deny people their individual right to guilt and individual responsibility for the sins of the world. Without individual guilt, there can be no identity, no innocence, and no humanity.

When God speaks out of the Whirlwind, he silences Job without answering his complaints. Job bows and forgives God. Like Satan, Nickles thinks incorrectly that Job will reject his newly reconstituted life. The play's ending, in which Job and Sarah are reconciled, has been controversial since the play's publication. Critics who deride the playwright do so because *J. B.* does not focus the Job story on God and his majesty. Instead, MacLeish gives humanity center stage and insists in this humanistic drama that Job and Sarah's choice of life comes from within, where God is.

Linda L. Labin

Further Reading

Campbell, Shannon O. "The Book of Job and MacLeish's *J. B.*: A Cultural Comparison." *English Journal* 61 (May, 1972): 653-657. Clarifies the connections between the Old Testament story and the poet's unique approach to it.

Donaldson, Scott, and R. H. Winnick. *Archibald MacLeish: An American Life.* Boston: Houghton Mifflin, 1992. Comprehensive and sympathetic account of MacLeish's life and work, including his friendships and literary achievements. Helps explains why he is all but forgotten in the twenty-first century.

Falk, Signi Lenea. *Archibald MacLeish.* New York: Twayne, 1965. A thorough analysis of the poet's major contributions to poetry and drama. Suggests connections between MacLeish and other twentieth century poets.

MacLeish, William H. *Uphill with Archie: A Son's Journey.* New York: Simon & Schuster, 2001. MacLeish's son recalls his father as a brilliant, talented, and unusually lucky man and describes his efforts to make his father proud of him.

Roston, Murray. "MacLeish's *J. B.*" In *Biblical Images in Literature*, edited by Roland Bartel. Nashville, Tenn.: Abingdon Press, 1975. Analyzes the supernatural elements in *J. B.* in contrast to the ordinary modern scene of horror.

Sanders, Paul S., ed. *Twentieth Century Interpretations of the Book of Job: A Collection of Critical Essays.* Englewood Cliffs, N.J.: Prentice-Hall, 1968. An excellent collection of critical articles on the Old Testament book of Job, including one by Richard B. Sewall, who calls Job the symbol of undeserved suffering.

Jack of Newbery

Author: Thomas Deloney (1543?-1600)
First published: 1597, as *The Pleasant History of John
    Winchcomb, in His Younger Days Called Jack of
    Newbery*
Type of work: Novel
Type of plot: Picaresque
Time of plot: 1509-1547
Locale: England

Principal characters:
JACK WINCHCOMB, a weaver
JACK'S MASTER'S WIDOW
JACK'S SECOND WIFE
HENRY VIII, the king of England
QUEEN CATHERINE, his wife
CARDINAL WOLSEY, the Lord Chancellor of England

The Story:

In the days of King Henry VIII, there lives in the English town of Newbery a young weaver named Jack Winchcomb. As a young man he is something of a prodigal, spending as much as he makes and having a reputation as a merry young fellow; he is known in all the county of Berkshire as Jack of Newbery. After his master dies, however, Jack changes his ways. His mistress, who acquires a fondness for the young man, entrusts to him the entirety of her husband's business. Jack becomes a careful man, both with his mistress's affairs and with his own, and he soon loses his reputation for prodigality. In its place, he acquires a reputation as an honest, hard-working, and intelligent businessman.

His mistress thinks so highly of Jack that she even makes him an adviser in affairs of the heart. His advice is of little value to her, however, for she makes up her mind, despite the difference in their years, to marry Jack. She tricks him into agreeing to further her marriage with an unknown suitor. When they arrive at the church, Jack finds that he is to be the bridegroom; thus Jack becomes her husband and the master of her house and business.

The marriage goes none too smoothly at first; despite her love for Jack, the woman does not like to be ordered about by the man who was once her servant. At last, however, they come to an understanding and live happily for several years, after which interval the good woman dies, leaving Jack master of the business and rich in the world's goods.

Not long after his first wife dies, Jack remarries, this time to a young woman. The wife is a poor choice, although he has the pick of the wealthy women of his class in the county. Not many months pass after the marriage, which was a costly one, before James, the king of Scotland, invades England while King Henry is in France. The justices of the county call upon Jack to furnish six men-at-arms to join the army raised by Queen Catherine. Jack chooses to raise a company of a hundred and fifty foot and horse, which he arms and dresses at his own expense in distinctive liveries. Jack rides at the head of his men. Queen Catherine is greatly pleased and thanks Jack personally for his efforts, although his men are not needed to achieve the English victory at Flodden Field. In reward for his services, Jack receives a chain of gold from the hands of the queen herself.

In the tenth year of his reign, King Henry makes a trip through Berkshire. Jack introduces himself in a witty way to the king as the Prince of the Ants, who is at war with the Butterflies, a sally against Cardinal Wolsey. The king is vastly pleased and betakes himself to Newbery, along with his train, where all are entertained by Jack at a fabulous banquet. After the banquet, the king views the weaving rooms and warehouses Jack owns. Upon his departure, the king wishes to make Jack a knight, but the weaver refuses the honor, saying he would rather be a common man and die, as he lived, a clothier.

In his house, Jack of Newbery has a series of fifteen paintings, all denoting great men whose fathers were tradesmen of one kind or another, including a portrait of Marcus Aurelius, who was a clothier's son. Jack keeps the pictures and shows them to his friends and workmen in an effort to encourage one and all to seek fame and dignity in spite of their humble offices in life.

Because of the many wars in Europe during King Henry's reign, trade in general is depleted. The lot of the clothiers and weavers is particularly bad; they join together and send leaders to London to appeal to the government on their behalf. One of the envoys they send is Jack. The king remembers Jack and in private audience assures him that measures will be taken to alleviate the hardships of the clothiers. Another man who did not forget Jack is the Lord Chancellor, Cardinal Wolsey. In an attempt to circumvent the king's promise, he has Jack and the other envoys thrown into prison for a few days. Finally, the duke of Somerset intervenes and convinces the cardinal that the clothiers mean no harm.

Some time later, an Italian merchant named Benedick

comes to the house of Jack to trade. While there, he falls in love with one of Jack's workers, a pretty young woman named Joan. She, however, pays no attention whatever to Benedick and asks a kinsman to tell the Italian not to bother her. When the kinsman does as he is asked, he angers the Italian, who vows to make a cuckold of the kinsman for his pains. With gifts and fair speech, the Italian finally has his way with the weaver's wife, although the woman is immediately sorry. She tells her husband, who has his revenge on the Italian by pretending that he will see to it that the Italian is permitted to go to bed with Joan. The Italian falls in with the scheme and finds himself put to bed with a pig, whereupon all the Englishmen laugh at him so heartily that he leaves Newbery in shame.

Jack's second wife is a good young woman, but she sometimes errs in paying too much attention to her gossipy friends. At one time, a friend tells her that she is wasting money by feeding the workmen so well. She cuts down on the quantity and the quality of the food she serves to the workers, but Jack, who remembers only too well the days when he was an apprentice and journeyman forced to eat whatever was placed in front of him, becomes very angry and makes her change her ways again. His workers are gratified when he says that his wife's friend is never to set foot in his house again.

At another time, Jack goes to London, where he finds a draper who owes him five hundred pounds working as a porter. Learning that the man, through no fault of his own, is bankrupt, Jack shows his confidence in the man by setting him up in business again. Friends warn him that he is sending good money after bad, but Jack's judgment proves correct. The man pays back every cent and later becomes an alderman of London.

Jack is always proud of his workers. One time a knight, Sir George Rigley, seduces a pretty and intelligent young woman who works for Jack. Jack vows that he will make it right for her. He sends the woman, disguised as a rich widow, to London. Not knowing who she is, Sir George falls in love and marries her. The knight is angry at first, but he soon sees the justice of the case and is very well pleased with the hundred pounds Jack gives the woman as a dower. Still knowing their places in life, Jack and his wife give precedence to Sir George and his new lady, even in their own house.

Critical Evaluation:

Very little is known about the pamphleteer and balladeer Thomas Deloney, the English writer whose works became precursors of the English novel. By trade a silk weaver, probably of Norwich, Deloney wrote topical ballads and, through his pamphlets, took part in the religious controversies of the

day. Even the date of his birth is not certain. Nevertheless, it seems certain that Deloney died early in 1600 after producing at least three "novels" (that is, episodic narratives) in a short but crowded life. He seems to have had more education than most weavers of the time, and he translated from Latin into his uniquely vigorous English. The ballads of the day were the newspapers of the period, and Deloney's apprenticeship, like that of so many novelists, might be said to have been in journalism. That was probably how he learned to write concisely and to choose popular subjects. He wrote broadside ballads on such subjects as the defeat of the Spanish Armada, great fires, the execution of traitors, and domestic tragedies, but current events were not Deloney's only ballad subjects. Using Holinshed and other sources, he drew on English history for subject matter. A collection of Deloney's ballads entitled *The Garland of Good Will* appeared in 1631, and earlier editions, such as those of his prose fictions, were probably read out of existence. More than once, Deloney's pamphlets and more than fifty ballads put him in trouble with the authorities, even sending him for a time to Newgate Prison. One ballad in particular, which showed disrespect for the queen, caused him serious difficulties.

Though widely read, Deloney's novels were scorned by the university-educated writers of the day as mere plebeian romances from the pen of a balladmaker, and it was not until the twentieth century that his merits as a writer were recognized. His three novels, all approximately the same length, appeared between 1597 and 1600. *Jack of Newbery* was probably the first one to be written and published. Each novel was in praise of a trade: *Jack of Newbery* of weaving, *The Gentle Craft* of shoemaking, and *Thomas of Reading* of the clothiers' trade.

Deloney's stories contain excellent pictures of contemporary middle-class London life, and they introduce a variety of quaint characters. The realism of the novels, however, is only in matters of setting and dialogue; probability is disregarded and wish-fulfillment fantasy prevails, for members of the hardworking trade class are inevitably rewarded for their diligence with large fortunes. The tales are rich with humor and told in a straightforward manner, with the exception of "ornamental" language used in some romantic passages.

Deloney may have been commissioned by the cloth merchants to compose a life of one of their order. Jack of Newbery was a real person who lived in Newbery under Henry VIII, but his history is merely traditional. Deloney, however, knew the town and had a gift for elaborating a tale with circumstantial facts and humorous episodes.

Despite its popularity in its own day, Deloney's fiction probably had little real effect on the subsequent development of English prose fiction, which had to wait a hundred years and more for the geniuses of Daniel Defoe and Samuel Richardson to get it off the ground. Yet *Jack of Newbery* may be considered the first really dramatic novel in English. The fictions of Thomas Nash and Robert Greene are witty and satirical, but they do not have the dramatic plots of Deloney's work. Sir Philip Sidney's *Arcadia* (1581) and John Lyly's *Euphues* (1578-1580) were only minor influences, if any, on Deloney, who seems to have been more impressed by the Elizabethan stage than anything else (the widow and the other characters display a sense of rhetoric in their dialogue reminiscent of the stage). Deloney's view of life was essentially dramatic, and the people he wrote about in *Jack of Newbery* and his other novels are people of action, people who set out to accomplish material things.

Deloney's focus is on the details of everyday life. Love, marriage, money, and food are the main topics of conversation. Materialist to his heart, he was fascinated by business and household matters. Like Charles Dickens, Deloney plunges into scenes that summarize dramatically an entire situation, painting a picture of an entire culture along the way. There are few irrelevant incidents in *Jack of Newbery*. The story of the middle-aged widow who falls in love with her young apprentice and the story of his subsequent adventures (including that concerning the king) are told with great enthusiasm. The widow is portrayed as a lusty, self-sufficient female, a woman who knows what she wants and goes after it. Jack is apparently as virtuous and industrious an apprentice as Ben Franklin, but he is not as innocent as he pretends and soon moves up in the world.

The tradesmen heroes such as Jack are idealized characters. Jack rises less from his own efforts than from those of the people around him. It almost seems that he is above certain efforts, resembling in this the king himself. The women in *Jack of Newbery* are the book's finest characterizations. In creating the gallery of female portraits, Deloney leaves behind him all of his rivals in the prose fiction of the time and approaches the best of Elizabethan stage comedy. Queen Catherine, the first Mistress Winchcomb, and other women in the story are colorful figures, alive with natural vitality. As the plots develop, the women remain in the midst of the action. Perhaps it is a man's world, but the wife seems to be responsible for her husband's success. Deloney knew and understood middle-class women and recorded their foibles and unique characteristics with a sharp eye and a precise pen. For the author, the good wife was one who was never idle but knew her place and did not "gad about." Thus Jack and his first wife make no headway at all until she decides to stay at home and manage the household.

The minor characters are well drawn, especially Randoll Pert. Recently out of debtor's prison, Pert becomes a porter to support his family. His description is delightful, and his antics add both comic and pathetic touches to the novel. The meeting of Jack and Pert at the Spread Eagle in London is superbly handled. The whole episode, including the part where Jack agrees not to collect five hundred pounds until Pert is sheriff of London, is excellent comedy.

Although the novel is episodic, it forms a coherent and dramatic whole and is filled with humorous scenes and witty dialogue. *Jack of Newbery* stands as a fine novel in its own right as well as the first example of its kind in English literature.

"Critical Evaluation" by Bruce D. Reeves

Further Reading

Jusserand, J. J. *The English Novel in the Time of Shakespeare.* Translated by Elizabeth Lee. London: T. Fisher Unwin, 1890. The classic study of early narrative tradition in English. Establishes an invaluable context for understanding the traditions Deloney inherited, including those of medieval romance, travel literature, euphuism, and pastoral. Discusses picaresque and realistic fiction and carries the study into the seventeenth century with the historical romance.

Ladd, Roger A. "Thomas Deloney and the London Weavers' Company." *Sixteenth Century Journal* 32, no. 4 (Winter, 2001): 981. Examines Deloney's novels *Jack of Newbery* and *Thomas of Reading* in relation to the writer's work as a silk weaver and his position as a yeoman in the guild of the London Weavers' Company. Discusses his novels' advocacy on behalf of his class and their idealized depiction of his craft.

Lawlis, Merritt E. *Apology for the Middle Class: The Dramatic Novels of Thomas Deloney.* Bloomington: Indiana University Press, 1960. Discusses *Jack of Newbery* in light of its dialogue. Concludes that the novel is replete with realistic detail, but that realism combines with confessional, satirical, and humorous modes. Deloney also employed euphuistic and jestbook styles, but he prepared the way for later realist writers.

_____. Introduction to *The Novels of Thomas Deloney.* Westport, Conn.: Greenwood Press, 1978. Places Deloney in his literary context, comparing his works to those of Ben Jonson, John Webster, and William Shakespeare. Deloney was the first in English prose fiction to employ dialect and malapropism. Includes an excellent index to all Deloney's novels.

Linton, Joan Pong. "*Jack of Newbery* and Drake in California: Narratives of English Cloth and Manhood." In *The Romance of the New World: Gender and the Literary Formations of English Colonialism.* New York: Cambridge University Press, 1998. Discusses the rise of the cloth trade in England as reflecting the transition from household economics to capitalism. Investigates Deloney's portrayal of the bourgeois hero, showing that it was not simply a nostalgic appropriation of the feudal model. Examines new ways in which Deloney defines manhood, showing that the novel participated in reshaping discourses of the self.

Wright, Eugene P. *Thomas Deloney.* Boston: Twayne, 1981. Includes an excellent introduction to *Jack of Newbery*, tracing its sources and plot and analyzing major themes. Contends that the novel is a cosmic apologia for workers in the cloth trade. Examines the relation of the novel to the contemporary social scene. Includes some discussion of narrative structure, character development, and imagery.

Jack Sheppard

Author: William Harrison Ainsworth (1805-1882)
First published: serial, 1839-1840, book, 1839
Type of work: Novel
Type of plot: Picaresque
Time of plot: 1702-1724
Locale: London and environs

Principal characters:
JACK SHEPPARD, a housebreaker and popular jailbreaker
JOAN SHEPPARD, his mother
OWEN WOOD, a London carpenter
MRS. WOOD, his wife
WINIFRED, their daughter
SIR ROWLAND TRENCHARD, an aristocrat
THAMES DARRELL, Sir Rowland's nephew and foster son of Owen Wood
JONATHAN WILD, a thief-taker
BLUESKIN, the devoted henchman of Jack Sheppard

The Story:

When Owen Wood goes to offer his condolence to Joan, the widow of Tom Sheppard, who was executed for stealing from Wood, he finds the woman living in misery near the Old Mint, a haven for mendicants, thieves, and debtors. Joan tells Wood that Van Galgebrok, a Dutch seaman and conjurer, prophesied that her baby, Jack, would be executed as his father was. The prophecy was based on the presence of a mole behind Jack's ear. Wood offers to take the infant out of the sordid environment in order to avert fulfillment of the prophecy, but the mother refuses to part with her child.

Left alone with the infant while Joan goes to the attic to get a key that her deceased husband ordered to be given to Wood, the carpenter is accosted by a mob led by Sir Rowland Trenchard, in pursuit of a young man named Darrell. In the confusion, Jonathan Wild, a thief-taker, picks up the key that Joan was to return to Wood.

While a great storm rages, Darrell, the fugitive, with a baby in his arms, is again pursued by Sir Rowland. The chase continues to the flooded Thames, where Darrell is drowned after a struggle with Sir Rowland. On his way home, Wood rescues the baby from drowning. Some falling bricks save him and the baby from Sir Rowland's wrath. Understanding little of the night's strange events, Wood takes the child home with him. He names the boy Thames Darrell.

Twelve years later, Wood takes Jack Sheppard as an apprentice in his carpenter shop, but he finds the boy indifferent and listless in his work. Thames, reared by the Woods, is a model apprentice. A third child in the household is Winifred, Wood's daughter, a charming, beautiful girl. The three twelve-year-olds are very fond of one another.

Mrs. Wood, a termagant, has long berated her husband for his kindness to Jack and to Joan Sheppard, who live modestly and respectably in Willesden. Following an episode in which Thames is injured while trying to prevent injury to Jack, Mrs. Wood reprimands Jack and predicts that he will come to the same end that his father met. Her chastisement is strong enough to arouse a spirit of criminality in Jack.

Wild, who had hanged Tom, boasts that he will hang the son as well. A resolute and subtle plotter, he works slyly to bring about the boy's ruin. One day, he gives Jack the key that he found on the floor of the Mint twelve years before. It is Wood's master key; his hope is that Jack will rob the carpenter. Investigating Thames's parentage, Wild learns also that Thames is the child of Sir Rowland's sister, Lady Alvira, whose husband Sir Rowland drowned and whose child he tried to destroy on the night of the great storm. Later, Lady Alvira was forced to marry her cousin, Sir Cecil Trafford. Lady Trafford is dying, in which event the estates will revert to her brother if she leaves no other heir. Wild promises Sir Rowland that he will remove Thames in order that Sir Rowland can inherit the entire estate. As a hold over the nobleman, he tells him also that he knows the whereabouts of Sir Rowland's other sister, Constance, carelessly lost in childhood to a Gypsy.

Wild and Sir Rowland trap Thames and Jack in Sir Rowland's house and accuse them of robbery. Imprisoned, Jack and Thames make a jailbreak from Old Giles's Roundhouse, the first of innumerable and difficult escapes for Jack, and the last for Thames, who is sent off to sea to be disposed of by Van Galgebrok, the Dutch seaman and conjurer.

Jack is soon fraternizing with the patrons of the Mint, much to the pleasure of the derelicts, prostitutes, and gamblers who gather there. It is in this environment that Joan sees Jack as the criminal he is. When she goes there to admonish her son to live a life of righteousness, she is answered by the taunts and sneers of the patrons, who remind her that she at one time enjoyed the life of the Mint. Jack, egged on by two prostitutes, spurns her pleas. Joan returns to her little home in Willesden to pray for Jack.

Wild had rid himself of Thames, an obstacle in his scheme to get control of the fortune of Sir Montacute Trenchard, Thames's grandfather. He now sets about to remove Sir Rowland as well. Plotting against the aristocrat, Wild has him arrested for treason in connection with a proposed Jacobite uprising against the crown.

Jack uses the key given to him by Wild to rob Wood's house. Caught and jailed in the Cage at Willesden as he is going to visit his mother, he soon escapes from the supposedly escape-proof structure. At his mother's house, Jack declares his undying love for her but announces that he cannot return to honest living. Questioned by Joan as to how long he will wait to execute his threat against Jack, Wild, who followed Jack to Willesden, answers boldly and confidently, "Nine."

Nine years later in 1742, Jack is the most daring criminal and jailbreaker of the day. By that time, the Woods are affluent citizens living in Willesden. Joan goes insane because of worry over Jack and has been committed to Bedlam, a squalid, filthy asylum. Sir Rowland is released from prison.

Thames, thrown overboard by Van Galgebrok, is picked up by a French fishing boat and carried to France, where he is employed by and subsequently commissioned by Philip of Orleans. Wild continues in his pleasures of execution and in collecting keepsakes of his grisly profession.

Jack and Blueskin, one of Wild's henchmen, quarrel with Wild because he will not help Thames get his rightful share of the estate that Sir Rowland confiscated, and Blueskin becomes Jack's loyal henchman. The two rob the Wood home again, Blueskin slashing Mrs. Wood's throat as she attempts to detain him.

Jack goes to see his mother, a haggard, demented object of human wreckage, in chains and on a bed of straw. Wild follows Jack to the asylum. During a brawl, Wild strikes Joan, and the blow restores the poor woman's senses. After her release from Bedlam, Wild divulges to Sir Rowland the fact that Joan is his long-lost sister and an heir to the Trenchard estates.

Wild disposes of Sir Rowland by bludgeoning him and throwing him into a secret well. Sir Rowland, almost dead from the beating, attempts to save himself by catching hold of the floor around the opening of the well, but Wild tramples his fingers until the nobleman drops to his watery grave. The thief-taker, still plotting to secure the Trenchard wealth, takes Joan captive, but she kills herself rather than be forced into a marriage with the villain. At her funeral, Jack is apprehended after a jailbreak that required passage through six bolted and barred doors and the removal of innumerable stones and bricks from the prison walls.

In the meantime, Thames returns from France to visit the Wood household. Through information contained in a packet of letters that reaches him in circuitous fashion, he learns that his father, the fugitive known only as Darrell, was the French Marquis de Chatillon. His paternity proved, he inherits the Trenchard estates as well. He then marries Winifred Wood.

After his seizure at his mother's funeral, Jack Sheppard is executed at Tyburn. As his body swings at the end of the rope, Blueskin cuts him down in an attempt to save his life. A bullet from Wild's gun passes through Jack's heart. The body is buried beside Joan in Willesden cemetery; in later years, the Marquis de Chatillon and his wife tend the grave and its simple wooden monument. Wild eventually pays for his crimes; he is hanged on the same gallows to which he sent Jack and his father.

Critical Evaluation:

William Harrison Ainsworth began creative writing as a youth in Manchester and published poetry, short stories, and a novel while he was studying to be a lawyer. After abortive careers in publishing and law, success came to him in 1834 with *Rookwood*, a best seller that made his name and that catapulted him to the top of London's literary scene. He followed this with *Crichton* (1837), which had respectable, although not large, sales.

Jack Sheppard, Ainsworth's third mature novel, was a spectacular success, eclipsing his first two novels in sales. The novel has its roots in the eighteenth century picaresque style of Tobias Smollett and Henry Fielding. This style moves the story along by recounting the adventures that a rogue has while traveling. The novel also follows in the tradition of the Newgate novel; its hero-namesake is a lowborn criminal. Finally, Ainsworth sets his novel in the past rather than telling a story about his contemporary society.

These three novelistic elements had proven their popularity with the early Victorian reading public when Ainsworth set out to write. Edward Bulwer-Lytton, already an established author, added to his popularity with the novels *Paul Clifford* (1830) and *Eugene Aram* (1832), which featured sensitive and intelligent heroes driven by circumstances to a criminal life. Ainsworth's *Rookwood* uses the Newgate theme of a glamorous criminal hero as well as the gothic features of sensationalism and mystery. When the sales of *Crichton*, a historical romance set in the sixteenth century French court, failed to match those of *Rookwood*, Ainsworth returned to the more popular Newgate formula. Crime stories continued to be read in the late 1830's: Charles Dickens' *Oliver Twist* (1837-1839), for example, began appearing before *Jack Sheppard*, and for four months the two novels were serialized together in *Bentley's Miscellany* (1839-1840).

Jack Sheppard's chief strength lies in its tight plotting. Ainsworth devoted considerable effort to planning the structure of his early novels, and this effort resulted in works that are coherent and fast-paced, and in which all the loose ends of the story line are tied up. In the case of *Jack Sheppard*, Ainsworth faced the problem of how to tell a story spanning twenty-two years without turning it into an increasingly monotonous recitation of adventure after adventure. He solved the problem by focusing on three periods in his hero's life, which he calls epochs. There is a short prologue, occurring in 1703, which introduces the main characters; then a few weeks in 1715, during which Jack turns to a life of crime; and finally six months in 1724, when the most exciting action takes place. The epochs are tied together with linking narratives, and an epilogue resolves the fates of the surviving characters. This strategy is effective in maintaining the reader's interest, but it is a modification of the picaresque tradition's episodic nature.

Ainsworth took pains to research thoroughly the histori-

cal background of his novels. As a result, his books have a strong sense of setting; the descriptions of buildings, clothing, and surroundings are vivid. His pages are populated with clearly drawn and believable historical figures. *Jack Sheppard* has all of these characteristics. Ainsworth was prepared, however, to change the past for the sake of his story. In this novel, for example, he turns the real Jonathan Wild, a historical figure of ambiguity, into an unmitigated villain.

Ainsworth shared with many of his contemporaries the belief that the characters in his works should be judged by the omniscient narrator. Using simple, black-and-white criteria, Ainsworth judges his characters as loyal or disloyal, brave or cowardly, noble or ignoble. Sometimes the author uses description to tell his readers what they should think of a character; sometimes he provides summary judgments. The author's voice is rarely unheard in Ainsworth's novels, whether as a moral judge or as a guide pointing out scenes. *Jack Sheppard* is no exception.

Ainsworth also wrote melodramatic episodes that were popular with his early nineteenth century audience. (*Jack Sheppard* was adapted for the stage in eight pirated versions—a measure of the novel's popularity.) He depicts the scene in which Wild throws Sir Rowland Trenchard into the well in especially lurid colors. Ainsworth fills his pages with examples of cruelty, violence, brutality, and murder. Sometimes this is effective and appropriate to the subject matter, but at other times it becomes an artistic flaw. Ainsworth focuses so closely on the details of Wild's cruelty (a depth of cruelty unusual by Victorian standards) that he fails to explain why the character is so malevolent. His failure to explain makes the character seem less real. (Several of Ainsworth's later novels also include characters whose villainy has no motives.)

Jack Sheppard reflects the concerns and interests of the society that produced it. Its historical approach was attractive at a time when the study of history was very popular. Its concern with urban violence and criminality came at a time when worries about maintaining public order in the streets were at the forefront of public debate. Its melodramatic passages were to the taste of a generation that liked terror and the exaggerated display of emotions.

At the height of his popularity, Ainsworth earned the princely sum of £1,500 a novel from his publishers, in addition to his handsome income from editing *Bentley's Miscellany* and *Ainsworth's Magazine*. Later generations of readers came to dislike Ainsworth's melodrama; after the mid-1850's, his novels ceased to sell and his career went into decline. Ainsworth knew that the tastes of his audience were changing, but he was unable to change with them. Instead, he continued to produce novels in the Newgate and picaresque traditions. When he at last began to write novels set in the nineteenth century, he was too late to regain his readership. By the end of his career, he was lucky to get as much as £50 for a novel.

"Critical Evaluation" by D. G. Paz

Further Reading

Carver, Stephen James. "Writing the Underworld: *Jack Sheppard*, a Romance, 1839." In *The Life and Works of the Lancashire Novelist William Harrison Ainsworth, 1805-1882*. Lewiston, N.Y.: Edwin Mellen Press, 2003. In part 3 of his book, Carver devotes several chapters to *Jack Sheppard*, describing it as "a sort of Hogarthian novel" and recounting the controversy that was touched off by the book.

Hollingsworth, Keith. *The Newgate Novel, 1830-1847: Bulwer, Ainsworth, Dickens, and Thackeray*. Detroit, Mich.: Wayne State University Press, 1963. One of the best studies of the tradition of stories about criminals. Places *Jack Sheppard* in that tradition, showing how Ainsworth is indebted to eighteenth century picaresque writers for many of his themes, images, and techniques. Contrasts that novel with Charles Dickens's *Oliver Twist*.

Sanders, Andrew. *The Victorian Historical Novel, 1840-1880*. New York: St. Martin's Press, 1979. One of the best studies of the historical novel in the nineteenth century. Explains the literary techniques that made *Jack Sheppard* Ainsworth's best novel.

Springhall, John. *Youth, Popular Culture, and Moral Panics: Penny Gaffs to Gangsta-Rap, 1830-1996*. New York: St. Martin's Press, 1998. Springhall studies how adults in both the nineteenth and twentieth centuries have denounced lower-class youth culture, including *Jack Sheppard* and other Victorian penny dreadful novels. Includes an appendix titled "*Jack Sheppard* in Victorian Popular Culture."

Sutherland, J. A. *Victorian Novelists and Publishers*. Chicago: University of Chicago Press, 1976. Sutherland includes Ainsworth's literary output as a major example in his well-written, thoughtful, and detailed examination of how business relationships between novelists and publishers affected the novels. He shows how *Jack Sheppard* propelled Ainsworth's career.

Worth, George J. *William Harrison Ainsworth*. New York: Twayne, 1972. A book-length critical study of Ainsworth's career. Describes the ways in which *Jack Sheppard* set the pattern of Ainsworth's writing style for the rest of his career.

Jacques the Fatalist and His Master

Author: Denis Diderot (1713-1784)
First published: Jacques le fataliste et son maître, 1796 (English translation, 1797)
Type of work: Novel
Type of plot: Picaresque
Time of plot: Mid-eighteenth century
Locale: Rural France

Principal characters:
JACQUES, a servant and former soldier
THE MASTER (unnamed), Jacques's employer
THE NARRATOR, the ostensible author of the novel
THE CAPTAIN, Jacques's military commander, who influences his fatalism
THE HOST, the talkative wife of the innkeeper of the Stag Inn
MME DE LA POMMERAYE, an aristocratic widow jilted by her lover
MARQUIS DES ARCIS, the unfaithful lover of Mme de la Pommeraye
DENISE, Jacques's most important love

The Story:

Jacques and his master are on a journey whose purpose and destination are unknown to the narrator. The latter even scolds the inquisitive reader for wanting to know such irrele-vant information as how the travelers met, what their names are, where they come from, or where they are going. Instead, the narrator merely informs the reader that, as the novel opens, the master is not saying anything, and that Jacques is repeating, for his master's benefit, the fatalist creed he learned from his captain. Everything that happens to people on earth, good or bad, Jacques explains, is foreordained, written on the great scroll "up above." As an appropriate example, his captain always adds that every bullet shot in battle has someone's name on it.

Jacques illustrates the truth of the captain's doctrine by noting the interconnected chain of events in his own life: He joined the army as the result of a quarrel with his father; soon after, in his first battle, he received "his" bullet, which shattered his knee; and had it not been for that bullet, he would probably never have fallen in love. That remark arouses the master's curiosity, and he asks his servant to tell him the story of his loves to make their journey more interesting.

The telling of that story, like the recurrent discussions of the doctrine of fatalism, constitutes a running theme throughout the novel. During the entire eight days of travel recounted in the novel, Jacques keeps trying to advance his story, but he is constantly interrupted and ultimately prevented from finishing it. The narrator provides a third running theme, periodically interrupting the narrative, as he does at the very outset, to engage the reader in discussions about storytelling in general and about the truth and morality of each story or interpolated tale that comes up during the journey.

The narrator's account of the journey is frequently interrupted by unexpected events, by digressions in dialogue between Jacques and his master and between the narrator and the reader, and by the telling of apparently unrelated tales volunteered by individuals they encounter on their journey. Some of the tales are brief but bizarre, such as the account of the relationship between Jacques's captain and his best friend, a relationship based on their mutual passion for fighting duels with each other whenever possible. Others are more elaborate and often comical, such as the story of a Monsieur Gousse who, wishing to live with his mistress unimpeded by his wife, devised a scheme by which he brings suit against himself to force the release of his furniture from his own home; he loses the suit and ends in jail. Still other tales depict the corruption in public morals, as in the tale of Father Hudson, a priest in charge of a monastery, who is considered by everyone in that town an excellent administrator of his institution but who successfully and in secret conducts a life of debauchery involving many women of the town.

The longest tale is told by the host of the Stag Inn, where Jacques and his master are obliged to stay for two nights because of inclement weather. The host, who is of peasant origin and exceptionally skillful as a storyteller, describes her

tale as that of a "strange marriage." The marriage is brought about by an elaborate plot of vengeance, patiently worked out by a widow, Mme de la Pommeraye, against the man who jilted her, the Marquis des Arcis. Mme de la Pommeraye bribes a woman and her attractive daughter, whose circumstances forced them both into a life of prostitution, to appear under assumed names in respectable company, where the Marquis des Arcis will be sure to make their acquaintance. The widow so maneuvers events that the smitten Marquis eagerly agrees to marry the daughter. Thereupon, Mme de la Pommeraye takes her vengeance by informing the Marquis of the true background of the woman he marries. Though shocked and angry at first, the Marquis decides that he can be happy with his new wife. That decision leaves Mme de la Pommeraye feeling cheated of her revenge.

During the last two days of the eight-day journey, Jacques makes rapid progress in the story of his loves, including the ribald tale of how he lost his virginity. He finally tells of his encounter with Denise, who nurses him after his knee surgery and with whom he falls in love. During those two days, the master tells Jacques the sad story of his one great love, whom he lost to a rival. At last they come to a village, where the master wishes to visit the son of the woman he once wooed and lost. As the master dismounts from his horse, he falls to the ground. Jacques admits that he purposely loosened the strap, causing his master to fall. The incident leads to the final debate between Jacques and his master on the question of fatalism and free will. In an unexpected outburst of violence, the master's victorious rival emerges from the house where his son is living and abruptly challenges the master to a duel. The rival is killed, the master flees, and Jacques is taken to jail as a material witness. Jacques's final reflections, in jail, are about the prospect of marrying his beloved Denise, followed by uneasy speculation as to whether he can escape the likely fate of all husbands—that of becoming a cuckold. Jacques then falls asleep, reminding himself of the futility of such speculation, since whatever befalls him will have been written "up above."

Critical Evaluation:

Denis Diderot, a prominent member of the group of leading thinkers and writers in eighteenth century France known as The Philosophers, expressed so many radical and controversial ideas about society and human nature in his novels, plays, and philosophical dialogues that he did not dare publish most of them out of fear of stringent government censorship. Instead, he circulated his works in manuscript among his trusted friends. Long after his death in 1784, those friends arranged for publication of his works.

Jacques the Fatalist and His Master was composed during the 1770's, when Diderot was over sixty. It was an experimental work in which Diderot tried to fuse his most controversial views about the writing of fiction, his boldest speculations about fatalism as a philosophy of life, and his opinions about the hypocritical conduct occasioned by the rigid moral values demanded by society. The experiment seemed designed to sum up his nearly forty years of reflection about life and literature. When it was finally published, in 1796, it was met with bewildered incomprehension at best and angry outrage at worst, for the text seemed almost perverse to its early readers in systematically thwarting their expectations of how a novel should be constructed and how characters should be shown to comport themselves. They were puzzled by the constant interruptions to the narrative thread that allowed no coherent story to emerge.

It was only in the last half of the twentieth century that readers both in France and elsewhere discovered and began to appreciate what it was that Diderot attempted in this culminating composition of his career. The narrator's interruptive discussions with the reader are now read as Diderot's declaration that fiction must avoid facile invention of heroic adventures in the interests of truth, a principle requiring him to shatter conventions of the novel. By deliberately presenting his novel's characters as inconsistent, neither wholly good nor wholly evil, neither purely rational nor purely irrational, Diderot was attempting to indict conventional novels for their oversimplified, one-dimensional characters that lacked true humanity. As for the endless chain of digressions, diversions, and changing scenes that prevent the main narrative from moving forward, they were Diderot's means, borrowed from Laurence Sterne's *Tristram Shandy* (1759-1767), of reminding readers that no life unfolds logically and coherently, free of interruptions or diversions, and that society is too complex, varied, and unpredictable to conform to preconceived patterns, whether attributable to God or to novelists. In Diderot's view, a novel must display the chaotic and unpredictable procession of events, behaviors, and motivations that characterize real life. Finally, since his unorthodox narrative techniques evoke the reader's laughter, Diderot seems to be arguing that the spectacle of life's chaotic unpredictability is best seen as an occasion for joyous delight in the vastness of human diversity.

This theme of chaotic unpredictability is announced by the title, which places the servant first and the master last and gives the servant a name and the master none. By calling Jacques a fatalist, the title also hints at his possible superiority of intellect over the master, since Jacques has at least reflected about the meaning of existence. This intellectual superiority of Jacques naturally produces moments of tension between the two, but the master's attempts to put Jacques "in his place" during these quarrels are always vehemently resisted, and each quarrel leads both back to the abiding truth that they need each other. This equality of mutual dependency was daring social doctrine for the times and is one of the ways in which this unusual novel can be seen as a forerunner of the French Revolution.

Unconventional moral themes are freely evoked in this novel, including the wide discrepancy in the sexual behavior of men and of women; the moral teachings of the Catholic Church; the randomness with which sinful behavior is sometimes punished and sometimes rewarded; and the equally capricious consequence of virtue, which can produce suffering as often as it produces a clear conscience. The novel mocks Jacques's fatalism by demonstrating how it distorts reality and by pointing out that Jacques himself often contradicts its tenets. Yet the novel also shows that fatalism has the power to console Jacques and enable him to accept evils he cannot prevent.

The interpolated tales in this novel exemplify the chaotic disorder of everyday life and illustrate concretely the novel's running themes. Indeed, careful analysis of the most celebrated tale in *Jacques the Fatalist and His Master*, that of Mme de la Pommeraye and her unfaithful lover, the Marquis des Arcis, reveals that it touches directly on every major theme of the entire novel: the problematical relations between the sexes; the morally perverse consequences of sin and virtue; and the comical unpredictability of human motivation, among others. This astonishing single tale embodies, for the thoughtful reader, the essence of what Diderot hoped to achieve with his farewell novel: a joyous celebration of the variety of human nature and the stunning but delightful unpredictability of human conduct.

Murray Sachs

Further Reading

Curran, Andrew. *Sublime Disorder: Physical Monstrosity in Diderot's Universe*. Oxford, England: Voltaire Foundation, 2001. Examines Diderot's fascination with anatomical monstrosity and analyzes how he represents the physically grotesque in his novels and other works. Includes bibliography and index.

Fellows, Otis. *Diderot*. Boston: Twayne, 1989. In this updated edition, the author was able to incorporate the later research on Diderot in general and on *Jacques the Fatalist and His Master*, which is discussed in the penultimate chapter, in particular.

Furbank, P. N. *Diderot: A Critical Biography.* New York: Alfred A. Knopf, 1992. Fine biographical study, which includes critical analyses of Diderot's writings. The study of *Jacques the Fatalist and His Master* in chapter 24 offers astute treatment of the philosophical issues and of the theories about fiction.

Goodden, Angelica. *Diderot and the Body.* Oxford, England: Legenda, 2001. A study of Diderot that focuses on his portrayal of the body. Examines Diderot's fiction and other works to describe his ideas about the relationship of the body to the mind, anatomy, ethical extensions of the body, sensuality, sexuality, and other concerns.

Loy, J. Robert. *Diderot's Determined Fatalist.* New York: King's Crown Press, 1950. The pioneering study that first opened up Diderot's experimental novel to intelligent critical evaluation of its qualities as a work of art and as a profound philosophical discussion of the nature of human existence.

Rex, Walter E. *Diderot's Counterpoints: The Dynamics of Contrariety in His Major Works.* Oxford, England: Voltaire Foundation, 1998. Examines Diderot's works in relation to his era, including analysis of *Jacques the Fatalist and His Master.* Includes bibliographical references and an index.

Vartanian, Aram. "*Jacques the Fatalist*: A Journey into the Ramifications of a Dilemma." In *Essays on Diderot and the Enlightenment in Honor of Otis Fellows.* Geneva: Librairie Droz, 1974. Exceptionally clear and elegant essay on Diderot's uncomfortable awareness of the contradictions in fatalism and determinism as philosophical systems.

Wilson, Arthur M. *Diderot.* New York: Oxford University Press, 1972. A thorough and scholarly critical study of Diderot's life and works. Chapter 46 has a fine discussion of *Jacques the Fatalist and His Master* as an exposition of Diderot's views on determinism and humanism.

Jane Eyre
An Autobiography

Author: Charlotte Brontë (1816-1855)
First published: 1847
Type of work: Novel
Type of plot: Domestic realism
Time of plot: 1800
Locale: Northern England

Principal characters:
JANE EYRE, an orphan
MRS. REED, the mistress of Gateshead Hall
BESSIE LEAVEN, a nurse
EDWARD ROCHESTER, the owner of Thornfield
ST. JOHN RIVERS, a young clergyman
MARY and DIANA RIVERS, his sisters

The Story:

Jane Eyre is an orphan whose parents died when she was a baby, at which time she passed into the care of Mrs. Reed of Gateshead Hall. Mrs. Reed's husband, now dead, was the brother of Jane Eyre's mother; on his deathbed, he directed his wife to look after the orphan as after her own three children. At Gateshead Hall, Jane experiences ten years of neglect and abuse. One day, a cousin knocks her to the floor. When she fights back, Mrs. Reed punishes her by sending her to the gloomy room where Mr. Reed died. There Jane loses consciousness, and the conflict causes a dangerous illness from which she is nursed slowly back to health by sympathetic Bessie Leaven, the Gateshead Hall nurse.

No longer wishing to keep her unwanted charge in the house, Mrs. Reed makes arrangements for Jane's admission to Lowood School. Early one morning, Jane leaves Gateshead Hall without farewells and is driven fifty miles by stage to Lowood, her humble possessions in a trunk beside her.

At Lowood, Jane is a diligent student and well liked by her superiors, especially by Miss Temple, one of the teachers, who refuses to accept without proof Mrs. Reed's low estimate of Jane's character. During the period of Jane's schooldays at Lowood, an epidemic of fever that causes many deaths among the girls leads to an investigation, after which there are improvements at the institution. At the end of her studies, Jane is retained as a teacher but she grows weary of her life at Lowood and advertises for a position as a governess. She is engaged by Mrs. Fairfax, housekeeper at Thornfield, near Millcote.

At Thornfield, the new governess has only one pupil, Adele Varens, a ward of Jane's employer, Mr. Edward Rochester. From Mrs. Fairfax, Jane learns that Mr. Rochester travels much and seldom comes to Thornfield. Jane is pleased with the quiet country life, with the beautiful old house and gardens, the book-filled library, and her own comfortable room.

While she is out walking one afternoon, Jane meets Mr. Rochester for the first time, going to his aid after his horse throws him. She finds her employer a somber, moody man, quick to change in his manner and brusque in his speech. He commends her work with Adele, however, and confides that the girl is the daughter of a French dancer who deceived him and deserted her daughter. Jane feels that this experience alone cannot account for Mr. Rochester's moody nature.

Mysterious happenings at Thornfield puzzle Jane. Alarmed by a strange noise one night, she finds Mr. Rochester's door open and his bed on fire. When she attempts to arouse the household, he commands her to keep quiet about the whole affair. She learns that Thornfield has a strange tenant, a woman who laughs like a maniac and stays in rooms on the third floor of the house. Jane believes that this woman is Grace Poole, a seamstress employed by Mr. Rochester.

Mr. Rochester attends many parties in the neighborhood, where he is obviously paying court to Blanche Ingram, daughter of Lady Ingram. One day, the inhabitants of Thornfield are informed that Mr. Rochester is bringing a party of house guests home with him. The fashionable Miss Ingram is among the party. During the house party, Mr. Rochester calls Jane to the drawing room, where the guests treat her with the disdain they think her humble position deserves. To herself, Jane already confessed her interest in her employer, but it seems to her that he is interested only in Blanche. One evening, while Mr. Rochester is away from home, the guests play charades. At the conclusion of the game, a Gypsy fortune-teller appears to read the palms of the lady guests. During her interview with the Gypsy, Jane discovers that the so-called fortune-teller is Mr. Rochester in disguise. While the guests are still at Thornfield, a stranger named Mason arrives to see Mr. Rochester on business. That night, Mason is mysteriously wounded by the inhabitant of the third floor. The injured man is taken away secretly before daylight.

One day, Robert Leaven comes from Gateshead to tell Jane that Mrs. Reed, now on her deathbed, asks to see her former ward. Jane returns to her aunt's home. The dying woman gives Jane a letter, dated three years earlier, from John Eyre in Madeira, who asked that his niece be sent to him for adoption. Mrs. Reed confesses that she wrote back informing him that Jane died in the epidemic at Lowood. The sin of keeping the news of her relatives from Jane—news that would have meant relatives, adoption, and an inheritance—becomes a burden on the conscience of the dying woman.

Jane goes back to Thornfield, which she now looks on as her home. One night in the garden, Rochester embraces her and proposes marriage. Jane accepts and makes plans for a quiet ceremony in the village church. She also writes to her uncle in Madeira, explaining Mrs. Reed's deception and telling him she is to marry Rochester. Shortly before the date set for the wedding, Jane has a harrowing experience, awakening to find a strange, repulsive-looking woman in her room. The intruder tries on Jane's wedding veil and then rips it to shreds. Rochester tries to persuade Jane that the whole incident is in her imagination, but in the morning she finds the torn veil in her room. When she and Mr. Rochester are saying their vows at the church, a stranger speaks up and declares the existence of an impediment to the marriage. He presents a document, signed by the Mr. Mason who was wounded during his visit to Thornfield, which states that Edward Fairfax Rochester married Bertha Mason, Mr. Mason's sister, in Spanish Town, Jamaica, fifteen years earlier. Rochester admits the fact and then conducts the party to the third-story chamber at Thornfield. There they find the attendant Grace Poole and her charge, Bertha Rochester, a raving maniac. Bertha was the woman Jane saw in her room.

Jane feels that she must leave Thornfield at once. She notifies Rochester and leaves early the next morning, using all of her small store of money for the coach fare. Two days later, she sets down on the north midland moors. Starving, she begs for food. Finally, she is befriended by the Reverend St. John Rivers and his sisters, Mary and Diana, who take Jane in and nurse her back to health. Assuming the name of Jane Elliot, she refuses to divulge any of her history except her connection with the Lowood institution. St. John Rivers eventually finds a place for her as mistress in a girls' school.

Shortly afterward, St. John Rivers receives word from his family solicitor that John Eyre died in Madeira, leaving Jane a fortune of twenty thousand pounds. Because Jane disappeared under mysterious circumstances, the lawyer is trying to locate her through the next of kin, St. John Rivers. Jane's identity is revealed through her connection with Lowood School, and she learns, to her surprise, that St. John Rivers and his sisters are really her cousins. She insists on sharing her inheritance with them.

When St. John Rivers decides to go to India as a missionary, he asks Jane to go with him as his wife—not because he loves her, as he frankly admits, but because he admires her and wants her services as his assistant. Jane feels indebted to him for his kindness and aid, but she hesitates and asks for time to reflect.

One night, while St. John Rivers is awaiting her decision, she dreams that Rochester is calling her name. The next day, she returns to Thornfield by coach. She finds the mansion gutted—a burned and blackened ruin. Neighbors tell her that the fire broke out one stormy night, set by the madwoman, who died while Rochester was trying to rescue her from the roof of the blazing house. Rochester was blinded during the fire and now lives at Ferndean, a lonely farm some miles away. Jane goes to him at once and shortly after marries him. Two years later, Rochester regains the sight of one eye, so that he is able to see his new child when it is placed in his arms.

Critical Evaluation:

Charlotte Brontë was always concerned that her work be judged on its own merits and not because of her gender. She continued to use her pseudonym even after her authorship was revealed, and in her letters she often referred to herself as Currer Bell. *Jane Eyre*, her first published novel, has been called feminine because of the Romanticism and deeply felt emotions of the heroine-narrator. It would probably be more correct to point to the feminist qualities of the novel, as reflected in a heroine who refuses to be placed in the traditional female position of subservience and who disagrees with her superiors, stands up for her rights, and ventures creative thoughts. More important, Jane is a narrator who comments on the role of women in society and the greater constraint imposed on them. Those feminine emotions often ascribed to in the character of Jane are found as well in Rochester, and the continued popularity of this work must suggest the enduring human quality of these emotions.

Brontë often discusses the lack of passion in her contemporaries' work and especially in that of Jane Austen, about whom she said, "Her business is not half so much with the human heart as with the human eyes, mouth, hands, and feet." Coldness, detachment, excessive analysis, and critical distance were not valued by Brontë. The artist must be involved in her subject, she believed, and must have a degree of inspiration not to be rationally explained. Such a theory of art is similar to that of the Romantic poets, an attitude no longer entirely popular by the mid-nineteenth century.

In *Jane Eyre*, Brontë chose the point of view of a first-person narrator, which suited both her subject matter and her artistic theory, The story is told entirely through the eyes of the heroine, a technique that enabled Brontë to deliver the events with an intensity that involves the reader in the passions, feelings, and thoughts of the heroine. A passionate directness characterizes Jane's narration: Conversations are rendered in direct dialogue, and actions are given just as they occur, with little analysis of event or character. In a half dozen key scenes, Brontë shifts to present tense instead of the

immediate past, so that Jane narrates the event as if it were happening at the very moment. After Jane flees Thornfield and Rochester, when the coachman puts her out at Whitcross where her fare runs out, she narrates to the moment: "I am alone . . . I am absolutely destitute." After a long description of the scene around her and her analysis of her situation, also narrated in the present tense, she reverts to the more usual past tense in the next paragraph: "I struck straight into the heath." Such a technique adds to the immediacy of the novel and further draws the reader into the situation.

Like all of Brontë's heroines, Jane has no parents and no family that accepts or is aware of her. She, like Lucy Snowe in *Villette* (1853) and Caroline Helstone in *Shirley* (1849), leads a life cut off from society, since family is the means for a woman to participate in society and community. Lacking such support, Jane has to face her problems alone. Whenever she forms a close friendship (Bessie at Gateshead, Helen Burns and Miss Temple at Lowood, Mrs. Fairfax at Thornfield), she discovers that nonkinship ties can be broken easily by higher authority, death, or marriage. Cutting her heroines off so radically from family and community gave Brontë the opportunity to make her women independent and to explore the Romantic ideal of individualism.

Jane Eyre is a moral tale, akin to a folk or fairy tale, with hardly any ambiguities of society, character, or situation. Almost all of Jane's choices are morally straightforward, and her character—though she grows and matures—does not change significantly. Her one difficult choice is to refuse to become Rochester's mistress and leave Thornfield. That choice is difficult precisely because she has no family or friends to influence her with their disapproval. No one will be hurt if she consents; that is, no one but Jane herself, and it is her own self-love that helps her to refuse.

Like a fairy tale, *Jane Eyre* is full of myth and superstition. Rochester often calls Jane his "elf," "changeling," or "witch"; there are mysterious happenings at Thornfield; Jane is inclined to believe the Gypsy fortune-teller (until Rochester reveals himself) and often thinks of the superstitions she has heard; the weather often presages mysterious or disastrous events. Most important, at the climax of the story, when Jane is about to consent to be the unloved wife of St. John Rivers, she hears Rochester calling her—at precisely the time, readers learn later, that he had in fact called to her. This event is never explained rationally and readers must accept Jane's judgment that it was a supernatural intervention.

Many symbolic elements pervade the novel. Often something in nature symbolizes an event or person in Jane's life. The most obvious example is the chestnut tree, which is split in two by lightning on the night that Jane accepts Rochester's marriage proposal, signifying the rupture of their relationship. The two parts of the tree, however, remain bound, as do Jane and Rochester despite their physical separation.

The novel is also full of character foils and parallel situations. Aunt Reed at Gateshead is contrasted with Miss Temple at Lowood; the Reed sisters at the beginning are contrasted with the Rivers sisters—cousins all—at the end; Rochester's impassioned proposal of love is followed by St. John's pragmatic proposition. Foreshadowing is everywhere in the book, so that seemingly chance happenings gain added significance as the novel unfolds, and previous events are echoed in those that follow. Because of the novel's artful structure and carefully chosen point of view, as well as the strong and fascinating character of Jane herself, *Jane Eyre*, if not a typical Victorian novel, remains a classic among English novels.

"Critical Evaluation" by Margaret McFadden-Gerber

Further Reading

Blom, Margaret Howard. *Charlotte Brontë*. Boston: Twayne, 1977. This introductory work asserts that *Jane Eyre* reflects Brontë's own contradictory struggle to be both independent and controlled by a man. Using biographical information as a springboard for analysis, the work examines Brontë's novels in separate chapters, including notes, an index, and a bibliography.

Bloom, Harold, ed. *Charlotte Brontë's "Jane Eyre."* Updated ed. New York: Chelsea House, 2007. Contains a biographical sketch of Brontë, plot summary, and analysis of the novel as well as critical essays. Some of the essays discuss Brontë's heroines and Jane's sexual awakening, contrast the characters of Jane, Blanche, and Bertha, and compare Jane to Cinderella.

Glen, Heather. *Charlotte Brontë: The Imagination in History*. New York: Oxford University Press, 2002. Describes how Brontë's novels engage with the social issues of her time. Devotes three chapters to analysis of *Jane Eyre*.

Imlay, Elizabeth. *Charlotte Brontë and the Mysteries of Love: Myth and Allegory in "Jane Eyre."* New York: St. Martin's Press, 1989. Discusses the relationships in the novel, focusing particularly on that of Jane and Rochester. Looks at the uses of myth and symbol in Brontë's depiction of relationships.

Kadish, Doris Y. *The Literature of Images: The Narrative Landscape from "Julie" to "Jane Eyre."* New Brunswick, N.J.: Rutgers University Press, 1987. Discusses the web of image and metaphor that governs *Jane Eyre* and transforms this realist novel.

King, Jeannette. *"Jane Eyre."* Philadelphia: Open University Press, 1986. An effective introduction to *Jane Eyre*, the book is arranged by literary elements with chapter headings such as "Characterization," "Language," and "Structure and Theme." Based on a tutorial approach in which readers are asked to reread certain chapters before reading discussion portions carefully and examining the passages.

Macpherson, Pat. *Reflecting on "Jane Eyre."* New York: Routledge, 1989. Macpherson's conversational style and humor make this an entertaining work of criticism. Offers extensive character examinations of Jane, Bertha, and St. John Rivers and suggests that Brontë is practicing biting social criticism behind the disarming disguise of feminine confession.

Michie, Elsie B., ed. *Charlotte Brontë's "Jane Eyre": A Casebook*. New York: Oxford University Press, 2006. Collection of essays providing numerous interpretations, including discussions of Jane's psychological development, the depiction of the psyche in the novel, an analysis of Jane in relation to contemporary debates about the role of the governess, and the novel's critical reception.

Nestor, Pauline. *Charlotte Brontë's "Jane Eyre."* New York: St. Martin's Press, 1992. Arguing that Jane does not control her own actions, this work of new feminist criticism rejects previous estimations of Jane as a feminist hero. Offers interesting analyses of the themes of motherhood, sexuality, and identity and surveys the work's historical background and criticism. Includes an index, notes, and a bibliography.

Plasa, Carl. *Charlotte Brontë*. New York: Palgrave Macmillan, 2004. Provides analyses of all of Brontë's novels and some lesser-known works. The examination of *Jane Eyre* is titled "'Incongruous Unions': Slavery and the Politics of Metaphor in *Jane Eyre*."

Thaden, Barbara Z. *Student Companion to Charlotte and Emily Brontë*. Westport, Conn.: Greenwood Press, 2001. Designed for students in the ninth grade and above. Provides biographical information about the two sisters, places their work in the context of their time, and discusses the plot development, settings, characters, themes, style, and criticism of *Jane Eyre* and the sisters' other novels.

Thomas, Sue. *Imperialism, Reform, and the Making of Englishness in "Jane Eyre."* New York: Palgrave Macmillan, 2008. Analyzes the novel in relation to the religious, political, and antislavery debates of Brontë's times.

Jasmine

Author: Bharati Mukherjee (1940-   )
First published: 1989
Type of work: Novel
Type of plot: Social realism
Time of plot: Mid-twentieth century to present
Locale: Hasnapur, India; Florida; New York; Iowa;
   California

Principal characters:
JASMINE, an Indian American immigrant
PRAKASH VIJH, her first husband
HALF-FACE, the captain of a shrimp boat
LILLIAN GORDON, a Florida woman who helps Jasmine
BUD RIPPLEMEYER, Jasmine's live-in partner
DU, Jasmine and Bud's adopted son
TAYLOR HAYES, Jasmine's employer and her last love
WYLIE HAYES, his wife
DUFF, their adopted daughter
SUKHWINDER, a radical Sikh

The Story:

An astrologer predicts that the young Jyoti (Jasmine's given Indian name) will be widowed and will live among foreigners. Horrified and unbelieving, the seven-year-old girl rejects her foretold future and then falls, injuring her forehead with a bundle of firewood she is carrying. The injury leaves a portentous star-shaped scar on her forehead.

Jyoti spends her youth in the village of Hasnapur, Punjab, India. When she is fifteen years old, she marries Prakash Vijh, and they form a partnership of love and mutual goals that focuses on a move to the United States. In America, they can expand and even supersede the limits of their traditional background—all in hope of beginning a repair business for computers, televisions, and other technological icons of the modern age.

Jyoti (which means "light") is rechristened by her husband as Jasmine—emblematic of his nonfeudal, modern perception of Indian women. Meanwhile, Prakash obtains admission to the Florida International Institute of Technology, and the two await visas to the United States. As they wait, against the backdrop of escalating religious tensions between Muslims and Hindus decades after the partition of British India into India and Pakistan, Jasmine and Prakash find themselves the victims of a bombing. Prakash is killed sacrificing himself by shielding his wife and saving her life.

Jasmine, combining a determination to honor her husband in a traditional way (burn his clothes and create a funeral pyre) and in a progressive way (continue his journey), sets off to the United States and tries to enter the country illegally (she is both underage and without a visa). Journeying on a European trawler, then a shrimper in the Caribbean, Jasmine's voyage ends at the Gulf of Florida. She is brutally raped by the shrimp boat's captain, Half-Face, in a rundown motel (an act initiated by a ruse of helping her). After the

rape, Jasmine resolves to kill herself, but in a moment of intense contemplation and a sense of an uncompleted mission—she has yet to burn her dead husband's clothes—she decides not to die. She takes a small knife given her by another refugee and slices her tongue—an ambiguous yet defiant gesture. Then, finding Half-Face asleep, her own mouth filled with blood, she leans down and slashes his throat, irreparably wounding him, while her open mouth showers him with blood.

A psychically transformed woman, Jasmine rises as if from the ashes and continues on her covert mission to honor Prakash and to make contact with his old professor. In Florida, Jasmine is rescued by a woman named Lillian Gordon, who provides Jasmine's basic needs, tends to her wounded tongue, and assists her in becoming as much an American as possible. Her new identity is tested by formerly unseen marvels, such as revolving doors and escalators. Lillian dubs her Jazzy—a more apt and hip American name, signifying another identity transformation for Jasmine.

Jasmine locates the professor and his wife and begins living with them. Through their friendship, she borrows money to obtain a falsified green card. With this key to a larger American society, Jasmine moves to New York and begins working for a young urban couple, Taylor and Wylie Hayes, as an au pair for their adopted daughter, Duff. Taylor calls Jasmine Jase—a frivolous and lighthearted nickname that defines their relaxed, adventurous, and platonic relationship that contains the seeds of something more. Jasmine remains with the family for two years.

Taylor and Wylie separate, and Jasmine is undecided about her next move. She spies a street vendor named Sukhwinder, whom she believes is her husband's killer. Fearful of repercussions and of the discovery of her illegal status, she abruptly leaves for Iowa. There she works with a banker named Bud Ripplemeyer, who falls in love with her. Jasmine moves in with him and becomes pregnant with his child. Bud's former wife resents Jasmine's intrusion into their lives, but eventually forgives the interloper. Bud serves both as protector (he is nearly thirty years older) and as stability for Jasmine, who is now known by the Anglicized name Jane in the conservative farming community.

One day, Bud is shot by a bereft farmer whose loans are handled by Bud's bank. Bud has to use a wheelchair for mobility, and Jane becomes his caregiver. Du, their dearly loved adopted teenage son from Vietnam, eventually leaves home to meet up with a dispossessed relative in the West. Jasmine, in a moment of clarity when she again sees Taylor and daughter Duff, leaves Bud to continue her voyage of selfhood, forming a new family with Taylor in California.

Critical Evaluation:

Considered a postcolonialist writer, Bharati Mukherjee has been both applauded and criticized for her stance on the necessary process of acculturation and the creation of identity for immigrants. Dispossessed, exiled, or self-proclaimed immigrants seek a new life or self-reinvention by moving to a new country—especially the United States.

Mukherjee has received several prestigious literary awards, including the National Book Critics Circle Award (1988), and, in addition to novels, has produced articles and book-length nonfiction. She seems to be at the center of a whirlwind of controversy involving the role of immigrant literature in multiculturalism, but she exists as a truly unique and individual writer who eschews ethnic stereotypes and political agendas.

In *Jasmine*, Mukherjee's title character transforms herself and is in turn transformed by her experiences and by the perceptions of others. She is a chameleon who defies categorization. This groundbreaking novel presents through its protagonist a dynamic attempt to create and mold identity in a process of change and in a refusal to be defined within the limits of a particular culture. For example, all of Jasmine's incarnations expand and explore her transformation as a woman and as an American: Jyoti is told she must accept a fate she denies; her name, Jasmine, rebels against traditional Indian values; Jazzy is a self-imposed, upbeat American girl; and Jase is the vision of an American woman who determines her own life, making unconventional and disturbing choices. With each new identity, Jasmine moves closer to self-actualization and complexity. She simultaneously merges with her current environment (or culture) and affects it.

At times, Jasmine as narrator has an ironic vision that informs the text with knowledge of her isolation and alienation, but at other times, she is a vulnerable human being who seeks to make sense of a world in which, for example, a terrorist bomb kills her husband, where brothers are satisfied with tinkering, and where men rape teenage girls with a sense of entitlement. Jasmine ultimately becomes a symbol for a transformed and transforming individual who epitomizes the mutating American consciousness infused with myriad cultures and voices. Furthermore, Jasmine's story chronicles not only the story of an immigrant but also of a woman who becomes empowered through her experiences, her dreams, and her transformation—her "shuttling between identities."

Mukherjee considers the immigrant's journey to be both difficult and exhilarating. In her view, immigrants must "murder" who they are to become dynamic and "in process." This view, in essence, is that of a modern multicultural America—a perspective that literary figures Huck Finn and Nick Carraway would not dispute. Both Huck and Nick "light out" for the West, just as Jasmine leaves Bud Ripplemeyer (who has become static in his inability to change) for California. The subsequent nonnuclear American family comprising Taylor (the urban American), Du (the Vietnamese adoptee), Duff (the adopted American girl), Bud's unborn child, and Jasmine, acts as metaphor for a nonuniform America—a truly multicultural composite.

The novel's narrative style underscores Mukherjee's themes. Fragmented and nonlinear in narration, *Jasmine* depicts an ever-evolving self—a self that is dynamic and self-reflective. In essence, through the nonlinear presentation of Jasmine's personality, the reader is exposed to all of Jasmine's identities—all at once. The narrative style is impressive—creating a consciousness simultaneously instead of chronologically. This narrative simultaneity further creates, as the novel progresses, a sense of many realities and many identities, each commenting on the others.

At various points in the novel, Mukherjee suggests that stasis is death and that the United States must continually transform itself. She has replaced the concept of America as a melting pot with that of a fusion chamber, in which a reciprocal process occurs—persons newly created and creating a new culture beyond itself—ever-changing and evolving. Certainly, Jasmine evolves: Each time she metamorphoses in name, she does in spirit and in core identity as well. Early in the novel, Jyoti (Jasmine's given name) declares "To want [to learn] English was to want more than you had been given at birth, it was to want the world." With this statement, the heroine seeks more power than her native culture allows—she wants a horizon that is America.

Mukherjee's concerns with identity and immigrant consciousness have influenced much South Asian and American literature and other writings. Her contributions cannot be overemphasized, and *Jasmine* remains her quintessential novel. It delineates her major theme: immigrants as settlers who have come to the United States to remake a nation, helping to invigorate and shape American life and consciousness and to create a consciousness that is eminently in process. However, to deal with the violence and hardships of acculturation, the self must be amorphous and nonstatic, and ready to embrace dreams, cope with otherness, and learn new ways of being. Thus, a new nation will be forged.

Sherry Morton-Mollo

Further Reading

Alam, Fakrul. *Bharati Mukherjee.* New York: Twayne, 1996. A book-length examination of Mukherjee's life, works, and overall accomplishments. Part of a series on South Asian writers.

Carter-Sanborn, Kristin. "We Murder Who We Were: *Jasmine* and the Violence of Identity." *American Literature* 66, no. 3 (September, 1994): 573-593. A complex reevaluation of the novel and its protagonist in terms of postcolonialist interpretations that argue that the author actually posits a colonialist mentality in her protagonist/heroine Jasmine.

Chua, C. L. "Passages from India: Migrating to America in the Fiction of V. S. Naipaul and Bharati Mukherjee." In *Reworlding: The Literature of the Indian Diaspora*, edited by Emmanuel S. Nelson. Westport, Conn.: Greenwood Press, 1992. Discussion of Mukherjee's and V. S. Naipaul's work is part of a collection of essays that analyze a variety of Indian expatriate writing, scrutinizing the major areas of the diaspora and the "haunting presence" of India in the process of "reworlding."

Dascalu, Cristina Emanuela. *Imaginary Homelands of Writers in Exile: Salman Rushdie, Bharati Mukherjee, and V. S. Naipaul.* Youngstown, N.Y.: Cambria Press, 2007. Places Mukherjee's fiction within the category of the literature of exile, analyzing it along with the works of other postcolonial authors.

Hoppe, John K. "The Technological Hybrid as Post-American: Cross-Cultural Genetics in *Jasmine.*" *MELUS* 24 (1999): 137-158. Initially disputes Kristin Carter-Sanborn's ideas of loss of agency in the protagonist's action, but then explores the function of technology in the novel as representative of the United States and its mutability.

Kuwahara, Kuldip Kaur. "Bharati Mukherjee's *Jasmine*: Making Connections Between Asian and Asian American Literature." *Journal of American Studies of Turkey* 4 (1996): 31-35. A general overview of *Jasmine* touching on several topics, such as the contradictory pairing of opposites—hope versus pain, East versus West, the real and the ideal—and allusions to Hindu female divinities and heroines in the Indian epic *Mahabharata*.

Mathur, Suchitra. "Bharati Mukherjee: An Overview." In *Feminist Writers*, edited by Pamela Kester-Shelton. Detroit, Mich.: St. James Press, 1996. Provides an overview of Mukherjee's thematic concerns and examines her position in the canon of American immigrant writers. Briefly discusses her four major novels, including *Jasmine*, and her short-story collections.

Morton-Mollo, Sherry. "Bharati Mukherjee." *A Reader's Companion to the Short Story in English*, edited by Erin Fallon et al. Westport, Conn: Greenwood Press, 2001. An overview of Mukherjee's work that features a biography, critical analysis (including of *Jasmine*), and authorial quotes.

Nelson, Emmanuel S., ed. *Bharati Mukherjee: Critical Perspectives.* New York: Garland, 1993. A collection of criticism addressing various topics and emphases in the works of Mukherjee, such as her use of violence, eroticism, and metamorphosis as metaphor.

Ruppel, F. Timothy. "'Re-inventing Ourselves a Million Times: Narrative, Desire, Identity, and Bharati Mukherjee's *Jasmine.*" *College Literature* 22 (February, 1995): 181-192. Asserts that the novel "resists closure" and "suggests a strategy of continual transformation" for the survival of the dispossessed and immigrant. Discusses the lack of linear narrative as a counter-narrative to prescribed historical interpretations of self.

Schlosser, Donna. "Autobiography, Identity, and Self-agency: Narrative Voice in Bharati Mukherjee's *Jasmine.*" *English Language Notes* 38, no. 2 (2000): 75-93. This journal article focuses on the role of the first-person narrative in *Jasmine*. Also examines how this narrative affects characters' identities and sense of self.

Jason and the Golden Fleece

Author: Unknown
First published: Unknown
Type of work: Folklore
Type of plot: Adventure
Time of plot: Antiquity
Locale: Greece

Principal characters:
JASON, the prince of Iolcus
KING PELIAS, his uncle
CHIRON, the centaur who raised Jason
ÆETES, the king of Colchis
MEDEA, his daughter

The Story:

In ancient Greece there lives a prince named Jason, son of a king who had been driven from his throne by a wicked brother named Pelias. To protect the boy from his cruel uncle, Jason's father takes him to a remote mountaintop, where he is raised by Chiron the Centaur, who is half man and half horse. When Jason grows to young adulthood, Chiron the Centaur tells him that Pelias seized his father's crown. Jason is destined to win back his father's kingdom.

Pelias is warned by an oracle to beware of a stranger who will visit with one foot sandaled and the other bare. Jason loses one sandal in a river he crosses on his way to Iolcus, where Pelias rules. When Pelias sees the young man, he pretends to welcome him but secretly plots to kill him. At a great feast, he tells Jason the story of the golden fleece.

In days past, a Greek king called Athamus had banished his wife and taken another, a beautiful but wicked woman who had persuaded Athamus to kill his own children. A golden ram swooped down from the skies, however, and carried the children away. The girl slipped from his back and fell into the sea, but the boy came safely to the country of Colchis, on the shores of the Black Sea. Here, the boy had allowed the king of Colchis to slaughter the ram for its golden fleece. The gods were angered by these happenings and placed a curse on Athamus and all of his family until the golden fleece was returned from Colchis.

As Pelias tells Jason the story, he sees that the young prince is stirred, and is not surprised when Jason vows that he will bring back the golden fleece to Iolcus. Pelias promises to give Jason his rightful throne when he returns from his quest; Jason trusts Pelias and agrees to the terms. He next gathers about him many of the great heroes of Greece: Hercules, the strongest and bravest of all; Orpheus, whose music soothes savage beasts; Argus, who with the help of Juno built the wondrous ship *Argo*; Zetes and Calais, sons of the North Wind; and many other brave men. The Argonauts set off in high hopes of a successful end to their quest.

The voyagers encounter numerous dangers on their journey. Hylas, Heracles' squire, is drawn into a spring by a nymph and is never seen again by his comrades. They next visit Salmydessa, where they meet the blind king, Phineus, who is tortured by harpies, loathsome creatures, with the faces of women and the bodies of vultures. Zetes and Calais chase the creatures across the skies, and when the heroes leave, the old king lives in peace.

Phineus had warned the heroes about the clashing rocks, the Bosporus, through which they must pass to reach Colchis. As they approach the rocks, they are filled with fear, but Juno holds the rocks back, and they sail past the peril. They row along the shore until they come to the land of Colchis.

Æetes, the king of Colchis, swears never to give up the treasure, but Jason vows that he and his comrades will do battle with Æetes. Then Æetes consents to yield the treasure if Jason manages to yoke to the plow two huge fire-breathing bulls and sow the field with dragon's teeth. When giant warriors spring up from each tooth, Jason has to slay each one. Jason agrees to the trial.

Æetes has a beautiful daughter named Medea, who falls in love with the handsome Jason, and she brews a magic potion that gives Jason godlike strength; thus it happens that he is able to tame the wild bulls and slay the warriors. Æetes promises to bring forth the fleece the next day, but Jason suspects the worst and warns his comrades to have the *Argo* ready to sail.

In the night, Medea secures the seven golden keys that unlock the seven doors to the cave where the golden fleece hangs, and she leads Jason to the place. Behind the seven doors, he finds a hideous dragon guarding the treasure. Medea's magic causes the dragon to fall asleep, allowing Jason to seize the fleece.

Fearing for her life because she has helped the stranger against her father, Medea sails away from her father's house with Jason and the other heroes. After many months and a circuitous voyage around the known world, they reach their homeland, where Jason places the treasure at the feet of Pelias. The fleece, however, is no longer golden. Pelias gets angry and refuses to give up his kingdom, but in the night

Medea causes him to die. Afterward, Jason becomes king and the enchanter Medea reigns by his side.

Critical Evaluation:

The journey of the Argonauts may well be one of the oldest of Greek adventure myths. Homer alludes to it, and it is placed in the generation preceding the Trojan War; the roster of heroes includes Telamon, the father of Ajax, and Peleus, the father of Achilles. Despite the age of this myth, the earliest extensive literary account is found in Pindar's *Pythian Ode 4* (in *Epinikia*, 498-446 B.C.E.; *Odes*, 1656), and it was not until the third century B.C.E. that the myth received formal expanded treatment by Apollonius Rhodius, who revived the epic genre on a small scale in line with the aesthetic codes of Hellenistic poetry. His romantic effort, the *Argonautica*, was the model for other versions of the quest, and it greatly influenced Roman epic poets, notably Vergil and Valerius Flaccus. Most knowledge of the myth derives from Apollonius's version. Jason's adventure, nevertheless, is included in *Bibliotecha*, the invaluable second century Greek collection of myths often attributed to Apollodorus.

Like most myths, the search for the fleece was subject to the rationalizing minds of classical writers; the geographer Strabo theorized, for example, that the Argonauts were on an expedition in search of alluvial gold. That Jason travels to Colchis on the Black Sea coast, after passing through the dangerous waters of the Bosporus, suggests that the story was in some way connected with Greek trading expeditions outside the Mediterranean and perhaps with the colonization of far-flung lands by Greek voyagers. In literary terms, its folktale theme of a sea journey to inhospitable lands in quest of a valuable prize was the model for the adventures of Odysseus, Hercules, Theseus, and others. Typical of such tales is the accomplishment of an impossible task and the confrontation with death and various incarnations of the Other—especially the female, the foreign, and the fantastic—all to prove nobility of birth and the right to reign. The retrieval of the fleece is therefore not the primary subject of this myth but the occasion; it is a device by which the hero becomes involved in a quest to prove his heroic qualities. The story of the Argonauts depicts the maturation of the youth into a hero.

Thus, for example, when Jason lands on the island of Lemnos in the Aegean Sea and discovers that it is inhabited only by women, he is initially tempted to stay and enjoy the delights on offer from queen Hypsipyle and her sisters. The revelation, however, that the women had murdered their husbands because they had married Thracian brides serves to alert Jason to the dangers of staying on the island and to remind him of his heroic duty to continue the quest.

The harpies, "snatchers of souls" who are half woman and half bird, are other examples of the threat to heroic virtue posed by hybrid creatures, female powers, and the realm of the dead. Driving the harpies from Phineus represents a triumph over these dangers. It is shortly after this that the *Argo* must pass through the clashing rocks, signifying the passage from the realm of the living into the world of the dead. The trip to Colchis is the equivalent of the hero's traditional descent into the underworld and the confrontation with death. According to one version, Jason is swallowed by the dragon guarding the fleece and then disgorged, signifying his conquest of death.

The conjoining of Jason's expedition with the story of Medea is one of the most intriguing elements of the story. Book 3 of Apollonius's poem contains the arrival at Colchis and Medea's falling in love with Jason, which is exploited for its romantic possibilities. Unlike Homer's *Iliad* (c. 750 B.C.E.; English translation, 1611), in which Hera and Athena are at odds with Aphrodite, the *Argonautica* portrays them as allies who instigate the mischievous Eros, or Cupid, to fire a dart into the heart of Princess Medea. Torn between filial loyalty and her uncontrollable passion, she soon yields to love. Her escape with Jason, and their eventual arrival at Iolcus in book 4, includes the murder of Medea's brother, Absyrtus, and the necessary expiation on Circe's island, Aeaea. Apollonius has Jason kill Absyrtus through Medea's treachery; in the earlier version, Medea herself murders her brother and scatters the butchered remains over the sea to delay the pursuing Colchians, who must gather the pieces for burial.

In earlier versions, the liaison of Jason and Medea may have been presented as a charged encounter between the Greek and the non-Greek, or barbarian, with all the thrills and dangers that accompanied such a violation of boundaries. The brutality of Medea's treatment of her brother points to the potential dangers for Jason in being associated with such an entity. This aspect is examined by Euripides in his play *Medea*, in which Medea's capacity for murderous violence and heartless revenge reaches a climax when she kills Jason's sons and his new bride.

The exact return route supposedly taken by the Argonauts had been disputed in ancient times. Doubtless the various versions are based on the trade routes begun in the Mycenaean age. Apollonius takes the Argonauts from the mouth of the River Phasis on the Black Sea to the Ister (Danube), overland to the Adriatic, where they are confronted by Absyrtus; then to the Eridanus (possibly the Po) and the Rhone, to the Tyrrhenian Sea and Circe's island. Other accounts include a return using the same route by which they came;

sailing east up the Phasis to the world-encircling River Ocean, then southwest to Africa and overland to the Mediterranean (Pindar's version); and sailing up the Phasis, through Russia, and over northern sea routes past Britain and through the Pillars of Hercules. There were very likely several versions of the return, or *nostos*, narrative available to poets, who could tailor their renditions to the taste of their particular audiences. This part of the story also affords further opportunities to depict exotic realms and peoples. As is the case with the returns from Troy, however, the journey home is difficult and does not always end in happiness.

The role of the object of the quest, the golden fleece, is open to varying interpretations. Some believe that the quest alludes to the search for precious minerals, such as gold, by Greek traders who were eager to bring foreign goods and materials back to their growing communities. Others suggest that mysterious, healing qualities were attributed to the object, which would tie in with the meaning of Jason's name in Greek, which means "healer." The centaur, Chiron, who raises him, is himself highly skilled in the medicinal arts, with knowledge of healing herbs and plants. This theme is also connected with Medea, who possesses knowledge of magic plants and potions and uses them on several occasions to further Jason's interests.

It is ironic that Jason, the healer, should prove unable to heal the breach that opens up between himself and Medea. As Euripides recounts, when Jason cruelly rejects the woman who sacrificed all she had—and even murdered—for him, she devises the perfect vengeance: to deprive Jason of the things he loves most by killing not only the girl he intends to marry but also Jason and Medea's sons. Thus, like the *Argo*'s voyage, the story of Jason eventually comes full circle. Overcome with grief, loneliness, and shame after the death of his sons and fiancé, he returns to the rotting hulk of the *Argo*, which he had beached at Corinth. There he dies after being struck by one of its falling beams. Such unexpected deaths are not unusual for heroes, but Jason's death is especially ignominious. The tale thus forms a striking contrast to the *Odyssey*, which concludes with the happy reunion between Odysseus and Penelope and the restoration of order in the royal household.

Jason-like heroes are seen not only in the many local legends of ancient Greece but also in history, as in Alexander's Asian conquests, which are subsequently romanticized. Comparisons may be drawn between Jason and Celtic heroes, and between the fleece and the grail. In 1867, William Morris revived the original myth with a seven thousand-line Victorian epic, *The Life and Death of Jason*, and in 1944, Robert Graves wrote a novel about the search for the fleece, *The Golden Fleece* (1944; also known as *Hercules, My Shipmate*, 1945).

"Critical Evaluation" by E. N. Genovese;
revised by David H. J. Larmour

Further Reading

Bacon, Janet Ruth. *The Voyage of the Argonauts*. Boston: Small, Maynard, 1925. A classic study of the myth of Jason and the golden fleece, in which Bacon follows the Argonauts through their extended history with literary evidence and illustrations. Provides excellent interpretations of the myth, including maps of the voyage and other illustrations.

DeForest, Mary Margolies. *Apollonius' "Argonautica."* New York: Brill, 1994. DeForest examines the significance of the golden fleece in the myth of Jason, as well as relationships between the characters. Makes a symbolic comparison of Medea to the golden fleece. Includes an extensive bibliography and a detailed index.

Papanghelis, Theodore, and Antonios Rengakos. *A Companion to Apollonius Rhodius*. Boston: Brill, 2001. A collection of essays on Apollonius Rhodius's version of *Jason and the Golden Fleece* that includes insightful discussions of the figure of Jason, similarities with the wanderings of Odysseus, and the motif of the golden fleece.

Pinsent, John. *Greek Mythology*. New York: Peter Bedrick Books, 1982. Pinsent interprets the meaning of the Jason myth through the symbols found in literature and art. Includes a number of Greek art illustrations.

Severin, Tim. *The Jason Voyage*. New York: Simon & Schuster, 1985. Severin embarks on the voyage of the Argonauts with a twentieth century crew. He captures the atmosphere and time of Jason's voyage and provides excellent archaeological details, evidence, and explanation of the origins of the myth. Also examines the reasons behind the timelessness of the legend of the golden fleece.

Thomas, Carol G. *Finding People in Early Greece*. Columbia: University of Missouri Press, 2005. Thomas amasses and analyzes an array of evidence to suggest that Jason was a historical figure and that his mythological legend was based on historic reality.

Wood, Michael. "Jason and the Golden Fleece." In *In Search of Myths and Heroes: Exploring Four Epic Legends of the World*. Berkeley: University of California Press, 2005. This book accompanies a program that aired on the Public Broadcasting Service, in which Wood travels to numerous locales to explore the Jason myth and other legends. Discusses why the story continues to capture the imagination.

Jazz

Author: Toni Morrison (1931-   )
First published: 1992
Type of work: Novel
Type of plot: Historical
Time of plot: 1920's
Locale: Virginia; Harlem, New York City

Principal characters:
VIOLET TRACE, a beautician
JOE TRACE, her husband and a cosmetics salesperson
DORCAS MANFRED, Joe's young lover
ALICE MANFRED, Dorcas's aunt
FELICE, Dorcas's friend
ROSE DEAR, Violet's mother
WILD, Joe's mother
GOLDEN GRAY, a light-skinned African American
TRUE BELLE, Violet's grandmother
HUNTERS HUNTER, Golden Gray's father and Joe's hunting mentor

The Story:

A three-month affair between Joe Trace and the young Dorcas Manfred ends when Joe shoots Dorcas at a party. At the young woman's funeral, Joe's wife, Violet Trace, is nicknamed Violent after she tries to cut the face of the corpse. For months, Violet and Joe grieve. They have only a photograph of Dorcas. The narrator believes that another scandalizing threesome is about to occur, as Dorcas's friend, Felice, visits the couple.

The childless, withdrawn Violet had once collapsed in the street. At another time she had intended to take someone else's baby home. Violet's public craziness differs greatly from the determined and vocal woman she used to be. After Dorcas's funeral, Violet even cast out the parrot who told Violet he loved her.

Violet herself recalls the funeral and its aftermath and wonders where her old, strong self has gone. She tortures herself about the things Joe may have done with Dorcas, revealing her own earlier relationship with Joe.

Violet is now remembering her childhood in Virginia: Her father can only visit the family occasionally, and secretly, because of Reconstruction (a period after the American Civil War). When he does visit, though, he always brings presents for his wife, Rose Dear, and their five children. Unfortunately for the family, Violet's father also belongs to a political party that opposes white landowners. Eventually, Rose Dear is dispossessed of her home and its contents because of his involvement with that party.

True Belle, Violet's grandmother, leaves Baltimore to care for her daughter and grandchildren. Eventually, Rose Dear drowns herself in a well. True Belle feeds the children stories of Golden Gray, the mixed-race boy that Violet never meets but is nevertheless crazy about. Violet believes her

husband, Joe, had been a substitute for Golden Gray, just as Violet had been a sort of substitute for Joe's mother, Wild.

In 1906, Joe and Violet travel by train to New York City, like numerous others from the American South. Twenty years later, Joe and Violet are barely speaking. Joe has given up his jobs, and Violet thinks of the woman who attacked Dorcas's dead body in the coffin as someone other than herself.

Joe still grieves for Dorcas and tries to fix in his mind his first meeting with her. He cannot even recall how he felt about his life with Violet in Vesper County, Virginia, before they left the South. He had first met Dorcas in 1905, when delivering a cosmetics order to a customer who was visiting her family. Earlier, he had seen Dorcas buying candy. In the room he rented every Thursday from his neighbor Malvonne, Joe talked with Dorcas about the South and the mother from whom he wanted a sign of acknowledgment. He also had comforted Dorcas, whose own parents had been killed in the East St. Louis riots of July, 1917.

Alice Manfred is watching a march with her nine-year-old niece, Dorcas, a march being held to protest the death of two hundred people in the East St. Louis riots. Alice, whose sister and brother-in-law had been killed in the riots, has just taken in Dorcas—who does not say a word to her aunt about her parents' deaths, and will never do so.

Now seventeen years old, Dorcas has been seduced by the music of the city and constrained by the discipline of her aunt. At one party she attends with her friend Felice, Dorcas is acknowledged but then dismissed by a boy she likes. It turns out that Joe is just the person she needs in her life.

Soon after Dorcas is killed by Joe, Violet visits Alice to ask her about her young niece who, unlike Violet, had light, creamy skin. Alice allows Violet to take a photograph of Dorcas home with her and then begins to thinks about the strength of many black women. She mends Violet's coat lining and thinks about her own unarticulated fury at a husband who had taken off with another woman and who had died seven months later.

Violet remembers her sudden hunger for motherhood from ten years earlier. She still has a doll hidden under her bed.

In spring, 1926, Joe still has the blues. He remembers the family who had adopted him in Virginia when he was a baby. As a child, he had given himself his own surname—Trace—after his adoptive mother had told him his parents had vanished without a trace. At the age of fourteen, he had tried to track down his mother, Wild. Joe now begins to think of how he had tracked Dorcas in the city, much like his earlier quest. He characterizes his relationship with Dorcas as having been Edenic.

The narrator tells what she knows of True Belle, who had worked for a Virginia plantation owner's daughter, Vera Louise, before the Civil War. When Vera Louise became pregnant—by a local black youth, Hunters Hunter—she was disowned by her parents and moved with True Belle to Baltimore; here, the yellow-haired Golden Gray had been born. True Belle had been forced to leave her own daughters behind with an aunt.

At the age of eighteen, Golden Gray, with directions from True Belle, sets out to find his father. Hunters Hunter has never been told of his existence. The narrator draws on literary stereotypes in imagining Golden Gray's quest and the young man's discovery of the pregnant and injured Wild, who is about to give birth to Joe.

In rural Virginia, the elusive black woman, Wild, is the source of many local superstitions. Field workers hear her laughter in the cane, and pregnant women worry that her presence might affect their unborn, but Hunters Hunter knows she is real and that Wild and Golden Gray are together.

Joe remembers looking for signs of his mother—a flock of redwings, rustling sugar cane, smoke-sugared air, a scrap of song—and he finds an entrance to a cave. The cave shows evidence of habitation—silver brushes, a doll, and Golden Gray's clothing, but no Wild. In 1925, he thinks about this cave as he seeks out Dorcas.

Dorcas is thrilled with her new boyfriend, Acton. Joe had empowered her, whereas Acton is demanding and self-centered. At a crowded party with Acton, Dorcas knows Joe will come for her, but when she is shot in the shoulder, she refuses to identify Joe or go to the hospital.

Dorcas's photograph has been returned to Alice, and mu-sic is in the air as Felice, carrying a race record for her aunt, visits Joe and Violet to tell more about Dorcas, including her last words. Like Wild and Violet, Felice is a dark-skinned black. Her visits comfort Violet and Joe, as if she is the child they never had. Joe begins to work again, and the couple find their true selves.

Critical Evaluation:

Set in New York in 1926, Toni Morrison's *Jazz* takes the reader back through the rural and city histories of the two main characters, Violet and Joe Trace, to make sense of their actions in the present. Historically, *Jazz* alludes to the great migration of African Americans from the South to the North, to returned veterans of World War I who cannot get respect or the work they deserve, to the Reconstruction period after the Civil War, and most emphatically, to the Harlem Renaissance, with its jazz and literature.

Jazz comprises ten sections in which the unnamed narrator characterizes the city and discusses what she knows of the lives of Joe and Violet. Subsections in each chapter are focalized through Joe, Violet, Dorcas, Alice, and Felice. The subsections fill out the narrator's improvisations, take them somewhere else, embellish them, and often contradict them. Various events, loves, and losses that have shaped the characters are repeated or given significance with differences in meaning, range, and depth. The last line of one section is usually picked up in the opening of the next. The idea of the South as the Promised Land for former slaves is also improvised upon by the narrator, who adores the city, and through Joe and Dorcas's love affair. Joe thinks of Dorcas as his Eden, believing he has eaten the first apple and its core.

The narrator is energized by the contradictions, bravado, and vibrancy of the city, and she often begins a section or a subsection with a riff on its excitement, diversity, changeability, and sheer spectacle. Like all Morrison novels, *Jazz* demands the reader's attention, so that she or he can follow the threads or motifs of the text and the shifts in time.

Music, central to the structure and themes of the novel, includes snatches of jazz lyrics and many allusions to blues and jazz and their focus on love and loss. Jazz, the narrator says, can be exhilaratingly dangerous or, as the middle-class Alice Manfred initially claims, dirty and lowdown.

Some reviewers of *Jazz* were puzzled by the novel's narrator. She seems to be a gossipy, lonely older woman, a voyeur who may be a member of the Salem Baptist Church Women's Club and a customer of Violet the beautician. Like most of her neighbors, the narrator seems to have a rural background. She provides the reader with facts but her interpretations, often based on books or films of the day, are often wrong. For example, in the sixth section, she believes that Golden Gray, the light-colored African American, would have shunned the black girl who is Joe's mother. As Joe's thoughts confirm later, Golden Gray and Wild become a couple.

The theme of lost love is as important in jazz music as it is in this novel. Many characters lose their parents to the consequences of racism, which in turn affects the children's lives, too. Violet's father is mostly absent because of his politics, and the family, particularly Rose Dear, pays for his absence. Rose Dear, too, lost her mother to the demands of slavery and the selfishness of True Belle's mistress, once slaves were liberated. Vera Louise withheld wages from True Belle until the latter convinced her she was dying. Joe's parents vanished, Dorcas's parents were killed during a riot, and Felice's parents worked away from home while Felice lived with her grandmother. Despite their parents' unavoidable absence, the characters carry a sense of guilt as well as anger and lack of self-worth into their new lives in the city.

At the center of the novel is the elusive Wild, who is Joe's mother, Golden Gray's companion, and the source of rural beliefs of various kinds. She may represent the black woman who is every African American's ancestor. She cannot be seen but can be heard in a laugh, in a rustle of crops, in the weather, or in characters like Violet or Felice.

Christine Ferrari

Further Reading

Eichelberger, Julia. *Prophets of Recognition: Ideology and the Individual in Novels by Ralph Ellison, Toni Morrison, Saul Bellow, and Eudora Welty.* Baton Rouge: Louisiana State University Press, 1999. A fascinating study that considers how Morrison's characters search for individual identity through a desire for or sometimes refutation of power. For undergraduate and graduate students. Includes a literature review.

Fultz, Lucille P. *Toni Morrison: Playing with Difference.* Urbana: University of Illinois Press, 2003. Examines Morrison's approach to differences (for example, black and white, male and female, wealth and poverty) in her intricate narratives.

Furman, Jan. *Toni Morrison's Fiction.* Columbia: University of South Carolina Press, 1996. Offers a comprehensive introduction to Morrison's novels with a strong chapter on *Jazz.*

Gates, Henry Louis, Jr., and K. A. Appiah, eds. *Toni Morrison: Critical Perspectives Past and Present.* New York: Amistad, 1993. Reviews, essays, and articles on Morrison's writing, including *Jazz.* An invaluable resource by two well-known scholars.

Rodrigues, Eusebio L. "Experiencing *Jazz.*" *Modern Fiction* 39, nos. 3/4 (Fall/Winter, 1993): 733-754. An excellent reading of Morrison's novel as a kind of jazz performance in itself.

Stein, Karen F. *Reading, Learning, Teaching Toni Morrison.* New York: Peter Lang, 2009. An excellent primer for students just beginning their studies of Morrison and her works. Includes a chapter on *Jazz* as well as an introductory chapter about the background to Morrison's fiction.

Tally, Justine, ed. *The Cambridge Companion to Toni Morrison.* New York: Cambridge University Press, 2007. A comprehensive work that offers several scholarly chapters on *Jazz* and includes a guide to further reading.

Van der Zee, James, Owen Dodson, and Camille Billops. *The Harlem Book of the Dead.* Dobbs Ferry, N.Y.: Morgan & Morgan, 1978. Morrison's idea for *Jazz* came from Van Der Zee's photograph of an unknown girl said to have been shot by her "sweetheart." This collection contains photographs of deceased African Americans that were taken in New York funeral homes in the 1920's. Includes a foreword by Morrison.

Walker, Alice. "If the Present Looks Like the Past, What Does the Future Look Like?" In *In Search of Our Mother's Gardens.* London: Women's Press, 1984. In this classic text, Walker explores the way "colorism" can exclude the black-woman ancestor, which may be relevant to understanding the characters of Wild and Golden Gray in Morrison's *Jazz.*

Jealousy

Author: Alain Robbe-Grillet (1922-2008)
First published: La Jalousie, 1957 (English translation, 1959)
Type of work: Novel
Type of plot: Antistory
Time of plot: Probably the early 1950's
Locale: Unnamed

Principal characters:
THE UNNAMED NARRATOR, the owner of a banana plantation
A . . . , the narrator's wife
FRANCK, the owner of a neighboring plantation

The Story:

The narrator suspects his wife, A . . . , of infidelity with their neighbor Franck. The narrator and Franck own banana plantations; they and their wives form a little enclave of French colonialism in the tropics, with common concerns about crops, the weather, and the unreliability of native workers. Most important, they share emotions of boredom and loneliness. For Franck and A . . . , the consequence is an affair—at least, so it seems. For the narrator, the consequence is the intense jealousy produced by his suspicions.

Franck and his wife, Christiane, were frequent dinner guests of the narrator and his wife in the past. Christiane seems not to get along well with A . . . ; that, together with her child's reported illness and her own vague ailments, keep her away, although her husband continues to visit. At one of these dinners, Franck mentions that he has to go to town the next week to see about various business matters, principally getting a new truck. The subject of motor trouble came up in earlier conversations, along with the difficulty of obtaining adequate repair and the unreliability of native drivers. Franck suggests that A . . . might like to accompany him for a day of shopping. She gladly accepts; they agree to leave at six-thirty in the morning and be back by night.

Franck and A . . . leave at the agreed time but do not return by nightfall. Instead, they show up the next day, saying that car trouble forced them to spend the night in town while waiting for a repair. This excuse seems untrue because of the glances the two exchange, Franck's suspiciously casual manner, the absence of purchases by A . . . , and their double-entendres (for example, Franck asks A . . . to forgive him for being a "bad mechanic," with the implication that their sexual encounter was not as thrilling as expected).

The narrator spies on his wife several times. Once he observes her from the veranda through the bedroom window secretly writing a letter—presumably to Franck. Other times he watches her comb her hair, get into Franck's car to go to town, and get out of the car upon returning with a suggestive lingering at the car window. He also watches the work of a gang of laborers repairing a small bridge and observes his property, including the rows of banana trees.

The narrator's observations are embedded within his constant role as voyeur—a not-entirely-objective observer, a roving camera eye whose meticulously objective impressions carry an emotional subtext that charges inconsequential events with latent meanings. The most pointed of these is the killing of a nasty-looking, poisonous centipede. At one of Franck's dinner visits, the centipede is noticed crawling up a wall; A . . . is horrified by it, and Franck immediately kills it with a rolled-up napkin, leaving an oddly shaped stain on the wall. This story is told several times with minor variations—in one of which it occurs not in the narrator's house but in the hotel room where A . . . and Franck spend the night. It is still from the jealous husband's subjective point of view that this version of the episode is related in the form of a fantasy. The narrator does not prove his suspicions of his wife's adultery. The novel ends very much as it began, with nothing really resolved.

Critical Evaluation:

In the usual understanding of the term, there is no "story" in this novel. The author's method of narration is deliberately designed to challenge conventional reader expectations. Events in the novel do not follow in a straight line from beginning to end; the pattern is more a convolution of episodes repeated again and again with minor variations, out of which there emerges a partially realized story.

A synopsis of *Jealousy*, therefore, sounds strange, with good reason. The type of novel exemplified by *Jealousy*, and of which Alain Robbe-Grillet is both the principal theorist and practitioner, is termed New Novel or "antinovel." Even considering the innovations in the novel by major twentieth century novelists such as James Joyce, Franz Kafka, and William Faulkner, the New Novel is, in many ways, without precedent. From the 1950's through the 1970's especially, it represented an extremely provocative, internationally influential approach to the craft of fiction by French writers such as Michel Butor, Natalie Sarraute, Claude Simon, and Robbe-Grillet.

Born in 1922, Robbe-Grillet came to intellectual maturity in a mid-twentieth century France divided by vicious political antagonisms and shattered by war but also animated by tremendous artistic and intellectual creative activity, such as the Theater of the Absurd, abstract expressionist painting, and existentialist philosophy—especially the last. Existentialism's main assertions—that the human is a radically free agent; that the universe has no meaning; that "meaning" itself is a perceptual construct validated only by action—became articles of faith for the French intellectual left during the 1940's and 1950's. Many writers derived themes of alienation or despair from such premises, but for Robbe-Grillet, the meaninglessness of life is simply a neutral fact. Meaning is the pattern imposed by consciousness upon experience; reality cannot be understood apart from our perceptions of it, which are always subjective no matter how objective they may seem. For Robbe-Grillet, the role of the novelist is not to seek out truths on such subjects as life, character, or morals but to challenge the reader's uncritical acceptance of such myths. The meaning of a Robbe-Grillet novel is to be sought in the techniques by which he subverts the very notion of meaning while creating an intriguing fictional structure that shimmers like a mirage with enigmatic significance.

The most basic and profound of these techniques is the fragmentation of linear time-sequence. This is a central feature of all his fiction and is especially prominent in *Jealousy*. Narrated entirely in present tense, the action consists of a repetitive pattern of the narrator's principal impressions: A . . . 's brushing her hair and writing a letter; several possibly flirtatious interactions between her and Franck at dinner and lunch; her departure and return; and the killing of the centipede. Repeated in the manner of a fugue, with small but noticeable variations, they describe a circle, or better a Moebius strip, in which the events of the beginning, middle, and end are parts of a constantly unfolding present.

Complementing the absence of a linear plot is the foregrounding of minor incidents and details. Among the many examples, the killing of the centipede is the most significant: Trivial though it is, this is the most dramatic and memorable event in the novel—the one outbreak of intuitive action, or impropriety, or violence. The narrator's consciousness records, with cameralike objectivity, the minute details of A . . . 's and Franck's gestures; the comings and goings of servants; the stain left by the centipede; various other stains and surface blemishes, such as a bit of peeling paint on the veranda rail; the exact layout, row by row, of the banana trees; and the shadow cast by the southwest corner column of the veranda, which, by its variations, marks the passage of time. The detailed, geometric precision of such descriptions is the most arresting feature of the novel—so much so that it may seem that Robbe-Grillet is concerned more with objects than with people. His early critics in France were inclined to praise him for just such an objectivism.

To an extent, his preoccupation with objective description grows out of his radical critique of fictional form. He has no use for the conventions by which the character is made to seem convincing, the events real, and the story true. For him, the form and purpose of a novel begin and end with structure. The intricate pattern of such descriptions, with their repetitions and serial permutations, thus constitutes a kind of meaning, in the manner of a modernist musical composition or an abstract painting. Much of Robbe-Grillet's critical acclaim, for this novel and for others, reflects the extent to which he has apparently succeeded in displacing humanist concerns with purely formalist ones.

Although *Jealousy* is not exactly a slice of life, it nevertheless creates a memorable and disturbing impression of human psychology. The title in the original French, *La Jalousie*, is a pun that links the narrator's psychology to the mode of narration. The tropical plantation house does not have glass windows, but blinds, or "jalousies," to keep out the sun while allowing the circulation of air; it is through the slats of these blinds that the narrator spies on his wife. The ingenuity of Robbe-Grillet's formal designs partly explains their artistic power, but not entirely. Filtered through the narrator's consciousness, they leave no imprint. The reader cannot be objectively sure that any impropriety occurred: The narrator's descriptions are cool and detached but also obsessive—the objective correlatives of a mind given to fantasy, infinite regression, and paranoid suspicion. Thus, without anything remotely resembling characterization, a kind of silhouette image of a morbidly jealous man emerges from the text by tone and implication.

Robbe-Grillet said of his narrators that they generally are men engaged "in an emotional adventure of the most obsessive kind, to the point of often distorting their vision." Much of his power as a novelist lies in just this ability to create unsettling psychological portraits out of ostensibly neutral, objective material—perhaps not camera images so much as images projected by a magic lantern from the unconscious and framed ironically by the most lucid, elegant prose.

Charles F. Duncan

Further Reading

Babcock, Arthur E. *The New Novel in France: Theory and Practice of the Nouveau Roman*. New York: Twayne, 1997. An overview of the literary movement of which Robbe-Grillet was a prominent proponent, analyzing his fiction and the work of other "new novelists."

Barthes, Roland. "Objective Literature: Alain Robbe-Grillet." In *Two Novels by Robbe-Grillet: "Jealousy" and "In the Labyrinth,"* translated by Richard Howard. New York: Grove Press, 1965. Important introductory essay to the standard English-language edition of *Jealousy* by the leading French structuralist critic and proponent of objective literature.

Fletcher, John. *Alain Robbe-Grillet*. New York: Methuen, 1983. Good monographic overview of Robbe-Grillet's fiction and critical theory. The section on *Jealousy* emphasizes the psychological aspects of the narrator's consciousness rather than the structural patterns of his descriptions.

Hellerstein, Marjorie H. *Inventing the Real World: The Art of Alain Robbe-Grillet*. Selinsgrove, Pa.: Susquehanna University Press, 1998. Describes how Robbe-Grillet's novels and films are influenced by painters' and printmakers' visual perceptions and by their use of space to create artistic illusions. Includes an analysis of *Jealousy*.

Jefferson, Ann. *The Nouveau Roman and the Poetics of Fiction*. New York: Cambridge University Press, 1980. A survey of the French New Novel that covers Robbe-Grillet in several chapters and includes an analysis of *Jealousy*. Describes Robbe-Grillet's narratives as "unnatural" and places his work within the context of the French New Novel movement of the 1950's and 1960's.

Leki, Ilona. *Alain Robbe-Grillet*. Boston: Twayne, 1983. A thorough, readable survey of the author's life and works. The chapter on *Jealousy* suggests that the narrator's paranoid psychology is produced by a generalized fear of dispossession and loss of control, not only of his wife but also of his house and property.

Morrissette, Bruce. *Alain Robbe-Grillet*. New York: Columbia University Press, 1965. Short but excellent monograph by Robbe-Grillet's premier critic. Extremely perceptive commentary on *Jealousy*, with a nice balance between formalist and humanist interpretative reading.

Smith, Roch C. *Understanding Alain Robbe-Grillet*. Columbia: University of South Carolina Press, 2000. An introductory guide to Robbe-Grillet's work and theories that aims to make him less bewildering to readers. Discusses the characterization, narration, plots, and other elements of Robbe-Grillet's fiction.

Stoltzfus, Ben. *Alain Robbe-Grillet: The Body of the Text*. London: Associated University Presses, 1985. Stoltzfus contends that Robbe-Grillet exaggerates images of sex and violence in his novels in order to expose and undermine them. Includes a bibliography and index.

Jennie Gerhardt

Author: Theodore Dreiser (1871-1945)
First published: 1911
Type of work: Novel
Type of plot: Naturalism
Time of plot: Last two decades of the nineteenth century
Locale: Chicago; Columbus, Cleveland, and Cincinnati, Ohio

Principal characters:
JENNIE GERHARDT
WILLIAM GERHARDT, her father
MRS. GERHARDT, her mother
SEBASTIAN GERHARDT, her brother
SENATOR BRANDER, Jennie's first lover
VESTA, Jennie's daughter
MRS. BRACEBRIDGE, Jennie's employer in Cleveland
LESTER KANE, a carriage manufacturer and Jennie's second lover
ROBERT KANE, Lester's brother
MRS. LETTY PACE GERALD, a widow, Lester's childhood sweetheart, and later his wife

The Story:

Jennie Gerhardt, a beautiful and virtuous eighteen-year-old, is one of six children of a poor, hard-working German family in Columbus, Ohio, in 1880. Her father, a glassblower, is ill, and Jennie and her mother are forced to work at a local hotel in order to provide for the younger children in the family. Jennie does the laundry for the kind and handsome Senator Brander (he is fifty-two at the time) and attracts his eye. Senator Brander is kind to Jennie and her family. When he is able to keep Jennie's brother Sebastian out of jail for stealing some needed coal from the railroad, Jennie, full of gratitude, allows him to sleep with her. Senator Brander, struck by Jennie's beauty, charm, and goodness, promises to marry her. He dies suddenly, however, while on a trip to Washington.

Left alone, Jennie discovers that she is pregnant. Her father, a stern Lutheran, insists that she leave the house, but her more understanding mother allows her to return when her father, once in better health, leaves to find work in Youngstown. Jennie's child is a girl, whom she names Vesta. At Sebastian's suggestion, the family moves to Cleveland to find work. While her mother looks after Vesta, Jennie finds a job as a maid in the home of Mrs. Bracebridge. One of Mrs. Bracebridge's guests, Lester Kane, the son of a rich carriage manufacturer, finds Jennie temptingly attractive. When he tries to seduce Jennie, the girl, though greatly attracted to him, manages to put off his advances.

Mr. Gerhardt is injured in a glassblowing accident and loses the use of both of his hands. Again, the family needs money badly, and Jennie decides to accept Lester's offer of aid for her family. The price is that she become his mistress, go on a trip to New York with him, and then allow him to establish her in an apartment in Chicago. Although Jennie loves Lester, she knows that he does not intend to marry her because his family will be horrified at such an alliance, but, once again, she sacrifices her virtue because she feels that her family needs the offered aid. After Jennie becomes Lester's mistress, he gives her family money for a house. Jennie is afraid, however, to tell Lester about the existence of her daughter Vesta.

Jennie and Lester move to Chicago and live there. Her family begins to suspect that, contrary to what Jennie told them, she and Lester are not married. When Mrs. Gerhardt dies several years later, Jennie moves Vesta to Chicago and boards the child in another woman's house. One night, Jennie is called because Vesta is seriously ill, and Lester discovers Vesta's existence. Although upset at first, when Jennie tells him the story, Lester understands and agrees to allow Vesta to live with them. Some time later, while Lester is staying at the apartment to recover from an illness, his sister Louise visits and discovers the relationship, which she reports to the Kane family upon her return to Cincinnati. Lester and Jennie soon move to a house in Hyde Park, a middle-class residential district in Chicago. Mr. Gerhardt, now old and ill and willing to accept the situation between Jennie and Lester, also comes to live with them and to tend the furnace and the lawn.

Although they are constantly aware of the increasing disapproval of Lester's family, Jennie and Lester live happily for a time. Lester's father, violently opposed to the relationship with Jennie, whom he never met, threatens to disinherit Lester if he does not leave her. Lester's brother Robert urges his father on and attempts to persuade Lester to abandon Jennie. Nevertheless, Lester feels that he owes his allegiance as well as his love to her, and he remains with her in spite of the fact that they are snubbed by most of Lester's society connections.

When Lester's father dies, still believing that his son's relationship with Jennie demonstrates irresponsibility, he leaves Lester's share of the estate in trust with Robert. Lester is given three alternatives: He can leave Jennie and receive all his money; he can marry Jennie and receive only ten thousand dollars a year for life; or he can continue his present arrangement with the knowledge that if he does not either abandon or marry Jennie within three years, he will lose his share of the money. Characteristically, Lester hesitates. He resigns from his managerial position in the family business and takes Jennie to Europe, where they meet Mrs. Letty Pace Gerald, a beautiful and accomplished widow who was Lester's childhood sweetheart and who is still fond of him. In the meantime, Robert expands the carriage business into a monopoly and eases Lester into a subordinate position. When Lester returns to Chicago, he decides to attempt to make an independent future for himself and Jennie. He puts a good deal of money into a real estate deal and loses it. Mrs. Gerald also moves to Chicago in pursuit of Lester.

After old Mr. Gerhardt dies, Jennie finds herself in a difficult situation. Lester, out of the family business because of her, is finding it more difficult to earn a living. Mrs. Gerald and Robert's lawyers keep pressing her to release him, claiming this suggestion is for his own economic and social good. Jennie, always altruistic, begins to influence Lester to leave her. Before long, both are convinced that separation is the only solution so that Lester can return to the family business. Finally, Lester leaves Jennie, setting up a house and an income for her and Vesta in a cottage an hour or so from the center of Chicago.

Once more established in the family business, Lester marries Mrs. Gerald. Six months after Lester leaves Jennie,

Vesta, a fourteen-year-old girl already showing a good deal of sensitivity and talent, dies of typhoid fever.

Jennie, calling herself Mrs. Stover, moves to the city and adopts two orphan children. Five years pass. Jennie, although still in love with Lester, accepts her quiet life. At last, she is able to cope with experience in whatever terms it presents itself to her, even though she is never able to impose her will on experience in any meaningful way. One night while in Chicago on business, Lester is stricken by severe cardiovascular illness and sends for Jennie; his wife is in Europe and cannot reach Chicago for three weeks. Jennie tends Lester throughout his last illness. One day he confesses that he always loved her and that he made a mistake by permitting the forces of business and family pressure to make him leave her. Jennie feels that his final confession, his statement that he should never have left her, indicates a kind of spiritual union and leaves her with something that she can value for the rest of her life. Lester dies. Jennie realizes that she will now be forced to live through many years that can promise no salvation, no new excitement—that will simply impose themselves upon her as have the years in the past. She is resolved to accept her loneliness because she knows there is nothing else for her to do.

Jennie goes to see Lester's coffin loaded on the train. She realizes then, even more clearly, that the individual is simply a figure, moved about by circumstance. Virtue, beauty, moral worth cannot save anyone, nor can evil or degeneracy. One simply yields and manages the best one can under the circumstances of one's nature, one's society, and one's economic situation.

Critical Evaluation:

Theodore Dreiser began writing his second novel, *Jennie Gerhardt*, in 1901, soon after the publication of *Sister Carrie* (1900). As in the earlier work, Dreiser's main theme is the individual's struggle to find happiness in an uncaring, often cruel world. In this struggle, all is chance. One might have a slight advantage if born into a wealthy family (as Lester Kane is), but this does not guarantee success. On the other hand, a person born without material advantages must struggle to make up for the lack.

From the beginning, Jennie faces obstacles that her brother Sebastian does not. The wages she receives from helping her mother as a scrubwoman in a fashionable hotel in downtown Columbus, Ohio, are much less than men receive for comparable work. She and her mother take in laundry to supplement their income. At the time, few honest jobs allow women to earn a living wage. This puts Jennie at a great risk because she has to enter Senator Brander's hotel room to pick up and deliver his laundry. The beautiful eighteen-year-old Jennie is vulnerable to Brander not only because of her age and social class but also because of her gender. During the last half of the nineteenth century, women engaged in domestic work, whether in hotels or private homes, were often targeted by men with less than honorable intentions. Jennie soon learns that her sexuality has value and can be exchanged for trinkets, clothes, and, finally, money.

By exchanging her virginity for Sebastian's bail, Jennie not only becomes pregnant but also becomes caught in a trap from which she never escapes. The possibility of marriage and a happy life with someone of her own class made impossible, she struggles as best she can. Given her situation, Jennie succeeds amazingly well. She lives comfortably in Chicago for several years with the man she loves, traveling extensively in America and Europe and enjoying the material comforts of wealth. Even after her separation from Lester, her basic needs are guaranteed by a trust fund he sets up for her. She has a nice house, food (she grows "stout"), and her daughter's companionship. Fate rears its ugly head, and Vesta is taken away by typhoid fever. Still unwilling to surrender to despair, Jennie takes in two foster children.

Jennie's constant struggle for survival makes this novel perhaps an even better example of literary naturalism than its predecessor, *Sister Carrie*, but Jennie's is not the only struggle in the novel. Lester tries to find his place in life, balanced between his own happiness and the dictates of his family's social position. Even when he seems successful (wealth, marriage to Letty Pace), his happiness is not guaranteed. In fact, his material success brings the cause of his demise. Lester's rich lifestyle includes the finest foods and drinks. He becomes very obese and unhealthy. Symbolically, his material success overfills his physical body, stretching his form and clogging his arteries. Fate is unpredictable and can attack the individual in many ways. Lester dies not in a gutter but in a luxurious Chicago hotel, smothered to death by his own good fortune. Lester's fondness for gambling during his marriage to Letty symbolizes fate's role in life. His favorite game is roulette—spinning the wheel of fortune.

Dreiser uses a different set of images for Jennie, whom he describes as "a pale gentle flower," "a rare flower," or "like a rudderless boat on an endless sea." Flower and boat metaphors are common in literary naturalism and echo Stephen Crane's description of the title character in *Maggie: A Girl of the Streets* (1893), a girl who "blossomed in a mud puddle," and the "rudderless" boat in his sixth poem from *The Black Riders, and Other Lines* (1895). Dreiser also refers to Jennie several times as a "wayfarer," an image Crane uses in the poem "The Wayfarer" in *War Is Kind* (1899) to suggest that people have no control over their destinies and that even a seemingly inconsequential decision can have disastrous results. Dreiser foreshadows Jennie's unluckiness in life by giving the Gerhardt family address as 13th Street in Columbus and 1314 Lorrie Street in Cleveland.

In Dreiser's naturalistic vision, nature has no concern for an individual's happiness, and those who look to religion for assistance get no relief. Jennie's father is a devout Lutheran, but still his family is torn apart by harsh social and economic conditions. Dreiser's original title for *Jennie Gerhardt* was "The Transgressor." Against whom or what did Jennie transgress—God, society, nature? Dreiser asks the reader to question Jennie's sins, but in the end the reader cannot condemn her choices. "How could the poor girl, amid such unfortunate circumstances, do otherwise than she did." Dreiser's statement implies no favorable alternatives.

Jennie Gerhardt has not enjoyed a high place in literary history and is usually put aside for *Sister Carrie* and Dreiser's later novel with working-class themes, *An American Tragedy* (1925). Perhaps this is the result of social attitudes toward events in the book. Readers want to sympathize with Jennie, but society tells them that the sins she falls into— sleeping with Brander and Lester—are wrong. During the great wave of social "improvement" in the first decade of the twentieth century, this issue caused Dreiser difficulty in publishing the work, and he had to soften its message considerably before the book was printed in 1911. Changes made for that edition have allowed critics to find weaknesses (such as Jennie's lack of psychological development) that were less telling in Dreiser's original manuscripts. Fortunately, the original text (now referred to as the Pennsylvania edition) has been restored and published, but readers should be aware that criticism written before the original text's publication in 1992 might be distorted by reliance on the bowdlerized version.

Jennie Gerhardt fits thematically with other works in which women are forced to go against Christianity's teachings to survive, including Daniel Defoe's *Moll Flanders* (1722), Crane's *Maggie: A Girl of the Streets*, Upton Sinclair's *The Jungle* (1906), and Dreiser's own *Sister Carrie* and *An American Tragedy*.

"Critical Evaluation" by Geralyn Strecker

Further Reading

Cassuto, Leonard, and Clare Virginia Eby, eds. *The Cambridge Companion to Theodore Dreiser.* New York: Cambridge University Press, 2004. A collection of twelve essays focusing on the novelist's examination of American conflicts between materialistic longings and traditional values. Includes essays on Dreiser's style, Dreiser and women, and Dreiser and the ideology of upward mobility. The references to *Jennie Gerhardt* are listed in the index.

Dreiser, Theodore. *Jennie Gerhardt.* Edited by James L. W. West III. Philadelphia: University of Pennsylvania Press, 1992. This restored version reclaims Dreiser's original intentions for the novel. Includes informative introduction, explanatory notes, a map, illustrations of pages from Dreiser's manuscript, and other useful materials.

Gogol, Miriam, ed. *Theodore Dreiser: Beyond Naturalism.* New York: New York University Press, 1995. Ten essays interpret Dreiser from the perspectives of new historicism, poststructuralism, psychoanalysis, feminism, and other points of view. Gogol's introduction advances the argument that Dreiser was much more than a naturalist and deserves to be treated as a major author.

Juras, Uwe. *Pleasing to the "I": The Culture of Personality and Its Representations in Theodore Dreiser and F. Scott Fitzgerald.* New York: Peter Lang, 2006. Juras examines how the two authors depicted the newly emerging concept of personality, defined as the outward presentation of self, in their work. Includes a discussion of *Jennie Gerhardt*.

Lingeman, Richard. *Theodore Dreiser: At the Gates of the City, 1871-1907.* New York: G. P. Putnam's Sons, 1986.

_____. *Theodore Dreiser: An American Journey, 1908-1945.* New York: G. P. Putnam's Sons, 1990. The standard biography offers information on the writing and biographical context of *Jennie Gerhardt* in volume 1 and information on its revision, publication, and critical reception in volume 2.

Loving, Jerome. *The Last Titan: A Life of Theodore Dreiser.* Berkeley: University of California Press, 2005. This engrossing survey of the author's life and work is a welcome addition to Dreiser scholarship. Focuses on Dreiser's work, including his journalism, discussing the writers who influenced him and his place within American literature.

Pizer, Donald. *The Novels of Theodore Dreiser: A Critical Study.* Minneapolis: University of Minnesota Press, 1976. The section on *Jennie Gerhardt* establishes information about the novel's sources and composition. Gives biographical details suggesting that Jennie was modeled after Dreiser's sister Mame. Valuable discussion of structure, characterization, and themes.

West, James L. W., III, ed. *Dreiser's "Jennie Gerhardt": New Essays on the Restored Text.* Philadelphia: University of Pennsylvania Press, 1994. A collection giving historical background and new interpretations of the novel in its restored version.

Jerusalem Delivered

Author: Torquato Tasso (1544-1595)
First published: Gerusalemme liberata, 1581 (English
   translation, 1600)
Type of work: Poetry
Type of plot: Epic
Time of plot: Middle Ages
Locale: The Holy Land

Principal characters:
GODFREY DE BOUILLON, leader of the Crusaders
CLORINDA, a female warrior
ARGANTES, a pagan knight
ERMINIA, princess of Antioch
ARMIDA, an enchantress
RINALDO, an Italian knight
TANCRED, a Frankish knight

The Poem:

For six years the Crusaders remain in the Holy Land, meeting with success. Tripoli, Antioch, and Acre are in their hands, and a large force of Christian knights occupies Palestine. Yet there is a lassitude among the nobles; they are tired and satiated with fighting. They cannot generate enough warlike spirit to continue to the real objective of their Crusade, the capture of Jerusalem. In the spring of the seventh year, God sends the Archangel Gabriel to Godfrey de Bouillon, ordering him to assemble all his knights and encouraging him to begin the march on Jerusalem. Obeying the Lord's command, Godfrey calls a council of the great nobles and reminds them stirringly of their vows. When Peter the Hermit adds his exhortations, the Crusaders accept their charge, and all preparations are made to attack the Holy City.

Within the walls of Jerusalem the wicked King Aladine hears of the projected attack. At the urging of Ismeno the sorcerer, he sends soldiers to steal the statue of the Virgin Mary, hoping to make the Christian symbol a Palladium for Jerusalem. The next morning, the statue disappears. Enraged when he cannot find the culprit who spirited away the statue, Aladine orders a general massacre of all his Christian subjects. To save her coreligionists, the beautiful and pure Sophronia confesses to the theft. Aladine has her bound to the stake. As her guards are about to light the fire, Olindo, who long loved Sophronia in vain, attempts to save her by confessing that he himself stole the statue.

Aladine orders them both burned. While they are at the stake, Sophronia admits her love for Olindo. They are saved from burning, however, by the arrival of Clorinda, a beautiful woman warrior who knows that both are admitting the theft to save the other Christians from death. Released, Sophronia and Olindo flee the city. Clorinda is a great warrior who scorns female dress. On a previous campaign she had met Tancred, a mighty Christian noble. Tancred fell in love with her; but she rejected his love. On the other hand, Erminia of Antioch was enamored of Tancred when he took her city, but Tancred feels only friendship for her.

The Christians come within sight of Jerusalem. A foraging party encounters first a small force under Clorinda. She is so valorous that she defeats them. The king of Egypt, whose army is advancing to the aid of Jerusalem, sends Argantes to parley with Godfrey. The Crusader chief haughtily rejects the overtures of the Egyptians, and Argantes angrily joins the infidel defenders of the Holy City. Although the Crusaders meet with some initial successes, Argantes is always a formidable opponent.

Satan is annoyed at the prospect of the fall of Jerusalem. He induces Armida, an enchantress, to visit the Christian camp and tell a false story of persecution. Many of the knights succumb to her wiles and eagerly seek permission to redress her wrongs. Godfrey is suspicious of her, but he allows ten knights chosen by lot to accompany her. In the night forty others slip away to join her, and she leads the fifty to her castle, where she changes them into fishes. Their loss is a great blow to Godfrey because the pagans are slaying many of his men.

Rinaldo, one of the Italian knights among the Crusaders, seeks the captaincy of a band of Norwegian adventurers. Gernando, who seeks the same post, quarrels with him, and in a joust Gernando is killed. For this breach of discipline Rinaldo is banished.

When Argantes challenges to personal combat any champion in the Crusaders' camp, Tancred is chosen to meet him. On the way to the fight, Tancred sees Clorinda and stops to admire her. Otho, his companion, takes advantage of his bemusement and rushes in ahead to the battle. Otho is defeated by Argantes and taken prisoner. Then Tancred, realizing what happened, advances to meet the pagan knight. Both men are wounded in the mighty, day-long duel. They retire to recuperate, agreeing to meet again in six days.

When Erminia hears of Tancred's wounds, she puts on Clorinda's armor and goes to his camp to attend him. He hears of her coming and waits impatiently, thinking his beloved Clorinda is approaching. Erminia is surprised by the sentries, and in her maidenly timidity she runs away to take refuge with a shepherd. When the supposed Clorinda does not arrive, Tancred goes in search of her and comes to the castle of Armida, where he is cast into a dungeon. Godfrey receives word that Sweno, prince of Denmark, who was occupying Palestine, was surprised by pagan knights and killed with all his followers. The messenger announces that he is divinely appointed to deliver Sweno's sword to Rinaldo. Although Rinaldo is still absent, Godfrey sets out to avenge the Palestine garrison.

Godfrey and his army fight valiantly, but Argantes and Clorinda are fighters too powerful for the shaken Christians to overcome. Then Tancred and the fifty knights, who were freed from Armida's enchantment, arrive to rout the pagans. Godfrey learns that the missing men were liberated by Rinaldo. Peter the Hermit is then divinely inspired to foretell the glorious future of Rinaldo.

In preparation for the attack on Jerusalem, the Christians celebrate a solemn mass on the Mount of Olives before they begin the assault. Wounded by one of Clorinda's arrows, Godfrey retires from the battle while an angel heals his wound. The Christians set up rams and towers to break the defense of the city.

At night Clorinda comes out of the city walls and sets fire to the great tower by which the Christians are preparing to scale the wall. She is seen, however, by the Crusaders, and Tancred engages her in combat. After he runs his sword through her breast, he discovers to his sorrow that he killed his love. He has time to ask her pardon and baptize her before her death.

Godfrey is taken in a vision to heaven where he talks with Hugh, the former commander of the French forces. Hugh bids him recall Rinaldo, and Godfrey sends two knights to find the banished Italian. On the Fortunate Islands the messengers discovers the Palace of Armida where Rinaldo, now in love with the enchantress, is dallying with his lady love. The sight of the two knights quickly reminds him of his duty. Leaving his love, he joins the besieging forces of Godfrey.

With the arrival of Rinaldo, the Christians are greatly heartened. Then the Archangel Michael appears to Godfrey and shows him the souls of all the Christians who died in the Crusades. With this inspiration, the Crusaders redouble their efforts to capture Jerusalem. The walls of the city are breached. Tancred meets Argantes and kills him in single combat. Finally the victorious invaders storm through the streets and sack the Holy City. When the Egyptians arrive to help the pagan defenders of Jerusalem, they, too, are beaten and their king is slain by Godfrey. Armida, all hope gone, surrenders herself to Rinaldo, who is the most valorous of the

conquerors. After the fighting is over, Godfrey and all his army worship at the Holy Sepulchre.

Critical Evaluation:

Torquato Tasso had two objectives in writing *Jerusalem Delivered*: one religious, to exhort the Christian peoples of Europe to crusade against the heathen; the other literary, to write a new epic fusing the heroic epic and chivalric romance, conforming to classical theory. Different forces operated within him. He was a devout Catholic, product of the Counter-Reformation and of Jesuitical education. He was also the product of court life at Ferrara, a center of chivalry and romantic tradition. Moreover, he was part of literary circles in Ferrara and Paris that were committed to the rules of pre-Christian writers.

Jerusalem Delivered is a Christian epic in its subject matter (the First Crusade), sentiment, and plot. Its poetic focus, however, is on the love stories. It is a new kind of epic, in the classical tradition but replacing pagan mythology with Christian figures and pagan magic with Christian miracle. It intermingles sober fact with invention, imposing classical majesty on chivalric and romantic material. Under the influence of Dante, it is an epic in the vernacular.

The main characters (except for Rinaldo) and events are historically authentic, but Tasso adds fictional episodes in which his imagination can find free expression, especially in the love scenes and battle and single combat scenes. He adds supernatural forces, divine and evil, intervening on behalf of the Christians and pagans.

The miraculous had a special appeal for Tasso, which he found in close relation to real experience. He held the traditional view of magic as the work of devils, but he did not confine it to them. He gave it a new interpretation, linking it to unintelligible human fears and dreads.

The importance of love appears early in the epic in the willingness of Sophronia and Olindo to die for each other. Love, capable of transcending human limitation, gives rise to complex situations: Pagan Erminia is frustrated by her love for the Christian Tancred; Christian Tancred falls in love with another pagan, the Amazon Clorinda. The pagan witch Armida is in love with the Christian Rinaldo, who finally succumbs to her seductions, then renounces her, only to be reconciled as she converts to Christianity.

Tasso's characters are complex. They are convincing human beings but also stern and mighty warriors. They have shortcomings and are differentiated. The ideal lies not in any one character (although Godfrey, with his talents as leader and with his common sense and control, is the closest to the ideal Christian warrior). Godfrey is the one chosen to receive divine help. Tancred is the ideal courtier—courteous, free from envy, patient, a good swordsman, reflective but able to act. Rinaldo is the proud adventurer and romantic. He is restless, quick-tempered, formidable in battle, and supremely honorable. He is finally disciplined to the Christian cause. The pagans are different from those in romances; they are not evil but mostly honorable men and worthy warriors. They are, however, misguided.

The debate over allegory in *Jerusalem Delivered* began almost as soon as it appeared in public. Tasso almost immediately began to comment on his work. In *Allegoria dei poema* (1581), he says that there is allegory in the poem but that the literal might be enough. He later adds that readers may make multiple readings. He also says that he did not think about any allegory at first but that, pondering about it later, realized it was there, but that not all details have allegorical meaning.

The principal allegory relates to the body politic. In the disintegration of the Christian forces in the first half of the epic, and the subsequent taking of control by Godfrey, with divine help (a reflection of Tasso's authoritarian convictions), the allegory is clear. The woods where Tancred and Erminia are lost and the Enchanted Forest produced by the evil Ismeno, protected by demons and exorcised by Rinaldo, are symbols of intellectual error and confusion. The wanderings of the characters and the circuitous reasons of Ismeno reinforce this meaning. Significantly, many episodes take place at night or in darkness. Tancred represents incontinent love, like the historical Tancred that was Tasso's source. He pursues wrong love—Erminia in Clorinda's armor. His wanderings represent false goals.

The Crusade is essentially a war between Good, watched over and aided by God, and Evil, watched over and aided by Satan. The providence of God is displayed by his periodic interventions: He brings about Godfrey's selection as commander of the Christian forces and sends Michael to him with instructions for beginning the Crusade. Periodically He sends one of the angels to advise and even to help in repelling the demons. His agent, Peter the Hermit, plays a key role, too, in inspiring and counseling the Christians. On the other side, Satan sends his demons to aid the pagan army and employs the services of the magician Ismeno and the enchantress Armida to confuse the Christians.

Regeneration and redemption by the miracle of grace are significant themes. Much of the first half of the epic dwells on the disintegration of the Christian forces, their revitalization beginning with the assumption of command by Godfrey. Subsequently the Christians make their arduous passage through dangers, fears, and seductions on their way to victory. Individuals are redeemed. Clorinda, born of Christian parents but a zealous pagan, on dying learns of her Christian roots and is baptized a Christian. Rinaldo, after seduction by Armida, awakens anew to the crusading vision. Even the pagan seductress, Armida, released from her hatred and finding a higher love, is converted and baptized.

Jerusalem Delivered is generally recognized as one of the best Christian epics, and Tasso is generally recognized as the greatest Italian poet of the late Renaissance. The poem is testimony to Tasso's goals, as a part of the Counter-Reformation, of expressing his religious ideas and, as a poet, of composing a poem in the epic form. His reformed idea of Christian heroism is colored by his love of passionate personalities and a pleasure in varied and vivid action—combining seriousness and love of life.

"Critical Evaluation" by Thomas Amherst Perry

Further Reading

Bowra, C. M. "Tasso and the Romance of Christian Chivalry." In *From Virgil to Milton*. New York: Macmillan, 1961. Analyzes the plot elements of *Jerusalem Delivered* to demonstrate how Tasso integrated romance with Christian sentiment. Finds the poem to be the product of the Counter-Reformation and a court life steeped in chivalric tradition.

Cavallo, Jo Ann. *The Romance Epics of Boiardo, Ariosto, and Tasso: From Public Duty to Private Pleasure*. Toronto, Ont.: University of Toronto Press, 2004. An analysis of *Jerusalem Delivered* is included in this history of the Italian Renaissance romance epic. Compares this work to epic poems by Ludovico Ariosto and Matteo Mario Boiardo, who, like Tasso were part of the Este court.

Fichter, Andrew. "Tasso: Romance, Epic, and Christian Epic." In *Poets Historical: Dynastic Epic in the Renaissance*. New Haven, Conn.: Yale University Press, 1982. Suggests that Tasso's purpose was to construct a true Christian epic with the formal properties of the classical epic. The theme of regeneration provides the required unity.

Giametti, A. Bartlett. "Tasso." In *The Earthly Paradise and the Renaissance Epic*. Princeton, N.J.: Princeton University Press, 1966. Summarizes the plot, with special attention to Tasso's sensuous treatment of the lovers. Argues that Tasso attempts to incorporate classical and romantic materials into a Christian point of view.

Greene, Thomas M. "The Counter-Reformation: Tasso." In *The Descent from Heaven*. New Haven, Conn.: Yale University Press, 1963. With frequent quotations from *Jerusalem Delivered*, suggests that this poem is composed of several elements: a framework of history, echoes of earlier poets, lyricism, a feeling for sensuous beauty, the flavor of court life, a formal self-consciousness, the moral climate of the Counter-Reformation, and Platonism.

Looney, Dennis. *Compromising the Classics: Romance Epic Narrative in the Italian Renaissance*. Detroit, Mich.: Wayne State University Press, 1996. Analyzes the "radical neoclassicism" in *Jerusalem Delivered* and in other Italian Renaissance romance epics by Ariosto and Boiardo. Demonstrates how these poets adapted the ro-

mance epic by imitating classic epics as well as pastorals, satires, and other literary genres.

Zatti, Sergio. *The Quest for Epic: From Ariosto to Tasso*. Edited by Dennis Looney, translated by Sally Hill and Looney. Toronto, Ont.: University of Toronto Press, 2006. Zatti, an Italian literary critic, traces the development of the epic poem in the fifteenth and sixteenth centuries. He focuses on *Jerusalem Delivered* and Ariosto's *Orlando Furioso*.

The Jew of Malta

Author: Christopher Marlowe (1564-1593)
First produced: c. 1589; first published, 1633
Type of work: Drama
Type of plot: Tragedy
Time of plot: Fifteenth century
Locale: Malta

Principal characters:
BARABAS, a Jewish merchant
ABIGAIL, his daughter
ITHAMORE, his slave
FERNEZE, the governor of Malta

The Story:

Barabas, a Christian-hating merchant of Malta, receives in his countinghouse a party of merchants who report the arrival of several vessels laden with wealth from the East. At the same time three Jews arrive to announce an important meeting at the senate. The import of the meeting is that the Turkish masters of Malta demand tribute long overdue. The Turkish grand seignior purposely lets the payment lapse over a period of years so that the Maltese will find it impossible to raise the sum demanded. The Maltese have a choice of payment or surrender. The Christian governor of the island, attempting to collect the tribute within a month, decrees that the Jews will have to give over half of their estates or become Christians. All of the Jewish community except Barabas submits to the decree of the governor. The governor seizes all of Barabas's wealth as punishment and has the Jew's house turned into a Christian convent.

Barabas, to avoid complete ruin, purposely fails to report part of his treasure hidden in the foundation of his house. Then he persuades his daughter, Abigail, to pretend that she has converted to Christianity so that she might enter the convent and recover the treasure. Abigail dutifully enters the nunnery as a convert and subsequently throws the bags of money out of the window at night to her waiting father.

Martin Del Bosco, vice-admiral of Spain, sails into the harbor of Malta for the purpose of selling some Turkish

slaves he has aboard his ship. The governor is reluctant to allow the sale because of the difficulties he is having with the grand seignior. Del Bosco, by promising military aid from Spain, persuades the governor to defy the Turks and to permit the sale.

Barabas buys one of the slaves, an Arabian named Ithamore. During the sale, Barabas fawns upon Don Lodowick, the governor's son, and Don Mathias. He invites the two young men to his house and orders Abigail, now returned from the convent, to show favor to both. In his desire for revenge, Barabas arranges with each young man, separately, to marry his daughter. He then sends forged letters to Don Lodowick and Don Mathias and provokes a duel in which the young men are killed. Meanwhile, Barabas trains his slave, Ithamore, to be his aide in his plot against the governor and the Christians of Malta.

As a result of her father's evil intentions, Abigail returns to the convent. Barabas, enraged, sends poisoned porridge to the convent as his gesture of thanks on the Eve of St. Jacques, the patron saint of Malta. All in the convent are poisoned, and Abigail, before she dies, confesses to Friar Jacomo, disclosing to him all that Barabas did and all that he plans to do. When the Turks return to Malta to collect the tribute, the governor defies them and prepares for a siege of the island.

Meanwhile the friars, in violation of canon law, reveal the

information they gained from Abigail's confession. Barabas, again threatened, pretends a desire to become a convert and promises all of his worldly wealth to the friars who will receive him into the Christian faith. The greediness of the friars causes differences to arise among them; Barabas takes advantage of this situation and with the help of Ithamore strangles a friar named Bernardine. He then props up Bernardine's body in such a way that Friar Jacomo knocks it down. Observed in this act, Friar Jacomo is accused of the murder of one of his clerical brothers.

Ithamore meets a strumpet, Bellamira, who, playing upon the slave's pride and viciousness, persuades him to extort money from his master by threatening to expose Barabas. His master, alarmed by threats of blackmail, disguises himself as a French musician, goes to the strumpet's house, and poisons Bellamira and Ithamore with a bouquet of flowers. Before their deaths, they manage to communicate all they know to the governor, who, despite his preoccupation with the fortifications of Malta, throws Barabas into prison. By drinking poppy essence and cold mandrake juice, Barabas fakes death. His body is placed outside the city. Reviving, he joins the Turks and leads them into the city. As a reward for his betraying Malta, Barabas is made governor. He now turns to the conquered Maltese, offering to put the Turks into their hands for a substantial price. The Maltese accept the deal.

Under the direction of Barabas, explosives are set beneath the barracks of the Turkish troops. Then Barabas invites the Turkish leaders to a banquet in the governor's palace, after arranging to have them fall through a false floor into cauldrons of boiling liquid beneath. The Turkish troops are blown sky-high, but the Christian governor, who prefers to seize the Turkish leaders alive, exposes Barabas's scheme. The Jew of Malta perishes in the trap he set for the Turks.

Critical Evaluation:

Barabas dominates *The Jew of Malta*; the other characters are merely sketched. The plot of the play seems to have come wholly from the fertile mind of Christopher Marlowe, whose exotic plots and romantic heroes set a pattern that was followed by subsequent Elizabethan playwrights, including William Shakespeare. *The Jew of Malta* begins well, but it degenerates into an orgy of blood after the second act. Although Marlowe may have found his initial inspiration for the story and its hero in the person of Juan Michesius, recorded in Philippus Lonicerus's *Chronicorum Turcicorum* (1578) and in Sebastian Munster's *La Cosmographie Universelle* (1575), it is clear from a comparison with the aforementioned works that the character of Barabas owes at least as much to the tradition of Italian revenge tragedy, to the En-

glish morality plays, and to Marlowe's own preferences in characterization as demonstrated in *Doctor Faustus* (1588), in *Tamburlaine the Great, Part I* (1587), and in *Tamburlaine the Great, Part II* (1587). Considered the most important English dramatist before Shakespeare, Marlowe was of a social background similar to that of his illustrious successor, although Marlowe's formal schooling was more extensive than Shakespeare's. Marlowe's theatrical career, however, was unfortunately much briefer. Marlowe constructed his greatest plays around characters obsessed with one thing or another; for them, the obsession itself is all-important, not particularly its object. Marlowe has been given credit for raising the formerly stilted and academic English theater to the level of both serious and entertaining art.

Although *The Jew of Malta* is written in Marlowe's most masterful and fully developed style, it remains an enigmatic and difficult play because of the unevenness of its structural impact and emotional effect. Perhaps this is inevitable in the very combination of the morality drama with the drama of personality; it is hard to maintain Barabas as both a typical figure of evil and a sympathetic, understandable person in his own right. T. S. Eliot considered it a farce, characterized by "terribly serious even savage comic humor." What is certain is its thematic resemblance to Marlowe's other great plays. Marlowe's plays share a concern with exploring the limits of human power. In *The Jew of Malta*, a self-made hero rises to power from lowly origins and brings about his own end by an obsessive passion. The play is unified by this hero's personality alone. Moreover, *The Jew of Malta* is Marlowe's first Machiavellian play, the first in which the word "policy" appears. As he speaks at the play's opening, Niccolò Machiavelli embodies in general and final fashion the vices that Barabas's history will reenact: unbounded greed, accompanied by a complete absence of conscience or moral scruples. In many senses, a major theme of the play is amorality rather than immorality—the amorality displayed by the governor as a representative of the political realm or by the friars as representative Catholics, as well as by Barabas himself as a type of the commercial sphere.

The Jew of Malta is critically difficult because of its apparent structural disjunction, as it moves from an emphasis on Barabas's mind and motivations in the first part to a concentration solely upon his evil actions in the second. In the first part, familiar Marlovian themes are presented. Barabas's Machiavellian egocentrism is apparently justified by the hypocrisy of his Christian enemies; the splendor of his wealth is delineated in appropriate mercantile detail. The scene between Barabas and the governor develops the satirical tone, as it seems to contrast the hypocrisy of the Maltese

Christians with the Jew's overt wickedness, their greed with his—an extension of the quarrel between Christians and infidels in *Tamburlaine the Great, Part II.* Barabas nearly captures the sympathies of the audience by making the audience believe that he will suffer from Ferneze's decree; that decree is manifestly unjust.

In the second part, as the play moves from what the noted critic M. C. Bradbrook calls the "technique of verse" to the "technique of action," the audience sees Barabas's subterfuge more clearly; he appears as a completely villainous Machiavellian. Marlowe therefore no longer presents introspective revelations of Barabas's mental and emotional processes but turns instead to concentrate on verbal and narrative reversals in the last three acts. The primary interest becomes clever stage situations and adroit manipulation of the narrative, as, for example, when Barabas constantly reverses his overt meaning by his tagged-on asides. The entrapment of Lodowick and Mathias, of the two friars, of Ithamore and Bellamira, and the final series of double-crosses among Ferneze; Calymath, the son of the grand seignior; and Barabas are obviously influenced by the revenge tragedy tradition. The plot of *The Jew of Malta*, then, is largely episodic, constructed through the "symmetrical pairing" of a series of figures around that of Barabas: the three Jews at the beginning, the abbess and the nun, Mathias and Lodowick, Friar Bernardine and Friar Jacomo, Bellamira and Ithamore, Calymath and Del Bosco.

The focus of the play is Barabas's own character. He is at one and the same time, according to the critic David M. Bevington, the "lifelike Jewish merchant caught in a political feud," an "embodiment of moral vice," and the "unrepenting protagonist in [a] homiletic 'tragedy.'" Once the audience's initial sympathies for Barabas have vanished, the audience sees him only as a heinous culprit who unintentionally fashions his own downfall. The complications of his evil schemes and his ultimate inability to control those around him who, in their own lesser ways, are also evil schemers, are what bring about his downfall. It would be a mistake to consider Barabas as an epitome of a race persecuted by prejudice; he shows, at the very beginning, that he himself has no more respect for Jews than he does for Christians or Turks. Abigail, before entering the convent for the second time, this time in earnest, makes this point when she says, "But I perceive there is no love on earth,/ Pity in Jews, nor piety in Turks." Barabas, instead, proclaims himself "a sound Machiavell," as the prologue predicts, when he instructs Ithamore in the ways of evil: "First, be thou void of these affections,/ Compassion, love, vain hope, and heartless fear." It is supremely ironic that he calls Ithamore his "second self," since in the end Barabas

murders the slave, figuratively revealing the self-destructive bent of his evil. On a larger scale, the same irony pervading the entire play is proclaimed in the absurdly righteous closing words of Ferneze: "So, march away; and let due praise be given/ Neither to Fate nor Fortune, but to Heaven." Heaven has little hand in this story; instead, the hand of the pessimistic atheist Marlowe leaves its prints everywhere.

"Critical Evaluation" by Kenneth John Atchity

Further Reading

Bartels, Emily C. "Malta, the Jew, and the Fictions of Difference: Colonialist Discourse in Marlowe's *The Jew of Malta*." *English Literary Renaissance* 20 (1990): 1-16. An excellent Marxist reading of the text that posits imperialism as the controlling discourse and Malta as the object of the colonizer's lust.

Bowers, Fredson Thayer. *Elizabethan Revenge Tragedy: 1587-1642.* Gloucester, Mass.: P. Smith, 1959. Asserts that Barabas fails as a tragic hero because he avenges a material wrong with murder, because his motives are petty and treacherous, and because his demise is unconnected to his revenge.

Cheney, Patrick, ed. *The Cambridge Companion to Christopher Marlowe.* New York: Cambridge University Press, 2004. Collection of essays, including discussions of Marlowe's life, his place in the twenty-first century, his literary style, gender and sexuality in his work, and his reception and influence. Julia Reinhard Lupton provides an analysis of *The Jew of Malta*.

Deats, Sara Munson, and Robert A. Logan, eds. *Placing the Plays of Christopher Marlowe: Fresh Cultural Contexts.* Burlington, Vt.: Ashgate, 2008. Includes several essays about *The Jew of Malta*, including a discussion of the drama's father-daughter relationship, actor Edmund Kean's performance in the play, and "misbelief and false profession" in the play.

Hopkins, Lisa. *Christopher Marlowe, Renaissance Dramatist.* Edinburgh: Edinburgh University Press, 2008. An introduction to Marlowe's plays, discussing their themes, theatrical contexts, and performance histories from 1587 through 2007; Marlowe's relationship to William Shakespeare; and Marlowe's theatrical achievements. The references to *The Jew of Malta* are listed in the index.

Oz, Avraham, ed. *Marlowe.* New York: Palgrave Macmillan, 2003. Collection of essays about Marlowe's plays, including "Marlowe, Marx, and Anti-Semitism" by Stephen Greenblatt, "'So Neatly Plotted, and so Well Perform'd': Villain as Playwright in Marlowe's *The Jew of*

Malta" by Sara Munson Deats and Lisa S. Starks, and "Economic and Ideological Exchange in Marlowe's *Jew of Malta*" by David H. Thurn.

Rothstein, Eric. "Structure as Meaning in *The Jew of Malta*." *Journal of English and Germanic Philology* 65 (1966):

260-273. Views the play as ironic parody and demonstrates this reading through an analysis of language and action. The play parodies the Bible, the pastoral, the code of friendship, and Catholicism, using Barabas to expose the weaknesses of other characters.

Joe Turner's Come and Gone

Author: August Wilson (1945-2005)
First produced: 1986; first published, 1988
Type of work: Drama
Type of plot: Historical realism
Time of plot: August, 1911
Locale: Pittsburgh, Pennsylvania

Principal characters:
SETH HOLLY, a boardinghouse owner
BERTHA HOLLY, Seth's wife
BYNUM WALKER, boardinghouse tenant and a conjure man
RUTHERFORD SELIG, white traveling salesman known as the People Finder
JEREMY FURLOW, boardinghouse tenant who recently arrived from the South
HERALD LOOMIS, boardinghouse tenant who is searching for his wife
ZONIA LOOMIS, Herald and Martha's daughter
REUBEN MERCER (SCOTT), a boy who lives next door to the boardinghouse
MATTIE CAMPBELL, boardinghouse tenant who is abandoned by her man
MOLLY CUNNINGHAM, boardinghouse tenant
MARTHA (LOOMIS) PENTECOST, Herald Loomis's wife

The Story:

One Saturday morning, Seth Holly is sitting in the kitchen looking out at Bynum, who is performing a ritual of sacrificing pigeons. After Bynum enters the house, so does Rutherford Selig. Bynum asks Selig if he has found the Shiny Man; then, Bynum relates his story of having met a Shiny Man who shared with him the secret of life and of his deceased father, who appeared and showed him how to find his song.

After Selig leaves, four people enter in quick succession: Jeremy, a boarder who has been jailed overnight for vagrancy; Herald Loomis and his daughter, who are seeking a room; and Mattie Campbell, who is looking for Bynum. Each is also searching for something else: Jeremy is looking for a woman to spend time with, Loomis is searching for his wife Martha, and Mattie desires Bynum's assistance so that her man, Jack Carper, will return to her. Bynum tells Loomis that he needs to see Selig, the People Finder; he tells Martha that Jack is not bound to her because their babies died and that someone else is searching for her. Jeremy approaches Mattie, and they decide to spend time together.

Outside, Zonia plays and sings. She meets Reuben and tells him that she and her father are searching for her mother. Reuben tells Zonia that Bynum is a conjure man who buys pigeons from him. The pigeons once belonged to Reuben's friend Eugene, whose dying request was that Reuben set the pigeons free.

The following Saturday morning, Seth talks to his wife about his discomfort with Loomis. Their discussion turns toward Martha Pentecost, a former tenant who is probably Martha Loomis. When Selig returns, Loomis gives him money to find Martha Loomis. Bertha tells Loomis that he has wasted his money, for Selig is not really a people finder; he only finds those whom he himself has taken away.

The next morning, after Jeremy informs Seth that Mattie is going to move in with him, Bynum tries to explain to Jeremy the value of a woman in a man's life. Molly Cunningham comes by the boardinghouse, seeking a room. Jeremy is immediately attracted to her; as a result, he thinks he understands what Bynum has been saying.

That Sunday evening, as all of the boardinghouse residents are present except Loomis, Seth suggests that they dance the juba, an African American call-and-response dance that contains some African residuals. Loomis returns while they are dancing and, hearing the word "Holy Ghost," insists that they stop. During an act of rage and rebellion, he goes into a trance. Speaking in tongues and dancing, Loomis relates that he sees bones rising out of the water. Encouraged by Bynum, he reveals that the bones, which are walking on water, sink, yet when waves wash the bones on shore, they have flesh. The bones people lie on the shore; then, they simultaneously stand. Loomis attempts to stand as well but cannot. Bynum picks up the vision, telling Loomis that the bones people are walking. Bynum coaxes Loomis, but, still unable to stand, Loomis collapses.

The next morning, Seth tells Bertha that Loomis has to leave. When Seth approaches him, Loomis states that he has paid for another week; consequently, he is allowed to remain until Saturday. Having entered the kitchen, Molly and Mattie share their stories of being abandoned by their men. After Mattie leaves for work, Jeremy enters and tells Seth that he has been fired; he and Molly run off together.

Seth and Bynum play dominoes as Bynum sings the blues song "Joe Turner's Come and Gone." Loomis enters and objects to the song. Bynum identifies Loomis as one of Joe Turner's men and tells him that he has forgotten his song. Loomis relates his story of being enslaved by Turner for seven years, being released, and returning home to find his wife gone and his daughter living with his mother-in-law. He has spent four years searching for his wife. Loomis then identifies Bynum as one of the bones people.

The following morning, Bertha, in an effort to comfort Mattie over Jeremy's departure, offers advice about men and love and tells her that her time is coming. When Loomis enters, Mattie asks him about his vision. There is an attraction between them, but when Loomis tries to touch Mattie, he discovers that he cannot.

Reuben and Zonia discuss two supernatural events from the previous evening: The wind spoke to Bynum, and Seth's dead mother, Miss Mabel, appeared to Reuben, reminding him that he promised Eugene to let the pigeons go. The conversation turns to Loomis's search for Zonia's mother so that he can find his place in the world. The two take an interest in each other; they kiss, and Reuben promises to search for Zonia when he grows up.

Zonia and Loomis leave the boardinghouse. A short time later, Martha enters with Selig. Loomis returns and gives Zonia to Martha. When Martha thanks Bynum for finding her child, Loomis becomes angry. Accusing Bynum of bind-

ing him, Loomis brandishes a knife. Bynum explains that he bound the child to her mother and that Loomis has bound himself by not finding his song. Martha interrupts, telling Loomis to look to Jesus. Defiantly, Loomis insists that no one needs to bleed for him; he slashes himself and rubs himself with his blood. Realizing his self-sufficiency, Loomis is finally able to stand. When Loomis turns and leaves, Mattie follows. Bynum calls after him, telling him that he is shining like new money.

Critical Evaluation:

Joe Turner's Come and Gone was the fourth play to be produced in August Wilson's ten-play cycle focusing on the lives of African Americans over the course of the twentieth century. Each play is set in a different decade, and *Joe Turner's Come and Gone* represents the 1910's. In the play, Wilson addresses the cultural and familial loss that resulted from the turn-of-the-century Great Northern Migration, in which many African Americans left the agrarian South and moved to the industrialized North. Considered the most symbolic of the cycle's ten plays and therefore the most difficult to stage, *Joe Turner's Come and Gone* was Wilson's favorite, for it contains all of the important elements of the cycle as a whole.

The final scenes of acts 1 and 2 illustrate Wilson's central theme: the importance of understanding one's cultural and personal past in order to survive the present. When Herald Loomis rejects the juba, the African-influenced dance, because of the mention of the phrase "Holy Ghost," he enters into his own trance-like vision of the bones people. His vision is a summary of the history of Africans Americans; it is a representation of the Middle Passage, the departure of Africans from one shore, the loss in the water of those who did not survive the crossing, and the arrival (rebirth) whole—in the flesh—on another shore. The vision is a representation not only of the Middle Passage but also of slavery and the postbellum forced servitude that many, such as Loomis, endured.

Because Loomis is unwilling to accept his cultural, historical, and personal pasts, he is unable to stand with those who rise and walk at the end of act 1. In the second act, however, Loomis confronts the personal demons of his past by telling his story of being unjustly incarcerated, finding his wife, and realizing the limitations of Christianity in his life. Then, in a ritualistic act that echoes the juba scene, he slashes himself and discovers that he can stand. Coming to terms with his African, African American, and personal pasts, Loomis finds his song—his way of being in the world.

Important to Wilson's concept of African American survival is the forging of the African and the American identity. The work's introduction, titled "The Play," emphasizes that the migrant characters are "newly freed *African* slaves," "foreigners in a strange land," who are seeking to "reconnect." One of their needs is to reconnect with Africa, which involves the merging of the African and the African American. One way this is addressed in the play is through religious traditions.

Loomis's rejection of anything related to Christianity appears to suggest a rejection of the Western Christian tradition; however, many critics have noted that Loomis's actions can be interpreted as the merging of that tradition with African tradition. Loomis rejects the African-inspired juba because of its African American reference to the Holy Ghost; however, like the juba participants, he becomes entranced, and in an African-like state of possession, he has a vision that is reminiscent of Ezekiel's biblical vision of the Valley of Dry Bones. In Loomis's transformation into the Shiny Man, "the One Who Goes Before and Shows the Way," at the play's end are echoes of the biblical John the Baptist. The self-cleansed Loomis, having found the god within, is poised—as Herald—to lead the way for other African Americans to find their way in the New World.

Seeking and finding that which has been lost is a prominent theme in the play. A majority of the characters are seeking to reconnect with someone: Bynum is seeking the Shiny Man; Loomis is seeking Martha; Mattie is seeking Jack Carper; and Jeremy and Molly, who both have lost their spouses, are looking for kindred spirits. A number of these reconnections point to the familial losses caused by the Great Northern Migration; however, one of the overlooked motifs in *Joe Turner's Come and Gone* is family. Although the permanence of the adult male-female relationships remains unresolved, the scene featuring Reuben and Zonia suggests that love, or positive male and female relationships, will be sought and found in the future.

The seeking-and-finding motif also includes the need to reconnect with one's self or one's purpose in life. This search is represented in the play through the motifs of song and storytelling. Bynum's father finds his purpose through the Healing Song. Jeremy plays the guitar yet is without his song. Bynum, through the help of the first Shiny Man and his father, finds his song, his purpose of binding people together (his Binding Song), whereby he ensures that the lost can be found. He, in turn, helps others find their purpose in life, their way in the world, their song. Bynum is the most prominent storyteller in the play; however, it is through Bertha's storytelling that Mattie finds her self. *Joe Turner's Come and*

Gone points to the need for African Americans to acknowledge both their African and their African American cultural and personal pasts by reconnecting with history, African heritage, cultural and religions traditions, others, and self.

Paula C. Barnes

Further Reading

Elam, Harry, Jr. *The Past as Present in the Drama of August Wilson*. Ann Arbor: University of Michigan Press, 2004. *Joe Turner's Come and Gone* is discussed in each chapter of this study; however, particularly insightful is the chapter, "Ogun in Pittsburgh," which addresses Wilson's incorporation of elements of the African spiritual traditions and argues that Herald Loomis is a representation of Ogun, an African god of fire.

Harris, Trudier. "August Wilson's Folk Traditions." In *August Wilson: A Casebook*, edited by Marilyn Elkins. New York: Garland, 1994. An important article for its discussion of Wilson's revision and expansion of African American secular and religious folklore, as well as of his use and inversion of both Christian and Western mythology.

Hay, Samuel A. "*Joe Turner's Come and Gone*." In *August Wilson*, edited by Christopher Bigsby. Cambridge, Mass.: Cambridge University Press, 2007. Argues that one of three influences for the play is the book of Job; draws striking parallels between the lives of Job and Loomis.

Pereira, Kim. "*Joe Turner's Come and Gone*: Seek and Ye Shall Find." In *August Wilson and the African-American Odyssey*. Urbana: University of Illinois Press, 1995. Posits that the blending of the African and Christian cultures is central to the search of each of the play's characters for their selves; examines how the major characters resolve the conflict between African and Christian identity.

Shannon, Sandra D. "Finding One's Song: *Joe Turner's Come and Gone*." In *The Dramatic Vision of August Wilson*. Washington, D.C.: Howard University Press, 1995. Builds from the theme that finding one's song is a metaphor for the search for identity; discusses how the play's adult characters undertake their search within Wilson's African worldview. Included is an insightful discussion of the four female characters.

Wolfe, Peter. "Songs That Bind and Glow." In *August Wilson*. New York: Twayne, 1999. Argues that one of the themes of the play is people needing people by examining various character pairings. Also useful is the discussion of characters' names and how they aid in audiences' understanding.

John Brown's Body

Author: Stephen Vincent Benét (1898-1943)
First published: 1928
Type of work: Poetry
Type of plot: Epic
Time of plot: 1859-1865
Locale: United States

Principal characters:
JOHN BROWN, a rebel leader
JACK ELLYAT, a soldier from Connecticut
CLAY WINGATE, a soldier from Georgia
LUKE BRECKINRIDGE, a Southern mountaineer
MELORA VILAS, Jack's beloved
SALLY DUPRÉ, Clay's fiancé
LUCY WEATHERBY, Sally's rival
SHIPPY, a Union spy
SOPHY, a hotel employee

The Poem:

The muse that is America is made of mountains and deserts, clipped velvet lawns and skyscrapers, buffalo and cowboys. It is also the place to which slave ships come. The captain of one of these ships tells the mate to get the captives on deck while the weather remains good. The mate reports that one of the black men claims to be a king, and the mate worries about losing more of the female slaves. As he walks into the hold with a lantern in his hand, the mate dreams of washing off the stench of the blackness of the ship.

Jack Ellyat, a Connecticut youth, has premonitions of trouble as he walks with his dog in the mellow New England Indian summer. He and his family are abolitionists, in favor of making slavery illegal in the United States. In Ellyat's hometown of Concord, the people feel the influence of writers Ralph Waldo Emerson and Henry David Thoreau as they talk about an ideal state. In Boston, Minister Higginson and Dr. Howe wait for reports of a project planned for Harpers Ferry. In Georgia, young Clay Wingate also receives a premonition of impending disaster and great change.

John Brown thinks he has been chosen by God to free slaves. He leads a force of his own sons, escaped slaves, and free blacks to seize the United States arsenal at Harpers Ferry, Virginia. The first man killed in the fracas is Shepherd Heyward, a free black man. Dangerfield Newby, born a slave, becomes the next to fall. The townspeople later cut off his ears as souvenirs. The bullets continue to fly and men continue to die. As the grievously wounded Oliver Brown, one of John's sons, begs for someone to put him out of his misery, his father tells him to die like a man. Federal troops under Robert E. Lee subdue the Brown party in fifteen minutes; all has ended but the slow, smoldering hatred and the deaths to come.

At Wingate Hall in Georgia, all is peaceful. Sally Dupré and Clay Wingate expect to marry. Meanwhile, Cudjo, the majordomo of the Wingate plantation, hears of the Harpers Ferry raid and of John Brown. He opines that the business of African Americans is not the business of white Americans. In Connecticut, Mrs. Ellyat prays for Brown.

Brown is tried at Charles Town, Virginia. During the trial, he denies the complicity of anyone but himself and his followers in the raid. He insists that he is God's instrument and that he will forfeit his life to further the ends of justice. A legend grows around his name that mushrooms upon his execution. Brown's body rests in its grave, but his spirit haunts the consciences of North and South alike.

There is a surrender of Fort Sumter. Representatives of the Confederate States of America elect gaunt, tired Jefferson Davis as their president. Lank, sad-faced Abraham Lincoln, the frontier wit and small-time politician, is president of the United States of America. He orders men to be drafted to fight. Wingate, loyal to the South, joins the Black Horse Troop and rides to the war as Ellyat marches off with the Connecticut volunteers.

Raw soldiers of North and South meet at the Battle of Bull Run under the direction of Generals McDowell, Johnston, and Beauregard. Congressmen and their ladies arrive from Washington, D.C., to watch the expected Union victory. While they watch, the Union lines break and men flee in panic. A movement to negotiate with the Confederacy for peace begins in the North. Lincoln is alarmed, but he remains steadfast.

Ellyat is discharged from service after Bull Run. Later he joins the Illinois volunteers in Chicago and acquires the nickname Bull Run Jack. Near Pittsburg Landing, in Tennessee, he runs during a surprise attack by the Confederates. He is captured but escapes again during a night march. Hungry and weary, Ellyat arrives at the Vilas farm, where he remains in hiding and falls in love with Melora Vilas. At last, he leaves the farm to seek the courage he had lost near Pittsburg Landing, but not before Melora becomes pregnant by him. He is recaptured soon afterward.

Meanwhile, Wingate returns to Georgia on leave. At Wingate Hall, the war seems far away, for the Confederate ships that successfully run through the Union blockade of Southern ports bring luxuries. Lucy Weatherby, a Virginian whose sweetheart had been killed at Bull Run, attends a dance at Wingate Hall and replaces Sally Dupré in Clay's affections. Spade, a slave on the nearby Zachary plantation who has dreamed of a free life in the North, escapes.

New Orleans is captured by the Union, thereby dealing a heavy blow to the South. Davis and Lincoln begin to bow under the burdens of the war. Union general George McClellan opens his Peninsular campaign while the Confederacy's Robert E. Lee inflicts defeat after defeat on the Army of the Potomac. Ellyat goes to a prison in the Deep South.

The fortunes of the Union sink to their lowest ebb after the Confederate victory at the Second Battle of Bull Run while the spirit of John Brown is generally invoked by editors and preachers. Lincoln issues the Emancipation Proclamation. In the meantime, the escaped slave Spade makes his way north and swims across a river to freedom. When he finally reaches the land of the free, he is railroaded into a labor gang. General McClellan is relieved by General Burnside, who, in turn, is relieved by General Hooker, as commander of the Army of the Potomac. Ellyat, now ill, is returned to the North in an exchange of prisoners of war.

Slowly the Confederacy begins to feel the effects of the blockade and the terrible costs of war. Wingate has thoughts of his next leave—and of Lucy. Ellyat spends the dark winter of 1862-1863 convalescing at his home in the cold Connecticut hills. He is due to report to the Army of the Potomac as soon as his recovery is complete. In Tennessee, Melora gives birth to a baby boy.

Generals Grant and Sherman lead the Union forces to victory in the West; Vicksburg is surrounded. Hunger and anti-inflation riots break out in Richmond, the capital of the Confederacy. America, meanwhile, is expanding. New industries spring up in the North, and the West is being settled. In Richmond, Shippy, a Union spy posing as a peddler, promises Sophy, a servant at the Pollard Hotel, that he will bring her some perfume from the North. Sophy knows that Wingate and Lucy had stayed together in the hotel. Luke Breckinridge, Sophy's rebel suitor, is a member of a patrol that stops Shippy to search him. When they find incriminating papers in his boots, Luke gloats, for he is jealous of Shippy.

Stonewall Jackson dies by the guns of his own pickets, while Lee, desperate for provisions, invades the North. Ellyat

is in the Union army that meets Lee at Gettysburg. He falls wounded during the battle but finds his courage. After three days of bloody fighting at Gettysburg, Lee falls back to Virginia. Then Vicksburg surrenders, splitting the South in two. Nearly defeated, the South continues to fight doggedly. Union general Sheridan marches through the Shenandoah Valley, leaving it bare and burned. Petersburg is besieged. Luke, along with thousands of other rebel troops, deserts the Confederate army. As he heads back toward his home in the mountains, he takes Sophy with him. Melora and her father, John Vilas, travel from place to place in search of Ellyat; they become a legend in both armies. General Sherman captures Atlanta and continues to march on to the sea. During his march, Wingate Hall catches fire accidentally and burns to the ground. Clay Wingate is wounded in a rearguard action in Virginia. The war comes to a close when Lee surrenders to Grant at Appomattox.

The war is over but it will not go away. Spade, no longer hopeful about life in the free North, hires out as a farm laborer in Cumberland County, Pennsylvania. Wingate returns to his ruined home in Georgia, where Sally is waiting. In Connecticut, Ellyat hears stories of strange gypsy travelers who are going from town to town looking for a soldier who was the father of the child of the woman who drives the creaking cart. One day he is standing beneath the crossroads elms when he sees a cart come slowly up the hill. He waits for Melora.

Critical Evaluation:

Stephen Vincent Benét came to national prominence with the publication of *John Brown's Body.* The work remains that for which he is best known. The poem is one of the few American poetic works that reach epic proportions; its length of nearly fifteen thousand lines qualifies it as an epic in the classical sense, and ranks it, in form and purpose, with the great epics of Western literature. Although the poem as a whole is traditional in its classic structure, it is distinctly and uniquely American in its atmosphere, imagery, style, and symbolism.

The work originated during Benét's stay in Paris in the 1920's at a time when the lost generation expressed disillusionment with the United States. Unlike his colleagues, Benét found that his separation from the United States had only deepened his love for his country. With his poem, he aimed to celebrate the American heritage.

The significance of the American Civil War to American history is expressed in various ways in the work. Benét holds a moderate Northern view of the conflict. In the prelude, "The Slaver," Benét emphasizes the economic motives behind slavery but condemns both the South and the North for profiting from human bondage. Benét portrays John Brown as a foolish and reckless man by dwelling on the deaths of two free blacks at the start of Brown's raid on Harpers Ferry. However, Benét also sees Brown as an instrument of history, a stonelike figure who will batter the wall of slavery and change the scheme of things. Brown accomplished nothing while alive, but his moldering body would generate the spirit that destroyed slavery.

Within the poem, Benét describes his work as a cyclorama, a series of large pictures of the United States spread around the reader, who views them from the center. The major unifying element in this cyclorama is the spirit of Brown. His memory grows into the legend that gives hope and inspiration during the dark days of the Civil War.

The second unifying thread in the loosely woven eight books is provided in the characters of Northerner Jack Ellyat and Southerner Clay Wingate. Other minor characters help round out the scheme, whereby all the regions and social groups of a huge nation are represented: Melora Vilas and her father typify the border states and the expanding West; Lucy Weatherby is the Southern coquette; Luke Breckinridge is the independent mountaineer; Jake Diefer is the settled farmer; Spade is the runaway slave; Cudjo is the loyal slave; and Shippy is the Northern spy. By tracing the fortunes of such diverse people, Benét dramatizes not only how the war affects their lives but also how their lives shape the nation.

While Benét does not fully explore the complexities of the Northern family and their way of life, he provides a richer picture of Southern life. The Southern slaves are portrayed in all the complexity, ambiguity, and irony of their situation, though with a touch of racism that undoubtedly reflects the era in which Benét wrote. The Wingates embody the dilemma of the genteel Southern aristocratic family. Benét saw the mind of the South as largely feminine—implied by his choice of heroic couplets for most of the Wingate episodes. The more masculine accents of blank verse and long loose line are employed for the Northern episodes and the narration of the main action.

Benét reveals himself as a master of style in *John Brown's Body*. He demonstrates expert control of blank verse, heroic couplets, and long five- and six-beat lines. The latter lines solve the problem of finding a verse suitable for contemporary speech that bedeviled poets of Benét's era. Benét's diction and imagery also are striking, with sensory detail and rich metaphor. *John Brown's Body* is a great American poem in theme as well as in style. It is not surprising that the poem became a popular success, and that the work remains widely read by Americans.

Revised by Caryn E. Neumann

Further Reading

Capps, Jack L., and C. Robert Kemble. Introduction to *John Brown's Body*, by Stephen Vincent Benét. New York: Holt, Rinehart and Winston, 1968. The editors identify Benét's sources, mark recurring motifs in the poem, identify and annotate the names of persons and places, and identify literary quotations and allusions in the text.

Fenton, Charles A. *Stephen Vincent Benét: The Life and Times of an American Man of Letters, 1898-1943*. 1958. Reprint. Westport, Conn.: Greenwood Press, 1978. Discusses Benét's sources for *John Brown's Body*, his writing habits, and the contemporary critical and popular responses to the poem.

Izzo, David Garrett, and Lincoln Konkle, eds. *Stephen Vincent Benét: Essays on His Life and Work*. Jefferson, N.C.: McFarland, 2003. The first half of the book contains essays about Benét's life, including his son's recollections of the writer and his marriage and friends. The rest of the essays examine Benét's work, including discussions of Benét and the development of American historical poetry and of the novel in the context of the Civil War.

Stroud, Parry E. *Stephen Vincent Benét*. New York: Twayne, 1962. Contains a long chapter praising *John Brown's Body* as an epic poem of historical and philosophical significance. Discusses its clusters of imagery, notably those involving Phaeton and his chariot, stones, and seeds; its contrasting realistic depiction of war and romantic conception of love; and its varied meters—blank verse, versatile long line, and poetic prose.

John Halifax, Gentleman

Author: Dinah Maria Mulock (1826-1887)
First published: 1856
Type of work: Novel
Type of plot: Domestic realism
Time of plot: 1795-1834
Locale: Rural England

Principal characters:
JOHN HALIFAX, one of nature's gentlemen
URSULA, his wife
MURIEL JOY,
GUY,
EDWIN,
WALTER, and
MAUD, their five children
ABEL FLETCHER, John's benefactor
PHINEAS FLETCHER, his disabled son, and the narrator
LORD RAVENEL, a landowner

The Story:

When Phineas Fletcher and his father, Abel, first see John Halifax, they are immediately struck with his honest face and behavior; although the boy is only fourteen years old and an orphan, he will accept help from no one. Instead, he prefers to make his own way, even though it means that he is always half-starved. Phineas is only sixteen years old and is disabled; he would have enjoyed having John for a companion, but Abel Fletcher, a wealthy Quaker, puts the boy to work in his tannery. Although Abel is a Christian and wants to help others, he knows that the boy will be better off if he helps himself. Then, too, there is a class distinction between Phineas and John that even Abel cannot entirely overlook.

Phineas and John become good friends; the orphan is the only friend Phineas ever loves as a brother. John rises rapidly in the tannery because of his honesty and his willingness to work at any job. He also has the ability to handle men, an ability ably proved when a hungry mob tries to burn down the Fletcher home and the mill that the Quaker owns. John arranges to have the workers get wheat for their families, and from then on, they are loyal to him through any crisis.

When they are in their early twenties, Phineas and John take a cottage in the country so that Phineas might have the advantage of the country air. While there, they meet a lovely girl, Ursula March, who took her dying father to the same spot. John is attracted to the modest girl from the beginning, but since she is a lady, he believes that he cannot tell her of his feelings. After the death of her father, it is learned that she is an heiress. She is therefore even more unattainable for John. When Ursula is told of John's feelings for her, however, she, knowing his true character, is happy to marry him. Everyone is shocked but Phineas, and Ursula's kinsman, a dissolute nobleman, refuses to give her her fortune. John will not go to court to claim the fortune as is his legal right as Ursula's husband.

After the death of Abel, Phineas lives with John and Ursula and their children, the oldest of whom, Muriel, is a lovely blind girl. Abel made John a partner in the tannery, but because John does not like the tanyard and it is losing money, he sells it and puts the money into the operation of the mill. Times are often hard during the next few years, but eventually, for political reasons, Ursula's kinsman releases her fortune. After settling a large amount on his wife and children, John uses the rest to lease a new mill and expand his business interests. His hobby is a steam engine to turn the mill, and before long, he begins to be successful. The family moves to a new home in the country and lives many long years there in peace and happiness. John becomes influential in politics, especially in connection with the Reform Bill and the abolition of slavery. He makes powerful enemies, too, but his concern is always for what is right. He becomes a wealthy man during this time, and his family moves to a more opulent home.

The steam engine, built and put into operation, gives John new advantages. Nevertheless, he provides generously for his workmen so that they will not suffer because of the efficiencies of the machine. Then tragedy strikes the family. Shortly after the birth of Maud, their last child, Muriel dies. It is a sorrow from which John never completely recovers. The years bring other troubles. When two of his sons fall in love with the governess of their little sister, they quarrel bitterly and the loser, Guy, leaves home and goes abroad. After two or three years, they learn that Guy nearly killed a man in Paris and fled to America. From that time on, Ursula ages, for Guy is her favorite son.

Shortly afterward, Lord William Ravenel reveals to John that he is in love with Maud. Not only is Lord Ravenel the son of a worldly family, he also leads a useless and sometimes Byronic life. John will not listen to the man's pleas, and Lord Ravenel, agreeing that he is unworthy of Maud, leaves without telling her of his love. John revises his opinion of the man somewhat when, after the death of his father, Lord Ravenel gives up his inherited fortune to pay his father's debts. After this incident, Lord Ravenel is not heard from for many years. Maud does not marry. Her parents know that she never lost her affection for Lord Ravenel, although she does not know that he returned her feelings.

Years pass. The married children give John and Ursula grandchildren. John could have had a seat in Parliament, but he rejects it in favor of others. He continues to do good with his money and power, even when suffering temporary losses. He always longs for his lost blind child, just as Ursula longs for her missing oldest son. Their own love grows even deeper as they reach their twilight years. John often suffers attacks that leave him gasping in pain and breathless, but in order to spare his family any unnecessary worry, he keeps this information from all but Phineas.

Then comes the wonderful news that Guy is coming home. All the family rejoices, Ursula more than any other. They have six anxious months when his ship seems to be lost at sea, but at last Guy arrives. He was shipwrecked but eventually makes his way home. With him is Lord Ravenel. Both men did well in America but lost everything in the shipwreck. This seems of little importance in the happy reunion. John now realizes that Lord William Ravenel proved himself worthy of Maud, and the two lovers are at last allowed to express their love for each other. Guy, too, begins to show interest in a childhood friend, and another wedding in the family seems likely.

John feels that his life is now complete, his peace and happiness being broken only by longing for his dead child. He is soon to join her. One day he sits down to rest, and his family finds him in the peaceful sleep of death. That night, as she sits by her husband's body, Ursula feels that she cannot live without him; later the children and Phineas find her lying dead beside her husband. They are buried side by side in the country churchyard.

Critical Evaluation:

Of the more than twenty novels that Dinah Mulock wrote, *John Halifax, Gentleman*, was by far the most popular, not only during her own lifetime but also well into the twentieth century. Toward the end of that century, critical interest turned to those among her novels that deal with gender issues

from a woman's point of view, among them *Olive* (1850) and *Agatha's Husband* (1853), and to some of her nonfictional work, such as *A Woman's Thoughts about Women* (1858). Mulock herself married late, in 1865; for a period in her early life she was responsible for supporting her family financially after her father, a nonconformist preacher, had been committed as insane.

Some of this personal experience of successful independence permeates *John Halifax, Gentleman*. It was, however, also a period when the British Victorian dream was closest to the American Dream, when people believed that anyone could make it to the top through sheer hard work and good character. Samuel Smiles's best seller, *Self-Help*, appeared a few years after Mulock's novel, in 1859. Both works owe a great deal to Thomas Carlyle, who posited the idea of new meritocracy in the form of a sort of neofeudal industrialism.

The breakdown of the old English class structures is clearly portrayed in *John Halifax, Gentlemen*. Central to this account is the figure of John Halifax, who is orphaned and destitute at the beginning of the novel. His belief that he is already a gentleman never wavers, nor does his life's ambition to manifest this to the world. He first convinces Abel Fletcher, who as a Quaker is already committed to a more democratic worldview. Then he convinces Ursula March, who loves him before she knows he is an apprentice tanner. Her guardian, Richard Brithwood, is never convinced, but he is shown to be part of a degenerate upper class whose claims to being the ruling class are morally bankrupt. His wife, Lady Caroline, is more sympathetic but equally morally bankrupt, and Mulock shows her to be literally destitute at the end. John also stands up to Lord Luxmore, Lady Caroline's father, during a corrupt election. In this episode, Mulock demonstrates her ability to describe both character clashes and socioeconomic ones. William Ravenel's renunciation of his title and estate is a sign of his moral worthiness to become part of the new Halifax family.

The debate on what constitutes a gentleman was conducted in a number of contemporary novels, the one chronologically nearest to Mulock's book being *North and South* (1854-1855) by Elizabeth Gaskell, one of her acquaintances. Gaskell's novel deals with a woman learning to accept a self-made man as an equal. Mulock manages to explicate the man's mind. Charles Dickens deals with the same issue in *Great Expectations* (1860-1861) but in a much less straightforward fashion. Mulock hints in the character of Guy that inherited wealth (or the promise of it) can be corrupting, but she allows him to redeem himself. Dickens portrays much more openly the corruption of wealth not earned through hard work, and in *Hard Times* (1854), he parodies the self-made Josiah Bounderby. In fact, it has been argued that since John's only record of ancestry is that his father was a gentleman, he is merely retrieving a lost rank.

Mulock, like Gaskell and Dickens, defines the term "gentleman" as a Christian man, within the context of a largely undogmatic, uninstitutionalized Christianity. This puts the norm well outside the traditional Church of England "squirearchy."

The case of the rise of a new middle-class meritocracy illustrates well Mulock's very straightforward views and their portrayal. As illustrated by the Reform Act and the emancipation of slaves, progress is coming. Mulock never portrays the evils of industrialism, keeping the setting determinedly pastoral. In fact, one of the stated subtexts to the novel is Phineas Fletcher's own ancestor of the same name, a Caroline poet whose *The Purple Island* (1633) is quoted as the epitome of pastoral idyll. John seeks to capture that idyll at his first rural dwelling, Longfield. As his status in life rises, however, he feels, despite Ursula's objections, that he should move to a grander house.

Mulock never resolves the apparent paradox of the impossibility of the pastoral in a life of increasing wealth, since it is her firm Roman philosophy that wealth brings public duty, and duty comes even before love, let alone pastoral seclusion. That is her moral platform.

John, for no clear reason, refuses political office, in much the same way as Mulock, unlike Mrs. Gaskell, refused political debate. By setting the story one generation back from her own, she is dealing, in fact, with issues that had largely been settled. Her preference is to concentrate on domestic issues, and it is in this that her enduring attraction as a writer lies. Although certain plot sequences are stereotyped and predictable, among them the blind daughter, the child's death, the mother's boy who errs, and the brothers' quarrel, there is nevertheless real observation, resulting in a convincing study of family relationships. The absence of any sort of united family in Mulock's own life may have created a desire in her for a fictional one, but she is realistic enough to know that changelessness, the pastoral dream of *otiosa*, is ultimately impossible. Suffering and unrest always lie lurking, whether for the poor or for the rich.

Indeed, as a result of the narrative viewpoint, that of Phineas, the novel constantly reminds the reader of sickness. Although in his adult years Phineas's poor health is never alluded to, he vowed never to marry so as not to pass on his genetic disease, and this androgynous stance comments ironically at times on the sexual passions that touch the other characters. Phineas is a man of peace, without pretension,

and he mediates Mulock's admiration for strength, action, and heroism, above all in his friend and brother John. He thereby ensures a totally sympathetic narrative account of this ideal Victorian.

"Critical Evaluation" by David Barratt

Further Reading

Altick, Richard D. *The Presence of the Present: Topics of the Day in the Victorian Novel.* Columbus: Ohio State University Press, 1991. Covers a large number of Victorian novelists, showing how they used everyday materials and experiences to satisfy readers' interest in the contemporary scene and ordinary social life. Includes specific discussions of *John Halifax, Gentleman.*

Brantlinger, Patrick. *The Spirit of Reform: British Literature and Politics, 1832-1867.* Cambridge, Mass.: Harvard University Press, 1977. An excellent discussion of the novel in chapter 5, "The Entrepreneurial Ideal," identifies the strengths and weaknesses of Mulock's social idealism. Includes index.

Dennis, Barbara. *The Victorian Novel.* New York: Cambridge University Press, 2000. Designed for students, this book explains the political and social contexts of the Victorian novel, advises how to read these books, and surveys critical approaches to these novels. Includes a brief excerpt from *John Halifax, Gentleman* and assignments for students.

Gilmour, Robin. "Dickens and the Self-Help Idea." In *The Victorians and Social Protest*, edited by John Butt and I. F. Clarke. Newton Abbot, England: David and Charles, 1973. Much of the chapter is a detailed comparison between *Great Expectations* and *John Halifax, Gentleman.* Includes bibliography and index.

_____. *The Idea of the Gentleman in the Victorian Novel.* London: Allen & Unwin, 1981. Gilmour sees *John Halifax, Gentleman* as "the classic novel of self-help . . . in its purest, least critical form." Notes the idea of retrieval of status and the way that John's self-culture is colored by sexual desire and social ambition. Includes index.

Kaplan, Cora. *Victoriana: Histories, Fictions, Criticisms.* Edinburgh: Edinburgh University Press, 2007. Examines the present-day interest in Victorian fiction and culture. Includes a discussion of Mulock's novel *Olive.*

Mitchell, Sally. *Dinah Mulock Craik.* Boston: Twayne, 1983. A useful life-and-works study, with a good section on *John Halifax, Gentleman.* Includes bibliography and index.

Jonathan Wild

Author: Henry Fielding (1707-1754)
First published: 1743, as *The History of the Life of the Late Mr. Jonathan Wild the Great*; revised, 1754
Type of work: Novel
Type of plot: Social satire
Time of plot: Late seventeenth century
Locale: England

Principal characters:
JONATHAN WILD, a "great man"
LAETITIA, his wife
COUNT LA RUSE, a rogue
THOMAS HEARTFREE, a good man
MRS. HEARTFREE, his good wife

The Story:

Jonathan Wild has been prepared by nature to be a "great man." His ancestors were all men of greatness, many of them hanged for thievery or treason. Those who escaped were simply shrewder and more fortunate than the others. Jonathan, however, is to be so "great" as to put his forefathers to shame.

As a boy, he reads about the great villains of history. He learns little at school; his best field of study is picking the pockets of his tutors and fellow students. When he is seventeen years old, his father moves to town, where Jonathan is to put his talents to even better use. There he meets the Count La Ruse, a knave destined to be one of the lesser "greats." La Ruse is in prison for debt, but Jonathan's skill soon secures his friend's freedom. Together they have many profitable ventures, picking the pockets of their friends and of each other. However, neither becomes angry when the other steals from him, for each respects the other's abilities.

For unknown reasons, Jonathan travels in America for seven or eight years. Returning to England, he continues his life of villainy. Since he is to be a truly "great" man, he cannot soil his own hands with too much thievery because there is always the danger of the gallows if he should be apprehended. He gathers about him a handful of lesser thieves who take the risks while he collects most of the booty. La Ruse joins him in many of his schemes, and the two friends continue to steal from each other. This ability to cheat friends shows true "greatness."

Jonathan admires Laetitia Snap, a woman with qualities of "greatness" similar to his own. She is the daughter of his father's friend, and she, too, is skilled in picking pockets and cheating at cards. In addition, she is a lady of wonderfully loose morals. No matter how hard he tries, Jonathan cannot get Laetitia to respond to his passion. The poor fellow does not at first know that each time he approaches her, she is hiding another lover in the closet. Had he known, his admiration would have been even greater.

Jonathan's true "greatness" does not appear until he renews his acquaintance with Mr. Heartfree, a former schoolmate. Heartfree will never be a "great" man because he is a good man. He cheats no one, holds no grudges, and loves his wife and children. These qualities make him the sort of person Jonathan likes to cheat. Heartfree is a jeweler; he becomes moderately prosperous through hard work and honest practices. With the help of La Ruse, Jonathan is able to bring Heartfree to ruin. They steal his jewels and his money and hire thugs to beat him unmercifully, all the time convincing the good man that they are his friends.

La Ruse approaches the greatness of Jonathan by leaving the country after stealing most of their booty. Poor Heartfree is locked up for debt after the two scoundrels ruin him. Then Jonathan performs his greatest act. He also has a strong passion for Mrs. Heartfree, a good and virtuous woman, and he persuades her that her husband asked him to take her and some remaining jewels to Holland until her husband could obtain his release. He talks so cleverly that the woman does not even tell her husband good-bye, although she loves him dearly. Instead, she puts her children in the hands of a faithful servant and accompanies the rogue on a ship leaving England immediately.

When a severe storm arises, Jonathan is sure that death is near. Throwing caution aside, he attacks Mrs. Heartfree. Her screams brings help from the captain. After the storm subsides, the captain puts Jonathan adrift in a small boat. The captain does not know that Jonathan is a "great" man and not destined to die in an ignoble fashion. After a while, he is rescued. He returns to England with tall tales of his adventure, none of which are the least bit true.

In the meantime, Heartfree begins to suspect his friend of duplicity. When Jonathan returns, he is for a time able to persuade Heartfree that he did everything possible to help the jeweler. He tells just enough of the truth to make his story acceptable; for "in greatness," the lie must always contain some truth. Jonathan, however, goes too far. He urges Heartfree to attempt an escape from prison by murdering a few guards. Heartfree sees his supposed friend as the rogue he is and denounces Jonathan in ringing tones. From that time on, Jonathan lives only to bring Heartfree to complete destruction.

While Jonathan is plotting Heartfree's trip to the gallows, Laetitia's father finally gives his consent to his daughter's marriage to the rogue. It takes only two weeks, however, for his passion to be satisfied; then the couple begin to fight and cheat each other constantly.

After his marriage, Jonathan continues in all kinds of knavery. His most earnest efforts are directed toward sending Heartfree to the gallows. At last, he hits upon a perfect plan. He convinces the authorities that Heartfree plotted to have his wife take the jewels out of the country in order to cheat his creditors. Mrs. Heartfree did not return to England. Although Jonathan hopes she is dead, he thinks it better to have her husband hanged at once in case she should somehow return. Before Heartfree's sentence is carried out, however, Jonathan is arrested and put in jail. He is surprised by a visit from Laetitia. She comes only to revile him. She was caught picking pockets and is also a prisoner. Her only wish is that she can have the pleasure of seeing Jonathan hanged before her turn comes to die on the gallows.

On the day that Heartfree is to be hanged, his wife returns. After many adventures and travel in many lands, she comes back in time to tell her story and to save her husband from hanging. She brings with her a precious jewel that was given to her by a savage chief she met on her travels. Heartfree is released, and his family is restored to prosperity. It is otherwise with Jonathan, whose former friends hasten to hurry him to the gallows. On the appointed day he is hanged, leaving this world with a curse for all humanity. His wife and all his friends are hanged, save one. La Ruse is captured in France and broken on the wheel. Jonathan was a "great" man because he was a complete villain.

Critical Evaluation:

Jonathan Wild appeared almost two decades after the real master criminal of that name had been hanged and a year after the fall from power of the corrupt British prime minister Robert Walpole, who was frequently likened to Wild. Henry Fielding did not intend to write another biography of Wild, who was no longer at the forefront of public interest, nor was there any point in reiterating the points of similarity between Wild and Walpole, which had been pointed out by so many others, most unforgettably by Fielding's friend and fellow Tory John Gay in *The Beggar's Opera* (1728). It is true that

shortly before his death Fielding revised his novel, removing a number of references to Walpole. However, even in its original form, *Jonathan Wild* was not primarily an attack on Walpole or on his Whig party, which remained in power after his departure from the government. Instead, Fielding's book is philosophical in nature, an examination of two ways of life, which may be contrasted through the use of one familiar character from the annals of crime and a whole set of characters from the author's imagination. Fielding wanted to show his readers that, whatever their circumstances, they had the power to choose between being "great," and ending in misery, and being "good," which would lead them to happiness or at least to inner peace.

As the full title of the book indicates, Wild represents the first alternative. His hero is Alexander the Great, and he sets himself to become "great." His purpose in life is not only to obtain power over as many people as possible but also to prove to himself that he is superior to everyone else. Thus he cheats the wily count and betrays the members of his gang not merely to enrich himself or even to inspire fear in others, but, more important, to give himself an excuse for admiring his own intelligence.

On the other hand, in keeping with his name, Thomas Heartfree is generous to a fault, giving and forgiving. Honest himself, he expects others to be the same. As a result, as Fielding says, he seems to be the natural victim of "great" men such as Wild, who consider "goodness" to be just another name for "silliness." It is not surprising that Wild and his confederates take advantage of Heartfree. What at first seems more puzzling is Wild's determination to annihilate the inoffensive Heartfree, who on the face of it is a far less worthy opponent than a clever crook such as the count.

However, given the polarity on which Fielding has based his novel, Wild's need to destroy Heartfree is understandable. If indeed human beings are inherently selfish, then Wild is right in his view of the world, and Heartfree is insignificant. However, Wild is threatened by the possibility that another view is correct, that represented by Heartfree. Like many other eighteenth century thinkers, Fielding was an adherent of Anthony Ashley Cooper, the Third Earl of Shaftesbury, who in his *Characteristicks of Men, Manners, Opinions, Times* (1711) argued not only that it is natural for human beings to have "affections" for others but also that people are born with a "moral sense" that enables them to distinguish between right and wrong. Following Shaftesbury, Fielding presents Heartfree as a "natural" man and Wild as an "unnatural" representative of the human species whose interpretation of life is fatally flawed.

Wild's obsession with getting rid of Heartfree, then, is motivated by his need to prove himself "natural" and his own worldview correct. Surely, Wild wants to believe, he will someday find happiness. What he does not realize, however, is that, like Alexander the Great regretting that there were no more worlds to conquer, Wild is enslaved by his own will. Nothing satisfies him. Every trick calls for another, even cleverer; every betrayal accomplished demands the next; and every sexual conquest is fast forgotten in the need for the next. In fact, in his relationships with women, Wild admits his weakness. As he himself is tricked and cheated by the likes of Molly Straddle, he feels more like a slave to his own desires than the master he wills himself to be.

As the novel progresses, it becomes increasingly apparent that even in the public arena, where he seems so successful, Wild is not truly free. He may be able to wrest control over the criminal world from another "great" man, but he cannot overcome the foolish desire to adorn himself, thus alienating his followers. As a result, when society decides that Wild is no longer of more value outside prison than in, there is no shortage of people to betray him. In fact, however, Wild has already been betrayed, both by his own weakness and by his misreading of the world.

Fielding's statement about the antipathy of great men toward "liberty" is thus revealed as doubly ironic. While on one level it reminds readers that Walpole used censorship to drive Fielding and his plays from the stage, the comment has a broader application. While the "great" believe themselves at liberty to do whatever they wish, they do not have the moral independence that Heartfree and his wife experience, even in their darkest hours. Fielding has already proven his point about virtue and happiness, even before he works out a providential happy ending for the Heartfrees and their family.

Admittedly, one can hardly expect total consistency from a writer whose own philosophy was so peculiar a compound of Deism, Christianity, and Platonism and whose own habit of mind was so playfully ironic. Fielding's disquisitions on Fortune, for example, contradict each other. Similarly, it is not clear whether he expects those who are neither villains nor saints, but only half-hearted and easily swayed, to suffer like Wild or to be pardoned by a divinity as generous as Heartfree. What is clear, however, is that in this novel Fielding takes up the weapon that "great" men employ to deceive the world and instead uses language as "good" men do, in the service of virtue and truth.

"Critical Evaluation" by Rosemary M. Canfield Reisman

Further Reading

Battestin, Martin C. *A Henry Fielding Companion*. Westport, Conn.: Greenwood Press, 2000. A comprehensive reference book covering Fielding's life and work. Includes sections on where he lived, his family, literary influences, his works, themes, and characters. Bibliography and index.

Battestin, Martin C., with Ruthe R. Battestin. *Henry Fielding: A Life*. London: Routledge & Kegan Paul, 1989. A standard biography, detailed but highly readable. Includes a chronological bibliography of Fielding's works and letters.

Dircks, Richard J. *Henry Fielding*. Boston: Twayne, 1983. Argues that Fielding's target was not Robert Walpole but what Walpole represented. Includes chronology, notes, and annotated bibliography.

Irwin, William Robert. *The Making of Jonathan Wild: A Study in the Literary Method of Henry Fielding*. Hamden, Conn.: Archon Books, 1966. The first book-length study of the novel and still an important source. Discusses biographical and historical background, ethical import, and genre.

Nokes, David. *"Jonathan Wild."* In *Henry Fielding*, edited by Harold Bloom. New York: Chelsea House, 1987. Comparing the novel to some modern works, Nokes points out subtleties that he feels other critics have overlooked. Interesting introductory comments place the novel in its historical context.

Pagliaro, Harold E. *Henry Fielding: A Literary Life*. New York: St. Martin's Press, 1998. An excellent, updated account of Fielding's life and writings, with chapter 3 devoted to his novels and other prose fiction. Includes bibliographical references and an index.

Paulson, Ronald. *The Life of Henry Fielding: A Critical Biography*. Malden, Mass.: Blackwell, 2000. Paulson examines how Fielding's literary works—novels, plays, and essays—all contained autobiographical elements. Each chapter of the book begins with an annotated chronology of the events of Fielding's life; also includes a bibliography and index.

Rawson, Claude, ed. *The Cambridge Companion to Henry Fielding*. New York: Cambridge University Press, 2007. A collection of essays commissioned for this volume, which includes an examination of Fielding's life, major novels, theatrical career, journalism, Fielding and female authority, and Fielding's style, among other topics. Chapter 5 is devoted to an analysis of *Jonathan Wild*.

_____. *Henry Fielding, 1707-1754: Novelist, Playwright, Journalist, Magistrate—A Double Anniversary Tribute*. Newark: University of Delaware Press, 2008. A collection of essays by Fielding scholars to mark the two-hundred-fiftieth anniversary of his death in 1754 and the tercentenary of his birth in 1707. The essays cover all aspects of Fielding's life and work.

Shesgreen, Sean. *Literary Portraits in the Novels of Henry Fielding*. De Kalb: Northern Illinois University Press,

1972. Shesgreen argues that Fielding reveals character as much through description, both physiological and psychological, as through action and dialogue. Unlike the fully developed characters in his later works, those in *Jonathan Wild* are types, representing extremes in what is intended to be a moral allegory.

Jorrocks' Jaunts and Jollities

Author: Robert Smith Surtees (1803-1864)
First published: 1838
Type of work: Novel
Type of plot: Wit and humor
Time of plot: 1830's
Locale: England and France

Principal characters:
JORROCKS, a grocer and sportsman
MR. STUBBS, a Yorkshireman
THE COUNTESS BENVOLIO

The Story:

When they go out to hunt, the members of Jorrocks' Surrey fox hunt do not always keep their minds on the sport. As they gather, their talk includes shouts to the dogs, quotations on the price of cotton, advice on horses, and warnings of bank policies. While waiting for the dogs to run the fox closer, they all eagerly pull out bread and meat from their roomy pockets.

One morning, a new man joins the veteran Surrey hunters. He is plainly an aristocrat. The others are paunchy and stooped, but he is thin and straight. His handsome mount contrasts sharply with their skinny nags. They all watch him enviously. He is evidently new in Surrey, for he drives his horse at a fast clip through the bottomlands, heedless of the numerous flints. The riders are glad when he retires from the chase with a lame horse.

As he leaves, Jorrocks rushes up with the news that the stranger is no less a personage than a Russian diplomat. The whole hunt joins in heartily wishing him back in Russia for good.

In town, Jorrocks runs into agreeable Mr. Stubbs, a foot-loose Yorkshireman. He invites Stubbs to the hunt on Saturday morning. As long as Jorrocks pays the bills, the Yorkshireman is glad for any entertainment. On the appointed foggy morning, Jorrocks is on time. He is riding his own bony nag and leading a sorry dray horse for his guest. The fog is so thick that they bump into carriages and sidewalk stands right and left. The Yorkshireman would have waited for the fog to lift, but doughty Jorrocks will tolerate no delay.

Mrs. Jorrocks has a fine quarter of lamb for supper, and her husband was sternly ordered to be back at five-thirty sharp. Jorrocks is never late for a meal.

On the way, Jorrocks's horse is nearly speared by a carriage pole. The resourceful hunter promptly dismounts and chatters a bit with a coach driver. When he remounts, he has a great coach lamp tied around his middle. Thus lighted, the two horsemen get safely out of town.

The hunt that day holds an unexpected surprise for both of them. Jorrocks put his horse at a weak spot in a fence to show off a little for his younger friend. He wants to sail over in good time and continue after the fox. Instead, he lands in a cesspool. His bright red coat is covered with slime and mud for the rest of the day. The Yorkshireman, however, notes that Jorrocks carries on until the end of the hunt and gets home in time for his lamb dinner.

As usual, Jorrocks goes hunting in Surrey on a Saturday. When his horse goes lame, he stops at the smith's shop for repairs, and his five-minute delay makes him lose sight of the pack. Consequently, he loses out on a day's sport. As he sits brooding in a local inn and threatening to withdraw his subscription to the Surrey hunt, Nosey Browne enters. Jorrocks is delighted to see his old friend and willingly accepts an invitation to a day's shooting on Browne's estate.

A few days later, he collects the Yorkshireman and sets out eagerly for the shooting. He is saddened to find that Nosey's estate is little more than a cramped spot of ground covered with sheds and other outbuildings. Squire Cheatum, learning that Nosey is bankrupt, forbids his neighbor to hunt in his woods; Jorrocks, therefore, is forced to hunt in the yard behind the sheds. Soon he sees a rabbit. In his excitement, he takes a step forward and shoots the animal. As he is about to pick up his prize, a gamekeeper arrives and accuses him of trespassing. After an extended argument, it is shown that Jorrocks's toe was, at the moment of shooting, over the line on Squire Cheatum's land, and so the wrathful Jorrocks is fined more than one pound.

Jorrocks will not accept calmly a fine that is so obviously unfair. He hires a lawyer and appeals the case to the county court. On the day of the trial, Jorrocks beams as his attorney pictures him as a substantial citizen with a reputation for good works. He squirms as the squire's lawyer describes him as a cockney grocer infringing on the rights of countryfolk. At the end, the judges wake up and sustain the fine.

After the fox hunting season ends, Jorrocks accepts an invitation to a stag hunt. The Yorkshireman comes to breakfast with him on the appointed morning. Jorrocks leads him down into the kitchen, where the maid sets out the usual fare. There are a whole ham, a loaf of bread, and a huge sausage. There are muffins, nine eggs, a pork pie, and kidneys on a spit. Betsy is stationed at the stove, where she deftly places mutton chops on the gridiron.

As the two friends eat, Mrs. Jorrocks comes in with an ominous look on her face. She holds up a card, inscribed with a woman's name and address, that she found in her spouse's pocket. Jorrocks seizes the card, throws it into the fire, and declares that it is an application for a deaf and dumb institute.

The men set out for the hunt in Jorrocks's converted fire wagon. Ahead of them is a van carrying a drowsy doe. They are shocked to learn on arriving that their "stag" is that same tame deer imported for the day. She has to be chased to make her stop grazing on the common. Jorrocks's disappointment is complete when he learns that he was invited only for his contribution to the club fund.

Abandoning the hunt for a while, Jorrocks takes a boat trip to Margate with the Yorkshireman. The expedition is also a failure, for he leaves his clothes on the beach when he goes for a swim and the tide engulfs them. The unhappy grocer is forced to go back to London in hand-me-downs.

Jorrocks, seeing numerous books for sale at fancy prices, determines to write a four-volume work on France that will sell for thirty pounds. With little more ado, he collects the Yorkshireman and sets out for Dover. He is charmed with Boulogne because the French are merry and the weather is sunny. On the coach to Paris, Jorrocks met the Countess Benvolio, as he calls her in cockney fashion. The countess is quite receptive to the rich grocer. She seems to be a beautiful, youthful woman, until she goes to sleep in the coach and her teeth drop down. Once in Paris, Jorrocks is snugly installed as the favored guest in her apartment. He begins to collect information for his book.

The countess is avid for presents, and before long, Jorrocks begins to run short of money. He tries to recoup at the races, but the Frenchmen are too shrewd for him. Finally, he offers to race fifty yards on foot with the Yorkshireman perched on his shoulders, against a fleet French baron who is to run a hundred yards. Jorrocks takes a number of wagers and gives them to the countess to hold. He wins the race easily. He regains his breath and looks about for the countess, but she has disappeared.

With little money and being unable to speak French, the Englishmen take quite some time to return to the countess's apartment. By the time they arrive, a gross Dutchman is installed as her favorite. When Jorrocks tries to collect his wagers, she presents him with a detailed board bill. Pooling his last funds with the Yorkshireman's hoard, he is barely able to pay the bill. Chastened by his sojourn among the French, Jorrocks returns to England.

Critical Evaluation:

Immensely popular with its first readers, *Jorrocks' Jaunts and Jollities* remains a minor classic of British fiction, although overshadowed by the early work of Robert Smith Surtees' more famous contemporary, Charles Dickens. Many critics have noted the similarities between Surtees' sporting novel and Dickens's first masterpiece, *Pickwick Papers* (1836-1837). Unfortunately for Surtees, his younger contemporary went on to become the most celebrated novelist of his day, moving beyond the picaresque tradition that informs these two early works and taking with him a reading public that could not get enough of Dickens's blend of social realism and Victorian sentimentalism. Although he continued to write for several decades after *Jorrocks' Jaunts and Jollities* appeared in 1838, Surtees never again achieved the popular following he enjoyed for this delightful look at the adventures of a goodhearted grocer whose penchant for sport leads him across Britain and to the Continent in search of adventure.

Much of the strength, and many of the weaknesses, associated with *Jorrocks' Jaunts and Jollities* can be traced to the form of its initial publication in *New Sporting* magazine. Forced to relate his tale in a series of vignettes that could stand alone for readers of the periodical, Surtees sometimes sacrifices unity of plotting for the sense of completeness in individual scenes. When the individual stories are read as parts of a single novel, readers find themselves wondering at times about the causal relationships between parts; the sense of the well-plotted novel, central to later works of the nineteenth century (for example, the complexities of publications by Dickens or Thomas Hardy) is noticeably absent. Instead, Surtees is forced to rely on readers' engagement with Jorrocks as the bait that will lure them from one chapter to the next. Fortunately for the author, his sporting hero does have many endearing qualities, and succeeding generations found his adventures humorous and engaging, thus ensuring a continued readership for the work.

The initial publication as a serial work also leads Surtees to repeat incidents, if not verbatim, then certainly by type. Because of the time lapse between the appearance of individual installments, what was funny to readers in one issue could be counted on to appeal to their sense of mirth several months later, and one should not fault the novelist for relying on stock situations for his humor. Reading *Jorrocks' Jaunts and Jollities* as a novel, in a much shorter time than the two years it took to publish the tale in serial form, highlights the weaknesses of plotting and the sense of indirection created by the episodic nature of the story.

The choice of *New Sporting* as the place of publication also had an impact on the story. Readers of that magazine were drawn to it by their love of the sporting life, and Surtees does all he can to fulfill their expectations for fiction that will satisfy their interest and teach them something about sport and travel in a leisurely, genial fashion. Many of the episodes are set within a day's ride of London, and Surtees' descriptions of the various locales in which Jorrocks has his adventures are meticulous. Readers not only could get a good laugh at the exploits of the good-natured grocer-turned-sportsman but also could learn about potential sites for their own sporting exploits.

Jorrocks' Jaunts and Jollities is no mere travelogue or sporting digest, however; despite the limitations placed on him by the form of publication, Surtees uses his story as a means of social commentary. The novel is a gentle satire on topics of special interest to the British public: the sham and duplicity of people who pretend to be something other than what they are; the evils of small-minded populaces such as the one at Newmarket, which receives especially odious treatment by the author; and the inferiority of French life and culture, a topic often held up for ridicule to a reading public already prejudiced against their neighbors across the English Channel.

Surtees' models for *Jorrocks' Jaunts and Jollities* are the great masters of eighteenth century fiction: Henry Fielding, Tobias Smollett, and Laurence Sterne. Like Fielding and Sterne, Surtees is more interested in creating character types

whose adventures are emblematic of larger, universal patterns of behavior. Like them, too, he has a comic view of humanity, seeing humankind as essentially good but susceptible to corruption in a society where excess of any kind may lead one into danger. Like all three of his predecessors, Surtees relies on the importance of incident and the loose episodic structure made popular in picaresque fiction to capture and maintain readers' interest. Although Jorrocks is no rogue, he shares affinities with those rapscallions who move from one adventure to another, escaping through good fortune only to fall victim to another snare from which they will be rescued only through ingenuity or grace. Perhaps the closest parallel exists between *Jorrocks' Jaunts and Jollities* and Sterne's *A Sentimental Journey Through France and Italy* (1768); in that novel, as in Surtees' work, the hero wanders, apparently without aim, through the countryside of his native land and the country across the English Channel, falling victim to men and women intent on drawing personal gain from his misfortune. Like Sterne, Surtees uses the journey motif as a means of calling attention to the evils and follies of people from various walks of life. Through Jorrocks, his opinionated yet lovable mouthpiece, Surtees provides a commentary on the humbugs and hypocrites who stand in the way of happiness for the person of good will.

"Critical Evaluation" by Laurence W. Mazzeno

Further Reading

Cooper, Leonard. *R. S. Surtees*. London: Arthur Baker, 1952. Biographical study of the novelist. Comments on *Jorrocks' Jaunts and Jollities* are interspersed throughout the narrative of Surtees' career; explains the composition process and the relationship of fictional characters and situations to the author's life.

Gash, Norman. *Robert Surtees and Early Victorian Society*. New York: Oxford University Press, 1993. General study of Surtees' ability to dramatize and comment on social situations in the early decades of the nineteenth century. Relates details of *Jorrocks' Jaunts and Jollities* to larger social issues that interested the novelist throughout his career.

Hamilton, Alex. Introduction to *Jorrocks' Jaunts and Jollities*, by Robert Smith Surtees. London: Cassell, 1968. Excellent commentary on the significance of the novel in Surtees' career; also explains how it served as the stimulus for later, similar productions, especially those by Charles Dickens and Anthony Trollope.

Neumann, Bonnie Rayford. *Robert Smith Surtees*. Boston: Twayne, 1978. General introduction to the novelist's career. Includes a scholarly examination of *Jorrocks' Jaunts and Jollities*, focusing on Surtees' development of his title character as a spokesperson for the author's views about society and its values; describes ways in which Surtees distinguishes genuine emotions from hypocrisy and sham.

Welcome, John. *The Sporting World of R. S. Surtees*. New York: Oxford University Press, 1982. General survey of Surtees' career. Comments on the development of characters in *Jorrocks' Jaunts and Jollities* and on the novel's publication history.

Joseph Andrews

Author: Henry Fielding (1707-1754)
First published: 1742, as *The History of the Adventures of Joseph Andrews, and of His Friend Mr. Abraham Adams*
Type of work: Novel
Type of plot: Social realism
Time of plot: Early eighteenth century
Locale: England

Principal characters:
JOSEPH ANDREWS, a footman to Lady Booby
PAMELA ANDREWS, his sister and the wife of Squire Booby
LADY BOOBY, Squire Booby's aunt
FANNY, Joseph's sweetheart
MRS. SLIPSLOP, Lady Booby's maid
PARSON ADAMS, the parson of Booby parish and a friend of Joseph Andrews

The Story:

For ten or eleven years, Joseph Andrews was in the service of Sir Thomas Booby, the uncle of Squire Booby, who was married to the virtuous Pamela, Joseph's sister. When Lord Booby dies, Joseph at first remains in the employ of Lady Booby as her footman. This lady, much older than her twenty-one-year-old servant and apparently little disturbed by her husband's death, is attracted to the pleasant-mannered, handsome young man. Joseph, however, is as virtuous as his famous sister, and when Lady Booby's advances become such that even his innocence can no longer overlook their true nature, he is as firm in resisting her as Pamela was in restraining Squire Booby. The lady is insulted and discharges Joseph on the spot, despite the protests of Mrs. Slipslop, her maid, who is herself attracted to the young man.

With very little money and even fewer prospects, Joseph sets out from London to Somersetshire to see his sweetheart, Fanny, for whose sake he holds firm against Lady Booby's advances. On the first night of his journey, Joseph is attacked by robbers, who steal his money, beat him soundly, and leave him lying naked and half dead in a ditch. A passing coach stops when the passengers hear his cries, and he is taken to a nearby inn.

Joseph is well cared for until the innkeeper's wife discovers that he is penniless. He is recognized, however, by a visitor at the inn, his old tutor and preceptor, Parson Adams, who is on his way to London to sell a collection of his sermons. He pays Joseph's bill out of his own meager savings; then, dis-

covering that in his absentmindedness he forgot to bring the sermons with him, he decides to accompany Joseph back to Somersetshire.

They start out, alternately on foot and on the parson's horse. Fortunately, Mrs. Slipslop overtakes them in a coach on her way to Lady Booby's country place. She accommodates the parson in the coach while Joseph rides the horse. The inn at which they stop next has an innkeeper who gauges his courtesy according to the appearance of his guests. When he insults Joseph, Parson Adams, despite his clerical cassock, challenges the host, and a fistfight follows that extends to a tussle between the host and Mrs. Slipslop. When the battle finally ends, Parson Adams comes off looking the bloodiest, since in her excitement the host doused him with a pail of hog's blood.

The journey continues, this time with Joseph in the coach and the parson on foot, for with typical forgetfulness the good man left his horse behind. Nevertheless, because he walks rapidly and the coach moves slowly, he easily outdistances his friends. While he is resting on his journey, he hears a woman shriek. Running to her rescue, he discovers a young woman being cruelly attacked by a burly fellow. The parson belabors the attacker with such violence that he fells him. As a group of fox hunters rides up, the ruffian rises from the ground and accuses Parson Adams and the woman of being conspirators in an attempt to rob him. The parson and the woman are quickly taken prisoners and led off to the sheriff.

On the way, the parson discovers that the young woman he aided is Fanny. Having heard of Joseph's unhappy dismissal from Lady Booby's service, she was on her way to London to help him when she was so cruelly molested.

After some uncomfortable moments before the judge, the parson is recognized by an onlooker, and both he and Fanny are released. Upon going to the inn where Mrs. Slipslop and Joseph are staying, Joseph and Fanny are overjoyed to see each other. Mrs. Slipslop is displeased to see Joseph's display of affection for another woman and drives off in the coach, leaving Parson Adams and the young lovers behind.

None of the three has any money to pay the bill at the inn. With indomitable optimism, Parson Adams goes to visit the clergyman of the parish to borrow the money, but he is unsuccessful. Finally, a poor peddler at the inn gives them every penny he has, which is just enough to cover the bill. They continue their trip on foot, stopping at another inn where the host is more courteous than any they have met and more understanding about their financial difficulties. Still farther on their journey, they come across a secluded house at which they are asked to stop and rest. Mr. and Mrs. Wilson are a charming couple who give their guests a warm welcome. Mr. Wilson entertains the parson with the story of his life, telling them that in his youth he was attracted by the vanity of London life, squandered his money on foppish clothes, gambling, and drinking, and eventually was imprisoned for debt. He was rescued from this situation by the kindly cousin whom he later married. The two retired from London to this quiet country home. They have two lovely children and their only sorrow, but that a deep one, is that a third child, a boy with a strawberry mark on his shoulder, was stolen by Gypsies and was never heard of again.

After a pleasant visit with the kindly family, the travelers set out again. Their adventures are far from over. Parson Adams suddenly finds himself caught in the middle of a hare hunt, with the hounds inclined to mistake him for the hare. Their master goads on the dogs, but Joseph and the parson are victorious in the battle. They find themselves face-to-face with an angry squire and his followers; but when the squire catches sight of the lovely Fanny, his anger softens, and he invites the three to dine.

Supper is a trying affair for the parson, who is made the butt of many practical jokes. Finally, the three travelers leave the house in great anger and go to an inn. In the middle of the night, some of the squire's men arrive, overcome Joseph and the parson, and abduct Fanny. An old acquaintance of Fanny, Peter Pounce, meets the party of kidnappers, however, and rescues Fanny.

The rest of the journey is relatively uneventful, but when they arrive home further difficulties arise. Joseph and Fanny stay at the parsonage and wait eagerly for their wedding banns to be published. Lady Booby also arrives in the parish, the seat of her summer home. Still in love with Joseph, she exerts every pressure of position and wealth to prevent the marriage. She even has Fanny and Joseph arrested. At this point, however, Squire Booby and his wife Pamela arrive. Booby insists on accepting his wife's relatives as his own, even though they are of a lower station, and Joseph and Fanny are quickly released from custody.

All manner of arguments are presented by Pamela, her husband, and Lady Booby in their attempts to turn Joseph aside from his intention of marrying Fanny. Her lowly birth makes a difference to their minds, now that Pamela made a good match and Joseph was received by the Boobys. Further complications arise when a traveling peddler reveals that Fanny, whose parentage until then was unknown, is the sister of Pamela. Mr. and Mrs. Andrews are summoned at this disclosure, and Mrs. Andrews describes how, while Fanny was still a baby, Gypsies stole the child and left behind them a sickly little boy she brought up as her own. Now it appears that Joseph is the foundling. A strawberry mark on Joseph's chest, however, soon establishes his identity. He is the son of the kindly Wilsons. Both lovers being now secure in their social positions, nothing further can prevent their marriage, which takes place soon afterward to the happiness of all concerned.

Critical Evaluation:

Joseph Andrews has been called the first realistic novel of English literature. Henry Fielding turned aside from the episodic sentimental writing of the age to give an honest picture of the manners and customs of his time and to satirize the foibles and vanities of human nature. In particular, he ridiculed affectation, whether it stemmed from hypocrisy or vanity. Although the structure of the novel is loose and rambling, the realistic settings and the vivid portrayal of English life in the eighteenth century more than compensate for this weakness.

Joseph Andrews is many things: a parody of Samuel Richardson's *Pamela* (1740-1741), a sentimental tale of virtue rewarded; a realistic portrayal of the English road in the eighteenth century; a resetting of the values of comic epic poetry in prose that resulted in what Fielding calls a "comic epic romance," by which he had in mind the model of Miguel de Cervantes' *El ingenioso hidalgo don Quixote de la Mancha* (1605, 1615; *Don Quixote de la Mancha*, 1612-1620); and an experiment in social satire. Fielding blended all these characteristics masterfully.

Fielding, along with Richardson, is sometimes called the

father of the English novel because he ventilated the concept of narrative itself; his brilliant plotting in *Tom Jones* (1749) and the desultory Odyssean travels of Joseph Andrews are contrasting patterns for realizing a broadly imagined action rich in human nature. *Joseph Andrews* is one of the earliest examples of literature's successful extension of mimetic possibilities beyond the models of classical antiquity and folklore. The novel is a mixed genre, being composed of tale, parable, ballad, and epic. The mixture, however, becomes a whole greater than its parts with true innovators such as Fielding.

What holds Fielding's novel together is its cosmic exposure of appearance. Wherever Joseph and Parson Adams go, their naïveté and innocence make them inadvertent exposers of affectation, that most ridiculous form of "appearance" among human beings. Affectation invites derision and must be exposed: The effect is morally healthy but, even more to the point, mimetically revealing. Behind appearance lie the "true springs of human action." The essence of individuals is often better than their appearance, although their vanity may commit them to affectation. Parson Adams is a lovable character mainly because a heart of gold beats under his pedantries and vanities. His naïve trust in human goodness and his unshakable belief in practiced Christianity define the true man: The real Adams is better than his affectations. Similarly, when Joseph is robbed, beaten, and stripped of his clothes, Fielding takes the opportunity to demonstrate the fact that true human charity may emanate from a person whose appearance and life history would seem to mark him incapable of any kindness: "The postilion (a lad who has since been transported for robbing a hen-roost) . . . voluntarily stripped off a greatcoat, his only garment; at the same time swearing a great oath, for which he was rebuked by the passengers, that he would rather ride in his shirt all his life, than suffer a fellow passenger to lie in so miserable a condition."

Fielding trusts in his satiric method—the exposure of affectation and the questioning of appearance—because he senses that it will not ground his comic vision in despair or cynicism. He avoids the satiric manner of Jonathan Swift, whose contempt for human imperfections of character and principle drove him to contempt for human beings in general. Fielding maintains a love of life itself, an essential state of mind for an artist who presumes to epic achievements in the imaginative grasp of social reality. Swift could never have written Fielding's great comic novel *The History of Tom Jones, a Foundling*, with its tolerant but objective picture of human nature. *Joseph Andrews* is a preface, in theme and style, to that more carefully plotted masterpiece.

As tolerant as Fielding is of human nature, he is also capable of making biting judgments. As the critic Walter Allen pointed out, Fielding is not a misanthrope like Swift, but he is a tough-minded moralist who will pass harsh judgment when it is called for. He was, after all, a court judge in real life. Parson Trulliber is a case in point. Fielding has Parson Adams fall into the mud with Trulliber's pigs, but this embarrassment is typical of the many other physical beatings and discomforts that the good parson suffers throughout the novel. They are emblematic of Fielding's mild judgment of Adams's clerical vanity. Once the mud is washed off, the naïve but true Christian in Parson Adams is all the more shiningly revealed. Things are exactly the opposite with Trulliber. His Christianity is completely superficial; Parson Adams's innocent request for fourteen shillings of charity is met by cries of thief. Once Trulliber's false Christianity is exposed, he is all hogs' mud underneath. This is established from the beginning of his encounter with Parson Adams, whom he mistakes for a hog merchant. Trulliber sees and feels with the eyes and temperament of a hog. He is stingy with food as well as money and quick to belligerence like his angry pigs. The only way he can defend himself against Parson Adams's accusation that he is not a good Christian is by clenching his fist. The most telling irony is Trulliber's contempt for Parson Adams's appearance. Because Trulliber's Christianity is all surface, it is he, not Parson Adams, who is dripping in hogs' mud from first to last.

Through the stripping away of affectation and appearance, Fielding pursues the essential humanity in his characters and is so successful that, by the end of the novel, he can indulge in burlesque without dehumanizing. Two chapters from the end, Parson Adams, thinking he is about to rescue Fanny from rape, finds himself wrestling with Slipslop, whom he mistakes for the rapist. Aroused to his mistake by Slipslop's huge bosom and Lady Booby's entrance, he staggers back to what he mistakenly thinks is his own room and lies down beside Fanny. In the morning, Joseph discovers them lying together. Everything is explained, and everyone is appeased. Even Slipslop seems to have enjoyed the "attention" of both the rapist (Beau Didapper) and her attacker, the parson. All of this is pure farce, a broad joke to usher in the warmly comic conclusion of the novel. It is a measure of Fielding's fictive power that he can people a story with characters rich enough to shift from burlesque to comedy without compromising their credibility. In fact, both plot and character seem to benefit from the author's comic exuberance.

"Critical Evaluation" by Peter A. Brier

Further Reading

Battestin, Martin C. *A Henry Fielding Companion*. Westport, Conn.: Greenwood Press, 2000. A comprehensive reference book covering Fielding's life and work. Includes sections on where he lived, his family, literary influences, his works, themes, and characters. Bibliography and index.

_____. *The Moral Basis of Fielding's Art: A Study of "Joseph Andrews."* Middletown, Conn.: Wesleyan University Press, 1959. Battestin examines the corrective nature of satire in the novel. A particularly useful chapter examines the quest theme in relationship to the novel's structure.

Dircks, Richard J. *Henry Fielding*. Boston: Twayne, 1983. Offers a general introduction to the author's life and work. The third chapter, "Experiments in Prose Fiction," includes a detailed discussion of themes, characterization, and structure in *Joseph Andrews*.

Mack, Maynard. "*Joseph Andrews* and *Pamela*." In *Fielding: A Collection of Critical Essays*, edited by Ronald Paulson. Englewood Cliffs, N.J.: Prentice-Hall, 1962. Mack examines Fielding's use of Richardson's novel *Pamela*, which inspired *Joseph Andrews*, noting ways in which Fielding uses the comic mode and his training as a dramatist to create a novel that is far more than a mere parody of *Pamela*.

Pagliaro, Harold E. *Henry Fielding: A Literary Life*. New York: St. Martin's Press, 1998. An excellent, updated account of Fielding's life and writings, with chapter 3 devoted to his novels and other prose fiction. Includes bibliographical references and an index.

Paulson, Ronald. *The Life of Henry Fielding: A Critical Bi-ography*. Malden, Mass.: Blackwell, 2000. Paulson examines how Fielding's literary works—novels, plays, and essays—all contained autobiographical elements. Each chapter of the book begins with an annotated chronology of the events of Fielding's life; also includes a bibliography and index.

Rawson, Claude, ed. *The Cambridge Companion to Henry Fielding*. New York: Cambridge University Press, 2007. A collection of essays commissioned for this volume, which includes an examination of Fielding's life, major novels, theatrical career, journalism, Fielding and female authority, and Fielding's style, among other topics. Chapter 4 is devoted to an analysis of *Joseph Andrews*.

_____. *Henry Fielding, 1707-1754: Novelist, Playwright, Journalist, Magistrate—A Double Anniversary Tribute*. Newark: University of Delaware Press, 2008. A collection of essays by Fielding scholars designed as a tribute to the two-hundred-fiftieth anniversary of his death in 1754 and the tercentenary of his birth in 1707. The essays cover all aspects of Fielding's life and work.

Spilka, Mark. "Comic Resolution in *Joseph Andrews*." In *Henry Fielding: Modern Critical Views*, edited by Harold Bloom. New York: Chelsea House, 1987. Spilka shows how Fielding ties the farcical events at Booby Hall to his themes of vanity and hypocrisy in order to create an artistic whole.

Wright, Andrew. *Henry Fielding: Mask and Feast*. Berkeley: University of California Press, 1966. In three chapters, Wright discusses Fielding's conscious artistry in the narrative of *Joseph Andrews*, the novel's relationship to the epic, and Fielding's use of characterization.

The Journal of a Tour to the Hebrides with Samuel Johnson, LL.D.

Author: James Boswell (1740-1795)
First published: 1785
Type of work: Diary

Principal personages:
JAMES BOSWELL, the author, a young Scottish lawyer
SAMUEL JOHNSON, his aging friend, the great essayist, biographer, poet, and critic
LORD AUCHINLECK, Boswell's father, a noted Scottish judge

In August, 1773, James Boswell finally succeeded in persuading his distinguished friend Samuel Johnson to accompany him on a tour of his native Scotland, a country for which the learned Dr. Johnson's scorn was legendary. Boswell kept a detailed journal for most of their journey together, and he published it, in a version edited and revised with the help of the Shakespearean scholar, Edmund Malone, in 1785, as a companion volume to Johnson's own account, *A Journey to the Western Islands of Scotland*, that had appeared in 1775. Boswell's original journal was discovered with many of his other private papers, giving the modern reader the opportunity to examine a considerably franker account than the one that was first issued to the public.

The Journal of a Tour to the Hebrides is a fascinating travelogue, an unusually full record of life in the Scottish highlands and on the remote islands of the Hebrides, a character sketch of Johnson, and, like Boswell's other diaries, a mirror of his personal idiosyncrasies. Boswell seems especially anxious to show the respect and the deference with which his friend was greeted by his countrymen; he wanted to prove to Johnson and to the world that the Scots were indeed capable of being scholars and gentlemen, closely in touch with the world of learning, and, being a Scot himself, he naturally felt pride in having the privilege of introducing so great a figure to the professors and noblemen of his homeland.

Perhaps the greatest appeal of Boswell's account lies in the absolute naturalness of style and content. Discussion of the quality of the food and of the beds at every inn along the way is interspersed with Johnson's comments on whatever volumes of prayers, sermons, or poems he was able to procure and with accounts of long conversations between the scholar and many of his hosts on religion, philosophy, politics, and literature. As the trip went on, Boswell tended to fall farther and farther behind in his account, and throughout the journal he casually tossed in collections of Johnsoniana after having forgotten the specific occasions of many of the doctor's comments. He chose, too, to stop his narrative at intervals to give geographical and historical details.

Boswell is brutally frank, in his unpublished account, about the character of some of their hosts. He is relatively sympathetic when treating the weakness of Donald MacLeod, a young kinsman of the chief of the MacLeod clan of Dunvegan, on the Isle of Skye, who took their money to town to have it changed and squandered a portion of it on his own refreshment, much to his later chagrin and shame. The arrogance and lack of hospitality of Sir Alexander Macdonald, whose manners seemed to Boswell entirely out of keeping with his station in life, are treated much more harshly. Boswell gives a particularly amusing account of their visit to the duke and duchess of Argyll at Inverary. The duchess refused so much as to acknowledge his presence, because he had opposed her in a celebrated lawsuit, but she and her husband welcomed Johnson cordially.

Johnson appears throughout the journal as a man remarkably willing to adapt to circumstances, however uncomfort-

able they might be; it was Boswell, many years his junior, who was most disturbed by the lack of clean bedding and who was almost overcome by fright when they ran into a storm as they traveled from one island to another in a small boat. Dr. Johnson teased the young daughters of his hosts, flattered and complimented the elderly ladies, and, for the most part, restrained himself from severely attacking those with whose views he differed violently, especially on such questions as the once burning issue of the authenticity of James MacPherson's Ossian poems, published, Johnson thought fraudulently, as translations from the Gaelic.

One of the most delightful episodes in the journal is Boswell's description of Johnson's meeting with Boswell's father, Lord Auchinleck, a staunch Whig and Presbyterian. Johnson was an equally dogmatic Tory, whose sympathies with the Jacobite cause led him to inquire with great interest about the activities of "Bonny Prince Charlie" when he escaped to Skye after the disastrous battle of Culloden; he was so loyal a member of the Church of England that he read his own prayers throughout most of his trip rather than participate in Presbyterian services. Boswell cautioned Johnson to avoid the controversial topics of politics and religion whenever possible, and the encounter of the two men the young lawyer revered most was, for a time, smooth. However, the "collision," as Boswell calls it, finally came. A medal with Oliver Cromwell's portrait on it was the cause, introducing the subject of Charles I and the Tories, with the inevitable results. Boswell discreetly withholds the details of the argument, but he does mention that afterward his father dubbed Johnson "Ursa Major," the great bear. In spite of their altercation, however, the two aging gentlemen apparently parted on terms of mutual respect, if not of friendship, and Boswell appears well-satisfied at having brought them together.

Boswell's portrait of himself in this account is less revealing than that in *Boswell's London Journal 1762-1763* (1950); age had apparently curtailed some of his frankness and unselfconsciousness, but even here, in the original diary, although not in the published version, he describes in some detail his spiritual experiences in several of the old ruins he visited, and he records with chagrin how quickly his resolutions for increased temperance and self-control were overcome by the offer of a fresh bowl of punch. His concern for his wife, whom he left at home in Edinburgh, runs throughout his pages, and he had what proved to be false premonitions of disasters befalling her and their children. His uxoriousness did not, however, curtail his roving eye for the various young ladies he and Johnson met on their travels.

Among the most interesting sections of the book for the modern reader are those that describe in detail the daily life of the heads of the various clans that inhabited the western islands. The civilized manners of the MacLeods of Raasay had made their daughters welcome at fashionable gatherings in Edinburgh and London, yet the lords and their young heirs were acquainted with the most menial tasks involved with the running of their estates. The wide reading of many of the Highlanders, especially of the clergymen, and the education of the young people also surprised the travelers, and Johnson on one occasion presented an arithmetic book to a bright young girl with whose family he lodged. However, the primitiveness of many of the tenants of the great landholders is presented in sharp contrast to the sophistication of their masters.

The Journal of a Tour to the Hebrides, like Boswell's other biographical and autobiographical writings, has had and will continue to have great appeal for readers, primarily for the spirit of life that infuses every page. Servants, obscure clergymen, elderly Scotswomen, and youthful lords come to life vividly as do Boswell and Johnson themselves, and the naturalness of Boswell's style makes his work contemporary and fascinating throughout.

Further Reading

Bate, W. Jackson. *Samuel Johnson*. New York: Harcourt Brace Jovanovich, 1975. Offers an insightful comparison between Johnson's travel account and Boswell's journal. Explains how Boswell's writings constitute a biographical memoir and record of conversation rather than a straightforward narration of events.

Brady, Frank. *James Boswell, the Later Years: 1769-1795*. New York: McGraw-Hill, 1984. Brady's coverage of Boswell's journal is annotated, indexed, thoroughly researched, and enthusiastically written. Examines Boswell's moral and psychological character, with fascinating accounts of his morbid curiosity.

Bronson, B. H. "Johnson, Traveling Companion, in Fancy and Fact." In *Johnson and His Age*, edited by James Engell. Cambridge, Mass.: Harvard University Press, 1984. Reviews the differences between the published version and the actual journal that Boswell kept, which appeared in 1936. Underscores Boswell's efforts to use the journal as a rehearsal for *The Life of Samuel Johnson, LL.D.*, which was published in 1791.

Delaney, Frank. *A Walk to the Western Isles: After Boswell and Johnson*. New York: HarperCollins, 1993. A chronicle of Delaney's journey that retraced the 1773 Scotland trip taken by James Boswell and Samuel Johnson. Contains beautiful photographs and illustrations. Re-creates the time, place, and intellectual environment in which the two scholars cemented their friendship.

LaScelles, Mary. *Notions and Facts: Johnson and Boswell on Their Travels*. Oxford, England: Clarendon Press, 1972. Re-creates Boswell's attempts to capture Johnson's response to unaccustomed circumstances. Reviews the circle of friends and contacts who arranged the tour.

Pittock, Murray. *James Boswell*. Aberdeen, Scotland: AHRC Centre for Irish and Scottish Studies, 2007. A detailed examination of Boswell's published and unpublished works. Pittock demonstrates how Boswell deliberately wrote ambiguously about himself and the major events of his time; he discusses how Boswell's writing was influenced by his sympathies with Catholicism, Scotland, and Jacobitism.

Rogers, Pat. *Johnson and Boswell: The Transit of Caledonia*. New York: Oxford University Press, 1995. Focuses on both Boswell and Johnson's accounts of their trip to the Hebrides. Rogers examines their journey from the perspective of eighteenth century travel writing and places their accounts of the trip within an intellectual, cultural, and literary context.

Turnbull, Gordon. "Generous Attachment: The Politics of Biography in the *Tour of the Hebrides*." In *Modern Critical Views: Dr. Samuel Johnson and James Boswell*, edited by Harold Bloom. New York: Chelsea House, 1986. Examines the political risks that Boswell took in exposing Scotland to Samuel Johnson and in exposing Samuel Johnson to Scotland.

A Journal of the Plague Year

Author: Daniel Defoe (1660-1731)
First published: 1722, as *A Journal of the Plague Year: Being Observations or Memorials of the Most Remarkable Occurrences, as Well Publick as Private, Which Happened in London, During the Last Great Visitation in 1655*
Type of work: Novel

Unlike Daniel Defoe's other books and novels, *A Journal of the Plague Year* is rarely read as a whole, although a number of writers, such as Virginia Woolf, testify to its impact. It is more likely than Defoe's novels, however, to be included in college anthologies of English literature, where its presence is justified as appropriate for reprinting in extracts by its episodic construction and by its historical significance. Both grounds indicate the nature and worth of the whole work. On every page, the book shows more clearly than *Moll Flanders* (1722), or any of the other episodic novels posing as true accounts, the intricate and slow development of the English novel. As the English novel developed, writers moved away from sermons, romances, and polemics and established a formal tradition that continued for some two centuries. Defoe's reputation as the founder of the English novel rests as much on *A Journal of the Plague Year* as it does on *Robinson Crusoe* (1719) or *Roxana* (1724).

The first problem in the development of the novel was to establish a working relationship between fact and fiction. The traditional novel still uses realistic narration to assist readers in the willing suspension of disbelief. Defoe's invention was to use statistics. Tabulated on the pages of *A Journal of the Plague Year* are the weekly death bills or returns from the ninety-seven parishes in the city of London and the sixteen or so in Southwark and outside the city limits. The tables are disposed artfully throughout the work, instead of appearing as appendices, and they are surrounded by further realistic particulars. In a very short time, the reader is in a region of rumor that Defoe first solemnly reports, then rationally dismisses or qualifies. Rumor is the middle ground between statistics and the imagination, and Defoe is careful to allow readers to believe it or not, as they wish. Readers accept such folklore at face value, perhaps, because gossip is more entertaining than truth. The first sentence of *A Journal of the Plague Year*, for example, specifies September, 1664, as the date the narrator first heard the rumor that the plague had come to Holland for the second year running. The first paragraph then expands with rumors about its place of origin: "they say . . . some said . . . others . . . all agreed."

The full title of *A Journal of the Plague Year* contains a bland lie that indicates the second way Defoe encouraged the reader's imagination to work. "Observations or Memorials" sufficiently confuses the distinction between what was recorded at the time and what was remembered later. Defoe's sources, beyond the death bills, were not extensive, and his memories were secondhand. His imagination, however, was fertile. He carefully controlled and encouraged the imagination by the threefold organization of his work. Contrary to the word "journal" in the title, the book is not a daily record. Time references shift from September to August and over the whole summer of the plague. Instead of daily entries, Defoe uses time references, from September, 1664, to December, 1665, as ways of beginning and concluding his narrative, ending with the doggerel quatrain that celebrates the narrator's deliverance. Within the work, he preserves a gradual movement of the plague from the western to the eastern parts of the city, ending with a central holocaust, and scattered throughout the work readers find his tables of statistics. The geographical, the chronological, and the numerical progress of the plague is not followed consistently. The jumps in geography and time make one want to restore logical order to the work and thereby turn it into a literal "journal," at the same time risking loss of its imaginative qualities. Much about the plague's effects and progress is left to the imagination, as the author intends.

Defoe's imagination proceeds mechanically but energetically by considering a general topic and its related topics one at a time. Therefore, readers get several pages of increasingly horrific detail about the practices of nurses, then a catalog of various kinds of quacks, fortune-tellers, prophets, and necromancers who flourished during that awful summer. The section on women in childbirth, for example, coolly divides their tragedies into those who died in childbirth with and without the plague, and the former are further subdivided into those who died before giving birth, or in the middle of giving birth, or before the cord was cut. Defoe's narrator could see little of these matters for himself, but "they say" and "I heard" fill up the paragraphs one after another until all possible contingencies have been covered.

Defoe's imagination works with three classes of corroborative detail: the quick summary, the brief anecdote, and the extended story. The summary paragraph often introduces a series of brief anecdotes but sometimes stands alone, as in his brief recital of the killing of forty thousand dogs and two hundred thousand cats as a precaution against the spread of the plague. There are many brief anecdotes, such as the frequently anthologized account of purifying a purse, that exhibit at once the commonsense caution Defoe admires, the honesty of the Londoner, and the belief that the plague was spread by contaminated air. The longest of the stories, filling about one-tenth of *A Journal of the Plague Year*, is that of the three men and their company who spent the summer camping in Epping Forest. Defoe tells the story at length to show what happened to Londoners who left the city and retired to places where his narrator could not follow them.

Defoe's subject was epic in scope: A great metropolis is slowly strangled by a hidden enemy. The size of his subject gives ample scope for the inclusion of all sorts of material, but his handling of it is typically original. Instead of a heroic poem, readers are presented with the sober account of an average Londoner. The Londoners who stayed in London are the heroes of Defoe's book—those from the Lord Mayor to beggars who did not abandon their city. The narrator is simply identified by the subscription of "H. F." throughout the novel (possibly an allusion to Defoe's uncle, Henry Foe) and is described as a saddler engaged in the American trade. This, like all trade and manufacturing, ended with the onslaught of the plague in June, 1665, and left his narrator free to observe the reactions of his townsfolk.

Defoe's choice of narrator serves to control his material. Presenting the terrible soberly, the narrator offers views on the prevention of the plague. For example, the narrator is critical of shutting up the living with the sick when one plague victim is found in the house. The opinions of the narrator, however, seem contradictory in two respects. The first is purely technical; the saddler recommends shutting up one's house at the beginning of the plague but acknowledges that supplies have to be brought by servants and thus the plague spreads. He shuts up his house and servants but wanders through the streets even to the death pits (he observes that one in his parish of Aldgate holds 1,114 corpses when full); he must wander in order to write his journal. Except for a period of three weeks when he is conscripted as an examiner, he remains an observer and thus uncharacteristic of London's energetic and resource-

ful citizens. The populace's organization is practical, and the narrator lauds the Londoners' community spirit during the plague and bewails its passage as the plague diminishes.

In a second respect, the ambivalence of the narrator is more striking. He lauds common sense and courage where he finds it but looks for the salvation of the city in divine providence during the despair most felt at the end of September, when deaths numbered more than ten thousand weekly. Then, suddenly, the weekly bills showed a dramatic decrease. To whom should go the praise? Defoe is equivocal, in much the same way that he solemnly introduces the scandalous history of Moll Flanders as a moral tract. This ambivalence may be called the true foundation of the English novel, a recital of fictions that rings true.

Further Reading

Backscheider, Paula R. *Daniel Defoe: His Life*. Baltimore: Johns Hopkins University Press, 1989. Scholarly and well-written, this biography is remarkably detailed in every aspect of Defoe's life and career. This refreshing cache of information is a work of history with few forays into literary criticism.

Defoe, Daniel. *A Journal of the Plague Year*. Edited by Paula Backscheider. New York: W. W. Norton, 1992. The definitive modern edition of Defoe's novel.

Flanders, W. Austin. "Defoe's *Journal of the Plague Year* and the Modern Urban Experience." In *Daniel Defoe: A Collection of Critical Essays*, edited by Max Byrd. Englewood Cliffs, N.J.: Prentice-Hall, 1976. Investigates Defoe's concern with the moral challenges that confront the urban dweller. Discusses Defoe's imaginative exploration of those challenges.

Nicholson, Watson. *The Historical Sources of Defoe's "Journal of the Plague Year."* Boston: Stratford, 1919. Reprint. Port Washington, N.Y.: Kennikat Press, 1966. Illustrated by extracts from the original documents in the Burney collection and the manuscript room in the British Museum. Of particular importance are the excerpts from the original sources, which are included. The comparisons of the novel with actual events and the careful examination of the errors found in Defoe's work offer an opportunity to scrutinize aspects of the novel that are often ignored by literary critics.

Novak, Maximillian E. *Daniel Defoe, Master of Fictions: His Life and Ideas*. New York: Oxford University Press, 2001. A biographical study by a leading Defoe scholar that focuses on Defoe's writings. Includes an analysis of *Robinson Crusoe*, *Moll Flanders*, and other novels, as well as discussion of his works in other genres.

Richetti, John J. *Daniel Defoe*. Boston: Twayne, 1987. An excellent introduction to Defoe's life and works. Includes bibliography.

_____. *Life of Daniel Defoe: A Critical Biography*. Malden, Mass.: Blackwell, 2005. A thorough look at Defoe's writing within the context of his life and opinions, including an analysis of his fiction and political and religious journalism. Richetti focuses on Defoe's distinctive literary style.

West, Richard. *Daniel Defoe: The Life and Strange, Surprising Adventures*. New York: Carroll and Graf, 1998. West covers all aspects of Defoe: the journalist, novelist, satirist, newsman, and pamphleteer, as well as the tradesman, soldier, and spy. Written with considerable flair by a journalist and historian of wide-ranging experience.

Zimmerman, Everett. *Defoe and the Novel*. Berkeley: University of California Press, 1975. Chapter 5, "*A Journal of the Plague Year*: Fact and Fiction," is a study of the evolution of Defoe's style and in particular his reaction to the demands entailed in fictionalizing a then-recent historical event.

Journal to Eliza

Author: Laurence Sterne (1713-1768)
First published: 1904
Type of work: Diary

Principal personages:
YORICK, Sterne's alter ego, the writer of the journal
ELIZA DRAPER, the object of his sentimental passion

Laurence Sterne's *Journal to Eliza* has been considered by unsuspecting readers as conclusive evidence that its author was a lachrymose sentimentalist. Yet anyone familiar with *Tristram Shandy* (1759-1767) and *A Sentimental Journey Through France and Italy* (1768) will recognize touches of that humorous view of eighteenth century sentimentalism that makes Sterne's novels so appealing.

Sterne was neither a parodist nor a satirist in the usual sense. He seems, in fact, to have enjoyed dramatizing his emotions on numerous occasions, and he could not have created some of his finest fictional scenes without real sensitivity to nuances of feeling. Nevertheless, an ironic humorist always occupied one corner of his mind, ready to appear at any moment to undercut the effect of a particularly touching episode. He was always aware of the ridiculous aspects of human behavior, and he appropriately adopted the name of one of literature's most famous jesters for his alter ego. It is as Parson Yorick that he sheds copious tears over the departure of his beloved Eliza and, in *A Sentimental Journey Through France and Italy*, invokes her name to protect him from the amorous intrigues that await him at every coach station.

The *Journal to Eliza* is not an easy work to analyze; numerous readers have puzzled over its tone. Is it to be considered an autobiographical document, a purely literary creation, or something between the two? Sterne met Eliza Draper, the wife of an employee of the East India Company, in 1767, the year before his death. Extant letters suggest that he fancied himself in love with her, while she regarded him as a friend but no more. It was not out of character for Sterne to indulge himself in a literary romance that existed primarily in his imagination. Some of the letters he wrote his wife before their marriage are almost identical to the effusions of his journal, and he later addressed other ladies who struck his fancy in similar terms. Whatever his feelings may have been, Sterne was the same man who was composing the brilliantly witty *A Sentimental Journey* during the last months of his life, and it is difficult to believe that he did not perceive the essential absurdity of some of his outpourings of emotion in the *Journal to Eliza*.

Yorick's diary, which is really an extended letter, begins just after Eliza has left for India with her husband. He has promised his "Bramine" that he will record his activities and his feelings every day, and he begins with extravagant protestations of grief at her departure. Few external events find a place in the journal; Yorick visits friends, travels from London to his country home, and, in the latter part of the book, anticipates a visit from his estranged wife and their daughter, but most of the pages are filled with accounts of the parson's illness and the torments of his sorrowing soul.

His laments over a solitary dinner are typical of the ludicrous sentimentality of the work:

I have just been eating my Chicking, sitting over my repast upon it with Tears—a bitter Sause—Eliza! but I could eat it with no other—when Molly spread the Table Cloth, my heart fainted within me—one solitary plate— one knife—one Glass! O Eliza; 'twas painfully distressing. . . .

The disjointed phrases, the apostrophes to the absent lady, the potent emotional effects of everyday objects characterize the style of the entire journal. The work abounds in tears. Yorick weeps over his dinner, over Eliza's picture, over dreams of her; he joins their friend Mrs. James in lamenting his pale, wan countenance, and he sobs with his maid, Molly, who comments emotively on how much Mrs. Draper is missed. Sterne is a master of the language of overwrought emotions, and it is not surprising that some readers have taken him completely seriously.

There are, however, clues along the way that suggest that Yorick's laments are not quite what they seem. It is typical that the writer who filled *Tristram Shandy* with bawdy double entendres should make much of the fact that Yorick's illness, brought on by grief at Eliza's leaving, has been diagnosed as venereal disease. He protests vehemently "'tis impossible, at least to be that, replied I—for I have had no commerce whatever with the Sex—not even with my wife, added I, these 15 years." This is not the kind of comment one expects to find in a truly "sentimental" work. Yorick's apology for bringing up the subject simply enhances the humor of the situation: "'Tis needless to tell Eliza, that nothing but the purest consciousness of Virtue, could have tempted Eliza's friend to have told her this Story—Thou are too good my Eliza to love aught but Virtue—and too discerning not to distinguish the open character, which bears it, from the artful and double one which affects it." Immediately after this statement, Sterne the novelist comes to the fore: "This, by the way, would make no bad anecdote in T. Shandy's Life." Other references to his writing later in the journal provide reassuring intervals of everyday life in the morass of sentiment.

Yorick begins his journal in April, and the entries for that month are long and impassioned. Sterne evidently became less interested in his romance in May; the daily comments are briefer and more perfunctory, although there is an occasional burst of emotion: "Laid sleepless all the night, with thinking of the many dangers and sufferings, my dear Girl! that thou art exposed to—." At the end of the month, Yorick records his journey from London to his country cottage, where he nurses himself, fancies Eliza beside him in every picturesque spot in his garden, and daydreams of a sequence of events that would allow them to marry.

The entries for early June initiate a new autobiographical episode that is the chief focus of the rest of the journal. Yorick receives a letter from his daughter Lydia announcing that she and her mother, who is throughout the book referred to as Mrs. Sterne, will visit him to discuss financial arrangements to enable them to retire to France permanently. The monetary details, discussed at length, are probably fairly accurate, as is the resentment with which Yorick predicts that the ladies will carry off all his household possessions: "In short I shall be pluck'd bare—all but of your Portrait and Snuff Box and your other dear Presents." It is, perhaps, significant of Sterne's state of mind that the entries for the month after the receipt of Lydia's letter are much longer and more emotional than those that preceded it. There is considerable discussion about the happy expression of concern about the forthcoming visit, and one is tempted to speculate that Sterne is using the journal less as a literary game and more as a means of putting his mind at ease. In any case, he seems finally to have grown tired of the project toward the end of the summer. The July entries are fond but increasingly less frequent and, on August 4, Yorick writes that his family is soon to arrive and that their presence will put an end to his diary. A single paragraph, dated November 1, concludes the work. Mrs. Sterne is to retire to France with an annuity of 300 guineas a year, and Yorick is free to think again of Eliza:

But What can I say,—What can I write—But the Yearnings of heart wasted with looking and wishing for thy Return—Return—Return! my dear Eliza! May heaven smooth the Way for thee to send thee safely to us, and joy for Ever.

The *Journal to Eliza* has attracted considerable attention as a biographical document, though it is one of somewhat dubious value, and as a work illustrating eighteenth century sentimental writing. It falls far below *Tristram Shandy* and *A Sentimental Journey*, however, in literary interest; the unceasing protestations of love, grief, and despair inevitably become monotonous, as Sterne himself seems to have discovered. Readers will, however, continue to turn to the journal for the insights it gives into the author's peculiar genius.

Further Reading

Anderson, Howard. "Sterne's Letters: Consciousness and Sympathy." In *The Familiar Letter in the Eighteenth Century*, edited by Howard Anderson, Philip B. Daghlian, and Irvin Ehrenpreis. Lawrence: University of Kansas Press, 1966. While this study focuses primarily on Sterne's letters, Anderson also considers the *Journal to Eliza*, analyzing Sterne's literary style.

Cash, Arthur H. "Eliza: 1766-1767." In *Laurence Sterne: The Later Years*. London: Methuen, 1986. Volume 2 of this two-volume critical biography describes Sterne's love for the married Eliza Draper and interprets his motives for writing the journal. Contains several passages from the work, with biographical details explaining them.

Keymer, Thomas, ed. *The Cambridge Companion to Laurence Sterne*. New York: Cambridge University Press, 2009. Collection of specially commissioned essays analyzing all of Sterne's works and their key issues of sentimentalism, national identity, and gender. Some of the essays consider Sterne's life, milieu, literary career, and his subsequent influence on modernism.

Kraft, Elizabeth. *Laurence Sterne Revisited*. New York: Twayne, 1996. Provides a short biography and then devotes individual chapters to specific works, including *Journal to Eliza*. The final chapter assesses Sterne's changing critical reputation.

Madoff, Mark S. "'They Caught Fire at Each Other': Laurence Sterne's Journal on the Pulse of Sensibility." In *Sensibility in Transformation: Creative Resistance to Sentiment from the Augustans to the Romantics*, edited by Syndy McMillen Conger. Rutherford, N.J.: Fairleigh Dickinson University Press, 1990. Examines Sterne's treatment of the eighteenth century idea of sensibility.

Ross, Ian Campbell. *Laurence Sterne: A Life*. New York: Oxford University Press, 2001. A thorough and well-researched biography. Includes information on Sterne's relationship with Eliza Draper and the circumstances that produced the journal.

Thomson, David. *Wild Excursions: The Life and Fiction of Laurence Sterne*. New York: McGraw-Hill, 1972. Examines how Sterne's life and his relationship with Eliza Draper, evidenced by the *Journal to Eliza*, show him to be a modern figure struggling with good nature, animal appetite, and intellectual detachment. Includes illustrations.

Van Leewen, Eva C. *Sterne's "Journal to Eliza": A Semiological and Linguistic Approach to the Text*. Tübingen, Germany: Narr, 1981. Although some of the material in this study is geared to specialists, there is much for the general reader, and the thorough table of contents makes it easy to select useful sections, such as those on genre.

A Journey to the Centre of the Earth

Author: Jules Verne (1828-1905)
First published: Voyage au centre de la terre, 1864 (English translation, 1872)
Type of work: Novel
Type of plot: Science fiction
Time of plot: May-September, 1863
Locale: Hamburg, Germany; Iceland; an extensive cave system far below the earth's surface

Principal characters:
OTTO LIDENBROCK, a professor of chemistry and mineralogy at the Johanneum college
AXEL, his young nephew, the narrator
GRAÜBEN, the object of Axel's affections
HANS BJELKE, an Icelandic guide
ARNE SAKNUSSEM, a sixteenth century Icelandic alchemist

The Story:

Professor Lidenbrock, a polymathic teacher at the prestigious Johanneum College in Hamburg, purchases a copy of the *Heimskringla* (a record of Icelandic kings) at a second-hand bookstore. In this copy, he finds an encrypted runic manuscript and deciphers the cryptogram, which proves to be the work of a celebrated (fictitious) alchemist, Arne Saknussem. The decrypted text claims that the center of the earth might be reached by means of one of the several craters of the extinct volcano Snaefell in Iceland.

Lidenbrock suggests to his nephew Axel that they should mount an expedition to follow in Saknussem's footsteps and journey to the center of the earth. Axel is initially horrified, but he is persuaded to risk the enterprise by a girl named Graüben, whose affection he craves and who judges that it will make a hero of him. Axel and his uncle then set sail for Reykjavik, eager to get there by the first of July, when the angle of the sun's rays will indicate the correct crater.

After conferring with local scholars, Lidenbrock hires a taciturn guide, Hans Bjelke, and assembles an extensive collection of scientific instruments. The members of the party then make their way to Snaefell, where a sign specified by Saknussem's manuscript informs them into which crater they must descend. As they do so, they make various geological observations, but the expedition seems doomed to failure when they run out of water. They are saved when they find a hot spring, the downward course of which they begin to follow.

Eventually, the expeditionaries reach a series of caves beneath the Atlantic Ocean, at a depth previously believed to be the lower limit of the earth's crust; instead of encountering the molten rock of the mantle, however, the travelers follow the mazy series of galleries down to an interior sea illuminated by a wan light produced by some kind of natural electrical phenomenon. On the shore of this sea, they find a fungal forest and other vegetable relics of Earth's Secondary Epoch. They improvise a raft and set sail upon the sea, witnessing a contest between a plesiosaur and an ichthyosaur in the water.

By mid-August, the three travelers calculate that they are somewhere beneath England. Their raft is wrecked by an electrical storm, and they find further relics of eras that are long past on the earth's surface, including a giant humanoid skull. Soon afterward, they glimpse a living giant tending a herd of mastodons. The travelers repair their raft, but when they try to blast their way through a rocky obstruction they provoke a major seismic disturbance and are nearly killed. Instead of dying, however, they are borne hectically upward by a flood of water and eventually expelled from the Italian volcano Stromboli. From there, they make their way home.

Critical Evaluation:

English-language readers of *A Journey to the Centre of the Earth* initially contended with extremely corrupt translations of the work. The first such translation was published in the United Kingdom in 1871 by Griffith and Farren and reprinted by numerous American publishers from 1877 onward. A much better translation was serialized in the *Philadelphia Evening Telegraph* in 1874, but the 1877 publishers chose the earlier, corrupt version. This version substituted "Jack" and "Professor Hardwigg" for the names of the two main characters and distorted the text out of all recognition, to the extent of improvising melodramatic incidents absent from Jules Verne's text and entirely out of keeping with his project. Several other variants appeared subsequently on both sides of the Atlantic, most of them abridged but not otherwise corrupted; the best and fullest translation was made by William Butcher for the Oxford University Press edition of 1992.

Meanwhile, the second French edition of the text, issued in 1867, was revised and expanded from the original. Much of the scientific information contained in the first edition was borrowed, sometimes almost verbatim, from Louis Figuier's

La Terre avant le déluge (1863; *The World Before the Deluge*, 1866), but Figuier issued a new edition of his book in 1867 that took account of recent developments and controversies in paleontology occasioned by discoveries of ancient human bones and artifacts by Jacques Boucher de Perthes and by the work of the English geologist Charles Lyell. Whereas the first edition of Figuier's book had located the origins of humankind in the Garden of Eden, the second substituted an evolutionary account in which primitive humans equipped with stone tools lived alongside mammals that had since become extinct; this led Verne to add the scene involving the giant humanoid herdsman to his novel.

Figuier, who was later to edit *La Science illustrée*—a popular science magazine that also featured a good deal of early science fiction—made no objection to Verne's borrowings and seems to have been delighted that his popularizing work was being reproduced and amplified. However, a plagiarism suit was launched against the first edition of Verne's novel by Léon Delmas, who had published a story about a subterranean descent provoked by a cryptogram in the September, 1863, issue of *La Revue contemporaine*; the suit was eventually abandoned.

A Journey to the Centre of the Earth was the second volume of what eventually became an extended series of *voyages extraordinaires* (extraordinary voyages) penned by Verne and published by P.-J. Hetzel, who had put him under contract to produce approximately a quarter of a million words per year to be published in a new periodical, *Le Magasin d'education et de récréation*, and subsequently in handsome illustrated volumes. The serials and books produced in consequence of this contract—which endured throughout his career—made Verne internationally famous. *A Journey to the Centre of the Earth* was the first novel in the series to win considerable popular and critical success; an advance copy sent by Hetzel to George Sand inspired her to write a hollow earth story of her own, *Laura: Voyage dans le cristal* (1864; *Journey Within the Crystal*, 1992; also as *Laura: A Journey into the Crystal*, 2004), in which Earth is imagined as a gargantuan geode filled with crystals.

A Journey to the Centre of the Earth was one of the most imaginatively adventurous of the *voyages extraordinaires*, to the extent that it qualifies as an early venture into proto-science-fiction. The notion of survivals from prehistoric eras continuing to thrive in protected enclaves was to be reemployed many times, although Verne's use of it is a trifle half-hearted and he was careful to leave open the possibility that some of these images were hallucinatory. The idea that the earth might be hollow was by no means original to Verne, however, having been suggested several times before, most notably by the astronomer Edmond Halley, and featured in numerous previous literary texts.

The geological and paleontological discoveries made by Professor Lidenbrock in the course of his descent through the earth's strata were as firmly based in the science of the day as Louis Figuier could contrive, but that science made a considerable leap between 1863 and 1867, and the amended account was, inevitably, to be far surpassed in later years. For that reason, the text's scientific content has become an artifact of mainly historical interest, but the narrative remains a zestful tale of unprecedented adventure and retains all its readability. In the context of the history of imaginative literature, the novel is uniquely important for the earnest determination with which it depicts the methodical process of observation and deduction undertaken by the professor with the aid of then-modern scientific instruments. Scientific inquisitiveness, served by ingenious technology and logical expertise, is located at the heart of the endeavor, although Verne was wise to choose a relatively naïve character, ever-ready to receive enlightenment from his older and wiser uncle, to perform the narrative function of standing in for readers.

Because Hetzel had made his reputation publishing collections of books and periodicals for children—although his new magazine was not as restricted in its intended appeal as his earlier ventures had been—the fact that *A Journey to the Centre of the Earth* employed a youthful narrator encouraged the notion that it ought to be seen as a children's book; its early translations were certainly marketed in that fashion in Britain and America. Verne did not intend it to be a children's book, however, and he certainly made no attempt to tailor the tenor of his didactic discourse to younger readers. Although some of his translators did that in his stead, in a more-or-less brutal fashion, the fuller and better translations give a much better idea of the extent of the author's research, the scope of his speculations, and the originality of his literary method.

There had never been a book like *A Journey to the Centre of the Earth*, and although Verne followed it with a handful of other adventure stories of similar boldness, he seems to have been strongly advised by Hetzel to restrain his imagination and stay within more mundane and easily comprehensible bounds. Most of his imitators, who established "extraordinary voyages" as a prolific late-nineteenth century subgenre, adopted the same restricted method, and it was not until the twentieth century emergence of the new genres of scientific romance and science fiction—which gladly claimed Verne as a significant ancestor and *A Journey to the Centre of the Earth* as one of their most important exemplars—that the true significance of the novel began to be fully appreciated. It

can now be seen not merely as a foundation stone of modern science fiction but also as a work whose determination to import robust scientific speculation and disciplined scientific method into a vivid adventure story, with a considerable degree of literary elegance, was rarely matched in the next hundred years.

Brian Stableford

Further Reading

Butcher, William. *Verne's Journey to the Center of the Self: Space and Time in the Voyages Extraordinaires.* New York: Macmillan, 1990. An elaborate account of Verne's work that makes much of the exemplary quality of *A Journey to the Centre of the Earth*—as might be expected from one of the novel's more responsible translators.

Evans, Arthur B. *Jules Verne Rediscovered: Didacticism and the Scientific Novel.* Westport, Conn.: Greenwood Press, 1988. Comprehensive study of Verne's proto-science-fiction works, relating them to the burgeoning field of the popularization of science, which progressed faster and more elaborately in France than anywhere else.

_____, ed. "A Jules Verne Centenary." *Science Fiction Studies* 32, part 1 (March, 2005): 1-176. A collection of essays and a roundtable discussion summarizing the current state of Verne scholarship, including a useful annotated bibliography of translations of the author's work and a commentary on the various kinds of distortion contained therein, both by Evans.

Evans, I. O. *Jules Verne and His Work.* London: Arco, 1965. A succinct critical biography, of particular interest because its author was the editor of the very extensive "Fitzroy Edition" of Verne's works, issued by Arco, which included many previously untranslated works that Evans himself rendered into English.

Fitting, Peter, ed. *Subterranean Worlds: A Critical Anthology.* Middletown, Conn.: Wesleyan University Press, 2004. Although it contains samples of text from the relevant works, this is more a history of its theme than an anthology and is very scrupulous in that regard. Chapter 12 deals specifically with *A Journey to the Centre of the Earth*, but the book is valuable for its provision of a literary context for the novel and some discussion of its influence.

Unwin, Timothy A. *Jules Verne: Journeys in Writing.* Liverpool, England: Liverpool University Press, 2005. Considers Verne to be an important contributor to the "nineteenth-century experimental novel"; offers a useful account of the sources from which Verne obtained the scientific information contained in the novel.

Journey to the End of the Night

Author: Louis-Ferdinand Céline (1894-1961)
First published: Voyage au bout de la nuit, 1932
   (English translation, 1934)
Type of work: Novel
Type of plot: Naturalism
Time of plot: World War I and after
Locale: France, Africa, and the United States

Principal characters:
FERDINAND BARDAMU, a rogue
LÉON, his friend
MADELON, a woman engaged to Léon

The Story:

Ferdinand, an indifferent student of medicine in Paris, is anarchistic in his reaction to authority and emphatically pacifistic. Immediately prior to World War I, he is expounding his cynical disregard for nationalistic pride in a café. Down the street comes a colonel at the head of a military band. The music and the uniforms capture Ferdinand's fancy, and in spite of his declarations he rushes off to enlist. During the fighting he is a runner, constantly exposed to scenes of savage brutality and to great danger on his errands. On one mission he meets Léon.

When Ferdinand suffers a slight wound in his arm, he is given convalescent leave in Paris. There he meets Lola, an American Red Cross worker who idolizes the French. She romanticizes his wound, becomes his temporary mistress, and fills him with stories of the United States. When she comes to think of Ferdinand as a coward and a cynic, she leaves him.

The thought of losing Lola is more than Ferdinand can bear. When his mind gives way, he is sent to a variety of mental hospitals, where he quickly learns to ingratiate himself with the psychiatrists by agreeing with everything they say. His tactics at last procure his release as cured but unfit for active duty.

In Paris, he leads a precarious life, but he betters his existence by acting as a go-between for Musyne, a dancer who is greatly sought after by rich Argentine meat dealers. The thought of all that beef to be sold at high prices is too much for Ferdinand, and after some months with Musyne, he leaves for colonial Africa. During the voyage, he becomes the scapegoat of the passengers but flatters them shamelessly to avoid being flung overboard.

In French West Africa, he is assigned to a trading post far in the interior. He makes the ten-day trip by canoe into the hot, lush jungle, where his trading post turns out to be a shack anchored by two big rocks. The mysterious trader he comes to relieve is, frankly, a thief, who tells Ferdinand that he has no goods left to trade, very little rubber, and only canned stew for provisions. The rascal gives Ferdinand three hundred francs, saying it is all he has, and leaves in the direction of a Spanish colony. Only after he leaves does Ferdinand realize that his predecessor was Léon.

After several weeks of fever and canned stew, Ferdinand leaves the trading post, which he accidentally burns, and his only baggage is the three hundred francs and some canned stew. His overland safari is a nightmare. His fever rises dangerously high, and during much of the trip he is delirious. His porters steal his money and leave him with a Spanish priest in a seaport. The priest, for a fee, delivers him to a captain of easy scruples. Ferdinand, still sick, is shanghaied on a ship bound for the United States.

When he attempts to jump ship in New York, he is caught by the immigration authorities. Pretending to be an expert on flea classification, he is put to work in a quarantine station catching and sorting fleas for the Port of New York. After gaining the confidence of his chief, he gets sent into the city to deliver a report, although technically he is still under detention. In New York, he looks up Lola, now older but still attractive, who gives him a hundred dollars to get rid of him. With the money he takes a train to Detroit. Soon he is employed by the Ford Motor Company.

In Dearborn he falls in love with Molly, who lives in a brothel. Each day, he escorts her to the bordello in the early evening. Then he rides streetcars until she is through for the night. On one of his nightly trips, he meets Léon again. Léon is unhappy in America because he cannot learn enough English to get along. He has to be content with a janitor's job. Ferdinand learns that Léon also wishes to return to France.

Although he loves Molly very much, Ferdinand leaves her and Detroit to go back to Paris. Completing his medical course, he is certified as a doctor, and he settles down to practice in a poor neighborhood. His patients rarely pay him. Mostly he is called for abortion cases.

One day, the Henrouilles summon him to attend the old grandmother who lives in a hut behind their house. They hate to spend the money necessary to feed the old woman, and

Madame Henrouille offers Ferdinand a thousand francs if he will certify that the grandmother is insane. Through conscience or fear, Ferdinand refuses. Then Léon is called on the same case. He agrees to set a bomb next to the old woman's hut so that she will kill herself when she opens the door. Clumsy Léon bungles the job; he accidentally detonates the bomb and loses his sight.

With the help of the Abbé Protiste, the family works out a scheme to get rid of the old woman and Léon. They propose to send the two to Toulouse, where there is a display of mummies. Léon will be a ticket seller and old Madame Henrouille will be the guide. For persuading Léon to accept the proposition, Ferdinand receives a thousand francs.

Ferdinand's practice grows smaller. At last, he goes to the Montmartre section of Paris, where for a time he is pleased with his job as supernumerary in a music hall. The Abbé Protiste looks him up after some months and offers to pay his expenses to Toulouse, where Ferdinand is to see if Léon is likely to make trouble for the Henrouilles on the score of attempted murder.

In Toulouse, Ferdinand learns that Léon is regaining his sight. He also is engaged to Madelon. The old lady is a vigorous and successful guide. Ferdinand dallies a little with the complaisant Madelon but decides to leave before their intimacy is discovered. Old Madame Henrouille falls, or is tripped, on the stairs and is killed. It is a good time for Ferdinand to leave—hurriedly.

Dr. Baryton runs a genteel madhouse. By great good luck Ferdinand is hired on his staff. He ingratiates himself with his employer by giving him English lessons. Dr. Baryton reads Thomas Macaulay's *History of England from the Accession of James II* (1849-1861) and becomes so enamored of English things that he departs for foreign lands and leaves Ferdinand in charge. Shortly afterward, Léon shows up, broke and jobless. He ran away from Madelon. Ferdinand takes him in and gives him a job.

Madelon comes looking for Léon and haunts the hospital gate. Hoping to appease her, Ferdinand arranges a Sunday party to visit a carnival. In the party are Léon, Madelon, Ferdinand, and Sophie, Ferdinand's favorite nurse. After a hectic day they take a taxi home. On the way Léon declares he no longer loves Madelon. The spurned woman takes out her revolver and kills him. Ferdinand knows that it is time for him to move on once more.

Critical Evaluation:

"His real self as you saw it in a war," says the narrator and antihero of this novel, of another of its characters. This phrase is central to a long, rambling, and rather improbable account of one man's life during and after World War I. The narrator, Ferdinand Bardamu, has a life out of a picaresque novel. He goes from one scrape to another, his narrow escapes as often as not taking him from the frying pan into the fire. By the same token, by using his wits, he sometimes is blessed with good luck. Chance and luck rule this novel and, by implication, the world.

Bardamu may often be confused and stunned in the many crises of his life, but in the telling of them, he is never at a loss. He is a man who has reflected intensely upon his experiences and has come to these conclusions regarding them. Readers may not like these conclusions—Bardamu is an incurable cynic—but readers can recognize, enjoy, and even honor them. Actually, Bardamu is less cynic than misanthrope, and one recalls the provocative definition of a misanthrope as someone who thinks too well of people. Bardamu has been deeply wounded in his idealism. One day, he is marching off to glory, awash in patriotic fervor; the next, he finds himself in the thick of horrendous war. What makes this betrayal all the more bitter is that he knew better even before he joined up. Having found that his sardonic armor does not protect him from a passing fit of patriotism, Bardamu has two choices: to allow emotions to deafen the voice of calculation or to redouble his efforts to guard against unpleasant surprises. The novel shows Bardamu, in the second mode, surrounded by people rendered dangerous by the first. The presence of one lone fleck of humanity in a sea of madness is not without its comic aspect.

In the slaughter of World War I, many notions of proper conduct perished. Louis-Ferdinand Céline was among the first to announce this staggering change of heart, and he found a generation ready to listen to it. This novel's immediate success testifies to its currency, and its continuing appeal speaks of Céline's genius. Bardamu is crippled, emotionally and spiritually, by the war, but the resolution and the alacrity with which he continues to show what he learned about survival inspire as well as entertain. He lies, he cheats, he steals, but there is an inevitability about his every act. No one else is any better; he is not born rich; and he is of military age when the war breaks out. To Céline, the blame needs to be placed squarely where it belongs: on society, or humanity as a species, but certainly not upon the shoulders of an individual.

Bardamu has a way of interspersing his narrative with lectures on the meaning of the latest episode. He seems to be telling his story in order to help readers realize the way things really are. There is no way out, no exit from the insanity. It is appropriate that Bardamu finds employment in a mental hospital. His journey may take him to the end of night, but it cannot carry him beyond. Metaphorically, night is always falling, and nightmares always loom. There is no dawn for humanity that is not false. Bardamu's only light is the light of the truth, always present even as one or another character is lying.

While being absolutely in tune with its times, *Journey to the End of the Night* also has a place in tradition. Literature has many other works of war and bitter disillusionment. Unfriendly critics of Céline object to the hatefulness of his characters and the narrowness of his vision, but, within the limitations he set himself, he works as a master.

"Critical Evaluation" by David Bromige

Further Reading

Bouchard, Norma. *Céline, Gadda, Beckett: Experimental Writings of the 1930's*. Gainsville: University Press of Florida, 2000. Maintains that works by Céline, Carlo Emilio Gadda, and Samuel Beckett have stylistic characteristics that would later be associated with postmodernism, such as a changed relationship to language, a burlesque worldview, and a "decentered" narrative.

Hewitt, Nicholas. *The Life of Céline: A Critical Biography*. Malden, Mass.: Blackwell, 1999. Provides analysis of Céline's life and work and places both within the context of French cultural, social, and political history. Includes bibliographical references and an index.

Knapp, Bettina. *Céline, Man of Hate*. Tuscaloosa: University of Alabama Press, 1974. Discusses hate in Céline's works. Presents a fuller and more complex Céline than one might expect from this book's title.

Ostrovaky, Erika. *Céline and His Vision*. New York: New York University Press, 1967. Uses Céline's pronouncements and speculations on the art of the novel to elucidate his work. Attempts to pull his various books together into a unified reading. Explores Céline's treatment of death in *Journey to the End of the Night*, noting how death is disparaged and how the author distinguishes among kinds of dying.

Quinn, Tom. *The Traumatic Memory of the Great War, 1914-1918, in Louis-Ferdinand Céline's "Voyage au bout de la nuit."* Lewiston, N.Y.: Edwin Mellen Press, 2005. Examines how Céline's traumatic experiences in and memories of World War I helped shape the novel.

Scullion, Rosemarie, Philip H. Solomon, Thomas C. Spear, eds. *Céline and the Politics of Difference*. Hanover, N.H.: University Press of New England, 1995. Collection of eleven essays examining Céline's life and work, including "The (Con)Quest of the Other in *Voyage au bout de la nuit*" by Jennifer Forrest.

Solomon, Philip H. *Understanding Céline*. Columbia: University of South Carolina Press, 1992. Examines the central themes and structures of Céline's novels, focusing on the self-reflective nature of his work. The first chapter is a general overview of his writings, with subsequent chapters focusing on the novels and a final chapter on his poetry, pamphlets, and plays. Includes a biography, chronology, bibliography, and index.

Thiher, A. *Céline: The Novel as Delirium*. New Brunswick, N.J.: Rutgers University Press, 1972. Points out how often people suffer from fevers in Céline's works and the feverish nature of his prose. Discusses the sense of matter disintegrating that pervades *Journey to the End of the Night*.

Thomas, Merlin. *Louis-Ferdinand Céline*. New York: New Directions, 1980. Places Céline in his historical period and discusses his books in relation to his life. Argues that *Journey to the End of the Night* not only concerns death but also survival.

Vitoux, Frederic. *Céline: A Biography*. Translated by Jesse Browner. 2d ed. New York: Marlowe, 1995. A thorough biography based on new information, including unpublished letters and documents and the first interviews to be conducted with Celine's widow. Vitoux is unapologetic but fair in his account of Céline's anti-Semitism and other unattractive aspects of the writer's personality.

The Journey to the West

Author: Wu Chengen (c. 1500-c. 1582)
First published: Xiyou ji, 1592 (abridged English translation, *Monkey,* 1942; English translation, 1977-1983)
Type of work: Novel
Type of plot: Fantasy
Time of plot: Seventh century
Locale: Realms of the gods

Principal characters:
MONKEY, a monster with miraculous powers
THE BUDDHA, the founder of Buddhism and Lord of the Western Paradise
KUAN-YIN, a Bodhisattva (commonly known as the Goddess of Mercy)
HSÜAN TSANG or TRIPITAKA, a Chinese Buddhist priest
T'AI TSUNG, the great Chinese emperor of the T'ang Dynasty
PIGSY and SANDY, monsters and Tripitaka's disciples

The Story:

In the beginning there is a rock. The rock gives birth to a stone egg, and the egg develops into the shape of a monkey. The monkey becomes alive and plays with other monkeys. He is made their king.

One day, troubled by the thought of death, he bids farewell to the monkey tribe and sets out on a journey to seek immortality. He becomes a pupil of the Patriarch Subodhi, from whom he learns seventy-two transformations and the cloud trapeze. When he shows off his newly learned magic of transformation by changing into a pine tree, this public display of magic enrages his master, who disowns him. Monkey goes back to his cave, but now he does not have to travel over mountains and rivers. One leap carries him head over heels for 108,000 leagues.

He kills the demon who molested his "little ones" during his absence. He gets the magic iron staff from the Sea Treasury of the Dragon King. The weapon can shrink, at his will, to the size of an embroidery needle. Despite all of these powers, however, his allotted life span of 342 years comes to an end. In a dream he is taken to the Land of Darkness. Furiously, he crosses out his name in the Registers of Death, together with whatever names of other monkeys he can find.

His meddling at the Palace of the Dragon King and the Court of Death is reported to the Jade Emperor. Monkey is summoned to Heaven so that he can be constantly watched. At first he is happy to have an appointment from the emperor, but upon learning how humble his position as groom in the heavenly stables really is, he returns to his monkeys.

As a rebel, he calls himself "Great Sage, Equal of Heaven," and he defeats the heavenly hosts sent off to arrest him. The Jade Emperor consents to appoint him to the rank he wishes. Then he crashes the Peach Banquet, to which he was not invited. By the joint effort of the gods he is caught and imprisoned in the crucible of Lao Tzu, where for forty-nine days he is burned with alchemical fire before he escapes. It seems that nothing can stop him until the Buddha comes to help the heavenly powers. Monkey is placed under a five-peaked mountain, originally the five fingers of the Buddha's hand, where he is to serve his penance.

The Buddha wishes that some believer from sinful China would come to the Western Continent to fetch the True Scriptures. Kuan-yin volunteers to help someone accomplish this. The someone is Hsüan Tsang. His father, a young scholar, was murdered while on his way to take up his duties as governor of Chiang-chou. The murderer, a ferryman, assumes the dead man's name and takes his wife and office. The wife would have committed suicide were it not for her unborn child. Immediately after the boy is born, she ties him to a plank with a letter written in blood tucked to his breast and pushes the plank into the river. The child is picked up by the abbot of a temple, who learns the tragic story of the boy's birth from the blood letter.

Hsüan Tsang is brought up as a monk. He does not know of his parentage until he is eighteen years old; then he meets his mother and makes plans to avenge his father. The false governor is executed, on the spot where he committed his evil deed. Suddenly a body comes floating up through the water. It is Hsüan Tsang's father, whom everyone thought dead but who was saved by the Dragon King of the River. Thus the family is reunited. Hsüan Tsang chooses to remain a monk.

Emperor T'ai Tsung of T'ang makes a visit to the World of Darkness. He promises to celebrate a great mass for the salvation of the hungry ghosts, and Hsüan Tsang is chosen to preside over the ceremonies. Kuan-yin, appearing in the disguise of a ragged priest, interrupts the service by pointing out that there are Three Baskets (or Tripitaka) of Mahayana scriptures for a pilgrim to bring from India. Then she reveals herself in her glory and vanishes. Hsüan Tsang volunteers to undertake the quest in spite of the length and perils of the journey. His request is granted, and he is given a new name, Tripitaka.

He passes several dangers before he arrives at the mountain where Monkey was imprisoned for five hundred years, waiting for the man who, according to Kuan-yin, will release him and whom he is to follow, to protect, and to obey as his master. When Tripitaka says a prayer, the seal of the prison is lifted into the air, and Monkey is freed.

Three other monsters receive similar instructions from Kuan-yin to wait for the priest of T'ang at three different places. They do not know what the man looks like, so they have to be defeated in battle before they can be convinced to join the pilgrimage. A young dragon devours Tripitaka's horse, but, learning his mistake, he allows himself to be changed into a horse to serve the priest. Pigsy, a banished marshal of the heavenly hosts, now reincarnated in the shape of a pig, is driven away from his human wife and father-in-law. The last to join is Sandy, a man-eating monster with red hair and a blue face, also a banished heavenly marshal.

Monkey and Pigsy sometimes create trouble. Pigsy is cowardly, lazy, self-indulgent, clumsily shrewd, and jealous of the much more powerful Monkey. Nevertheless, he seems to be Tripitaka's favorite. The brilliant Monkey cannot be a paragon of obedience, and on several occasions, he quarrels with his master. The priest, however, needs only to say a certain spell, and the fillet on the monkey's head begins to hurt him by becoming tighter. He was tricked into wearing the cap with the fillet, and now he cannot take it off. This is the only control Tripitaka, with Kuan-yin's help, holds over the unruly Monkey.

The travelers pass the kingdom of Crow-cock, where a Lion Demon murdered the king and, disguised as the monarch, usurped the throne. The ghost of the dead king asks help from Tripitaka. After the king is fished up from a well and miraculously revived, the usurper is forced to flee. He turns out to be the gelded lion in the service of the Bodhisattva Manjusri. The travelers also come to Cart-slow Kingdom, where Taoists are the privileged class and Buddhists are persecuted. Monkey challenges three Taoist magicians, who won the full confidence of the king, to a contest of miracles. The first magician cannot recover his head, chopped off in the contest, and he falls dead, leaving the corpse of a headless tiger. The second magician is found to be only a white deer, now dead, since he is not able to close his ripped-open belly. The third is fried to death in boiling oil, leaving in the cauldron the bones of a ram. Monkey survives every one of the ordeals.

Monkey and Pigsy change into a boy and a girl for the Great King of Miracles, who demands annual human sacrifice. Although the monster proves no match for Tripitaka's disciples, he captures the priest and brings him down to the River That Leads to Heaven. There the monster, caught at last in Kuan-Yin's basket, turns out to be a golden fish. A big turtle carries Tripitaka across the river. The turtle was perfecting himself for more than one thousand years, but he is worried because he cannot yet achieve human form. Tripitaka promises to ask the Buddha about the turtle's wish.

The travelers finally arrive in the Blessed Region of the Buddha, find the scriptures, and begin to carry them to China. Tripitaka, however, forgets to ask about the turtle's prospects. Annoyed, the turtle makes a dive, leaving the pilgrims, who are riding on his back to recross the river, and the scriptures in the water. The pilgrims are all saved, but a part of the scriptures is lost. This is the "eighty-first calamity."

Carried back to paradise after completing their mission, Tripitaka and Monkey are both made Buddhas, and Pigsy is promoted to be Cleanser of the Altar. Sandy, Golden-Bodied Arhat, and the white horse, who also aided Tripitaka, are set among the eight senior Heavenly Dragons. Buddhism prospers in China.

Critical Evaluation:

The Journey to the West was inspired by the pilgrimage of the Chinese priest Hsüan Tsang to India in the seventh century. Except for the priest and a few other historical personages, the novel is fantastic, with the whole mythical universe as its background. It is interpreted as a satire, with the rebellious monkey against the bureaucratic heavenly government, and as an allegory, what Westerners might consider a Buddhist version of John Bunyan's Christian adventure tale, *The Pilgrim's Progress* (1678, 1684). For centuries, however, the Chinese—adults and children alike—have loved this absurd story of monsters simply because of its imagination, humor, and delightful nonsense. Arthur Waley translated thirty out of the original one hundred chapters, omitting many of the calamities the pilgrim and his disciples encounter. The story before the start of the pilgrimage is preserved almost in its entirety, and this alone makes interesting reading.

Wu Chengen was a sixteenth century magistrate as well as a novelist. Starting his hundred-chapter novel with Monkey's birth in the creation myth, Wu Chengen has made him a divine hero on an unflinching quest for immortality, to which the subsequent pilgrimage is but the final chapter. Waley used *Monkey* as the title of his partial yet witty translation of the book. The novel represents the "dual modes of myth and comedy." Most fully developed myths in the novel have some relation to the story of Monkey, and these include the creation, the quest for immortality, the journey to the underworld, the fall from grace, the divine mercy, the mission, the redeeming pilgrimage, and the apotheosis.

Nevertheless, Monkey is not the only hero in the pilgrimage. He and Pigsy are a pair of complementary characters. When Monkey is alone, his adventures are not as interesting as those in which Pigsy joins him. In addition, the five pilgrims almost achieve a harmony of personalities among themselves after reaching the Crow-cock Kingdom. On their way they are transformed from isolated victims of fate into united victors in faith. In the Cart-slow Kingdom, they not only help themselves but they also become the destined saviors of suffering people.

This harmony of personalities among the pilgrims is vitally related not only to character development but also to the union of the dual modes of myth and comedy in the novel. The characters of Monkey and Pigsy, for example, gradually balance each other, while in the plot, Pigsy often provides a comic relief to temper Monkey's mythic adventures. The pilgrims' quest in the physical world is also a quest within their personalities. As the quest continues, the relations among them become more and more harmonious. It is chiefly through the harmony of their personalities that they at last attain their goal.

In Monkey's fearless quest for immortality, his determination almost becomes a kind of destiny. In his heroic striving, he reaches a height of spiritual awareness at which time stands still. In most journey themes in world literature, the end revisits the beginning. The quest of Monkey also goes in a cycle, in which the perpetual process can be identified with the final goal. The Buddha himself tells the pilgrims that even the Mahayana scriptures ought to be left behind in a quest for enlightenment. The plot of the quest, therefore, is like a circle that has no end; the important part of the pilgrimage is the pilgrimage, not so much the recovery of the scriptures.

Myth and comedy are further related by the author's lyrical vision of life and the lyrical style of his narrative. Nature is charged with human feeling in the story, which uses some of the lively conventions of the oral traditions, such as the recurring exclamation, "Dear Monkey!" Humor and myth are joined, for example, in the pilgrims' last calamity on the river; the author uses an old Chinese folk motif to reach the mythic number of eighty-one. This is also a joke at the expense of storytellers, who tend to miscount their calamities during their oral performances.

Further Reading

Bantly, Francisca-Cho. "Buddhist Allegory in the *Journey to the West*." *Journal of Asian Studies* 48, no. 3 (1989): 512-524. Analyzes and explains Buddhist allegorical elements interwoven into this novel.

Ch'en, Shou-yi. *Chinese Literature: A Historical Introduction*. New York: Ronald Press, 1961. Discusses the structure of the work and traces the literary development of the presumed author.

Hsia, C. T. *The Classic Chinese Novel*. New York: Columbia University Press, 1968. Reprint. Ithaca, N.Y.: Cornell University, East Asia Program, 1996. Critical analysis of six major classical Chinese works, including *The Journey to the West*. Gives historical background for the novel and traces similarities to and divergences from the epic pilgrimage of Hsüan Tsang to India, which provides its historical basis.

Hsia, C. T., and T. A. Hsia. "New Perspectives on Two Ming Novels: *Hsi Yu Chi* and *Hsi Yu Pu*." In *Wen-lin: Studies in the Chinese Humanities*, edited by Tse-tung Chow. Madison: University of Wisconsin Press, 1968. Provides historical background in its comparison of *The Journey to the West* to another novel of the era.

Jenner, William J. F., trans. *The Journey to the West, by Wu Chengen*. 3 vols. Hong Kong: Commercial Press, 1994. Jenner's complete translation of the novel includes an extensive scholarly introduction and notes that address the allegorical significance of the book.

Li, Qiancheng. *Fictions of Enlightenment: "Journey to the West," "Tower of Myriad Mirrors," and "Dream of the Red Chamber."* Honolulu: University of Hawaii Press, 2004. Examines how the Buddhist quest for enlightenment has been transformed into narrative in *The Journey to the West* and in two other works of classic Chinese fiction.

Liu, Wu-chi. *An Introduction to Chinese Literature*. Bloomington: Indiana University Press, 1966. Chapter 16 discusses *The Journey to the West* as a supernatural novel that is as much a product of folk tradition as of the author's creative imagination. Examines the structure of the novel and concludes that it is a good-natured satire of human foibles and bureaucratic stupidity.

So, Francis K. H. "Some Rhetorical Conventions of the Verse Sections of *Hsi-yu-chi*." In *China and the West: Comparative Literature Studies*, edited by William Tay et al. Hong Kong: Chinese University Press, 1980. Analyzes the verse sections, which use all the major genres of poetry in Chinese literature, in *Journey to the West*.

Subbaraman, Ramnath. *Beyond the Question of the Monkey*

Imposter: Indian Influence on the Chinese Novel, "The Journey to the West." Philadelphia: Department of Asian and Middle Eastern Studies, University of Pennsylvania, 2002. Subbaraman examines "some of the remarkable plot similarities" between *The Journey to the West* and two Indian epics, the *Ramayana* and the *Mahabharata.*

Wang, Jing. *The Story of Stone: Intertextuality, Ancient Chinese Stone Lore, and the Stone Symbolism in "Dream of the Red Chamber," "Water Margin," and "The Journey to the West."* Durham, N.C.: Duke University Press, 1992. Compares and contrasts the use of stone symbolism in *The Journey to the West* and the two other literary works, describing how this symbolism originates in Chinese myth and folklore.

The Joy Luck Club

Author: Amy Tan (1952-   )
First published: 1989
Type of work: Novel
Type of plot: Social realism
Time of plot: Twentieth century
Locale: China and San Francisco

Principal characters:
JING-MEI (JUNE) WOO, the protagonist
SUYUAN WOO, Jing-mei's mother
ROSE HSU JORDAN, a homemaker
AN-MEI HSU, Rose's mother
WAVERLY JONG, a businesswoman
LINDO JONG, Waverly's mother
LENA ST. CLAIR, an architect
YING-YING ST. CLAIR, Lena's mother

The Story:

After Suyuan Woo passes away, her daughter, Jing-mei, is asked by her mother's friends to take her mother's place as a member of their Joy Luck Club, a group of friends who play Mah-Jongg together. At first, Jing-mei is reluctant to join the club. She is not very good at Mah-Jongg and not particularly interested in hearing her "aunties" talk about the past. Once she accepts, however, she begins to learn more about her mother's past and about the twin daughters her mother left in China. She also learns about her aunties' lives and about their daughters.

The aunties describe their childhood experience in China and their journey to the United States. An-mei Hsu recalls how her mother was mistreated by her husband's family after his death, and how she was disowned by Popo, her mother, for marrying Wu Tsing, who already had a wife and two concubines. When Popo became very sick, An-mei's mother nevertheless returned home to take care of her. An-mei later learned from a servant, Yan Chang, that her mother had been raped by Wu Tsing and tricked into the marriage, and that she was physically abused and emotionally tortured by Wu Tsing's wife and concubines.

Lindo Jong was a child bride. Her husband, Tyan-yu, was several years younger than she and even more immature. When Huang Taitai, Tyan-yu's mother, became angry with Lindo for not bearing the family a son, Lindo told her that from a meeting she had with the ghosts of the family's ancestors she was warned to leave the family to prevent calamity from descending on them. That trick enabled Lindo to leave Huang Taitai's house without disgracing her own family. The money Huang Taitai gave her was enough for her to go to America.

Ying-ying St. Clair was born to a well-to-do family, and she was brought up with strict rules about how to behave properly. Both her mother and Amah, the maid, believe that a "girl can never ask, only listen"; while a "boy can run and chase dragonflies, because that is his nature . . . a girl should stand still." In the legendary figure Chang-o, the Moon Lady, Ying-ying finds a companion and someone she can trust, but after Ying-ying makes a secret wish to Chang-o while watching a play, she is shocked to find out that the person who plays Chang-o is a man.

The aunties' daughters also tell their stories about the cultural conflicts they experienced growing up in America. Waverly Jong was Chinatown's chess champion when she was a child, but because she did not like the way her mother bragged about her achievement, she stopped playing. Lately, Waverly was fighting her mother over the way she treats her boyfriend, Rich Shields; it seems that her mother considers neither Rich nor Waverly's former Chinese husband good enough.

Lena St. Clair is tired of hearing her mother talk about how her marriage with Harold Livotny is unbalanced. She eventually comes to think that her mother was right all along and that she and her husband do not have an equal relationship. Lena is as important as Harold in the architectural firm Livotny and Associates but is not paid accordingly; yet they split the household bills and expenses evenly in half.

In the story "Half and Half," Rose Hsu Jordan sees a parallel between what happens to her brother Bing and what happens to her marriage. When Rose was a teenager, she was once given the responsibility to take care of her younger brothers while the family was vacationing on a beach. A misunderstanding between Rose and her father results in Bing's disappearance. From that incident, Rose learns that fate is shaped "half by expectation, half by inattention." Just as she knows now that she never expects to find Bing, Rose now also knows she will not find a way to save her marriage to Ted Jordan, who not only does not respect her being a housewife but also has an affair with another woman.

Jing-mei Woo is the spokesperson for both her and her mother. When Jing-mei was a child, Suyuan believed that her daughter was a prodigy and hired a piano teacher for her. Jing-mei was not very excited about playing piano, however, and did not practice hard. After a disastrous appearance on a talent show, Jing-mei has a big altercation with her mother, after which she never touches the piano again. After her mother dies, Jing-mei develops a sentimental attachment to the piano, and one day she plays Robert Schumann's piano pieces "Pleading Child" and "Perfectly Contented" a few times and discovers that they are "two halves of the same song."

When the aunties give Jing-mei an envelope with twelve hundred dollars and tell her to go to China to meet her twin sisters, she starts to understand the ontological significance of having taken her mother's place at the Mah-Jongg table—on the East, where things began. In the last story of the book, "A Pair of Tickets," Jing-mei Woo describes her trip to China in search of her "lost" twin sisters. When she finally meets them, Jing-mei can see that together they look just like their mother.

Critical Evaluation:

The development of Asian American literature can be divided into two periods. The first period was marked by the writers' interest in an autobiographical approach to identify their relationship with mainstream American culture and to establish an increased awareness of their other cultural heritage. The second period began with the publication of Amy Tan's *The Joy Luck Club* in 1989, which heralded the emergence of a large group of Asian American writers who were interested in experimenting with various literary genres and styles in search of a medium that could reflect and depict their experience accurately. Besides rekindling hope for many Asian American writers, the success of *The Joy Luck Club* pushed publishers' doors a bit wider. The book was succeeded in 1991 by Tan's second successful novel, *The Kitchen God's Wife*, and, that same year, by Gish Jen's *Typical American*, David Wong Louie's collection of short stories *Pangs of Love* (which won the Los Angeles Times 1991 Book Prize for first fiction), Frank Chin's *Donald Duk*, and Gus Lee's autobiographical novel *China Boy*.

In *The Joy Luck Club*, Tan intermingles intercultural and intergenerational conflict. The mothers who immigrated to the United States from China and still have very strong cultural ties to their old home want to raise their children in the traditional Chinese way. Their Chinese American daughters, however, feel trapped between traditional Chinese culture and mainstream American society, between their aspirations for individual freedom and their desire to satisfy familial and social obligations, and between their false and their true identities. The daughters eventually conclude that they are as American as they are Chinese.

Tan spoke of her constant search "to find a harmony between the self and the world." Her thematic preoccupation with balance and harmony in *The Joy Luck Club* is revealed by chapter titles such as "Half and Half," "Two Kinds," "Four Directions," "Double Face," and "A Pair of Tickets" and in her skillful use of structure. The book begins with the mothers' stories about their experiences in China and emigrating to the United States, and it ends with their conclusion that, much as they would like to believe they are still completely Chinese, they, too, now have two faces, a Chinese face and an American one. The daughters, on the other hand, come to the realization that "Once you are born Chinese, you cannot help but feel and think Chinese."

Jing-mei Woo is first reluctant to join the Joy Luck Club, and she only halfheartedly accepts her Chinese name, though she mentions that it is "becoming fashionable for American-born Chinese to use their Chinese names." She is not aware, however, that it is impossible for her to find her true identity without reclaiming her relationship with her ethnic cultural heritage. Only after joining the Joy Luck Club can she begin to understand her mother. The trip to China finally enables her to see that, together with her sisters, they look just like their mother: her "same eyes, her same mouth, open in surprise to see, at last, her long-cherished wish."

Tan's use of ancient Chinese myths and legends in *The Joy Luck Club* works well with her thematic concerns. In the story "The Moon Lady," for example, Ying-ying St. Clair, who is told that woman is "yin, the darkness within where untempered passions" lie and that man is "yang, bright truth lighting our minds," finds a friend in Chang-o, the Moon Lady. According to the legend, Chang-o took medicine that belonged to her husband and was sent to the moon as punishment. Tan uses Ying-ying's story and the mythical story to lament the way women were treated in a feudalist society and to suggest that that way should be rejected in traditional Chinese culture.

Qun Wang

Further Reading

Adams, Bella. *Amy Tan*. New York: Manchester University Press, 2005. Analyzes *The Joy Luck Club* and three other novels, examining their depiction of identity, history, and reality. Provides a critical overview of Tan's works.

Bloom, Harold, ed. *Amy Tan's "The Joy Luck Club."* Philadelphia: Chelsea House, 2002. Collection of interpretative essays about the novel, including discussions of its depiction of mother-daughter relationships and storytelling, a comparison of the novel with Maxine Hong Kingston's *Tripmaster Monkey*, and Tan's essay "The Language of Discretion."

Chan, Jeffery Paul, Frank Chin, Lawson Fusao Inada, and Shawn H. Wong. "An Introduction to Chinese-American and Japanese-American Literatures." In *Three American Literatures*, edited by Houston A. Baker, Jr. New York: Modern Language Association of America, 1982. Arguing from the viewpoint that white supremacist thinking controls American culture, the authors detail the origins of a distinctly Asian American literature, a category not readily recognized by critics. The stereotype of the Asian American "dual personality" is rejected.

Chin, Frank. "Come All Ye Asian American Writers of the Real and the Fake." In *The Big Aiiieeeee! An Anthology of Chinese American and Japanese American Literature*, edited by Jeffery Paul Chan et al. New York: Meridian, 1991. Discusses Tan's, Maxine Hong Kingston's, and David Henry Hwang's use of ancient Chinese myths and legends in their works.

Kim, Elaine H. "'Such Opposite Creatures': Men and Women in Asian-American Literature." *Michigan Quarterly Review* 29, no. 1 (Winter, 1990): 68-93. Kim briefly discusses mother-daughter relations in *The Joy Luck Club* in her examination of the different ways in which Asian American men and women portray gender and ethnicity in their writing.

Ling, Amy. *Between Worlds: Women Writers of Chinese Ancestry*. New York: Pergamon Press, 1990. Takes a feminist look at Asian American women writers' contribution to the development of Asian American literature. Includes a section on *The Joy Luck Club*.

Souris, Stephen. "'Only Two Kinds of Daughters': Inter-Monologue Dialogicity in *The Joy Luck Club*." *MELUS* 19, no. 2 (1994): 99-123. Uses Wolfgang Iser's reader-response theory in discussing how the novel requires the reader's active involvement to create the meaning.

Tan, Amy. Interview by Barbara Somogyi and David Stanton. *Poets and Writers* 19, no. 5 (September 1, 1991): 24-32. In an informative interview, Tan talks about the origins of *The Joy Luck Club*, its autobiographical elements, and its portrayal of mother-daughter issues.

Wiener, Gary, ed. *Women's Issues in Amy Tan's "The Joy Luck Club."* Detroit, Mich.: Greenhaven Press, 2008. Provides background and biographical information about Tan, as well as critical essays discussing the novel's depiction of gender and ethnic identity, female empowerment, stereotypes of immigrant women, and other women's issues.

Wong, Sau-ling Cynthia. *Reading Asian American Literature: From Necessity to Extravagance*. Princeton, N.J.: Princeton University Press, 1993. Takes a thematic approach to the study of contemporary Asian American literature. Discusses the significance of Tan and *The Joy Luck Club* in the history of Asian American literature.

Jubilee

Author: Margaret Walker (1915-1998)
First published: 1966
Type of work: Novel
Type of plot: Historical realism
Time of plot: 1840-1870
Locale: Georgia and Alabama

Principal characters:

ELVIRA "VYRY" DUTTON, a young biracial woman born into slavery
JOHN MORRIS DUTTON (MARSTER JOHN), plantation owner and Vyry's natural father
SALINA DUTTON (BIG MISSY), his wife
JOHNNY DUTTON (YOUNG MARSTER), their son
LILLIAN DUTTON MACDOUGALL (MISS LILLIAN), their daughter
ED GRIMES, the Dutton plantation's overseer
RANDALL WARE, a free African American blacksmith and Vyry's first husband
INNIS BROWN, a farmer, Vyry's second husband
BROTHER EZEKIEL, a black preacher and link to the Underground Railroad
JIM, Vyry and Randall's son
MINNA, Vyry and Randall's daughter
HARRY, Vyry and Innis's son
JIM,
MAY LIZA,
CALINE, and
AUNT SALLY, slaves on the Dutton plantation

The Story:

As a small child, Vyry is taken to the cabin where her mother lies dying, her body worn out from constant childbearing. Mammy Sukey cares for Vyry for several years as she grows up on the Dutton plantation, until Big Missy (Salina, the plantation's mistress) and Grimes, the overseer, order the child to work in the Big House as Miss Lillian's maid. The day she starts working as a maid, Vyry sees six new slaves being brought in, one of whom is sick with plague. The disease spreads, and five other slaves die, including Vyry's beloved Mammy Sukey.

Vyry and Lillian had played together as small children, but Vyry shows no aptitude for working as her maid. When she breaks a dish, Salina hangs her up by her thumbs in a closet. Vyry is rescued only when Lillian tells Marster John what has happened upon his return from a trip and John takes her down. Salina especially hates Vyry because the slave's resemblance to Lillian reminds Salina of her husband's dalliances. John is more easygoing than his wife, but, traveling for his political career, he leaves most plantation management to Salina and to Grimes, both of whom hate black people wholeheartedly.

After Vyry's brush with death, John sends Vyry to live with Aunt Sally, the Big House cook. Vyry works as Sally's helper and becomes an excellent cook herself. Growing up on the isolated plantation, she learns how the antebellum southern world treats people of color. She sees dogs loosed to maul a runaway slave to death and two old black men locked into a shed that Grimes then sets on fire because they can no longer earn their keep. Aunt Sally is sold away because Salina fears poisoning.

Vyry takes over Sally's kitchen duties. As her mentor had, she sings to dispel her problems. When Randall Ware does some work on the plantation, he meets Vyry, who has become a competent young woman of sixteen. They fall in love. Randall starts to visit Vyry surreptitiously at night. Brother Ezekiel can marry them only in a "broomstick" ceremony. Over the next few years, they have two children. Randall tries to buy Vyry's freedom, but the attempt goes wrong and puts him in danger. He asks Vyry to flee north with him. On the appointed night, Vyry reaches the riverbank meeting place too late. Grimes has her brutally whipped when she returns.

John Dutton breaks his leg in a carriage accident in early 1860. After several pain-filled weeks, he dies. His son Johnny enlists in the Confederate army right after his West Point graduation. He likes being an officer but is mortally wounded at Chickamauga. Lillian's husband, a reluctant enlistee, also dies in battle. Randall Ware joins General Dodge's Union forces in Illinois. Miss Salina puts her remaining money into Confederate bonds to prove her patriotism. General Grant's march through Georgia misses the Dutton place, but, as Yankee guns fire in the distance, Salina dies from a stroke.

By now, only Vyry and a few house slaves are left on the plantation; everyone else has run away. In May, 1865, Union troops visit the Dutton plantation. Their commander reads the Emancipation Proclamation to the remaining slaves. With the troop is Jim, a former Dutton houseboy who had brought Johnny home when he was wounded, and Innis Brown, a freed slave. Jim tells Vyry that he saw Randall Ware, very ill, in Atlanta and that he is probably dead now. The soldiers ransack the house and fields. That night, one of them attacks Vyry, but Innis drives him off then sleeps in the cabin doorway, guarding Vyry and her children. The next day, they find Miss Lillian unconscious in the house. She eventually awakens, but she has suffered a head injury that has affected her mind.

Jim leaves with May Liza and Caline. Innis urges Vyry to go away with him. She equivocates, saying she is waiting for Randall to return and for Lillian's relatives to come. Lillian can no longer care for herself or her children.

Once Lillian's aunt arrives, Vyry, Jim, Minna, and Innis set out in an old wagon, seeking a place to build a farm and house. After crossing into south Alabama, they find a site in the low country. They plant crops in the rich soil and build a cabin, but the Chattahoochee River rises, flooding them out. Moving on, they find some land to farm as sharecroppers. Their son Harry is born while they live there; Innis is the only person on hand to help with the birth. When they discover the oppressive terms of their work, they move on. After Innis builds a fine new house outside Troy, the Ku Klux Klan burns it down; the family barely escapes with their lives. Five years after Emancipation, the family is homeless again, sleeping in a wagon.

Terrified by the Ku Klux Klan attack, Vyry resists building another house. Their fortunes change when she peddles eggs and vegetables in town and hears a scream. The cry is from a woman in childbirth. The woman's frightened young husband begs Vyry to help. After the baby's birth, the couple's gratitude overcomes their shock at the light-skinned emergency midwife being black. In fact, the neighborhood welcomes the new "granny" with a houseraising and a quilting bee.

Meanwhile, Randall Ware, still alive, has returned to Dawson to reclaim his smithy and his life. As a literate and informed black man, he takes part in reconstruction politics, but the Ku Klux Klan beats him over a piece of land he owns. Vyry's son Jim, now a fifteen-year-old, constantly clashes with his stepfather about farm chores. Mr. Porter, the husand of Lillian's aunt, visits Vyry and Innis on his way to Georgia. He notices that Jim's back is raw from a whipping, and when he later meets Randall in Dawson, he tells him of his observation. Randall decides he needs to see for himself and goes to Alabama to visit Vyry and his children.

Vyry is astonished to see Randall again. The reunion goes well, but now she must choose between two husbands. She decides to stay with Innis. After ascertaining that the whipping was a one-time event, Randall offers to take Jim home with him and send the boy to school. Jim joyously agrees. Jim and Randall leave on the train the next morning. Vyry looks forward to the future in her new house and tells Innis that they will soon have another baby.

Critical Evaluation:

Jubilee was the first significant novel to tell the story of the Civil War and Reconstruction from a slave's perspective. It took a century after the actual events occurred for such a book to be written and published—itself a commentary on American society in the intervening years. The book was thirty years in the making. Margaret Walker worked on it while earning bachelor's and advanced degrees, marrying, giving birth to four children, teaching at Jackson State College, and writing well-received poetry. She said that the novel was stronger for her having "lived it" through life experiences as well as simply writing it.

Jubilee is based on the life of Walker's great-grandmother as related by her daughter, the author's grandmother. To these story elements, which she heard in childhood, Walker added intensive research in folklore and history, tracing family birth records and using other primary sources. At the same time, she applied her poetic talents and humanistic outlook to the storytelling. *Jubilee* was completed as part of the requirements for Walker's doctorate in creative writing from the University of Iowa in 1965.

Reviewers' reactions at the time of the novel's initial publication were mixed. Several critics called it uneven, saying that passages of pedestrian prose and unfiltered historical information undercut its literary value. Other reviewers praised the novel's achievement as a portrayal of plantation life through the eyes of the slaves who made it possible. As time passed, the criticisms of the work's literary merit faded. As the canon of African American literature expanded, it became clear that neither the romantic nor the heroic style, both of which had often been used in novels about the Civil War, were suitable approaches to the black experience of slavery and oppression. As an epic work of historical realism, *Jubilee* was a trailblazer.

Walker brought poetry and metaphor to the book. Each chapter opens with a short poem, a traditional African American spiritual, or a folk saying from the era represented. Chapter titles, too, are often evocative, including "Death is a mystery that only the squinch owl knows" and "A noise like thunder . . . a cloud like dust." Brother Ezekiel's sermons, coding the Israelites' captivity in Egypt as a parallel to his listeners' enslavement, express the spiritual underpinnings that sustained Vyry.

The major thematic thread of *Jubilee* is freedom. In Vyry's early life, freedom is only a distant dream. She hopes for it and dreams of it, but, when Randall's plans to buy her freedom come to nothing, she is not surprised. She knows that Randall's freedom is severely limited by oppressive Georgia laws and customs. When Emancipation comes, her longed-for freedom brings dilemmas. Even facing the prospect of "forty years in the wilderness," though, it is better to be free than a slave. Vyry and Innis can at least work toward a better future for themselves and their children.

Subtly interwoven with the freedom theme is one of social pressure. Vyry, although she is not formally educated, tests everything she hears through the filters of experience and reason, deciding things for herself. In contrast, the Duttons are captives of the "conventional wisdom" of their peers and their society. As a result, they make bad decisions: Salina invests in worthless Confederate bonds, and Lillian's husband enlists even against his own principles.

Jubilee explores the importance of a home. Even though the Dutton plantation is not a true home to Vyry, she makes her cabin into a home for her children that is so warm and secure that Innis wants to join the household. In their Reconstruction-era wanderings, Innis and Vyry must find a safe place to build their home before the rest of their dreams can come true. Linked with this search is the archetypal figure of the strong and nurturing black woman. The orphaned Vyry would not have survived without the unselfish care of Mammy Sukey and Aunt Sally. Nor would Miss Lillian and her children have survived without Vyry staying to care for

them until Lillian's aunt came. A reader does not see either Salina or Lillian carrying out a mother's role. The only white woman in the story who fulfils such a role is Lillian's aunt, Miss Lucy, who as a merchant's wife has never owned slaves.

Jubilee is an important novel not only for the story it tells but also because of its influence on subsequent American fiction. Its appearance and success paved the way for later narratives of the black experience under slavery, including such significant works as Alex Haley's *Roots* (1976) and Toni Morrison's *Beloved* (1987). *Jubilee*, published in the decade of the Civil Rights movement's greatest victories, marked the incorporation of African American experience into mainstream American literature.

Emily Alward

Further Reading

Carmichael, Jacqueline Miller. *Trumpeting a Fiery Sound: History and Folklore in Margaret Walker's "Jubilee."* Athens: University of Georgia Press, 2003. Extensive study of *Jubilee*'s use of folk and historical elements, its structure and narration, and the responses of critics.

Dieng, Babacar. "Reclamation in Walker's *Jubilee*." *Journal of Pan African Studies* 2, no. 4 (June, 2008): 117. Evaluates Walker's achievements as a historian. Portrays the novel as changing American culture's perception of African American life under slavery.

Leveeq, Christine. "Black Women Writers and the American Neo-Slave Narrative: Femininity Unfettered." *African American Review* 35 (Spring, 2001): 136. Long article analyzing the works of Walker and five other women novelists. Views these novels as revisions of the history of slavery from a female perspective, which encompasses family, identity, and freedom.

Walker, Margaret. *Conversations with Margaret Walker.* Edited by Maryemma Graham. Jackson: University Press of Mississippi, 2002. Reprints interviews conducted with the author over a twenty-four-year period. Discusses controversies in the public sphere as well as in the literary realm.

_____. *How I Wrote "Jubilee," and Other Essays on Life and Literature.* New York: Feminist Press, 1990. The title essay centers on the author's search for source material. Others illuminate her life and approach to art and discuss major African American writers who influenced her.

Jude the Obscure

Author: Thomas Hardy (1840-1928)
First published: 1895
Type of work: Novel
Type of plot: Philosophical realism
Time of plot: Nineteenth century
Locale: Wessex, England

Principal characters:
JUDE FAWLEY, a stonemason
ARABELLA DONN, a vulgar country girl
SUE BRIDEHEAD, Jude's cousin and a freethinker
LITTLE FATHER TIME, Jude's son by Arabella
RICHARD PHILLOTSON, a schoolmaster
DRUSILLA FAWLEY, Jude's great-grandaunt

The Story:

When he is eleven years old, Jude Fawley says good-bye to his schoolmaster, Richard Phillotson, who is leaving the small English village of Marygreen for Christminster to study for a degree. Young Jude is hungry for learning and yearns to go to Christminster, too, but he has to help his great-grandaunt, Drusilla Fawley, in her bakery. At Christminster, Phillotson does not forget his former pupil. He sends Jude some classical grammars, which the boy studies eagerly.

Anticipating a career as a religious scholar, Jude apprentices himself at the age of nineteen to a stonemason engaged in the restoration of medieval churches in a nearby town. Returning to Marygreen one evening, he meets three young girls who are washing pigs' chitterlings by a stream bank. One of the girls, Arabella Donn, catches Jude's fancy, and he arranges to meet her later. The young man is swept off his feet and tricked into marriage, but he soon realizes that he married a vulgar country girl with whom he has nothing in common. Embittered, he tries unsuccessfully to commit suicide; when he begins to drink, Arabella leaves him.

Once he is free again, Jude decides to carry out his original intention. He goes to Christminster, where he takes work as a stonemason. He hears that his cousin, Sue Bridehead, lives in Christminster, but he does not seek her out because his aunt warned him against her and because he was already a married man. Eventually, he meets her and is charmed. She is an artist employed in an ecclesiastical warehouse. Jude connects with Phillotson, who is again a simple schoolteacher. At Jude's suggestion, Sue becomes Phillotson's assistant. The teacher soon loses his heart to his bright and intellectually independent young helper, and Jude is hurt by evidence of intimacy between the two. Disappointed in love and ambition, he turns to drink and is dismissed by his employer. He goes back to Marygreen.

At Marygreen, Jude is persuaded by a minister to enter the church as a licentiate. Sue, meanwhile, wins a scholarship to a teachers' college at Melchester; she writes Jude and asks him to visit her. Jude works at stonemasonry in Melchester to

be near Sue, even though she tells him she promised to marry Phillotson after completing her schooling. Dismissed from college after an innocent escapade with Jude, Sue influences him away from the church with her unorthodox beliefs. Shortly afterward, she marries Phillotson. Jude is despondent and returns to Christminster, where he comes upon Arabella working in a bar. Jude hears that Sue's married life is unbearable. He continues his studies for the ministry and thinks a great deal about Sue.

Succumbing completely to his passion for Sue, Jude at last forsakes the ministry. His Aunt Drusilla dies, and at the funeral, Jude and Sue realize that they cannot remain separated. Sympathizing with the lovers, Phillotson releases Sue, who now lives apart from her husband. The lovers go to Aldbrickham, a large city where they will not be recognized. Phillotson gives Sue a divorce and subsequently loses his teaching position. Jude gives Arabella a divorce so that she might marry again.

Sue and Jude now contemplate marriage, but they are unwilling to be joined by a church ceremony because of Sue's dislike for any binding contract. The pair lives together happily, and Jude continues his simple stonework. One day, Arabella appears and tells Jude that her marriage did not materialize. Sue is jealous and promises Jude that she will marry him. Arabella's problem is solved by eventual marriage, but out of fear of her new husband, she sends her young child by Jude to live with him and Sue. This pathetic boy, nicknamed Little Father Time, joins the unconventional Fawley household.

Jude's business begins to decline, and he loses a contract to restore a rural church when the vestry discovers that he and Sue are unmarried. Forced to move on, they travel from place to place and from job to job. At the end of two and a half years of this itinerant life, Jude and Sue have two children of their own and a third on the way. Jude, in failing health, becomes a baker; Sue sells cakes in the shape of Gothic ornaments at a fair in a village near Christminster. At the fair, Sue meets

Arabella, who is now a widow. Arabella reports Sue's poverty to Phillotson, who is once more the village teacher in Marygreen.

Jude takes his family to Christminster, where the celebration of Remembrance Week is underway. Utterly defeated by failure, Jude still loves the atmosphere of learning that pervades the city.

The family has difficulty finding lodgings and is forced to separate. Sue's landlady, learning that Sue is an unmarried mother and fearful that she might have the trouble of childbirth in her rooming house, tells Sue to find other lodgings. Sue becomes bitter, and she tells Little Father Time that children should not be brought into the world. When she returns from a meal with Jude, she finds that the boy hanged the two babies and himself. She collapses and gives premature birth to a dead baby.

Her experience brings about a change in Sue's point of view. Believing she sinned and wishing now to conform, she asks Jude to live apart from her. She also expresses the desire to return to Phillotson, whom she believes, in her misery, to be still her husband. She returns to Phillotson, and the two remarry. Jude is utterly lost and begins drinking heavily. In a drunken stupor, he is again tricked by Arabella into marriage. His lungs fail; it is evident that he will die soon. Arabella will not communicate with Sue, whom Jude desires to see once more, and so Jude travels in the rain to see her. The lovers have a last meeting. She then makes complete atonement for her past mistakes by becoming Phillotson's wife completely. This development is reported to Jude, who dies in desperate misery of mind and body. Fate grew tired of its sport with a luckless man.

Critical Evaluation:

An extraordinary transitional figure who straddled the Victorian and twentieth century literary worlds, Thomas Hardy was initially an undistinguished architect whose novels and poems became his chief profession. Although his rustic characters and some of his poems exhibit a humorous touch, most of his creations are permeated by a brooding irony reflecting life's disappointments and a pessimistic belief that human beings are victims of an impersonal force that darkly rules the universe. Hardy divided his novels into three groups: novels of ingenuity, such as *Desperate Remedies* (1871); romances and fantasies, such as *A Pair of Blue Eyes* (1872-1873); and novels of character and environment. This class includes his best and most famous works, *Tess of the D'Urbervilles* (1891), *The Return of the Native* (1878), *Far from the Madding Crowd* (1874), *The Mayor of Casterbridge* (1886), and *Jude the Obscure*.

First published in a modified form as a serial in *Harper's*, *Jude the Obscure* came to be considered by many critics to be Hardy's best novel. It was the outraged initial reception accorded *Jude the Obscure* that turned Hardy from the novel to concentrating on his poetry. Reception ranged from moral outrage to indignation that the book was not as spectacularly evil as touted, and Hardy's disgust with the public was bitter and enduring.

The best explanation of the book was stated by Hardy in his preface, where he declared that the work was intended "to tell, without a mincing of words, of a deadly war waged between flesh and spirit; and to point the tragedy of unfulfilled aims." To these could be added two other important themes: an attack on convention and society and an examination of human beings' essential loneliness.

Exhibiting the flesh-spirit division is, of course, Jude's conflicting nature. His relationship with Arabella represents his strong sexual propensities, while his attraction to intellectual pursuits and his high principles reveal his spiritual side. His obsession with Sue is a reflection of both sides of his personality; for while he is compelled by her mind and emotion, he is also drawn to her physically. At the crucial moments of his life, Jude's fleshly desires are strong enough temporarily to overwhelm his other hopes. His two major goals are checked by this flaw, for his initial attempt at a university career is halted when he succumbs to Arabella and his plans for the ministry end when he kisses Sue and decides that as long as he loves another man's wife he cannot be a soldier and servant of a religion that is so suspicious of sexual love.

"The tragedy of unfilled aims" is forcefully present in both Jude and Sue. For years Jude, in a truly dedicated and scholarly fashion, devotes himself to preparing to enter Christminster (Hardy's name for Oxford). Even after he frees himself from the sexual entanglement with Arabella, his hopes for an education are doomed, for the master of the college who bothers to reply advises him to "remain in your own sphere." Through no fault of his own and despite his seeming ability, he is continually denied what he so desperately seeks. The fact of his birth as a poor person is unchangeable, and Jude must accept its results.

His second great desire, a spiritual (as well as sexual) union with Sue, is also doomed. When Jude first sees Sue's picture, he thinks of her as a saint, and he eventually derives many of his maturing intellectual concepts from her. His passion for Sue is true and full; yet Sue's deeply flawed character necessitates her self-destruction as well as Jude's destruction. She drains Jude while simultaneously serving as a source of his growth, for she is irresponsible, cold, and cruel.

She is an imperfect being, afraid not only of her physical side but also of her very ideas. She tells Jude that she does not have the courage of her convictions, and when he adopts her iconoclastic stance, she abandons it and demonstrates how conventional she really is. Her pagan shouts, her free thought, her brave spirit prove as much a sham as Christminster's promises. Her tragedy—the gap between what she is and what she might have been—is not hers alone but is shared by Jude and becomes his.

As an attack on convention and society, *Jude the Obscure* focuses on three major areas: the British university system, marriage, and religion. Jude's exclusion from Christminster is an indictment of the structure of an institution that allegedly symbolizes the noble part of the human mind yet actually stands only for a closed, tightly knit club. In its criticism of marriage, a union that Hardy said should be dissolvable by either side if it became a burden, the novel reveals how false is the view of marriage as a sacred contract. Marriage, as in Jude's merger with Arabella, is often the fruit of a temporary urge, but its harvest can be lifelong and ruinous. Sue's fear of marriage also suggests that the bond can be one of suffocation.

Perhaps most important are the novel's charges against Christianity. The fundamental hollowness and hypocrisy of Christianity, Hardy asserted, damn it. A farmer thrashes Jude for lovingly letting the birds feed, and the sounds of the beating echo from the church tower that the same farmer had helped finance. Hardy's scorn for such inconsistencies abounds throughout the book, and he proposes that the only valuable part of Christianity is its idea that love makes life more bearable.

Mirroring the development of these themes is the final impression that the book is also a cry of loneliness. Jude's hopelessness is in the final analysis a result of his alienation not only from Arabella and Sue but also from his environment. Used in connection with Jude, the word "obscure," in addition to conveying his association with darkness, his lack of distinction in the eyes of the world, and his humble station, suggests that he is not understood and that he is hidden from others and only faintly perceptible. In Hardy's world, the happiest people are those who are most in touch with their environment, a condition that usually occurs in the least reflective characters. Jude, however, is always grasping for the ideal and ignoring the unpleasantness around him as much as he can; this inevitably leads to isolation. Hardy hints that such is the price human beings must pay for the refusal unquestionably to accept their status.

All the ills that Hardy ascribes to this world are merely a reflection of the ills of the universe. Human beings ruin society because they are imperfect and caught in the grip of a fatal and deterministic movement of the stars. In defense of his dark outlook, Hardy writes: "If a way to the better there be, it demands a full look at the worst." In a philosophy that he termed evolutionary meliorism, Hardy further amplifies this concept in both a brighter and a more disastrous vein. That philosophy proposes that not only may human beings improve but they must find the way to that better condition if they are to survive.

"Critical Evaluation" by Judith Bolch

Further Reading

Boumelha, Penny, ed. *"Jude the Obscure," Thomas Hardy.* New York: St. Martin's Press, 2000. Collection of essays analyzing the novel from a variety of modern perspectives, including discussions of sexual ideology, narrative form, and male relations in the novel and "Jude Fawley and the New Man."

Butler, Lance St. John. *Thomas Hardy.* New York: Cambridge University Press, 1978. A short introductory study that deals with the issue of flesh versus spirit in *Jude the Obscure*. Butler claims that the quality of the novel lies in its plotting.

Gatrell, Simon. *Thomas Hardy and the Proper Study of Mankind.* Charlottesville: University Press of Virginia, 1993. Discusses the way Hardy treats the theme of the conflict between the sexes and notes that Hardy believes sexual union to be the essence of marriage.

Hardy, Thomas. *"Jude the Obscure": An Authoritative Text, Backgrounds and Sources, Criticism.* Edited by Norman Page. New York: W. W. Norton, 1978. Contains, in addition to the text of the novel, six contemporary reviews, comments from Hardy's letters, and ten twentieth century critical essays. These deal with *Jude the Obscure* as a distinctively progressive novel and as a tragedy, the novel's poetic power, its pessimism and meliorism, its imagery and symbolism, and Hardy's portrait of Sue Bridehead.

Hawkins, Desmond. *Hardy: Novelist and Poet.* New York: Barnes & Noble, 1976. In this biocritical study, Hawkins maintains that the significance of the changing partnerships in *Jude the Obscure* is the fact that the two lesser characters, Arabella and Phillotson, represent the more conventional, tolerant, conformist elements in society, while Jude and Sue are unconventional, rebellious, and critical of the social order.

Kramer, Dale, ed. *The Cambridge Companion to Thomas Hardy.* New York: Cambridge University Press, 1999. An introduction and general overview of all Hardy's work and specific demonstrations of Hardy's ideas and literary skills. Individual essays explore Hardy's biography, aesthetics, and the impact on his work of developments in science, religion, and philosophy in the late nineteenth century. The volume also contains a detailed chronology of Hardy's life and Kramer's essay "Hardy and Readers: *Jude the Obscure*."

Mallett, Phillip, ed. *The Achievement of Thomas Hardy*. New York: St. Martin's Press, 2000. A collection of essays that analyze some of the novels and other works and discuss Hardy and nature, the architecture of Hardy, and the presence of the poet in his novels, among other topics. Includes bibliography and index.

Page, Norman, ed. *Oxford Reader's Companion to Hardy*. New York: Oxford University Press, 2000. An encyclopedia containing three hundred alphabetically arranged entries examining Hardy's work and discussing his family

and friends, important places in his life and work, his influences, critical approaches to his writings, and a history of his works' publication. Also includes a chronology of his life, lists of places and characters in his fiction, a glossary, and a bibliography.

Tomalin, Claire. *Thomas Hardy*. New York: Penguin, 2007. This thorough and finely written biography by a respected Hardy scholar illuminates the novelist's efforts to indict the malice, neglect, and ignorance of his fellow human beings. Tomalin also discusses aspects of his life that are apparent in his literary works.

Vigar, Penelope. *The Novels of Thomas Hardy: Illusion and Reality*. London: Athlone Press, 1974. Emphasizes that *Jude the Obscure* achieves its intense psychological verisimilitude from its many short scenes and episodes in which the abstractions of feeling are transcribed into observable actions and events.

Julius Caesar

Author: William Shakespeare (1564-1616)
First produced: c. 1599-1600; first published, 1623
Type of work: Drama
Type of plot: Tragedy
Time of plot: 44 B.C.E.
Locale: Rome

Principal characters:
JULIUS CAESAR, dictator of Rome
MARCUS ANTONIUS, his friend
MARCUS BRUTUS, a conspirator against Caesar
CAIUS CASSIUS, another conspirator against Caesar
PORTIA, wife of Brutus and Cassius's sister
CALPURNIA, Caesar's wife

The Story:

At the feast of Lupercalia all Rome rejoices, for the latest military triumphs of Julius Caesar are being celebrated during that holiday. Nevertheless, tempers flare and jealousies seethe beneath the public gaiety. Flavius and Marallus, two tribunes, coming upon a group of citizens gathered to praise Caesar, tear down their trophies and order the people to go home and remember Pompey's fate at the hands of Caesar.

Other dissatisfied noblemen discuss with concern Caesar's growing power and his incurable ambition. A soothsayer, following Caesar in his triumphal procession, warns him to beware the Ides of March. Cassius, one of the most violent of Caesar's critics, speaks at length to Brutus of the dictator's unworthiness to rule the state. Why, he demands, should the name of Caesar be synonymous with that of Rome when there are so many other worthy men in the city?

While Cassius and Brutus are speaking, they hear a tre-

mendous shouting from the crowd. From aristocratic Casca they learn that before the mob Marcus Antonius three times offered a crown to Caesar and three times the dictator refused it. Thus do the wily Antonius and Caesar catch and hold the devotion of the multitude. Fully aware of Caesar's methods and the potential danger that he embodies, Cassius and Brutus, disturbed by the new turn of events, agree to meet again to discuss the affairs of Rome. As they part, Caesar arrives in time to see them, and suspicion of Cassius enters his mind. Cassius does not look contented; he is too lean and nervous to be satisfied with life. Caesar much prefers to have fat, jolly men about him.

Cassius's plan is to enlist Brutus in a plot to overthrow Caesar. Brutus is one of the most respected and beloved citizens of Rome; were he in league against Caesar, the dictator's power could be curbed easily. It will, however, be difficult to turn Brutus completely against Caesar, for Brutus is an honorable man and not given to treason, so that only the most drastic circumstances would override his loyalty. Cassius plots to have Brutus receive false papers that imply widespread public alarm over Caesar's rapidly growing power. Hoping that Brutus might put Rome's interests above his own personal feelings, Cassius has the papers secretly laid at Brutus's door one night. The conflict within Brutus is great. His wife Portia complains that he did not sleep at all during the night and that she found him wandering, restless and unhappy, about the house. At last he reaches a decision. Remembering Tarquin, the tyrant whom his ancestors banished from Rome, Brutus agrees to join Cassius and his conspirators in their attempt to save Rome from Caesar. He refuses, however, to sanction the murder of Antonius, which is being planned for the same time—the following morning, March 15—as the assassination of Caesar.

On the night of March 14, all nature seems to misbehave. Strange lights appear in the sky, graves yawn, ghosts walk, and an atmosphere of terror pervades the city. Caesar's wife, Calpurnia, dreams she sees her husband's statue with a hundred wounds spouting blood. In the morning, she tells him of the dream and pleads with him not to go to the Senate that morning. When she almost convinces him to remain at home, one of the conspirators arrives and persuades the dictator that Calpurnia is unduly nervous and that the dream is actually an omen of Caesar's tremendous popularity in Rome, the bleeding wounds a symbol of Caesar's power extending out to all Romans. The other conspirators arrive to allay any suspicions Caesar might have of them and to make sure that he attends the Senate that day.

As Caesar makes his way through the city, more omens of evil appear to him. A paper detailing the plot against him is thrust into his hands, but he neglects to read it. When the soothsayer again cries out against the Ides of March, Caesar pays no attention to the warning.

In the Senate chamber, Antonius is drawn to one side. Then the conspirators crowd about Caesar as if to second a petition for the repealing of an order banishing Publius Cimber. When he refuses the petition, the conspirators attack him, and he falls dead of twenty-three knife wounds.

Craftily pretending to side with the conspirators, Antonius is able to reinstate himself in their good graces. In spite of Cassius's warning, he is granted permission to speak at Caesar's funeral after Brutus delivers his oration. Before the populace, Brutus frankly and honestly explains his part in Caesar's murder, declaring that his love for Rome prompted him to turn against his friend. The mob cheers him and agrees that Caesar was a tyrant who deserved death. Then Antonius

rises to speak. Cleverly and forcefully, he turns the temper of the crowd against the conspirators by explaining that even when Caesar was most tyrannical, everything he did was for the people's welfare. The mob becomes so enraged over the assassination that the conspirators are forced to flee from Rome.

The people's temper gradually changes and they split into two camps. One group supports the new triumvirate of Marcus Antonius, Octavius Caesar, and Aemilius Lepidus. The other group follows Brutus and Cassius to their military camp at Sardis.

At Sardis, Brutus and Cassius quarrel constantly over various small matters. In the course of one violent disagreement, Brutus tells Cassius that Portia, despondent over the outcome of the civil war, killed herself. Cassius, shocked by this news of his sister's death, allows himself to be persuaded to leave the safety of the camp at Sardis and meet the enemy on the plains of Philippi. The night before the battle, Caesar's ghost appears to Brutus in his tent and announces that they will meet at Philippi.

At first, Brutus's forces are successful against those of Octavius. Cassius, however, is driven back by Antonius. One morning, Cassius sends one of his followers, Titinius, to learn if approaching troops are the enemy or Brutus's soldiers. When Cassius sees Titinius unseated from his horse by the strangers, he assumes that everything is lost and orders his servant Pindarus to kill him. Actually, the troops were sent by Brutus; rejoicing over the defeat of Octavius, they are having rude sport with Titinius. When they return to Cassius and find him dead, Titinius also kills himself. In the last charge against Antonius, Brutus's soldiers, tired and discouraged by events, are defeated. Brutus, heartbroken, asks his friends to kill him. When they refuse, he commands his servant to hold his sword and turn his face away. Then Brutus falls upon his sword and dies.

Critical Evaluation:

The first of William Shakespeare's so-called Roman plays—which include *Coriolanus* (pr. c. 1607-1608, pb. 1623) and *Antony and Cleopatra* (pr. c. 1606-1607, pb. 1623)—*Julius Caesar* also heralds the great period of his tragedies. The sharply dramatic and delicately portrayed character of Brutus is a clear predecessor of Hamlet and of Othello. With *Titus Andronicus* (pr., pb. 1594) and *Romeo and Juliet* (pr. c. 1595-1596, pb. 1597), *Julius Caesar* is one of the three tragedies written before the beginning of the sixteenth century. It is, however, more historical than Shakespeare's four great tragedies—*Hamlet, Prince of Denmark* (pr. c. 1600-1601, pb. 1603), *Othello, the Moor of Venice* (pr.

1604, pb. 1622), *Macbeth* (pr. 1606, pb. 1623), and *King Lear* (pr. c. 1605-1606, pb. 1608)—being drawn in large part from Sir Thomas North's wonderfully idiomatic translation of Plutarch's *Bioi paralleloi* (c. 105-115; *Parallel Lives*, 1579). A comparison of the Shakespearean text with the passages from North's chapters on Caesar, Brutus, and Antonius reveals the remarkable truth of T. S. Eliot's statement: "Immature poets borrow; mature poets steal." In instance after instance, Shakespeare did little more than rephrase the words of North's exuberant prose to fit the rhythm of his own blank verse. The thievery is brilliant.

Shakespeare's originality, found in all his historical plays, is similar to that of the great classical Greek playwrights Aeschylus, Sophocles, and Euripides. They, too, faced a dramatic challenge very unlike that of later writers, who came to be judged by their sheer inventiveness. Just as the Greek audience came to the play with full knowledge of the particular myth involved in the tragedy to be presented, the Elizabethan audience knew the particulars of events such as the assassination of Julius Caesar. Shakespeare, like his classical predecessors, had to work his dramatic art within the restrictions of known history. He accomplished this by writing "between the lines" of Plutarch, offering insights into the mind of the characters that Plutarch does not mention and which become, on the stage, dramatic motivations. An example is Caesar's revealing hesitation about going to the Senate because of Calpurnia's dream, and the way he is swayed by Decius into going after all. This scene shows the weakness of Caesar's character in a way not found in a literal reading of Plutarch. A second major "adaptation" by Shakespeare is a daring, dramatically effective telescoping of historical time. The historical events associated with the death of Caesar and the defeat of the conspirators actually took three years; Shakespeare condenses them into three tense days, following the unity of time (though not of place).

Although prose is used in the play by comic and less important characters or in purely informative speeches or documents, the general mode of expression is Shakespeare's characteristic blank verse, which consists of five stressed syllables, generally unrhymed. The iambic pentameter, a rhythm natural to English speech, has the effect of making more memorable lines such as Flavius's comment about the commoners, "They vanish tongue-tied in their guiltiness," or Brutus's observation, "Men at some time are masters of their fates." As in most of his tragedies, Shakespeare follows a five-part dramatic structure, consisting of the exposition (to act 1, scene 2), complication (act 1, scene 2, to act 2, scene 4), climax (act 3, scene 1), consequence (act 3, scene 1, to act 5, scene 2), and denouement (act 5, scenes 3 to 5).

The main theme of *Julius Caesar* combines the political with the personal. The first deals with the question of justifiable revolutions and reveals with the effectiveness of concentrated action the transition from a republic of equals to an empire dominated by great individuals such as Antonius, influenced by the example of Caesar himself, and Octavius, who comes into his own at the end of the play. The personal complication is the tragedy of a noble spirit involved in matters it does not comprehend. Despite the title, Brutus, not Caesar, is the hero of this play. It is true that Caesar's influence motivates Marcus Antonius's (also called Mark Antony), straightforward and ultimately victorious actions throughout the play and accounts for his transformation from an apparently secondary figure into one of stature. It is, however, Brutus, as he gradually learns to distinguish ideals from reality, who captures the sympathy of the audience. Around his gentle character, praised at last even by Antonius, Shakespeare weaves the recurrent motifs of honor and honesty, freedom and fortune, ambition and pride. Honor as it interacts with ambition is the theme of Brutus's speech to the crowd in the forum: "As Caesar loved me, I weep for him; as he was fortunate, I rejoice at it; as he was valiant, I honour him, but, as he was ambitious, I slew him." After the deed, Brutus comments, "Ambition's debt is paid." One of the great, dramatically successful ironies of the play is that Antonius's forum speech juxtaposes the same two themes: "Yet Brutus says he was ambitious/ And Brutus is an honourable man." By the time Antonius is finished, the term "honour" has been twisted by his accelerating sarcasm until it has become a curse, moving the fickle crowd to call for death for the conspirators.

The conjunction of Brutus and Antonius in this scene reveals the telling difference between their dramatic characterizations. Whereas Caesar may have had too much ambition, Brutus has too little; Brutus is a man of ideals and words, and therefore he cannot succeed in the arenas of power. Cassius and Antonius, in contrast, are not concerned with idealistic concepts or words such as honor and ambition; yet there is a distinction even between them. Cassius is a pure doer, a man of action, almost entirely devoid of sentiment or principle; Antonius is both a doer of deeds and a speaker of words—and therefore prevails over all in the end, following in the footsteps of his model, Caesar. To underline the relationships among these characters and the themes that dominate their actions, Shakespeare weaves a complicated net of striking images: the monetary image, which creates tension between Brutus and Cassius; the tide image ("Thou are the ruins of the noblest man/ That ever lived in the tide of times") connected with the theme of fortune; the star image (Caesar compares himself, like Marlowe's Tamburlaine, to a fixed star while Cassius says, "The fault, dear Brutus, is not in our stars,/ But in ourselves, that we are underlings"); and the image of wood and stones used to describe the common people by those who would move them to their own will.

In yet another way, *Julius Caesar* marks the advance of Shakespeare's artistry in its use of dramatic irony. In this play, the Shakespearean audience itself almost becomes a character in the drama, as it is made privy to knowledge and sympathies not yet shared by all the characters on the stage. This pattern occurs most notably in Decius's speech interpreting Calpurnia's dream, showing the ability of an actor to move men to action by well-managed duplicity. The pattern is also evident when Cinna mistakes Cassius for Metellus Cimber, foreshadowing the mistaken identity scene that ends in his own death; when Cassius, on two occasions, gives in to Brutus's refusal to do away with Antonius; and, most effectively of all, in the two forum speeches when Antonius addresses two audiences, the one in the theater (who know his true intentions), and the other the Roman crowd whose ironic whimsicality is marked by its startling shift of sentiment. The effect of the irony is to suggest the close connection between functional politics and the art of acting. Antonius, in the end, defeats Brutus—as Bolingbroke defeats Richard II— because he can put on a more compelling act.

"Critical Evaluation" by Kenneth John Atchity

Further Reading

Batson, Beatrice, ed. *Shakespeare's Christianity: The Protestant and Catholic Poetics of "Julius Caesar," "Macbeth," and "Hamlet."* Waco, Tex.: Baylor University Press, 2006. Collection of essays that assess the influence of Catholicism and Protestantism on the three tragedies. Includes discussions of Providence and "cobbling souls" in *Julius Caesar*, and the problem of self-love in Shakespeare's tragedies and in Renaissance and Reformation theology.

Bloom, Harold, ed. *William Shakespeare's "Julius Caesar."* New York: Chelsea House, 1988. Nine essays on various aspects of the play by distinguished Shakespeare critics of the 1970's and 1980's. Marjorie Garber's essay on the significance of dreams and Michael Long's on the social order are particularly worthwhile.

Davies, Anthony. *Shakespeare, Julius Caesar.* New York: Cambridge University Press, 2002. Guidebook designed for advanced level students of English literature. Provides a commentary on the text; discusses the play's historical, cultural, and social contexts and use of language; offers a survey of critical interpretation.

Dean, Leonard F., ed. *Twentieth Century Interpretations of "Julius Caesar."* Englewood Cliffs, N.J.: Prentice-Hall, 1968. Informative collection of short articles by leading mid-twentieth century Shakespeare critics. Dean's introduction gives an overview of earlier criticism. Various articles provide character studies, analyze language, and supply literary-historical background.

Miles, Geoffrey. "'Untired Spirits and Formal Constancy': *Julius Caesar.*" In *Shakespeare and the Constant Romans.* New York: Oxford University Press, 1996. Examines the depiction of constancy in *Julius Caesar* and Shakepeare's other Roman plays. The Romans considered constancy a virtue, and Miles traces the development of this ethical concept from ancient Rome through the Renaissance. He then analyzes the ambiguity of this virtue in Shakespeare's depiction of the constant Brutus.

Thomas, Vivian. *"Julius Caesar."* London: Harvester Wheatsheaf, 1992. Concise study of *Julius Caesar* that reflects various postmodernist approaches to Shakespeare and provides a thorough analysis of the play's stage history, style, and relationship to its principal source, Plutarch's *Parallel Lives.* Includes an extensive bibliography.

Traversi, Derek. *Shakespeare: The Roman Plays.* Stanford, Calif.: Stanford University Press, 1963. Chapter two of this classic study focuses on the moral and political themes of *Julius Caesar.* Following the text closely and in detail, Traversi probes the interplay of contrasting personalities and motives that generated a political tragedy with universal significance.

Wilson, Richard, ed. *Julius Caesar.* New York: Palgrave, 2002. Ten essays provide a range of interpretations, including feminist, new historicist, psychoanalytic, and Marxist readings of the play. Includes discussions of the crisis of the aristocracy, collective violence and sacrifice, blood as a trope of gender, and reading character in *Julius Caesar.*

Zander, Horst, ed. *"Julius Caesar": New Critical Essays.* New York: Routledge, 2005. The essays include discussions of *Julius Caesar* and current historiography; the play's critical legacy; plot construction, characterization, and the vicissitudes of language in the play; and *Julius Caesar*'s relation to Shakespeare's other Roman tragedies.

July's People

Author: Nadine Gordimer (1923-   )
First published: 1981
Type of work: Novel
Type of plot: Psychological realism
Time of plot: Soon after 1980
Locale: Rural South Africa

Principal characters:
MAUREEN SMALES, a Johannesburg wife and mother, a
    political liberal
BAMFORD "BAM" SMALES, her husband, an architect, also a
    liberal
JULY, their male servant

The Story:

July, incongruously both servant and host, brings morning tea to Maureen and Bamford Smales where they are sleeping with their three children in a one-room mud hut with only a piece of sack cloth for a door. A small truck, bought for hunting holidays for Bam's fortieth birthday, brought the Smales family six hundred kilometers across the veld in a journey that took three days and nights. The revolutionary forces trying to wrest power from the whites in South Africa caused the family to flee Johannesburg with their servant July to his rural settlement, which is populated only by his relatives. Maureen and Bam's feelings about the revolution are mixed. It brings danger to them as privileged whites, but on the other hand it represents a possible end to the racist system they do not endorse.

Noticing one of the huts contains mining artifacts, Maureen thinks about her childhood as the daughter of a shift boss for the mines. A photographer once snapped a picture of Maureen and Lydia, her family's servant. Years later she saw the photograph in a book. The photograph captured their social relationship, one that Maureen was too young at the time to discern herself: the black servant carrying the white girl's school bag.

One day, without asking, July rides off in the truck, with his friend Daniel driving. Upset, not knowing where July went or why, Maureen and Bam begin bickering about why they failed to leave South Africa while there was still time, about whether their attitude toward the politics of South Africa is realistic, and about each other's character. That night, after the children and Bam fall asleep, Maureen goes outside in the dark to shower in the rain. Before returning to the hut, she notices the lights of the truck returning. July returns with supplies and reports of shortages at the store and fighting at the mines not far from the settlement. Daniel teaches July to drive the truck, and July explains its presence to people in nearby villages by saying he took it from his Johannesburg employers. There is no longer any white authority in the area to worry July.

Maureen and July argue about who should keep the truck's keys, but the argument reveals deeper conflicts. July makes it clear he was always their "boy," and Maureen, angered at his representation of their fifteen-year relationship, strikes back by asking how he could leave Ellen, the woman he lived with in Johannesburg, in the midst of the fighting. The reversal of roles between July and the Smales family is complete. July walks away, with the keys, his head moving "from side to side like a foreman's inspecting his workshop or a farmer's noting work to be done on the lands." July has the power to make the Smales family leave the settlement or to allow them to stay.

Bamford helps July mend farm tools and install a water tank for the settlement, whose water supply is the river. He shoots warthogs and fishes to help supply his and July's family with food. Maureen and Bam are dependent, however, on July for nearly everything. They are able to pay with the notes they brought from the bank. During their stay, they listen to a radio, hearing reports of martial law, fighting, and closed airports. Maureen and Bam's children get along fine with the other children of the village, playing with them, picking up their habits and some of their language.

After they were living in the settlement for more than three weeks, a representative from the chief tells July to bring the Smales family to see him. The chief asks about the fighting in the cities and wants Bam to show him how to use his gun and to help him fight any who come to take over the surrounding villages. Bam responds that the chief should not fight against the black revolutionaries. One day the Smales family joins the rest of July's relatives as a music box is set up for entertainment; when they return to the hut, Bam's gun and ammunition are missing. Bam is devastated by the loss of the second of his two possessions—first the truck, then the gun. Maureen goes to July to tell him to get the gun back. July tells her Daniel might have taken the gun because he went off to join the revolutionaries. One afternoon, when Bam and the children are fishing at the river, Maureen hears a helicopter land nearby; she runs toward it, leaving behind the sounds of her husband and children.

Critical Evaluation:

Awarded the Nobel Prize in Literature in 1991, Nadine Gordimer has published nonfiction, more than two hundred short stories, and eleven novels. Born in South Africa, Gordimer sets most of her fiction in that country and as a consequence deals with apartheid, the racist system of government that lasted until 1991. Her eighth novel, *July's People*, deals with the possibility of a successful black revolution against the white power structure. The revolution is the background of the novel, not the central focus. As with her other novels, *July's People* concentrates on individual lives, not the broad politics. Gordimer centers her attention on Maureen Smales, a twenty-nine-year-old Johannesburg wife and mother. As the novel opens, a revolution is in progress and the Smales family takes refuge with July, their male servant, in a rural settlement. The novel traces the sudden role reversal between Maureen, who for fifteen years employed July, and July, who suddenly takes control not only of his life but also of the Smales family. The role reversals of Maureen and July serve as the microcosm for the supposed effects of the revolution. The title of the novel is deliberately ambiguous: The phrase "July's people" appears twice in the novel, the first time referring to the Smales family and the second time to July's extended family in the settlement. Once in the novel the narrator refers to "July's white people," distinguishing them from his relatives.

Although the novel lets the reader understand July's position, Maureen is central. A privileged citizen in South Africa, she deplores apartheid and feels her treatment of July as a servant for fifteen years is beyond reproach. Maureen and Bam pay him for his services, give him living quarters in their yard, send home presents to his family, start a special bank account for him with a hundred rands in honor of ten years of service, and never question his relationship with Ellen, the woman who lives with him in Johannesburg. The novel reveals that July feels he is not treated with dignity. Maureen gives him their cast-offs and orders him about, seemingly oblivious to some of his hardships. He has every Wednesday and every second Sunday off but has leave to visit his wife and children in the rural area only every other year.

Once Maureen lives in his home, she realizes what it is like to be dependent, not to have status. For example, she cannot walk far for fear of being seen by someone who might report the presence of whites in the area. (July, as a black South African, for years had to follow very strict laws governing where he was permitted to live, work, and travel.) Necessities—food and shelter—come mainly from July's willingness to supply them, and his willingness could end at a moment's notice, just as a new white farm owner in South Africa had the power to tell black farmworkers born on the farm to leave.

Maureen's whole life begins to fall apart. Her children do not seem to need her care. She feeds them from the supplies July brings, but otherwise they take care of themselves, spending time with the other children of the village. She does not recognize her husband as the same man she lived with in Johannesburg, and she bickers with him, pointing out his character flaws. She herself changes. When her civilized life is stripped to the primitive, she sees her past as a pose. She is not content with her present either. She finds life in the rural area degrading; she has no function there.

In his home area, when July realizes power has passed from Maureen to him, his language becomes more assertive. In fact, during the last conversation he has in the novel with Maureen, July uses his own language, a language Maureen cannot understand. That language, in the settlement, is the language of power. Maureen thinks that she and July communicate well, understand each other. Maureen was mistaken for fifteen years; the agreeableness of July is the response of one who knows his position in South Africa. He never forgets he is the servant who can stay in the city only as long as Maureen signs his pass book each month.

Although the broader story of *July's People* may be the revolution in South Africa, the central story is the discovery by one woman of how deluded she has been about her own life, about her treatment of July, and about her liberal stance regarding South African politics. *July's People* is Gordimer's first novel to center all the action on the home ground of the blacks in South Africa. Although Maureen is the protagonist, she can only be understood through an understanding of July. Gordimer tells Maureen's story and in doing so reveals July's.

The closing of the novel does not clarify Maureen's future. Will she be successful in gaining access to the helicopter? Who is in the helicopter? Americans who come to rescue their countrymen from the revolution? Cubans who come to aid the revolutionaries? The ending does make clear that Maureen wants to abandon her past life in Johannesburg and her present life in July's settlement. That her running can lead to a better life is suspect, but it does suggest she realizes the failure of her past.

Marion Petrillo

Further Reading

Bodenheimer, Rosemarie. "The Interregnum of Ownership in *July's People*." In *The Later Fiction of Nadine Gordimer*, edited by Bruce King. New York: St. Martin's Press,

1993. Sees the novel as revealing the hollowness of a materialistic life. Removed from their privileged society, detached from their material possessions, Bamford and Maureen lose their selfhood.

Caminero-Santangelo, Byron. "Subjects in History: Disruptions of the Colonial in *Heart of Darkness* and *July's People*." In *African Fiction and Joseph Conrad: Reading Postcolonial Intertextuality*. Albany: State University of New York Press, 2005. Examines the relationship between Gordimer's novel and Conrad's *Heart of Darkness*.

Clingman, Stephen. *The Novels of Nadine Gordimer: History from the Inside*. Winchester, Mass.: Allen and Unwin, 1986. Places Gordimer's first eight novels in the context of South African society and politics. Clingman sees the major themes of *July's People* as racial and class revolution and also a revolution in language and sexual roles.

Dojka, Stephanie. "*July's People*: She Knew No Word." In *Joinings and Disjoinings: The Significance of Marital Status in Literature*, edited by JoAnna Stephens Mink and Janet Doubler Ward. Bowling Green, Ohio: Bowling Green State University Popular Press, 1991. Sees the deterioration of the marriage of the Smaleses as an indication that white institutions based on exploitation must be dismantled; the marriage is successful at July's expense.

Neill, Michael. "Translating the Present: Language, Knowledge, and Identity in Nadine Gordimer's *July's People*." *Journal of Commonwealth Literature* 25, no. 1 (1990): 71-97. Sees the novel as being not so much about the revolutionary future as about the difficulties of the South Africa of the novel's present. Analyzes how language, knowledge, and identity break down with a change of culture.

Roberts, Ronald Suresh. *No Cold Kitchen: A Biography of Nadine Gordimer*. Johannesburg: STE, 2005. Examines Gordimer's life and work, placing them within the context of South African history and the many authors and other people she has known.

Smith, Roland. "Masters and Servants: Nadine Gordimer's *July's People* and the Themes of Her Fiction." In *Critical Essays on Nadine Gordimer*, edited by Roland Smith. Boston: G. K. Hall, 1990. Centers on Maureen's recognition of the flaws of her liberalism. Sees a main theme of the novel as the inability of whites and blacks to communicate.

Temple-Thurston, Barbara. *Nadine Gordimer Revisited*. New York: Twayne, 1999. Examines all of Gordimer's novels, finding common themes of revolution, sexuality, gender, Africanness, race, and other issues and charting the development of her narrative form and technique. Chapter 4 focuses on an analysis of *July's People* and *Burger's Daughter*.

Uledi Kamanga, Brighton J. "Cracks in the Wall: The Decline of Apartheid in *July's People* and *My Son's Story*." In *Cracks in the Wall: Nadine Gordimer's Fiction and the Irony of Apartheid*. Trenton, N.J.: Africa World Press, 2002. Focuses on Gordimer's depiction of apartheid in South Africa in her short stories and novels published before 1994. Traces how her fiction chronicles apartheid from its introduction in the late 1940's to its abolition in the early 1990's.

Juneteenth

Author: Ralph Ellison (1914-1994)
First published: 1999; revised as *Three Days Before the Shooting*, 2010
Type of work: Novel
Type of plot: Psychological realism
Time of plot: Early to mid-twentieth century
Locale: Washington, D.C., the American South, and the American Midwest

Principal characters:
REVEREND ALONZO HICKMAN
SENATOR ADAM SUNRAIDER (BLISS)

The Story:

The Reverend Alonzo Hickman and members from his congregation descend on Washington, D.C., to confront Senator Adam Sunraider, who has made a name for himself with his race-baiting speeches. The congregation believes it can "save" Sunraider from himself, since he, as a boy named Bliss, once belonged to their church. Unbeknownst to them,

Sunraider's racist rants are part of his plan to spur passive blacks into revolutionary action. The church members attend a session of Congress to hear one of the senator's racist speeches.

The congregation's plans to redeem Sunraider are foiled when he is shot by one of its members, an angry young boy named Severen. As Sunraider lies on the Senate floor, he begins to remember his life. He continues his reveries as he is taken to the hospital, and Hickman interrupts and corrects some of Sunraider's recollections. In the hospital, Hickman sits at the bedside of the fatally wounded senator. Delirious, hallucinating, the senator offers up a mea culpa and "confession" but, at the same time, castigates Hickman for his role in Sunraider's fate. Sunraider passes out but while unconscious flashes back to his childhood as Bliss, when he knew Hickman as Daddy Hickman.

Daddy Hickman promises Bliss ice cream if he will climb into a wooden coffin. Hickman, a preacher, has decided that the only way to unite the black and white races in America is to put on a "revival" show featuring a young white boy, Bliss, rising from the coffin as a new Christ. Bliss is a typical young boy; he is afraid of the darkness of the closed coffin. Hickman tells him he can take his Easter bunny into the casket with him, but Bliss will enter only if he can bring his teddy bear with him because, he says, "bears ain't afraid of the dark."

Sunraider continues to relive his childhood at random, recalling events in no particular order. As Bliss, he stands up to a group of African American bullies by beating them at a game of the dozens and hitting one of the boys in the forehead with a stone (recalling David's battle with Goliath). The most traumatic and significant event of Bliss's childhood, the one that drives him away from Hickman and his congregation, occurs at one of the revival shows: As Bliss is rising from the coffin on cue, a red-haired woman from the crowd rushes the stage, attempts to grab him, and calls him "Cudworth," claiming to be his mother. The black women in the congregation pull her away and rush Bliss off to a safe hiding place. Although he does not get a good look at the woman's face, Bliss never forgets her red hair. After he runs away, he decides to film his adventures across the South and the Midwest. However, his real motive for making the film is that he hopes, one day, to find the red-haired woman.

After the revival show but before Bliss leaves for good, Hickman tries to placate the boy by taking him to see a movie. Hickman dislikes this new form of entertainment since it tempts people not only to confuse illusion and reality but also to prefer the former to the latter. Hickman's reserva-

tions turn out to be well founded. The film they see features a red-haired Mary Pickford, and Bliss, who has never been in a theater before, is so transported by the experience that he believes he is actually in the film with the actress. Worse, he believes she is his mother. From that moment on, he goes from movie house to movie house, shoots film in town after town, searching for the red-haired woman.

Still a young boy and as a white preacher speaking in the voice of black Baptists, Bliss is intoxicated with his powers of persuasion; he becomes a miniature version of Hickman. He meets and falls for a young black girl named Laly, but all he dreams of is making her over into someone else. Just as Hickman made him a "black" boy with white skin, so Bliss believes he can transform Laly—and himself—into an Indian princess and prince. That dream quickly dissipates when local ruffians—having observed Bliss and his assistants, Donelson and Karp, taking pictures and shooting film—threaten them at gunpoint.

As Sunraider drifts in and out of consciousness, Hickman undergoes his own crises. He feels guilty for not preventing Severen from shooting Sunraider and for betraying both his congregation and Bliss by putting so much faith in, and responsibility on, a child. Hickman's true motives for raising Bliss as a preacher and a symbol of racial reconciliation are related to the mystery of Bliss's birth. Hickman's brother, Bob, was once involved in an illicit affair with the red-haired woman. When she became pregnant, she panicked and informed the police that she'd been raped by Bob. Bob was arrested, but, before he could be tried in court, a lynch mob hanged him. The red-haired woman, desperate to shield her lie, gave birth in secrecy and, one night, brought the newborn to Hickman's cabin. Wracked with guilt, she begged him to take the child as compensation for his dead brother. Hickman, outraged, grabbed her by the throat, intending to strangle her. She did not resist, telling him he had every right to kill her. However, Hickman could not bring himself to murder the mother of his nephew. He relented, took the child, invented a cover story (a black man traveling with a white child, he told everyone that he was the child's servant), and began his ministry.

Critical Evaluation:

In many respects, *Juneteenth* is as much the work of John Callahan, Ralph Ellison's literary executor, as it is of Ellison himself. Culled from over two thousand pages of manuscripts, the posthumously edited and published novel reflects what Callahan surmised to be Ellison's intentions. Ellison began writing *Juneteenth*, his second novel, the year before the publication of his acclaimed 1952 debut, *Invisible Man*.

As the years went by, however, the second novel never appeared. In the late 1960's, Ellison bought a house in upstate New York where he could focus on the novel. Unfortunately, a catastrophic fire destroyed the house and manuscripts in 1967. Devastated, Ellison started over, and by the 1970's felt confident enough to share large portions of the work with fellow writers such as Saul Bellow. For over twenty years, friends, editors, and the literary community awaited the publication of Ellison's sophomore novel. It never came, and when he died in 1994 most people assumed Ellison would remain a one-hit wunderkind. It was only when Callahan announced that he had found a treasure trove of manuscripts, all apparently different sections of what was to have been an epic novel, that it became clear Ellison's second novel could still be published. *Juneteenth* was published in 1999; an expanded and revised version of the novel was published in 2010 with the title *Three Days Before the Shooting*.

In *Juneteenth*, Ellison raised the stakes of the "great experiment" that is the United States of America, plumbing the depths of paternity, maternity, and miscegenation to highlight the absurdities of racial politics absolutely dependent on appearances. Thus, misidentifications, masks, and racial "passing" drive the narrative. The central leitmotif of visual impairment as the normal state of racially conditioned Americans is anchored by the metaphor of film, a popular form of mass illusion. At the same time, Bliss/Sunraider's penchant for rhetoric is figured as the very framework of his life as an evangelical child prodigy who becomes a muckraking senator. Meanwhile, Hickman fears that his deployment of religious showmanship in the service of social and political ends (such as racial reconciliation, civil rights, and integration) has done just as much harm as has Sunraider's misguided attempt to foment a black revolution by becoming an over-the-top racist. Hickman's guilt over his actions keeps him at Sunraider's bedside in the hospital. Both have much to confess to and atone for, though it is too late to save the life of either the assassinated Sunraider or the assassin Severen.

In a novel in which the central mystery turns on birth, Ellison demonstrates some sympathy for the unnamed red-haired woman. Hickman explains to Bliss that this woman has kidnapped children before, that she has not been "right in the head" since she fell out of a tree as a teenager after she started menstruating. Because her mother refused to tell her why she was bleeding, she came to believe that her blood was actually her dead children. Although this story is itself fairly misogynistic, it functions in the novel as a lie, a fairytale, to shield Bliss from both Hickman's relationship to the woman and a darker truth: Bliss's mother gave him up as recompense for her role in the death of Hickman's brother.

Finally, Ellison deploys the myth of Icarus and Daedalus to underscore a theme resonating through both *Invisible Man* and *Juneteenth*: that flight from social and personal responsibility is impossible. The red-haired woman's flight to Hickman's cabin to deliver up Bliss does not sever her ties with her son. Hickman's flight from one revival to another does not alleviate him of the gnawing realization that he is exploiting both his congregation and Bliss. Bliss's flight across Middle America neither distances him from the image of the red-haired woman in his memory nor closes the distance between him and the "real" red-haired woman he pursues. In one of Sunraider's last hallucinations, he observes skeet shooters on a cliff picking off pigeons. He notices that the pigeons who survive do not attempt to fly higher, beyond the range of the guns. Instead, they swoop down, below the level of the cliff, and thus elude death. This counterintuitive strategy replicates that of the unnamed narrator in *Invisible Man*. He, too, escapes death during the riot that closes the novel by living underground, trying to figure out how to return topside as a socially responsible man.

Tyrone Williams

Further Reading

Aithal, S. Krishnamoorthy. "*Juneteenth*: A Novel for the New Millennium." *American Studies International* 38, no. 3 (October, 2000): 115-121. Focuses on the humanity and complexity of Hickman's relationship to Bliss. Argues that Ellison uses irony to explore the ways that both Hickman and Bliss attempt to overcome the burden of American history by trying to meet each other outside the realms of their particular expertise: culture and politics.

Applebome, Peter. "Ralph Ellison's Elusive Novel, *Juneteenth*." *Crisis (The New)* 106, no. 2 (March/April, 1999): 38-39. Based on an interview with editor John Callahan, this article discusses the cultural and literary events that led up to the anticipated publication of *Juneteenth*.

De Santis, Christopher C. "*Juneteenth*, by Ralph Ellison." *Review of Contemporary Fiction* 19, no. 3 (September, 1999): 172-173. Emphasizes that *Juneteenth* challenges simple notions of race and identity as its essentially musical structure moves back and forth across dizzyingly constructed and discarded identities.

Jones, Malcolm. "Visible Once Again." *Newsweek* 133, no. 21 (June 24, 1999): 69. Argues that as good as the novel is, characterized by Ellison's refusal to give in to simple binary oppositions regarding culture and race in America, it is burdened by Ellison's self-consciousness that he was writing the long-anticipated follow-up to *Invisible Man*. Nonetheless, Ellison was unique in wedding high and low culture by combining literary culture with music (blues and jazz)—not to show off but because he is a fan of both art forms.

O'Meally, Robert G. "How Can the Light Deny the Dark?" *Atlantic Monthly* 284, no. 1 (July, 1999): 89-90. Summarizes the history behind the publication of *Juneteenth*, as well as O'Meally's relationship to Ellison, focusing specifically on the folk cultural elements in the novel as well as in *Invisible Man*.

Pinsker, Sanford. "America, Race, and Ralph Ellison." *Sewanee Review* 108, no. 2 (Spring, 2000): lix-lxxiii. Reads *Juneteenth* as essentially a tone poem, a fragment among the thousands of unpublished pages left behind by Ellison. For Pinsker, the major problem with the novel is the lack of psychological development of Bliss and the decision by Callahan to render what was apparently going to be a postmodern work as a more traditional novel.

Shank, Barry. "Bliss, or Blackface Sentiment." *boundary 2* 30, no. 2 (Summer, 2003): 46-63. Argues that, in both *Invisible Man* and *Juneteenth*, Ellison interrogates the productive and limited possibilities of blackface. Insofar as blackface describes not only the minstrel tradition but also the very nature of American culture—that what is native in American culture is, in large part, black—it is the source of the myth of distinct black and white cultures and identities.

The Jungle

Author: Upton Sinclair (1878-1968)
First published: 1906
Type of work: Novel
Type of plot: Social realism
Time of plot: Early twentieth century
Locale: Chicago

Principal characters:
JURGIS RUDKUS, a stockyards worker
DEDE ANTANAS, Jurgis's father
ONA, Jurgis's wife
ANTANAS, child of Jurgis and Ona
ELZBIETA, Ona's stepmother
JONAS, Elzbieta's brother
MARIJA, Ona's orphan cousin

The Story:

While he is still a peasant boy in Lithuania, Jurgis Rudkus falls in love with a gentle girl named Ona. When Ona's father dies, Jurgis, planning to marry her as soon as he has enough money, comes to America with her family. Besides the young lovers, the emigrant party is composed of Dede Antanas, Jurgis's father; Elzbieta, Ona's stepmother; Jonas, Elzbieta's brother; Marija, Ona's orphan cousin; and Elzbieta's six children. By the time the family arrives in Chicago, they have very little money. Jonas, Marija, and Jurgis at once get work in the stockyards. Dede Antanas tries to find work, but he is too old.

They decide that it will be cheaper to buy a house on installments than to rent. A crooked agent sells them a ramshackle house with a fresh coat of paint that he describes to his ignorant customers as new. Jurgis finds his job exhausting, but he thinks himself lucky to be making forty-five dollars a month. At last, Dede Antanas also finds work at the plant, but he has to give part of his wages to the foreman in order to secure his job.

Jurgis and Ona save enough money for their wedding feast and are married. Then the family finds that they need more money. Elzbieta lies about the age of her oldest son, Stanislovas, and he, too, gets a job at the plant. Ona is already working. Dede Antanas works in a moist, cold room, where he develops consumption. When he dies, the family has scarcely enough money to bury him. Winter comes, and everyone suffers in the flimsy house. When Marija loses her job, the family income diminishes. Jurgis joins a union and becomes an active member. He goes to night school to learn to read and to speak English.

At last, summer comes with its hordes of flies and oppressive heat. Marija finds work as a beef trimmer, but at that job the danger of blood poisoning is very great. Ona has a baby, a fine boy, whom they call Antanas after his grandfather. Winter comes again, and Jurgis pulls a tendon in his ankle while attempting to avoid a rampaging steer at the plant. Compelled to stay at home for months, he becomes moody. Two more of Elzbieta's children leave school to sell papers. When

Jurgis is well enough to look for work again, he can find none, because he is no longer the strong man he was. Finally, he gets a job in a fertilizer plant, a last resort, for men last only a few years at that work.

One of Elzbieta's daughters is now old enough to care for the rest of the children, and Elzbieta also goes to work. Jurgis begins to drink. Ona, pregnant again, develops a consumptive cough and is often seized with spells of hysteria. Hoping to save her job, she allows herself to be seduced by her boss, Connor. When Jurgis learns what she did, he attacks Connor and is sentenced to thirty days in jail. Having time to think in jail, Jurgis sees how unjustly he is treated by society. No longer will he try to be kind, except to his own family. From now on, he will recognize society as an enemy rather than as a friend.

After he serves his sentence, Jurgis goes to look for his family. He finds that they lost the house because they could not meet the payments and moved. He finds them at last in a rooming house. Ona is in labor with her second child, and Jurgis frantically searches for a midwife. By the time he finds one, Ona and the child are past saving. Now he has only little Antanas to live for. He tries to find work. Blacklisted in the stockyards for his attack on Connor, he finally finds a job in a harvesting machine factory. Soon after, he is discharged when his department closes down for a lack of orders.

Next he goes to work in the steel mills. In order to save money, he moves near the mills and comes home only on weekends. One weekend he comes home to find that Antanas drowned in the street in front of the house. In order to flee his inner demons, his remorse, and his grief, he hops a freight train and rides away from Chicago. He becomes one of the thousands of hobos and workers; his old strength comes back in healthful, rural surroundings.

In the fall, Jurgis returns to Chicago. He gets a job digging tunnels under the streets. Then a shoulder injury makes him spend weeks in a hospital. Discharged with his arm still in a sling, he becomes a beggar. By luck he obtains a hundred-dollar bill from a drunken son of a packing owner. When he goes to a saloon to get it changed, however, the barkeeper tries to cheat him out of his money. In a rage, Jurgis attacks the man. He is arrested and sent to jail again. There he becomes acquainted with a dapper safecracker, Jack Duane, whom he met during his last incarceration. After their release, Jurgis joins Duane in several muggings and becomes acquainted with Chicago's underworld. At last, he is making money.

Jurgis becomes a political worker. About that time, the packing plant workers begin to demand more rights through their unions. When packinghouse operators will not listen to union demands, there is a general strike. Jurgis goes to work

in the plant as a scab and is given a managerial position. One night, however, he meets Connor and attacks him again. After getting out on bond and learning that Connor is well connected, Jurgis flees from the district to avoid a penitentiary sentence. On the verge of starvation, he finds Marija working as a prostitute. Jurgis is ashamed to think how low he and Marija fell since they came to Chicago.

Jurgis leaves, despondent, but he happens upon a socialist meeting. He experiences something like a religious transformation. At last, he knows how the workers can find self-respect. He finds a job in a hotel where the manager is a socialist. It is the beginning of a new life for Jurgis, the rebirth of hope and faith.

Critical Evaluation:

The Jungle is indisputably Upton Sinclair's best and most influential book. He was, nevertheless, never entirely happy with its reception. While it contributed to the passage of the Pure Food and Drug Act in 1906 and other consumer protection legislation, his intent was to lay bare the capitalist system and demonstrate the need for democratic socialism. This message was largely ignored.

The Jungle's critique of capitalism is unrelenting. Sinclair depicts a world that is dominated, as his title suggests, by might rather than right, a world that pits everyone against everyone else and metes out rewards on the basis of clout rather than merit. People are lured to the cities in droves and then discarded when they no longer serve the purposes of the powerful. They are maimed, forced to work in unsafe and unsavory conditions, and pushed, psychologically and physically, well past their breaking points.

Even as Sinclair describes the wedding feast in the opening chapter, he mixes images of gaiety and trays of piping-hot food with vignettes that chronicle the hardships of those forced to work as canners, picklers, beef boners, and general laborers. These workers' tales are tragic, yet the workers refuse to admit defeat.

Jurgis personifies their defiance, constantly vowing to work harder and refusing to accept the systemic causes of his sufferings. He dedicates himself to achieving the American Dream and is convinced that through his own resolve and determination he can provide for his family and loved ones and rise through the system.

Characterizing Jurgis as a strict individualist who believes that anyone can succeed, Sinclair makes a direct appeal to his nonsocialist readers. The characters in *The Jungle* are not slackers; they are working men and women with simple dreams and expectations who are more than willing to contribute their fair share.

The Jungle / SINCLAIR

To bring his point home, Sinclair depicts a family more than willing to make sacrifices in order to become full-fledged members of the larger social order. Even Jurgis's father, who is clearly too old to endure the ruthless conditions of the factory, pours his energies into securing employment so the family can afford the basic necessities and provide the youngsters a proper education.

From the beginning, it is clear to the readers that Jurgis and his family are fighting against the odds. Each new detail makes it abundantly clear that the system tempts people with unrealistic dreams and then erects insurmountable barriers to prevent the attainment of those dreams. Instead of a promised land, the family finds a land where greed and exploitation rule. It is not only the greed of the factory owners that the family encounters but also that of the owners' lackeys who sell repossessed tract homes as new, the judges and politicians who have long since abandoned any moral scruples, and the slumlords who live in splendor while their tenants are surrounded by filth and disease. Added to this mix are the churches and the missions that are callously indifferent to the conditions the poor endure, and, quite often, contribute to their suffering.

For the first two-thirds of the book, however, Jurgis is ill-equipped to comprehend the realities that surround him. Until the time of Antanas's death, he clings to a vague belief that, despite their setbacks, he and the remaining family members will somehow be able to save enough money to allow them a comfortable life and to revive "their habits of decency and kindness."

Once he loses his son, however, he loses the last vestige of hope. He steels himself against emotions and heads for the country. He recovers his health there but finds that even those farmers who are willing to help him (and many are not) treat their work animals better than they do their hired hands. Jurgis resorts to guile and thievery as a way to make ends meet. He cannot, however, silence his conscience, and after coming to terms with the painful losses that he already endured, returns to the city and resumes his search for a better life.

Although the most memorable and horrifying scenes in the book are those that center on the meatpacking industry, Sinclair goes to great lengths to demonstrate that conditions in other industries are no better. Whether Jurgis is working at Packingtown, at the Harvester Works, at the steel mills, or in the city's underground tunnels, he is treated with indifference and contempt and, when supply exceeds demand, summarily discharged, "turned out to starve for doing his duty too well." The brutalization is underscored by Sinclair's use of numerous analogies that compare the individuals to wild and hunted animals and of parallels between the fate of the innocent livestock and the fate of the common working person. Factory life is variously compared to an inferno, a bubbling cauldron, and a medieval torture chamber, where it is considered good sport to extract the last ounce of flesh from the hapless workers. The factory, however, is only a reflection of society's disregard for democratic values and its indifference to truth and justice.

This, not the vile conditions and practices of the meatpackers, is Sinclair's primary message. It is not, however, the message that the majority of his readers received. Coming as it did on the heels of the embalmed beef scandal exposed by William Randolph Hearst in 1899, the book merely added to the clamor for stricter regulation of the meatpacking industry, and Sinclair's larger purpose was ignored.

In part, the fault was Sinclair's. Rather than integrating his call for democratic socialism into the fiber of the novel, he tacks it on almost like an addendum; it lacks authenticity. In describing Jurgis's conversion, he somehow loses sight of Jurgis, reducing him to spectator status, and does not fill the void that this creates with any memorable presence. Sinclair was aware of the flaws that weakened the last third of the novel and, at one point, even suggested ending the novel with Antanas's death and then publishing a sequel. One might wish that his publisher had agreed. It would have strengthened *The Jungle* and allowed Sinclair the time to develop his critique of the role the political and judicial system plays in the disempowerment of the average citizen. Whether it would have made his socialist appeal any more compelling, however, is a moot point.

"Critical Evaluation" by C. Lynn Munro

Further Reading

Arthur, Anthony. *Radical Innocent: Upton Sinclair*. New York: Random House, 2006. A well-researched, balanced, and thorough portrait of Sinclair that tracks the ups and downs of his career and personal life. Includes sixteen pages of black and white photos.

Bloodworth, William A., Jr. *Upton Sinclair*. Boston: Twayne, 1977. Portrays Sinclair as a literary rebel who weds art and ideology and sacrifices the last four chapters of *The Jungle* in his attempt to introduce hope into an otherwise dismal world. Analyzes the novel as a contemporary tragedy, paying attention to the conservative biases inherent in the message.

Bloom, Harold, ed. *Upton Sinclair's "The Jungle."* Philadelphia: Chelsea House, 2002. Collection of essays about Sinclair and *The Jungle*, including discussions of Sinclair as a muckraker, the narrative strategy and suppressed conclusion of "America's first proletarian novel," the "two lives" of Jurgis Rudkus, and comparisons of *The Jungle* with George Orwell's *Animal Farm* and Jack London's *The Call of the Wild*.

Harris, Leon. *Upton Sinclair: American Rebel*. New York: Thomas Y. Crowell, 1975. Depicts Sinclair as the most influential, but not the best, writer in the United States because he changed the way Americans viewed themselves, their rights, and their expectations. Includes bibliography.

Mattson, Kevin. *Upton Sinclair and the Other American Century*. Hoboken, N.J.: John Wiley & Sons, 2006. Published during the centenary of *The Jungle*'s publication, Mattson's biography places Sinclair's life within the context of social, cultural, economic, and political events, expanding upon previous biographies.

Mookerjee, R. N. *Art for Social Justice: The Major Novels of Upton Sinclair*. Metuchen, N.J.: Scarecrow Press, 1988. Argues that Sinclair's novels must be assessed as an extension of his social activism and desire to communicate with the masses. Examines Sinclair's use of a documentary style and defends Sinclair's characterization, noting that in addition to Jurgis, Sinclair manages to give heroic status to both Marija and Elzbieta.

Scott, Ivan. *Upton Sinclair: The Forgotten Socialist*. Lewiston, N.Y.: Edwin Mellen Press, 1997. A sound scholarly biography, drawing extensively on the Sinclair collection at the Lilly Library at the University of Indiana. In his introduction, Scott makes a good case for Sinclair's importance; chapters 1 and 2, "The Formation of Genius" and "*The Jungle*," respectively, are especially useful.

Sinclair, Upton. *"The Jungle": An Authoritative Text, Contexts and Backgrounds, Criticism*. Edited by Clare Virginia Eby. New York: Norton, 2003. In addition to the text of the novel, this edition contains information about the history of the meatpacking industry, social conditions in the Chicago stockyards, the life of immigrant workers, and other essays and documents that place the novel in its historical, social, and political contexts. Eight other essays provide critical interpretations of the novel, including discussions of its documentary strategy, depiction of gender, and Jurgis's conversion.

Yoder, Jon A. *Upton Sinclair*. New York: Frederick Ungar, 1975. Analyzes the reasons Sinclair's works have been neglected and why Sinclair deemed *The Jungle* a failure. Explains the underpinnings of Sinclair's vision of democratic socialism.

The Jungle Books

Author: Rudyard Kipling (1865-1936)
First published: The Jungle Book, 1894; *The Second Jungle Book*, 1895
Type of work: Short fiction
Type of plot: Fables
Time of plot: Nineteenth century
Locale: India

Principal characters:
MOWGLI, an Indian boy
FATHER WOLF
MOTHER WOLF
SHERE KHAN, the tiger
AKELA, the leader of the wolf pack
BAGHEERA, the black panther
BALOO, the bear
KAA, the rock python
THE BANDAR-LOG, the monkey people
HATHI, the elephant
MESSUA, a woman who adopts Mowgli for a time
MESSUA'S HUSBAND
BULDEO, a village hunter
GRAY BROTHER, a young wolf

The Story:

Shere Khan, the tiger, pursues a small Indian boy who strays from his native village, but Shere Khan is lame and misses his leap upon the child. When Father Wolf takes the boy home with him to show to Mother Wolf, Shere Khan follows and demands the child as his quarry. Mother Wolf refuses. The tiger retires in anger. Mowgli, the frog, for such he is named, is reared by Mother Wolf along with her own cubs.

Father Wolf takes Mowgli to the Council Rock to be recognized by the wolves. Bagheera, the panther, and Baloo, the bear, speak for Mowgli's acceptance into the Seeonee wolf pack. Therefore, Mowgli becomes a wolf. Baloo becomes Mowgli's teacher and instructs him in the lore of the jungle. Mowgli learns to speak the languages of all the jungle people. Throughout his early life, the threat of Shere Khan hangs over him, but Mowgli is certain of his place in the pack and of his friends' protection; someday when Akela, the leader of the wolves, misses his kill, the pack will turn on him and Mowgli. Bagheera tells Mowgli to get the Red Flower, or fire, from the village to protect himself. When Akela misses his quarry one night and is about to be deposed and killed, Mowgli attacks all of the mutual enemies with his fire sticks and threatens to destroy anyone who molests Akela. That night, Mowgli realizes that the jungle is no place for him, and that someday he will go to live with men. That time, however, is still far off.

One day, Mowgli climbs a tree and makes friends with the Bandar-Log, the monkey tribe, who because of their stupidity and vanity are despised by the other jungle people. When the Bandar-Log carries off Mowgli, Bagheera and Baloo go in pursuit, taking along Kaa, the rock python, who loves to eat monkeys. Mowgli is rescued at the old ruined city of the Cold Lairs by the three pursuers, and Kaa feasts royally upon monkey meat.

One year during a severe drought in the jungle, Hathi the elephant proclaims the water truce; all animals are allowed to drink at the water hole unmolested. Shere Khan announces to the animals gathered there one day that he killed a man, not for food but from choice. The other animals are shocked. Hathi allows the tiger to drink and then tells him to be off. Then Hathi tells the story of how fear came to the jungle and why the tiger is striped. It is the tiger who first kills man and earns the human tribe's unrelenting enmity; for his deed, the tiger is condemned to wear stripes. For one day a year, the tiger is not afraid of man and can kill him. This day is called, among jungle people, the Night of the Tiger.

One day, Mowgli wanders close to a native village, where he is adopted by Messua, a woman who lost her son some years before. Mowgli becomes a watcher of the village herds; from time to time, he meets Gray Wolf, his brother, and hears the news of the jungle. Learning that Shere Khan intends to kill him, he plans with Akela and Gray Brother to kill the tiger. They lure Shere Khan into a gully and then stampede the herd. Exiled by stoning from the village because he is believed to be a sorcerer who speaks to the animals, Mowgli returns to the jungle, resolved to hunt with the wolves for the rest of his life.

Buldeo, the village hunter, follows the trail of Mowgli,

Gray Brother, and Akela. Mowgli overhears Buldeo say that Messua and her husband are imprisoned in their house and will be burned at the stake. Messua's husband saved some money, and he has one of the finest herds of buffaloes in the village. Knowing that the imprisonment of Messua and her husband is a scheme for the villagers to get their property, Mowgli plans to help his friends. Entering the village, he leads Messua and her husband beyond the gates in the darkness. Then the jungle people began to destroy, little by little, the farms, the orchards, and the cattle, but no villager is harmed because Mowgli does not desire the death of any human. Finally, just before the rains, Hathi and his three sons move into the village and tear down the houses. The people leave, and thus the jungle is let into the village.

Kaa takes Mowgli to Cold Lairs to meet the guardian of the king's treasure, an old white cobra who expresses a desire to see Mowgli. The old cobra shows them all the treasure; when he leaves, Mowgli takes a jeweled elephant goad, a king's ankus, with him, even though the cobra says it brings death to the person who possesses it.

Back in the jungle, Mowgli throws the ankus away. Later that day, he goes with Bagheera to retrieve the ankus and discovers that it is gone. They follow the trail of the man who picked it up and find that altogether six men who had possession of the ankus died. Believing it to be cursed, Mowgli returns the ankus to the treasure room in the Cold Lairs.

Sometimes fierce red dogs called dholes travel in large packs, destroying everything in their paths. Warned of the approach of the dholes, Mowgli leads the marauders, by insults and taunts, toward the lairs of the Little People, the bees. Then he excites the bees to attack the dholes. The destruction of the red dogs that escape the fury of the bees is completed by the wolves lying in ambush a little farther down the river, which flows under the cliffs where the Little People live; it is the last battle of old Akela, the leader of the pack when Mowgli was a little boy. He crawls out slowly from under a pile of carcasses to bid Mowgli good-bye and to sing his death song.

The second year after the death of Akela, Mowgli is about seventeen years old. In the spring of that year, Mowgli knows that he is unhappy, but none of his friends can tell him what is wrong. Mowgli leaves his own jungle to travel to another, and on the way he meets Messua. Her husband died and left her with a child. Messua tells Mowgli that she believes he is her own son lost in the jungle years before and that her baby must be his brother. Mowgli does not know what to make of the child and the unhappiness he feels. When Gray Brother comes to Messua's hut, Mowgli decides to return to the jungle. On the outskirts of the village, however, he meets a girl coming down the path. Mowgli melts into the jungle and watches the girl. He knows at last that the jungle is no longer a place for him and that he returns to the man-pack to stay.

Critical Evaluation:

Although originally published separately, *The Jungle Books* are usually combined into one volume. For most readers, *The Jungle Books* tell the story of Mowgli, the boy raised by wolves to become ruler of the jungle, only to have to return to the human world as an adult. Mowgli's adventures in fact take up only eight of the fifteen stories that make up *The Jungle Books*, but those eight stories captivate the reader's imagination in a way that the others do not. Mowgli's story is essentially a reworking of an ancient folklore theme, the child raised by animals. In most versions of this motif, human society remains the frame of reference; the child's animal existence is simply a prelude to his or her reintegration into humanity. In contrast, Kipling places Mowgli in the context of a complete jungle society, which appears more attractive than the few glimpses of the human world allowed into the stories. Although Mowgli's return to the outside world is predicted in the first of the stories, it is his development within the animal world that interests the author. Kipling wrote one story about Mowgli as an adult in the human world, but he did not choose to include it in *The Jungle Books*.

The animal world in the Mowgli stories has been described as a post-Darwinian Eden, with Mowgli as Adam given dominion over the animals. Animal existence is rough, with survival dependent on the individual's strength and cunning, and even the revered leader of the wolf pack, Akela, must constantly demonstrate his fitness. That a helpless human child in such an environment could survive infancy, let alone grow to dominate all other jungle creatures, seems an impossible fantasy. Kipling makes it more plausible by reversing expectations. It is the savage jungle that is governed by order and law, while the "civilized" humans are bound by no law and little morality. Humans attack their own out of superstitious fear of witchcraft or out of greedy desire for gold. To Mowgli, gold seems useless—it cannot be eaten and is too soft to use as a tool or weapon.

In contrast, each animal has its place under the law of the jungle. All know what is required and what is prohibited, both for themselves and for others. With the singular exception of Shere Khan, each animal obeys the law with scrupulous care. The law, with its prohibition on killing humans, protects the infant Mowgli. His eventual mastery of the law in all its nuances grants him authority over the jungle animals.

Kipling's jungle law is in many ways little more than a codification of (carnivorous) animal instincts, which accounts for its universal applicability. As various critics have written, the insistence on law and order reflects late-nineteenth century concepts about the formation of stable societies and the legal basis of imperial rule.

Born to English parents in India, learning Hindi before he learned his mother tongue, Kipling found himself as child and adult without a stable place in either Indian or British society. At the age of six, he was sent away from his family to be schooled in England, where he lived with an abusive caretaker. Later, he endured life in an English boarding school designed to prepare boys for military life, for which he was personally unfitted. As a young man, he returned to India as a newspaperman, reporting on the Anglo-Indian community.

To Kipling, personal experience and professional observation demonstrated the vulnerability of the individual in an unregulated, chaotic world. The law, with its strictures on behavior and on social relationships, offered a means to offset the precarious condition of life as he knew it and incidentally provided a place for everyone regardless of background.

Mowgli is accepted by the animal world, but he can never completely become part of it. In the final Mowgli story, the python Kaa cites the law: "Man goes to man at the last, though the jungle does not cast him out." Mowgli, caught between two worlds, is an extension of the author into his work. Kipling's own childhood was less than idyllic; Mowgli's life would compensate. In the jungle, Mowgli experiences a world of freedom made possible, ironically, by the strictness of a law that grants even an in-between child protection. Moreover, Mowgli's position as an outsider enables him to learn as much as the jungle can teach; he masters far more of the jungle law than any animal.

The Anglo-Indian community into which Kipling was born and which he chronicled as a journalist also had reason to feel its position precarious. On behalf of the crown, a comparative handful of British soldiers, bureaucrats, and ordinary citizens ruled millions of Indians. Just how tenuous that rule could be was demonstrated by the Indian Mutiny of 1857-1858, an event that continued to reverberate forty years later. Kipling alludes to the Indian Mutiny in "The Undertakers," one of *The Jungle Books*' non-Mowgli stories.

Only by a strict adherence to imperial law, and by the subject peoples' recognition of the laws, could order prevail in such a colonial empire. Kipling's jungle law serves as a model for effective colonial administration, just as Mowgli's complete immersion in and knowledge of the culture of those he will later rule is Kipling's model for the ideal colonial education. The other stories in *The Jungle Books* elaborate the vision of a hierarchical world, one in which harmony prevails when socially ordained boundaries are respected. Still essentially beast fables, these stories are more realistic in depicting animal protagonists without the ability to communicate with humans. While several, such as "Rikki-Takki-Tavi," are interesting in their own right, they function in the context of *The Jungle Books* primarily as foils to Mowgli's experiences.

"Critical Evaluation" by A. Waller Hastings

Further Reading

Allen, Charles. *Kipling Sahib: India and the Making of Rudyard Kipling*. London: Little, Brown, 2007. A biography focusing on Kipling's life from his birth until 1889, including his thirteen years in India, which were the inspiration for much of his writing. Allen traces the experiences of Kipling's parents in India, the Indian culture into which Kipling was born, and the state of the country when he returned in 1882 to begin his literary career by working on a newspaper in Lahore.

Bauer, Helen Pike. *Rudyard Kipling: A Study of the Short Fiction*. New York: Twayne, 1994. Analyzes the stories in *The Jungle Books* and Kipling's other short fiction. Discusses the stories' themes of isolation, work, the British Empire, childhood, the supernatural, and art. Includes Kipling's comments on writing and excerpts from a formalist and a postcolonial analysis of Kipling.

Blount, Margaret. *Animal Land: The Creatures of Children's Fiction*. New York: William Morrow, 1975. Analyzes the Mowgli stories as variants on the school story. Discusses the inversion of moral order between the animal and human worlds.

Dillingham, William B. *Rudyard Kipling: Hell and Heroism*. New York: Palgrave Macmillan, 2005. Dillingham maintains that other biographers and critics have neglected Kipling's deeply pessimistic worldview and his complex code of heroism. He focuses on these aspects of Kipling's personality to analyze the writer's life and some of his works, including a discussion of *The Jungle Books* in chapter 4.

Frey, Charles, and John Griffith. *The Literary Heritage of Childhood: An Appraisal of Children's Classics in the Western Tradition*. Westport, Conn.: Greenwood Press, 1987. Analyzes Mowgli as a character situated between two cultures, unable to fit into either fully, and connects Mowgli's situation to Kipling's position in regard to Indian and English society.

Hagiioannu, Andrew. "Mowgli's Feral Campaign: *The Jungle Books* and the Americanisation of Empire." In *The Man Who Would Be Kipling: The Colonial Fiction and the Frontiers of Exile*. New York: Palgrave Macmillan, 2003. Analyzes the political ideas, narrative style, and historical meanings in *The Jungle Books* and Kipling's other colonial fiction. Examines the impact of India, the United States, South Africa, and the British Empire on these works.

McBratney, John. "Imperial Subjects, Imperial Space in Kipling's *Jungle Book*." *Victorian Studies* 35, no. 3 (Spring, 1992): 277-293. Detailed examination of the Mowgli stories in relation to contemporary categories of race and ethnicity. McBratney argues that the stories are an attempt to create in fiction a society in which distinctions of caste and race do not operate; Kipling is a "quiet rebel" against prevailing racial ideas.

McClure, John A. *Kipling and Conrad: The Colonial Fiction*. Cambridge, Mass.: Harvard University Press, 1981. Examines *The Jungle Books* in relation to the politics of imperialism. The Mowgli stories offer Kipling's conception of the ideal education for imperial rule. The beast fable structure obscures the flaws in his concept.

Murray, John. "The Law of *The Jungle Books*." *Children's Literature* 20 (1992): 1-14. Provides a good summary of earlier writings on Kipling's concept of law and argues that this concept must be understood in the context of group survival against inimical forces rather than as natural or ethical law.

Juno and the Paycock

Author: Sean O'Casey (1880-1964)
First produced: 1924; first published, 1925
Type of work: Drama
Type of plot: Satire
Time of plot: 1922
Locale: Dublin

Principal characters:
"CAPTAIN" JACK BOYLE, a ne'er-do-well
JUNO BOYLE, his wife
JOHNNY BOYLE, their son
MARY BOYLE, their daughter
JOXER DALY, the captain's pal
JERRY DEVINE, Mary's suitor
CHARLIE BENTHAM, a schoolteacher
MRS. MAISIE MADIGAN, a neighbor
"NEEDLE" NUGENT, a tailor

The Story:

Waiting for Captain Boyle to come in from his morning visit to the pub, Mary Boyle and her mother, Juno, discuss the newspaper account of the murder of Robbie Tancred, a fanatic Irish Republican. Johnny Boyle, who was shot in the hip and lost an arm fighting against the Free State, leaves the living room after denouncing the two women for their morbid insensitivity. Juno scolds Mary for participating in the Trades Union Strike, especially at a time when the family is in debt for food, but Mary defends her activities, and her brother's as well, as matters of principle.

When Jerry Devine rushes in with a message from Father Farrell, who found a job for Boyle, Juno sends Jerry to look for her husband at his favorite bar. Soon afterward she hears her husband and his crony, Joxer Daly, singing on the stairs. She hides behind the bed curtains so as to catch them talking about her. Disclosing herself, she frightens Joxer away and berates her husband for his laziness and malingering. Jerry returns and delivers his message to Boyle, who immediately develops a case of stabbing pains in his legs. Juno, not deceived, orders him to change into his working clothes. She then leaves for her own job.

Jerry accosts Mary, complains of her unfriendliness, and once again proposes to her. Although Jerry offers her love and security, Mary refuses him, and both leave in a huff.

Ignoring his wife's instructions to apply for the job, Boyle, leisurely proceeding to get his breakfast, is rejoined by Joxer. Absorbed in their talk, they refuse to acknowledge a loud knocking at the street door, though the continuance of it seems to upset Johnny. Their rambling discourse on family life, the clergy, literature, and the sea is interrupted by Juno and Mary, who returned with Charlie Bentham, a schoolteacher and amateur lawyer, to announce that a cousin bequeathed two thousand pounds to Boyle. Boyle declares that he is through with Joxer and the like, whereupon Joxer, who

was hiding outside the window, reappears, expresses his indignation, and leaves.

Two days later the two cronies are reconciled, Joxer having served as Boyle's agent for loans based on expectations of the inheritance. The entrance of Juno and Mary with a new gramophone is followed by that of Bentham, now Mary's fiancé. Over family tea, Bentham explains his belief in theosophy and ghosts. Johnny, visibly upset by this conversation about death, leaves the room but quickly returns, twitching and trembling. He is convinced that he saw the bloody ghost of Robbie Tancred kneeling before the statue of the Virgin.

The arrival of Joxer with Mrs. Madigan, a garrulously reminiscing neighbor, smooths over the incident. A party featuring whiskey and song ensues. The revelry is interrupted by Mrs. Tancred and some neighbors, on their way to Tancred's funeral. Soon thereafter the merriment is again dispelled, this time by the funeral procession in the street. A young man, an Irregular Mobilizer, comes looking for Johnny, whom he reproaches for not attending the funeral. He orders Johnny to appear at a meeting that had been called to inquire into Tancred's death. Two months later, Juno insists on taking Mary to the doctor, for the young woman seems to be pining away over Bentham, who has disappeared.

After the women leave, Joxer and Nugent, a tailor, slip into the apartment. Having learned that Boyle will not receive the inheritance, Nugent comes to get the suit that he sold to Boyle on credit. Taking the suit from a chair, Nugent scoffs at Boyle's promise to pay and his order for a new topcoat as well. Joxer, who sneaks out unseen, returns, hypocrite that he is, to commiserate with Boyle. Mrs. Madigan, who also hears that Boyle will not receive his inheritance, arrives to collect the three pounds she lent him. Rebuffed, she appropriates the gramophone and leaves, followed by Joxer.

News of Boyle's misadventure spreads rapidly; two men arrive to remove the new, but unpaid-for, furniture. Mrs. Boyle runs out to find her husband. Mary having returned, Jerry Devine comes to see her. Again he proposes. Although he is willing to forget that Mary jilted him for Bentham, he recoils at her admission that she is pregnant.

Left alone with the two moving men, Johnny imagines that he feels a bullet wound in his chest. At that moment two armed Irish Irregulars enter the apartment and accuse Johnny of informing on Tancred to the gang that murdered him. Ignoring Johnny's protestations of innocence and loyalty, the men drag him out. A little later, Mrs. Madigan notifies Mary and Juno that the police are waiting below, requesting that Juno identify a body. Juno and Mary leave, vowing never to return to the worthless Boyle.

Soon Boyle and Joxer stumble into the abandoned apartment, both very drunk and unaware of Johnny's death or Juno and Mary's desertion. Joxer stretches out on the bed; Boyle slumps on the floor. With thick tongues they stammer out their patriotic devotion to Ireland, and Boyle deplores the miserable state of the world.

Critical Evaluation:

Sean O'Casey's plays mark the culmination, in drama, of the Irish Renaissance. Drama of the Irish Renaissance began as a part of the European movement toward realistic theater in opposition to the French romantic drama but diverged from the dramaturgic techniques of Henrik Ibsen and George Bernard Shaw. Believing that continental and English dramas were too intellectualized, O'Casey, along with his compatriots William Butler Yeats and John Millington Synge, tried to make Irish drama individualistic and realistic by adding heavy doses of Irish local color. Formlessness—ignoring formal dramatic technique to reflect the vigor and vitality of life—was O'Casey's unique contribution to the Irish movement. In *Juno and the Paycock* he reached a new peak of realism. He dispensed with an elaborate plot, ideas, and consistency of character, content merely to show Irish characters in action.

Captain Jack Boyle is such a character. "The whole worl's in a state of chassis (chaos)!" he declares; he is the "paycock" (peacock) of the play. The background of "chassis"—in particular the turbulence of the civil wars that wracked Ireland during the first quarter of the twentieth century—is in O'Casey's great trilogy of realistic plays about violence and strife in Dublin. The plays are *The Shadow of a Gunman* (1923), *Juno and the Paycock*, and *The Plough and the Stars* (1926).

Civic disorder provides the atmosphere of general bitterness and tension as well as determines the fate of the son, Johnny, in *Juno and the Paycock*, the most domestic of the three plays. What happens to the Boyle family is largely the product of their own actions, but, because they embody personal qualities that are common to the Irish, the Boyles are representative. Their actions illuminate the follies, evils, and strengths of the national character in a time of turmoil.

Twice, in the early moments of the play, Mary tells her mother that "a principle's a principle," once in reference to her own support of a fellow striker and once in regard to her crippled brother's nationalistic activities. A short time later Johnny repeats the same slogan to Juno, but this time she answers it emphatically: "Ah, you lost your best principle, me boy, when you lost your arm; them's the only sort o' principles that's any good to a workin' man." That exchange sets up the thematic dichotomy of the play: abstract moral principles, based on generalized causes such as nationalism, Marxism, or religion, versus a practical morality based on human loyalties, needs, and sympathies. The abstractions are used either as justifications for violence or as rationalizations for no action at all.

Captain Boyle is a veritable catalog of Irish weaknesses. His capacity for strong drink is exceeded only by his capacity for self-deception and pompous moralizing. Most of his time is spent in idle chatter and drinking with his equally irresponsible crony, Joxer Daly. If offered honest work, Boyle has a sudden attack of leg pains. He continually complains about the moral state of the world ("is there any morality left anywhere?" he asks Joxer), but he refuses any involvement with the problems of others ("We've nothing to do with these things, one way or t'other"). Boyle is nevertheless charming; he sings, he recites poetry, and, when not in a drunken stupor, he speaks with style and vigor. He has opinions on every current political, social, and religious subject and, although they are trite, they are not stupid. If he is never exactly lovable, he is at least likable at the beginning of the play; these defects do not seem too harmful and, most important, he is very funny. His early scenes with Joxer are masterpieces of comic repartee.

The audience's attitude toward Boyle changes during the course of the play. As the action progresses it becomes clear that his buffoonery has serious implications. When his daughter's unwed pregnancy is revealed, he rises to heights of moral indignation as though she did it as a personal insult to him ("when I'm done with her she'll be a sorry girl!"). He continues to squander money on credit, in spite of the serious damage it does to the household. At the end of the play, he and Joxer come in very drunk and do a repeat of their earlier routine; what was previously funny becomes grotesque. The consequences of his braggadocio are too real and serious to laugh at a second time. Dramatically this mixture of tragedy and farce is powerful. Thematically O'Casey suggests that many of those "lovable" Irish failings, so celebrated in popular myth and song, may, on closer inspection, prove to be dangerous and destructive.

Although Boyle's faults may be the most blatant, the kind of self-righteousness he exhibits infects others in the play. Jerry Devine's abstract pieties prevent him from marrying Mary because she is a "fallen woman." It is strongly hinted that the death of Robbie Tancred is the inevitable result of his politics. The men who take Johnny make sure that he "has his beads" so that the proper religious proprieties will not be missing from his murder. All of the men in the play cling to their narrow patterns of thought and rigid moral postures, and they fail in every situation that requires practical, humane responses. Thus, instead of "freedom," their ideas produce confusion, violence, and pain.

The men are a damning influence, and the women in *Juno and the Paycock* are a redeeming one—although, even for them, there are important lessons to be learned. The difference is that they are capable of learning and growing because they react to personal needs and sorrows, not abstractions. At the play's beginning, Mary chides her mother about the need for "principles," but by the end of it, having been impregnated and deserted by Charlie Bentham and rejected by Jerry, she comes to understand and accept human weakness without bitterness. As she says to Jerry: "I don't blame you . . . your humanity is as narrow as the humanity of the others."

Juno Boyle is the supreme embodiment of compassionate action. Throughout the play it is evident that her strength has kept the Boyle household intact. Juno has nevertheless been tainted by the atmosphere of the times and the prospect of easy money. She is casual about Boyle's defects, intolerant of her children's feelings and opinions, and somewhat callous toward those outside the family. She feels no special sympathy for her bereaved neighbor, Mrs. Tancred, and even plays her new phonograph while the rituals of mourning are going on nearby. After Juno faces the loss of the money, her husband's betrayal, Mary's pregnancy, and Johnny's execution, she gains a new insight into her fellow man and a deeper, more sympathetic humanity. She overcomes her grief for Johnny, casts aside her political and moral prejudices ("Why didn't I remember that when he wasn't a Diehard or a Stater, but only a poor dead son!"), leaves Boyle, accepts the burden of Mary and her unborn child, and hopefully assumes the "biggest part o' the trouble."

Whether or not the strength evidenced by Juno is enough to overcome the weaknesses, follies, and evils the men ex-

hibit is not answered in the play. In the end it depends upon whether or not it is possible to give a positive response to Juno's final, plaintive prayer: "Sacred Heart o' Jesus, take away our hearts o' stone, and give us hearts o' flesh! Take away this murdherin' hate, and give us Thine own eternal love!"

"Critical Evaluation" by Keith Neilson

Further Reading

Ayling, Ronald. *Sean O'Casey.* Nashville, Tenn.: Aurora Press, 1970. Contains selected O'Casey criticism with valuable comments on *Juno and the Paycock.* Considers O'Casey's poetic gifts, his use of symbols, his socialism, and his place in the Irish dramatic movement.

Hogan, Robert. *The Experiments of Sean O'Casey.* New York: St. Martin's Press, 1960. A synthesis of dramatic theory and theatrical technique. Argues that in his Dublin trilogy, O'Casey is continually expanding his technical capacities and that *Juno and the Paycock* is a stage in his continuing experimentation.

Kilroy, Thomas, ed. *Sean O'Casey: A Collection of Essays.* Englewood Cliffs, N.J.: Prentice-Hall, 1975. Excellent selection from leading Irish, British, and American critics who discuss O'Casey's politics, dramatic technique, and development. The critics offer differing assessments of his achievement as a political dramatist.

Krause, David. *Sean O'Casey: The Man and His Work.* New York: Macmillan, 1975. One of the best studies of O'Casey's dramatic genius and the complex engagement between his milieu and his dramatic work. Describes the economic, political, and religious tensions in Dublin in his time, his involvement with Irish revolutionary movements, the Gaelic League, and the Irish Labor Movement.

McDonald, Ronan. *Tragedy and Irish Literature: Synge, O'Casey, Beckett.* New York: Palgrave, 2002. Compares the work of three Irish playwrights, analyzing how their culture of suffering, loss, and guilt is reflected in their drama.

Murray, Christopher. *Sean O'Casey: "The Shadow of a Gunman," "Juno and the Paycock," "The Plough and the Stars."* London: Faber, 2000. An analysis of the plays in O'Casey's Dublin trilogy, placing these works within the context of Irish society and theater in the 1920's.

_____. *Sean O'Casey: Writer at Work, a Biography.* Dublin: Gill & Macmillan, 2004. Biography focusing on O'Casey's literary career, tracing the development of his writing from his early nationalist work to his later socialist writings.

Owens, Cóilín D., and Joan N. Radner, eds. *Irish Drama: 1900-1980*. Washington, D.C.: Catholic University of America Press, 1990. Places *Juno and the Paycock* in the context of the Irish dramatic movement. Provides a clear general introduction to the critical issues in the play, a bibliography, and comprehensive annotations to the text.

Stewart, Victoria. *About O'Casey: The Playwright and the Work*. London: Faber and Faber, 2003. Describes the political and social conditions in Ireland that led to O'Casey's association with the Abbey Theatre and his subsequent literary career. Includes interviews with O'Casey and theater people who worked with him.

Jurgen
A Comedy of Justice

Author: James Branch Cabell (1879-1958)
First published: 1919
Type of work: Novel
Type of plot: Fantasy
Time of plot: Middle Ages
Locale: Poictesme, France

Principal characters:
JURGEN, a middle-aged pawnbroker
DAME LISA, his wife
DOROTHY LA DÉSIRÉE, his childhood sweetheart
QUEEN GUENEVERE
DAME ANAÏTIS
CHLORIS, a Hamadryad
QUEEN HELEN OF TROY
MOTHER SEREDA
KOSHCHEI, the maker of things as they are

The Story:

In the old days, a middle-aged pawnbroker named Jurgen says a good word for the Prince of Darkness. In gratitude, the Prince of Darkness removes from the earth Dame Lisa, Jurgen's shrewish wife. Some time later, Jurgen hears that his wife returned to wander on Amneran Heath; consequently, the only manly thing for him to do is to look for her.

It is Walpurgis Night when Jurgen meets Dame Lisa on the heath. She leads him to a cave, but when he follows her inside, she disappears and Jurgen finds a centaur instead. Jurgen inquires for his wife. The centaur replies that only Koshchei the Deathless, the maker of things as they are, can help Jurgen in his quest. The centaur gives Jurgen a beautiful new shirt and starts off with him to the Garden between Dawn and Sunrise, the first stopping place of Jurgen's journey to find Koshchei.

In the garden, Jurgen finds Dorothy la Désirée, who was his first sweetheart and who retains all the beauty he praised in his youthful poetry. She no longer knows him, for she is in love only with Jurgen as he was in youth, and he cannot make her understand that in the real world she, too, is middle-aged and commonplace. Sadly he parts from her and finds himself suddenly back in his native country.

His friend the centaur becomes an ordinary horse. Jurgen mounts and rides through a forest until he comes to the house of Mother Sereda, the goddess who controls Wednesdays and whose job it is to bleach the color out of everything in the world. By flattery, Jurgen persuades her to let him live over a certain Wednesday in his youth with Dorothy la Désirée. When the magic Wednesday ends, however, Dorothy la Désirée turns into the old woman she really is, and Jurgen quickly departs.

He wanders again to Amneran Heath and enters the cave to look for Koshchei and Dame Lisa. There he finds a beautiful girl who says that she is Guenevere, the daughter of King Gogyrvan of Glathion. Jurgen offers to conduct her back to her home. When they arrive at the court of King Gogyrvan, Jurgen, pretending to be the duke of Logreus, asks for the hand of Guenevere as a reward for her safe return, but she is already promised to King Arthur. Jurgen stays on at court. He makes the discovery that he still looks like a young man; the only trouble is that his shadow is not his shadow; it is the shadow of Mother Sereda.

King Arthur's envoys, Dame Anaïtis and Merlin, arrive to take Guenevere to London. Jurgen watches her depart for

London without feeling any sorrow because of a magic token Merlin gives him. Dame Anaïtis invites Jurgen to visit her palace in Cockaigne, the country where time stands still. There Jurgen participates with her in a ceremony called the Breaking of the Veil, to learn afterward that it was a marriage ceremony and that Dame Anaïtis is now his wife. Dame Anaïtis, a myth woman of lunar legend, instructs Jurgen in every variety of strange pleasures she knows.

Jurgen visits a philologist, who tells him that he, too, is a legend; consequently, he cannot remain long in Cockaigne. When the time comes for him to leave the country, Jurgen chooses to go to Leuke, the kingdom where Queen Helen and Achilles rule. Jurgen's reason for wishing to go there is that Queen Helen resembles Dorothy la Désirée.

In Leuke, Jurgen meets Chloris, a Hamadryad, and marries her. He is still curious about Queen Helen, however, and one evening he enters her castle and goes to her bedchamber. The sleeping queen is Dorothy la Désirée, but he dares not touch her. Her beauty, created from the dreams of his youth, is unattainable. He leaves the castle and returns to Chloris.

Shortly afterward, the Philistines invade Leuke and condemn all its mythical inhabitants to limbo. Jurgen protests because he is flesh and blood, and he offers to prove his claim by mathematics. Queen Dolores of the Philistines agrees with him after he demonstrates his proof to her by means of a concrete example. However, he is condemned by the great tumblebug of the Philistines for being a poet.

After Chloris is condemned to limbo, Jurgen goes on to the hell of his fathers. There he visits Satan and learns that Koshchei created hell to humor the pride of Jurgen's forefathers. Then he remembers that he is supposed to be looking for Dame Lisa. Learning that she is not in hell, he decides to look for her in heaven. Mistaken for a pope by means of the philologist's charm, he manages to gain entrance to heaven, but Dame Lisa is not there. St. Peter returns him to Amneran Heath.

On the heath, he again meets Mother Sereda, who takes away his youth and returns him to his middle-aged body. Actually, it is a relief to Jurgen to be old again. Then for the third time, he enters the cave in search of Dame Lisa. Inside he finds the Prince of Darkness who took her away. The Prince is really Koshchei; Jurgen is near the end of his quest. He asks Koshchei to return Dame Lisa to him.

Koshchei again shows him Guenevere, Dame Anaïtis, and Dorothy la Désirée, but Jurgen will not have them. He had his youth to live over, and he committed the same follies. He is content now to be Jurgen the pawnbroker. Koshchei agrees to return Jurgen to his former life, but he asks for the centaur's shirt in return. Jurgen gladly gives up the shirt.

Koshchei walks with him from the heath into town. As they walk, Jurgen notices that the moon is sinking in the east. Time is turning backward. It is as if the past year never was. He approaches his house and sees through the window that the table is set for supper. Inside, Dame Lisa sits sewing and looking quite as if nothing ever happened.

Critical Evaluation:

The famous 1922 obscenity trial over *Jurgen* has probably drawn away too much attention from literary issues of the novel's style and organization, but the attempted censorship does provide a clue to the book's continuing importance. Like James Joyce's *Ulysses* (1922), published only three years after *Jurgen* and also the subject of an obscenity case, *Jurgen* dares to lampoon all the sacred beliefs of Anglo-American ideology. It mocks human beings' belief in their own importance, romantic notions of male-female relationships, belief in an afterlife, faith in cosmic justice, idealistic ideas of human motives, and the well-meaning idea of literary censorship. It mocks, however, in an upbeat, comic, and sometimes wistful tone. Cabell's "Gallantry" is the most lighthearted form of cynicism ever conceived.

Cabell agreed with his critics that he opposed the prevalent naturalism of his time. It is true that Cabell diligently avoids realistic detail in his narrative, yet in one respect—his cynical treatment of human motives—he is in fact naturalistic. The novel is characterized by psychological realism while maintaining a veneer of romanticism in its incidents and motifs, which are drawn mostly from myth, folklore, and medieval romances. Because Cabell refuses to lie about the human heart, *Jurgen*, again like *Ulysses*, remains contemporary. Cabell's honesty ensures that it does not appear dated.

The gaily disillusioned and cynical tone of the book is mainly a result of Cabell's view of the sordidness of human motives. Because Jurgen is portrayed lying to himself about his own character and motives, Cabell's irony and satire apply as much to the title character himself as they do to the characters he dupes and uses.

The ironic tone is also a constant reminder that this is a satirical farce, an artifice of words, and that Cabell in no sense believes in the world he has created. In this respect, he contrasts with those fantasy writers who maintain a serious tone and, by pretending to believe in their creations, lay claim to a transcendent importance that Cabell calls into question. His skeptical modernism is the opposite of Christian Neoplatonism.

The author's tone should not divert attention from his staggering inventiveness and his ability to adapt and to develop characters and motifs from myth, legend, and folklore. Cabell, who was familiar with a wide range of sources, was surely one of America's most learned authors.

A first-time reader, even if familiar with some of Cabell's source material, is apt to become confused because of the multitude of the characters, settings, and incidents in *Jurgen*. The allegorical point of the rather episodic plot is simple, however. Jurgen learns to abandon his regrets because his forays into his past reveal that his youthful ideals, especially about people, were all illusions and his dreams therefore impossible to fulfill, even when he is given a second chance with the advantage of foreknowledge.

The plot revolves around three excursions Jurgen makes into a cave in search of his lost wife. In the second excursion, he relives a year of his youth, which he spends mainly in three realms: Glathion, Cockaigne, and Leuke. Glathion is modeled on Arthurian romance, Cockaigne on medieval legends of a land of plenty, and Leuke on Greek mythology. Because medieval romance often served as a vehicle for religious allegory, Guenevere, the woman he seduces in Glathion, becomes a symbol for the beauty of simple religious faith. When Jurgen loses Guenevere, he seeks solace in the arms of another woman of Arthurian legend, Anaïtis, the Lady of the Lake, who is symbolic of passion and with whom he journeys to the land of sensual delight. Continuous sexual overstimulation soon becomes cloying, however, and he tricks Anaïtis into sending him to Leuke, where he hopes to come face to face with the ideal of perfection, symbolized by Helen of Troy.

In the central chapter—entitled "Economics of King Jurgen"—Cabell suggests a metaphor through which the governing principle of the novel can be understood. Just as Helen is within his grasp, Jurgen refrains from attempting to possess her, because he now understands that perfection (and, by implication, fulfillment) is an illusion created by temporal and physical distance from the object of desire. Rather than risk disillusionment, he withdraws, preferring to remain in the comfort of his unattainable dreams.

In deliberately declining to face truth, Jurgen necessarily chooses a kind of double-think, clinging to beliefs that at the deepest level he knows to be false. Disturbingly, Cabell seems to be suggesting that this is the nature of all cherished human beliefs about a universe that ultimately refuses to be explained coherently by any philosophy or model. Cabell presents Jurgen's double-think as a compromise between reality and the comforting illusions used to maintain sanity. Compromise is the basis of Gallantry. Jurgen proceeds through an allegorical series of dissatisfactions. He seeks to replace his lost faith with sensual pleasure; when that proves cloying, he seeks after ideal beauty, but he eventually abandons that quest, too.

Like most allegories, *Jurgen* is heavily laden with symbolic objects. The phallic symbols of Jurgen's sword, lance, and scepter were the offensive elements that occasioned the obscenity trial—though only a sophisticated reader already attuned to such possibilities would actually notice them. In other words, people already had to be "corrupt," by the censors' definition, in order to be "corrupted" by the material. The earthiness of the novel is less interesting and less profound than the two central objects that reinforce Cabell's philosophy: the shirt of Nessus and the shadow of Mother Sereda, both of which Jurgen wears for the duration of his one-year excursion into the past, and both of which he loses when his odyssey ends. The shirt, which in the classical myth of Hercules was supposed to ensure Hercules' devotion to his wife but which turned out to be poisonous, represents the youthful charm Jurgen uses to deceive and seduce women. The ominous shadow, which prevents Jurgen from entering wholeheartedly into any of his enterprises, seems to represent his awareness of the impossibility of recovering the past or reaching fulfillment, effectively summing up the novel's theme.

"Critical Evaluation" by James Schiavoni

Further Reading

Attebery, Brian. *The Fantasy Tradition in American Literature: From Irving to Le Guin.* Bloomington: Indiana University Press, 1980. Places Cabell in the larger context of American literature, comparing and contrasting him specifically with science fiction writer Edgar Rice Burroughs. A perceptive and groundbreaking study.

Carter, Lin. *Imaginary Worlds: The Art of Fantasy.* New York: Ballantine Books, 1973. Discusses Cabell and *Jurgen* in relation to a tradition extending from the ancient epics to literature of the early 1970's. An appreciation rather than a rigorous analysis.

Davis, Joe Lee. *James Branch Cabell.* New York: Twayne, 1962. Treats *Jurgen* as a volume in Cabell's series *The Biography of the Life of Manuel* and ranks him with such internationally known writers as George Bernard Shaw and André Gide. The obvious starting point for anyone interested in Cabell.

Fiedler, Leslie A. "The Return of James Branch Cabell: Or, The Cream of the Cream of the Jest." In *James Branch Cabell: Centennial Essays,* edited by M. Thomas Inge and Edgar E. MacDonald. Baton Rouge: Louisiana State University Press, 1983. An informal essay praising

Cabell for writing what Fiedler ironically labels "juvenile trash" (as opposed to "high art"). *Jurgen* is also discussed in many of the other essays in this collection.

Ginés, Montserrat. "James Branch Cabell: Quixotic Love, the Exercise of Self-Deception." In *The Southern Inheritors of Don Quixote.* Baton Rouge: Louisiana State University Press, 2000. Ginés analyzes the work of five southern writers—Cabell, Mark Twain, William Faulkner, Eudora Welty, and Walker Percy—whose fiction expressed the ideals and spirit of Don Quixote. He describes how the writers were sympathetic to idealistic characters who tilted at windmills, and he points out the similarities between the Spain of Miguel de Cervantes and the social and economic conditions of the American South.

McDonald, Edgar. *James Branch Cabell and Richmond-in-Virginia.* Jackson: University Press of Mississippi, 1993. MacDonald, a senior Cabell scholar, provides a detailed, authoritative biography that focuses on how Cabell was influenced by living in Richmond, Virginia, in the late nineteenth and early twentieth centuries. Includes an excellent bibliography.

Riemer, James D. *From Satire to Subversion: The Fantasies of James Branch Cabell.* New York: Greenwood Press, 1989. Evaluates a handful of Cabell's best fantasies, including *Jurgen*, and concludes that he successfully merges satire and subversion. Useful secondary bibliography.

K

Kaddish for a Child Not Born

Author: Imre Kertész (1929-   )
First published: Kaddis a meg nem született gyermekért, 1990 (English translation, 1997)
Type of work: Novella
Type of plot: Psychological realism
Time of plot: Twentieth century
Locale: Hungary

Principal characters:
B., the narrator, a Jewish Hungarian writer
HIS FORMER WIFE, a Jewish dermatologist, born after the Holocaust
DR. OBLATH, a philosopher and academic
THE PROFESSOR, a concentration-camp inmate

The Story:

The narrator, B., is a Jewish Hungarian writer and a Holocaust survivor. Sometime near the end of the communist period in Hungary, he attends an academic retreat at a mountain resort. Avoiding the social atmosphere of dinner, B. goes for a walk in the woods one night and runs across Dr. Oblath, a philosopher. The two men begin walking together, although B. is not sure if he sought this company or meant to avoid it. They begin an academic discussion of life, philosophy, and survival, and then Dr. Oblath asks B. whether he has a child. He is childless himself, apparently the consequence of lost opportunity, and worries about being alone in his old age. B., by contrast, is childless by choice: He refuses to create another person who might suffer as he has. Even as he reflects on the life he has not inflicted on a child, however, he wonders what the lost child might have been like: A dark-eyed, freckled girl? A stubborn, blue-eyed boy?

B.'s reflections turn to his marriage, its failure, and his former wife, a woman he categorizes as a "beautiful Jewess." She was born after the war, the child of Auschwitz survivors. She and B. met at a party, when she approached him to discuss one of his books. With nearly every mention of his wife, B. brings back the memory of that first night, her beauty, and the look of her approaching him for the first time.

At the party, a group of Holocaust survivors begin discussing their experiences, each telling the others where he had been taken during the war. B. dreads having to respond, but the conversation ends before it comes around to him when a member of the group mentions Auschwitz. Auschwitz is determined by the other survivors to be unbeatable in a recounting of horrors, the worst of all the death camps, and ultimately inexplicable. The latter attitude upsets

B., who argues that Auschwitz must be explained because it existed, that evil is rationally motivated. What he finds difficult to understand is the behavior of those who were able to do good, even in the concentration camps. B. remembers one inmate, the Professor, who protected B.'s food ration and delivered it to B. at the risk of his own life.

Afterward, B. and his wife-to-be continue the conversation, falling first into bed and then into marriage. She finds in B. a chance to understand and embrace her own Jewishness and to redeem her parents' suffering. She tells B. that she became a doctor because of her mother's premature and inexplicable death from illnesses contracted in the camps. Now, she tries to rescue B. from his suffering, a project she continues even after their divorce, for she continues to meet with B. and to write him prescriptions.

Prior to his marriage, B. lived without roots and without family. While his peers started families and bought homes, he continued to live in a prefabricated apartment, with everything provided for him. He observes that there is a similarity between his time as an inmate in a concentration camp, the time after liberation when he still lived in the camp, and his life in apartments: In all three cases, he became accustomed to his environment rather than creating it. B's new wife is younger, unscarred, and wants to create rather than simply adapt.

When the question of children comes up, B's wife assumes his refusal to father offspring is a problem that she can fix. She sees it as the result of a wound she can heal. B., too, thinks at first that with time and effort he will be able to change his mind. When he sees an unhappy family on a streetcar, however, he realizes that he will never be willing to inflict the unhappiness of childhood, especially a childhood like his, on another person.

B.'s recollections turn further back, to his childhood. He remembers when he—a secular, assimilated Budapest Jew—first encountered the "real" Jews of the countryside, his observant relatives. He describes his fright at seeing his aunt sitting bald before a mirror, learning only later that religious women shave their heads and wear wigs. He notes that he paid little attention to his Jewishness as a child, realizing its importance only after being Jewish became dangerous.

B. revisits the places of his childhood, including his grandparents' apartment block and his old boarding school. The school, once a grand home, has been turned into apartments, and families live in squalor in the former classrooms. B. remembers his school days, when there was no difference between Christians and Jews; all students recited the same neutral prayers in German. He compares the school director's weekly ritual of publicly assessing each student's behavior to the *Appel* of the camps. He later learns that the school director died in Auschwitz.

In the end, B's memories destroy his marriage. His wife confronts him late one night and tells him that she has to flee the marriage and that she has found someone else. She is grateful to B. for helping her understand her parents' experience, and she has tried to save him from his depression, but she has given up. She sees him as poisoning and destructive and has decided to leave him for a man who is not Jewish. B. is outraged that he is expected to be outraged, and he shouts that being a Jew is a blessing, for it sent him to Auschwitz, an experience he will have forever. As B. closes his memoir, he writes that he once saw his former wife with two children, a dark-eyed freckled girl and a stubborn blue-eyed boy. He is alone with his misery and memories.

Critical Evaluation:

Kaddish for a Child Not Born is an answer to a question. The answer—"No!"—appears again and again. The question, "do you have a child?" seems harmless, but it invokes difficult memories and problems for B. The novella is presented as a reflection on the question and B.'s related memories, compiled from notes just as communism is ending in Hungary and channeled as a stream-of-consciousness response to the question by the narrator.

Imre Kertész received the Nobel Prize in Literature in 2002; he was the first Hungarian to do so. The Nobel announcement particularly cited a trilogy comprising *Sorstalanság* (1975; *Fateless*, 1992; also as *Fatelessness*, 2004), *A kudarc* (1988; fiasco), and *Kaddish for a Child Not Born*. The announcement portrayed these books as shining exam-

ples of maintaining individual thought in a time when people are subjugated. Kertész was the first Holocaust writer to receive a Nobel Prize in Literature; Elie Wiesel received the Peace Prize in 1986. Kertész's work is beginning to be translated into English and to be used pedagogically, alongside Wiesel's *Un di Velt hot geshvign* (1956; *Night*, 1960), Primo Levi's *Se questo è un uomo* (1947; *If This Is a Man*, 1959; revised as *Survival in Auschwitz: The Nazi Assault on Humanity*, 1961), and other standards of Holocaust literature.

Born in Budapest, Hungary, and raised in a secular family, Kertész was deported to Auschwitz in the spring of 1944, when he was a fifteen-year-old student. He was selected for survival and work and then, as the war ended, was marched across Europe to the concentration camp at Buchenwald. The camp was liberated in May, 1945. Kertész returned to Budapest and began work as a journalist, but he lost his job in 1951. Under the Hungarian communist regime, he worked as a German-Hungarian translator. He began writing in the 1960's, but the repressive government prevented him from publishing until the 1970's.

All of Kertész's work is about the Holocaust. In his acceptance speech before the Nobel committee, he said that the Holocaust, as a break in civilization, is present in all postwar European art. This comment was perhaps meant to address Theodor Adorno's assertion that there can be no art after Auschwitz. Modern European artists, such as B.'s wife, live in the shadow of the Holocaust and cannot help but be affected by it.

Kertész's B. engages the European intellectual tradition of Franz Kafka, Jean-Paul Sartre, and Rainer Maria Rilke. He places Hitler (referred to only by his initial) within that tradition, debating Hitler's philosophies as he would those of any academic. While B. engages this tradition, his own past prevents him from joining it completely. It is absurd, B. thinks, to use the same word—"writer"—to describe himself and to describe these other figures.

The trilogy that *Kaddish for a Child Not Born* concludes is very specifically about the Holocaust. *Fateless* is an event-by-event account of time in the camps that concludes with the protagonist's survival and a glimmer of hope. *Kaddish for a Child Not Born* is a different story—that of the survivor years later, when the burden of survival weighs as heavily as the events he survived.

Kertész's survivor-narrator does not tell a story of hope, rebirth, or defiance. B. rejects such stories, refusing to have a child just to celebrate life and survival. Rather, he simply survives—he exists through his days from birth until death, seeing life as a time more of waiting than of purpose. For B., the very act of writing hastens death: With his pen, he says, he is digging a grave in the air—the same phrase he uses to describe his relatives' end over the chimneys of Auschwitz. While *Fateless* is about life, *Kaddish for a Child Not Born* is about death.

The Jewish prayer of the title, the Kaddish, is not about death. Although it is recited for the dead, the prayer itself is a celebration and sanctification of God. There is a tradition that a Jewish boy is born to say Kaddish for his father, and one says the Kaddish longer following the death of a parent than for any other loss. Something has happened out of order when a parent must say Kaddish for a child. The title raises the question, Who is mourning in the story, and who is being mourned? B. will have no one to mourn for him. His Kaddish, his glorification of God, could be for his lost opportunity, for his childhood, for his family, or for himself.

There are other, historical, Holocaust accounts—from Simon Wiesenthal and Elie Wiesel, for example—of victims who said Kaddish for themselves. Perhaps this will be B.'s fate. Perhaps he does not care. His resignation, his insistence on the rationality of evil and the explicability of Auschwitz, is a challenge to Wiesel's mystical approach to the Holocaust. *Kaddish for a Child Not Born* was written at a time when Wiesel, a religious, rural Jew, was becoming more prominent.

After Kertész's Nobel Prize was announced, he received a package from the memorial center at Buchenwald. In it was a copy of a camp record from February 18, 1945, that listed one Imre Kertész as having died. In a sense, it was Kertész's second death; he lied about his age and occupation upon entering the camp, sacrificing the real Imre to stay alive. Kertész does not say whether he said Kaddish for himself over either death.

Laura Shumar

Further Reading

Adelman, Gary. "Getting Started with Imre Kertész." *New England Review* 25, nos. 1/2 (2004): 261-279. Useful introduction to the author's work and life.

Braham, Randolph L. *The Politics of Genocide: The Holocaust in Hungary.* Detroit, Mich.: Wayne State University Press, 2000. Historical account of the Hungarian experience of the Holocaust and its effects on the nation and its people.

Hoffman, Lawrence A., et al. *Tachanun and Concluding Prayers.* Vol. 6 in *My People's Prayer Book: Traditional Prayers, Modern Commentaries.* Woodstock, Vt.: Jewish Lights, 2002. Includes a discussion of the Kaddish, its liturgical role, and its evolution into a mourner's prayer.

Kertész, Imre, and Ivan Sanders. "Heureka." *PMLA* 118, no. 3 (May, 2003): 601-614. Kertész's acceptance speech from the Nobel Prize banquet. He addresses the problems of memory of the Holocaust and discusses the presence of the Holocaust in European art.

Vasvári, Louise O., and Steven Tötösy de Zepetnek, eds. *Imre Kertész and Holocaust Literature.* West Lafayette, Ind.: Purdue University Press, 2005. Twenty-three chapters about Kertész's life, his work, and the Holocaust in Hungary.

Kalevala

Author: Elias Lönnrot (1802-1884)
First published: 1835 (English translation, 1888)
Type of work: Poetry
Type of plot: Saga
Time of plot: Mythological times
Locale: Finland and Lapland

Principal characters:
VÄINÄMÖINEN, the Son of the Wind and the Virgin of the Air, the singer-hero
ILMARINEN, the smith-hero
LEMMINKÄINEN, the warrior-hero
LOUHI, ruler of Pohjola, the North Country
AINO, a young Lapp maiden
JOUKAHÄINEN, a Laplander, Aino's brother
KULLERVO, an evil, sullen, and very powerful slave
THE DAUGHTER OF LOUHI, Ilmarinen's wife
MARJATTA, a holy woman

The Poem:

After his mother created the land, the sun, and the moon out of sea duck eggs, Väinämöinen is born, and with the help of Sampsa Pellervoinen he makes the barren land fruitful, sowing seeds and planting trees. By the time Väinämöinen is an old man, he gained great fame as a singer and charmer. When a brash young man named Joukahäinen challenges him to a duel of magic songs, Väinämöinen wins easily and forces the young man to give him his sister Aino for a wife. Aino is greatly saddened, however, at having to marry an old man, and so she drowns herself, to Väinämöinen's sorrow. He looks all over the sea for her and finds her at last in the form of a salmon, but in that form she escapes him forever.

In time he hears of the beautiful daughters of Louhi in the far North Country, and he decides to seek them out. On the way to Pohjola, the land of Louhi, his horse is killed by the bold young man whom he defeated in the duel of songs, and Väinämöinen is forced to swim to Pohjola. Louhi, the witch, finds him on the beach, restores his health, tells him that he will have to forge a magic Sampo (a mill that grinds out riches) in order to win a daughter, and then sends him on his way.

Väinämöinen finds one of Louhi's daughters seated on a rainbow and asks her to become his wife. She gives him three tasks to do. After completing two, he is wounded in the knee while trying to complete the third. The wound, which bleeds profusely, is healed by a magic ointment prepared under the directions of an old man skilled in leechcraft. Väinämöinen goes home and raises a great wind to carry Ilmarinen, the mighty smith who forged the sky, into the North Country to make the Sampo for Louhi. Ilmarinen forges the Sampo, but still Louhi's daughter refuses to marry and leave her homeland. Ilmarinen, who is also in love with the maiden, goes sadly home.

A gallant youth, Lemminkäinen, is famous for winning the love of women. Having heard of Kyllikki, the flower of Saari, he determines to win her for his wife. When he arrives in Esthonia she refuses him, and he abducts her. They live happily together until one day she disobeys him. In retaliation he goes north to seek one of Louhi's daughters as his wife. In Pohjola, Lemminkäinen charms everyone except an evil herdsman whom he scorns. Like Väinämöinen, he is given three tasks and performs the first two without much difficulty; but while trying to complete the third he is slain by the evil herdsman. Alarmed by his long absence, his mother goes searching for him, finds him in pieces at the bottom of a river, and restores him finally to his original shape.

Meanwhile, Väinämöinen is busy building a ship by means of magic, his third task for Louhi's daughter; sud-

denly he forgets the three magic words needed to complete the work. He searches everywhere for them and is almost trapped in Tuonela, the kingdom of death. Then he hears that the giant Vipunen might know them. When they meet, Vipunen swallows him, but Väinämöinen causes the giant so much pain that the creature is forced to release him and reveal the magic charm. With the charm Väinämöinen completes his ship and again sets sail for Pohjola.

Ilmarinen, learning of Väinämöinen's departure, starts after him on horseback. When they meet they agree to abide by the maiden's choice. On their arrival at Pohjola, Louhi gives Ilmarinen three tasks to perform: to plow a field of snakes, to capture a bear and a wolf, and to catch a great pike. Ilmarinen performs these tasks. Since Väinämöinen is old, Louhi's daughter chooses Ilmarinen for her husband. There is great rejoicing at the marriage. Väinämöinen sings for the bridal couple. A gigantic ox is slain and mead is brewed, and the bride and groom are both instructed in the duties of marriage. At last Ilmarinen takes his new bride to his home in the south.

Lemminkäinen is not invited to the festivities because of his quarrelsome nature, and he is therefore angry. Although his mother warns him of the dangers he will have to face on the journey and of Louhi's treachery, he insists on going to Pohjola. With his magic charms he is able to overcome all dangers along the way. In Pohjola, Louhi tries to kill him with snake-poisoned ale, but Lemminkäinen sees through the trick. Then he and Louhi's husband engage in a duel of magic that ends in a tie. Finally they fight with swords and Lemminkäinen slays Louhi's husband. Lemminkäinen then turns into an eagle and flies home. In fear of retribution he takes his mother's advice and goes to live for several years on an obscure island where the only inhabitants are women whose warrior husbands are away from home.

Forced to flee when the time comes for the husbands to return, Lemminkäinen sets out for his own land in a boat. The craft turns over and he is forced to swim to shore. Upon arriving home, he finds the country desolate and his mother missing. At last he discovers her hiding in the forest. Swearing to avenge himself on the warriors of Pohjola who desolated the land, he sets sail with Tiera, a warrior companion, but Louhi sends the frost to destroy him. Although Lemminkäinen manages to charm the frost, he and his companion are shipwrecked and forced to retreat.

The wife of Kalervo is carried off by her brother-in-law, Untamoinen, who then lays waste to Kalervo's land. In the cradle, Kullervo, born to Kalervo's wife, swears to be avenged on his uncle. Kullervo grows up strong, but so stupid and clumsy that he breaks or ruins everything he touches. He tries to kill his uncle and his uncle tries to kill him. Finally, the uncle gives him to Ilmarinen. Ilmarinen's wife immediately dislikes the boy and gives him a loaf of bread with a stone in it. In return, while Ilmarinen is away from home, Kullervo has her killed by wild beasts. He then flees into the forest, where he finds his parents and lives with them for a long time. He performs all his chores badly. After a time he sets out on a journey. Two women having refused him, he rapes a third, only to learn that she is his sister. In anguish, she kills herself, and Kullervo returns home in sorrow. When his family rejects him, he sets off to attack Untamöinen. After killing his uncle he returns to find his family dead and the countryside desolate. He wanders off into the forest and kills himself by falling on his sword.

Ilmarinen, after weeping for his dead wife, makes up his mind to make another in his forge. He fashions a woman out of gold and silver, but she remains cold and lifeless; so Ilmarinen goes north again to Pohjola. When Louhi refuses to give him a wife, he abducts one of her daughters. This wife soon proves unfaithful, and in anger he turns her into a seagull.

Väinämöinen is thinking about the Sampo, that magic mill. Determined to steal it from Louhi, he builds a ship and Ilmarinen forges a sword for him, and the two heroes start for Pohjola. On the way Lemminkäinen calls to them from the shore and asks to accompany them. They take him along. During the voyage the boat strikes a giant pike. Väinämöinen kills the great fish and from its bones fashions a harp with which he sings everyone in Pohjola to sleep. With the help of an ox the three heroes take the Sampo and sail for home. When Louhi awakens, she sends fog and wind after the heroes. During the storm Väinämöinen's harp falls overboard.

Louhi and her men follow in a war boat. The two boats meet in a great battle. Although Väinämöinen is victorious, Louhi drags the Sampo from his boat into the lake. There it breaks into pieces, most of which sink to the bottom. Only a few smaller pieces float to shore. After making violent threats against Kalevala, Louhi returns home with only a small and useless fragment of the Sampo. Väinämöinen collects the pieces on the shore and plants them for good luck; the land becomes more fruitful. Having searched in vain for his lost harp, Väinämöinen makes another of birchwood, and his songs to its music give joy to everyone.

Vexed because her land is barren after the loss of the Sampo, Louhi sends a terrible pestilence to Kalevala, but Väinämöinen heals the people by magic and salves. Next Louhi sends a great bear to ravish the herds, but Väinä-

möinen kills the savage beast. Then Louhi steals the moon and the sun, which came down to earth to hear Väinämöinen play and sing. She also steals the fire from all the hearths of Kalevala. When Ukko, the supreme god, kindles a new fire for the sun and the moon, some of it falls to earth and is swallowed by a fish in a large lake. Väinämöinen and Ilmarinen finally find the fish, and Ilmarinen is badly burned. The fire escapes and burns a great area of country until it is at last captured and returned to the hearths of Kalevala. Ilmarinen, recovered from his burns, prepares great chains for Louhi and frightens her into restoring the sun and the moon to the heavens.

Marjatta, a holy woman and a virgin, swallows a cranberry, whereupon a son is born to her in a stable. The child is baptized as the king of Carelia, despite Väinämöinen's claim that such an ill-omened child should be put to death. Angered because the child proves wiser than he, Väinämöinen sails away to a land between the earth and the sky, leaving behind him, for the pleasure of his people, his harp and his songs.

Critical Evaluation:

The stories contained in the *Kalevala* stem from Finnish folktales that are many centuries old. However, it is important to remember that the *Kalevala* that now exists took shape only in 1835. This was when Elias Lönnrot published a compilation of folktales he spent years gathering and arranging. Lönnrot did not invent any of the stories in the *Kalevala*, but he did codify and edit them so that they would flow into each other in a smooth narrative that would make up a unified aesthetic whole. Lönnrot was no doubt influenced in his compilation of the *Kalevala* by the Finnish nationalism of his day (Finland was ruled by Russia until 1917). Finland was one of many European countries that experienced a nationalistic revival in the nineteenth century, and throughout Europe folk legends were an important part of this revival.

The *Kalevala* is a cohesive story, but it contains dozens of individual tales within the central narrative. The stories are legends, not historical fact. The adventures of Väinämöinen, Ilmarinen, and Kullervo are fantastic and mythical. Nevertheless, the epic chronicles a development through time that can be termed historical. Like the Hindu epic *The Mahabharata* (c. 400 B.C.E.-200 C.E.; English translation, 1834) and the Babylonian creation story "Enuma elish," the *Kalevala* starts at the beginning of time, with the creation of the cosmos itself, and then tells the story of the Adamlike Väinämöinen, who in many ways epitomizes basic human strivings and yearnings. As further generations are born and the epic's list of characters lengthens, the narrative moves on in a historical progression to more complex strivings and conflicts, ending with the birth of Marjatta's child, who heralds a new order of being. The *Kalevala* is the ontogenesis of humankind.

Väinämöinen has to be accounted the major character of the *Kalevala*, yet he is in many ways an enigmatic and unfulfilled figure. Like the biblical Adam and the Greek hero Prometheus, he is the first to do many things, but he never finds earthly happiness, particularly with regard to women. He repeatedly meets younger men, among them Joukahäinen and Ilmarinen, who do better with the opposite sex and who also represent more active, vitalistic forces than Väinämöinen does, whatever his intelligence and ingenuity. Väinämöinen's practical failure, though, is compensated by his musical gifts, which have to do not only with performance and entertainment but also with a fundamental shaping of the universe through beauty. Väinämöinen's sorrow is transfigured into aesthetic power.

Kullervo, like Väinämöinen and, indeed, many of the *Kalevala*'s heroes, is not a conventionally sympathetic protagonist. This epic is different from many others, however, in that its protagonists are not so much paragons of humanity as they are people suffering ordinary human misfortune in extraordinary ways. Kullervo's short and savage life is doomed to tragedy, yet he clearly desires alleviation for his sense of being ill at ease in the world. Kullervo's combination of bravery and stupidity is reminiscent of the biblical Samson or the Greek Hercules; like these heroes, his martial prowess finally falls victim to an earthly luck that even the most pugnacious of men cannot control.

Ilmarinen represents another archetypal kind of hero. He is the smith whose ability to forge human beings out of inanimate material can be read as a metaphor for creative force. Like Väinämöinen's poignant melodies, Ilmarinen's smithy exemplifies the attempt to order an often chaotic and random world. Ilmarinen's failure to forge a wife for himself is a parable of the limited human ability to exercise a full creative power in the cosmos. Ilmarinen's great achievement, the Sampo, is an interesting feature of the *Kalevala*. The Sampo is a talisman, a token of great deeds, a symbol of wealth and glory, and a proof of heroic achievement. However, it is more than merely an inanimate object, for it produces wealth and can bring prosperity and happiness. The Sampo is practical as well as symbolic, and it may well reflect the harsh realities of a tribal society in a cold climate where there was little time for leisure and little role for mere ornaments.

One of the salient features of the *Kalevala* is its lyrical evocation of the Finnish landscape, which is, however, not portrayed romantically or sentimentally. In comparison with many other so-called primary epics compiled largely out of

oral tales, the *Kalevala* avoids easy idealizations and gratifying closures. The landscape, vast and desolate yet starkly beautiful, is always surrounded with an air of remoteness and mournful if majestic pathos. The *Kalevala* does not concern only deeds of war or brute strength; its heroes are for the most part intellectuals and craftsmen, and the poem has a spiritual depth that transcends its apparently "primitive" atmosphere.

The ending of the *Kalevala* expresses this spirituality in an even more recognizable fashion. The birth of the child to the virgin Marjatta is clearly meant to parallel the birth of Christ to the Virgin Mary, and it also takes place in a stable. The final acknowledgment of defeat by Väinämöinen in his confrontation with the newly born child is an allegory of the replacement of the mythic world of the *Kalevala* with the world of redemption and hope represented by Christ. In this world, though, the legends and folktales compiled by Lönnrot will always have a special significance for the Finnish nation. Lönnrot's efforts gave the world a work that is a national epic and, at the same time, a considerable repository of mythic spirituality.

"Critical Evaluation" by Nicholas Birns

Further Reading

Ahokas, Jaakko. *A History of Finnish Literature*. Bloomington: Indiana University Press, 1973. Demonstrates the importance of Lönnrot's compilation of traditional Finnish folktales in providing the impetus for the formation of a Finnish literary tradition.

Branch, Michael. "Finnish Oral Poetry, *Kalevala*, and *Kanteletar*." In *A History of Finland's Literature*, edited by George C. Schoolfield. Lincoln: University of Nebraska Press in cooperation with the American-Scandinavian Foundation, 1998. Offers information about the epic and Lönnrot.

Ervast, Pekka. *The Key to the "Kalevala."* Edited by John Major, translated by Tapio Joensuu. Nevada City, Calif.: Blue Dolphin, 1999. Originally published in Finland in 1916, Ervast's book explains the "mysterious knowledge" and esoteric meaning of the *Kalevala*.

Honko, Lauri. *Religion, Myth, and Folklore in the World's Epics: "The Kalevala" and Its Predecessors*. Berlin: Mouton de Gruyter, 1990. Collection of scholarly essays that takes a comparative and analytical focus. Occasionally difficult, but worthwhile for its illumination of how much intellectual reflection and debate the *Kalevala* is capable of inspiring among scholars.

Jones, Michael Owen. *The World of the "Kalevala": Essays in Celebration of the 150 Year Jubilee of the Finnish Na-*

tional Epic. Los Angeles: University of California, Folklore and Myth Publications, 1987. By far one of the best general books on the *Kalevala*. Provides a clear and cogent description of the story of the epic as well as of its significance in Finnish literary history and cultural life.

Kailo, Kaarina. "Gender and Ethnic Overlap in the Finnish *Kalevala*." In *Of Property and Propriety: The Role of Gender and Class in Imperialism and Nationalism*, edited by Himani Bannerji, Shahrzad Mojab, and Judith Whitehead. Toronto, Ont.: University of Toronto Press, 2001. Kailo examines the depiction of women and the indigenous Sami/Lapps in the *Kalevala*. She maintains that the epic laid an ideological foundation for the representation of gender, class, and ethnicity in subsequent Finnish literature.

Pentikäinen, Juha Y. *"Kalevala" Mythology*. Edited and translated by Ritva Poom. Bloomington: Indiana University Press, 1999. Detailed analysis of the *Kalevala*, including discussions of its genesis, worldview, and place in Finnish history and mythology. Chapter 4 focuses on Lönnrot as both "the individual and the national myth," and there are many other references to him throughout the book.

Sawin, Patricia G. "Lönnrot's Brainchildren: The Representation of Women in Finland's *Kalevala*." *Journal of Folklore Research* 25, no. 3 (1988): 187-217. A feminist examination of the epic. Examines such characters in the story as Aino, the daughter of Louhi, and Marjatta, and discusses the way they express and epitomize gender roles. Despite the overall domination of the epic by a patriarchal vision, Sawin isolates many occasions in which women are able to assert themselves.

Kamouraska

Author: Anne Hébert (1916-2000)
First published: 1970 (English translation, 1973)
Type of work: Novel
Type of plot: Historical
Time of plot: 1838-1839
Locale: Sorel, Kamouraska, Quebec City, and Montreal, Canada

Principal characters:
ELISABETH D'AULNIÈRES, a young woman
MARIE-LOUISE D'AULNIÈRES, her teenage mother
ANTOINE TASSY, Elisabeth's first husband
CAROLINE TASSY, his mother
JÉRÔME ROLLAND, Elisabeth's second husband
GEORGE NELSON, Elisabeth's lover
ADÉLAÏDE,
LUCE-GERTRUDE, and
ANGÉLIQUE, Elisabeth's aunts
AURÉLIE CARON, a servant and prostitute

The Story:

Elisabeth d'Aulnières, the only child of Marie-Louise d'Aulnières, a widowed teenager, has been reared by three unmarried aunts, whose imaginations are formed by romance reading and by piety. The household of Elisabeth's childhood has been a feminine abode, notable by its absence of men. Shielded from the raw facts of life, Elisabeth has been taught that babies are dumped into the beds of ladies by "Indians." In her daydreams, marriage is a swirling collage: the marriage at Cana of Galilee in the Gospels, the bride of Lammermoor in Sir Walter Scott's 1819 novel, and the romantic French folk song "À la claire fontaine."

Elisabeth's aunts prepare their niece lovingly for the governor's ball, where her beauty attracts the eye of Antoine Tassy, the squire of Kamouraska, a picturesque village four hundred miles from Elisabeth's home in Sorel. Antoine's mother, Caroline, asks Madame d'Aulnières for the hand of Elisabeth, and the proposed match is considered advantageous, despite the young squire's admitted bad reputation.

The two are married.

Madame Tassy counsels her new daughter-in-law to ignore the drunkenness and debauchery of the squire, whom she pronounces basically "a good man." Despite the affluence of the Tassys, their home is austere, dominated by the mother-in-law, a harsh woman with a club foot who insists on simple meals, rough clothing, and a Puritanical simplicity of residence. She dismisses all emotional displays.

After the birth of two sons, Elisabeth can no longer endure her husband's drunkenness, carousing, and brutality.

She retreats to her former home in Sorel and the protection of her three adoring aunts. There she meets George Nelson, an American physician practicing in Sorel. Nelson is from a royalist family that has converted to Catholicism so thoroughly that his brother is now a Jesuit priest, while his sister is an Ursuline nun. Nelson, however, soon undergoes a religious crisis when his sister appears to lose her faith on her deathbed. Consequently, he chooses to devote his life to science and to the alleviation of suffering in his vocation as a doctor.

Nelson is called to treat the ailing Elisabeth, whose nerves are frazzled by the violence of her husband and whose body is depleted by the birth of two children so closely. A forbidden love between these two lonely individuals develops quickly. Because only death can end a marriage, escape for Elisabeth means that Antoine must die. Nelson convinces himself that Antoine's eradication is as necessary as the destruction of a sickness in one of his patients. When Elisabeth gives birth to a third child, which she attends with special love, she is certain that he is the son of Nelson.

Although they daydream of a duel in which the lover Nelson will overcome the husband Antoine, Elisabeth and Nelson realize this would be too risky and too scandalous. Still, Antoine must be killed. Nelson, a physician vowed to preserve life, hesitates to commit the act himself. Promising a rich reward, the lovers first send the disreputable Aurélie Caron with poison to lure Antoine to his death. Overcoming her initial fears of divine vengeance, Aurélie sets forth. In Kamouraska, Antoine joins her for what he anticipates will be a night of drunken revelry. The poisoning, however, is incomplete, and only makes him ill. Aurélie returns to Sorel, her mission unaccomplished.

Nelson finally recognizes that the deed must be his. He leaves for Kamouraska in his easily recognizable American sleigh, moving his horse too quickly through the winter ice and snow, sometimes losing his way and being redirected by the locals along the road. After murdering Antoine, he leaves a heavy trail of blood, particularly noted in the wayside inn where he and his horse pass the night. The innkeeper and his wife do not believe his explanation that he was forced to lodge his horse and carriage the previous night in a slaughterhouse. They conclude that he is a murderer.

Though Nelson returns to Sorel having accomplished the deed, he can no longer accept his reward. His act of violence, in deviance of his oath as a physician, has turned him against the woman who inspired the deed. Now he laments to his assistant that he ever met "the damned woman who has ruined me." Instead of returning to the arms of Elisabeth, he flees across the border into the United States. Despite attempts by Canadian authorities, he escapes extradition and is never heard of again.

Elisabeth is briefly imprisoned in Montreal and faces a trial. With only the perjured testimony of her aunts and with the hesitancy of the Quebec courts to convict well-born women of capital crimes, she is exonerated. Still, she is "soiled goods." She eventually is rescued from disgrace by Jérôme Rolland, notary of Quebec City, who marries her even while reminding her that he is her savior. Elisabeth perseveres through eighteen loveless years of respectability as Madame Rolland. Always a dutiful wife, she gives birth to eight children. Now, as Jérôme lies dying, she faithfully assists his nurse, Florida, and keeps vigil at his bedside, all the while remembering Dr. Nelson, the only man she has ever loved.

Critical Evaluation:

Kamouraska is a scenic Quebec village on the south shore of the St. Lawrence River. Its name comes from the Algonquin word meaning "where rushes grow at the water's edge." Even today, residents recall the brutal murder in 1839 of the region's leading citizen and the sensational trial that followed. The victim was distantly related to novelist Anne Hébert's mother, and as a child Hébert spent time in Kamouraska with relatives. Long intrigued by these real but distant events, Hébert also was writing in the afterglow of the centennial celebration of Canadian Confederation (1960). All of Canada was preoccupied with national heritage, remembering bloody wrongs as well as heroic deeds. The plot of *Kamouraska* is generally faithful to historical events, though names are changed and a few details are embellished for dramatic purposes.

Though Hébert's narrative flows coherently, her technique is intricate, her prose poetic. She manipulates time through a stream-of-conscious technique that takes the reader into the mind of Elisabeth d'Aulnières. Events unfold not chronologically but thematically, through a slow interior development. Elisabeth, half asleep and fatigued from tending her dying second husband, is tormented by past memories rushing into her semiconsciousness. The poetry is in Hébert's rich, allusive language; she savors the place names of Quebec, the villages passed, as life itself flows as a carriage constantly plunging through the ice and snow from Sorel to Kamouraska.

The publication of *Kamouraska*, a best seller in Canada, was an important event for Canadian letters. Claude Jutra's 1973 film *Kamouraska*, with a script partially written by Hébert, also was acclaimed in Canada, though it was rarely shown in the United States. Interpreters of Canadian literature have noted that a characteristic, in both the novel's English and French forms, is the correspondence between psychological and external physical atmospheres. Novelist Margaret Atwood has written that in Canadian novels the only season seems to be winter and that the lonely, snow-devastated landscapes are states of mind as well as locales. The harsh climate and uncompromising land play as significant a role in *Kamouraska* as do the haunted minds of the characters. The slain body of Antoine Tassy is discovered in a block of ice, surrounded by frozen blood. These chilling images have led some readers to designate the novel the Canadian *Doktor Zhivago* (the 1957 novel by Boris Pasternak) and its portrait of a fragile aristocratic society has encouraged others to compare it to Margaret Mitchell's *Gone with the Wind* (1936).

American literary critic Edmund Wilson, who has given Canadian literature its due, observes a claustrophobic feature, a psychic asphyxiation, in Québécois fiction. Family and community often function as conscience and jailor. In other Hébert writings—the germinal short story "Le Torrent" (1950), for example—Quebec is perceived as a consuming mother figure maiming her children. Her weapons of oppression are many, the marriage of convenience being one of the most effective. A familiar theme of continental French literature, the misfortunes of marriage, is as central in Hébert's writings as it is in the novels of nineteenth century French novelist Honoré de Balzac. In *Kamouraska*, Elisabeth accepts the endless duties of Canadian women, especially the duty to provide heirs to populate the frozen land. An inescapably repressive Québécois domesticity and an inescapable marriage to a cruel man compel this gently reared woman to plot murder. It is Elisabeth alone, deserted by her lover and her companion in crime, who must stand trial, only to be rescued from infamy by yet another man and a second household prison.

Elisabeth's family, the solemn spinster aunts who resemble the three fates of mythology and a mother who has been a widow since the age of seventeen, forms a protective shield when Elisabeth's life is on trial. Superstitious and god-fearing though they may be, these women perjure themselves so that their charge will escape execution. Though Elisabeth's life is spared and her second marriage provides some refuge, she must wear a mask of innocence for the rest of her life. When she is forty years old, her second husband, even on his deathbed, reminds her that she is a murderer whom he had rescued from purgatory. She realizes only too well that her genuine life ended in that far-off time when the only man she ever loved had fled across the border into the United States. The eight children she has with Jérôme Rolland account for

less than the one child fathered by Nelson. Her marriage to Rolland seems a kind of tomb in which she had been buried alive. The men in her life form a strange triptych, her victims as well as her oppressors: the squire of Kamouraska, Tassy, a corpse frozen in the snow; her American lover Nelson, a fugitive cursing the day he had met her; and Rolland, living with the knowledge that only a cold resignation had been given in exchange for his love.

Quebec was once widely referred to as "the priest-infested province to the North," nurtured by a Jansenist Catholicism in which determinism was a prominent feature. Elisabeth, despite her religious upbringing, the echoes of the catechism still filling her thoughts and her sense of being "so much kindling for the eternal flames," had been drawn irresistibly into the arms of her doctor-lover. In retrospect, her crimes seem to have been foreordained, as was her birth in these "few acres of snowy waste that England once took from France."

Allene Phy-Olsen

Further Reading

Kroller, Eva-Marie, ed. *The Cambridge Companion to Canadian Literature.* New York: Cambridge University Press, 2004. Hébert's work is not covered in detail, but these essays provide necessary context for understanding her contribution to both Québécois literature and that of Canada as a whole.

Pallister, Janis L., ed. *The Art and Genius of Anne Hébert: Essays on Her Works.* Madison, N.J.: Fairleigh Dickinson University Press, 2001. A collection of essays in both English and French, concentrating on the complexities of Hébert's work. A substantial book with an extensive bibliography.

Russell, Delbert W. *Anne Hébert.* Boston: Twayne, 1983. A volume in the notable Twayne author's series. Although there are few biographical facts—Hébert was always reclusive—the thorough analyses of her fiction and poetry published before 1983 are helpful.

Skallerup, Lee, ed. *Anne Hébert: Essays on Her Works.* Toronto, Ont.: Guernica Editions, 2009. One of the relatively few English-language critical examinations of Hébert's work, from a variety of twenty-first century viewpoints.

Wilson, Edmund. *O, Canada: An American's Notes on Canadian Culture.* 1965. Reprint. New York: Octagon Books, 1976. The first internationally recognized literary critic to seriously evaluate Canadian writing within a world context. Wilson's observations remain pertinent.

Kenilworth
A Romance

Author: Sir Walter Scott (1771-1832)
First published: 1821
Type of work: Novel
Type of plot: Romance
Time of plot: 1575
Locale: England

Principal characters:
DUDLEY, the earl of Leicester
RICHARD VARNEY, his master of horse
AMY ROBSART, Dudley's wife
EDMUND TRESSILIAN, a Cornish gentleman and a friend of
    Amy Robsart
WAYLAND SMITH, his servant
THE EARL OF SUSSEX
QUEEN ELIZABETH
SIR WALTER RALEIGH
MICHAEL LAMBOURNE, the nephew of Giles Gosling and
    an innkeeper
DOCTOR DOBOOBIE, alias Alasco, an astrologer and
    alchemist
DICKIE SLUDGE, alias Flibbertigibbet, a bright child and a
    friend of Wayland Smith

The Story:

Michael Lambourne, a ne'er-do-well in his early youth, returns from his travels. While drinking and boasting in Giles Gosling's inn, he wagers that he can gain admittance to Cumnor Place, a large manor where an old friend is now steward. It is rumored in the village that Tony Foster is keeping a beautiful young woman prisoner at the manor. Edmund Tressilian, another guest at the inn, goes with Lambourne to Cumnor Place. As Tressilian suspects, he finds the woman there to be his former sweetheart, Amy Robsart, apparently a willing prisoner. He also encounters Richard Varney, her supposed seducer, and the two men engage in a sword fight. Lambourne, who decides to ally himself with his old friend, Tony, intervenes.

Contrary to Tressilian's suspicion, Amy is not Varney's mistress but the wife of Varney's master, the earl of Leicester. Varney only served as the go-between and accomplice in Amy's elopement. Leicester, who is competing for Queen Elizabeth's favor with the earl of Sussex, fears that the news of his marriage to Amy will displease the queen; he therefore convinces Amy that their marriage must be kept secret.

Tressilian returns to Lidcote Hall to obtain Hugh Robsart's permission to bring Varney to justice on a charge of seduction. On his way, he employs Wayland Smith as his manservant. Smith formerly served as an assistant to Dr. Doboobie, an alchemist and astrologer. Tressilian later visits the earl of Sussex, through whom he hopes to petition either the queen or the earl of Leicester in Amy's behalf. During that visit, Wayland saves Sussex's life after the earl was poisoned.

When the earl hears Tressilian's story, he presents the petition directly to the queen. Confronted by Elizabeth, Varney swears that Amy is his lawful wife, and Leicester, who is standing by, confirms the lie. Elizabeth then orders Varney to present Amy to her when she visits Kenilworth the following week.

Leicester sends a letter to Amy asking her to appear at Kenilworth as Varney's wife. She refuses. In order to have an excuse for disobeying Elizabeth's orders regarding Amy's presence at Kenilworth, Varney has Alasco, the former Dr. Doboobie, mix a potion that will make Amy ill without killing her. This plan is thwarted, however, by Wayland, who was sent by Tressilian to help her. She escapes from Cumnor Place and with the assistance of Wayland makes her way to Kenilworth to see Leicester.

When she arrives at Kenilworth, the place is bustling in preparation for Elizabeth's arrival that afternoon. Wayland takes Amy to Tressilian's quarters, where she writes Leicester a letter telling him of her escape from Cumnor Place and asking his aid. Wayland loses the letter, and through a misunderstanding, he is ejected from the castle. Disappointed that Leicester does not come to her, Amy leaves her apartment and goes into the garden. There she is discovered by the queen, who, judging Amy to be insane because of her contradictory statements, returns her to the custody of Varney, her supposed husband.

Leicester decides to confess the true story to the queen, but Varney is afraid for his own fortunes if Leicester falls from favor; he convinces the earl that Amy was unfaithful to him and that Tressilian is her lover. Leicester, acting on Varney's lies, decides that death will be just punishment for Amy and her lover. Varney takes Amy back to Cumnor Place and plots her death. When Leicester relents and sends Lambourne to tell Varney that Amy must not die, Varney kills Lambourne so that he might go through with Amy's murder. Leicester and Tressilian fight a duel; but before either can harm the other, they are interrupted by Dickie Sludge, the child who stole Amy's letter. Leicester reads the letter and realizes that Amy was faithful to him and that the complications of the affair were caused by Varney's machinations.

Leicester immediately goes to the queen and confesses the whole story. Elizabeth is angry, but she sends Tressilian and Sir Walter Raleigh to bring Amy to Kenilworth. They arrive too late to save her. She falls through a rigged trapdoor and plunges to her death.

Tressilian and Raleigh seize Varney and bring him to prison. There Varney commits suicide. Elizabeth permits the grief-stricken Leicester to retire from her court for several years but later recalls him to her favor. Much later in life, he remarries, and he eventually meets his death as a result of poison he intended for someone else.

Critical Evaluation:

To a historical novelist such as Sir Walter Scott, vivid and accurate settings were invaluable tools for summoning a past age. Nowhere in his novels is his masterful use of setting more central to theme and meaning than in *Kenilworth*. In this novel of love and intrigue in Elizabethan England, the moral statements dramatized by the story are strengthened by their association with either of the two places where all the major action occurs—Cumnor Place and Kenilworth. Both places are described in highly charged images and richly symbolic language. Cumnor Place is like a gilded prison. Lavishly decorated, its rooms sumptuously comfortable and filled with expensive finery, it is nevertheless designed as a place of detainment and hiding. In one vivid, eerie passage, Scott describes its specially designed oaken shutters and thick drapes, which allow the rooms to be ablaze with light without the slightest flicker showing to an observer on the outside. Leicester uses this strictly private place as the hiding place for his wife and as a place of escape from court life for himself. He travels to Cumnor Place in disguise, and while there he sheds the finery that identifies and validates him at court.

By contrast, Kenilworth is a public manor house. With the entire court and nobility preparing for the royal entertain-ments, it exhibits all the pomp and splendor of a regal palace; it is literally exploding with feverish activity. The atmosphere at Kenilworth is one of unreality; in his initial picture of the place, Scott describes a row of guards along the battlements who are intended to represent King Arthur's knights—but uncannily, some are real men, some mere pasteboard figures, and it is impossible to distinguish from a distance which are which. A more sinister and frightening instance of the confusion between illusion and reality occurs when Elizabeth encounters Amy in the garden; unable to understand her replies given her supposed understanding of the situation, the queen assumes that Amy is one of the wandering actresses planted throughout the grounds to pay her homage, who has forgotten her lines in embarrassment or fright.

The two major characters—Leicester and Amy—are torn between these two places, and close beside each of them throughout their trials are their personal servants, whose relationships with them point up a major theme in the novel, that of the moral connection or interdependency between masters and their servants; a master, being responsible for his choice of servants, may be judged to a large extent by their attitudes and behavior. Therefore, when Varney interviews Michael Lambourne as a prospective employee for himself—and ultimately for Leicester—he is very pleased with Lambourne's list of desirable qualities in a courtier's servant, which includes "a close mouth" and "a blunt conscience." These are Varney's qualifications exactly, to which are added cunning, greed, and consuming ambition. The proper scheme of things is turned topsy-turvy early in the story in the symbolically prefigurative scene in which Varney persuades his master to disguise himself as a servant, while he impersonates the master. Leicester's moral guilt is clear when he recognizes his servant's true nature yet keeps him in service; he calls Varney a devil, but he is a devil indispensable to the earl's ambitious plans. In contrast to Leicester's and Varney's standards of a good servant are those of the admirable Tressilian, who warns Wayland Smith against knavery, pointing out that transgression committed "by one attending on me diminishes my honour." In addition to Wayland, Amy's maidservant offers another example of a loyal servant who reflects her mistress's worth; Janet Foster is totally devoted, even to the dangerous extreme of aiding her lady's escape from Cumnor Place in defiance of her father, Amy's jailer.

Scott said once that the sight of a ruined castle or relic of the medieval period made him wish to construct the life and times represented by the ruin. In *Kenilworth*, he demonstrates his imaginative powers in setting a vivid scene and creating compelling characters that bring the past to life.

Further Reading

Hayden, John O., ed. *Scott: The Critical Heritage.* New York: Barnes & Noble, 1970. Provides information on the original reception of *Kenilworth*, presenting reviews dating from 1805 to an 1883 article on Scott written by Mark Twain. Also provides a thorough guide to the critical and literary treatment of Scott in the twentieth century.

Henderson, Diana E. "Bards of the Borders: Scott's *Kenilworth*, the Nineteenth Century's Shakespeare, and the Tragedy of *Othello*." In *Collaborations with the Past: Reshaping Shakespeare Across Time and Media.* Ithaca, N.Y.: Cornell University Press, 2006. Argues that William Shakespeare is fundamental to the structure and vision of the novel, focusing on the similarities between the novel and *Othello*.

Hillhouse, James T. *The Waverley Novels and Their Critics.* New York: Octagon Books, 1970. A collection of critical reviews, including criticism by Scott himself and reviews of *Kenilworth* after its publication. Also includes critical interpretations of Scott and *Kenilworth* in the fifty years following his death.

Irvine, Robert P. "The State, the Domestic, and National Culture in the Waverley Novels." In *Enlightenment and Romance: Gender and Agency in Smollett and Scott.* New York: Peter Lang, 2000. Analyzes the fiction of Scott and Tobias Smollett within the context of the emergence of social sciences and the dominance of novels written by female writers in the eighteenth century. Describes how the authors adapted the feminine romance and the domestic novel to assert control over the narrative structure of their novels.

Johnson, Edgar. *Sir Walter Scott: The Great Unknown.* 2 vols. New York: Macmillan, 1970. Considers the historical significance of *Kenilworth*, with particular emphasis on Scott's treatment of royalty. Concludes that the subject matter and the setting are perfectly matched.

Lincoln, Andrew. "The Condition of England: *Ivanhoe* and *Kenilworth*." In *Walter Scott and Modernity.* Edinburgh: Edinburgh University Press, 2007. In his examination of Scott's novels and poems, Lincoln argues that these were not works of nostalgia; instead, Scott used the past as a means of exploring modernist moral, political, and social issues.

Macintosh, W. *Scott and Goethe: German Influence on the Writings of Sir Walter Scott.* Port Washington, N.Y.: Kennikat Press, 1970. Compares *Kenilworth* with William Shakespeare's *Othello* and Johann Wolfgang von Goethe's *Egmont*. Summarizes Goethe's opinion of Scott's writing.

Shaw, Harry E., ed. *Critical Essays on Sir Walter Scott: The Waverley Novels.* New York: G. K. Hall, 1996. Collection of essays published between 1858 and 1996 about Scott's series of novels. Includes journalist Walter Bagehot's 1858 article about the Waverly novels and discussions of Scott's rationalism, storytelling and subversion of the literary form in his fiction, and what his work meant to Victorian readers.

Kidnapped
Being Memoirs of the Adventures of David Balfour in the Year 1751

Author: Robert Louis Stevenson (1850-1894)
First published: 1886
Type of work: Novel
Type of plot: Adventure
Time of plot: 1751
Locale: Scotland

Principal characters:
DAVID BALFOUR, a young man
EBENEZER BALFOUR OF SHAWS, his uncle
MR. RANKEILLOR, a lawyer
ALAN BRECK STEWART, a Jacobite adventurer

The Story:

When David Balfour's father dies, the only inheritance left his son is a letter to Ebenezer Balfour of Shaws, his brother and David's uncle. Mr. Campbell, the minister of Essendean, delivers the letter to David and tells him that if things do not go well between David and his uncle he is to return to Essendean, where his friends will help him. David sets off in high spirits. The house of Shaw is a great one in the Lowlands of Scotland, and David is eager to take his rightful place in the family from which his father, for some unknown reason, separated himself.

As he approaches the great house, he begins to grow apprehensive. Everyone of whom he asks the way has a curse for the name Shaws and warns him against his uncle. When he arrives at the place, he finds not a great house but a ruin with one wing unfinished and many windows without glass. No friendly smoke comes from the chimneys, and the closed door is studded with heavy nails.

David finds his Uncle Ebenezer even more forbidding than the house, and he begins to suspect that his uncle cheated his father out of his rightful inheritance. When his uncle tries to kill him, he is convinced of Ebenezer's villainy. His uncle promises to take David to Mr. Rankeillor, the family lawyer, to get the true story of David's inheritance, and they set out for Queen's Ferry. Before they reach the lawyer's office, David is tricked by Ebenezer and Captain Hoseason into boarding the *Covenant*, and the ship sails away with David a prisoner, bound for slavery in the American colonies.

At first, he lives in filth and starvation in the bottom of the ship. The only person who befriends him is Mr. Riach, the second officer. Later, he finds even some of the roughest seamen to be kind at times. Mr. Riach is kind when he is drunk but mean when sober, whereas Mr. Shuan, the first officer, is gentle except when he is drinking. It is while he is drunk that Mr. Shuan beats Ransome, the cabin boy, to death because the boy displeased him. After Ransome's murder, David becomes the cabin boy, and for a time his life on the *Covenant* is a little better.

One night, the *Covenant* runs down a small boat and cuts her in two. Only one man is saved, Alan Breck Stewart, a Scottish Highlander and Jacobite with a price on his head. Alan demands that Captain Hoseason set him ashore among his own people, and the captain agrees. When David overhears the captain and Mr. Riach planning to seize Alan, he warns Alan of the plot. Together, the two of them hold the ship's crew at bay, killing Mr. Shuan and three others and wounding many more, including Captain Hoseason. Alan and David became fast friends and remain so during the rest of their adventures. Alan tells David of his part in the rebellion against King George and of the way he is hunted by the king's men, particularly by Colin of Glenure, known as the Red Fox. David is loyal to the monarch, yet out of mutual respect, he and Alan swear to help each other in time of trouble.

It is not long before they have occasion to prove their loyalty. The ship breaks apart on a reef. David and Alan, separated at first, soon find themselves together again, deep in the part of the Highlands controlled by Alan's enemies. When Colin of Glenure is murdered, the blame falls on Alan. If they are caught, they will both hang. They begin to work their way to the Lowlands to find Mr. Rankeillor, their only chance for help. They hide by day and travel by night. Often they go for several days without food. They are in danger not only from the king's soldiers but also from Alan's own people, for there is always the risk that a trusted friend will betray them for the reward offered. However, David is able to learn the meaning of loyalty. Many of Alan's clan endanger themselves to help the hunted pair.

When David is too weak to go on and wants to give up, Alan offers to carry him. They finally reach Queen's Ferry and Mr. Rankeillor. At first, Mr. Rankeillor is skeptical when he hears David's story, but it begins to align so well with what he hears from others that he becomes convinced; he tells David that his father and his Uncle Ebenezer both loved the same woman, whom David's father won. Because he was a kind man and because Ebenezer took to his bed over the loss of the woman, David's father gave up his inheritance as the oldest son in favor of Ebenezer. The story helps David realize why his uncle tried to get rid of him. Ebenezer knows that his dealings with David's father will not stand up in the courts, and he was afraid that David came for his inheritance.

With the help of Alan and Mr. Rankeillor, David is able to frighten his uncle into offering him two-thirds of the yearly income from the land. David does not want to submit his family name to public scandal in the courts, and he knows he can better help Alan if the story of their escape is kept quiet, so he agrees to the settlement. In this way, he is able to help Alan reach safety and pay his debt to his friend.

Critical Evaluation:

Robert Louis Stevenson directed many of his works to young readers in deference to nineteenth century Romanticism's idealization of the innocence of childhood and the fecundity of children's imaginations. He believed strongly that youngsters were an important segment of the reading public. *Kidnapped* was originally published as a serial in a boys' magazine, and Stevenson first won fame as a novelist with the children's adventure story *Treasure Island* (1881-1882, serial; 1883, book). *A Child's Garden of Verses* (1885) also falls in this category.

A large part of the popular appeal of *Kidnapped* lies with the historical-romantic nature of the plot. The novel revolves around a historical incident, the murder of Colin Campbell, the Red Fox of Glenure, and other historical figures appear, among them King George. Thus the nonhistorical but pivotal events of the plot—David Balfour's trials and Alan Stewart's escapades, which constitute the largest part of the novel—are tied to actual history. This intertwining of history and fantasy has the effect of personalizing history and making fantasy credible.

Another factor that enhances the verisimilitude of *Kidnapped* is Stevenson's narrative technique. David tells his story in the first person. As a consequence, the reader develops a close rapport with the narrator and sympathizes with his plight. Most important, the first-person narrative makes the story highly plausible.

To some extent, Stevenson emphasizes plot over characterization; his goal is above all to entertain, to transport the reader from mundane, daily existence to a believable world of excitement and adventure. To create this effect, Stevenson combines the extraordinary with the commonplace. David's kidnapping, Alan's rescue, and the shipwreck combines with such more commonplace occurrences as family hostilities, the life of sailors, and Scottish feuds. This combination produces an exceptionally convincing tale.

Stevenson does not ignore the impact of character development, however. By juxtaposing David, the canny Lowlander, with Alan, the proud Highlander, he brings two opposing value systems together into a compatible relationship. David and Alan have contradictory points of view and antithetical sociopolitical commitments; yet they work together and form a lasting bond on the basis of friendship and loyalty that transcend their differences. Here Stevenson the novelist is at his best, forsaking dogma and ideology in favor of humanistic values.

Stevenson is a master storyteller. He weaves this tale around the great and the small, the rich and the poor, virtuous men and scoundrels, and each character is truly drawn. A stolen inheritance, a kidnapping, a battle at sea, several murders—these are only a few of the adventures that befall the hero. It is easily understood why *Kidnapped* is a favorite with all who read it.

Further Reading

Ambrosini, Richard, and Richard Dury, eds. *Robert Louis Stevenson: Writer of Boundaries*. Madison: University of Wisconsin Press, 2006. Collection of essays examining all of Stevenson's work. References to *Kidnapped* are listed in the index.

Buckton, Oliver S. "Mr. Betwixt-and-Between: History, Travel, and Narrative Indeterminacy in *Kidnapped*." In *Cruising with Robert Louis Stevenson: Travel, Narrative, and the Colonial Body*. Athens: Ohio University Press, 2007. Examines the influence of Stevenson's travels on his fiction and nonfiction works.

Calder, Jenni. *Robert Louis Stevenson: A Life Study*. New York: Oxford University Press, 1980. Claims that Stevenson could not have written *Kidnapped* or *Treasure Island* if he had not had the life experiences he had. Discusses the characters of David Balfour and Alan Breck Stewart and concludes that the novel's success rests on the credibility of Balfour's character.

_____. *Stevenson and Victorian Scotland*. Edinburgh: Edinburgh University Press, 1981. Includes a number of articles that refer to *Kidnapped*. Christopher Harvie's "The Politics of Stevenson" examines settings in Stevenson's novels and his development of a rich Scottish dialogue, as well as the role that Scottish politics play in *Kidnapped*. W. W. Robson, in "On *Kidnapped*," analyzes the way the vernacular and the character interaction are affected by the intersection of time and place.

Harman, Claire. *Myself and the Other Fellow: A Life of Robert Louis Stevenson*. New York: HarperCollins, 2005. A substantial biography of Stevenson, covering the writer's early family life, his writing and travels, and his curious but successful marriage. Includes bibliography and index.

Zharen, W. M. von. "*Kidnapped*: Improved Hodgepodge?" In *Children's Novels and the Movies*, edited by Douglas Street. New York: Frederick Ungar, 1983. Compares *Kidnapped* to motion picture productions of the novel, and considers the reason behind the changes made to the story. Discusses the reasons for the novel's appeal to children.

Kim

Author: Rudyard Kipling (1865-1936)
First published: 1901
Type of work: Novel
Type of plot: Adventure
Time of plot: Late nineteenth century
Locale: British India

Principal characters:
KIMBALL O'HARA (KIM), a street boy
A TIBETAN LAMA, Kim's teacher
MAHBUB ALI, a horse trader
COLONEL CREIGHTON, the director of the British Secret Service
HURREE CHUNDER MOOKERJEE, a babu

The Story:

Kim grows up on the streets of Lahore. His Irish mother died when he was born, and his father, a former color-sergeant of an Irish regiment called the Mavericks, died eventually of drugs and drink. He left his son in the care of a half-caste woman. Young Kimball O'Hara thereupon became Kim, and under the hot Indian sun, his skin grew so dark that one could not tell he was a white boy.

One day, a Tibetan lama, in search of the holy River of the Arrow that will wash away all sin, comes to Lahore. Struck by the possibility of exciting adventure, Kim attaches himself to the lama as his chela. That night, at the edge of Lahore, Mahbub Ali, a horse trader, gives Kim a cryptic message to deliver to a British officer in Umballa. Kim does not know that Mahbub Ali is a member of the British secret service. He delivers the message as directed and then hides in the grass and watches and listens until he learns that his message means that eight thousand men will go to war.

Out on the big road, the lama and Kim encounter many people of all sorts. Conversation is easy. Kim is particularly interested in one group, an old lady traveling in a family bullock cart attended by a retinue of eight men. Kim and the lama attach themselves to her party. Toward evening, they see a group of soldiers making camp. It is the Maverick regiment. Kim, whose horoscope says that his life will be changed at the sign of a red bull in a field of green, is fascinated by the regimental flag, which is just that: a red bull against a background of bright green.

Caught by a chaplain, the Reverend Arthur Bennett, Kim accidentally jerks loose the amulet he carries around his neck. Mr. Bennett opens the amulet and discovers three papers folded inside, including Kim's baptismal certificate and a note from his father asking that the boy be taken care of. Father Victor arrives in time to see the papers. When Kim tells his story, he is informed that he will be sent away to school. Though he parts sadly from the lama, Kim is sure that he will soon escape. The lama asks that Father Victor's name and ad-

dress and the costs of schooling Kim be written down and given to him. Then he disappears. Kim, pretending to prophesy, tells the priests and soldiers what he heard at Umballa. They laugh at him, but the next day his prophecy comes true, and eight thousand soldiers are sent to put down an uprising in the north. Kim remains in camp.

One day, a letter arrives from the lama. He encloses enough money for Kim's first year at school and promises to provide the same amount yearly. He requests that the boy be sent to St. Xavier's for his education. The drummer who is ordered to keep an eye on Kim is cruel to his charge. When Mahbub Ali comes upon the two boys, he gives the drummer a beating and begins talking to Kim. While they are thus engaged, Colonel Creighton comes up and learns from Mahbub Ali, in an indirect way, that once he is educated Kim will be a valuable member of the secret service.

On his way to St. Xavier's, Kim spies the lama, who was waiting a day and a half to see him. They agree to see each other often. Kim is an apt pupil, but he dislikes being shut up in classrooms and dormitories. When vacation time comes, he goes to Umballa and persuades Mahbub Ali to let him return to the road until school reopens.

Traveling with Mahbub Ali, he plays the part of a horse boy and saves the trader's life when he overhears two men plotting to kill the horse dealer. At Simla, Kim stays with Mr. Lurgan, who teaches him a great many subtle tricks and games and the art of make-up and disguise. Just as Mahbub Ali said, he now learns the great game, as the work of the secret service is called. At the end of the summer, Kim returns to his studies at St. Xavier's, where he stays for three years.

At the end of that time, Mahbub Ali suggests to Mr. Lurgan and Colonel Creighton that Kim be permitted to go out on the road with his lama again. Kim's skin is stained dark, and he resumes the dress of a street boy. Given the password by Hurree Chunder Mookerjee, a babu who is another member of the secret service, Kim sets out with his lama.

Still seeking his river, the lama moves up and down India with Kim as his disciple. The two of them once more encounter the old woman they met on the road three years before. A little later, Kim is surprised to see the babu, who tells him that two of the five kings of the north were bribed and that the Russians sent spies down into India through the passes that the kings agreed to guard. Two men, a Russian and a Frenchman, are to be apprehended, and the babu asks for Kim's aid. Kim suggests to the lama a journey into the foothills of the Himalayas, and so he is able to follow the babu on his mission.

During a storm, the babu comes upon the two foreigners. Discovering that one of their baskets contains valuable letters, including a message from one of the traitorous kings, he offers to be their guide; in two days, he leads them to the spot where Kim and the lama are camped. When the foreigners tear almost in two a holy drawing made by the lama, the babu creates a disturbance in which the coolies, according to plan, carry off the men's luggage. The lama conducts Kim to the village of Shamlegh. There, Kim examines all the baggage that the coolies brought. He throws everything except letters and notebooks over an unscalable cliff. He hides the documents on his person.

In a few days, Kim and the lama set out again. At last, they come to the house of the old woman who befriended them twice before. When she sees Kim's emaciated condition, she puts him to bed, where he sleeps many days. Before he goes to sleep, he asks that a strongbox be brought to him. He deposits his papers in it, locks the box, and hides it under his bed. When he awakens, he hears that the babu arrived, and Kim delivers the papers to him. The babu tells him that Mahbub Ali is also in the vicinity. They assure Kim that he played his part well in the great game. The old lama knows nothing of these matters. He is happy because Kim brought him to his river at last, a brook on the old lady's estate.

Critical Evaluation:

Rudyard Kipling won the Nobel Prize in Literature in 1907 and received honorary degrees from both Harvard and Oxford, but he was an extremely controversial writer, not only during his lifetime but also after it. Kipling was admired by such literary giants as Henry James, Mark Twain, and T. S. Eliot. However, many critics who praised Kipling felt the need to preface their comments with an explanation or an apology; Ernest Hemingway commented that he liked "the good Kipling." The "bad" Kipling is seen as the defender of British imperialism who supported oppressors against native populations, espoused the idea of racial superiority, and re-

mained casually unaware of the value of the cultures the British Empire dismissed and dominated. Remarkably, Kipling manages to inspire great intensity of feeling long after that empire faded. Although *Kim* is not the most controversial of his works, it received widely disparate evaluations, both when it was first published in 1901 and in later criticism. It is perceived by some as a paternalistic, a stereotypical, and an unrealistic picture of India, whereas others find it a rich, sympathetic portrayal.

Kim is a complex book. It has elements of a boys' novel of adventure, a spy story, and a picaresque tale. Kipling himself once called *Kim* plotless. On a more serious level, it can be seen as a tale of initiation, a search for being and belonging, a quest. Because Kipling spent his first five years in Bombay, a time of great happiness for him, followed by six years of misery in England, where he was placed in a rigid, abusive household that he later described as the House of Desolation, *Kim* also has been viewed as a personal fantasy and a creation of a lost childhood idyll.

Setting is extremely important in *Kim*. The India that Kipling portrays stretches from Benares in the middle of the Indian peninsula to the Punjab and the Himalayas in the north. The story begins in Lahore with Kim sitting on the Zam-Zammah, the great gun that controls the north. The opening paragraphs introduce both India and the realities of the British presence there. In spite of the fact that Kim "consorted on terms of perfect equality with the street boys of the bazaar," he felt free to kick one of his companions off the gun "since the English held the Punjab and Kim was English." This opening may imply a belief in the superiority of the British, but as the novel moves to describe the bazaar in detail, it becomes obvious that Kim and Kipling relish life on the Indian streets. After Kim meets the lama, they travel through India following the path of the railroad, the Grand Trunk Road. In chapters 3 and 4 particularly, Kipling presents vivid portraits of people from different castes and backgrounds; the reader is introduced to the sights, sounds, and smells of many different places and peoples on the road. This rich variety caused some critics to call India itself the main character of the novel.

Kim does more than present a fascinating, exotic picture of India; it also is a story about a boy's search for identity. Kim, an Irish orphan, has taken on the characteristics of the Indian street boy. He seems an ideal hero for a boys' adventure tale—clever, brave, able to overcome all odds, a perfect blend of Oliver Twist and the Artful Dodger. He becomes more than just an adventure hero, however, because he faces not only physical and emotional challenges but also spiritual ones. His search begins after he meets the lama, a truly holy man, who desires to free himself completely from the evils and bonds of this world. Kipling represents the novel's theme of the quest, the lama seeks salvation. When Kim decides to join him on this adventure, he, too, decides that he must have a goal. Since his father said before he died that Kim's future would be secure when he finds a red bull on a green field, Kim chooses to search for this bull; the quest that begins as a boys' adventure eventually becomes a quest for himself.

His search is complicated by the different, seemingly contradictory, directions that are pointed out to him by the individuals he meets. The lama leads Kim, his chela or disciple, in one direction, on the search for the river, to a life of religion, spiritualism, asceticism. One part of Kim embraces this life as he follows the lama, whom he truly loves. His other guides prepare him to follow the great game, the network of British spies operating in India, and the boy is also fascinated with the intrigue and excitement of this world. Kim is caught between these two worlds, often wondering just who he is. On several occasions he restates a variation of the question, "Who is Kim?"

Kipling uses powerful symbols to represent the opposing ways and the paths that will lead Kim to them. Repeatedly, Kipling refers to the River, the Road, the Wheel, the Way, the Game. Animal imagery recurs frequently as well. The white stallion represents the British Empire, the bull his father's regiment, and Kim is often referred to as a pony. Colors, too, have symbolism. For the lama, red—the color of the bull—is the color of deceit.

Deeply involved in both worlds, Kim struggles to find his identity. On one hand, he has England, adventure, and the life of a spy and a sahib; on the other lies India, the life of the spirit, and the search for salvation. The novel's end provides no clear answer for Kim or for the reader. Although in the last chapter Kim tells the lama, "I am not a Sahib, I am thy chela," it seems obvious the great game has not released Kim.

"Critical Evaluation" by Mary Mahony

Further Reading

Allen, Charles. *Kipling Sahib: India and the Making of Rudyard Kipling.* London: Little, Brown, 2007. A biography focusing on Kipling's life from his birth until 1889, including his thirteen years in India, which were the inspiration for much of his writing. Allen traces the experiences of Kipling's parents in India, the Indian culture into which Kipling was born, and the state of the country when he returned in 1882 to begin his literary career by working on a newspaper in Lahore.

Bloom, Harold, ed. *Rudyard Kipling's "Kim."* New York: Chelsea House, 1987. An excellent introductory source gathering a cross section of essays providing extremely useful criticism. Analyzes character and theme, discusses Kipling's views on India, presents revisions from an earlier draft, and compares Kipling's views on the British Empire with those of E. M. Forster and George Orwell.

Dillingham, William B. *Rudyard Kipling: Hell and Heroism.* New York: Palgrave Macmillan, 2005. Dillingham maintains that other biographers and critics have neglected Kipling's deeply pessimistic worldview and his complex code of heroism. He focuses on these aspects of Kipling's personality to analyze the writer's life and some of his works, including a discussion of *Kim* in chapter 5.

Kipling, Rudyard. *"Kim": Authoritative Text, Backgrounds, Criticism.* Edited by Zohreh T. Sullivan. New York: W. W. Norton, 2002. In addition to the text of the novel, this edition reprints some of Kipling's other writings, including letters and portions of his autobiography. It also contains an excerpt from a biography of Kipling that describes the origins of *Kim* and two essays placing the novel within its historical context. Thirteen critical essays provide various interpretations of the novel and of Kipling's work, including discussions of Kipling's place in the history of ideas, storytelling in *Kim*, *Kim* as an imperialist novel, and *Kim* and Orientalism.

Nagai, Kaori. *Empire of Analogies: Kipling, India, and Ireland.* Cork, Ireland: Cork University Press, 2006. Analyzes Kim and the other Irish characters in Kipling's India stories. Nagai argues that Kipling was aware that nationalists in both India and Ireland found similarities in their colonial situations and used these analogies to advocate self-government and denounce British misconduct; Kipling's emphasis on Irish participation in the Raj can be interpreted as an "imperialist" counter-argument to these analogies.

Page, Norman. *A Kipling Companion.* London: Macmillan, 1984. Helpful introductory source providing a brief biography, chronology, and discussion of Kipling's world. Identifies historical figures and gives clear, insightful analyses of the novels, short stories, and poetry. Includes a useful annotated bibliography.

Rao, K. Bhaskara. *Rudyard Kipling's India.* Norman: University of Oklahoma Press, 1967. Evaluates Kipling's place as a writer about India and compares him with other British writers. Provides historical background and analyzes theme, setting, and character in *Kim*.

Shahane, Vasant. *Rudyard Kipling: Activist and Artist.* Carbondale: Southern Illinois University Press, 1973. Excellent introductory source. Provides chapter-by-chapter summary illustrating the novel's thematic unity and charting Kim's inner growth as he deals with his two separate worlds. Helpful in following the complex action in the novel. Provides a clear analysis of major symbols, setting, and character.

Sullivan, Zohreh. *Narratives of Empire: The Fictions of Rudyard Kipling.* New York: Cambridge University Press, 1993. A detailed analysis that stresses the quest of the lama and Kim, discusses theme and symbol, and provides a detailed character analysis and a clear explanation of the novel's religious background.

Kindred

Author: Octavia E. Butler (1947-2006)
First published: 1979
Type of work: Novel
Type of plot: Science fiction
Time of plot: June 9-July 4, 1976, and the early nineteenth century
Locale: Los Angeles and Maryland

Principal characters:
EDANA (DANA), an African American woman
KEVIN FRANKLIN, her white husband
RUFUS WEYLIN, Dana's white ancestor in antebellum Maryland
TOM WEYLIN, Rufus's father, a slave owner
ALICE GREENWOOD, Dana's black ancestor in antebellum Maryland

The Story:

Dana and Kevin are moving into their new home in suburban Los Angeles in 1976 when Dana suddenly disappears for a few seconds. She experiences a few hours in an unidentified time and place, where she saves a small boy from drowning, only to have the boy's father aim a gun at her. She feels disoriented and then finds herself back in her apartment, wet and muddy. Kevin has seen her vanish and reappear across the room, and yet he finds it hard to believe that she has traveled elsewhere.

A second incident allows Dana to better understand what is happening to her. Once again, she vanishes from her California home and finds herself rescuing the same boy, now a few years older and this time in danger from a fire. She learns that she is in Maryland and it is 1815, so the color of her skin marks her as a slave, since she has no free papers. Dana also realizes that the boy, Rufus, and his free black neighbor, Alice, are her ancestors, as she has read their names in her family bible. As night falls, Dana seeks refuge at Alice's house, only to witness the brutal beating of a black slave man visiting his free black wife, Alice's mother, without permission. The man's white assailants are Patrollers, forebears of the Ku Klux Klan, and one of them attacks Dana, ultimately sending her back to twentieth century Los Angeles.

Dana and Kevin make preparations after the first two voyages, having determined that Rufus somehow calls Dana to him whenever his life is in danger and that Dana returns

home when she feels grave danger to herself. The next time Dana feels herself losing consciousness, Kevin holds onto her and is thus transported with her to Maryland. The year is 1819, and Rufus has become a difficult twelve-year-old who enjoys Dana's company but shows streaks of his emotionally distant father. Dana must pretend to be Kevin's slave, and she is astonished by how easily both manage their roles. They remain for about two months, until Rufus's father, Tom Weylin, catches Dana teaching two slave children to read and attacks her. Her life in danger, Dana returns to Los Angeles.

Dana finds herself alone, her white husband trapped in the past in his role as slave owner. Eight days later in 1976, and five years later in antebellum Maryland, Dana returns to find Rufus being severely beaten in a fistfight with a black man. Rufus's opponent is Isaac, Alice's slave husband, and he is nearly killing Rufus for raping his wife and trying to sell him down the river. Dana saves Rufus's life and nurses him back to health with the help of some modern over-the-counter medicines she has brought back with her. Dana's fourth journey into the past lasts two months and is full of reflections on the nature of slavery.

Kevin has gone north, so, without his protection, Dana becomes a house slave on the Weylin plantation, although Rufus promises to mail a letter to Kevin informing him of her return. Dana learns how slaves are made when she finds her letter unmailed and runs away. Quickly caught, Dana receives a horrific beating, but she is unable to time travel because she knows her life is not in real danger. Beaten and subdued, Dana begins to lose touch with her identity as a twentieth century African American writer and to experience the subtleties of oppression built into the system of slavery.

Dana observes her ancestors, Rufus and Alice, and even becomes involved in their relationship when Rufus asks Dana to convince Alice not to resist his advances, since he will possess her sexually with or without her consent. Dana watches as Alice, who received a beating far worse than Dana's when she was caught as a runaway, becomes her owner's sexual slave. After two months, Kevin returns to the plantation, and he and Dana are leaving when they encounter Rufus. Rufus points a gun at them and when he means to use it, the two travel back to 1976.

Dana's fifth trip to antebellum Maryland finds Rufus laying face down in a puddle, drunk and ill. Dana treats his illness with Excedrin but is unable to help his father, who dies of what appears to be a heart attack. In a rage because he believes Dana allowed Tom Weylin to die, Rufus sentences Dana to fieldwork, where she briefly experiences the physical brutality practiced on field slaves. Dana soon returns to the house, but, when Rufus sells a slave specifically because he has spoken to Dana, she takes matters into her own hands and cuts her wrists, returning herself to Los Angeles.

Dana's final voyage occurs on July 4, 1976, America's bicentennial. For the first time, Rufus does not appear to be in immediate danger when she finds him, although the fact that Dana has time-traveled suggests that he is considering suicide. He immediately takes Dana to see Alice, who has hanged herself because she believed that Rufus had sold her children, whom he actually secreted with family in order to further subdue Alice. When Rufus, desperately lonely, attempts to rape Dana, she briefly thinks how easy it would be to allow herself to become a victim before stabbing Rufus repeatedly. Rufus fights back, and this time, when Dana returns to twentieth century California, she is without her left arm, which has remained in the space between Rufus's desperate grasp at her arm and the wall of her home.

Critical Evaluation:

At the time of her death in 2006, Octavia E. Butler was considered the most successful African American woman science-fiction writer. She won two Nebula and two Hugo awards, science fiction's highest honors. Her work is highly respected in mainstream literary circles, and she is the only science-fiction writer ever to have been awarded a MacArthur Fellowship.

Butler wrote twelve novels, creating complex imaginative worlds peopled by hybrid characters who challenge the boundaries of race, gender, sexuality, and history. Her most important works include the Patternist series (1976-1984), which treats mental enslavement of regular humans by telepaths, and the *Xenogenesis* series (1987-1989), which features a postapocalyptic Earth in which humans must merge with aliens for survival. Her acclaimed short story collection, *Bloodchild* (1995), explores themes of power and control in various configurations.

As an African American woman raised by a single mother in an ethnically diverse, struggling neighborhood, Butler was fundamentally concerned with questions of identity, especially of gender, race, and class. Her writing repeatedly returns to themes of power and enslavement, often placing humans in symbiotic relationships with other beings. *Kindred* is her only novel to explicitly treat the institution of chattel slavery in the antebellum South.

Butler has explained that she first got the idea for *Kindred* when she heard a young African American saying that sometimes he wanted to kill the old African Americans who were complacent about unequal race relations but that doing so would entail killing his own parents and ancestors. *Kindred* is very much about facing family histories by understanding the decisions black people have made throughout the history of the United States, which is fundamentally based on the institution of slavery.

Kindred is difficult to categorize by genre, since it includes elements of both the slavery narrative and science fiction. The theme of time travel, common in science fiction, is used as a mechanism to place twentieth century characters in the situation of slavery, although the science of Dana's travel is never explained. Less graphic in its depictions of brutality than most slave narratives, *Kindred* nevertheless has enormous emotional power since Dana experiences the institution of slavery from the perspective of a twentieth century person with whom a reader can identify. The novel has been read as a neoslave narrative and has been compared to Toni Morrison's *Beloved* (1987) and Margaret Walker's *Jubilee* (1966) in working within this small subgenre. It can also be usefully placed within the much broader category of literature of memory. Butler herself categorized the novel as simply a "grim fantasy."

Like most Butler novels, *Kindred* explores power dynamics in complex ways. The two interracial couples at the novel's emotional core are doubles in that they include a white man and an African American woman. Dana and Alice look very similar, which is unsurprising in that Alice is Dana's direct ancestor. Although Rufus and Kevin do not look particularly alike, they are linked in that on one of her returns to Los Angeles, Dana mistakes Kevin for Rufus and attacks him.

Rufus and Alice's relationship is one of slavery and oppression in which Rufus seems to hold all the power. He is able to take away Alice's freedom, and he rapes her repeatedly, impregnating her with several children. Through ongoing physical and emotional abuse, Rufus thinks he has succeeded in making Alice his own, yet Alice never entirely submits to him, and her suicide can be read as her final upsetting of their power balance.

Kevin and Dana's relationship is a loving marriage into which they both enter freely, yet, even in 1976, they often face prejudice against their interracial union. Their time travel shows them that their relationship dynamic is also susceptible to uneven power relations, since it is surprisingly easy for them to play the parts of slave owner and slave. Indeed, small details from descriptions of the Franklins' 1976 relationship are cast in a new light by the way they interact in the past; for example, Kevin's present-day suggestions that Dana type his manuscripts (she hates to type) or get rid of some of her books (she loves her books) can be seen as a white man subtly disempowering an African American woman.

The main theme of the novel is the insidious nature of slavery throughout American history. When in Maryland, Dana admires Alice's steely resolve in keeping a part of herself untouched by Rufus, since Dana feels the brutality of slavery wearing down her twentieth century feminist resolve with alarming speed. She also realizes that slave owners are just as easily made as slaves. Dana had imagined that Rufus, caught between his bad-tempered, abusive white father and the highly literate black woman who appears regularly to save his life might question the ethics of owning slaves. Instead, Rufus continues in his father's footsteps and even makes the fatal mistake of attempting to rape Dana.

Dana's loss of her arm when she kills Rufus and returns home represents the loss of her innocence in believing that race relations are different in the present. However, her experiences and those of her husband are given a hopeful tinge in the epilogue, as Kevin and Dana visit together the site of the Weylin plantation. Little trace remains of the people they knew in the past, but records show that the children of Rufus and Alice were not sold with the plantation, suggesting that they escaped continued enslavement. Hagar, another of Dana's ancestors, lived to be freed by the Emancipation Proclamation.

Pamela Bedore

Further Reading

Ampadu, Lena. "Racial, Gendered, and Geographical Spaces in Octavia Butler's *Kindred*." *CEAMAGazine* 17 (2004): 70-78. Analyzes the representation and thematic importance of literacy and sexuality in *Kindred*.

Butler, Octavia E. "An Interview with Octavia E. Butler." Interview by Charles Rowell. *Callaloo* 20, no. 1 (1997): 47-66. Detailed interview that includes Butler's advice for burgeoning writers and information about the genesis of *Kindred*.

Long, Lisa A. "A Relative Pain: The Rape of History in Octavia Butler's *Kindred* and Phyllis Alesia Perry's *Stigmata*." *College English* 64, no. 4 (2002): 459-483. Discussion of how these two novels embody the experience of slavery in their characters and thus their readers, with attention to using these texts in teaching at the college level.

Rushdy, Ashraf H. A. "Families of Orphans: Relation and Disrelation in Octavia Butler's *Kindred*." *College English* 55, no. 2 (1993): 135-157. Reads *Kindred* as an exploration of the complexities of memory and kinship for twentieth century African American culture.

Steinburg, Marc. "Inverting History in Octavia Butler's Postmodern Slave Narrative." *African American Review* 38, no. 3 (2004): 467-476. Argues that *Kindred* shows marriage to be a form of slavery and that it complicates the relationship between literacy and the empowerment of slaves.

Yaszek, Lisa. "'A Grim Fantasy': Remaking American History in Octavia Butler's *Kindred*." *Signs: Journal of Women in Culture and Society* 28, no. 4 (2003): 1053-1066. Shows that using science-fiction motifs, such as time travel and the alien other, allows Butler to create a nuanced vision of American history.

Kinflicks

Author: Lisa Alther (1944-   )
First published: 1975
Type of work: Novel
Type of plot: Bildungsroman
Time of plot: 1960's and early 1970's
Locale: Tennessee, Boston, and Vermont

Principal characters:
VIRGINIA "GINNY" BABCOCK BLISS, a young woman
MRS. BABCOCK, Ginny's dying mother
JOE BOB SPARKS, Ginny's football-star boyfriend
CLEM CLOYD, Ginny's motorcycle-riding boyfriend
EDNA (EDDIE) HOLZER, Ginny's lover
IRA BLISS, Ginny's husband
WENDY BLISS, Ginny and Ira's daughter
HAWK, an Army deserter whom Ginny befriends

The Story:

Ginny Babcock Bliss's mother is dying of a blood-clotting disorder, and Ginny comes back to Hullsport, Tennessee, to stay with her. Ginny leaves her husband, Ira Bliss, behind in Vermont, with their two-year-old daughter, Wendy. In fact, Ira made Ginny leave their home after finding her with another man. Ginny thinks back on the steps of her life leading up to where she is at the time. Some of her memories are like the home movies, or "kinflicks." She occasionally thinks about growing up with her two brothers, but she is more concerned with the past twelve years, from her first serious boyfriend through the few years of her marriage.

Her first boyfriend was Joe Bob Sparks, a football star with very little intelligence. Their times together were happier for him than for her; she dated him primarily because he was popular and dating was what everyone did. Ginny's next boyfriend was Clem Cloyd, a motorcycle hoodlum whom she knew since childhood. Her parents strongly disapproved of her relationship with Clem and looked for a way to break them up. Again, Ginny was not in love with Clem; instead, he was someone with whom she experimented sexually and whom she used to rebel against her parents. Their relationship ended when Ginny was seriously injured in a fall from Clem's motorcycle.

After the accident, Ginny's parents decided to get her away from Hullsport by sending her to Worthley, a highly reputable women's college in Boston. Ginny objected to this move, but she went anyway, probably because she had no compelling reason to stay in Tennessee and because protesting took too much energy. At Worthley, Ginny met Miss Helena Head, a philosophy professor who became her mentor. Under Miss Head's tutelage, Ginny became increasingly interested in philosophy and cultural events. She threw herself into her studies and pondered the questions of the great philosophers. She abandoned her emotional life for a mental one, as Miss Head had done, and thought about everything with detachment.

Another woman who lived in Ginny's dormitory challenged Ginny during this cerebral stage. Eddie Holzer, an earthy, rebellious student, began discussing with Ginny the ideas of philosophers, arguing that denying the world of emotion was just as limiting as denying the world of the mind. Their friendship became even stronger when another woman on their hall tried to commit suicide and Ginny did not know what to do. Eddie took control of the situation and comforted Ginny. Eventually, Ginny and Eddie fell in love. When Ginny told Miss Head about their affair, then tried again to approach the world philosophically, Ginny became so distraught that Eddie decided they should both leave Worthley.

The two women lived for a time in an apartment in Boston, using money Ginny received from a trust fund. The trust fund was a problem, however, because the factory that Ginny's family owned made ammunition, and Eddie and Ginny opposed the Vietnam War. They finally calculated the proportion of the money earned from making defense materials and sent that amount to charity, living on the rest.

Eddie and Ginny later moved to Vermont and planned to live off the land. Eddie's relaxed attitude was not conducive to farm work, so the two struggled until friends moved in and helped them. Unfortunately, the four women began to have trouble with local people who wanted to hunt on their property. When the women protested, the locals killed their cow. The women strung barbed wire to try to keep the hunters, who used snowmobiles, off their land. One night as the locals partied on the women's lake, Eddie jumped on a snowmobile and drove toward them. She was decapitated when she ran into the barbed wire.

After grieving for a period of time, Ginny married a man from town, a man she knew before Eddie's death. She said that she needed some order in her life. As was the case with her earlier relationships with men, her marriage to Ira was anything but blissful. He wanted a stereotypical wife and an extremely ordered life. Ginny lived as a rebel and a bohemian. The two had a daughter, Wendy, whom Ginny loved.

One day as Wendy napped indoors and Ginny sat by the pool, a bearded man came up. Ginny learned that he was called Hawk and that he was a U.S. Army deserter. Their friendship developed, and Hawk tried to teach Ginny about meditation. Their rituals became increasingly bizarre, and one night Ira came back from a meeting and caught them asleep together in what appeared to be a sexual position. He ran Ginny off, telling her never to return. Ginny's memories of these events alternate with visits to her mother's hospital bed, with trying unsuccessfully to save some baby birds, and with visits to Joe Bob Sparks and Clem Cloyd, both currently married. Mrs. Babcock, too, was exploring the past, especially her marriage to her late husband and the rearing of their children.

Two other patients at the hospital where Ginny's mother is being treated, a nun and a Jewish immigrant from Europe, often discuss the meaning of suffering and the existence of God. Their arguments contribute to Ginny's confusion.

Ginny gives her mother blood transfusions, but Ginny's blood cannot save Mrs. Babcock. After her mother's death, Ginny tries to commit suicide by tying a rock to her leg and jumping off a pier, but she lands on a boat. She finally decides not to kill herself. In the end, she leaves the cabin on her parents' property, with no idea where she is going.

Critical Evaluation:

Lisa Alther's first published novel, *Kinflicks*, functions on three levels. First, it is a cultural history of America from the 1960's to the 1970's. Second, it is a maturation novel of a young American woman during that time. Third, it is a philosophical novel that explores the value of life and questions whether suffering, death, and life have meaning.

As a cultural history, *Kinflicks* looks at the effect the war in Vietnam had on the United States. As Ginny becomes more aware of the war, she loses her innocence. She moves from being a flag-twirling teenager who dates a gum-chewing football star to being a lesbian, vegetarian war protester who joins the revolution against the establishment. Like other Americans, she can no longer conform to traditional patriotic and family values, such as settling down to be a housewife and mother; even after she marries and has a child, she becomes intimate with an Army deserter. The Vietnam War changed America forever.

As a maturation novel, *Kinflicks* examines Ginny's search for an identity. This search is symbolized by her hairstyles, which always reflect someone else. For example, while dating the football player, she wears a ponytail. She teases her

hair when she dates the biker, then puts it in a bun to imitate Miss Head. Eddie takes down the bun and braids Ginny's hair like her own. In short, Ginny always takes on the identity of the person she is with.

It is worth noting that Ginny is trying to find her way in a patriarchy, but she finds meaning only in her relationships with other women and girls—her mother, Miss Head, Eddie, and Wendy. Her relationships with men always seem to be disrupted by sex and sexual problems.

One of Ginny's fears is that she will take on her mother's personality and her burdens. She needs to escape her mother's influence to avoid such a fate. In the end Ginny comes full circle, returning to her home after marrying and becoming a mother. Ginny, however, does not resign herself to that life, and the way that she gets there ensures that she is not following in her mother's footsteps. In the end, she is not sure who she is because she has no referent by which to define herself.

Finally, *Kinflicks* explores deeper questions. With Ginny, the reader considers conformity, then nonconformity, then conformity again. The novel moves between a false order and an unsatisfying rebellion against order. Ginny cannot decide whether to give in to passion, as she does with Eddie, or to remain unmoved, as she does under the influence of Miss Head. The arguments between the nun, who believes that God makes the noble suffer to ready them for heaven, and the Jewish man, who protests that no decent God could have let the Holocaust happen, could almost be the arguments in Ginny's own mind. She wonders whether her mother's suffering has any meaning. When Ginny contemplates suicide, she wonders whether life has meaning. Alther does not resolve these issues for the reader. She raises the questions in an intelligent and thought-provoking manner.

Early reactions to *Kinflicks* were mixed. Most scholars who discuss the book see it as feminist. A problem with the novel is that readers may consider it dated. As an examination of the United States during the time of the Vietnam War, it is valuable. It also explores universal themes: maturation, the meaning of life, death, and suffering, and human relationships.

Kinflicks is also a witty and entertaining novel. Its episodic, almost picaresque qualities remind one of such classics as Henry Fielding's *The History of Tom Jones* (1749) and Mark Twain's *Adventures of Huckleberry Finn* (1884). Certainly some of Alther's material is autobiographical. More important, the novel is a biography of America as it moved from the innocence of the 1960's to the attempt to regain order after the Vietnam War.

M. Katherine Grimes

Further Reading

Braendlin, Bonnie Hoover. "New Directions in the Contemporary Bildungsroman: Lisa Alther's *Kinflicks*." *Women and Literature* 1 (1980): 160-171. Asserts that Alther's book is a new type of maturation novel because it emphasizes the woman rather than the man. She says the book alternates between the picaresque and the confessional modes, the first being patriarchal and the second matriarchal, as Ginny struggles between freedom and security.

Ferguson, Mary Anne. "The Female Novel of Development and the Myth of Psyche." *Denver Quarterly* 17 (Winter, 1983): 58-74. Ferguson discusses the myth of Psyche and Cupid in *Kinflicks* and works by Eudora Welty and Erica Jong. She also examines Ginny's relationship with her mother as it parallels Ginny's development as heroine.

_____. "Lisa Alther: The Irony of Return?" *Southern Quarterly* 21 (Summer, 1983): 103-115. Ferguson analyzes Ginny's relationship with her mother, including Ginny's attempt to imitate her mother by following her into death. She also focuses on Ginny's rebellion against the South and her return to it.

Hall, Joan Lord. "Symbiosis and Separation in Lisa Alther's *Kinflicks*." *Arizona Quarterly* 38 (Winter, 1982): 336-346. Hall examines Ginny's behavior as symbolically related to her mother's blood: As Mrs. Babcock's blood cells turn upon themselves, Ginny wonders whether she is like a cell functioning in a larger organism. Hall asserts that Ginny can find freedom only when she becomes part of a larger community.

Hart, Vada. "Woebegone Dykes: The Novels of Lisa Alther." In *Beyond Sex and Romance? The Politics of Contemporary Lesbian Fiction*, edited by Elaine Hutton. London: Women's Press, 1998. This analysis of the lesbian characters in Alther's novels is included in a collection of nine essays providing feminist and lesbian interpretations of lesbian fiction.

Levy, Barbara. "Lisa Alther: Playing for the Laugh—Comic Control in *Kinflicks*." In *Ladies Laughing: Wit as Control in Contemporary American Women Writers*. Amsterdam: Gordon and Breach, 1997. Alther is one of seven women writers whose work is analyzed in this study of how the writers use wit as a means of engaging their readers.

Peel, Ellen. "Subject, Object, and the Alternation of First- and Third-Person Narration in Novels by Alther, Atwood, and Drabble." *Critique* (Summer, 1989): 107-122. Peel describes the techniques of Alther's fiction, favorably comparing her work to that of novelists Margaret Atwood and Margaret Drabble.

A King and No King

Authors: Francis Beaumont (c. 1584-1616) and John Fletcher (1579-1625)
First produced: 1611; first published, 1619
Type of work: Drama
Type of plot: Tragicomedy
Time of plot: Indeterminate
Locale: Armenia and Iberia

Principal characters:
ARBACES, king of Iberia
TIGRANES, king of Armenia
GOBRIAS, Lord-Protector of Iberia and Arbaces' father
BACURIUS, an Iberian nobleman
MARDONIUS, an honest old captain in Arbaces' army
BESSUS, a cowardly braggart
LYGONES, an Armenian courtier, Spaconia's father
ARANE, Queen-Mother of Iberia
PANTHEA, her daughter
SPACONIA, an Armenian lady, Tigranes' sweetheart

The Story:

Arbaces, the valiant young king of Iberia, ends a long war against Armenia by defeating in single combat Tigranes, the king of that country. Arbaces, although a hero in war, is also an intensely passionate man; honest and outspoken Mardonius comments that he is capable of the wildest extremities of emotion and that he can move through the entire emotional range with the greatest speed. Inflamed by his victory, Arbaces illustrates the qualities Mardonius ascribes to him. In a series of blustering speeches he shows himself to be inordinately proud. When Mardonius takes him to task for boasting, he becomes, after a few gusts of ranting, temporarily contrite and amiable, and he resolves to give his beautiful, virtuous sister Panthea, whom he did not see since her childhood, in marriage to the defeated but valorous Tigranes. Tigranes protests because he already plighted his troth to Spaconia, a lady of his own land.

Messages, arriving from Gobrias, in whose care the government of Iberia was left, tell that a slave sent by Arane to poison Arbaces was taken and executed. Instead of flying into a rage, Arbaces, in a burst of magnanimity and pity, forgives the queen mother's unnatural act. Thus he swings from the objectionable boastfulness of moments before to the opposite emotional pole.

Meanwhile, Tigranes, who is to accompany Arbaces home as a prisoner, arranges with Bessus, a fatuous and cowardly captain in the Iberian army, for him to convey Spaconia to Iberia and secure for her a place as one of Panthea's ladies-in-waiting. There, according to Tigranes' plan, it is to be Spaconia's task to set the princess's heart against a match with him.

In Iberia, where Arane was put under guard for her attempt on Arbaces' life, Panthea is deeply torn between her love for her mother on the one hand and her loyalty and devotion to the king, her brother, on the other. Although the reason for Arane's crime is unexplained, her conversation with Gobrias reveals that there are secrets between them having an important bearing on her relationship with Arbaces. Bessus, accompanied by Spaconia, arrives with messages from the king, including a pardon for Arane. Importuned by the courtiers, the braggart gives an amusing account of the duel between Arbaces and Tigranes, contriving to make himself the central figure. Panthea, interrupting Bessus's tale frequently, reveals agonized concern for her brother's safety. Even though she did not yet see him, she nevertheless feels a powerful attraction to him. Spaconia then reveals to Panthea her reason for coming to Iberia, and the virtuous princess vows to reject the proposed match with Tigranes.

After a triumphal passage through the city, Arbaces and his company arrive at the court. When Panthea presents herself to her brother, Arbaces, overwhelmed by her beauty, falls hopelessly in love with her at first sight. Frantically he tries to convince himself that she is not really his sister but a lady of the court; however, he is unable to escape the guilty feeling that he is the victim of an incestuous love.

At last, succumbing to his passion, he kisses her; then, overcome with guilt and shame, he violently orders the weeping Panthea imprisoned. As time passes, however, his love for Panthea increases, and at last he begs Mardonius to act as his bawd. When Mardonius indignantly rejects Ar-

baces' plea, the king turns to Bessus, whom he finds more willing to undertake such a task. Revolted by Bessus's ready acquiescence, and probably also by the image of himself that he saw in the minion, Arbaces swears to keep his sin within his own breast in spite of the torture his desire inflicts upon him.

Bessus, meanwhile, discovers that the reputation for bravery he created for himself has serious drawbacks. Now that he is worthy of challenge, he is called to account by all of the gentlemen he insulted before leaving for the wars. He dismisses the second of his 213th challenger when Bacurius appears, demanding satisfaction for a past wrong. Bessus, attempting to put him off, pleads a lame leg; but Bacurius, recognizing the braggart's cowardice, browbeats him unmercifully and takes away his sword. Bessus, after enlisting the aid of two professional swordsmen who are in reality as absurd and as cowardly as he, allows himself to be convinced by a very peculiar exercise in logic that he is, after all, a valiant man. He is on the way to deliver this news to Bacurius when he encounters Lygones, who journeyed from Armenia in search of his daughter Spaconia. Believing him to be Spaconia's seducer, Lygones gives Bessus a drubbing before the braggart can explain. Parting from Lygones, bruised Bessus locates Bacurius, who, over Bessus's loud protests that he is no coward, mocks his logic and cudgels his two hired companions. During this time Lygones locates Spaconia and Tigranes in prison; and he learns joyfully that his daughter, whom he thought guilty of a disgraceful alliance with Bessus, is actually to be married to Tigranes and thus is to become the queen of Armenia.

Indirectly urged on by Gobrias and nearly mad with desire, Arbaces visits Panthea in her prison and at once begs her to yield and not to yield herself to his lust. Although she rejects his proposal, she confesses that she, too, feels unsisterly desire for him. After they part, Arbaces attempts to govern himself but finally concluded wildly that he can bear the situation no longer. He resolves to murder Mardonius, ravish Panthea, and then kill himself. At that moment, however, Gobrias and Arane reveal their secret: Arbaces is really the son of Gobrias. As an infant he was adopted for political reasons by the barren Arane, who later conceived and bore Panthea. He is thus no king. Gobrias, however, who protected his son against Arane's attempts to dispose of him so that Panthea can rule and who subtly encouraged Arbaces' love for Panthea, finds his complicated plan a success. Arbaces, now totally without pride of majesty, is overjoyed to learn that he is an impostor. His and Panthea's passion now becomes legitimate, and by marrying her he will once more assume the crown. Thus a happy ending is brought about, and to fill the moment completely Tigranes and Spaconia are released from prison and reunited.

Critical Evaluation:

This Francis Beaumont and John Fletcher play is richer in texture and plot than *The Maid's Tragedy* (1610-1611), which is less ambitious and tends to satisfy itself with a simple tragic plot. In *A King and No King*, however, the matter is somewhat more complicated by parallelisms between the major theme and the conduct of lesser figures. Like many of the Jacobean tragicomedies, the play is set in a foreign land, at the highest levels of aristocratic power, and one of the major figures, as in *The Maid's Tragedy*, has just successfully defended his country from the enemy. In this case, the contest comes down to single combat between Arbaces, the king of Iberia, and Tigranes, the king of Armenia. Arbaces wins but intends to act magnanimously by wedding his sister Panthea to the conquered king. There are obvious signs, however, that Arbaces is not an entirely stable character, and he is given to public declamations of his political and military prowess, which are comically echoed in the conduct of one of his lieutenants, Mardonius, a cowardly, loud-mouthed fool. Mardonius, a wiser, courageous soldier, chastises both men and seems to be able to talk some sense into the king, but there is always a feeling that the king is inclined to wild swings of mood and conduct, which culminate in his sudden infatuation with his sister, who returns his ardor. Their passion throws the two of them into a desperate indecision which is only resolved by the revelation that they are not, in fact, related to each other. This comes just in time to forestall a bloodbath of considerable proportion.

Thus the play satisfies its description as a tragicomedy. The play begins with all the potential for serious damage, and flirts with the possibility of carnage until very late, when it turns both in structure and in narrative into a comedy when the king learns that he is, in fact, not by birth the king and, more happily, discovers that the woman with whom he is dangerously infatuated is not his sister and therefore can be his wife. They can live happily ever after, not only as lovers but also as rulers, since she is of royal birth. Played against this agonizing extravaganza of uncontrolled and menacing arbitrariness is the parallel, proper love affair of Tigranes, the defeated king, and his loved one, Spaconia, which provides opportunity for the lyric expression of legitimate love, ironically echoing the immorality of the royal pair.

Royal lunacy is only barely balanced by the good sense of Mardonius, by the quiet patience and courage of the defeated Tigranes, and by Spaconia. On the other hand, the posturings of Bessus are something of a comic parallel to the repetitive

boasting of his king. It all looks a bit silly, and a close look reveals a kind of contrived madness, closer to fantasy than to real life, but Jacobean tragicomedy is often inclined to excess. The romantic expostulations of Arbaces and Panthea, taken on the inflated level of high drama, allow for a rich manipulation of poetic language, made all the more credible by the fact that both parties, tempted as they are to consummate their love, are torn deeply by the awareness of the forbidden nature of their love. What somewhat undermines this power is the revelation of their real situation, with its rather dubious implicit suggestion that unconsciously they know all along that their love is proper.

Quite as successful, if not more so, is the tale of Bessus, bluntly realistic in its exposure of a braggart who goes too far too often and still has enough gall to attempt to talk his way out of the beating he deserves. On a more serious level, he is used to prick the conscience of the king, when he eagerly agrees to facilitate any incestuous affair that the king may have in mind, and, in so doing, reveals to the monarch how morally low he sinks. The comic aspect of his story, however, is a good example of how these playwrights are able to relieve the afflatus of high declamatory language with blunt simplicities, and, in so doing, give the tragic matter a credibility in a world of common conduct.

For a modern reader, the ridiculous nature of the plot and the excessive conduct of the characters, especially the king, may blind one to the great success of the language. It is easiest appreciated in the Bessus material, with its quick, realistic ironies and insults, and it may be that this work is, in the main, the contribution of Fletcher. Harder to appreciate are the poetic intensities of the passages of deep feeling expressed by the king and his putative sister, both in tandem and in soliloquy. Here, the material has considerable power, if attention is paid, and it is sometimes suggested that it occasionally reaches the quality of William Shakespeare's work. It is usually presumed that Beaumont is responsible for this poetic material. This matter of authorship is of lesser concern; the real question is how well these two men used the rather ludicrous motifs of Jacobean drama to make reasonably good theater and sometimes glorious language.

The seemingly vicious, and sometimes ridiculous excess of this typical Jacobean play should not, however, be dismissed out of hand as a simple example of bad theatrical taste. Many critics see the enthusiasm for violent, arbitrary conduct; for gratuitous cruelty; for the disdain for the lower orders, women, and the older generation; and for the exercise of irresponsible power by the rulers of the day as not very far from the truth of the times. The pessimism flaunted in a play like this may be, in part, simply an artistic expression of the prevailing social, political, and moral sensibility. Significantly, this form of tragicomedy had an influence on the drama that followed it.

"Critical Evaluation" by Charles Pullen

Further Reading

Braunmuller, A. R., and Michael Hattaway, eds. *The Cambridge Companion to English Renaissance Drama.* 2d ed. New York: Cambridge University Press, 2003. This collection of essays discussing various aspects of English Renaissance drama includes numerous references to Francis Beaumont and John Fletcher and information about *A King and No King.*

Frost, David L. *The School of Shakespeare.* New York: Cambridge University Press, 1968. A discussion of the various ways in which playwrights who knew and admired Shakespeare made use of his work. There is a chapter on his effect on Beaumont and Fletcher.

Misener, Arthur. "The High Design of *A King and No King.*" *Modern Philology* 38 (November, 1940): 123-154. Questions how morally serious these playwrights were, or if they were simply interested in providing sensational scenes.

Oliphant, E. H. C. *The Plays of Beaumont and Fletcher.* New Haven, Conn.: Yale University Press, 1927. Standard, dependable discussion of the canon, with some detailed discussion of *A King and No King.*

Ornstein, Robert. *The Moral Vision of Jacobean Tragedy.* Madison: University of Wisconsin Press, 1965. Ornstein argues that such frightful things—physical, moral, and political—happen in this sort of play that it is difficult for a contemporary reader to understand the context, and his book attempts to put this problem in perspective.

Sprague, Arthur Colby. *Beaumont and Fletcher on the Restoration Stage.* New York: Benjamin Blom, 1965. Sprague maintains that one of the best ways to understand a work of art is to examine how another historical period interprets and uses the material. Beaumont and Fletcher were not only an influence on Restoration drama but were also very popular, in their own right, on the Restoration stage.

King Horn

Author: Unknown
First transcribed: c. 1225
Type of work: Novel
Type of plot: Romance
Time of plot: Sixth century
Locale: England and Ireland

Principal characters:
HORN, a chivalrous young prince dispossessed of his kingdom
QUEEN GODHILD, his mother
ATHULF, his brother
FIKENHILD, his treacherous friend
AYLMAR, king of Westernesse
RYMENHILD, his daughter, in love with Horn
MODI, king of Reynes, Horn's enemy and another suitor for Rymenhild's hand
THURSTON, an Irish king
BERILD and HARILD, his sons
REYNILD, his daughter
ATHELBRUS, steward to King Aylmar

The Story:

Horn, the fairest youth ever born, is bright as glass and white as a flower; his color is rose-red, and he has no equal in any kingdom. When Horn is fifteen years old, his father, King Murry of Suddene Isle of Man, is killed by invading Saracens. His mother, Queen Godhild, finds refuge under a rock, where she prays for Horn's safety. Because of Horn's fairness, the Saracens spare him, setting him adrift with twelve companions, among them his brother Athulf and the wicked Fikenhild, on a ship that they expect will sink. The youths land safely on the shore of Westernesse, where good King Aylmar receives them kindly and takes a special liking to Horn. Aylmar's daughter, Rymenhild, is also attracted to Horn and asks the steward, Athelbrus, who is in charge of Horn's instruction, to bring him to her room. Disturbed at this command, Athelbrus brings Athulf instead. Mistaking him for Horn, Rymenhild tells Athulf that she loves him. When she discovers that Athelbrus tricked her, she threatens to have him hanged, whereupon Athelbrus brings Horn to her. Rymenhild asks him to marry her, but Horn refuses, saying that he is a foundling and unworthy. At this rebuff, Rymenhild falls in a swoon. Horn takes her in his arms, kisses her, and asks her to have her father make him a knight so that he might marry her.

King Aylmar knights Horn and permits him to knight his companions. As soon as Horn is knighted, Rymenhild wants him to marry her; but Horn says that he must first prove his merit as a knight. Rymenhild gives him a ring engraved with her name and tells him that if he looks at the ring and thinks of her, he will overcome all enemies. On a handsome black steed, Horn sets forth on his quest. He quickly finds and slays at least one hundred Saracens. The next day, Rymenhild tells him that she dreamed that a great fish escaped from her net. The significance of her distressing dream is clear when Fikenhild, envious of Horn, tells King Aylmar that Horn is planning to kill him and marry Rymenhild. He says that Horn is at the moment in bed with Rymenhild. Aylmar, rushing into his daughter's chamber, finds Horn embracing Rymenhild. The king orders Horn to leave the castle. Before departing, Horn instructs Athulf to guard Rymenhild. He tells Rymenhild that he expects to be back in seven years; if he does not return by that time, she is to take another husband.

Horn goes to Ireland, where he meets two princes, Harild and Berild. He tells them that his name is Cutberd, and they take him to their father, King Thurston. The time is Christmas. Soon a giant comes from heathendom to offer a challenge from paynims who arrived in the land. One of them offers to fight any three of the Irish knights. The king appoints his sons, Harild and Berild, as well as Cutberd. Cutberd offers to take on the challenger alone. Having fought with Cutberd, the champion says that he encountered only one man his equal, King Murry of Suddene. Shuddering, Horn realizes that he is facing his father's murderer. He looks on his ring, thinks of Rymenhild, and smites the champion through the heart. The paynims turn to run to the boat, but Horn and his companions follow and kill them all. Harild and Berild are killed in the fighting. Thurston offers his daughter Reynild in marriage to Horn and plans to make the young knight heir to the throne. Horn replies that he will serve the king for seven years. At the end of that time, if he wants his reward, including the princess for his wife, he will ask for it.

Back in Westernesse, Rymenhild hears nothing of Horn. King Modi of Reynes (Turness in northern Lancashire),

Horn's enemy, wants to marry her. She sends a messenger to find Horn. The messenger succeeds in his mission, but on his return he drowns and his body washes up at Rymenhild's door. Horn, meanwhile, asks King Thurston to help him regain Rymenhild. In return, he promises his brother Athulf as husband for Reynild. Thurston gives him a ship, but when Horn arrives in Westernesse he finds Rymenhild's wedding to King Modi in progress. A palmer tells him that the bride wept. Horn changes clothes with the palmer, disguises his features with dirt, and goes to the wedding feast, where he asks the bride for wine. Rymenhild gives him wine in a bowl as if he is a thirsty beggar. Horn refuses, saying he is a fisherman who came to see if the net he set seven years ago took a fish. He says that he wants to drink to Horn from horn. Rymenhild gives him wine in a drinking horn, and Horn drops in it the ring that Rymenhild gave him. Rymenhild sees the ring and asks if Horn is dead. Horn replies that he died aboard ship after asking him to tell her of his death. Rymenhild throws herself on her bed and prepares to kill herself with the knife she hid there to kill both Modi and herself that night. Horn wipes the dirt from his face and tells her that he is Horn, her true lover. Rymenhild runs to tell Athulf, who jumps for joy. Returning to the wedding party with his Irish warriors, Horn kills King Modi and his followers. After convincing King Aylmar that Fikenhild slandered him, Horn tells the king that he will return to Suddene and regain his kingdom, then marry Rymenhild. Horn recovers his kingdom from the Saracens and finds that his mother is still alive.

While Horn is gone, Fikenhild, through bribery and by intimidating the king, is able to carry Rymenhild off to his castle. Warned of this in a dream, Horn returns to Westernesse, only to hear that Fikenhild married Rymenhild. Disguised as harpers, Horn and his men gain access to Fikenhild's castle, where he kills Fikenhild, hacks him to pieces, and rescues Rymenhild. He makes Athelbrus, the good steward, king of Reynes in place of Modi, and he takes Athulf to Ireland to marry Reynild. Then Horn takes Rymenhild to Suddene and there makes her his queen.

Critical Evaluation:

King Horn represents a literary genre, the romance, that had its inception in France during the second half of the twelfth century. This new genre immediately spread to England and remained popular in both countries for about a century. While it never achieved the status of serious literature, it afforded light entertainment for the rural gentry and, possibly, for small numbers of the nobility and the merchant class. Medieval romances can be classified into three types: the hero-alone type, which *King Horn* represents; the family-based pattern; and the epic romance. *King Horn* also belongs to the subgenre that deals with the child exile—a type especially provocative of sympathy from the audience.

The romance developed from the *chanson de geste*, which had, in turn, grown from the Germanic epic. While the romance bears traces of its immediate and remote predecessors, however, it differs in its emphasis. That is, while the epic and *chanson de geste* primarily focused on military feats, the romance centered on the search of individuals for their place in society. When Horn asks King Aylmar of Westernesse to knight him, for example, he is asking for an authentic place in this foreign kingdom. Moreover, Horn is not content to be a knight in name only but must prove the validity of his position by his deeds. He exhibits great prowess in slaying the Saracens, but his prime motive in so doing is to win Rymenhild's hand by establishing himself as a proven defender in her land. Conversely, his use of an alias while in Ireland indicates that he does not desire permanent affiliation with that country.

Most critics consider the medieval romance unsophisticated in style, theme, and structure. Its meter is crude, its characters are flat, and its plot is predictable. It contains few, if any, symbols, and offers no insight for further reflection. Its very simplicity, however, served a purpose for its original audience. Members of the country gentry, who were beneath the nobles on the social ladder and members of the rising merchant class, may have felt somewhat insecure regarding their power and position in society. This was probably especially true of the women—who constituted most of the romance's audience—who had little genuine power or position in any class. By representing extremes of good and evil, rather than simulating realistic persons with complex personalities, romance characters and their actions offered clear-cut examples of how to behave in an ordered society. The kingdom of Aylmar, for example, is one of order and propriety. Aylmar graciously opens his home to the children from Suddene, but when Finkenhild falsely accuses Horn of sleeping with Rymenhild, the king has no choice but to banish the latter, whom he sees as a threat to a society where every activity has its prescribed time and circumstance. Although Horn is wrongly treated, he obediently leaves Westernesse, with no apparent intention of vindicating himself or seeking revenge. His obedience to authority is rewarded by his eventual marriage to Rymenhild, whereas Finkenhild's deceit is punished by his loss of the princess.

To ensure the specific nature of the audience's reactions, romance poets make it clear at the outset whether a given character is good or bad. The poet of *King Horn* states as early as line 14 that Horn is "bright as the glass/ white as the flower."

Since these similes describe the Virgin Mary in some lyrics of the same period, it is made obvious that Horn is pure and virtuous. All of his actions, including the murder of Modi, are meritorious. Finkenhild, on the other hand, is referred to in line 28 as "the worst," and everything he does is evil.

The romance not only provides paradigms of desirable conduct but also seeks to inculcate in the audience accepted societal values. To this end, they are structured around predictable plots whose repetition reinforces values the audience already accepts, whether consciously or unconsciously. The typical plot is one in which a good king dies and leaves a son, whose responsibility it becomes to save his father's kingdom from external or internal enemies. A beautiful heroine functions as the son's motive and reward for virtuous and heroic behavior. Finally, the son's marriage to the heroine results in the restoration of the late father's land, bringing full closure to the story. In *King Horn*, the enemies are Scandinavians, whom, possibly to give the poem a flavor of the crusading era, the poet calls Saracens. Throughout his sojourn in Ireland, Horn's valor is inspired by his love for Rymenhild, and their marriage reestablishes his father's line in Suddene. The action of the poem thus extols the values of order, fidelity, bravery, and lineage, all of which were previously honored and are now strengthened.

Because they were frequently sung or recited as well as read, it was imperative for romances to be memorable and pleasing. *King Horn*'s rhyming couplets give it a lyrical quality, and synecdoches (the use of a whole to represent a part or a part to represent the whole) make it vivid and retainable. Line 112, for example, conveys the agony of the banished children through the phrase "wringinde here honde" (wringing their hands). Similarly, the poet expresses all of Godhild's loss and despair when he says that "Under a roche [rock] of stone/ Ther heo [she] livede alone."

Although the writers of medieval romance did not achieve the wit of Chaucer or the perception of the Pearl Poet, they provided entertainment and escape for those who read or listened to their works. Like later authors of romances, they did not strive to offer novel ideas but sought only to reinforce conventional, widely accepted values and behaviors.

"Critical Evaluation" by Rebecca Stingley Hinton

Further Reading

Barnes, Geraldine. *Counsel and Strategy in Middle English Romance*. Cambridge, England: D. S. Brewer, 1993. Barnes discusses the nature and functions of kingdoms and advisory bodies described in romances. Includes research on the audiences of the romance.

Cannon, Christopher. "The Spirit of Romance: *King Horn, Havelok the Dane*, and *Floris and Blancheflour*." In *The Grounds of English Literature*. New York: Oxford University Press, 2004. As part of his study of early English literature, Cannon analyzes *King Horn* and other medieval works to demonstrate how they were influences for subsequent English writing.

Cooper, Helen. "Magic That Doesn't Work." In *The English Romance in Time: Transforming Motifs from Geoffrey of Monmouth to the Death of Shakespeare*. New York: Oxford University Press, 2004. Cooper makes several references to *King Horn* in her study of recurrent motifs in English romantic literature of the Middle Ages and Renaissance. Most references are in the section on magic, while other citations are listed in the index.

Knight, Stephen. "The Social Function of the Middle English Romances." In *Medieval Literature: Criticism, Ideology, and History*, edited by David Aers. New York: St. Martin's Press, 1986. Knight divides the medieval romance into three subgenres and describes each in detail.

Ramsey, Lee C. *Chivalric Romances: Popular Literature in Medieval England*. Bloomington: Indiana University Press, 1983. Provides background on the history and development of the medieval romance. Ramsey discusses elements common to all romances and includes information on the genre's audience.

Riddy, Felicity. "Middle English Romance: Family, Marriage, Intimacy." In *The Cambridge Companion to Medieval Romance*, edited by Roberta L. Krueger. New York: Cambridge University Press, 2000. Riddy places *King Horn* within the context of the Middle English romance.

Spearing, A. C. *Readings in Medieval Poetry*. New York: Cambridge University Press, 1987. Begins by discussing the relationship between self-perception and modes of language, then applies this material to various works, including *King Horn*. Spearing compares the medieval romance to twentieth century film.

Zesmer, David M. *Guide to English Literature from "Beowulf" Through Chaucer and Medieval Drama*. New York: Barnes & Noble, 1961. Includes a brief analysis of the romance and identifies the geography in *King Horn*.

King Johan

Author: John Bale (1495-1563)
First produced: 1539(?); first published, 1538
Type of work: Drama
Type of plot: Historical
Time of plot: Early thirteenth century
Locale: England

Principal characters:
ENGLAND, a widow
KING JOHAN
NOBILITY,
CLERGY,
CIVIL ORDER, and
COMMONALTY, betrayers of King Johan
SEDITION
DISSIMULATION
PRIVATE WEALTH
USURPED POWER
POPE INNOCENT III
TREASON
VERITY
IMPERIAL MAJESTY
STEPHEN LANGTON, a churchman and statesman
CARDINAL PANDULPHUS

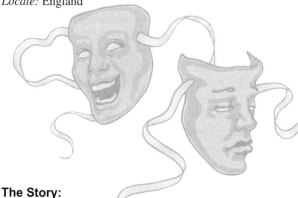

The Story:

England complains to King Johan that she was stripped of her rights and her wealth by the rapacious clergy who drove her husband, God, from the realm. King Johan promises to right her wrongs but is mocked by Sedition, the comic vice and the foremost agent of the Church. Sedition, demonstrating the way in which he and the Church subvert the government of kings, introduces Dissimulation, his right-hand man. Dissimulation works with Private Wealth and Usurped

Power. Private Wealth is the darling of the religious orders; he gives strength to Usurped Power, who sustains the arrogance of popes.

King Johan defies Sedition and his cohorts. He calls Nobility, Clergy, and Civil Order to him and prevails on them for their support. Nobility and Civil Order give theirs willingly, but Clergy is reluctant. King Johan was too harsh on him. When the king reminds him of the temporal rights of rulers as outlined in the Gospel, Clergy, still reluctant, consents.

The allegiance of the three is short-lived, however, for Sedition and his minions have little trouble convincing them that the actual power of Rome is stronger than any abstract claim based on the Gospel. Besides, the Church has the sole right of interpreting the Gospel. Nobility, Clergy, and Civil Order are forsworn.

King Johan, now bereft of his three strongest allies, places all of his hopes on Commonalty, his one sure support. Commonalty, the true child of England, is brought to King Johan by his mother, and the king is dismayed to learn that he is both impoverished and blind. He is impoverished, his mother explains, because the Church stole all his goods; his blindness symbolizes his spiritual ignorance, an ignorance in which he is kept by the conspiracy of Clergy who is supposed to open his eyes. For all his failings, Commonalty still is faithful to the king who always sees to his welfare. He willingly reasserts his faith.

In the end, however, he is no more staunch than his more exalted brothers. Clergy has too strong a hold on him, and he, too, becomes a victim of Sedition's plots.

King Johan now stands alone in his attempt to save the widow England. Assured now of the king's vulnerability, the pope sends his agents to bring the king to his knees. King Johan's old enemy, Stephen Langton, the archbishop of Canterbury, returns. The interdict is proclaimed with bell, book, and candle, and the vindictive Cardinal Pandulphus arrives to enforce it.

King Johan stands firm, defying the pope to do his worst. Claiming that he will not betray England, he turns to history and the scriptures to defend his rights; he points out the ways in which the Church perverts the true faith and he cites the corruptions of the holy orders. Sedition mocks him and promises that his defiance will end.

End it does, for the pope gathers a strong alliance and threatens to invade England. Rather than see his country devastated and his people killed, King Johan submits. He surrenders his crown to the pope and receives it back as a fief of the Holy See. When England protests, she is reviled by Sedition and his aides.

King Johan rules for a number of years as the vassal of the pope. If he tries to assert his power, Sedition and his agents are on hand to thwart it. Treason runs through the land with impunity, and when the king tries to punish him, he pleads benefit of clergy and is released. Nevertheless, King Johan is determined to hang him.

Cardinal Pandulphus and Sedition conceive a plan to curb King Johan's power. Cardinal Pandulphus will not release England from the interdict until King Johan hands over to the Papacy a third of his lands as a dowry for the bride of Richard, his late brother. Although King Johan protests, Cardinal Pandulphus insists on these harsh terms. Providentially, the king is released when it is announced that Julyane, the lady in question, is dead.

The forces of the Church are now determined to get rid of King Johan completely. Dissimulation, in the guise of Simon of Swinsett, a monk, concocts a poison cup from the sweat of a toad. When he offers Johan the draught, the king forces the monk to drink first and then drains the cup. Both die in agony.

Upon the death of King Johan, Verity appears and proclaims that all the evils attributed to King Johan are false, the lies of slandering monks. He lists all of the good things the king did for the benefit of the common people and asserts that, for three hundred years, that good was undone by the corrupt Church. Now, he announces, Imperial Majesty arrives to crush the Church and save the widow England.

Imperial Majesty confronts Nobility, Clergy, and Civil Order. Verity points out to them the error of their ways, and, contrite, they swear their eternal allegiance to Imperial Majesty. England is safe from the evils of Rome.

Critical Evaluation:

John Bale, bishop of Ossory and one of the most outspoken champions of the English Reformation, claimed to have written some forty plays in his lifetime. Of these, five are extant; of these five, the allegorical *King Johan* is the most important. Although far too long and tedious for dramatic effectiveness, being in structure two plays or one play in two parts, it is interesting as a scathing and uncompromising attack on the Church of Rome and as a version of history different from that usually accepted. Challenging those historians—Polydore Virgil in particular—who made King Johan a knave, Bale depicts the king as a virtuous protector of the realm, who is betrayed by the covetousness and viciousness of the Church. History may be altered and revised to suit Bale's cause, but the fact that he uses it at all is of concern, for *King Johan* announces the beginning of the great tradition of the English history play. It shows the transition from the old to the new—an allegorical play using the techniques of the medieval morality (Sedition, for instance, is an example of the morality "vice"), but using them to dramatize historical events.

King Johan well illustrates Bale's position as a follower of the so-called New Learning as espoused by Cambridge reformers during the reign of Henry VIII. Two of these reformers particularly link Bale to that group. William Tyndale's book on Christian obedience (1528) sets out the theme that Bale followed. To both Tyndale and Bale, King Johan was a king who was prevented from the exercise of his royal duty by the usurping power of an anti-Christian Papacy. Thomas Cranmer, another member of the Cambridge Protestant circle, gave this play its first performance, in his house on January 2, 1539.

Reformation in England consisted of dissolving many monasteries and religious houses of England and of removing the pope as the Church's recognized head. In matters of doctrine, Henry VIII was conservative. He retained the mass and sacraments, and, although he permitted the Bible to be translated into English and allowed the vernacular liturgy, he tended to reject many of the Lutheran doctrines and those of the more radical reformers in Switzerland. Of all the Protestant sects, Bale attacks only the quasi-anarchical Anabaptists. He attacks monks strongly, as would be expected in Henry's England, but goes on to rail against the Mass, sacraments, relics, bells, vestments, and other "papist" accouterments retained by Henry. All this fits in well with the more radical reformation that reached England after Henry's death. Led by Cranmer and others, the Protestants of the old Cambridge school were riding high during the reign of Edward VI. The beliefs of Edward's time were presaged by Bale's play, but it is surprising to see such sentiments expressed so strongly when Henry VIII was alive and vigorous. This play, then, gives the reader a full picture of one part of religious belief during the reign of Henry VIII, a belief that was later to come powerfully into its own.

Bale also expresses in *King Johan* a significant idea that usually is called "Erastianism" after Thomas Erastus but is more correctly ascribed to Marsiglio of Padua. Marsiglio held that the church was not an equal of the state but instead was subject to civil authority as an arm of the state, like the army or any bureaucracy. Tied up in this concept is the idea of empire. England was an empire rather than a kingdom, and the concept that England was autonomous is at the heart of both Bale's *King Johan* and Henry VIII's Reformation. It was Henry who first declared that England owed no allegiance to any other organization, and the reign of his daughter Elizabeth can partly be understood as an attempt to make Henry's dream of Imperial Majesty into a reality.

Further Reading

Adams, Barry B., ed. Introduction to *King Johan*, by John Bale. San Marino, Calif.: Huntington Library, 1969. Adams comments on the manuscripts and early editions of the play, reviews sources Bale used in composing his drama, and discusses the theatrics and versification and the play's relationship to sixteenth century drama.

Blatt, Thora B. *The Plays of John Bale: A Study of Ideas, Technique, and Style*. Copenhagen: G. E. C. Gad, 1968. Blatt provides information on extant manuscript sources, comments on structure and style, and reviews history of productions. She attributes the play's popularity to the fact that it was the first English drama to "introduce characters from national history on the stage."

Cavanagh, Dermot. "Reforming Sovereignty: John Bale and Tragic Drama." In *Interludes and Early Modern Society: Studies in Gender, Power, and Theatricality*, edited by Peter Happé and Wim Hüsken. Amsterdam: Rodopi, 2007. Collection of essays interpreting the interlude, a popular form of drama in sixteenth century England. Cavanagh's essay on Bale analyzes the representation of political power in Bale's plays.

Happé, Peter. *John Bale*. New York: Twayne, 1996. A critical overview of Bale's life and works, with chapter 5 devoted to an analysis of *King Johan*. Happé argues that Bale was a political writer as well as a religious writer and his religious plays were "encoded" statements about sixteenth century English politics.

_____, ed. *The Complete Plays of John Bale*. 2 vols. Dover, N.H.: Boydell & Brewer, 1985-1986. The introduction to volume 1 provides useful information about Bale's career, gives details of production and printing, and analyzes sources and analogues. Happé comments on the language and versification and gives background about the religious controversy that inspired this drama.

Pafford, J. H. P., ed. Introduction to *King Johan*, by John Bale. New York: Oxford University Press, 1931. The introduction provides extensive details about the manuscript, sources, text, and language. Most useful for specialists, but informative for general readers.

Shrank, Cathy. "John Bale and Reconfiguring the 'Medieval' in Reformation England." In *Reading the Medieval in Early Modern England*, edited by Gordon McMullan and David Matthews. New York: Cambridge University Press, 2007. Shrank's examination of Bale's work is included in a collection of essays that describe how early modern English writers, editors, and scholars reconstructed medieval culture.

Taylor, Andrew W. "The Reformation of History in John

Bale's Biblical Dramas." In *English Historical Drama, 1500-1660: Forms Outside the Canon*, edited by Teresa Grant and Barbara Ravelhofer. New York: Palgrave Macmillan, 2008. While acknowledging the importance of William Shakespeare's history plays, these essays focus on dramas by lesser-known authors, seeking to establish "alternative paradigms of early modern historical drama."

Walker, Greg. *Plays of Persuasion*. New York: Cambridge University Press, 1991. A lengthy chapter on *King Johan* discusses the history of performances during the Renaissance, the political dimensions of the drama, and Bale's use of polemical language. Walker examines the play as a tool for influencing Henry VIII.

King John

Author: William Shakespeare (1564-1616)
First produced: c. 1596-1597; first published, 1623
Type of work: Drama
Type of plot: Historical
Time of plot: Early thirteenth century
Locale: England and France

Principal characters:
JOHN, the king of England
PRINCE HENRY, his son
ARTHUR OF BRETAGNE, the king's nephew
WILLIAM MARESHALL, the earl of Pembroke
GEFFREY FITZ-PETER, the earl of Essex
WILLIAM LONGSWORD, the earl of Salisbury
HUBERT DE BURGH, chamberlain to the king
ROBERT FAULCONBRIDGE, an English baron
PHILIP FAULCONBRIDGE (THE BASTARD), his half-brother, the natural son of King Richard I
CARDINAL PANDULPH, the papal legate
LEWIS, the dauphin of France
ELEANOR, King John's mother
CONSTANCE, Arthur's mother
BLANCH OF CASTILE, King John's niece

The Story:

King John of England indignantly rejects the message of the French envoy, Chatillon, that Philip, king of France, has decided to support the claim of young Prince Arthur—the son of John's deceased older brother Geffrey—for the throne of England. At the same time, the Faulconbridge brothers bring their domestic quarrel to the king's court: Philip (identified throughout the play as the "Bastard") complains that his younger brother Richard has claimed his lands. Philip decides, however, to surrender his claim and to seek success on his own initiative after acknowledging that he is the son of the late King Richard I, John's brother. Embarrassed, Philip's elderly mother admits that Richard was indeed his father.

At the French court, King Philip of France and the duke of Austria vow to fight on behalf of Arthur's claim, while Arthur, in exchange for their military support, is willing to for-

give Austria for having killed his uncle, King Richard. Chatillon reports that the English forces are marching to Angiers, led by John, who has brought along his formidable mother, Eleanor of Acquitaine, as well as the Bastard. John enters to demand that France support his right to the English throne, but King Philip upholds Arthur's claim.

At the besieged city of Angiers, its spokesman, the Citizen, explains from the city walls to the two armies that the town is loyal to the English king and insists that it will admit the king, once the true king is decided upon. The Citizen offers a peaceful compromise solution to the tense situation— that Lewis the dauphin and Blanche of Spain should wed. Eleanor agrees to this plan, while Arthur's mother Constance is distressed because the plan will exclude her son's claim to the throne. In the play's most famous speech, "Mad world, mad kings, mad composition," the Bastard professes to be amazed at the cynical peace agreed upon by the politicians; the world, he explains, is ruled by "That smooth-faced gentleman, tickling Commodity" (that is, self-interest).

Constance is outraged by the report of the proposed marriage of Lewis and Blanche and denounces Austria for agreeing to it. Pandulph, the papal legate, demands that John drop his objection to the pope's candidate for the archbishopric of Canterbury, and he enjoins Philip to defend the Church against England. Philip thus promptly breaks his new alliance with John. John tells Hubert to keep Arthur under his control and quietly hints to Hubert that he should arrange Arthur's death, describing the boy as "a very serpent in my way."

Philip reports that France has been defeated: Its fleet is scattered, Angiers is lost, and Arthur has been captured. Constance, now clearly under mental duress, pathetically laments that she knows she will never see her son again. Pandulph tells Lewis that John, by winning, has lost: He will not know rest until Arthur is dead, at which time Lewis can claim the throne.

Hubert shows Arthur his order from John to put out Arthur's eyes. Arthur appeals to Hubert's mercy and reminds him of their previously friendly relationship, successfully persuading Hubert to relent. The innocent Arthur is then forced to improvise a succession of arguments to persuade Hubert not to kill him, and Hubert is touched by pleas such as "I would to heaven/ I were your son, so you would love me, Hubert."

At court, the nobles discourage John from staging a second coronation, and Hubert falsely reports Arthur's death to the king. A messenger reports that France has invaded England and that Eleanor and Constance are both dead. John now blames Hubert for Arthur's death, although he had suggested it, and he clearly becomes disoriented by the news of his mother's death. The king cruelly orders the death of a local prophet, Peter of Pomfret, merely for having predicted the end of his reign. At this low point, Hubert reveals that has actually spared Arthur's life.

While attempting to escape from captivity by disguising himself as a ship's boy, Arthur jumps from the walls and dies. Finding the boy's broken body, the nobles scoff at Hubert's claim to have spared Arthur. They proceed to blame Hubert for murder and John for having ordered it. When he enters to report that Arthur still lives, Hubert is struck with emotion when he is shown the boy's body. Anguished but still loyal to John, the Bastard bears the body away.

John offers obedience to the papal legate. Pandulph replies that he will quell the storm that he has raised. The Bastard explains how the nobles found Arthur's body. Despite

John's reconciliation with Rome, Lewis refuses to withdraw his claim to Arthur's title, now that he has married Blanche. The Bastard reports that John is now in arms but claims that John is haunted by Death ("in his forehead sits/ A bare-ribbed Death").

John, now sick with fever and heavy in heart, explains that he will seek refuge at Swinstead Abbey. Wounded in battle, Melun, one of the French nobles, warns the English nobles to submit to John, explaining that the duplicitous Lewis will condemn them to death if the French win the battle. A messenger reports to Lewis that Melun is dead, the English nobility has defected, and the French ships have foundered: An English victory is now assured. Hubert seeks the Bastard to report to him the defection of the English nobles back to John—and that John has been poisoned by a monk.

Prince Henry, John's son, is present when his father dies. In a final irony, it appears that England will be governed by a boy after all. The Bastard vows revenge on John's murderer and swears fealty to the late king in heaven. Pandulph brings an offer from peace from Lewis, while Prince Henry explains that John will be buried in Worcester. The Bastard concludes the play by insisting that England can only be conquered when it wounds itself first.

Critical Evaluation:

King John is an anomaly among William Shakespeare's history plays. While eight of the ten history plays deal with the dynastic struggles of the fifteenth century, this isolated play is devoted to the troublesome reign of King John in the early thirteenth century. Like the other single history, *Henry VIII* (pr. 1613, pb. 1623), *King John* touches on the quarrel of an English sovereign with the Papacy. The play, like the monarch it depicts, seems to struggle to find its focus; now seldom performed, it offers little by way of emotional uplift. The great scenes of royal pageantry no longer inspire audiences, although the play was a popular favorite for the Victorians. It also provides great insight into the parallel worlds of dynastic and domestic disputes, but its cynical view of politics perhaps offers insufficient surprises to a modern audience. The play has much to say about power and self-assertion, but John's incompetence as a ruler leaves a void at the center of the play.

John's inconsistency as a ruler and dramatic character are largely offset by a fictional character, the Bastard Faulconbridge, who in the first act is revealed to be the illegitimate son of the late King Richard, Coeur de Lion, whose strong presence he has clearly inherited. The Bastard becomes the moral center of the play, but, while his loyalty to John makes him an exemplary loyal citizen, it also underscores the limitations of his pragmatism, which causes him to refrain from condemning John for the death of Prince Arthur.

The play is an unrelenting expose of cynical political acts. From the start, even John's mother, Eleanor, admits that John holds the kingship more by possession than by right (the crown should fall to Arthur, the heir of John's older brother, Geffrey). However, Arthur and his manipulative mother, Constance, are compromised by their willingness to let France invade England to assert his right to the throne. In the longest scene of the play act 2, scene 1, the city of Angiers is threatened both by English and French troops. Both Philip of France and John are outsmarted by the Citizen of Angiers, who proposes a dynastic marriage between the dauphin and Blanche of Spain as a compromise that spares the city from destruction.

There is further intrigue when the papal legate, Pandulph, berates John for his failure to pay "Peter's pence" and threatens to excommunicate John and even to call for his assassination. In an exchange that echoes Henry VIII's quarrel with the Papacy in the 1530's, John refuses to be bullied by an "Italian priest" or a "meddling priest." He even (anticipating Henry VIII's claim to that title) calls himself the "supreme head" of the English Church. Shakespeare chooses not to depict John as a proto-Protestant, as sixteenth century writers such as John Bale had done, and the most famous event in John's reign, John's submission to the nobles with the signing of the Magna Carta, is not even mentioned.

When Philip is forced by Pandulph to renounce his alliance with John, Blanche recognizes that she has lost the power she sought to gain through her marriage. A greater female victim than Blanche is Constance, who understands immediately when she hears news of Arthur's capture by the English that her son's death will be the inevitable consequence. The news of the capture apparently drives her mad, and her mad scene in act 3, scene 4, was an audience favorite in the nineteenth century. Constance is also a shrill manipulator—like John's mother, who, in the opening scenes of the play, is depicted as the power behind John's throne. The announcement of Eleanor's death in act 4 leaves John disoriented, and he goes to his death without ever recovering a sense of direction.

It is the plight of women and children in *King John* to be bullied and defeated. In the most dramatically effective scene of the play, act 4, scene 1, John's henchman Hubert orders a pair of executioners to murder Arthur. Arthur's pleading succeeds in winning over Hubert, who relents and even offers to protect Arthur from John. When Arthur dies later in the act, not by royal violence but by his own attempt to jump from a wall to freedom, there is a grotesque scenic contrast between the conversation of a group of nobles, who believe that Arthur has already been murdered by John, and the pathetic claim by Hubert to have spared the boy's life—all while the body lies in plain view.

John's incompetence as king and emotional ruin are clearly evident in act 5, when John symbolically gives his crown to Pandulph in obedience to the Papacy (the legate promptly hands it back) and then hands over political authority to the Bastard. Although John has been reconciled to the pope, it is clear that Lewis will not relent in his opposition to John. John, having been poisoned by a monk, dies pathetically in the play's final scene.

King John is far from a popular play, but Shakespeare's dramatization of the reign of the unhappy John has a modern edge. John's England suffers from a moral vacuum in its political life; John is not so much a machiavellian villain as a frightened, desperate man who can barely hold on to a throne that never was properly his. The virtuous characters, such as Arthur, are themselves too weak or immature to deserve power, while the less admirable characters are motivated not so much by evil as by confused attempts to do the right thing. Pandulph owes his allegiance to the pope, while King Philip of France seems as weak-willed as John. The death of his mother, Eleanor, disorients John, while the threat to the life of Arthur sends his mother, Constance, into madness and death.

The moral center of the play, the Bastard Faulconbridge, is admirable in his determination to rise by his own merits, but, although he correctly diagnoses the political disease as "Commodity," he finally places loyalty to John over morality. For all the anxiety in England about placing a child on the throne, England gains a child king when John dies by poisoning. The new king is Henry III, John's son, rather than Arthur. *King John* does not rise to Shakespeare's highest dramatic or poetic levels, but it clearly deserves greater attention than it has usually received, and it has proven to be effective onstage.

"Critical Evaluation" by Byron Nelson

Further Reading

Chernaik, Warren. "Gain, Be My Lord: *King John*." In *The Cambridge Introduction to Shakespeare's History Plays.* New York: Cambridge University Press, 2007. Provides an overview of the plot, characters, uncertainties, and other aspects of *King John*. Other chapters in this anthology discuss Renaissance ideas about history, describe the genre and conventions of the history play, and survey the critical reception of Shakespeare's historical dramas.

Eliot, John R. "Shakespeare and the Double Image in *King John*." In *Shakespeare Studies*, edited by J. Leeds Barroll. Vol. 1. Cincinnati, Ohio: University of Cincinnati Press, 1965. Focuses on the historical and literary sources of the play.

Honigmann, E. A. J., ed. *The Arden Shakespeare: King John*. Cambridge, Mass.: Harvard University Press, 1962. In addition to the text of *King John*, this volume contains more than seventy pages of introductory material that considers the play's sources, its production history, and the meaning of the text itself. Appendixes deal with the play's sources and problems with the text.

Lloyd Evans, Gareth. *The Upstart Crow: An Introduction to Shakespeare's Plays*. London: J. M. Dent and Sons, 1982. A comprehensive discussion of the dramatic works of Shakespeare. While the major emphasis is on critical reviews of the plays, there are also discussions of sources, as well as material on the circumstances that surrounded the writing of the plays.

Partee, Morriss Henry. *Childhood in Shakespeare's Plays*. New York: Peter Lang, 2006. Examines the depiction of child characters in *King John* and some of Shakespeare's other plays. Challenges the idea that Shakespeare regarded children as small adults, demonstrating that he did not portray children as either unnaturally precocious or sentimentally innocent.

Pierce, Robert B. *Shakespeare's History Plays: The Family and the State*. Columbus: Ohio State University Press, 1971. A general discussion of Shakespeare's history plays. *King John* is considered as a transitional play between the early history plays and the later tetralogy of plays about Richard II, Henry IV, and Henry V, which Pierce considers to be far greater works.

Piesse, A. J. "*King John*: Changing Perspectives." In *The Cambridge Companion to Shakespeare's History Plays*, edited by Michael Hattaway. New York: Cambridge University Press, 2002. Describes *King John* as a "provocatively problematic play" and examines why the play has generated "fierce debate" and a "flurry of critical writing on its behalf" in the late twentieth century.

Ribner, Irving. *The English History Play in the Age of Shakespeare*. Rev. ed. London: Methuen, 1965. Examines history plays from the Elizabethan era, assessing Shakespeare's contributions in the field. Discusses the development and sources of the genre.

King Lear

Author: William Shakespeare (1564-1616)
First produced: c. 1605-1606; first published, 1608
Type of work: Drama
Type of plot: Tragedy
Time of plot: First century B.C.E.
Locale: Britain

Principal characters:
KING LEAR OF BRITAIN
KING OF FRANCE
DUKE OF CORNWALL
DUKE OF ALBANY
EARL OF KENT
EARL OF GLOUCESTER
EDGAR, Gloucester's legitimate son
EDMUND, Gloucester's illegitimate son
GONERIL,
REGAN, and
CORDELIA, Lear's daughters

The Story:

King Lear, in foolish fondness for his children, decides to divide his kingdom among his three daughters. Grown senile, he scoffs at the foresight of his advisers and declares that each girl's statement of her love for him will determine the portion of the kingdom she receives as her dowry. Goneril, his oldest daughter and the duchess of Albany, speaks first. She says that she loved her father more than eyesight, space, liberty, or life itself. Regan, the duchess of Cornwall, announces that the sentiment of her love was expressed by Goneril, but that Goneril stopped short of the statement of

Regan's love. Cordelia, who secretly confides that her love is more ponderous than her tongue, tells her father that because her love is in her heart, not in her mouth, she is willing to sacrifice eloquence for truth. Lear angrily tells her that truth alone should be her dowry and orders that her part of the kingdom be divided between Goneril and Regan. Lear's disappointment in Cordelia's statement grows into a rage against the earl of Kent, who tries to plead for Cordelia with the foolish king. Because of Kent's blunt speech, he is given ten days to leave the country. Loving his sovereign, he risks death by disguising himself and remaining in Britain to care for Lear in his infirmity.

When Burgundy and France come as suitors to ask Cordelia's hand in marriage, Burgundy, learning of her dowerless fate, rejects her. France, honoring Cordelia for her virtues, takes her as his wife, but Lear dismisses Cordelia and France without his benediction. Goneril and Regan, wary of their father's vacillation in his weakened mental state, sets about to establish their kingdoms against change.

Lear is not long in learning what Goneril's and Regan's claims of love for him really mean. Their caustic comments about the old man's mental and physical feebleness furnish Lear's fool with many points for philosophical recriminations against the king. Realizing that his charity to his daughters makes him homeless, Lear cries in anguish against his fate. His prayers go unanswered, and his daughters' abuse hastens his derangement.

The earl of Gloucester, like Lear, is fond of his two children. Edmund, a bastard, afraid that his illegitimacy will deprive him of his share of Gloucester's estate, forges a letter over Edgar's signature, stating that the sons should not have to wait for their fortunes until they are too old to enjoy them. Gloucester, refusing to believe that Edgar desires his father's death, is told by Edmund to wait in hiding and hears Edgar make assertions that could easily be misinterpreted against him. Edmund, furthering his scheme, tells Edgar that villainy is afoot and that Edgar should not go unarmed at any time.

To complete his evil design, he later advises Edgar to flee for his own safety. After cutting his arm, he then tells his father that he was wounded while he and Edgar fought over Gloucester's honor. Gloucester, swearing that Edgar will not escape justice, has his son's description circulated so that he might be apprehended.

Edmund, meanwhile, allies himself with the dukes of Cornwall and Albany to defend Britain against the French army mobilized by Cordelia and her husband to avenge Lear's cruel treatment. Edmund wins Regan and Goneril completely by his personal attentions to them and sets the sisters against each other by arousing their jealousy.

Lear, wandering as an outcast on the stormy heath, is aided by Kent, disguised as a peasant. Seeking protection from the storm, they find a hut where Edgar, pretending to be a madman, took refuge. Gloucester, searching for the king, finds them there and urges them to hurry to Dover, where Cordelia and her husband will protect Lear from the wrath of his unnatural daughters.

Because he attempts to give succor and condolence to the outcast Lear, Gloucester is blinded when Cornwall, acting on information furnished by Edmund, gouges out his eyes. While he is at his grisly work, a servant, rebelling against the cruel deed, wounds Cornwall. Regan kills the servant, but Cornwall dies later as the result of his wound. Edgar, still playing the part of a madman, finds his father wandering the fields with an old retainer. Edgar, who refrains from revealing his identity, promises to guide his father to Dover, where Gloucester plans to die by throwing himself from the high cliffs.

Goneril becomes bitterly jealous when widowed Regan is able to receive the full attention of Edmund, who was made earl of Gloucester. She declares that she would rather lose the battle to France than lose Edmund to Regan. Goneril's hatred becomes more venomous when Albany, whom she detests because of his kindliness toward Lear and his pity for Gloucester, announces that he will try to right the wrongs done by Goneril, Regan, and Edmund.

Cordelia, informed by messenger of her father's fate, is in the French camp near Dover. When the mad old king is brought to her by the faithful Kent, she cares for her father tenderly and puts him in the care of a doctor skilled in curing many kinds of ills. When he regains his reason, Lear recognizes Cordelia, but the joy of their reunion is clouded by his repentance for having misunderstood and mistreated his only loyal daughter.

Edgar, protecting Gloucester, is accosted by Oswald, Goneril's steward, on his way to deliver a note to Edmund. In the fight that ensues, Edgar kills Oswald; he then delivers the letter to Albany, in which Goneril declares her love for Edmund and asks that he kill her husband. Gloucester dies, feeble and broken-hearted after Edgar reveals himself to his father. Edmund, who commands the British forces, takes Lear and Cordelia as prisoners. When they are led to prison, he sends along written instructions for how they are to be treated.

Albany, aware of Edmund's ambition for personal glory, arrests him on a charge of high treason. Regan intercedes for her lover but is rebuffed by Goneril. Regan is suddenly taken ill and carried to Albany's tent. When Edmund, as is his right, demands a trial by combat, Albany agrees. Edgar, still in disguise, appears and in the fight mortally wounds his false brother. Goneril, learning from Albany that he knows of her plot against his life, is desperate. She goes to their tent, poisons Regan, and kills herself.

Edmund, dying, reveals that he and Goneril ordered Cordelia to be hanged and her death to be announced as suicide because of her despondency over her father's plight. Edmund, fiendish and diabolical always, is also vain. As he lies dying, he looks upon the bodies of Goneril and Regan and expresses pleasure that two women are dead because of their jealous love for him.

Albany dispatches Edgar to prevent Cordelia's death, but he arrives too late. Lear refuses all assistance when he appears carrying her dead body in his arms. After asking forgiveness of heartbroken Kent, whom he recognizes at last, Lear, a broken, confused old man, dies in anguish. Edgar and Albany alone are left to rebuild a country ravaged by bloodshed and war.

Critical Evaluation:

Despite the three-hundred-year-old debate regarding the lack of unity in the plot of *King Lear*, it is one of the most readable and gripping of William Shakespeare's dramas. The theme of filial ingratitude is presented clearly in the depiction of two families, whom circumstances eventually bring together as the two narrative lines converge. *King Lear* is not only an absorbing drama but a disturbing one. The beauty of diction and the overwhelming pathos of the treatment given to innocence and goodness add to the poignancy of the emotional play. Like all great tragic dramas, the story of Lear and his folly purges the emotions by terror and pity.

King Lear's first entrance in act 1 is replete with ritual and ceremony. He is full of authority and assurance as he makes his regal way through the ordered court. When he reveals his intention to divide his kingdom into three parts for his daughters, he exudes the confidence generated by his long reign. The crispness and directness of his language suggests a power that, far from senility, demonstrates the stability and certainty of long, unchallenged rule. From that point on, the play acts out the destruction of that fixed order and the emergence of a new, tentative balance.

In the opening scene, Lear speaks as king and father. The absolute ruler decides to apportion his kingdom to his three heirs as a gift rather than bequest. In performing this act, which superficially seems both reasonable and generous, Lear sets in motion a chain of events that exposes his vulnerabilities not only as a king and a father but also as a man. Shakespeare shows that it is foolish to divest oneself of power and responsibility and yet expect to retain the trap-

pings of authority. This is exactly what Lear does when he relies with ill-placed confidence on the love of his daughters. He asks too much and he acts too precipitously, but he is punished by an inexorable universe out of all proportion to his errors in judgment.

When he asks his daughters for a declaration of love, as a prerequisite for a share of the kingdom, he is as self-assured a parent as he is an overbearing monarch. He credits the facile protestations of love by Goneril and Regan because they are what he wants to hear and because they conform to the ceremonial necessities of the occasion. Cordelia's honest response, born of a greater love, are out of keeping with the occasion. Lear does not look beneath the surface. He lets ritual appearances replace internal reality; in fact, he refuses to distinguish between the two.

The asseverations of Goneril and Regan soon emerge as the cynical conceits they really are, but by then Lear banished Cordelia and the loyal Kent, who sees through the sham. Lear is successively and ruthlessly divested of all the accoutrements of kingship by his villainous daughters, who eventually reduce him to the condition of a ragged, homeless madman. Paradoxically, it is in this extremity on the heath with Edgar and the fool that Lear comes to a knowledge of himself and his community with humanity that he never achieved while enjoying the glories of power. Buffeted by the natural fury of the storm, which is symbolic of the chaos and danger that come with the passing of the old order, Lear through his madness sees the common bond that connects him to the rest of humanity.

The experience of Lear is, on a more manageable, human level, mirrored in the Gloucester subplot. Gloucester, too, suffers filial ingratitude, but not one raised to a cosmic level. He, too, mistakes appearance for reality in trusting the duplicitous Edmund and disinheriting the honest Edgar, but his behavior is more clearly the outgrowth of an existing moral confusion, which is reflected in his ambivalent and unrepentant affection for his illegitimate son. His moral blindness leads to physical blindness when his faulty judgment makes him vulnerable to the villains. In his blindness, he finally sees the truth of his situation, but his experience remains that of a father and a man.

Lear's experience parallels Gloucester's in that his figurative madness leads to a real madness in which he finally recognizes what he lacks. He sees in the naked Edgar, himself a victim of Gloucester's moral blindness, the natural state of man, stripped of all external decoration, and he realizes that he ignored the basic realities of the human condition. His experience finally transcends Gloucester's, however, because he is a king, preeminent among men. He not only represents the hazards of kingship but also the broadly human disposition to prefer pleasant appearances to troubling realities. Because of his position, however, Lear's failure brings the whole political and social order down with him.

Lear violates nature by a culpable ignorance of it. The result is familial rupture, physical suffering, and existential confusion. Brought low, Lear begins to fashion a new salutary view of himself, human love, and human nature. In his insanity, Lear assembles a bizarre court of mad king, beggar, and fool that reasserts the common bonds of all men. Once he achieves these realizations, the play's evil characters, so carefully balanced against the good in Shakespeare's precarious world, begin to kill each other off and succumb to the vengeance of regenerated justice.

It is, however, a mark of Shakespeare's uncompromising view of reality that there is no simple application of poetic justice to reward the good and punish the wicked. The good die, too. Edgar finishes off his brother in a trial by combat, and the machinations of Goneril and Regan result in the destruction of both, but the redeemed Lear and Cordelia, the perfection of selfless love, also die. That Lear should die is perhaps no surprise. The suffering he endures in his confrontation with the primal elements does not allow an optimistic return to normal life and prosperity. He looks into the eye of nature and there is nothing left for him but to die.

The death of Cordelia is more troublesome because she is the perfectly innocent victim of the evil and madness that surround her. She dies gratuitously, not because of any internal necessity of the plot but because the message to save her arrives too late. The dramatist creates his own inevitability to represent the ruthless consequences of the evil and chaos that are loosed. When Lear enters with the dead Cordelia, he accomplishes the final expiation of his unknowing.

Out of these sufferings and recognitions comes a new moral stasis. Nevertheless, the purged world does not inspire great confidence that it will attain stability in the future. When Kent, who is old, refuses kingship, Edgar assumes authority, but despite his rectitude there is an unsettling doubt that he has the force or stature to maintain the new order in this volatile world where evil and chaos always exist not far beneath the surface.

"Critical Evaluation" by Edward E. Foster

Further Reading

Bloom, Harold. "Nothing Begets Nothing: *King Lear.*" In *William Shakespeare*, edited by Bloom. Philadelphia: Chelsea House, 2004. An analysis of the play by a noted literary critic.

Booth, Stephen. *"King Lear," "Macbeth," Indefinition, and Tragedy.* New Haven, Conn.: Yale University Press, 1983. In part 1, "On the Greatness of *King Lear*," much of the discussion focuses on the repeated false endings of the play. Booth also has an important appendix on the doubling of roles in Shakespeare's plays, especially in *King Lear.*

Flower, Celeste. *Shakespeare: King Lear.* New York: Cambridge University Press, 2002. Guidebook designed for advanced-level students of English literature. Provides a commentary on the text; discusses the play's historical, cultural, and social contexts and use of language; offers a survey of critical interpretation.

Halio, Jay L. *Critical Essays on "King Lear."* New York: Twayne, 1995. Contains a selection of some of the best essays on *King Lear*, including several on the "two-text hypothesis," the play in performance, and interpretation. The introduction surveys contemporary trends in criticism.

Hamilton, Sharon. *Shakespeare's Daughters.* Jefferson, N.C.: McFarland, 2003. Analyzes the father-daughter relationship in selected plays. "Plighted Cunning, Playing the Good Girl Role: *The Taming of the Shrew* and *King Lear*" discusses how Goneril and Regan deceive their father by pretending to be dutiful daughters. "Daughters Who Forgive and Heal" focuses on Cordelia, as well as Marina in *Pericles* and Perdita in *The Winter's Tale.*

Kahan, Jeffrey, ed. *King Lear: New Critical Essays.* New York: Routledge, 2008. The essays include discussions of "The Reshaping of *King Lear*" by R. A. Foakes, the evolution of the play's texts, *King Lear* and early seventeenth century print culture, nature and justice in the play, and "What Does Shakespeare Leave out of *King Lear*?" by Jean R. Brink.

Leggatt, Alexander. *King Lear.* Harvester New Critical Introductions. Hemel Hempstead, England: Harvester-Wheatsheaf, 1988. Includes a brief discussion of the stage history and critical reception as well as a thorough examination of the play's dramatic idiom and characters.

Mack, Maynard. *"King Lear" in Our Time.* Berkeley: University of California Press, 1965. Surveys the play's historical background, sources, and aspects of its staging. Provides many perceptive critical comments on the action and its significance.

Rosenberg, Marvin. *The Masks of King Lear.* 1972. Reprint. Newark: University of Delaware Press, 1993. Examines the significance of each scene and the "polyphony" of the characters, with extensive reference to the history of *King*

Lear on the stage and of the earliest recorded performances. Discusses the so-called Lear myth.

Shakespeare, William. *The Tragedy of King Lear: With Classic and Contemporary Criticisms*. Edited by Joseph Pearce. San Francisco: Ignatius Press, 2008. In addition to the text of *King Lear*, this edition reprints classic criti-

cal essays about the play written by John Keats, Samuel Johnson, and A. C. Bradley as well as new essays. Some of the new essays explore nature and convention, chaos and order, comic elements and tragic necessity, and the uncertainty of faith in the play.

King Solomon's Mines

Author: H. Rider Haggard (1856-1925)
First published: 1885
Type of work: Novel
Type of plot: Adventure
Time of plot: Nineteenth century
Locale: Africa

Principal characters:
ALLAN QUATERMAIN, an English explorer
SIR HENRY CURTIS, his friend
CAPTAIN JOHN GOOD, Curtis's friend
UMBOPA, a Zulu, in reality Ignosi, hereditary chieftain of the Kukuanas
TWALA, the ruler of the Kukuanas
GAGOOL, a native sorceress

The Story:

Returning to his home in Natal after an unsuccessful elephant hunt, Allan Quatermain meets Sir Henry Curtis and his friend, retired Captain John Good, aboard ship. Sir Henry inquires whether Quatermain met a man named Neville in Bamangwato. Learning that he did, Sir Henry explains that Neville is his younger brother, George, with whom he quarreled. When Sir Henry inherited his parents' estate, George took the name Neville and went to Africa to seek his fortune. He was not heard from since.

Quatermain says that Neville reportedly headed for King Solomon's Mines, diamond mines reputed to lie far in the interior. Ten years before, Quatermain met a Portuguese man, José Silvestre, who tried unsuccessfully to cross the desert to the mines and dragged himself into his camp to die. Before he died, José gave him a map showing the location of the treasure. It was written on a piece of a shirt that belonged to his relative, another José Da Silvestre, three hundred years before. Silvestre saw the mines but died in the mountains while trying to return. His servant brought the map back to his family, and it was passed down through succeeding generations of the Silvestre family. By the time the ship reached Natal, Quatermain agrees to help Sir Henry find his brother.

In Natal, Quatermain gets the equipment together, and the trio choose the five men who are to accompany them. Besides the driver and the leader for the oxen that are to pull their cart, they hire three servants: a Hottentot named Ventvogel and two Zulus, Khiva and Umbopa. Umbopa

explains that his tribe lives far to the north in the direction in which they are traveling and that he is willing to serve for nothing if he might go with the party. Quatermain is suspicious of the native's offer, but Sir Henry agrees to take Umbopa as his servant.

On the journey from Durban, they lose Khiva when, trying to save Captain Good from attack by a wounded bull elephant, the native is torn in two by the rampaging animal. At Sitandra's Kraal at the edge of the desert, the men leave all the equipment they cannot carry on their backs. Quatermain's plan is to travel at night to avoid the heat of the sun and to sleep during the day. On the third day out, however, the men can find no shelter from the heat. They decide that trekking is more comfortable than trying to rest. They are out of water by the fourth day, but on the following day, Ventvogel discovers a spring. Refreshing themselves, they start off again that night. At the end of the next night, they reach the lower slope of a mountain marked on the map as Sheba's left breast. On the other side of the mountain lies King Solomon's road, which is supposed to lead to the diamond mines.

The climb up the mountain is not an easy one. The higher they ascend, the colder it grows. At the top of the ridge, they find a cave and climb into it to spend the night. Ventvogel freezes to death before morning. Ventvogel is not the only dead man in the cave. When it grows light the next morning, one of the party sees the body of a white man in its rocky recesses. Quatermain decides that it is the body of the first José Silvestre, preserved by the cold.

Leaving the bodies in the cave, the remaining men start down the mountain slope. As the mist clears, they can distinguish fertile lands and woods below them. Reaching King Solomon's road, they follow it into the valley. The road is a magnificent engineering feat that crosses a ravine and even tunnels through a ridge. In the tunnel, the walls are decorated with figures driving in chariots. Sir Henry declares that the pictures were painted by ancient Egyptians.

When Quatermain and his party descend to the valley, they stop to eat and rest beside a stream. Captain Good undresses to shave and bathe. Suddenly, Quatermain realizes that they are being observed by a party of natives. As the leader of the band, an old man, steps up to speak to them, Quatermain sees that he greatly resembles Umbopa.

Were it not for Captain Good's peculiarities, the four men would surely have been killed. Luckily, Captain Good's false teeth, bare legs, half-shaven face, and monocle fascinated the savages so that they are willing to believe Quatermain's story that he and his friends descended from the stars. To make the story more credible, he shoots an antelope with what he declares is his magic tube. At Quatermain's insistence, the old man, whose name is Infadoos, agrees to lead the men to Twala, king of the Kukuanas. After a three-day journey, Quatermain and his party reach Loo, where Twala is holding his summer festival. The white men are introduced to the hideous one-eyed giant before an assemblage of eight thousand of his soldiers.

Before Twala's annual witch hunt begins that evening, the four travelers have a conference with Infadoos. They learn from him that Twala and his son, Scragga, are hated for their cruelty. Umbopa then reveals that he is, in reality, Ignosi, son of the rightful king, whom Twala murdered. On the death of her husband, his mother fled across the mountains and desert with her child. As proof of his claim, Ignosi displays a snake tattooed around his middle. The snake is the sign of Kukuana kingship.

All the men, including Infadoos, agree that they will help him overcome Twala and gain the throne. Infadoos declares that he will speak to some of the chiefs after the witch hunt and win them to Ignosi's cause. He is certain that they could have twenty thousand men in their ranks by the next morning.

That night, Gagool and her sister sorceresses help Twala search out more than a hundred of his men charged with evil thoughts or plots against their sovereign. When, in their wild dances, one of them stops before any one of the twenty thousand soldiers who are drawn up in review, the victim is im-

mediately stabbed to death. In her blood thirst, Gagool does not hesitate to stop in front of Ignosi. Quatermain and his friends fire their guns to impress Twala and persuade him that Ignosi's life should be spared.

Infadoos is true to his word. He brings all the chiefs he can muster, and Ignosi again exhibits the tattoo around his waist. The men fear he might be an impostor, however, and ask for a further sign. Captain Good, who knows from his almanac that an eclipse of the sun is due, swears that they will darken the sun the following day.

King Twala continues his festival and has his maidens dance before him the next afternoon. When they finish, he asks Quatermain to choose the most beautiful; his custom is to have the loveliest of the dancers slain each year. Foulata is selected, but before she can be killed, the white men interfere on her behalf. As they do so, the sun begins to darken. Scragga is mad with fear and throws his spear at Sir Henry, but the Englishman is luckily wearing a mail shirt, a present from Twala. Seizing the weapon, he hurls it back at Scragga and kills him.

Quatermain and his friends, including Infadoos and the girl, take advantage of the eclipse to flee from the town with the chiefs who rallied to them. Approximately twenty thousand men prepare for battle on a hill about two miles from Loo. Twala's regiments, some thirty thousand soldiers, attack the next day. They are driven back and then set upon by their enemies who, driving at them from three directions, surround and slaughter many of the Kukuanas. The vanquished Twala is slain in a contest with Sir Henry, who lops off his head with a battle ax.

In return for the help that his white friends give him, the new king, Ignosi, orders Gagool to lead them to King Solomon's mines, which lie in the mountains at the other end of the great road. Deep into the hills they go, past three enormous figures carved in the rock, images that Quatermain believes might be the three false gods for whom Solomon went astray. To reach the treasure room, they passed through a cave that Gagool calls the Place of Death. There, seated around a table, are all the dead kings of the Kukuanas, petrified by siliceous water dripping upon them.

While the men stand dumbfounded by the sight, Gagool, unobserved, moves a lever that causes a massive stone to rise. On the other side of it are boxes full of diamonds, gold coins, and ivory. As the men stand gloating over the treasure, Gagool creeps away. She releases a lever to bring down the door, but Foulata catches her before she can escape. Gagool stabs the girl fatally, but before she can pass under the door, it drops and crushes her.

For several hours, Quatermain and his friends believe that

they are buried alive, for they have no idea where to find the secret of the door. At last, in the dark, they find a lever that discloses a subterranean passage. Through it, they find their way once more to the outside and to Infadoos, who is waiting for them.

A few weeks later, some of Ignosi's men guide them out of Kukuanaland, across the mountains, and on the first stage of their trip back across the desert. The only treasure they have with them is a handful of diamonds Quatermain stuffed into his pockets before they found a way out of the treasure room.

Their guides, who know of a better trail than that by which the travelers came, lead them to an oasis from which they can pass on to other green spots along their way. On their return trip they find a small hut near the bank of a stream. Sir Henry's lost brother, George, is in it. He was badly injured by a boulder two years before and was not able to travel since that time. Quatermain and his friends support George across the desert to Sitandra's Kraal and then on to Quatermain's home. According to their agreement before setting out on the expedition, the diamonds are divided. Quatermain and Captain Good each keep a third, and they give the rest of the stones to George, Sir Henry's brother.

Critical Evaluation:

This story of the search for King Solomon's legendary lost treasure, hidden in the land of the Kukuanas, provides absorbing reading for children and adults alike. The slaughter provoked by the cruelty of King Twala and the character of the ancient sorceress, Gagool, make *King Solomon's Mines* a book that is not soon forgotten. This, the first great African adventure novel, set the pattern for a host of jungle stories to follow, from Edgar Rice Burroughs's *Tarzan* epics (the first of which was published in 1912) to serious novels such as Joseph Conrad's *Heart of Darkness* (1899) and Saul Bellow's *Henderson the Rain King* (1959).

H. Rider Haggard chooses his heroes for maximum dramatic effect. Allan Quatermain, the narrator, is the thorough professional. He is a moderate, practical, cost-conscious man, courageous when he has to be but quite willing to avoid danger if given the option; he is a firm believer in brain over brawn. Sir Henry Curtis is the more typical hero. Where Quatermain is rational and careful, Curtis is emotional and extravagant. Quatermain is the mechanical expert, especially with guns, but Sir Henry is most at home with primitive weapons and becomes fearsome in hand-to-hand combat. In short, Sire Henry is the natural warrior; it is he who kills the one-eyed villain, King Twala.

Captain John Good, the former naval officer, is the one hero who seems out of place in the depths of Africa. He is fastidious and fussy. His personal quirks and unusual accessories—such as his monocle, his false teeth that "snap" into place, his formal attire, and his delicate white legs—provide the necessary comic relief. Late in the novel, however, these humorous details become crucial plot elements when Good's half-shaved face and bare legs are taken as signs of divinity by the hostile natives. Although the characterizations are neither deep nor complex, they are vivid and thoroughly convincing.

Haggard also keeps the plot simple and the language plain, as Quatermain states in offering his "apologies for my blunt way of writing . . . simple things are always the most impressive, and books are easier to understand when they are written in plain language." The plot is organized around the most basic adventure formula—the treasure hunt—and has all the necessary ingredients: a mysterious map; an exotic, even mythic, destination; an unknown, dangerous terrain; and a pair of grotesque, diabolical villains. Haggard carefully develops his story by subjecting his heroes to a series of crises that become progressively more dangerous, more extreme, and more fantastic.

No matter how exotic these adventures become, the author keeps them believable with his matter-of-fact language and his careful, realistic use of detail. Calling upon his own youthful experiences in Africa, Haggard supports every incident with relevant particulars. Quatermain, the thoroughly seasoned professional, uses the best equipment, detailed accurately, and demonstrates his expertise in dozens of small ways: handling animals, negotiating with natives, organizing and directing their hunts, and supervising the day-to-day safari routine. As the men encounter more unusual environments, Haggard continues to reinforce his narrative with concrete details. The natives' equipment, social and military organizations, tribal customs, and religious rituals are described with precision. Even the most fantastic sequences in the novel—the exploration of Solomon's mines, the discovery of the giant figures and the Place of Death, the search through the treasure room, and the escape through the underground tunnel—are explained minutely and logically by historical speculation, biblical references, and native folklore. Since the novel takes place in an area that was, at the time, as yet unexplored, the book seems "authentic," and many of its first readers even thought that the story was true.

As one of the first and best of the popular modern adventure novelists, Haggard understood the basic rule of escapist fiction: If the imaginative adventure is to succeed, the world the reader escapes to must be as real as the one he lives in, however improbable the particular events may be.

Further Reading

Butts, Dennis. Introduction and notes to *King Solomon's Mines*, by H. Rider Haggard. New York: Oxford University Press, 1989. Butts's introduction discussing the historical background and literary reception of the novel is concise and informative. He notes the novel's familiar structure as a folktale. Includes bibliography.

Chrisman, Laura. *Rereading the Imperial Romance: British Imperialism and South African Resistance in Haggard, Schreiner, and Plaatje.* New York: Oxford University Press, 2000. Examines how Haggard and other writers used the romance genre to express ideological issues of British imperialism in South Africa. Chrisman's analysis of Haggard's novels focuses on his novels *King Solomon's Mines* and *Nada the Lily.*

Cohen, Morton. *Rider Haggard: His Life and Works.* London: Hutchinson University Library, 1960. Scrupulously documented and judiciously restrained in its appreciation of Haggard as a writer. Provides rich historical context for the composition of *King Solomon's Mines.*

Fraser, Robert. *Victorian Quest Romance: Stevenson, Haggard, Kipling, and Conan Doyle.* Plymouth, England: Northcote House/British Council, 1998. Examines Victorian romance novels, including *King Solomon's Mines,* in which protagonists searched for lost or buried pasts. Fraser demonstrates how the writers used these novels to raise questions about their own cultures and beliefs.

Higgins, D. S. *Rider Haggard: The Great Storyteller.* London: Cassell, 1981. Excellent, accessible biography, with limited literary analysis and thorough historical context and publishing history.

Katz, Wendy R. *Rider Haggard and the Fiction of Empire: A Critical Study of British Imperial Fiction.* New York: Cambridge University Press, 1987. Suggests Haggard's considerable cultural significance as an imperial propagandist. Discusses his philosophy of life and commitment to empire through an analysis of *King Solomon's Mines* and other works.

Monsman, Gerald Cornelius. *H. Rider Haggard on the Imperial Frontier: The Political and Literary Contexts of His African Romances.* Greensboro, N.C.: ELT Press, 2006. Monsman disagrees with other critics who have described Haggard as an apologist for imperialism, demonstrating how his work subverts Victorian imperialist culture by endorsing African religion, autonomous female characters, and racial mixing. Chapter 3, "Diamonds and Deities: The Spoils of Imperialism," focuses on *King Solomon's Mines,* and many other references to the book are listed in the index.

Sandison, Alan. *The Wheel of Empire: A Study of the Imperial Idea in Some Late Nineteenth and Early Twentieth Century Writers.* London: Macmillan, 1967. A provocative chapter on the intellectual foundations laid down by Charles Darwin, Georg Wilhelm Friedrich Hegel, and Karl Marx leads to the assertion that Haggard adapted to modern thought more readily than did Rudyard Kipling, Joseph Conrad, or John Buchan. Thus he escaped the vice of racial prejudice so prevalent among writers on empire.

Stiebel, Lindy. *Imagining Africa: Landscape in H. Rider Haggard's African Romances.* Westport, Conn.: Greenwood Press, 2001. Focuses on Haggard's depiction of land and landscapes in his African novels, including *King Solomon's Mines.* Stiebel argues that Haggard created an idealized Africa that reflected the fears and desires of late-Victorian Britain.

The King, the Greatest Alcalde

Author: Lope de Vega Carpio (1562-1635)
First published: El mejor alcalde, el rey, 1635 (English translation, 1918)
Type of work: Drama
Type of plot: Tragicomedy
Time of plot: Sixteenth century
Locale: Spain

Principal characters:
SANCHO, a poor laborer
NUNO, a farmer
ELVIRA, his daughter
DON TELLO DE NEIRA, a nobleman
FELICIANA, his sister
PELAYO, a swineherd
DON ALFONSO VII, the king of Leon and Castile

The Story:

Sancho, a poor peasant, is in love with an equally poor girl, Elvira, the daughter of a farmer named Nuno. When the old man gives Sancho permission to wed his daughter, he insists that Sancho also secure the consent of Don Tello, master of all the surrounding lands, and of Don Tello's sister, Feliciana. In obedience to Nuno, Sancho goes with Pelayo, a swineherd, to the castle to ask his lord's approval of the marriage. Both Don Tello and his sister Feliciana readily give their consent and their blessing, and they declare that they themselves will attend the wedding.

When Don Tello sees the beautiful Elvira, however, he is filled with such passion for her that he decides to postpone the wedding and take Elvira to satisfy his own lust before giving her to Sancho for his wife. Dismissing the priest, he tells the assembled guests that the wedding must wait until the next day. Sancho and Elvira feels themselves already married, however, since the priest heard them declare their true love for each other, and Sancho plans to go to Elvira's room that night. When Elvira opens her door, she confronts not her lover but Don Tello and his attendants, all masked, who carry her off to the castle.

Sancho and Nuno, learning of this betrayal, are ready to die. Nuno cautions Sancho not to despair, however, for he knows his daughter will die rather than lose her honor. Nuno knows his daughter well. Although Don Tello pleads with her and threatens her, she will not give herself to him. Feliciana begs him to remember his good name and his honor and not to force the girl.

Sancho and Nuno, going to Don Tello, pretend that they hear but cannot believe that he stole Elvira away. Don Tello pretends also that he is outraged at such a story and would whip those who tell such lies to defame his honor. However, when Elvira enters the room, Don Tello flies into a rage and orders Sancho and Nuno beaten to death. They flee for their lives. Don Tello vows that he will force Elvira to submit to him or be killed. Again Sancho wants to die, but once more Nuno persuades him that there is still hope. He sends Sancho and Pelayo to the court of Alfonso, the king of Castile, for the king is a good man and well known for his justice in dealing with high and low alike.

When the king hears Sancho's story, he immediately writes a letter to Don Tello, ordering him to release Elvira at once. Don Tello ignores the letter and declares that on his own land his people will do only his will. Pelayo assures Sancho that Don Tello did not yet possess Elvira, for he would have obeyed the king were his lust satisfied. Sancho and Pelayo go again to the king, to tell him that Don Tello did not obey his orders. The king promises to go in person

to Don Tello and force him to return Elvira to her father and husband-to-be. He intends to go in disguise, taking with him only two attendants.

Don Tello, filled with wild rage and passion at Elvira's refusal to accept him, swears that he will take her by force. Nuno speaks with her through the bars of the room where she is confined and tells her that Sancho went for help, and she promises again to die rather than lose her virtue. When Sancho and Pelayo return with word that the king is sending help, Nuno is not much encouraged, for he knows that Don Tello keeps his castle well guarded and cannot be overcome by only three men. What Nuno does not know is that the king himself is coming, though Pelayo is hard put to it to keep the secret.

When King Alfonso arrives, he questioned Nuno's servants and is convinced that Sancho and Nuno tell the truth. Then he goes in disguise to Don Tello's castle. There he is rudely received by that haughty nobleman. At last the king reveals himself and orders Elvira brought before him. Elvira tells the king of her pure love for Sancho, of having obtained her father's and Don Tello's permission, of her seizure by Don Tello and his men, and, finally, of her lost honor. Don Tello carried out his vow. He ordered her taken into a wood and there, even though she fought until she was weak, he raped her. She declares that she can never know joy again, for her honor is lost forever.

The king orders Don Tello beheaded, both for his treatment of the innocent girl and for his failure to obey the king's command sent in his earlier letter. Although Feliciana pleads for her brother, the king refuses to be moved by her tears. Don Tello confesses that he deserves the penalty, for he sinned twice, against his own honor and against the king. Then the king pronounces his final sentence. He will wed Elvira to Don Tello, then execute him. As his widow Elvira will inherit half his lands and gold. These will be her dowry when she marries Sancho. Feliciana he will take to court, to wait on the queen until a noble husband can be secured for her. The peasants bless the king's wisdom and actions for he rights their wrongs as far as is humanly possibly.

Critical Evaluation:

The King, the Greatest Alcalde, which Lope de Vega Carpio wrote in 1620-1623, belongs, along with the earlier *Fuenteovejuna*, written 1611-1618, to the best work of one of the most remarkable literary men of all time. Like Samuel Johnson, Lord Byron, and the composer Franz Liszt, Vega Carpio is as much of a "personality" as he is an artist. Born of humble parents, he became a soldier, a sailor in the Spanish Armada (taking part in the ill-fated expedition of 1588), a duelist, an exile, a lover of innumerable ladies and the husband of two, a priest of passionate if temporary convictions, an arbiter of the theater, and reputedly the writer of about eighteen hundred plays and other dramatic works, less than one-third of which have survived. A contemporary of William Shakespeare, he is often compared to the English bard for his breadth of vision, his vitality, his role in the creation of a national theater, and the similar innyard-type theater (the *corral*) for which he wrote. As is perhaps inevitable for such a prolific dramatist, however, his artistry falls short of Shakespeare's. It cannot be said of his role in Spanish dramaturgy, as Johnson said of John Dryden's influence on English poetry, that he found it brick and left it marble; perhaps, however, it can be said that he found it sand and left it brick.

Vega Carpio wrote with a disdain for classical precedent and an open appeal for popular approval. "When I set out to write a play," he observed, "I lock up all the rules under ten keys, and banish Plautus and Terence from my study. . . . For I write in the style of those who seek the applause of the public, whom it is but just to humor in their folly, since it is they who pay for it." The Spaniards called him *monstruo de la naturaleza*, or "the freak of nature," for his plays have the vices of their virtues: Bubbling with inventiveness, energy, and variety, they are also often careless in their construction, shallow in their characterization, and uneven in their poetic power.

The King, the Greatest Alcalde exhibits both the virtues and the vices and exemplify Vega Carpio's dramatic outlook. The play, a tragicomedy, is a mixture of love story and realism. Sancho and Elvira are closely related to the Corydons and the Phyllises of pastoral tales in their rustic, idealized love for each other and in the miseries they must endure before they are finally reunited. They are, however, observed with a realism and a pessimism that take due note of the branding power of evil in the world. "There is no interest beneath the sun by which an honest woman may be won," Feliciana assures Don Tello, underestimating the savage determination of her brother. In the standard pastoral tale, the honest woman would remain chaste to the end, despite all temptations and menaces, but Vega Carpio realizes that life is not like that, and Elvira is raped before the king can restore her to Sancho. The primary interest of the play, however, is Vega Carpio's treatment of social forces, especially the interaction among the peasants, the feudal lord Don Tello, and the king.

In *The King, the Greatest Alcalde*, Vega Carpio reveals an unalloyed admiration for the peasant class unlike that in any other dramas of the time, including Shakespeare's. In the twentieth century, Marxist critics seized on such plays as this one and *Fuenteovejuna* as examples of Vega Carpio's "proletariat" theater, which portrays an oppressed and hearty peasantry struggling against a corrupt and depraved aristocracy. There certainly is a discernible tendency toward idealization of the peasants. Sancho's opening paean to nature and his elevated sentiments throughout mark him as a noble character indeed, far more noble, certainly, than the outwardly refined Don Tello. Sancho himself feels that "in the passion of the heart" he is a lord, and the king is highly impressed with Sancho's eloquence. Just as important, the king is taken with the honest and open nature of the peasants whom he questions about Don Tello's villainy: "The guilelessness of these folk is the most convincing proof," he remarks.

Lords such as Don Tello were intermediate in the social structure between the peasants and the king (Vega Carpio gives virtually no hints of a middle class). Spain, in this period, was still in transition between a feudal and a national governmental structure, and Don Tello makes a fatal miscalculation as to how much power he retains in the new structure. Traditionally, the peasants living within the province of a lord are subject to his absolute authority in all matters of daily life (such as marriage). "You serve Don Tello in his flocks, who rears his powers over these lands, and is supreme through all Galicia," Nuno tells Sancho. Apparently, Don Tello's permission to marry is no longer strictly required, though Nuno strongly advises his future son-in-law to ask for permission anyway in the hope of receiving a generous gift. Don Tello can indeed be generous when he is in the mood, but he is also arrogantly proud of his undisputed authority. Living quite distant from the king, he accepts no remote challenges to his authority. Even when presented with a direct order in writing from the king he asserts his independence: "I reign here and here I do my will as the king does his in Castille. My forebears never owed land to him—they won it from the Moors." Only when the king personally appears before Don Tello does the once haughty lord crumble and acknowledge his higher authority.

The king himself is presented as the only recourse, this side of God, for the injustices heaped on the peasants. From the outset, he is their special friend. As one of Don Tello's courtiers warns him, "Alfonso was reared in Galicia . . . and for that reason they say he will never close his door to any Gallegan, though never so humble his birth." Indeed, the first view of the king reveals him asking his own courtiers whether there are any suppliants waiting with appeals to him; as he confesses, he is unable to resist the poor. As an indication of his lack of pretentiousness, Alfonso (unlike Don Tello) is unostentatiously dressed; when Sancho is first admitted he must ask a lord which person is the king. This unpretentiousness, however, does not in the least diminish the king's real importance and power, for he is nothing less than God's regent on earth. His face, Sancho declares to him, is the "Image of God," and "you reflect his glory!" Later, a humbled Don Tello admits that he has "offended God—God and the King!"

The motif of the king in disguise is a fairly common theatrical and literary device with high dramatic potential (Sir Walter Scott uses a disguised Richard the Lion-Hearted in his 1819 novel *Ivanhoe* to great effect, for example). Vega Carpio uses it not only for its suspense value but also as an emblem of his attitude toward the king. When Alfonso tells Sancho that he intends to intervene personally in the matter, disguised as an alcalde, or justice of the peace, the youth fears that the king is humbling himself by concerning himself so much with a peasant's honor, and he urges instead that the king simply dispatch an alcalde to the scene. Alfonso, however, conscious of his judicial as well as his executive role, replies, "The King, the greatest Alcalde!"

It must be noted that this play is not free from the flaws that mar the playwright's other, less important work. The poetry often sags, and the lyrical passages, apart from the fact that they sound faintly incongruous in the mouths of Sancho and Elvira, often become artificial and declamatory. There are, moreover, inconsistencies of characterization. Don Tello's passionate desire for Elvira is condemned by her as mere lust, yet at the opening of the play Sancho says repeatedly that his own love for Elvira is based entirely on her physical beauty and is, in fact, in direct proportion to it: "May your beauty grow, so that in me may grow the love I bear!" Vega Carpio's hasty writing also betrays itself in careless construction, as when Elvira, in the final scene of the play, declares that she was taken out to a wood "a fourth league removed" and raped; yet only one scene earlier she is still untouched and still fleeing from Don Tello.

These flaws may be among the reasons why the plays of Vega Carpio are seldom performed outside his own country. Without question, however, he is an important and influential playwright. The dramatic vitality and skillful inventiveness of his plays, despite their frequent lapses, make for exciting reading and playing. He was to influence such other, more highly regarded dramatists as Jean Racine and Molière, as is seen in the kingly intervention in *Tartuffe* (1664). Vega Carpio's concern with the social importance and dignity of the peasant, who was conventionally represented in drama as a fool or a clown (such as Pelayo), marks his plays, thematically, as far ahead of their time.

"Critical Evaluation" by Laurence Behrens

Further Reading

Cañadas, Ivan. *Public Theater in Golden Age Madrid and Tudor-Stuart London: Class, Gender, and Festive Community.* Burlington, Vt.: Ashgate, 2005. Compares English Tudor and Spanish Golden Age drama, focusing on theatrical conventions, social significance of the plays, and reception of audiences in London and Madrid. Examines Lope Vega Carpio's peasant honor plays, including *The King, the Greatest Alcalde.*

Chandler, Richard E., and Kessel Schwartz. *A New History of Spanish Literature.* Baton Rouge: Louisiana State University Press, 1961. An excellent survey of the development of Spanish drama. Provides a helpful explanation of Vega Carpio's art.

Hays, Francis C. *Lope de Vega.* New York: Twayne, 1967. Acquaints English-speaking readers with Vega Carpio's life, career, and the new dramatic art of his comedies. Contains an effective formula for comprehending the elements of Vega Carpio's comedies.

Northup, George Tyler. *An Introduction to Spanish Literature.* 3d rev. ed. Chicago: University of Chicago Press, 1960. A helpful presentation of the Spanish *comedia.* Includes a chapter devoted to Vega Carpio and his dramatic school.

Samson, Alexander, and Jonathan Thacker, eds. *A Companion to Lope de Vega.* Rochester, N.Y.: Tamesis, 2008. Twenty-one essays provide various interpretations of Vega Carpio's life and work. Includes discussions of Vega Carpio and the theater of Madrid, his religious drama, his chronicle memory plays, his comedies, and Vega Carpio as icon.

Vega Carpio, Lope de. *Four Plays by Lope de Vega.* Translated by John Garrett Underhill. Westport, Conn.: Hyperion Books, 1978. Contains an English translation of *The King, the Greatest Alcalde* that is mainly in verse. The volume has an introduction and critical essay by Jacinto Benavente.

Wright, Elizabeth R. *Pilgrimage to Patronage: Lope de Vega and the Court of Philip III, 1598-1621.* Lewisburg, Pa.: Bucknell University Press, 2001. Chronicles how Vega Carpio used his publications and public appearances to win benefactors at the court of Philip III. Describes how his search for patrons shaped his literary work and how the success of his plays altered the court's system of artistic patronage.

Kiss of the Spider Woman

Author: Manuel Puig (1932-1990)
First published: El beso de la mujer araña, 1976
    (English translation, 1979)
Type of work: Novel
Type of plot: Social realism
Time of plot: 1975
Locale: Argentina

Principal characters:
MOLINA (LUIS ALBERTO MOLINO), a gay prisoner
VALENTÍN ARREGUI PAZ, a political prisoner
MARTA, Valentín's girlfriend

The Story:

Molina, an effeminate gay window dresser in Argentina, is growing discontented with the frivolous life he leads with his friends; he wants a lifelong partner. He becomes friends with a heterosexual waiter named Gabriel, who is married, but he knows the relationship will not lead to a romantic attachment. When he is convicted on charges of corrupting a minor, he is sentenced to eight years in prison without the possibility of parole.

Valentín is a journalism student in love with Marta, a beautiful and well-educated member of the upper class in Argentina. He is also secretly a member of the underground movement that seeks to overthrow the corrupt and oppressive military regime of the country. When he tells Marta of his involvement, she forces him to choose between her and the movement. Even though he loves Marta, he feels he has a responsibility to stand up to injustice, and he leaves her. In the movement, he has another girlfriend, named Lidia.

Valentín is never as deeply involved as many who are in the political rebellion, but he agrees to help Dr. Americo escape the country by giving him his own passport. Americo is one of the oldest living members of an earlier movement for true democracy. At the airport after making the exchange, Valentín is arrested. He is put in Molina's cell.

At first, Valentín despises Molina. He thinks his effeminacy is a disgusting display of irresponsibility in the face of the sacrifices his friends in the movement are willing to make. Nevertheless, he does find Molina at least entertaining. Molina's great talent is in telling stories, especially the tales he remembers from romantic films.

The film that Molina likes the most is a story set in Paris during World War II. Leni, a French chanteuse, learns that Michelle, the cigarette girl in her club, although a member of the French underground movement against the Germans, fell in love with a German soldier, by whom she is pregnant. Perhaps to help Michelle, or perhaps because of her own growing interest, Leni decides to accept the offer of Werner, the German officer in charge of counterintelligence, and visits

his chateau. Meanwhile, thugs in the French underground learn of Michelle's betrayal and kill her. Then they seek to coerce Leni to take Michelle's place and to obtain the map to the German arsenal. When Leni learns of the German atrocities, she agrees to help. However, Werner convinces her that the Germans are really seeking to release the masses from the control of the elite in society, and she ends up killing the head of the French underground. She is then shot and dies in Werner's arms, singing.

Though he is entertained, Valentín denounces the film as Nazi propaganda. Molina protests that life itself is painful and must be filled with dreams. When Valentín insists, over his protests, that Molina take the larger helping of food, Molina becomes ill and goes to the infirmary. When he returns, he continues telling film stories, and the two men become closer. They continue to argue over what it means to be a man and over the possibilities for change in the world.

Molina recounts another film, this time a horror film with romantic overtones. People are becoming zombies. The beautiful heroine learns that her husband's first wife, who is now trying to help her escape, is a zombie, too. Molina's telling of the story is confused, and he mixes up many details.

Molina is called to see the warden, who reminds him that Molina's mother is quite ill and that he will be released sooner if he gets Valentín to reveal secrets about the revolutionaries. Molina goes back to the cell with several bags of wonderful food, supposedly a gift from his mother. Next it is Valentín's turn to become sick from the prison food, which was poisoned both times, and he gets terrible diarrhea. He is mortified and amazed when Molina cleans him without complaint.

A new prisoner is brought into the cell across from them, and Valentín reveals that the new inmate is the Dr. Americo he tried to help. The warden complains that Molina is not getting enough information, so Molina suggests that he be released in the hope that Valentín, who by now likes him, will suddenly reveal more. The warden agrees.

That evening Molina tells a new story about a beautiful woman on a tropical island ensnared in a web that grows from her own body. She nurses back to health a shipwrecked man, who then sees a tear streaming down her face. The two men have an important conversation in which Molina reveals that he is in love with Valentín. Valentín, in turn, shows that he respects Molina and recognizes his kindness. On this last evening of Molina's confinement, they have sexual relations.

The next morning, Valentín tells Molina how to contact his revolutionary friends and asks him to pass along a message. Molina is frightened, but he decides to take this bold step. On the outside, he is reunited with his friends, who call him Luisa, and with his long-suffering mother. After a few days, he contacts Lidia and a meeting is arranged. Molina is followed by the police, however, and the revolutionaries kill him when they think he betrayed them.

In prison, Valentín is once again tortured, this time so severely that he is taken to the infirmary. A sympathetic nurse gives him a large shot of morphine, and Valentín slips into a dream that combines his own memories of Marta with Molina's memories of romantic movies.

Critical Evaluation:

Made into a stage play, a Hollywood feature film, and a very successful Broadway musical, this novel is Manuel Puig's most famous. Some say that it is also his most accomplished, using all his characteristic techniques in a way that remains accessible to the ordinary reader and coupling them with themes that are the closest to the author's heart.

Puig was born in rural Argentina in 1932 and attended the University of Buenos Aires and film school. In 1956, he moved to London and then Rome, where he worked as an assistant film director. He returned to Buenos Aires and worked as a director for a year but then moved to New York, where he took up permanent residence. His novels reflect his early life in the rural countryside, where he spent most of his time watching films made during the 1930's and 1940's. His experience with the simple people with whom he matured shaped the sorts of characters he includes in his novels. His studies and his travels, however, prepared him for the sophisticated techniques and daring themes that make his writing stand out in contemporary literature.

Kiss of the Spider Woman is a story without a narrator, and much of it reads like a movie script without definite indications of who is speaking. The variety of types of discourse is part of Puig's charm as a writer, and *Kiss of the Spider Woman* includes dream sequences, remembrances of film clips, official police reports, snatches of letters, interviews, and, most strangely, interminable footnotes. The effect is to force the reader to become involved in the act of creation, as if Molina is there recounting a story for the reader to visualize. In reading the novel, one is actually having an experience similar to that of the characters; one is lifted out of the chair and taken to many imaginary places. Using such metafictional techniques, Puig thus calls attention to the book as a product, as something put together by a real person.

Of more importance, however, are the novel's themes, which were so disturbing to the Argentine government that the book was banned until the military government was overthrown. Puig himself had more hope for influencing relations between individuals than for changing society itself, but in this novel he makes an attempt to marry the two. Molina, as a gay male in Argentina, has always been an outcast in society. To compensate for that exclusion from the world of significance, he and his friends live their lives in romantic illusion. Valentín, on the other hand, dedicates himself to the Marxist ideal of a classless society. In pursuit of that goal, the needs of any one individual are seen as less important than those of the larger, anonymous group. In their cell, the two men must find some accommodation for these two conflicting approaches to life. Valentín comes to accept a broader definition of masculinity, and Molina learns that he can assume responsibility for changing an unjust society.

Although Puig's treatment of this topic is unique, especially within South American literature, he was criticized by members of the homosexual community for choosing a stereotypically effeminate spokesperson for the gay male. He was also criticized by various feminists for the stereotypical, and practically invisible, role that women play in the novel. However, Puig includes much information that educates the reader on the challenges faced by the homosexual community. As a gay man himself, Puig said that he included the controversial footnotes, which offer an abbreviated history of psychoanalytic interpretations of the meaning of homosexuality, to bring the information to the attention of a large reading public that might not otherwise give it much consideration. By concluding that supposed history with an unknown psychiatrist, Puig more or less puts himself in the picture and speaks through that "character." Significantly, this last speaker seems to lay the groundwork for the sort of political action that Molina ultimately decides to undertake.

On the structural level, the scientific footnotes distance the reader from the story and offer a reminder that the entertainment being provided, much like the films that Molina recounts, will ultimately dissolve into thin air. The problems that the story depicts, however, will not. The reader is also reminded that there are different types of truth, just as there are the various types of discourse embodied in the book.

There is the supposedly objective truth of science and the more inclusive truth that can be adequately explored only in art.

"Critical Evaluation" by John C. Hawley

Further Reading

Bacarisse, Pamela. *Impossible Choices: The Implications of the Cultural References in the Novels of Manuel Puig.* Calgary, Alta.: University of Calgary Press, 1993. An excellent critical study of Puig's work, in which Bacarisse focuses on the references to American films and to other elements of popular culture in his writings. Includes bibliography and index.

Balderston, Daniel, and Francine Masiello, eds. *Approaches to Teaching Puig's "Kiss of the Spider Woman."* New York: Modern Language Association of America, 2007. Although intended for teachers, the essays in this book contain useful analytical information for students and others who are interested in learning more about *Kiss of the Spider Woman.* Includes discussions of "entangled setting, stories, and secrets," narrative voices, and the construction of meaning in the novel; the novel's reception; the film adaptation of the novel; and revolution and sexuality in Argentina in the 1960's and 1970's.

Boccia, Michael. "Versions (Con-, In-, and Per-) in Manuel Puig's and Hector Babenco's *Kiss of the Spider Woman,* Novel and Film." *Modern Fiction Studies* 32, no. 3 (1986): 417-426. Discusses Puig's fascination with film and the history of the novel's development as it went from book to screen. Notes how the plot turns on an inversion of the relationship of the two men.

Chabot Davis, Kimberly. *Postmodern Texts and Emotional Audiences.* West Lafayette, Ind.: Purdue University Press, 2007. Analyzes the novel and film adaptation of *Kiss of the Spider Woman* focusing on their combination of sentimentality and postmodernism. Chabot Davis maintains this combination intensifies political engagement by moving audiences to identify emotionally with people across a range of genders, sexual identities, races, and ethnicities.

Colas, Santiago. *Postmodernity in Latin America: The Argentine Paradigm.* Durham, N.C.: Duke University Press, 1994. Puig is included in this study of postmodern literature, which also examines the writings of Julio Cortázar and Ricardo Piglia. Colas devotes two chapters to *Kiss of the Spider Woman,* placing the novel within the context of Argentine politics.

Echavarrén, Roberto. "Manuel Puig: Beyond Identity." *World Literature Today* 65, no. 4 (1991): 581-585. Discusses the novel as Puig's most radical effort at gay liberation. This issue of *World Literature Today* contains many other articles celebrating Puig's life and works.

Levine, Suzanne Jill. *Manuel Puig and the Spider Woman: His Life and Fictions.* Madison: University of Wisconsin Press, 2001. A full-length biography by one of Puig's translators. Levine combines her personal knowledge of Puig with her research to focus on the intersections of his life and his art.

Review of Contemporary Fiction 11, no. 3 (1991). This special edition of the journal, published on the occasion of Manuel Puig's early death, contains tributes from other writers and provocative articles that examine *Kiss of the Spider Woman* as unique among prison literature.

Rice-Sayre, Laura. "Domination and Desire: A Feminist-Materialist Reading of Manuel Puig's *Kiss of the Spider Woman.*" In *Textual Analysis: Some Readers Reading,* edited by Mary Ann Caws. New York: Modern Language Association of America, 1986. Demonstrates how the novel explores the connections between emotion, politics, and sexuality. Notes how Puig condemns society as based upon aggression and humiliation and proposes a respect for difference.

Tittler, Jonathan. *Manuel Puig.* New York: Twayne, 1993. Provides an excellent account of the writing of *Kiss of the Spider Woman,* summarizes its plot, and discusses critical responses to it. Situates the book among Puig's other works and describes it as his most complete novel because it addresses his principal issues in the most satisfying way.

The Kitchen God's Wife

Author: Amy Tan (1952-   )
First published: 1991
Type of work: Novel
Type of plot: Autobiographical
Time of plot: 1925-1990
Locale: San Francisco Bay Area; Shanghai, China, and environs

Principal characters:
WINNIE LOUIE, a Chinese immigrant
PEARL LOUIE BRANDT, her daughter
HELEN KWONG, her friend
WEN FU, her first husband
JIMMY LOUIE, her second husband
GRAND AUNTIE DU, Helen's elderly aunt
LONG JIAGUO, Helen's first husband
PEANUT, Winnie's cousin

The Story:

Since the death of Jimmy Louie, the father of Pearl Louie Brandt, Pearl and her mother, Winnie Louis, have had a difficult relationship, and Pearl has not told her mother about her struggle with multiple sclerosis. Winnie's friend Helen Kwong tells Pearl that she knows about her multiple sclerosis and threatens to reveal it to Winnie if Pearl does not disclose it herself by the Chinese New Year.

Helen's aunt, Grand Auntie Du, soon dies, leaving Pearl an altar to the Kitchen God. Because Pearl has never heard of the Kitchen God, Winnie tells her his story. She explains that the Kitchen God was once a rich man with a hard-working wife. However, he had abandoned his wife and wasted all the money. Finally reduced to a beggar, the man received charity from a kind woman, only to learn she was his wronged wife. Embarrassed, he jumped into a fire and burned to death. As a reward for admitting that he had been wrong, the Jade Emperor asked him to spy on families and report whether they deserve good luck or bad. Winnie expresses distaste for the Kitchen God and removes him from the altar, promising she will replace him with a more appropriate god.

A few days later, Helen gives Winnie some news: Winnie's first husband, Wen Fu, has died. Seeing this as an opportunity to tell the truth about the past, Helen gives Winnie the same ultimatum she had given to Pearl, telling her to share her secrets with her daughter. Winnie initially resists, but after some thought she invites Pearl to her house and tells her life story.

In 1925, Winnie is a young Chinese girl named Jiang Weili. After her mother runs away, Weili's wealthy father sends her away to live with her uncle and aunts. Several years later, at a public play, Weili and her cousin Peanut meet a confident, charismatic man named Wen Fu, who arranges a marriage with Weili. Weili's father bestows upon her a dowry of money and furniture that will belong to her alone; it also will be the only money she receives for the rest of her life.

Wen Fu is a pilot in the air force, so he and Weili must move to Hangzhou so that he can fight the invading Japanese. Wen Fu begins to abuse Weili, raping and humiliating her every night. Weili also meets and becomes friends with Hulan (Helen), who is married to Long Jiaguo, a vice captain. As World War II begins, the pilots and their wives must move to different parts of China, first Yangzhou, then Nanking, and finally Kunming. In Nanking, Wen Fu appropriates and wastes some of the dowry money that Weili had set aside for an emergency. They escape from Nanking just before the Japanese invade. In Kunming, Wen Fu's behavior toward Weili worsens. At one point, he confronts her in public, forcing her to kneel and apologize. Nobody intervenes on her behalf.

Weili gives birth, and the baby becomes strange because of Wen Fu's abuse. She dies after Wen Fu refuses to allow a doctor to treat her dysentery. While Weili is in the hospital giving birth to their next child, Danru, Wen Fu allows his mistress to live in their home. The mistress becomes pregnant, leading Weili to ask for a divorce. Wen Fu refuses to sign the papers.

Weili, Wen Fu, Hulan, and Jiaguo attend a dance given by the American Volunteer Group. There, they meet a Chinese American translator, Jimmy Louie, who gives Hulan and Weili American names, Helen and Winnie. Jimmy and Weili dance. At home, an enraged Wen Fu forces Weili, at gunpoint, to make up divorce papers, then he rapes her. The next morning, she takes the papers and leaves with Danru, but Hulan reveals her whereabouts to Wen Fu, forcing Weili to return.

Four years later, the war ends. Weili and Wen Fu return to her father's house in Shanghai to find it in disrepair. Hoping for advice on escaping her marriage, Weili seeks out Peanut, who has abandoned her marriage to become a communist in a house of like-minded women. On the way, Weili meets Jimmy and has a long conversation with him, during which

Jimmy reveals that he wishes to marry her. With Peanut's help, Weili and Danru escape and live with Jimmy. Weili sends Danru to stay with Hulan and Grand Auntie Du so that he will be safe from Wen Fu. Both Danru and Jiaguo die in an epidemic.

Wen Fu uses Danru's death as an excuse to have Weili arrested for stealing his son. Because Weili cannot produce her divorce papers, she is found guilty and sent to prison. She is there for a year before Auntie Du procures her release by hinting to prison officials that Weili is related to powerful communists, who are about to take over Shanghai.

Weili sends Jimmy a telegram with the news of her release from prison, and he sends back money and a U.S. visa. She buys airplane tickets, but still wants to secure her divorce from Wen Fu. She and her friends trick him and force him to sign the paper, but he follows Weili home afterward, destroys the document, and rapes her at gunpoint. Nine months later, in the United States, Pearl is born.

Winnie finishes telling her story to daughter Pearl, leaving unresolved the question of whether Wen Fu is Pearl's father. Pearl reveals her own secret, her multiple sclerosis. She, Helen, and Winnie plan a trip to China to find medicine for Pearl. Winnie finds an unnamed goddess—the Kitchen God's Wife, renamed Lady Sorrowfree—to replace the Kitchen God on Pearl's altar.

Critical Evaluation:

Amy Tan, born in Oakland, California, as the daughter of two Chinese immigrants, gained both popular and critical acclaim by writing about relationships between Chinese immigrants and their American-born children. *The Kitchen God's Wife*, Tan's second novel, shares many incidents with the life of her mother, Daisy Tan, who had escaped an abusive marriage to come to the United States.

The Kitchen God's Wife is written in first person from two different perspectives. Pearl Louie Brandt's voice introduces the novel and takes up the narrative again near the end, providing a frame narrative for her mother's story. The bulk of the novel, however, is Winnie Louie's story and is told in her voice. Winnie often interrupts her own story to explain Chinese words, to ask for Pearl's approval, or to compare her understanding of the past with that of Helen Kwong, her close friend. These interruptions serve to emphasize that Winnie is finally telling her own story after being silenced for most of her life; they also remind the reader that the story is being told orally, allowing the novel to draw on the traditional talk-story. Talk stories constitute an oral genre that transmits crucial cultural information within a family context, a particularly appropriate genre for a novel that also retells a tale in the

oral tradition, that of the Kitchen God. Finally, by reminding the readers that they are "listening in" on a story that Pearl is hearing, Winnie's self-interruptions create a cozy family setting that contrasts strongly with the harsh realities of Winnie's first marriage.

Tan's style in the frame narrative adheres closely to standard American English, but during Winnie's narrative, Tan attempts to re-create the vivid and compelling, if imperfect, English spoken by her mother. To this end, she uses an abundance of descriptive detail, along with simple sentences with occasional syntactic irregularities and a few Chinese words that do not translate exactly. These strategies serve both to strengthen the reader's sense of Winnie's character and to validate the kind of English that she speaks. Some critics have objected to Tan's use of Chinese-seeming details as reinforcing a stereotyped American image of China, but others maintain that—by critiquing the role of the United States in World War II; by allowing Peanut, a communist, to take a positive role; and by highlighting Winnie's marginalized position even in the United States—the novel poses a challenge to those stereotypes.

The Kitchen God's Wife also is a feminist retelling of the Kitchen God's story. In the original story, the focus is on the Kitchen God, who is not only forgiven but also rewarded for his bad behavior, while his wife is an unnamed figure who never speaks and whose suffering is never redressed. In contrast, *The Kitchen God's Wife* allows the abused wife to tell her own story and recognizes her strength. Wen Fu, the real-life equivalent of the Kitchen God, is portrayed as a monster, whom Winnie attempts to forgive but ultimately cannot. Where the Kitchen God's wife is casually cast aside, Winnie achieves agency by actively rejecting her husband on several occasions.

Other feminist themes also appear in the novel. Wen Fu's abuse of Winnie is supported by a patriarchal Chinese society that gives the husband authority over his wife. Winnie's friends and neighbors refuse to intervene when she is abused in public, and they ignore her complaints, even when her daughter is dying. In contrast, Wen Fu is believed, unquestioningly, when he confronts Winnie in court and claims she is a thief, a kidnapper, and a neglectful mother. In the novel, resistance to patriarchy comes primarily from positive relationships among women; the support of female friends is necessary to relieve Winnie's sufferings. Although Jimmy Louie plays a role in helping Winnie to escape her marriage, it is her female cousin Peanut who provides her with the encouragement and advice that she needs to leave Wen Fu. Winnie is released from jail with the help of Grand Auntie Du, and it is Auntie Du, Helen, and their friend Betty who help her to get her revenge on Wen Fu. Even Wen Fu's concubine, whom patriarchal standards suggest Winnie should see as a rival, surreptitiously becomes a friend. At other times, however, women work to uphold the status quo, as when Helen reveals Winnie's hiding place to an enraged Wen Fu.

As Winnie speaks, she is drawing on her own memories, aware that there are gaps in both her memory and her knowledge. By admitting that Helen would tell these stories differently, Winnie acknowledges that differences in perspective may influence the way that history is remembered; still, she insists on the validity of her own marginalized experiences. She knows that official versions of the truth, like Wen Fu's story in court, can be used against her, and she partly counteracts this "official" truth by telling her own story. This story had been silenced both in China and in the United States. In China, it had been repressed by the unquestioned power of Wen Fu's voice. In the United States, Winnie cannot tell her story because of a complex combination of factors, including the language barrier, her immigrant status, and a myopic American culture in which there is little scope for understanding her experiences. Ultimately, she tells her story in a domestic, private space and only to Pearl, but by telling it, she bridges the cultural distance between herself and her American-born daughter.

Nancy Foasberg

Further Reading

Adams, Bella. *Amy Tan*. New York: Manchester University Press, 2005. This study of Tan's work includes an excellent introduction and a chapter on *The Kitchen God's Wife*. Adams argues that Winnie's difficulty in telling her own story creates a powerful critique of the forces that would silence her.

Bloom, Harold, ed. *Amy Tan*. New York: Bloom's Literary Criticism, 2009. A collection of some of the most important articles on Tan, including several on *The Kitchen God's Wife*. Provides a range of perspectives on many topics in Tan's work in general and *The Kitchen God's Wife* in particular.

Ho, Wendy. *In Her Mother's House: The Politics of Asian American Mother-Daughter Writing*. Walnut Creek, Calif.: AltaMira Press, 1999. Includes two chapters that address Tan's fiction specifically: "Losing Your Innocence but Not Your Hope: Amy Tan's Joy Luck Mothers and Coca-Cola Daughters," and "The Heart Never Travels: The Incorporation of Fathers in the Mother-Daughter Stories of Maxine Hong Kingston, Amy Tan, and Fae Myenne Ng."

Huntley, E. D. "*The Kitchen God's Wife*." In *Amy Tan: A Critical Companion*. Westport, Conn.: Greenwood Press, 1998. This critical study of Tan's work devotes a chapter to an analysis of each of her novels, including *The Kitchen God's Wife*. In each case, an alternate reading is also provided.

Snodgrass, Mary Ellen. *Amy Tan: A Literary Companion*. Jefferson, N.C.: McFarland, 2004. A reference work in which Tan's novels, characters, and themes are arranged alphabetically, providing in each case an overview and a bibliography for further research. The appendixes include a chronology and a glossary of Chinese words used in her fiction.

Tan, Amy. *The Opposite of Fate: A Book of Musings*. New York: G. P. Putnam, 2003. A collection of Tan's essays on writing. Among other topics, she describes *The Kitchen God's Wife* as the story of her mother's life and discusses her status as a renowned Chinese American writer.

The Kite Runner

Author: Khaled Hosseini (1965-   )
First published: 2003
Type of work: Novel
Type of plot: Bildungsroman and historical realism
Time of plot: 1960's to early twenty-first century
Locale: Afghanistan, Pakistan, and the United States

Principal characters:
AMIR, an Afghan boy
HASSAN, his family's servant
ALI, Hassan's father
BABA, Amir's father
RAHIM KHAN, Baba's friend
ASSEF, a neighborhood bully
SORAYA, Amir's wife
SOHRAB, Hassan's son

The Story:

Amir lives with his father, Baba, in Kabul, Afghanistan. His mother, who had died during childbirth, had left behind a collection of Sufi literature. From early childhood, Amir likes to read stories from her books to his servant and playmate, Hassan. While Amir is privileged and able to go to school, Hassan is busy with housework. However, in their free time they are good friends. To commemorate these happy times, Amir carves their names on a pomegranate tree.

Living in a single-parent home, Amir yearns for his father's attention and gets jealous of Hassan when his father bestows favors on Hassan, favors like arranging cosmetic surgery for his harelip. Amir's desire for his father's affection also stems from his father's indifference toward his son's interest in books. When it is time for the local kite-flying contest, Amir gets excited because he knows that his father will be watching him with genuine interest.

Hassan is excited about the contest, too, and after Amir wins, Hassan runs and catches the prizewinning kite for his friend. Unfortunately, the neighborhood bully, Assef, and his companions stop Hassan and demand the kite from him. Hassan does not surrender the kite and is physically assaulted and raped by Assef. Amir sees the assault but, fearing confrontation with the bully, does nothing—an act of betrayal that will affect Amir into adulthood and forever change his relationship with Hassan.

Both Amir and Hassan know the social gap that defines their identities. In Afghan culture, Amir is a Pashtun and Hassan is a Hazara, which makes him a servant. Religious difference also sets them apart, even though they both are Muslim: Amir is Sunni, and Hassan is Shia. Pashtuns, the majority ethnic group in Afghanistan, make fun of Hazaras, a minority ethnic group, treating them as pariahs. Children taunt Hassan's father, Ali, as "a slant-eyed donkey," and Assef insults Hassan as a "flat-nosed" Hazara who does not belong in Afghanistan.

Amir is not disturbed with his servant-master friendship until the kite incident. Even as a twelve-year-old kid, he is old enough to know that he has not been good. Hassan's presence reminds him of his own guilt, so he asks his father to get new servants. Baba refuses but, instead, frames Hassan, accusing him of theft; Hassan and his father leave Kabul. A few years later, because of the Russian invasion, Baba and Amir secretly leave Kabul, too. They cross the border into Pakistan after a difficult journey and emigrate to the United States.

Baba adjusts to the cultural and economic challenges of living in the United States and is happy with Amir's educational success. Amir had majored in English to pursue a writing career, his childhood dream. On weekends, he helps his father sell at the local flea market, where he meets Soraya, the daughter of an expatriate Afghan general. Amir and Soraya soon fall in love, and Amir's father makes lavish arrangements for a grand wedding. Baba, who has been suffering from cancer, dies one month after the wedding.

Amir and Soraya are happy together, but they remain childless for many years. Twenty years later Amir is a successful novelist in the United States. An old friend of his father, Rahim Khan, calls Amir on the phone and invites him to Pakistan. Amir meets him and soon learns that Baba had sold his home to Rahim. Rahim had then brought back Hassan and his family to live with him. Unfortunately, in Rahim's absence, Talibs had come to the house and shot Hassan and his wife; their son, Sohrab, ended up in an orphanage.

Rahim also reveals that Hassan was actually Baba's son, and Amir's half-brother. Amir is outraged by this belated discovery, but he also recalls his own guilt. Thus, he embarks on a dangerous journey to Afghanistan to atone his past sins and to rescue Sohrab, his nephew.

Afghanistan is now under the oppressive control of the Taliban. After a great deal of searching, Amir meets a Talib, who agrees to arrange a meeting with Sohrab. Amir goes to the appointed place and recognizes Assef, the neighborhood bully from their younger days, who is now a Talib; Assef practically owns Sohrab. Assef says he will release Sohrab only if Amir will engage in one-on-one physical combat with him, and win. In this mismatched fight, Amir is seriously injured. Sohrab hits Assef in the eye with something fired from his slingshot, and Amir and Sohrab manage to escape.

Sohrab and Amir flee to Pakistan, and Amir is hospitalized. He plans to return to the United States with Sohrab after he recovers from his injuries, but because he is not a legal guardian of the child, he cannot obtain a U.S. visa for him. A lawyer advises Amir that to legally adopt Sohrab, it would be necessary to place Sohrab in an orphanage. When Amir reveals this plan to Sohrab, the child is devastated and feels betrayed; Amir had promised him that he would never send him to an orphanage. Sohrab attempts suicide, and Amir finds his nephew's body in the bathroom, covered with blood. Amir screams for help and vows to become a devout Muslim if God will spare Sohrab's life. Sohrab lives, but he no longer talks or smiles.

Finally, Amir is able to return to the United States with Sohrab after Soraya obtains a humanitarian visa for the child. The couple do their best to make Sohrab happy in his new home, and Amir forbids his father-in-law from ever referring to Sohrab as a Hazara. Later, Sohrab shows signs of a faint smile as Amir runs after a prizewinning kite.

Critical Evaluation:

The Kite Runner is Khaled Hosseini's first novel. Born in Kabul, Hosseini draws heavily on his own experiences to create the setting for the novel; the characters, however, are fictional. Hosseini's plot shows historical realism, as the novel includes dates—for chronological accuracy, including the time of the changing regimes of Afghanistan. Amir's happy childhood days fall under the peaceful and affluent era of King Zahir Shah's reign, a time when Amir and his friend, Hassan, could themselves feel like kings of Kabul, carving their names into a tree. In 1973, Dawood Khan becomes the president of Afghanistan. This era is reflected in the novel when the local bully, Assef, harasses Amir with his brass knuckles and hopes that Hazaras will be eliminated.

The Russian invasion in 1981 turns Kabul into a war zone, forcing many residents, including Baba and Amir, to escape to Pakistan. Even after the Russians had left the country, the unrest had continued. In 1996, the Talibs had come to power. In the novel, Rahim Khan tells Amir that Talibs had banned kite fighting in 1996 and that in 1998, Hazaras had been massacred.

The novel's complex plot consists of several conflicts that evoke sympathy for characters who are unjustly victimized. The story begins with the internal conflicts of Amir—a wealthy child—who enjoys Hassan's friendship but is also jealous of him and ends up cheating him. An external conflict occurs between the protagonist, Amir, and the antagonist, Assef. Amir goes to Afghanistan to rescue his nephew Sohrab, as "a way to be good again," but encounters Assef, a vindictive and cruel enemy from the past, and now a ruling Talib.

A final conflict shows the gap between the legal system and the human rights of orphans as victims of war, a gap that leads to Sohrab's attempted suicide. Intrinsic to the conflicts in the novel is the unjust victimization of the innocent—a theme evoking the import of human rights across international boundaries.

Hosseini succeeds in striking the right balance between tragic emotion and optimism. For example, the narrator drops clues that Sohrab will talk again "almost a year" after his suicide attempt. Similarly, Sohrab's faint smile in the novel's last scene is a clue that he will be happy with his new guardians. Hosseini's imagery also is powerful and layered with meaning. For example, Sohrab hitting Assef with slingshot fire is a befitting image that shows the triumph of the weak and lowly over the high and mighty—a modern David and Goliath tale.

Another successful aspect of the novel is characterization. When Amir's character transforms, he is willing to risk his life for Sohrab. In contrast, Assef claims a religious conversion but shows no change of character. Some critics find fault with Hosseini's one-dimensional characterization of Assef as a stereotyped Talib who is inhumane and tyrannical. However, the novel is written from a first-person narrator's viewpoint. Amir is the narrator for twenty-four chapters, and Rahim Khan narrates the events of the past in chapter 16. Both narrators can report only their respective experiences, and both paint a tragic picture of Taliban atrocities.

Unique to Hosseini is his artistic ability to blend the literary tradition of the Western novel with the Persian literature of the Sufis. The novel includes consistent references to the Persian legend of Rostam and Sohrab, which comes from Persian poet Firdusi's *Shahnamah* (c. 1010), the poetic epic of Afghanistan, Iran, and other Persian-speaking countries. These references serve to exemplify the novel's theme, a classic one, of the quest for the father. Other parallels with the Persian epic are *The Kite Runner*'s ironic revelations about the past, the novel's war-zone setting, and the novel's tragic irony associated with the ignorance of many of its characters. Tragic irony is a vehicle for revelation, and it also serves as a rhetorical strategy to validate the narrator's claim: "I've learned . . . [how] the past claws its way out." Likewise, tragic irony becomes a rhetorical strategy for comparing and contrasting characters' behaviors as they manipulate knowledge and claim ignorance in their relationships. For example, Amir's childish ploys to get rid of Hassan and his father, Ali, culminate in a tragic scene, in which "Hassan knew . . . everything. . . . He knew I had betrayed him and yet he was rescuing me once again." Hassan would not expose to Baba that Amir was actually a liar and a cheater. This marks a critical moment in Amir's life because he realizes that he loves Hassan, "more than he had loved anyone else"; still, Amir cannot confess the truth and will never again see Hassan.

The Kite Runner is a powerful story about two boys whose friendship is threatened by deception and betrayal yet withstands the pressures of cultural barriers and legal boundaries. Their childhood memories of happy days outlast their tragic separation, and the steadfast loyalty of Hassan defines the theme of this novel as one of true friendship.

Mabel Khawaja

Further Reading

Aubry, Timothy. "Afghanistan Meets the Amazon: Reading *The Kite Runner* in America." *PMLA* 124, no. 1 (2009): 25-43. An analysis of data collected from reader reviews of *The Kite Runner* on the Web site Amazon.com. Presents divergent interpretations. Also discusses the relevance of the novel in a post-September 11, 2001, political environment in the United States.

Bloom, Harold, ed. *Khaled Hosseini's "The Kite Runner."* New York: Bloom's Literary Criticism, 2009. Comprehensive study guide on *The Kite Runner* with essays written especially for students in grades 9 through 12. Part of the Bloom's Guides series of analyses of classic works of literature.

Goldblatt, Patricia D. "Exploring Ethics: The Role of Multicultural Narrative." *MultiCultural Review* 16, no. 2 (2009): 40-44. This source provides a summary and literary analysis of *The Kite Runner* and two other novels. Each analysis is followed by suggested teaching techniques that encourage students to search for deeper meaning in interpreting the respective works.

Hosseini, Khaled. "Kabul's Splendid Son: Interview with Khaled Hosseini." *Mother Jones* 34, no. 3 (2009): 74-75. This magazine article includes a brief biographical sketch of Hosseini. In the interview, Hosseini deplores the impoverished condition of Afghans living in a war-torn country.

_____. *The Kite Runner.* New York: Riverhead Books, 2005. This edition of the novel begins with a number of quotations from leading newspapers and magazines praising Hosseini's art of storytelling. The book also includes a reader's guide with discussion points and questions based on a reading of the novel.

Katsoulis, Melissa. "Kites of Passage: New Fiction." *The Times* (London), August 30, 2003. A brief review of Hosseini's novel *The Kite Runner* in a renowned British periodical.

Thomson, Patricia. "Honoring a Friend: Roberto Schaefer, ASC, Helps Bring the Best-selling Novel *The Kite Runner* to Screen." *American Cinematographer* 88, no. 11 (November, 2007): 57-61. An informative article about the motion picture based on the novel. Includes color visuals of characters and scenes from the film as well as details about special cinematic effects and filming locations.

The Knight of the Burning Pestle

Author: Francis Beaumont (c. 1584-1616)
First produced: 1607; first published, 1613
Type of work: Drama
Type of plot: Comedy
Time of plot: Early seventeenth century
Locale: England and Moldavia

Principal characters:
GEORGE, a London greengrocer
NELL, his wife
RALPH, an apprentice to George
VENTUREWELL, a London merchant
JASPER MERRYTHOUGHT, his apprentice
MASTER HUMPHREY, a slow-witted youth
LUCE, Venturewell's daughter
MERRYTHOUGHT, a carefree old gentleman

The Story:

A production in a London theater is abruptly interrupted when George, a greengrocer, declares that he wants to see a new kind of play, one in which the common man of London is glorified. Sitting beside him in the audience, George's wife, Nell, further suggests that there be a grocer in the play and that he kill a lion with a pestle. The indulgent speaker of the prologue agrees to these demands after George offers his apprentice, Ralph, to play the part of the commoner-hero. The play begins.

For presuming to love Luce Venturewell, the daughter of his master, apprentice Jasper Merrythought is discharged. Old Venturewell chooses Master Humphrey, a foolish young citizen, for his daughter, but Luce, in league with Jasper, tells

the gullible Humphrey that to win her love he must abduct her and take her to Waltham Forest, where she plans to meet Jasper. In the audience, Nell, the grocer's wife, comments that Humphrey is a fine young man.

In a grocer's shop, Ralph reads a chivalric romance and, yearning for the olden times, determines himself to become a knight-errant. He enlists his two apprentices, Tim and George, to be his foils: the one, his squire, the other, his dwarf. Dubbing himself the Knight of the Burning Pestle, Ralph explains the rules of knight-errantry to his amused followers. Nell, pleased with Ralph's first appearance on the stage, clamors for his immediate return.

Jasper goes home and collects his patrimony—all of ten

shillings—from his indigent but carefree father, old Merry-thought. Mrs. Merrythought, sick of hard times, packs her few valuables into a small chest and, with her younger son, Michael, leaves home to seek a better fortune. In the pit, George and Nell grow impatient for the reappearance of Ralph, their prodigious apprentice. Simple-minded Humphrey tells old Venturewell of Luce's whimsical conditions for their marriage, and the old man consents to the plan. Mrs. Merrythought and Michael, traveling afoot, arrive in Waltham Forest. While resting, they grow frightened and run away when Ralph, as the Knight of the Burning Pestle, appears with his retainers. George and Nell, from their places at the edge of the stage, shout a welcome to Ralph. Ralph, assuming that Mrs. Merrythought fled from some evil knight, follows her in order to rescue her from her distress. Jasper, arriving in the forest to meet Luce, picks up the casket containing Mrs. Merrythought's valuables. Nell, scandalized, declares that she will tell Ralph what Jasper did. When Mrs. Merrythought reports her loss to Ralph, he, in extravagantly courteous language, promises to assist her in regaining her valuables. George and Nell commend themselves for having trained such a polite and virtuous apprentice.

Humphrey and Luce come also to the forest, where they find Jasper waiting. Jasper, after thrashing Humphrey soundly, departs with Luce. George and Nell, sorry for Humphrey, offer to call back Ralph to fight Jasper. The protests of the theater boy notwithstanding, the grocer and his wife want to change the plot to see Jasper properly punished. Ralph immediately abandons his search for Mrs. Merrythought's valuables and sets out after the runaways. Overtaking them, he challenges Jasper in the language of knight-errantry. Nell, at this juncture, exhorts Ralph to break Jasper's head. Jasper, taking Ralph's pestle from him, knocks down the Knight of the Burning Pestle. George tries to explain Ralph's defeat by saying that Jasper is endowed with magical powers.

Ralph, his retainers, Mrs. Merrythought, and Michael put up for the night at the Bell Inn in Waltham. When they mistake the inn for a castle, the innkeeper indulgently joins them in their make-believe. Humphrey, meanwhile, returns to old Venturewell, to whom he complains of his treatment at the hands of Jasper. Irate, Venturewell goes to old Merrythought and threatens to kill Jasper. George and Nell at this point are so taken with the plot of the play that they believe it to be real. Old Merrythought, carefree as usual, pays no heed to Venturewell's vengeful threats. That night, while Luce is asleep in Waltham Forest, Jasper decides to test her love for him. Drawing his sword, he arouses the girl with threats that he intends to kill her because her father discharged him. Nell excitedly urges George to raise the London watch, to

prevent what appears to her to be certain violence. As Luce trustingly submits to Jasper's threats, Venturewell, Humphrey, and their men appear and rescue her. Jasper, hopeful that he might somehow explain his behavior to Luce, follows them.

Next morning, at the Bell Inn, Ralph, unable to pay the reckoning, is threatened by the landlord. George gives Ralph twelve shillings so that he can pay. Mrs. Merrythought and Michael, disenchanted, go home. Ralph, still in search of romantic adventure, is directed by the innkeeper to a barbershop in the town, where, he says, a giant named Barbaroso commits enormities every day. At this point Mrs. Merrythought returns to the stage, only to be dragged off by George and Nell, who cannot wait to see Ralph's fight with the barber.

Ralph, after challenging the barber to mortal combat, knocks him down. While he begs for mercy, Ralph directs his retainers to liberate the barber's victims. One is a knight whose face is covered with lather. Another is a man on whom the barber did minor surgery. As other victims appear, the barber is spared on the condition that he no longer subject humans to such indignities. George and Nell beam with pride at Ralph's conquest of the giant Barbaroso, and Nell allows Mrs. Merrythought and Michael to appear on the stage.

Mrs. Merrythought despairs because she is unable to get old Merrythought to have a serious thought. Nell, furious at the old man's carefree indifference, orders a beer to calm her temper. Then the action of the play becomes somewhat too pedestrian for the tastes of George and Nell. The couple next request that Ralph be involved in a truly exotic adventure. Ralph suddenly finds himself an honored guest at the court of Moldavia. Courteously rejecting Princess Pompiana's favors, he declares that he was promised to Susan, the daughter of a cobbler in London. George gives Ralph a handful of small coins to distribute as largess to the royal household. Nell commends Ralph's loyalty and patriotism in preferring a London girl to a princess of a foreign land.

Luce, meanwhile, is confined to her room with the prospect of marriage to Humphrey in three days' time. Mrs. Merrythought seeks aid, unsuccessfully, from old Venturewell. Venturewell receives a letter of repentance from Jasper, allegedly written by the youth as he lay dying of a broken heart, with the request that his body be conveyed to Luce. Hard upon the letter comes a coffin, which is carried to Luce's room. Jasper, quite alive, springs from the coffin, makes explanations to Luce, places her in the coffin, and has it removed from the room. He hides in the closet. Venturewell, still vengeful, orders the coffin to be delivered to old Merrythought, who by this time is penniless although still merry. George, no respecter of plot, demands that Ralph appear again. Ralph, in the guise of Maylord, presents the month of May to the city of London.

Jasper, meanwhile, covers his face with flour and, appearing as a ghost, tells old Venturewell that he will never see his daughter again. Thoroughly frightened and repentant of his past actions, the old man thrashes Humphrey, who came to see Luce, and sends him away. George and Nell, their interest flagging, demand a diversion in which Ralph will be the center of attention. Ralph appears as a highly efficient captain leading a parade of London volunteers.

The coffin containing Luce is delivered to old Merrythought, who continues to be indifferent. When Jasper appears and reveals Luce's presence, the young people prevail upon old Merrythought to take back Mrs. Merrythought and Michael. Venturewell, still mindful of Jasper's ghost, tells old Merrythought that he forgives all Jasper's transgressions. Jasper and Luce then confront Venturewell, who offers them his blessings. George and Nell, unaware of dramatic proprieties, ask for the stage death of Ralph so that the play can end properly. Ralph, with a forked arrow through his head, delivers an absurd speech about Princess Pompiana and Susan. Highly pleased with the sad ending, Nell invites the audience to partake of tobacco and wine at her house.

Critical Evaluation:

Francis Beaumont, the son of a knight, could well have been cruel in a dramatic treatment of the ordinary citizens of London, but in *The Knight of the Burning Pestle*, he reveals, beneath the hilarious burlesque of the plot, a warm sympathy for and a large understanding of the London lower middle classes, as represented by George, the greengrocer; his wife Nell; and Ralph, their apprentice. An outstanding feature of the play is the farcical audience participation. This device, a startling innovation in 1607, survives to the present day in semidramatic situations of broad humor. *The Knight of the Burning Pestle* was probably written under the influence of the keen interest taken by the literate of James I's time in Spanish prose fiction; surely Beaumont had heard of, if he had not read, Miguel de Cervantes' *Don Quixote de la Mancha* (1605, 1615), echoes of which mark the play.

The prologue to the 1635 Beaumont and Fletcher Folio reprint of *The Knight of the Burning Pestle* makes clear that Beaumont's comedy was innovative when it was first presented about 1607. At that time the theatergoers' rage was all for satires full of "invective . . . touching some particular persons." This mock-heroic play, with its parody of romantic bombast and its warm treatment of the London lower middle class, enjoyed little success until it was revived about 1635; then the aristocratic court audience delighted in its wordplay,

wit, and ingenious construction. *The Knight of the Burning Pestle* has three plots cleverly unified in one: a frame-story concerning George the grocer, his outspoken wife Nell, and his cloddish apprentice Ralph; a mock-romantic play, *The London Merchant*, which parodies stock conventions and concerns Jasper Merrythought, the witty apprentice who loves Luce, Venturewell's comely daughter; and finally a parody of chivalric romances, featuring the apprentice Ralph, now cast as "the right courteous and valiant knight," whose actions are a travesty to heroic traditions.

As Knight of the Burning Pestle, Ralph utters archaic, confused, hyperbolic language as he goes about his business of knight-errantry. Instead of performing brave, wonderful deeds, he confronts a monster who is in reality a barber; instead of being a noble warrior, he is in reality a grocer's boy who is faithful to his profession; instead of marrying a beautiful princess, he remains faithful to his cobbler's maid, Susan. In the end, instead of succeeding, he dies; indeed, he does not even die on stage but walks off with a forked arrow through his head.

Thus the play successfully parodies the whole gamut of romantic and heroic conventions. In addition to Ralph's misadventures, other stock elements of the theater are employed in satirical jest. Jasper and Humphrey are the traditional "rival wooers"; Jasper and Michael are the "double sons." George and Nell consistently support the wrong lover, as they display their lack of artistic sense. Venturewell, the rich London merchant, portrays the typical protective father-figure, just as Luce is the typical independent-minded daughter. Nevertheless, Beaumont's parody of stock theatrical situations and personalities never descends to the level of insult. His intent is to "move inward delight, not outward lightness . . . soft smiling, not loud laughing." Despite this modest disclaimer, *The Knight of the Burning Pestle* is Beaumont's most amusing, inventive comedy.

Further Reading

Appleton, William E. *Beaumont and Fletcher: A Critical Study*. Winchester, Mass.: Allen & Unwin, 1956. Discusses the play as a brilliant burlesque whose humaneness makes it unique. Attributes its initial failure on the stage to Beaumont's misjudging his audience.

Beaumont, Francis. *The Knight of the Burning Pestle*. Edited by Sheldon P. Zitner. New York: Manchester University Press, 1984. A scholarly edition whose lengthy introduction includes a detailed commentary and a review of the play's stage history. Discusses the play's antecedents and innovations.

Bradbrook, Muriel C. *The Growth and Structure of Elizabe-*

than Comedy. London: Chatto & Windus, 1962. A classic study of comic drama from its beginnings at midcentury to 1616, when William Shakespeare died. Many references to Beaumont place his works in the thematic and structural context of the period.

Braunmuller, A. R., and Michael Hattaway, eds. *The Cambridge Companion to English Renaissance Drama.* 2d ed. New York: Cambridge University Press, 2003. This collection of essays discussing various aspects of English Renaissance drama includes numerous references to Beaumont and information about *The Knight of the Burning Pestle.*

Clark, Sandra. *Renaissance Drama.* Cambridge, England: Polity, 2007. This accessible overview of Renaissance drama places Beaumont and his plays, including *The Knight of the Burning Pestle,* in their broader historical context.

Greenfield, Thelma N. *The Induction in Elizabethan Drama.* Eugene: University of Oregon Press, 2001. A study of the frame, or play within a play, device in drama of the period. Greenfield believes that in *The Knight of the Burning Pestle* Beaumont demonstrates the most successful use of the technique, particularly as a means of character development.

The Knights

Author: Aristophanes (c. 450-c. 385 B.C.E.)
First produced: *Hippēs*, 424 B.C.E. (English translation, 1812)
Type of work: Drama
Type of plot: Satire
Time of plot: Fifth century B.C.E.
Locale: Athens

Principal characters:
DEMUS, a slave master, a personification of the Athenian people
DEMOSTHENES, slave of Demus
NICIAS, another slave
CLEON THE PAPHLAGONIAN, a favorite slave and a personification of the Athenian tyrant Cleon
A SAUSAGE SELLER, later called Agoracritus

The Story:

Demus, a selfish and irritable old man, a tyrant to his slaves, purchases a tanner, nicknamed the Paphlagonian. This slave, a fawning, foxy fellow, quickly ingratiates himself with his new master, to the dismay of all the other slaves in Demus's household, Demosthenes and Nicias in particular. As a result of the Paphlagonian's lies, Demosthenes and Nicias receive many floggings. The two at one time consider running away but decide against this course because of the terrible punishment they will receive if caught and returned to their owner. They also consider suicide, but in the end they decide to forget their troubles by tippling. Going for the wine, Nicias finds the Paphlagonian asleep in a drunken stupor.

While the drunken man sleeps, Nicias steals the writings of the sacred oracle that the Paphlagonian guards carefully. In the prophecies of the oracle, Demosthenes and Nicias read that an oakum seller should first manage the state's affairs; he should be followed by a sheep seller, and he in turn should be followed by a tanner. At last the tanner would be overthrown by a sausage seller.

As they are about to set out in search of a sausage seller, a slave of that butcher's trade comes to the house of Demus to sell his wares. Nicias and Demosthenes soon win him over to their cause, flattering him out of all reason and assuring him that his stupidity and ignorance fit him admirably for public life. When the Paphlagonian awakens, he loudly demands the return of the oracle's writings. The sausage seller, however, is able to fight him with success. Spectators become involved. Some of the citizens protest against the Paphlagonian's unjust accusations of the sausage seller. Others claim that the state is falling into ruin while this shameless name-calling continues. Others accuse the Paphlagonian of deafening all Athens with his din. The sausage seller accuses the Paphlagonian of cheating everybody. A few citizens gloat that someone even more arrogant and dishonest than the Paphlagonian is found in the person of the sausage seller. Others fear that this new demagogue will destroy all hope of defending Athens from her enemies.

While the citizens clamor, the sausage seller and the Paphlagonian continue to out-boast, out-shout, and out-orate each other. The sausage seller says that he will make meat-balls out of the Paphlagonian. Demus's pampered slave threatens to twitch the lashes off both the sausage seller's eyes. Demosthenes breaks in to suggest that the sausage seller inspect the Paphlagonian as he would a hog before butchering it.

At last both began to call for Demus, asking him to come out of his house and decide the merits of their claims. When he answers their calls, both boast of a greater love to do him service. Convinced by the assurances of the sausage seller, Demus decides to dismiss the Paphlagonian and demands that his former favorite return his seal of office. The two continue their efforts to bribe Demus for his favor. At last the rivals run to consult the oracles, to prove to Demus the right of their contentions.

Each brings back a load of prophetic writings and insists upon reading them aloud to Demus. In their prophecies they continue to insult one another, at the same time flattering Demus. The sausage seller relates a dream in which Athena comes down from Olympus to pour ambrosia upon Demus and the sourest of pickles upon the Paphlagonian.

Demus sends them off on another foolish errand, laughing meanwhile because he duped both of them into serving him. At last the sausage seller convinces the Paphlagonian that he has the right of stewardship by the word of an ancient oracle in whom both believe. Having won his victory, the sausage seller, now calling himself Agoracritus, begins to browbeat his new master and to accuse him of stupidity and avarice. He boasts that he will now grow wealthy on bribes the Paphlagonian formerly pocketed. To show his power, he orders Cleon the Paphlagonian to turn sausage seller and peddle tripe in the streets.

Critical Evaluation:

The Knights satirizes Athenian politics in the form of an allegory. Although not named in the play, the two slaves in the opening scene are recognizable as representing the Athenian generals Demosthenes and Nicias. These were prominent figures in the Peloponnesian War (431-404 B.C.E.) between Athens and Sparta. The two generals were upstaged and humiliated by the demagogue Cleon. A particular incident that is mentioned frequently in the play is Cleon's intervention at a late stage in the battle for Spartan-controlled Sphacteria. Later, Cleon arrogantly took full credit for the Athenian victory. Aristophanes depicts these three political figures as slaves of a fickle and gullible master Demus (from the Greek world *demos*, "people"). The political rivalries among these figures from Athenian history are thus depicted—in a comic reduction—as a kind of domestic squabble with which most Athenians could identify.

Cleon dominated Athenian politics after Pericles died of the plague in 429 B.C.E. Although there is evidence that he was a capable leader, Aristophanes and many contemporaries saw Cleon as little more than a political manipulator who directed the will of the people in the assembly, which decided on all matters of policy, by appealing to the people's basest instincts. Accordingly, to secure the favor of his master Demus, the Paphlagonian tanner (Cleon operated a leather industry) uses bribes and shamelessly manipulates oracles. Not surprisingly, in late fifth century Athens there were countless charges among leaders of bribery and of abuse of authority, including the fabrication of forged oracles to support one political program or another.

The Peloponnesian War and the proposals for winning or ending the conflict form the dramatic backdrop for *The Knights*, but the play is not simply a critique of contemporary politics. The focus is on the personality of Cleon, who is represented as a foreign-born slave. In fact, the name of Cleon is used only once in the play, in a remark by the chorus, but from various clues the audience certainly knew who was the object of Aristophanes' ridicule. Two years before *The Knights* was produced, Cleon was offended by Aristophanes' unrelenting criticism (in his *Babylonians*, a play now lost) and threatened the poet with a lawsuit. Cleon's object was to silence the comic poet. Very soon afterward, by way of answer, *The Knights* appeared, filled with vicious, personal criticism of Cleon's character. The Paphlagonian is a vulgar, loud, unscrupulous, and totally obnoxious character. These traits, along with the depiction of Cleon as a calculating and ruthless politician, suggest that *The Knights* reveals more about the poet's personal loathing of Cleon than about the political debates of the time.

The dramatic structure of the play depends on a fantastic contest in which the Paphlagonian experiences a humiliating fall from grace in the eyes of his master. In order to rid themselves of the obnoxious Cleon-figure, who wins the favor of Demus with lies and trickery (and, significantly, by claiming credit for the work of others), his fellow slaves concoct a plan. Most of Aristophanes' plays depend for their central plot on some such plan, termed a great idea, by means of which an unpleasant situation is to be remedied. In this play the great idea is suggested by an oracle, stolen from the Paphlagonian, revealing that he will ultimately be supplanted in the city by a sausage seller. The content of the oracle may seem somewhat inconsistent with the allegory that Aristophanes constructs, since the sausage seller will presumably be a free man and not one of the household slaves. The outstanding qualification of the sausage seller, who happens to appear, is that he is even more shameless and calculating than the slave he is supposed to overthrow. He is also of bad family, virtually illiterate, and otherwise disreputable. Aristophanes could certainly have chosen a worthier alternative to Cleon. It suits his comic message, however, that the sausage seller, precisely because he is so vile, is the perfect person to remove the Paphlagonian from his master's affections and take charge of Demus.

Once the sausage seller is examined and approved, much of the rest of the play is concerned with the contest. The chorus of dashing knights, who provide the title for the play, represent a class in Athenian society that might ordinarily support the program of Cleon. Despite flattery and threats from the Paphlagonian, these knights stoutly support Demosthenes, Nicias, and the sausage seller in their struggle to win the favor of Demus. The first part of the contest is little more than a war of shouted boasts, in which the sausage seller seems almost at a loss, and yet he is victorious. The rivals soon turn their attention to winning over the Council. The sausage seller outdoes the Paphlagonian in utter shamelessness and bribery. The final part of the competition is the direct appeal to Demus. As befits the allegory, all of the methods used to flatter Demus are thinly veiled representations of techniques used by politicians to manipulate the Athenian people.

With the final victory of the sausage seller, Aristophanes offers a surprise for his audience. The allegory of a disreputable contest between slaves for the attention of their master gives way to an open political message. The sausage seller, now bombastically named Agoracritus (the people's choice), transforms Demus and extracts a promise from him that from now on he will be more sensible and less gullible to the manipulative influence of politicians such as Cleon. The paradoxical result, that the depraved protagonist manages to reform Demus, is an inconsistency. *The Knights* moves with ease, however, between humble household allegory and weightier political satire, suggesting a larger message that proper management of the household resembles the proper governance of a city.

"Critical Evaluation" by John M. Lawless

Further Reading

Aristophanes. *Knights*. Edited and translated by Alan H. Sommerstein. Warminster, England: Aris & Phillips, 1981. Provides scholarly introduction, bibliography, Greek text, facing English translation, and commentary keyed to the translation. Sommerstein's translation supersedes most earlier versions.

De Luca, Kenneth M. *Aristophanes' Male and Female Revolutions: A Reading of Aristophanes' "Knights" and "Assemblywomen."* Lanham, Md.: Lexington Books, 2005. In his analysis of the two plays, De Luca maintains they are both about democracy and democratic revolutions, and he shows how Aristophanes handles these themes differently in each play.

Dover, K. J. *Aristophanic Comedy*. Berkeley: University of California Press, 1972. Useful and authoritative study of the plays of Aristophanes. Chapter 7 provides a synopsis of the play, discussion of the use of allegory, notes on theatrical production, and important comments on political themes in the play. An absolutely essential starting point for study of the plays.

Murray, Gilbert. *Aristophanes: A Study*. Oxford, England: Oxford University Press, 1933. Contains valuable insights into the plays. Chapter 2 discusses the figure of Cleon as he is represented in *The Knights* and other plays of Aristophanes.

Rothwell, Kenneth S., Jr. "The Literary Fragments of Aristophanes' *Knights*, *Wasps*, and *Frogs*." In *Nature, Culture, and the Origins of Greek Comedy: A Study of Animal Choruses*. New York: Cambridge University Press, 2007. Rothwell analyzes *The Knights* and other comedies in which Aristophanes featured animal choruses. He maintains that these animal characters may be a conscious revival of an earlier Greek tradition of animal representation.

Silk, M. S. *Aristophanes and the Definition of Comedy*. New York: Oxford University Press, 2002. Silk looks at Aristophanes not merely as an ancient Greek dramatist but as one of the world's great poets. He analyzes *The Knights* and the other plays to examine their language, style, lyric poetry, character, and structure.

Spatz, Lois. *Aristophanes*. Boston: Twayne, 1978. A reliable introduction to Aristophanes for the general reader. Chapter 5 discusses the problems of the play and comments on characterization and the figure of Cleon.

Whitman, Cedric. *Aristophanes and the Comic Hero*. Cambridge, Mass.: Harvard University Press, 1964. A standard work on the Aristophanic protagonist. Chapter 3, "City and Individual," offers a valuable study of the play.

The Known World

Author: Edward P. Jones (1950-   )
First published: 2003
Type of work: Novel
Type of plot: Historical, Magical Realism, and social
    criticism
Time of plot: 1830-1861
Locale: Manchester County, Virginia

Principal characters:
HENRY TOWNSEND, a slave owner, and also a former slave
AUGUSTUS and MILDRED TOWNSEND, Henry's parents,
    former slaves
WILLIAM ROBBINS, a white plantation owner
PHILOMELA, Robbins's black mistress
MOSES, slave foreman of Henry's farm
CALDONIA TOWNSEND, Henry's wife
JOHN SKIFFINGTON, county sheriff
MINERVA, his slave, raised as a daughter
COUNSEL SKIFFINGTON, Skiffington's cousin
ELIAS FREEMAN,
CELESTE FREEMAN,
STAMFORD CROW BLUEBERRY, and
ALICE NIGHT, slaves on the Townsend farm
FERN ELSTON, a light-skinned black schoolteacher
ODEN PEOPLES,
HARRY TRAVIS, and
BARNUM KINSEY, sheriff's deputies

The Story:

Moses, the favorite slave of Henry Townsend—a former slave himself—remembers his life as a foreman on Henry's farm. Moses especially remembers how he had shared Henry's ambitions and aspirations. Moses had deliberately disaffiliated with the other slaves with whom he had been forced to share quarters, including his son and his son's mother, and after Henry's untimely death, Moses had hoped to replace his boss as the new husband of Henry's wife, Caldonia. Even though Moses had been more than able to run the entire farm, he could not convince Caldonia, the new boss, that he could do so.

It is now years earlier. Henry's high status is the outcome of his relationship with William Robbins, a white plantation owner. Robbins and Henry develop a father-son relationship rather than a master-slave relationship; appreciating Henry's potential, Robbins makes it possible for Henry to achieve freedom and acquire his own farm and his own slaves. Robbins also has a black mistress, Philomela, a slave with whom he has two children. Although Robbins loves Philomela, he fails to understand that his life with her is corrupted by her status as a slave; Philomela's goal is to escape to freedom.

Similarly, Henry fails to understand that he is replicating the evils of slavery on his own farm, even as he assumes his regime will be a significant improvement over the regime of any white slaveholder. In reality, Henry is just as neglectful,

punitive, and insensitive to the human rights of his slaves. In one case, Henry had one of the sheriff's deputies, the Cherokee Oden Peoples, slice his slave Elias Freeman's ear as discipline after Elias had tried to run away; Henry also allows one of his young black slaves to be worked to death in a neighboring field.

Fern Elston, a former slave who is so light skinned she could pass as white, is also a slaveholder, impervious to the ironies of her situation; Fern, however, never attempts to pass for white. She makes her living as a teacher of the local black children, including Henry when he was a boy. When she forms an erotic bond with one of her slaves, however, the power she enjoys as a slaveholder makes it impossible for this love to be truly reciprocated.

Henry dies, and Moses expects to take his place as farm owner; he is unable to do so because Henry's high status had been dismantled upon his death. Henry's father, Augustus Townsend, who had assumed that his own freedom would be honored and that his son's success would continue to afford protection, is sold back into slavery through the machinations of Deputy Harry Travis, who delivers him to illegal slave traders. Deputy Peoples, whose wife also is a slave, had helped to sell Augustus back into slavery. Only a third deputy, the alcoholic Barnum Kinsey, had retained an uncorrupted conscience, but he had been overruled by the others.

Unlike his deputies Travis and Peoples, Sheriff John Skiffington is a high-minded, educated man who refuses to own slaves on principle. He and his wife receive a little black girl named Minerva as a wedding present, but they raise her as their daughter instead. The mind-set of Manchester County, however, affects their relationship with Minerva. Although they love her, and although she loves them, her status as their "property" is such that she chooses to break for freedom. While Skiffington is unsuccessful in his attempts to recover Minerva, he does capture Moses, who has run away to the house of Henry's mother, Mildred Townsend.

Although he tries to distance himself from the institution of slavery, Skiffington eventually becomes indistinguishable from his own racist deputies. Suffering from a toothache and feeling overwhelmed by the first rumblings of a changing society, Skiffington insults Mildred with racial slurs, then guns her down. The downfall of the once noble Skiffington shocks even his far less ethical cousin, Counsel Skiffington, who, having lost his wife and his land, had just returned from a long, strange trip outside the county. Counsel Skiffington's journey through the Deep South had been an education in the nature of evil, and it culminated in his witnessing of his own cousin's fall from grace. Counsel himself had by this time gone bad; now, he is certain that he will reap monetary profit by murdering his cousin and arranging it to look as if the murdered Mildred had been responsible. Also by this time, Augustus has died while enslaved in the Deep South.

One of the Townsend-farm slaves, however, the clever Alice Night, whose addled demeanor allows her to wander the countryside unhindered, has made a successful break for freedom. Other slaves, such as the mystical Stamford Crow Blueberry and the devoted couple Elias and Celeste Freeman, also successfully escape the farm. In the meantime, Moses, back on the Townsend farm, is humiliated and hobbled, and his hopes are thoroughly dashed. The system in which he had hoped to succeed is destined for destruction.

Critical Evaluation:

Largely set in the mythical Manchester County, Virginia, in the years before the American Civil War, Edward P. Jones's *The Known World* moves back in time and ultimately forward, into a changed United States. Some stories also take readers north to Washington, D.C., and New York, but then return to the Deep South and the Southwest. The lives and stories of numerous characters, both black and white, are intertwined in significant ways. The major stories center on characters associated with the black slaveholder Henry Townsend.

One of the major achievements of this novel, which won the Pulitzer Prize in fiction in 2004 and the prestigious International IMPAC Dublin Literary Award in 2005, is its skillful interweaving of narratives on slavery and its consequences. These narratives, some anecdotal, others extended, are all encompassed within a thoughtful, meditative perspective that assimilates authentic historical detail, psychological realism, mystical or magical incidents, and a viewpoint that speaks beyond the specific historical situation to contemporary issues and to the human condition in general.

The theme of slavery is developed with considerable nuance and complexity. Jones's many stories—involving black slaves, white slaves, poor whites, wealthy white landowners, light-skinned blacks, and even European immigrants—all explore issues of freedom and slavery in ways that include but also move beyond race. The corruptions of power are color blind, but Jones's inclusion of black slaveholders of black slaves further complicates the novel.

Jones explores the paradox at the heart of Manchester County through stories that show how the social codes of the time had been far from fixed; the simplistic opposition of black and white is subverted by relationships that cross the boundaries of racial segregation, especially family relationships. Parent-child relationships and husband-wife relationships develop in a way that do not observe the formal racial codes of the time. Within the confines of the relationship between a black owner and a black slave, other deeper bonds of affection also develop, demonstrating the arbitrary and unsustainable operation of the socioeconomic institution of slavery.

In addition to looking at the ways in which race relations are far from rigid, Jones uses the stories of Henry and other black slaveholders to explore the psychological and moral consequences of an upward social mobility. This mobility allows a member of a subjugated class to succeed in the very system that will continue to oppress the majority of his or her people; this newly empowered person becomes one of the oppressors. Jones, however, does not present only those relationships that have been twisted by a master-slave dynamic; a significant aspect of the novel is the way the slaves on Henry's farm will find freedom from the entire social structure. One inspiring example is the spiritual conversion of the passionate Stamford Crow Blueberry. His conversion during a rainstorm gives him a new generosity of spirit and leads him to found a home for orphans after the Civil War.

A stronger example of this escape from a world of masters and slaves is the strange slave Alice Night. While appearing disoriented, she emerges as a canny and visionary artist who uses her habit of wandering to secure a route to freedom in the North. The sad outcome of the self-interested Moses, who loses his humanity in his cynical struggle to move up into the established slave-based society of Manchester County, is contrasted to the open-hearted spiritual optimism of slaves such as Stamford, Alice, and Elias and Celeste Freeman. This narrative thread suggests that, even within a context of oppressive power, there still exists the potential for freedom and transformative change.

The second, equally important theme in this novel is suggested by its title. One meaning of the title is represented by an old wooden map that hangs on the wall of Sheriff Skiffington's jailhouse. Inscribed as "The Known World," this map is in reality completely outdated, analogous to the situation of the county Skiffington serves; his county is also incomplete and in error, and it has a skewed and truncated knowledge of the world. This definition of "the known world" indicates the way in which Manchester County has represented a partial and mistaken social consensus.

Another visual representation of "the known world" is a tapestry that Alice creates once she escapes to Washington, D.C. This extraordinary work of art represents an omniscient, godlike perspective of her former home in Manchester County. Her tapestry evokes not just one limited moment but, like the novel itself, evokes past, present, and future; it encompasses knowledge beyond one moment in time. Alice's vision of time is like that of the novel itself; both the tapestry and the novel suggest that time will eventually "tell," and that the unfolding of history will reveal more than what one present moment could possibly "know." There is considerable dramatic irony in the novel's depiction of a society that, while unable to envision a future different from its known past, will nevertheless find itself in that yet-to-be-known future. That society's economic and social structure will have changed to such an extent that the county itself will disappear.

Jones's patient, thoughtful narrative demonstrates the truth that what is considered eternal in Manchester County before the Civil War would be in a short time discarded; but the narrative indicates also a universal truth, one that can apply to any society undergoing a crisis of transformation.

Margaret Boe Birns

Further Reading

Beasley, Conger, Jr. "A Luminous Look at an Obscure World: Much-Praised Novel Focuses on Black Slave Owners in America." *National Catholic Reporter*, March 12, 2004, p. 15. Beasley, in this secular publication, praises *The Known World* both for its depiction of character and for its visionary power.

King, Richard H. "The Known World." *Rethinking History*, June, 2005, 355-380. A major discussion of the way in which *The Known World* fits into the post-1960's genre of the slave novel. Examines and discusses what the novel teaches about slavery in the American South.

Maslin, Janet. "His Brother's Keeper in Antebellum Virginia." Review of *The Known World*, by Edward P. Jones. *The New York Times*, August 14, 2003. This brief, perceptive article praises Jones for his wisdom, effective understatement, and wide range of perspective in his writing.

Mason, Wyatt. "Ballad for Americans: The Stories of Edward P. Jones." *Harpers Magazine*, September, 2006, pp. 87-92. A thoughtful, thorough, and appreciative analysis of a number of Jones's stories, including those in the novel *The Known World*.

Pinckney, Darryl. "Gone with the Wind." *The New York Review of Books*, October 21, 2004, pp. 14-18. A brief but perceptive discussion of *The Known World* as a revisioned and intimate kind of historical novel.

Ryan, Tim A. "Mapping the Unrepresentable: Slavery Fiction in the New Millennium." In *Calls and Responses: The American Novel of Slavery Since "Gone with the Wind."* Baton Rouge: Louisiana State University Press, 2008. *The Known World* is discussed in a chapter on slavery fiction in the twenty-first century, with special reference to the novel's depiction of racial codes as both fixed and fluid.

Vida, Vendela, ed. "ZZ Packer Talks with Edward P. Jones." In *The Believer Book of Writers Talking to Writers*. San Francisco: McSweeney's, 2008. African American writer ZZ Packer interviews Jones in this collection of conversations between writers and their mentors.

Krapp's Last Tape

Author: Samuel Beckett (1906-1989)
First produced: 1958; first published, 1958
Type of work: Drama
Type of plot: Absurdist
Time of plot: An evening
Locale: Krapp's den

Principal character:
KRAPP, a sixty-nine-year-old man

The Story:

In a circle of light surrounded by darkness, Krapp sits at a table in his den. Pale and clownlike in appearance, he has a bulbous purple nose and wears old black trousers, a dirty white shirt with a black vest, and oddly oversized dirty white boots. His gray hair is messy, and he needs a shave. It is his sixty-ninth birthday. Krapp fumbles in his pocket, withdraws an envelope, and takes out a small bunch of keys. He goes to his desk where he unlocks a drawer and removes a recording tape. After peering at the tape he puts it back and unlocks the second drawer, taking out a banana. Krapp strokes the banana, peels it, and puts the end in his mouth, meanwhile staring into space. Finally he eats the banana and drops the peeling. In gestures suggesting a clown's comic pantomime, he paces back and forth, slips on the peeling, then nudges the banana peel off stage with his toe. He takes out another banana, fondles it suggestively, peels it, tosses the peeling, and puts it in his mouth. Then he thinks of something. Krapp sticks the banana in his pocket and leaves the scene. A few moments later he returns with a ledger.

Scanning the ledger, for the first time Krapp speaks aloud. "Box . . . three . . . spool . . . five." He studies the ledger in which he records the contents of tapes he makes each year on his birthday and searches through his boxes of tapes. The one he is looking for is from his thirty-ninth birthday. A ledger note refers to his mother's death, an unexplained black ball, "the dark nurse," bowel problems, and a "memorable equinox." It ends "farewell to love." Krapp plays the tape and hears his younger self describe a birthday spent drinking, then returning to his room to write and eat bananas. This younger voice seems self-satisfied and expresses the smug belief that, at thirty-nine, he is at the height of his powers. The voice of Krapp at thirty-nine goes on to talk about listening to a still earlier tape of himself from ten or twelve years before. Krapp in his twenties was living with someone named Bianca. Krapp at thirty-nine sneers at his younger self and calls these sentimental memories "gruesome." He laughs at the lofty aspirations of his younger self, and Krapp at sixty-nine joins in the derisive laughter. Other events noted are his father's death and the end of an affair.

Krapp switches off the tape. He seems disturbed. Abruptly he walks out. This time three corks pop. When he returns he begins to sing drunkenly until he starts coughing. When Krapp resumes listening to the tape, he hears himself describing his mother's death. At the word "viduity" he stops the tape and looks puzzled. He can no longer remember the meaning of this word he once used. He goes searching for a dictionary and brings it back to the table. He looks up the meaning of the word and finds that it means "widowhood." It also refers to a black bird. This seems to amuse him. He continues listening. His younger voice tells of sitting outside by a canal while his mother is dying and of wishing it were over. He is eying an attractive nursemaid when he notices the window blind go down on his mother's window, a sign she died. As he sits in the park along the canal, he is throwing a small black ball for a stray dog. Now he pauses. The dog paws his hand and he lets it take the ball. Krapp says he will never forget the feeling of the dog's mouth gently taking the ball from his hand moments after his mother's death.

At this point Krapp hears himself at thirty-nine beginning to tell of some revelation or meaningful insight. Impatiently he switches off the tape, fast-forwards it, turns it on briefly, then switches it off and fast-forwards again. He does this three times until a particular passage catches his attention. The voice speaks of an erotic past moment. Krapp listens, pauses, and rewinds the tape in order to hear it again. The voice describes his being with a woman in a small boat on a lake. They were swimming. Now she lies on the bottom of the boat, her eyes closed against the bright sun. He notices small details: a scratch on her leg from picking gooseberries, the way she barely opens her eyes to look at him. Wild iris growing in the water bends before the movements of the boat and makes a sighing sound. He lies down with her. The boat rocks gently.

When the voice resumes after a short pause, Krapp switches off the tape. Once more he goes out of sight. This time there is a sound of whiskey being poured into a glass. When he returns, Krapp walks somewhat unsteadily, but he takes out a clean reel of tape and prepares to make a recording to mark his sixty-ninth birthday. He begins by deriding his younger self. Then he falls into a reverie, forgets to speak, shuts off the tape, begins to speak, and realizes he forgot to turn it on again. He seems distracted. In his mutterings Krapp refers to a publication, "Seventeen copies sold," a book he wrote. His associations move to women, Effie Briest, a figure in a German novel he read, and someone named Fanny, an old prostitute, who visited him a couple of times and flattered his failing virility. He derides this most recent sexual encounter as better than being kicked in the crotch.

Krapp turns again to the past. He speaks of going to vespers as a boy when he dozed and fell off the church pew, of gathering holly in the country in the west of Ireland, and of hiking with his dog in the mountains. Momentarily doubts about his life assail him but he chides himself for dwelling on the past, which he refers to as "All that old misery." Still, the memory of the woman in the boat haunts him. He removes the new tape and reinserts the one from his thirty-ninth birthday. He replays the scene in the boat. This time, however, he does not turn it off. Then the voice stops and the tape runs on in silence as Krapp stares at nothing.

Critical Evaluation:

One of the principal authors of the theater of the absurd, Samuel Beckett was born and grew up in Ireland, where he studied languages at Trinity College. As a young man he traveled to the Continent and eventually settled in Paris. Although *Krapp's Last Tape* was originally written in English, he wrote most of his works first in French and translated them into English. Besides plays, Beckett wrote and published novels, shorter fiction, and poetry. During World War II he served as a member of the French resistance and had to go into hiding to survive. He was awarded the Nobel Prize in Literature in 1969.

In *Krapp's Last Tape*, an older man reviews his life and confronts his isolation and inability to love. Krapp's failures as a human being are glaringly evident, but the audience may also identify with him. Like a mime or a circus clown, Krapp wrings his audience out with contrary emotions. He is laughable and pathetic, grotesque and human. Within the small framework of a one-act monologue, in the soiled comedic figure of Krapp, Beckett creates a complex reality. Describing *Krapp's Last Tape* as absurdist theater is subject to interpretation. Unlike more extremely absurdist Beckett plays such as *En attendant Godot* (1952; *Waiting for Godot*, 1954) or "Fin de partie" (1957; *"Endgame"*), the play is fairly realistic. Krapp's comic appearance and the way it contrasts with his sad life is, however, absurdist. Here is an ordinary human being who aspired to be a writer but with slight success, suf-

fered the death of parents, and failed in love. He wrestled (not too vigorously) with alcoholism. He is experiencing a lonely old age and, to judge by the title of the play, will soon experience death. The circle of light in which he operates is a symbol of his existence, a tiny spot in a vast darkness.

Beckett chooses to picture Krapp as a down-at-heels clown. As a clown Krapp is absurd rather than tragic. The human condition, projected from Krapp's example, is absurd. Through Krapp the audience sees the individual as a posturing little spark in time, soon extinguished. Krapp himself is uneasy and disgusted with this role. When he listens to his younger voice on tape speaking of a visionary night on a jetty, he becomes impatient and switches off the tape. Other than his drinking, only the fact that he replays the section of the tape dealing with the scene in the boat implies that Krapp is touched by a sense of loss. The audience never knows for sure what Krapp is feeling. To create the illusion of meaning Krapp begins his annual ritual of making a birthday tape, but this time he fails to find value in the exercise. He has nothing to add, for in the end his life has come to nothing. The "memorable equinox" turns out to have been the beginning of the end. Beckett uses the stark setting and the contrast between the spotlight in which Krapp moves and the darkness beyond to give a concrete representation of Krapp's situation. The repetition of threes gives Krapp's actions a ritualistic character. For example, he goes offstage three times to drink, and he looks at his watch three times. The audience is presented with Krapp at three different times in his life.

The play is set during "a late evening in the future." It has been suggested that this avoids the anachronism of recording tape being available at an earlier date. Setting the play in the future also serves as an omen, imbuing the play with a mood of dark presentiment.

Krapp's ceremonial recording of his own life, as if for some posterity never realized, is in some ways a parody of the writer's life. His life work, however, turns out to be the taped version of his life, and he is both author and audience, a narcissistic circle. No wonder the play ends in silence as the blank portion of the tape unspools. The ending of the play is bleak, but it also has a cleansing stoicism. Krapp is a moving human figure.

Barbara Drake

Further Reading

Esslin, Martin. *The Theatre of the Absurd*. 3d ed. New York: Vintage Books, 2004. Points out that Beckett, who is sometimes considered the finest novelist of the last half of the twentieth century, is also sometimes considered to be the finest playwright of the period. His plays are valuable because they represent a simpler version of his work. Also puts his work in the intellectual and the social context of the period.

Fletcher, John. *Samuel Beckett: "Waiting for Godot," "Endgame," "Krapp's Last Tape."* London: Faber & Faber, 2000. A critical guide designed to introduce readers to the three plays. Contains analysis of the plays' language, structure, characters, and features of performance and a select bibliography.

Gontarski, S. E. *The Intent of Undoing in Samuel Beckett's Dramatic Texts.* Bloomington: Indiana University Press, 1985. A chapter on *Krapp's Last Tape* connects the revision process to an evolving interpretation of the play. Includes selected bibliography.

_____, ed. *On Beckett: Essays and Criticism.* New York: Grove Press, 1986. Essays by various scholars, including Ruby Cohn's "Beckett Directs: *Endgame* and *Krapp's Last Tape*," which discusses Beckett's adeptness at staging.

Kenner, Hugh. *Samuel Beckett: A Critical Study.* New ed. Berkeley: University of California Press, 1973. Important study of Beckett. Kenner consulted with Beckett in writing it. Does not focus on *Krapp's Last Tape*, but the preface provides valuable insight into Beckett's attitude toward his work.

Knowlson, James. *Damned to Fame: The Life of Samuel Beckett.* New York: Simon & Schuster, 1996. Knowlson, Beckett's chosen biographer, provides a meticulously detailed book, containing much new material as well as detailed notes and a bibliography.

McDonald, Rónán. *The Cambridge Introduction to Samuel Beckett.* New York: Cambridge University Press, 2006. Chapter 3 of this concise overview of Beckett's life and work includes a discussion of *Krapp's Last Tape.*

MacMillan, Dougald, and Martha Fehsenfeld. *From "Waiting for Godot" to "Krapp's Last Tape."* Vol. 1 in *Beckett in the Theatre.* New York: Riverrun Press, 1988. Devotes a chapter to *Krapp's Last Tape.* Discusses changes Beckett made from early to later drafts. Extensive interpretation of the play in relation to production.

Reid, Alec. *All I Can Manage, More than I Could: An Approach to the Plays of Samuel Beckett.* Dublin: Dolmen Press, 1968. Accessible and valuable source on Beckett's plays, with information about publication and first production and synopses. Also contains introductory essays on Beckett and his innovative work in broadening the scope of modern drama.

Worth, Katharine. *Samuel Beckett's Theatre: Life Journeys.* New York: Clarendon Press, 1999. A look at the production history and psychological aspects of Beckett's plays, including *Krapp's Last Tape.*

The Kreutzer Sonata

Author: Leo Tolstoy (1828-1910)
First published: *Kreytserova sonata*, 1889 (English translation, 1890)
Type of work: Novel
Type of plot: Social realism
Time of plot: Late nineteenth century
Locale: Russia

Principal characters:
VASYLA POZDNISHEF, a Russian aristocrat
MADAME POZDNISHEF, his wife
TRUKHASHEVSKY, the lover of Madame Pozdnishef

The Story:

One spring night a railway train speeds across Russia. In one of the cars a sprightly conversation about the place of women, both in public and in the home, is in progress among a group of aristocrats. One of the listeners finally breaks into the conversation with the statement that Russians marry only for sexual reasons and that marriage is a hell for most of them unless they, like himself, secure release by killing the other

party to the marriage. With that remark he leaves the group and retires to his own seat in the car. Later on, he tells his story to his seat companion.

His name was Pozdnishef, and he is a landed proprietor. As a young man, he learned many vices, but he always kept his relationships with women on a monetary basis, so that he would have no moral responsibility for the unfortunates with whom he came in contact. His early life taught him that people of his class did not respect sex. The men viewed women only in terms of pleasure. The women sanctioned such thoughts by openly marrying men who became libertines; the older people allowed their daughters to be married to men whose habits were known to be of a shameful nature.

At the age of thirty, Pozdnishef fell in love with a beautiful woman of his own class, the daughter of an impoverished landowner in Penza. During his engagement he was disturbed because she and he had so little about which to converse when they were left alone. They would say one sentence to each other and then become silent. Not knowing what should come next, they would fall to eating bonbons. The honeymoon was a failure, shameful and tiresome at the beginning, painfully oppressive at the end. Three or four days after the wedding they quarreled, and both realized that in a short time they grew to hate each other. As the months of marriage passed, their quarrels grew more frequent and violent. Pozdnishef became persuaded in his own mind that love was something low and swinish.

The idea of marriage and sex became an obsession with him. When his wife secured a wet nurse for their children, he felt that she was shirking a moral duty by not nursing her offspring. Worse, Pozdnishef was jealous of every man who came into his wife's presence, who was received in his home, or who received a smile from his wife. He began to suspect that his wife had taken a lover.

The children born to Pozdnishef and his wife were a great trouble to him in other ways as well. They were continually bothering him with real or fancied illnesses, and they broke up the regular habits of life to which he was accustomed. They were new subjects over which he and his wife could quarrel.

In the fourth year of their marriage, the couple reached a state of complete disagreement. They ceased to talk over anything to the end. They were almost silent when they were alone, much as they were during their engagement. Finally the doctors told the woman she could have no more children with safety. Pozdnishef felt that without children to justify their relations, the only reason for their life together was the children already born who held them like a chain fastening two convicts.

In the next two years, the young woman filled out and bloomed in health, after the burden of bearing children was taken from her. She became more attractive in the eyes of other men, and her husband's jealousy sharply increased.

Madame Pozdnishef had always been interested in music, and she played the piano rather well. Through her musical interest, she met a young aristocrat who turned professional musician when his family fortune dwindled away. His name was Trukhashevsky. When he appeared on the scene, the Pozdnishefs had already experienced several crises in their marriage. The husband at times considered suicide, and the wife tried to poison herself. One evening, after a violent scene in which Pozdnishef told his wife he would like to see her dead, she rushed to her room and swallowed an opium compound. Quick action on the part of the husband and a doctor saved her life, but neither forgot her desperate attempt.

One evening Trukhashevsky came to Pozdnishef's home in Moscow. He and Madame Pozdnishef played during the evening for a number of guests. The first piece they played together was Ludwig von Beethoven's *Kreutzer* Sonata. The first movement, a rapid allegro, worked upon the highly strung emotions of the husband until he began to imagine that there was already an understanding between the musician and his wife. The idea so obsessed him that he could hardly wait until the other man was out of the house. Never in his life had music affected Pozdnishef in that manner. Between it and his jealousy, he was almost violently insane.

Two days later, Pozdnishef left Moscow to attend a meeting. He went away fearful of what might happen while he was gone. On the second day of his absence, Pozdnishef received a letter from his wife saying that the musician called at the house.

Jealousy immediately seized the husband. He rushed back to Moscow as fast as carriage and train could carry him. He arrived at his home after midnight. Lights were burning in his wife's apartment. Taking off his shoes, he prowled about the house. He soon discovered the musician's overcoat. He went to the nursery and the children's rooms but found everyone there asleep. Returning to his study, he seized a dagger and made his way to his wife's apartment. There he found his wife and the musician seated at a table, eating. He rushed at the man, who escaped by ducking under the piano and then out the door. Pozdnishef, beside himself with anger and jealousy, seized his wife and stabbed her. When she dropped to the floor, he ran from the room and went to his study. There he fell asleep on a sofa.

A few hours later his sister-in-law awakened him and took him to see his dying wife. Shortly afterward the authorities carried Pozdnishef away to prison. He went under police escort to his wife's funeral. It was only after he looked at the waxen face of the corpse that he realized he committed a murder. Then, at his trial, Pozdnishef was found innocent because he murdered while in the heat of anger at finding his wife unfaithful to him.

Now judged insane, Pozdnishef declares that if he had it to do over, he would never marry. Marriage, he insists, is not for true Christians with strong sensibilities and weak moral restraints.

Critical Evaluation:

One of the strangest of Leo Tolstoy's works, *The Kreutzer Sonata* is almost entirely a raving monologue concerning sex and marriage. The sources for *The Kreutzer Sonata*, first published in 1889 in lithograph, are said to be autobiographical. An idea for the short novel initially came from a friend of Tolstoy, who told him about meeting a stranger on a train who, during the course of a long journey, related an account of his wife's infidelity. The story intrigued Tolstoy, who began working the idea into a story he was writing on the complexities arising out of the conflict between chastity and sexual love. About a year after he began this project, Tolstoy happened to go to a musical. Among the pieces performed that evening was the *Kreutzer* sonata (1803). This piece deeply affected Tolstoy, and he was inspired to incorporate it into his novel.

The autobiographical aspects of the novel center on the dilemma Tolstoy experienced after his conversion in his later years to a life of asceticism and chastity. He was revolted by his former life, which he saw as one of indulgence, greed, and lust. In trying to change his nature, he became obsessed by his desires, in particular, his sexual desires and the spiritual unrest arising from them. His obsession included his wife, Sonya; consequently, their final years together were, for the most part, miserable. On his deathbed, Tolstoy refused to see her, and although no one could claim that he, like the protagonist in *The Kreutzer Sonata*, murdered his wife, her heart was broken.

Since the publication of *The Kreutzer Sonata*, critics, in their assessment of the novel, have run the gamut from praise to disgust. Anton Chekhov wrote that "it is hardly possible to find anything of equal importance in conception and beauty of execution." Others have read it as a diatribe against sexuality rather than a work of fiction. Tolstoy himself once called it a negative, malicious work, and his wife complained, during the period Tolstoy was writing it, that he no longer was doing creative work.

Today, the critical scales might be balanced by reading the novel not only as a diatribe against lust but also as a mesmerizing, gothic portrayal of a husband ravaged with jealousy. The short novel takes place on a train and, for the most part, inside a carriage in which the narrator and another passenger, Vasyla Pozdnishef, sit throughout the long night drinking glasses of strong tea, smoking, and talking—that is,

Pozdnishef talks and the narrator listens. Earlier, a woman, a lawyer, a tradesman, and a clerk enter the carriage and, in desultory fashion, begin talking about subjects that later become the center of the novel—sexual love, infidelity, jealousy, chastity, and marriage.

Outside Pozdnishef's monologue, there is little action. At one point, before dawn, the conductor comes by to remove a burned candle. Tea is made and drunk. They smoke. They change their positions—cross a leg, lean forward. The effect of little or no action outside the monologue is similar to being locked into the same, confining space as the characters. One is on the train, so to speak, and unable to get off. Listening to a deranged, although intelligent, man's obsessive tale is not everyone's idea of a pleasant journey. In a manner of speaking, Tolstoy imprisons the reader with the narrator in a situation in which there is no alternative but to listen if one wants to find out what happened and why.

Pozdnishef's monologue works on several levels. It is both a classic case of jealousy, dramatically and inextricably leading to murder, and also a polemic on sexual mores. The novel suffers from the latter—Pozdnishef's doctrinaire digressions on sexual mores. His bitter, impersonal view of marital love is chilling. He attributes falling in love to an excess of rich foods and to dressmakers' skills. Although he is not a misogynist (he claims that man corrupted woman with his filthy passions), he claims that women enslave men through their sexuality.

What rescues the novel from didacticism, however, is the riveting drama, interwoven among the monologues, of the jealous husband caught in a tapestry of his own weaving. Pozdnishef introduces the violinist, Trukhashevsky, to Madame Pozdnishef. He encourages him to come to their home and participate in musicals with her, as she is an enthusiastic pianist. Thus he sets into motion sexual jealousy, a passion flaming out of his control to its tragic end. In this characterization, Tolstoy's skill is superb. Listening to his attractive wife and the young violinist play the *Kreutzer* sonata, Pozdnishef imagines a pulsating, romantic liaison between them, and his rage mounts.

Tolstoy's character, Pozdnishef, is equal to the best of a long list of nervous neurotics teetering on the edge of psychotic behavior. In *The Kreutzer Sonata*, Pozdnishef is portrayed as continually horrified, exasperated, painfully struck, or ashamed. He calls himself swinish, depraved, malicious, and evil. In telling his story, Pozdnishef is agitated, tense, and irritable. His eyes glitter and his movements are abrupt; he emits strange sounds, not quite human. He talks obsessively.

He is a type familiar to nineteenth century readers from

writers such as E. T. A. Hoffmann and Edgar Allan Poe, who excelled in the psychological horror story. In these macabre tales, the character's body and soul or mental and instinctive drives are dissected, the rift or schism between body and spirit is exposed, and the personality is revealed to be founded on fear, cruelty, and madness. Pozdnishef is such a personality and, in portraying him, Tolstoy's skill is unsurpassed.

Although Tolstoy created a remarkable character, his jeremiads on sexual mores weaken the plot. His didacticism threatens to overwhelm his narrative skills. The result is a flawed novel, but one of strange and compelling interest.

"Critical Evaluation" by Alice L. Swensen

Further Reading

Bayley, John. "What Is Art?" In *Leo Tolstoy*, edited by Harold Bloom. Edgemont, Pa.: Chelsea House, 1986. Discusses Tolstoy's ideas about the function and moral purpose of art, with special reference to *The Kreutzer Sonata*. Contains many other excellent essays pertinent to understanding Tolstoy's ideas about art, love, and sex.

McLean, Hugh. *In Quest of Tolstoy*. Boston: Academic Studies Press, 2008. McLean, a professor emeritus of Russian at the University of California, Berkeley, and longtime Tolstoy scholar, compiled this collection of essays that examine Tolstoy's writings and ideas and assess his influence on other writers and thinkers. Includes discussions of the young Tolstoy and women and Tolstoy and Jesus, Charles Darwin, Ernest Hemingway, and Maxim Gorky.

Maude, Almyer. *The Life of Tolstoy*. New York: Oxford University Press, 1953. Maude, Tolstoy's English friend and translator, produced tasteful and accurate English translations of Tolstoy's writings. This biography is outstanding because of Maude's close association with the Russian author and his opportunities to consult Tolstoy in person. Contains many references to *The Kreutzer Sonata*.

Orwin, Donna Tussig, ed. *The Cambridge Companion to Tolstoy*. New York: Cambridge University Press, 2002. Collection of essays, including discussions of Tolstoy as a writer of popular literature, the development of his style and themes, his aesthetics, and Tolstoy in the twentieth century. References to *The Kreutzer Sonata* are listed in the index.

Shirer, William L. *Love and Hatred: The Troubled Marriage of Leo and Sonya Tolstoy*. New York: Simon & Schuster, 1994. Devotes an entire chapter to *The Kreutzer Sonata*, analyzing how it reflects the real-life marital relationship of the Tolstoys, and how its publication created further marital friction. Contains many excellent rare photographs.

Smoluchowski, Louise. *Lev and Sonya: The Story of the Tolstoy Marriage*. New York: G. P. Putnam's Sons, 1987. A revealing study of the tempestuous marriage of the Tolstoys, which lasted from 1862 to 1910. Discusses the marriage's powerful influence on the Russian author's ideas about love and marriage, as reflected in such works as *Anna Karenina* (1875-1877; English translation, 1886) and *The Kreutzer Sonata*.

Tolstoy, Leo. *What Is Art?* Translated by Almyer Maude. Indianapolis, Ind.: Bobbs-Merrill, 1960. Originally published in Russian in 1896, this great, neglected work was the fruit of decades of intensive thought and study. Tolstoy condemned art designed to entertain the idle upper classes, a belief he dramatized in *The Kreutzer Sonata*.

Kristin Lavransdatter

Author: Sigrid Undset (1882-1949)
First published: 1920-1922; includes *Kransen* (1920;
  The Bridal Wreath, 1923), *Husfrue* (1921; *The
  Mistress of Husaby*, 1925), *Korset* (1922; *The Cross*,
  1927)
Type of work: Novel
Type of plot: Historical realism
Time of plot: Fourteenth century
Locale: Norway

Principal characters:
KRISTIN LAVRANSDATTER
LAVRANS BJÖRGULFSÖN, Kristin's father and the owner of
  Jörundgaard
RAGNFRID IVARSDATTER, Kristin's mother
ULVHILD and RAMBORG, Kristin's sisters
ERLEND NIKULAUSSÖN, the owner of Husaby
SIMON ANDRESSON, the son of a neighboring landowner
LADY AASHILD, Erlend's aunt
NIKULAUS (NAAKVE),
BJÖRGULF,
GAUTE,
SKULE,
IVAR,
LAVRANS,
MUNAN, and
ERLEND, the sons of Erlend and Kristin

The Story:

Lavrans Björgulfsön and his wife, Ragnfrid Ivarsdatter, are descended from powerful landowners. Although Kristin was born at her father's manor, Skog, she spends most of her childhood at Jörundgaard, which falls to Lavrans and Ragnfrid upon the death of Ragnfrid's father. Kristin's childhood is exceedingly happy.

A second daughter, Ulvhild, is crippled at the age of three. Lady Aashild, a declared witch-wife, is sent for to help the child. Kristin becomes well acquainted with Lady Aashild that summer.

When she is fifteen years old, Kristin's father betrothes her to Simon Andresson of Dyfrin. One evening, Kristin slips away to bid good-bye to a childhood playmate, Arne Gyrdson. On her way home, Bentein, Sira Eirik's grandson, accosts her. She escapes after a fight with him, physically unharmed but mentally tortured. Later that year, Arne is brought home dead after fighting with Bentein over Bentein's sly insinuations regarding Kristin. Kristin persuades her father to put off the betrothal feast and permit her to spend a year in a convent at Oslo.

Soon after entering the Convent of Nonneseter, Kristin and her bed partner, Ingebjorg Filippusdatter, go into Oslo to shop, accompanied by an old servant. When they become separated from the old man, they are rescued by a group of men riding through the woods. In that manner Kristin meets Erlend Nikulaussön, the nephew of Lady Aashild. In July, Kristin and Erlend meet once more at the St. Margaret's Fes-

tival and that night vow to love each other. The following morning, Kristin learns from Ingebjorg of Eline Ormsdatter, whom Erlend stole from her husband, and by whom Erlend had two children. Later that summer, while visiting her uncle at Skog, Kristin and Erlend meet secretly, and Kristin surrenders to Erlend. During the following winter, Kristin and Erlend manage to meet frequently. In the spring, Kristin tells Simon of her love for Erlend and her desire to end their betrothal. He agrees, much against his will. Lavrans and Ragnfrid unwillingly accept Kristin's decision.

When Erlend's kinsmen bring suit for Kristin's hand in marriage, Lavrans refuses. During the winter Erlend and Kristin plan to elope to Sweden. While they are making their plans at Lady Aashild's home, Eline overtakes them. Discovered by Erlend when she is trying to give poison to Kristin, she stabs herself. Erlend and Sir Bjorn, Lady Aashild's husband, put her on a sled and take her south to be buried. Kristin returns home.

The following spring Erlend's relatives again make a bid for Kristin's hand, and worn out with suffering—Ulvhild's death and Kristin's unhappiness—Lavrans agrees to the betrothal. During Erlend's visit at Whitsuntide, Kristin becomes pregnant. On the night of the wedding, Lavrans realizes that Kristin already belongs to Erlend. He gives to Erlend what Erlend already possesses.

After her marriage Kristin moves to Erlend's estate at Husaby. She is quick to notice the neglect everywhere evident. In the next fifteen years she bears Erlend seven sons—Nikulaus, Björgulf, Gaute, the twins Ivar and Skule, Lavrans, and Munan. At the same time she struggles to save her sons' inheritance by better management of Husaby. Erlend, however, is intent on becoming a great man; he sells land to pay his expenses and grants tenants free rent in exchange for supplies for his military musters.

Simon Andresson lives at Formo with his sister Sigrid and his illegitimate daughter, Arngjerd. Simon makes suit to Lavrans for Kristin's youngest sister, Ramborg. The following year Lavrans dies, followed two years later by Ragnfrid. Kristin's part of the inheritance is Jörundgaard.

There is much unrest in the country at that time. A boy, Magnus VII, is named king of both Sweden and Norway, and during his childhood, Erling Vidkunsson is made regent of Norway. When Magnus reaches the age of sixteen, Sir Erling resigns, and soon Norway has little law or order. During those years of unrest, Erlend conspires to put another claimant on the throne of Norway. Arrested, he is tried for treason by a king's-men's court. Erlend survives, but he has to forfeit all of his lands.

Erlend goes with Kristin and his sons to Jörundgaard to live, but he cares little for farming or for the people of the dale, and the neighbors avoid Jörundgaard. As the boys grow to manhood, Kristin becomes fearful for their future. In her desire to further their fortunes, she and Erlend come to harsh words, and she tells him he is not a fit lord of Jörundgaard. He leaves her and goes to Haugen, the farm where Lady Aashild spent her last days. Although she longs to have Erlend back, Kristin believes that she is in the right and struggles along with the help of Ulf, a servant, to make Jörundgaard produce.

The following winter her brother-in-law Simon dies as a result of a cut on the arm, sustained while separating two drunken fighters. Before he dies, he asks Kristin to go to Erlend and settle their quarrel. Kristin promises to do so. Ramborg gives birth to her son six weeks early and, upon Simon's death, names the child Simon Simonsson.

Kristin keeps her promise and goes to Haugen to ask Erlend to return to Jörundgaard, but he refuses. She stays at Haugen that summer and then returns home to her sons. Finding herself pregnant again, she sends her sons to tell her husband. When the child is born, Erlend still does not come to her. The child dies before it is three months old. Soon thereafter, when Bishop Halvard comes to the parish, Jardtrud, Ulf's wife, goes to him and charges Ulf with adultery with Kristin. Lavrans, unknown to the rest of the family, rides to Haugen to get his father. Erlend returns immediately with his son, but in a scuffle in the courtyard, he is wounded and dies. The same year Munan dies of a sickness that goes around the parish. Thus Kristin is left with six sons, each of whom must make his way in the world.

Ivar and Skule, the twins, take service with a distant kinsman. Ivar marries Singe Gamalsdatter, a wealthy young widow. Nikulaus and Björgulf enter the brotherhood at Tautra. Gaute falls in love with Jofrid Helgesdatter, heiress of a rich landowner. The two young people elope and are not married until the summer after the birth of their child, Erlend. During that winter, they live at Jörundgaard, and after their marriage, Kristin relinquishes the keys of the manor to Jofrid. Lavrans takes service with the Bishop of Skaalholt and sails to Iceland.

Kristin feels out of place in her old home after she is no longer mistress there. She decides to go to Nidaros and enter a convent. In the year 1349, after Kristin is in the cloister for about two years, her son Skule goes to see her. From him she receives the first news of the Black Plague. The disease soon engulfs the whole city, carries off her two sons in the convent, Nikulaus and Björgulf, and finally causes Kristin's own death.

Critical Evaluation:

Sigrid Undset was one of many European writers in the twentieth century who felt a strong attraction to traditional Catholicism. Undset differed, though, from writers such as T. S. Eliot, G. K. Chesterton, and Charles Maurras, who supported reactionary political regimes and were opposed to the personal autonomy characteristic of the modern era. Undset was not opposed to twentieth century liberalism and individualism. She saw personal autonomy as expressing a human dignity consonant with Christian conception of the potentially exalted character of humanity that, though inevitably sinful, was redeemed by the sacrificial love of Jesus Christ.

This delight in individualism can be seen in Undset's portrayal of the character of Kristin Lavransdatter. Kristin is no plaster saint. She has human desires, human passions, and human failings. She also is a pious Christian throughout the course of the work, although her religious dedication only reaches its full consummation in the last portion of the trilogy, *The Cross*, when she formally enters a convent. Undset indulges in no melodramatic contrast between pagan sin and Christian devotion. She recognizes that, in a society as totally Christian as medieval Norway, Christianity tended to embrace the full range of human attributes and behaviors, even if it could not have officially condoned them all. Kristin's drives and passions may be gently chided by the clerical authorities in the book, but they are not constrained. Indeed, the defiance of social norms that Kristin displays at the beginning of the book (for instance, in her premarital relationship with Erlend Nikulaussön) is also displayed at the end of the book, when her passionate spirit diverges from the social norm in another direction (selfless devotion to the Church).

The significance of the character of Erlend is often missed by critics. Erlend's inadequacies as a man and as a husband are evident. Before he marries Kristin, he sires an illegitimate child by another woman. After their marriage, he has numerous affairs. He mismanages and mortgages his property to advance his unrealistic personal interests. At first, the reader infers that Kristin has made a disastrous match and that her religious devotion is a repudiation of Erlend's wayward secular morality. The truth, on consideration, is more complicated. Erlend, like Kristin, will not tolerate the limits placed upon him by stolid, unimaginative, run-of-the-mill people. Erlend's appetite can lead to ignoble and disagreeable behavior, but it also possesses a kind of zeal that has much akin to Kristin's own spiritual fire. If anything, Kristin's clear moral superiority to Erlend can be seen less as a religiously motivated gesture on the part of the author than as a feminist critique of male adventurism and self-serving charisma. It is in the middle section of the trilogy, *The Mistress of Husaby*, that the ambiguities of Erlend's character are most fruitfully displayed. Erlend agitates to replace the Swedish hegemony over Norway with rule by a native Norwegian noble. This conspiracy fails in worldly terms and is judged by Kristin to be a distraction from the truly primary spiritual goals of human life. Kristin's perspective is reminiscent of Beatrice's view of Dante Alighieri's political intrigues in Florence in Dante's *Paradiso* (c. 1320; English translation, 1802). The conspiracy does reflect a praiseworthy desire on the part of Erlend to make life better for his people and to strive for the general good. Erlend's Norwegian nationalism was hardly unattractive to Undset, who was twenty-three years old when Norway finally gained independence from Sweden in 1905. Kristin might have had a less tragedy-filled life had she married a more placid and dutiful man, such as her devoted suitor Simon Darre (who always remains constant to Kristin even after she marries another man), but her passions and ambitions would have been less fulfilled.

Erlend's house, Husaby, also plays an important role in the book, especially in contrast and in comparison with Jörundgaard, the house of Kristin's father, Lavrans Björgulfsön. Put simply, Jörundgaard is more of a homestead, and Husaby is more of a manor. Jörundgaard represents the simplicities of childhood, and Husaby represents the challenges, the rewards, and the sorrows of being a mature adult. Much attention is paid to how Kristin renovates Husaby and restores it to its proper rank and station in the region. However, when Kristin is old and widowed, it is to Jörundgaard that she

returns, finding in its raw and windswept reaches a proper haven for her battered spirit.

It is neither the characters nor the houses of the novel, however, with which the reader must first relate. It is the setting of the book itself: medieval Norway. Almost incalculably remote to most English-speaking readers, Undset's setting threatens to dwarf the human protagonists of the book in a wealth of exotic detail. It is Undset's great achievement that this does not occur. Undset's fidelity to historical detail far exceeds that of the garden-variety historical novelist, yet the book is never wooden or fusty in its depiction of the past. Although the reader develops an interest in medieval Norway for its own sake, Undset's character portraits are so powerful that eventually the reader takes the setting in stride and evaluates the characters within their given context much as he or she would do when reading a novel concerning contemporary life. Undset's objective historical accuracy is far greater than that of nineteenth century romantic historical writers (such as Sir Walter Scott). She is far less interested than they, however, in bringing the heroic spirit of the past to bear upon the perceived mediocrities of her time. Undset believes, rather, that people should value the past for its own sake but realize that the same conflicts that ensnare and beset contemporaries also have afflicted their predecessors. In her broadmindedness in acknowledging the range of brilliance and shortsightedness, generosity and evil, of which women and men are capable, Undset succeeds in animating the distant past.

"Critical Evaluation" by Nicholas Birns

Further Reading

Allen, Walter Gore. *Renaissance in the North*. London: Sheed & Ward, 1946. Contains an informative essay on Undset's conversion to Catholicism at the age of forty-two, discussing its influence on both her contemporary-based and medieval-based works.

Bayerschmidt, Carl F. *Sigrid Undset*. New York: Twayne, 1970. Argues that Undset emphasized the empirical side of Christianity rather than the dogmatic. Includes a comprehensive biography.

Brunsdale, Mitzi. *Sigrid Undset: Chronicler of Norway*. Oxford, England: Berg, 1988. A comprehensive and wholly contemporary revaluation of Undset's canon, placing her firmly within a Norwegian historical and cultural context. Especially informative on the often neglected minor characters in *Kristin Lavransdatter*.

Gustafson, Alrik. "Christian Ethics in a Pagan World: Sigrid Undset." In *Six Scandinavian Novelists*. Minneapolis:

University of Minnesota Press, 1968. Places Undset within the context of European and Scandinavian modernism. Shows how her Christianity differentiated her from other modernist authors, but also suggests that the spiritual dilemmas faced by the characters in *Kristin Lavransdatter* have their counterparts in the modern age.

Lytle, Andrew. *Kristin*. Columbia: University of Missouri Press, 1992. This loving tribute to Undset's masterwork summarizes the plot and testifies to the book's moral values and its enduring emotional core. Filled with a tender affection for the book's central character.

Maman, Marie. *Sigrid Undset in America: An Annotated Bibliography and Research Guide*. Lanham, Md.: Rowman and Littlefield, 2000. A useful resource for English-speaking students. Maman has compiled bibliographies of American publications featuring information about Undset, placing them into four categories: reviews and articles about Undset's novels set in the Middle Ages, materials about Undset's contemporary novels, other articles, and book chapters about the writer. Also includes a bibliography of autobiographical material found in Undset's own works.

Mishler, William. "The Epic Novelists: Undset, Duun, Uppdal, Falkberget." In *A History of Norwegian Literature*, edited by Harold S. Naess. Lincoln: University of Nebraska Press, in cooperation with the American-Scandinavian Foundation, 1993. Analyzes Undset's works and places them within the broader context of Norwegian epic fiction.

Winsnes, A. H. *Sigrid Undset: A Study in Christian Realism*. Translated by P. G. Foote. New York: Sheed and Ward, 1953. A study of Undset as a writer in the realist tradition. Interprets, among other things, Undset's tendency to indulge in lengthy descriptions and analyses of mental states.

L

The Labyrinth of Solitude
Life and Thought in Mexico

Author: Octavio Paz (1914-1998)
First published: El laberinto de la soledad: Vida y
pensamiento de México, 1950; revised and enlarged,
1959 (English translation, 1961)
Type of work: Social criticism

Widely acknowledged as the greatest poet of his time in Mexico, Octavio Paz led a life that in many ways was typical of the Mexican intelligentsia he describes in *The Labyrinth of Solitude*. He published more than thirty books of poetry, fought with the Loyalists in Spain, and served his country as a diplomat. Deeply involved in the future of the Mexican land, he fitted himself out for defining it to the world by engaging in a career that included experiences of both intense action and intense contemplation.

The Labyrinth of Solitude was first published in 1950 by Jesús Silva Herzog's famous and influential magazine *Cuadernos Americanos*. The version that came to North Americans in 1961 through Lysander Kemp's translation is based on a second edition, revised and expanded, published by the Fondo de Cultura Economica in 1959. This book is in effect the result of labors that spanned a decade, labors that show themselves best in Paz's understanding of his own implications: The labyrinth he describes is the modern world.

Paz begins with an analysis of the phenomenon of the pachucos, those youths of Latin descent who during the 1940's and 1950's alarmed the cities of the American Southwest with their "antisocial" behavior, their peculiar dress, and their hostile acts and attitudes. He sees the pachuco as standing between Mexican culture and U.S. culture, in a limbo, unable to accept the values of either, equally alienated from both. Moreover, says Paz, the pachuco has, without understanding them, reasons for his attitude. Both cultures have cut themselves off from the flux of life, have failed in their separate ways to reconcile the individual and the universe. Unable to partake of communion, both the Mexican and the North American have thus become spiritual orphans, impris-

oned in the sterility of solitude. If the Mexican seclusion is similar to stagnant water, Paz says, North America is similar to a mirror. Neither contains life anymore.

The forces that confine the North American are summarized in the three sets of laws to which Paz pays due attention: the seventeenth century religious code of Calvinism, the eighteenth century political code of the Founders, and the nineteenth century moral code of the American Victorians. Caged by these sets of laws, North Americans have let themselves become ciphers, handling the universe easily by simply denying any part of it that might conflict with these codes. North Americans, therefore, live in a wholly artificial world, creating psychological mothers and fathers out of the delusions of Panglossism (Pangloss is the fictional philosopher who states that this is the best of all possible worlds). Mexicans, on the other hand, have no such delusions, but see themselves more or less clearly in their orphanhood, without a mother and without a father.

For a Mexican, life is a combat in which the role of an isolated individual can only be defensive. The Mexican's interior turbulence is a torture, and his or her exterior defensiveness destroys even the possibility of the communion that might bring happiness. Hence the Mexican's world is hollow, self-consuming, masochistic, and more or less devoid of love, for what love a Mexican knows is merely a form of narcissism. Paz says that Mexicans refuse to progress beyond themselves, to free themselves, to expose themselves to the outside world. If North American happiness exists only in illusions, Mexican happiness exists only in remotest theory.

Relief comes to a certain extent with the fiesta, a uniquely Mexican plunge into chaos from which the group emerges purified and strengthened, a drunken rapture during which people briefly confront themselves. The fiesta, however, cannot wholly offset the lack of communion; it is too impermanent, short-lived, and unstable. Mexicans oscillate between intimacy and withdrawal, shouting and silence, fiesta and wake, without ever surrendering to anything but themselves. Despite fiestas, Mexicans never really transcend their solitude.

Paz sees this solitude in Mexico as largely the result of the reform movement, which, following so many years after independence, finally disrupted both the Aztec and the colonial traditions. The new Spanish American nations are not new, he claims. Instead, they are static or decadent societies, remnants of older, more integrated cultures. Reform was thus an attempt at social reanimation. Its method, however, was based not on indigenous realities but on abstract and geometrical reasoning imported from Europe. The most profound effect of Mexico's liberal Constitution of 1857 was therefore the creation of a split between the individual Mexican and the native past. Mexicans became inevitably, at the moment of that split, orphaned from themselves.

The revolution that came after reform may be seen as a movement meant to overcome this orphanhood, to reconquer the past, to assimilate it, and to make it live in the present. Paz finds particular significance in the Zapatistas, whose program to reinstitute the ancient systems of land tenure epitomized the revolution on its ideological side. The revolution was above all, however, a "fiesta of bullets," the orgiastic celebration of a total Mexico daring at length to be, and to be in communion with itself.

Mexico's success in maintaining this communion after the shooting stopped has been, for various historical reasons, sharply limited. The essential solitude that Paz describes in his earlier chapters still stands, of course, as tragic as ever, with its accompanying problems. These problems are not merely Mexican; they are universal. In Paz's view the crisis of time is not the opposition of two great and different cultures but an inward struggle of one civilization that, unrivaled, is shaping the future of the whole world. Each person's fate involves all of humanity. Thus, Mexicans cannot solve their problems as Mexicans, for they are involved in matters that are universal, not merely national.

The existence of "underdeveloped" countries and of totalitarian "socialist" regimes in the twentieth century Paz regards as equally anomalous, equally scandalous, equally symptomatic of the social chaos that is the outward and visible sign of the labyrinth of solitude. Too often, an undeveloped country attempting to emerge from its economic prison becomes merely another victim of totalitarianism. The real

cure for chaos and sterility, says Paz, must therefore lie in an outgrowing and a rejection of those false divinities that rule the modern world: endless, infinite work and fixed, finite, chronometric time.

People today pretend they are always wide awake when they are thinking, but this is not true; usually thinking leads one into the nightmare of reason. After the nightmare is over one may realize that one was dreaming, not wide awake, and that dreams of reason are unbearable. With this in mind one may then close one's eyes to dream again. The only alternatives to the continuing frustration of labyrinthine solitude are suicide or some new kind of creative involvement and participation, the exercise of loving imagination in communion with the rest of the world.

The Labyrinth of Solitude is a wise book. Years spent in Paris did not seduce Paz into succumbing to the pathetic charms held out by existentialism. In this work he avoids the promulgation of a doctrine, achieving instead the kind of essential statement that one should expect from a poet. Anyone who thinks about the world in which people live and what that world does to people should find the book stimulating; it also provides perhaps the best gloss available on Paz's poetic work.

Further Reading

Alves, Abel A. "History, Mexico, the United States, and Humanity in the Writings of Octavio Paz." *CLIO: A Journal of Literature, History, and the Philosophy of History* 20, no. 1 (Fall, 1990): 53-63. Surveys the main themes of *The Labyrinth of Solitude*, including gender roles and Mexican history. Demonstrates how Paz believes that Mexicans can achieve an understanding of the present through an examination of the past.

Bell, Steven. "Contexts of Critical Reception in *El laberinto de la soledad*: The Contingencies of Value and the Discourse of Power." *Siglo XX / 20th Century* 20, nos. 2/3 (1992): 101-124. Examines the changing critical reception that Paz's essay has received over the years. Discusses Paz's view of power as male-centered.

Caistor, Nick. *Octavio Paz*. London: Reaktion Books, 2007. Biographical work presents analysis of Paz's essays and other writings. Describes Paz's participation in efforts to bring utopian revolution to Mexico while at the same time refusing to accept doctrinaire political ideologies.

Katra, William H. "Ideology and Society in *El laberinto de la soledad*, by Octavio Paz." *Chasqui* 15, nos. 2/3 (1986): 3-13. Offers a fairly harsh reading of Paz's essay. Argues that it gives rise to some misconceptions about Mexican society and the roles of men and women in that society.

Klein, Leonard S., ed. *Latin American Literature in the Twentieth Century: A Guide*. New York: Frederick Ungar, 1986. A section on *El laberinto de la soledad* discusses how Paz identifies concealment, or the use of a mask, as a symptom of the identity crisis suffered by modern Mexicans.

Quiroga, José. *Understanding Octavio Paz*. Columbia: University of South Carolina Press, 1999. Presents analyses of Paz's writings, with one chapter devoted to a lengthy examination of *The Labyrinth of Solitude*. Describes Paz's works as "open narratives" that explore the relationship between Paz and his readers.

Rosman, Silvia Nora. "On Being Mexican, for Example: Octavio Paz and the Dialectics of Universality." In *Being*

in *Common: Nation, Subject, and Community in Latin American Literature and Culture*. Lewisburg, Pa.: Bucknell University Press, 2003. Focuses on two of Paz's nonfiction works published in the 1950's, *The Labyrinth of Solitude* and *El arco y la lira* (1956; *The Bow and the Lyre*, 1971), discussing how they address the singularity of Mexican identity and are precursors to modern concepts of globalization.

Wilson, Jason. *Octavio Paz*. Boston: Twayne, 1986. Section on *The Labyrinth of Solitude* shows how Paz universalized his personal experiences of alienation to create a theory of the noncenteredness of modern Mexicans. Following the inspiration of the Surrealists, Paz saw love as the only escape from the prison of the modern world.

Lady Chatterley's Lover

Author: D. H. Lawrence (1885-1930)
First published: 1928
Type of work: Novel
Type of plot: Psychological realism
Time of plot: 1910-1920
Locale: English Midlands and London, England; Venice

Principal characters:
LADY CONSTANCE CHATTERLEY, a young woman of intelligence and latent sensuality
SIR CLIFFORD CHATTERLEY, her husband, a baronet, paralyzed in World War I
OLIVER MELLORS, Sir Clifford's gamekeeper, an ex-soldier and former blacksmith
BERTHA COUTTS, Mellors's wife, a vicious harridan
IVY BOLTON, a widow and nurse, Sir Clifford's personal caregiver
MALCOLM REID, Constance's father, a member of the Royal Academy of Arts
MICHAELIS, an Irish playwright, briefly Constance's lover
TOMMY DUKES, old army friend of Sir Clifford

The Story:

Constance Chatterley feels that her life is empty and pointless. A well-educated young woman in her mid-twenties, Connie had married Sir Clifford Chatterley in 1917 when he was on leave from the army and then tried to remain cheerful and encouraging during the two years he spent recovering from severe wounds suffered when he returned to battle in France. Now that Clifford is paralyzed from the waist down, Connie's life with him is primarily restricted to Wragby, the Chatterley family estate in the English Midlands, where she assists him with the short fiction he is producing with the aim of satisfying "a lame instinct for publicity." She finds the life of a baronet's wife to be stultifying in spite of her wish to be of support to her husband. She finds

the grimy coal towns of the Midlands soulless and ugly and fears that her separation from sensual experience is leading toward a very premature numbing of her still-embryonic passionate nature.

Aside from a brief interlude in Germany when she was eighteen, and her contact with Sir Clifford before his injury, Connie has had no opportunity to develop a sense of real sexual intimacy. Her growing restlessness and feelings of futility, combined with her distaste for many of the obligations of a landed aristocrat's wife, render her susceptible to the invitation of an Irish playwright, Michaelis, to begin an affair, but his "small boy's frail nakedness" and his calculated, commercial approach to art dishearten Connie. She tries to find something positive in her relationships with Sir Clifford and with "Mick," but she feels there must be more to a life with a man. As a means of making some kind of connection to a more vital aspect of life, and in response to her revulsion at the mechanized, money-mad world in which she lives, she begins to spend time in the woods around Wragby. One day, on a walk in the wilderness, she comes upon the cottage of Oliver Mellors, Sir Clifford's gamekeeper.

Mellors, who is almost forty, is very much at home in the wild; he is a former scholarship student and former soldier who grew up in Tevershall, a nearby coal town. He is separated from his wife, Bertha Coutts, and has a daughter who lives with his mother. Connie gradually begins to appreciate Mellors's sensitivity and intelligence. Although their early contacts are frequently contentious, Mellors grows steadily more sympathetic about Connie's unhappiness and, in the course of his comforting her, the two become involved sexually. Both of them recognize the terrible consequences of an affair, but the passionate attraction they share continues to draw them together as they discover that there is much more than just an erotic bond between them. Meanwhile, Ivy Bolton, a widow and nurse, is hired to help Sir Clifford with the basic tasks of his life, and this further enables Connie and Mellors to spend time together.

As Connie and Mellors become more deeply involved, Connie resolves to spend an entire night with the gamekeeper in his cottage in the woods. In a symbolic sense, this marks a turning point in Connie's life. She begins to consider the possibility of having a child, of leaving Clifford, and of beginning a new life with Mellors, who remains very much aware of the obstacles they face.

Connie's sister Hilda arrives at Wragby in preparation for a visit to the Continent that the women are to make with their father, and Mellors, blunt and direct as always, immediately alienates Hilda. Connie takes Mellors's side, and in doing this, she realizes that she is no longer really dependent on the opinions of others—either men or women—that have previously ordered her life. In her travels with her sister and father, Connie is not particularly engaged by either London or Paris because she is preoccupied with the possibility of joining Mellors; Venice, their holiday destination, seems to her frivolous and shallow. Back in England, Mellors has to deal with the return of his estranged wife, who, apparently not entirely mentally stable, is trying to reclaim a place in his life, as they had not been officially divorced after she deserted him.

In Venice, Connie tells her father that she is pregnant, and a plan is proposed in which Connie would tell Sir Clifford that Duncan Forbes, an artist, is the child's father. Forbes is willing to cooperate if necessary. In London, Connie's father

has a jovial meeting with Mellors, but then Mellors savages Forbes's paintings, speaking with characteristic candor and insight, an indication of the absurdity of the entire scheme. Connie attempts to carry out the deception, but in the course of her discussion with Sir Clifford when she returns to Wragby, her displeasure with all of the demands of a "proper" society, one that requires that appearances be maintained regardless of the human cost, drives her to a complete disclosure of her relationship with Mellors.

Sir Clifford, both enraged and distraught, obstinately refuses to grant Connie a divorce. Connie leaves Wragby to stay with Hilda in Scotland, and Mellors finds work on a farm, where he hopes to accumulate some savings while he and Connie wait for his divorce from Bertha to become official, for his and Connie's child to be born, and for the possibility that Sir Clifford might decide to grant Connie a divorce. Mellors writes a letter to Connie from the farm, where he feels comfortable and among friends; in the letter he expresses his hope that in spite of their problems, the intensity of their love, which brought "a flame into being," can sustain them until they can achieve a more permanent union in the future.

Critical Evaluation:

Lady Chatterley's Lover, a novel that D. H. Lawrence completed two years before his death, when he was already quite ill, might not be the culmination of his career as a writer, but it is a drawing together of the essential themes of his work. Between October, 1926, and January, 1928, Lawrence wrote three versions of the manuscript, polishing and revising the structure and language of the book in an attempt to convey his social, political, and artistic concerns as precisely and powerfully as he could. He realized that he would not be able to find a conventional publisher in England to issue the book, because he was determined to write about the erotic experiences of Connie Chatterley and Oliver Mellors using every word and image that the subject required, so he printed the first edition privately with the Italian firm of Giuseppe Orioli. Appearing six years after James Joyce's *Ulysses* (1922) and six years before Henry Miller's *Tropic of Cancer* (1934), *Lady Chatterley's Lover* was subject to the same vilification as those other two milestones of twentieth century literature. *Lady Chatterley's Lover* was not legally sold in Great Britain in an unexpurgated edition until 1960.

Throughout Lawrence's earlier work, the portrayals of various male characters tend toward an emphasis either on the physical nature of their being or on their cerebral agility—they are either men of the earth, rooted in elemental forces but limited in terms of linguistic dexterity, or men of the air, whose mental facilities are not adequate compensation for an absence of what Lawrence called "blood consciousness." In the short story "The Shades of Spring," Lawrence describes a gamekeeper who has a very vigorous physical presence and an intuitive understanding of the natural world but cannot articulate the splendor of his realm for the woman with whom he lives. In "The Blind Man" Lawrence delineates a brilliant, sophisticated barrister who is a sexual neuter and whose fragile veneer is crushed by a physical overture of friendship. These men, and many others in his writing, are Lawrence's expression of the defects of character inherent in men of the modern age, who had been damaged or stunted by what he regarded as an overly mechanized, relentlessly pecuniary, and dreadfully classist society.

In creating Oliver Mellors, Lawrence attempted to combine the strengths of a man who is at home in the natural world and who has awareness of his own body and pleasure in its capacity for sensual response with one who has eloquence in discussing it. Mellors has the style, education, manners, and confidence of a member of the upper class, but he despises the effects of class consciousness and division. The necessary complexity, as well as the unavoidable contradictions, seen in the character of Mellors have made him an object of critical controversy since the novel was published.

After the initial hysterical reaction to Lawrence's vividly explicit descriptions of sexual activity subsided, the divergent strains of Mellors's personality, and of Connie Chatterley's, compelled critical attention. There is a poignancy in the urgency with which Lawrence invests Mellors with many of his own ideas about art and life, frequently permitting Mellors to become engulfed by passionate declarations that mock the reserve and restraint of more circumspect novelists. Lawrence gives Mellors his own origins in coal-mining country; his own fluency with the Derby vernacular, which Mellors uses as a shield and a weapon; his own love for the English landscape, which Mellors sees with the image-making power of Lawrence's poetry; his own considerable erudition; and his own highly questionable beliefs about the instinctual truth of the skin and the senses. Similarly, his depiction of Connie Chatterley as a woman awakened by her sexual experiences with Mellors but also as a woman with "an immense respect for thought" who steadily grows toward an independence of outlook, opinion, and personal resolution has been the subject of considerable critical controversy, particularly in the light of some feminist scholarship that sees Mellors as a crude projection of phallic deity and Connie Chatterley as a kind of male power fantasy of a compliant, easily aroused, grateful woman.

As indicated by the continuing divergence in commentaries on *Lady Chatterley's Lover*, the relationship at its center remains engrossing. Lawrence was a master at creating the tone and inflection of conversation, and Connie and Mellors emerge as psychologically plausible, their behavior convincing, as much through their talk as through their erotic involvement. Their relationship resonates with the authenticity of vividly drawn, substantial human beings who achieve an intensity of existence unavailable to either one singly or, by implication, with anyone else. It is not perfection that Lawrence is reaching for with them, but possibility. As Lawrence, speaking with authorial conviction but from within the sphere of Connie's thoughts, writes:

And here lies the vast importance of the novel, properly handled. It can inform and lead into new places the flow of our sympathetic consciousness, and it can lead our sympathy away in recoil from things gone dead. Therefore, the novel, properly handled, can reveal the most secret places of life.

Leon Lewis

Further Reading

Britton, Derek. *"Lady Chatterley": The Making of the Novel*. Winchester, Mass.: Unwin Hyman, 1988. Provides a detailed look at the events of Lawrence's life from 1925 until the completion of the novel.

Burack, Charles Michael. *D. H. Lawrence's Language of Sacred Experience: The Transfiguration of the Reader*. New York: Palgrave Macmillan, 2005. Maintains that Lawrence structured *Lady Chatterley's Lover*, *The Rainbow* (1915), *The Plumed Serpent* (1926), and *Women in Love* (1920) as if they were religious initiation rites intended to evoke new spiritual experiences for their readers.

Cushman, Keith, and Earl G. Ingersoll, eds. *D. H. Lawrence: New Worlds*. Madison, N.J.: Fairleigh Dickinson University Press, 2003. Collection of essays aims to present reinterpretations of Lawrence's work. Topics addressed include Lawrence's influence on late twentieth century British fiction, debate regarding Lawrence's English identity, and myth in *Lady Chatterley's Lover*.

Fernihough, Anne, ed. *The Cambridge Companion to D. H. Lawrence*. New York: Cambridge University Press, 2001. Collection of essays offers interpretations of Lawrence's work from various perspectives. Includes the essay "Work and Selfhood in *Lady Chatterley's Lover*," by Morag Shiach.

Holbrook, David. *Where D. H. Lawrence Was Wrong About*

Woman. Lewisburg, Pa.: Bucknell University Press, 1992. Discusses Lawrence's depictions of women characters in his major fiction. A long, concluding chapter argues that Lawrence fails in his attempt to portray Connie Chatterley as a free woman.

Squires, Michael. *The Creation of "Lady Chatterley's Lover."* Baltimore: Johns Hopkins University Press, 1983. Provides detailed discussion of the development of the novel through the three versions that Lawrence wrote.

Squires, Michael, and Dennis Jackson, eds. *D. H. Lawrence's "Lady": A New Look at "Lady Chatterley's Lover."* Athens: University of Georgia Press, 1985. Contains twelve essays covering the novel's social and intellectual significance, artistic techniques, and historical context as well as its relationship to Lawrence's other works.

Worthen, John. *D. H. Lawrence: The Life of an Outsider.* New York: Counterpoint, 2005. Compelling and readable biography by a distinguished Lawrence scholar. Includes photographs.

Wright, T. R. *D. H. Lawrence and the Bible*. New York: Cambridge University Press, 2000. Argues that the Bible plays a significant role in almost all of Lawrence's works and analyzes Lawrence's use of biblical allusions and themes. Includes discussion of *Lady Chatterley's Lover*.

The Lady from the Sea

Author: Henrik Ibsen (1828-1906)
First produced: Fruen fra havet, 1889; first published, 1888 (English translation, 1890)
Type of work: Drama
Type of plot: Psychological realism
Time of plot: Nineteenth century
Locale: A small town in northern Norway

Principal characters:
DOCTOR WANGEL, a physician
ELLIDA, his second wife
BOLETTA and HILDA, his daughters by his first marriage
ARNHOLM, a schoolmaster
LYNGSTRAND, a sculptor
A STRANGER

The Story:

There is no real affection between Ellida Wangel and her two stepdaughters, Boletta and Hilda. Ellida married their father, Doctor Wangel, several years before, soon after the death of his first wife. She met him in the seacoast town that was her home, which she loved because it was near the sea. In fact, the sea had always dominated her life, and she feels stifled in her new home, which is surrounded by mountains.

Arnholm, Boletta's former tutor, pays a visit to the Wangel home. He had known and loved Ellida before her marriage to Doctor Wangel, but she had refused his suit because she was already betrothed to another. As the two old friends talk, a traveling sculptor, Lyngstrand, stops to tell them of a group he hopes to model. Lyngstrand has been at sea, where he met a sailor who told him a strange story. The sailor had married a woman who had promised to wait for him, but three years earlier he had read that his wife had married another man. The sailor told Lyngstrand that his wife was still his, that he would have her even though she had broken her vows.

This strange tale moves Ellida, seems even to frighten her. She is moody after hearing it, which makes her husband think she is unhappy because she is away from the sea. He offers to move his family to the seashore so that Ellida can regain her peace of mind, but Ellida knows that a move will not bring her happiness, whereas it certainly would make him and the girls unhappy to leave their home. She tells him the real cause of her misery. Some years before, she had come under the spell of a sailor whose ship was in port for only a few days. He, too, loved the sea and seemed to be part of it. Indeed, he and Ellida seemed to be animals or birds of the sea, so closely did they identify themselves with the vast waters. When the sailor murdered his captain, he was forced to flee. Before he left, he took a ring from his hand and one from hers, joined them together, and threw them into the sea. He told her that this act joined them in marriage and that she was to wait for him. At the time, she seemed to have no will of her own and to be completely under his spell. Later, she regained her senses and wrote to tell him that she did not consider the joining of the rings a lasting bond. He ignored her letters, however, and continued to tell her that he would come back to her.

Ellida tells her husband that she had forgotten the sailor until three years ago, when she was carrying the doctor's child. Then, suddenly, the sailor seemed very close to her. Her child, who lived only a few months, was born—or so she believed—with the eyes of the sailor. She has felt such guilt that from that time on she has not lived with her husband as his wife. The anguish she has suffered is affecting her mind, and she fears that she will go mad. She loves her husband, but she is drawn to the man of the sea whom she has not seen in ten years.

Doctor Wangel tries to comfort his wife, but he is also worried about her sanity. One day, a stranger appears in their garden. He is the sailor, come to claim Ellida. He tells her that he has come to hold her to the vow she had taken years before. Ellida says that she could never leave her husband, but the stranger will not listen. The doctor tells the man that he will never allow his wife to leave him and that the stranger cannot force her to go against her will. The stranger responds that he would never force her but that she will come to him of her own free will. Those words, "of her own free will," seem to fascinate Ellida. She repeats them over and over and gains strength from them. The stranger leaves, saying that he will return for her answer the next night; if she refuses to join him then, she will never see him again.

Ellida begs her husband to save her from the stranger. He tries to persuade her that her mind has been conditioned by Lyngstrand's story of the sailor and his unfaithful wife, and he also reminds her that the sailor does not even look as she had remembered him. Ellida will not be comforted, however. She concludes that there is only one way she can make the right decision and save her sanity: The doctor must release her from her marriage vows, not by divorce but verbally. Then she will be free to choose between her husband and the stranger. She says that she has never been free, for first she was under the will of the stranger and then she has been under the will of her husband.

The doctor refuses her request because he thinks he must save her from the stranger and from herself. He feels that the stranger exerts an evil influence over her, and he wants to save her from disaster. He promises her, however, that after the stranger leaves, he will release her from her vow to him and give her the freedom she wishes.

The next night, the stranger comes again as promised, and Ellida and her husband meet him in the garden. When the stranger asks Ellida to come with him of her own free will, the doctor orders the stranger to leave the country or be exposed as a murderer. The stranger shows them a pistol and says that he will use it to take his own life rather than give up his freedom.

Ellida again tells her husband that he must release her from her marriage vows; although he can keep her body tied down, he cannot fetter her soul and her desires. Seeing that she is right and that his refusal will drive his wife out of her mind, the doctor tells her that he will release her from her commitment to him. When she sees that he loves her enough to put her happiness above his own, she turns to the stranger, who is pleading with her to leave with him on the ship standing offshore, and tells him that now she can never go with him. The stranger, realizing that there is something between these two that is stronger than his will, leaves, promising never to return.

Ellida assures her husband that her mind is whole once more and that she will never again long for the stranger or the sea. The unknown no longer has any power over her, for at last she has made a decision of her own free will. Because she has been free to choose or reject the stranger, his fascination is gone. Now she can go with her husband and live with him again as his wife. She knows too that she can now win the affection of his daughters and come to think of them as her own. Ellida will never again feel like the wild, eager birds of the sea. In binding herself forever to the land, she will find freedom.

Critical Evaluation:

In the last phase of his career, Henrik Ibsen turned from the realistic social plays of his middle period toward a more psychological and, eventually, symbolic drama. He also shifted his emphasis from characters who are "normal," if extreme, to those more obviously "abnormal." He became fascinated by what he called the "trolls" or "demons" present in the back of the mind—that is, the irrational, subconscious side of the human personality that could erupt and dominate the actions of the most apparently stable individuals. Although there are important aspects of this transition in some of Ibsen's earlier plays, such as *Vildanden* (pb. 1884; *The Wild Duck*, 1891) and *Rosmersholm* (pb. 1886; English translation, 1889), it was in *The Lady from the Sea* that he first overtly dramatized this new preoccupation with the "demonic." *The Lady from the Sea* may lack the stature of Ibsen's major plays, both in the level of its craftsmanship and in the depth of its perceptions, but it remains a pivotal play in his development and also offers one of the author's most fascinating female characters.

Ellida Wangel, "the lady from the sea," is an intelligent, sensitive, vivacious, sensuous woman. She is also, clearly, on the edge of an emotional breakdown. She feels oppressed by her domestic routine and alienated from her immediate surroundings. Her husband loves her but is unable either to understand her or to communicate with her. Ellida respects and feels gratitude toward him, but, because she feels her marriage to have been a "business arrangement," she is unable to confide in him or to respond to him emotionally. She is even more isolated from his daughters, Boletta and Hilda, who treat Ellida as an intruder. They make this evident by celebrating their dead mother's birthday behind her back.

Such a stifling environment is, of course, common to many of Ibsen's great heroines—among them Nora Helmer, Mrs. Alving, Gina Ekdal, and Hedda Gabler—but only in *The Lady from the Sea* does it actually threaten to drive a woman to madness. Ellida's grasp on reality is precarious. She cannot forget that her own mother died in an asylum, and she is irrationally drawn to the sea; she is obsessed with the memory of her dead son, whose eyes, she believes, "changed with the seas." Her mood shifts are abrupt and erratic; she cannot even remember what people look like when they are out of her sight.

The focus of Ellida's obsession is, of course, the mysterious sailor whom she met before meeting Wangel. Although the vow she made to him was unsanctioned by law, Ellida cannot disregard it. She has felt his presence ever since her marriage to Wangel, and especially since the death of her son. The final crisis is provoked by his return to claim her as his "bride."

When he does appear, however, Ellida's reaction is a curious one, for she does not recognize him until she looks him directly in the eyes. It is not the stranger for whom Ellida longs but what he has come to represent to her. The sea, not the sailor, is the primary symbol, and it suggests the life of the imagination, of daring (the stranger once killed a man), of experience, and of total personal and spiritual fulfillment. The risk, however, is self-destruction. The real contest, all three participants realize, lies not in any contention over the physical possession of Ellida but within the mind and heart of the woman herself. "The root of that fascination lies in my own mind," she tells Wangel, "what can you do against that?"

Wangel finally realizes that even if he forces her to remain with him, he will lose her to insanity. As a trained and sensitive doctor, he also sees that she will be destroyed if she goes with the stranger. Caught on the horns of this dilemma, he makes a desperate and, for him, soul-wrenching decision: He gives her the absolute freedom to make her own choice and be responsible for the consequences of it.

Those two words, "freedom" and "responsibility," give Ellida power over herself, and they resolve the play. Three factors free her from the stranger's power: Hilda's emotional reaction to the news that Ellida may be going away suggests to Ellida the real possibility of a relationship with the girls, Wangel's obvious agonizing over his decision proves the depths of his devotion, and her own restored responsibility has given her the strength to look directly at the stranger.

Once she sees things clearly, the choice is not difficult. Because Ellida is allowed—indeed, forced—to take control of her own life, she does so, thus not only resolving her marital difficulties but also, more important, regaining her mental and emotional stability.

Further Reading

Binding, Paul. *With Vine-Leaves in His Hair: The Role of the Artist in Ibsen's Plays*. Norwich, England: Norvik Press, 2006. Examines the character of the artist-rebel in *The Lady from the Sea* and four other Ibsen plays. Demonstrates how this character represents the tensions of society at the time Ibsen was writing.

Durbach, Errol. *"Ibsen the Romantic": Analogues of Paradise in the Later Plays*. Athens: University of Georgia Press, 1982. Argues that the marriage depicted in *The Lady from the Sea* is a positive counterpart to the marriages Ibsen portrays in *Et dukkehjem* (pr., pb. 1879; *A Doll's House*, 1880) and *Hedda Gabler* (pb. 1890; English translation, 1891).

Haugen, Einar. *Ibsen's Drama: Author to Audience*. Minneapolis: University of Minnesota Press, 1979. Provides a superb general introduction to Ibsen's works and their place in European cultural history. Includes discussion of *The Lady from the Sea*.

Holtan, Orley I. *Mythic Patterns in Ibsen's Last Plays*. Minneapolis: University of Minnesota Press, 1970. Presents a thorough discussion of the psychological, philosophical, and mythic aspects of *The Lady from the Sea*, arguing that the play should be regarded from the perspective of myth or allegory.

Jacobsen, Per Schelde, and Barbara Fass Leavy. *Ibsen's Forsaken Merman: Folklore in the Late Plays*. New York: New York University Press, 1988. Discussion of Ibsen's use of folklore motifs addresses the similarities between Ellida Wangel and such mythological creatures as mermaids and seal maidens.

McFarlane, James, ed. *The Cambridge Companion to Ibsen*. New York: Cambridge University Press, 1994. Collection of essays addresses a wide variety of topics, such as Ibsen's dramatic apprenticeship; his historical dramas, comedies, and realistic problem dramas; and his working methods. Includes discussion of *The Lady from the Sea*.

Moi, Toril. "The Art of Transformation: Art, Marriage, and Freedom in *The Lady from the Sea*." In *Henrik Ibsen and the Birth of Modernism: Art, Theater, Philosophy*. New York: Oxford University Press, 2006. Refutes the traditional definition of Ibsen as a realistic and naturalistic playwright and describes him as an early modernist.

Robinson, Michael, ed. *Turning the Century: Centennial Essays on Ibsen*. Norwich, England: Norvik Press, 2006. Collection of essays published in the journal *Scandinavica* from the 1960's to the early twenty-first century. Includes discussions of Ibsen's style, his language, and the reception of his plays in England. One essay analyzes *The Lady from the Sea*.

Templeton, Joan. *Ibsen's Women*. New York: Cambridge University Press, 1997. Examines the women characters in Ibsen's plays and their relationships to the women in the playwright's life and career. Chapter 8 includes an analysis of *The Lady from the Sea*.

Weigand, Herman J. *The Modern Ibsen: A Reconsideration*. 1925. Reprint. Salem, N.H.: Ayer, 1984. Provides an excellent introduction to Ibsen's later plays. Contains a good discussion of *The Lady from the Sea* that praises the subtlety of the psychological portrayal of the main character.

The Lady of the Lake

Author: Sir Walter Scott (1771-1832)
First published: 1810
Type of work: Poetry
Type of plot: Historical
Time of plot: Sixteenth century
Locale: Scottish Highlands

Principal characters:
JAMES OF DOUGLAS, a banished nobleman
ELLEN DOUGLAS, his daughter
MALCOLM GRAEME, a nobleman loved by Ellen
RODERICK DHU, a rebel Highland chief
JAMES FITZ-JAMES, a nobleman of royal birth
ALLAN-BANE, a minstrel

The Poem:

As he follows a stag during a hunt, James Fitz-James becomes lost in the Highlands. He wanders around until he comes to Loch Katrine, a beautiful lake surrounded by steep mountains. There he meets the lovely Ellen, who tells him that his coming was foretold by Allan-Bane, an ancient minstrel who serves her father. When she offers the hunter food and shelter for the night, Ellen does not volunteer her name or anything of her family history, and out of courtesy he does not ask questions. Fitz-James is disturbed, however, because the young woman bears a marked resemblance to members of the Douglas clan, a family banished by the king. When he departs the next morning, he still knows nothing about the young woman whose beauty and grace have deeply touched his heart.

Fitz-James is correct in his fear that Ellen is of the Douglas clan. Her father is James of Douglas, once a powerful friend of the king but now hunted and with a price on his head. He and Ellen and his sister are protected by Roderick Dhu, a rebel against the king and the leader of a large and powerful Highland clan. Roderick Dhu wants Ellen's hand in marriage, but although she honors him for the aid he has given her father, she detests him for his many cruel and merciless deeds. He kills and plunders at will, trying to avenge

himself on the king and the Lowlanders who, he believes, have robbed him and his people of their land and wealth. Among the men he hates is Malcolm Graeme, a young nobleman, Ellen's former suitor, whom she loves. After Ellen's refusal of his proposal, Roderick Dhu calls his clan together to fight Malcolm and the other supporters of the king. He claims that he fears Malcolm will lead the king to Douglas's hiding place.

Like lightning, burning beacons and swift-riding messengers carry through the Highlands word that the clan is gathering. Young grooms leave their brides at church doors, and boys replace fathers who have died since the last gathering. The women and children are placed on a lonely and protected island for safety, for a fierce and dangerous battle is to be fought. A hermit monk prophesies that whichever side spills the first foe's blood will be the victor. The prophecy suits Roderick Dhu, whose men have seen a spy lurking in the mountains and even now have lured the stranger into paths that will lead him into a trap. He will be killed by Roderick Dhu's men, and thus the Highlanders will be assured of victory.

James of Douglas leaves Ellen. Although he does not tell her his destination, she knows that he is going to give himself up to the king in order to prevent the bloodshed of a great battle. After he goes, Allan-Bane tries to cheer Ellen by telling her that his harp sings of glad tidings, but she will not hear him. As she sits grieving, Fitz-James appears again. Ellen knows that he has been tricked by Roderick Dhu's men, for no one could gain entrance to a place so hidden and secret without their knowledge. Fitz-James, refusing to heed her warning, asks her to return to the court with him. She refuses, telling him of her love for Malcolm Graeme. Fitz-James then removes from his finger a ring that was given to him by the king and explains to her that the king owes him a favor and will grant any request made by the bearer of the ring. A safe journey through the Lowlands is also promised to anyone wearing it. Fitz-James places the ring on Ellen's finger and then departs quickly.

His guide leads him through the mountain paths until they come upon a crazed woman who sings a warning song to Fitz-James. The guide thrusts his sword into her, and Fitz-James then kills the guide. He goes to the side of the crazed woman, who, before she dies, tells him that Roderick Dhu killed her lover and caused her to lose her sanity. Fitz-James vows that he will meet Roderick Dhu and avenge the woman. Having been warned by her as well as by Ellen, he travels on cautiously. When he stumbles on a sentry stationed by a watch fire, the sentry calls him a spy, wanted by Roderick Dhu, but offers him rest and safety, for the laws of the clansmen demand courtesy even to one's enemies. The guard promises to lead Fitz-James safely through Roderick Dhu's lines and—even though Fitz-James calls Roderick Dhu a coward and a murderer—keeps his word. When they reach a place of safety, the sentry reveals himself as Roderick Dhu. His promise fulfilled, he then challenges Fitz-James to a duel. In personal combat Roderick Dhu proves the stronger, but Fitz-James, who is more skilled, overcomes the rebel. Then Fitz-James blows his horn and calls his men to carry Roderick Dhu to a prison cell.

In the meantime, James of Douglas has gone to the court to give himself up. First, however, he takes part in some games being staged that day and wins every event he enters. The whisper goes through the crowd that only a Douglas could possess such skill and strength. Douglas then offers himself to the king as a ransom for his friends and clansmen. When the king orders him thrown into prison, the people side with Douglas and are ready to rise against the king, but Douglas quiets them, for he will not act against his monarch. He allows himself to be taken, and the king sends messengers to the Highlanders with word that there is no need to fight; Douglas has surrendered and Roderick Dhu is a prisoner.

Ellen, accompanied by Allan-Bane, goes to the court to seek the release of her father. The ring that Fitz-James has given her guarantees her safety along the way. Before news comes that a truce has been arranged, Allan-Bane goes to Roderick Dhu's cell and sings to him of a fierce battle that has been fought. Roderick Dhu dies with a smile, for he believes that his clansmen have fought bravely.

Ellen prepares for her audience with the king, and Fitz-James comes to her quarters to conduct her to the court. When they arrive, she notes that everyone bows before Fitz-James; not until then does she realize that Fitz-James is in reality the king. He tells her to claim the favor promised by the ring, but it seems there is nothing left for her to ask. The king has already restored her father to favor, and Roderick Dhu is dead, so she cannot plead mercy for him. She tries to stammer something about Malcolm Graeme, and the king reads her heart, calling Malcolm to her side. He forgives Malcolm for trying to aid the rebels and redeems the ring Ellen wears by joining her with her beloved.

Critical Evaluation:

After the unexpected popularity of *The Lay of the Last Minstrel* (1805), Walter Scott began *The Lady of the Lake* but laid it aside in favor of *Marmion: A Tale of Flodden Field* (1808), which was again a success with his readers. *The Lady of the Lake* is now regarded as a better poem than either *The Lay of the Last Minstrel* or *Marmion* and is probably read more often. After writing it, Scott created several other long poems of the same kind. His next, *The Vision of Don Roderick* (1811), failed to satisfy the expectations raised by his former efforts and was made to look all the worse when a previously little-known poet named Lord Byron came out in 1812 with the first half of his electrifying *Childe Harold's Pilgrimage*, which dealt not with the Scottish past but with the English present.

Unwilling as yet to be shunted aside, Scott persevered with *Rokeby* (1813), a poem set in Yorkshire. He had little firsthand knowledge of that area and lacked the intuitive understanding of its people that had make his Scottish poems so popular; *Rokeby*, therefore, is the worst of his failures. Scott's *The Bridal of Triermain* (1813) is the first of many nineteenth century poems with an Arthurian theme. *The Lord of the Isles* (1815) and *Harold the Dauntless* (1817) have Scottish themes and each has some fine elements, but neither equals *The Lady of the Lake*. By the time they appeared, Scott had lost confidence in his abilities as a poet and was instead committed to a series of influential but anonymous historical novels, of which the first is *Waverley: Or, 'Tis Sixty Years Since* (1814; begun in 1805). It is his novels for which Scott has become best known by present-day readers.

Scott's poems were written at a time when poetry was still a more prestigious literary form than prose. At the time of his birth, in 1771, there were few good poets in English literature, and none of them were Scots. Robert Burns, whom Scott met as a boy, became famous for his short poems, called lyrics, which were often set to music. Burns and other poets of his time turned away from the impersonal moralizing and philosophical reflection previously typical of literary practice and emphasized the pleasure or pain of intense but momentary emotions. This same concentration on the inner states of the poet proved increasingly more congenial to readers during the stressful years of the Napoleonic Wars than did Scott's restraint.

The Lady of the Lake was published in 1810, while the conflict with Napoleon was at its height. As a result of the war, British tourists could not visit France and Italy on the extended jaunts that previously had been popular, and travel to Scotland increased. In prewar times, few Englishmen had thought of Scotland as a scenic destination, but, trapped at home by international strife, British readers were attracted to literature that enhanced the scenic and historic value of their own island. After 1815, when the Battle of Waterloo had been fought and Napoleon subdued for the final time, the English rushed to revisit places in other European countries that they had been unable to reach since the beginning of the troubles with France in 1789. The popularity of Scotland fell off to a considerable extent, and Scott's popularity as a poet fell with it.

Although Scott is known for re-creating actual great events, *The Lady of the Lake* is only marginally historical. Unlike some of Scott's other poems and novels, it lacks a fierce concluding battle. The most historically based character is the disguised hunter at the beginning of the poem, James Fitz-James. In canto 6, stanza 26, it is revealed that he is actually James V (1512-1542), king of Scotland. The reign of James V, begun in 1524, was notable for his oppression of the Douglas clan, for his defense of the Catholic faith in opposition to that of newly arisen Protestantism, and for his popularity with the Scottish people. James's daughter and successor was Mary, Queen of Scots, who was held prisoner for years by Elizabeth I of England and eventually executed by her.

None of the other characters in *The Lady of the Lake* has a historical identity. James of Douglas, Malcolm Graeme, Roderick Dhu, and Allan-Bane are plausible but fictitious creations of Scott's imagination. One has only to compare them with similar characters in Scott's two earlier poems to discover how much his ability to create characters improved over time. Ellen Douglas is an attractive heroine and the title

character (see 1, 17). The lake of the title is Loch Katrine, a beautiful spot in the Trossachs northwest of Sterling. Although it previously had been ignored, Loch Katrine achieved great fame through the publication of Scott's poem, and its continuing renown is still in evidence. Perhaps no other poem in the English language has immortalized a scene so effectively.

Not surprisingly, *The Lady of the Lake* is particularly noted for its descriptive passages, but one should not overlook the quality of its interpolated lyrics, including "Hail to the Chief" (2, 19-20), "Coronach" (3, 16), and "Hymn to the Virgin" (3, 29). The last of these (based in part on Luke 1:28) has been set to music as "Ave Maria."

"Critical Evaluation" by Dennis R. Dean

Further Reading

Cockshut, A. O. J. *The Achievement of Walter Scott.* London: Collins, 1969. Presents a reasonable, centrist introduction to the man and his work. Chapters on Scott's major poems precede those dealing with his novels and other works.

Daiches, David. *Sir Walter Scott and His World.* London: Thames and Hudson, 1971. Competently written, well-illustrated introduction to Scott includes good views of the landscapes and other settings made famous by *The Lady of the Lake.*

Felluga, Dino Franco. *The Perversity of Poetry: Romantic Ideology and the Popular Male Poet of Genius.* Albany: State University of New York Press, 2005. Examines the nineteenth century reception of Romantic poetry, focusing on the work of Scott and Lord Byron. Demonstrates how Scott's poetry was represented as a "panacea" for the era's utilitarianism, capitalism, industrialism, and democracy.

Gamer, Michael. "'To Foist Thy Stale Romance': Scott, Antiquarianism, and Authorship." In *Romanticism and the Gothic: Genre, Reception, and Canon Formation.* New York: Cambridge University Press, 2000. Analysis of Scott's poetry is part of a larger discussion of works by Romantic writers that demonstrates how these authors were influenced by many of the conventions of earlier gothic literature.

Goslee, Nancy Moore. *Scott the Rhymer.* Lexington: University Press of Kentucky, 1988. Offers one of the few serious critiques of Scott's long poems undertaken since modern techniques of analysis were developed. Includes separate chapters on *The Lay of the Last Minstrel, Marmion,* and *The Lady of the Lake.*

Johnson, Edgar. *Sir Walter Scott: The Great Unknown*. 2 vols. New York: Macmillan, 1970. Critical biography is among the most important modern books available on Scott. Contains unsurpassed discussions of his major poems, including *The Lay of the Last Minstrel*, *Marmion*, and *The Lady of the Lake*.

Lincoln, Andrew. *Walter Scott and Modernity*. Edinburgh: Edinburgh University Press, 2007. Examines Scott's novels and poems and asserts that these were not works of nostalgia; instead, Scott used the past as a means of exploring modernist moral, political, and social issues. Includes discussion of *The Lady of the Lake*.

Lady Windermere's Fan

Author: Oscar Wilde (1854-1900)
First produced: 1892; first published, 1893
Type of work: Drama
Type of plot: Comedy of manners
Time of plot: Nineteenth century
Locale: London

Principal characters:
LADY WINDERMERE, a proper woman
LORD WINDERMERE, her husband
LORD DARLINGTON, a man-about-town
MRS. ERLYNNE, an adventurer
LORD AUGUSTUS LORTON, Mrs. Erlynne's fiancé

The Story:

On Lady Windermere's birthday, Lord Windermere presents her with the gift of a beautiful, delicately wrought fan with her name, Margaret, engraved on it. She intends to carry the fan at a ball she is giving that evening, a ball to which everyone of importance in London has been invited. That afternoon, the duchess of Berwick calls on Lady Windermere to tell her friend of a rumored affair between Lord Windermere and Mrs. Erlynne, a fascinating but notorious woman not received in the best houses. According to the duchess's story, Lord Windermere has for some months been supplying Mrs. Erlynne with funds for her support. The old dowager suggests that Lady Windermere take immediate steps to learn the nature of the relationship between the two.

Lady Windermere, upset, is determined to find out if there is any truth to the gossip. She finds a locked bankbook in her husband's desk, and, ripping it open, discovers evidence of her husband's duplicity, a record of checks issued to Mrs. Erlynne over a long period of time. Angry and hurt at Lord Windermere's apparent failure to appreciate love and virtue, she turns on him the moment he appears. His main concern is annoyance that his wife has dared tamper with his property behind his back. He informs her that his relations with Mrs. Erlynne are perfectly honorable, that she is a fine but unfortunate woman who wishes to win the regard of society once more. Moreover, Lord Windermere explicitly orders his wife to send Mrs. Erlynne an invitation to the ball. When Lady Windermere refuses, her husband writes an invitation. An-

gered at his act, Lady Windermere threatens to strike Mrs. Erlynne with her new fan if she dares cross the threshold of Windermere House.

When Mrs. Erlynne appears at the ball, Lady Windermere loses her resolution and lets the fan drop to the floor. The guests, believing that Mrs. Erlynne has been invited by Lady Windermere herself, accept her. She is lionized by all the men, and the women, curious because of the many stories they have heard, want to see at first hand what she is really like. Among Mrs. Erlynne's special admirers is Lord Augustus Lorton, the duchess of Berwick's disreputable brother, to whom she has just become engaged to be married.

Mrs. Erlynne is not the only woman greatly admired that evening. Lord Darlington is persistently attentive to Lady Windermere. Having sharply turned Lord Darlington's advances down, Lady Windermere becomes despondent when she unexpectedly catches sight of her husband and Mrs. Erlynne in rapt conversation.

Without waiting to see her guests out, Lady Windermere writes a letter informing Lord Windermere that she is leaving his house forever. She gives the letter to a servant to deliver and leaves for Lord Darlington's apartment.

Mrs. Erlynne, who with Lord Augustus has remained behind to talk with Lord Windermere after the other guests have gone, discovers the letter Lady Windermere has written, and the thought of that lady's rash act brings back old memories. Twenty years before, Mrs. Erlynne had written a similar letter to her husband and had left him and their child for a lover who later deserted her. Her years of social ostracism have made her a stranger to her own daughter. Perhaps, however, she can keep her daughter from making the same mistake; Lady Windermere should never feel the remorse that her mother, Mrs. Erlynne, has known.

Mrs. Erlynne takes Lady Windermere's letter before Lord Windermere can see it and hurries to Lord Darlington's apartment, first persuading Lord Augustus to take Lord Windermere to his club and keep him there for the rest of the night. In Lord Darlington's rooms, without revealing her identity, Mrs. Erlynne manages to persuade Lady Windermere to think of her child and go back to her husband. Out of the depths of her own bitter experience, Mrs. Erlynne insists that Lady Windermere's first duty is not to her husband but to her child.

As Lady Windermere is leaving, Lord Darlington returns, accompanied by Lord Windermere, Lord Augustus, and several cohorts. Ready to face the men, Mrs. Erlynne counsels Lady Windermere to slip behind a curtain to await a fortuitous moment for escape. Upon learning of Lord Augustus's presence, Mrs. Erlynne goes into the next room, hoping to avoid detection. Lord Windermere soon discovers his wife's fan and faces Lord Darlington with it. Giving Lady Windermere the opportunity to exit, Mrs. Erlynne appears suddenly from the adjoining room with the explanation that she had taken the fan, mistaking it for her own, when she left Windermere House. Her explanation saves Lady Windermere at the cost of her own reputation. Lord Windermere is furious, for he feels that he has in good faith befriended and helped a woman who is beneath contempt, and Lord Augustus turns away.

The next morning, having realized that, by some strange irony, the "bad" woman has accepted public disgrace in order to save the "good" one, Lady Windermere defends Mrs. Erlynne to her husband, who persists in disparaging the adventurer. Frustrated by Lord Windermere's demand that she not see Mrs. Erlynne again, Lady Windermere poises herself to explain all. Then Mrs. Erlynne arrives to return the fan, but she refuses to reveal herself to her daughter, not wanting to shatter Lady Windermere's illusions. Taking advantage of the simultaneous arrival of Lord Augustus and her coach, Mrs. Erlynne asks her now-cold suitor to escort her out; he does so and then accepts her explanation that his own interests had taken her to Lord Darlington's rooms. When he returns to the Windermeres to share his good news, Lord Windermere tells him that he is marrying a very clever woman. Lady Windermere insists that he is marrying a good woman.

Critical Evaluation:

Oscar Wilde, the celebrated dandy of the Victorian fin de siècle, described *Lady Windermere's Fan*, his first financially successful theater piece, as "one of those modern drawing-room plays with pink lampshades." Although such a classification might initially appear to be frivolous, when this remark is placed in the context of Mrs. Erlynne's statement, "I have never admitted that I am more than twenty-nine, or thirty at the most. Twenty-nine when there are pink shades, thirty when there are not," it can be seen that Wilde viewed his play as generously contributing to society's ability to pose what the careful observer might call an illusion. Wilde's own description demonstrates how his play marshals witty epigrams to dismiss itself as fluff, foster society's illusions about itself, and reveal—to those careful about construing his meaning—how what is seen is pure fabrication. With or without pink shades, Mrs. Erlynne is nearing forty, but given her society's values, to present herself as forty would severely limit her options.

Mrs. Erlynne will hardly limit her options unnecessarily, since Wilde wishes her—as a fallen woman and beautiful adventurer—to represent the role he would have art play in the world. For the timid, such as Lord and Lady Windermere, who can function adequately only in a world of illusion, art hides the truths that would ravage their lives while saving them from ruinous mistakes by living those mistakes for them. For those reckless enough to know more, art can help them to understand and find peace with the complexities and compromises necessary to achieve wider vision and greater—as Wilde would put it—individualism.

Mrs. Erlynne sees and understands more than any of the other characters in *Lady Windermere's Fan*, which she can do because she has fallen. She has seen and embraced the other side of life, so she can face the reality of both good and evil, dealing with each appropriately without letting society's definitions rule her. She can cross the line because she has already crossed the line and survived. She can blackmail Windermere and bamboozle Lord Augustus because she does not fear falling anymore. She can get what she wants from those who have the power to refuse her—although they choose not to—in contrast to the duchess of Berwick, who, tied up in society's knots, must get what she wants by dominating her powerless daughter and devastating other inexperienced women through gossip and cynical sexism.

This contrast between Mrs. Erlynne and the duchess reveals the beauty of the freedom Mrs. Erlynne has. She can live her own life while allowing others to live theirs. If, in Lord Darlington's apartment, she decides Lady Windermere's fate for her, she does so with the understanding of the fate Lady Windermere would prefer for herself but thinks she has lost. If she decides Lord Augustus's fate, she does so knowing that he believes "she is just the woman for me. Suits me down to the ground." When she gets each of them what they want, she does so fully aware that she is compromising some of her own needs but meeting others. She can thus sacrifice without eliciting from them a guilty sense of debt: "Then pay your debt by silence. That is the only way in which it can be paid."

Because she can compromise, she can find a certain contentment in a future abroad, which Lord Darlington, who gives up and leaves the country in a fit of romantic torpor, lacks the maturity to understand. She can take pleasure in a man who loves her. In contrast, when Lord Darlington is rejected by Lady Windermere, "all other women in the world become absolutely meaningless" to him. The dandy's delights, which Lord Darlington had previously avowed, disintegrate in the face of defeat. Lord Darlington has only assumed the dandy's pose, not learned to live it. Mrs. Erlynne, on the other hand, knowing full well that life consists of nothing but poses, can deftly lie to snatch victory from the reversals that structure the play as a whole.

Mrs. Erlynne's consummate gift for lying with total awareness and fully conscious control not only distinguishes her from the rest of her society but also most clearly identifies her with Wilde's realm of art. Wilde has courage enough to break free from earlier theorists who sought to validate art on the basis of its access to fictional truth, to a truth that goes beneath and beyond ordinary perceptions of reality. Wilde is not afraid to face the truth that all societies base themselves on an ideology of lies and that cultures cannot be preserved and purified through truth—which is seldom conclusively definable and often downright harmful—but only through lies, though not typical, everyday, vapid lies, such as the exchanges among the guests when they first arrive at the ball, although those have their place. What are needed are artful, daring, perceptive lies that create new possibilities for a social order that allows as many people as possible the chance to live more happily than before.

Wilde recognizes that lies will always rule the world, so instead of attempting to conquer self-serving and decayed lies with an unconvincing "truth," he proposes surpassing them with better and more beautiful lies that will lead to a more general good. The belief that Lady Windermere holds at the end of the play, that Mrs. Erlynne is a very good woman, remains debatable as truth. Wilde takes great care to show Mrs. Erlynne rejecting her newly discovered maternal instincts and threatening Lord Windermere that she will

"mar every moment of [Lady Windermere's] life" should he divulge Mrs. Erlynne's identity. Such a scene helps the audience to resist sentimentalizing Mrs. Erlynne as Lady Windermere does. Nevertheless, one must question whether Mrs. Erlynne really means her threat or whether this is just another pose to accomplish a goal. If she means it, then she might be considered truly bad, but if she is lying, then she is truly very good. *Lady Windermere's Fan* forces the audience to recognize the logical impossibility of clearly separating good from evil and offers a marvelous illustration of what Wilde proposes as the ideological role of art.

"Critical Evaluation" by David B. Arnett

Further Reading

Brooks, Cleanth, and Robert B. Heilman. *Understanding Drama: Twelve Plays*. New York: Holt, 1948. Includes an indispensable act-by-act analysis of *Lady Windermere's Fan* that points to problems in the play's characterization and motivation and measures the work against defined genres.

Cohen, Philip K. *The Moral Vision of Oscar Wilde*. Rutherford, N.J.: Fairleigh Dickinson University Press, 1978. Discusses *Lady Windermere's Fan* in terms of a societal shift from Old Testament to New Testament values.

Fortunato, Paul L. "Consumer Fashion and Modernist Aesthetics in *Lady Windermere's Fan*." In *Modernist Aesthetics and Consumer Culture in the Writings of Oscar Wilde*. New York: Routledge, 2007. Examination of *Lady Windermere's Fan* is part of a larger discussion of Wilde as a "consumer modernist" whose concern with surface ornament and ephemeral public image would become fundamental characteristics of twentieth century modernism.

Kileen, Jarlath. *The Faiths of Oscar Wilde: Catholicism, Folklore, and Ireland*. New York: Palgrave Macmillan, 2005. Discussion of Wilde's work focuses on his lifelong attraction to Catholicism. Explores the influence of his Protestant background, and his antagonism toward it, on his work.

McKenna, Neil. *The Secret Life of Oscar Wilde*. London: Century, 2003. Controversial and groundbreaking biography focuses on the influence of Wilde's sexuality, and of homosexuality in the Victorian era, on his life and work. Includes illustrations.

Pearce, Joseph. *The Unmasking of Oscar Wilde*. London: HarperCollins, 2000. Examines Wilde's emotional and spiritual searching, including his fascination with Catholicism.

Powell, Kerry. *Oscar Wilde and the Theater of the 1890's.* New York: Cambridge University Press, 1990. Sets Wilde's work within its theatrical and social contexts. The chapter devoted to *Lady Windermere's Fan* provides the basis for comparisons made throughout the book.

Sammells, Neil. *Wilde Style: The Plays and Prose of Oscar Wilde.* New York: Longman, 2000. Argues that the primary aesthetic of Wilde's work is not art but style. Describes how his society comedies, including *Lady Windermere's Fan*, became more stylized over time.

The Lady's Not for Burning

Author: Christopher Fry (1907-2005)
First produced: 1948; first published, 1949
Type of work: Drama
Type of plot: Comedy
Time of plot: c. 1400
Locale: The small market town of Cool Clary

Principal characters:
RICHARD, an orphaned clerk
THOMAS MENDIP, a discharged soldier
HEBBLE TYSON, mayor of Cool Clary
MARGARET DEVIZE, his sister
NICHOLAS and HUMPHREY, her sons
ALIZON ELIOT, Humphrey's fiancé
JENNET JOURDEMAYNE, an alleged witch

The Story:

Thomas Mendip wants to be hanged, but he can get no one to take an interest in his case because everyone in Cool Clary is interested in a woman accused of witchcraft—specifically, of having turned old Skipps, the rag and bone man, into a dog. Thomas begs the mayor's clerk, Richard, to get him an audience with the mayor so that he can confess his crime, but Richard has other things on his mind. The mayor's nephew, Humphrey Devize, has been betrothed to Alizon Eliot, and the girl is due to arrive any minute. No one has time for a fool who wants to be hanged.

Alizon is one of six daughters, and her father had feared that he had too many girls to marry off. He had placed Alizon in a convent, but after he married off his other daughters easily enough, he changed his mind about her, and now he has promised her to Humphrey. Humphrey's brother Nicholas has read in the stars that Alizon belongs to him, however, and so he knocks his brother down, hoping to kill him and take Alizon for himself. Humphrey, although not dead, lies still—he has not knocked himself down, so he will not pick himself up. Their mother, Margaret Devize, sister of the mayor, sometimes thinks motherhood is too much for any woman. Since the boys have become untidy from lying in the rain and mud, she fears that Humphrey's appearance might discourage Alizon, which it does.

When Mayor Hebble Tyson finds Thomas waiting to be hanged, he is very much upset. Hebble is tired of strangers dropping into town with such ridiculous requests; it is all very irregular. Suspecting that someone is making a mockery of his authority, he threatens to have Thomas tortured if he does not go away and stop his bother. Thomas, however, holds out for hanging. He confesses to killing old Skipps and a worthless pander. He does not expect to get the favor of hanging for nothing; he knows the rules, all right.

Thomas's interview with Hebble is interrupted by an announcement from Nicholas that a witch is waiting to see the mayor. Poor Hebble, upset at the news, insists that he will not have his dignity mocked. The witch is a beautiful young woman named Jennet Jourdemayne, a wealthy orphan whose property will be confiscated if she is condemned for witchcraft. Jennet thinks the accusations against her are a joke; she has been accused of turning old Skipps into a dog and of other evil deeds. She has come to Hebble for the protection of his laughter at the crimes of which the mob outside accuses her. Hebble, not amused, sends for the constable to arrest her. Thomas tries to divert attention from Jennet to himself by insisting that he murdered Skipps and the pander, but no one pays any attention to him; he is poor and decidedly strange. He even tells all assembled that the end of the world will come that night. All he gets for his pains is to be thrown into the cellar with Jennet, to await her burning the next day.

Hebble and his associates have a problem on their hands: Jennet will admit nothing, and Thomas will not stop confessing. Thomas is a poor former soldier, and Jennet has property; she has to be the guilty one. At last Hebble has an idea. Hebble and his associates will leave Jennet and Thomas alone together while Hebble and the others listen at an open door. Hebble expects that, thinking themselves alone, the unfortunate pair will confess—she to witchcraft and he to innocence. The two are brought forth from the cellar, Thomas still wearing the thumbscrews that have been used to try to make him stop confessing. When they are left alone, Jennet tells Thomas of her father, a scientist who gave his life to his dreams. She will have no such nonsense. Facts and facts alone will rule her life—until tomorrow, when she will be burned. Fancy and imagination, she says, have caused her present trouble. Overhearing this conversation, Hebble is convinced that Jennet is a witch. At any rate she is wealthy, and her property will go to the city when she is burned.

From the conversation Hebble also learns that Thomas wants to be hanged because he finds life mean and dull. Therefore his punishment is to be to spend the night in joy and revelry at the party celebrating the betrothal of Humphrey and Alizon. Thomas will not agree to attend the party, however, unless Jennet is allowed to go with him. Dressed in one of Margaret's old gowns, Jennet is sent to the party, where Humphrey, the bridegroom-to-be, no longer wants Alizon. Since Humphrey will not claim her, neither will Nicholas. Unknown to them both, Alizon has found that she loves Richard and that Richard returns her love. They slip away and are married by the priest who found Richard in the poor box when he was just a tiny baby.

Unhappily for Thomas, he has fallen in love with Jennet and she with him. He has no wish to be in love; life is miserable enough. Jennet, on the other hand, does not want to renounce her factual world for one of love and fancy. Jennet knows that Thomas has not committed murder, that he heard the mobs accusing her of turning Skipps into a dog and said he murdered the ragman only to divert suspicion from her. Humphrey goes to Jennet and offers to get her free from the charge of witchery if she will entertain him in her cell that night. Although her body loves the thought of living, her mind and heart rebel, and she turns down his offer. She loves Thomas too much to take life at such a price.

Fortunately for all, old Skipps is found alive. Hebble, still coveting Jennet's property, will not be satisfied, but a softhearted justice allows Thomas and Jennet to slip out of town in the dark. Thomas hates to face living again, but he decides to forgo the pleasure of dying for another fifty years and spend the time waiting with Jennet.

Critical Evaluation:

The English dramatist Christopher Fry restored poetry and humor to the modern stage. From 1948 to 1970, Fry wrote a quartet of comedies, *The Lady's Not for Burning*, *A Yard of Sun* (pr., pb. 1970), *Venus Observed* (pr., pb. 1950),

and *The Dark Is Light Enough* (pr., pb. 1954), each related to a season of the year. The first written and probably the most successful of the quartet is *The Lady's Not for Burning*, the play associated with springtime. The simple mention of a particular season carries with it the burden of traditional connotation. Spring suggests fertility, rebirth, new love, and the giddiness of spring fever. Summer suggests growth, heat, and languidness; autumn, ripeness, harvest, and maturity. Winter is inevitably associated with coldness and death. Fry uses this imagery in traditional contexts, but he also plays with the seasonal references in ironic contexts.

The Lady's Not for Burning is set in April, and the characters frequently remark upon the weather and how it affects their states of mind. The play begins in a fit of spring fever, with all the characters' actions seeming quite mad. Alizon quizzes Richard as to the nature of males, whom she finds so strange that she is surprised when they actually speak English. Richard blames the madness of men on the "machinations of nature;/ As April does to the earth." Alizon is delighted with the analogy: "I wish it were true/ Show me daffodils happening to a man!" Precisely at this point Nicholas enters to claim Alizon as his bride, declaring that he has killed his twin brother and rival, Humphrey, in a bed of daffodils. Not surprisingly, Humphrey is not dead in the least and is found lying on his back, picking daffodils. As the action becomes more complicated, Margaret Devize, in motherly fashion, finally declares to her brother that the younger generation is all "in the same April fit of exasperating nonsense." The silly but mostly harmless spring fever of the younger generation contrasts with the absurd and dangerous behavior of the elders.

The Lady's Not for Burning teeters between rebirth and stagnation. The year in which the play is set, "1400 either more or less exactly," traditionally marks the end of the Middle Ages and the beginning of the modern world in England. The elders of the town of Cool Clary are stuck in a medieval worldview in which the unusual is dangerous and the status quo must be preserved.

The Lady's Not for Burning is a quixotic comedy, one in which the comic heroes, as does Don Quixote of Miguel de Cervantes' famous novel, flee into "madness" in order to escape the madness of an authoritarian society. The youthful lovers—Jennet and Thomas, Richard and Alizon—cannot transform the ludicrous society of Hebble Tyson and the Devizes, a society in which material gain is the predominant virtue, so they must escape from it. The escape in this play resembles the severance from parental authority that youth must accomplish before reaching maturity. The younger characters are in tune with the mad delight and love of an

"April anarchy," so they must flee from those who are out of tune and who cannot recognize the rebirth that spring brings.

Margaret and Hebble declare their distaste for spring quite emphatically, and they cannot see the possibility for redemption in their midst. The redeemers are outsiders and will remain so: Alizon, the child of nature who "appeared overnight/ As mushrooms do" and was given to God; Richard, no one's child, who was not born but "was come across"; Jennet, the alchemist's daughter, who is called a witch because she speaks French to her poodle and dines with a peacock; and Thomas Mendip, the disillusioned soldier, who wants to be hanged because "each time I thought I was on the way/ To a faintly festive hiccup/ The sight of the damned world sobered me up again." Humor is not tolerated in this most rigid of societies; it is seen as tiresome and incompatible with good citizenship.

Laughter, however, is what Jennet seeks, and it is laughter, "the surest touch of genius in creation," with which Thomas Mendip cheers her when things look bleakest. Only in each other can the lovers create a festive society. The world, however, does not change because of their love, as Thomas declares to Jennet. Although their festive society does not triumph, the play ends on a wish: "Good morning.—And God have mercy on our souls." The ironic absurdity of the existing society does not destroy the idealism and desire of the protagonists for harmony. *The Lady's Not for Burning* is a youthful comedy—one that looks forward with hope.

Christopher Fry wrote *The Lady's Not for Burning* shortly after the end of World War II, when the austerities of wartime were still very much a part of English life. The lushness of the play's poetic language and the fancy of its romantic setting were fashioned to appeal to the audience's longing for relief from drab reality. The war-weariness of Thomas Mendip is a reminder of the harshness of what was, when the play was first performed, recent history. The verbal wit and sensuous imagery of Fry's language satisfied a hunger for sophisticated drama in the generation coming home from World War II. *The Lady's Not for Burning*, first produced in a regional theater in 1948, was transferred to London's West End in 1949 in a highly successful production directed by and starring John Gielgud. The play was subsequently produced on Broadway.

Fry's poetic drama was eclipsed in the 1960's with the revival of the harsh naturalism of Britain's "angry young men" and the experimentation of the absurdists. Although perhaps not as poetically impressive as T. S. Eliot's dramas, Fry's seasonal comedies have a much stronger theatrical appeal, undoubtedly drawn from the playwright's long association with the theater as actor, director, and dramatist. *The Lady's Not for Burning* helped to define the theatrical accomplishment of the mid-twentieth century in the English-speaking world.

"Critical Evaluation" by Jane Anderson Jones

Further Reading

Donoghue, Denis. "Christopher Fry's Theatre of Words." In *The Third Voice: Modern British and American Verse Drama*. Princeton, N.J.: Princeton University Press, 1959. Deplores the eccentricity of Fry's language in the early plays, including *The Lady's Not for Burning*.

Jessup, Frances. *Christopher Fry: A Dramatic Reassessment of the Fry/Eliot Era of British Verse Drama*. Palo Alto, Calif.: Academic Press, 2009. Chronicles Fry's life and analyzes his plays. Describes how, for a brief period after World War II, Fry was a central figure in the British theater; his plays sparked a revival of British verse drama and reinvigorated Christian belief.

Leeming, Glenda. "Christopher Fry: Poetic Drama in Conventional Setting." In *Poetic Drama*. New York: St. Martin's Press, 1989. Chapter on Fry's work is part of a larger discussion that traces the development of twentieth century verse drama from William Butler Yeats and T. S. Eliot to W. H. Auden, Christopher Isherwood, and Fry. Emphasizes how the imagery in *The Lady's Not for Burning* evokes and insists upon the beauty of the natural world.

_____. "Condoning Creation in *The Lady's Not for Burning*." In *Christopher Fry*. Boston: Twayne, 1990. Describes Fry's sources for the play and focuses discussion on its characters and imagery.

Nightingale, Benedict. "Christopher Fry, British Playwright in Verse, Dies at Ninety-Seven." *The New York Times*, July 5, 2005. Obituary provides an overview of Fry's life and career.

Roy, Emil. *Christopher Fry*. Carbondale: Southern Illinois University Press, 1968. Contains a chapter on each of Fry's plays until 1968 as well as discussion of Fry's language, his imagery, and his "outlook and ideas." Addresses the literary influences on *The Lady's Not for Burning*, the play's themes and plot structure, and its motifs of alchemy, martyrdom, and seduction.

Stanford, Derek. *Christopher Fry*. Rev. ed. London: Longmans, Green, 1962. Includes a brief biographical sketch and a discussion of each of Fry's plays written before 1962. Emphasizes Fry's intuition of the presence of the mystery that informs mortality.

The Lais of Marie de France

Author: Marie de France (c. 1150-c. 1215)
First transcribed: Lais, c. 1167 (English translation, 1911)
Type of work: Poetry

The Poem:

The Lay of Guigemar. In the days of King Arthur, Guigemar, a knight who loves no lady, is injured by an arrow with which he has shot a white doe. In human speech, the doe tells Guigemar that he will have no relief from his hurt until he finds a woman who will suffer as never woman has before and for whom he will suffer as well. Binding his wound with the hem of his shirt, Guigemar boards an empty ship that he comes across in the harbor. He falls asleep and awakens in another land, where he is discovered by the queen, a young woman whom her old lord keeps as a prisoner. The queen takes him home, conceals him, and heals him, and the two become lovers. They live happily for a year and a half. As tokens of their love, the queen ties a knot in the hem of Guigemar's shirt that only she can untie and Guigemar fastens a girdle about the queen's waist that only he can unbuckle. They pledge that they will never take other lovers who are unable to unfasten the knot or the buckle.

When the king discovers Guigemar, he allows him to leave on the ship in the hope that it will perish at sea. He imprisons the queen in a tower, where she stays for two years. One day, finding the door unlocked, she goes to the harbor and boards an empty vessel; the ship carries her to the shore of a warlike prince, Meriadus, who lodges her with his unmarried sister and tries to win her love. Because he cannot loosen the buckle on the girdle she wears, Meriadus brings to her a knight who has a mysterious knot tied in his shirt. The knight is Guigemar. After the knot and the buckle have been loosed, Guigemar wants to take the queen away, but Meriadus will not let her go. Guigemar joins forces with Meriadus's enemy to lay siege to the prince's castle; they capture the castle when its defenders became weak with hunger, burn it, and kill Meriadus. The lovers then depart in triumph.

The Lay of Chaitivel. In Nantes in Brittany lives a beautiful lady who is loved by four knights. She is undecided which knight she likes best, and she sends presents and messages to all. Each carries her favor and cries her name in the lists. During an Easter tournament, three of the knights are slain and the fourth is severely wounded. All four of the knights are brought on their shields to the lady. Distressed, she has the three slain knights buried in an abbey and nurses the wounded knight back to health. Mourning for the three dead knights, she tells the fourth knight that she is going to make a lay about their deaths and his terrible wounds and call it "The Lay of the Four Sorrows." The knight suggests that she instead call it "The Lay of the Dolorous Knight." His three comrades are past suffering, he declares, but he receives every day only a few courteous, empty words from the lady and no love. The lady agrees that this is a good title. However, some still call it "The Lay of the Four Sorrows."

The Lay of Eliduc. In Brittany, Eliduc, having lost favor with the king because of false rumors, is forced to leave the country. After he and Guideluec, his wife, pledge their faith to each other, Eliduc takes a ship to Totenois. There, he helps an aged king defeat a prince who wants to marry the king's daughter, Guilliadun. The king gives Eliduc reward and honor, and the princess gives him her love. Although Eliduc reminds himself of his wife at home, he neglects to mention his wife to the princess.

In time, Eliduc's own king, needing help against an enemy, sends for his return. At home, Eliduc's wife is delighted to see him, but Eliduc is sad. He then returns to the country of Totenois and sends word to the princess to meet him. They leave secretly on a ship. During a heavy storm at sea, one of the men cries that the princess is the cause of the storm because Eliduc has deserted his wife at home. When the man wants to throw the princess overboard, Eliduc hits him with an oar and casts him into the sea. The princess faints when she hears that Eliduc is married, and all aboard the ship believe her to be dead. Going ashore in Brittany, they carry her to a chapel, intending to give her burial rites. Eliduc leaves her at the altar and returns home to his wife.

Eliduc is in such a downcast mood that his wife decides to learn the cause. When Guideluec finds the princess, she is overcome at the sadness of her death, even though she realizes that Eliduc loves the maiden. When she sees a weasel revive its dead mate by putting a red flower in his mouth, she takes the flower, uses it to revive the girl, and tells her that she will release Eliduc from his marriage vows. She takes the princess to her home, releases Eliduc, and becomes an abbess.

Eliduc and the princess marry and live happily for a time, but finally they part, and each takes holy orders. The princess goes to the abbess, who receives her as a sister. Eliduc and the princess send messages back and forth between the convent and the monastery, each encouraging the other in the holy life. Their repentance is lasting.

The Lay of Laüstic. In the town of Saint Malo, in Brittany, a bachelor knight falls in love with his friend's wife. Although they seldom meet, the two at last become lovers. Because their houses stand side by side, they are able to gaze at each other and to pass messages and gifts through the window casements. When the knight's friend asks his wife why she spends her nights watching at the window, she says that she is listening to the nightingale. Her husband has his servants trap the bird, and then he wrings its neck and throws it in her lap. The wife, sad because she can no longer use the bird as an excuse to see her lover, embroiders the story of the nightingale's fate on rich silk cloth, wraps the bird in the cloth, and sends it to her lover. The doleful knight has a little chest made of gold and precious stones for the body of the bird and carries it everywhere with him.

The Lay of Sir Lanval. Because of trouble with the Picts and Scots, King Arthur is lodging at Caerleon-on-Usk in Wales. There, at Pentecost, he bestows honors and lands on all except Sir Lanval, the son of a king in a distant country whom Arthur despises. Too proud to ask his lord for his due, Lanval remains poor.

Riding unattended in a meadow near a stream, Lanval dismounts because his horse is trembling. He lets the horse graze while he tries to sleep. Two maidens wearing purple mantles appear and tell Lanval that their mistress has summoned him. He finds a beautiful maiden lying on a richly covered bed in a silken pavilion with a golden eagle on top. She is dressed in white linen with a mantle of ermine trimmed in purple. When she offers Lanval her love, provided that he tell no one of her existence, he accepts. She gives him rich clothing and a purse that is never empty. Now wealthy, Lanval redeems captives, clothes poor minstrels, comforts strangers, and is completely happy. The beautiful maiden appears whenever he calls her.

At a party in the royal orchard, Lanval ignores the queen and thirty of her most beautiful maidens because they look like kitchen wenches to him. Calling Lanval to her, the queen offers him her love. Lanval refuses, saying that he will not betray his lord. Angrily, the queen retorts that Lanval must despise women, but Lanval tells her that his love is richer than any other and that the meanest of his love's maidens excels the queen in goodness and beauty. The queen flees, weeping, to her chamber.

When Arthur returns, the queen tells him that Lanval had sought her love and that she had refused him. At her refusal, she declares, Lanval reviled her and said that his love is set on a lady whose meanest wench is fairer than the queen. Arthur swears that he will burn or hang Lanval if he cannot deny his boast before his peers.

Because he has revealed his lady's existence, Lanval loses contact with her. He wants to die, but instead he is compelled to appear before the court of barons. The barons say that they will look at Lanval's lady and decide if she is more beautiful than the queen. If she is, there will be no trial. Because Lanval cannot produce her, the barons prepare to pass judgment on him. At that moment, two beautiful maidens, followed by two even more beautiful maidens, appear and announce that their lady is approaching. They are so beautiful that many say the queen has already lost. Soon Lanval's lady appears, riding a white horse and wearing white with a purple mantle. Every man marvels at her beauty and cares no more for mortal women. She says that Lanval has never craved the love of the queen but that he had spoken hastily. The barons are overcome by her beauty, and Arthur suggests that she stay a while at court. She declines and, together with Lanval, she rides away forever, perhaps to Avalon.

The Lay of the Two Lovers. A king in Normandy has a fair daughter whom he does not wish to give in marriage. He proclaims that no one shall wed her except he who carries her to the pinnacle of a great and perilous mountain. Many try and fail. The girl falls in love with a slender young man and obtains from her aunt a magic potion that will enable him to reach the mountaintop. Armed with this potion, the youth asks for and receives the king's permission to carry the girl to the pinnacle. To lighten his load, the maiden fasts for several days beforehand, and on the journey she wears only her smock. The youth sets out bravely, refusing to drink the potion in the presence of the watchers. As he carries her higher, the maiden urges him to take the potion, but he refuses; he finally falls dead of exhaustion. Flinging away the flask of potion, the girl dies of grief, holding her lover in her arms. When a search party led by the king finds them dead, the king is distraught. The lovers are buried in a marble coffin on the mountain where they died. Wherever the magic potion has touched the barren ground, healing herbs spring up.

The Lay of Bisclavret. At the insistence of his wife, who demands an explanation of his absence from home three nights a week, Bisclavret, a baron in Brittany, reveals that he is a werewolf. He tells his wife that when he assumes the shape of a wolf he hides his clothing in a hollow stone near a chapel and that if he were to lose his clothing he would not be able to return to a man's shape. The wife, who is afraid of her husband, sends for a knight who has long loved her unrewarded. She tells him that her husband is a werewolf and asks him to steal her husband's clothing from its hiding place. He does so and marries the wife after Bisclavret seems to be lost forever from the world of men.

More than a year later, the king, hunting in the woods, is surprised by a wolf that fawns on him, and he takes the animal home as a pet. Bisclavret makes an admirable pet until his wife's second husband comes to court, when he springs for his rival's throat. The king calls the wolf off, but when Bisclavret's wife comes to court, he bites off her nose. The king's men beat the wolf, but they do not kill him, for a wise counselor points out that the wolf's malice has been directed at only the woman and her husband. Questioned by the king, the woman reveals the truth. He makes her return her first husband's clothing, but Bisclavret ignores the garments. The counselor then suggests putting the wolf alone in a room with the clothing, and when this is done Bisclavret returns to his human form. The king, delighted, restores Bisclavret's fief, and the wife and her second husband leave the country.

The Lay of Le Fresne. When the wife of a knight in Brittany bears twin sons, the wife of another knight spreads the story that twin children always have two fathers. A year later, that woman has twin girls. Because she was the one who spread the word about the supposed double paternity of twins, she is afraid to reveal that she has given birth to twins herself. At first, she considers killing one of the infants. Later, she has a serving maid take one of the babies, wrapped in sanguine silk and with a rich ring tied to her wrist, and leave her in an ash tree near a church. The child is found and reared by an abbess, who calls her Le Fresne, which means "ash."

When the beautiful Le Fresne is grown, a knight, Gurun, falls in love with her and persuades her to run away with him to his castle. There they live happily until the knights of the realm persuade Gurun to put Le Fresne away and take a wife. At last he agrees to marry another beautiful girl named La Codre, which means "hazel." Although Gurun's servants are angry with him, Le Fresne accepts this development with grace and decks her lord's bed with the sanguine silk in which she was found as a child. After the wedding, La Codre's mother brings her daughter to the bridal bed and recognizes the silk as that in which she wrapped her other twin daughter when she sent her away. She questions Le Fresne, who shows her the ring that was tied to her wrist when she was abandoned. The mother obtains her husband's forgiveness, and the archbishop dissolves the marriage between Gurun and La Codre. Le Fresne marries her lord, and La Codre soon finds another husband.

The Lay of the Honeysuckle. King Marc banishes his nephew Tristan for having fallen in love with the queen, Isolde. Tristan goes to his native South Wales, but before long he returns to Cornwall to be near the queen. Living in the forest, he seeks shelter from friendly peasants. Hearing that King Marc plans to keep high court at Tintagel, Tristan enters a wood through which he knows Isolde will pass. He cuts a wand from a hazel tree, peels it, carves his name on it, and sets it in the road, where the queen finds it. To her alone, it is a message that Tristan is waiting and that, like the honeysuckle and the hazel tree, they are eternally inseparable. She sends her knights aside and enters the wood with her maiden, Brangwaine. Isolde finds Tristan and spends a joyful hour with him. She then tells him that she is trying to reconcile Marc to him. After they part, Tristan returns to Wales, where he makes a new lay.

The Lay of Equitan. King Equitan, a great but not wise lover, decides to win the love of his seneschal's wife. Although she refuses at first, Equitan finally wins her and they exchange rings. When Equitan's people urge him to marry, the wife hears the news and comes to him in tears. Equitan assures her that he will never marry unless her husband were to die and he might marry her. This declaration quickly brings a plan to mind. The wife asks Equitan to arrange it so that she will be bled with her husband at their castle; she will prepare a bath for both and make her husband's so hot that he will die. The king agrees and rides to the chase with the seneschal, after which the surgeon bleeds them. Beside each bed, the wife places a bath, her husband's boiling. When the husband delays his appearance, the wife and Equitan look tenderly at each other while they sit waiting on the seneschal's bed by the steaming bath. The husband returns, brushes aside the maiden guarding the door, and finds his wife and the king in each other's arms. The king, jumping up, springs into the fatally hot bath. Enraged, the seneschal throws his wife into the same bath, where they both die.

The Lay of Milun. Milun, a famous knight in South Wales, receives word from an unknown maiden that she will give him her love. Milun accepts, and she bears him a son. Fearing her father, the girl keeps the birth secret, and Milun's servants carry the baby to his mother's sister, who is married to a lord in Northumberland. With the child are sent letters and his father's signet ring, to be given to him when he comes of age. Then Milun goes in search of reward in a foreign country, and the child's mother is given in marriage to an old lord.

Returning to South Wales, Milun is sad to learn that his love is married, but he is happy to know that they are not far apart. He sends to her a swan with a letter concealed in a feather. She is instructed to answer the letter but to keep the bird unfed for three days before she wants the letter returned.

She does as she is asked, although she is compelled to wait a month before she can get parchment and ink. The swan then flies home to be fed and delivers her letter. For twenty years, the swan serves as messenger between the lovers, who never see each other during that time.

In Northumberland, the son, now grown, is known as the Knight Peerless. His aunt tells him of his origin and gives him the signet ring. His fame spreads to Brittany, where Milun hears of the unknown young knight and determines to joust with him to preserve his own fame. Milun crosses the sea and meets the youth in tournament, where the boy unhorses him. When Milun's helmet is knocked off, his white hair and beard are revealed, at which the Knight Peerless dismounts and apologizes to his elder. When Milun asks the young man's name, the knight tells him his story and shows Milun the ring. Father and son are joyfully united, and the son promises to kill his mother's husband. When they arrive in Brittany, a messenger meets Milun with the happy news that his love's husband is dead. Milun and his son go to the mother, and the youth has the joy of seeing his parents wed.

The Lay of Yonec. In Britain, a rich old man marries a beautiful young woman whom he guards for seven years in a castle. One day, she cries out in despair that old tales about young wives married to old lords finding lovers cannot be true. In a few minutes, a falcon alights at her window, enters the room, and turns into a handsome knight. He says that his name is Eudemarec and that he has come at her call. The two immediately become lovers.

The husband becomes suspicious because his wife suddenly appears to be so happy. He pretends to leave and sets his older sister to watch his wife. When she learns the secret and tells her brother, the husband sets sharp blades in the window to kill the hawk. The next time Eudemarec alights there, he receives his death wound. He flutters, bleeding, to his love's bed, tells her that he will die, and promises that she will bear a son, Yonec, who will avenge both his death and her suffering. The wife follows the hawk out the window and tracks him by the trail of blood until she finds him dying. He gives her a ring that he says will cause her husband to leave her alone. He also gives her a sword as a gift to his son. When the proper time comes, she is to go with her husband and son to an abbey, where they will see a tomb. There she is to tell her son of his father and give him the sword.

In time, these events come to be. At the abbey, the wife tells Yonec of his father and gives him the sword before she falls dead on Eudemarec's tomb. The son then takes the sword and cuts off the old man's head. Because Eudemarec was king of the land, the people proclaim Yonec their lord as he leaves the church.

Critical Evaluation:

Probably connected with the court of the Anglo-Norman king Henry II of England, Marie de France is credited with the creation of the *lai*, or lay, as a literary genre. Her lays are Celtic stories she had heard recounted and sung in the Breton language and that she chose to preserve in written verse form in the Anglo-Norman dialect of Old French. They are narratives with frequent lyrical and moral overtones and occasional brief intrusions by the author to express her own opinions. Their popular appeal to readers, both in Marie's time and today, has gained for their author recognition as the first important female literary figure of the Western world.

Familiar with the classical and vernacular literature circulating in Britain and Western Europe during the second half of the twelfth century, Marie de France synthesizes in her verse tales the narrative tradition of northern France and the courtly love lyrics of the southern troubadours. Knightly activities and adventures such as hunting parties, tournament jousts, mercenary military engagements, and the wielding of weapons, which were the essence of Old French *chansons de geste* and the medieval romances, figure prominently in the *Lais*. These events are never gratuitous; rather, they occur because they have a direct effect on the central love relationship, for each of Marie's *lais* is, above all, a love story. Each *lai* presents a different scenario that offers a new perspective on the subject.

In her depiction of love and its intricacies, Marie uses a number of literary themes. One of the most popular motifs is that of the *mal mariée* (mismatched wife). In the first story, Guigemar's lover is married to a wealthy old man who, because of jealousy, has locked her away. The reader is not surprised that the wife falls instantly in love with the handsome wounded knight. Similarly, Yonec's mother is married to an old man who had taken her as his wife for the purposes of begetting an heir. The reader, medieval or modern, is sympathetic to her illicit affair with the bird/man. Mismarriage is also implied in the *lais* of Laüstic and Milun, although mismarriage is not essential to the plot of either. Reversal of this theme, the mismatched husband, appears in *The Lay of Equitan* and *The Lay of Bisclavret*.

Lack of self-control is illustrated in several of the stories. In *The Lay of the Two Lovers*, the young lover, overconfident of his strength, will not stop to drink his energizing potion while attempting to ascend the mountain with his bride-to-be in his arms, and he dies of the physical strain. In three of the tales, overindulgence in sexual pleasure on the part of adulterous lovers results in detection of the affairs by the cuckolded husbands, leading to the separation or even the deaths of the lovers. In contrast, the patience and composure of Le

Fresne, Milun, and Eliduc's first wife bring about happiness for all concerned.

All twelve stories rest on the premise that love brings with it suffering in the form of physical and emotional distress. In *The Lay of Guigemar*, Marie de France declares, "Love is an invisible wound within the body, and, since it has its source in nature, it is a long-lasting ill." In the first story, love is symbolized by the rebounding arrow that strikes Guigemar in the thigh. In *The Lay of Yonec*, it is the lack of love that keeps the young wife awake. Separation from the beloved is the worst of all the woes sustained by the lovers in *The Lais of Marie de France*. Their anguished longing is portrayed with poignancy and delicate lyricism. Several of the estranged couples are reunited, but some must endure permanent despair.

Supernatural elements, particularly those characteristic of Celtic legend, are present in several of the *Lais*. Since much of the natural world was as yet unexplained in the twelfth century, the medieval mind easily accepted the possibility of human transformation into wolves or birds, visits from otherworldly beings, animals that talk, magic potions, and magic boats that sail without a crew. Whenever paranormal activity occurs in the *Lais*, it always moves the story forward; such activity is not portrayed with the intention of dismaying the reader.

The author of the twelve *lais* presents a composite picture of love that is strikingly more modern than the concept of courtly love established by the Provençal troubadours. For Marie de France, true love can exist only between equals—persons of the same age, social status, and education. Moreover, both members of a couple must possess the same courtly qualities as each other, and they must be completely loyal to each other. Although never overtly expressed, it is implicit in the stories that God condones such love, even when, through circumstances, the love is necessarily illicit or adulterous. As in the well-known legend of Tristan and Isolde, true love in the *Lais* is a product of destiny, and the love is eternal.

Symmetry and balance are evident in the structure and style of the *Lais*. In the only manuscript containing all twelve stories, long tales are followed by short ones; the opening and closing tales, both extended ones, end with the triumph of love in this life, whereas the two middle tales end with the union of the lovers in death. In one story a lonely knight is loved by an otherworldly female; in another story, an imprisoned lady is visited by a supernatural bird/man lover. The *Lais* are replete with polarities of vices and virtues: cupidity and charity, deceit and loyalty, generosity and greed, excess and moderation, egotism and altruism.

Obviously, moral lessons can be inferred from such narratives. In her prologue to the tales, Marie discusses ancient texts that, on close scrutiny, reveal subtle truths. It is clear in the prologue, however, that the author's primary purpose is to relate interesting stories and, by doing so, preserve them and her own name for posterity. She insists that her tales are not fictitious, and she frequently lends them veracity by including precise geographical locations and by associating events with specific dates in the Church calendar. Her concise writing is occasionally punctuated with analytical or descriptive passages vital to proper comprehension of the narrative. Unlike many medieval texts, Marie de France's *lais* contain no obscurities. They are the products of a gifted young writer and consummate storyteller; they will doubtless continue to delight readers everywhere, just as they did in the twelfth century.

"Critical Evaluation" by Judith L. Barban

Further Reading

Bloch, R. Howard. *The Anonymous Marie de France*. Chicago: University of Chicago Press, 2003. Analyzes all of Marie de France's writing, including the *Lais*. Argues that she was a self-conscious, sophisticated writer who was aware of her role in the preservation of French cultural memory and of the effects of her writing within an oral tradition.

Bruckner, Matilda Tomaryn. "Marie de France." In *French Women Writers*, edited by Eva Sartori and Dorothy Zimmerman. Westport, Conn.: Greenwood Press, 1991. Discusses the themes and chronology of the *Lais* and provides a concise survey of critical writings on the work, noting its importance in feminist studies.

Burgess, Glyn Sheridan. "Chivalry and Prowess in the *Lais* of Marie de France." *French Studies* 37 (April, 1983): 129-142. Argues that the *Lais* are primarily an upper-class phenomenon presenting twelfth century knights in the context of their social superiors. Examines the vocabulary that Marie adopts for various courtly virtues.

_____. *"The Lais of Marie de France": Text and Context*. Athens: University of Georgia Press, 1987. Provides one of the best general analyses of the *Lais* available, addressing such matters as chronology, chivalry, character analysis, vocabulary, and the status of women in the poems. Includes an extensive bibliography.

Burgess, Glyn Sheridan, and Keith Busby. Introduction to *The Lais of Marie de France*. New York: Penguin Books, 1986. Presents an overview of the extant manuscripts and discusses the composition as well as the major themes and impact of the work. Includes a comparison of the *lai* with other medieval genres.

Chamberlain, David. "Marie de France's Arthurian *Lai*: Subtle and Political." In *Culture and the King: The Social Implications of the Arthurian Legend*, edited by Martin Shichtman and James Carley. Albany: State University of New York Press, 1994. Presents an interpretation of *The Lay of Sir Lanval*, pointing out the importance of irony, iconography, and humor in the story.

Clifford, Paula. *Marie de France: Lais*. London: Grant & Cutler, 1982. Offers succinct discussion of love and destiny in the *Lais*, with background information on Marie de France and her contribution to twelfth century literature.

Ferrante, Joan M. "The French Courtly Poet: Marie de France." In *Medieval Women Writers*, edited by Katharina M. Wilson. Athens: University of Georgia Press, 1984. Analyzes the stories in the *Lais* from the perspective of love and personal relations. Provides information on Marie's other works and includes Ferrante's own English translation of the Yonec tale.

Mickel, Emanuel J. *Marie de France*. New York: Twayne, 1974. Intended for the general reader, this is a good introduction to many aspects of the *Lais*. Includes information on Marie's possible identity and the sources of her works, some historical background, and concise discussion of each poem.

Whalen, Logan E. *Marie de France and the Poetics of Memory*. Washington, D.C.: Catholic University of America Press, 2008. Analyzes the rhetorical use of description and memory in the *Lais* and in Marie de France's other works.

Lalla Rookh
An Oriental Romance

Author: Thomas Moore (1779-1852)
First published: 1817
Type of work: Poetry
Type of plot: Love
Time of plot: c. 1700
Locale: India

Principal characters:
AURUNGZEBE, the emperor of Delhi
LALLA ROOKH, Aurungzebe's daughter
FERAMORZ, a young poet of Kashmir
ABDALLA, the king of Lesser Bucharia
ALIRIS, the young king of Bucharia and Abdalla's son disguised as Feramorz
FADLADEEN, a chamberlain of the harem

The Poem:

Aurungzebe, the emperor of Delhi, entertains Abdalla, who recently abdicated his throne to his son Aliris and is on a pilgrimage to the Shrine of the Prophet. Aurungzebe has promised his daughter Lalla Rookh (Tulip Cheek) in marriage to Aliris. The lonely princess is to journey to Kashmir, where she and Aliris will meet and be married.

Lalla Rookh's caravan, of the finest and most comfortable equipment, is manned by the most loyal and efficient of servants, the entire cavalcade having been sent by Aliris to conduct his bride to him. Among the servants sent by Aliris is a young poet of Kashmir, Feramorz. Feramorz captivates all the women with his beauty and charming musical ability as he sings and recites to the accompaniment of his kitar. Lalla Rookh, not immune, becomes enamored of the young poet.

Fadladeen, the chamberlain traveling as Lalla Rookh's protector, is a bumptious, all-knowing, perspicacious authority on any subject: food, science, religion, and literature. His criticism is so detailed and harsh that the person being assessed is reduced to feeling like a virtual ignoramus. Fadladeen criticizes Feramorz's poem "The Veiled Prophet of Khorassan," which tells the story of Azim and Zelica, young lovers who live in the province of Khorassan.

In the story, after Azim goes off to fight in the wars in Greece, Zelica is enticed into the harem of Mokanna, the "veiled prophet of Khorassan," in the belief that she will gain admission into Paradise; there she will be reunited with Azim, whom she believes has been killed in the Greek wars. Mokanna is a dastardly, cruel ruler who has gained the throne through magic. When Azim learns, in a dream, of Zelica's plight, he returns to his country to join the army of the veiled prophet. Discovering the truth of his vision of Zelica's unhappy state, he joins the troops of an enemy caliph and fights against Mokanna.

Mokanna, defeated, commits suicide by plunging into a vat of corrosive poison. Zelica, feeling remorse for having become Mokanna's wife and sadness at seeing her young lover but not being able to be his, puts on the veil of Mokanna and confronts the caliph's army, with the intention of being mistaken for Mokanna and being killed. Azim does mistake her for Mokanna and attacks her; before she dies of her wounds, her identity is revealed and the lovers exchange vows of devotion and forgiveness. Azim grows old grieving by Zelica's grave, where he finally dies after another vision in which Zelica appears and tells him she is blessed.

Feramorz, unaccustomed to criticism, is taken aback by Fadladeen's reaction to this beautiful love poem. Fadladeen is caustic. He belabors the subject of long speeches by the characters in the story, contrasts Feramorz's poem with the fluency and tone of poems of other writers of the day, and analyzes the meters of specific lines in the poem. Feramorz does not attempt to tell another story for some days.

Finally, encouraged to sing by Lalla Rookh, he begins his second poem only after an appealing look at Fadladeen as he explains that this tale, "Paradise and the Peri," is in a lighter and humbler vein than the first. In the poem, the peri, wishing to be admitted to Paradise, is told to bring as her passport the gift most treasured by heaven. Her first offering is a drop of blood from a dying Indian patriot; this unacceptable gift is followed by the last sigh of an Egyptian maiden as she dies of grief at the loss of the lover whom she has nursed through the plague. Rejected for this gift, the peri is finally admitted to Paradise when she presents the penitential tear of a hardened criminal of Balbec. The criminal's tear had been shed as he heard a child's prayer. Fadladeen is even more outspoken in his criticism of Feramorz's second story. He refuses to be halted in his critical onslaught, despite Lalla Rookh's attempt to intervene.

By the time the party arrives in Lahore, Lalla Rookh realizes not only that she is in love with Feramorz but also that the handsome singer is in love with her, and she resolves that he should not be admitted to her presence again. Although the heart she is to give to her bridegroom will be cold and broken, it must be pure.

As they journey on, the travelers come upon the ruins of an ancient tower, a structure that arouses the curiosity of the entire group. Fadladeen, who has never before been outside Delhi, proceeds learnedly to show that he knows nothing whatever about the building. Despite Lalla Rookh's admonition that Feramorz not be called to identify the ruins for them, he is brought before her. The tower, he says, is all that remains of an ancient Fire-Temple, built by Ghebers, or Zoroastrian Persians, who fled to the site from their Arab conquerors in order to have liberty in a foreign country rather than persecution in their own land.

This historical detail gives rise to Feramorz's third song, "The Fire-Worshippers." In this story, Hafed, the leader of the resisting Gheber forces in the mountains, falls in love with Hinda, the daughter of the Arabian emir who has come to rout the insurrectionists. Hafed, his identity concealed, gains access to Hinda's quarters and wins her love before he is captured by the Ghebers. The Arabs defeat the Ghebers in a sudden attack, and Hafed sacrifices himself on a funeral pyre. As Hinda watches from a distance, she plunges into a lake and is drowned.

On this occasion Fadladeen decides to forgo criticism of Feramorz's tale. Rather, Fadladeen decides to report this profane story to Aliris. Fadladeen hopes in this manner to bring about punishment for Feramorz and to secure for himself a place in Aliris' court.

In the tranquil, beautiful valley of Hussun Abdaul, Feramorz sings his last song, "The Light of the Haram," an account of married love reconciled after a misunderstanding between husband and wife. The "Light of the Haram" is Sultana Nourmahal, the favorite wife of the emperor Selim, son of the great Acbar. During the celebration of the Feast of Roses, Nourmahal quarrels with Selim. The couple's period of sadness and remorse because of their harsh words to each other ends when Nourmahal learns a magic song from an enchantress, Namouna. Masked, Nourmahal sings the song to Selim at the emperor's banquet, and they are reunited in undying love for each other.

After considerable hardship, the party crosses the mountains that separate Kashmir from the rest of India. At a temple where they rest, the young king arrives to welcome his bride into his kingdom. Lalla Rookh, seeing his face in full view for the first time, faints. The king is the young singer, Feramorz. He has traveled disguised as a poet because he wished to win Lalla Rookh's love.

Learning the identity of the man whose songs he has criticized so caustically, Fadladeen recants immediately and declares that Aliris is the greatest poet of all time. In his new position of prestige, bestowed on him by Aliris, Fadladeen recommends the whip for anyone who questions Aliris's poetic ability. To her dying day, Lalla Rookh never calls the king by any name other than Feramorz.

Critical Evaluation:

Lalla Rookh, one of Romantic Great Britain's literary sensations, is a prose narrative that frames four successive episodes. The setting is Lalla Rookh's journey from Delhi to Kashmir. The irony of her story is her love for Feramorz, the young and handsome poet who tells verse tales to entertain the entourage sent by her husband-to-be, Aliris; only after much agitation of spirit does Lalla Rookh discover that Feramorz is Aliris in disguise.

The frame of the journey and the storytelling places *Lalla Rookh* structurally in the tradition of *The Canterbury Tales* (1387-1400) by Geoffrey Chaucer. In the four poems, Thomas Moore's musical gifts tap a rich vein of lyricism in the English language, revivifying the aural qualities of written verse. The first tale, "The Veiled Prophet of Khorassan," told in heroic couplets, combines the Romantic era's fascination with the gothic and with the East. Moore transforms history to tell the story of two ill-fated lovers destroyed by the evil magician Mokanna, a gothic villain who entraps a pure and virtuous heroine. The veiled prophet was the historical figure al-Muqanna (Hashim ibn Hakim), who led a revolt against the Abbasid caliphs between 775 and 780 C.E. in the mountains of what later became known as Uzbekistan. The tragedy of Zelica and her nightmarish sufferings draws on a familiar theme of death by mistaken identity, not unlike the melodrama found in contemporary opera. The ending, with Azim praying by Zelica's grave, must have appealed to the sentimental literary tastes of the time.

The second tale, "Paradise and the Peri," is written in a very different vein and displays Moore's gift for song. As in William Blake's *Songs of Innocence and of Experience* (1794), the easy, elegant tone and accessible language of this piece disguises the seriousness of its moral theme. The piece looks forward to the sentimental Victorian ideal of the purity of children.

By Moore's time, the English in India had become acquainted with the Parsis, descendants of those who had escaped to India during the Arab conquest of Zoroastrian Persia in the seventh century. Moore takes another turn in tone and execution when he uses this as his grim subject in "The Fire-Worshippers," in which there are no happy endings. The star-crossed lovers are parted forever, and warring nations will never make peace. For contemporaneous readers, this tragic drama evoked a sense of remote history and satisfied their pleasure in weeping copious tears over inexorable twists of fate.

The fourth poem, "The Light of the Haram," deals with the doting love of the Mughal emperor for his wife, Nur Mahal (later Nur Jahan). With this tale of Aurungzebe's grandfather, the reader is returned to Mughal India, where the work began with Aurungzebe receiving Abdalla at his court. Reflecting contemporary British familiarity with India and Persia, Moore's stories are drawn from either Persian literature and tradition or from the Persianized court culture of Mughal India.

The whimsical Moore introduces a satirical note into an otherwise serious text. Critical of Feramorz's poetry as melodramatic and exaggerated, the pedantic Fadladeen brings the fanciful and exotic storytelling heavily down to earth. He dismisses the ghastly Mokanna as "an ill-favoured gentleman, with a veil over his face." A charlatan who knows little about poetry or religion, he thinks himself qualified to pronounce upon both. In this character, Moore, who had suffered personally from the vituperative literary criticism of Sir Francis Jeffrey (1773-1850) in the *Edinburgh Review*, may have seized the opportunity to retaliate by pricking the bubble of critical pretentiousness.

The most fruitful way for readers to evaluate *Lalla Rookh* is to see it as Moore's contemporaries saw it. The reading public had anticipated the work's publication for six years. When the first readers of *Lalla Rookh* opened their copies in May, 1817, they found that Moore had not disappointed them in satisfying their voracious taste for all things Eastern. They had just learned of places like Bukhara, to which no European had been since the time of Queen Elizabeth I; the name of Kashmir evoked images of incomparable natural beauty, of perfumed gardens and limpid lakes. New scholarship had revealed the East for the first time to British readers, travelers had been writing exotic accounts, and poets knew the great theme of the time was the mysterious, remote, and opulent "Orient." When the conquering British reached Delhi in 1803, the Taj Mahal in Agra and other fascinating examples of Indo-Islamic architecture became known to the West through paintings and engravings. Moore's readers had already heard of Mughal India and the splendor of its Persianized culture. They had read William Beckford's *Vathek: An Arabian Tale* (1786) and countless gothic novels set in the East as well as the translations by Sir William Jones of the Persian poetry of Hafez. Literary Britain was eager for more in such a book as *Lalla Rookh*.

Moore's readers reveled in the evocative power of the Eastern names and the images of wealth, power, and exotic beauty that Moore conjured up. Since the time of the heroic drama *Aureng-Zebe* (pr. 1675) by John Dryden, they would have known about the sixth and last of the great Mughal emperors, Aurungzebe. Moore's readers were aware of the story of the love of Jahangir, the fourth great Mughal emperor, for Nur Mahal; they had recently been introduced to Persian folklore and the history of the conflicts between the Arabs and the pre-Islamic Persians. Moore's detailed footnotes from respected authorities authenticated for his readers the images of the remote East, of "all Bocára's vaunted gold" and of "all the gems of Samarcand," of which they had read in Jones's translations.

Just as the Prince Regent indulged himself by building

his Royal Pavilion at Brighton—a Taj Mahal on the English Channel coast—Moore indulged his readers by bringing them the quintessential Romantic poem about the sumptuous East, replete with sensuous images of nightingales, roses, perfumed fountains, and shimmering gossamer veils. Moore's readers could learn of the world of the remote East through the enchanted verses of *Lalla Rookh* and enjoy the love story of concealed identity in which all is well that ends well.

"Critical Evaluation" by Donna Berliner

Further Reading

Birley, Robert. "Thomas Moore: *Lalla Rookh*." In *Sunk Without Trace: Some Forgotten Masterpieces Reconsidered*. London: Rupert Hart-Davis, 1962. Discusses the reputation of *Lalla Rookh*, both in its own time and in the twentieth century.

Haddad, Emily A. *Orientalist Poetics: The Islamic Middle East in Nineteenth-Century English and French Poetry*. Burlington, Vt.: Ashgate, 2002. Moore's poetry is among the work discussed in this examination of the key role of Orientalism in the development of nineteenth century English and French poetry.

Kelly, Linda. *Ireland's Minstrel: A Life of Tom Moore—Poet, Patriot, and Byron's Friend*. New York: I. B. Tauris, 2006. Uses Moore's newly published journals and other materials to provide an up-to-date account of his life and work. Chapter 14 focuses on *Lalla Rookh*.

Mack, Robert L. Introduction to *Oriental Tales*. New York: Oxford University Press, 1992. Provides information on the tradition of Orientalism in British literature.

McMahon, Sean. *The Minstrel Boy: Thomas Moore and His Melodies*. Cork, Ireland: Mercier Press, 2001. Biography depicts Moore as an Irish patriot whose songs fostered a new sense of Irish nationalism.

Nolan, Emer. *Catholic Emancipations: Irish Fiction from Thomas Moore to James Joyce*. Syracuse, N.Y.: Syracuse University Press, 2007. Chronicles the history of Irish literature from the Catholic political resurgence in the 1820's to the publication of Joyce's *Ulysses* in 1922, showing how Moore and other nineteenth century writers created new narrative forms that were later adapted by Joyce.

Schwab, Raymond. *Oriental Renaissance: Europe's Rediscovery of India and the East, 1680-1880*. Translated by Gene Patterson-Black and Victor Reinking. New York: Columbia University Press, 1984. Discusses the development of British interest in things "Oriental."

Vail, Jeffery W. *The Literary Relationship of Lord Byron and Thomas Moore*. Baltimore: Johns Hopkins University Press, 2001. Argues that Moore, not Percy Bysshe Shelley, was the dominant influence on Byron's life and work. Describes the two poets' friendship, which resulted in Moore's biography of Byron.

Lancelot
Or, The Knight of the Cart

Author: Chrétien de Troyes (c. 1150-c. 1190)
First published: Lancelot: Ou, Le Chevalier à la charrette, c. 1168 (English translation, 1913)
Type of work: Poetry
Type of plot: Romance
Time of plot: c. sixth century
Locale: Logres and Gorre, Great Britain

Principal characters:
ARTHUR, the king of Britain
LANCELOT, King Arthur's greatest knight
GUINEVERE, the wife of King Arthur
GAWAIN, the nephew of King Arthur
MELEAGANT, a treacherous knight
BADEMAGU, the king of Gorre and the father of Meleagant

The Poem:

Chrétien begins his romance by declaring that he writes at the command of his patroness, Marie, the countess of Champagne, who has provided him with the basic elements of the story. On Ascension Day, a strange knight appears before King Arthur's court and challenges him to send Queen Guinevere into the forest with a champion to defend her against him. If the queen's defender wins, the knight will return the many subjects of Arthur whom he holds captive. Sir Kay, having persuaded the king in advance to grant a request, demands that he be named as the queen's escort. Gawain, critical of the king's rash promise and skeptical of Kay's ability, leads a group of knights after them into the woods, where he finds Kay's riderless horse. He sees another, unknown knight in pursuit of the queen on a broken-down horse and lends him a fresh horse.

When Gawain catches up to the knight again, the horse has died, and the knight must continue his quest in a cart driven by a dwarf who claims knowledge of the queen's whereabouts. The cart is of a type that is reserved for transporting convicted criminals to their places of execution, and the knight hesitates briefly, until love conquers reason and he shames himself by entering the cart. Gawain rides along beside the cart to a castle where a damsel welcomes them to spend the night. Their host abuses the knight for riding in a cart, and warns him against sleeping in a perilous enchanted bed. He insists on accepting the risk, and survives a mysterious assault from a flaming lance. The next morning, having glimpsed the queen and her abductor pass by in a procession, they encounter a damsel who will help them find the evil knight, whom she identifies as Meleagant of Gorre, a land from which no visitor has ever returned.

The land of Gorre may only be reached by two approaches, the dangerous Underwater Bridge and the even more dangerous Sword Bridge. Gawain chooses the former, and the other knight chooses the latter. On the way, the unnamed knight has a series of adventures that establish his exceptional chivalric prowess and also his great love for the queen. Lost in meditation on his beloved as his horse drinks at a ford, he does not even notice the knight defending the ford, who knocks him into the water before he regains his senses and quickly defeats the guardian. The heroic knight then has a second encounter with a host and a castle; in this case, the damsel makes him rescue her from a feigned attack and extracts a promise that he will sleep with her, a promise he upholds without touching her. Along his route, the knight discovers a comb with Guinevere's blond hairs in it and nearly faints. His final adventure on the way to the Sword Bridge takes place in a cemetery containing the future resting places of Arthur's knights. He raises a massive stone lid from his own tomb, revealing inscriptions that confirm his role as the queen's rescuer and the liberator of the prisoners of Gorre.

The knight finally reaches the Sword Bridge, which is literally a giant sword. He removes the armor from his hands and feet to better grip the sword's blade, and he is seriously wounded as he crawls across it. The knight challenges Meleagant; Meleagant's father, King Bagdemagu, advises his son to simply return the queen. Meleagant, however, accepts the anonymous knight's challenge, agreeing to meet

him in combat the next morning. Because of his injuries, the knight initially gets the worst of the fight.

Observing the combat from a tower, the queen reveals to one of her damsels that the unknown knight is Lancelot. When the damsel calls out to Lancelot that Guinevere is watching, his strength is increased and he easily gains the advantage, but the fight is ended when Bademagu and then Guinevere ask Lacelot to spare Meleagant's life. Meleagant nevertheless remains unrepentant and refuses to surrender his captives, so the two combatants agree to fight again in a year's time at Arthur's court.

Lancelot finally comes to the queen, but he is coldly rebuffed. After he leaves to find Gawain, rumors of the queen's death and Lancelot's suicide circulate, causing Guinevere to regret her treatment of Lancelot. When they are reunited, she explains her initial scorn as a response to his brief hesitation before entering the cart, and they arrange to meet that night at the window to her bedroom. Lancelot breaks the iron bars on the queen's window and spends the night with her, unaware that he has cut his hands on the bars and left bloodstains on her sheets. Meleagant takes the blood as evidence that the injured Kay, who was sleeping in a chamber nearby, has been in the queen's bed. He charges Kay with committing treason against Arthur and charges Guinevere with adultery. Lancelot defends them against the accusations in a trial by combat, again defeating Meleagant and again being stopped short of complete victory by Bagdemagu's pleas.

Meleagant arranges for Lancelot to be ambushed and imprisoned, and Gawain, who has been narrowly rescued from drowning at the Underwater Bridge, escorts Guinevere back to Camelot. The woman guarding Lancelot lends him a horse and armor and allows him to leave his captivity temporarily to participate in a tournament at Noauz. As an anonymous knight in red armor, Lancelot demonstrates his ability to the extent that Guinevere guesses his identity, and she tests her suspicion by sending him orders to fight alternately with cowardice or with valor. He wins the tournament and returns to his imprisonment.

Meleagant's sister, whom Lancelot aided earlier, finds and releases him in time for the champion to confront Meleagant for a third and final battle, and the poem ends with the celebration of Meleagant's death. A final note reveals that the ending of the romance was written by a clerk named Godefroy, who completed it according to Chrétien's instructions from the point at which Lancelot returned to the tower after the tournament.

"The Story" by C. M. Adderley

Critical Evaluation:

Chrétien de Troyes is the originator of the Arthurian romance, combining the pseudo-historical chivalric exploits of King Arthur and his knights with the romantic conventions of courtly love. Chrétien's *Lancelot* was the third of his five romances. It contains the first mention of Camelot, establishes Lancelot as the greatest of the knights, and, most important, provides the first account of Lancelot's love affair with Arthur's queen, Guinevere.

Chrétien claims in the prologue to the poem that the "sense and subject matter" were given to him by Countess Marie of Champagne, his patroness. Precisely what that sense and matter consisted of is unknowable, but Marie also appears to have been the patroness of Andreas Capellanus, author of *The Art of Courtly Love* (c. 1180), and her request may well have been that Chrétien use his narrative to provide an illustration of Capellanus's principles. Early critics speculated that Chrétien, who elsewhere sharply condemns extramarital love affairs as immoral, found the task uncongenial. If true, this would explain his failure to finish the poem himself (leaving the final thousand lines, nearly one-seventh of the total narrative, to be written by Godefroy de Lagny), as well as the occasional hints of an amused and even satirical attitude on the part of the narrator toward his characters.

Much of the early scholarship relating to *Lancelot* focused on locating Chrétien's sources. Scholars concluded that the basic plot was assembled from two ancient stories. One was a Celtic myth of the abduction and rescue of a woman. The other was a tale known in folklore as the Fair Unknown in which an anonymous individual establishes his identity in society and emerges as a champion. The numerous extra events and characters added by Chrétien to these two basic plots were typically dismissed as incoherent, further indicating the author's lack of interest in writing the poem.

Later critics reversed this early consensus that the work was poorly written and demonstrated that the poem is much more complex in structure and theme than had been supposed. The romance is now generally taken to be carefully constructed, complete, and in the form the author wished. The scene in which Lancelot and Guinevere confess their love forms its center. The overall structure of the work is widely admired as an interlaced series of symmetrical scenes that parallel and echo one another, exemplifying the technique that Chrétien calls *molt bele conjointure*, or "beautifully ordered composition." It is no longer generally dismissed as a miscellany of random adventures.

Chrétien's ambiguous depiction of courtly love in *Lancelot* has come to be interpreted as evidence of his sophisticated command of narrative technique instead of being attributed to confusion or personal ambivalence: The author carefully avoids taking either a naïvely positive or a cynically negative position, instead allowing for a range of possible responses as readers gather and interpret the various threads of the story in their own manner. Critics now find ambiguity and contradiction at virtually every level of the poem, and they admire Chrétien's artistry in revealing and analyzing these difficulties rather than simply assuming that he was unable to gloss them over smoothly.

The conflict between love and reason that makes Lancelot hesitate before entering the dwarf's cart is emblematic of a series of conflicts between different social and moral imperatives that appear throughout the story. While Lancelot clearly chooses love and rejects reason, as the ideal courtly lover always must, the narrator refrains from explicitly endorsing or contesting his action, limiting himself to a more-or-less objective report of what the knight did. However, the narrator's apparent obliviousness to these moral and ethical conflicts does not preclude readers from forming judgments about the characters. Lancelot is represented in the poem as the greatest of Arthur's knights, but also as guilty of treason in committing adultery with the queen. Paradoxically, the poem shows that his great prowess as a warrior is inextricably linked to his great love for Guinevere, his invaluable service to Arthur directly enabled by his treason against Arthur. The character of Guinevere is also open to debate, as her love for Lancelot appears sometimes as a great romantic passion and at other times as calculating and manipulative.

These mixed and ambiguous messages demand interpretive decisions from a reader through the poem, and the critical history of the work demonstrates that good readers have reached different, and often opposed, conclusions about how to understand them. Lancelot's unquestioning subservience to Guinevere's whims may make him a perfect courtly lover or may reveal him to be weak and foolish. When he discovers her ivory comb with half a handful of golden hair caught in it, Lancelot begins to "adore" the hair and put all his "faith" in it; when he finally comes to the queen's bed, he approaches it as a "holy relic" and even an "altar" to be worshiped. These applications of religious imagery to the description of a romantic, specifically sexual, and adulterous love may be seen by some readers as emphasizing the force and beauty of that love. Other readers might see this religion of love as blasphemous, implicitly condemning Lancelot's worship of worldly lust over his Christian faith. Yet other readers may find the narrator's tone best described as lightly ironic—amused at the exaggerated feelings of lovers but far from condemning them. Chrétien never makes these underlying tensions or interpretive cruces explicit, however—nor does he allow the characters to discuss or consider them: Readers must discern these issues for themselves and draw their own conclusions.

Chrétien's intricate plotting, subtle explorations of psychology and emotion, and development of complex, rounded characters have led many critics to declare him the father of the modern novel. He deserves credit for laying the foundation for virtually all subsequent Arthurian romances, and his presentation of the quintessential romantic triangle of Lancelot, Guinevere, and Arthur has proven so rich and compelling that, eight centuries later, it remains one of the most widely known stories in Western literature: Hardly a year goes by without a novelist or filmmaker attempting to tell it yet again.

"Critical Evaluation" by William Nelles

Further Reading

Brewer, Derek. "The Presentation of the Character of Lancelot: Chrétien to Malory." In *Arthurian Literature*, edited by Richard Barber. Vol. 4. Totowa, N.J.: D. S. Brewer, 1984. A classic discussion, frequently reprinted, of the character of Lancelot in Chrétien's romance in relation to his portrayal in other medieval works.

Duggan, Joseph J. *The Romances of Chrétien de Troyes*. New Haven, Conn.: Yale University Press, 2001. Focuses on the common characteristics of Chrétien's romances, such as the importance of kinship and genealogy, his art of narration, and his depiction of knighthood.

Frappier, Jean. "Chrétien de Troyes." In *Arthurian Literature in the Middle Ages*, edited by R. S. Loomis. Oxford, England: Clarendon Press, 1959. A brief and reliable general overview by one of the leading scholars of Chrétien's works.

Kelly, Douglas. *Sens and Conjointure in the "Chevalier de la Charrette."* The Hague, the Netherlands: Mouton, 1966. One of the key documents in the modern rehabilitation of Chrétien's artistic reputation. Analyzes the romance's style and structure in close detail, dispelling the earlier negative critical consensus about its aesthetic merit.

Lacy, Norris J., and Joan Tasker Grimbert, eds. *A Companion to Chrétien de Troyes*. New York: D. S. Brewer, 2005. Collection of essays that provide useful general discussions of Chrétien's sources, historical contexts, and the reception and influence of his work. Includes an essay on *Lancelot*, "*Le Chevalier de la Charrette*: That Obscure Object of Desire, Lancelot" by Matilda Tomaryn Bruckner.

Lupack, Alan, ed. *The Oxford Guide to Arthurian Literature and Legend*. New York: Oxford University Press, 2005. A very good background resource for exploring Chrétien's sources and successors; contains brief chapters on each of his works.

Maddox, Donald. *The Arthurian Romances of Chrétien de Troyes: Once and Future Fictions*. New York: Cambridge University Press, 1991. Includes a detailed study of the key functions played by the customs of Logres and Gorre in *Lancelot*.

Topsfield, L. T. *Chrétien de Troyes: A Study of the Arthurian Romances*. New York: Cambridge University Press, 1981. An accessible and thorough discussion of all of the romances.

Walters, Lori J., ed. *Lancelot and Guinevere: A Casebook*. New York: Routledge, 2002. Contains four essays devoted entirely to Chrétien's version of the two characters (including Brewer, cited above), and several others of related interest.

Language, Truth, and Logic

Author: A. J. Ayer (1910-1989)
First published: 1936; second edition, 1946
Type of work: Philosophy

A. J. Ayer's *Language, Truth, and Logic* was the first systematic presentation in English of the doctrines of logical positivism. While a student at Oxford University, Ayer spent the academic year 1932-1933 in Vienna attending the lectures and meetings of a group of philosophers, mathematicians, and scientists who called themselves the Vienna Circle. He quickly absorbed the basic tenets of the Vienna Circle and wrote *Language, Truth, and Logic* shortly after his return to England.

Ayer accepts the traditional empiricist view of philosophers such as David Hume that all genuine propositions either are analytic (in the sense, for Ayer, of being true solely by virtue of linguistic rules) or are empirically verifiable. Since analytic propositions are true in virtue of the meanings of the words composing them, they cannot be used to make factual assertions about the world. The tautological proposition "Either it is raining or it is not" is analytic in this sense, and it therefore says nothing about actual weather conditions. Because analytic propositions are true by virtue of meaning alone, Ayer believes, they can be known independently of experience; that is, they are knowable a priori.

In addition to tautologies and conceptual truths (for example, "Red is a color"), according to Ayer, the set of analytic propositions includes the necessarily true propositions of logic and mathematics. Traditional empiricists and Ayer maintain that propositions that are not analytic, and so are not true solely by virtue of linguistic rules, cannot be known a priori; they cannot be known by pure reason alone. It requires perceptual experience or some sort of empirical investigation to determine whether such propositions are true or false. Because these propositions are not true solely in virtue of linguistic rules, they have factual content and thus can be used to make informative assertions about the way things are in world.

Traditional empiricism was thus primarily a claim about knowledge and justification: The only propositions that can be known without empirical investigation are ones that are true by definition (for Ayer and other logical positivists, by virtue of linguistic rules), so any informative proposition can be known only on the basis of perceptual experience. In other words, the empiricists denied the rationalist claim that a priori knowledge of the world is possible.

With the principle of verification, Ayer and the logical positivists take empiricism to the semantic level by focusing on meaning rather than knowledge. This principle says that, in order to be meaningful, a proposition that is not analytic must be empirically verifiable. It must be possible, that is, to specify what sort of perceptual experiences would demonstrate that the principle is true or false. Propositions that do not satisfy this criterion of meaningfulness are declared by Ayer and the logical positivists to be meaningless and devoid of cognitive significance. Ayer's version of verificationism does not require that the proposition be conclusively verifiable. His version more modestly requires only that there be possible sensory experiences that are relevant to the question of whether a statement is true or false. Furthermore, in Ayer's version of the principle of verification, it is not necessary for verification to be practically possible; it is enough that verification could be carried out in principle.

With the principle of verification in place, Ayer goes on to argue that much of traditional metaphysical philosophy is not merely false but also meaningless nonsense. Metaphysics, as traditionally conceived, attempts to determine the nature of the world in itself, the reality "behind" the phenomenal world given in perceptual experience. The metaphysician, using pure a priori reasoning, claims to penetrate the veil of appearance and to arrive at the truth regarding the ultimate nature of reality. Ayer argues that metaphysical assertions, which are intended to be genuine assertions about the way the world is in itself, cannot be cognitively significant since they purport to describe that which cannot be an object of human experience. For example, theological claims such as "God exists" are regarded by Ayer as not merely false but also meaningless nonsense since there is no empirical evidence that could either confirm or refute that claim. The controversy between realists and idealists about the existence and nature of the external world, to take another example, is judged by Ayer to be a meaningless debate since no possible empirical evidence could decide the issue one way or the other. Realists maintain that there is a mind-independent physical world that causes perceptual experiences, while idealists assert that the world consists of minds and their ideas. Ayer points out that this whole controversy is meaningless since, he asserts, the evidence derived from the senses could never decide which of these two theories is correct.

The principle of verification guides Ayer regarding the proper task of philosophy. For Ayer, the role of philosophy is to use logic to clarify and analyze the concepts and propositions of science and common sense. Rather than engaging the fruitless debate between realists and idealists about the external world, Ayer suggests that philosophers look at the meaning of commonsense assertions about the external world in the light of the principle of verification.

According to Ayer, statements about physical objects are equivalent to statements about actual and possible experiences. To say, for example, that there is a chair in the next room means that, if someone were to go into the room, that person would have perceptual experiences of a chair. This view, which Ayer calls phenomenalism, is not intended to be a metaphysical theory about the ultimate nature of reality: He is not asserting that reality is essentially composed of minds and experiences. Such a theory would be just more meaningless metaphysics. Ayer's phenomenalism is, rather, a theory about the meaning of statements about physical objects. His analysis is intended to capture the empirically verifiable content of statements about physical objects. Philosophy as conceived by Ayer is not, then, a body of knowledge. It is, rather, the activity of analyzing and clarifying the propositions of science and everyday life.

One of the more notorious doctrines of *Language, Truth, and Logic* is Ayer's emotivist analysis of ethical propositions. Ayer believes that ethical assertions, such as "Stealing is wrong," are not analytic in the sense of being true by virtue of meaning alone. They are also not empirically verifiable: No perceptual experience could verify that stealing is wrong. Thus, Ayer's verificationism would seem to imply that ethical assertions should be regarded as meaningless nonsense. Given the importance of such statements in human life, this implication of the principle of verification seems to present a serious objection to that principle. Ayer deals with this problem by developing an emotivist theory of meaning. This theory says that ethical claims should not be interpreted as having factual or cognitive significance but rather as having emotive significance. They are not genuine assertions that are either true or false. Instead, they are exclamations that express a speaker's emotions and attitudes toward actions and persons. To say, then, that stealing is wrong is to express one's disapproval of stealing.

In 1946, Ayer wrote an extensive introduction for the second edition of *Language, Truth, and Logic* in which he defended the main doctrines of the book. In the ten years following the publication of the first edition, the principle of verificationism, the view that metaphysical assertions are meaningless, and Ayer's emotivism had all come under attack. Despite his vigorous defense, logical positivism's influence was already waning, and by the mid-1950's it had been eclipsed in the English-speaking world by ordinary-language philosophy, W. V. O. Quine's scientific naturalism, and Ludwig Wittgenstein's later work. Although logical positivism is no longer a living philosophical movement, *Language, Truth, and Logic* remains a superb introduction to doctrines that exerted an enormous influence on the evolution of twentieth century analytic philosophy.

David Haugen

Further Reading

Ayer, A. J. *Philosophy in the Twentieth Century.* New York: Random House, 1982. Includes Ayer's own evaluation of the central doctrines of logical positivism and puts the movement in the context of twentieth century philosophy.

_____, ed. *Logical Positivism.* New York: Free Press, 1959. A valuable collection of key papers by members of the Vienna Circle and by other logical positivists.

Friedman, Michael. *Reconsidering Logical Positivism.* New York: Cambridge University Press, 1999. A collection of essays focusing on the origin and development of logical positivism by a noted expert in the history of early analytic philosophy.

Griffiths, A. Phillips. *A. J. Ayer: Memorial Essays.* New York: Cambridge University Press, 1992. An excellent collection of essays on Ayer's philosophy, published shortly after his death in 1989.

Hahn, Edwin Lewis, ed. *The Philosophy of A. J. Ayer.* Library of Living Philosophers 21. Chicago: Open Court, 1999. Contains essays on Ayer's philosophy, as well as Ayer's replies. A valuable resource.

Jørgensen, Jørgen. *The Development of Logical Empiricism.* Chicago: University of Chicago Press, 1951. An account of some of the central doctrines of logical positivism by a Danish philosopher who participated in some of the meetings of the Vienna Circle.

Soames, Scott. *Philosophical Analysis in the Twentieth Century.* Vol. 1. Princeton, N.J.: Princeton University Press, 2003. Part 4 of this volume includes a penetrating discussion of the verifiability criterion of meaning, as well as discussions of the positivist views on necessity, a priori knowledge, and the emotivist account of ethics. Highly recommended.

Largo Desolato

Author: Václav Havel (1936-   )
First produced: 1985; first published, 1985 (English
    translation, 1987)
Type of work: Drama
Type of plot: Absurdist
Time of plot: Late 1970's or early 1980's
Locale: Prague

Principal characters:
PROFESSOR LEOPOLD NETTLES, a philosopher
EDWARD, his friend and his wife's companion
SUZANA, Leopold's wife
FIRST SIDNEY, a mill worker
SECOND SIDNEY, a mill worker
LUCY, Leopold's lover
BERTRAM, a friend of Leopold
FIRST CHAP, a government agent
SECOND CHAP, a government agent
FIRST MAN, the agents' assistant
SECOND MAN, the agents' assistant
MARGUERITE, a student

The Story:

In scene 1, Professor Leopold Nettles sits on the couch in his living room, watching the front door. After a while he walks to the door, peers through its peephole, and listens at the door as if expecting someone; he appears tense. After a long pause, the curtain drops.

Scene 2 repeats scene 1 exactly. Scene 3 begins in the same way, but it continues until the doorbell rings and Nettles jumps. After he recognizes the man at the door, he opens the door and Edward, his friend and his wife's companion, enters. The two engage in small talk, mostly about Leopold's digestion and nerves; Edward expresses concern that Leopold is drinking too much and that he has not gone outside in some time. Suzana, Leopold's wife, returns from shopping and asks Leopold about his activities of the day. He details his morning's tidying and fixing of breakfast. Suzana chastises him for eating his eggs with a silver teaspoon. She then leaves, and Leopold and Edward resume their conversation. Leopold appears very anxious and concerned that he will soon be arrested, although he does not reveal where he thinks he will be taken or by whom.

The doorbell rings again, startling Leopold. Two workers from a paper mill, First Sidney and Second Sidney, whom Nettles met two years ago but had forgotten, have come to request that Leopold take some sort of action, described only in the vaguest of terms. The two Sidneys declare themselves fans of Leopold and claim that many people are looking to him for direction. The doorbell rings again, and Lucy, Leopold's mistress, enters; the ensuing conversation repeats much of what has already been said. The two Sidneys, having overstayed their welcome, eventually leave, promising to return with writing paper and imploring Leopold to maintain

his courage. When Leopold and Lucy are finally alone, Lucy also encourages Leopold to resume his writing and suggests that her love should be an inspiration to him. Leopold remains unresponsive, and the curtain falls.

When scene 4 begins, it is night. Leopold's friend Bertram is sitting on the sofa. Like Edward in scene 3, he asks Leopold about his drinking and his nerves and alludes to Leopold's inactivity. He repeats that many people are concerned about Leopold, and, like the two Sidneys, presents himself as an emissary representing Leopold's supporters. Bertram refers to uncertainties and possible danger, suggesting that Leopold's anxieties are related to past actions and future consequences. Lucy emerges from Leopold's bedroom, causing Bertram some embarrassment. After Bertram leaves, Lucy insists on talking with Leopold about their affair, which Leopold refuses to acknowledge. Lucy asserts that she has entered the relationship in order to stimulate him to some sort of intellectual activity, but now she feels used; Leopold claims he is incapable of love. Their discussion is interrupted by the doorbell and the appearance of First Chap and Second Chap, government agents representing the source of Leopold's fears. The Chaps have Lucy removed by the First Man and the Second Man; they then inquire about Leopold's activities.

The Chaps have come to offer a resolution to Leopold's difficulties, which are revealed to have come about because of an essay he published called *Ontology of the Human Self.* If Leopold will sign a statement saying that he is not the same Professor Nettles who wrote the essay, he will be exonerated and the matter will be dropped. The Chaps assure Leopold that many others in similar predicaments have accepted such offers. Leopold, however, is visibly disturbed and requests time to consider his decision. The scene ends with Leopold sitting on the couch, wrapped in a blanket.

Leopold is alone at the beginning of scene 5. He alternately paces, checks the front door's peephole, takes vitamins from a collection of vials on the table, and retires to the bathroom to wash his face. Suzana enters with shopping bags, and their conversation parallels that of the third scene. Leopold describes the visit of the previous night and the Chaps' offer. Suzana is angered that Leopold would even consider accepting and exits to her room. Leopold repeats the actions of the opening of the scene.

Next, Edward arrives and questions Leopold about his digestion, his drinking, and the events of the previous night. Leopold continues to pace, take vitamins, and leave the room to wash his face. The two Sidneys arrive with writing paper and suitcases full of documents from the mill. They repeat their encouragement and support. Bertram arrives, and he, the two Sidneys, Suzana, and Edward repeat lines from earlier scenes, all calling on Leopold to act. Leopold orders them out, and, as the curtain falls, he can be heard running water in the bathroom. The doorbell rings again.

Scene 6 continues from where scene 5 ends. Leopold emerges from the shower to answer the door. The caller, Marguerite, is a philosophy student who admires his work; like Lucy, she offers her love as an inspiration to Leopold, and it appears that Leopold has decided to replace Lucy with Marguerite. They are interrupted by the doorbell and the reappearance of the two Chaps. Leopold announces that they might arrest him, for he refuses to sign their paper and relinquish his identity; however, the Chaps reply that they have not come to arrest him or to require his signature, but to inform him that his case has been postponed indefinitely. Leopold begs to be arrested rather than to continue in limbo with an uncertain future. As the curtain falls, he has collapsed on the floor. Scene 7 repeats the opening scene.

Critical Evaluation:

Largo Desolato, the title of which is taken from a string quartet by Alban Berg, is the most autobiographical of Václav Havel's dramatic works. Havel, a playwright, philosopher, and political activist who later served as president of Czechoslovakia (1989-1992) and first president of the Czech Republic (1993-2003), was imprisoned in 1979 by the Communist regime in Czechoslovakia (which took control of the country in 1968) for his opposition to totalitarianism and his leadership of the dissident group Charter 77. Havel was released in 1983, without having served his entire sentence, but remained under police surveillance and the constant threat of

reincarceration. He composed *Largo Desolato* in 1984. It is an absurdist drama that draws on repetition of action and dialogue to produce an unsettling and sometimes humorous effect.

The character Leopold Nettles, a philosopher who has published a controversial essay, *Ontology of the Human Self*, appears to have undergone an imprisonment and release similar to Havel's, and he lives in fear of future punishment. Although much is left open to interpretation, one can conclude from the title of the essay that Leopold's crime is that he has insisted on individuality in a world that demands its sacrifice. The destruction of individual identity is apparent from the names of several characters: First Sidney, Second Sidney, First Chap, Second Chap, First Man, and Second Man. The workers and the government agents are interchangeable cogs in the mechanism of bureaucracy and totalitarianism. In fact, what the state requests of Nettles is self-annihilation, a denial of authorship that entails the creation of a fictitious Nettles-the-author-and-public-enemy and that would rob Leopold of his sense of identity.

The theme of the individual in conflict with the system, which occurs throughout Havel's plays, has its antecedents in the works of two earlier Prague writers, Franz Kafka and Jaroslav Hašek. In Kafka's novels, the protagonists find themselves both alienated from and manipulated by impenetrable bureaucracies; any effort to retain a sense of self and survive within the system results in failure and destruction of self. In Hašek's classic Czech novel *The Good Soldier Švejk* (1921-1923), the title character repeatedly undermines the system by carrying its false logic to extremes. In *Largo Desolato*, Havel's protagonist exists within a similarly oppressive system that could destroy his identity, but Leopold recognizes the flaw in the logic of oppression: In imprisoning him, the system would only increase his reputation and sphere of influence. Once Leopold has decided against recanting his work, he has achieved a personal victory, but that victory is undermined by the system's retraction of its offer, which renders his decision meaningless and leaves him in the same position as when the play began.

The ambiguous conclusion and the circular structure of the play are characteristic of absurdist drama, particularly the work of Samuel Beckett, and Beckett and Havel are frequently compared. Both rely on repetition of action and dialogue, yet to different effects. While Beckett places his characters in incomprehensible settings, outside recognizable time and place, Havel situates his drama in realism. Leopold's apartment is a typical apartment; his daily routines are quite ordinary. This normality, however, is mere illusion, and that is Havel's point: The home is no safe haven from the oppression of the totalitarian state, and the appearance of order, characterized through mundane activities such as preparing meals, tidying rooms, and grooming, only camouflages the ubiquity of government control over individual lives.

Even more than the action, the dialogue reinforces this theme. Characters speak in stock phrases and clichés whether they are discussing daily routine, emotional intimacy, or politics. Havel heightens the effect through a technique called "time slips," in which different characters repeat the lines or actions of other characters. For example, the two Chaps begin their apparent interrogation by asking exactly the same questions of Leopold as does his friend Bertram; Leopold's conversation with Lucy, which marks the decline in their relationship, is repeated almost verbatim with Marguerite, suggesting the beginning of an affair. At the end of scene 5, the words of the two Sidneys, Edward, Bertram, Suzana, and Lucy form a chorus as each remarks, "Some hero." Speech and action thus become nonsensical; relationships appear superficial; barriers between the external world and the internal world disintegrate. In Beckett's plays, characters create their own realities through language. In Havel's work, language threatens to imprison the characters in a reality that has slipped from their control. The clichés, circular reasoning, and bureaucratic language employed by all the characters represent the extent to which the control of the state has infiltrated their daily lives.

Largo Desolato lends itself to several interpretive approaches. It can be viewed as autobiographical, as a political work critical of Communism, or as an absurdist play. Its appeal to Western scholars derives from its thematic universality and its reflection of late twentieth century concerns with the interrelationships among language, self, and truth. Of his own work, Havel has stated, "Drama's success in transcending the limits of its age and country depends entirely on how far it succeeds in finding a way to its own place and time." Regarded by many as his most successful play, *Largo Desolato* depicts life in Communist Czechoslovakia in a manner that allows those who enjoy democracy to recognize themselves and the problems of their own societies.

K Edgington

Further Reading

Goetz-Stankiewicz, Marketa. *The Silenced Theatre: Czech Playwrights Without a Stage*. Toronto, Ont.: University of Toronto Press, 1979. Comprehensive study locates the Czech theater of the absurd in a Czech rather than a Western European literary tradition. Chapter 2 features discussion of Havel's early plays *Zahradni slavnost* (pr., pb. 1963; *The Garden Party*, 1969) and *Vyrozumění* (pr. 1965; *The Memorandum*, 1967), which introduce themes also evident in *Largo Desolato*.

Havel, Václav. "Stories and Totalitarianism." In *Open Letters: Selected Writings, 1965-1990*. Edited and translated by Paul Wilson. New York: Alfred A. Knopf, 1991. Presents a discussion of Havel's views on the relationship between literature and politics.

Kriseova, Eda. *Václav Havel: The Authorized Biography*. Translated by Caleb Crain. New York: St. Martin's Press, 1993. Biography explores Havel's development as a writer in conjunction with his political activism. A brief chapter on *Largo Desolato* details the autobiographical elements of the play.

Pontuso, James F. *Václav Havel: Civic Responsibility in the Postmodern Age*. New York: Rowman & Littlefield, 2004. Focuses on Havel's political philosophy and demonstrates how these ideas are expressed in his plays.

Rocamora, Carol. *Acts of Courage: Václav Havel's Life in the Theater*. Hanover, N.H.: Smith and Kraus, 2004. Chronicles Havel's involvement in the Czech theater during three decades of Communism and the risks he and others undertook to produce his plays. Includes discussions of his ten full-length and eight one-act plays.

Skloot, Robert. "Václav Havel: The Once and Future Playwright." *Kenyon Review* 15, no. 2 (Spring, 1993): 223-231. Takes a critical look at Havel's later plays, including *Largo Desolato*. Valuable essay presents a dissenting voice in a field of largely adulatory response to Havel's work.

Soderberg, Douglas. "Life Under Absurdity: Václav Havel's *Largo Desolato*." In *Critical Essays on Václav Havel*, edited by Marketa Goetz-Stankiewicz and Phyllis Carey. New York: G. K. Hall, 1999. Analysis of *Largo Desolato* is part of a collection of essays that discuss Havel's individual plays and his career in the theater as well as his involvement in Czech politics.

Vladislav, Jan, ed. *Václav Havel or Living in Truth: Twenty-two Essays Published on the Occasion of the Award of the Erasmus Prize to Václav Havel*. London: Faber & Faber, 1987. Rich collection of essays by sixteen of Havel's contemporaries provides a variety of insights into influences on Havel as a dramatist and the significance of his work artistically, philosophically, and politically.

The Last Chronicle of Barset

Author: Anthony Trollope (1815-1882)
First published: 1867
Type of work: Novel
Type of plot: Domestic realism
Time of plot: Mid-nineteenth century
Locale: Barsetshire, England

Principal characters:
MR. CRAWLEY, the curate of Hogglestock
MRS. CRAWLEY, his wife
GRACE CRAWLEY, their daughter
MR. PROUDIE, bishop of Barchester
MRS. PROUDIE, his wife
HENRY GRANTLY, Grace's suitor
LILY DALE, Grace's friend
JOHN EAMES, Lily's suitor

The Story:

The citizens in the community of Hogglestock are upset because Mr. Crawley, the curate, has been accused of stealing a check for twenty pounds. In Archdeacon Grantly's home, where there is concern that Henry Grantly might marry Grace Crawley, the curate's schoolteacher daughter, emotions are running high.

Bishop Proudie and his wife are set against the unfortunate Crawley. Mrs. Proudie, who exerts great power over her husband, persuades the bishop to write a letter to Mr. Crawley, forbidding him to preach in his church until the case is settled one way or another. When Mr. Crawley refuses the injunction in a letter of reply, Mr. and Mrs. Proudie quarrel regarding his answer. Mr. Proudie then sends for Mr. Crawley, asking him to come to the bishop's palace at once. Mr. Crawley arrives, hot and tired from his very long walk to to the palace, and simply repeats what he has stated in his letter. He then departs, leaving the bishop and his wife amazed at his boldness.

Mr. Crawley is not kept from performing his duties at the church on Christmas morning. Because he cannot recall how he came into possession of the money in question, he tells his wife that he believes he must belong either in jail or in Bedlam (an insane asylum). At last, Henry Grantly decides to ask Grace Crawley to marry him even though to do so is to go against his parents' wishes. At the same time, Lily Dale, Grace Crawley's friend, is being wooed by young John Eames, a clerk in the Income Tax Office in London and a suitor, once rejected, whom Lily's mother favors. Eames is the friend of a London artist named Conway Dalrymple, who is painting a portrait of Miss Clara Van Siever, a mutual friend, in the sitting room of Mrs. Dobbs Broughton. Meanwhile, the aged Mrs. Van Siever is engaged in forcing Dobbs Broughton to pay money he owes to her.

Not long afterward, John Eames meets Henry Grantly. Neither likes the other at first. Eames meets Lily in Lady Julia de Guest's home, where Grace is also visiting, and he discusses his unfavorable meeting with Henry Grantly in front of Grace. When Henry proposes to Grace, she refuses him and returns home to be with her father during his trial. Lily tells Eames that she plans to die an old maid, her heart having been broken by Adolphus Crosbie, a former suitor.

Mr. Toogood, a distant relative, is to defend Mr. Crawley in his trial regarding the stolen check. John Eames is brought into the Crawley case by Mr. Toogood, who wants Eames to go to Florence and attempt to persuade Mr. Arabin, an influential clergyman, to come to Mr. Crawley's rescue. There is another reason Arabin should return to England: Mrs. Arabin's father, Mr. Harding, is ailing and growing weaker each day.

Conway Dalrymple works on Miss Van Siever's portrait, which is still a secret from Dobbs Broughton, in whose house it is being painted. Broughton has ordered the artist out of his house, but Mrs. Broughton wants the picture painted, regardless of her jealous husband's reactions.

The clerical commission summoned by Bishop Proudie reaches no decision concerning Mr. Crawley. The commission members resolve that nothing should be done until the civil courts have decided his case. Archdeacon Grantly tries to engage the help of Lady Lufton to prevent the marriage of his son to Grace Crawley, but Lady Lufton refuses. The archdeacon finally promises that he will no longer oppose the marriage if Mr. Crawley is found innocent of any crime.

Dobbs Broughton is being pressured for money by old Mrs. Van Siever. Clara Van Siever is to marry Musselboro, Broughton's former partner, but Dalrymple is still hoping to marry Clara. He is putting the last touches to Clara's portrait when Mrs. Van Siever enters the Broughton house; at her word, he destroys the painting. Over Clara's objections, Mrs. Van Siever announces that her daughter is to marry Musselboro. After the Van Sievers leave, Musselboro arrives with news that Dobbs Broughton has killed himself that morning. Clara and Dalrymple resolve to face Mrs. Van Siever's wrath together.

Mrs. Proudie continues her fight to have Mr. Crawley removed. After a quarrel with her husband, she retires to her room and dies there of a heart attack. True to the resolution imposed on him by Mrs. Proudie before her death, Mr. Crawley preaches a final sermon in his church and never again enters it as curate.

On the Continent, John Eames learns from Mrs. Arabin the cause of Mr. Crawley's troubles. Mrs. Arabin, who had received the check from a tenant, had turned it over to Mr. Crawley without telling her husband, the dean, of the transaction. She has only recently heard of the charges against Mr. Crawley, and she is hurrying home to England to do what she can to straighten out the matter. In the meantime, Mr. Toogood traces the theft of the check to the tenant who had forwarded it to Mrs. Arabin.

Mr. Toogood and Henry Grantly take the good news to Mr. and Mrs. Crawley. When she hears their story, Mrs. Crawley, who has defended her husband from the beginning, breaks into tears. The messengers have to explain the situation carefully to Mr. Crawley, who cannot at first believe that his innocence is about to be proved. When Mr. Harding, the aged incumbent vicar of St. Ewold's parish, dies, Archdeacon Grantly offers that position to Mr. Crawley as a recompense for all he has suffered. In midsummer, Grace Crawley becomes Mrs. Henry Grantly.

John Eames does not marry Lily Dale after all, for Lily is unable to make up her mind about him; Dalrymple, however, marries Clara Van Siever as he had planned. Musselboro, after losing Clara, proceeds to marry the widow of his old partner, and Mrs. Broughton's sorrows are thus brought to an end.

Critical Evaluation:

The Last Chronicle of Barset is the last of a series of novels that Anthony Trollope wrote about the ecclesiastical community in the fictional county of Barsetshire, based on the Anglican Church life in and around Salisbury in southwestern England in the mid-nineteenth century. It was preceded by *The Warden* (1855), *Barchester Towers* (1857), *Doctor Thorne* (1858), *Framley Parsonage* (1860-1861, serial; 1861, book), and *The Small House at Allington* (1862-1864, serial; 1864, book). Many of the characters appear in all six novels, so the ideal way to read this novel is as the conclusion of Trollope's accumulated tale of nineteenth century social and professional life, particularly among clergymen and their families.

Trollope was aware of the possibility that any of the Barsetshire novels might be read outside that context, however, and each of the books provides sufficient information as the story progresses for it to be read alone. Repetition of incidents from previous novels is a common practice in Trollope's works, but one that can be irritating at times for readers who are not accustomed to detailed repetitions of matters they may view as long since settled. This is part of a more serious difficulty common to nineteenth century novels in general: They tend to be very long, as during the time when they were written, narrative alone was not considered to be adequate for the experience of reading novels. There was a taste for novels of extraordinary length in a society that had plenty of time for reading, given its lack of other forms of entertainment. In addition, many novels, including *The Last Chronicle of Barset*, were originally published in magazines in serial form, a few thousand words at a time. The authors knew that readers might easily forget details between readings, and so they repeated important information.

In this novel, Trollope provides comment on the narrative as it takes its leisurely time unfolding. The story is told with considerable detail and much measured, sophisticated, philosophical rumination by the wise narrator. The novel is also a contemplation of ethical and social insight and an opportunity for witty, sometimes satirical, commentary on the eccentricities and cruelties of supposedly civilized characters. Trollope does not attack the structures of British society or of the Anglican Church, which follows similar patterns of privilege. What he is against is the way in which power often falls into the hands of ambitious, thrusting careerists who are more interested in exercising power for personal gain and satisfaction than they are in benefiting the Church or its parishioners.

It can be argued that in the twenty-first century *The Last Chronicle of Barset* is as pertinent as ever, given its exploration of the ways in which power is often grasped by the least capable members of society. Mrs. Proudie is the most blatant example of this misplaced power. She is powerful not because of any official position she possesses but because of her influence over her husband, who has, despite his intellectual and personal limitations, managed to become the bishop of Barset. In the earlier novels, Trollope has much to say about the politics of Bishop Proudie's appointment and his malpractice of the office under the malign influence of his wife. Mrs. Proudie exercises the same irresponsible conduct in this novel as she attempts to drive Mr. Crawley from his pulpit long before his guilt or innocence has been determined.

The Last Chronicle of Barset is less concerned with the

internal politics of ecclesiastical life than are the previous works in the series; it is focused instead on two further themes that interest Trollope—character and the eccentric nature of human conduct. The plot is dependent on the slight fact of the Arabins' absence on the Continent and their misunderstanding of what Crawley's problem is. Once they know the facts of the matter, the mystery is solved. The novel's real theme is how Crawley, those around him, and those with power over him cope with the idea that this penurious cleric would steal money, however small the sum might be. The matter is complicated by Crawley's intransigently honest character and his financial and personal situation. Prone to depression, worn out by years of poverty and despair, he is fragile, emotionally and intellectually. A brilliant ecclesiastical scholar but lacking in the political and social skills to make his way in the Church, he has wound up at the bottom of the institution, working hard and constantly with his poor parishioners but with a fixed sense of outrage at the lack of recognition he receives and his inability to provide for his family. He is a man difficult to patronize, given his high skills and intelligence, and he is prideful in his righteousness. For all his pride, however, he is also a man of considerable humility, which does him great harm when Arabin denies the check. Crawley gives up, presuming that Arabin must be telling the truth, since his friend's word must necessarily be better than his own. Crawley comes to believe that he must be wrong, that he must have somehow taken the check improperly, although he has no memory of doing so.

A variation on this battle of personal honor is shown in Crawley's daughter's determination to refuse to marry the man she loves if her father is legally proven to be a thief. The ramifications of that decision move through the community, as the love affair impinges on the family relations of her prospective in-laws, themselves prominent members of the ecclesiastical society. Not the least interesting is the way in which the entire society, so closely connected by professional power and intermarriage, reacts to and is affected by Crawley's plight. He is a man whom the members of the community have, in the main, conveniently patronized and attempted to ignore in his serious financial struggles, but whom they feel inclined to judge, for good or ill. *The Last Chronicle of Barset* is a close study of a good man who is his own worst enemy, but it is also an involved exploration of the problem of how people live together in close-knit social structures, and how, sometimes, they simply make a muddle of life, given the inclinations of human nature. It is also a charming love story and a tale of family affections in situations of both sorrow and pleasure—an example of how Trollope generously cultivates a multiplicity of themes in his novels.

"Critical Evaluation" by Charles Pullen

Further Reading

apRoberts, Ruth. *The Moral Trollope*. Athens: Ohio University Press, 1971. Discussion of Trollope's efforts as a moralist is informative for an understanding of *The Last Chronicle of Barset*.

Bridgham, Elizabeth A. *Spaces of the Sacred and Profane: Dickens, Trollope, and the Victorian Cathedral Town*. New York: Routledge, 2008. Describes how Trollope and Charles Dickens use the setting of Victorian cathedral towns to critique religious attitudes, business practices, aesthetic ideas, and other aspects of nineteenth century English life.

Bury, Laurent. *Seductive Strategies in the Novels of Anthony Trollope, 1815-1882*. Lewiston, N.Y.: Edwin Mellen Press, 2004. Focuses on seduction in all of Trollope's novels, arguing that seduction was a survival skill for both men and women in the Victorian era. Demonstrates how Trollope depicted the era's sexual politics.

Edwards, P. D. *Anthony Trollope*. London: Routledge & Kegan Paul, 1968. Short study of Trollope's work includes a section on *The Last Chronicle of Barset*. Uses extracts from the novels to discuss specific topics. A good starting place for research.

Markwick, Margaret. *New Men in Trollope's Novels: Rewriting the Victorian Male*. Burlington, Vt.: Ashgate, 2007. Examines Trollope's novels to trace the development of his ideas about masculinity. Argues that Trollope's male characters are not the conventional Victorian patriarchs and demonstrates how his works promoted a "startlingly modern model of manhood."

_____. *Trollope and Women*. London: Hambledon Press, 1997. Examines how Trollope could simultaneously accept the conventional Victorian ideas about women while also sympathizing with women's difficult situations. Demonstrates the individuality of his female characters. Discusses his depiction of both happy and unhappy marriages, male-female relationships, bigamy, and scandal.

Mullen, Richard, and James Munson. *The Penguin Companion to Trollope*. New York: Penguin, 1996. Comprehensive guide describes all of Trollope's novels, short stories, travel books, and other works. Discusses plot, characters, background, tone, allusions, and contemporary references and places the works in their historical context.

The Last Days of Pompeii

Author: Edward Bulwer-Lytton (1803-1873)
First published: 1834
Type of work: Novel
Type of plot: Historical
Time of plot: 79 C.E.
Locale: Pompeii

Principal characters:
GLAUCUS, a wealthy young Greek
ARBACES, the Egyptian priest of Isis
IONE, his Greek ward
APAECIDES, her brother
NYDIA, a blind flower-seller

The Story:

Late one afternoon in the ancient city of Pompeii, the fashionable rich young men are congregating for the daily rite of the public baths. Among them are Clodius, a foppish Roman, and Glaucus, a popular young Greek. Together the two stroll toward the baths, mingling with slaves bearing bronze buckets and idlers gowned in purple robes. Along the way, they see the beautiful blind flower seller, Nydia. She, too, is from Greece, and for that reason Glaucus takes an interest in her. It is still too early for the baths, so the two friends walk along the seafront as Glaucus describes a Neapolitan woman of Greek birth with whom he has fallen in love. Unfortunately, he has lost contact with the woman and is now morose. While they talk, Arbaces, the evil-looking Egyptian priest of Isis, intercepts them. The two young men are barely able to conceal their dislike for the Egyptian.

Arbaces secretly defies the Romans and the Greeks and prays for the day when Egypt will once again be powerful. He reveals to a lesser priest his interest in the brother and sister Apaecides and Ione, his wards. He hopes to make a priest of Apaecides, and he plans to marry Ione. The siblings had been in Naples, but recently Arbaces has brought them to Pompeii, where he can influence them.

Glaucus meets Ione at a party. She is the young woman he had seen and lost in Naples. At the same time, Arbaces develops his hold over Apaecides, who is growing more and more confused after coming into contact with the sophistries of the corrupt priest of Isis. Meanwhile, Nydia, the flower seller, is falling hopelessly in love with Glaucus.

It happens that Glaucus and Clodius are loitering in the establishment of Burbo, the wine seller, when Burbo and his wife are beating Nydia, their slave. Glaucus, hearing the woman's cries, buys her from her owners, planning to give her to Ione. Nydia realizes that Glaucus can never love her after he gives her a letter to deliver to Ione. In this letter, he accuses Arbaces of false imputations. On reading the letter, Ione decides to go at once to the palace of the priest and face him with Glaucus's charges.

Knowing the danger to Ione at the palace, Nydia warns both Ione's brother and Glaucus. Glaucus hurries to the palace to confront the priest. An earthquake interrupts the quarrel between the two men, and a statue of the goddess Isis falls from a pedestal, striking Arbaces. Glaucus and Ione run from the building to join the throng in the street. Alone and deserted, the blind slave weeps bitterly.

The earthquake causes little damage, and the people of Pompeii take up again the threads of their lives. Apaecides becomes a convert to Christianity, and Glaucus and Ione remain together.

Julia, daughter of a wealthy freedman named Diomed, is also in love with Glaucus and seeks to interfere between him and Ione. She goes to the house of Arbaces, where she and the priest plot together. Arbaces has a drug prepared to be administered to Glaucus; under its influence, Glaucus runs from his house into a cemetery in a demented stupor. Apaecides and Arbaces then arrive at the cemetery. They quarrel, and Arbaces stabs Apaecides, killing him. Then, hoping to kill Glaucus indirectly, the priest summons the crowd and declares that Glaucus in his drunken rage has killed Apaecides. Glaucus and a Christian who attempts to defend him are arrested. They are condemned to be given to wild beasts at the upcoming public games.

After the funeral of her brother, Ione resolves to declare her belief in the innocence of Glaucus. Before she can carry out her plan, however, Arbaces seizes her and carries her off to his palace. The only one who knows of Arbaces' guilt is a priest who is also his prisoner, but Arbaces has not reckoned with Nydia, who as a dancing woman at his palace has learned most of his secrets. Nydia contacts the priest imprisoned by Arbaces and agrees to carry his story to the authorities. Unfortunately, she too is captured. She persuades a slave to carry the message to Sallust, a friend of Glaucus, but the message is delivered while Sallust is drunk, and he refuses to read it.

The day on which Glaucus is to die in the arena arrives.

The games begin with gladiatorial combat, which the members of the crowd watch listlessly; they are bored because the deaths do not come fast enough or with enough suffering. After one combat, the crowd condemns an unpopular gladiator to death; his body is dragged across the arena and placed on the heap with those previously slain. A lion is turned loose in the arena with Glaucus, but, unfortunately for the crowd's amusement, the lion creeps with a moan back into its cage. Before the animal can be prodded into action, Sallust appears and demands the arrest of Arbaces. A slave had called his attention to Nydia's letter, which he had thrown aside the night before. After reading it, he had hurried to lay his information before the praetor. The mob, not to be cheated after Glaucus is set free, demands that Arbaces be thrown to the lion.

Then the famous volcanic eruption of Mount Vesuvius begins. The whole gladiatorial scene becomes chaos as terrified thousands pour out of the doomed amphitheater, crushing the weakest in their hurry to escape. Looting begins in the temples. Nydia reaches Glaucus, and together they hurry to the house of Arbaces to find and save Ione. Arbaces dies there in an earthquake that closely follows the eruption. Smoke and ash in the air make it too dark to see, but Nydia, accustomed to darkness, is able to lead Ione and Glaucus through the streets. At last Glaucus, Ione, and Nydia gain the safety of the seaside and put out to sea in a small ship. They fall asleep in the boat that night, and in the morning Glaucus and Ione discover that the heartbroken Nydia has cast herself into the sea.

Critical Evaluation:

Edward Bulwer-Lytton wrote *The Last Days of Pompeii* before he inherited his family estate, in the days when he was forced to make his living as a hack writer. His mother, who disapproved of his marriage, refused to support him in the manner to which he had hoped to become accustomed. He had made his name with mildly scandalous novels of high society and with crime thrillers. *The Last Days of Pompeii* was a calculated move upmarket, into the genre of historical romance, which had proved not only popular but also respectable thanks to the endeavors of Sir Walter Scott.

Bulwer-Lytton began to write *The Last Days of Pompeii* in a more conscientious spirit than he had applied to his earlier works, and he put a great deal of effort into the background research. He paid a lengthy visit to the partly excavated city, which had by then become a popular stopping-off point for European tourists. Although subsequent research has provided much more information about the era in which the novel is set, and about Pompeii itself, the lavishly footnoted reconstruction of everyday life in the city that Bulwer-Lytton provides in the early chapters of his novel are as good and as full as could have been expected at the time.

Bulwer-Lytton presumably thought this research work was justified, because he had great hopes for the novel. The idea was full of potential; in setting out to write the book he was forearmed with a ready-made climax far more spectacular than any that had recommended itself to Scott: the eruption of Vesuvius and the devastation of Pompeii. Regardless of whether he chose to represent this event as an act of God, punishing the wickedness of the decadent Romans, it was there to be invoked as a deus ex machina whose fallout could destroy the villainous characters and provide the virtuous with a magnificently narrow escape.

The book became one of the best sellers of the Victorian era and obtained a new lease on life when it was reprinted in a cheap format in the mid-nineteenth century as one of the earliest "railway novels." It cannot be said, however, that Bulwer-Lytton exploited the story's melodramatic potential to the full. The story seems to lose its way toward the end, and the volcanic eruption—when it arrives—is described in a cursory and distinctly halfhearted fashion. It may be that the pressure of financial necessity made the author determined to get the final part of the text over and done with. It is also possible that Bulwer-Lytton found his story an increasingly uncomfortable straitjacket and hurried through the final chapters.

The most interesting aspect of the text is the role played by Arbaces. He is cast as the villain and is duly destroyed in the climax, but the author seems far more interested in the priest's cynical view of the world than in the careful piety of the Christian characters. Beneath his hypocritical pose as a priest of Isis, Arbaces practices his true faith, which substitutes the "Necessity of Nature" for the gods and includes an occult "secret wisdom." This places him within a long tradition of Bulwerian mystics, which also included the enigmatic Volktman in *Godolphin* (1833) and the central characters of *Zanoni* (1842) and *A Strange Story* (1861).

Bulwer-Lytton remained uneasily skeptical about the occult, but it always fascinated him, and the rejection implied by his allocation of villainous roles to these charismatic magicians rings false. His endeavors in this regard were much appreciated by some, including the Theosophist Helena Blavatsky, who borrowed heavily from Bulwer-Lytton's occult fiction in compiling her "secret wisdom." Bulwer-Lytton was equally skeptical about orthodox religion and Victorian morality. This skepticism is also evident in *The Last Days of Pompeii*, most obviously in the priggish fashion in which Glaucus announces his eventual conversion to Christianity.

This ambivalent quality is all the more interesting by virtue of its being somewhat hidden. Victorian puritanism ruthlessly repressed the fascination that English writers might otherwise have found in contemplation of pagan antiquity; Bulwer-Lytton's description of the orgies that take place in the secret chambers of the temple of Isis is very carefully censored. The author's fascinations, some considered incorrect in his time, always seem to be seething beneath the surface of the narrative, rather like the pent-up fires of the volcano. Some of this impatience is revealed in what looks suspiciously like an act of wanton cruelty, when the author flings the unfortunate Nydia into the sea to die a suicide simply because there is no clear happy ending ready to receive her.

The "confused and perplexed" character of Arbaces, formed by the "spirit of discontented pride," is a far closer reflection of Bulwer-Lytton's own personality (and his fierce resentment of his temporary disinheritance) than anything to be found in the character of the hero, Glaucus, or in that of the ascetic Apaecides. Bulwer-Lytton was not in the least attracted to the kind of Christianity that could rejoice in humility, and he despised those who could take comfort from the belief that the end of the world might arrive at any moment in a flurry of fire and brimstone. In order to secure publication and an adequate measure of popularity, however, he had no alternative but to meet the expectations of his audience by bringing Glaucus into the Christian fold.

As a depiction of the classical world, *The Last Days of Pompeii* has been superseded by more recent research, and its melodramatic potential is at best only partially fulfilled. As a specimen of the way in which one era's contemplation of another can reveal all kinds of insights and prejudices, however, it remains an interesting and valuable work.

"Critical Evaluation" by Brian Stableford

Further Reading

Campbell, James L., Sr. *Edward Bulwer-Lytton*. Boston: Twayne, 1986. Surveys Bulwer-Lytton's career, the influences on his work, and his fictional output. Analyzes the elements that contributed to the writing of *The Last Days of Pompeii* and describes the novel as a sensationalistic costume romance rather than a serious exploration of Roman history.

Christensen, Allan Conrad, ed. *The Subverting Vision of Bulwer Lytton: Bicentenary Reflections*. Newark: University of Delaware Press, 2004. In addition to Angus Easson's essay "'At Home' with the Romans: Domestic Archaeology in the *Last Days of Pompeii*," presents discussions of Bulwer-Lytton's reputation, his crime novels and other works, and his relationship with his wife.

Fleishman, Avrom. *The English Historical Novel: Walter Scott to Virginia Woolf*. Baltimore: Johns Hopkins University Press, 1971. Examines the English tradition of historical fiction from its beginnings to the start of World War II. Discussion of *The Last Days of Pompeii* praises the novel's depiction of Roman society and its use of Roman history to examine nineteenth century political controversy.

Mitchell, Leslie. *Bulwer Lytton: The Rise and Fall of a Victorian Man of Letters*. New York: Hambledon and London, 2003. Biography recounts the events of Bulwer-Lytton's life and seeks to rehabilitate his reputation as an author, which has suffered since World War I. Organized according to the themes of the subject's life and work rather than chronologically.

Sutherland, J. A. *Victorian Novelists and Publishers*. Chicago: University of Chicago Press, 1976. Examines how business relationships between authors and publishers affected the Victorian novel. Describes the negotiations between Bulwer-Lytton and his publishers that preceded the writing of *The Last Days of Pompeii* and explains how the finished product differed from the author's expectations.

The Last of the Mohicans
A Narrative of 1757

Author: James Fenimore Cooper (1789-1851)
First published: 1826
Type of work: Novel
Type of plot: Adventure
Time of plot: 1757
Locale: Northern New York State

Principal characters:
NATTY BUMPPO, a frontier scout known as Hawkeye
CHINGACHGOOK, Hawkeye's friend
UNCAS, Chingachgook's son
MAJOR DUNCAN HEYWARD, an English soldier and
    Hawkeye's friend
MAGUA, a renegade Huron
CORA MUNRO, daughter of the commander of Fort William
    Henry
ALICE MUNRO, her half sister

The Story:

Major Duncan Heyward has been ordered to escort Cora and Alice Munro from Fort Edward to Fort William Henry, where the young women's father, Colonel Munro, is commandant. Also in the party is David Gamut, a Connecticut singing master. On their way to Fort William Henry, they do not follow the military road through the wilderness. Instead, they place themselves in the hands of a renegade Huron known as Magua, who claims that he can lead them to their destination by a shorter trail.

It is afternoon when the little party meets the woodsman Hawkeye and his Delaware Mohican friends Chingachgook and his son Uncas. To their dismay, they learn that they are but an hour's distance from their starting point. Hawkeye deduces that Magua has been planning to lead the party into a trap. His Mohican comrades try to capture the renegade, but Magua flees into the woods. At Heyward's urging, Hawkeye agrees to guide the travelers to their destination. After the horses are tied and hidden among rocks along a river, Hawkeye produces a hidden canoe from among the bushes and paddles the party to a rock at the foot of Glenn's Falls. There they prepare to spend the night in a cave.

That night, the party is surprised by a band of Iroquois led by Magua. Hawkeye, Heyward, and the rest might have a chance of victory, but unfortunately their ammunition, which was left in the canoe, has been stolen by one of the enemy. Their only hope then lies in the possibility of future rescue, for the capture of the little group is a certainty. Hawkeye, Chingachgook, and Uncas escape by floating downstream, leaving the Munro sisters and Major Heyward to meet the savages.

Captured, Cora and Alice are allowed to ride their horses, but their captors force Heyward and David to walk. Although they take a road paralleling the one that leads to Fort William Henry, Heyward cannot determine the destination the Indians have in mind. Drawing close to Magua, he tries to per-

suade him to betray his companions and deliver the party safely to Colonel Munro. The Huron agrees on the condition that Cora be given to him to live with him among his tribe as his wife. When she refuses, the enraged Magua has everyone bound. He is threatening Alice with his tomahawk when Hawkeye and his friends creep up silently on the band and attack. The Iroquois flee, leaving several of their dead behind. The party, under David's guidance, sings a hymn of thanksgiving and then pushes onward.

Toward evening, they stop at a deserted blockhouse to rest. Many years before, it had been the scene of a fight between the Mohicans and the Mohawks, and a mound still shows where bodies lay buried. While Chingachgook keeps watch, the others sleep, and then at moonrise they continue on their way. It is dawn when Hawkeye and his charges draw near Fort William Henry. They are intercepted and challenged by a sentinel of the French under Montcalm, who is about to lay siege to the fort. Heyward is able to answer him in French, and they are allowed to proceed. Chingachgook kills and scalps the French sentinel. Then, through the fog that has risen from Lake George and through the enemy forces that throng the plain before the fort, Hawkeye leads the way to the gates of the fort.

On the fifth day of the siege, Hawkeye, who has been sent to Fort Edward to seek help, is intercepted on his way back, and a letter he carries is captured. Webb, the commander of Fort Edward, has refused to come to Munro's aid. Under a flag of truce, Montcalm and Munro hold a parley. Montcalm shows Webb's letter to Munro and offers honorable terms of surrender. Colonel Munro and his men will be allowed to keep their colors, their arms, and their baggage if they vacate the fort the next morning. Helpless to do otherwise, Munro accepts these terms. During one of the parleys between the English and the French, Heyward is surprised to see Magua in the camp of the French. He was not killed during their earlier skirmish.

The following day, the vanquished English leave Fort William Henry and start for Fort Edward. Under the eyes of the French and their Indian allies, they pass across the plain and enter the forest. Suddenly an Indian grabs at a brightly colored shawl worn by one of the women from the fort. Terrified, she pulls the shawl closer and wraps her baby in it. The Indian darts to her, grabs the infant from her arms, and dashes the child's head against a rock. Then, under the eyes of Montcalm, who does nothing to hold back his savage allies, a monstrous slaughter begins. Cora and Alice, entrusted to David Gamut's protection, are in the midst of the killing when Magua swoops down upon them and carries Alice away. Cora runs after her sister, and faithful David follows her. They are soon atop a hill, from which they watch the slaughter of the garrison.

Three days later, Hawkeye, leading Heyward, Munro, and his Indian comrades, tracks the young women and David with the help of Cora's veil, which had caught on a tree. Heyward is concerned above all for the safety of Alice. The day before the massacre, he had been given her father's permission to court her.

Hawkeye, knowing that hostile Indians are on their trail, decides that they should save time by traveling across the lake in a canoe that he has discovered in its hiding place nearby. He is certain that Magua has taken the Munro sisters north, where he plans to rejoin his own people. Heading their canoe in that direction, the five men paddle all day, at one point having a close escape from some of their enemies. They spend that night in the woods, and the next day they turn west in an effort to find Magua's trail.

After much searching, Uncas finds the trail of the captives. That evening, as Hawkeye and his party draw near the Huron camp, they meet David Gamut wandering about. He tells his friends that the Indians think him crazy because of his habit of breaking into song, and they allow him to roam the woods unguarded. Alice, he says, is being held at the Huron camp, and Cora has been entrusted to the care of a tribe of peaceful Delawares a short distance away.

Heyward, disguising his face with paint, goes to the Huron camp in an attempt to rescue Alice while the others set about to help Cora. Heyward has been in the camp but a short time, posing as a French doctor, when Uncas is brought in, a captive. Called to treat a sick Indian woman, Heyward finds Alice in the cave with his patient. He is able to rescue her by wrapping her in a blanket and declaring to the Hurons that she is his patient, whom he is carrying off to the woods for treatment. Hawkeye, attempting to rescue Uncas, enters the

camp disguised in a medicine man's bearskin he has stolen. He cuts Uncas loose and gives him the disguise, and the woodsman borrows David Gamut's clothes. The singer is left to take Uncas's place while the others escape, for Hawkeye is certain that the Indians will not harm David because of his supposed mental condition. Uncas and Hawkeye flee to the Delaware camp.

The following day, Magua and a group of his warriors visit the Delawares in search of the escaped prisoners. The chief of the Delawares decides that the Hurons have a just claim to Cora because Magua wishes to make her his wife. Under inviolable Indian custom, the Huron is permitted to leave the camp unmolested, but Uncas warns him that in a few hours he and the Delawares will follow his trail.

During a bloody battle, Magua flees with Cora to the top of a cliff. There, pursued by Uncas, Magua stabs and kills the young Mohican; he is then, in turn, sent to his death by a bullet from Hawkeye's long rifle. Cora, too, is killed by a Huron. Amid deep mourning by the Delawares, she and Uncas are laid in their graves in the forest. Colonel Munro and Heyward conduct Alice to English territory and safety. Hawkeye returns to the forest. He has promised to remain with his sorrowing friend Chingachgook forever.

Critical Evaluation:

The Last of the Mohicans is the second title published in what was to become a series of five works known collectively as the Leatherstocking Tales. When James Fenimore Cooper published the first of these "romances," as he called them (to distinguish them from the somewhat more realistic contemporary novels), he had no plan for a series with a hero whose life would be shown from youth to old age and death. In *The Pioneers: Or, The Sources of the Susquehanna* (1823), Natty Bumppo, or Leatherstocking, is in his early seventies. Responding to a suggestion from his wife, Cooper in *The Last of the Mohicans* went back to Natty's early thirties, when he was called Hawkeye. The great popularity of *The Last of the Mohicans* led Cooper then to move chronologically beyond *The Pioneers* and to picture in *The Prairie: A Tale* (1827) the last of Natty's life when he was in his eighties, living as a trapper and finally dying on the Great Plains far from his early home.

At the time, Cooper did not intend to revive Natty in further books. One minor romance of the forest, *The Wept of Wish-Ton-Wish: A Tale* (1829), was followed by a stream of nautical novels, sociopolitical novels, and nonfictional works of social and political criticism. In 1840, Cooper finally responded to the pleas of literary critics and readers and revived the hero whose death he had so touchingly portrayed at the end of *The Prairie*. In *The Pathfinder: Or, The Inland Sea* (1840), Natty Bumppo is called Pathfinder, and the action shifts from land to the waters of Lake Ontario and back again. Pleased by the resounding praise he gained for having brought back his famed hero, Cooper then decided to write one final romance about him. In *The Deerslayer: Or, The First War-Path, a Tale* (1841), Natty is in his early twenties and goes by the nickname Deerslayer.

In 1850, Cooper published a new edition of all five Leatherstocking Tales arranged according to the order of events in Natty Bumppo's life: *The Deerslayer, The Last of the Mohicans, The Pathfinder, The Pioneers, The Prairie*. For this edition, he wrote a preface in which he remarked (prophetically, as it turned out): "If anything from the pen of the writer of these romances is at all to outlive himself, it is, unquestionably, the series of *The Leatherstocking Tales*." Despite many complaints, particularly from Mark Twain and later critics, about Cooper's style, plots, story structure, characterization, and dialogue, the Leatherstocking Tales continue to be read, both in the United States and in many other countries, and they seem assured of a long life to come.

In Cooper's day, *The Last of the Mohicans* was the most popular of the five tales, and it has continued to be so. Structurally, the novel is superior to the other tales, with three major plot actions and a transitional though bloody interlude (the massacre after the surrender of Fort William Henry). Cooper depicts romantic love conventionally. His portrayal of Duncan Heyward and the Munro sisters, Cora and Alice—who carry most of the love interest in *The Last of the Mohicans*—shows little originality. They are all genteel characters, and they speak in a stiff, formalized manner. Duncan is gentlemanly, and the two "females" (as Cooper repeatedly refers to them) are ladylike. Cooper contrasts Cora and Alice as he does the members of other pairs of women who keep turning up in his books. Cora, the dark one, is passionate, independent, unafraid, even defiant; blond Alice is timid and easily frightened into faints—she resembles the sentimentalized helpless girls of popular early nineteenth century fiction.

Cooper does much better with his forest characters. Hawkeye is talkative, boastful, superstitious, scornful of the book learning he does not possess, and inclined to be sententious at times. He is also, however, brave, resourceful, and loyal to his two Indian friends. His French nickname, La Longue Carabine, attests to his shooting skill. He is religious but sometimes seems more pantheistic than Christian in any formal sense. Hawkeye's arguments with David Gamut contrast his generalized beliefs and Gamut's narrow Calvinism. With his dual background of white birth and early education

by Moravian missionaries on one side and his long experience of living with the Indians on the other, he is, as French novelist Honoré de Balzac called him, "a moral hermaphrodite, a child of savagery and civilization."

Chingachgook and Uncas are idealized representatives of their race. As "good" Indians, they are dignified, taciturn, even noble despite their savage ways, which Hawkeye excuses as being simply their native "gifts." Uncas is lithe, strong, and handsome, and he reminds the Munro sisters of a Greek statue. Magua is the "bad" Indian, sullen, fierce, cunning, and treacherous. His desire to take Cora as his wife is motivated by his wish to avenge a whipping once inflicted on him at the order of Colonel Munro.

In addition to the love story that leads to the marriage of Heyward and Alice, the book depicts an interesting relationship between Cora and Uncas, who wants to marry her. Cooper has been accused of evading the theme of miscegenation by killing off both Cora, who is part black, and Uncas. Another important theme in the book is suggested by the title. Chingachgook is left mourning for his son, the last of the Mohican sagamores. He grieves also because he foresees the eventual vanishing of his race. Both he and Hawkeye despair as they envision the end of their way of life in the American wilderness. Implicit in much of the novel is the opposition of savagery and civilization, with Hawkeye realizing that civilization will triumph.

Although it is easy to complain of Cooper's faulty style, his verbosity, his heavy-handed humor, his improbable actions, the insufficient motivation of his characters, and the inconsistency and inaccuracy of his dialogue, many readers willingly suspend their disbelief or modify their critical objections in order to enjoy the rush of action that makes up so much of *The Last of the Mohicans*. They sorrow over the deaths of Cora and Uncas, and their sympathies go out to Chingachgook and Hawkeye for the loss of what has meant so much in their lives. Moreover, readers continue to enjoy Cooper's descriptions of the natural beauties of the northeastern wilderness as it was in the eighteenth century.

"Critical Evaluation" by Henderson Kincheloe

Further Reading

Barker, Martin, and Roger Sabin. *The Lasting of the Mohicans: History of an American Myth*. Jackson: University Press of Mississippi, 1995. Discusses how Cooper's novel has acquired mythic status through numerous film and television adaptations, including animated versions. Asserts that each adaptation provides a new interpretation of the idea of the American frontier.

Cooper, James Fenimore. *The Last of the Mohicans: A Narrative of 1757*. Albany: State University of New York Press, 1983. Beautiful edition of the novel includes the definitive text, a historical introduction, sixteen illustrations, commentary from the early nineteenth century, and exhaustive explanatory notes and textual commentary.

Franklin, Wayne. *James Fenimore Cooper: The Early Years*. New Haven, Conn.: Yale University Press, 2007. Well-written, informative work—the first part of a planned two-volume biography—covers Cooper's life from birth until his move from the United States to Europe in 1826. Describes his personal life as well as the events surrounding the writing and publishing of *The Last of the Mohicans*.

Krauthammer, Anna. *The Representation of the Savage in James Fenimore Cooper and Herman Melville*. New York: Peter Lang, 2008. Focuses on Cooper's and Melville's creation of Native American, African American, and other non-European characters, including the characters of Magua and Chingachgook in *The Last of the Mohicans*. Discusses how these characters were perceived as "savages," both noble and ignoble, by American readers.

McWilliams, John. *"The Last of the Mohicans": Civil Savagery and Savage Civility*. New York: Twayne, 1995. Excellent starting place for students of the novel provides information on the literary and historical contexts in which the work was written as well as discussion of topics such as the novel's style and genre, its depictions of race and gender, and Cooper's use of history. Supplemented with a chronology of Cooper's life and works.

Peck, H. Daniel, ed. *New Essays on "The Last of the Mohicans."* New York: Cambridge University Press, 1992. Introductory critical guide presents reassessments of the novel from social, historical, feminist, and psychological perspectives. An editor's introduction provides information on the work's composition and critical reception.

Person, Leland S., ed. *A Historical Guide to James Fenimore Cooper*. New York: Oxford University Press, 2007. Collection of essays includes a brief biography by Wayne Franklin and a survey of Cooper scholarship and criticism. *The Last of the Mohicans* is discussed in "Cooper's Leatherstocking Conversations: Identity, Friendship, and Democracy in the New Nation," by Dana D. Nelson. Features an illustrated chronology of Cooper's life and important nineteenth century historical events.

Rans, Geoffrey. *Cooper's Leather-Stocking Novels: A Secular Reading*. Chapel Hill: University of North Carolina Press, 1991. Discusses why interest in Cooper's works has lasted so long. The chapter on *The Last of the Mohicans*, "The Death of a Nation, the Denial of a Genre," focuses on the fact that the Indians' superiority does not protect them from annihilation.

The Last of the Wine

Author: Mary Renault (1905-1983)
First published: 1956
Type of work: Novel
Type of plot: Historical
Time of plot: 430-402 B.C.E.
Locale: Athens and the Aegean Sea

Principal characters:
ALEXIAS, a young Athenian
MYRON, his father
LYSIS, Alexias's mentor and lover
XENOPHON, Alexias's friend and later Athenian leader
SOKRATES, a famous philosopher
PLATO (ARISTOKLES), a student of Sokrates
PHAEDO, a disciple of Sokrates
KRITIAS, an orator, politician, and member of the Thirty Tyrants, an acquaintance of Alexias's family
ALKIBIADES, a controversial politician and military leader
ANYTUS, a politician and one of the accusers of Sokrates

The Story:

Alexias is born prematurely at a most unpropitious time: The Athenian statesman Pericles has died, the Athenians are embroiled in skirmishes with the Spartans, and a plague threatens Athens. When Alexias's father Myron is called to military duty, he orders that the puny baby be killed, but the household, distracted by the death of Myron's brother and his male lover, spares the child.

Alexias grows into childhood and adolescence as a typical Athenian boy of good family: He attends school accompanied by his tutor, makes friends such as his schoolmate Xenophon, develops strength as a runner, and blooms into a handsome youth. His beauty attracts a large number of suitors. With the help of the famous philosopher Sokrates, Alexias commits himself erotically to Lysis, a handsome athlete and one of Sokrates' disciples.

When Alexias is fifteen years old, sacred statues of Hermes (square pillars of stone topped by busts of Hermes, often with prominent phalli) are mutilated—a portent of disaster. On the evening of this sacrilege, Myron hosts a meeting of his club. Serving wine at the feast, Alexias observes guests such as Theramenes and Kritias, who are later to play significant roles in Athenian politics. Kritias spills wine on Theramenes to mask fondling the boy. Alexias also overhears a discussion of Alkibiades, a charismatic orator and Myron's treasured friend.

Because Alkibiades may have been responsible for the desecration of the Herms, he is disgraced. However, he still manages to join a campaign to conquer Sicily. When he is recalled from the front to face trial, he escapes instead to Sparta. Meanwhile, Myron is rumored to have been killed in the catastrophic Sicilian expedition.

When Sparta breaks a truce with Athens, Alexias serves in the military guard under Lysis's command. Despite the war, the Isthmian Games are held, and Alexias wins his race. However, his hopes for competing in the Olympic Games are dashed when his heart is damaged by physical exertion. Myron proves to have survived the Sicilian campaign but to have been enslaved. He escapes his enslavement but returns home demoralized to find a depleted estate. The governing Council of Four Hundred is established, and Alexias and Lysis join the Athenian navy. While in Samos, they participate in the naval coup against the oligarchs there.

Next, the once-exiled Alkibiades returns triumphantly to Athens and is elected supreme leader. Alexias serves under his command in the war against Sparta, whose troops are commanded by General Lysander. In 405 B.C.E., the Athenians are slaughtered in the battle of Aegospotami. After a Spartan siege and ensuing famine, Myron serves as one of the negotiators for peace with Sparta. The terms of Athens' surrender are harsh: Not only are its defenses destroyed, but the city is also occupied by Spartan troops.

Kritias seeks to establish a ruling body known as the Thirty Tyrants. He has moderate politicians such as Theramenes assassinated, and he kills Myron. Alexias takes revenge, slaying Kritias and escaping with Lysis to Thebes. Allied with the Thebans, Athenians regain control of their city, but Lysis is killed in battle. A year later, Alexias watches a torch-light race that signifies the passing of the sacred fire, a symbol of Athenian civilization. He also hears Anytus attack Sokrates, who is among the spectators and drinking wine with his disciples.

"The Story" by Elizabeth R. Nelson; revised by Nikolai Endres

Critical Evaluation:

The Last of the Wine continues to fascinate readers for a number of reasons. As a historical novel, it is based on a multitude of rich sources. Particularly user-friendly, the text includes a map of ancient Greece, chronological table, glossary, and notes on the principal characters. Mary Renault diligently researched Socrates and his world, as well as their reconstruction by Plato and the historians Xenophon, Herodotus, Thucydides, Plutarch, Diogenes Laertius, Macrobius, Atenaeus, and others. Before putting pen to paper, Renault also visited Athens, Piraeus, Crete, Delos, Knossos, and Marathon, and she spent long hours in various European museums devoted to Greek culture. All this research helped Renault visualize battles at sea, Spartan armor, the beautiful male body, Greek vineyards, athletic contests, and geographic peculiarities.

As a result, *The Last of the Wine* vividly portrays a climax in Athenian history, beginning with the reign of Pericles (c. 490-429 B.C.E.), epitomized by the building of the Parthenon, and ending tragically with the execution of Socrates for allegedly corrupting young people and failing to honor the established gods (399 B.C.E.). Together with its sequel *The Mask of Apollo* (1966), the novel offers a detailed view of the Socratic circle, with intimate portraits of the "traitors" Alcibiades and Critias; of the title characters of many Platonic dialogues, such as Euthydemus, Menexenus, Charmides, Phaedo, and Lysis; of the playwrights Agathon, Aristophanes, and Euripides; of the historian Xenophon; of the orator Lysias; of the star actor Theodoros; of the philosopher Aristotle; and of Anytus, the chief accuser at Socrates' trial.

Renault provides readers with unique anecdotes, firmly anchored in historical evidence yet virtually forgotten to posterity. Aristokles, known to history by his nickname, Plato, exercises as a first-class wrestler and, as young man in Corinth, once composed poetry. To modern-day readers, he is better remembered for excluding mimetic poetry from his ideal republic. Phaedo, to whom Socrates would lovingly explain the immortality of the soul while awaiting the final days of his life, began his career as a prostitute in a bathhouse after being sold into slavery. Even the normally calm Socrates occasionally lost his temper, but behind his ugly, satyrlike exterior, he exuded godlike wisdom.

As the novel's title implies, social erosion and decay are imminent, as Athens is compared to sweet wine about to turn to sour vinegar. The protracted Peloponnesian War (431-404 B.C.E.) marked the end of Athens' hegemony. Renault draws attention to this defeat by contrasting the Greeks with their ultimate conquerors, the Romans. While the Greeks amassed great accomplishments in philosophy, science, culture, and the arts, the Romans would set out to explore new frontiers and eventually rule the entire known world. In *The Last of the Wine*, the Roman Empire is prefigured at the Pankration (a mixture of boxing and wrestling), when Lysis fights the wrestler Sostratos, a giant, monstrously powerful man. The graceful Greek athlete of the palestra will give way to the brute strength of the arena gladiator.

Political issues are raised in the presentation of Alcibiades. To Alexias, Alcibiades seems so tall and beautiful as to epitomize a divinity accustomed to worship, but he squanders his stellar potential and fails to achieve the good life. Alcibiades turns out to be a citizen so overcome by self-interest that he does not fit into a democratic city. In 415 B.C.E., he goads the Athenians into a megalomaniacal excursion to Sicily, where the Athenian fleet is annihilated.

Thus, in Renault's hands, hubristic aspirations prove self-defeating in the very act of attaining their objectives. Renault thus uses her portrayal of ancient events to sound a warning against the great tyrants and warmongers of the twentieth century, including Adolf Hitler, Joseph Stalin, Benito Mussolini, Francisco Franco, and South African prime minister Heinrich Verwoerd. (South Africa, where Renault emigrated in 1948, was a deeply undemocratic county, having implemented strict apartheid laws to secure white supremacy.)

Renault also employs symbolism, notably in the portrayal of wine, which provides joy and headache, love and loss. In classical Greece, wine was part of a young man's rite of passage. Drinking wine and giving the present of the drinking cup represented admission to the world of adulthood. Women, on the other hand, were forbidden to drink wine. Alexias stands as a model for wine cups bearing the salutation "Alexias the Beautiful." Lovers drink wine to pledge their commitment to Eros. Renault's title further alludes to a Greek custom, called *kottabos*, of tossing the wine remaining in a cup to form the name of a lover or to divine an omen. Socrates drinks but never gets drunk, while Alcibiades is known for drinking unimaginable quantities of wine. Myron cherishes Alcibiades' gift of a wine cup, but he later destroys it when Alcibiades betrays his country. In the last scene, Socrates enjoys wine with his friends, but later he will be made to drink hemlock.

Renault is famous for her sympathetic depiction of Greek love. Her previous publication, *The Charioteer* (1953), is a gay novel, but it is set in the clinical and sterile world of a hospital. In *The Last of the Wine*, the Greek setting enables Renault to depict same-sex love in a frank, celebratory, and social context. Alexias narrates his views not only of contemporary controversies but also of *paiderastia*, an erotic relationship practiced by elite Athenians that united an *erastes*—an older, mature, and experienced man—and an *eromenos*—a beloved boy before the growth of his beard. The *eromenos* derived from his mentor educational values and often offered his body for the gratification of the *erastes*'s sexual needs. Together, the two would pursue athletics, discuss politics, and defend their country in war.

Often, a lover would follow his beloved in death by committing suicide. Alexias's uncle ingests hemlock when his lover Philon is dying from the plague because they want to make their last journey together. Although an *erastes* often had a wife, the *erastes-eromenos* relationship was considered preferable to heterosexuality because it guaranteed the youth's initiation as a worthy member of the city-state. Alexias marries, but only his attachment with Lysis is emotionally meaningful. *The Last of the Wine* is thus also a bildungsroman, charting Alexias's growth as an erotic and political citizen.

"Critical Evaluation" by Nikolai Endres

Further Reading

Abraham, Julie. "Mary Renault's Greek Drama." In *Are Girls Necessary? Lesbian Writing and Modern Histories*. New York: Routledge, 1996. Abraham's study of lesbian writers includes a chapter on Renault in which she discusses *The Last of the Wine* and other works, focusing on the relationships between such discourses as history and writing, masculinity and the state, gayness and citizenship, narrative and disruption, and skepticism and sex.

Dick, Bernard F. *The Hellenism of Mary Renault*. Carbondale: Southern Illinois University Press, 1972. An essential book on the classical background of Renault's work; Dick's comments, which received Renault's personal approbation, treat topics ranging from Renault's use of language to the authenticity of her historical backgrounds to themes and symbols in the novels.

Endres, Nikolai. "Mary Renault." In *British Writers*, edited by Jay Parini. Supplement 9. Detroit, Mich.: Charles Scribner's Sons, 2004. A complete assessment of Renault's corpus, including her five apprentice works or nurse romances, her gay novel *The Charioteer*, and her eight works of mythological and historical fiction; also provides biographical background and a lengthy bibliography of further reading.

Hoberman, Ruth. "Masquing the Phallus: Genital Ambiguity in Mary Renault's Historical Novels." In *Gendering Classicism: The Ancient World in Twentieth-Century Women's Historical Fiction*. Albany: State University of New York Press, 1997. A feminist interpretation of historical fiction set in ancient Greece and Rome, describing how Renault and five other women writers challenge the misogynist classical tradition and gender classicism to reclaim a denied cultural heritage and to correlate power and the phallus.

Kopelson, Kevin. *Love's Litany: The Writing of Modern Homoerotics*. Stanford, Calif.: Stanford University Press, 1994. One chapter compares Renault's work with Marguerite Yourcenar's *Memories of Hadrian*; provides a historicist, feminist, and queer reading that relies on the work of Michel Foucault and Sigmund Freud. Investigates Renault's role as "factual historian" and "erotic fantasist."

Moore, Lisa L. "Lesbian Migrations: Mary Renault's South Africa." *GLQ: A Journal of Lesbian and Gay Studies* 10, no. 1 (2004): 23-46. Evaluates Renault's work as a pioneer lesbian writer who disavowed gay rights, who deemed male artists to be superior to women, who benefited from South African apartheid, and who therefore holds a controversial place in postcolonial race and immigration studies.

Sweetman, David. *Mary Renault: A Biography*. New York: Harcourt Brace Jovanovich, 1993. Detailed biography with strong personal references providing illuminating commentary on all of Renault's novels and clarifying the introduction of gay love in the *The Last of the Wine* as both historically and thematically correct.

Wolfe, Peter. *Mary Renault*. New York: Twayne, 1969. The first full-length examination of the writer, both a plea for critical recognition of Renault as an important twentieth century novelist and a critical analysis of her work.

Zilboorg, Caroline. *The Masks of Mary Renault: A Literary Biography*. Columbia: University of Missouri Press, 2001. Combines biographical and literary methods; analyzes Renault's novels from the perspective of queer theory, arguing that the depiction of transgressive sexual identities is a common feature of Renault's fiction. Includes bibliography and index.

The Last Picture Show

Author: Larry McMurtry (1936-   )
First published: 1966
Type of work: Novel
Type of plot: Narrative
Time of plot: 1950's
Locale: Texas

Principal characters:
SONNY, a high school football player
DUANE, his best friend
CHARLENE SUGGS, Sonny's girlfriend
JACY FARROW, Duane's girlfriend
SAM THE LION, a pool-hall owner
LOIS FARROW, Jacy's mother
RUTH POPPER, the football coach's wife

The Story:

Sonny is a football player in his last year of high school, living in Thalia, a small town in Texas. He lives with his best friend, Duane, and dates Charlene Suggs. Sonny is not very fond of Charlene and is in love with Duane's girlfriend, Jacy Farrow, but Charlene is the only available girl in school. Sonny's days consist of sleeping through school, driving a butane truck, and hanging out at a pool hall owned by Sam the Lion, the veritable town elder. The only other thing to do in town is watch movies at the local movie theater,

where most of Sonny and Duane's dates with Charlene and Jacy take place. Sonny also regularly keeps Billy company. As Billy is mentally disabled, Sam the Lion takes note of Sonny's generous nature toward Billy and is less critical of Sonny than of the other boys in town.

Duane concerns himself with trying to make love to Jacy and is wholly intent on marrying her after high school. Duane, however, is from a poor family, while Jacy's family is far wealthier. Jacy is peripherally aware that she will never marry Duane, but Duane is caught up in being in love and is resolved to make it work. Duane spends most evenings after school working on an oil drill, while Jacy concerns herself with preparing for college and leaving Thalia forever.

Sonny, Duane, and Jacy are sexually frustrated, and they constantly push the boundaries between their desires and what is socially acceptable. The entire town, in fact, is sublimely aware of sexual frustration, and the populace is rife with sexual controversy. Jacy's mother, Lois Farrow, is known to be engaged in an affair with a man named Abilene, a local pool shark and Duane's boss. The high school's football and basketball coach, Coach Popper, is ostensibly a closeted homosexual, despite being married and more than willing to point out and berate other possible homosexuals. Popper's wife, Ruth, is so neglected that she and Sonny soon begin an affair of their own after Coach Popper asks Sonny to take Ruth to a doctor, a task for which Coach Popper himself cannot make time.

As part of her attempt to pave the way to post-Thalia life, Jacy begins to hang out with wealthier kids in Wichita Falls. There, she thinks she falls in love with a boy named Bobby Sheen and quickly makes plans to replace Sheen's girlfriend, Annie-Annie. Duane, rightfully suspicious, beats up the boy responsible for taking Jacy to Wichita Falls, an attention seeker named Lester Marlow. After the beating, Lester tells Duane about Bobby Sheen, though Duane is loathe to believe him. Lester runs to tell his friends that he was jumped by Duane and Sonny, and Lester's friends arrive in Thalia to take revenge.

Fed up with everything, Sonny and Duane decide to make an excursion into Mexico to get drunk and find whores. When the local waitress Genevieve and Sam the Lion find out about their plan, they give the boys money for the trip, each knowing that something in both Sonny and Duane has fundamentally changed. In Mexico, the two are exposed to things they never imagined, including a pornographic film involving a dog. Sonny eventually winds up with a pregnant whore, and the next day he and Duane return to Texas, almost completely broke and as unfulfilled as they were the day before. On arriving back in Thalia, Sonny is struck with the news that Sam the Lion has passed away.

Shortly following Sam the Lion's funeral, the high school seniors embark on a trip to San Francisco, where Jacy finally decides to let Duane make love to her. Duane, unfortunately, is unable to perform in his first attempt, but the next day he manages to succeed. Jacy, however, is unhappy with the arrangement and resolves to break up with Duane once and for all. Duane is heartbroken, while Jacy relishes the chance to pursue Bobby Sheen uninhibited. Unbeknownst to Jacy,

Bobby Sheen has married Annie-Annie, a fact that Jacy's mother takes slight pleasure in revealing to her daughter. Back in Thalia, Jacy decides to seduce Abilene to spite her mother. Abilene essentially uses her, and Jacy is left with a feeling of emptiness and disgust. Strangely, it is Jacy's mother that provides her with comfort and advice.

Afterward, Duane decides to enlist in the Army and prepares to leave Thalia, still very much in love with Jacy. In the absence of Sam the Lion, the few businesses of Thalia seem to fall apart, and it is announced that the movie theater will close soon. With Duane leaving, Bobby Sheen married, and Abilene having rejected her, Jacy seduces Sonny. As a result, Sonny ends his affair with Ruth Popper by simply no longer showing up for their rendezvous. Duane naturally takes offense at Sonny's relationship with Jacy, and an argument culminates in a fight in which Duane breaks a beer bottle on Sonny's head, seriously damaging one of Sonny's eyes. Sonny spends a few days in the hospital, reconnecting with his partially estranged father.

Sonny convinces himself that he was meant to marry Jacy, and Jacy gladly accepts his proposal. Jacy, however, is aware that her parents will stop at nothing to annul any marriage and leaves a note detailing when and where the wedding will take place. Predictably, following the wedding, Sonny and Jacy are stopped by local police and held until Jacy's parents arrive. Jacy's father takes her home, while Lois Farrow offers Sonny a ride. During the drive back to Thalia, Lois comes clean about her relationship with Sam the Lion. Sonny understands Sam was Lois's true love, and he and Lois depart with a greater respect for each other.

Duane returns home from Army boot camp, en route to Korea, and he and Sonny reconnect. The two share a meal and then watch the final movie at the local theater, not wanting to miss Thalia's last picture show. They head to Fort Worth for one last night of drinking, and each spends the night with a whore. The next day, Duane ships off, and Sonny is aware that his old life is almost over. A while later, Billy errantly steps in front of a truck while he is sweeping the streets. He is run over and killed. Sonny explodes in a moment of anger, and, as unsure of himself now as he has ever been, he attempts to find solace in the arms of Ruth Popper. He is surprised to find that she accepts him with open arms.

Critical Evaluation:

A stalwart of contemporary American writers, Larry McMurtry won the Pulitzer Prize in literature in 1986 for *Lonesome Dove*, arguably his greatest work. He is a renowned writer of Westerns and contemporary dramas. The town of Thalia, which appears in *The Last Picture Show* and several other works, is strongly based upon his hometown of Archer City, Texas, and much of his writing is semi-autobiographical.

Lovingly dedicated to McMurtry's hometown, *The Last Picture Show* realistically, bluntly, and often tragically portrays the lives of unremarkable people in an unremarkable town. McMurtry's propensity to quickly and frequently change perspective from one character to another essentially makes Thalia a character in and of itself and emphasizes the inevitably close knit nature of a small town's populace. There are no secrets in Thalia, and the book makes no attempt to hide any.

The Last Picture Show is a novel partly about coming of age and partly about reflections of small town life but also wholly about the pursuit of love and sex. Indeed, upon its release in 1966, it was fairly controversial as a result of the unabashedly frank manner in which it depicts sex in several forms. Adultery, premarital sex, group sex, homosexuality, pedophilia, statutory rape, and even bestiality all make appearances in the novel. There is little in the manner of a progressive plot, save for Sonny, Duane, and Jacy's pursuit of sex, and nearly all of the subplots concern themselves with the sexual pursuits of minor characters. The lack of a traditional goal allows McMurtry to concentrate on the one thing that is important to all of the characters of *The Last Picture Show*: living life.

As he does in his other works, McMurtry develops and explores minor characters with as great care as he does the primary protagonists and antagonists. McMurtry's ability to jump from character to character with ease is central to this strategy, and it enables him to incorporate subplots that pay off significantly by the end of the book. A deprived preacher's son is exposed as a potential pedophile; an effeminate teacher is wrongly accused of being homosexual; the masculine coach inadvertently reveals his homosexual tendencies. All these threads are hinted early in *The Last Picture Show*, and all are resolved by the final chapter.

Of particular note is Sam the Lion, whom McMurty uses to set the overall stage for Sonny's narrative in particular. Sam operates as Sonny's mentor and conscience. Sam is also, initially, representative of the town of Thalia itself, and McMurtry reflects this by noting that all of the businesses on Thalia's lonely main street are owned by Sam. It is Sam who cares for Billy, while Sonny befriends Billy. It is Sam who identifies with Sonny's affair with Ruth Popper, having had a vibrant affair with Lois Farrow when he was younger. It is no accident that Sam dies when Sonny and Duane, fed up with Thalia, leave for their jaunt to Mexico. Sam's death occurs roughly midway through the book, and just as his presence is used to pressure Sonny in the first half of the novel, his absence has the same effect in the second half. Sam was the one person in town who interacted with everyone else, and by the end of *The Last Picture Show* Sonny has subtly taken his place.

While the book seems to meander as a result of McMurtry's deliberate narrative choices, its tone remains remarkably consistent. It is in McMurtry's blunt manner of presenting somewhat alarming facts of life, including the pedophile incident and a chapter almost completely dedicated to a group of young boys attempting to have sex with a cow, that *The Last Picture Show* truly shines. These things happen, and McMurty is not shy in writing about them. The novel is widely reputed to be heavily autobiographical, making the depictions of such events resonate with an even greater honesty. McMurtry's style passes no judgment and presents his story matter-of-factly. As with *Lonesome Dove*, the truth hidden in the fiction is a strong point.

Jeffrey K. Golden

Further Reading

Busby, Mark. *Larry McMurtry and the West: An Ambivalent Relationship*. Denton: University of North Texas Press, 1995. An overall analysis of McMurtry's work. Attempts to explain McMurtry's preference for depicting Texas in a less-than-ideal light, including in *The Last Picture Show*.

Jones, Robert Walton. *Larry McMurtry and the Victorian Novel*. College Station: Texas A&M University Press, 1994. A study of the influence of Victorian literature on the works of McMurtry, particularly on *The Last Picture Show* and *Lonesome Dove*. Provides a detailed analysis concerning how individual characters act within their societies and the roles they play.

Reilly, John M. *Larry McMurtry: A Critical Companion*. Santa Barbara, Calif.: Greenwood Press, 2000. Reads McMurtry's novels—from *Horseman, Pass By* (1961) to the second sequel to *The Last Picture Show*, *Duane's Depressed* (1999)—in detail. Discusses the evolution of the characters of *The Last Picture Show* and the novel's importance as a contemporary Western.

Whipple, Robert, Jr. "*The Last Picture Show*: Characters." In *Beacham's Encyclopedia of Popular Fiction*, edited by Kirk H. Beetz. Vol. 10. Osprey, Fla.: Beacham, 1996. A short analysis of the many characters of *The Last Picture Show*. Examines how each relates to the small town of Thalia.

The Last Puritan
A Memoir in the Form of a Novel

Author: George Santayana (1863-1952)
First published: 1935
Type of work: Novel
Type of plot: Social realism
Time of plot: Early twentieth century
Locale: Connecticut, Massachusetts, and England

Principal characters:
OLIVER ALDEN, the last Puritan
PETER ALDEN, his father
HARRIET ALDEN, his mother
FRAULEIN IRMA SCHLOTE, Oliver's governess
JIM DARNLEY, Oliver's friend
ROSE DARNLEY, Jim's sister
MARIO VAN DE WEYER, Oliver's cousin
EDITH VAN DE WEYER, another cousin
BOBBY, Jim's illegitimate son

The Story:

Young Peter Alden has been educated in the United States, but he leaves Harvard before completing his studies and goes abroad with a tutor. After he comes of age and receives his inheritance, he wanders aimlessly about the world, studying occasionally. He is in his early middle years before he completes any one course. Licensed to practice medicine, his practice is limited to himself, for he has burdened himself with many ills, some real but most imaginary. At one point he consults Dr. Bumstead, a psychiatrist whose main concern is Peter's money. Dr. Bumstead convinces Peter that a home and a wife would be the best treatment possible, and, as a consequence, Peter marries the doctor's daughter, Harriet. They have one child, Oliver.

Little Oliver is a Puritan from the beginning. He accepts things as they are, never complaining, never wondering why. He has no child playmates because his mother fears that other children might be dirty or vulgar. Furthermore, Oliver hears no stories, songs, or prayers, as Mrs. Alden is determined that he not be filled with nonsensical ideas. Oliver's father, who spends most of his time traveling, is no more than a polite stranger to his son.

Fraulein Irma Schlote, a German, becomes Oliver's governess, and from her he has what little brightness there is in his childhood. On their long walks together, Irma instills in Oliver his first feelings of a love of nature and a love for the German language. Even with Irma, however, Oliver remains a stoic little Puritan. If he is tired or his foot hurts as they walk, he feels there is no use to complain—they have come for a walk, and they must finish that walk. One must do one's duty, even if it is unpleasant. As he grows older, Oliver comes to hate human weakness with the hatred of a true Puritan.

When Oliver is fifteen, he goes to high school, where he excels in scholarship and in athletics because it is his duty

to do everything that the school demands. During one holiday season, Oliver joins his father on his yacht. There he meets Jim Darnley, the yacht's captain, who had been a British sailor before he became involved in a scandal. Jim is an entirely new type of person in Oliver's world. Oliver knows that the sailor is worldly and has no sense of duty, but strangely enough, Oliver comes to consider Jim his dearest friend.

After his graduation from high school, Oliver joins his father and Jim in England. There, while visiting Jim's family, he learns to respect Jim's minister father and to enjoy the company of Rose, Jim's young sister. He learns also that Jim has an illegitimate child, Bobby, who lives with Mrs. Bowler, his tavern-keeping mother.

While in England, Oliver also meets his distant cousin Mario Van de Weyer, a worldly young man who is dependent on his rich relatives for his education and livelihood. Oliver is puzzled by Mario, who has nothing, not even much real intelligence, yet is happy. Oliver, who has everything, is not consciously happy; he merely lives as he feels it is his duty to live.

Before they leave England, Oliver's father commits suicide because he has come to believe that Oliver needs to be free of him and—as much as possible—of his mother as well. Rather than see the boy torn between his conflicting duties to both parents, Peter takes his own life.

Back in the United States, Oliver enters Williams College. While playing football, he breaks his leg, and in the infirmary he is visited by his cousin Mario and another cousin, Edith Van de Weyer. Mario is attending Harvard on Oliver's money, and he seems to feel no reluctance about living extravagantly on his cousin's bounty. Oliver begins to think of Edith as a possible wife. Like his father, he does not consider love an important element in marriage, but he feels it is his duty to marry and have children.

In his last year of college, Oliver transfers to Harvard University. There he spends a great deal of time with Mario until his cousin is forced to leave college because he has been caught with a young woman in his room. When Oliver goes to Edith's home to tell her what has happened to Mario, he finds that Edith's family members have already heard the story from Mario and have forgiven him. Oliver also learns that Edith has great affection for Mario, but because Oliver thinks a match between himself and Edith a sensible one, he proposes to her anyway, forgetting to mention love. Edith refuses him; she knows that marriage with Oliver would be a dutiful experience only, and she wants more than duty.

When he has finished college, Oliver takes a cruise around the world. He then settles in England and lives for a time near Jim Darnley's family. War is coming closer, but Oliver feels no duty toward either side. Mario the romantic, in contrast, enlists at once. The war becomes more personal for Oliver when he learns that Jim has been killed. Jim's death seems to him proof of war's useless waste. More practically, Jim's death means that Bobby and Rose are now Oliver's responsibility.

When the United States enters the Great War, Oliver feels that it is his duty to go home and join the armed services. He enlists in the U.S. Army, and after his training, he is sent to fight in France. Before he goes to the front, he writes to Rose Darnley and asks her to marry him at once, so that she will receive benefits as his widow if he is killed. Rose, like Edith, wants love, and she refuses to marry him. She knows, too, that Oliver should never marry, because love should be unreasoning and illogical at times, conditions that Oliver can never accept.

After Rose's refusal, Oliver seems free for the first time. No one needs him any longer. Jim is dead, and Mario is in the army and provided for in case of Oliver's death. Oliver has also made sure that Bobby is secure financially. Edith is engaged to be married, and Rose is provided for in Oliver's will. All of his life he has acted in accordance with duty—in his parental relations, in school, and in the army. At least he will not be a dutiful husband. Now he need be true only to himself. That night he sleeps peacefully.

Oliver is killed while in the service, but not in battle. He is a post-Armistice casualty, the victim of a motorcycle accident. His will tells the story of his life. He has left ample, but not extravagant, provisions for Mario, Rose, Mrs. Darnley, Fraulein Irma, and Bobby. He has left the bulk of his fortune to his mother because he believed it his duty to provide for her.

Oliver Alden lived his life as a true Puritan, doing what must be done without flinching, taking little pleasure in worldly things, yet not withdrawing from the world. He did not believe in Puritanism, for he knew that those who live selfishly are often happier than he had been. He was not a prig. He had been a Puritan in spite of himself, and for that reason, perhaps, the last true Puritan.

Critical Evaluation:

George Santayana's *The Last Puritan* offers a probing critique of the Romantic philosophy of Ralph Waldo Emerson and Arthur Schopenhauer as well as a caustic treatment of what Santayana identifies as the Puritan strain in pre-World War I American upper-class society. Santayana's only novel shows the influence of at least three major sources: first, the insightful but somewhat cynical philosophical treatment of religion by William James; second, the novels of Henry James, with their probing explorations of American and European society; third, the biting social satire of Samuel Butler's *The Way of All Flesh* (1903). Although Santayana gradually grew toward affirming the Roman Catholic faith, he spent most of his life denouncing religious sentiments and championing a materialistic view of life, a view rooted in what people can experience here and now in life. *The Last Puritan* reflects a tension between Santayana's loathing of religion and his fascination for principles of spirituality and beauty.

The Last Puritan begins with a description of a Boston resident named Mr. Nathaniel Alden, a half brother of Peter Alden, who later becomes the father of Oliver Alden, the central figure of the novel. While Nathaniel and Oliver never meet, Nathaniel's rigid, stingy, coldhearted ways seem to foreshadow all that will prove debilitating in Oliver. The Alden family has descended from a line of Puritans turned Unitarians, a group determined to maintain a high moral tone even though they have abandoned any sense of a personal God and prefer a vague philosophical view of deity. Unitarians accept all religions, provided they are not taken too seriously. Like his father, who was murdered for his ruthless treatment of his tenants, Nathaniel loathes human weakness; upon discovering moral shortcomings in his ward, Peter, Nathaniel sends him away, never to see his face again. Nathaniel is the epitome of religious facade and pretense, of a lifestyle lacking all sense of feeling, especially human compassion.

Although Peter Alden, Oliver's father, proves to be a womanizer and a drug addict, Oliver turns out to be quite free of these tendencies. As the narrator notes, "All sensation in Oliver was, as it were, retarded; it hardly became conscious until it became moral." This tendency in Oliver so stifles his life that he finds himself incapable of relating to a potential wife, such as his cousin Edith Van de Weyer or his best friend's sister, Rose Darnley, both of whom reject Oliver because they know he is incapable of loving. That Oliver should die not in the battles of World War I but in his effort to avoid a motorcycle driver speeding on the wrong side of the road symbolizes how much of his life he spends in avoiding possible problems only to encounter worse ones—including the wasting of his own life. As the narrator notes, living longer would have been useless to Oliver Alden because he lacked the capacity to enjoy life. As a young man with all of the advantages of wealth and education and culture at his disposal, Oliver was incapable of experiencing life as more than a duty, a moral obligation to be endured with stoic discipline.

While Santayana seems to have aimed much of his criticism at the Puritan pseudoreligious work ethic, he also seems to have taken special pleasure in debunking the Romantic philosophy of Emerson and Schopenhauer. These two Romantic philosophers were much more reserved than some of their contemporaries, such as Walt Whitman, Friedrich von Schiller, and Johann Wolfgang von Goethe, whose writings Oliver Alden does not like. While preparing to attend Harvard, Oliver stops at Concord to admire the landmarks associated with his hero Emerson, and later he stays in a room thought to have once been used by that philosopher. Like Emerson, Oliver admires nature and looks to it as the ultimate source of revelation and beauty, and also like Emerson, Oliver fails to see that the best part of life cannot be actualized without commitment to choices. Oliver drifts through life in a theoretical mode that rarely touches the world in which most people live. He is not unconcerned about others, nor is he consciously arrogant or selfish, but he fails to discover how to move beyond his own little sphere of sensibility. Oliver's life has great capacity for good, as his cousin Caleb Wetherbee indicates when he prophesies that Oliver may soon feel a call into ministry. Much later in the novel, Rose Darnley also notes Oliver's capacity for a religious vocation, but she does so in a context that underscores his unsuitability for normal, domestic life in marriage. As the novel emphasizes, Oliver lacks the boldness and commitment necessary to make himself more than an idealistic young man with high expectations that the world will never meet.

The strength of *The Last Puritan* lies in its insightful exploration of human failings and disappointments. At times the style of the book is almost poetic. Many of Santayana's characters in this novel are capable of surprising action, in-

triguing, and memorable. Although not as stylistically fluid as the works of Henry James, Santayana's *The Last Puritan* is at least as rich in insights into human personalities as are James's works. The primary weakness of the novel lies in its blatant dismissal of religious ideals as being of any worth and in the novel's presentation of irresponsible and selfish people as offering a higher standard than the Puritans offered. This latter problem is caused primarily by the author's limited point of view. The novel itself, as a work of art, is certainly one of the most memorable American novels of the 1930's.

"Critical Evaluation" by Daven M. Kari

Further Reading

Kirby-Smith, H. T. *A Philosophical Novelist: George Santayana and "The Last Puritan."* Carbondale: Southern Illinois University Press, 1997. Describe Santayana's various literary styles, argues for the significance of his philosophical writings as a form of literature, provides a psychological portrait of the author, and defends him against the often harsh attacks of literary critics. Chapters 8 and 9 provide an analysis of the novel.

Lachs, John. *George Santayana*. Boston: Twayne, 1988. Provides a useful framework for the interpretation of Santayana's life and philosophical works. Includes an informative chronology and bibliography.

Levinson, Henry Samuel. *Santayana, Pragmatism, and the Spiritual Life*. Chapel Hill: University of North Carolina Press, 1992. Discusses the philosophical issues at the core of *The Last Puritan*. Describes the novel as an exploration of the failure of Romantic, Emersonian philosophy to teach action as the basis for enlightenment.

McCormick, John. *George Santayana: A Biography*. 1987. Reprint. New Brunswick, N.J.: Transaction, 2003. Detailed, readable biography surveys Santayana's life and writings. Includes discussion of *The Last Puritan*.

Price, Kenneth M., and Robert C. Leitz III, eds. *Critical Essays on George Santayana*. Boston: G. K. Hall, 1991. Collection of scholarly essays includes nine contributions that discuss *The Last Puritan*. Useful for serious students of Santayana's works.

Singer, Irving. *George Santayana, Literary Philosopher*. New Haven, Conn.: Yale University Press, 2000. Examines Santayana's writings, demonstrating his ability to turn personal alienation into the creative elements that recur in his work. Chapter 3 provides an analysis of *The Last Puritan*.

The Last Temptation of Christ

Author: Nikos Kazantzakis (1883-1957)
First published: Ho teleutaios peirasmos, 1955
   (English translation, 1960)
Type of work: Novel
Type of plot: Psychological realism
Time of plot: First century C.E.
Locale: Israel

Principal characters:
JESUS, a carpenter of Nazareth
SIMEON, his uncle, a rabbi
BARABBAS, a bandit
MARY MAGDALENE, a prostitute
SIMON PETER,
ANDREW,
JAMES,
JOHN,
PHILIP,
JUDAS ISCARIOT,
THOMAS, and
MATTHEW, Jesus' disciples

The Story:

Israel is occupied by the forces of the Roman Empire. In his village of Nazareth in Galilee, Jesus has just finished building a cross ordered by the Romans when Judas Iscariot, a member of the rebel group called the Zealots, comes to ask his help. Judas's leader, known simply as the Zealot, has been sentenced to be crucified that same day. Judas believes that the Zealot is the Messiah promised to the Jews by the ancient prophets, the man who will save Israel, and that if the people rise up against the Romans to prevent his execution, the Zealot will reveal himself as the Messiah and cast the Romans out of Israel.

Jesus refuses to take part in the rebellion, which he knows the Romans will crush. He has long suspected that he himself is the Messiah, but he is terrified of crucifixion, and he is angry that the role God has chosen for him will deny him the earthly joys beloved by all men in ancient Israel: a hearth, a home, a loving wife, and children. When he was younger he loved Mary Magdalene, but the hand of God kept them apart, and Jesus blames himself for Mary's descent into sin.

Jesus' fear and anger have led him to rebel against God, and as part of that rebellion he has built the cross for the execution of the Zealot. He delivers the cross to the Romans and helps to set it in place. The people of Nazareth are stunned, and the planned rebellion never occurs. After the crucifixion, the people call Jesus a traitor, and Jesus, ashamed, sets out for a distant monastery, where he stays for some months. There he gives himself to God and begins his ministry.

For some months, Jesus wanders Galilee and Judea, preaching the Gospel. At Capernaum he saves Mary Magdalene from a mob under the sway of Barabbas, the bandit and Zealot. He is baptized by John the Baptist, then he goes into the desert and wrestles with Satan, who appears to him as a serpent with the eyes and breasts of a woman. Satan offers Jesus the world and, in particular, Mary Magdalene, whom Jesus, the man, still loves. Jesus resists, hoping that he has conquered temptation, but Satan promises to see him again at Passover.

Jesus continues preaching, performing miracles, and gathering followers. In Cana he cures the daughter of Rufus, the Roman centurion of Nazareth, of a mysterious disease. In Bethany, he raises Lazarus from the dead. In Jerusalem, he turns the money changers out of the temple. There, on Jesus' own orders, Judas betrays him to the hypocritical Pharisees, who arrest him for blasphemy. Lacking the legal authority to punish prisoners, the Pharisees turn Jesus over to the Roman ruler of Judea, Pontius Pilate, and they demand that Jesus be crucified. Pilate, no stranger to the ruthless suppression of troublemakers, complies.

On the cross, Jesus experiences his last temptation. In agony, his head swimming, he shouts, "My God, my God!" but he faints before he can finish. While he is unconscious, an angel comes to him and tells him that his crucifixion has been a dream, a test of his resolve. The angel explains that the disciples have all run away, and that Jesus' reward for his suffering is to be the earthly joys that have for so long been denied him. The angel leads him to Mary Magdalene and her servant. Jesus and Mary make love, but a short time later Mary is stoned to death by an angry mob. Jesus returns to Bethany, where he marries Lazarus's sister, Mary. He later enters into a bigamous relationship with Mary and her sister, Martha.

The years pass, and Jesus prospers. Mary and Martha give him many children. As an old man, near death, Jesus is visited by his aged disciples, including Judas, who reviles him as a traitor. Jesus realizes that the angel who led him down from the cross was really Satan in disguise and that all his years of happiness with Mary and Martha are an illusion conjured up by Satan to sway Jesus from his divine purpose. In an instant he finishes his cry, "My God, my God, why hast thou forsaken me?" and is transported back onto the cross, thereby completing his divine mission.

Critical Evaluation:

Born in 1883 on the Greek island of Crete, then a possession of Turkey, Nikos Kazantzakis was sent to a monastery on nearby Naxos at the age of four when his home island was torn by armed rebellion against the Turks. Franciscan monks introduced him to Western thought and to the spiritual heroism personified by Christ. Kazantzakis began a quest for spiritual perfection that led him to reject Christianity for a series of saviors. He became a follower first of the German philosopher Friedrich Nietzsche (1844-1900), then of the Indian philosopher and founder of Buddhism, Siddhārtha Gautama (c. 566-c. 486 B.C.E.), then of the Russian revolutionary leader Vladimir Ilich Lenin (1870-1924), and, finally, of the ancient Greek hero Odysseus, before returning to Catholicism in late middle age. The dominant theme of his major works—all published after Kazantzakis's fifty-eighth birthday—is the necessity of struggling against the temptations of the flesh in order to achieve spiritual enlightenment. From his personal struggles sprang his questions about Christ; these questions are explored in *The Last Temptation of Christ*.

From its first publication, *The Last Temptation of Christ* has been a highly controversial novel; the German edition was placed on the Vatican's list of forbidden books, the *Index librorum prohibitorum*, in 1954, and an English-language film version, released in 1988, scandalized Christians around the world. Kazantzakis saw Christ, like the other heroes in his life, as engaged in the struggle for freedom—freedom from limitations imposed by family, freedom from the pleasures of the flesh, freedom from political entities, and freedom from the fear of death. He came to believe that Christ, given human flesh and human experiences, removed from his heavenly home by three decades of life on earth, must have felt the same doubts and desires that other people feel, and he must have struggled to overcome these doubts and desires. In orthodox Christian terms, this position is heretical, but like the Puritan poet John Milton, Kazantzakis believed that choice is essential to virtue. For Kazantzakis, the wonder of Christ's sacrifice lies less in his divinity than in his humanity; the stronger Christ's attraction to temptation, the more meaningful is his ultimate choice to reject it.

The result of Kazantzakis's exploration is a moving portrait of Christ as a man struggling toward union with God. Kazantzakis filled in from his own imagination the human details typically missing from sacred texts. The novel begins, for example, with Jesus' tortured dreams, his subconscious and human struggles between flesh and spirit, and it ends with his agonized fantasies on the cross. Unlike the Gospel, which mentions only one incident in which the twelve-year-old Jesus amazed the elders in the Temple of Jerusalem with his wisdom, the novel describes Jesus' early life in detail. Kazantzakis gives Jesus a father struck by lightning and completely disabled. The Gospel does not mention Joseph after the incident in the Temple. Kazantzakis also gives Jesus a domineering mother desperate for grandchildren.

Once Jesus' ministry has begun, his disciples, all save Judas, who is weak and vacillating, bicker among themselves incessantly and achieve only a shallow, worldly understanding of Jesus' divine message. Judas himself becomes not the archetypical traitor vilified throughout Christian history but instead a great patriot who saves Jesus from the wrath of Barabbas, who stays with him even while the others deny him, and who is chosen to betray Jesus because he alone can be trusted to follow orders and because he alone has the strength and courage to perform such a dangerous—but necessary—mission.

Kazantzakis tightens the familiar plot of the Passion, bringing causal relations to events left disconnected in the Gospel. For example, when word reaches Jerusalem that Jesus has raised Lazarus from the dead, Caiaphas, the high priest of the Pharisees, plots with Barabbas to murder Lazarus, thereby destroying evidence of Jesus' divinity. It is for this crime that Barabbas is to be executed when the mob chooses him, instead of Jesus, to be spared from the cross.

Aside from the final chapters, in which Christ experiences his last temptation, Kazantzakis's most interesting additions to the story in the Gospel appear in the parables. Given his belief that Christianity is the religion of divine love, Kazantzakis writes new endings for several parables—endings more in keeping with his own vision of a forgiving, all-inclusive Christ. In his new version of the parable of the wise and foolish virgins, both the wise and the foolish are invited to the wedding feast; neither is excluded. In the parable of the rich man, Dives, and the beggar, Lazarus, God allows Dives into heaven at the request of the forgiving Lazarus. Kazantzakis's Christ tempers justice with mercy throughout the novel.

In a 1954 letter to a friend, Kazantzakis insisted that *The Last Temptation of Christ* was a "laborious, sacred, creative endeavor to reincarnate the essence of Christ, setting aside the dross—falsehoods and pettiness which all the Churches and all the cassocked representatives of Christianity have heaped upon His figure, thereby distorting it." The Christ portrayed by Kazantzakis in the novel is a highly personal vision, but it is nonetheless a compelling one.

Craig A. Milliman

Further Reading

Bien, Peter. *Kazantzakis: Politics of Spirit*. 2 vols. Princeton, N.J.: Princeton University Press, 1989-2007. Volume 1 focuses on the evolution of Kazantzakis's personal philosophy up to the point of his publication in 1938 of *The Odyssey: A Modern Sequel*. Volume 2 completes this definitive biography, describing the period of Kazantzakis's life in which he wrote *Zorba the Greek* and *The Last Temptation of Christ*.

_____. *Nikos Kazantzakis, Novelist*. Bristol, England: Bristol Classical Press, 1989. Useful introduction to Kazantzakis's work includes an appraisal of his importance as a novelist, discussion of his worldview, and analysis of *The Last Temptation of Christ* and other major novels.

Dombrowski, Daniel A. *Kazantzakis and God*. Albany: State University of New York Press, 1997. Analyzes Kazantzakis's novels and other works to describe his religious vision, interpreting his ideas in terms of contemporary "process theology." Explains how Kazantzakis combined his ideas about God with a Darwinian belief in the evolution of all creatures—including God.

Dossor, Howard F. *The Existential Theology of Nikos Kazantzakis*. Wallingford, Pa.: Pendle Hill, 2001. Discusses Kazantzakis's ideas about religion, describing how Kazantzakis created a personal theology based on his existential belief that human beings are mortal and must live as if they are heading toward death.

Levitt, Morton P. *The Cretan Glance: The World and Art of Nikos Kazantzakis*. Columbus: Ohio State University Press, 1980. Beginning with *Freedom or Death*, one of Kazantzakis's few novels set on his home island of Crete, discusses the development of Crete as metaphor in the author's major novels, including *The Last Temptation of Christ*.

Middleton, Darren J. N., ed. *Scandalizing Jesus? Kazantzakis's "The Last Temptation of Christ" Fifty Years On*. New York: Continuum, 2005. Collection of essays is devoted to various aspects of Kazantzakis's novel and the film adaptation, with an essay by the film's director, Martin Scorsese, titled "On Reappreciating Kazantzakis."

Middleton, Darren J. N., and Peter Bien, eds. *God's Struggler: Religion in the Writings of Nikos Kazantzakis*. Macon, Ga.: Mercer University Press, 1996. Collection of essays explores the theme of religion in Kazantzakis's works, including a Greek Orthodox interpretation of his religious ideas and a discussion of mysticism in his writings. An essay by John S. Bak, "Christ's Jungian Shadow in *The Last Temptation*," discusses the novel.

Owens, Lewis. *Creative Destruction: Nikos Kazantzakis and the Literature of Responsibility*. Macon, Ga.: Mercer University Press, 2003. Detailed study of Kazantzakis's writings describes how the author was influenced by the philosophy of Henri Bergson. Argues that Kazantzakis believed destruction is a necessary prerequisite of renewed creative activity.

The Last Tycoon

Author: F. Scott Fitzgerald (1896-1940)
First published: 1941
Type of work: Novel
Type of plot: Social realism
Time of plot: 1930's
Locale: Hollywood, California

Principal characters:
MONROE STAHR, a film producer
KATHLEEN MOORE, his mistress
PAT BRADY, Stahr's partner
CECILIA BRADY, his daughter

The Story:

Cecilia Brady is flying to California for a summer vacation from college. On the plane she meets Wylie White, an alcoholic screenwriter, and Schwartz, a ruined film producer.

Monroe Stahr, the partner of Cecilia's father, is also aboard, though traveling as Mr. Smith. When the plane is grounded in Nashville, Tennessee, Schwartz sends a note to Stahr warning him about Pat Brady, Cecilia's father. When the plane takes off again, Schwartz stays behind and commits suicide.

Stahr had been the boy wonder of the motion-picture industry. He had been in charge of a studio in his twenties and almost dead from overwork at thirty-five. Indeed, he is half in love with death for the sake of his dead wife, Minna Davis, a great star with whom he was deeply in love. Since her death, he has worked harder than ever, often remaining in his office around the clock. In contrast to Stahr, Brady is mean and selfish. Lacking taste and understanding little of the technical end of the industry, Brady acquired his share of the studio through luck and has retained it through shrewdness.

One night, while Cecilia is visiting the studio, an earthquake occurs, rupturing a water main and flooding the back lot. Stahr, working with his troubleshooter, Robinson, to clear away the mess, sees a film-set sightseer perched on top of a huge idol, a piece of a set that has come loose and is now floating in the flood. The girl reminds him of his dead wife, and he tries to discover her identity. That night, Cecilia falls in love with Stahr, but she feels that her attachment is hopeless.

A self-made man and paternalistic employer, Stahr personally manages almost every detail at the studio. Though he is not an educated man, he has raised the artistic level of motion pictures and does not hesitate to make good films that might lose money. As a result, he has incurred the distrust of the studio's stockholders, who see filmmaking only as a business. Their distrust of the producer is, however, mixed with genuine respect for his many abilities.

In addition to dealing with opposition from the stockholders, Stahr is concerned because the studio's writers are the target of Communist union organizers; he works closely with his writers and wants them to trust him. Wylie White, in particular, enjoys the producer's favor, although he resents Stahr. White is hoping to marry Cecilia for the sake of her father's influence. Typical of Stahr's interest in his employees is his investigation of the attempted suicide of a cameraman, Pete Zavras. Stahr learns that Zavras has been unable to find work because of a rumor that he is going blind. Stahr is able to put an end to the rumor by providing Zavras with a statement from an eye doctor.

Stahr is successful in locating the young woman he saw on the back lot after the earthquake; her name is Kathleen Moore. At first she is reluctant to meet him, but eventually they have a brief, passionate affair. Stahr learns that she was once the mistress of a deposed monarch and that she is about to marry the man who rescued her from that situation when it became difficult. Stahr realizes that marriage to Kathleen could give him the will to go on living. While he hesitates,

her fiancé arrives ahead of schedule, and she goes through with the marriage from a sense of obligation. Cecilia, knowing nothing of these matters, is still desperately hoping to attract Stahr's attention, all the more so after she discovers her father in a compromising situation with his secretary. At Stahr's request, Cecilia arranges a meeting between Stahr and a Communist union organizer. Stahr gets drunk before they meet, however, and tries to beat the man up.

At this point, F. Scott Fitzgerald's manuscript ends, but the rest of the story may be pieced together from the author's notes. Because the studio is in financial difficulties, Brady tries to push through a wage cut. Stahr, opposing this plan, travels to the East Coast to convince the stockholders to postpone the wage slash. Brady cuts the salaries and betrays the writers while Stahr is ill in Washington, D.C. Although he breaks with Brady after that, Stahr agrees to go along with Brady's plan for a company union, chiefly because Stahr feels personally responsible for the welfare of his employees. Wylie White has also turned on Stahr.

Kathleen and Stahr resume their relationship, and when Brady tries use his knowledge of the affair to blackmail Stahr, the producer threatens him with information about the death of Brady's wife. Fitzgerald considered having Brady persuade Robinson to undertake Stahr's murder, but he apparently rejected this idea in favor of having Brady inform Kathleen's husband, a film technician involved with the union organizers, of Kathleen's affair with Stahr. This leads to a lawsuit against Stahr for alienation of affection, but Stahr is somehow saved by Zavras, the cameraman.

Stahr becomes alienated from Kathleen and is no longer able to dominate his associates at the studio. Nevertheless, he continues to oppose Brady. Finally, Stahr feels that he has to eliminate Brady before Brady has him killed. After hiring gangsters to murder Brady, Stahr flies east to provide himself with an alibi; he changes his mind on the plane, however, and decides to make a phone call to stop the killers at the next airport. The plane crashes before he can carry out his intention. Fitzgerald was uncertain about including an episode in which the plane's wreckage is plundered by three children who discover it, the idea being that the children's individual personalities would be reflected by the items they steal.

Stahr's funeral is a powerful, detailed, ironic arraignment of Hollywood sham. It includes an incident in which a has-been cowboy actor is invited to be a pallbearer by mistake and consequently enjoys a return of good fortune. Cecilia later has an affair, probably with Wylie White, and then suffers a complete breakdown. At the end of the novel, the reader learns that she has been telling the story while a patient in a tuberculosis sanatorium.

Critical Evaluation:

After the overwhelming success of his autobiographical novel, *This Side of Paradise* (1920), and his fourth novel, *Tender Is the Night* (1934), which describes the precipitation of what he later termed "emotional bankruptcy," F. Scott Fitzgerald settled in Hollywood. There, he died while pursuing a fruitless career as a screenwriter. *The Last Tycoon*, Fitzgerald's last and unfinished novel, is a sobering picture of society written by a man who had experienced both ends of prosperity's spectrum.

Although Fitzgerald intended this novel to be "an escape into a lavish, romantic past that perhaps will not come again in our time," the fragmentary novel has at least two qualities that transcend its nostalgia: the manner in which the narrative is handled and the characters' views of society. Cecilia Brady functions as both narrator and character and is able to piece the story together by collecting fragments from people involved in various incidents. By means of a retrospective device revealed in the novel's projected outline, however, she is shown to be as limited in her view of American society as anyone else in the novel connected with the motion-picture industry. It is this limited viewpoint that gives unity between plot and theme to the novel as well as credibility to the characters.

Fitzgerald's decision to use Cecilia Brady instead of a detached narrator allows him to reveal only those elements of reality that he deems thematically essential. Reality is filtered through life in Hollywood; Hollywood, in turn, is revealed only in relation to Stahr, and Cecilia reveals only the aspects of Stahr's life that she finds interesting. The narrator functions as a personification of the illnesses of Hollywood life; the illnesses manifest themselves physically in the form of her tuberculosis.

The major significance of this unfinished novel is the evidence in its stylistic daring and social criticism that Fitzgerald was far from through as a novelist. The moral subtleties of Stahr's characterization recall Fitzgerald's greatest achievement, *The Great Gatsby* (1925). Like the hero of that novel, Stahr becomes involved with the underworld to preserve a dream. The difference between Gatsby's illusion of Daisy and Stahr's professional integrity is the measure of Fitzgerald's own hard-won maturity as a writer and man.

Further Reading

Bloom, Harold, ed. *F. Scott Fitzgerald*. New York: Chelsea House, 2006. Updated edition of an essay collection originally published in 1985 presents analysis of *The Last Tycoon* as well as Fitzgerald's other novels.

Bryer, Jackson R., Alan Margolies, and Ruth Prigozy, eds. *F. Scott Fitzgerald: New Perspectives*. Athens: University of Georgia Press, 2000. Collection presents scholarly criticism as well as personal essays by some of Fitzgerald's friends, including Budd Schulberg and publisher Charles Scribner III. An essay by Robert A. Martin discusses the subject of Fitzgerald's use of history in *The Last Tycoon*.

Bryer, Jackson R., Ruth Prigozy, and Milton Stern, eds. *F. Scott Fitzgerald in the Twenty-first Century*. Tuscaloosa: University of Alabama Press, 2003. Collection of essays contains an informative overview of Fitzgerald's career and an essay that discusses *The Last Tycoon* in relation to the final developments in his writing style.

Curnutt, Kirk. *The Cambridge Introduction to F. Scott Fitzgerald*. New York: Cambridge University Press, 2007. Provides a concise overview of Fitzgerald's life and work, including discussions of the author's composition process and the major themes, characters, plots, and motifs found in his novels. Also addresses the critical reception of Fitzgerald's works at the time they were published as well as the views of present-day Fitzgerald scholars.

Ebel, Kenneth. *F. Scott Fitzgerald*. Rev. ed. Boston: Twayne, 1977. Good introductory resource includes biographical information; readings of Fitzgerald's novels, stories, and articles; and critical responses to his works. Includes discussion of *The Last Tycoon*.

Ford, Edward. *Rereading F. Scott Fitzgerald: The Authors Who Shaped His Style*. Lewiston, N.Y.: Edwin Mellen Press, 2007. Focuses on the influences that other writers had on Fitzgerald's work, particularly European authors such as Alain-Fournier. Includes a chapter devoted to *The Last Tycoon*.

Hook, Andrew. *F. Scott Fitzgerald*. London: Edward Arnold, 1992. Presents an accessible reading of Fitzgerald's work. A chapter on *The Last Tycoon* draws from Fitzgerald's letters, in which he discusses his intentions and plans for the novel.

Prigozy, Ruth, ed. *The Cambridge Companion to F. Scott Fitzgerald*. New York: Cambridge University Press, 2002. Collection of essays examines a wide variety of topics, including Fitzgerald's critical reputation, the portrayal of women in his fiction, Fitzgerald and Hollywood, and other aspects of his life and work.

The Late George Apley
A Novel in the Form of a Memoir

Author: John P. Marquand (1893-1960)
First published: 1937
Type of work: Novel
Type of plot: Naturalism
Time of plot: Late nineteenth and early twentieth
　centuries
Locale: Boston

Principal characters:
GEORGE APLEY, a proper Bostonian
JOHN, his son
ELEANOR, his daughter
CATHARINE, his wife
MR. WILLING, George Apley's biographer

The Story:

George William Apley is born on Beacon Hill in Boston on January 25, 1866. The Apleys are an old family in Massachusetts. Thomas, known in the old records as Goodman Apley, emigrated from England to America and settled in Roxbury in 1636. Goodman Apley's son, John, graduated from Harvard in 1662. From his time, there has been an Apley at Harvard in each succeeding generation. John Apley's son, Nathaniel, established himself in Boston. A later Apley, Moses, became a shipping master and laid the foundation of the Apley fortune. Moses Apley was George Apley's grandfather.

George Apley grows up in a quiet atmosphere of wealth and social position. He learns his parents' way of living calmly and with fortitude. In an orderly way, he is introduced to the polite world, at first through visits to relatives and later through study at Harvard. His Harvard days are probably the high point of his life. His parents send him to Harvard in part to help him firmly establish those qualities of gentlemanly behavior that they and private grammar school together have tried to encourage in him. George's parents are anxious that he should make friends with the right people.

At Harvard, George is carefully instructed in the ways of high-minded gentlemen. The success of this training is evident in a theme that he writes in which he describes a Boston brothel in terms expressing his repulsion and shock. In the gymnasium, George wins distinction as a boxer. Moreover, he becomes a member of the board of the campus humor magazine, the *Harvard Lampoon*. He is also taken into the Club, an honor his father appreciates greatly. In his junior and senior years, he takes part in the musical extravaganzas of the Hasty Pudding Club. In spite of these activities, George never neglects his studies, and he is known as a respectable student with grades placing him in the middle of his class at graduation.

While in college, George falls in love with an impossible woman, Mary Monahan. Their affair is cut short by the

Apleys and is never referred to publicly. Shortly after the breakup, George's parents prescribe a sea voyage for him. When he returns home, he takes up the study of law and becomes a member of the board of the Boston Waifs' Society. As part of George's instruction in the shrewd business manners and knowledge of the Apleys, he is sent to work with his uncle William for one summer. William senses that his nephew will never make a good businessman and advises that George should go into law or be made a trustee of other people's money, not his own. As a result George, like many of his friends, never goes into business actively.

In February, 1890, George follows his parents' wishes and becomes engaged to the suitable Catharine Bosworth. After he is married, his father-in-law and his own father see to it that the young couple have a house as well as a summer cottage. The two mothers are equally solicitous. George discovers that he has married not only Catharine but the rest of her family as well. When Catherine and George have their first child, the naming of the boy becomes a subject for debate in both their families. The name John, common to both families, is finally chosen. Their second child is a daughter, Eleanor.

As the years pass, George devotes his time to charitable groups, to learned societies, and to writing for his clubs. One of his papers, "Jonas Good and Cow Corner," is said to be among the best papers read before the Browsers in fifty years.

Shortly after George's sister, Amelia, is married, George's father dies of a stroke. He leaves one million dollars to Harvard, other large sums to various charities, and the remainder of his fortune in trust for his family. George has to pay a sum of money to a woman who claims that she bore George's father a son; although he does not believe the charge, he pays rather than allow scandal to touch the family.

George invests in a place known as Pequod Island, and he takes his friends there when he wants to get away from

Boston. On the island, he and his friends condescend to share their campfire with their guides. Envisioned by George as a male retreat, the island is soon overrun with literary lights of the times, invited by George's wife and sister.

As his son grows up, George notes the increasing tendency on the part of the younger generation to be wild and careless with money. Later, George begins to believe that he and his generation have let much slip, and he is particularly dismayed that the "Irish element" is taking over Boston. He lends his support to the Save Boston Association, as he considers his membership an Apley duty. He also studies bird lore and philosophy and takes as much personal interest as possible in the affairs of his children. When his mother dies in 1908, George counts her death as one of his most poignant tragedies.

When his son enters Harvard, George takes a new interest in the university and notes many changes he does not like. He finds his daughter's marriage not completely satisfactory because Eleanor does not induce her husband to give up his job for a position in the Apley mills and to take up residence near her family. During World War I, George is proud of his son for his service at the front. When John marries a girl of good connections after the war, George is doubly pleased.

In his later years, George comes into opposition with a man named O'Reilly, whom George plans to have brought before criminal court on charges of extortion. O'Reilly, however, tricks George into a scandal. George intends to have the whole case cleared in court, but before the trial, he receives a note from his onetime sweetheart, Mary Monahan. After an interview with her, he settles the case quietly and buys off his opponents.

In 1928, George becomes a grandfather. As soon as the baby is born, George telegraphs the elite prep school Groton to include his grandson's name among its entrance applicants.

In his final years, George takes an interest in the new novels, condemning those that he finds too blatant in their descriptions of sex and fighting against the inclusion of some of them in the collections of Boston libraries. He hides his own copy of D. H. Lawrence's *Lady Chatterley's Lover* (1928) in a safe to keep his daughter from seeing it. He defies Prohibition as an abuse of his rights, using the services of a private bootlegger on principle, he says, because it is important to help break such an unjust law. He also believes that the colossal fortunes being gathered by the uneducated should be handed over to the government.

In the autumn of 1929, George and his wife make a trip to Rome, where they visit George's cousin Horatio Apley, recently appointed to a diplomatic post there. George is thus absent from the United States when the stock market crash comes. His financial affairs do not suffer greatly, but his health is increasingly poor, and he begins to plan his will and his funeral. George Apley dies in December, 1933.

Critical Evaluation:

The Late George Apley, considered by many to be the best of John P. Marquand's novels, was a turning point in its author's career. For fifteen years prior to its publication, Marquand had, as a "slick" popular writer, enjoyed considerable commercial success but no critical recognition. *The Late George Apley*, however, was immediately recognized as an important book, and its author was promoted by the critics from "popular" to "serious" writer. This elevation was certified when the novel earned for Marquand the Pulitzer Prize in 1938. Throughout the remaining years of his writing career, Marquand confirmed and further consolidated his reputation, although he never completely abandoned the commercial marketplace.

The Late George Apley is the first of a trilogy of novels in which Marquand minutely describes and analyzes the social patterns, behaviors, mores, and conflicts in upper-class Boston society during the rapidly changing period from 1880 to 1920. This novel depicts that part of old Boston society with Puritanical antecedents and commercial traditions; the second of the books, *Wickford Point* (1939), shows the decline of Bostonians with Transcendentalist ancestors and artistic pretensions; and the last, *H. M. Pulham, Esquire* (1941), examines the Boston businessman as he tries to accommodate his geographical and class inheritances to the pressures of the contemporary world.

In each of these books, Marquand explores the ways in which social forms and cultural assumptions left over from the past bind those in the present and how, in short, those environments that have evolved to ensure familial and social protection, identity, and continuity become prisons for the individuals who inherit them. This is most obvious in *The Late George Apley*. George's father, Thomas, represents the old nineteenth century individualistic businessman. He is highly intelligent, austere, rigid, hardworking, and uncompromising. His relationship with his son is reserved and formal, almost institutionalized, although he shows concern and, on occasion, affection for the boy. The doubts that are to plague his son are foreign to Thomas. He knows who he is and what his roles are as father, as businessman, as member of the community, and as an Apley. When he and George have their only real public disagreement, the older man emphatically quashes George's fuzzy democratic ideas: "You and I do not stand for the common good. We stand for a small class; but you don't see it. . . . Nobody sees it but me and my contemporaries." Thomas, however, is saved from robber baron status by his sincere Puritan "stewardship" ethic; he truly believes that the Apley position and fortune are signs of Godly favor and that the family's money must be conserved and shared with the community—but only on terms dictated by that "small class" of superior people at the top of the social pyramid.

George Apley envies his father's certainty and strength but cannot emulate him personally. Early in his life, he accepts the verdict of his uncle William, and subsequently Thomas, that he is "not a businessman," that he is "too easy-going" and "erratic," and so accepts permanent placement as an investment counselor (for other people's money), lawyer, and civic leader. George assumes from the beginning that his environment is the only one he "could have survived in," but neither he nor the reader can ever be sure. He is never able to test his well-meaning mediocrity; he is given the opportunity neither to succeed nor to fail but only to fit into a predetermined groove.

In his youth, George makes a few feeble attempts at nonconformity: He chooses some dubious friends, questions a few Apley dogmas, and, most important, has a brief, intense love affair with a young middle-class Irish Catholic woman. The affair is squelched, of course; George is sent on a Grand Tour, and Mary Monahan becomes a sad memory (until the end of the book). Throughout his life, George is plagued by the sense that he is trapped, living a life filled with activity but devoid of action or meaning. The most important events of his life are family disputes: what to name the baby, how to prevent cousin John from divorcing his wife, where to bury cousin Hattie, whether or not to move the rosebushes.

George's few attempts to find even momentary respite from his milieu fail before they begin. He travels abroad but carries Boston with him. "I am a raisin," he says, "in a slice of pie which has been conveyed from one plate to another." He buys an island as a masculine retreat from Bostonian formality and its guardians, the womenfolk, and before he knows it, the ladies arrive and "Boston has come to Pequod Island." Throughout his life, he suspects that he cannot escape the "net" (young John's phrase) of an environment that stifles more than it supports, and shortly before his death, he acknowledges it. Worst of all, he realizes that it has cost him the one important thing that he might have had from his life: happiness.

Like his father before him, George tries to pass the Apley ethic down to his own son. John rebels more directly and emphatically than his father did, however. His social and political views baffle and alarm George. John pushes the rebellion further by refusing to join his father's firm, by going to New

York City, and by marrying a divorced woman. He is much more attuned to the modern world than is his father, and his experiences in battle during World War I help him to mature and become more sophisticated. In the end, however, John proves to be his father's son; he returns to Boston and sets up housekeeping at Hillcrest, the family estate. George dies secure in the knowledge that the Apley niche in Boston remains filled; the cycle continues.

The Late George Apley is more than a sad story of the environment's tyranny over individuals. For all of the bleakness of its conclusions, the novel is very entertaining and amusing. The comedic and satiric center of the novel lies in its narrator, Mr. Willing. Marquand decided to tell the story as "a novel in the form of a memoir" for two reasons: first, to parody the then-common subliterary genre of the "collected papers," and second, and more important, to filter the information about the Apleys through the mind and language of a character even more dogmatically committed than the Apleys are to the proper Bostonian vision of life.

Willing understands none of George Apley's incipient rebellions or his son's more blatant social improprieties. Much of the novel's rich humor and gentle satire comes from his fussy, polite, pseudoliterary apologies and rationalizations for any errant Apley behavior. In the end, in spite of Willing's stuffy shortsightedness, the reader comes to know and understand George Apley very well; although amused and saddened by his weaknesses and narrowness, the reader is finally tolerant of, and sympathetic toward, the late George Apley.

"Critical Evaluation" by Keith Neilson

Further Reading

Auchincloss, Louis. "John P. Marquand." In *Writers and Personality*. Columbia: University of South Carolina Press, 2005. Discussion of Marquand is part of novelist Auchincloss's examination of how writers' temperaments, interests, and other personality traits are reflected in their fiction.

Bell, Millicent. *Marquand: An American Life*. Boston: Little, Brown, 1979. Analyzes *The Late George Apley* as an accurate depiction and study of the Bostonian world its author loved and resented. Summarizes the mainly hostile reviews the work received in Boston periodicals when it was published.

Gross, John J. *John P. Marquand*. New York: Twayne, 1963. Discusses *The Late George Apley* as a work reflecting Marquand's concerns about the increasing atomization of contemporary society and about the tendency of some to take old New England values, including frugality and charity, too far.

Kazin, Alfred. "John P. Marquand and the American Failure." *The Atlantic Monthly*, November, 1958. Notes that Marquand, a genteel satirist, is ideally positioned in *The Late George Apley* as an observer. Asserts that Apley's abandonment of his Irish girlfriend represents the dilemma of many Americans who wish to defy convention but find it difficult to do.

Marquand, John P. "Apley, Wickford Point, and Pulham: My Early Struggles." *The Atlantic Monthly*, September, 1956. Marquand comments on his decision to parody the epistolary novel by employing as narrator a preposterous, pompous, obtuse, and conceited biographer.

Tuttleton, James W. *The Novel of Manners in America*. Chapel Hill: University of North Carolina Press, 1972. Contains a thumbnail biography of Marquand that shows the importance of social influences on his writings. Discusses *The Late George Apley* as an exposure of the Boston Brahmin caste system and the tragedy of its perpetuation.

Whipple, Robert D., Jr., ed. *Essays on the Literature of American Novelist John P. Marquand, 1893-1960*. Lewiston, N.Y.: Edwin Mellen Press, 2004. This collection, intended for a general academic audience, presents essays on varied topics, such as the roles of women in Marquand's fiction and how Marquand dealt with his success. Includes an analysis of *The Late George Apley*.

The Laugh of the Medusa

Author: Hélène Cixous (1937-   )
First published: "Le Rire de la méduse," 1975 (English translation, 1976)
Type of work: Literary criticism

Hélène Cixous, in "The Laugh of the Medusa," advocates new ways of thinking and writing about women and literature. The essay has become a staple of feminist criticism because of its incisive critique of patriarchal politics, its endorsement of a feminist philosophy that is grounded in poststructuralism and psychoanalytic theory, and its modeling or representation of the possibilities of *écriture féminine* ("feminine writing")—what Cixous calls white ink. "The Laugh of the Medusa" is also a call to arms, urging women to reclaim their bodies and, by extension, their desires and identities through writing.

Concerned with traditional representations of women by men in literature and other scholarly texts, Cixous begins her analysis by invoking the classical figure of Medusa, but she does so by refiguring how Medusa has been represented through the ages. In this way, Cixous reclaims her. Traditionally, Medusa has been portrayed as a physical and moral monster; with snakes in place of hair, Medusa turns the men who look upon her to stone. However, Cixous's Medusa laughs, which is both a joyful and a disruptive act that can lead to new directions for women's (feminist) writing. From the first paragraph, women's writing is positioned as both liberating and intervening.

Phallocentrism, a male-dominated, masculine-coded linguistic and philosophical system—or, to put it more simply, male bias—keeps women from accessing their own stories. Without this access, women lack knowledge of the multiple ways to be; women, thus, have no body and are thus nobody. It is imperative, Cixous argues, that a woman must, broadly speaking, "write her self" and "put herself into the text— as into the world and into history—by her own movement." Essentially, Cixous calls upon women to assert themselves in writing and in the world by leaving their literary imprint, and she speaks in terms associated with revolution. Among Cixous's aims are to "break up" and "destroy" and "to foresee the unforeseeable, to project." Thus, her agenda in "The Laugh of the Medusa" is to call into question and break from the existing literary and social order and to embrace a new vision for women and literature through the form and content of her own essay.

Cixous has been criticized for what some see as essentialist tendencies in her work, meaning that she perceives women as biologically determined and universally similar. While Cixous does reference psychoanalysts like Sigmund Freud and Jacques Lacan, she moves away from their absolutism. Instead, she emphasizes plurality and multiplicity. Cixous, in arguing that there is no "general" or "typical" woman, focuses her study on what women have in common: a history of exclusion and a legacy of limited agency and visibility.

Cixous discusses the female body and women's sexuality in connection with writing for several reasons: Women are driven away both from their own bodies and from their own sexualities, sexuality informs and works in tandem with writing, and women's sexuality and women's writing are distinctly female. That which is beautiful in women's lived experiences and in writing cannot be fully expressed or claimed until the taboo is lifted on women's corporeal desires and sexualities—a taboo that makes women feel ashamed of their bodies, and their work. More important, Cixous declares, by reclaiming their bodies, women will take back what is rightfully theirs.

The conception of women and writing, wherein Cixous fuses the body and the mind, dismantles the Cartesian notion of a mind/body split. Cixous is invested in unifying the figure of woman by making her whole, and so her theoretical stance is opposed to the binary opposition of mind and body. She underscores the affirmative nature of her enterprise and refutes the notion, proposed by Freud, that women are lacking power (and, by extension, worth or value) without the phallus and are, as Cixous clarifies, "deprived" and "wounded." In this conception, the symbolic power of the phallus leaves women disempowered because it entraps them between two "horrifying" myths: the Medusa and the abyss. Cixous suggests that, because men have been the mythmakers in Western culture, it is imperative that women assume the role of mythmaking and revise the existing narratives so that "history [can] change its meaning." Rather than accept Medusa as the monster who defines femininity, Cixous resituates Medusa, causing her to be both "beautiful" and, symbolically, "laughing." This laughter is disruptive and playful, and it mirrors the abstract principles Cixous sets out for women's writing, the agenda of which will disrupt existing ideologies and established texts and exude playfulness and joyfulness in the process.

Unlike phallocentrism, Cixous argues, women's writing cannot be pinned down. However, it is clear that Medusa the monster gives way in Cixous's essay to the beautiful, laughing, loving, and flying mother figure. For Cixous, writing is both an intellectual and a bodily act that takes into account female desire, experience, sisterhood, and love. The body is featured as the trope par excellence. To a lesser extent, Cixous uses the image of water to describe women's writing. Water has long been associated with femininity (that is, women's cycles, life-giving properties) and feminism (that is, encompassing nature, unfixed qualities, transformative nature, multiple characteristics). What is most classically

feminist, though, about Cixous's essay is her admonition to women that they should have a choice: They should choose, for example, whether or not to become mothers (and, for Cixous, becoming a mother is an esteemed responsibility).

The experimental style of "The Laugh of the Medusa" mirrors its content: Cixous puts into practice her theory of white ink. In her notion of white ink, she embraces aspects of female experience that have been denigrated: sexuality, sisterhood, and motherhood. White ink, a metaphor for *écriture féminine*, is likened to the "good mother's milk." In this way, white ink is marked writing; it designates the writing from the female body that Cixous advocates. As such, white ink is associated with breast milk. It is nourishing although, abstractly, difficult to define and read because it is almost invisible. White ink appears as experimental writing because it thwarts traditional forms and subject matter in its objective of capturing female experience, psychology, and desire. It is more closely associated with the psychoanalytic realm of the imaginary/semiotic, a place associated with the womb and the baby's experience of and connection with the mother's body, where all desires and needs are met and the baby is unified with the mother. Conversely, the black ink of phallocentrism is associated with the psychoanalytic realm of the symbolic, where behavior and meanings are ordered according to a male system of rules and punishment. Because writing is, in some way, a record of a life lived, Cixous sanctions white ink and feminist theory by producing a feminist essay that is radical in both its content and form.

Women need to write in their own language about their own lives. This radical tenet leads Cixous to explain that the metaphor of flying belongs to women solely: Women have had to fly stealthily in the past to "possess anything," but now they can fly openly, even soar, in language. In other words, women need to liberate themselves in writing and through writing. In short, white ink and Cixous's feminist politics will require a reorienting of self and reading strategies: The objective of "The Laugh of the Medusa" is to "break up the [supposed] 'truth' with laughter.'"

Julie Goodspeed-Chadwick

Further Reading

Barry, Peter. *Beginning Theory: An Introduction to Literary and Cultural Theory*. 2d ed. New York: Manchester University Press, 2002. A helpful introduction to literary theory that provides an excellent and elegant overview of various critical theories. Chapter 6, a feminist criticism, contextualizes Cixous's work. Includes a good suggested-readings list.

Benstock, Shari, Suzanne Ferriss, and Susanne Woods. *A Handbook of Literary Feminisms*. New York: Oxford University Press, 2002. A concise introduction to feminist theory that offers a short discussion on literary theory, language, and Cixous's ideas on *écriture feminine*.

Blyth, Ian, with Susan Sellers. *Hélène Cixous: Live Theory*. New York: Continuum, 2004. In this book examining Cixous's theoretical writing, the authors contextualize her body of work, including "The Laugh of the Medusa."

Cixous, Hélène. *White Ink: Interviews on Sex, Text, and Politics*. New York: Columbia University Press, 2008. This book comprises interviews with Cixous. Chapter 6, "My Text Is Written in White and Black, in 'Milk and Night,'" is an insightful interview that touches on "The Laugh of the Medusa."

Guerin, Wilfred L., et al. *A Handbook of Critical Approaches to Literature*. 5th ed. New York: Oxford University Press, 2005. Although the discussion on Cixous is abbreviated, the section on feminism and psychoanalysis may provide some useful background.

Jacobus, Lee A., and Regina Barreca. *Hélène Cixous: Critical Impressions*. Amsterdam: Gordon & Breach, 1999. This anthology of essays originated from a special journal issue on Cixous in *LIT: Literature Interpretation Theory*. See the pertinent essays "The Medusa's Slip: Hélène Cixous and the Underpinnings of Écriture Féminine" by Anu Aneja and "Hélène Cixous: A Space Between—Women and (Their) Language" by Pamela A. Turner.

Zajko, Vanda, and Miriam Leonard. *Laughing with Medusa: Classical Myth and Feminist Thought*. New York: Oxford University Press, 2006. This book features a particularly interesting assortment of essays connected by their focus on classical myth—such as that surrounding Medusa—and feminism.

Laughter
An Essay on the Meaning of the Comic

Author: Henri Bergson (1859-1941)
First published: Le Rire: Essai sur la signification du comique, 1900 (English translation, 1911)
Type of work: Philosophy

Laughter, Henri Bergson's profound essay on the nature and source of laughter, grows out of his concern with the nineteenth century mechanization of life. For Bergson, life is ever in flux through time and space, and any divergence from this principle of flux, any attempt to fix or concretize life, is removed from life. Bergson's famous principle of *élan vital*, the vital life force that underlies all living things, leads to the central motif of his theory of comedy, that "the mechanical encrusted upon the living" promotes laughter. Any time a living thing takes on attributes of death or mechanization or rigid automatism, it ceases to be wholly alive and inspires social laughter. Comedy, in Bergson's view, is a social gesture designed to promote organic health in the social body. Laughter, by ridiculing social outsiders, effects in those laughed at a desire to purge themselves of unsocial traits. Comedy attempts to return to life those half-alive people on society's fringes whose "failure" to adapt themselves impairs social well-being.

Bergson opens chapter 1, a general discussion of comedy, with three fundamental observations on the nature of the comic spirit: "the comic does not exist outside the pale of what is strictly human," an "absence of feeling . . . usually accompanies laughter," and laughter's "natural environment . . . is society." Laughter's function is social: It "must have social signification." People only laugh, Bergson asserts, at things that in some way they have stamped as theirs. People do not laugh at landscapes, for instance, but at humans or at animals in which people see human elements. Nor can people laugh at things without putting aside their emotions. People may laugh at one they pity, but their pity must first be silenced. Emotion stifles laughter; intellect kindles it. Viewing life disinterestedly, people can disengage their emotions, permitting life to impress them as comic. Finally, laughter occurs in company with others; one does not often laugh in isolation.

A man who stumbles and falls as he runs along the street

becomes an object of laughter because of his "rigidity" or "momentum," his clumsiness, or as Bergson terms it, "lack of elasticity through absentmindedness and a kind of physical obstinacy." This involuntary comic movement caused by mechanical inelasticity is a failure to adapt oneself to circumstance, an inability to be flexible and responsive to change. It may be external, as when people fail to notice a chair being pulled away from behind, or internal, as with the absentminded individual whose mind is so engaged with things other than the present place and time that he or she cannot function. In either case, the more natural the cause of inelasticity the more comic the effect will be. With Don Quixote, for example, whose absentmindedness is largely due to his belief in an imaginary world, lies the whimsical madman with a systematic absentmindedness "organized around one central idea." It is therefore doubly comic when he falls into a well while gazing at a star.

Vice may so affect comic characters that the rigidity of a fixed idea of, for example, avarice or jealousy infects their personalities to the extent that they personify avarice or jealousy. The vice exists rather than the person, who becomes an automaton, and the character is comic "in proportion to his ignorance of himself." Awareness of others' laughter corrects people's manners, compelling people to try to appear less ridiculous, but self-correction cannot occur when ignorance of one's absurdity remains.

Society imposes on its members the necessity to adapt to circumstance. Life offers two forces, tension and elasticity, that enable people to avoid routine or empty habit and to encourage a constant effort toward "reciprocal adaptation." Society fears eccentricity, which presupposes a separatist tendency in the individual, and endeavors to harmonize individual wills. Routine harmony may not exist, however, so society demands a continual readjustment of individual egos. Society therefore must prod the slumbering individual, who respects the group but lets his or her adjustment drift into dead conformity, as well as guide the eccentric, who gravitates toward nonsocial values. Laughter is the social gesture by which society imposes its lessons upon the eccentric or the conformist; laughter satisfies aesthetic and utilitarian aims.

Having outlined this formula for the comic spirit, Bergson then details the sequence of comic forms, from a clown's horseplay to the most refined effects of comedy. The comic element resident in forms derives from the opposition of soul—supple and in perpetual motion—to matter—inertly resistant to movement. When matter or body succeeds, for example, in capturing fleeting states of being of the face, it petrifies the "outward life of the soul" in a material, "mechanical operation" and achieves a comic effect.

It is this admixture of the human and the mechanical that accounts for the comic element of gesture and movement. The more the "attitudes, gestures and movements of the human body" remind one of a machine the more they are laughable. Whenever mechanism appears in the human body, as in the gestures of a public speaker, the repetition elicits the comic response. When attention focuses on form instead of matter, on body instead of soul, comic response occurs. Physical comedy, then, is a parody of the mechanization of human life.

In chapter 2, Bergson turns to the comic element in situations and in words. He again finds the comic residing in the dualism of the mechanical and the human. Acts or events that give, in a single combination, the "illusion of life and the distinct impression of a mechanical arrangement" produce comedy. The ultimate formulas for the comic state are repetition, inversion, and reciprocal interference of series. Repetition reflects a mathematical or symmetrical ordering of life. Inversion is simply the reversal of roles, as when a prisoner lectures a judge. Reciprocal interference describes a situation, belonging simultaneously to different series of events, yet capable of two entirely different interpretations. The classic Who's on first? dialogue is an example. The laughter of words also falls under the same three headings. Again, whenever the living quality, the suppleness, of language is contrasted to the rigid mechanism of language, laughter searches out this automatism and corrects it.

Chapter 3 examines the comic element of character. Bergson asserts that laughter has a social meaning, expresses a special lack of adaptation to society, and cannot exist apart from humanity. Characters who remove themselves from society are fundamentally comic; such characters illustrate the basis of comedy, which begins with a "growing callousness to social life." Comedy does not necessarily direct itself at moral faults; rather it usually aims to correct social aloofness.

Bergson places comedy midway between life and art. Art expresses true reality. Society constructs its values on the superficial perceptions of ordinary people, but art deals with deeper realities. Comedy, because it accepts a social, utilitarian goal—the correction of the social outsider—lies close to life. Comedy also aims to please, however, and may require more accurate perception than that available to everyone; therefore, comedy belongs to art. Comedy differs from tragedy in that the latter seeks the individual, the unique, while comedy presents the general, the type. Comedy depicts general characters, universals of humanity, categorizing people by surface distinctions and by the roles of everyday life. The comic poet observes inductively and surveys people for external, general eccentricities. Such a writer never endeavors to portray alienation for fear of engaging the emotions, hence endangering the comic element. Comedy tries to isolate the superficial and telling facet of character, the mechanical, and then creates types. Tragedy examines the depths of the individual, gives an impression of life, and develops out of the emotions. The tragic poet's characters are in a sense extensions of his or her own personality—in contrast to the comic character, the tragic character arises deductively, from within, rather than from without.

Comedy therefore is not disinterested, as is genuine art. Comedy accepts social life as a natural environment; it even obeys an impulse of social life. In this respect it rejects art, which is a reaction against society.

Further Reading

Atkinson, Camille. "What's So Funny?" *Philosophy Today* 50, no. 5 (Winter, 2006): 437-443. Atkinson examines the nature of laughter from a philosophical perspective and includes a discussion of Bergson's incongruity theory.

Bergson, Henri. *The Creative Mind: An Introduction to Metaphysics.* Translated by Mabelle L. Andison. 1946. Reprint. Mineola, N.Y.: Dover, 2007. Bergson discusses his views of metaphysics and science, relative to comedy; the role of the mechanical, especially in gestures, as a device for humor; and intuition, absolutes, language, and logic relative to humor. Part 1 of the introduction and chapters 3, 4, and 5 are particularly useful.

Carr, H. Wildon. *Henri Bergson: The Philosophy of Change.* 1912. Reprint. Boston: Adamant Media, 2004. Brief presentation of Bergson's philosophic views on life, intellect and matter, instinct and intelligence, intuition, freedom, mind and body, and creative evolution. Those unacquainted with Bergson's work should read this classic work before reading *Laughter.*

Guerlac, Suzanne. *Thinking in Time: An Introduction to Henri Bergson.* Ithaca, N.Y.: Cornell University Press, 2006. Although her accessible introduction to Bergson's philosophy focuses on works other than *Laughter,* Guerlac does discusses the book in chapter 6.

Prusak, Bernard G. "*Le Rire* à nouveau: Rereading Bergson." *Journal of Aesthetics and Art Criticism* 62, no. 4 (Fall, 2004): 377-388. Prusak examines the book as a "metaphysics" of laughter. Argues that although Bergson's metaphysics "distorts" his account of comedy, the book still contains valuable insights about the nature of laughter.

Sypher, Wylie. Introduction to *Laughter: An Essay on Comedy,* by George Meredith. 1956. Reprint. Baltimore: Johns Hopkins University Press, 1980. An extensive, readable, and interesting comparative analysis of George Meredith's essay on comedy and Bergson's *Laughter.* Reviews the foundations of Bergson's complicated notions on comedy and the mechanical.

Taylor, Mark C. *Erring: A Postmodern A/theology.* Chicago: University of Chicago Press, 1984. This discussion of comedy, language, and laughter—particularly in chapter 7—is an excellent analogy to Bergson's philosophy on these subjects. A comparison of Bergson's philosophy of laughter to that of Taylor reveals astonishing similarities. For advanced readers.

Lavengro
The Scholar, the Gypsy, the Priest

Author: George Henry Borrow (1803-1881)
First published: 1851
Type of work: Novel
Type of plot: Autobiographical
Time of plot: Nineteenth century
Locale: England, Scotland, and Ireland

Principal characters:
LAVENGRO, a scholar, journalist, and tinker
JOHN, his brother
JASPER PETULENGRO, his gypsy friend
MRS. HERNE, an old crone
THE FLAMING TINMAN, a bully of the roads
ISOPEL BERNERS, Lavengro's companion
PETER WILLIAMS, an evangelist
WINIFRED, his wife

The Story:

Lavengro is the son of an army officer who fought against Napoleon, and the boy spends his early years at army garrisons in various parts of England, Scotland, Ireland, and Wales. When he is six years old, Lavengro discovers Daniel Defoe's *Robinson Crusoe* (1719), a book that stimulates his imagination and arouses in him a desire to read and to study languages. One day, while wandering on the outskirts of a garrison town, he meets a group of Romany, or gypsies, who threaten to do him harm. They draw back, however, when he shows them a tame snake that he is carrying. The gypsies, becoming friendly, nickname him Sapengro, or snake tamer. A young gypsy named Jasper declares that he and Sapengro will always be brothers. Lavengro also meets a man at the gypsy camp whom he will eventually see hanged fifteen years later at Newgate prison.

A few years later, the boy begins the study of Latin. About the same time, his father is ordered to Edinburgh, Scotland, and while living there Lavengro is involved in several bickers, or fights, with his schoolmates; he also learns the sport of mountain climbing. In 1815, Lavengro's father is ordered to Ireland, and there Lavengro attends a seminary at Clonmel and studies more Latin and Greek; in incidental fashion, he also learns to speak Irish. His brother John is made an ensign and is transferred to a post a few miles away. After Britain signs a peace treaty with the French, however, opportunities for military employment are few. As John has always wanted to paint, the young man's father allows him to go to London to study art.

Lavengro again meets Jasper, his gypsy friend, and discovers that Jasper's last name is Petulengro. Jasper is now a Romany kral, or gypsy king, as well as a horseshoer, pugilist, jockey, and soothsayer. Through Jasper, Lavengro makes the acquaintance of a malignant old crone named Herne, who hates him because she believes that he is stealing the Romany tongue. It is Jasper who has named him Lavengro, which means "word-master," because he has learned the gypsy language so rapidly. All the gypsies depart for London, except Mrs. Herne, who goes to Yorkshire. Lavengro remains at home with his parents while his father tries to decide what to do with him. It is finally agreed that Lavengro will enter a solicitor's office to study law. Lavengro, however, neglects his law studies while he learns Welsh and translates the poetry of Ab Gwilym. About the same time, Lavengro obtains a Danish book and learns to read it by first studying the Danish Bible. One day, Lavengro is sent to deliver a thousand pounds to a magistrate, and he has a very entertaining conversation with the man concerning the art of self-defense. In spite of the magistrate's

fondness for boxing, however, he refuses a match with Lavengro.

Lavengro meets Jasper again and puts on the gloves with him for a friendly bout. Later, he returns home and discovers that his father is seriously ill. His brother John also arrives home just before their father dies. Shortly afterward, Lavengro goes to London to seek his fortune as a writer, taking with him a letter of introduction to a noted publisher. The publisher seems delighted to be able to employ him but is not interested in such things as Lavengro's translations of the songs of Ab Gwilym and of Danish songs. Lavengro is informed that the reading public scoffs at works such as those. Instead, the publisher recommends that he write a story modeled on a work that has sold well.

While walking through the London neighborhood of Cheapside one day, Lavengro climbs onto the balustrade of a bridge in order to see something below. An old woman selling apples nearby thinks that he is trying to commit suicide and begs him not to fling himself over. Lavengro learns that the old lady has a partiality for a book about the "blessed" Mary Flanders, and thereafter he returns from time to time to visit with her.

Lavengro is invited to dinner at the publisher's house one Sunday, and he discovers that the publisher does not believe in eating meat or drinking wine. After dinner, the publisher tells Lavengro what his new assignment is to be: He is to prepare a collection of the stories of the lives and trials of famous criminals incarcerated at Newgate. In addition, he is to translate the publisher's book of philosophy into German and to write an article about it for the *Review*.

In the company of an acquaintance named Francis Ardry, Lavengro visits many of the underworld spots of London. The experiences he has there, together with the research he does in preparing his series of stories on criminals, give him a wide and practical knowledge of the underworld. Then Lavengro's brother comes to London and introduces him to a painter of the heroic. The peculiar thing about this painter's pictures is the short legs of all the people depicted in them.

When Lavengro has finished writing his stories of crime, he takes them to the publisher, who is displeased because Lavengro has omitted several of the publisher's favorite criminal histories. Lavengro goes to visit the apple-woman again, and his despondent appearance leads her to think that he has been caught stealing—Lavengro has never told the apple-woman about his profession. He talks her into letting him read her cherished copy of the life of Mary Flanders.

The publisher's speculations fail, and Lavengro is left without money, but he eventually obtains all the wages that were due him. Taggart, the publisher's assistant, tells Lavengro that Glorious John, another printer, will publish Lavengro's ballads and the songs of Ab Gwilym, but Lavengro never offers his ballads to Glorious John. In mid-winter, he goes again to visit the apple-woman and finds that she has moved her stall to the other side of the bridge. He promises to take her book and trade it in for a Bible; however, he loses the book and has nothing to trade. He decides to purchase a Bible and never let her know about his negligence.

About this time, Lavengro saves an Armenian from pickpockets. The Armenian wishes him to translate some Armenian fables into English, but Lavengro refuses. The Armenian, who has inherited one hundred thousand pounds from his father, is intent upon doubling the amount through speculation. The Armenian runs into a bit of luck and comes into possession of two hundred thousand pounds. Lavengro's advice to the Armenian is to take his fortune and fight the Persians.

When his money runs short, Lavengro decides to do the translations for the Armenian, but the man has already departed to invest his money in a war against the Persians. Lavengro leaves London after having some small success writing fiction. He meets and talks with many and various people on his travels about England. On his rambles, he hears stories concerning the Flaming Tinman, who holds a great repute as a fighter and who has forced Jack Slingsby, another tinker, out of business with threats of death. Lavengro meets Slingsby and buys out his business. He decides to become a tinker himself in the hope of meeting the Flaming Tinman.

One day while he is mending pots and pans, Lavengro encounters Mrs. Herne and Leonora, a thirteen-year-old girl who is traveling with the old woman. Leonora brings him cakes made by Mrs. Herne, and after eating one of them he becomes seriously ill. When the evil old crone comes to gloat over him, he realizes that the cakes had been poisoned. Then the sound of wheels frightens the old woman away, and Lavengro is saved by the timely arrival of Peter Williams, a traveling Welsh preacher, and Winifred, his wife. Peter Williams tells Lavengro the sad story of his life and relates how he was led to commit a sin against the Holy Ghost, a sin for which there is no redemption. Peter has become a preacher to warn other people against the unforgivable sin. Lavengro journeys with Peter and his wife as far as the Welsh border, where he leaves them to join Jasper Petulengro and his band of gypsies.

Jasper tells Lavengro that Mrs. Herne hanged herself because of her failure to poison him. Because Jasper is a blood kinsman of Mrs. Herne, it is required by Romany law that he obtain revenge from Lavengro. Lavengro, however, has really been only indirectly responsible for the old woman's death, a fact of which Jasper is well aware. The two young men retire to a place where they can fight, and there Jasper receives full satisfaction when he makes Lavengro's nose bleed.

Soon after his friendly tussle with Jasper, Lavengro meets the Flaming Tinman, Moll, his wife, and Isopel Berners, the daughter of a gypsy mother and a noble father and now a free woman of the roads. Isopel is responsible for Lavengro's victory in a brawl with the Flaming Tinman, for she has told him to use his right hand and to strike at the bully's face. The Flaming Tinman and Moll depart, leaving the territory to Lavengro the tinker, but Isopel remains behind with her belongings. The story of the Flaming Tinman's defeat is soon known throughout the neighborhood, and Lavengro becomes a hero of the roads. At a public house, he meets a priest whom he calls the Man in Black. The priest and Lavengro have many conversations concerning religion and the attempt to establish Catholicism in England.

On a wild, stormy night, Isopel and Lavengro help a coachman to right his overturned coach. Later, the coachman tells them the story of his life, a tale that proved to Lavengro that in those days romance journeyed on the highways and adventure waited around the turn of any English lane.

Critical Evaluation:

Lavengro may or may not be an autobiographical novel. George Henry Borrow was trained in law and traveled widely. His primary interest, however, was literature. How much of himself he put into that literature—and how much he fantasized—is irrelevant, because the writing stands on its own merits. Although he contributed to the *Newgate Calendar*—a compilation of stories of infamous crimes—Borrow is best known for his works about gypsy life: *The Zincali: An Account of the Gypsies in Spain* (1841), *Lavengro*, and *The Romany Rye* (1857). The fact that Borrow was well traveled and proficient in languages may account for some of his knowledge of and easy entrée into non-Anglo cultures, hence his familiarity with esoteric customs.

As Borrow depicts it, Romany life certainly differs from Western European life. *Lavengro*, in the Romany tongue, means "philologist"—a student of languages. In Borrow's novel, the lust for language amounts to a lust for life—a theme carried more or less explicitly through his other novels. Knowledge of languages is the key to a gypsy's survival, since the gypsy is by definition a nomad and must adapt to differing linguistic circumstances on a moment's notice. Linguistic facility is thus at a premium, and Borrow's novel is aptly titled to suggest the central ingredient in a gypsy's life.

One consequence of the peripatetic Romany life, however, is a selective skepticism toward political and religious institutions. Here, *Lavengro* delivers the message clearly: Popery, radicalism, and anything inimical to the Church of England were abhorrent, Romany customs notwithstanding. Gypsies can adapt to and live within a system while still maintaining their own customs and integrity, but because their way of life is dissident, they cannot tolerate dissidents in their own ranks, as these individuals endanger the safety of the Romany community. Borrow has not been given proper credit for this astute political insight, for he demonstrates it rather than preaches it.

To nineteenth century readers, Borrow's *Lavengro* was at least a curiosity and at most a perplexity. It depicted a totally foreign way of life—something exotic and appealing yet simultaneously repugnant for its unconventional ways. Even today, Western readers may be caught in a similar dilemma. Although *Lavengro* possesses a compelling fascination, the novel nevertheless depicts an experience largely alien to Western readers because the Romany are essentially a private people with their own customs and values. Assimilation with the dominant culture is incompatible with Romany life. This novel can help Western readers understand the features that human beings hold in common as well as appreciate the differences between cultures.

Further Reading

Hollingsworth, Keith. *The Newgate Novel, 1830-1847: Bulwer, Ainsworth, Dickens, and Thackeray.* Detroit, Mich.: Wayne State University Press, 1963. Offers one of the best discussions available of the English tradition of stories about criminals. Examines the references in *Lavengro* to John Thurtell, a childhood acquaintance of Borrow, whose sensational murder trial and execution in 1823 left many traces in literature.

Hyde, George. "Borrow and the Vanity of Dogmatising: *Lavengro* as Self-Portrait." *Cambridge Quarterly* 32, no. 2 (2003): 161-173. Presents a reevaluation of Borrow's literary reputation and discussion of the autobiographical nature of the novel.

Knapp, William I. *Life, Writings, and Correspondence of George Borrow, Based on Official and Other Authentic Sources.* 2 vols. 1899. Reprint. Detroit, Mich.: Gale Research, 1967. Study of Borrow's life remains one of the best sources on the author. Relates the narrative of *Lavengro* to verifiable events in Borrow's early life.

Meyers, Robert R. *George Borrow.* New York: Twayne, 1966. Provides an objective and realistic assessment of *Lavengro* as account of gypsy culture, description of the gypsy language, and autobiography. Emphasizes Borrow's indebtedness to the Bible, to *Robinson Crusoe*, and to the eighteenth century picaresque tradition of Henry Fielding, Tobias Smollett, and Laurence Sterne.

Nord, Deborah Epstein. "In the Beginning Was the Word: George Borrow's Romany Picaresque." In *Gypsies and the British Imagination, 1807-1930.* New York: Columbia University Press, 2006. Examines the British obsession with gypsies by analyzing the works of Borrow and several better-known writers. Demonstrates how British writers have used gypsy characters and stories to explore cultural and racial differences as well as national and personal identity.

Shorter, Clement. *The Life of George Borrow.* New York: E. P. Dutton, 1928. Enthusiastic account of Borrow's life and writings emphasizes the way *Lavengro* reflects Borrow's linguistic abilities. A good starting point for students of Borrow's work.

Stonyk, Margaret. *Nineteenth-Century English Literature.* New York: Schocken Books, 1984. Includes an excellent discussion of *Lavengro* that shows how the novel uses dialogue to reveal hypocrisy, describes its outrageous characters, and comments on how the work's seemingly random organization repelled its early audience.

Willems, Wim. "George Borrow (1803-81): The Walking Lord of Gypsy Lore." In *In Search of the True Gypsy: From Enlightenment to Final Solution.* Translated by Don Bloch. London: F. Cass, 1997. Focuses on the search for the origins of contemporary ideas about gypsies and includes an examination of Borrow's fiction.

The Lay of Igor's Campaign

Author: Unknown
First transcribed: Slovo o polku Igoreve, c. 1187
    (English translation, 1919)
Type of work: Poetry
Type of plot: Romance
Time of plot: Late twelfth century
Locale: The Russian steppes

Principal characters:
IGOR, the prince of Novgorod-Seversk
PRINCE VSEVOLOD, his brother
PRINCE VLADIMIR, his son
PRINCE SVATOSLAV, his nephew
THE GREAT PRINCE OF KIEV

The Lay of Igor's Campaign, a heroic romance, is the earliest great work of Russian literature. Moreover, it is the only surviving heroic poem of the Russian Middle Ages, and it is one of the few pieces of literature known to have appeared in Russia before the nineteenth century. The poem, of which the author is unknown, is admired by most educated Russians both for its place in the Russian tradition and for its literary excellence. Although it is relatively unknown outside Russia, it has been widely translated.

The subject matter of *The Lay of Igor's Campaign* is typically medieval: the expedition, defeat, capture, and escape of a knightly warrior—Prince Igor of Novgorod-Seversk (not to be confused with Novgorod the great, a much more famous and important city of old Kievian Russia). Igor's antagonists were the Kumans, a race of pagan nomads who inhabited the southern steppes around the Don River. Three other princes and their troops accompanied Igor's contingent: Igor's brother, Prince Vsevolod; Igor's son, Prince Vladimir; and Igor's nephew, Prince Svatoslav. However, while it is an early work, and while it did not appear in a culture notable for its literary and artistic achievements, and while it is a heroic tale of warriors and battle, the poem is far from being a primitive and unsophisticated work. Like the other medieval national epics to which it is sometimes compared, *The Lay of Igor's Campaign* is the product of a very skillful artist whose insight and poetic skills are of the highest order. In fact, the art of this Russian poem strikes one as being in some respects subtler than that of the nation's romantic epics; it has been said with some justice that the sophisticated, symbolic technique of the lay has a striking kinship with modern poetic techniques.

The history of the poem is somewhat obscure. It was probably written about 1187, but memory of it was soon lost, and it remained unknown until 1795, when Count Alexei Ivanovich Musin-Pushkin, a distinguished literary amateur, discovered a manuscript copy of the poem. He purchased what was probably a sixteenth century codex from a former official of a recently dissolved monastery. *The Lay of Igor's Campaign* was one of several manuscript items included in the codex, which had been in the monastery library. The text was published in 1800, but little was known at that time about interpreting and editing early Russian texts, and the edition was marred by errors and misinterpretations. Moreover, the sixteenth century scribe who had copied the text into the codex was himself unfamiliar with the twelfth century Russian language, and thus the manuscript itself was far from accurate. Before a second edition of the poem could be prepared for the printer, the manuscript was damaged by fire when Napoleon burned Moscow in 1812. Modern scholars have succeeded in repairing much of the damage of time, but nevertheless certain brief passages in the poem remain obscure. It should be noted also that for a time some scholars assumed that the story of the discovery of the poem in 1795 was a hoax and that the poem was a modern forgery. However, a portion of the poem has been found quoted verbatim in a manuscript made in 1307, and thus it has been certified that the poem is genuine.

The unknown author of the lay composed his masterpiece late in the twelfth century, about one or two years after the events of which he writes had occurred. This date can be determined by certain matters that are mentioned in the text. It is known that the characters and the events of the narrative are historical, for the story can be checked in surviving medieval chronicles. So far as can be determined from the poem, the author was a layman, very likely a soldier, who was the companion of some prince of Kievian Russia, perhaps of Igor himself. The poet was a city dweller but was familiar with the life of the steppes. He was also familiar with the literature and oral traditions, such as they were, of his times. One can tell from references in the text that a tradition of heroic oral poetry existed in the generations before the author of *The Lay of Igor's Campaign* wrote. The author refers to and quotes one of those older poets, Bayan the Bard.

The poem was not written by a professional singer; that is, although the author did not hesitate to use the techniques of oral poetry to achieve many of his poetic effects, the lay is a purely literary work, and it is written to be read. The spirit of the poem, it should be noted, is secular, heroic, and, crucially, patriotic. Russia as much as Igor is the hero of the piece. While the poem is nominally a Christian work, Christianity is only an incidental element in it. The older pagan nature worship of pre-Christian Russia has a much more integral place in the imagery and the tone of the poem than does Christianity.

Although often called a heroic poem, *The Lay of Igor's Campaign* is not a heroic tale per se. It is really quite difficult to classify, for while a heroic narrative is the foundation of the piece, much of it is a lyric lament for the feudal discord that characterized the poet's age; moreover, much of the time the author's objective seems to admonish the princes responsible for the feuds and troubles of Kievian Russia, and to that extent the lay is an inspired piece of political oratory. One must conclude that the work is a blend of the narrative, the lyric, and the hortatory. Further, it is not a poem in the strict sense but a prose poem. Although it may be sung, *The Lay of Igor's Campaign* is not composed in verse. The rhythm of the language is not that of verse, and the work is not composed in lines but in the rhythmical prose typical of the old Russian liturgy. Nevertheless, the work is emphatically poetic in its complex and vivid use of imagery, metaphor, and simile, and the total effect of the work can only be described as powerfully poetic.

Structurally, the poem falls into eight sections. The first is the poet's prologue, in which the author comments on the literary usage of the past and the departures he will make to achieve his own literary ends. The second deals with the determination of Igor and his brother to make their expedition. The third describes the advance across the steppes and Igor's initial success. The fourth is about the defeat and capture of the Russian forces. At this point the scope of the poem expands dramatically. The poet begins to dramatize the meaning of Igor's defeat to the Russian people. In the fifth section, the poet begins a lyrical-oratorical digression, first in his own voice and then in the voice of the Great Prince of Kiev. The prince, not yet aware of the disaster of Igor, has had a prophetic and symbolic dream of ill omen. Next, in the sixth section, the poet apostrophizes to nine other princes, asking them to end their quarrels and to join together to save Igor and Russia. This section is followed, in section seven, by a lyric lament by Igor's wife on the walls of her city. The poem ends (section eight) with a brief account of Igor's escape from the Kumans and a closing apostrophe by the poet.

This structure is supported by a pattern of metaphor, symbol, and imagery based primarily on nature: the sun, light and darkness, the land, the rivers, plants, winds, and the ancient nature gods. The men of the poem, their actions, their emotions, and the political, military, and social forces in the world of the poem, are all perceived and expressed in terms of this nature imagery and symbolism. In the end, the picture that *The Lay of Igor's Campaign* presents is one of a totally integrated world in which there is no distinct line of separation between the world of people and the world of nature. For example, the expedition begins amid ominous eclipses of the sun, and the light-darkness idea is complicated throughout the narrative until, at the end, Igor escapes his captors under cover of darkness. Also, at the sight of Igor's defeat, the trees bow down in grief. Throughout the poem the foreboding and anxious voices of nature can be heard moving in the wind and the rivers, and as Igor escapes, he holds a thankful dialogue with the pro-Russian river Donets while he sneeringly mocks the anti-Russian river Stugna. For all the lay's complexity of parts, when it is seen as a whole, it has, as do all great works of art, an overall simplicity and power that no serious reader can miss.

Further Reading

Gudzii, N. K. *History of Early Russian Literature.* 2d ed. Translated by Susan Wilbur Jones. New York: Macmillan, 1949. Classic resource reviews the textual history of the work and comments on the issue of its authenticity. Examines the tale in its historical context with respect to the Old Russian chronicles and reflects on its references to nature, pagan gods, and folk elements.

Howes, Robert C. Introduction to *The Tale of the Campaign of Igor.* New York: W. W. Norton, 1973. Provides probably the most thorough and readily accessible treatment of the work in English. Includes solid historical background, examination of the poem, and commentary on nature, religion, and the role of the hero.

Mann, Robert. *The Igor Tales and Their Folkloric Background.* Karacharovo, Russia: Birchbark Press of Karacharovo, 2005. Provides English translations of the Igor tales and other folktales that parallel the Igor story. Discusses the evidence that demonstrates the tales were not written down until the thirteenth century.

Milner-Gulland, Robin. "Old Russian Literature and Its Heritage." In *The Routledge Companion to Russian Literature*, edited by Neil Cornwell. New York: Routledge, 2001. Places *The Lay of Igor's Campaign* within the context of other early works of Russian literature.

Muchnic, Helen. *An Introduction to Russian Literature.* Rev. ed. New York: Dutton, 1964. Presents an examination of *The Lay of Igor's Campaign* that discusses the presumed character of the anonymous poet as well as the nature of the poetry itself.

Pronin, Alexander. *History of Old Russian Literature*. Frankfurt: Posev, 1968. Three discussions of *The Lay of Igor's Campaign* include brief historical context, a genealogical chart of the major characters, and a simple section-by-section analysis.

Tschizewskij, Dmitrij. *History of Russian Literature from the Eleventh Century to the End of the Baroque*. The Hague, the Netherlands: Mouton, 1971. Includes a section on *The Lay of Igor's Campaign* that focuses on its poetic elements, such as metaphors, imagery, and sounds. Notes the predominance of auditory and color images in the poem.

The Lay of the Last Minstrel

Author: Sir Walter Scott (1771-1832)
First published: 1805
Type of work: Poetry
Type of plot: Historical
Time of plot: Mid-sixteenth century
Locale: Scottish border

Principal characters:
LADY BUCCLEUCH, Lord Branksome's widow
MARGARET, her daughter
MASTER OF BUCCLEUCH, her son
LORD CRANSTOUN, Margaret's lover
SIR WILLIAM OF DELORAINE, a knight in Lady Buccleuch's service
THE DWARF, Lord Cranstoun's page
GHOST OF MICHAEL SCOTT, a wizard

The Poem:

An old minstrel, allegedly the last of his kind, wanders through the Scottish borders some time in the eighteenth century, lamenting the lost past; he asks for hospitality in Branksome Hall, the residence of the duchess of Buccleuch, and pays for his keep by singing a romance about her sixteenth century ancestors.

Lord Buccleuch has been killed in battle with the English, but his widow and children are well protected in Branksome Hall by a group of knights who had followed their dead leader. Although a truce has been declared, there are still skirmishes between the English and the Scots throughout the border country.

The widow, Lady Buccleuch, is the daughter of a magician; before he had died, he taught her to talk with the spirits.

One night, the lady hears the spirits predicting that the stars will show no favor to Branksome castle until pride should die and make love free. She presumes that this omen is meant for her, because her daughter, Margaret, loves the young Lord Cranstoun, who has fought against Lord Buccleuch. Lady Buccleuch swears nevertheless that Margaret shall never wed a foe of the family, no matter what the spirits might say. She sends William of Deloraine to Melrose Abbey to secure the mystic book of Michael Scott, a famous wizard who is buried in the abbey crypt. She orders William not to look into the book, on peril of his life.

The porter at the abbey leads the knight into to the wizard's tomb: Deloraine, the bravest of knights in battle, shivers with dread as he looks down at the body of the magician, which is as well-preserved as if he had not been dead for a day. When the knight takes the book from the dead wizard's hand, he seems to frown. As Deloraine leaves the vault, he hears noises reminiscent of the laughter and sobbing of friends.

While Deloraine is on his way back from the abbey, Margaret slips out of the castle to meet her lover, Lord Cranstoun, who is accompanied by the Dwarf, who had attached himself to the lord some time before and now refuses to leave him. The Dwarf, also known as Goblin, serves him as a page. The Dwarf warns the lovers of the approach of a horseman; it is Deloraine, returning from his mission. Margaret runs away and the two knights fight. Deloraine is seriously wounded.

Cranstoun orders the Dwarf to take Deloraine to Branksome Hall so that his wounds can be properly tended. The Dwarf finds the book but cannot open it until he has smeared the cover with the wounded man's blood. While he is reading one of the spells described in the book, an unseen hand strikes him on the cheek and knocks him down; the book snaps shut and cannot be opened again. The Dwarf hides it under his cloak, then proceeds to Branksome Hall with the wounded Deloraine.

At the castle, the Dwarf sees the young master of Buccleuch. Changing himself and the boy into dogs, he leads the child into the woods. There, after they have resumed their real shapes, the child is captured by the English soldiers patrolling the border. His absence remains undiscovered at the castle, because the Dwarf returns and assumes the child's shape, and then proceeds to make mischief. Lady Buccleuch, busy tending the wounds of her faithful knight, fails to notice the child's strange behavior.

The sentinels in the castle sight signal fires, indicating that the English are gathering to attack the Scots. Messengers are hurriedly dispatched to summon friendly clansmen to the defense of Branksome Hall. In the confusion, the Dwarf, still in the form of the master of Buccleuch, escapes from the knight assigned to watch him.

The English arrive before the castle and make their demands. They want William of Deloraine turned over to them, accusing him of murdering the brother of one of their group. They also demand that two hundred English knights be quartered in Branksome, in order to prevent the Scots from carrying out raids on the English side of the border. If these demands are not met, they declare, the castle will be stormed and the heir of Buccleuch will be sent to the English court to serve as a page.

Lady Buccleuch refuses these demands. She proposes that Deloraine should meet the brother of the slain man in combat, to settle the dispute in knightly fashion. Initially, the English leaders refuse and then begin preparing to attack the castle when one of their number brings word that Scottish clansmen are approaching the castle. Fearful of being outnumbered, the English accept the proposal for a settlement by mortal combat between the two knights concerned, or by the wronged man and a substitute for Deloraine should his wounds not be healed in time.

Other knights argue over the right to represent Deloraine, who is still weak from his wounds, but at the last minute, a knight appears in Deloraine livery and armor, ready to fight. The fight lasts some time, and both knights lose a great deal of blood before the Englishman falls. The victor, standing triumphantly over his fallen rival, does not remove his visor. The spectators are amazed to see Deloraine approaching from the castle. The supposed Deloraine is revealed to be Lord Cranstoun, who has stolen Deloraine's armor so that he might defend the hall and save Margaret's brother. At first, Lady Buccleuch refuses to receive him, but remembers the prophecy of the spirits and concedes that she must forget pride and allow love to prevail. She consents to give her daughter to the knight who had been her husband's enemy, and swears that she will return the book to Michael Scott's tomb.

At the wedding feast, the Dwarf continues to make trouble. To undo the mischief he causes, the assembled minstrels sing songs of days gone past. As the last song dies away, the banquet hall grows suddenly dark. A flash of lightning strikes the Dwarf, who vanishes. Deloraine is terrified, having seen the form of the dead wizard in the unearthly light. Lady Buccleuch renounces the magic of her father, and the knights undertake pilgrimages to pray for Michael Scott's soul.

Critical Evaluation:

In the original preface to this poem, Sir Walter Scott claimed, modestly, that *The Lay of the Last Minstrel* was primarily intended to illustrate life in the Scottish borders in the middle of the sixteenth century, but the new introduction and elaborate notes he added to the poem in the 1830 edition of his collected poetry—issued by his friend and business partner James Ballantyne—tell a different story. Scott explains the autobiographical and economic circumstances that led to its composition, and he footnotes the history and folklore on which the poem is based.

One of the significant revelations of the notes is that the name of Lord Buccleuch, whose widow is featured in the poem, had been Sir Walter Scott, one of a whole series of Scotts implicit in the history of Branksome; the author also fancied himself (without any real evidence) as a descendant of the thirteenth century natural philosopher Michael Scott, who obtained the inevitable reputation for wizardry attached to anyone in that era capable of rational thought; the poem is therefore as much a celebration of the author's own presumed genealogy as anything else.

Scott was an unorthodox scholar, and his notes explain at some length that his personal researches and literary endeavors had detracted considerably from the law career that he was supposed to be pursuing. In particular, he had long labored on the compilation of a collection of traditional ballads, *Minstrelsy of the Scottish Border* (1802-1803; 3 volumes), supplementing Thomas Percy's classic collection of *Reliques of Ancient English Poetry* (1765), which had made popular again some of the most famous Scottish ballads. He had also dabbled in translation of German ballads and had written a few short imitations, but *The Lay of the Last Minstrel* was his first substantial literary composition. It was published three years before he ventured into publishing and nine years before he turned to writing novels.

Understandably, Scott's 1830 introduction is a trifle defensive about what he had to consider as apprentice work, commenting that the once enchanting ballad measure had become "hackneyed and sickening," and that a long work formulated in relentlessly regular quatrains had a grating effect on the mind. Printed poetry is intended to be formally pronounced in the mind rather than directly digested in the fashion of prose, so that the reader might obtain the benefits of rhythm and rhyme. However, Scott fully appreciated the world of difference that there was between reading and listening, and he was anxious that metrical devices whose primary purpose had been to assist the memory of a reciter might be reckoned superfluous in an era when the printed page made memorization redundant.

Scott's fears proved largely unfounded. His subsequent success as poet, largely based on pastiche lays (simple narrative ballads), clearly demonstrates that the reading public still had an appetite for such artifice, and that it was not yet of merely antiquarian interest. The fluency developed in the writing of *The Lay of the Last Minstrel* served him well in subsequent endeavors of a similar sort. Times have changed markedly since then, but they did not do so rapidly, and Scott's endeavors—alongside the endeavors of Samuel Taylor Coleridge and Robert Southey in England—provided significant examples for such successors as Lord Byron and Alfred, Lord Tennyson, who far exceeded what Scott considered to be the risky length of *The Lay of the Last Minstrel* in ventures tending to epic dimensions.

Given these considerations, *The Lay of the Last Minstrel* must be credited not only for its boldness as a seemingly hazardous venture, and for the skill with which the project had been completed, but also for the proof it provides that success is possible. It also should be credited for proving that self-indulgent eccentricities—its scrupulous gathering of esoteric research materials and its digressions developing those materials—can enhance rather than detract from the enjoyment of such a work. In his later work, especially his novels, Scott—believing that the tide of history was running against superstition—tones down the supernatural intrusions that his fascination for traditional folklore continually encouraged him to accommodate in his works. Instead, he meekly represents the supernatural as false belief; but one of the joys of pastiche, so far as he was concerned, is the freedom to accommodate the supernatural more wholeheartedly.

This license allowed Scott to present Michael Scott as the full-blooded wizard that wild rumor considered him to be, rather than the valiant scholar he really was, and to make the historical vagabond Gilpin Horner into the goblin that he was reputed to be. This license also allowed Scott to add his own measure of nightmarish detail to the tales in question. Readers now know that the tide of history turned again, and thus have cause to be grateful for that endeavor. While readers are free to doubt that the poem offers a reliable illustration of life on the Scottish borders in the sixteenth century, its status as a classic of supernatural literature is completely assured.

"Critical Evaluation" by Brian Stableford

Further Reading

Cockshut, A. O. J. *The Achievement of Walter Scott.* London: Collins, 1969. A succinct but solid general introduction to Scott and his work that neatly places *The Lay of the Last Minstrel* in the broad context of Scott's literary production.

Davis, Lloyd. "The Story in History: Time and Truth in Scott's *The Lay of the Last Minstrel.*" *Clio* 18, no. 3 (1989): 221-238. An assiduous exploration and evaluation of the historical detail fleshed out in the notes to the 1830 edition of *The Lay of the Last Minstrel.*

Felluga, Dino Franco. *The Perversity of Poetry: Romantic Ideology and the Popular Male Poet of Genius.* Albany: State University of New York Press, 2005. An examination of the nineteenth century reception of Romantic poetry, focusing on the work of Scott and Lord Byron. Explores the manner in which Scott's poetry was represented as a panacea for the era's utilitarianism, capitalism, industrialism, and democracy.

Gamer, Michael. "'To Foist Thy Stale Romance': Scott, Antiquarianism, and Authorship." In *Romanticism and the Gothic: Genre, Reception, and Canon Formation.* New York: Cambridge University Press, 2000. An analysis of Scott's poetry and works by other Romantic writers, attempting to demonstrate the influence of the conventions of earlier gothic literature.

Goslee, Nancy Moore. *Scott the Rhymer.* Lexington: University Press of Kentucky, 1988. Includes separate chapters on *The Lay of the Last Minstrel* and other pastiches, providing one of few serious critiques of Scott's long poems undertaken since modern techniques of analysis were developed, and thus warranting serious attention.

Johnson, Edgar. *Sir Walter Scott: The Great Unknown.* 2 vols. New York: Macmillan, 1970. Intended to commemorate the two hundredth anniversary of Scott's birth, Johnson's critical biography remains one of the most important modern books on Scott. Has detailed discussions of his major poems, including *The Lay of the Last Minstrel.*

Lincoln, Andrew. "Towards the Modern Nation: *The Lay of the Last Minstrel, Marmion, The Lady of the Lake,* and *Waverly.*" In *Walter Scott and Modernity.* Edinburgh: Edinburgh University Press, 2007. Lincoln argues that Scott's poems and novels are not works of nostalgia, but that Scott uses depictions of the past to explore modernist moral, political, and social issues.

Lazarillo de Tormes

Author: Unknown
*First published: La vida de Lazarillo de Tormes y de
 sus fortunas y adversidades*, 1553 (English
 translation, 1576)
Type of work: Novel
Type of plot: Picaresque
Time of plot: Sixteenth century
Locale: Spain

Principal character:
LAZARILLO DE TORMES, a picaro

The Story:

Lazarillo's surname comes from the peculiar circumstance of his birth: His mother happened to stay the night at the mill where his father was employed, and Lazarillo was born on the mill floor just over the river Tormes, after which he was named. He has reached his ninth year when his father is caught taking flour from customers' sacks. After being soundly punished, the father joins an army that is preparing to move against the Moors. He becomes a mule driver for a gentleman soldier and is killed in action. Lazarillo's mother opens an eating house near a nobleman's estate, where she soon makes the acquaintance of Zayde, a black groom. Zayde begins to visit the widow and her son frequently; at first Lazarillo is afraid of the black man, but he quickly learns that Zayde's visits meant food and firewood. One consequence is a bit displeasing: Lazarillo acquires a small, dark brother to look after.

The nobleman's steward begins to notice that horseshoes and brushes, as well as other supplies used in the stables, are going missing. When he is asked directly about the thefts, Lazarillo tells all that he knows of Zayde's peccadillos. In punishment, Zayde is soundly flogged, and boiling fat is poured on his ribs. To avoid further scandal, Lazarillo's mother sets up a new eating house in a different neighborhood.

When Lazarillo is fairly well grown, his mother apprentices him to a blind man who wants a boy to lead him about. The elderly blind man is shrewd and tough. As he and Lazarillo are leaving the city, they pass by a stone statue of a bull. The blind man tells the boy to put his ear to the statue and listen for a peculiar noise, and when Lazarillo obeys, the old man knocks the boy's head sharply against the stone, hard enough so that his ears ring for three days. Lazarillo is thus forced to learn a few tricks for himself in order to survive.

Lazarillo notices that when the two of them squat over a fire to cook a meal, the blind man keeps his hand over the mouth of his wine jug. Surreptitiously, Lazarillo bores a tiny hole in the jug so that, lying down, he can let the liquid trickle into his mouth. He then plugs the hole with beeswax. The old man grows suspicious, and when he feels all over the surface of the jug, he finds the hole because the wax has melted. Giving no sign of what he has discovered, the next night he again puts the jug in front of him and Lazarillo again lies down next to it, expecting to drink wine once more. Suddenly the old man raises the jug and brings it down on Lazarillo's face with such great force that all the boy's teeth are loosened. On another occasion, Lazarillo seizes a roasting sausage from the spit and substitutes a rotten turnip. When the blind man bites into what he expects to be sausage, he roars with rage and scratches the boy severely with his long nails.

Lazarillo resolves to leave his master. Guiding the old man along the shores of a brook, Lazarillo positions him behind a stone pillar and then tells him that he must run and leap to clear the water. The old man gives a mighty jump, cracks his head on the stone, and falls down senseless. Lazarillo leaves town quickly.

His next master is a penurious priest who engages Lazarillo to assist at Mass. Unfortunately, the priest watches the collection box like a hawk, and Lazarillo has no chance to filch a single coin. For food, the priest allows him an onion every fourth day. If it were not for an occasional funeral feast, the boy would starve to death. The priest keeps his fine bread securely locked in a chest, and eventually Lazarillo is lucky enough to meet a strolling tinker who makes him a key to open the lock. To avoid suspicion when he eats the priest's bread, he gnaws each loaf to make it look as if rats had gotten into the chest. The alarmed priest nails up all the holes in the chest securely, but Lazarillo makes new holes. Then the priest sets numerous traps for the rats, from which Lazarillo eats the cheese. The puzzled priest is forced to conclude that a snake is stealing his bread.

Fearing a search while he is asleep, Lazarillo keeps his

key to the chest in his mouth while he is in bed. One night the key shifts, and as he breathes he blows air through the keyhole. The resulting whistle wakes the priest, who, seeing the key, seizes a club and breaks it over Lazarillo's head. After his head has been bandaged by a kind neighbor, Lazarillo is dismissed. Hoping to find employment in a larger city, he leaves to seek further fortune in Toledo.

One night in the city, while his pockets are full of crusts he has begged on the streets, a careless young dandy, a real esquire, engages Lazarillo as a servant. Thinking himself lucky to have a wealthy master, Lazarillo follows the young man to a bare, mean house that has scarcely a stick of furniture. After waiting a long time for a meal, the boy begins to eat his crusts. To his surprise, his master joins him. The days go by, both of them living on what Lazarillo can beg.

At last the esquire procures a little money and sends Lazarillo out for bread and wine. On the way, he meets a funeral procession. The weeping widow loudly laments her husband and cries out that the dead man is going to an inhospitable house where there is no food or furniture. Thinking that the procession is going to take the corpse to his esquire's house, Lazarillo runs home in fear. His master disabuses him of his fear and sends him back out on his errand.

At last the master leaves town, and Lazarillo is forced to meet the bailiffs and the wrathful landlord. After some difficulty, he persuades the bailiffs of his innocence and is allowed to go free.

His next master is a *bulero*, a dealer in papal indulgences, who is an accomplished rogue. Rumors begin to spread that his indulgences are forged, and even the bailiff accuses him publicly of fraud. The wily *bulero* prays openly for his accuser to be confounded, and forthwith the bailiff falls down in a fit, foaming at the mouth and growing rigid. The prayers and forgiveness of the *bulero* are effective, however, and little by little the bailiff recovers. From that time on the *bulero* earns a rich harvest selling his papal indulgences. Lazarillo, wise in roguery, wonders how the *bulero* has worked the trick, but he never finds out.

Four years of service with a chaplain who sells water enables Lazarillo to save a little money and buy respectable clothes. At last he is on his way to some standing in the community. On the strength of his new clothes, he is appointed to a government post that will furnish him an income for life. All business matters of the town pass through his hands.

The archpriest of Salvador, seeing how affluent Lazarillo has become, gives a woman from his own household to be Lazarillo's wife. The woman makes a useful wife, for the archpriest frequently gives them substantial presents. Lazarillo's wife repays the holy man by taking care of his wardrobe; however, evil tongues wag, and the archpriest asks Lazarillo if he has heard stories about his wife. Lazarillo discloses that he has been told that his wife had borne three of the archpriest's children. The archpriest advises him sagely to think of his profit more and his honor less. Lazarillo is content, for surely the archpriest is an honorable man.

Lazarillo eventually becomes so influential that it is said that he can commit any crime with impunity. His happiness increases when his wife presents him with a baby daughter. The good lady swears that the infant is truly Lazarillo's child.

Critical Evaluation:

In the fifteenth and sixteenth centuries, the Spanish novel began to develop into a modern form. This early novel form—particularly during the sixteenth century, the Spanish Golden Age—evolved into four types. The earliest was the novel of chivalry. *Amadís de Gaul*, written in about the mid-fourteenth century but not published until 1508, is one of the best known of this type. Next in chronological order was the dramatic novel—a novel in dialogue—of which Fernando de Rojas's *La Celestina* (1499; *Celestina*, 1631) is the prime example. The other two types appeared at approximately the same time, the mid-sixteenth century. One was the pastoral novel, the first and greatest being Jorge de Montemayor's *La Diana* (1559; *Diana of George of Montemayor*, 1598). The other was the picaresque novel, exemplified by *Lazarillo de Tormes*.

The anonymous *Lazarillo de Tormes* is generally conceded to be the earliest and the best of the picaresque novels. Episodic in form, the picaresque novel's narrative is usually told in the first person, the story dealing with the life of a picaro, or rogue, who is narrator and protagonist. In spite of much scholarly investigation, the origins of the terms "picaresque" and "picaro" are still in doubt, and etymological research has so far proved fruitless. "Picaro," however, is understood to designate a wandering knave, a poor adventurer, who lives by his wits on the fringes of a class-conscious society and who must subordinate the luxury of ethics to the necessities of survival. Since the picaro typically serves several masters sequentially and in the course of his service observes their weaknesses and those of others, the picaresque novel becomes an ideal vehicle for depicting a wide cross section of society and, with its satirical tone, manages to attack broad segments of that society in the process. The picaresque elements of satire, parody, caricature, and the like are not unique to picaresque novels, however. These traits also exist in earlier literature—such as *El libro de buen amor* (1330; *The Book of Good Love*, 1933), by Juan Ruiz, the archpriest of Hita, and Rojas's *La Celestina*—that influenced the development of the picaresque novel. Still, it is in the picaresque novel that society is held up to most careful scrutiny and receives the most scathing denunciation.

In addition, *Lazarillo de Tormes* is often thought, by virtue of its form, to be autobiographical. The likelihood that this is the case, however, is slim. The anonymous author refers to Latin authors (improbable for a real-life Lazarillo) and reveals a distinct influence of the philosopher Erasmus (equally improbable for Lazarillo, whose formal education might charitably be described as lacking). The intrinsically fascinating adventures of Lazarillo need no autobiographical buttress. The instant and enduring popularity of the novel—three editions from 1554 alone are extant—is testimony to its compelling qualities as literature. So, too, is the fact of its translation into many languages: French, English, Dutch, German, and Italian versions of *Lazarillo de Tormes* appeared within less than seventy years of the work's first publication, and others followed. Imitation is another gauge of the novel's popularity and influence: In addition to Alain-René Lesage's *Histoire de Gil Blas de Santillane* (1715-1735; *The History of Gil Blas of Santillane*, 1716, 1735; better known as *Gil Blas*, 1749, 1962), among many others, two sequels to *Lazarillo de Tormes* were written. Perhaps the ultimate accolade, however, was that the novel was placed on the Catholic Church's list of forbidden books, the *Index librorum prohibitorum*, for its anticlericalism, an element of the work that is routinely attributed to the influence of Erasmus.

As a character, Lazarillo is not original, cut from the whole cloth of the author's imagination. Before becoming the novel's protagonist, he was a character in folklore, with his name appearing in early proverbs and anecdotes. In fact, a quarter century before *Lazarillo de Tormes* was published, Lazarillo had a cameo role in Francisco Delicado's novel *La Lozana Andaluza* (1528; *Portrait of Lozana: The Lusty Andalusian Woman*, 1987), which features a *pícara*, a female rogue after the *La Celestina* model. Following *Lazarillo de Tormes*, however, Lazarillo himself became such a staple that the name itself became a generic term for those who guide the blind.

The most important aspect of *Lazarillo de Tormes*, however, is its satire, and the targets of this satire are lined up like ducks in a shooting gallery. All told, Lazarillo serves seven masters before becoming his own master, so to speak. The story is thus divided into seven *tratados* (treatises or chapters), each dealing with a particular employer. The first is the blind beggar; the next, a priest; the third, a nobleman; the fourth, a friar; the fifth, a seller of indulgences; the sixth, a chaplain; the last, a constable. After narrating his unconven-

tional background, Lazarillo launches his attack on social stratification, beginning with the blind man and continuing through the penniless nobleman and the constable; his harshest commentary, however, is reserved for the clergy—priest, friar, seller of indulgences, and chaplain—whose duplicity and venality are a constant source of amazement and embarrassment to him. Lazarillo's implicit and explicit criticism of the clergy constitutes the preponderant thrust of the novel. His observations are astute, and the account accurately reflects contemporary conditions. Nevertheless, in such perceptivity lies a challenge to the status quo, a challenge that those in power were obliged to suppress, as they did by banning the novel.

Above all, *Lazarillo de Tormes* conveys a mood, a temper, a tenor: a cynical antidote to the idealistic worldviews, secular or religious, that characterized the medieval age of faith. In this sense, the novel is refreshing, breathing clear air into a musty, closed era. It wafts a clarity that should, but does not, make the blind man see, the exploiter turn philanthropist, the self-seeking cleric become true shepherd, and so on. The unalloyed power of this novel in fact stems from its lack of malice: It deplores corruption, but it does not hate.

Although it focuses on the lower levels of society, the novel is not intended to reform. Although it attacks clerical depredations, it is not sacrilegious. Still, *Lazarillo de Tormes* is, in the last analysis, more than a bitter tale of personal privation. It is a realistic commentary—a foil to the competing idealism of chivalric romances—on life as it is actually lived by common people who have neither privilege nor power. Beyond cynicism and despair, the novel offers hope for better things to come, since Lazarillo ultimately gets his foot on the bottom rung of the ladder to respectable success. As town crier, he has a steady, assured income, even if his wife is a hand-me-down mistress of the archpriest of Salvador. Lazarillo is willing thus to compromise. The reader is inclined to respect Lazarillo's judgment in this and other matters of the art of survival.

"Critical Evaluation" by Joanne G. Kashdan

Further Reading

Alter, Robert. *Rogue's Progress: Studies in the Picaresque Novel*. Cambridge, Mass.: Harvard University Press, 1964. Discusses several picaresque novels, beginning with *Lazarillo de Tormes*, and, by stretching the meaning of "picaresque," traces the form's survival into the twentieth century.

Bjornson, Richard. *The Picaresque Hero in European Fiction*. Madison: University of Wisconsin Press, 1977.

Presents an expansive survey of picaresque literature in Spain, Germany, England, and France. Asserts that the author of *Lazarillo de Tormes* was among the first to realize "the novel's potential as a serious form of literary expression."

Camino, Mercedes Maroto. *Practising Places: Saint Teresa, Lazarillo, and the Early Modern City.* Atlanta: Rodopi, 2001. Provides a close interpretation of *Lazarillo de Tormes* as part of an examination of the culture of early modern Spain through literature, paintings, and the history of urban areas.

Deyermond, A. D. *"Lazarillo de Tormes": A Critical Guide.* London: Grant & Cutler in association with Tamesis Books, 1975. Discusses the novel in its social and religious context, and analyzes the novel's structure, style, and imagery. An indispensable resource. Includes an annotated bibliography.

Fiore, Robert L. *Lazarillo de Tormes.* Boston: Twayne, 1984. Good starting point for the general reader devotes a chapter to the novel's disputed authorship and concludes by praising the work as being "universal in scope." Includes chronology and annotated bibliography.

Maiorino, Giancarlo. *At the Margins of the Renaissance: "Lazarillo de Tormes" and the Picaresque Art of Survival.* University Park: Pennsylvania State University Press, 2003. Argues that *Lazarillo de Tormes* originated in the "culture of indigence" that existed at the margins of Spanish Renaissance society and demonstrates how the work challenged that society's authoritarian ambitions.

Sánchez, Francisco J. *An Early Bourgeois Literature in Golden Age Spain: "Lazarillo de Tormes," "Guzmán de Alfarache," and Baltasar Gracián.* Chapel Hill: North Carolina Studies in the Romance Languages and Literatures, 2003. Chronicles the emergence of a middle-class literature in Golden Age Spain, focusing on the picaresque novels *Lazarillo de Tormes* and Mateo Alemán's *Guzmán de Alfarache* (1599) and on the works of Baltasar Gracián. Describes how these works represented bourgeois values and sensibilities and how they treated contemporary notions of person, culture, and life.

Leaves of Grass

Author: Walt Whitman (1819-1892)
First published: 1855
Type of work: Poetry

"America" is the first word of Walt Whitman's 1855 preface to *Leaves of Grass*, but this most American of poetic achievements is also the most universal. "The United States themselves are essentially the greatest poem," Whitman says, a belief that informs *Leaves of Grass* and led Whitman to redefine "poem" in such a way as to change forever the face of poetry.

Whitman paid for the publication of the first version of *Leaves of Grass* and even set some of the type himself. It is a slim volume, containing a preface and twelve poems, each several pages in length, sprawling across the pages, and looking quite unlike the neatly rhymed and metered poems then popular with readers. Whitman revised and expanded the book six times and reprinted it twice more. The final and most complete version of *Leaves of Grass*, published while Whitman was near death (1891-1892), includes hundreds of pages and dozens of poems. Through its various versions, *Leaves of Grass* always remained a unified whole, and several themes and stylistic innovations remain constant.

Whitman believed that his lyrical epic poem about a new land required a new voice. *Leaves of Grass* represents a major innovation in poetic form. It is the first great nineteenth century work in English in what has come to be called free verse, poetry without obvious rhyme or meter. Whitman draws on other poets' experiments with unrhymed, nonmetrical poetry and on the sonorous rhythms of the King James version of the Bible, but he develops the form in volume and expressive power. Free verse—long lines and loose rhythmic structure—became the perfect vehicle for poems with themes of identity, nationality, and transcendence.

At best, the poems of *Leaves of Grass* are brilliantly rhythmic, with an eloquent use of the American language to describe ordinary experience. In "The blab of the pave, tires of carts, sluff of boot-soles," for example, colloquial diction and onomatopoeia re-create the sights and sounds of the streets. Whitman takes risks by presenting himself as a typical American working man, "one of the roughs" and a democratic Everyman, but also as a poet of frank sexuality. This image of the poet as sensuous Everyman represents the masterly centerpiece of all the versions of *Leaves of Grass*, that long poem that Whitman did not title in 1855 but that he eventually called "Song of Myself." In the 1855 edition, Whitman's name does not appear on the title page but it appears in the poem: "Walt Whitman, an American, one of the roughs, a kosmos,/ Disorderly fleshy and sensual . . . eating drinking and breeding."

"Myself" in the poem is and is not Whitman, for the poem is at once personal and an elevation of the individual to the mythic. A central idea of "Song of Myself" is that the cycle of life constantly renews itself and so triumphs over death: "The smallest sprout shows there really is no death."

Whitman is preeminently a poet of joy and of the intersection of body and soul: "I and this mystery here we stand." Individual identity therefore becomes at once fragile and transcendent. The individual dies and "life" goes on. By recognizing and absorbing this knowledge, Whitman says, all may feel unity with life and so triumph over death.

Early in "Song of Myself," Whitman introduces leaves as a metaphor, likening the grass to a flag, handkerchief, child, and hieroglyphic, "the beautiful uncut hair of graves" and "so many uttering tongues." By using metaphor, Whitman helps the reader see grass differently. Like the speaker, who is an ordinary man, grass represents an ordinary creation so plentiful it is likely to go unnoticed. However, just as in a democracy every voice is important, in *Leaves of Grass* every leaf is a reminder of the beauty and transcendence of life.

Like *Leaves of Grass* as a whole, "Song of Myself" progresses toward its climax by dilating and contracting on a number of themes and images. Section by section, this poem includes many subtle and not-so-subtle modulations in tone. Sometimes these shifts occur from one section to the next, from, for example, "twenty-eight young men bathe by the shore" (section 11) to "the butcher-boy puts off his killing-clothes" (section 12). Over the larger structure of the poem, Whitman's expression ranges from passages of personal emotion such as "To touch my person to some one else's is about as much as I can stand" (section 27) to descriptive passages that, while also intensely emotional, find their focus outside the speaker's consciousness, as in "The spotted hawk swoops by" (section 89).

The sections of the poem shuttle constantly between general and specific, between description and emotion, and between the body and the soul. These shifts are appropriate to the theme of endless renewal, but "Song of Myself" also moves toward a conclusion in which the poet disappears

into the cycle of life, and readers are left to find their own way.

The roughness and sensuality of *Leaves of Grass* offended and even frightened many of Whitman's early readers. "Song of Myself" in particular still has the power to surprise and even shock, as when Whitman says in section 24, "The scent of these arm-pits aroma finer than prayer," words that still dismay some readers. Sexuality is the common denominator of human beings, and Whitman wants to strip away pretense (represented by clothing) to reveal the naked body, which is also the naked soul, for soul and body are one: "Behold," he says in "Starting from Paumanok," "the body includes and is . . . the soul."

In addition to long poems such as "Song of Myself," the smaller poems in *Leaves of Grass* also contribute to the book's unity. Many readers have found homoerotic imagery in Whitman's celebration of "adhesiveness" and "manly love," though Whitman himself denied that connection. In "I Saw in Louisiana a Live Oak Growing," which first appears in *Leaves of Grass* in 1860, Whitman uses the live oak tree as an image of solitary strength; unlike the tree, the speaker says he could not live "without a friend or lover near." In another major poem that appears in every version of *Leaves of Grass*, "The Sleepers," Whitman provides counterpoint to the joyous optimism of "Song of Myself" when he describes the narrator going from bedside to bedside like an angel overseeing suffering humanity. The imagery of "The Sleepers" takes on a special poignancy from the fact that, long after he wrote this poem, Whitman cared for hospitalized soldiers during the American Civil War. When his brother, George, was listed among those wounded at the Battle of Fredericksburg, he headed south to look for him; George's wound was slight, but Whitman stayed on in Washington, D.C., to visit the sick and wounded soldiers in the military hospitals.

Whitman's charitable work in the hospitals allowed him to participate in the war without fighting and to express his complex amorous and charitable feelings toward men. These feelings surface in *Leaves of Grass*:

I stand in the dark with drooping eyes
    by the worst-suffering and most restless,
I pass my hands soothingly to and fro a
    few inches from them,
The restless sink in their beds,
    they fitfully sleep.

"The Sleepers" is a difficult, visionary poem, full of troubled and troubling imagery, as in the line "The wretched features of the ennuyés, the white features of corpses." The poem has the quality of a nightmare but might more accurately be characterized—as it was by Whitman's friend and first biographer, Richard M. Bucke—as "a representation of the mind during sleep" moving rapidly over loosely connected images. The central metaphors are darkness and sleep, which stand for confusion and death. In the end, however, just as night disappears into sunrise, death must disappear into life and the poem returns to the affirmative voice of "Song of Myself."

"Crossing Brooklyn Ferry," added to *Leaves of Grass* in 1856, describes the immortality of the individual across the sweep of time. As the speaker rides a ferryboat across the East River, he contemplates the crowd on the boat, the flow of the water, and the motion of the boat, finding in them a transcendent continuity: "It avails not, time nor place—distance avails not,/ I am with you, you men and women of a generation, of ever so many generations hence." When he is gone, other people will look at the crowd and think the same thoughts he is thinking. These others will in that sense become him. By accepting one's own identity, by trusting life and the soul's natural impulses, one can be happy and recognize the interrelationship with all of life, past, present, and future.

"Out of the Cradle Endlessly Rocking," published first in 1871 in a separate volume of poems entitled *Passage to India*, and later incorporated into the expanded 1881 edition of *Leaves of Grass*, is a poem of reminiscence. The speaker looks back on his boyhood to a time when, near the ocean, he is awakened from innocence to an empathetic experience of a male mockingbird's loss of his mate. This empathy leads him directly to an enlightened state that gives him a sense of his identity and his vocation as a poet, or a bard. By revising "Out of the Cradle Endlessly Rocking," Whitman brings the italicized sections representing the mockingbird's song to an increasingly subtle onomatopoeia, which unites the bird's song and the poet's words just as the poet's empathy for the bird's loss has united them through the bird's song. "My own songs awaked from that hour," the speaker says.

"When Lilacs Last in the Dooryard Bloom'd," Whitman's great elegy for Abraham Lincoln, also first appears in *Passage to India*, before it become part of *Leaves of Grass* in 1881. Just as "Out of the Cradle Endlessly Rocking" weaves together a bird's song, ocean, beach, and memory, "When Lilacs Last in the Dooryard Bloom'd" uses three key symbols—the blooming lilac, the "western fallen star," and the warbling of a thrush in a swamp—to mourn the death of Lincoln: "Lilac and star and bird twined with the chant of my soul." Whitman adored Lincoln as the preserver of the Union, and in this poem he pays homage to Lincoln's greatness and comes to terms with his tragic death.

In "A Passage to India," the title poem of the 1871 collection of that name, Whitman celebrates the great breakthroughs in communication during his lifetime: the Suez Canal, which opened access to the East; the transcontinental railroad, which made travel across the United States easier; and the laying of telegraph cables across the Atlantic and Pacific oceans, which made virtually instantaneous international communication possible. Whitman himself describes that the poem concerns the way evolution unfolds "cosmic purposes."

Leaves of Grass is a work of integration and wholeness. Through its dozens of poems and many revisions, the central themes of the work—the transcendence of the individual through knowledge of the wholeness and continuity of life, the naturalness of death, and the beauty of the living world—serve to describe the joy Whitman took in his own American century.

Thomas Lisk

Further Reading

Allen, Gay Wilson. *A Reader's Guide to Walt Whitman.* New York: Farrar, Straus & Giroux, 1970. A succinct survey intended to be an introductory work for readers and students. A good place to start a study of Whitman.

_____. *The Solitary Singer: A Critical Biography of Walt Whitman.* Chicago: University of Chicago Press, 1985. First published in 1955, this biography remains one of the best life-and-works sources available on Whitman.

Belasco, Susan, Ed Folsom, and Kenneth M. Price, eds. *"Leaves of Grass": The Sesquicentennial Essays.* Lincoln: University of Nebraska Press, 2007. Twenty essays reassess the collection more than 150 years after its 1855 publication. Includes discussions of the work's historical context, the poetry marketplace, the visionary and visual in Whitman's poetics, and the centennial celebration of the book's publication.

Folsom, Ed, ed. *Walt Whitman: The Centennial Essays.* Iowa City: University of Iowa Press, 1994. A collection of essays in honor of the centennial of Whitman's death. Provides a good overview of trends in literary criticism of *Leaves of Grass*.

Kaplan, Justin. *Walt Whitman: A Life.* New York: Simon & Schuster, 1980. An elegant, deeply imagined biography that focuses on Whitman and his times.

Kummings, Donald D., ed. *A Companion to Walt Whitman.* Malden, Mass.: Blackwell, 2006. Examines Whitman's life, the cultural and historical context of his works, his use of language, his writing style, and the reception and legacy of his writings. Some of the essays analyze individual poems in *Leaves of Grass*.

Maslan, Mark. *Whitman Possessed: Poetry, Sexuality, and Popular Authority*. Baltimore: Johns Hopkins University Press, 2001. Analyzes Whitman's poetry in relation to nineteenth century theories of sexual hygiene, sexual desire, poetic inspiration, and political representation.

Miller, James E. *"Leaves of Grass": America's Lyric-Epic of Self and Democracy*. New York: Twayne, 1992. An excellent introduction to the background, themes, and style of *Leaves of Grass*. Especially helpful on the work's structure.

Pearce, Roy Harvey, ed. *Whitman: A Collection of Critical Essays*. Englewood Cliffs, N.J.: Prentice-Hall, 1962. A collection of articles gathered primarily for use by students. Contains interesting material, including poet William Carlos Williams's "An Essay on *Leaves of Grass*."

Sowder, Michael. *Whitman's Ecstatic Union: Conversion and Ideology in "Leaves of Grass."* New York: Routledge, 2005. Analyzes the religious elements in the first three editions of the collection, reading the poems within the context of antebellum evangelicalism. Argues that Whitman, like the evangelical preachers, sought to induce ecstasy and provide new definitions of identity.

The Left Hand of Darkness

Author: Ursula K. Le Guin (1929-   )
First published: 1969
Type of work: Novel
Type of plot: Science fiction
Time of plot: Hainish Cycle 93, Ekumenical year 1490-1497
Locale: The planet Gethen (also known as Winter)

Principal characters:
GENLY AI, the envoy from Ekumen to Gethen
THEREM HARTH REM IR ESTRAVEN, a Karhidish noble and official
KING ARGAVEN XV, ruler of the country of Karhide on Gethen
THE COMMENSALS, top officials of Orgota, a country on Gethen

The Story:

Genly Ai, the Ekumen's envoy to the planet Gethen/Winter, is dealt a setback in his mission to recruit Gethen to the Ekumen when Therem Harth rem ir Estraven, formerly Ai's ally, withdraws support. Estraven has fallen from favor with Karhide's King Argaven XV because his efforts to avoid a war between his country and the neighboring nation of Orgoreyn have caused the king to lose *shifgrethor*, a complex Karhidish version of honor. Estraven tries to explain to Ai that his new coolness toward the Ekumen is a ploy to keep his dishonor from infecting the Ekumen's mission, but Ai, a stranger to the intricate subtleties of *shifgrethor* and still unused to Gethen's politics, fails to see anything but betrayal in Estraven's actions.

Ai's alien nature haunts his mission. He is unused to the planet's intense cold, its complex cultural codes, and, most of all, its unique form of human sexuality. Gethenians are ambisexual, uninterested four-fifths of the time, then intensely sexual during "kemmer," when they might manifest as male for a kemmer or two, then female during the next cycle. Ai persists in trying to interpret Gethenians as men

or women, even though intellectually he knows better. The Gethenians face a similar problem in that they view Ai's persistent maleness as a perversion.

Ai meets with the king on the day Estraven is banished from the country. Argaven, although suspicious of the Ekumen and Ai, nevertheless gives the envoy freedom to travel throughout Karhide. Ai uses his freedom to explore, and he meets with the Handdara Foretellers, who practice a meditative religion based on unlearning what culture has taught them. For the price of two rubies, the Foretellers undertake to answer Ai's question, Will Gethen join the Ekumen within five years? Their answer, after a harrowing ceremony, comes back as a single word—yes.

Ai applies for admission to the neighboring country of Orgoreyn, where Estraven has fled after his banishment. Estraven's influence gains him swift entry, and Ai immediately notices differences between the nations: Karhide is feudal and anarchic; Orgoreyn is socialistic and totalitarian.

Ai's first night in Orgoreyn is disrupted by raiders from Karhide, involved in the same Sinoth valley land dispute that has cost Estraven his position. Ai's escape from the raiders puts him in contact with the Orgota, who strike him as an excessively passive people, in contrast to the highly individualistic and passionate Karhiders. He spends a night locked in a grain bin with others displaced by the raid, then is recognized by officialdom and given a vehicle and a pass to take him to the capital city, Mishnory, where he is welcomed by Commissioner Shusgis.

For a while, Ai is feted by the Commensals who rule Orgota, but then subtle changes occur. Estraven, living in the capital, recognizes that no news of Ai's presence has been communicated to the rest of the country. His diplomatic experience has taught him that, in this country ruled by secret police, this is a bad sign, and he hurries to warn Ai. The envoy distrusts Estraven too much to take immediate action, however, so when government agents come to arrest him in the night, they face no opposition.

Ai is taken first to Kunderer Prison, where he is drugged and questioned for days on end. Then officials load him onto a truck with dozens of other prisoners and send him on a nightmarish journey to a voluntary farm. The envoy nearly dies on the journey; the truck is unheated, the prisoners are not fed, and, at the standard rate of twenty-five miles per hour—not including long, inexplicable stops—the trip takes many days to accomplish.

Once at the farm, Ai is fed inadequately, worked moderately, and again subjected to repeated inquisitions. The drugs administered to him during the interrogations prove toxic to his alien system, and soon he lies comatose for days after each session.

Estraven has followed Ai through Orgota, using falsified papers. Despite his seeming treachery, Estraven believes entirely in Ai's mission, and, in the underground ways of Gethen, has been working ceaselessly for Ai's benefit. He buys provisions for a long winter journey and then, posing as a guard, carries the unconscious Ai out of Pulefen Farm.

To make their escape, the two must cross the Gobrin Ice, an almost impossible journey in winter. They have enough food for seventy-eight days and approximately eight hundred miles to cover. During the journey, which throws Ai and Estraven into extremely close contact and taxes both to their physical limits, Estraven goes into kemmer, his sexual phase. It is this that finally brings the two together, as Ai realizes the sexual prejudice that has kept him from seeing Estraven as fully human.

By the end of their journey, they have used up all their supplies and have been without food for three days. When they finally reach Karhide, Estraven sends Ai to sell the valuable stove they used on the journey and then use the money to buy transmission time from a local radio station to call his ship out of orbit. While Ai is doing this, Estraven is betrayed by an old acquaintance. He flees for the border, is shot by the guards, and dies in Ai's arms.

Saddened, but determined not to let his friend's death destroy their mutual goal, Ai approaches King Argaven once more and secures Karhide's decision to enter the Ekumen. After the Ekumen ship lands and final details have been settled, Ai journeys to Estraven's home, where he meets his friend's child and tells him of "other worlds out among the stars—the other kinds of men, the other lives."

Critical Evaluation:

Ursula K. Le Guin has described *The Left Hand of Darkness* as a thought experiment, a place where she changed the world in her imagination, then observed how this change affected her understanding of human nature. The book was written in 1969, near the start of the late twentieth century women's movement, when women were struggling with the issues of what is essential about their gender and what seemingly gender-driven behaviors are the results of cultural adaptation. The novel won two prestigious awards, the Hugo and the Nebula, both given for excellence in the genre of science fiction.

Drawing on her background in mythology and anthropology, Le Guin incorporates several different points of view in chapters that retell the mythical tales of the planet and other chapters written as scientific reports from the Ekumen's first, anonymous corps of observers. All deal with the concepts of duality and unity, and seek to explain how the Gethenians' unique sexual nature has influenced their civilization and worldview.

Some critics, including science-fiction writer Stanisław Lem, have taken Le Guin to task for creating androgynous beings who seem more male than female. She has challenged these critics to show her a single action performed by a character in the novel that had to be performed by a specifically male or female character. At the same time, she has noted, the novel does not show many characters engaging in activities that have traditionally been regarded as feminine, such as child rearing. Le Guin has also lamented the lack of a genderless pronoun in the English language that would have allowed her to avoid calling the Gethenians "he" and "him."

Without a male/female split to suggest an intrinsically dualistic worldview to the Gethenians, they have created a society that, in many ways, seeks to see all in one. Genly Ai at one moment muses, "Perhaps you are as obsessed with wholeness as we are with dualism." Because this world is seen through Genly Ai's eyes, readers can perceive how different it is from their own experience. Ai cannot shake his desire to see Gethenians as male or female, nor can he feel comfortable with someone who does not give him some sexual regard. He continually describes Estraven using feminine qualities as the basis for his dislike, calling the other "womanly, all charm and tact and lack of substance." This shifts during their flight across the Gobrin Ice, when Estraven enters kemmer. He asks Ai about women, bringing the envoy to realize that gender is "the heaviest single factor in one's life" and that he knows nothing of a woman's life, that women are, in fact, "more alien to me than you are."

While Le Guin exposes disturbing trends in the ways culture shapes gendered behavior, she does not advocate life without duality. As Ai and Estraven realize, even in the absence of a second gender, humans will always face the gap between self and other. Le Guin insists, however, that humans seek the creative tension between opposites that comes when both sides of a duality are honored. She shows the importance of this as she compares the two religions of Gethen: the Handdara, which actively explores the dark unknowns of human existence, and the Yomeshta, which insists that light is the only truth. The Handdara religion has made Karhide anarchic and individualistic, but essentially human. The Yomeshta, worshiping Orgota, have created a socialistic bureaucracy in which the individual is completely subordinated to the public good. As a result, the Orgota commit acts of great barbarity without any thought of conscience.

The shadow as metaphor for other also surfaces as Ai and Estraven labor across the Gobrin Ice. The weather changes to a white mist, and the shadows disappear, leading Ai to realize that without the shadows he cannot see the dangers that lie in his path: the crevasses, the rotten ice, the cracks. He draws the Daoist yin-yang symbol for Estraven, finally understanding in a deep way the need for duality in the world and the ability of one human being to contain both light and shadow, working in creative harmony.

Le Guin's depiction of the world of Gethen in minute and realistic detail further adds to the thematic material of the novel. Winter is both a cruel reality of the planet and a mythological setting for the journey Gethenians make from an isolated and relatively static planet to a planet preparing to join an alliance of similarly human, yet largely alien, brethren. Genly Ai's journey, beginning and ending in spring, takes both him and Gethen from a flowering abundance to near destruction and back, into a springtime of regeneration and re-creation.

Susan E. Keegan

Further Reading

Bernardo, Susan M., and Graham J. Murphy. *Ursula K. Le Guin: A Critical Companion.* Westport, Conn.: Greenwood Press, 2006. Provides biographical information on the author as well as analyses of her works. Chapter 3 is devoted to discussion of *The Left Hand of Darkness.*

Bloom, Harold, ed. *Ursula K. Le Guin.* New York: Chelsea House, 1986. Collection of previously published essays is arranged chronologically, tracing the general critical reception of Le Guin's novels.

_____. *Ursula K. Le Guin's "The Left Hand of Darkness."* New York: Chelsea House, 1987. Collection of nine previously published essays examines the novel from a variety of perspectives, including feminism and speech-act theory. Martin Bickman's essay on the novel's unity persuasively counters earlier charges that the Gethenians' ambisexuality is irrelevant to the plot.

Cadden, Mike. *Ursula K. Le Guin Beyond Genre: Fiction for Children and Adults.* New York: Routledge, 2005. Examines Le Guin's work for children, young adults, and adults, tracing the similarities in her handling of these genres. Includes an interview in which Le Guin discusses her writing practices and the origins of some of her works.

Cummins, Elizabeth. *Understanding Ursula K. Le Guin.* Columbia: University of South Carolina Press, 1990. Chapter 3 compares *The Left Hand of Darkness* to Le Guin's other novels about the results of Hainish experiments. Includes a good annotated bibliography.

Ketterer, David. "*The Left Hand of Darkness*: Ursula Le Guin's Archetypal Winter Journey." In *New Worlds for Old: The Apocalyptic Imagination, Science Fiction, and American Literature.* Garden City, N.Y.: Anchor, 1974. Looks at Le Guin's use of myth in the novel, especially as it concerns her depictions of duality and mystical unity. Ketterer was the first to describe the mythology of winter as contained in the book.

Le Guin, Ursula K. *The Language of the Night: Essays on Fantasy and Science Fiction.* Edited by Susan Wood. Rev. ed. New York: HarperPerennial, 1993. In the important essay "Is Gender Necessary?" Le Guin critiques her own novel as a feminist experiment—not wholly successful—in which she tried to discover the essence of humanity by eliminating gender.

Rochelle, Warren. *Communities of the Heart: The Rhetoric of Myth in the Fiction of Ursula K. Le Guin.* Liverpool, England: Liverpool University Press, 2001. Focuses on Le Guin's use of myth as a form of rhetorical persuasion. Compares the author to other "romantic/pragmatic rhetoricians" such as Ralph Waldo Emerson, Henry David Thoreau, and Walt Whitman.

Spivack, Charlotte. *Ursula K. Le Guin.* Boston: Twayne, 1984. Provides thorough discussion of all of Le Guin's

works through the early 1980's. Examination of *The Left Hand of Darkness* includes sections on its narrative structure, its use of mythology, the political and religious themes in the novel, and its critical reception.

The Legend of Good Women

Author: Geoffrey Chaucer (c. 1343-1400)
First published: 1380-1386
Type of work: Poetry

Principal characters:
CHAUCER, the dreamer
CUPID, the god of love
ALCESTE, the wife of Admetus, the king of Pherae
CLEOPATRA, the queen of Egypt
THISBE, the beloved of Pyramus
DIDO, the queen of Carthage
HYPSIPYLE, the queen of Lemnos, who is betrayed by Jason
MEDEA, the princess of Colchis, who is betrayed by Jason
LUCRETIA, a Roman matron raped by Tarquin
ARIADNE, a Cretan princess betrayed by Theseus
PHILOMELA, an Athenian princess raped by Tereus
PHYLLIS, a Greek maiden betrayed by Demophon
HYPERMNESTRA, the daughter of Danaüs, the king of Egypt

The Legend of Good Women, a poem recounting the stories of women from history and myth who were martyrs to love, is written in the tradition of medieval love poetry. Unlike Geoffrey Chaucer's masterpieces, *Troilus and Criseyde* (c. 1382) and *The Canterbury Tales* (1387-1400), this work only occasionally rises above the limitations imposed by the artificial conventions of the times and is, therefore, somewhat inferior to these other works. Chaucer's greatness as a poet resulted less from his ability to perfect the current modes of writing than from his capacity to transcend them. Although his debt to contemporary thought and literary practice was considerable, his lasting position among English writers depends largely on his gift for bringing reality to a literature that was customarily unrealistic. In *The Legend of Good Women*, however, he constructed a framework so restrictive as to prevent his being able to infuse it with the richness and subtle shadings of human existence.

The most engaging part of the poem is the prologue, in which Chaucer expresses his elation at the arrival of spring and his delight in roaming through the meadows, listening to

the small birds, and gazing at the flowers. He is especially attracted to the daisy, which he can observe for hours without becoming bored. One spring day, after a walk in the fields, he falls asleep and has a vision in which the god of love and the beautiful Alceste, dressed in the colors of the daisy, appear before him. Cupid denounces the dreamer for having committed heresy against the laws of love in writing of Criseyde's infidelity and translating the *Romaunt of the Rose* (c. 1370), with its disparaging remarks about womankind. Cupid's companion (the same Alceste whom Hercules rescued from Hades after she had given her life to redeem her husband from death) rises to the poet's defense by contending that he, having appropriated his plots from other writers, has acted out of ignorance, not malice. She concludes that he might gain Cupid's forgiveness by writing a legendry of wives and maidens who have been faithful in love all of their lives.

The prologue is filled with literary devices popular in the fourteenth century. The religion of love—which had its sins, penances, self-abnegation, and sanctity, as well as the figures of Cupid and Alceste, somewhat analogous to God and the Virgin Mary—closely paralleled the Christian religion. The daisy had recently replaced the rose as the symbol of love. Chaucer touches on the question of whether the flower or the leaf is superior, apparently a hotly debated issue in courtly circles, but the poet does not commit himself. The dream-vision used here had been a very popular device ever since the appearance of the *Romaunt of the Rose*, and Chaucer himself employed it in several works. Despite this elaborate machinery, which today is mainly of historic interest, the prologue has about it a universal appeal; cheerfulness, humor, and a tinge of ironic detachment preserve it from mediocrity. Also delightful is Chaucer's expression of pleasure in nature.

According to the prologue, Chaucer planned to write twenty tales about good women. He finished eight and left a ninth just short of completion. The theme of all the legends is the fidelity of women in love. All the heroines suffer for, and the majority die for, their love. All are treated as wholly admirable, even saintly, without regard to the illicit nature of some of the relationships presented. Events in their lives that are not concerned with their fidelity are omitted or hastily summarized. With the exception of the first two legends, the women suffer as the result of the treachery of men, who are generally thoroughgoing villains.

The longest and one of the best of the legends retells the story of Dido's love for Aeneas. After Aeneas lands on the Libyan coast, he meets Venus, his mother, who instructs him to go to the court of Dido, the queen of Carthage. Dido greets him cordially and, knowing of his flight from Troy, feels great pity for the disinherited hero. With her pity comes love, and to comfort and entertain Aeneas during his visit, she provides everything her riches can command.

One day, when Aeneas, Dido, and her retinue are hunting, a thunderstorm bursts upon them. Everyone rushes for shelter, and Dido and Aeneas find themselves together in a cave. There the perfidious Aeneas protests his love for her, and she, after much importuning, has pity and yields herself to him. For a time afterward, Aeneas does everything a courtly lover should, but finally, becoming weary, he makes plans to leave. When Dido notes his lessened ardor and asks him what is wrong, he tells her of a vision he has had (a pure fabrication, Chaucer implies) in which his father has reminded him of his destiny to conquer Italy. Ignoring Dido's pleas, Aeneas steals away to his ships without her. As soon as she discovers his absence, she has her sister build a funeral pyre upon which she stabs herself, using Aeneas's sword.

Chaucer's principal source for this tale was Vergil's *Aeneid* (c. 29-19 B.C.E.; English translation, 1553), to which he made only slight modifications in the plot but substantial changes in characterization. Dido, who in Vergil's telling does not escape censure, is made blameless by Chaucer, mainly by his elaboration of the scene in the cave. By minimizing the intervention of the gods and degrading Aeneas's motives, Chaucer turns Vergil's pious Aeneas into a mere seducer. He thus transforms a story of tragic struggle between love and duty into one of man's treachery and woman's loyalty.

Chaucer's source for "The Legend of Lucretia" was Ovid's *Fasti* (c. 8 C.E.; English translation, 1859), which he followed quite closely. To prove the virtues of his wife, Lucretia, Collatinus offers to accompany Tarquin, the king's son, to Rome to see her. Secreted outside her chamber door, they find her spinning among her servants and expressing concern for her husband's safety. Tarquin, observing her beauty, conceives a great desire for her. The next day, his lust increasing, he determines to return to Collatinus's house and seduce Lucretia. Stealing into her room at night, he threatens her at the point of a sword and, while she lies in a swoon, rapes her. After he leaves, Lucretia dresses in mourning, calls her friends about her, and tells them what has happened. Declaring that her husband shall not gain a foul name from her guilt, she stabs herself.

"The Legend of Hypsipyle and Medea" recounts the double treachery of Jason. On his expedition to recover the Golden Fleece, Jason stops at the island of Lemnos, where he and Hercules meet Queen Hypsipyle and conspire to win her for Jason. While Jason counterfeits modesty, Hercules extols his virtues, thus ensnaring Hypsipyle, who consents to marry Jason. After using her wealth and begetting two children with her, Jason leaves Hypsipyle. He ignores her letter imploring him to return, but she remains true to him and dies of a broken heart.

After Jason arrives at Colchis, he is entertained by King Aeetes, and Medea, the king's daughter, becomes enamored of him. She tells him that the Golden Fleece can be secured only with her help. They agree to marry, and Jason makes a solemn promise never to be untrue. Later, after the expedition is successful, Jason again proves false, leaving Medea to marry Creusa.

Toward the end of *The Legend of Good Women*, Chaucer's work indicates a definite weariness with his subject. By adhering to his original plan, he had written tales with a tiresome sameness about them. Committed to depicting perfect women and, in most instances, evil men, he found it difficult to develop his characters. A further deterrent to good characterization was his effort to keep the tales brief; as a result, some are little more than plot summaries. Because he lavished more attention on Dido than on his other heroines, hers is the most lifelike portrait. There are, however, good touches in the other female characters, including, for example, the pathos of Lucretia in her death scene and the mingled fear and courage of Thisbe. Chaucer's men are, however, little more than abstractions.

These tales mark a step toward Chaucer's later work. In *The Legend of Good Women*, he first used the decasyllabic couplet that he afterward employed so successfully in *The Canterbury Tales*. Moreover, juxtaposing *The Legend of Good Women* with *Troilus and Criseyde* was good preparation for the subtler contrasts of the Marriage Group. It is possible that Chaucer abandoned the work because of growing absorption with *The Canterbury Tales*. Whatever the case, *The Legend of Good Women* is an interesting transitional work with merits of its own.

Further Reading

Boitani, Piero, and Jill Mann, eds. *The Cambridge Companion to Chaucer*. 2d ed. New York: Cambridge University Press, 2003. Collection of essays includes discussions of Chaucer's style, the literary structure of his works, the social and literary scene in England during his lifetime, and his French and Italian inheritances. An essay by Julia Boffey and A. S. G. Edwards examines *The Legend of Good Women*.

Chaucer, Geoffrey. *The Legend of Good Women*. Translated by Ann McMillan. Houston: Rice University Press, 1987. Provides a literal modern English translation of Chaucer's Middle English verse. Includes an informative general introduction and useful suggestions for further reading on the subject of medieval women.

Collette, Carolyn P., ed. *"The Legend of Good Women": Context and Reception*. Rochester, N.Y.: D. S. Brewer, 2006. Collection of essays applies a variety of late medieval cultural approaches to interpretation of the poem. Includes discussion of the poem's manuscript and print history as well as the influence of stories about Amazons, Thebes, and Troy upon the work.

Frank, Robert Worth, Jr. *Chaucer and "The Legend of Good Women."* Cambridge, Mass.: Harvard University Press, 1972. First full-length study of the poem remains one of the best sources on this work for the general reader. Focuses on narrative technique and argues that the poem represents a stylistic turning point in Chaucer's development.

Holton, Amanda. *The Sources of Chaucer's Poetics*. Burlington, Vt.: Ashgate, 2008. Examines the literary sources for *The Legend of Good Women* and five of *The Canterbury Tales*, describing how Chaucer adapted these sources to create his own narrative, speech, rhetoric, and figurative language.

Kiser, Lisa J. *Telling Classical Tales: Chaucer and "The Legend of Good Women."* Ithaca, N.Y.: Cornell University Press, 1983. Argues that the work is really more about Chaucer's basic views of literature than about his views of love. Includes discussions of medieval theories of literature and an analysis of Chaucer's use of sources.

Lynch, Kathryn L. *Chaucer's Philosophical Visions*. Rochester, N.Y.: D. S. Brewer, 2000. Focuses on Chaucer's knowledge of and interest in late medieval English Scholasticism and other forms of philosophy, and how his works reflect his philosophical visions. Chapter 5 discusses *The Legend of Good Women*.

Percival, Florence. *Chaucer's Legendary Good Women*. New York: Cambridge University Press, 1998. Presents a comprehensive interpretation of the poem, placing it within the context of medieval literary, political, and cultural traditions.

Rowe, Donald W. *Through Nature to Eternity: Chaucer's "The Legend of Good Women."* Lincoln: University of Nebraska Press, 1988. Surveys relevant contexts and earlier criticism and argues that the poem has a circular or cyclical structure rather than being merely a series of loosely related portraits. Interprets the nine legends as a complete, coherent, and artistically successful whole.

The Legend of Sleepy Hollow

Author: Washington Irving (1783-1859)
First published: 1820
Type of work: Short fiction
Type of plot: Tall tale
Time of plot: Eighteenth century
Locale: New York State

Principal characters:
ICHABOD CRANE, a schoolteacher
KATRINA VAN TASSEL, an heiress
ABRAHAM VAN BRUNT (BROM BONES), a young squire

The Story:

Near Tarrytown on the Hudson River is a little valley populated by Dutch folk that seems to be the quietest place in the world. A drowsy influence hangs over the place and people so that the region is known as Sleepy Hollow, and the lads who live there are called Sleepy Hollow boys. Some say that the valley is bewitched.

A schoolteacher named Ichabod Crane arrives in the valley, looking like a scarecrow because of his long, skinny frame and his snipelike nose. As is customary, Crane circulates among the homes in Sleepy Hollow, boarding with the parents of each of his pupils for one week at a time. Fortunately for him, the valley's larders are full and the tables groan with food, for the schoolmaster has a wonderful appetite. He is always welcome in the country homes because in small ways he has contrived to make himself useful to the farmers. He takes care to appear to be patient with the children, and he loves to spend the long winter nights with the families of his pupils, exchanging tales of ghosts and haunted places, while ruddy apples roast on the hearths.

The main figure said to haunt Sleepy Hollow is a man on horseback without a head. The villagers speculate that the specter is the apparition of a Hessian horseman who lost his head to a cannonball; whatever it may be, the figure is often seen in the countryside during the gloomy winter nights. The specter is known to all as the Headless Horseman of Sleepy Hollow.

A fan of the writings of Salem Witch Trial chronicler Cotton Mather and a believer in ghosts, haunts, and spirits of all description, Ichabod is often filled with fear as he walks home after an evening of storytelling. His only source of courage at those times is his loud and nasal voice, which makes the night resound with many a sung psalm.

The schoolteacher picks up a little extra money by holding singing classes. One student who captures his fancy is the plump and rosy-cheeked Katrina Van Tassel. She is the only child of a very substantial farmer, a fact that contributes to her charms for the ever-hungry Ichabod. Since she is not only beautiful but also lively, she is a great favorite among the lads in the neighborhood.

Abraham Van Brunt—Brom for short—is Katrina's favorite squire. Known for his tall and powerful frame, the locals have taken to calling him Brom Bones. A lively lad with a fine sense of humor and a tremendous amount of energy, Brom scares away Katrina's other suitors. Brom Bones is a formidable rival for the gaunt and shaggy Ichabod. Brom would like to carry their battle over Katrina into the open, but the schoolteacher knows better than to tangle with him physically. Brom can do little more than play practical jokes on the lanky Ichabod.

One fall evening, the whole countryside is invited to a quilting frolic at Mynheer Van Tassel's farm. Ichabod borrows a horse for the occasion from his current host. The horse, called Gunpowder, is as gaunt as Ichabod himself but still possesses a spark of spirit. The two of them are a sight as they trot happily to the party. Everything Ichabod sees on the Van Tassel farm pleases him. He revels in the pretty picture painted by fields full of shocks of corn and pumpkins, granaries stuffed with grain, and meadows and barn lots filled with sleek cattle and plump fowl. The farm is clearly the most prosperous holding for miles around. Ichabod thinks that, upon winning the hand of Katrina, he could perhaps sell the farm and, with the proceeds, move farther west.

The party is merry and exciting, punctuated by grand feasts and lively dances. Ichabod is enraptured by the cakes, pies, meats, and tea. He joins in the dancing, feeling himself to be at his best when he dances with Katrina. Later, he listens to the men exchange Sleepy Hollow ghost stories on the porch. As the evening wanes and the others leave, he tarries in an attempt to pay court to Katrina. Before long, however, he leaves the Van Tassels crestfallen at his lack of success and starts home on the gaunt Gunpowder. As he rides along in the darkness, all the evening's stories of ghosts return to haunt Ichabod, and he becomes even more dismal. In the darkness, he thinks he sees dim shapes and hears soft moans.

When Ichabod finally approaches the bridge over Wiley's Swamp, his horse Gunpowder balks and will not respond to Ichabod's urgent commands; then, across the marsh, through the dark evening, Ichabod sees something huge and misshapen. He calls out to the figure, which refuses to answer him. Ichabod's hair stands straight on end, and he keeps to the road, thinking it must be too late to turn back. The strange figure keeps pace with him, whether he goes fast or slow, and before long Ichabod believes the dark shape to be a headless horseman holding his head on the pommel of his saddle. Ichabod soon loses his nerve and whips Gunpowder to a gallop; as they rush down the dark road, his saddle loosens and he nearly loses his grip, but he hugs the horse around the neck. He is so scared that he cannot even muster the courage to sing a psalm.

When Ichabod reaches the church bridge, where by tradition the headless specter should disappear in a flash of fire and brimstone, he hears the horseman close upon him. As he turns to look, the spirit seems to throw his head at the schoolmaster. Ichabod tries to dodge, but the head bursts against his skull and tumbles him from his mount. In the morning, a shattered pumpkin is found near the bridge. Gunpowder is found grazing at the farmer's gate nearby. Ichabod, however, is never seen in Sleepy Hollow again, although later reports are heard that he has relocated. In the valley, they say that Brom Bones, long after marrying Katrina, laughs heartily whenever the story is told of the Headless Horseman.

Critical Evaluation:

Washington Irving, the first professional writer in the United States, was by inclination an amused observer of people and customs. By birth, he was in a position to be that observer; the son of a New York merchant in good financial standing, he was the youngest of eleven children, several of whom helped Irving take prolonged trips to Europe for his health and fancy. He was responsible for the evolution and popularity of two genres in American literature: the regional, legendary tale and the historical novel. "The Legend of Sleepy Hollow" belongs to the first genre. The two best-known of Irving's stories are "Rip Van Winkle" (1819) and "The Legend of Sleepy Hollow," both of which appeared originally in *The Sketch Book of Geoffrey Crayon, Gent.* (1819-1820), a collection of tales and familiar essays. Both stories were adapted by Irving from German folklore to a lower New York State setting and peopled with Dutch American farmers.

On one level, "The Legend of Sleepy Hollow" reveals Irving's love for and use of folklore. As he had in "Rip Van Winkle," Irving employed the fictional folklorist Diedrich Knickerbocker as an external narrator looking back on old tales. Ichabod Crane is an outsider, a Yankee schoolmaster among the canny Dutch farmers. As such, Crane becomes the butt of local humor and the natural victim for Brom Bones's practical jokes. Most of the humorous sallies of the Sleepy Hollow boys are in the vein of good-natured ribbing, but Brom's practical jokes are somewhat more serious because of the rather unequal rivalry between Brom and Ichabod for the hand of Katrina Van Tassel.

Several dichotomies are established in the story between Ichabod and the local men. On the one hand, Ichabod is of Connecticut stock, a New Englander, and an educated man, in contrast with the locally bred Sleepy Hollow men. He scorns the rougher male pursuits of the local men of Dutch heritage and instead spends his time working his way into the hearts of the women. He is a representative of the larger America that lurks outside the confines of Sleepy Hollow, a walking figure of the need of the growing United States to acquire and assimilate every element of the continent in its reach for Manifest Destiny. As is often the case in folklore, the local parties are validated and the interloper is vanquished.

"The Legend of Sleepy Hollow" operates on more than one level, however. As in "Rip Van Winkle," the primary tone in "The Legend of Sleepy Hollow" is irony. "Rip Van Winkle" may be a story about a man who drinks from a flagon and sleeps for twenty years in the mountains, but it may also be a story about a man fleeing an insulting wife and shirking his responsibilities as a husband and father. Similarly, "The Legend of Sleepy Hollow" may be a story about an enterprising young man who is vanquished by a spectral figure on a dark autumn night. However, to a careful reader, the story is more than that. Throughout the text, almost all of the observations made by the narrator about Crane and his encounters with Katrina Van Tassel, Brom Bones, and the purported horseman, are ironic and tongue-in-cheek.

Although Crane presumably tries not to hurt his weaker students, he has no compunction about doubling the punishment to others, in defiance of pedagogical objectivity. Ichabod fancies himself an amazing vocal talent, yet the text makes it clear that his singing is horrible, just as his dancing is such a sight that the servants gather to ogle him. Although he tries to make himself useful to farmers, it is always to the ones with full larders and pretty daughters who receive his aid. His love of superstition may also reveal the kind of schoolmaster he is; this observation is particularly borne out by his admiration for the Puritan writer Cotton Mather, whose 1693 book *The Wonders of the Invisible World* served as an apology for the abuses of the Salem witch trials of 1692.

Ichabod is a ravenous eater in the story. His appetite is

both literal and figurative. Beyond his physical need to consume, his hunger demonstrates avariciousness and greed. Even his interest in Katrina has very little to do with any kind of romantic attraction to her and much more to do with her father's possessions and—more to the point—the food her father can provide. His feelings for Katrina are especially piqued after he has seen her father's great wealth; indeed, the story makes very clear that the extent of Crane's amorous feelings for Katrina extend only so far as her father's wealth. He seems to regard her as a food to be consumed, considering her a tempting "morsel," "plump as a partridge," and "ripe and melting and rosy cheeked as one of her father's peaches." This conflation of food with sexual and romantic imagery continues when Ichabod attends a feast at the Van Tassel household and observes pigeons "snugly put to bed" and "ducks pairing cosily in dishes, like snug married couples."

When considering his courtship of her, Ichabod's thoughts are not of Katrina or what her feelings for him might be; rather, he considers her father's lands and plans how he might dispose of them and use the cash gained from the sale. What is more, Katrina is overtly more interested in Brom Bones than in Crane. Although the narrator refers to her as a coquette, the text never once indicates that she gives Crane reasons to suspect she might entertain romantic notions toward him. When he seeks to ply his troth, she rejects him soundly enough that he leaves more like a man skulking after having raided a hen-roost than like a triumphant knight. The supernatural elements of the story are further questioned when a traveling farmer finds out that Crane has left Sleepy Hollow, studied for the bar, and become a politician and justice.

On a figurative level, Crane's gluttony and greed may again reference the growth of American Manifest Destiny; old folkways and beliefs must fall beneath the encroaching new American way of life. Crane's defeat and subsequent flight from Sleepy Hollow are, in a sense, a victory for the old Dutch American world. Katrina has married another Dutch man, who settles down with her without leaving the valley and without disrupting the farm or the ancient way of life of the old Dutch denizens of New York.

"Critical Evaluation" by Scott D. Yarbrough

Further Reading

Anthony, David. "'Gone Distracted': Sleepy Hollow, Gothic Masculinity, and the Panic of 1819." *Early American Literature* 40, no. 1 (March, 2005): 111-144. Demonstrates how "The Legend of Sleepy Hollow" reflects male anxiety about the economy in the years leading up to and following the Panic of 1819.

Bowden, Mary Weatherspoon. *Washington Irving*. Boston: Twayne, 1981. Good introduction to Irving's work. Bowden examines the first edition of "The Legend of Sleepy Hollow" within the context of its place and importance in *The Sketch Book of Geoffrey Crayon, Gent.*

Burstein, Andrew. *The Original Knickerbocker: The Life of Washington Irving*. New York: Basic Books, 2007. Critical biography that situates Irving's work within its social and political context, describing how Irving created an American literature. Includes photographs.

Greven, David. "Troubling Our Heads About Ichabod: 'The Legend of Sleepy Hollow,' Classic American Literature, and the Sexual Politics of Homosocial Brotherhood." *American Quarterly* 56, no. 1 (March, 2004): 83-110. Focuses on the representation of masculinity in the story, examining its depiction of nineteenth century male heterosexuality, fraternity, and anxiety about compulsory marriage.

Hedges, William L. *Washington Irving: An American Study, 1802-1832*. Westport, Conn.: Greenwood Press, 1980. Seeks to substantiate Irving's relevance as a writer, define his major literary contributions, and detail aspects of his intellectual environment. Presents "The Legend of Sleepy Hollow" as proof that Irving was a pioneer in the renaissance of American prose fiction.

Jones, Brian Jay. *Washington Irving: An American Original*. New York: Arcade, 2008. Chronicles Irving's life and literary career, giving Irving credit for being the first American to make a living as a writer.

Roth, Martin. *Comedy and America: The Lost World of Washington Irving*. Port Washington, N.Y.: Kennikat Press, 1976. Surveys Irving's American period of creativity, including "The Legend of Sleepy Hollow," demonstrating that his last experiment creates a comic vision of America.

Rubin-Dorsky, Jeffrey. *Adrift in the Old World: The Psychological Pilgrimage of Washington Irving*. Chicago: University of Chicago Press, 1988. Critical revisionist view of Irving and his work primarily in psychological terms. Dissects Irving's personal problems and political orientation as reflected in his writings, particularly in a substantive chapter discussing "The Legend of Sleepy Hollow."

Tuttleton, James W., ed. *Washington Irving: The Critical Reaction*. New York: AMS Press, 1993. Solid collection of sixteen essays that survey the breadth of Irving's work from early sketches to his final biographies. Two essays, Terence Martin's "Rip and Ichabod" and Daniel Hoffman's "'The Legend of Sleepy Hollow,'" scrutinize the story and view it as a unique creation.

The Leopard

Author: Giuseppe Tomasi di Lampedusa (1896-1957)
First published: Il gattopardo, 1958 (English
   translation, 1960)
Type of work: Novel
Type of plot: Historical
Time of plot: 1860-1910
Locale: Sicily

Principal characters:
DON FABRIZIO CORBERA, the prince of Salina
TANCREDI FALCONERI, his nephew and ward, an
   opportunist
PRINCESS MARIA STELLA, Don Fabrizio's wife
PAOLO,
FRANCESCO PAOLO,
CAROLINA,
CONCETTA, and
CATERINA, five of their seven children
DON CALOGERO SEDÀRA, a provincial mayor
ANGELICA, his daughter
COUNT CARLO CAVRIAGHI, Concetta's suitor
FATHER PIRRONE, a chaplain in the Salina household
THE CAVALIERE AIMONE CHEVALLEY DI MONTERZUOLO,
   a Piedmontese politician

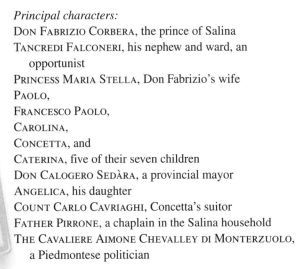

The Story:

In 1860, Sicily, a land reduced to political apathy by centuries of conquest and foreign rule, is being invaded by Giuseppe Garibaldi's red-shirted volunteers. Don Fabrizio, prince of the ancient feudal house of Salina, waits to see whether Garibaldi is only another upstart adventurer or a patriot dedicated to the unification of Italy under *il galantuomo*, the Piedmontese king Victor Emmanuel. A tawny-haired man of passive disposition, great physical energy in the hunting field, strong sensual appetites, and some reputation as an amateur astronomer, the prince rules his family and the peasants on his estates with unconscious arrogance. Although his allegiance is to King Francis II, his common sense tells him that the Bourbon regime in Naples is tottering and will soon fall. At the same time, he is too shrewd and worldly-wise to expect that the Risorgimento will greatly transform a way of life that has been molded by Byzantine tax collectors, Berber emirs, Spanish viceroys, the Catholic Church, and the Bourbons. Faced with the necessity of choosing a side, he hesitates and, in the end, does nothing. For him, while all Italy is being shaken, life goes on very much as before. He ignores his pious wife, dislikes his heir, keeps a mistress close at hand for his bodily needs and a browbeaten chaplain for his soul's salvation, and watches the stars.

The only person for whom the prince has any real affection is his penniless, scapegrace nephew Tancredi, prince of Falconeri, in whom he finds a reflection of his own restless youth. Ironically, his fondness for the boy turns out to be his

salvation. When Tancredi goes off to join Garibaldi in the hills, Don Fabrizio gives him a roll of gold pieces. This act of love and family feeling has political consequences, for when the Garibaldists triumph, Don Fabrizio finds himself regarded as a supporter of their cause.

As for Tancredi, he bobs like a cork on the wave of the future. His philosophy, as he explains it to his uncle, is simple: If people like he and his uncle do not join in the cause, the rebels will form a republic; thus, if the princes do not want real change, they must help the rebels to make change. Tancredi fights with Garibaldi in the hills, takes a commission in the Piedmontese army before Garibaldi and his ragged followers are defeated by *il galantuomo*'s troops at Aspromonti, and, to recoup his family fortunes, courts and marries the beautiful daughter of a rich, vulgar provincial upstart.

Don Fabrizio meets the future three times. The first is in the person of Don Calogero Sedàra, the mayor of Donnafugata, who in the time of the Risorgimento buys, trades, and sells so shrewdly that before long his revenues almost match those of the Salina estates. The second occasion is the time of the plebiscite for unification. Don Fabrizio, knowing that there can be no return to the old ways, advises those who ask his opinion to vote yes. Secretly he knows that a number have voted against unification, but when the votes are counted in Donnafugata, 512 out of 515 votes are yes votes—the wily mayor has stuffed the ballot box. The third time Don Fabrizio meets the future is again in the person of Don Calogero, when Don Fabrizio has to swallow his pride and go to the town hall to ask the mayor formally for the hand of the mayor's daughter Angelica in the name of his nephew, Tancredi Falconeri. In earlier times, the Salinas had exercised droit du seigneur over handsome girls like Angelica; in the new Italy, spendthrift young noblemen try to marry them. Don Fabrizio is made no happier by the knowledge that his daughter Concetta also loves Tancredi and has now lost him to the daughter of a grasping, ambitious peasant father and a mother who once tended pigs.

When the Cavaliere Aimone Chevalley di Monterzuolo asks Don Fabrizio to accept a post as senator in the new kingdom, the prince, being what he is, feels this to be no particular honor and pretends not to understand whether "senator" is a title of honor or a decoration. Chevalley is sincerely disturbed, whereupon the prince undertakes to explain his attitude, the one occasion Don Fabrizio allows himself to speak openly and bitterly about the history of Sicily and the character of Sicilians, who never want to improve because they think themselves already perfect and whose vanity is greater than their misery. He explains that he is caught between the old world and the new, and he feels ill at ease in both. Moreover, he is without illusions and lacks the talent for self-deception, a necessary quality for guiding others. He is unable to blend personal interest with vague public aims and ideals. Don Fabrizio ends his remarkable discourse on time, mutability, and knowledge of tragic destiny enclosed in the ambiguities of the past by suggesting that Don Calogero Sedàra, a man for the future, be named to the new senate.

In 1888, Don Fabrizio dies. He had been the survivor of a way of life that was feudal and despotic but in many ways fruitful and good; he had lived to see the new class of money and bourgeois power exercising its authority with brutal realism. By 1910, Tancredi is dead and Angelica a dashing widow. Don Fabrizio's spinster daughters, Carolina, Concetta, and Caterina, live in pious seclusion amid religious relics and souvenirs of the past. Concetta realizes too late that she lost Tancredi to Angelica because of her own pride and folly, and that it had been a futile love that had caused her to reject Tancredi's friend Count Carlo Cavriaghi when he wooed her. In a final gesture, she throws out on a rubbish heap the moth-eaten pelt of Bendicò, a Great Dane that had been her father's favorite dog. As it falls from the open window into the courtyard, it assumes for a moment the appearance of a dancing quadruped with long whiskers and one foreleg raised as if in imprecation—a ghastly travesty of the Salina crest.

Critical Evaluation:

The fundamental theme of Giuseppe Tomasi di Lampedusa's *The Leopard* is death—the death of a civilization, of an era, and, eventually, of the hero of the novel. From the novel's opening line, taken from the traditional "Ave Maria" prayer, the narrative moves through a series of passages that describe various declines. The novel's first scene begins with *Nunc et in hora mortis nostrae* (Now and in the hour of our death) and takes place in the hero's palace near Palermo. The drawing room's decor, a mélange of rococo style and Roman mythology, offers an odd backdrop for a Christian service, but the contradictions inherent in this scene set the tone for the narrative's basic themes.

The novel's story encompasses some twenty-eight years in the lives of Sicily, the new united Italy, and Prince Don Fabrizio Corbera, who is a transitional figure himself, a symbol of the old order's reaction to the new world. Don Fabrizio, like Sicily and Italy, is a tangle of paradoxes. He is proud, conscious of his aristocratic heritage, a cultivated, sensitive, and sensuous man who regrets seeing the past give way to the future. At the same time, he realizes that change and death are inevitable and inescapable; if he is unable to summon great enthusiasm for the new Italy, he nevertheless accepts the transformations that are taking place in the country, in his family, and in himself as he ages.

Don Fabrizio finds comfort in his sons, in his nephew Tancredi, and in the stars. As an amateur astronomer, Don Fabrizio has gained a certain amount of notoriety; moreover, his research satisfies his need for stability amid the flux he sees around him on earth. Beyond his sons, his nephew, and the stars, he finds little of interest or fulfillment. His onetime passion for his wife—ironically named Maria Stella (Mary Star)—has long since faded into quiet affection and occasional mild contempt. Much of the novel, therefore, concerns how Don Fabrizio reacts to the changes in Sicily and the ways in which Tancredi adapts to the new society and its conditions.

Early in the novel's first chapter, there appears a symbol that establishes the tone of what is taking place in Sicily and foreshadows some of the tragedy that befalls Don Fabrizio. He and his villa caretakers discover, in a grove of trees on Don Fabrizio's estate, the body of a young soldier who had been wounded in a skirmish with Garibaldi's rebels. In its state of ugly decomposition, the corpse brings home the cruel reality of war as well as the unpleasant death of the old Bourbon monarchy for which the soldier died.

The image of the dead soldier reappears, directly or somewhat transformed, at later points in the novel. Don Fabrizio recalls the corpse when his tenant farmers present him with some newly slaughtered lambs; when he is hunting, he sees the lacerated corpse of a rabbit, which inspires him to ponder the similar futility of human life and death. Near the end of the story, Don Fabrizio's obsession with the dead soldier's body resurfaces as he thinks about his son Paolo's fatal equestrian accident and his own forthcoming death, and acknowledges how everyone faces the same fate.

In a discussion with the Cavaliere Aimone Chevalley di Monterzuolo, a representative of the Piedmontese government of unification, Don Fabrizio declines to serve as a senator, citing Sicily's fundamental collective death wish. Instead, in a gesture of enlightened resignation, he recommends Don Calogero Sedàra, an ambitious provincial mayor of peasant stock, for the senate post.

To a great extent, *The Leopard* focuses on coming to terms with life and the disappointment it brings, and with death. For Don Fabrizio, there is considerable regret. In the novel's penultimate chapter, just before Don Fabrizio expires, he calculates that very little of his seventy-three years has been real living; most of it has been pain and boredom. His final moments contain a certain logic, however: Death appears to the sensuous prince as a beautiful woman whom he has long courted and with whom he has long been familiar. Death comes to Don Fabrizio in the guise of his love of beauty and sensuality, but also as something and someone he has seen in the stars.

Ironically, some of Don Fabrizio's fondest memories are of Tancredi, the nephew who, by marrying Angelica Sedàra, has compromised with modern Italy. Tancredi (ironically named for a legendary hero of the Crusades) understands that the old order is passing and that survival is better than complete extinction. His marriage is of the kind familiar to European aristocracy since the Renaissance, when hereditary nobility began to see the necessity of union with the more prosperous emerging middle classes. Tancredi's marriage, like that of his uncle, begins in passion, but also in Tancredi's consciousness of the need to accept the fact that the bourgeoisie and the people inevitably will have roles in modern society. The former two Sicilies will be united as one with the new Italian monarchy; Don Fabrizio understands that he is the last of his line and that Garibaldi and those like him—the new revolutionaries—have won the struggle for change.

The last chapter of *The Leopard* is a lugubrious epilogue, a coda that takes place in 1910, twenty-two years after the death of the novel's hero. The focus of this chapter is demythologization on two levels. First, many of the Christian relics that Don Fabrizio's daughters have collected in the family chapel are judged by the Church to be profane. Then, in the novel's final image, one of the daughters at last throws the mummified remains of Bendicò, what is left of the prince's faithful dog, on the trash heap. Thus the image of the leopard, the symbol of the Salina line, disintegrates into the pitiful bits of what was Bendicò, whose final gesture, as the carcass flies from a villa window, is a curse.

"Critical Evaluation" by Gordon Walters

Further Reading

Bondanella, Peter, and Andrea Ciccarelli, eds. *The Cambridge Companion to the Italian Novel*. New York: Cambridge University Press, 2003. Tomasi di Lampedusa and *The Leopard* are mentioned in a number of essays in this volume, but the majority of the discussion is found in two chapters: "Alessandro Manzoni and Developments in the Historical Novel," by Olga Ragusa, and "The Italian Novel in Search of Identity: Lampedusa and Pasolini," by Manuela Bertone.

Cupolo, Marco. "Tomasi di Lampedusa's *Il gattopardo* and Postwar Italian Political Culture." In *Risorgimento in Modern Italian Culture: Revisiting the Nineteenth-Century Past in History, Narrative, and Cinema*, edited by Norma Bouchard. Madison, N.J.: Fairleigh Dickinson University Press, 2005. Examines how the Risorgimento, the nineteenth century movement to create a unified Italian nation, has been depicted in films and novels, including *The Leopard*.

Della Coletta, Cristina. *Plotting the Past: Metamorphoses of Historical Narrative in Modern Italian Fiction*. West Lafayette, Ind.: Purdue University Press, 1996. Study of Italian historical fiction begins with an examination of the aesthetic and philosophical questions raised in Alessandro Manzoni's essay "Del romanzo storico" (1845; on the historical novel) and then analyzes *The Leopard* and two other historical romances to demonstrate how Italian novelists adapted Manzoni's legacies and reshaped the genre.

Donadio, Rachel. "The Leopard Turns Fifty." *The New York Times Book Review*, July 13, 2008. Takes a fresh look at *The Leopard* on the fiftieth anniversary of its original publication with a review of a new American edition published to commemorate the event.

Gilmour, David. *The Last Leopard: A Life of Giuseppe Tomasi di Lampedusa*. 1988. Reprint. London: Eland, 2007. Biography provides an incisive portrait of the author, depicting him as a deeply skeptical man, similar to his fictional counterpart, Don Fabrizio in *The Leopard*. Also discusses *The Leopard* in its historical and aesthetic context, recounting the controversy the novel's publication generated among Italy's literati.

Hampson, Ernest. *Tomasi di Lampedusa's "Il gattopardo": An Introductory Essay*. Market Harborough, England: University Texts, 1996. Useful guide to *The Leopard* analyzes the extent to which Tomasi de Lampedusa's personal experiences in Sicily influenced the novel as well as the impact of the Risorgimento on Sicily's ruling class.

Discusses the novel's complex, symbolic imagery and its theme of death.

Marías, Javier. "Giuseppe Tomasi di Lampedusa in Class." In *Written Lives*. Translated by Margaret Jull Costa. New York: New Directions, 2006. Offers a brief biography of Tomasi di Lampedusa.

Les Misérables

Author: Victor Hugo (1802-1885)
First published: 1862 (English translation, 1862)
Type of work: Novel
Type of plot: Social realism
Time of plot: c. 1815-1835
Locale: France

Principal characters:
JEAN VALJEAN, later known as Father Madeleine
FANTINE, a woman befriended by Valjean
COSETTE, her daughter
MONSIEUR JAVERT, the inspector of police
MARIUS PONTMERCY, in love with Cosette
MONSIEUR THÉNARDIER, known also as Jondrette, a rogue
EPONINE THÉNARDIER, his daughter

The Story:

In 1815 in France, a man named Jean Valjean is released after nineteen years in prison. He had been sentenced to a term of five years because he stole a loaf of bread to feed his starving sister and her family, but the sentence was later increased because of his attempts to escape. During his imprisonment, he astonished others by his exhibitions of unusual physical strength.

Freed at last, Valjean starts out on foot for a distant part of the country. Innkeepers refuse him food and lodging because his yellow passport reveals that he is a former convict. Finally, he comes to the house of the bishop of Digne, a saintly man who treats him graciously, feeds him, and gives him a bed. During the night, Jean steals the bishop's silverware and flees. He is immediately captured by the police, who return him and the stolen goods to the bishop. With no censure, the priest not only gives Valjean what he had stolen but also adds his silver candlesticks to the gift. The astonished gendarmes release the prisoner. Alone with the bishop, Valjean is confounded by the churchman's attitude, for the bishop asks only that he use the silver as a means of living an honest life.

In 1817, a beautiful woman named Fantine lives in Paris. She gives birth to an illegitimate child, Cosette, whom she leaves with Monsieur and Madame Thénardier to rear with their own children. As time goes on, the Thénardiers demand more and more money for Cosette's support, yet they treat the child cruelly and deprive her even of necessities. Mean-

while, Fantine goes to the town of M—— and obtains a job in a glass factory operated by Father Madeleine, a kind and generous man whose history is known to no one, but whose good deeds and generosity to the poor are public information. He had arrived in M—— a poor laborer, and through a lucky invention he was able to start a business of his own. Soon he built a factory and employed many workers. After five years in the city, he was named mayor and is now beloved by all the citizens. He is reported to have prodigious strength. Only one man, Javert, a police inspector, seems to watch him with an air of suspicion.

Javert was born in prison. His whole life is influenced by that fact, and his fanatical attitude toward duty makes him a man to be feared. He is determined to discover the facts of Father Madeleine's previous life. One day he finds a clue while watching Father Madeleine lift a heavy cart to save an old man who had fallen under it. Javert realizes that he has known only one man of such prodigious strength, a former convict named Jean Valjean.

Fantine has told no one of Cosette, but knowledge of her illegitimate child spreads and causes Fantine to be discharged from the factory without the knowledge of Father Madeleine. Finally, Fantine becomes a prostitute in an effort to pay the increasing demands of the Thénardiers for Cosette's support. One night, Javert arrests her while she is walking the streets. When Father Madeleine hears the details of her plight and learns that she has tuberculosis, he sends Fantine to a hospital and promises to bring Cosette to her. Just before the mayor leaves to get Cosette, Javert confesses that he has mistakenly reported to the Paris police that he suspects Father Madeleine of being the former convict, Valjean. He says that the real Valjean has been arrested at Arras under an assumed name. The arrested man is to be tried in two days.

That night, Father Madeleine struggles with his own conscience, for he is the real Valjean. Unwilling to let an innocent man suffer, he goes to Arras for the trial and identifies himself as Valjean. After telling the authorities where he could be found, he goes to Fantine. Javert arrives to arrest him. Fantine is so terrified that she dies. After a day in prison, Valjean escapes.

Valjean, some time later, is again imprisoned by Javert, but once more he makes his escape. Shortly afterward he is able to take Cosette, now eight years old, away from the Thénardiers. He grows to love the child greatly, and they live together happily in the Gorbeau tenement on the outskirts of Paris. When Javert once more tracks them down, Valjean escapes with the child into a convent garden, where they are rescued by Fauchelevant, whose life Valjean had saved when the old peasant had fallen beneath the cart. Fauchelevant is now the convent gardener. Valjean becomes his helper, and Cosette is put into the convent school.

Years pass. Valjean leaves the convent and takes Cosette, her schooling finished, to live in a modest house on a side street in Paris. The old man and the girl are little noticed by their neighbors. Meanwhile, the blackguard Thénardier had brought his family to live in the Gorbeau tenement. He now calls himself Jondrette. In the next room lives Marius Pontmercy, a young lawyer estranged from his aristocrat grandfather because of his liberal views. Marius is the son of an officer whose life Thénardier had saved at the battle of Waterloo. The father, now dead, had asked his son someday to repay Thénardier for his deed. Marius never suspects that Jondrette is really his father's benefactor. When the Jondrettes are being evicted from their quarters, however, he pays their rent from his meager resources.

During one of his evening walks, Marius meets Cosette and Valjean. He falls in love with the young woman as he continues to see her in the company of her white-haired companion. At last he follows her to her home. Valjean, noticing Marius, takes Cosette to live in another house. One morning, Marius receives a begging letter delivered by Eponine Jondrette. His neighbors are again asking for help, and he begins to wonder about them. Peeping through a hole in the wall, he hears Jondrette speak of a benefactor who would soon arrive. When the man comes, Marius recognizes

him as Cosette's companion. He later learns Cosette's address from Eponine, but before he sees Cosette again he overhears the Jondrettes plotting against the man whom he believes to be Cosette's father. Alarmed, he tells the details of the plot to Inspector Javert.

Marius is at the wall watching when Valjean returns to give Jondrette money. While they talk, heavily armed men appear in the room. Jondrette then reveals himself as Thénardier. Horrified, Marius does not know whom to protect, the man his father had requested him to befriend or the father of Cosette. Threatened by Thénardier, Valjean agrees to send to his daughter for more money, but he gives a false address. When this ruse is discovered, the robbers threaten to kill Valjean. Marius throws a note of warning through the hole in the wall as Javert appears and arrests all but Valjean, who makes his escape through a window.

Marius finally locates Cosette. One night she tells him that she and her father are leaving for England. He tries, unsuccessfully, to get his grandfather's permission to marry Cosette. In despair, he returns to Cosette and finds the house where she had lived empty. Eponine meets him there and tells him that his revolutionary friends have started a revolt and are waiting for him at the barricades. Cosette has disappeared, so he gladly follows Eponine to the barricades, where Javert had been seized as a spy and bound. During the fighting, Eponine gives her life to save Marius. As she dies, she gives him a note that Cosette had given her to deliver. In the note, Cosette tells him where she can be found.

In answer to her note, Marius writes that his grandfather will not permit his marriage, that he has no money, and that he would be killed at the barricades. Valjean discovers the notes and sets out for the barricades. Finding Javert tied up by the revolutionists, he frees the inspector. The barricades fall. In the confusion, Valjean comes upon the wounded Marius and carries him into the Paris sewers.

After hours of wandering, Valjean reaches a locked outlet. There, Thénardier, unrecognized in the dark, meets him and agrees to open the grating in exchange for money. Outside, Valjean meets Javert, who takes him into custody. Valjean asks only that he be allowed to take Marius to his grandfather's house. Javert agrees to wait at the door, but suddenly he turns and runs toward the river. Tormented by his conscientious regard for duty and his reluctance to return to prison the man who had saved his life, he drowns himself in the River Seine.

When Marius recovers, he and Cosette are married. Valjean gives Cosette a generous dowry, and for the first time Cosette learns that Valjean is not her real father. Valjean tells Marius only that he is an escaped convict, believed dead, and he begs to be allowed to see Cosette occasionally. Gradually, Marius banishes him from the house. Marius then learns from Thénardier that Valjean had rescued Marius at the barricades. Marius and Cosette hurry to Valjean's lodgings, to find him on his deathbed. He dies knowing that his children love him and that all his entangling past is now clear. He bequeaths the bishop's silver candlesticks to Cosette, with his last breath saying that he has spent his life in trying to be worthy of the faith of the bishop of Digne. He is buried in a grave with no name on the stone.

Critical Evaluation:

Essentially a detective story, *Les Misérables* is a unique combination of melodrama and morality. It is filled with unlikely coincidences, with larger-than-life emotions and giantlike human beings, yet it all manages to ring true and to move the reader. An epic of the people of Paris, with a vital and fascinating re-creation of the swarming Parisian underground, the novel suggests the crowded, absorbing novels of Charles Dickens and Fyodor Dostoevski. The main theme of humanity's ceaseless combat with evil clearly emerges from the suspenseful plot, while the book as a whole gives a dramatic picture of the ebb and flow of life.

Victor Hugo claimed that the huge book was a religious work, and certainly religion does play an important part in the story. The struggle between good and evil is foremost in the tale. Another theme of equal importance is that of fate or destiny. To whatever extent one attempts to chisel the "mysterious block" of which one's life is made, Hugo writes, the "black vein of destiny" reappears continually. One can never be certain what fate has in store until the last breath of life disappears. Mortals never are safe from the tricks of destiny, from the seemingly endless struggle.

The breathless pace of the novel probably has accounted for its tremendous popularity. The story is filled with dramatic and surprising action, many of the scenes ending with suspenseful episodes. Despite its digressions, the story moves quickly and with excitement, as the characters race across the countryside and through the narrow streets and alleys of Paris. The characterizations, while on a grand—even epic— scale, are lifelike and believable. Many of the characters seem possessed by strange obsessions or hatreds, but Hugo makes it clear that they have been warped by society and their earlier lives. Although a Romantic novel, *Les Misérables* has much in common with the naturalistic school that came into being a few decades later.

Perhaps the most terrifying and fascinating of all the characters who populate the book's pages is Inspector Javert. Javert is clever but not intelligent. He is consumed by the malice that often dwells within the narrow, ignorant individual. He can conceive of no point of view other than his own. Sympathy, mercy, and understanding require an insight that he does not possess. For him there is no such thing as an extenuating circumstance. He clings with mindless, insane tenacity to his belief in duty. At his hands, justice is warped beyond recognition. Through him, Hugo shows the dark side of virtue.

The casual reader may be moved by the author's search for justice in *Les Misérables*, and still others may admire the novel's complex structure. Like so many of the greatest literary works, *Les Misérables* can be enjoyed many times by different kinds of readers, and on many different levels.

An important, if implied, theme of *Les Misérables* is the attainment of salvation through good works. Many of the characters of the novel give charity to those less fortunate. The dramatic opening scenes in which the convict Jean Valjean learns of goodness through the charity of the priest establishes the importance of this theme. Later, Valjean and Cosette give anonymous charity to others. Marius, in his goodness, gives charity to the disreputable Thénardier family.

Other biblical virtues are dramatized in the novel, but none so effectively as love. By love, Hugo means not only romantic love but also love of humanity, the love of a kindhearted human being for another human being, the love that must be connected with genuine charity. Valjean learns what love is during the course of the novel. "The bishop has caused the dawn of virtue on Jean's horizon; Cosette worked the dawn of love." Hugo makes it clear that one cannot exist without love, for if one tries, that person becomes warped and less than human. Valjean grows as a person, and he becomes a good and honorable man after he has found the love of the helpless little girl. By devoting his life to her, he finds the necessity of a meaning outside his own life. Valjean comes to value his own existence more because the girl is dependent upon him and loves him.

The novel covers a time span of more than twenty years— from the fall of the first Napoleon to the revolts of a generation later. The most exciting scenes, described with breathless precision and dramatic flair, are those at the barricades. The characters are swept up in an action bigger than they are. Skillfully, Hugo weaves Marius, Javert, Eponine, and the others into the battles along the streets of Paris. Always, Hugo's eye catches the details of the passing spectacle, from the old woman who props up a mattress in front of her window to stop the stray bullets to the dynamic flood of humanity coursing down the boulevards. It is here that Hugo's skill as a master of narrative is fully displayed. Never, however, does he lose sight of the pathos of the individuals' struggles;

the reader never forgets the principal characters and their plight amid the chaotic scenes. Hugo balances between the two elements that compose his masterpiece. The final scenes of the novel move relentlessly to their conclusion. Perhaps Dostoevski probed deeper or Dickens caught the humor of life more fully, but Hugo was their equal in his ability to portray the individual heartache and tenderness, the human struggle of those caught up in the forces of history.

Hugo knew how to write effectively and with simplicity of the common joys and sorrows of the average man and woman. His poetry and novels have always been popular, although they have at times been out of critical favor. The public mind was much moved by the generosity of his ideas and the warmth of their expression; *Les Misérables* is still a favorite book with many people around the world. Much of Hugo's poetry and drama is no longer read or produced, but *Les Misérables* and *The Hunchback of Notre Dame* (1831) will endure.

"Critical Evaluation" by Bruce D. Reeves

Further Reading

Brombert, Victor. *The Romantic Prison: The French Tradition.* Princeton, N.J.: Princeton University Press, 1978. Points out that in *Les Misérables* the most significant reference to Hell is its embodiment in the sewers of Paris, through which Jean Valjean carries Marius as the final part of his quest—through death to resurrection.

_____. *Victor Hugo and the Visionary Novel.* Cambridge, Mass.: Harvard University Press, 1984. A sophisticated study of Hugo's fiction. Notes Hugo's use of digressive patterns and impersonal, realistic narration. Draws on a wealth of French criticism.

Frey, John Andrew. *A Victor Hugo Encyclopedia.* Westport, Conn.: Greenwood Press, 1999. A comprehensive guide to the works of Hugo. Addresses Hugo as a leading poet, novelist, artist, and religious and revolutionary thinker of France. The balance of the volume contains alphabetically arranged entries discussing his works, characters, and themes, as well as historical persons and places. Includes a foreword, biography, and bibliography.

Grant, Richard B. *The Perilous Quest: Image, Myth, and Prophecy in the Narratives of Victor Hugo.* Durham, N.C.: Duke University Press, 1968. An exhaustive study of Hugo's use of image, myth, and prophecy. Notes, among other images and uses of myth, the christological references to Jean Valjean, who finds redemption in saving others.

Grossman, Kathryn M. *"Les Misérables": Conversion, Revolution, Redemption.* New York: Twayne, 1996. Recounts the historical events leading up to the novel's publication, discusses the importance of the book, describes how Hugo's political and philosophical ideas are expressed in the work, and analyzes the character of protagonist Jean Valjean. Includes bibliographical references and an index.

Houston, John Porter. *Victor Hugo.* Rev. ed. Boston: Twayne, 1988. An indispensable starting guide to the works—drama, poetry, and novels—and life of Hugo.

Porter, Laurence M. *Victor Hugo.* New York: Twayne, 1999. A study of Hugo and his works, providing a biography, a chapter analyzing *Les Misérables*, and discussions of his plays and poetry. Includes a bibliography and an index.

Raser, Timothy. *The Simplest of Signs: Victor Hugo and the Language of Images in France, 1850-1950.* Newark: University of Delaware Press, 2004. Raser analyzes the relationship of Hugo's works to French architecture and other visual arts, examining Hugo's aesthetics and politics and how he uses language to describe time, place, and visual details.

Robb, Graham. *Victor Hugo.* New York: W. W. Norton, 1998. Thorough biography reveals many previously unknown aspects of Hugo's long life and literary career. Robb's introduction discusses earlier biographies. Includes detailed notes and a bibliography.

Roche, Isabel. *Character and Meaning in the Novels of Victor Hugo.* West Lafayette, Ind.: Purdue University Press, 2007. Focuses on Hugo's creation of characters, placing his novels within the broader context of nineteenth century French fiction.

Vargas Llosa, Mario. *The Temptation of the Impossible: Victor Hugo and "Les Misérables."* Princeton, N.J.: Princeton University Press, 2007. A fascinating look at Hugo's writing of *Les Misérables*, including an examination of the work's structure and narration.

Let Us Now Praise Famous Men

Author: James Agee (1909-1955)
First published: 1941
Type of work: Journalism

In 1936, poet-writer James Agee and photographer Walker Evans, who had been working with the U.S. Farm Security Administration, were commissioned by the staff of *Fortune* magazine to develop an article on cotton tenantry that would include photographs. *Fortune* wanted a visual and verbal record of the daily lives of white sharecroppers. As the two carried out their assignment, they found it developing into a much larger project. Ultimately, they were forced to return to their jobs much sooner than they wished, and the work they had done was refused publication by those who had commissioned it.

By this time, 1941, Agee and Evans had envisioned *Let Us Now Praise Famous Men*, complete in itself, as part of a larger work to be called "Three Tenant Families." The other part remained a vision. In its published form, the book consists of sixty-two photographs followed by a lengthy text, partly factual, partly imaginative, all extremely detailed. As a narrative of fact, a regional study, a moving moral document, a lyric meditation on life and art, and an exercise in style, *Let Us Now Praise Famous Men* is one of the most remarkable books of the twentieth century.

First, as in a play script, Agee lists the members of the three families whose lives animate the book; he also includes their ages and relationships. Agee lists himself among the "casts" as a spy traveling as a journalist, and he lists Evans as a counterspy traveling as a photographer. Listed also are William Blake, Louis-Ferdinand Céline, Ring Lardner, Jesus Christ, and Sigmund Freud, as unpaid agitators.

Many critics considered the book a structural failure. It has no apparent pattern of development. Agee begins by explaining that the project is corrupt, obscene, terrifying, and mysterious. He realizes painfully that he is spying into the private misery of the sharecroppers, that their lives will thus be exposed as passing entertainment to the curious and casual reader, and that he is being paid for doing this work. Determined to show the sacredness and dignity of each life down to the smallest detail, he approaches his subjects with boundless love and humility.

Agee records three incidents—"Late Sunday Morning," "At the Forks," and "Near a Church"—that are so moving to him that they render him almost inarticulate. He somehow manages to write about these incidents simply and vividly. In the first, a white foreman intrudes into the local black community and forces three African Americans to sing for Agee and Evans. In the second, Agee asks directions of a sick young man, his worn wife, and a mentally disabled older man. Near a church that Evans wishes to enter to take photographs, Agee accidentally frightens a young black couple by running up behind them. In each case, he empathizes so strongly with each individual that he feels sympathy and understanding for the foreman even though he humiliates the black singers; he feels sick with joy and gratitude when the wife at the forks shows sufficient confidence in him to smile slightly; he feels the fear of the young couple and the utter impossibility of ever communicating his intentions clearly to them.

A Country Letter, which begins part 1, and which Agee wrote while sitting up late at night, contains some of the most beautiful lyric prose of the entire book. It is unified, developed, and complete in itself. Agee speaks of his tenants specifically, but he places them and their flimsy homes against a backdrop of the earth and the universe so that they and their problems, their joys and sorrows, become representative of all; and the theme running through the piece is of aspirations and ideals dulled and lost, worn down by the hard necessities of living, of the flame of life that sinks down almost to an ember as they ask themselves how they are thus caught.

Parts 1 and 2 are primarily factual. Agee introduces the people and clarifies their complex family relationships. The order of their waking up and getting breakfast is described in detail. Agee explains simply the attempts of the men to find other work during slack times on the farm and the kinds of jobs available to them. The chapter on money is an objective and devastating account of the tenant farmers' financial situation. The section on shelter is almost one hundred pages. Agee details the setting of one tenant home, the surrounding fields, the spring, the garden, and the outbuildings, including the contour and quality of the soil, the angle of the path, the flavor of the water, the shape and size of the building, the boards and nails holding them together, and the odds and ends found inside them. Systematically, he examines, as with a microscope, the house itself, its outside structure and materials, the space underneath the house, including the dampness, the insects, and the odors; then, inside, he details the front bedroom, where he sleeps, the rear bedroom, where the family sleeps, the kitchen and storeroom, and the space beneath the roof. For each room he describes the walls, floor, placement of furniture, the furniture itself and the contents of each drawer down to bits of dust, the items on the furniture and pinned to the walls, the insects inhabiting the bed, the wasps in the beams of the roof, the textures and odors, and the imagined hopes and feelings of the people whose home it is.

Agee's description of the house is of a living thing, flimsy and inadequate, but alive and placed, like the people, against the curve of the earth and sky. He describes the homes of the other two families also, but chiefly to point out their differences from the first. The final part of this section is devoted to the life present other than human: the dogs, cats, cows, mules, pigs, snakes, insects, birds, and trees. These lives, too, are described with respect and consideration, with humor, and with an appreciation of the beauty to be found in them.

Part 2 is devoted to sections on clothing, education, and work. Agee lists the items of clothing worn by the men and women on Sundays, Saturdays, and workdays. He describes in particular detail a suit of overalls and the shirt worn with them, their cut, pockets, stitching, straps, color, and texture when new, when partly worn out, and when completely worn out, differentiating carefully between the three stages; and again he makes the clothes almost alive, an outer skin, part of the person who wears them.

The section on education, considered brilliant by some critics, is an angry analysis of the failure of schools and teachers not only in the South but also in other areas to educate the young properly, and of society's forcing on them work with no bearing on their lives and values that are meaningless and harmful.

In "Work," Agee gives a step-by-step description of the raising of cotton, from the preparation of the soil through the sowing, cultivating, and harvesting of the crop. Such work is extremely laborious and is done with primitive, inadequate tools. The entire family participates in the labor and in the anxious waiting for harvest, which will determine the meager incomes of the sharecroppers. The next part of the book, "Intermission," is illustrative of the confused structure of the text. It deals with a questionnaire sent to Agee by a noted journal and Agee's answers to that survey.

Part 3, "Inductions," goes back in time to the first meetings between Agee and Evans and the three families involved in their work. In particular, the section describes Agee's first night in the Gudgers' home, how he came to be there, what they said and ate, and how they all reacted to the prospect of Agee and Evans living with them.

From this point on, the book consists of short pieces: descriptions of a graveyard, of Squinchy Gudger and his mother, of Ellen Woods; a poem, the first line of which gives the book its title; and a section, "Notes and Appendices," containing various notes, chiefly on American photographer Margaret Bourke-White, and a listing of Anglo-Saxon monosyllables.

The concluding piece describes a call, possibly of a small fur-bearing animal, probably a fox, heard one night from the Gudgers' front porch. The call is answered by another animal, and as the two continue to call back and forth, Agee and his friend speculate on the animals and their locations. Finally, within himself, Agee experiences the joy of hearing the world and nature talk, and he experiences the grief that comes from the inability to communicate.

The faults of the book arise from its very virtues: Agee's love and compassion for people result not only in vivid, lyric prose but also in verbosity and repetition. When the book first appeared, some critics thought Agee's prose arrogant, mannered, precious, and nonsensical; others found it confused and adolescent. Obsessed though the author was with his own complex reactions to his subjects and the rest of the world, and his failure to convey all that he felt, he nevertheless gives a picture of himself and of the tenants and their lives in a way that is vivid and overwhelming. At times, the writer's sensibility would be almost unbearable if it were not of a high moral order. *Let Us Now Praise Famous Men* breaks through the limits of reality to convey meanings and insights that are rich and strange. Its personal revelations are of great moral significance.

Further Reading

Bergreen, Laurence. *James Agee: A Life*. New York: E. P. Dutton, 1984. An exceptional biography, well written and researched, providing a balanced view of Agee as a writer and as a person. Includes photographs, notes, bibliographies of works by and about Agee, and an index.

Folks, Jeffrey J. "James Agee's Quest for Forgiveness in *Let Us Now Praise Famous Men*." In *From Richard Wright to Toni Morrison: Ethics in Modern and Postmodern American Narrative*. New York: Peter Lang, 2001. Folks studies the relationship of literature to contemporary ethical dilemmas in selected works in American literature, including *Let Us Now Praise Famous Men*.

Humphries, David T. "Divided Identities, Desiring Reporters in Zora Neale Hurston's *Mules and Men* and James Agee and Walker Evans's *Let Us Now Praise Famous Men*." In *Different Dispatches: Journalism in American Modernist Prose*. New York: Routledge, 2006. Humphries analyzes how Agee and other writers who published books between World War I and II employed elements of journalism to create innovative texts, a type of creative nonfiction.

Kramer, Victor A. *Agee and Actuality: Artistic Vision in His Work*. Troy, N.Y.: Whitston, 1991. A valuable resource for understanding Agee's aesthetics and the controlling themes of his works. Also discusses Agee's focus on details and "the real."

_____. *A Consciousness of Technique in "Let Us Now Praise Famous Men": With Thirty-one Newly Selected Photographs*. Albany, N.Y.: Whitston, 2001. Kramer focuses on the complex techniques that both Agee and Evans used to create *Let Us Now Praise Famous Men*. Contains thirty-one photographs not included in the original published version of the book.

_____. *James Agee*. Boston: Twayne, 1975. This well-written work remains one of the more valuable sources on Agee for the nonspecialist, useful for its analyses, bibliography, and chronology of the author's life.

Lofaro, Michael A., ed. *Agee Agonistes: Essays on the Life, Legend, and Works of James Agee*. Knoxville: University of Tennessee Press, 2007. Compilation of seventeen essays, divided into four parts, addressing Agee's influences and syntheses as well as his films, literature, and correspondence. Also features photographs, newly found correspondence, and a remembrance by Agee's daughter.

Madden, David. "James Agee's *Let Us Now Praise Famous Men*: The Cruel Radiance of What Is." In *Touching the Web of Southern Novelists*. Knoxville: University of Tennessee Press, 2006. Madden analyzes the lives and works

of writers of the American South, including Agee, and examines how these same writers have inspired his own work.

Spiegel, Alan. *James Agee and the Legend of Himself*. Columbia: University of Missouri Press, 1998. This critical study of Agee's writing offers especially sound insights into the role that childhood reminiscence plays in the author's nostalgia. The extensive discussion of *Let Us Now Praise Famous Men* represents one of the best interpretations of this work.

Stott, William. *Documentary Expression and Thirties America*. 1973. Reprint. Chicago: University of Chicago Press, 1986. In this classic work, Stott examines the documentary impulse of the 1930's in the United States, analyzing journalism, sociology, photography, radio broadcasts, and other media to determine their influence upon literature and the arts. Devotes two chapters to *Let Us Now Praise Famous Men*, one discussing Evans's photographs and the other describing Agee's text.

Tindall, George Brown. "The Lost World of Agee's *Let Us Now Praise Famous Men*." In *James Agee: Reconsiderations*, edited by Michael A. Lofaro. Knoxville: University of Tennessee Press, 1992. Examines the literary and sociological interest of the 1930's in the southern rural poor, a trend that fostered Agee's and Evans's work.

Wagner-Martin, Linda. "*Let Us Now Praise Famous Men*—and Women: Agee's Absorption in the Sexual." In *James Agee: Reconsiderations*, edited by Michael A. Lofaro. Knoxville: University of Tennessee Press, 1992. Examines the emphasis Agee places on the Gudger women, his awareness of their sexuality, and his own role as a voyeur.

Letter from Birmingham City Jail

Author: Martin Luther King, Jr. (1929-1968)
First published: 1963
Type of work: Social criticism

Letter from Birmingham City Jail is perhaps the finest literary achievement of the Reverend Martin Luther King, Jr. It is indeed the most profound defense of his nonviolent program for the Civil Rights movement in the United States. Early in 1963, African American leaders in Birmingham, Alabama, had invited King to lead a local demonstration against segregation. King led a nonviolent protest march that resulted in his arrest on Good Friday, April 12, 1963.

The following day, a full-page advertisement, "A Call for Unity" that was signed by eight white clergy, appeared in the *Birmingham News*, challenging the appropriateness of King's "outside" involvement, questioning the necessity of demonstrations, and calling for "negotiation" instead. King responded with what came to be called *Letter from Birmingham City Jail*, which he had written on the margins of the newspaper and on toilet paper and had smuggled from the jail. After eight days of incarceration, King was released. His letter was subsequently published in several periodicals. The events of Birmingham (owing in part to the effectiveness of King's letter) proved to be turning points in the Civil Rights movement.

King's article-length letter opens with a brief introduction that establishes a firm but irenic, or moderate, tone. Though jailed unjustly, King does not lash out angrily at his critics. Instead, he addresses them in disarming fashion, characterizing them as sincere men of "good will." After this introduction, King answers one by one the charges that had been leveled against him by the eight ministers, the first criticism being that he was an outsider meddling in local affairs. He explains that his role as president of the Southern Christian Leadership Conference demands that he assist local organizations that call upon him. Second, he argues that his work is like that of the biblical prophets and apostles who had traveled far afield to challenge injustice and to bring the "gospel of freedom." Third, he cites the principle of corporate solidarity, pointing out that the United States is a single nation whose citizens are bound in purpose and future. He states profoundly, "Injustice anywhere is a threat to justice everywhere."

King then takes exception to the idea that demonstrations are too unsettling and that patient negotiation with political leaders would be a more acceptable path to racial equality. He admits that direct action disturbs the community, but he insists that segregation and racial prejudice are even more disturbing. He provides ample details to show that racial injustice is an ongoing evil in Birmingham. King writes that negotiation is in fact his goal but that demonstrations are necessary to create the tension that forces the issues into negotiation. His own experience and the testimony of history show that "freedom is never voluntarily given by the oppressor." With a staggering flurry of examples, he illustrates the suffering of African Americans and insists that waiting for a more convenient season is not a viable option. The reader is forced to concede that serious injustices must be addressed without delay.

Next, in answering the charge that he and his fellow demonstrators are law breakers, King offers a defense of civil disobedience that stands in the tradition of Henry David Thoreau and Mahatma Gandhi. With impeccable logic he cites well-known philosophers and theologians to show the difference between just laws and unjust laws. Furthermore, he applauds famous examples of civil disobedience from the Bible and from history. He closes this section by starkly contrasting the legal but immoral acts of Adolf Hitler with the illegal but commendable acts of those who aided European Jews before and during World War II.

King follows up his logical argument for civil disobedience with a more personal and emotional appeal to the "moderates" who stand for equality in principle but who are unwilling to support direct actions that disturb the status quo. He pleads for immediate and concrete moves toward justice and racial integration. He refuses the label of "extremist," claiming that he stands in the middle between two extremes in the African American community. He insists that his position is more advantageous than either complacent acquiescence or violent activism. King, however, is willing to own the label of "extremist" when it registers his identification with other important extremist persons such as Jesus Christ, Saint Paul, Martin Luther, John Bunyan, Abraham Lincoln, and Thomas Jefferson.

More than moderates in general, it is the white church that. disappoints King. He reveals his painful experiences of rejection that resulted in his disillusionment with white Christianity. He deduces that, unlike the early church, the present church is "a weak, ineffectual voice with an uncertain sound." Appealing to its conscience, its sense of right and wrong, and to divine will, King challenges the church to participate actively and wholeheartedly in the historic African American freedom movement. The rhetoric of this section (like other parts of the letter) reflects King's roots in the tradition of African American preaching. Although it is a written document, the letter is quite similar in style to oral discourse: the use of repetition, stock phrases, affective language, and figurative language. King shows himself to be a master of oral technique. The figures of speech, the emotional tone, and the large number of concrete examples invite the reader to enter King's world and to participate in his vision.

In a final point of disagreement with the eight clergymen, King chides them for their naïve commendation of Birmingham police. According to King, the police should not be commended, because in spite of their restraint they had mistreated a number of men, women, and children during and after the demonstration. Instead of praising the police, King praises the brave demonstrators who endured ridicule, remained calm in the face of provocation, and in some cases suffered personal injury. As in earlier parts of the letter, King names specific persons who are worthy of the title heroes.

In conclusion, King apologizes for writing such a lengthy letter. He begs forgiveness from his critics if he has overstated his case and from God if he has understated it. Finally, King offers a brief word of conciliatory hope toward his opponents, reaching out the hand of friendship to his fellow ministers. His optimistic vision for the future, his trust in democracy, and his confidence in the indomitable character of his people are evident here and throughout the letter.

King's most remarkable rhetorical accomplishment in *Letter from Birmingham City Jail* is its effective tone. He consistently maintains an astonishing balance between measured restraint and constant pressure, between humility and boldness. His repeated references to his imprisonment and to the suffering of the African American community create in the reader a consciousness of injustice and deep sympathy for the marginalized.

However, King never appears to be seeking special treatment or pity; he asks only for justice and equality. He displays no air of superiority, but neither does he cower in fearful hesitancy. Imprisoned, he writes with the mood of a free man. Denounced, he responds with charity toward his detractors. Without status, he writes with statesmanlike moral authority. Finally, the letter reflects seasoned theological reflection, a fully developed philosophy, and a sophisticated understanding of social and political realities.

Lee Roy Martin

Further Reading

Bass, S. Jonathan. *Blessed Are the Peacemakers: Martin Luther King, Jr., Eight White Religious Leaders, and the "Letter from Birmingham Jail."* Baton Rouge: Louisiana State University Press, 2001. A complete history of the circumstances surrounding King's work in Birmingham and the circumstances surrounding his writing of the letter.

Calloway-Thomas, Carolyn, and John Louis Lucaites, eds. *Martin Luther King, Jr., and the Sermonic Power of Public Discourse.* 1993. New ed. Tuscaloosa: University of Alabama Press, 2005. Nine essays, varying in approach, study King's style of oral rhetoric and examine five of his most famous works. Part of the Studies in Rhetoric and Communication series.

Colaiaco, James A. "The American Dream Unfulfilled: Martin Luther King, Jr., and the 'Letter from Birmingham Jail.'" *Phylon* 45, no. 1 (1984): 1-18. A thorough study of the letter, with primary emphasis on King's philosophical process and political strategy.

Garrow, David J. *Bearing the Cross: Martin Luther King, Jr., and the Southern Christian Leadership Conference.* 1989. Reprint. New York: Perennial Classics, 2004. A balanced biography of King that is based upon interviews, King's personal files, and Federal Bureau of Investigation transcripts. Reveals King's strengths, weaknesses, and philosophy of nonviolent direct action.

King, Martin Luther, Jr. *Why We Can't Wait.* 1963. Reprint. New York: Signet Classic, 2000. King's account of the events in Birmingham, Alabama, in 1963. Includes *Letter from Birmingham City Jail.* Also includes a new afterword by the Reverend Jesse Jackson.

Tiefenbrun, Susan. "Semiotics and Martin Luther King's 'Letter from Birmingham Jail.'" *Cardozo Studies in Law and Literature* 4, no. 2 (Autumn, 1992): 255-287. An advanced study that utilizes linguistic approaches. Tiefenbrun argues convincingly that King's primary rhetorical strategy is based on the semiotic principle of similarity and difference.

Letters from an American Farmer

Author: Michel-Guillaume Jean de Crèvecœur (1735-1813)
First published: 1782
Type of work: Essays

When, in 1759, Voltaire published his *Candide: Ou, L'Optimisme* (*Candide: Or, All for the Best*, 1759), Michel-Guillaume Jean de Crèvecœur was already planning to cultivate his garden hewn out of the Pennsylvania frontier. Like Voltaire's naïve hero, Crèvecœur had seen too much of the horrors of the civilized world and was more than ready to retire to his bucolic paradise, where for nineteen years he lived in peace and happiness until the civilized world intruded on him and his family with the outbreak of the American Revolution.

The twelve essays that make up his *Letters from an American Farmer* are, ostensibly at least, the product of a hand unfamiliar with the pen. The opening letter presents the central theme quite clearly: The decadence of European civilization makes the American frontier one of the great hopes for a regeneration of humanity. Crèvecœur wonders why people travel to Italy to "amuse themselves in viewing the ruins of temples . . . . half-ruined amphitheatres and the putrid fevers of the Campania must fill the mind with most melancholy reflections." By contrast, Crèvecœur delights in the humble rudiments of societies spreading everywhere in the colonies, people converting large forests into pleasing fields and creating thirteen provinces of easy subsistence and political harmony. He has his interlocutor say of him, "Your mind is . . . a Tabula rasa where spontaneous and strong impressions are delineated with felicity." Similarly, he sees the American continent as a clean slate on which people can inscribe a new society and the good life. It may be said that Crèvecœur is a Lockean gone romantic, but retaining just enough practical good sense to see that reality is not rosy. The book is the crude, occasionally eloquent, testimony of a man trying desperately to convince himself and his readers that it is possible to live the idealized life advocated by Jean-Jacques Rousseau.

With a becoming modesty, appropriate to a man who learned English at age sixteen, Crèvecœur begins with a confession of his literary inadequacy and the announcement of his decision simply to write down what he would say. His style, however, is not smoothly colloquial. Except in a few passages in which conviction generates enthusiasm, one senses the strain of the unlettered man writing with feeling but not cunning.

The first image Crèvecœur presents is perhaps a bit too idyllic for modern tastes. He dandles his little boy on the plow as his wife sits at the edge of the field knitting and praising the straightness of the furrows, while birds fill the air with summer melodies. "Who can listen unmoved to the sweet love tales of our robins told from tree to tree?" This is, nevertheless, the testimony of a man who for nineteen years actually lived at the edge of the wilderness, three hundred miles from the Atlantic. He was no Henry David Thoreau at Walden Pond, within easy walking distance of friends, family, and a highly developed New England culture at Concord. He was, instead, a responsible man who cleared 371 acres of land and raised enough crops and animals to provide for his family, black workers, and all peaceful strangers who chanced to appear at his door. Also unlike Thoreau (with whom he inevitably invites comparison), Crèvecœur was acutely aware of his social responsibilities and enormously proud of the ways in which they could be fulfilled in the New World.

Crèvecœur's third epistle, "What Is an American?" caught the attention of Benjamin Franklin and the Europeans of the Age of Enlightenment:

[America] is not composed, as in Europe, of great lords who possess everything, and of a herd of people who have nothing. Here are no aristocratical families, no courts, no kings, no bishops, no ecclesiastical dominion, no invisible power giving to a few a very visible one; no great manufacturers employing thousands, no great refinements of luxury. The rich and the poor are not so far removed from each other as they are in Europe. . . . We are the most perfect society now existing in the world.

Enthusiastic as this description is, it is not as extravagant as it might seem; Crèvecœur does not claim that the American colonists have founded the best of all possible worlds. He is, for example, acutely aware that religious influence gradually declines as one goes west and that, instead of liberating, this decline reduces humanity to a perfect state of war, each against each. Crèvecœur rejoices, however, that there are almost no concentrated religious sects preying on each other in America: "Zeal in Europe is confined . . . a grain of powder enclosed; here it burns away in the open air, and consumes without effect."

Furthermore, not every man succeeds after arriving in the New World—only the sober, the honest, the industrious. In his "History of Andrew, the Hebridean," Crèvecœur presents a case history of the Horatio Alger hero in primitive America, the story of a simple illiterate Scot who, after four years of sweat and toil, became a prospering freeholder. Franklin had occasion to caution his friends in France that Crèvecœur's was a highly colored account.

Part of the coloring is contributed by the pervasive nature imagery. The freedom and beauty of birds seem to symbolize the condition Europeans might achieve when immersing themselves in nature. Crèvecœur describes hours spent in quiet admiration of the hummingbirds, tells regretfully of shooting a kingbird to rescue bees, and describes the feeding and care of quail in the winter. Insects, too, fascinate him; he keeps a hornet's nest in the house. The letter on rattlesnakes and copperheads is horrendous and awesome. Crèvecœur tells of copperheads enticing birds by the power of their eyes, of a defanged rattler trained as a pet, of a pair of snakes in mortal combat. Most curious of all is the account of a farmer who kicked away a snake that had thrust its fangs into his boot. After pulling off his boots that night, he suddenly became violently ill, writhed horribly, and died. His son, inheriting the boots, suffered the same fate. A neighbor, next in succession, almost died, too, but was saved when a shrewd doctor located the poison-filled fangs stuck in the boot. Crèvecœur in these passages reveals an exciting narrative power.

Apart from the agricultural life inland, Crèvecœur praises most the industry and sobriety of the coastal fishing communities at Nantucket and Martha's Vineyard, where "perfect equanimity prevails." At Nantucket, five thousand prosperous people inhabit a place that in Europe would have housed a few simple fishermen. Their Yankee ingenuity and sound business sense have enabled them to build—beginning with one whale boat—a whaling fleet that ranges even to the South Seas. Martha's Vineyard is already the "nursery" of seamen for the entire East Coast. So detailed is Crèvecœur's description of the whalers' chase, the ferocity of the whale's struggle, the dangers from sharks and thrasher whales, the processing of blubber into whale oil—in short, the entire experience—that one wonders how Herman Melville could have overlooked it in compiling the extracts in *Moby Dick* (1851).

Crèvecœur finds Nantucket a model community in that it contains only one minister (a Presbyterian—the Quakers, much to Crèvecœur's delight, do not have special ministers), two doctors, one lawyer (seldom employed), no soldiers, and no governors.

> Happy the people who are subject to so mild a government; happy the government which has to rule over such harmless and such industrious subjects! . . . I wish I had it in my power to send the most persecuting bigot I could find in —— to the whale fisheries; in three or four years you would find him a much more tractable man and therefore a better Christian.

Colonial Nantucket is apparently not perfect, however; the Quakers persist in their ungrammatical English, do not tolerate any deviation from their sober customs and homespun dress, and sternly prohibit music, singing, and dancing. "Such an island . . . is not the place where gay travellers should resort in order to enjoy the variety of pleasures the more splendid towns of this continent afford." Crèvecœur also reports, obviously misled by some notorious gossip, that the women are addicted to opium. "But," he philosophizes, "where is the society perfectly free from error and folly?"

Crèvecœur's criticism is reserved for the most European of American cities, which he calls Charles-Town: "gayest in America . . . centre of our beau monde." Lawyers, planters, and merchants make up the population, all addicted to dangerous excesses of all kinds. At the heart of this social corruption, Crèvecœur finds the brutal institution of slavery. He tells the horrifying tale of his chance encounter with a slave who had been driven to kill an overseer. The slave's punishment was to be suspended from a tree in a cage for two

days. Vicious birds had already plucked out his eyes and bared his cheekbones. No sooner were the birds dispersed than swarms of insects covered him. The miserable man begged for water and hoped it was poisoned. "Gracious God!" cries Crèvecœur, "to what end is the introduction of so many beings into [such] a mode of existence! . . . Is there then no superintending power who conducts the moral operations of the world?"

Some of Crèvecœur's faith is restored by the spectacle of the humble, kind, and generous aspect of William Bartram, a Quaker botanist, who employs free black men as salaried workers on his plantation and welcomes them as companions at his table and worshipers at the Friends' meetinghouse.

Letters from an American Farmer ends in ominous tones of impending tragedy. Unwilling to commit his allegiance to either the British or the colonists, Crèvecœur finds it necessary to flee:

> Must I in order to be called a faithful subject, coolly and philosophically say it is necessary for the good of Britain that my children's brains should be dashed against the walls of the house in which they were reared; that my wife should be stabbed and scalped before my face; that I should be either murdered or captivated?

To escape such a fate, Crèvecœur develops an intricate plan to take his family to join an American Indian settlement in the uncultivated wilderness (a plan that he never actually carried out). It is tragically ironic that this mild Frenchman's absolute certainty of the blessings of life in the colonies should be so violently shattered after nineteen years of expending all his energies to make a decent life possible. It is appropriate that his final impulse is to immerse himself deeper into nature by joining the Indians. Whatever flaws it may have, *Letters from an American Farmer* is among the most sympathetic and thoughtful of all eighteenth century analyses of frontier life and its shaping influence on the emerging American character.

Further Reading

Arch, Stephen Carl. "The 'Progressive Steps' of the Narrator in Crèvecœur's *Letters from an American Farmer*." *Studies in American Fiction* 18 (Autumn, 1990): 145-158. Separates Crèvecœur from the character of James and traces James's progression through the work as closely related to the "epistolary form" and the "dialogic structure." James is not the main character in an American Dream, but a character threatened by the dangers of revolution.

Carlson, David J. "Crèvecœur's *Letters from an American Farmer.*" In *The Oxford Handbook of Early American Literature*, edited by Kevin J. Hayes. New York: Oxford University Press, 2008. Provides in-depth discussion of Crèvecœur's essays.

_____. "Farmer Versus Lawyer." *Early American Literature* 38, no. 2 (2003): 257-279. Argues that *Letters from an American Farmer* is a political allegory that examines crucial tensions in the philosophy of classic liberalism and in the social contract theory.

Cook, Elizabeth Heckendorn. "The End of Epistolarity: *Letters from an American Farmer.*" In *Epistolary Bodies: Gender and Genre in the Eighteenth-Century Republic of Letters*. Stanford, Calif.: Stanford University Press, 1996. Chapter focusing on *Letters from an American Farmer* is part of a larger analysis of eighteenth century epistolary narratives that places these works within the context of eighteenth century print culture, new models of readership, emerging ideas about the social contract between readers and writers, and techniques of mechanical reproduction.

Hanson, Victor Davis. *The Land Was Everything: "Letters from an American Farmer."* New York: Free Press, 2000. A professor of classical literature and sixth-generation orchard keeper uses Crèvecœur's work as a model for this collection of essays about the death of the family farm. Argues that the domination of farming by corporate agribusiness has obliterated the rural culture that was once the bedrock of American democracy.

Philbrick, Thomas. *St. John de Crèvecœur.* Boston: Twayne, 1970. Offers a general and comprehensive introduction to Crèvecœur's life and work, including two major sections on *Letters from an American Farmer.*

Winston, Robert P. "'Strange Order of Things!': The Journey to Chaos in *Letters from an American Farmer.*" *Early American Literature* 19, no. 3 (Winter, 1984/1985): 249-267. Examines the structure of *Letters from an American Farmer* and finds elements of romance that anticipate the work of novelists James Fenimore Cooper, Nathaniel Hawthorne, and Herman Melville. Describes how Crèvecœur identifies an idyllic world and a demoniac one and struggles to find a compromise between the two.

Ziff, Larzer. *Writing in the New Nation: Prose, Print, and Politics in the Early United States.* New Haven, Conn.: Yale University Press, 1991. Chapter 2 explores Crèvecœur's life, the epistolary nature of *Letters from an American Farmer*, and Crèvecœur's attempts to find a middle ground between old and new cultures.

Letters to His Son

Author: Lord Chesterfield (1694-1773)
First published: 1774
Type of work: Epistolary literature

On the periphery of literature exists a valuable and fascinating genre, the personal letter. Like the private diary, the personal letter reveals an individual and an age far more intimately than any other form of writing. Probably no era practiced the epistolary art more widely than the eighteenth century and no person more skillfully than the fourth earl of Chesterfield. Although the earl had served his country unimpeachably as a member of Parliament, lord lieutenant of Ireland, and ambassador to Holland, it is generally conceded that Lord Chesterfield would have remained an inconspicuous figure in the eighteenth century historical scene had it not been for the unintended publication of some four hundred letters he wrote to his illegitimate son, Philip Stanhope. No doubt the very fact that these letters were private, intended to develop the education and manners of a young man who was expected to take a significant place in government and cultivated society, endows them with a frankness and honesty that betrays the cultivated self-seeking and hypocritical morality of the upper-class society of the time. Eugenia Stanhope, whose secret marriage with young Philip was only one of the many disappointments Lord Chesterfield suffered at the hands of his intractable son, was so incensed at being excluded from the earl's will that, against the family's wishes, she sold the letters for a little more than fifteen hundred pounds, thus infuriating English society and securing for Lord Chesterfield minor but recognized importance in the history of English prose.

The early letters are charmingly didactic essays addressed

to a preadolescent boy whom the writer hoped would become "not only the best scholar but the best bred boy in England of your age." "Dear boy," they all begin, and then proceed to shape little lessons on language, literature, geography, history, and good manners. They conclude with admonitions to obey his seventy-year-old tutor, Maittaire, and with promises of "very pretty things" to reward him for industrious study. There is irony in Lord Chesterfield's explanation of irony—"Suppose that I were to commend you for your great attention to your book, and for your retaining and remembering what you have once learned; would you not plainly perceive the irony, and see that I laughed at you?" Reasons for such laughter were to come, but it was never bitter or audible ("there is nothing so illiberal, and so ill-bred as audible laughter"). Lord Chesterfield's optimism and faith in rationalism may have diminished somewhat, but it was never extinguished completely. After his failure in making an outstanding figure of young Philip, he began the whole process over again in 1761 with his godson, to whom he wrote almost three hundred letters in one decade, published posthumously as *Letters to His Godson* (1890).

It was not the early letters to his son but the later ones—addressed to "My Dear Friend"—that aroused controversy after the letters were published. A strong believer in John Locke's educational theory that a mind is wax to be molded into shape by environmental influences, Lord Chesterfield sent his son at the age of fourteen not to a university but on the Grand Tour, accompanied by a new tutor, the Reverend Walter Harte. The boy was supplied with letters of introduction into the highest social circles of great European cities, and he was spied upon by the earl's agents and pursued by the affectionate but earnest epistles of an anxious father. How earnest they were can be gauged from this excerpt written to Lausanne in 1746: "I do not so much as hint to you how absolutely dependent you are on me; and that, as I have no womanish weakness for your person, your merit must and will be the only measure of my kindness." It would nevertheless be unfair to charge that even if the father had never displayed warmth, love, or understanding, his kindness far exceeded the boy's merit.

The controversy concerned Lord Chesterfield's realistic observations on those aspects of life that he constantly urges his son to explore:

Search, therefore, with the greatest care, into the characters of those whom you converse with; endeavor to discover their predominant passions, their prevailing weaknesses, their vanities, their follies, and their humours, with all the right and wrong, wise and silly springs of hu-

man actions, which make such inconsistent and whimsical beings of us rational creatures. . . . This is the true knowledge of the world; and the world is a country which nobody ever yet knew by description; one must travel through it oneself to be acquainted with it.

Having traveled that country well himself, Lord Chesterfield could advise his son with cynical sophistication. A man who never knew love and who married for a dowry to repair his fortunes, he wrote:

Women are merely children of a larger growth. . . . A man of sense only trifles with them. . . . They will greedily swallow the highest [flattery], and gratefully accept the lowest . . . [but] They have, from the weakness of men, more or less influence in all courts. It is therefore necessary to manage, please and flatter them.

It is this worldly self-interest that constitutes the dominant tone of the letters; as Lord Chesterfield declares, "Without some dissimulation no business can be carried on at all." There is no trace of mysticism or sentimentality about him: "Religion must still be allowed to be a collateral security, at least, to Virtue." Yet virtue, apparently, is not an end in itself. Rather, it is a means to worldly success—a dependable means, if Lord Chesterfield's own career based on honesty and integrity is any measure. Worldly success is the goal, and though "learning, honour, and virtue are absolutely necessary to gain you the esteem and admiration of mankind, politeness and good breeding are equally necessary to make you welcome and agreeable in conversation and common life." Elsewhere, Lord Chesterfield urges his son to be neat and clean, to avoid obesity, to care for his teeth, and never under any circumstances to stick his finger into his nose. The ultimate purpose was that young Stanhope should become—at the very least—a successful diplomat; but the principal objective of that occupation was "to get into the secrets of the court at which he resides" through any means, including flattery or intimacy with a king's or minister's mistresses.

On the Continent, publication of *Letters to His Son* was met with acclaim, the greatest admirer probably being Lord Chesterfield's old friend Voltaire, who stated, "I am not certain that it is not the best book on education which has ever been written." In England, however, the reaction was sternly condemnatory, even virulent. One periodical declared that, as a man, Lord Chesterfield was "certainly solely actuated by pride, vanity, and ambition," and in her own letters Mary Wortley Montagu expressed her belief that "tho' many admired, no one ever esteem'd Lord Chesterfield."

Further Reading

Chesterfield, Philip Dormer Stanhope, Lord. *Lord Chesterfield's Letters*. Edited by David Roberts. 1992. Reprint. New York: Oxford University Press, 2008. Provides an informative introduction to the correspondence between Lord Chesterfield and his son, and reprints the letters with helpful annotations.

Franklin, Colin. *Lord Chesterfield: His Character and Characters*. Brookfield, Vt.: Ashgate, 1993. Presents Lord Chesterfield's other writings, pieces on contemporary people and events, which were never published or meant to be published. Includes commentary and annotations.

Shellabarger, Samuel. *Lord Chesterfield and His World*. 2d ed. Boston: Little, Brown, 1951. Biography emphasizes the intimate connection between Lord Chesterfield's conduct and teaching and the rationalism of his time. Offers an enjoyable and illuminating picture of the life of a man whose primary motivation was worldly ambition.

Leviathan
Or, The Matter, Forme, and Power of a Commonwealth Ecclesiasticall and Civill

Author: Thomas Hobbes (1588-1679)
First published: 1651
Type of work: Politics

In considering the "matter, forme, and power" of the commonwealth, or state, Thomas Hobbes does far more than describe governments as he finds them. His goal is to explain the origin of political institutions and to define their powers and right limits. To this end he draws an analogy between the art of nature, which produces humanity, and the art of humanity, productive of the commonwealth. In drawing the analogy he first explains humanity, giving to the description a thoroughly mechanistic bias. He then proceeds to explain the state as humanity's artful creation, designed to put an end to the war of all against all.

The state, "that great Leviathan," is but an "Artificial Man," writes Hobbes. The sovereign is an artificial soul, the officers of the state are artificial joints, reward and punishment are nerves, and wealth and riches are strength. The people's safety is the business of the artificial man; the laws are its reason and will; concord, its health; sedition, its sickness; and civil war, its death.

All human ideas originate in sense, according to Hobbes—that is, they are derived from sense impressions. All sensation is a result of external bodies pressing upon the sense organs. Imagination is "nothing but decaying sense," the effect of sense impressions after the external body has ceased to press upon the organs. If one wants to emphasize the past cause of the impression, one calls the fading image a "memory" image. If one wants to emphasize the image as one not now related to any present cause, one calls it "fancy" or "imagination."

Hobbes, led by his mechanistic psychology, denies content to such a term as "infinite." He argues that when one says something is infinite one merely shows that one cannot conceive its boundaries. Consequently, such a term as "God" is used not to conceive any being but only to honor something incomprehensible.

Common names, such as "man," "horse," and "tree," may be applied to a number of individual things, yet there is nothing universal but names. In making this claim Hobbes is denying the Platonic belief that individual objects share a certain common character, or universal, in virtue of which they are similar. According to Hobbes, then, reasoning is simply the manipulation—the addition and subtraction—of names.

The passions are the "interior beginnings of voluntary motions," writes Hobbes. Given that Hobbes argues that everything can be understood in terms of bodies in motion, it is not surprising that even the emotions are, to him, simply motions inside the body. Motion toward something is desire; motion away, aversion. Hobbes defines the other passions in terms of these two basic motions.

After considering the intellectual virtues and defects, the two kinds of knowledge (knowledge of observed fact and the conditional knowledge of science), and the powers and manners of people, Hobbes turns his analytical mind to religion. Religion, he writes, is a human invention, the result of ignorance and fear. Religious power and dogma are used to serve the interests of the priests. Given these views, it is not surprising that Hobbes was constantly in trouble at home and abroad and was attacked from the pulpit for generations.

When Hobbes declares that people are by nature equal, he does so with no tone of ringing idealism. He means only that the differences among people are not so marked as are the similarities, and he means also that there is no natural sanction for one person's assuming authority over another. People are similar, so sometimes two persons come to desire the same thing; if they cannot both enjoy the object of their desire, they become enemies and war over the object. According to Hobbes, fights have three principal causes: competition, diffidence, and glory. While people have no common power over them to keep them all in check, they are in "that condition which is called Warre; and such a warre, as is of every man, against every man." There are many inconveniences to war, and the fact that in a state of war there is no injustice (since there is no natural law governing action) in no way makes that state of affairs satisfactory. In order to secure peace, people enter into certain agreements by which the people bring about a transferring of rights. It is possible for people to make such agreements, or contracts, because they have certain natural rights to use their power however they choose in order to preserve themselves.

Having discussed people, their nature, and their rights, Hobbes argues, in the second part of *Leviathan*, that the commonwealth is brought into being in order to enable people to escape from the state of war. Loving liberty and dominion over others, humans agree to make some person sovereign over them all to work for their peace and benefit. The sovereign is not bound by the contract or covenant; the contract is among those who are to be ruled. If the ruler turns out to be a despot, it must be remembered that it is better to be ruled in a commonwealth than to be in a state of nature and, consequently, a continual state of war.

Hobbes considers three kinds of commonwealth: monarchy, democracy, and aristocracy, the last of which is ruled by an assembly of part of the commonwealth. There are certain advantages to the monarchal form of government, according to Hobbes: A monarch combines the private interest and the public interest. A monarch is better able to consult with those whose knowledge the monarch needs. The only inconstancy with which a monarch has to live is his or her own. A monarch cannot disagree with him- or herself; and although it is sometimes inconvenient to have power vested in one person, particularly when the monarch may be an infant because of succession, the disadvantages are no greater than they are in other forms of government.

The subjects in a commonwealth are not entirely subject to the sovereign. The basic principle is that they cannot be compelled to act against the natural inclination toward self-preservation that the commonwealth is supposed to serve. They cannot be bound to injure themselves or to wage war—although this is a dubious right, given that the sovereign is free to imprison or execute them for disobedience. If the sovereign is not able to protect the subjects, the subjects are absolved of obedience to the sovereign.

The civil law of a commonwealth is made up of all those rules that prescribe what is right and wrong for the subjects; since the commonwealth itself is no lawmaker, the sovereign must be the legislator. The sovereign is not subject to civil law, and only the sovereign can abrogate the law. Because an undeclared law is no law at all, and because law is not binding unless it is clearly commanded by the sovereign, the sovereign must make the law known and understood, and the sovereign must see to it that it is known as the law. The only laws that need not be published are laws of nature, and they can be contained in one sentence: "Do not that to another, which thou thinkest unreasonable to be done by another to thy selfe."

Hobbes regards crime as resulting from some defect of the understanding, some error of reasoning, or some force of the passions. He declares that "no law, made after a Fact done, can make it a Crime," and that although ignorance of natural law is no excuse, ignorance of civil law may excuse one, provided one has not had the opportunity to hear the law declared. Punishment is not fundamentally retributive in Hobbes's scheme: "A Punishment, is an Evill inflicted by publique Authority, on him that hath done, or omitted that which is Judged by the same Authority, to be a Transgression of the Law; to the end that the will of men may thereby the better be disposed to obedience."

Like anything made by people, a commonwealth can perish. Its infirmities result from what Hobbes calls an "Imperfect Institution"—errors in the creation of the commonwealth. Perhaps the sovereign is not given enough power, or everyone is allowed to be a judge, or conscience is authoritative in moral judgment, or supernatural inspiration is given precedence over reason, or the sovereign is held to be subject to civil law, or it is supposed that everyone has some absolute property that the sovereign cannot touch, or it is supposed that sovereign power can be divided. Other difficulties, such as the lack of money, the presence of monopolies and corrupt politicians, the popularity of certain subjects, the greatness of a town, or the invasion by a foreign power, can lead to the dissolution of the commonwealth.

Part 3 of *Leviathan* is concerned with showing the relations between a Christian commonwealth and commonwealths in general. Hobbes uses hundreds of biblical references, as interpreted by him, to support his conclusion that it is possible to reconcile obedience to God with obedience to a civil sovereign, for the sovereign either is or is not a Christian. If the sovereign is a Christian, then, even if the sovereign may sometimes err in supposing that some act is God's will, the proper thing for the subject, who has no right to judge, is to obey. If the sovereign is an infidel, then the subject must obey because the law of nature justifies the sovereign's power in a commonwealth, and to disobey would be to disobey the laws of nature, which are the laws of God. No church leader, even a pope, can rule the sovereign; this situation is not contrary to God's law, for the church works through civil government.

The concluding section of *Leviathan*, "Of the Kingdome of Darknesse," argues that spiritual darkness has not been completely eliminated from the church—by which Hobbes means the Roman Catholic Church. His principal attack on the church of Rome is based on his claim that it misinterprets the Scripture in order to justify the assumption of temporal power by the popes.

Although Hobbes maintains that his entire argument is based on a study of nature and of humanity's natural inclinations, it is clear that a large part of his discourse is an expression of his own preference for absolute monarchy. On this account he tends to overlook the possibility of restraining the power of a sovereign through democratic procedures. Nevertheless, *Leviathan* is a remarkable attempt to explain and justify the institution of government, and it remains one of the masterpieces of political thought.

Further Reading

Brandon, Eric. *The Coherence of Hobbes's "Leviathan": Civil and Religious Authority Combined*. London: Continuum, 2007. Focuses on Hobbes's ideas about how to eliminate the causes of civil war and internal strife. Argues that Hobbes's arguments are based on philosophical materialism and the more radical religious ideas of the Reformation.

Butler, Todd Wayne. "Imaging the Body Politics: Hobbes and His Critics." In *Imagination and Politics in Seventeenth-Century England*. Burlington, Vt.: Ashgate, 2008. Discussion of Hobbes's writings, including *Leviathan*, is part of a larger examination of the relationship between individual thought and collective political action in the philosophies of Hobbes and his contemporaries.

Johnston, David. *The Rhetoric of "Leviathan": Thomas Hobbes and the Politics of Cultural Transformation*. Princeton, N.J.: Princeton University Press, 1986. Provides a detailed reading of *Leviathan*, with a focus on the work's genesis and its metaphysical and theological themes.

Mace, George. *Locke, Hobbes, and the "Federalist" Papers: An Essay on the Genesis of the American Political Heritage*. Carbondale: Southern Illinois University Press, 1979. Places the philosophical work of both Hobbes and John Locke in the context of the founding of the United States. Argues that *The Federalist* reflects a view that is more Hobbesian than Lockean and that Hobbes was the greater thinker of the two.

Martinich, A. P. *A Hobbes Dictionary*. Malden, Mass.: Blackwell, 1995. Defines more than one hundred key concepts in Hobbes's philosophy. Includes biographical information and chronologies of Hobbes's life and works as well as events in English history related to Hobbes.

Newey, Glen. *Routledge Philosophy Guidebook to Hobbes and "Leviathan."* New York: Routledge, 2008. Provides a brief biography of Hobbes, an overview of *Leviathan*, and individual chapters describing the philosophical concepts discussed in the book, including Hobbes's ideas about human nature, the state of nature, contract and consent, and religious liberty and toleration.

Rogers, Graham Alan John, and Alan Ryan, eds. *Perspectives on Thomas Hobbes*. New York: Oxford University Press, 1988. Collection of essays includes comparisons of the philosophies of Hobbes and René Descartes and discussions of Hobbes's concepts of the social contract, justice, and the state of nature.

Sorrell, Tom, ed. *The Cambridge Companion to Hobbes*. New York: Cambridge University Press, 1996. Reference book edited by a leading British Hobbes scholar presents essays on various aspects of Hobbes's life and on his ideas about such subjects as politics, morality, law, mathematics, and religion.

Springborg, Patricia, ed. *The Cambridge Companion to Hobbes's "Leviathan."* New York: Cambridge University Press, 2007. Collection of essays examines the work, including discussions of Leviathan, the mythical beast; Hobbes's moral philosophy, ideas on civil strife, and covenant theology; the book's reception; and Hobbes and his contemporaries.

The Liar

Author: Pierre Corneille (1606-1684)
First produced: Le Menteur, 1643; first published, 1644
　(English translation, 1671)
Type of work: Drama
Type of plot: Farce
Time of plot: Seventeenth century
Locale: Paris

Principal characters:
DORANTE, a student newly arrived in Paris
GERONTE, his father
CLITON, his valet and confidant
ALCIPPE, his friend, engaged secretly to Clarice
PHILISTE, a friend to both Alcippe and Dorante
CLARICE, a young woman engaged to Alcippe
LUCRECE, her friend and fellow conspirator
SABINE, the maid and confidant of Lucrece

The Story:

Dorante, a young gallant who has come to Paris to get his social education and not to take a wife (as his father, Geronte, wishes), hires as his mentor Cliton, a valet who has military and amatory connections. The young man wishes to be schooled in the ways of the world, though the only advice he ever takes from Cliton is to spend freely. Quite by planned accident, Clarice, tired of waiting for her lethargic lover, Alcippe, to conclude their secret arrangements to marry, trips onto the waiting arm of the newly arrived student. Although a rustic, Dorante immediately accommodates himself to the situation and exchanges euphemistic compliments with the young coquette, much to his valet's despair. The brazen liar captivates not only Clarice but also her companions— especially Lucrece, who is silent throughout—with his false accounts of the wars in which he has fought and the deeds he has accomplished in Germany during the last four years.

The arrival of Alcippe puts the young women to flight, but not before Alcippe sees Clarice talking to his old friend Dorante. Dorante then quite ecstatically informs his companions that he has had amazing amatory adventures during his month's stay in Paris. Last night, for example, he entertained a beautiful lady and five companions on five boats with four choirs of instruments playing all night and with dancing until dawn after a sumptuous repast of six courses, and so on. Cliton attempts to break into this mad monologue, but with no result, for Dorante's philosophy is to tell big lies about wars and adventures in order to be believed.

Dorante's stories are so plausible and his manner so persuasive that the two young ladies fall in love with him. His friend Alcippe burns with jealousy because he thinks that his fiancé was on the barge with Dorante the previous night, and his friend Philiste is completely mystified when he tries to reconcile the tales with what he later finds to be the unvarnished and unromantic truth. The one flaw in the liar's plans is that in his conversation with Cliton, who has gained information about the young women from a coachman, Dorante has confused Clarice with Lucrece.

Into this confused web of mendacity and misplaced affections comes the good-natured Geronte, who, without his son's knowledge, presses the young man's suit for marriage with the daughter of an old friend. The young woman is Clarice, ready and willing to be wooed after all the time she has spent waiting for Alcippe's advances. The old man and Clarice contrive a meeting that evening under her balcony and incognito, though she doubts that she can judge her suitor's character from such a distance and under such unintimate circumstances. A friend then suggests that she receive him at Lucrece's house and as Lucrece.

Alcippe, consumed with jealousy, angrily accuses Clarice of infidelity. Although she denies his charges, she refuses to seal their engagement with two kisses, her hand and her faith. Alcippe, thinking himself the injured party, swears revenge.

Meanwhile, the tolerant father retracts his offer of his son's hand in marriage to Clarice because the young scoundrel has invented a touching story to escape the wedding planned for him. The story, a cloak-and-sword melodrama, concerns his marriage to a poor girl whose father found them alone; in his anxiety to disguise their presence his gun went off, his sword was broken, his barricade smashed, and her reputation threatened—what could he do but marry sweet Orphise? Cliton's despair changes to admiration now that he realizes how useful his master's ability at lying can be. Although Cliton tries to explain to Dorante his mistake about the shy, virtuous, and quiet Lucrece, with whom Dorante has not spoken, the bewitched swain swears he will keep his appointment under the balcony. Alcippe writes a letter breaking off his friendship with Dorante and demanding satisfaction. In one short day, his second in the big city, the provincial student has quarreled, made love, and reported a marriage. To lie effectively, Cliton observes, one must have a good memory.

Confronted by his accuser, Dorante tells Alcippe and Philiste that he has known Clarice for several years and is not interested in her. He has, he says, taken a beautiful married woman with him on the barge, a woman whom Alcippe could not possibly know. He cautions Alcippe not to believe all he hears and not to be led by the green-eyed monster. When Philiste reveals to Alcippe that the young dandy arrived only the day before from the college at Poitiers—proof that although he might be valorous, his reported deeds are imaginary—Alcippe asks the innocent scoundrel's pardon.

By the time she has exchanged places on the balcony with Lucrece, Clarice also knows about the lies Dorante has told. Lucrece thinks his actions a sign of love. Confronted, Dorante denies all accusations save one; he declares that he pretended marriage in order to wed his Lucrece—at this point there is consternation on the balcony—whom he will marry that next day as proof of his sincerity. By group action he is ordered hence, so shocked are the young ladies at his effrontery—or naïveté.

Dorante now promises Cliton that he will not lie anymore, or at least he will give a signal when he does. He then immediately lies by saying that the rumor of his fight with Alcippe is true and that the unfortunate challenger has been left for dead. He lies again when he claims that the secret of Alcippe's recovery lies in the magic of a Hebrew word. Hebrew, he claims, is one of his ten languages. He lies also to Sabine, the servant, in order to get back in Lucrece's good graces, and he invents new names so that his father can send his nonexistent daughter-in-law his good wishes; the duped father is pleased to learn a grandchild is even now six months along. His lies are countered by the lies of the clever Sabine, who lies for money and keeps herself in constant employment by delivering letters and arranging assignations.

By now neither Dorante, Lucrece, nor Clarice knows whom they love. Clarice declares herself in favor of Alcippe, whose father finally settles the marriage arrangements. Dorante then observes that Clarice has been only flirtatious and curious, while the real Lucrece—he declares that he fell in love with the name and henceforth changed the face to fit it—is much deeper. Dorante's father, declaring as he does so that he will never again help his scoundrel of a son, arranges quite docilely for his marriage. Lucrece, who swears she will love the liar when she can believe him, is suddenly converted to belief when she sees that his avowals are true in spirit. Cliton has known as much all along.

Critical Evaluation:

Pierre Corneille composed works for the aristocratic ladies and gentlemen of the seventeenth century. He was ac-

claimed by many critics to have brought new levels of psychological realism and elegance of language into French comedy; he rejected, for example, the pastoral tradition of disguising noble or gentle characters in shepherds' clothing in *Mélite: Ou, Les Fausses Lettres* (pr. 1630; English translation, 1776), which portrays gentlepersons of the gallant world of the 1620's and 1630's. The lively dialogue that characterizes Corneille's comedies is especially dazzling in *The Liar*. Corneille's penchant for creating verse was manifested before he began composing the French neoclassical twelve-syllable Alexandrine lines that are so sparkling in *The Liar*; Corneille won prizes in Latin versification in both 1618 and 1620.

The Liar played a significant role in the development of French comedy because it moved away from the farcical techniques and the obscenities of earlier comedies. In accordance with the French classical style, emphasizing reason, order, and clarity, *The Liar* portrays life and manners in Paris. In the first scene of act 1, Dorante's valet, Cliton, gives a realistic account of the Parisian manner of living. By pointing out that all types of people inhabit Paris, Cliton presents the central theme of reality versus appearances; the valet's idea that appearances are often deceptive because people enjoy pretending to be what they are not shows his keen perception about people.

The Liar, which is based on Juan Ruiz de Alarcón's *La verdad sospechosa* (pb. 1630; *The Truth Suspected*, 1927), contains elements that show the influence of Spanish drama, with its emphasis on the themes of instability, confusion, and misunderstandings and the comic relationship of valet and master. Corneille presents the theme of instability through his depiction of the falseness of appearances. For example, Clarice wants to discern between appearance and reality in act 2, scene 2, when she speaks to Isabelle about Dorante, whose father has just proposed her marriage to his son. While wondering if Dorante's gracious appearance could possibly mask vices, she realizes that the eyes can deceive the lover, given that many handsome lovers possess vile hearts.

Another variation on the theme of instability is found in deception. Dorante practices deception when he invents stories about his being a soldier and about his marriage to a well-bred lady carrying an unborn child. The protagonist tells the first story in order to gain favor with the beautiful Clarice, who he thinks is Lucrece. He relates the second story because his father proposes Dorante's marriage to Clarice to Clarice's father, who reacts favorably to the proposal. This pattern of deception becomes so familiar to Dorante that distinction between truth and deception seems impossible.

The theme of instability is also manifested in the conflict

of illusion and reality. This conflict is especially significant to *The Liar* because the play features considerable confusion of identity. Dorante's confusion as to the identities of Clarice and Lucrece is a source of jealousy between Dorante and Alcippe, who are both attracted to Clarice; this rivalry is accentuated because Dorante believes that his beloved is named Lucrece.

Although Dorante is unaffected by Alcippe's declaration of love for Clarice, Dorante's creation of a fictitious background to impress his beloved causes Alcippe to become jealous. Since Alcippe acts on the assumption that the reputation Dorante has created for himself is accurate, Alcippe is a comic character; his jealousy gives rise to various ridiculous rages directed toward Philiste and Clarice. The fact that Clarice, who does not give credence to Alcippe's rages, remains calm underlines his comic role. By underscoring Alcippe's ridiculousness, Corneille makes the audience more aware of the comic nature of the irony of the situation: Alcippe and Dorante really do love the same woman. The rivals' jealousy is dramatically effective. Although Alcippe's jealousy is based on illusion, this emotion illustrates the playwright's use of dramatic irony, in which the truth is hidden from the character but clear to the audience. The presentation of the rivals' jealousy in the form of comic irony is characteristic of Corneille's work, which often combines truth and deception, reality and illusion, in a refined manner.

The irony produced by the confusion of identity is further developed when Dorante's father, Geronte, suggests to his son that Dorante become engaged to Clarice, a suggestion that causes the protagonist, unaware that Clarice is his beloved, to invent the lie that he is already married. Alcippe then challenges his rival to a duel. Dorante, still unaware of his rivalry with Alcippe, relates to Cliton that he has killed a man in a duel. This confession leads to comic tension when Dorante learns of Alcippe's previous betrothal to Clarice. Pointing out that he has already successfully courted Clarice, Alcippe unknowingly promotes the rivalry between himself and Dorante; the presentation of Dorante's imagined victory in a duel over his real rival gains comic authenticity. Dorante's illusionary role of rival thus becomes his comic misunderstanding of the truth.

Corneille's play reflects the influence of its Spanish origins, but the French version places the accent on the comic elements rather than on the moral aspects of the story. This is reflected in the relationship between the master and his valet. Corneille converts the valet from Ruiz de Alarcón's play, whose role was to judge his master's behavior, into a witty person capable of astute observation and helpful advice. For example, Cliton's reaction to his master's untruthfulness is considerably less emphatic than that of his Spanish counterpart. Corneille gives Cliton his own identity, as distinct as his master's.

Corneille's adaptation of the baroque theme of instability to the orderly French classical style is especially evident in the play's conclusion. Instead of being a victim forced into marrying someone he does not love, Dorante logically fulfills his "false" reputation, triumphantly transforming himself into the role of lover.

"Critical Evaluation" by Linda Prewett Davis

Further Reading

Abraham, Claude. *Pierre Corneille*. Boston: Twayne, 1972. Provides an introductory overview of Corneille's life and works, with quotations from the works translated into English. Includes a brief biographical sketch that helps explain the evolution of the playwright's works.

Adam, Antoine. *Grandeur and Illusion: French Literature and Society, 1600-1715*. Translated by Herbert Tint. New York: Basic Books, 1972. Shows the relationship between French society in the seventeenth century and French literature of the era. Discusses the history of the theater in France.

Brereton, Geoffrey. *French Comic Drama: From the Sixteenth to the Eighteenth Century*. New York: Methuen, 1977. Comprehensive study presents a meaningful history of the comic genre that spans three centuries and discusses the relationship of comic theater works to their epochs. Includes discussion of *The Liar*.

Ekstein, Nina. *Corneille's Irony*. Charlottesville, Va.: Rookwood Press, 2007. Provides a detailed examination of the use of irony in Corneille's plays, describing the different types of irony he employs and how each type functions in specific plays.

Longstaffe, Moya. *Metamorphoses of Passion and the Heroic in French Literature: Corneille, Stendhal, Claudel*. Lewiston, N.Y.: Edwin Mellen Press, 1999. Argues that the works of Corneille, Paul Claudel, and Stendhal share a common aspiration for human dignity. Compares the writers' treatments of the ideal of the heroic and the relations between men and women.

Mallinson, G. J. *The Comedies of Corneille: Experiments in the Comic*. New York: Manchester University Press, 1984. Gives a thorough analysis of Corneille's comic plays in terms of composition and style. Shows how in *The Liar* Corneille shifts the emphasis from the original Spanish source, creating the neoclassical French version.

Liber Amoris
Or, The New Pygmalion

Author: William Hazlitt (1778-1830)
First published: 1823
Type of work: Autobiography

Because William Hazlitt was a writer, it was not enough that he found himself passionately attracted to his landlord's daughter; he had to write about it. *Liber Amoris: Or, The New Pygmalion* appeared in 1823, slightly disguised by initials in place of names, as the anonymous account of a writer's foolish passion, but it was not long before the secret was out. A reviewer for the magazine *John Bull*, claiming that the review in *The Times* of London, which was favorable, had been written by Hazlitt himself, attempted to picture the young woman in the book as a young, innocent child and Hazlitt as an "impotent sensualist."

Hazlitt quite properly gave his work a subtitle, for his passion led him into flights of creative imagination whereby he sought to give his beloved traits of character and depth of feeling to match her physical charms. His conversations with the landlord's daughter, delightfully transcribed at the beginning of the work, show Hazlitt to have been as much dazzled by his own literary facility in describing her charms as he was with the charmer herself when she was seated on his lap returning his kisses. By the time the affair ended—after he had discovered that she was no more than a flirt, and not an innocent one at that—what impressed him most was that she was not what she had seemed. What she had seemed to be is what, in his writer's imagination, he had made her; what he discovered, when he realized her true nature, was that reality does not copy the images of poets, even when they write a *Liber Amoris*.

The Pygmalion theme is never explicitly developed in the book, but Hazlitt speaks of Sarah as "the statue." In the first of his letters to C. P., Esq., written from Scotland, Hazlitt says in a footnote, "I have begun a book of our conversations (I mean mine and the statue's) which I call *Liber Amoris*." Later, in letter 13, the penultimate letter of part 2, he writes to Peter George Patmore again about Sarah: "Since I wrote to you about making a formal proposal, I have had her face constantly before me, looking so like some faultless marble statue, as cold, as fixed and graceful as ever statue did."

Liber Amoris begins with a series of conversations, apparently the result of Hazlitt's attempt to re-create the substance and feeling of amatory moments spent with Sarah. After that, a series of letters to Patmore carries the narrative forward as it tells of Hazlitt's hopes and doubts while in Scotland awaiting a divorce from his wife. The book closes with some letters to J. S. K., which, unlike the letters to Patmore, were never actually sent but composed solely to complete the book.

Hazlitt became acquainted with Sarah Walker after his separation from his wife. Sarah, the second daughter of Hazlitt's landlord, Micaiah Walker, a tailor, was then in her late teens, and, according to the account in *Liber Amoris*, Sarah let Hazlitt kiss her the first time they met. During the first week of their acquaintance, she sat upon his knee, and, as he wrote, "twined your arms round me, caressed me with every mark of tenderness consistent with modesty."

Later, Hazlitt was to tell Sarah's father that she had made a habit of sitting on his knee and kissing him. The father had supposed that the occasion upon which he had surprised the two lovers together was the only time such a thing had occurred, but Hazlitt, trying to win sympathy for himself when he could not convince Sarah to marry him, assured Walker that "it was a constant habit; it has happened a hundred times since, and a thousand before. I lived on her caresses as my daily food, nor can I live without them."

The conversations are convincing and lively, more self-revealing than Hazlitt probably supposed. They show a man convinced of his ability to charm with language one whom he had so often kept busy with embraces. From Sarah's brief answers, it is clear that she found Hazlitt something of a chatterbox and wished that he would pay more attention to the physical side of love and less to the spiritual and literary aspects of the experience.

For Hazlitt the overwhelming problem of his affair with Sarah was how to reconcile their hours of intimacy with her refusal to marry him or, at least, to live with him "in friendship." He asked her for an answer; he asked his friends; he asked her mother and father. Sarah had given him the answer all along, but he lacked the ability to recognize its truth: "I told you my regard could amount to no more than friendship." Sarah's friendship was that of a healthy young woman who enjoyed being fondled by the lodgers in her father's house, whereas Hazlitt had the conventional notion that a young woman who seems innocent and demure makes love only because she wishes to accept a proposal of marriage.

The course of the affair is simply told. Hazlitt met the tailor's daughter, kissed her on their first meeting, and held her on his lap. The entertainment continued for hundreds of performances. Hazlitt spent a good part of the time expressing his love in elaborate, literary ways that Sarah, for the most part, failed to appreciate. He repeatedly tried to win from her a declaration of love to match his own, but she insisted that he could never be more than a friend to her. He gave her various books—including several he had written—and a small bronze figure of Napoleon, which she treasured because it reminded her of a man she had cared for, a nobleman who considered the social distance between himself and Sarah too great to be bridged.

After Hazlitt went to Scotland to await his divorce, he wrote entreating letters to Sarah, which were either not answered or answered perfunctorily. Hazlitt expressed his doubts and hopes at great length in letters to his friend Patmore.

Upon returning to London after having obtained the divorce, Hazlitt again tried to persuade Sarah to marry him. On the pretext that he had insulted her in a quarrel before his journey, when he had suggested vaguely that she was easy in her favors, she not only refused to marry him but also returned the books and the statuette, which he promptly smashed. He finally discovered that she was playing the same game with another gentleman, C——, and that she had been doing so during the very period when he thought he had her embraces to himself alone. His final opinion of her, contrasting with his first image of her, was that she was "a practiced, callous jilt, a regular lodging-house decoy, played off by her mother upon the lodgers, one after another, applying them to her different purposes, laughing at them in turns, and herself the probable dupe and victim of some gallant in the end."

Despite Hazlitt's literary flights shown in both the conversations and the letters, *Liber Amoris* is a convincing and compelling account of an ordinary love affair. The style is mannered, in the fashion of a time when literary elaboration of ordinary passion was as much a sport as holding the landlord's daughter on one's knee. Beneath the poetry and the banter, however, there is something of the English spirit and attitude, which gives a dignity to what would otherwise be too trivial to warrant description, whatever the joys and pains of the participants. Hazlitt shows himself to be a divided man, worldly enough to realize that Sarah, for all her demureness, allowed him liberties that she could not have al-

lowed were she all she seemed to be, yet romantic enough and idealistic enough to suppose that somehow the fault was in himself and that all he had to do was to make himself worthy of her love and esteem. In this division of self Hazlitt shows himself to be the romantic Englishman, at once cynical and hopeful.

It is not enough to say that the portrait of Hazlitt and his "statue" is convincing and typical. Considered as a piece of literary work, *Liber Amoris* is remarkable because it sustains interest with such slight material. What accounts for Hazlitt's success is the spirit of the piece, for it is amusing, lively, sophisticated, and revealing of human foibles. It is a minor piece, and perhaps it is better to remember Hazlitt as a critical essayist; yet it is from such minor pieces that English literature acquires its distinctive flavor and enduring charm.

Further Reading

Beaty, Frederick L. *Light from Heaven: Love in British Romantic Literature*. DeKalb: Northern Illinois University Press, 1971. Describes how, in *Liber Amoris*, Hazlitt develops the romantic notion of love as a hallucination. Argues that the work was Hazlitt's attempt to punish and purge himself.

Butler, Marilyn. "Satire and the Images of Self in the Romantic Period: The Long Tradition of Hazlitt's *Liber Amoris*." In *Spirits of Fire: English Romantic Writers and Contemporary Historical Methods*, edited by G. A. Rosso and Daniel P. Watkins. Rutherford, N.J.: Fairleigh Dickinson University Press, 1990. Asserts that although *Liber Amoris*, the agonized record of a man in the grip of a sexual obsession, has been regarded as an artless Romantic autobiography, the work's satirical elements reveal themselves if it is read alongside Thomas De Quincey's *The Confessions of an English Opium Eater* (1821).

Cook, Jon. *Hazlitt in Love: A Fatal Attachment*. London: Short, 2007. Provides a lively account of Hazlitt's infatuation with Sarah Walker, which led him to divorce his wife and write *Liber Amoris*.

Natarajan, Uttara, Tom Paulin, and Duncan Wu, eds. *Metaphysical Hazlitt: Bicentenary Essays*. New York: Routledge, 2005. Collection of essays focuses on Hazlitt as a philosophical essayist. *Liber Amoris* is discussed in Philip Davis's piece "Hazlitt and the Selfishness of Passion."

Priestley, J. B., and R. L. Brett. *William Hazlitt*. Plymouth, England: Northcote House/British Council, 1994. Reprints two separate earlier brief volumes on Hazlitt's work, including Priestley's 1960 essay in which he interprets *Liber Amoris* from a Jungian perspective, noting how the book exemplifies Hazlitt's characteristically personal obsession in his writing.

Wardle, Ralph M. *Hazlitt*. Lincoln: University of Nebraska Press, 1971. Uses Hazlitt's letters to his friend Patmore during the *Liber Amoris* affair to show his development as a writer.

Wu, Duncan. *William Hazlitt: The First Modern Man*. New York: Oxford University Press, 2008. Comprehensive biography argues that Hazlitt was essentially a modern writer who created the essay form as it is now practiced. Includes discussion of the writing of *Liber Amoris*.

Lie Down in Darkness

Author: William Styron (1925-2006)
First published: 1951
Type of work: Novel
Type of plot: Psychological realism
Time of plot: Mid-twentieth century
Locale: Virginia

Principal characters:
PEYTON LOFTIS, a deceased young woman
MILTON LOFTIS, her father
HELEN LOFTIS, her mother
HARRY MILLER, Peyton's husband
DOLLY BONNER, Milton's mistress
CAREY CARR, Helen's minister

The Story:

Peyton Loftis has committed suicide in New York City. A hearse awaits her body at a train station for a transfer that will carry it to the distant cemetery. Her mother, Helen, shares a limousine with the family's minister; her father, Milton, shares another car with his mistress, Dolly. As the body is delivered and taken to the cemetary, the survivors reflect upon the past.

Milton Loftis is an alcoholic and an unfaithful husband. Helen is cold, neurotic, self-righteous, unforgiving, and intolerant of weakness. The couple has two children only to fulfill their sense of obligation to the social mores of the day. Their elder daughter, Maudie, is severely handicapped physically and emotionally. Their younger daughter, Peyton, is stunningly beautiful, much beloved by her father, and consequently hated by her mother. As the Loftises' marriage disintegrates, the bond between father and daughter strengthens, several times lapsing into quasi-incestuous behavior.

Milton adores Peyton, who reciprocates his feelings. She is not an innocent party, though her age makes her a victim. She knows sex play, if not its boundaries, very well. She dresses skimpily, calls her father by such loving names as "Dear Bunny," leans and sits on him, snuggles and hugs him tightly, and whispers and giggles into his ear. Once, she even kisses him full on the lips, under the guise of playfulness. At one point, Peyton asks her father to leave her room so that she can change her clothes, but he lingers, making clear the depth of his passion. Milton never sexually engages Peyton, but each touch is sexually charged. Peyton is sexually attracted to her father, but she confines her actions to teasing and innuendo.

Milton finds outlets for his forbidden love in alcohol and his mistress, Dolly Bonner. Helen seeks out her minister Carey Carr, who has, at best, a shaky faith and who does not like people well enough to offer wise counsel or care what happens to them. Helen's rigidity and her compulsions cause her constantly to attempt to bring order into the family morass, but to no avail.

Critical Evaluation:

After writing the first portion of *Lie Down in Darkness*, William Styron realized that he was too heavily under the influence of his guiding lights, William Faulkner and James Joyce. He decided to put his work aside temporarily, hoping to find his own distinct voice. Indeed, his instincts appear to have been accurate, as critics have written voluminously on particular scenes that are derivative of other works. The plot is likely to be familiar to readers of southern fiction: It tells of a deeply flawed, dysfunctional family of four in mid-twentieth century Virginia. It is despairing and nihilistic, devoid of hope. The novel starts in deep despair and goes deeper into the abyss. It begins at the end, as the hearse awaits Peyton's body. Peyton's story unfolds during the long journey from train station to grave site. There are many complications along the way. The hearse breaks down, it gets stuck in a rutted dirt path, and participants in a religious revival flood the roads, further delaying the procession.

Despite its potentially derivative nature, *Lie Down in Darkness* is distinctly different from the works of earlier writers. For example, Styron tries an innovative approach to narration and to plot development. With the funeral cortege as a constant backdrop, he is able to hand the narrative to assorted people and to employ shifts in time and place without losing continuity or cohesiveness. At each gap in the progression, he has a different narrator take the reins. At the first delay, the narrator is impartial, unidentified, simply relating one aspect of Peyton's life. Subsequent lapses are narrated by major characters. Readers can thus gain intimate knowledge of multiple points of view, reserving judgment until all the facts are known.

Each monologue begins with an event in Peyton's life, such as a typical Sunday dinner, her sixteenth birthday party, Christmas two years later, a college football game, or her marriage. Each event ends disastrously. Peyton's own monologue is reserved for last. In the hands of a less skilled writer, this structure could have been a recipe for failure, but Styron is meticulous, and he has been praised for the architecture of the novel. Form and style make *Lie Down in Darkness* successful. Styron switches from one narrative point of view to another with ease, bringing readers into the minds of his characters and making each character at least partly sympathetic. Greater understanding of motivations and individual pathologies helps create a sense that no one is evil per se. Most of the characters are despairing, lonely, and seeking meaning. Styron balances their narrations so delicately that the structure does not seem contrived. Always, in the background, the funeral cortege crawls along toward eternal darkness.

Gay Pitman Zieger

Further Reading

Baumbach, Jonathan. "Paradise Lost: *Lie Down in Darkness* by William Styron." In *The Landscape of Nightmare: Studies in the Contemporary Novel*. New York: New York University Press, 1965. Places the novel in the context of southern gothic literature. Useful for comparisons of Styron with William Faulkner and other writers of the genre.

Casciato, Arthur D., and James L. W. West III, eds. *Critical Essays on William Styron*. Boston: G. K. Hall, 1982. A good basic resource for scholars and students; makes available some of the more useful work published on Styron.

Cologne-Brookes, Gavin. *The Novels of William Styron: From Harmony to History*. Baton Rouge: Louisiana State University Press, 1995. Examines the influence of the modernist movement on Styron's novels, exploring his psychological themes and analyzing his shifting patterns of discourse. Chapter 1 focuses on *Lie Down in Darkness*.

Hadaller, David. *Gynicide: Women in the Novels of William Styron*. Madison, N.J.: Fairleigh Dickinson University Press, 1996. Explores the treatment of women in Styron's fiction, with special emphasis on his handling of women's deaths and the meaning of these deaths. Argues that Styron's depictions force readers to question a society that victimizes women. Chapter 2 focuses on *Lie Down in Darkness*.

Ross, Daniel W., ed. *The Critical Response to William Styron*. Westport, Conn.: Greenwood Press, 1995. A collection of previously printed reviews and articles, as well as original essays, that chronologically trace the critical reception to Styron's novels.

Styron, William. *Letters to My Father*. Edited by James L. W. West. Baton Rouge: Louisiana State University Press, 2009. A compilation of the letters, more than one hundred, which Styron wrote to his father between 1943 and 1953, detailing the son's "adventures, his works in progress, and his ruminations on the craft of writing." Includes a "prefatory memoir" by Styron's wife, Rose Styron.

West, James L. W., ed. *William Styron: A Life*. New York: Random House, 1998. A well-researched study, exploring the autobiographical details in Styron's novels. An essential work for anyone who wishes to understand Styron and his writing.

The Life and Extraordinary Adventures of Private Ivan Chonkin

Author: Vladimir Voinovich (1932-   )
First published: Zhizn' i neobychainye priklyucheniya
    soldata Ivana Chonkina, 1975 (English translation,
    1977)
Type of work: Novel
Type of plot: Satire
Time of plot: Summer, 1941
Locale: Krasnoye, Soviet Union

Principal characters:
IVAN CHONKIN, a Russian soldier guarding a military
    plane
NYURA BELYASHOVA, the postmistress, Chonkin's lover
KUZMA GLADISHEV, a pseudoscientist raising hybrid plants
IVAN GOLUBEV, a manager of the collective farm
CAPTAIN MILYAGA, a secret-police officer

The Story:

At the end of May, 1941, amid rumors of war, the short, bowlegged Red Army private Ivan Chonkin is sent to the village of Krasnoye to guard an airplane that was forced to land near the village. Chonkin is a poorly educated lad. He has trouble understanding questions properly and asks himself impertinent questions, such as whether Stalin has two wives. He is met in Krasnoye by inquisitive and distrustful villagers, including Nyura Belyashova, a postmistress. They are perplexed by the purpose of Chonkin's mission, since his looks do not inspire respect.

Facing the plane, Chonkin does not know what to think or do. He knows that a sentry is forbidden to eat, drink, smoke, laugh, sing, talk, or relieve himself while on duty, but he soon breaks this rule. He is pleasantly surprised to see Nyura working on her potatoes. He is immediately attracted to her and helps her in her work. Nyura is all alone in the world, and she is loved only by her cow Beauty and her pig Borka. Chonkin's friendliness is enough for her to reciprocate. She invites him to a modest dinner, and he accepts, despite sentry rules. He moves into her modest house. He even rolls the plane into her yard.

After ten days, Chonkin feels right at home guarding the plane, but he begins to worry as he receives no communications from his superiors about a post that seems to be permanent. He was sent to Krasnoye with sufficient rations for only one week. Chonkin turns for advice to Kuzma Gladishev, a pseudoscientist working on a potato-tomato hybrid. Gladishev is a learned and erudite man—a wooden outhouse in his garden has a sign on it reading "water closet" in English. Chonkin asks Gladishev to write a letter for him to his commander asking for unlimited rations and a new uniform. Nyura never delivers the letter, however, fearing that the army will recall Chonkin, even though he forces her to make love several times each night and day.

One day, Chonkin is told by a villager named Burly that

Nyura has been having sex with her hog. The enraged Chonkin decides to leave Nyura, and she, embarrassed and hurt, lets him go without attempting to reconcile with him. Chonkin has a terrible dream that night, sleeping in hay by the plane. Among the terrifying images he experiences is that of Nyura's wedding to a young man. After waking up, Chonkin is invited by Gladishev to share food and beverages, declaring proudly that they are made of fecal matter. Chonkin makes up with Nyura just as the Germans attack their country.

At a meeting in Krasnoye, people discuss the war in utter confusion while grabbing any goods they can. The Communist Party members protest, demanding that the townsfolk return their party cards because assembly without party control is forbidden. The local party leader clings to Communist slogans, but the people do not listen to him. Most of them leave before the end of his speech, except for Chonkin, who is still confused by the question of the origins of man, which he had been discussing with Gladishev. Chonkin looks for Nyura, while worrying that the army may send for him now that the country is at war.

The villagers keep arguing and trying to reason with one another. They listen to a speech by a man with a Georgian accent, wondering if he is Joseph Stalin. The speech calls upon all Soviet citizens to defend their country.

Nyura's cow eats Gladishev's hybrid plants. He responds by trying to kill both the cow and Chonkin. Gladishev writes a letter to Captain Milyaga, the village's secret-police officer, accusing Chonkin of desertion and treason and demanding that he be arrested and shot. Milyaga gives an order for the arrest of Chonkin. In the meanwhile, Milyaga must deal with an old man in the village named Stalin, who is suspected of being the real Stalin or being related to him.

Milyaga's men go to arrest Chonkin, fearing that they may face an entire gang of traitors. Chonkin, standing by the plane, threatens to shoot them, worrying that they have come to capture the plane he has been charged with guarding. He manages to arrest them all. Milyaga comes to see why his men have not returned with Chonkin, and Chonkin arrests him too. The private then visits Ivan Golubev and offers to help run the collective farm with the men he has arrested, since most of the local men have been mobilized by the army. Drinking heavily, Golubev agrees and sends a report in advance to his superiors that the prisoners are working well on the potato harvest.

Still drunk, Chonkin returns to the plane and falls asleep in Nyura's home. Milyaga seizes the opportunity to free himself, but in the darkness he is struck unconscious by a member of a strike force sent to unravel the confusing situation in Krasnoye. When he comes to, Milyaga thinks he has been captured by German soldiers and tries to speak to them in his broken German. The members of the strike force, in turn, believe they have captured a German soldier. They attempt to interrogate the secret-police officer with their scant German. Milyaga is shot.

Chonkin and Nyura are still defending the plane, but the strike force destroys it. Chonkin and Nyura are dazed in the attack but not killed. The general of the strike force is amazed to find that the plane was guarded not by a gang but only by a man and a woman. These two were able to resist a whole regiment of the strike force. The general expresses his gratitude to Chonkin for his bravery and presents him with a decoration on the spot, but when the general is reminded that Chonkin is supposed to be arrested as a traitor, he rescinds his gratitude and decoration and arrests the private. As Chonkin is led away, Nyura cries and reaches for him, but Chonkin yells to her that he will be back.

Critical Evaluation:

The Life and Extraordinary Adventures of Private Ivan Chonkin offers abundant satire on the Soviet state from the top down, as do all the works of Vladimir Voinovich. Voinovich became a leading Russian satirist in the 1970's. The satire is manifold but mostly political in nature. It is directed at the incompetence of Stalin, as well as that of provincial and local leaders. Voinovich concentrates on their sycophancy, lack of integrity, cruelty toward their fellows, fanaticism, and ignorance. For example, in the novel, the editor of the local newspaper makes sure that Stalin's name is mentioned twelve times in each article.

Voinovich satirizes the Soviet judicial system through the trial of Chonkin, which he does not understand at all. The chief prosecutor commits suicide after condemning Chonkin to death without any proof, saying, "Please consider my life

invalid." The Red Army is criticized mercilessly for incompetence. For example, while attacking the Soviet plane that the soldiers believe is German, the strike force forgets to ignite their Molotov cocktails before throwing them. Chonkin, meanwhile, reassures Nyura not to worry because they will get their deposit on the bottles back later. There are many such incidents in the novel.

Sometimes, Voinovich's satire turns into absurdity, as in Gladishev's effort to grow potatoes and tomatoes on the same plant, in his making food and drinks from feces, in rumors of Nyura's having sex with a pig, and in Chonkin making love several times each day and night. These improbable happenings, however, fit into the overall oddity of the novel, emphasizing the points the author is making.

Symbolically, the plane's forced landing in the backwaters of the hinterland on the eve of the war mirrors the lack of security of the state at a fateful moment. Chonkin's confusion about the place in which he finds himself, his lack of understanding of his mission, and his superiors' forgetting about him reflect the inadequate workings of the state. The sexual prowess of the protagonist symbolizes the virility of the common people, and Nyura's undying love for him speaks to the basic goodness of the Russian people. Voinovich also uses symbolism in an ironic sense, as in the names he chooses for Golubev (a cruel man whose name suggests a dove) and Milyaga (suggesting a dear, good-natured person). He also incorporates humor, mainly in the way villagers use local idioms in their conversations, often misunderstanding what they have been told. When Gladishev threatens to kill the cow, he has no powder in his rifle, because he has used it for fertilizer. One officer orders a junior commander to place himself under arrest. Such humorous events help relieve the barbarity of other events depicted in the novel.

Voinovich is a master of characterization. The protagonist, Chonkin, is an antihero, resembling such other antiheroes as those portrayed in Jaroslav Hašek's *Osudy dobrého vojáka Švejka za sv tove války* (1921-1923; *The Good Soldier: Švejk*, 1930; also as *The Good Soldier Švejk and His Fortunes in the World War*, 1973) and Georg Büchner's *Woyzek* (pb. 1879, pr. 1913). Elements of mistaken identity in the novel also resemble aspects of Nikolai Gogol's *Revizor* (pr., pb. 1836; *The Inspector General*, 1890). Chonkin behaves as is to be expected of a poorly educated citizen, and he takes advantage of circumstances, thinking primarily of his own needs. He does not occupy himself with political matters, but his actions and those taken against him serve the novel's political satire.

Nyura is a woman without love, who clings to the opportunity for a relationship when it arises with Chonkin. Even though she is better educated than he is, she tolerates his irrational outbursts and continues to love him. The leaders portrayed in the novel, from the general to the collective farm chairman, are constantly bumbling, in a way that mirrors the failures of the entire state. Gladishev is the best example of this bumbling. He is not aware that he is a ludicrous figure, declaring, "If I perish, I ask to be considered a Communist." He embodies the false scientific policies prevailing in Stalin's time.

Golubev runs his collective farm without understanding it, but when he refuses to allow harvesting in rainy weather, he is accused of treason. He is brave enough to return his party card. Captain Milyaga, the head of the local secret police, uses his authority expeditiously, at times cruelly, yet he becomes a victim of his own inadequacy and pays the price for it. All these characters and many others contribute to a colossal satire of an entire system. They also enliven the novel, making for good reading in addition to offering delightful satire.

Voinovich's satire is not entirely negative. To be sure, he castigates the Soviet system for not helping the people or defending the country under attack. He also, however, expresses sympathy for common folks such as Chonkin and Nyura, as well as the hope that eventually things may improve, as may be seen in Chonkin's assurance at the end of the novel that he will be back.

Vasa D. Mihailovich

Further Reading

Matich, Olga, and Michael Helms, eds. *The Third Wave: Russian Literature in Emigration.* Ann Arbor, Mich.: Ardis, 1983. Study of Voinovich and other Soviet émigré writers, discussing both their works and their biographies.

Milivojevic, Dragan. "The Many Voices of Vladimir Voinovich." *Rocky Mountain Review of Language and Literature* 30, no. 2 (1979): 55-62. General but useful discussion of Voinovich's satire.

Porter, R. C. "Vladimir Voinovich and the Comedy of Innocence." *Forum for Modern Language Studies* 16, no. 2 (1980): 97-108. Examines Voinovich's treatment of common Russians, who are often portrayed comically but deliver a potent satiric message in his work.

Szporluk, Mary Ann. "Vladimir Voinovich: The Development of a New Satirical Voice." *Russian Literary Quarterly* 14 (Winter, 1976): 99-121. Details the emergence of Voinovich as a leading satirist in post-Stalin Russian literature.

Terras, Victor. *A History of Russian Literature.* New Haven, Conn.: Yale University Press, 1991. Succinct discussion of Voinovich's role as a leading Russian dissident.

Wakamiya, Lisa Ryoko. *Locating Exiled Writers in Contemporary Russian Literature: Exiles at Home.* New York: Palgrave Macmillan, 2010. Study of exiled Russian writers who, like Voinovich, returned to Russia after the fall of the Soviet state and sought to redefine the nature of Russian literary identity in a post-Communist era.

Life and Times of Michael K

Author: J. M. Coetzee (1940-   )
First published: 1983
Type of work: Novel
Type of plot: Allegory
Time of plot: Early 1980's
Locale: South Africa

Principal characters:
MICHAEL K, a gardener
ANNA K, his mother
A DOCTOR, who cares for Michael K during his internment at Kenilworth

The Story:

Michael K is born with a harelip in Cape Town, South Africa. His mother, Anna K, shelters him from other children and takes him with her to work: Anna tends the house of a wealthy white family, the Buhrmans, who live in Sea Point, near Cape Town. At an early age, because of his deformity and his slowness of speech and thought, K is placed in a state-run institution called Huis Norenius. At fifteen, he becomes a gardener for the state, slowly rising through the ranks to gain increasing autonomy. K does not have friends other than his mother, and he is most at ease alone.

When K is thirty-one, his mother is in the hospital and South Africa is at civil war. After Anna is released from the hospital, she is too weak to care for herself, and K returns to live with her in her broom closet under the stairs in a decrepit hotel. Anna tells K of her plan to return to her birthplace on a farm in the district of Prince Albert. K agrees to the plan, quits his job, and attempts to secure a permit that will allow them to travel; the permit will not arrive for two months, if at all. As they wait, the war increases in pitch.

After their hotel is ransacked, K and his mother move into the vacant Burhman apartment until fear of discovery overtakes them; K makes one last attempt to determine the status of his permit application to no avail. K and his mother strike out on foot toward the farm, with K pushing his feeble mother in a wheelbarrow, but they are turned back at a checkpoint.

Days later, they set off again by back roads, hoping to avoid surveillance. Anna's health deteriorates further, and when they arrive in Stellenbosch, a small city east of Cape Town, K admits her to a hospital. After two days in the hospital, Anna dies; K, after wandering the hospital grounds dazed, is given a box containing his mother's ashes and asked to leave.

K leaves Stellenbosch, heading north toward Paarl. He avoids checkpoints and convoys until he is accosted and robbed by a lone Nationalist soldier. Afterward, he decides his purpose is to bury Anna's ashes at her birthplace.

On his way through the mountains, K is discovered by police near Worcester and taken into custody. He is herded onto a train and forced to help clear the track of debris they encounter. After the train lets him off in Touwe River, K makes his way to Prince Albert.

In Prince Albert, K locates the farm he believes is the one his mother remembered and finds it deserted. He lives on the farm for a time, indulging in the freshwater there, and scatters his mother's ashes carefully in the field. He finds pumpkin, bean, and corn seeds at the farm, plants them, and tends his new garden carefully.

As K settles into this life, the grandson of the Visagie family that owns the farm arrives, a military deserter. The grandson assumes K is a hired hand and immediately begins to treat K as a servant. Eventually, he sends K with some money to Prince Albert for supplies; K leaves with the money and heads instead higher into the Swartberg mountains.

K lives for a time in the mountains without food or water until, at the very edge of starvation, K descends to Prince Albert, where he is arrested and taken to jail. He is charged with

traveling without documentation, infringing curfew, and being drunk and disorderly and is taken to Jaakalsdrif, a resettlement camp.

In Jaakalsdrif, K is forced to work again; the labor begins to take its toll on his body. After a time, police raid the camp during some kind of riot, ushering in even more inhumane living conditions. As acts of violence and criminal neglect increase, K escapes again.

K returns to the Visagie farm. Finding no sign of the grandson, he sets about replanting and tending his meager crop. Months pass, and K regains his health and confidence until revolutionaries arrive. Most of K's crops are eaten and destroyed. Despite K's fears, peace returns to the farm, and some of his fruit grows and ripens. K eats it with great satisfaction and joy.

K continues to live on the farm for a long time and begins to show increasing signs of crippling malnourishment. After a rainstorm forces him to find shelter, he is again discovered by soldiers, who believe him to be aiding revolutionaries. K is taken into custody, and the farmhouse is destroyed.

K is taken to a hospital in Kenilworth, a rehabilitation camp, where a doctor becomes obsessed with the mystery of K as he attempts to help K recover. K refuses to eat hospital food or to reveal anything substantial about himself. Soon after news arrives that Kenilworth is to be turned from a rehabilitation camp into an internment camp, K escapes. The doctor decides not to report K missing and muses at length in his journal about the profound effect K has had on him.

After his escape, K returns to Sea Point and meets wandering vagrants who want to take him in. At nightfall, as K is preparing to sleep, he imagines a life like the one he lived for a time on the Visagie farm. He thinks that he would like to return to it.

Critical Evaluation:

Life and Times of Michael K was awarded the British Man Booker Prize for Fiction in 1983, as was J. M. Coetzee's later novel *Disgrace* (1999), marking the only time a single author has been given the award more than once. In 2003, Coetzee was awarded the Nobel Prize in Literature, which recognized him for his morally and ethically charged examinations of South African culture, especially of the implications and effects of apartheid (state-sanctioned racial segregation and oppression).

Many of Coetzee's earlier works, including *Dusklands* (1974), *In the Heart of the Country* (1977), and *Waiting for the Barbarians* (1980), are considered by critics and reviewers to be allegorical to some extent; *Life and Times of Michael K* is no exception. Coetzee has at times been criticized in South Africa for his allegorical impulse, which his critics have believed to obscure his resistance to the Nationalist apartheid regime of 1948 to 1994. Those critics felt that he had an obligation to make this resistance explicit rather than implicit in his fiction. Other critics, however, have argued that Coetzee's ethical aims for his fiction are more complex than mere political commentary.

Although the political landscape and time line of *Life and Times of Michael K* are purposefully vague, there are many details that imply an allegorical near-future South Africa where exaggerated apartheid-like conditions exist. The "travel permits" K needs reflect the "pass laws" of apartheid designed to facilitate segregation by limiting the movements of nonwhites within South Africa. Although there were not explicit "rehabilitation" or "internment" camps in South Africa in 1983, there were strict zoning regulations based on race.

The state institution for "children with disabilities" that K attends as a youth and that primes him for a life of manual labor mirrors the curriculum of black schools during apartheid. When K is captured at one point, he is labeled "CM—40—NFA—Unemployed"; the *CM* means "colored male," one of the three possible racial categories under apartheid's Population Registration Act of 1950. If one accepts the clues that K is indeed black (which a few critics do not), then the pieces of allegory fall convincingly in place; the plight and journey of Michael K become an allegory for the plight of every victim of South African apartheid.

As emblematic of every black or "coloured" man in South Africa, K's story could take on a predictable arc, similar to those of many tales of postcolonial oppression. Every setback K encounters can be seen as a reflection of his race. K's harelip could be interpreted as an exaggerated sign of the stigma of black skin; his silence and slowness could be attributed to an oppressor's view of the mental capacity of people of color. The economic conditions surrounding K and his mother are poor, as evidenced by the hospitals they visit and their living conditions; it is unclear if these conditions are due to the war or to their race. The allegory continues as K is repeatedly detained or impeded; he is captured and forced to labor; he flees and hides; he lives off the land; he is recaptured and flees again. K's plight reads like a modern slave narrative.

While K himself is a character immersed in an allegorical world, many critics argue that the role of the allegorical protagonist is one that he constantly evades. In a more traditional allegory, K would become a revolutionary and work to overthrow the power structure of the colonial oppressors. Instead, K resists the pull of allegory and chooses not to participate in or be defined by power structures in any way.

The power of the colonizers is often exerted on K in the form of language, and K's resistance often takes the form of silence. For example, K foils the medical officer at Kenilworth, who becomes obsessed with reaching him, by refusing to explain himself. That the doctor—a colonial agent, since hospitals are agencies of the state—wants to help save K's life makes no difference; K does not want to be defined by any terms other than his own. The power of language is readily apparent when K is named by different authorities at various times: He is named first "Michael Visagie" and later "Michaels." He does not resist these names, for they do not matter to him; in an existential line of thinking, simply being is enough for K. What he is or what he is called does not matter.

Another moment where K chooses action to evade power structures occurs when he kills a goat to eat at the Visagie farm and finds the act distasteful. The farm is a colonial structure; Dutch and British colonists acquired the land, settled on it, and raised livestock. Although he cannot articulate his feelings, K has no urge to eat what the colonials eat and no urge to acquire or stockpile; he merely wants to subsist. He only wants what he can cultivate; he wants not to farm but rather to garden. His nature mirrors his desires to remain untouched by political doctrine and untouched by histories—either of the colonizer or of the colonized. Although K's resistance in *Life and Times of Michael K* is subtle, it illuminates the inherent problems with any political system in South Africa, where Coetzee sees no satisfactory option of a way to live.

Alan C. Haslam

Further Reading

Attridge, Derek. "Against Allegory: *Waiting for the Barbarians* and *Life and Times of Michael K*." In *J. M. Coetzee and the Ethics of Reading*. Chicago: University of Chicago Press, 2004. A theoretical explanation of the allegorical narrative framework of *Life and Times of Michael K*; reads K as an antiallegorical figure.

Attwell, David. "Contexts: Literary, Historical, Intellectual." In *J. M. Coetzee and the Politics of Writing*. Berkeley: University of California Press, 1993. A thorough introduction to the complex themes of Coetzee's work and its relation to South Africa.

_____. "Writing in the Cauldron of History: *Life and Times of Michael K* and *Foe*." In *J. M. Coetzee and the Politics of Writing*. Berkeley: University of California Press, 1993. Detailed description of Coetzee's expression of Michael K's desire to escape political pressures; argues that, although immersed in history, K manages to remain untouched by it.

Gordimer, Nadine. "The Idea of Gardening: *Life and Times of Michael K* by J. M. Coetzee." In *Critical Essays on J. M. Coetzee.* New York: G. K. Hall, 1998. Review of the novel that provides an accessible and insightful introduction to the themes it explores.

Head, Dominic. "Gardening as Resistance: *Life and Times of Michael K.*" In *J. M. Coetzee.* New York: Cambridge University Press, 1997. Describes how *Life and Times of Michael K* undermines the tradition of political involvement in historical novels by representing the life of someone who resists all contact with social forces.

Marais, Michael. "The Hermeneutics of Empire: Coetzee's Postcolonial Metafiction." In *Critical Perspectives on J. M. Coetzee,* edited by Graham Huggan and Stephen Watson. New York: St. Martin's Press, 1996. A highly theoretical essay examining the work of Coetzee, *Life and Times of Michael K* in particular. Argues that Coetzee's novels cannot be easily categorized as either postcolonial or postmodern but rather resist and reside within both literary modes.

Life Is a Dream

Author: Pedro Calderón de la Barca (1600-1681)
First produced: La vida es sueño, 1635; first published, 1636 (English translation, 1830)
Type of work: Drama
Type of plot: Melodrama
Time of plot: Sixteenth century
Locale: Poland

Principal characters:
BASILIO, king of Poland
SEGISMUNDO, his son
ASTOLFO, Basilio's nephew and a duke of Muscovy
ESTRELLA, the infanta, Basilio's niece
CLOTALDO, a Polish general
ROSAURA, a Russian noblewoman disguised as a man
FIFE, her servant

The Story:

One night, in the wild, mountainous country between Poland and Russia, a Russian noblewoman, Rosaura, and her servant, Fife, find themselves in distress. Their horses have bolted, and they fear that they will have to complete the remainder of their journey on foot. They are traveling to the royal court of Poland, and Rosaura is disguised as a man for protection as they make their way through the barbarous frontier country. Their weary way brings them at last to a forbidding fortress. There they overhear a young man, chained to the doorway of the castle, deliver a heart-rending soliloquy in which he laments the harshness of his life. Rosaura approaches the youth, who greets her eagerly, with the excitement of one who has known little of sympathy or kindness during his brief span of years. At the same time, he warns her to beware of violence. No sooner has he spoken these words than a shrill trumpet blast fills the night. Rosaura tosses her sword to the captive before she and Fife hide themselves among the rocks.

Clotaldo, a Polish general and the keeper of the youth, gallops up to the young man. Seeing the sword in his prisoner's hand, he orders his men to seek the stranger who must be lurking nearby. Apprehended, Rosaura explains that she and Fife are Russian travelers on their way to the Polish court and that they are in distress because of the loss of their horses. Fife inadvertently hints that Rosaura is really a woman. Clotaldo, however, is most interested in the sword, for he recognizes the weapon as one he had owned years before and that he left in the keeping of a young noblewoman with whom he had been deeply in love. He comes to the conclusion that Rosaura must be his own son, but, torn between his sworn duty to his king and his paternal obligation toward his supposed son, he decides at last to say nothing for the time being. The fact that Rosaura possesses the sword obligates him to protect the travelers and to escort them safely through the mountains.

Meanwhile, in King Basilio's royal castle, the problem of succession to the Polish throne is to be decided. To this purpose, the king welcomes his nephew Astolfo and his niece Estrella. The problem of the succession exists because it is generally believed that the true heir, King Basilio's son, died with his mother in childbirth many years before. The need for a decision is pressing; both Astolfo and Estrella are supported by strong rival factions that, in their impatience, are threatening the peace of the realm.

King Basilio greets his niece and nephew with regal ceremony and then startles them with the news that his son, Segismundo, is not really dead. The readings of learned astrologers and horrible portents that had accompanied Segismundo's birth had led the superstitious king to imprison the child in a mountain fortress for fear that otherwise the boy might grow up to be a monster who would destroy Poland. Now, years later, King Basilio is not sure that he did the right thing. He proposes that Segismundo be brought to the court in a drug-induced sleep, awakened after being dressed in attire befitting a prince, and observed carefully for evidence of his worthiness to wear his father's crown. Astolfo and Estrella agree to the proposal.

In accordance with the plan, Segismundo, who dresses in rough wolf skins in his captivity, is drugged, carried to the royal castle, and dressed in rich attire. When he awakes, he is disturbed to find himself suddenly the center of attention among obsequious strangers. Force of habit causes him to recall sentimentally his chains, the wild mountains, and his former isolation. Convinced that he is dreaming, he sits on the throne while his father's officers and the noble courtiers treat him with the respect due his rank. When they tell him that he is the heir to the throne, he is mystified and somewhat apprehensive, but before long he begins to enjoy his new feeling of power.

Clotaldo, his former guard and tutor, appears to confirm the fact that Segismundo is really the prince. The young man then demands an explanation of his lifelong imprisonment. Clotaldo patiently explains King Basilio's actions in terms that Segismundo might understand, but the youth, blinded by the sudden change in his fortunes, can see only that he has been grievously mistreated by his father. Declaring that he will have revenge for his unwarranted imprisonment, he seizes Clotaldo's sword, but before he can strike the old general, Rosaura appears out of the crowd, takes the weapon from him, and reproves him for his rashness.

Segismundo, in a calmer mood, is introduced to Astolfo, whose courtly bearing and formal speech the prince cannot bear. Sick of the whole aspect of the court, he orders the guards to clear the audience hall. Again, however, he is mollified, this time by the appearance of Estrella and her ladies-in-waiting. Unaccustomed to feminine society, he behaves in a boorish manner, even attempting to embrace Estrella. The courtiers advise him to behave in a manner befitting a prince, and Astolfo, who hopes to marry his beautiful cousin, cau-

tions Segismundo about his behavior toward the princess. Unfamiliar with the formalities of court life, Segismundo loses his patience. Holding all present responsible for his long exile, he reminds them of his exalted position and defies anyone to touch Estrella. When Astolfo does not hesitate to take her by the hand, Segismundo seizes Astolfo by the throat.

At this crucial moment in Segismundo's test, King Basilio enters the throne room and sees his son behaving like a wild beast. Crushed, he fears that the predictions about him were accurate after all. Segismundo faces his father with shocking disrespect and presses for an explanation of his imprisonment. When the king tries to prove that the young man's future was written in the stars, Segismundo scoffs at the folly of a man's putting responsibility for his actions on the disinterested heavens. Then he curses his father and calls on the guards to seize the king and Clotaldo. At a trumpet blast, however, the soldiers quickly surround Segismundo himself and take him prisoner.

Having failed the test of princehood, Segismundo is drugged and returned in chains to the mountain fortress. In his familiar surroundings once more, he has full opportunity to reflect on his recent experiences. When he speaks to Clotaldo about them, the old general tells him that all had been a dream. Since the prince was drugged before he left the fortress and before he returned, he is quite convinced that he has suffered an unpleasant dream. Clotaldo assures him that dreams reveal the true character of the dreamer. Because Segismundo has conducted himself with violence in his dream, there is great need for the young man to bridle his fierce passions.

Meanwhile Rosaura, aware of Segismundo's plight and anxious to thwart the ambitions of Astolfo, who had once promised to marry her, stirs up a faction to demand the prince's release. The rebels invade the mountains and seize the fortress; they fail, however, to seize Clotaldo, who has already returned to the royal castle to report to King Basilio. When the rebel army carries the sleeping Segismundo out of the fortress and awakens him with trumpet blasts, the unhappy prince will not be persuaded that his new experience is real, and he doubts the assurance that he has been rescued from his imprisonment. The rebel leader finally convinces him that it would be well for him to join the dream soldiers and fight with them against King Basilio's very real army, which is approaching.

Clotaldo is taken prisoner by Segismundo's forces, but the young prince, remembering the advice to curb his passions, orders the old general's release. A great battle then takes place in which Segismundo proves his princely valor and chivalric bearing. King Basilio, defeated but refusing Clotaldo's and Astolfo's pleas to flee to safety, in admiration surrenders his crown to his son.

As king of Poland in his own right, Segismundo orders the marriage of Astolfo to Rosaura, who has, in the meantime, been revealed as Clotaldo's daughter. Estrella becomes Segismundo's queen, and the young king makes Clotaldo his trusted adviser.

Critical Evaluation:

Before Pedro Calderón de la Barca's *La vida es sueño* was freely adapted by Edward Fitzgerald in 1853, it had been known to most English and European readers through the medium of French translations from the original Spanish. In spite of their richness of imagination, however, Calderón's plays are still little known outside the Spanish-speaking world. All of this playwright's work has vigor and brilliance; in *Life Is a Dream*, for example, he uses his Polish setting and period as freely as William Shakespeare uses the seacoast of Bohemia or the forest of Arden. A gothic quality in the mountain scenes suggests the popular atmosphere of much eighteenth century fiction, and the play offers considerable psychological insight into character as well. This work admirably reveals the personality of its writer, who was a soldier, an ardent patriot, an artist, and a devout son of the Catholic Church.

Life Is a Dream, which has also been translated into English as *Such Stuff as Dreams Are Made Of*, is one of the masterpieces of world literature, as relevant today as when it was first performed in 1635. Its power, along with the sheer beauty of its verse, lies in the questions it asks but never answers. The play's richness of meaning can be inferred from the various categories into which critics and scholars have placed it; it has been called Christian, romantic, philosophical, existentialist, absurdist, and tragic theater.

The drama is organized around three great soliloquies by Segismundo that not only further the action but also exemplify the dominant themes of the play. The first, spoken by Segismundo while he is still in chains, imprisoned in his tower, centers on his lack of freedom compared with other creatures of the earth; the second is the famous "life is a dream" speech, in which Segismundo can no longer distinguish between reality and dream; and the third focuses on Segismundo's decision to act and act well, no matter whether he is awake or asleep.

The dramatic interplay of light and shadow in the play's imagery reflects Segismundo's confusion between reality and dream. For example, the abrupt change he experiences from the perpetual twilight of his tower to the hurtful brilliance of the court is the stuff of nightmares for Segismundo. Ironically, the bright light of the court should symbolize knowledge and wisdom, but in the play its harshness, which blinds Segismundo, represents the cruelty of a king who is blinded in turn by his own self-image and mistaken beliefs. Segismundo finds the light of truth in his dark tower.

The paradoxes of the imagery mirror the ambiguities of the themes of the play. A principal theme is that of the triumph of free will. Out of fear, at Segismundo's birth King Basilio rejected the concept of free will and robbed his son of his freedom, but Segismundo finds that only by controlling his will can he achieve the freedom he seeks. Segismundo, at the end of the work, has triumphed over his baser nature, but he has had to give up the woman he loves. The denouement, although it ties up the loose ends of the plot, is far from being the happy ending of a typical romance. When Segismundo's final action is to imprison in his tower for rebellion a soldier who helped to set him free, an ironic cycle is completed.

Much has been written of the metaphysical nature of the work. Calderón has long been considered the foremost idea-oriented dramatist of the Spanish language. Many critics label him one of the first existentialists. *Life Is a Dream* takes place in no particular time, and therefore in every time, and Segismundo can be seen to represent every human being forced to find the right way in a shadow world, imprisoned and oppressed by forces unknowable and uncontrollable, and fettered by ignorance and base instincts. No matter how strong the philosophical underpinnings of the work, however, it should not be forgotten that Segismundo is also strong as a dramatic character. He is very much a flesh-and-blood person, and his love for Rosaura is clear. This makes his giving her up a greater sacrifice, not just the politic and dutiful gesture of some hypothetical model of the good ruler.

A sense of personal loss is evident in this play. Segismundo has lost his childhood and adolescence. He also recovers what was lost: his identity. All the other major characters' lives are colored by the question of what might have been. Such melancholy explains their unwillingness to act in an uncertain world. This fear is given beautiful poetic expression in Segismundo's comparison of life to a flowering almond tree whose blooms, appearing too soon, wither and die at the first slightly cold wind.

One character in the play does not fit into this mold of passivity in the face of loss: Rosaura. She has lost her lover, Astolfo, but she decides to seek, not accept, her fate and go after him. Defying convention, disguised as a man, she travels to Poland and ends up serving in Segismundo's army. She is an elemental force whose actions turn Segismundo's, Clotaldo's, Astolfo's, and Estrella's lives upside down. Her determination and will are juxtaposed, on a higher level, to the cowardice of Basilio. Basilio has spent his whole life, and ruined his son's, trying to flee his supposed preordained fate. He realizes his error when, on fleeing the battlefield, he stumbles across the dead body of Rosaura's servant, who, thinking to avoid death on the battlefield, had run straight into it.

Philosophy, characterization, emotions, and action are all realized in the masterful poetic tapestry of *Life Is a Dream*. The Romantics considered Calderón to be the greatest of all lyrical dramatists, and the 3,315 verses of the play could be used as a textbook on how to write verse drama. The evaluation of Spanish Golden Age drama has gone through many changes over the years, depending on prevailing literary and political winds, but appreciation of *Life Is a Dream* has been unchanging. It is a complex, intricate work that cannot easily be slotted into any comfortable critical niche.

"Critical Evaluation" by Charlene E. Suscavage

Further Reading

Benabu, Isaac. *Reading for the Stage: Calderón and His Contemporaries*. Rochester, N.Y.: Tamesis, 2003. Analyzes playtexts for works by Calderón and contemporary playwrights. (A playtext is the text usually read by the theater company at the beginning of a play's production and provides the playwright's directions for staging the work.) Among the topics discussed are the religiosity of Spanish theater in the Golden Age and Calderón's devotional comedies.

Heigl, Michaela. *Theorizing Gender, Sexuality, and the Body in Calderonian Theater*. New Orleans, La.: University Press of the South, 2001. Focuses on the transvestites, scolds, sodomites, monsters, and other "deviant" characters in Calderón's plays, demonstrating how they embody the idea of excess and subvert the boundaries between the sexes and between different social classes. Argues that these characters represent the inherent corruption and perversion in society.

Parker, A. A. *The Mind and Art of Calderón: Essays on the Comedias*. Edited by Deborah Kong. New York: Cambridge University Press, 1988. One of the critics responsible for renewed interest in and new interpretations of Spanish Golden Age theater provides in-depth discussion of Calderónian theater.

Rodríguez Cuadros, Evangelina. "Pedro Calderón de la Barca." In *The Cambridge History of Spanish Literature*, edited by David T. Gies. New York: Cambridge University Press, 2004. Presents an overview of Calderón de la Barca's life and places his work within the broader context of Spanish literature.

Thacker, Jonathan. *A Companion to Golden Age Theatre*. Rochester, N.Y.: Tamesis, 2007. Good introduction to Spanish Golden Age theater examines the work of Calderón and other playwrights. Describes the different types of plays produced in this era and traces the growth and maturation of Spanish theater.

Wilson, Margaret. *Spanish Drama of the Golden Age*. New York: Pergamon Press, 1969. Offers a basic introduction to Spanish Golden Age drama. Compares Calderón's plays with those of his contemporaries and reaches conclusions about the work that are different from those of many critics.

The Life of Marianne

Author: Marivaux (1688-1763)
First published: La Vie de Marianne, 1731-1741 (English translation, 1736-1742)
Type of work: Novel
Type of plot: Psychological realism
Time of plot: Late seventeenth century
Locale: France

Principal characters:
MARIANNE, COUNTESS OF ——, a virtuous orphan
MONSIEUR DE CLIMAL, Marianne's benefactor and Madame de Valville's brother
MONSIEUR DE VALVILLE, Marianne's fiancé
MADAME DE VALVILLE, his mother
MADEMOISELLE VARTHON, a young woman loved by Valville
MADEMOISELLE DE TERVIRE, now a nun

The Story:

Shortly after renting a country house near Rennes, the narrator states, he came upon several notebooks in the house containing the story of a lady, presented in her own handwriting. At the request of his friends, he agreed to edit and publish her account. Marianne, the name the lady in the autobiography gives herself, is a countess, about fifty years of age at the time of her writing. She explains that she is describing her past because a dear friend has entreated her to tell the full story of her life.

While still an infant, Marianne is orphaned in an attack by brigands on the coach in which she and her parents are traveling. She is the only survivor of this brutal encounter, and as a result her identity is unknown. Passersby rescue the child and put her in the care of the sister of the local priest. Marianne remains the ward of that kind person until she is fifteen years of age, at which time, while she and her foster mother are visiting Paris, misfortune comes to her again. An epidemic breaks out, and all of those intimately concerned with Marianne's welfare are fatally stricken.

Soon another benefactor appears, Monsieur de Climal, who offers to aid her out of charitable piety. By this time, Marianne is a beautiful young woman, and Climal shows his fondness by buying her expensive clothing and arranging for her lodging with a widowed shopkeeper, Madame Dutour. Marianne objects strongly to the bourgeois atmosphere of her new home, but her circumstances give her no other choice.

One day, on a religious holiday, she dresses in her finery and strolls about the city after church. The young men ogle her; one in particular is especially attracted to her and she to him, although no words pass between them. Bemused and distracted by the encounter, Marianne steps into the path of a moving carriage and is knocked down. Her young admirer, Monsieur de Valville, comes immediately to her aid. At the time, neither learns the other's identity, for Monsieur de Climal arrives and jealously insists on taking his charge home.

Beside himself, Climal declares his undying love and offers to set Marianne up in an apartment. Proudly refusing this hypocritical proposal and also his protection, she goes to live in a nearby convent. Meanwhile, Valville sets about to learn her name and whereabouts. Successful in his search, he arrives at the convent soon after Marianne has acquired a loving benefactress, who turns out to be his mother. When Madame de Valville learns of the mutual attraction between her son and Marianne, she agrees that they could well be in love, but she counsels delay in the affair. In the meantime, Climal has succumbed to a fatal illness; as an act of repentance, he

has bequeathed one-third of his estate to Marianne. The remainder is to go to his nephew, Valville.

As soon as Valville's noble and influential relatives find out about Marianne's dubious parentage and her brief stay with a shopkeeper, they take steps to prevent the young couple from marrying. In an elaborate abduction scheme, they succeed in luring Marianne away from the convent. They then tell her that she has two choices: to become a nun or to marry a young man they will provide. In the hope of gaining time, she agrees to talk with the prospective bridegroom, but she informs her captors that she will wed no one but Valville. At that moment, Madame de Valville and her son catch up with the plot and arrive to defend Marianne. At last the relatives, convinced of Marianne's strength of character, nobility, and worthiness, withdraw their objections to the marriage, and plans for the wedding are made. Within a few weeks, Marianne is to leave the convent and become a bride.

A chance call upon friends brings Mademoiselle Varthon to the attention of Valville. During a brief illness Marianne is confined, and Valville becomes infatuated with Mlle Varthon, who promptly tells Marianne of her love for the young man. Deeply grieved by her son's infidelity, Madame de Valville assures Marianne of her own love and affection, which she continues to shower upon the unfortunate young woman. Death ends Madame de Valville's acts of kindness a short time later, however, and once more Marianne is alone in the world.

To take Marianne's mind off her misfortunes and to give her some perspective on the many curious things that happen to human beings, a nun who has become very friendly with her suggests that Marianne should hear the story of the nun's life. Depressed and lonely, Marianne agrees to listen to the nun's account.

The nun, the daughter of Monsieur de Tervire and Mademoiselle de Tresle, learned early in life that her father was dead. Sometime later, her mother married a grand seigneur of the court, and the young girl was left to the care of a farmer. Although her mother sent money for her support and promised again and again to bring her daughter to live with her in Paris, the invitation was constantly delayed. When Mlle de Tervire was seventeen years of age, Baron de Sercour sought her hand in marriage. An unscrupulous trick by the baron's heir disgraced the bride-to-be, however, and the marriage never took place. Madame de Dursan then became the young woman's foster mother. She willed her estate to Mlle de Tervire, but an estranged son turned up as Madame de Dursan was dying, and the will was changed. When Madame de Dursan's relatives refused to give Mlle de Tervire one-third of the property, as had been promised, she decided to go to Paris. On the stagecoach, she met a Madame Darcire. Ultimately, Mlle de Tervire discovered that Madame Darcire knew the young woman's mother well. From a lawyer, they learned that Madame la Marquise, the mother, had been persuaded to turn her estates over to her son. He then took all the property and abandoned his mother to poverty. Furious at this turn of events, Mlle de Tervire went to her sister-in-law and demanded that her half brother take proper care of their parent. The nun ended her story with the recounting of a disastrous love affair and her ultimate decision to take the veil.

After years of tribulation, Marianne finally marries Valville. She also learns that she is of noble birth.

Critical Evaluation:

Marivaux's eleven-volume tale about the vicissitudes of a young woman thrust upon the world with no clear-cut social identity ranks with Samuel Richardson's *Pamela: Or, Virtue Rewarded* (1740-1741) and *Clarissa: Or, The History of a Young Lady* (1747-1748) as one of the first modern psychological novels. It is a pity that Marivaux did not finish the work; it was completed by Marie-Jeanne Riccoboni. The unfinished novel stops before the nun finishes her story and before Marianne is jilted, suffers various tribulations, and at last marries Valville.

Writing in the early decades of the eighteenth century, Marivaux used a variety of devices already common in the fiction of the day to give his work an air of verisimilitude. Using the device of the memoir and telling the story in the epistolary form were both well-tried techniques that helped readers accept the story as plausible and the behavior of the characters as realistic.

Marivaux is successful in creating lifelike characters because, unlike many of his predecessors and contemporaries, he concentrates on the exploration of emotion rather than on development of action. He goes beyond a number of novelists of his time to achieve a sense of realism by including language spoken by commoners, a device scorned by earlier writers who attempted to maintain standards of decorum prescribed by neoclassical theories of literature in vogue at the time. Marivaux often uses the language of the streets when appropriate for the scene and situation he is depicting. As a result, a number of his characters become individualized through their language, an accomplishment that links the author with the realistic tradition.

The writer's major success in *The Life of Marianne* is his creation of a heroine whose behavior seems psychologically sound. Marianne is a complex character who succeeds by her wits and charm rather than by social position. Throughout the story, she struggles to find her rightful place in society. She is unable simply to claim that right because her origins are unknown, so she must earn her social rewards by acting in such a way that those in the upper classes of society will accept her. Her efforts are not always successful, and often she stumbles because she makes poor decisions. She is not always a sound judge of character, nor does she always make the right choices, but she is resilient and resourceful. As she admits, she is often blessed by good fortune; circumstance and coincidence play no small role in extricating her from potentially devastating situations. She is not presented as perfect, however; Marivaux and his eighteenth century contemporaries make that distinction between their heroines and those of earlier ages, whose virtues are often so great that they become mere pasteboard figures rather than believable human beings. Marianne has her faults, but she also has a certain inner strength that allows her to appreciate her triumphs without becoming too elated and to deal realistically with her tragedies. This is especially true when she loses Valville to the vapid Mlle Varthon.

Although there is no evidence that Marivaux modeled his work on that of any of the English writers, clear parallels exist between Marianne and that paragon of resourcefulness, Daniel Defoe's Moll Flanders. Like Defoe, Marivaux structures his tale so that the elder Marianne tells readers of her life as a younger woman. Doing so allows her to serve, in the same fashion as Moll Flanders does, as commentator and judge of her own past behavior. Unlike Moll, Marianne is not forced to resort to a life of crime to preserve herself; however, the two women share a certain quality of self-awareness and an understanding that being true to oneself is often more critical to one's psychological health than being accepted in the eyes of society.

Because Marivaux did not finish *The Life of Marianne*, it is impossible to know exactly what he had planned for his heroine in her struggle to retrieve her good name and her heritage. Hints in the novelist's writings suggest that eventually she would have discovered the identity of her parents and been restored to her rightful place in society. Nevertheless, the materials available indicate that Marivaux is more interested in character development than in knitting together the disparate strands of plot; action, for him, seems simply an excuse for character revelation.

Perhaps the most significant contribution Marivaux makes to French literature stems from his decision to concentrate not on the nobility but on the middle classes. No writer before him had chosen as the subject for such an extended romantic tale a woman whose claim to nobility could be disputed. His focus throughout the eleven volumes is on the lower classes of society. He paints meticulous, favorable portraits of characters such as Madame Dutour, the simple shopkeeper with whom Marianne lives for a time. His interest in the common people of France precedes the work of the greatest of all French chroniclers of everyday life, the nineteenth century novelist Honoré de Balzac. So accurate and detailed are Marivaux's descriptions that one critic has asserted about *The Life of Marianne* that even Balzac "has done nothing better than this realistic study of a little bourgeois milieu."

"Critical Evaluation" by Laurence W. Mazzeno

Further Reading

Brady, Patrick. "Chaos, Complexity, Catastrophe, and Control in Marivaux's *La Vie de Marianne*." In *Disrupted Patterns: On Chaos and Order in the Enlightenment*, edited by Theodore E. D. Braun and John A. McCarthy. Atlanta: Rodopi, 2000. Examination of *The Life of Marianne* is included in a collection of essays devoted to the interpretation of European Enlightenment texts from the perspective of modern chaos theory.

Foster, James R. "Sentiment from Aphra Behn to Marivaux." In *The Eighteenth Century English Novel*, edited by Harold Bloom. Philadelphia: Chelsea House, 2004. Addresses Marivaux's work within the context of a discussion of the sentimental novel in England.

Greene, E. J. H. *Marivaux*. Toronto, Ont.: University of Toronto Press, 1965. Presents a detailed, sensitive reading of *The Life of Marianne* that examines Marivaux's artistic intentions, his handling of characterization, his adroit use of sentimentalism, and his hardheaded analysis of a corrupt society. Speculates on the reasons the novel was never finished.

Haac, Oscar A. *Marivaux*. New York: Twayne, 1974. Provides a general survey of the writer's achievements and discusses *The Life of Marianne* as an early example of the psychological novel. Pays special attention to Marivaux's development of major characters in the work.

Laden, Marie-Paule. *Self-Imitation in the Eighteenth-Century Novel*. Princeton, N.J.: Princeton University Press, 1987. Extended analysis of *The Life of Marianne* focuses on Marivaux's handling of narrative voice. Explains how he gives emotional and moral perspective to Marianne's adventures by having the heroine serve as both protagonist and commentator, since she writes as an older woman about her life as an ingenue.

Mander, Jenny. *Circles of Learning: Narratology and the Eighteenth Century French Novel*. Oxford, England: Voltaire Foundation, 1999. Study of narration and autobiography in the eighteenth century French novel focuses on works by Marivaux and Abbé Prévost. Includes discussion of *The Life of Marianne*.

Rosbottom, Ronald C. *Marivaux's Novels: Theme and Function in European Eighteenth Century Narrative*. Rutherford, N.J.: Fairleigh Dickinson University Press, 1974. Devotes two chapters to an analysis of *The Life of Marianne*. Focuses on the accommodations Marianne must make in order to succeed in society and the limits beyond which she cannot compromise her principles.

Russo, Elena. In *Styles of Enlightenment: Taste, Politics, and Authorship in Eighteenth-Century France*. Baltimore: Johns Hopkins University Press, 2007. Examines works by Marivaux and others to support the argument that while French Enlightenment writers and philosophers espoused theories of democracy, they also established strict and elitist standards of literary style and artistic expression.

Life of Pi

Author: Yann Martel (1963-　　)
First published: 2001
Type of work: Novel
Type of plot: Bildungsroman
Time of plot: 1970's
Locale: Pondicherry, India; the Pacific Ocean; Scarborough, Canada

Principal characters:
YANN MARTEL, author, primary narrator, and interviewer of Pi
PISCINE "PI" MOLITOR PATEL, the novel's main character and secondary narrator
RICHARD PARKER, a Royal Bengal tiger and Pi's companion across the Pacific
SANTOSH PATEL, Pi's father
MOTHER PATEL, Pi's mother
RAVI PATEL, Pi's brother
FRANCIS "MAMAJI" ADIRUBASAMY, Santosh's business contact and a lifelong friend to Pi
MR. SATISH KUMAR, Pi's biology teacher and close friend
FATHER MARTIN, parish priest and Pi's mentor in his Christian faith
SATISH KUMAR, a Sufi and Pi's mentor in his Muslim faith
THE FRENCHMAN, apparently the chef from the Japanese cargo ship *Tsimtsum*, who meets Pi on the Pacific Ocean
MR. TOMOHIRO OKAMOTO, retired senior investigator in the Maritime Department of the Japanese Ministry of Transport
MR. ATSURO CHIBA, junior investigator in the Maritime Department of the Japanese Ministry of Transport

The Story:

Life of Pi begins with an author's note written by a character named Yann Martel. Martel confesses that his previous novel received poor reviews and faded into obscurity and he lost interest in writing another novel. Martel sought inspiration in India, where he met a strange old man who directed him to Piscine "Pi" Molitar Patel. Pi's life story inspired Martel's new novel.

Piscene grows up in Pondicherry, India, the son of a zoo keeper. Young Piscine suffers as a boy because of his name, which sounds very close to the word "pissing." When Piscine changes schools, he takes the opportunity to rename himself "Pi" after the mathematical symbol, publically declaring his new name to all. With his new name, Pi enjoys a happy childhood, free from mockery, as he explores the zoo, makes many friends, and relishes life with his close-knit family.

An intelligent and deeply religious boy, Pi excels in the study of his native religion, Hinduism. Surprisingly, however, Pi explores two more of the world's major religions—Islam and Christianity—when his family vacations in Munnar. With the help of a Muslim mystic named Satish Kumar and a parish priest named Father Martin, Pi becomes

a devotee of both religions. As an old man, Pi will still practice the three faiths of Hinduism, Islam, and Christianity, making him a unique religious figure.

Pi's life in India ends when his father sells the zoo and moves the family to Canada. The family embarks across the Pacific Ocean on the Japanese cargo ship *Tsimtsum* with a menagerie of zoo animals to be sold to North American zoos. Unfortunately, the *Tsimtsum* sinks, taking Pi's family with it. Pi makes it safely onto a lifeboat, where, besides some vermin, his only companions are a zebra with a broken leg, a hyena, an orangutang, and a Bengal tiger named Richard Parker.

At first, Pi does not see the tiger, so he lives in fear of the hyena. Since Pi paid such close attention to everything his father said about wild animals, he manages to survive the hyena's predatory advances long enough to see it kill and eat the zebra and orangutang. Pi observes nature's cruelty with horror, realizing that he will become the hyena's next victim. Pi has virtually surrendered himself to the savage hyena when, suddenly, the tiger makes his presence known, easily destroying the hyena and saving Pi's life.

Pi remains adrift on the Pacific Ocean with a tiger for 227

days. He struggles to survive and overcome his sudden orphaning, his new grief, seasickness, endless waves, relentless storms, starvation, thirst, blazing sun, desiccative salt water, skin sores, utter loneliness, and despair, as well as the aggressions of an infamous predator. The vegetarian boy finds himself eating fish and turtles raw; the frightened boy tames a tiger; the devout disciple of three religions grapples with his faith in God, discovering indomitable strength therein. Pi surprises himself with the depth of his resolve to live, overcoming all obstacles with his powerful will.

While adrift, Pi has two remarkable encounters: He discovers a new, carnivorous species of algae, and—after going temporarily blind—he runs into another survivor from the *Tsimtsum*, a Frenchman adrift in his own lifeboat who has also gone blind. The Frenchman attacks Pi intending to eat him. Before he can kill Pi, however, he is attacked and eaten by the tiger.

The novel ends with the transcript of an interview between Pi and two investigators, Mr. Okamoto and Mr. Chiba, who are trying to determine what caused the *Tsimtsum* to sink. The men refuse to believe the more fantastical parts of Pi's story, such as Pi surviving 227 days on a lifeboat with a tiger or coincidentally running into the Frenchman. They demand that Pi tell them the real story of what happened, and he finally offers them an alternative version of his story.

Pi tells the investigators that the lifeboat held four human survivors: Pi, his mother, the French chef from the *Tsimtsum*, and a Japanese sailor with a broken leg. He claims that the Frenchman amputated the sailor's leg when it became infected and used the leg as fishing bait. When the sailor died, the Frenchman butchered the body and, in addition to using it for bait, ate some. This horrified Pi and his mother so much that Pi's mother periodically berated and attacked the chef for many days, until the chef killed her while Pi watched. Then, apparently consumed with grief and despair over killing Pi's innocent mother, the chef allowed Pi to kill him in revenge.

The investigators appear satisfied with the second version of Pi's story, though they are impressed with the parallels between the two versions. Pi points out that neither story helps them understand what caused the *Tsimtsum* to sink. Given that both stories are equally valid for the men's purposes, Pi asks which version they prefer. The men prefer the first, more mysterious and unusual story, the one with the animals. Mr. Okamoto includes the first version in his official report.

Critical Evaluation:

The central theme of Yann Martel's *Life of Pi* concerns religion and human faith in God. However, the novel pointedly refrains from advocating any single religious faith over an-

other. Instead, the novel investigates the nature of religious faith itself. This theme is embodied most clearly in the novel's protagonist, Pi Patel, who is a devout follower of three very different religions. Pi has studied and memorized the stories of all the various incarnations of the Hindu gods, maintaining shrines in his home to many of them. He also possesses a crucifix and a rosary, going to church on Sundays and praying to Jesus. Lastly, he owns and proudly uses a prayer rug, observing the call to prayer several times a day as a devoted Muslim. By comfortably following three of the world's major religions, Pi represents not just the possibility of peaceful coexistence between different faiths but also the belief that different religions are merely alternative paths to the same destination.

The specific doctrines of Pi's three faiths make very little difference to him. When comparing these religions to one another, Pi seems to conclude in his innocence that there need not be conflict between them. For him, each religion simply emphasizes what is most powerful and true in the others according to its own strengths. The religions resemble different chapters of one very long book, each chapter setting up and feeding into the next. The novel contrasts Pi's easy acceptance of his three faiths with the competition and arguments between the leaders of those faiths. In Munnar, while Pi is walking in a busy marketplace with his parents, they happen upon the pandit, imam, and priest who are the leaders of Pi's Hindu, Muslim, and Christian faiths, respectively. When the leaders discover that Pi has been following three different religions, each attempts to claim Pi for himself. They reason that one boy cannot follow three different paths, and they begin to debate which religion would be best for Pi. When the leaders demand that Pi choose one faith to the exclusion of all others, he blurts out, "I just want to love God," embarrassing the hot-headed religious leaders and putting a stop to their debate.

This tension between reason, logic, and argument, on one hand, and simple religious faith and the desire to love God, on the other hand, lies at the novel's core. The human capacity for reason is contrasted to religious faith repeatedly, nowhere more poignantly than in the chapters showing Pi adrift on the Pacific Ocean, where his faith, not his reason, enables Pi to survive:

> I was alone and orphaned in the middle of the Pacific hanging onto an oar, an adult tiger in front of me, sharks beneath me, a storm raging about me. Had I considered my prospects in the light of reason, I surely would have given up and let go of the oar, hoping that I might drown before being eaten.

Pi's refusal to consider his predicament "in the light of reason" opens up space for his faith in God to flourish, and this faith sustains him even through the darkest, most fearful moments. Fear, Pi realizes, is "life's only true opponent," and he holds back the fear with his faith, no matter what religion embodies that faith.

The novel also explores another meaning of faith—the human capacity to believe what is unbelievable. Pi's story challenges readers with plot twists that sound impossible. That Pi survives 227 days adrift on a lifeboat in the Pacific Ocean is remarkable enough; that he survives this time in the company of a Bengal tiger or that he happens to run into a floating island of carnivorous algae strains readers' ability to suspend their disbelief. A skeptical attitude toward the narrative is embodied by Mr. Okamoto and Mr. Chiba, who at first refuse to believe Pi's stories about a Bengal tiger and carnivorous algae. They insist that his story contradicts reality, to which Pi replies, "You want a story that won't surprise you. That will confirm what you already know. That won't make you see higher or further or differently. You want a flat story."

When Pi gives them the flat story they want, a story that fails to contradict what they are prepared to believe, the men become excited by the prospect that this second version is the truth. However, Pi is not finished with them or their skepticism. He demonstrates that the facts of both stories are irrelevant to the men's purpose of finding out what caused the *Tsimtsum* to sink, and he points out that the men are in a position to verify neither of the two versions. Then, he asks, "Which is the better story, the story with animals or the story without animals?" The men agree that the story with animals is superior, which prompts Pi to add, "And so it goes with God." This is faith, Pi seems to say. Since it is the nature of religious faith that it can never be proven, just as the facts of Pi's journey across the Pacific can never be verified, the question is not a matter of reason but of belief. Pi seems to argue that what should compel one to believe a story is whether the story is a good one—whether it helps readers "see higher or further or differently."

Paul Cockeram

Further Reading

Boyagoda, Randy. "Faith, Fiction, Flotsam." *First Things: A Monthly Journal of Religion and Public Life* 131 (May, 2003): 69-72. Critical review of *Life of Pi* that appreciates the story's power but argues that Martel's scattered views on religion weaken the book.

Cloete, Elsie. "Tigers, Humans, and Animots." *Journal of Literary Studies* 23, no. 3 (September, 2007): 314-333. Provides a complex analysis of the tiger's role in the novel, drawing upon major theories in literary studies to examine the representation of relationships between humans and animals.

Duncan, Rebecca. "*Life of Pi* as Postmodern Survivor Narrative." *Mosaic* 41, no. 2 (June, 2008): 167-183. Analyzes the novel's self-reflective, postmodern characteristics, paying special attention to the text's portrayal of Pi's subjective experience of trauma.

Dwyer, June. "Yann Martel's *Life of Pi* and the Evolution of the Shipwreck Narrative." *Modern Language Studies* 35, no. 2 (Fall, 2005): 9-21. Focuses on animal-human relations in the novel, comparing this work to other important works about animal-human relations such as *The Black Stallion* (1941).

Innes, Charlotte. "Robinson Crusoe, Move Over." *The Nation* 275, no. 6 (August, 2002): 25-29. Favorable review focusing on the novel's religious themes of both faith and doubt.

Krist, Gary. "Taming the Tiger." *The New York Times*, July 7, 2002, p. 5. Represents early and positive press, providing a thorough review with some analysis.

The Life of Samuel Johnson, LL.D.

Author: James Boswell (1740-1795)
First published: 1791
Type of work: Biography

Principal personages:
SAMUEL JOHNSON, author, critic, and lexicographer
JAMES BOSWELL, the biographer, Johnson's friend
DAVID GARRICK,
SIR JOSHUA REYNOLDS,
MR. THRALE,
MRS. THRALE,
DAVID HUME, and
OLIVER GOLDSMITH, members of the Johnson circle

James Boswell's life of Samuel Johnson has often been considered the greatest biography produced in the English language, and it has probably had more readers than any other biography written in English. Among the works published during Boswell's lifetime, *The Life of Samuel Johnson, LL.D.* stood out as the greatest for almost a century and a half. A new estimate of Boswell's work has had to be taken since 1950, however, for much of Boswell's writing was lost in manuscript until the 1920's. During the period between 1927 and 1949, Lieutenant Colonel Ralph Heyward Isham, a collector, brought together the Boswell papers that had been stored at Malahide Castle, near Dublin, Ireland, and the Forbes collection, which had accidentally passed into the hands of one of Boswell's executors and descended to the latter's heirs. Some of the papers were published by Isham, who sold the entire collection to Yale University in 1949 and 1950. The university began to publish volumes of the papers under the general title of *The Yale Editions of the Private Papers of James Boswell*. Through such collections of his writings as *Boswell's London Journal, 1762-1763* (1950), *Boswell in Holland, 1763-1764* (1952), and *Boswell on the Grand Tour: Germany and Switzerland, 1764* (1953), Boswell emerged as a splendid writer of journals. This fact, however, does not detract from his stature as the author of the biography of Johnson, nor will these more recently published works replace the biography as the most important of Boswell's books, although critical opinion may be modified to grant Boswell greater stature in literature than he once had.

Readers now know that *The Life of Samuel Johnson, LL.D.* is based on materials that Boswell had recorded in the copious journals he kept during the greater part of his adult life. This is not to say, however, that the biography is merely a transcription of materials from those journals. From present knowledge of the papers it can be seen that Boswell was an

artist in biography, choosing carefully what suited his needs and goals. Even those who feel that Boswell intrudes too much into the biography must now recognize that Boswell took some pains to omit much material about Johnson in which Boswell figured. Those who feel that Boswell intrudes too much into the work possibly overlook the fact that during Johnson's life, Boswell was Johnson's friend and spent from four hundred to five hundred days with his subject, thus becoming himself a part of Johnson's life and the Johnsonian environment.

Boswell's method was to record information about Johnson in his journals. Sometimes the material was recorded daily, but on occasion Boswell fell behind and had to rely on his memory—a phenomenal one—recalling events that had transpired in periods of four or five days and evenings. It is notable, too, that Boswell was careful to prompt Johnson into conversation, often asking what seem to present-day readers to be obvious or absurd questions in order to goad Johnson into making remarks worthy of record. One such question noted by critics is that in which Boswell asked Johnson what he would do if given the solitary care of a small infant; the question, seemingly absurd, led Johnson to reply in such fashion as to comment on the rearing and education of children and to set forth a philosophy of education. The more readers learn about Boswell and his work, the more they understand that he was not a mere transcriber, as critical legend held for some time; rather, he was a skillful writer who shaped his materials with great care. The casual reader may even miss some of the more obvious points of artistry in his work, such as notations on how Johnson looked and spoke when delivering comments and opinions.

Johnson was a man of many achievements. He singlehandedly brought forth the first recognized dictionary of the English language. He also made himself famous as a writer by means of his writings for *The Rambler* (1750-

1752), his drama *Irene: A Tragedy* (pr. 1749), his poetry, and his essays. As a moralist Johnson also won fame as the author of the didactic novel *Rasselas, Prince of Abyssinia: A Tale by S. Johnson* (1759). As a critic he was famous for his ten-volume work *Prefaces, Biographical and Critical, to the Works of the English Poets* (1779-1781; also known as *The Lives of the Poets*) and his preface to an edition of William Shakespeare's plays. People great and small admired Johnson, including many of the famous and remarkable Englishmen of his time, men such as David Hume, Sir Joshua Reynolds, Oliver Goldsmith, and David Garrick. In addition, Johnson was a picturesque, at times even ludicrous, figure, and this fact Boswell did not attempt to hide, giving himself the task of writing "not his panegyrick, which must be all praise, but his Life; which great and good as he was, must not be supposed to be perfect."

In further defense of his way of writing biography, Boswell states near the beginning of the biography:

I am fully aware of the objections which may be made to the minuteness on some occasions of my detail of Johnson's conversation, and how happily it is adapted for the petty exercise of ridicule by men of superficial understanding, and ludicrous fancy; but I remain firm and confident in my opinion, that minute particulars are frequently characteristick, and always amusing, when they relate to a distinguished man. I am therefore exceedingly unwilling that anything, however slight, which my illustrious friend thought it worth his while to express, with any degree of point, should perish.

Boswell realized, as readers know from what he said and wrote, that the function and art of biography is to focus on the subject and keep that person constantly before the reader. This Boswell does in his biography of Johnson. To do so he carefully gathered together more than what he knew first-hand of the man who was his friend and subject. He exercised diligence and care in collecting letters written by Johnson, including the text of his famous letter to Lord Chesterfield. He collected, too, letters written about Johnson, as well as anecdotes about his subject's life, trying at the same time to establish the authenticity of the reports he had of Johnson. These materials are presented in the biography in chronological order. If the results have some defects, the defects are more or less forgivable in view of their sparseness. Seldom did Boswell record facts that later biographers needed to correct.

The biography's account of Johnson's life before he met Boswell is relatively short. This fact may be excused on the

ground that Boswell used only the information about Johnson's early life that he could gather and trust. Naturally, he had a much larger fund of materials from the period during which he knew Johnson personally. Some critics have noted Boswell's reluctance to interpret. Of this reluctance, it must be said that interpretation was not Boswell's way. On occasion in the biography he generalizes on Johnson perceptively, but his preference, as he carefully states, is to present particulars rather than generalizations. The result is that Johnson is "alive" in *The Life of Samuel Johnson, LL.D.* as few biographical subjects are, with his personality and character borne out by his own spoken and written words. On occasion the reader may feel that Johnson's written words, usually letters, have been inserted where they fit none too well, seeming to interfere with the flow of the book. They are nevertheless a part of the scheme Boswell worked out and put together.

Samuel Johnson has been the subject of many biographies; five, for example, appeared after Johnson's death and before Boswell's work. Others have been written since, but none has ever equaled Boswell's *The Life of Samuel Johnson, LL.D.*

Further Reading

Bronson, Bertrand H. "Samuel Johnson and James Boswell." In *Facets of the Enlightenment*. Berkeley: University of California Press, 1968. Takes a negative view of Boswell's literary artistry, arguing against his dramatic abilities. Implies that Boswell's perspective was narrow, his style mechanical, and his great success accidental.

Clingham, Greg, ed. *New Light on Boswell: Critical and Historical Essays on the Occasion of the Bicentenary of "The Life of Johnson."* New York: Cambridge University Press, 1991. Collection of essays explores Boswell's literary and personal achievements and limitations. Noteworthy for the investigation of the critical and theoretical questions surrounding the notion of biographical representation.

Hart, Kevin. *Samuel Johnson and the Culture of Property.* New York: Cambridge University Press, 1999. Examines Johnson's literary legacy and reputation. Contends that Boswell's biography turned Johnson into a public monument, a piece of "cultural property." Also analyzes the works of other biographers and critics who helped create "The Age of Johnson."

Pittock, Murray. *James Boswell.* Aberdeen, Scotland: AHRC Centre for Irish and Scottish Studies, 2007. Presents a detailed examination of Boswell's published and unpublished works. Demonstrates how Boswell deliberately wrote ambiguously about himself and the major events of his time and discusses how Boswell's writing was influenced by his sympathies with Catholicism, Scotland, and Jacobitism.

Redford, Bruce. *Designing the Life of Johnson*. New York: Oxford University Press, 2002. Closely examines the manuscript of *The Life of Samuel Johnson, LL.D.*, pointing out the techniques and models Boswell used to create the famed biography.

Siebenschuh, William R. "*The Life of Johnson*." In *Form and Purpose in Boswell's Biographical Works*. Berkeley: University of California Press, 1972. Critical study focuses on Boswell's methods for dramatizing the primary factual materials in his biographical work, with particular emphasis on his gift for characterization, structure, and style.

Sisman, Adam. *Boswell's Presumptuous Task: The Making of the Life of Dr. Johnson*. New York: Penguin, 2002. Chronicles the seven-year period in which Boswell, who was facing many personal problems and suffering from depression, created the biography of his friend and mentor.

Life on the Mississippi

Author: Mark Twain (1835-1910)
First published: 1883
Type of work: Memoir

Principal characters:
THE NARRATOR, a former steamboat pilot
MR. BIXBY, the master pilot who trains him
HENRY, the narrator's brother, a clerk on the *Pennsylvania*
MR. BROWN, an unpleasant pilot on the *Pennsylvania*
THOMPSON (the poet) and ROGERS (the stenographer), the narrator's travel companions in 1882
"UNCLE" MUMFORD, a mate on the *Gold Dust*
ROBERT STYLES, a pilot on the *Gold Dust*
KARL RITTER, a German whom the narrator meets in Munich

The Story:

As a boy growing up in a Mississippi River town, the narrator has the common ambition of becoming a steamboatman. He especially wants to be a pilot. Later, while living in Cincinnati, he decides to make his fortune in the Amazon and buys passage on the steamboat *Paul Jones* to New Orleans, from where he intends to sail to the Amazon. After arriving in New Orleans, however, he discovers that he will not be able to continue his journey, so he looks for a new career. He lays siege to Mr. Bixby, pilot of the *Paul Jones*, and persuades the man to accept him as a cub pilot on the return voyage upriver.

The new pilot begins his education under Bixby's tutelage by steering the *Paul Jones* out of New Orleans and listening to Bixby call attention to monotonously nondescript points along the way. At midnight on his first day, he is rudely turned out of his bed to stand watch—his first intimation that piloting might not be quite as romantic as he had imagined.

His second such intimation comes when he learns that Bixby expects him to remember everything he is told. As the boat continues upriver, the narrator's new notebook fills with information, but his head remains empty.

After switching boats at St. Louis for the return trip, the cub pilot discovers that downstream navigation differs greatly from upstream navigation. In fact, each time he thinks he is mastering his new trade, Bixby piles on more facts for him to learn. He is expected to memorize the river's features and its shape, then he has to learn the river's depths and how to "read" it like a book. Eventually, the narrator thinks his education is complete, only to be told that he now has to learn how to read the river's fluctuating depths from its banks. His education continues.

The narrator relates the minutiae of piloting because he loves the profession more than any other. In the early days, he says, a steamboat pilot was the only completely unfettered human being on earth. That situation began changing before the Civil War, when the rapid increase in licensed pilots started cutting into wages. A handful of bold veterans reversed the trend by forming a professional association that forced the steamboat companies to restore their former wages. Shortly after, however, the war halted commercial steamboat traffic, and it never recovered because of postwar competition from railroads and tow barges.

A prime example of a master pilot with an exceptional memory, Bixby proves his skill by switching to the more difficult Missouri River, where he quickly earns a new license. Meanwhile, the young cub stays on the Mississippi and apprentices himself on the *Pennsylvania* under the despotic tutelage of Mr. Brown. His younger brother Henry has joined the *Pennsylvania* as a lowly clerk. One day, Brown assaults Henry, which provokes the narrator to beat Brown. The narrator thinks that with this act he has ruined his career, but kindly Captain Klinefelter approves of what he has done and even offers to put Brown ashore in New Orleans. Not feeling up to assuming Brown's piloting responsibilities, the cub himself stays ashore and then follows the *Pennsylvania* upriver on another boat. Near Memphis, Tennessee, he learns that the *Pennsylvania*'s boilers have exploded, killing 150 people, his own brother among them, and Brown has disappeared.

Eventually the narrator earns his license and becomes steadily employed as a pilot. Soon, however, the Civil War intervenes and brings his occupation to an end. Twenty-one years later—after going through a succession of careers—he decides to return to the Mississippi, and he enlists a poet named Thompson and a stenographer named Rogers to accompany him. At St. Louis, they board the *Gold Dust*, on which the narrator quickly begins discovering how much steamboating has changed. Traveling under a pseudonym, he sits quietly in the pilothouse and listens while the pilot, Robert Styles—who had once been his fellow cub—tries to impress him with outrageous lies before revealing that he had recognized him immediately.

As the *Gold Dust* travels south, the mate, "Uncle" Mumford, and other crew members recount the river's recent history and the impact of the Civil War on southern towns. The narrator observes how much navigational techniques have been modernized—a development that he feels has destroyed the river's romance.

As the boat nears Napoleon, Arkansas, the narrator tells his companions an amazing story about a German named Ritter whose last wish he had promised to fulfill by retrieving ten thousand dollars that Ritter had hidden in Napoleon and sending it to the son of a man whom Ritter had wronged. The

story arouses avarice among the narrator's companions until they learn that the entire town of Napoleon has been washed away by a flood.

At Vicksburg, Mississippi, the travelers switch to another steamboat that takes them to Baton Rouge, Louisiana, where they enter the "absolute South," where romantic influences in architecture remind the narrator of the debilitating influence that Sir Walter Scott's Romanticism has had on the region. In New Orleans, the narrator spends much of his visit with authors George Washington Cable and Joel Chandler Harris. He also meets Horace Bixby, who is now captain of the *City of Baton Rouge*. The narrator, Bixby, and other old-time pilots swap stories about former rivermen, including Captain Isaiah Sellers, from whom the narrator has appropriated his pen name, "Mark Twain." After returning to St. Louis on Bixby's boat, the narrator continues upriver to Hannibal, Missouri—his boyhood home. There he recalls poignant memories from his youth. He then travels north by boat to St. Paul, Minnesota, from where he later returns home by land.

Critical Evaluation:

Though usually classified among Mark Twain's five travel books, *Life on the Mississippi* defies neat categorization. Like much of the author's work, it is structurally flawed and uneven in tone; indeed, it even resists simple synopsis. Nevertheless, the book is generally recognized as one of Twain's finest works, a true classic about the great Mississippi River. It is, moreover, the immediate predecessor to his masterpiece, *Adventures of Huckleberry Finn* (1884).

The book's structural problems arise from its author's conflicting goals. A decade before Twain began the book, he entertained the idea of writing a standard work on the Mississippi River. The germ of this idea can be seen in the book's first three chapters, which describe the river's history and geographical peculiarities. As early as chapter 3, however, Twain's resolve to continue along these lines begins wavering, and he shifts direction by introducing an extract from a novel on which he had worked for several years. Taken from what would become chapter 16 of *Adventures of Huckleberry Finn*, this passage introduces Huck and Jim and depicts life on a great commercial river raft. A beautifully realized passage, it evokes the power and romance of the Mississippi and links the book directly to the novel.

Chapter 4 of *Life on the Mississippi* opens with what is generally acknowledged to be one of Twain's finest pieces of writing: an almost lyrical account of his two years as an apprentice steamboat pilot on the lower Mississippi. He originally composed most of the seventeen chapters that constitute this part of the book for magazine serialization. With the encouragement of his friends Joseph Twichell and W. D. Howells, the editor of *The Atlantic Monthly*, he wrote these articles in order to re-create the great age of steamboating. After they appeared in *The Atlantic Monthly* in 1876 as a series titled "Old Times on the Mississippi," he put aside his idea of writing a book on the Mississippi until six years later, when he succumbed to the itch to return to the river.

In early 1882, Twain spent just over a month on the Mississippi with his book publisher, James R. Osgood ("Thompson" in the narrative), and a Hartford, Connecticut, stenographer named Roswell Phelps ("Rogers"). Afterward, he returned home to Hartford and threw himself into writing what he believed must be a large book. After completing the introductory chapters, he naturally returned to his "Old Times" articles. These he lightly revised and supplemented with several new chapters—including those recounting his troubles with Mr. Brown.

Although chapters 4 through 20 of *Life on the Mississippi* are based on Twain's own experiences as a cub pilot from early 1858 through early 1859, they cannot strictly be regarded as autobiography. Twain's narrator writes in the first person, but the cub whom he depicts as his youthful self appears to be a much younger and more naïve person than the twenty-one-year-old Sam Clemens who had become an apprentice pilot. Twain's interest in writing these chapters is to describe the marvelous art of piloting and the wonders of the Mississippi River, not to recount his own life. Once he achieves these objectives, he dismisses the two years that he spent as a licensed pilot in one brief paragraph (chapter 21).

The balance of the sixty-chapter book recounts Twain's return to the Mississippi in 1882. Much of this section is straightforward travel narrative, but even this cannot be read as unadulterated autobiography. As with Twain's other travel books, much of this section is embroidered for entertainment and literary effect. More even than in the earlier chapters, the narrator speaks with the voice of Twain, but here, too, he never openly identifies himself as Mark Twain (or as Samuel Clemens), although he twice alludes to his famous pen name. Keeping the identity of his narrator vague—a technique that typifies most of Twain's travel writing—leaves him free to invent and embroider without the strictures of nonfiction.

Readers unaware of the extent to which Twain freed himself to invent may become confused in reading *Life on the Mississippi*. The second part of the book contains several frame stories that are pure fiction, but the author gives no hint of their nature. A prime example is the Karl Ritter episode, which blends so seamlessly into chapters 31 and 32 that one might mistakenly read the story as authentic. Another example occurs in chapter 52—"The Burning Brand"—to which Twain adds a realistic note by working in the name of his literary friend Charles Dudley Warner.

Although *Life on the Mississippi* should not be read as authentic autobiography, the book is filled with autobiographical interest. Its cub-piloting chapters help illuminate an important phase of Twain's early life, just as the book's later narrative at least approximates Twain's 1882 experiences. Of perhaps greater autobiographical significance, and of often superior literary interest, are the chapters concerning his return visit to Hannibal, Missouri. Chapters 53-56 take Twain deeper into his youth than anything he wrote until he seriously undertook his autobiography a quarter century later.

R. Kent Rasmussen

Further Reading

Camfield, Gregg. *The Oxford Companion to Mark Twain.* New York: Oxford University Press, 2003. Comprehensive collection of original essays presents discussion of Twain's individual works, covering topics such as themes, characters, language, and subjects that interested Twain. Includes an appendix on researching Twain that lists useful secondary sources and an extensive annotated bibliography of Twain's novels, plays, poems, and other writings.

Coulombe, Joseph L. "Moneyed Ruffians: The New American Hero in *Life on the Mississippi.*" In *Mark Twain and the American West.* Columbia: University of Missouri Press, 2003. Analyzes the book and some of Twain's other works to describe how he deliberately altered nineteenth century concepts of the American West. Examines the central role of the West in creating Twain's public persona.

Cox, James M. "*Life on the Mississippi* Revisited." In *The Mythologizing of Mark Twain*, edited by Sara deSaussure Davis and Phillip D. Beidler. Tuscaloosa: University of Alabama Press, 1984. Presents a persuasive argument that *Life on the Mississippi* converts the life of Samuel L. Clemens into the "myth" of Mark Twain.

Emerson, Everett. *Mark Twain: A Literary Life.* Philadelphia: University of Pennsylvania Press, 2000. Masterful work—a complete revision of Emerson's *The Authentic Mark Twain* (1984)—traces the development of Twain's writing against the events in his life and provides illuminating discussions of many individual works.

Hellwig, Harold H. *Mark Twain's Travel Literature: The Odyssey of a Mind.* Jefferson, N.C.: McFarland, 2008. Analyzes *Life on the Mississippi* and Twain's other travel literature, describing his depictions of time, place, and identity. Demonstrates how the travel literature reflects Twain's nostalgia for a disappearing America, his concern about Native American assimilation, and his own quest for personal and national identity. Argues that the theme of travel is also central to Twain's fictional works.

Kruse, Horst H. *Mark Twain and "Life on the Mississippi."* Amherst: University of Massachusetts Press, 1981. Excellent study that focuses on Twain's composition of *Life on the Mississippi.* Concludes that one of Twain's intentions was to help redeem the South from the Romanticism that brought on the Civil War.

Messent, Peter B. "Travel and Travel Writing: *Innocents Abroad, A Tramp Abroad, Roughing It, Life on the Missis-* sippi." In *The Cambridge Introduction to Mark Twain.* New York: Cambridge University Press, 2007. Provides a solid overview of Twain's travel writing, placing it within the context of his other works.

Rasmussen, R. Kent. *Critical Companion to Mark Twain: A Literary Reference to His Life and Work.* 2 vols. New York: Facts On File, 2007. Alphabetically arranged entries about the plots, characters, places, and other subjects relating to Twain's writings and life. Features extended analytical essays on Twain's major works, including *Life on the Mississippi*; an expanded and fully annotated bibliography of books about Twain; and a glossary explaining unusual words in Twain's vocabulary, including terms related to steamboating.

Ligeia

Author: Edgar Allan Poe (1809-1849)
First published: 1838
Type of work: Short fiction
Type of plot: Gothic
Time of plot: Early nineteenth century
Locale: Germany and England

Principal characters:
THE NARRATOR
LIGEIA, his first wife
LADY ROWENA TREVANION, his second wife

The Story:

The narrator begins by saying that he cannot remember when he first met Ligeia, and he knows nothing of her family except that it is old. Ligeia herself, once his wife, he can remember in every detail, and he relates their story.

Ligeia is tall and slender, ethereal as a shadow. Her face is faultless in its beauty, her skin like ivory, her features classic. Crowning the perfect face and body is raven-black, luxuriant hair. Her eyes, above all else, hold the key to Ligeia's mystery. Larger than most, those black eyes hold an expression unfathomable even to her husband. It becomes his all-consuming passion to unravel the secret of that expression.

In character, Ligeia possesses a stern will that never fails to astound him. Outwardly she is placid and calm, but she habitually utters words that stun him with their intensity. Her learning is immense. She speaks many languages, and in metaphysical investigations she is never wrong. Her husband is engrossed in a study of metaphysics, but it is she who guides him and unravels the secrets of his research. With Ligeia to assist him, he knows that he will one day reach a goal of wisdom undreamed of by others.

Then Ligeia falls ill. Her skin becomes transparent and waxen, her eyes wild, and he knows that she will die. The passion of her struggle against death is frightening. He has always known that she loves him, but in those last days she abandons herself completely to love. On what is to be the last day of her life, she bids him repeat to her a poem she had composed not long before. It is a morbid thing about death, about the conquering of Man by the Worm. As he finishes repeating the melancholy lines, Ligeia leaps to her feet with a shriek, then falls back on her deathbed. In a scarcely audible whisper, she repeats a proverb that has haunted her: that human beings do not yield to death save through the weakness of their own will. So Ligeia dies.

Crushed with sorrow, her husband leaves his desolate home by the Rhine and retires to an old and decayed abbey in a deserted region in England. He leaves the exterior of the building in its sagging state, but inside he furnishes the rooms lavishly and strangely. He has become the slave of opium, and the furnishings take on the shapes and colors of his fantastic dreams. One bedchamber receives the most bizarre treatment of all, and it is to this chamber that he leads his new bride, the blue-eyed Lady Rowena Trevanion, of Tremaine.

The room, in a high turret of the abbey, is of immense proportions. It is lighted by a single huge window, the pane of which has a leaden hue, giving a ghastly luster to all objects within. The walls, floors, and furniture are all covered with a heavy, arabesque tapestry showing black figures on pure gold. The figures change as one looks at them from different angles, their appearance being altered by an artificial current of air that constantly stirs the draperies.

In rooms such as this, the narrator spends a bridal month with Lady Rowena. It is easy to perceive that she loves him but little, and he hates her with a passion more demoniac than human. In his opium dreams, he calls aloud for Ligeia, as if he could restore her to the earthly life she has abandoned. He revels in memories of her purity and her love.

In the second month of their marriage, Rowena grows ill, and in her fever she speaks of sounds and movements in the bedchamber, fantasies unheard and unseen by her husband. Although she recovers, she has recurring attacks of the fever, and it becomes evident that she will soon succumb to her illness. Her imaginings become stronger, and she grows more insistent about the sounds and movements she perceives in the tapestries.

One night, Rowena becomes visibly weaker and unusually agitated. Seeking to calm her, her husband steps across the room to get some wine, but he is arrested midway by the sense of something passing lightly by him. Then he is startled to see on the gold carpet a shadow of angelic aspect. Saying nothing to Rowena, he pours the wine into a goblet. As she takes the vessel from him, he distinctly hears a light footstep on the carpet and sees, or thinks he sees, three or four drops of a ruby-colored liquid fall into the goblet from an invisible source.

Immediately after drinking the wine Rowena grows worse, and on the third night, she dies. As her husband sits by her shrouded body in that bridal chamber, he thinks of his lost Ligeia. Suddenly, he hears a sound from the bed on which the corpse of his wife lies. Going closer, he perceives that Rowena has a faint color in her cheeks. It is unmistakable—Rowena lives. Unable to summon aid, he watches her with mounting terror. Then a relapse comes, and she subsides into a death pallor more rigid than before. All night this phenomenon recurs—Rowena returns briefly from the dead, only to sink once more into oblivion. Each time, he sees again a vision of Ligeia.

Toward the morning following that fearful night, the enshrouded figure rises from the bed and totters to the center of the chamber. Terrified, the narrator falls at her feet. She unwinds the burial shroud from her head, and there streams down raven-black hair that did not belong to the living Rowena. The spectral figure then slowly opens her eyes. He cannot be mistaken. Staring at him are the full black eyes of his lost love, Ligeia.

Critical Evaluation:

First published in *The Baltimore American Museum* in September, 1838, "Ligeia" was included in Edgar Allan Poe's *Tales of the Grotesque and Arabesque* (1840). The final text appeared in *The Broadway Journal* in 1845. One of Poe's most famous tales, "Ligeia" is also among his most brilliantly written, and he himself once declared it his best. He considered it an "arabesque," a term he used to refer to tales that, while scarcely credible as depictions of realistic occurrences, are told seriously, without the tone of mockery or satire that he used in his so-called grotesques. Examples of the latter include "King Pest," with its fantastic group of characters, "every one of whom seemed to possess a monopoly of some particular portion of physiognomy," and "A Predicament," in which a lady writer tells in shuddering detail how she felt when the minute hand of a giant clock cut off her head. Later critics have called "Ligeia" a tale of terror, since the narrator is frightened and horrified by what he sees, or thinks he sees, at the story's end. Similar terror is experienced by Roderick Usher in "The Fall of the House of Usher" and by a number of Poe's other narrators who undergo harrowing experiences.

The narrator of "Ligeia," who should not in any way be autobiographically identified with the author, never tells his name, a device Poe employed often, as in "The Pit and the Pendulum," "The Tell-Tale Heart," "The Black Cat," and many other tales. Telling the story from a first-person point of view increases the final dramatic effect, a predetermined element that, as Poe said in his famous review of Nathaniel Hawthorne's *Twice-Told Tales* (1837), should always be the aim of a serious artist in short fiction.

Two themes in "Ligeia" appear elsewhere in Poe's tales. Psychic survival through reincarnation is the theme in an early tale, "Morella," in which a bereaved husband learns that his dead wife has taken over the body and the character of the daughter who was born just before the mother died. In the climactic closing scene of "Ligeia," the supposedly dead first wife, Ligeia, has (or seems to have) appropriated the body of the second wife, Rowena. A second theme, that of premature burial, appears in the early tale "Berenice" and in such later tales as "The Fall of the House of Usher" and "The Premature Burial."

"Ligeia" illustrates Poe's skill in achieving the unity of impression that, like his "predetermined effect," he considered of primary importance in telling a tale. Throughout, the tone of the narrator is intensely serious as he relates the story of his two marriages. He dwells on his love for and passionate adoration of the beautiful, mysterious, intellectual Ligeia. There is foreshadowing when he speaks of his suffering and of the loss "of her who is no more." The final scene is anticipated in several ways. The description of Ligeia at the beginning emphasizes "the raven-black, the glossy, the luxuriant, and naturally-curling tresses," and her eyes are repeatedly mentioned: "Those eyes! those large, those shining, those divine orbs!" The brief, hectic excitement of the second marriage, to the "fair-haired and blue-eyed Lady Rowena Trevanion, of Tremaine," is quickly followed by the husband's obsessed memories of "the beloved, the august, the beautiful, the entombed" Ligeia. In the second paragraph of the tale, Ligeia's beauty of face is described as "the radiance of an opium dream." This anticipates the actual opium dreams that result from the husband's addiction following his loss of Ligeia. Those dreams, which accompany his loathing and hatred of Rowena, are filled with Ligeia, and the intensity of the husband's longing for his lost love climaxes with her return at the story's end. When she opens her eyes, he is sure of her identity, and he shrieks, "These are the full, and the black, and the wild eyes—of my lost love— . . . of the Lady Ligeia!"

The theme of psychic survival is suggested first in the story's epigraph, with its final sentence, "Man doth not yield himself to the angels, nor unto death utterly, save only through the weakness of his feeble will." This theme first appears in the story when the narrator recalls having read this passage from Joseph Glanvill, which he quotes. He connects Glanvill's words with Ligeia when he speaks of her "intensity in thought, action, or speech" as "a result, or at least an index" of her "gigantic volition." After she falls ill, he is struck by "the fierceness of resistance with which she wrestled with the Shadow." Just before she dies, she asks him to repeat a poem she had written some days before, a symbolic poem portraying life as a tragic drama with "its hero, the conqueror Worm," which finally devours each actor. As he concludes the poem, Ligeia shrieks and pleads, "O God! O Divine Father! . . . shall this conqueror be not once conquered?" Her last murmured words echo Glanvill's: "Man doth not yield him to the angels, nor unto death utterly, save only through the weakness of his feeble will." Yet her own fierce will to live does not save her from death—or so her husband

thinks. He leaves Germany, moves to England, purchases a decaying abbey, extravagantly refurnishes its interior, and leads his new bride to the bedroom in the high turret. Though entombed, Ligeia continues to "wrestle with the Shadow." She fills her husband's memories, and in final triumph she replaces her blond successor. Or does she?

"Ligeia" has achieved considerable fame as the subject of many widely divergent interpretations. It has been argued that Ligeia is not a real woman but symbolically "the very incarnation of German idealism, German transcendentalism provided with an allegorical form." One critic has suggested that Ligeia never existed at all but has merely been imagined by the narrator, who is mad. Another has called her a witch, and still another a "revenant—a spirit who has spent immemorial lifetimes on earth." As for the husband, he has been termed a liar and even a murderer who kills Rowena, his second wife, by poisoning her with the "ruby drops" that fall into her wine glass.

Perhaps the most acceptable interpretation of the story is a literal one. The narrator marries the beautiful, brilliant Ligeia, and they live happily in Germany until she dies of a mysterious disease. He then marries Rowena in England but soon turns against her. Rowena suffers spells of illness, and her husband endlessly dreams of his lost Ligeia, for whom he longs deeply. His increasing use of opium causes his dreams to become so confused with reality that in a final frightening hallucination, he believes he sees standing before him the beloved dark-haired and large-eyed Ligeia, who has taken over the body of her fair-haired successor. By the strength of her intense will, Ligeia would thus have defeated Death, the Conquering Worm.

Dramatically, the scene achieves the effect for which the Glanvill quotation prepares readers. That the return of Ligeia is only imagined is also prepared for by the narrator's repeated references to his drug addiction:

> I had become a bounden slave in the trammels of opium. . . . I was habitually fettered in the shackles of the drug. . . . I was wild with the excitement of an immoderate dose of opium. . . . Wild visions, opium-engendered, flitted, shadow-like, before me . . . passionate waking visions of Ligeia . . . a crowd of unutterable fancies . . . had chilled me into stone.

In his numbed state he has regained his intensely desired Ligeia, but surely it is a drug-induced fancy that shocks him into shrieking the words that end the story.

"Critical Evaluation" by Henderson Kincheloe

Further Reading

Ackroyd, Peter. *Poe: A Life Cut Short*. London: Chatto & Windus, 2008. Ackroyd, a novelist, provides a very readable and concise chronicle of Poe's brief, unhappy life.

Basler, Roy P. "The Interpretation of 'Ligeia.'" In *Poe: A Collection of Critical Essays*, edited by Robert Regan. Englewood Cliffs, N.J.: Prentice-Hall, 1967. Classic essay presents a psychological study of "Ligeia" that interprets the work as an exploration of the narrator's rational and nonrational obsession and madness.

Fisher, Benjamin F. *The Cambridge Introduction to Edgar Allan Poe*. New York: Cambridge University Press, 2008. Presents an overview of Poe's literary career and writings and describes how his fiction advanced from gothic fantasies to more sophisticated explorations of human psychology. Includes discussion of "Ligeia."

Hayes, Kevin J., ed. *The Cambridge Companion to Edgar Allan Poe*. New York: Cambridge University Press, 2002. Collection of essays covers such topics as Poe's aesthetic theory, his humor, his place within the gothic tradition, and sensationalism in his work. Includes discussion of "Ligeia," particularly in the essay "Poe's Feminine Ideal," by Karen Weekes.

Jones, Daryl E. "Poe's Siren: Character and Meaning in 'Ligeia.'" *Studies in Short Fiction* 20, no. 1 (Winter, 1983): 33-37. Dismisses interpretations of "Ligeia" as a straightforward gothic tale or a tale of psychological realism and instead explores the title character as a siren, noting that the powers of a siren would explain Ligeia's strength as well as the narrator's weakness of will.

Levine, Stuart. "'Ligeia': Multiple Intention, Unified Effect." In *Edgar Poe: Seer and Craftsman*. DeLand, Fla.: Everett/Edwards, 1972. Argues that Poe uses Ligeia's beauty to establish an explicitly romantic aesthetic. Explores several reasons the story is difficult to interpret.

Magistrale, Tony. *Student Companion to Edgar Allan Poe*. Westport, Conn.: Greenwood Press, 2001. Introduction to Poe's life and works is designed for students and general readers. Includes a discussion of "Ligeia" in chapter 4, "Vampiric Love Stories."

Saliba, David R. "Formulaic Achievement: 'Ligeia.'" In *A Psychology of Fear: The Nightmare Formula of Edgar Allan Poe*. Lanham, Md.: University Press of America, 1980. Explores "Ligeia" as one of Poe's most successful nightmare pieces. Accepts the premise that the title character is a dream figure.

Light in August

Author: William Faulkner (1897-1962)
First published: 1932
Type of work: Novel
Type of plot: Psychological realism
Time of plot: 1930
Locale: Mississippi

Principal characters:
JOE CHRISTMAS, a light-skinned African American man
DOC HINES, his grandfather
MR. MCEACHERN, his foster father
JOANNA BURDEN, his benefactor and mistress
JOE BROWN, alias Lucas Burch, his partner
LENA GROVE, the mother of Brown's child
BYRON BUNCH, a man in love with Lena

The Story:

Joe Christmas is the illegitimate son of a dark-skinned circus trouper who was thought to be of African American descent and a white girl named Milly Hines. Joe's grandfather, old Doc Hines, kills the circus man, lets Milly die in childbirth, and puts Joe—at Christmas time, hence his last name—into an orphanage, where the children learn to call him "Nigger." Doc Hines then arranges to have Joe adopted by a religious and heartless farmer named McEachern, whose cruelties to Joe are met with a matching stubbornness that turns the boy into an almost subhuman being.

One day in town, McEachern takes Joe to a disreputable restaurant, where he talks to the waitress, Bobbie Allen. McEachern tells the adolescent Joe never to patronize the place alone. Joe goes back, however, to meet Bobbie at night, and the two become lovers. Night after night, while the McEacherns are asleep, Joe creeps out of the house and hurries to meet Bobbie in town.

One night, McEachern follows Joe to a country dance and orders him home. Joe knocks McEachern unconscious, whispers to Bobbie that he will meet her soon, and races to return home before McEachern can. There he gathers up all the money he can lay his hands on before he leaves to go into town. At the house where Bobbie is staying, he encounters the restaurant proprietor, his wife, and another man. The two men beat Joe, take his money, and leave for Memphis with the two women.

Joe moves on. Sometimes he works, but more often he simply lives off the money that women give him. He has sex with many women and nearly always tells them that he is black. Eventually, he arrives in Jefferson, a small town in Mississippi, where he gets work shoveling sawdust in a lumber mill. He finds lodging in a long-deserted cabin near the country home of Miss Joanna Burden, a spinster of Yankee origin who has few associates in Jefferson because of her zeal for bettering the lot of African Americans. She feeds Joe and plans to send him to a school for African Americans. Miss Burden and Joe become lovers, and they carry on their affair for three years. Her reactions to him range from sheer animalism to evangelism, as she tries to make Joe repent his sins and become a Christian.

A young man who calls himself Joe Brown arrives to begin working at the sawmill, and Joe Christmas invites Brown to share his cabin with him. The two begin to sell bootleg whiskey. After a while, Joe tells Brown that he is African American, and before long, Brown discovers the relationship between Joe and Miss Burden. When the two men's bootlegging business prospers, they buy a car and give up their jobs at the lumber mill.

One night, Joe goes to Miss Burden's room half determined to kill her. She attempts to shoot him with an antiquated pistol that does not fire, and Joe cuts her throat with his razor and runs out of the house. Later in the evening, Miss Burden's house is discovered to be on fire. When some townspeople enter the burning home and start to go upstairs to look for Miss Burden, Brown tries to stop them, but they brush him aside. They find Miss Burden's body in the bedroom and carry it outside before the house burns to the ground.

Through a letter that Miss Burden had earlier written and deposited at the Jefferson bank, the authorities learn of her New Hampshire relatives, whom they notify. Almost at once, word comes back from the relatives offering a thousand-dollar reward for the capture of her murderer. Brown tries to tell the story as he knows it, putting the blame on Joe Christmas, so that he can collect the money. Few believe his story, but he is held in custody until Joe Christmas can be found.

Joe Christmas remains at large for several days, but at last, with the help of bloodhounds, he is found. Meanwhile, old Doc Hines has learned of his grandson's crime, and he has

come with his wife to Jefferson. He urges the white people to lynch Joe, but his rantings go unheeded.

On the way to face indictment by the grand jury in the courthouse, Joe, handcuffed but not manacled to the deputy, manages to escape. He runs to a cabin and finds a gun. Some volunteer guards from the American Legion give chase and finally find him in the kitchen of the Reverend Gail Hightower, a former Presbyterian minister. Hightower is an outcast because people believe that his obsession with the gallant death of his grandfather in the Civil War drove his wife into dementia. Joe has gone to Hightower at the suggestion of his grandmother, Mrs. Hines, who had a conference with Joe in his cell just before his escape. She had been advised of this possible way of escape by Byron Bunch, Hightower's only friend in Jefferson. The Legionnaires shoot Joe, and then their leader mutilates him with a knife.

Brown now claims his reward. A deputy then takes him out to the cabin where he had lived with Joe Christmas. On entering the cabin, he sees Mrs. Hines holding a newborn baby. In the bed is a young woman, Lena Grove, with whom Brown had sex in a town in Alabama. Lena had started out to find Brown when she learned she was going to have a baby. Traveling most of the way on foot, she had arrived in Jefferson on the day of the murder and the fire. Directed to the sawmill, she had at once seen that Byron Bunch, to whom she had been sent, was not the same man as Lucas Burch, which is Brown's real name. Byron, a kindly soul, has fallen in love with her. Having identified Brown from Byron's description, Lena is sure that, in spite of his new name, Brown is the father of her child. She has given birth to the baby in Brown's cabin, where Byron has made her as comfortable as he could, with the aid of Mrs. Hines.

On learning about the baby, Brown jumps from a back window and escapes. Byron, torn between his desire to marry Lena and the wish to see her baby's rightful father take responsibility, tracks Brown to the railroad grade outside town and fights with him. Brown escapes aboard a freight train.

Three weeks later, Lena and Byron take to the road with the baby, Lena still searching for Brown. A truck driver gives them a lift as they make their way toward Tennessee. Byron is patient, but one night, he tries to get Lena to have sex with him. When she refuses, he leaves the little camp where the truck is parked. The next morning, however, he is waiting at the bend of the road; the truck stops for him, and he climbs up onto it.

Critical Evaluation:

William Faulkner was thirty-five when he published *Light in August* as the final explosive creation of the richest part of his artistic career, the time that saw the production of *Sartoris* (1929), *The Sound and the Fury* (1929), *As I Lay Dying* (1930), and *Sanctuary* (1931). Only *Absalom, Absalom!* (1936) would approach again the intensity and splendid richness of this, his tenth book published and the seventh in the series about the fictional Yoknapatawpha County. Armstid, who appears in the novel's first chapter, is the same farmer who appears as a character in *As I Lay Dying*; and Joanna Burden mentions Colonel Sartoris in her account of her own family's blood-spattered history. *Light in August* is Faulkner's longest work and, as critic Richard H. Rovere has noted, his most varied "in mood and character." It is perhaps equaled only by *The Sound and the Fury* as a penetrating and compelling analysis of southern society.

The style of this novel has often been criticized for its inconsistency and is often presented as an example of Faulkner's "undisciplined genius." Indeed, the work's stylistic characteristics are manifold and complex. Faulkner incorporates sudden changes of narrative tense, from present to past and back again, and abrupt shifts in point of view, ranging from the viewpoints of the major characters to viewpoints of characters who apparently have no part in the main action at all. Faulkner also utilizes stream-of-consciousness techniques similar to the emphasis on key images found in the works of Marcel Proust or to what James Joyce termed "radiating imagery," while creating long compound words, also a Joycean technique, such as "womanpinksmelling," "Augusttremulous," "stillwinged," and "womanshenegro." Epiphanies similar to those found in the works of Joyce also appear in the novel, as when Joe Christmas is caught in the glare of headlights after the murder of Joanna Burden.

Faulkner's emphasis on all the senses is similar to that found in the poetry of T. S. Eliot, while the simplicity of his imagery is evocative of the works of Robert Frost. Faulkner mixes these elements with a flamboyant poetic diction that is characteristic of the works of Wallace Stevens and includes the repetition of implicit interrogatives and phrases, such as "grown heroic at the instant of vanishment" and "two inescapable horizons of the implacable earth." In fact, his awkwardly repetitious use of manneristic expressions such as "by ordinary," "terrific," and the adverb "quite" seems to support the argument that the composition of this admitted masterpiece was at times hurried and even heedless.

The last two chapters of the novel—Hightower's rambling retrogression into Civil War history and the resumption of Lena's travels (this time with Byron)—achieve a sense of open-ended comprehensiveness that indicates Faulkner's epic concept of his novel. Furthermore, it is the universality of the epic genre that may account for the work's apparently

arbitrary grouping of stylistic elements. Faulkner uses every angle of insight, every avenue of perspective, every mode of entry to compel the reader into the world of the novel—a world complete with its own dimensions: of time and space, of emotions, and of events.

As an epic, *Light in August* falls into the genre of search epics. Joe Christmas is searching for a light that will give meaning to his existence, exploring, in turn, the light of McEachern's "home," the light of his adolescent town, the lamp of Bobbie Allen's room, the inordinate streetlights of nameless ghettos, the light of Joanna's candle, and, finally, the light of the flames of Joanna's burning house—the "light in August" around whose central, sinister radiance all the main characters' lives revolve. That burning light brings their identities into momentary and terrible focus, disillusioning Lena of her dreams of trust and security, forcing Lucas Burch and Gail Hightower to confront their cowardice, coercing Byron Bunch to throw in his lot irrevocably with his love, ending Joanna's ambiguously introverted life in perverted horror, and, with supreme irony, ultimately identifying Christmas through the reaction of the outraged town and, through this identification, ending his search in death.

The novel is also epic in its thematic scope, a scope embodied in the ambivalence of Joe Christmas himself, who, through no fault of his own, is tragically made to straddle two worlds—neither of which will accept him because of his relation to the other, neither of which he will accept because of his inherent inability to be singularly defined. The two worlds, as Faulkner steeps them through the very fiber of his novel, may be described as a kind of movable equation—an equation generally defined by the racial distinction between black and white. On one side, Christmas confronts his African American identity, death (as stasis), darkness or artificial light, evil, fire, the female, sleeping, insanity, sin, savageness, violence, secrecy, cunning and deceit, softness, the fugitive state, belief, and passivity. Opposed to these elements, but also mingling and combining with them in unpredictable and unmanageable patterns, are his white identity, life (as kinesis and fluid movement), light, good, the sun, the male, being awake and aware, control, righteousness, calm, openness, durability and determination, domestic security, knowing, and activity. "He never acted like either a nigger or a white man," one of his murderers comments at the end. Because Christmas could not find himself on either side of the equation, because his entire life was a confusion between the two sides, his epic quest ends in his own individual death and in the symbolic death of the community of Jefferson.

It is because Faulkner envisioned Christmas as an epic hero that he identified him with Christ, not only in name but also in his peculiar silences, his master-disciple relationship with Brown, his capture on a Friday, Joanna's resemblance to both Mary Magdalene and the Virgin Mary, his thirty years of private life (about which the narrator reveals nothing specific), his refusal to complain when beaten at the end, and the town's final comment that "it was as though he had set out and made his plans to passively commit suicide." *Light in August*, however, is christological only in the sense that it draws on Christian ideas to complicate and deepen the essentially secular, sociological myth that Faulkner constructs consistently in the entire saga of Yoknapatawpha County. *Light in August* professes only the religion of humanity, a religion that must function in a world "peopled principally by the dead," as Hightower, the rejected minister, remarks. This is a novel of "mighty compassion."

"Critical Evaluation" by Kenneth John Atchity

Further Reading

Brooks, Cleanth. "The Community and the Pariah." In *William Faulkner: The Yoknapatawpha Country*. 1963. Reprint. Baton Rouge: Louisiana State University Press, 2002. Essay discussing *Light in August* is part of one of the most valuable studies of Faulkner's fiction, particularly the works involving the fictional county he created.

Karl, Frederick R. *William Faulkner, American Writer: A Biography*. New York: Ballantine Books, 1989. Examines Faulkner's life with psychological, emotional, and literary precision. Focuses on the strengths on which Faulkner relied in his growth as a great American writer of the twentieth century.

Loichot, Valérie. *Orphan Narratives: The Postplantation Literature of Faulkner, Glissant, Morrison, and Saint-John Perse*. Charlottesville: University Press of Virginia, 2007. Discusses the works of writers from the United States and the Caribbean who wrote about the plantation culture after the abolition of slavery. Examines Faulkner's treatment of that world in *Light in August*.

Marius, Richard. *Reading Faulkner: Introduction to the First Thirteen Novels*. Compiled and edited by Nancy Grisham Anderson. Knoxville: University of Tennessee Press, 2006. Collection of the lectures that Marius, a novelist, biographer, and Faulkner scholar, presented during an undergraduate course. Provides an approachable introduction to Faulkner. Includes a chapter on *Light in August*.

Millgate, Michael, ed. *New Essays on "Light in August."* New York: Cambridge University Press, 1987. Presents a good introduction to the novel as well as a clarification of its structure; a consideration of the depictions of women, sexism, and racism in the work; and an exploration of Faulkner's understanding of "the difference between enduring and prevailing."

Porter, Carolyn. *William Faulkner*. New York: Oxford University Press, 2007. Concise and informative resource spans Faulkner's entire life but focuses on his most prolific period, from 1929 to 1940. Examines his childhood and personal struggles and offers insightful analyses of his major works. *Light in August* is discussed in chapter 2.

Romine, Scott. *The Narrative Forms of Southern Community*. Baton Rouge: Louisiana State University Press, 1999. Focuses on the paradoxical concept of southern community—how a place that is valued for its cohesiveness and moral stability is also riven by racial and class oppression. Examines *Light in August* and other works that try to negotiate these inherent tensions.

Towner, Theresa M. *The Cambridge Introduction to William Faulkner*. New York: Cambridge University Press, 2008. Accessible resource, aimed at students and general readers, provides detailed analyses of Faulkner's nineteen novels, discussion of his other works, and information about the critical reception of his fiction.

Lightning

Author: Santō Kyōden (1761-1816)
First published: Mukashigatari inazuma-byōshi, 1806
    (English translation, 1986)
Type of work: Novel
Type of plot: Romance
Time of plot: Fifteenth century
Locale: Japan

Principal characters:
SASAKI SADAKUNI, the feudal lord of Yamato Province
SASAKI KATSURA, his firstborn son, by his deceased first
    wife
SASAKI HANAGATA, his second son, by his present wife
KUMODE NO KATA or LADY SPIDER, Sadakuni's present
    wife and Hanagata's mother
ICHŌ NO MAE or LADY GINKGO, Katsura's wife
TSUKIWAKA or YOUNG-MOON, the son of Katsura and Lady
    Ginkgo
FUWA DŌKEN or ROAD-DOG, a steward to the House of
    Sasaki
FUWA BANZAEMON, Dōken's son
HASEBE UNROKU, a disloyal retainer
NAGOYA SABUROZAEMON, a loyal retainer
NAGOYA SANSABURB, his son
FUJINAMI or WISTERIA-WAVE, a dancer
SASARA SAMPACHIRŌ, a loyal retainer, also known as
    Namuemon
KURITARO or CHESTNUT-SON, Namuemon's son
KAEDE or MAPLE, Namuemon's daughter
YUASA MATAHEI, Fujinami's brother
UMEZU KAMON or GOOD-GATE, a recluse
SARUJIRO or MONKEY-SON, Sampachirō's servant
SHIKAZŌ or DEER, Sansaburō's servant

The Story:

    During the mid-fifteenth century, under the shogunate of Ashikaga Yoshimasa, lives a warrior lord by the name of Sasaki Sadakuni, lord of the Province of Yamato. He has two sons. One, twenty-five years old and named Katsura, is the son of Sadakuni's first wife; the other, twelve-year-old Hanagata, is the son of Sadakuni's second and present wife, Lady Spider. Katsura, a handsome young man, is taken into the luxurious and self-indulgent service of the shōgun at Kyoto. There, at the instigation of one of his retainers, Fuwa Banzaemon, Katsura falls in love with a dancer, Wisteria-wave, and he begins to lead a life of pleasure.

    A retainer of the House of Sasaki, Nagoya Sansaburō, is sent to Kyoto to present a treasured painting to the shōgun. Learning how matters stand with Katsura, he does his best to make the young lord mend his ways, but to no avail. Meanwhile, Banzaemon himself is discovered to be in love with Wisteria-wave, and he is discharged from feudal service. Sansaburō is sent back to the Sasaki provincial headquarters. At the same time, a loyal retainer, Sasara Sampachirō, kills Wisteria-wave and goes into hiding. On the same night, a

disloyal retainer, Hasebe Unroku, steals the treasured painting and disappears.

    The next day, Banzaemon's father, Road-dog, steward to the House of Sasaki, arrives as Sadakuni's emissary. He severely reprimands Katsura for his dissolute ways and discharges Katsura's retinue as being disloyal. Behind Road-dog's outwardly righteous actions, however, lies a deeper plan, a plot to take over his lord's domain with the connivance of Governor General Hamana. Knowing that Lady Spider hopes that her own son, Hanagata, will succeed to the lordship of Sasaki, Road-dog has joined forces with her. With the backing of an evil sorcerer, the two attempt to do away with Katsura's wife, Lady Ginkgo, and her son, Young-moon, who are living in the Sasaki villa in Heguri, guarded by Sansaburō and his father, Nagoya Saburozaemon. Although their plot fails, Sadakuni is deceived, and troops are dispatched against Lady Ginkgo and her young son.

    In the meantime, Banzaemon, who holds a grudge against Sansaburō, kills Saburozaemon. Sansaburō places Young-moon in the care of the boy's elderly nurse and helps them escape; he fights valiantly in defense of Lady Ginkgo, but in spite of his courage and efforts his lord's lady is abducted. He escapes into Kawachi Province. The old woman in charge of Young-moon meets with difficulty in escaping with her charge, but the boy is saved by Sasara Sampachirō, who has changed his name to Namuemon and has been hiding in Tamba Province.

Namuemon is still haunted by the spirit of the dead Wisteria-wave, whom he killed for the sake of his lord; his son, Chestnut-son, becomes blind, and his daughter, Maple, is haunted by a serpent. When it becomes known that Namuemon has been secretly watching Road-dog's movements with the idea of killing him, warriors are sent against Namuemon, who beheads his own son and then, in order that Young-moon's life might be spared, identifies the head as Young-moon's. Namuemon's daughter sells herself for the painting. Namuemon, with his wife and Young-moon, seeks refuge in Kawachi Province. Leaving the others in a place of safety, Namuemon then sets out to find his master, Katsura, and Katsura's wife, Lady Ginkgo.

Meanwhile, Lady Ginkgo, who has fallen into Road-dog's hands, is about to be murdered, but she is saved by a hero-recluse by the name of Umezu (Good-gate). Katsura, who has become an itinerant Buddhist priest, is about to meet his death at a temple festival in Omi Province when his life is saved by Monkey-son, Sansaburō's son who has become a street preacher.

After his delivery, Katsura is hidden in the home of Yuasa Matahei, Wisteria-wave's older brother and a painter living in Otsu. By chance, Namuemon is also staying there. Matahei becomes aware that Namuemon is his own sister's murderer, but at the same time he is deeply impressed by the quality of Namuemon's loyalty. Matahei's wife confesses that six years ago she had attempted to hang herself because a ruffian had robbed her of twenty pieces of gold. Namuemon not only saved her from death but also gave her twenty gold pieces to make up for her loss.

Torn between his wish for revenge and his gratitude toward Namuemon, Matahei draws his sword and cuts Namuemon's traveling hat instead of Namuemon's head; he then offers the sundered hat to Wisteria-wave's departed but still-vengeful spirit. With past wrongs thus redressed, Matahei shows his gratitude by bringing Namuemon to Katsura. At this point Hasebe Unroku appears on the scene and is recognized by Matahei's wife as the man who robbed her six years before. Namuemon forces Unroku to commit suicide to expiate his sins.

A traveling theatrical troupe arrives in the area, and among its members is Namuemon's daughter, Maple. Na-

muemon, now revealed as Sampachirō, meets his daughter, whose haunting by serpents has been healed by the painting she bought so dearly. Matahei, for the first time, realizes that he has attained the inner secret that he had striven for in his art—its magical power.

On the following day, Katsura and his party leave Otsu for Kawachi Province. Katsura acquires a book on military strategy and tactics from Good-gate, who saved Lady Ginkgo's life. Intending to seek the assistance of the new governor general, Katsumoto, the party arrives at Good-gate's secluded abode on Diamond Mountain to find that Katsumoto is already there and attempting to persuade Good-gate to accept the position of chief of military strategy. It is also revealed that Good-gate is related to Katsura by marriage. Katsura is reunited with Lady Ginkgo, who has been staying there under Good-gate's protection. With the backing of the governor general and Good-gate, Katsura prepares to return to his home province of Yamato.

Meanwhile, in Kyoto, Sansaburō, accompanied by his faithful servant Deer, has been searching for Fuwa Banzaemon and his gang in the brothels of the city. Finally he finds them, and, with the assistance of a courtesan and Good-gate, who had been a friend of his slain father, Saburozaemon, Sansaburō achieves his revenge. Good-gate, appointed the governor general's deputy, receives orders to go to the headquarters of the House of Sasaki. Requesting the attendance of Sadakuni's wife, Lady Spider, and his steward, Road-dog, as well, Good-gate tells Lord Sasaki Sadakuni that Katsura not only has mended his former ways but also has displayed great military valor. He requests that Sadakuni pardon his son and name Katsura his heir and successor; Sadakuni will then retire in Katsura's favor as head of the clan. Good-gate also reveals the plot concocted by Lady Spider and Road-dog to take over the House of Sasaki by conniving for the succession of the second-born, Lady Spider's son, Hanagata. Road-dog is then placed under arrest and locked in a caged carriage. His mission accomplished, Good-gate takes his leave amid the low and reverent bows of the members of the House of Sasaki.

Critical Evaluation:

Santō Kyōden, also known in the West by his artist's name of Kitao Masanobu, followed his early successes in print designing and fiction by concentrating his attention on the latter. He was the most versatile and gifted of the popular Edo (modern Tokyo) writers. In addition to the picture books and fanciful didactic *yomihon* reading books to which he turned under the pressure of Tokugawa censorship, he wrote many excellent *sharebon* (books of wit), sophisticated sketches of manners in the Yoshiwara and other pleasure quarters. Though these were limited in subject matter, their realistic dialogue technique greatly influenced the two leading kinds of realistic Edo fiction of the nineteenth century. This tendency toward realism is evident in *Lightning*.

Using the central themes of rivalry for succession to a great feudal house and the triumph of good over evil, right over wrong, Kyōden took his materials from traditional Kabuki plays and wrote *Lightning* with stage production in mind. The scenes change rapidly, and the plot is complicated by the appearance of a large number of secondary characters who disrupt the unity of the story. The principal theme thus tends to move away from the succession intrigues to a depiction of the feudal loyalty of a secondary character, Sasara Sampachirō. That this novel was soon produced on the Kabuki stage was a matter of course, and it was staged under various titles. The first was in Osaka in 1808, and then in Edo in 1809. As a novel, the work constitutes a unit in itself, but Kyōden wrote a sequel, the *Honchō sui-bodai zenden*, which was published in 1809. This later work, making greater use of syllabic meter, has little connection with the original and is thin in plot, but it carries the reader on through the author's sheer writing ability.

Like many of Kyōden's works, *Lightning* is written in a vigorous, popular style, simple and direct, and often melodramatic in plot. Because of the skillful handling of action and the true-to-life emotions of the characters, the novel was very well received in Japan. A somber history of vengeance, the novel abounds in violence, suicides, torture, combat, and rapid shifts of plot. It reads often like an early nineteenth century European Romantic novel, filled with gothic horrors and boiling emotions, but, at the same time, a lusty quality and a certain vigorous humor raise the book to a greater level of realism. Kyōden was considered one of the leaders in Japan in the development of the realistic school of fiction.

Although the plot is at times confusing, owing partly to the large number of characters, a vigor of style and narrative drive carries the action steadily forward. The minor characters tend to be stylized, boldly sketched figures, but the principal characters are much more realistically portrayed. *Lightning* possesses an almost cinematic sweep and power of movement, and the Western reader should not become sidetracked by attempting to follow every minute plot thread; the novel's romantic vision of feudal life in Japan is rendered in an exciting, enjoyable style.

Further Reading

Devitt, Jane. "Santō Kyōden and the Yomihon." *Harvard Journal of Asiatic Studies* 39, no. 2 (1979): 253-274. Discusses the life and works of Kyōden, with a focus on his central themes of the samurai class and its values.

Jenkins, Donald, et al. *The Floating World Revisited*. Honolulu: University of Hawaii Press, 1993. Catalog prepared for an art museum exhibit of *ukiyo-e*, or floating world art from late eighteenth century Edo, Japan, presents essays that discuss the art and literature of this time and place, including an essay about Kyōden.

Kern, Adam L. *Manga from the Floating World: Comicbook Culture and the Kibyōshi of Edo Japan*. Cambridge, Mass.: Harvard University Press, 2006. Study of the *kibyōshi*, or Japanese picture books, from the late eighteenth century places these works in their socioeconomic and historical contexts. Includes three annotated translations of picture books written and illustrated by Kyōden.

Korniki, Peter F. "*Nishiki no ura*: An Instance of Censorship and the Structure of a *Sharebon*." *Monumenta Nipponica* 32, no. 2 (1977): 153-188. Discusses the historical context of the work, the censorship of *sharebon*, or books of wit, and Kyōden's success with the genre.

Roddy, Stephen J. "Santō Kyōden's *Chōshin suikoden*: Representations of Violence and Honor in Tokugawa Fiction." In *Knight and Samurai: Actions and Images of Elite Warriors in Europe and East Asia*, edited by Rosemarie Deist and Harald Kleinschmidt. Göppingen, Germany: Kümmerle, 2003. Discussion of Kyōden's 1789 novel *Chōshin suikoden* addresses the depiction of samurai warriors in his work.

Santō Kyōden. *The Straw Sandal: Or, The Scroll of the Hundred Crabs*. Translated by Carmen Blacker. Folkestone, England: Global Oriental, 2008. New English translation of *Mukashigatari inazuma-byōshi*, the work earlier translated as *Lightning*. An informative introduction by Peter F. Korniki discusses the novel and its author.

Like Water for Chocolate
A Novel in Monthly Installments with Recipes, Romances, and Home Remedies

Author: Laura Esquivel (1950-   )
First published: Como agua para chocolate: Novela de entregas mensuales con recetas, amores, y remedios caseros, 1989 (English translation, 1992)
Type of work: Novel
Type of plot: Domestic realism and Magical Realism
Time of plot: Early twentieth century
Locale: Near Piedras Negras, Mexico, and the Mexico-U.S. border

Principal characters:
TITA DE LA GARZA, protagonist
PEDRO MUZQUIZ, Tita's boyfriend, who later marries Tita's sister
MAMÁ ELENA, Tita's mother
ROSAURA DE LA GARZA and GERTRUDIS DE LA GARZA, Tita's sisters
NACHA, the family's cook
JOHN BROWN, an American doctor
CHENCHA, the family's cook after Nacha's death
ESPERANZA MUZQUIZ, Rosaura's daughter
ALEX BROWN, Esperanza's husband
TITA'S GRANDNIECE, the story's narrator

The Story:

The grandniece of Tita de la Garza begins telling Tita's life story. Tita is the daughter of Elena de la Garza, an authoritarian and inflexible woman who, with an iron fist, rules the lives of her three daughters, Tita, Rosaura, and Gertrudis. Mamá Elena forbids Tita from marrying Pedro Muzquiz, arguing an old family tradition that insists on keeping the youngest female of a family from marrying, so that she can take care of her parents instead.

Pedro asks for Tita's hand, but Mamá Elena offers her middle daughter, Rosaura, to him instead. Pedro accepts this proposal, realizing it is the only way he can be close to Tita, his real love. Likewise, Rosaura accepts her mother's proposal of marriage to Pedro, knowing the damage it will cause her. Indeed, she is haunted by jealousy and the fear of losing Pedro.

Tita becomes the caregiver of the couple's first child, Roberto, when Rosaura is unable to feed him. Miraculously, Tita starts to produce breast milk, and she begins to feed the baby. Mamá Elena worries that Tita and Pedro are getting too close, so she sends Rosaura and Pedro to live in another town with their baby. Tita remains in the house, devastated and worried for the baby's well-being. Soon, Roberto has died of hunger. Tita, who is unable to cope with the grief, goes crazy. Full of sorrow, she hides in the dovecote, set up in the roof of the home, and remains there until Dr. John Brown, an American, convinces her to come down from the roof. Mamá Elena decides that Tita should be committed to an asylum, but John takes Tita to his home instead. With loving care, John nurses her back to health.

Tita returns to her home after learning that her mother has fallen ill, but not before promising John that she will marry him. Rosaura and Pedro also return to the house. Upon seeing each other, Tita and Pedro realize that their love is as strong as ever. Unable to contain themselves, they consummate their love, before John returns from a short trip. Tita also believes that she is pregnant with Pedro's baby. Tita does not want to be unfair to John, so she breaks up her engagement, realizing that she loves Pedro more than she loves John. Rosaura finds out about her sister and John's relationship and agrees to keep the secret as long as Pedro does not divorce her.

Rosaura gives birth to a daughter, named Esperanza (meaning "hope"). Years later, Rosaura tries to maintain family tradition by prohibiting Esperanza's marriage to Alex, John's son. Rosaura dies, and with the blessings of Tita and John, Esperanza and Alex get married. Tita and Pedro, on the night of the wedding, consummate their love, and die doing so. The ranch burns to the ground, and the only object that survives is Tita's cookbook-diary.

Esperanza and Alex's daughter, who has Tita's ability and passion for cooking, reads Tita's cookbook, noting that Tita will live on if somebody prepares her recipes. As the story goes, Tita comes to the world crying so much that her tears become ten pounds of cooking salt. She develops a strong connection to the kitchen, a connection that starts when her mother is unable to feed her as a baby and gives her to Nacha, the family's indigenous cook, to be cared for. Nacha not only takes care of Tita but also teaches her all the culinary secrets that she learned from her Mexican ancestors. From Nacha, Tita learns that cooking is a reflection of her feelings and, as a result, she has the power to affect the people who consume her meals.

At Rosaura and Pedro's wedding, Tita's cake makes everyone feel sad; later, they all vomit. Nacha dies during the wedding, probably sharing the sadness of all the other guests and realizing that she may never find love. (Nacha reappears as a ghostly figure to aid and guide Tita.) Chencha replaces Nacha as the family's cook. Like all the other women, she suffers the tyranny of Mamá Elena. Her life is difficult, not only for having to serve Mamá Elena; she also is raped by a group of revolutionary men. Still, she finds the love of her life, Jesus Martinez. Chencha becomes Tita's companion in the kitchen after Nacha dies.

Tita, physically desiring Pedro, prepares a meal for the whole family. After the meal, Tita's sister Gertrudis, unable to contain herself, rips off her clothes. A soldier, sensing her smell from a distance, rides his horse to her and takes her away. The meal that Tita had prepared was so powerful that Juan Alejandrez, the soldier, is unable to satisfy Gertrudis sexually, so he has to take her to a brothel at the U.S.-Mexico border near Texas. After some time, Gertrudis and Juan get back together and eventually return to the ranch.

Mamá Elena dies, and Tita is forced to keep a secret from Gertrudis, who is actually her half sister. Gertrudis's father was mulatto, or mixed-race, and was her mother's only true and impossible love. When Gertrudis has a mulatto child, Tita has to reveal the secret to save her sister's marriage.

Critical Evaluation:

Laura Esquivel's *Like Water for Chocolate* is written in the style of Magical Realism, similar to the style of Mexican writer Elena Garro. Like Garro's novel *Los recuerdos del porvenir* (1963; *Recollections of Things to Come*, 1969), *Like Water for Chocolate* employs a third-person narrator to tell the story of her dead family. The novel mixes two important elements of family life: love and food.

Esquivel called *Like Water for Chocolate* an installment novel, with family recipes structured according to the months of the year, beginning with January. Many more recipes, or "home remedies," are used in the book, combining with the narration. Esquivel's title comes from a saying common in some countries of Latin America: "Like water for chocolate," which means to be, literally and figuratively, "at a boiling point." In Mexico, for example, hot chocolate is often prepared by dissolving a tablet of chocolate in boiling water, not in milk (hence the expression). The novel's main character, Tita de la Garza, uses the expression metaphorically, to

signal how mad she is about having to remain in her house—as the youngest daughter—taking care of her mother while her sisters are free to live their lives.

Academically, the novel has been the subject of much analysis. It is required reading in many schools, colleges, and universities. This interest comes, in part, from the novel's seemingly common story—lovers who cannot get together—and a fast-paced plot. However, what sets the novel apart from a simple romance is the cycle of failed romances: Mamá Elena is kept away from her lover because he is poor and a mulatto; the family cook, Nacha, never finds a partner; Rosaura marries Pedro knowing that he loves Tita; and Dr. John Brown loves Tita but cannot marry her. More important is Pedro and Tita's romance. They finally find a moment of love, but die together, in ecstasy.

Another feature of the novel is its Magical Realism, intermingled with humor, life experience, and recipes. Magical Realism is a technique employed by many Latin American writers in which time-shifts, dreams, and surrealistic descriptions, as Helene Price says, "are recounted in a matter-of-fact tone, as if they were commonplace events. In other words, within the ontological parameters of the text, magical things really do happen."

Other themes in the novel have received critical analysis, including the relationships between mothers and daughters, the presence of women in the Mexican revolutionary army, and the position of women in society. The great success of the novel, and the 1992 film (1993 in the United States) of the same name, which also was a hit with audiences, led some critics to consider the novel a best seller. They argue, however, that best sellers aimed at women readers rarely propose social or cultural change. In fact, in *Like Water for Chocolate*, Tita never really challenges the rules of her mother, even though they affect her negatively. It seems that Tita just wants to be a good wife, a great mother, and an excellent cook. Other critics declare that Esquivel is appropriating the spaces assigned to women—the home and the kitchen—to subvert tradition, and gender roles. Instead of feeling imprisoned in her own kitchen, Tita uses that space as a place of self-fulfillment.

Susana Perea-Fox

Further Reading

Price, Helene. "Unsavoury Representations in Laura Esquivel's *Like Water for Chocolate*." In *A Companion to Magical Realism*, edited by Stephen M. Hart and Wenchin Ouyang. Rochester, N.Y.: Tamesis, 2005. Price argues that the novel, in using the style rather than the substance of Magical Realism, reveals the way in which Europeans, Americans, and even urban, middle-class Mexicans wish to perceive Mexican rural reality.

Willingham, Elizabeth Moore, ed. *Laura Esquivel's Mexican Fictions*. Fort Worth: Texas Christian University Press, 2009. This comprehensive collection includes a biographical essay, an essay introducing literary criticism of Esquivel's writings, her work in the context of Latin American women's fiction, and several analyses of *Like Water for Chocolate*, among her other works.

Zubiaurre, Maite. "Culinary Eros in Contemporary Hispanic Female Fiction: From Kitchen Tales to Table Narratives." *College Literature* 33, no. 3 (2006): 29-51. Argues that "kitchen tales" such as *Like Water for Chocolate* keep women out of the public arena, confining them to the kitchen and keeping them in roles such as "witches, virgins, nurturers, and mothers." Offers an alternative fiction, called table narratives, which consider women as culinary consumers rather than producers.

Liliom
A Legend in Seven Scenes

Author: Ferenc Molnár (1878-1952)
First produced: 1909; first published, 1909 (English translation, 1921)
Type of work: Drama
Type of plot: Fantasy
Time of plot: Early twentieth century
Locale: Budapest

Principal characters:
LILIOM, a merry-go-round barker
MRS. MUSKAT, his employer
JULIE, his wife
MARIE, her friend
WOLF, Marie's husband
MRS. HOLLUNDER, Julie's aunt
FICSUR, Liliom's friend
LINZMAN, the cashier whom Ficsur suggests robbing
LOUISE, daughter of Julie and Liliom

The Story:

Liliom is a barker for Mrs. Muskat's merry-go-round at an amusement park on the edge of Budapest. As a barker he is a great success, for he has a stock of funny jokes that keep the customers laughing, and he has a playful way with young women.

One day two young servants, Marie and Julie, come to ride the merry-go-round. To Mrs. Muskat's indignation, Liliom follows Julie onto the carousel and puts his arm around her. Mrs. Muskat warns Julie that if she ever comes near the merry-go-round again, she will be thrown out, as Mrs. Muskat does not wish to lose her license because of questionable behavior in the park. Liliom, however, tells Julie that she is welcome to come back anytime. Although Mrs. Muskat is reluctant to let Liliom go, she cannot ignore this insolence, and she dismisses him.

Liliom, to show his independence, announces that he is going to get some beer. While he is collecting his belongings, Marie discloses to Julie that she is in love with a man in a uniform—a porter, however, not a soldier. When Liliom returns, he turns Marie away and begins to discuss love with Julie, bragging and bullying all the while. Julie shows that she is deeply in love—she has forfeited her job by staying out late with Liliom. Two policemen looking for vagrants interrupt their conversation. After asking routine questions and warning Julie that Liliom is a notorious ne'er-do-well, the policemen continue on their rounds. Although Julie protests that she does not love Liliom, it is obvious that she does.

Liliom and Julie marry and then move into a run-down photographer's shop, operated by Mrs. Hollunder and her son, at the edge of the park. Mrs. Hollunder, Julie's aunt, provides them not only with shelter but also with food and fuel. She grumbles all the time, but she is good-hearted beneath her gruffness. Marie, meanwhile, is falling more deeply in love with Wolf, the porter. One day, while the two young women are exchanging confidences, Mrs. Hollunder comes in and says that Julie's other suitor, a widowed carpenter with two children and a respectable income, still wants to take her out of the poverty in which she lives. Julie tells her that she prefers to stay where she is. Mrs. Muskat comes and offers to take Liliom back, but he refuses. He and a friend named Ficsur have a scheme for getting a great deal of money, and he is no longer interested in his old job at the merry-go-round.

Ficsur is planning a robbery. Each Saturday, a cashier for a leather factory passes a nearby railway embankment carrying the money for the factory workers' wages in a leather bag. The plan is for Liliom to accost the man and ask him what time it is while Ficsur comes up from behind and stabs the man. Ficsur encourages Liliom to steal a knife from Mrs. Hollunder's kitchen. Julie, knowing that the two men are up to no good, begs Liliom not to go out with Ficsur, for she has arranged to have the carpenter come that evening and offer Liliom work. After Liliom has left, Mrs. Hollunder misses her knife and suspects Liliom of taking it. Julie lies for him, saying that she had gone through Liliom's pockets and found only a pack of cards.

Liliom and Ficsur arrive at the embankment just as the six o'clock train passes. Being early, they start a game of twenty-one, and Ficsur wins from Liliom his share of the loot they hope to take from the cashier. Liliom accuses Ficsur of cheating. Then their victim appears, and Liliom accosts him. As Ficsur is about to strike, however, the cashier seizes Ficsur's arm and points a pistol at Liliom's chest. Ironically, he has come from the factory, where he has just finished paying off the workers; if Ficsur had killed him, the robbers would have gotten no money. As the cashier calls out to two policemen in the distance, Liliom breaks away and stabs himself with the kitchen knife. The policemen attempt to take him to a hospital, but his condition is too critical. They carry him back to the photographer's studio, where he dies with Julie by his side, holding his hand.

As he is dying, Liliom has a vision. Two heavenly policemen come to him and tell him to follow them. They remind him that death is not the end, that he is not through with earth until his memory has also passed away. Then they lead him to the heavenly court assigned to suicide cases. There he learns that, after a period of purification by fire, suicides are sent back to earth for one day to see whether they have profited by their purification. Liliom is sentenced to sixteen years in the fires.

At the end of that time, Liliom is returned to earth, where he finds his wife and sixteen-year-old daughter, Louise, about to lunch in the garden of their dilapidated little house. They do not recognize Liliom. Julie gives him some food, and Louise tells him that her father, a handsome man, had gone to the United States before she was born and had died there. When Liliom accuses Julie's late husband of having

struck her, Julie denies that he ever mistreated her, and she dismisses Liliom as an ungrateful wretch. Liliom tries to please his daughter with card tricks and with a beautiful star that he has stolen from heaven, but Louise will have nothing more to do with him. As he leaves, he strikes her hard on the hand, but the blow feels as tender as a caress to her. Her mother tells her that there have been times when she, too, experienced that sort of reaction from a blow. Liliom leaves in the company of the two policemen, who shake their heads in profound regret at Liliom's failure.

Critical Evaluation:

Known primarily as a playwright outside his native Hungary, Ferenc Molnár was the most prolific and versatile Hungarian writer of the first half of the twentieth century. Educated in Budapest and Geneva, Molnár early deserted the study of law for journalism and, in a short time, was publishing novels, essays, poetry, and short stories. His second play, *Az ördög* (pr., pb. 1907; *The Devil*, 1908), was a great success, launching him on a theatrical and dramatic career that lasted almost forty years and brought him international recognition as a master of ingenious light comedy. His penchant for juxtaposing realistic, often urban and lower-class, characters and situations with the fantastic placed him at the cutting edge of avant-garde theater in the 1920's and 1930's, and his admirers saw in Molnár a genuine, if quixotic, champion of the common person. Although he continued to write until his death in 1952, his reputation suffered a rapid decline in the 1940's, from which it has not recovered. Critics generally agree that most of Molnár's plays exhibit a flair for comic dialogue and dazzling theatrical technique but lack substance, all too often substituting cleverness and the shock of the unexpected for serious engagement with social and moral issues.

A product of the earliest period of Molnár's career, *Liliom* has long been regarded as his finest work. Not only does it showcase his gift for developing comic situations, it also makes startlingly effective use of his characteristic and innovative blend of realism and fantasy. In these respects, it strongly resembles many of his less well regarded dramas. Although the writing here may be a bit finer, Molnár is often funnier and wittier elsewhere. What sets *Liliom* apart is a seriousness of purpose that is lacking in almost all of his other dramas. It is not merely an exercise in cleverness or an excuse for light entertainment but a sincere attempt to grapple with difficult moral and ethical questions without settling for an easy answer—a point that is emphasized by its ambiguous ending. Nowhere else in his oeuvre is Molnár so nearly serious, so seriously in earnest, as he is in *Liliom*.

Subtitled *A Legend in Seven Scenes*, the play proceeds according to the intuitive logic of an Eastern European folktale. By turns whimsical and violent, realistic and fanciful, dramatic and sentimental, its brilliant use of sudden and increasingly shocking reversals of expectation to move the action forward demonstrates Molnár's mastery of dramatic technique.

The play dramatizes twin themes: the inability of accepted Judeo-Christian standards of morality to accord with human nature and the fact that the ruling classes use those standards to control—to police—the masses of working men and women. This theme is initially expressed in the contrast between the deep and true love of Liliom and Julie and the relationship between Wolf and Marie. Julie somehow can withstand Liliom's verbal and physical abuse, as well as the sixteen years of widowhood and poverty his criminal lack of judgment and impulsive suicide force on her and his daughter. In contrast, the love that Wolf and Marie share is portrayed as emotionally shallow. They begin by holding hands and sitting silently on park benches together and end by formally calling each other "Mr. Beifeld" and "Mrs. Beifeld" to keep from quarreling so they can "get along with society folk." By conforming to the moral guidelines laid down by society, Wolf and Marie are socially and economically successful, but they cannot experience life or love fully, as Liliom and Julie do. This double theme is extended through the pervasive presence of the police—in both earthly and heavenly forms—who observe and regulate the morality of the actions and activities of the characters of the play from beginning to end.

Within the framework provided by the opposition of Liliom and Julie's relationship to Wolf and Marie's, and by the parallel of earthly and heavenly police, the play moves ahead swiftly through a series of increasingly severe reversals. The unexpected marriage of Liliom and Julie solves the problems created by their being in love, but that solution creates a new problem: It leaves them both unemployed. Mrs. Muskat's offer to rehire Liliom convinces him to abandon Julie for his old life until Julie's news that she is pregnant catalyzes both Liliom's rejection of Mrs. Muskat's offer and his ill-fated try at thievery, which in turn leads to suicide and then to a heavenly court that duplicates the order of the world below. In contrast to expressionist drama, the fusion of realism and the fantastic that dominates the play from this point forward does not externalize interior, psychological, or emotional states. Rather, it is a metaphysical extension of the real world, a kind of transcendent realism, presenting the afterlife in a simple, matter-of-fact manner rather than by means of distortion or exaggeration. The rules, the moral guidelines,

and the power to punish those who flout them are symbolized here, as in life, by the courts and the police.

Despite *Liliom*'s undeniable effectiveness in the theater and the brilliance of its dramatic technique and the craftsmanship of its design, the play's greatest achievement is the character of Liliom himself. Unpredictable, brash, rough, funny, proud, tender, stubborn, violent, unhappy—he transcends the ordinary limits of theatrical characters. His personality is so complex and contradictory, so true to the inconsistency of judgment and impulse that mark all human beings and their actions, that, like Hamlet and King Lear, he cannot be reduced to a symbol. The difference between William Shakespeare's great theatrical characters and Molnár's, however, is that Hamlet and King Lear can live outside the plays that bear their names, while Liliom cannot. Hamlet and Lear simply exist, contradictions and all, without enduring any authorial attempt at shaping our opinion of them, whereas Molnár tries to justify Liliom's moral ambivalence and to "damn the police," thereby confining his greatest character to the limits of the argument he makes in his play.

"Critical Evaluation" by R. A. Martin

Further Reading

Gassner, John. *Masters of the Drama*. 3d ed. New York: Dover, 1954. Classic work includes an excellent chapter on the German dramatist Gerhart Hauptmann and his followers that offers an account of Molnár's dramatic art, linking its fantastic and expressionist elements to the unusual blend of realism and romanticism pioneered by Hauptmann.

Gergely, Emro Joseph. *Hungarian Drama in New York: American Adaptations, 1908-1940*. Philadelphia: University of Pennsylvania Press, 1947. Provides a balanced, perceptive, highly informed account of Hungarian dramas adapted for the American stage. Features substantial and penetrating analyses of all of Molnár's major plays and discusses a number of his lesser works.

Kovacs, Lee. "*Liliom*." In *The Haunted Screen: Ghosts in Literature and Film*. 1999. Reprint. Jefferson, N.C.: McFarland, 2005. Focuses on the depiction of Liliom when he returns to earth as a ghost in Molnár's drama and in subsequent film adaptations of the play. Describes *Liliom* as a gothic ghost story that presents a "time-defined" and "task-driven" ghost.

Reményi, Joseph. *Hungarian Writers and Literature: Modern Novelists, Critics, and Poets*. Edited and with an introduction by August J. Molnár. New Brunswick, N.J.: Rutgers University Press, 1964. Contains an essay on

Molnár that assesses his plays in a literary rather than a dramatic context, examining them in terms of the seriousness and complexity of their themes, the author's deployment and use of symbols and imagery, and the adequacy of his style to his subject matter.

Sárközi, Mátyás. *The Play's the Thing.* London: White Raven Press, 2004. Biography of Molnár, written by his grandson, helps to place the playwright's works within the context of his life and times.

Várkonyi, István. *Ferenc Molnár and the Austro-Hungarian "Fin de Siècle."* New York: Peter Lang, 1992. Focuses on the work that Molnár produced before 1920. Argues that he forged a new literary style, based in realism, that enabled him to deal more effectively with the complex issues of social transformation, industrialization, and urbanization than could be done in the fundamentally Romantic style favored by other writers of the period.

Little Big Man

Author: Thomas Berger (1924-   )
First published: 1964
Type of work: Novel
Type of plot: Picaresque Western
Time of plot: 1852-1952
Locale: Western United States

Principal characters:
JACK CRABB, a survivor of adventures on the Great Plains and the Battle of Little Big Horn
OLD LODGE SKINS, a Cheyenne chief
GENERAL GEORGE ARMSTRONG CUSTER, leader of the U.S. Seventh Cavalry annihilated at the Battle of Little Big Horn
YOUNGER BEAR, a Cheyenne contemporary of Crabb
MRS. PENDRAKE, Crabb's stepmother
WILD BILL HICKOCK, famous gunslinger of the American West
ALLARDYCE T. MERRIWEATHER, a con man
RALPH FIELDING SNELL, an amateur historian who records Crabb's recollections

The Story:

In 1952, Ralph Fielding Snell, a middle-aged, jobless dilettante, lives off a modest stipend provided by his father. Snell fancies himself an expert on the American West and decides to tape the memories of Jack Crabb, a 111-year-old resident of a local rest home. Crabb claims to have met and witnessed many of the most famous American figures and events of the nineteenth century, including the Battle of Little Big Horn.

In 1852, an eleven-year-old Jack Crabb, his sister Caroline, his brother, and their parents depart Indiana for Utah, but, because of a misunderstanding, the wagon train is massacred in Nebraska, and Jack is taken hostage by a Northern Cheyenne tribe. He lives for the next five years as the adopted son of the chief, Old Lodge Skins. During his time with the Cheyenne, Jack evolves from an outsider to an accepted member of the tribe, and his relationship with Old Lodge Skins becomes increasingly intimate as the old man in-

structs the young one in both the traditions and the mythology of the tribe.

In his first battle against some Crow Indians, Crabb saves the life of another young warrior, Younger Bear, who is humiliated by his vulnerability and by the obligation that he now owes to Crabb. After the encounter, Crabb is given the name Little Big Man in honor of his valor and thus begins years of enmity with Younger Bear. In an ensuing battle with the U.S. cavalry, Crabb is returned to the white world and placed in the care of the Reverend Pendrake and his much younger wife in western Missouri. While Pendrake thunders on about sin and depravity, Crabb subtly comments on the reverend's gluttony and hypocrisy and becomes increasingly enamored of his attractive wife. At this time, he also meets an emancipated slave, Lavender. Crabb's domestic interlude ends when he discovers Mrs. Pendrake having sex with the owner of a soda parlor.

Crabb travels to Denver as a muleskinner and, after being ambushed, holds a series of other jobs. He pans for gold and when that fails opens a dry-goods business. On a trip with some cargo, he once more encounters the Cheyenne and has a brief reunion with Old Lodge Skins but returns to his business. During this period, he marries a woman named Olga and they have a son, Gus. Crabb's business slowly fades after he is swindled by his partners. The family wanders through more of the Western states until they are attacked by Cheyenne and Olga and Gus are abducted.

Crabb's peripatetic life continues until, now a hopeless drunk, he meets his lost sister, Caroline, and they hire on as muleskinners with a railroad party. Eventually, Crabb goes in search of his lost family. He stumbles on a Cheyenne woman giving birth, whom he protects and marries. They return to the tribe of his youth, and Crabb finds that Olga and Gus are now with Younger Bear. Crabb's sojourn with Cheyenne is abruptly destroyed when General Custer and his forces massacre most of the tribe at the Washita River. Crabb vows to kill Custer.

Once more, he wanders through the white world, traveling to San Francisco and back to Nebraska in search of Custer. He befriends Wild Bill Hickok and becomes a gunslinger and gambler, and he meets a prostitute named Amelia whom he believes is his niece. Attempting to support Amelia and keep her from prostitution, Crabb becomes a buffalo hunter. He meets a swindler named Allardyce T. Meriweather and shares in some of his confidence schemes. When he discovers Amelia is not his relative and has run off with a senator, Crabb takes up gold mining in the Black Hills. He once again meets his sister, whom he places in an asylum in Omaha. Eventually, he joins Custer's cavalry as a herder and scout. He follows the general to the Little Big Horn, where his life is saved by Younger Bear, who reunites him with the tribe.

Crabb's reunion with Old Lodge Skins is bittersweet, as the aged chief praises his last living son, discusses the battle and Custer's bravery, and predicts that Native Americans will decline and their way of life will be destroyed. After a series of migrations, the chief climbs up a hill and wills his own death.

Crabb's narrative is followed by a brief epilogue by Snell. The dilettante ponders the veracity of Crabb's story.

Critical Evaluation:

Little Big Man is widely considered to be Thomas Berger's greatest and most enduring novel. It was the recipient of the Western Heritage and the Richard and Hinda Rosenthal awards in 1965, and it was adapted into a major motion picture in 1970, starring Dustin Hoffman and Faye Dunaway. Despite the film's sensitive interpretation and critical success, a comparison of the two media reveals an important feature of Berger's achievement. Where the film valorizes the Cheyenne as noble savages and fundamentally superior human beings, the novel is careful to balance its view of the two ethnic groups it portrays. Crabb, although sympathizing more with the tribe, is unsparing in his comic criticism of each group's foibles and failings. One of the translations of the name for the Cheyenne is "human beings," and indeed Crabb learns important lessons from Old Lodge Skins about the nature of all people and their humanity, in spite of all their differences.

While the novel has been hailed as an example of everything from black humor to postmodern narrative, its roots are in a far older tradition, the picaresque. The dizzyingly episodic plot; the constantly wandering hero; and the appearance, disappearance, and reappearance of key characters such as Caroline, General Custer, Lavender, Alardyce T. Meriweather, and Younger Bear are all examples of key picaresque conventions. However, Crabb, as picaro, is perhaps the most interesting and complex of the novel's instantiations of these conventions. Picaros are more often than not orphans, figures who lose not only their families but also their places in the world and are forced to set out on their own at early ages. Because they are victims of the vicissitudes of life, their primary motivation is survival, and indeed survival is paramount for Crabb: He watches one friend or partner after another vanish or abruptly die, and in each case his position in society or his security is annulled. Picaros are usually rogue heroes, people who live more by wits and chicanery than by higher moral principles. Crabb's wry social comments and willingness to stretch truth and honesty to serve his own ends place him squarely in this rogue position.

More important, though, is that the picaro, because of his position as outsider and moral opportunist, sees the world in a radically different way from those around him. Crabb realizes that order, civilization, and fixed moral positions are illusory; for him, the world is full of tumult and chaos, and the notion of security is impossible. Thus Crabb, like all picaros, is an infinitely adaptable creature, a protean man who invents and reinvents himself repeatedly. His many social positions and professions—warrior, gunslinger, muleskinner, scout, businessman, buffalo hunter, and so on—underline his infinite changeability. These reinventions also permit him to wander through all levels and stations of life and provide a privileged glimpse of the vagaries of existence.

The novel also hearkens back to another early literary form, the captivity narrative. Such narratives are uniquely

American, though they have been adapted by other cultures because of their often sensational features. Originating with Mary White Rowlandson's *The Sovereignty and Goodness of God, Together with the Faithfulness of His Promises Displayed* (1682), the form deals with the abduction of white settlers by Native American attackers. Rowlandson repeatedly describes her three-month wanderings in the woods as removes through hell and her captives as demons, and the story helped establish the stereotype of the Native American as a godless heathen.

Berger, after reading literally hundreds of books on the West and on Native Americans, presented his protagonist's abduction as a salvation that entailed tutelage in an alternate, no less dignified, way of life than that of white settlers. For Crabb, return to "civilization" is inevitable but hardly desirable. The persistent imagery of lines, associated with white culture, and circles, associated with Native Americans, suggests the profoundly different points of view that each culture brings to the world.

The novel explores the whole myth of westward expansion as Manifest Destiny. The Western genre, as established by James Fennimore Cooper and later Owen Wister, Zane Grey, Jack Schaefer, and Louis L'Amour, has been called the quintessential American narrative form. The limitless expanse of the frontier often acts as a metaphor for limitless possibilities and freedom in the new nation of the United States. *Little Big Man* demythologizes the ethos of the West as a source of rugged individualism and cultural reinvigoration, and it examines the racial and cultural hegemony of one group's domination of another.

David W. Madden

Further Reading

Betts, Richard A. "Thomas Berger's *Little Big Man*: Contemporary Picaresque." *Critique: Studies in Contemporary Fiction* 23, no. 2 (1981): 85-96. One of a handful of essays that consider the novel in terms of the picaresque. Isolates a number of distinct picaresque conventions and traces them through the novel, concluding that *Little Big Man* is in the mainstream of the picaresque tradition.

Landon, Brooks. *Thomas Berger.* Boston: Twayne, 1989. Comprehensive, book-length study of Berger's oeuvre up to his fifteenth novel, *The Houseguest* (1988). The chapter on *Little Big Man* emphasizes the work's narrative construction, Crabb's distinct voice, and the theme of freedom. The 1989 Dell reprint of the novel also features a helpful introduction by Landon.

Madden, David W., ed. *Critical Essays on Thomas Berger.* New York: G. K. Hall, 1995. Features reprints of thirteen seminal articles and reviews, as well as a previously unpublished play by Berger, an extensive interview, and an article about another of his novels. A number of the articles discuss *Little Big Man* among other works, and Michael Cleary's "Finding the Center of the Earth: Satire, History, and Myth in *Little Big Man*" deals exclusively with the novel.

Schulz, Max F. "The Politics of Parody and the Comic Apocalypses of Jorge Luis Borges, Thomas Berger, Thomas Pynchon, and Robert Coover." In *Black Humor Fiction of the Sixties: A Pluralistic Definition of Man and His World.* Columbus: Ohio State University Press, 1973. Approaches *Little Big Man* as one of the most important examples of late 1960's black humor and emphasizes the novel's mordant comedy and its parodic dimensions.

Studies in American Humor 2, nos. 1/2 (1983). Edited by Brom Weber. This two-volume special issue devoted to Thomas Berger features twelve articles from some of the most important Berger scholars. Although there is no single article devoted exclusive to *Little Big Man*, some articles deal with it in terms of comedy, parody, and style.

The Little Clay Cart

Author: Sudraka (fl. c. 300-600 B.C.E.)

First produced: Mrcchakatika, between second century
  B.C.E. and sixth century C.E. (English translation, 1905)

Type of work: Drama

Type of plot: Tragicomedy

Time of plot: Fifth century B.C.E.

Locale: Ancient city of Ujjayini

Principal characters:

CHĀRUDATTA, an impoverished young Brahman

VASANTASENĀ, a courtesan in love with Chārudatta

MAITREYA, a poor Brahman, Chārudatta's friend

SAMSTHĀNAKA, King Pālaka's brother-in-law

ĀRYAKA, an exiled prince

SARVILAKA, a Brahman and a thief

MADANIKĀ, Vasantasenā's slave and confidant

The Story:

Chārudatta is a Brahman who has impoverished himself by spending his substance on the public welfare and in helping individuals who have sought his aid. Although dwelling in poverty in a broken-down house, he still enjoys a fine reputation in Ujjayini as an honest and upright man of rare wisdom. This reputation eases somewhat the fact that he has been deserted by most of his friends and is embarrassed by his lack of wealth.

Although married happily and the proud father of a small son, Rohasena, Chārudatta is enamored of Vasantasenā, a courtesan of great wealth and reputation who, having seen him at a temple, is also in love with him. One evening, as Chārudatta and his friend Maitreya sit discussing Chārudatta's misfortunes and the efficacy of devotion to the gods, Vasantasenā finds herself pursued by Samsthānaka, a half-mad brother-in-law of King Pālaka, and one of his henchmen. The men threaten to do violence to Vasantasenā, but she escapes from them in the darkness and finds safety in the house of Chārudatta, where a meeting between the two increases the love they already feel for each other. Before she leaves to return to her own palace, the courtesan entrusts a casket of jewelry to Chārudatta as an excuse to see him again.

During the night a thief, Sarvilaka, enters Chārudatta's house and steals the jewelry to buy his love, Madanikā, who is Vasantasenā's slave and confidant. The courtesan accepts the jewels and frees Madanikā to marry Sarvilaka, intending to see that Chārudatta should learn that the jewels have been recovered. In the meantime, Chārudatta sends a rare pearl necklace of his wife's to Vasantasenā to recompense the courtesan for the loss of her less valuable jewels. His friend Maitreya, fearing that Vasantasenā's attentions can bring only bad luck and disaster, cautions Chārudatta against doing so. Maitreya, knowing courtesans, believes that Vasantasenā is merely scheming to take from Chārudatta the few possessions he still has.

After leaving Vasantasenā's palace with his newly freed bride, Sarvilaka learns that his friend Prince Āryaka has been arrested by King Pālaka and placed in a dungeon. The king, neither a popular nor a just monarch, fears that the people might rise up, as a soothsayer has predicted, to place Prince Āryaka on the throne. After Sarvilaka succeeds in freeing the prince from prison, Āryaka seeks help from Chārudatta, who aids him in escaping the pursuing guards.

Vasantasenā, having become Chārudatta's mistress, meets his small son and gives him some jewels with which to purchase a golden toy cart to replace the unsatisfactory clay cart Chārudatta had been able to afford. She makes arrangements to meet Chārudatta in Pushpakarandaka Park, outside the city, for a day's outing, but by mistake she enters the wrong vehicle and finds herself in the gharry belonging to Samsthānaka, who still pursues her and is madly jealous of the love and favors she bestows freely upon Chārudatta. When Vasantasenā arrives at the park, she is discovered in the gharry by Samsthānaka, who at first is overjoyed at seeing her because he thinks she has come to him voluntarily. When she spurns him and declares her love for Chārudatta, Samsthānaka tries to make his henchmen kill her, but they refuse. Samsthānaka sends his followers away and chokes her himself. Believing her dead, he hides the body under a pile of leaves. Then, hoping to escape the penalty for his crime, Samsthānaka decides to go to a court and accuse Chārudatta of murdering Vasantasenā.

When Samsthānaka first appears at the court, the judges, who know him to be somewhat mad, refuse to see him or take him seriously, but when he threatens to go to King Pālaka, the judges become frightened and send for Chārudatta. Falsely accused, Chārudatta proclaims his innocence, but circumstances are against him. He admits having been in the park, and the jewels of Vasantasenā are found at his home, offering a motive for the poverty-stricken man to have killed her. The judges, in spite of Chārudatta's previous reputation, find him guilty. Although Chārudatta's status as a Brahman exempts him from the death penalty for any crime, King Pālaka orders Chārudatta put to death. No one knows that the body identified as Vasantasenā's was actually that of another woman or that Vasantasenā is not dead; befriended by a Buddhist monk, she is recovering near the park from Samsthānaka's attack.

Chārudatta is taken through the city by two executioners, who stop several times to announce the name of the condemned man and the nature of his crime. Although the people of the city love Chārudatta, they dare not intervene on his behalf, even though he steadfastly maintains his innocence. Samsthānaka's slave tries to tell that his master is really the one who committed the crime, but no one believes him, and so Chārudatta and his executioners, accompanied by a crowd, continue on their way to the place of execution, a cemetery south of the city.

The executioners, thinking to be merciful, offer to decapitate Chārudatta, but a miracle prevents their sword from touching him, and so they prepare the victim for the slow, agonizing death by impalement on a pike. Fortunately, Vasantasenā, seeing the excited crowd as she makes her way back to the city, intervenes in time to save Chārudatta. When she tells who really attacked her, Samsthānaka is arrested. The excitement does not end with that, however, for word comes that Chārudatta's wife, believing herself a widow, is about to cast herself upon a funeral pyre. Chārudatta reaches her in time to prevent her death, and she and Vasantasenā meet and accept each other. Word comes, too, that Prince Āryaka has deposed King Pālaka and is now king. One of his first deeds is to restore Chārudatta's fortune and make him an important official of the court. Chārudatta, still a man of conscience and charity, forgives Samsthānaka for his villainy and causes him to be set free.

Critical Evaluation:

Many critics have pointed out that Sudraka's *The Little Clay Cart* is more like Western drama than any other Sanskrit play, in structure, characterization, and tone. This may account for the fact that Indian critics have been less enthusiastic about the work than have those of the Western world. *The Little Clay Cart* is noteworthy for being the only known Sanskrit play to show a courtesan in love with a Brahman, as it is also the only known one to contain important characters from various strata of Hindu society rather than from the upper castes only. It is the realistic and vivid presentation of these characters that probably has appealed most to Western readers.

Hindu philosophy places less emphasis on individuals' power to alter their own lives or destinies than does Western, Christian philosophy. Throughout *The Little Clay Cart*, nearly all the characters speak of destiny and fate. Hindu thought also tends toward seeing life and history as circular, moving in cycles of such opposites as destruction and creation, growth and decay, rather than the Western view, which tends toward a linear interpretation. The title is a summation of this wheel-of-fortune concept, although the section of the drama dealing with the cart is extremely short. Chārudatta's young son has been playing with a gold cart belonging to a friend, and the friend wants it back. In his impoverished state, Chārudatta can afford only to have his servant make a clay cart for the boy. When Vasantasenā sees the boy crying for the gold cart, she gives him jewels with which to buy one for himself. Thus the circle is complete.

Many other circles are also seen in the plot. Āryaka, an exiled prince, is imprisoned but escapes. The mad king is killed and Āryaka becomes king. A gambler who has lost his money and owes much is rescued and becomes a friar. As all turns out well in the end, he is asked what ambition he might have, and he replies that, having watched the instability of human fortune, he prefers to remain a friar.

The overall circle that encloses all the rest is the story of Chārudatta and his lover, Vasantasenā. The Brahman has become poor because he has given away his fortune to help others in need. To add to his troubles, he is accused of the murder of Vasantasenā, whom he loves, and actually is very nearly executed before Vasantasenā appears and points out the attempted murderer, Samsthānaka, who is arrested while Chārudatta is freed. Āryaka, the new king, whom Chārudatta had protected when he escaped from prison, names him viceroy of the city of Kusavati.

The opening and closing dialogues by Chārudatta bring the total drama to its complete circle. In the beginning dialogue he is scattering grain for the birds and notes that when he was wealthy his offerings were of better quality; swans and cranes fed upon his terrace. Now even wrens shun the poor seed he throws into the tangled grass. In the ending dialogue he remarks that "destiny, as it plays with us, teaches us that the world is a union of opposites, an alternate recurrence of fortune and misfortune."

When presented properly, *The Little Clay Cart* is a delight. In a traditional staging of the drama, the story is acted out in mime, with no stage settings. A minimum number of props are used, and each may represent a number of things, from an altar to a tree or a carriage. The tempo is rapid, with one scene following the next so quickly that illusions created by the actions, gestures, and speeches of the players are of prime importance. The actions are carried out like a ritualized dance. Emotional reactions are played down, so that the viewer has a continuous feeling of repose and enjoyment at the finale. There is no catharsis as in Western drama.

Readers of *The Little Clay Cart* learn about the characters through what they say and what is said about them. No physical descriptions are given; one knows only that the courtesan is beautiful. The characters are from all walks of life, and the lines they speak are appropriate to their stations. Vasantasenā comes through as the strongest and most astute character; Samsthānaka is the most pompous and ridiculous. The play has much wit, humor, and buffoonery as well as wisdom, which appears in similes and metaphors, aphorisms and maxims.

Further Reading

Chakrabarti, Prakaschandra. *A Treatise on Śūdraka's "Mṛcchakaṭika."* Kathamandu, Nepal: Pilgrims Book House, 1999. Presents a critical introduction to the play, discussing, among other subjects, its characters and its theme of the conflict between good and evil.

Devaśarmā, Vśvanātha. *Shudraka.* New Delhi, India: Sahitya Akademi, 1999. Provides an introductory overview of Sudraka's life and discusses *The Little Clay Cart.*

Keith, Arthur Berriedale. *The Sanskrit Drama in Its Origin, Development, Theory, and Practice.* New York: Oxford University Press, 1964. Accessible and well-indexed guide to Sanskrit drama serves as a good starting place for further study.

Sharma, Sudarshan Kumar. *"Mṛcchakaṭika of Śūdraka: A Critical and Cultural Study.* Delhi, India: Parimal, 2005. Provides a biography of Sudraka and analyzes the philosophical, architectural, astronomical, and other cultural elements of *The Little Clay Cart.*

Sudraka. *The Little Clay Cart: An English Translation of the "Mṛcchakaṭika" of Śūdraka, as Adapted for the Stage by A. L. Basham.* Edited by Arvind Sharma. Albany: State University of New York Press, 1994. Basham, a prominent historian and Indologist, translated Sudraka's play, and his translation was adapted for the theater and staged in Australia in 1968. This book includes that translation as well as an introductory essay by Robert E. Goodwin that addresses how Western audiences can approach the play.

_____. *The Little Clay Cart (Mrcchakatika): A Hindu Drama Attributed to King Shudraka.* Translated by Arthur William Ryder. Cambridge, Mass.: Harvard University Press, 1905. Ryder's introduction provides an outline of the play's plot and discussion of his method of translation as well as an examination of the work's authorship.

Van Buitenen, J. A. B., trans. *Two Plays of Ancient India: "The Little Clay Cart," "The Minister's Seal."* New York: Columbia University Press, 1968. Van Buitenen's introduction presents a synopsis of the play and describes how the purported author of *The Little Clay Cart*, Sudraka, employed what may, in the context of ancient Sanskrit literature, be called "borrowing" privileges in the creation of the play, which is a completion of an earlier, incomplete work.

Little Dorrit

Author: Charles Dickens (1812-1870)
First published: 1855-1857, serial; 1857, book
Type of work: Novel
Type of plot: Social realism
Time of plot: 1820's
Locale: England

Principal characters:
LITTLE DORRIT, a young woman born and reared in a debtors' prison
WILLIAM DORRIT, her father
FANNY, her older sister
ARTHUR CLENNAM, Little Dorrit's friend
MRS. CLENNAM, Arthur's mother and Little Dorrit's employer
MONSIEUR BLANDOIS, a blackmailer
MR. MERDLE, a banker and Fanny Dorrit's father-in-law

The Story:

Amy Dorrit, who is better known as Little Dorrit, was born in the Marshalsea debtors' prison. Although her mother died soon after, the little girl and her older brother and sister have continued to live in the prison with their bankrupt father; he is the only member of the family not permitted to leave the prison. As she becomes older, Little Dorrit works as a seamstress. One of her clients is Mrs. Clennam, a widow who is also a businesswoman, although she has been confined to her room by illness for fifteen years. Mrs. Clennam's forty-year-old son, Arthur, had gone to the East twenty years earlier to join his father, who looked after the company's business there. After his father's death, Arthur Clennam returns. He tells his mother that he will take his part of the inheritance and fend for himself; he does not want to remain in the business with his miserly, grasping, and rather inhuman mother. Mrs. Clennam thereupon takes her old clerk, Flintwinch, into partnership with her.

While he is staying at his mother's house, Arthur notices Little Dorrit and is struck by her retiring disposition and sweet appearance. He learns that she lives in the Marshalsea prison, and he goes there and tries to help the Dorrit family. When he raises the possibility of getting Mr. Dorrit out of prison, everyone thinks such a thing is impossible, for Mr. Dorrit's affairs are in hopeless confusion; some of his debts are owed to the Crown through the Circumlocution Office, a place of endless red tape.

Arthur finds that he has a confederate in his endeavor to help Mr. Dorrit in a clerk named Pancks, an odd creature who collects rents for a landlord who is the father of Arthur's former fiancé, Flora. Pancks is aided in turn by John Chivery, the son of a turnkey at the Marshalsea, who is in love with Little Dorrit, and by Mr. Rugg, an elderly lawyer. In addition to helping Little Dorrit by trying to help her father and getting her brother out of trouble, Arthur helps her to get more sewing clients and provides small amounts of money to the Dorrit household in the prison.

Pancks discovers that Little Dorrit's father, who has been in prison for more than twenty years, is the only surviving heir to a large fortune, and when he collects that inheritance, he is finally released. Mr. Dorrit immediately sets himself up as a man of fortune, and he and his two older children are determined to live up to their new social position and try to forget the past. They decide that Arthur Clennam has insulted them by acting condescendingly toward them, and they refuse to have anything more to do with him. Only Little Dorrit remains unspoiled.

The Dorrit family travels to the Continent, where they can successfully carry out the fiction that they have never seen a debtors' prison and where they are admitted to the society of expatriate Britons. Fanny Dorrit, Little Dorrit's older sister, is pursued by Mr. Sparkle, the stepson of Mr. Merdle, who is reputed to be the richest and most influential banker in England. Although not in love with Sparkle, Fanny likes the prospect of marrying into a wealthy family. The Merdles, who see only that the Dorrits have a fortune, agree to the match, even though Mrs. Merdle is well aware of the fact that her son had fallen in love with Fanny when she was only an impecunious dancer in London.

After they are married, Fanny and her husband go to live in London. Mr. Dorrit visits them there and becomes a close friend of Mr. Merdle. The banker even proposes to help Mr. Dorrit increase his already large fortune through shrewd and well-paying investments. Mr. Dorrit, the former debtor, is elated by his new prospects.

Little Dorrit wonders at the changes in her family but remains her old self. She writes to Arthur at intervals, for, in addition to continuing to be grateful for all he has done to help her, she is in love with him.

Arthur remains in London, where he tries to discover the identities of the mysterious people who visit his mother. At the same time, he is trying to keep his own business solvent. Neither task is easy. On two occasions, Mrs. Clennam is visited by a Monsieur Blandois, whom Arthur knows to be a knave and possibly a murderer. He wonders what business his mother could have with such a person. He also distrusts Flintwinch, a grubbing, miserly fellow who mistreats his wife and has taken a great dislike to Arthur.

While trying to unravel the mystery, Arthur becomes bankrupt. Like many others, he has invested all of his and his company's money in Mr. Merdle's business ventures, believing them a safe and quick way to make a fortune. When Merdle and his bank fail, Arthur falls into debt and is sent to the Marshalsea debtors' prison, where he is assigned to Mr. Dorrit's old quarters. Mr. Rugg and Pancks do their best to make Arthur's imprisonment a short one, but he seems to have lost all desire to live. Only after Little Dorrit returns to England and takes up residence within the prison to comfort him as she had comforted her father does Arthur begin to recover.

Learning that Monsieur Blandois has disappeared from Mrs. Clennam's house, Pancks tracks the man down and brings him back to London. Mrs. Clennam realizes at this point that she has to reveal the truth unless she is willing to resign herself to paying blackmail to Blandois. Rising from her wheelchair and leaving her house for the first time in almost twenty years, she goes to the prison to tell Arthur that he is not her child and that she has for many years been keeping money from him and from Little Dorrit. Once restitution has been made, Arthur is released from prison. Shortly afterward, he and Little Dorrit are married.

Critical Evaluation:

Little Dorrit has been hailed as one of Charles Dickens's greatest novels and one of the major novels of the nineteenth century. Despite its prevailingly somber and gloomy character, the book was among the most popular of Dickens's novels during his lifetime.

The structure of the novel is rather complex, consisting as it does of two books, "Poverty" and "Riches." The first book comprises the events of the time when Mr. Dorrit is imprisoned for debt; the second, the events that take place after his sudden inheritance of a fortune. Interwoven through both parts are the romantic story of the gradually awakening love between Clennam and Amy Dorrit (which Clennam does not realize until near the end of the novel) and biting social criticism, as in the descriptions of the Circumlocution Office, its officials, and its obstructionism. Dickens originally intended to call the novel "Nobody's Fault," with the thesis that social decay, rather than the actions of individuals, is responsible for the misfortunes of the various characters.

Little Dorrit is, next to *David Copperfield* (1849-1850, serial; 1850, book), the most autobiographical of Dickens's novels. The author's father was imprisoned for debt in the Marshalsea in 1823 and 1834, and during his first term the boy Dickens stayed there on weekends while working in a blacking factory during the week, a routine he vividly describes in *David Copperfield*. Although the Marshalsea had been closed and torn down by the time Dickens wrote *Little Dorrit*, the atmosphere and geography of the place remained searingly vivid in his memory.

The metaphor of prison dominates the entire novel, not only as represented by the Marshalsea but also in many other incidents and objects. The novel opens with descriptions of the swindler Blandois in prison in Marseilles; a group of English citizens, including Clennam, the Meagles family, and Miss Wade, in quarantine; and the miserable Sunday in London preceding Clennam's reunion with his mother, which reminds him of his rigid Calvinist upbringing and unhappy childhood. These small prisons all precede the reader's introduction to the Marshalsea and the Dorrit family.

One of the more striking of the many prison images throughout the novel occurs at the opening of book 2, where the convent of Saint Bernard in the Swiss Alps is compared to a prison. The expatriate English colonies in Italian cities are their own kind of prison. When old Mr. Dorrit has a stroke at Mrs. Merdle's home during a banquet, he imagines himself back at the Marshalsea. The world of social climbing and assumed gentility is a prison, which Dickens uses to create one of his most comic characters, Mrs. General, a warden of social climbing who is brought into the Dorrit entourage to teach the young ladies proper manners. Mrs. Clennam and Miss Wade are among those characters who live in prisons of their own making; the character Tattycoram, for example, in a fit of temper, exchanges her relatively easy life as a servant to the Meagles family for the undisclosed bondage of life with Miss Wade. Both comic and pathetic at the same time is Flora Finching (based on Dickens's own first love, whom he later met again), whose long-ago engagement to Clennam

was broken off at his mother's insistence before his departure for the East, and who has now become fat and almost incoherently talkative.

By far the greatest prison, and the cause of so many of the smaller ones, is the Circumlocution Office, a mysterious branch of government where nothing gets done, everything is obstructed, and the officeholders receive their positions through family connections. The topicality of the description stems from investigations into Britain's conduct of the Crimean War. About the time Dickens began writing *Little Dorrit*, knowledge of the incompetence with which the war was directed had become common, and this incompetence was shown to have stemmed in large part from the tradition of staffing government bureaus and the higher positions in the military through family connections. Dickens includes a scathing exposé of this tradition in his description of one of Merdle's dinner parties, where Lord Barnacle (supposedly a portrait of Lord Palmerston, Britain's prime minister at the time) makes arrangements for Merdle's stepson (who marries Fanny Dorrit) to get a position with the Circumlocution Office. Those most victimized by this office are Clennam's business partner, Doyce, whose invention is swallowed up by the immense and mysterious bureaucracy; Clennam, who is abused by the office when he tries to find out why Mr. Dorrit has been imprisoned; and Dorrit himself, who has fallen through the cracks of the system. The exact duties of the Circumlocution Office are never described. Here Dickens can be considered to anticipate Franz Kafka's device of depicting an isolated individual at the mercy of an unfeeling and mysterious bureaucracy.

Social climbing is another prison in which many of the characters are trapped: Fanny Dorrit when she makes an advantageous match with Merdle's stepson; Pet Meagles when she marries the well-connected Henry Gowan, a dilettante artist who regards it as a matter of course that his in-laws pay his debts; and above all Mr. Dorrit, who is both comic and tragic in his attempts to put a veneer of distinction on his position as "Father of the Marshalsea" and later when he assumes the airs of an English lord. Clennam and Little Dorrit are exempt from this climbing, Clennam perhaps more because he does not care to take the trouble, but Little Dorrit because of her innate goodness and nobility.

Although this novel contains a wealth of memorable characters, Dickens portrays all of his principal ones obliquely. The villain, the blackmailing swindler Blandois, has two other disguises as Rigaud and Lagnier, for example, and in many cases it takes the reader a while to guess the identities of characters. In the opening of book 2, for instance, a group of travelers in the Alps is only gradually revealed to be the Dorrit entourage. Merdle's suicide, which marks the crash of his financial empire and the ruin of its investors (including Clennam and the Dorrit heirs), is treated with similar obliqueness. The various mysteries are clarified explicitly only in the three final chapters.

"Critical Evaluation" by R. M. Longyear

Further Reading

Grant, Allan. *A Preface to Dickens*. London: Longman, 1984. Provides an excellent introduction to Dickens's life and times, with especially good descriptions of the author's London, which forms the background to so many of his novels.

Hardy, Barbara. *Dickens and Creativity*. London: Continuum, 2008. Focuses on the workings of Dickens's creativity and imagination, arguing that these are at the heart of his self-awareness, subject matter, and narrative. *Little Dorrit* is discussed in chapter 5, "Talkative Men and Women in *Pickwick Papers*, *Nicholas Nickleby*, *Martin Chuzzlewit*, and *Little Dorrit*," and in chapter 9, "Forecast and Fantasy in *Little Dorrit*."

Jordan, John O., ed. *The Cambridge Companion to Charles Dickens*. New York: Cambridge University Press, 2001. Collection of essays presents information about Dickens's life and times as well as analyses of his novels and discussions of such topics as Dickens's use of language and gender, family, and domestic ideology in Dickens's work.

Novak, Daniel A. "Composing the Novel Body: Remembering the Body and the Text in *Little Dorrit*." In *Realism, Photography, and Nineteenth-Century Fiction*. New York: Cambridge University Press, 2008. Discussion of *Little Dorrit* is part of a larger work that examines the relationship between photography and literary realism in Victorian Britain by analyzing works of fiction.

Paroissien, David, ed. *A Companion to Charles Dickens*. Malden, Mass.: Blackwell, 2008. Collection of essays provides information about Dickens's life and work, including discussion of Dickens as a reformer, as a Christian, and as a journalist. *Little Dorrit* is examined in an essay by Philip Davis.

Rosenberg, Brian. *Little Dorrit's Shadows: Character and Contradiction in Dickens*. Columbia: University of Missouri Press, 1996. Examines the relationship between Dickens's ambivalent imagination and his creation of character, concentrating on *Little Dorrit*, which is "founded on contradiction." Argues that in *Little Dorrit* and other novels, contradiction and uncertainly are a primary reason for the distinctiveness and success of Dickens's characterization.

Shelston, Alan, ed. *Charles Dickens: "Dombey and Son" and "Little Dorrit"—A Casebook*. London: Macmillan, 1985. Collection of essays and observations includes, on *Little Dorrit*, a Marxist interpretation by T. A. Jackson, a psychological examination by Edmund Wilson, a close reading by Hillis Miller, and Lionel Trilling's classic appreciation.

Sucksmith, Harvey. Preface to *Little Dorrit*, by Charles Dickens. New York: Oxford University Press, 1979. Excellent essay traces the background and compositional history of the novel, preceding an edition of the text that includes variant readings and the author's preliminary notes and outline.

The Little Foxes

Author: Lillian Hellman (1905-1984)
First produced: 1939; first published, 1939
Type of work: Drama
Type of plot: Social realism
Time of plot: 1900
Locale: Alabama

Principal characters:
REGINA GIDDENS, a predatory woman
BENJAMIN HUBBARD and OSCAR HUBBARD, her brothers
HORACE GIDDENS, her husband
ALEXANDRA, daughter of Regina and Horace
BIRDIE HUBBARD, Oscar's wife
ADDIE and CAL, the Hubbards' servants

The Story:

In 1900, in a small Alabama town, three siblings are attempting to negotiate a lucrative deal that will bring northern manufacturing to the area so that the cotton crop will not have to be sent away for processing. Among these three, the accumulation of wealth takes precedence over family loyalty, decency, honor, and morality.

The two brothers, Oscar and Ben Hubbard, are heirs to their father's fortune; sister Regina is not named in the will. To ensure that she will be on equal footing with her brothers she marries a man of considerable wealth. Her husband, Horace Giddens, has been in a Baltimore hospital for months, recovering from a serious heart problem. It seems that the deal to bring the cotton mill to town will go through if Regina can come up with her one-third of the collateral within two weeks, money she hopes will come from Horace.

Oscar, the least bright of the siblings, secures his future by marrying Birdie, whose family has the most prosperous cotton fields in the area. Shortly after the wedding, Oscar's inherent meanness shines through. He accuses his wife of babbling nonsensically, of drinking too much (which is true), and of behaving foolishly. He even slaps her across the face when he feels she is undermining his schemes. Birdie is too timid and subdued to stand up to his abuses. Even her pleas for him to stop shooting small birds for sport are ineffectual. He throws the dead birds away rather than give them to poor and hungry black people. By this time, Birdie's family land has been bought by the Hubbards, leaving her with nothing but wistful hopes of a return one day to a more genteel South where family comes first. Ben is unmarried and dreams mostly of buying a horse farm with the money.

Addie and Cal, two subservient and powerless, but wise, black servants, comment on the evil around them; still, they continue to serve. Horace wants to name Addie in his will, but she points out that the money would never get to her. Such is the status of blacks in the South. There is no way for them to fight a corrupt legal system. Addie takes on the job of alerting Regina and Horace's daughter, Alexandra, to the machinations of the family.

Regina hosts a dinner party in honor of Chicago industrialist William Marshall, who is considering building a cotton mill in town. Regina is ruthless in her determination to gain power and wealth and is winning over the guest with her great charm. A major complication arises, though: Regina cannot produce her portion of the needed funds without her husband, Horace, so she sends daughter Alexandra to the hospital to convince her father to return home. Sadly, Horace still holds on to a glimmer of hope that someone may care for him.

Meanwhile, Birdie and Oscar's son, Leo, disliked even by Birdie, gains access to Horace's safe deposit box through a friend at the local bank and learns that Horace has more than enough in bonds to meet Regina's obligation. The plan is to take the bonds long enough to provide good-faith capital and to then return them before Horace has a chance to check the box. By this time, the family is already making plans for Leo

and Alexandra, first cousins, to wed, thereby grounding the family in further wealth. Leo and Alexandra, however, do not like each other.

Upon his return from the hospital, Horace catches on to the scheming and changes his will in such a way that his wife will be forever dependent upon her brothers. Horace and Regina quarrel furiously, leading Horace to suffer an attack. In reaching for his life-saving medicine, he sends the bottle crashing to the floor. Regina knows that a second bottle is in the upstairs bedroom, but she sits there passively while Horace struggles out of his wheelchair and heads for the stairs. He collapses and dies half-way up.

Critical Evaluation:

The Little Foxes is a tale of a greedy, grasping, family trying to create an empire by lying to each other; by using ruthless tactics; by violating the all-important concepts of southern family, love, and support; and by striking at each other like pit vipers. Lillian Hellman's play has been produced successfully in community theaters and in revivals since its debut in 1939. The universality of its multiple themes accounts for its longevity. The themes of injustices against people of color and ethnic minorities, against women, and against workers have remained constant. Capitalism appears at its worst, with hints at ways in which Marxism and communism might help to counter its evils.

Hellman also deals with opposites and conflicts: Family contention and rivalry; marriage for money or status rather than for love; manipulation as a way of life for getting what one wants; the old South of genteel aristocracy and the changes brought by the North; agrarian culture and industrialism; the freed slaves who have not gained true freedom or any serious respect; false fronts of family harmony covering thieving, conniving, unscrupulous behavior; and disregarding morality for personal gain.

The play's characters, though often despicable, are real, behaving as one would expect. They are richly drawn, if not multidimensional. Hellman can elicit some sympathy for the unsavory characters, considering the circumstances of their backgrounds, but mainly she makes audiences identify with the good people and marvel at how evil the bad can be. Having Regina sit quietly while her husband struggles to get his life-saving medication is a chiller, as is her announcement that she hopes he dies soon. Hellman's play shows unscrupulous business people happily tromping on others. Made clear as well are the attractions of the South for northerners, who know blacks will work for subsistence wages and will not threaten with union talk.

Hellman's prose is spare, direct, and to the point. She had

been convinced that drama best suited her style, given that she did not care for description. Indeed, even with the plays, she avoided stage directions and parenthetic asides, making each word count and have impact.

Hellman's work has special significance because it conveys her mind-set without espousing a cause. At no time does she take a political stand. She does not proselytize, though anyone knowing about her personal activism and associations can see her objections to a system that subverts the worker, takes little notice of the poor, and privileges the accumulation of money and power.

"Critical Evaluation" by Gay Pitman Zieger

Further Reading:

Estrin, Mark W., ed. *Critical Essays on Lillian Hellman.* Boston: G. K. Hall, 1989. Estrin's excellent twenty-seven-page introduction provides a good starting point for any student of Hellman and includes more than one hundred comprehensive notes. Also includes a thorough discussion of *The Little Foxes.*

Griffin, Alice, and Geraldine Thorsten. *Understanding Lillian Hellman.* Columbia: University of South Carolina Press, 1999. An examination of Hellman's major plays, discussing her style, her concern for moral issues, and her influence on other American playwrights. Chapter 3 contains an analysis of *The Little Foxes.*

Horn, Barbara Lee. *Lillian Hellman: A Research and Production Sourcebook.* Westport, Conn.: Greenwood Press, 1998. Provides an overview of Hellman's life, as well as a plot summary, history, and critical overview of *The Little Foxes.* Also includes sources for further study.

Martinson, Deborah. *Lillian Hellman: A Life with Foxes and Scoundrels.* New York: Counterpoint, 2005. An exhaustive biography of Hellman, based on Martinson's detailed research and her unprecedented access to the writer's close friends. A complete and even admiring portrait of Hellman.

Moody, Richard. *Lillian Hellman: Playwright.* New York: Pegasus, 1972. The first important book-length examination of Hellman's work, written by a prominent theater scholar. The long chapter on *The Little Foxes* scrutinizes the play as well as the circumstances surrounding its first Broadway production.

Rollyson, Carl. *Lillian Hellman: Her Legend and Her Legacy.* New York: St. Martin's Press, 1988. A comprehensive biography of the complex Hellman. Also includes an analysis of *The Little Foxes.*

The Little Prince

Author: Antoine de Saint-Exupéry (1900-1944)
First published: Le Petit Prince, 1943 (English translation, 1943)
Type of work: Children's literature
Type of plot: Allegory
Time of plot: World War II
Locale: The Sahara

Principal characters:
THE LITTLE PRINCE, an unusual child
THE PILOT, the narrator, who is stranded in the desert

The Story:

A golden-haired boy—a little prince—unexpectedly appears in the vast Sahara, where a pilot has landed his plane because of engine problems. The pilot is anxiously trying to fix the engine, for he has no food or water to survive for long. The boy politely asks the pilot to draw him a picture of a sheep. The pilot instead draws a picture from his own childhood: a boa constrictor with an elephant in its stomach. The boy, exasperated, concludes that adults cannot understand anything without numerous explanations. Only after the pilot draws a box with air holes in it is the boy happy. Both the pilot and the little prince understand that a sheep is inside the box.

Gradually, the man and the boy "tame" each other. The home from which the little prince has come is an asteroid, hardly larger than a house; it holds one rose, one baobab tree, and three volcanoes. The boy hopes to widen his knowledge by visiting much larger places, such as the planet Earth, and meeting the people, animals, and plants that live in those places. He is inwardly preoccupied, however, with the safety of his dearly loved rose.

The little prince tells the pilot about his visits to other tiny asteroids, where he met one single inhabitant on each: a king claiming to rule the universe, although he has no subjects; a conceited man who sees everyone as his admirer; a drunkard living in a stupor, drinking to forget his shame of being an alcoholic; a businessman greedily counting the stars as his own treasure; and a geographer who does not know the geography of his place and never leaves his office. The smallest planet he has visited, which turns very rapidly (with 1,440 sunsets per day), has no homes or people, yet the planet's lamplighter has no moment of rest as he constantly lights and puts out the only lamp, following old orders that make no sense. The little prince, who sees grown-ups as odd, respects the lamplighter for his dedicated, selfless work.

In the Sahara, the prince meets the fox, who reveals to him the major secrets of life. These secrets cannot be seen by the eyes, unless the heart is involved. When the prince wants to play, the fox explains that "connecting" takes time and patience; through such connecting, one rose among thousands becomes special. The fox explains also that one is forever responsible where love is involved, that words cause misunderstandings; that rites and rituals are significant but often forgotten, and that crucial matters are often ignored and not appreciated. These lessons help the little prince understand his own mistakes, and he decides to return home to protect his rose.

The boy meets the snake, who talks in riddles, and he understands the creature's power to send him back where he came from quickly. The little prince and the pilot are now both dying from thirst. In search of water, they walk through the starry night. On the verge of collapse, the pilot carries his little friend, not knowing whether they are even headed in the right direction. At dawn, when it is almost too late to save their lives, they find a deep, old well. The stars shimmer on the surface of the water. They drink, and the water tastes unusually sweet to them. Both the man and the boy sense the value of that moment. The pilot is sad; the prince feels fear mixed with joy, because of his decision to go home. The water feels like an earned gift. The prince comments that the beauty of the desert is in the knowledge that it hides such a well.

The prince tells his friend that he will be leaving the next day. Neither mentions the snake. When the little prince laughs to cheer his friend up, the laughter sounds like the jingle of a million little bells. He offers the pilot a farewell gift: From now on, when the pilot looks up on starry nights, he and only he will hear the little prince's laughter. It will be comforting for both of them to know that they have each other.

The next day, on the one-year anniversary of the little prince's arrival on Earth, the pilot comes to the same spot where he met the boy. There he glimpses the yellow flash of the snake as it bites the ankle of his little friend, and the boy falls quietly and gently onto the sand. Later, the little prince's body is nowhere to be found. The pilot finally fixes his engine and leaves for home, hoping that his friend is safely back at his home, too. In the years afterward, on starry nights the pilot hears the little prince's laugh and feels warm in his heart: Love is a powerful, invisible thread connecting people no matter how far apart in space and time they may be.

Critical Evaluation:

The Little Prince is one of the world's best-loved books. It has been translated into more than 180 languages (the most translated work in French literature) and has sold more than eighty million copies. It is autobiographical, poetic, and philosophical in nature, and it is charmingly illustrated in watercolors by the author. Novelist and aviator Antoine de Saint-Exupéry wrote the book, which was his last and became his most famous, in three months. The seeds of *The Little Prince* have since been found scattered in the author's many notes, sketches on napkins, and details in his other books depicting the contemporary world, which drew on his own flights and missions.

Saint-Exupéry's writings, which capture magnificent scenes and landscapes, and his actions as an aviator turned him into a hero during his lifetime. His disappearance during a flight—which he seemed to sense and announce in his novel *Vol de nuit* (1931; *Night Flight*, 1932)—served to perpetuate his status as a hero. His multifaceted personality (in addition to being a pilot and an author of fiction, he was a mathematician, an inventor, and a diplomat) has been portrayed in his own books and in those of countless other authors, who have written about him and his relations with numerous prominent people of his time, from the artists Salvador Dalí and Joan Miró to the actor Greta Garbo, the poet and playwright Maurice Maeterlinck, and the philosopher Martin Heidegger.

The original English translation of *The Little Prince* is just over ninety pages long. The book is divided into twenty-seven chapters. The story is told by the pilot, and both the pilot and the little prince voice the author's messages. The language is simple and symbolic, charged with extraordinary emotional intensity through poetic riddles and thought-provoking metaphors. The tone is factual and devoid of beauty as the author sketches the narrow world of "grown-ups," who are obsessed with self-importance, power, and money. Saint-Exupéry's purpose in this work is to teach "matters of consequence," those things that are crucial but often go unnoticed because the physical eyes are blind to them, preventing complete understanding of the meanings behind things.

The Little Prince is written in a condensed style that is overflowing with symbols, and full understanding of the author's meaning requires careful reading and pondering. Many scholars have published discussions of the specific meanings of the symbols and metaphors that appear in the work (especially baobabs and roses), which are open to various interpretations. The book has inspired writers of other works of prose fiction as well as dramatists, music composers, and filmmakers. The messages in *The Little Prince* are still being studied; both children and adults continue to decode Saint-Exupéry's thoughts and follow his dreams; among the messages they have uncovered is that nature opens its beauty and wisdom to those who search for peace, harmony, and meaning beyond the physical appearance.

In the book's dedication, Saint-Exupéry sets the tone and offers the reader guidance: He begs to be pardoned for dedicating the work to an adult, Leon Werth, his best friend in the whole world, who is hungry and cold in France. He then corrects himself and dedicates the work to Werth as a little boy, because children live in a better and more beautiful world than do adults, intuitively accepting more than can be seen with the eyes and logic only. Although it is dedicated to children, *The Little Prince* addresses fundamental ideas about life and human nature; its messages have made it a work of lasting value for all readers in all times.

Some scholars have noted that the story includes scenes that parallel events in the life of Jesus Christ, in particular the Last Supper. The episodes take the form of parables, with dialogue that has multifaceted meanings shrouded by mystery and wonder. The little prince's statements are often unfinished, trailing off as if his mind is in another world while his body is on Earth. Some of the pilot's comments hint at the autobiographical background of the work; some of the grown-ups described are real people whom he knew and whose life philosophies he opposed. It has been asserted that the main force that drove Saint-Exupéry's writing of this book was the love and pain he experienced in his relationship with his wife, not only because of the couple's own actions but also because of the turbulent times in which they lived.

Mirjana N. Mataric

Further Reading

Breaux, Adéle. *Saint-Exupéry in America, 1942-1943: A Memoir.* Rutherford, N.J.: Fairleigh Dickinson University Press, 1971. Covers the events of the time Saint-Exupéry spent in the United States during World War II. Includes discussion of his work on *The Little Prince.*

Capestany, Edward J. *The Dialectic of "The Little Prince."* Lanham, Md.: University Press of America, 1982. Searching study presents a chapter-by-chapter analysis of the book, focusing on Saint-Exupéry's use of myth.

Cate, Curtis. *Antoine de Saint-Exupéry: His Life and Times.* New York: Putnam, 1970. Comprehensive biography describes the author as a passionate pilot, inventor, mathematician, and diplomat. Provides a complete panorama of the times in which he lived and discusses the famous people he knew.

Harris, John R. L. *Chaos, Cosmos, and Saint-Exupéry's Pilot Hero: A Study in Mythopoeia.* Scranton, Pa.: University of Scranton Press, 1999. Discusses the unique qualities of Saint-Exupéry's writing and argues that scholars may overestimate the complexity of *The Little Prince.*

Higgins, James E. *"The Little Prince": A Reverie of Substance.* New York: Twayne, 1996. Provides information on the book's literary and historical contexts, including its critical reception. Offers an interpretation that emphasizes the "eye of innocence," "the landscape of metaphor," and Saint-Exupéry's explorations of the spirit and of responsibility.

Robinson, Joy D. Marie. *Antoine de Saint-Exupéry.* Boston: Twayne, 1984. Unusually thorough study is perhaps the best resource for the beginning student of Saint-Exupéry's works. Opens with three chapters devoted to Saint-Exupéry's childhood, his student and soldier years, and his career as an aviator, with subsequent chapters following the development of both his life and his writing.

Saint-Exupéry, Antoine de. *Saint-Exupéry: Art, Writing, and Musings.* Compiled by Nathalie des Vallieres. New York: Rizzoli International, 2004. Collection of Saint-Exupéry's photographs, letters, drawings, and private notebooks—compiled by Saint-Exupéry's great-niece—sheds light on his life and writings through both words and images.

Saint-Exupéry, Consuelo de. *The Tale of the Rose: The Passion That Inspired "The Little Prince."* Translated by Esther Allen. New York: Random House, 2001. Memoir by Saint-Exupéry's wife—the possible model for the little prince's coquettish flower—recalls her difficult marriage to the restless and sometimes irresponsible aviator and writer.

Schiff, Stacy. *Saint-Exupéry: A Biography.* 1994. Reprint. New York: Henry Holt, 2006. Presents substantial previously unavailable material on Saint-Exupéry's life and career, especially his experience as a war pilot. Draws on extensive interviews in considering the relationship between Saint-Exupéry the aviator and Saint-Exupéry the writer.

Little Women

Author: Louisa May Alcott (1832-1888)
First published: 1868-1869
Type of work: Novel
Type of plot: Didactic
Time of plot: Mid-nineteenth century
Locale: A New England village, New York City, and
 Italy

Principal characters:
MEG,
JO,
BETH, and
AMY, the March sisters
MRS. MARCH or MARMEE, their mother
MR. MARCH, their father
THEODORE LAURENCE or LAURIE, a young neighbor
PROFESSOR BHAER, a tutor, in love with Jo

The Story:

The March family lives in a small house next door to the Laurence mansion, where young Theodore Laurence, known as Laurie, and his aged grandfather have only each other for company. Old Mr. Laurence is wealthy, and he indulges every wish of his grandson, but often Laurie is lonely. When the lamps are lit and the shades are up in the March house, he can see the four March sisters, with their mother in the center, seated around a cheerful fire. He learns to know them by name before he meets them, and, in his imagination, he almost feels himself a member of the family.

The oldest is plump Meg, who has to earn her living as the governess of a group of unruly youngsters in the neighborhood. Next is Jo, tall, awkward, and tomboyish, who likes to write and who spends all her spare time devising plays and entertainments for her sisters. Then there is gentle Beth, the homebody, content to sit knitting by the fire or to help her mother take care of the house. The youngest is curly-haired Amy, a schoolgirl who dreams of someday becoming a famous artist like Michelangelo or Leonardo da Vinci. The sisters' father is away, serving as an army chaplain during the Civil War.

At Christmastime, the girls are confronted with the problem of what to do with the dollar that Marmee, as they call their mother, has said they might spend. At first, each thinks only of her own pleasure, but all end by buying a gift for Marmee instead. On Christmas morning, they insist on sharing their breakfast with the Hummels, a poor family in the neighborhood, and for this unselfishness they are rewarded when Mr. Laurence sends over a surprise Christmas feast consisting of ice cream and bonbons along with four bouquets of flowers for the table.

Many happy days follow, with Laurie becoming a part of the March family circle after he meets Jo at a fashionable New Year's Eve dance. In November, however, a telegram brings a message that the girls' father is critically ill. Mrs.

March does not know what to do. She feels that she should go to her husband at once, but she has barely five dollars in her purse. She is hesitant about going to her husband's wealthy, irascible relative Aunt March for help. Jo solves the problem by selling her long, beautiful chestnut hair, which has been her only vanity, for twenty-five dollars. She makes the sacrifice willingly, but that night, after the others have gone to bed, Meg hears Jo weeping softly. Gently, Meg asks if Jo is crying over her father's illness, and Jo sobs that it is not her father she is crying for now, but for her hair.

During Marmee's absence, dark days fall upon the little women. Beth, who has never been strong, contracts scarlet fever, and for a time it looks as if Jo is going to lose her dearest sister. They send for Marmee, but by the time she arrives, the crisis has passed and her little daughter is better. By the next Christmas, Beth is her old contented self again. Mr. March surprises them all when he returns home from the front well and happy. The little family is together once more.

Then John Brooke, Laurie's tutor, falls in love with Meg. This fact is disclosed when Mr. Brooke surreptitiously steals one of Meg's gloves and keeps it in his pocket as a memento. When Laurie discovers the glove and informs Jo, he is greatly surprised at her reaction; she is infuriated at the idea that the family circle might be disturbed. She is quite reconciled three years later, however, when Meg becomes Mrs. Brooke.

In the meantime, Jo herself has grown up. She begins to take her writing seriously and even sells a few stories, which helps with the family budget. Her greatest disappointment comes when Aunt Carrol, a relative of the Marches, decides she needs a companion on a trip to Europe and asks the more ladylike Amy, rather than Jo, to accompany her. Then Jo, with Marmee's permission, decides to go to New York City. She takes a job in New York as governess for a Mrs. Kirke, who runs a large boardinghouse. There she meets Professor

Bhaer, a lovable and eccentric German tutor, who proves to be a good friend and companion.

When Jo returns home, Laurie, who has always loved her, asks her to marry him. Jo, who imagines that she will always remain unmarried, devoting herself exclusively to her writing, tries to convince Laurie that they are not made for each other. He persists, pointing out that his grandfather and her family both expect them to marry. When she finally makes him realize that she will not be persuaded, he stomps off, and shortly afterward he leaves for Europe with his grandfather. In Europe, Laurie spends a great deal of time with Amy, and the two become close friends, so that Laurie is able to transfer to Jo's younger sister a great deal of the feeling he previously had for Jo.

Jo remains at home caring for Beth, who has never fully recovered from her earlier illness. In the spring, Beth dies, practically in Jo's arms, and after the loss of her gentle sister Jo is lonely indeed. She tries to comfort herself with her writing and with Meg's two babies, Daisy and Demi, but not until the return of Amy, now married to Laurie, does she begin to feel like her old self again. When Professor Bhaer stops to visit on his way to a university appointment in the Midwest, Jo is delighted. One day, as they share an umbrella during a downpour, he asks her to marry him, and Jo accepts. Within a year, old Aunt March dies and leaves her home, Plumfield, to Jo. Jo decides to open a boys' school there, where she and her professor can devote their lives to instructing the young.

So the little women have reached maturity, and on their mother's sixtieth birthday, they all have a great celebration at Plumfield. Around the table, at which there is but one empty chair, sit Marmee, her daughters and their husbands, and her grandchildren. When Laurie proposes a toast to his mother-in-law, she replies by stretching out her arms to them all and saying that she can wish nothing better for them than this present happiness for the rest of their lives.

Critical Evaluation:

Little Women has been condemned by critics as being little more than a moral battering ram aimed at nineteenth century adolescent girls, but Louisa May Alcott produced a work much larger in scope and more complex in feeling than such critics recognize. On the surface, the novel comprises a series of episodes depicting the four March girls' private battles with expectations concerning the moral conduct befitting good Christian young ladies. If the story of the Marches were merely that, however, it would not have sparked the level of controversy and analysis that it has, nor would it have remained so popular a book for children that libraries find it hard to keep copies on the shelves even in the twenty-first century.

Although it was Alcott's intention to demonstrate right behavior, her method of presenting a problem for each sister to solve without much adult influence makes the characters real and the situations believable. Each of the sisters harbors a weakness, as lovingly noted by Marmee, their conscience and gentle guide. Meg is vain and wishes to live in luxury; Jo can often be too spontaneous, direct, and temperamental; Beth is too timid; and Amy has a tendency to be pretentious. These character flaws may seem mild by present-day standards, but they are timeless benchmarks of youth from which Alcott draws out and measures each girl's growth. However predictable the outcomes, the March sisters' journeys to womanhood involve pain and hardship, humiliation, and even danger in the midst of the protective family nest.

The process of individual growth within the family is Alcott's focus. A realist, she does not develop any progressive notions in the novel that were impossible to pursue in Victorian-era America. Jo will not marry Laurie because these two characters' bold, adventuresome natures simply do not apply to the marriage conventions of the mid-nineteenth century. Alcott was a feminist, however, and she depicts the relentless self-denial of Victorian women as it was. Her purpose is echoed in Marmee's wish for her daughters to become happy, loved, dutiful wives and mothers. To accomplish this, they must sacrifice independence of thought and action, and that is what each girl does. Alcott does not gloss over the price they pay, nor does she neglect to show the personal rewards of happy married life and motherhood, self-discipline, and altruism.

The focus on these qualities makes the work timeless. The story opens in the early years of the Civil War, but little is said about Mr. March and his experiences as a chaplain at the front lines. Slavery is never mentioned, nor is Abraham Lincoln's assassination. It would be wrong to conclude that Alcott neglected such institutions and events out of disinterest or out of an assumed disinterest on the part of her readers. She served as a nurse during the war and knew intimately the suffering and tragedy that befell young men. Her father, Bronson Alcott, was a progressive educator, and Louisa was raised with an awareness of politics and social problems. Alcott smartly focuses the story on the family, the center toward which the March girls are drawn time and again for moral support and rejuvenation.

The story opens at Christmas, when the girls are sad and disappointed about their father's absence and their own poverty. Marmee gently reminds them that others suffer more, and the women troop to the poor Hummel household laden with their own Christmas breakfast. Their selflessness is rewarded with a sumptuous dinner courtesy of their neighbor,

Mr. Laurence. When Jo nearly lets Amy drown in the river after Amy has destroyed Jo's precious manuscript, Jo appeals to Marmee to help her control her anger. Marmee reveals her own struggle with rage and frustration, and from that point on, the two share a special bond. Jo has learned to separate her feelings from her actions. After Meg spends a week with wealthy friends whose lifestyle she envies, she returns home grateful for the simplicity and authentic love and comfort of her humble home. Meg has learned the high price of vanity. Amy, the baby of the family, does some rather extreme things to win the approval of her affluent schoolmates. A comic episode concerning pickled limes and public humiliation prompts her to realize the consequences of climbing the social ladder. Amy has learned that it is better to stand on the lower rungs in safety than to make it to the top and fall flat on her face. Beth's character is virtually undeveloped, and she changes the least of the four sisters. She is a touching reminder that some delicate souls are simply too vulnerable to remain for very long on this planet. Her death leaves its mark on the March family, particularly on Jo.

Jo, the most tenacious and free-spirited character, is also the most challenged to change. Her tempestuous behavior and childlike joy for living are appealing to readers. She chafes at the expectations of women in her day and vows to remain unmarried and fulfilled by her work as a writer. Neighbor Laurie, her charming and rebellious kindred spirit, grows to love her, and it seems that the two will end up together. Jo's vow is half fulfilled as she turns her back on the radical choice to marry her best friend and embark on a life of self-absorbed adventure. Instead, she marries Professor Bhaer and engages herself in work more suitable to women of the day by opening a school for boys. This choice may disappoint readers, but she and her sisters have fulfilled their mother's wish that they be married, loved, and valued by others, a theme that resonates throughout the story.

However idealistic and dependent the relationships may seem between the daughters and their parents and husbands, the family represents an unchanging core around which world events and personal calamity spiral. This family portrait contains both real-life conflicts with which any reader can sympathize and a model for the kind of family most readers privately long to be part of. The result is irresistible.

"Critical Evaluation" by Kim Dolce

Further Reading

Alberghene, Janice M., and Beverly Lyon Clark, eds. *"Little Women" and the Feminist Imagination: Criticism, Controversy, Personal Essays.* New York: Garland, 1999. Collection of essays offers feminist interpretations of the novel, including discussions of the depictions of men and families in the book.

Alcott, Louisa May. *Little Women, or, Meg, Jo, Beth, and Amy: Authoritative Text, Backgrounds and Contexts, Criticism.* Edited by Anne K. Phillips and Gregory Eiselein. New York: W. W. Norton, 2004. In addition to presenting the full text of the novel supplemented by explanatory annotations, this edition contains some of Alcott's correspondence and other archival materials, twenty-nine reviews of the work that first appeared in the nineteenth century, and seven essays on the work by present-day scholars.

Delamar, Gloria T. *Louisa May Alcott and "Little Women": Biography, Critique, Publications, Poems, Songs, and Contemporary Relevance.* Jefferson, N.C.: McFarland, 1990. Goes beyond a biography of Alcott to include a comprehensive bibliography of Alcott's works and analyses of her work. Includes critical analysis of *Little Women* and selections from letters by Alcott and her close associates.

Elbert, Sarah. *A Hunger for Home: Louisa May Alcott's Place in American Culture.* New Brunswick, N.J.: Rutgers University Press, 1987. Provides both biographical background and critical coverage, tracing the two predominant themes in *Little Women* and in Alcott's work generally: domesticity and feminism. The chapters "Writing *Little Women*" and "Reading *Little Women*" are particularly informative.

Keyser, Elizabeth Lennox. *"Little Women": A Family Romance.* New York: Twayne, 1999. Uses Freudian analysis and other interpretations of children's fantasies to describe the personal and artistic reasons Alcott created an idealized version of her own family in the novel. Argues that the book is not about Jo but about the relationships of all of the March sisters to one another and to their mother.

_____. *Whispers in the Dark: The Fiction of Louisa May Alcott.* Knoxville: University of Tennessee Press, 1993. Offers an intriguing analysis of Jo and Laurie's relationship as the Sleeping Beauty tale with gender roles reversed. Suggests that Alcott depicts Jo and Laurie as androgynous characters who together make a whole person, but whose wholeness could not exist in the Victorian era.

MacDonald, Ruth K. *Louisa May Alcott.* Boston: Twayne, 1983. Critical overview of Alcott's works includes a chapter titled "The March Family Stories" that covers not only *Little Women* but also its sequels: *Little Men* and *Jo's Boys.* Acknowledges the autobiographical basis of *Little Women* but also shows how the work departs from factual details of Alcott family life.

Showalter, Elaine. *Sister's Choice: Tradition and Change in American Women's Writing*. New York: Oxford University Press, 1991. Influential analysis of *Little Women* is part of a larger discussion of American women writers and the diversity of their language and literary vision in the context of race, ethnicity, and class.

Strickland, Charles. *Victorian Domesticity: Families in the Life and Art of Louisa May Alcott*. Tuscaloosa: University of Alabama Press, 1985. Presents a thoughtful exploration of the sentimental and its implications in Alcott's work. Suggests that her juvenile fiction offers the most radical departure from Victorian conventions. Connects to Alcott's own struggle with the sentimental ideals of child and parent in her own family.

Trites, Roberta Seelinger. *Twain, Alcott, and the Birth of the Adolescent Reform Novel*. Iowa City: University of Iowa Press, 2007. Analyzes the work of Alcott and Mark Twain to delineate how these two authors helped change the nature of American adolescence, viewing it as a time in which children express a great potential for change and reform. Includes discussion of *Little Women*.

The Lives of the Poets

Author: Samuel Johnson (1709-1784)
First published: 1779-1781, as *Prefaces, Biographical and Critical, to the Works of the English Poets*; revised edition 1781, as *The Lives of the Most Eminent English Poets*
Type of work: Biography and literary criticism

The essays contained in Samuel Johnson's *The Lives of the Poets* were composed as prefaces to a large collection of the works of English writers of the seventeenth and eighteenth centuries, and they are therefore primarily critical rather than biographical. Johnson related the known information about the lives of his subjects, but he was content to rely on facts gathered by earlier biographers, reserving his original thoughts for his critical commentary.

The more than fifty essays vary greatly in both length and detail. Johnson wrote extensive studies of men such as John Dryden, Alexander Pope, John Milton, and Jonathan Swift, whereas he only briefly summarized the achievements of minor figures whose names subsequently vanished from all but the pages of detailed literary histories. It is a tribute to the soundness of Johnson's judgment that the writers whom he considered important are those whose works continue to be highly regarded.

The collection is among Johnson's best, most readable works. The language he uses is characteristically stately, but his style is less formal than in some of his earlier writing. He occasionally departs from the easy narrative flow to offer a striking rhetorical passage in which balanced phrases and carefully constructed comparisons make his critical judgments memorable. One of his most famous "set pieces" is his contrast of the writings of Dryden and Pope:

The style of Dryden is capricious and varied, that of Pope is cautious and uniform; Dryden obeys the motions of his own mind, Pope constrains his mind to his own rules of composition. Dryden is sometimes vehement and rapid; Pope is always smooth, uniform, and gentle. Dryden's page is a natural field, rising into inequalities, and diversified by the varied exuberance of abundant vegetation; Pope's is a velvet lawn, shaven by the scythe, and levelled by the roller.

Most of the essays in *The Lives of the Poets* follow the same structural pattern. Johnson begins with an account of his subject's family and education, then summarizes the main events of his life and gives brief notes on the times and circumstances of the composition and publication of his major works. The biography concludes with critical commentary on specific poems and a final assessment of the poet's literary talents and faults.

Johnson's moral and literary standards formed a strong foundation for all his writings, and both the biographical and the critical portions of *The Lives of the Poets* reveal their author's characteristic point of view. The biographical sketch of a popular Restoration dramatist, for example, begins with this statement: "Of Thomas Otway, one of the first names in the English drama, little is known; nor is there any part of that little which his biographer can take pleasure in relating."

The characters and personalities of the poets were far more interesting to Johnson than facts and dates. He had begun his career as a biographer with a searching study of the motives that shaped the life of his friend Richard Savage, and in *The Lives of the Poets* he often manages to convey the essential qualities of a subject in a few words. Writing of the charming, if somewhat irresponsible, author of *The Beggar's Opera* (pr., pb. 1728), he notes: "[John] Gay is represented as a man easily incited to hope, and deeply depressed when his hopes were disappointed. This is not the character of a hero, but it may naturally imply something more generally welcome, a soft and civil companion."

Johnson's insights into the human personality are shown especially clearly in his life of Pope. He brings the brilliant, ambitious, often ailing and bad-tempered poet vividly before the reader, chiding the excessive sensitivity that made Pope viciously attack critics of his writing in satirical works such as *The Dunciad* (1728-1743) and led him to hold grudges against his "enemies" far longer than most people thought reasonable. Johnson also comments on one of Pope's rather amusing foibles:

> In all his intercourse with mankind he had great delight in artifice, and endeavored to attain all his purposes by indirect and unsuspected methods. He practised his arts on such small occasions that Lady Bolingbroke used to say, in a French phrase, that "he plaid the politician about cabbages and turnips."

Johnson points out Pope's more appealing characteristics as well, noting his loyalty to his friends and his respect and tenderness for his elderly parents, and he tries to suggest something of the state of mind brought about by Pope's physical disabilities, his small stature, his weakness, and his almost constant pain.

Although *The Lives of the Poets* reveals Johnson as a skillful analyst of the human personality, the book is still more interesting as a work of theoretical and practical criticism. His essay on the life of Abraham Cowley contains a famous discussion of metaphysical poetry in which Johnson defines the wit that was the essence of the technique of John Donne and his followers: "Wit, abstracted from its effects upon the hearer, may be more rigorously and philosophically considered as a kind of *discordia concors*; a combination of dissimilar images, or discovery of occult resemblances in things apparently unlike."

Johnson, who believed that great poetry should deal with

universal thoughts in general terms, felt that the achievement of the metaphysical poets was a minor one, and he quotes many lines to illustrate the absurdities often produced by their quest for novelty. He does, however, show appreciation of their intellectual efforts and grants that they occasionally succeeded: "Yet great labor, directed by great ability, is never wholly lost; if they frequently threw away their wit upon false conceits, they likewise sometimes struck out unexpected truth; if their conceits were far-fetched, they were often worth the carriage."

The life of Milton shows Johnson at once at his worst and at his best. His natural antipathy for allegory in general and pastoral allegory in particular led to his scornful dismissal of "Lycidas," the elegy that many consider one of the finest English lyrics:

> In this poem there is no nature, for there is no truth; there is no art, for there is nothing new. Its form is that of a pastoral, easy, vulgar, and therefore disgusting; whatever images it can supply are long ago exhausted; and its inherent improbability always forces dissatisfaction on the mind.

Johnson's succinct praise of *L'Allegro* and *Il Penseroso* (both 1631) conforms more closely to later views, however: "Every man that reads them, reads them with pleasure."

His extensive remarks on *Paradise Lost* (1667, 1674) are undeniably illuminating, for he recognizes and pays tribute to the epic's greatness, majesty, unity, and powerful theological foundation; however, he also examines closely what he feels to be a major flaw. All the characters except Adam and Eve are supernatural beings, and even these two are in a situation different from that of all other men and women: "The reader finds no transaction in which he can be engaged; beholds no condition in which he can by any effort of the imagination place himself; he has, therefore, little natural curiosity or sympathy." This comment shows clearly Johnson's conviction that literature should be, as Aristotle had declared, an imitation of life and a reflection of the real emotions of human beings. This viewpoint led Johnson to conclude, a little reluctantly:

> The want of human interest is always felt. *Paradise Lost* is one of the books which the reader admires and lays down, and forgets to take up again. None ever wished it longer than it is. Its perusal is a duty rather than a pleasure. We read Milton for instruction, retire harassed and overburdened, and look elsewhere for recreation; we desert our master, and seek for companions.

Although Johnson's general statements are the passages from *The Lives of the Poets* most often quoted, he actually devotes much of his attention to commentary on specific lines. He presents, for example, a detailed discussion of the individual stanzas of Thomas Gray's ode "The Bard," criticizing the poet's excessive alliteration, his use of "the puerilities of obsolete mythology," and the many clichés among his images.

Quotation of brief passages is especially effective in the life of Dryden, where Johnson cites many lines to illustrate the elegance and majesty as well as the pedantry and carelessness of the poet. He finds that Dryden "delighted to tread upon the brink of meaning, where light and darkness begin to mingle; to approach the precipice of absurdity, and hover over the abyss of unideal vacancy." Close examination of many passages leads Johnson to lament Dryden's carelessness, although he admires his great talent:

> Such is the unevenness of his composition that ten lines are seldom found together without something of which the reader is ashamed. Dryden was no rigid judge of his own pages; he seldom struggled after supreme excellence, but snatched in haste what was within his reach; and when he could content others, was himself contented.

A reading of *The Lives of the Poets* reveals why Johnson has become increasingly famous not only as the colorful personage immortalized by James Boswell but also as one of the best prose writers and ablest critics in English literary history. Although his many prejudices occasionally brought forth declarations that later critics came to consider absurd, his personal standards generally contributed to the lasting worth of his criticism. Johnson evaluated literature on the basis of its truth to life, and, since he understood better than most men what human beings think and feel, his judgments for the most part remain valid. He appreciated the appeal of the new and the unusual, but he reserved his highest praise for what he considered to be lastingly true and moving.

Further Reading

Burke, John J., Jr., and Donald Kay. *The Unknown Samuel Johnson*. Madison: University of Wisconsin Press, 1983. Provides an overview of Johnson's method and style of writing. Makes a distinction between professional writing and academic critique, and maintains that *The Lives of the Poets* is an example of the former.

Clingham, Greg. *Johnson, Writing, and Memory*. New York: Cambridge University Press, 2002. Examines Johnson's writing and places it within the context of eighteenth century ideas about literature, history, fiction, and law, discussing the challenges that these ideas pose to twentieth and twenty-first century critical theory. Chapters 4 and 5 provide an extensive analysis of *The Lives of the Poets*.

_____, ed. *The Cambridge Companion to Samuel Johnson*. New York: Cambridge University Press, 1997. Collection of essays includes discussions of Johnson and the arts of conversation, poetry, and the essay as well as examination of his political views. Includes an essay devoted to *The Lives of the Poets*.

Damrosch, Leopold, Jr. *The Uses of Johnson's Criticism*. Charlottesville: University Press of Virginia, 1976. Focuses on how Johnson's critiques in *The Lives of the Poets* have influenced subsequent literary studies.

Hart, Kevin. *Samuel Johnson and the Culture of Property*. New York: Cambridge University Press, 1999. Examines Johnson's literary legacy and reputation and analyzes the works of those biographers and critics who helped create the "Age of Johnson." Asserts that James Boswell's famous biography turned Johnson into a public monument.

Martin, Peter. *Samuel Johnson: A Biography*. Cambridge, Mass.: Harvard University Press, 2008. Provides a psychological profile of Johnson, focusing on aspects of his personality and life that are not covered in Boswell's biography, such as Johnson's insecurities, bouts of deep depression, and self-doubt.

Nath, Prem, ed. *Fresh Reflections on Samuel Johnson: Essays in Criticism*. Troy, N.Y.: Whitston, 1987. Collection presents a broad range of critical essays dealing with Johnson's writings, with particular emphasis on his critical style in *The Lives of the Poets*.

Wain, John, ed. *Johnson as Critic*. London: Routledge & Kegan Paul, 1973. Examines the factual accuracy of *The Lives of the Poets* and explores Johnson's critical expectations, his idealism, and the assumptions about poetry that he shared with his contemporaries.

Weinbrot, Howard D. *Aspects of Samuel Johnson: Essays on His Arts, Mind, Afterlife, and Politics*. Newark: University of Delaware Press, 2005. Individual essays examine Johnson as prose writer, poet, lexicographer, historical figure, and literary and political thinker. Chapter 11 describes the critical response to *The Lives of the Poets*.

Locksley Hall

Author: Alfred, Lord Tennyson (1809-1892)
First published: 1842
Type of work: Poetry
Type of plot: Dramatic monologue
Time of plot: Early nineteenth century
Locale: Near the coast of England

Principal characters:
THE NARRATOR, who remains unnamed
AMY, who has just broken their engagement
AMY'S PARENTS, who opposed the marriage
THE NARRATOR'S FATHER, killed in battle
THE NARRATOR'S UNCLE, lord of Locksley Hall
FRIENDS OF THE NARRATOR

The Poem:

An unnamed narrator has just returned to his childhood home of Locksley Hall. He asks a group of friends there to leave him in solitude so he may reflect on his past. He recalls his life in the large country house, which included leisurely contemplation and an education in the classics and science. The estate belongs to the narrator's uncle, who took him in after the death of his parents.

The narrator is now despondent because Amy, the woman he loves, has broken their engagement and plans to marry another man. She apparently made the decision at her parents' insistence on the grounds that the other man has more desirable prospects. After recalling in detail idyllic walks on the beach with Amy, the narrator denounces her bitterly and predicts that her husband will mistreat and neglect her. Unable to forget Amy, he questions the nature and endurance of love. Amy may find comfort from her husband's predicted aloofness in the love of a child, but the narrator imagines her hypocritically warning her own daughter of the dangers of yielding to one's emotions.

In order to forget Amy, the narrator resolves to turn to further adventures. Economic forces in his society deny him access to military glory or commercial success. He recalls the dreams of his younger years, when he saw infinite possibilities for both himself and others, including technological advances and the advent of an international government that would eliminate war. The future no longer seems so positive to the narrator in his present depressed mood, however. He makes dire predictions of a world overcome by an increasingly hungry population. Platitudes that have previously reassured him that all is for the best are powerless against his current emotions.

The narrator's friends sound a horn to call for him, and he is brought out of his reveries into the present. In a violent reaction to the returning memory of his lost love, he denounces all women as inferior to men and seeks a more distant escape from his stifling society. He will return to India, where his father fell in battle defending Britain's empire, or he may travel even farther. He dreams of exotic and isolated islands where he could lead a carefree life surrounded by the beauty of nature.

Once again, however, the dream fails him. He realizes that he will never be able to give up his own country. European culture, moving ahead with the advances of modern science, dominates the globe and offers him a life superior to any found elsewhere. With this triumphal conclusion, the narrator turns definitively away from Locksley Hall. He no longer cares what happens to the estate, as he prepares to seek happiness elsewhere.

Critical Evaluation:

The narrator's concerns in "Locksley Hall" parallel those of his nineteenth century society and evolve as literature did during Alfred, Lord Tennyson's lifetime. The personal love story at the beginning of the poem echoes the emotional and autobiographical mode of Romanticism, while the economic pressures underlying the speaker's plight invoke social problems that would become the focus of later realist and naturalist writing.

The Romantic tone of the opening section comes not only from its emphasis on the story of thwarted love but also from its description of nature. Locksley Hall stands near the coast, where the implied danger of ocean waves recalls the Romantic concept of sublime nature. References to birds, symbols exploited by Romantic writers as emblems of joy and freedom, surround the narrator's early days with Amy. As their love deepens, the narrator likens Amy's radiant face to the Northern Lights and her sighs to those of the wind. All these references follow the Romantic tradition of invoking imagery that coincides with the emotions of its characters.

The Romantic hero may be in harmony with nature, but he is also traditionally suffering. During the decade prior to the publication of "Locksley Hall," French novelists defined the frustration of a generation of young men who lacked the opportunities for glory that Napoleon Bonaparte's conquests had offered when he gained victories abroad for France. Stendhal, in his novel *Le Rouge et le noir* (1830; *The Red and the Black*, 1898), and Alfred de Musset, in *Confession d'un enfant du siècle* (1836; *Confession of a Child of This Century*, 1892), depicted protagonists frustrated in a shrinking economy. For Tennyson's hero, the British Empire plays an analogous role. His options are limited by his father's death in India.

The personal loss of his father is not the only reason for the narrator's despair. He is living in rapidly changing times, as Europe enters the age of industrialization. The accompanying social upheaval can be both beneficial and harmful. When he recalls his youthful optimism, the narrator evokes a vision of social and material advances. In the short term, however, he sees himself unable to succeed without the money and family support that are essential in a materialistic society.

Forty-four years after the publication of "Locksley Hall," Tennyson continued the story of its protagonist and his attendant social criticism in "Locksley Hall Sixty Years After" (1886). In this sequel, the speaker of the earlier poem has been consoled for the loss of Amy by his marriage to Edith, with whom he has had a son. Both mother and son have died, and the narrator returns again to Locksley Hall with his grandson. Like his grandfather, the grandson has been jilted by the girl he loved—Judith. Recalling his own experience, the grandfather asserts that this modern love could not be the equal of his own passion, just as society, ever more harsh and materialistic, uses its new technology to expand the atrocities of war.

In "Locksley Hall Sixty Years After," Tennyson again alternates between hope and despair for the future, but negative ideas are more numerous because the narrator has observed so much suffering during his life. "Locksley Hall" retains more of the young man's optimism. While he has rejected his fantasy of a simpler life at the fringes of European influence, the narrator renews his hope because of the expanding possibilities associated with advancing science.

In the final lines of "Locksley Hall," the narrator leaves the titular estate behind as a violent storm bears down on the area. The storm suggests simultaneously the destruction of Locksley Hall and the intensity of the narrator's passion. Furthermore, the narrator describes the wind as blowing toward the sea. Following it, he may again take the outward path that had led his country, and that may lead him, to greatness. This final triumphalism returns to the Romantic spirit of the opening of the poem but with a hope for a positive outcome at last.

Dorothy M. Betz

Further Reading

Alden, Raymond Macdonald. *Alfred Tennyson: How to Know Him.* Indianapolis, Ind.: Bobbs-Merrill, 1917. This early study compares the story to a novel, highlighting the hero's evolving emotions.

Bloom, Harold, ed. *Alfred, Lord Tennyson.* Modern Critical Views. New York: Chelsea House, 1985. An essay by A. Dwight Culler in this collection of Tennyson criticism compares the reaction of "Locksley Hall" to catastrophe to that of Tennyson's "Maud" (1855) and traces the origins of the monologue form in Arabian poetry.

Goslee, David. *Tennyson's Characters: "Strange Faces, Other Minds."* Iowa City: University of Iowa Press, 1989. Draws on readings by several other critics to reveal the weaknesses of the poem's narrator.

Hughes, Linda K. *The Manyfacèd Glass: Tennyson's Dramatic Monologues.* Athens: Ohio University Press, 1987. Dwelling on the role of time, this study sees the remembered past and visions of the future in "Locksley Hall" as defining both the poem's narrator and his society.

Kissane, James D. *Alfred Tennyson.* New York: Twayne, 1970. The chapter "The Dramatic Poet" outlines the independent persona of the narrator and the role of Locksley Hall itself as an emblem of his past.

Shaw, David W. *Alfred, Lord Tennyson: The Poet in an Age of Theory.* Twayne's English Authors Series 525. New York: Twayne, 1996. This general study presents the hero as Byronic and alternating between opposing emotions. Here, his violent feelings mask a failure to assume responsibility.

_____. *Tennyson's Style.* Ithaca, N.Y.: Cornell University Press, 1976. This study sees various stages of the poem progressively modifying the story.

Smith, Elton Edward. *Tennyson's "Epic Drama."* Lanham, Md.: University Press of America, 1997. This reading shows the hero progressing from negative jealousy to a positive and hopeful resolution.

Wright, F. W. Nielsen. *Tennyson, Locksley Hall Then and After, and "The Alexandrians, an Epic Poem": An Essay in Literary Derivation.* Wellington, New Zealand: Cultural and Political Booklets, 2007. Detailed study of the relationship between "Locksley Hall" and an epic poem of New Zealand.

Lolita

Author: Vladimir Nabokov (1899-1977)
First published: 1955
Type of work: Novel
Type of plot: Satire
Time of plot: 1910-1952
Locale: France and numerous small American towns

Principal characters:
HUMBERT HUMBERT, an intellectual from France
DOLORES HAZE, his stepdaughter
CHARLOTTE BECKER HAZE HUMBERT, her mother,
   Humbert's second wife
CLARE QUILTY, a playwright
RITA, Humbert's traveling companion
MISS PRATT, a girls' school headmistress
RICHARD F. SCHILLER, Dolly's husband
ANNABEL LEIGH, Humbert's first love
VALERIA HUMBERT, Humbert's first wife
JOHN RAY, JR., an academic and editor

The Story:

After the death by heart attack of Humbert Humbert, before he was to be tried for murder, his lawyer asks John Ray, Jr., Ph.D., to edit the accused murderer's last manuscript. It is titled "Lolita, or the Confession of a White Widowed Male." Dolores Schiller, the girl Humbert calls Lolita, dies giving birth to a stillborn daughter a few weeks after Humbert's fatal heart attack. Ray defends the manuscript against charges of pornography and claims it will become a classic in psychiatric circles.

Humbert's confession begins with a summary of his life from his birth in 1910 until his discovery of Lolita in 1947. He was born in Paris to an English mother and a Swiss father, who ran a luxurious hotel on the Riviera. At thirteen, he fell in love with Annabel Leigh, who was close to his age, and experienced unfulfilled lust. Four months later, Annabel died of typhus. He had been haunted by her memory until he found her essence reincarnated in Lolita. After studying English literature in Paris, Humbert became a teacher and discovered himself drawn to certain girls between the ages of nine and fourteen, whom he calls "nymphets." Trying to lead a conventional existence, he was married to Valeria from 1935 until 1939, when she left him for a White Russian taxi driver; she later died in childbirth.

Humbert then relates how, at the start of World War II, he moves to the United States. After his second stay in a mental institution, he seeks refuge in the small New England town of Ramsdale, where he rents a room from Charlotte Haze, a widow, after seeing her twelve-year-old daughter, Dolores, known as Lo to her mother and Dolly to her friends, and also sometimes called Lolita. The darkly handsome Humbert soon discovers that he resembles some singer or actor on whom Lolita has a schoolgirl crush. When the girl goes away to summer camp, Humbert decides that he cannot live without her. Then Charlotte leaves a note for Humbert in which she confesses her love for him and orders him to marry her or leave her home. They marry, and afterward he hints to her friends that he and Charlotte had had an affair thirteen years previously, and he begins to regard Lolita as his child. Humbert decides that he must somehow get rid of her mother, his wife, but he cannot bring himself to kill her.

Humbert's problem is solved when Charlotte breaks into his locked desk to read his journal and discovers his disdain for her and his lust for Lolita. As she is crossing the street, in an emotional turmoil, to mail some letters incriminating him (for protection, having read of his desire for her death), she is struck and killed by a car. Humbert recovers the letters, plays the role of a grieving widower, continues planting suggestions that he is Lolita's real father, and announces plans to take the girl on a trip west.

Humbert retrieves Lolita from her summer camp on the pretext that her mother is ill and takes her to a hotel called the Enchanted Hunters. As Humbert relates it, before he can break the news of her mother's death to her, Lolita seduces him and afterward reveals that she lost her virginity to the son of the camp director. Humbert is immediately consumed by guilt but continues to have sexual relations with her. When Lolita demands to call her mother, Humbert tells her that Charlotte is dead.

Humbert and Lolita begin traveling from motel to motel across the United States. Seeing how other adult men are attracted to the young girl, Humbert is constantly on his guard. He is also aware of the repercussions that await him if his criminal treatment of Lolita is discovered.

After a year and some twenty-seven thousand miles on the road, they return east to Beardsley, where Lolita attends a private girls' school. Miss Pratt, the headmistress, convinces

Humbert to let Lolita play the lead in the school's production of a new play, *The Enchanted Hunters*. Just before the play is to open, Lolita announces that she hates school and the play and wants to travel again. Humbert has been told that the playwright, Clare Quilty, a man whom Lolita has falsely identified as "some old woman," has been raving about the young actress. Humbert and Lolita set out again, and Humbert takes with him a gun once owned by Harold Haze, Lolita's father. He feels he might need it after he notices they are being followed by a red convertible and he discovers Lolita talking to a stranger who resembles Gustave Trapp, Humbert's cousin.

In the town of Elphinstone, Lolita develops a high fever and is hospitalized. Humbert becomes incapacitated by fever as well, and while he is ill, Lolita is checked out of the hospital by "her uncle, Mr. Gustave." Humbert spends the next four months searching for her and her abductor, tormented by the taunting clues left by his nemesis. In a northeastern bar, he meets Rita, an alcoholic, suicidal young woman; the two then travel together for two years. Eventually Humbert receives a letter from Lolita, now Mrs. Richard F. Schiller, and he goes to see her. She is living in the dismal town of Coalmont, pregnant and married to a young Korean War veteran. He is surprised at how much he still loves the haggard, seventeen-year-old housewife.

Lolita tells Humbert the identity of her abductor, Clare Quilty, and tells him how Quilty had wanted her to perform in pornographic home movies and had thrown her out when she refused. Humbert gives her four thousand dollars so that she and her husband can move to Alaska, and then he sets out to find Quilty. After returning to Ramsdale to sign over all his money and possessions to Lolita, Humbert tracks Quilty down in the town of Parkington and, after a lengthy confrontation, shoots and kills him.

Critical Evaluation:

Before the publication of *Lolita*, the Russian-born Vladimir Nabokov was not widely known in English-speaking literary circles; most of his early work had not yet been translated from Russian. After *Lolita* was rejected by four American publishers, Nabokov's French agent sent it to Olympia Press in Paris, which quickly published it. Although Olympia published many controversial works by writers such as Jean Genet, it was notorious for cheap editions of pornographic books, a fact of which Nabokov was ignorant at the time. The novel went virtually unnoticed until novelist Graham Greene praised it in London's *Daily Express*. When Putnam published the first American edition in 1958, it became a best seller. Many readers, expecting salacious fun,

were disappointed by the book's lack of overt sexual content and dismayed by its demanding style. Still others attacked it as immoral. Nabokov's fiction is not for passive readers who resist being drawn into the author's linguistic games. *Lolita* is considered one of this highly acclaimed writer's two greatest novels—*Pale Fire* (1962) is the other—and a masterpiece of American comic fiction.

Lolita is a highly literary work, filled with allusions to famous and little-known novels, poems, and plays. Many of the allusions are to Edgar Allan Poe, who, at twenty-seven, married his thirteen-year-old cousin. Poe wrote "Annabel Lee" (1849), a poem about a child love dead by the seaside. He also wrote "William Wilson" (1839), a tale of a psychological double, and invented the detective story. Nabokov works these and other allusions to Poe into his novel. There are also many references to *Carmen* (1845; English translation, 1878), not the Georges Bizet opera but the Prosper Mérimée novella about love, loss, and revenge and an imprisoned narrator. Another strong influence is James Joyce, whose ornate, self-aware, stylistic whimsy is reflected in *Lolita*. Joyce pioneered heavily allusive fiction, full of word games, and *Lolita* is full of puns, coinages (such as "nymphet"), neologisms, and foreign, archaic, and unusual words. It also features jokes such as the appearance of Vivian Darkbloom, the letters of whose name may be rearranged, changing one *o* to an *a*, to spell Vladimir Nabokov. *Lolita* is drunk on language; a typical sentence reads, "I spend my doleful days in dumps and dolors." In his afterword, Nabokov says the novel is about his love affair with the English language.

Lolita can be seen as a parody of such literary forms as autobiography, the confessional tale, the Romantic novel, the tale of the doppelgänger or double, and the detective story. As for the last of these, the reader knows from the beginning that Humbert has murdered someone but does not know more. Hints of the victim's identity are scattered throughout the novel, and Humbert even warns his readers to keep their eyes on the clues. Nabokov has fun with the detective element by having Quilty appear to Humbert wearing a Dick Tracy mask.

The doppelgänger device is central to the novel. Humbert Humbert sees the old lecher Clare Quilty as his evil double. Lolita has her double in Annabel Leigh (herself a reference to another and a joke about the youth of Edgar Allan Poe's wife). Humbert Humbert has two wives, both, in his eyes, contemptible. One dies in childbirth, as does Lolita. The three main characters have a multitude of names. Humbert thinks of the mysterious stranger as Trapp and McFate, Quilty's friends call him Cue, Humbert calls him Punch (as in Punch and Judy), and Lolita tries to convince Humbert that the playwright is a woman. Dolores Haze is Lo, Dolly, Lolita, Lola, and Mrs. Richard F. Schiller. She is a girl and a woman, a victim and a manipulator. Humbert's name is a double; he uses it for wordplay. It is mispronounced numerous ways by those he encounters (and once by him), and he is frequently called "Mr. Haze." His calling himself Edgar H. Humbert is typical of Nabokov's jokes within jokes. Humbert's editor is another double: The initials of John Ray, Jr., are J. R., or Jr. Beyond the gamesmanship, however, the novel conveys the pain the protagonists suffer.

One of the main targets of Nabokov's satire is Freudian psychology. Humbert admits, but glosses over, his mental instability and refuses to see himself as a stereotype or a case study. *Lolita* is thus a parody of the psychiatric simplicity of a case study, with Humbert sneering at those who would see his affair with Lolita as an attempt to rid himself of his obsession with Annabel, laughing at those who interpret the incestuous relationship in Oedipal terms. Humbert's attacks on Sigmund Freud can be taken seriously, for Humbert is not just a comic figure but also a tormented, guilt-ridden soul.

Humbert is a complex figure because he changes from a self-centered sexual pervert to something of a caring father. Even as Lolita loses her nymphet charms, he falls more deeply in love with her. Pregnant by another and worn out by poverty, she remains his ideal. His moral growth is shown by his lament over his having robbed Dolly Haze of the stable family life to which every child is entitled and having stolen her childhood for his selfish pleasures. He must kill Quilty, his double, to destroy the evil side of his nature. His confession, far from being pornography, is an attempt at a moral cleansing and illustrates the healing power of art.

This double-edged approach can also be seen in Nabokov's treatment of his adopted country. He satirizes the vulgar, commercialized side of American life through Lolita's love of junk food, trashy movies, and bland popular singers. Humbert writes of Lolita, "She it was to whom ads were dedicated: the ideal consumer, the subject and object of every foul poster." Nabokov makes fun of such topics as American progressive education: "What we are concerned with is the adjustment of the child to group life," says Miss Pratt. Humbert is more amused at than appalled by these excesses and sincerely loves the American landscape, the West in particular. *Lolita* was partially inspired by the summer trips Nabokov and his wife took over several years through forty-six U.S. states in pursuit of rare butterflies (the writer was also a prominent lepidopterist). The novel is a comic valentine to "the lovely, trustful, dreamy, enormous country."

Michael Adams

Further Reading

Bloom, Harold, ed. *Lolita*. Edgemont, Pa.: Chelsea House, 1993. Collection of nine essays addresses such topics as the effect of America on Humbert, necrophilia, the novel's attacks on Sigmund Freud, its parodic elements, and Nabokov's treatment of women.

Connolly, Julian W., ed. *The Cambridge Companion to Nabokov*. New York: Cambridge University Press, 2005. Collection of essays offers a good introduction to Nabokov's life and writings. Topics addressed include Nabokov as a storyteller, a Russian writer, a modernist, and a poet; also covered are his transition to writing in English and the reception of *Lolita*.

De la Durantaye, Leland. *Style Is Matter: The Moral Art of Vladimir Nabokov*. Ithaca, N.Y.: Cornell University Press, 2007. Focuses on *Lolita* but also looks at some of Nabokov's other works to discuss the ethics of art in Nabokov's fiction. Asserts that although some readers find Nabokov to be cruel, his works contain a moral message—albeit one that is skillfully hidden.

Field, Andrew. *VN: The Life and Art of Vladimir Nabokov*. 3d ed. New York: Crown, 1986. Critical biography recounts the events of Nabokov's life and places his works within personal and historical context. Includes discussion of *Lolita*, *Pale Fire*, *The Gift*, and other works.

Grayson, Jane, Arnold B. McMillin, and Priscilla Meyer, eds. *Nabokov's World: Reading Nabokov*. New York: Palgrave Macmillan, 2002.

_____. *Nabokov's World: The Shape of Nabokov's World*. New York: Palgrave Macmillan, 2002. Two-volume collection of essays written by an international group of Nabokov scholars provides comprehensive discussion of his work. Presents analyses of individual novels, including *Lolita*, as well as coverage of topics such as intertextuality in Nabokov's works and the literary reception of his writings.

Maddox, Lucy. *Nabokov's Novels in English*. Athens: University of Georgia Press, 1983. Interprets *Lolita* as an anatomy of an obsession, with Humbert romanticizing Lolita and America and discovering that both are flawed yet still endearing.

Nabokov, Vladimir. *The Annotated "Lolita."* Edited by Alfred Appel, Jr. Rev. ed. New York: Vintage Books, 1991. Presents the text of the novel accompanied by notes explaining the allusions and translating the French passages, with occasional comments by Nabokov. Also offers an informative editor's introduction.

Pifer, Ellen, ed. *Vladimir Nabokov's "Lolita": A Casebook*. New York: Oxford University Press, 2002. An interview with Nabokov and a collection of essays provide a range of approaches to the reading of *Lolita*, including discussions of the novel and the art of persuasion, the Americanization of Humbert Humbert, and *Lolita* and the poetry of advertising.

Vickers, Graham. *Chasing "Lolita": How Popular Culture Corrupted Nabokov's Little Girl All over Again.* Chicago: Chicago Review Press, 2008. Analyzes the sources of the Lolita character, the impact of the novel, and misunderstandings surrounding the character and the work. Examines film, stage, and other adaptations of the novel.

Wood, Michael. *The Magician's Doubts: Nabokov and the Risks of Fiction.* Princeton, N.J.: Princeton University Press, 1995. Close readings of Nabokov's works show the power and beauty of his language and the subtlety of his art. Chapter 5 examines the language of *Lolita*.

The Lone Ranger and Tonto Fistfight in Heaven

Author: Sherman Alexie (1966-   )
First published: 1993
Type of work: Short fiction
Type of plot: Realism and Magical Realism
Time of plot: 1976-1993
Locale: Spokane Indian Reservation and Spokane, Washington

Principal characters:
VICTOR POLATKIN, an American Indian, the main narrator
JUNIOR POLATKIN, his brother
THOMAS BUILDS-THE-FIRE, a storyteller
JAMES MANY HORSES, a terminal cancer patient
NORMA MANY HORSES, his wife

The Stories:

"Every Little Hurricane": Young Victor Polatkin recalls reservation hurricanes, watching fights and seeing an old American Indian man drown in a mud puddle. He also remembers the alcoholism enveloping his people. Victor also realizes that his drunken father and mother embody an unnamed hurricane deep enough to destroy everything.

"A Drug Called Tradition": A grown-up Victor, along with his brother Junior and Thomas Builds-the-Fire, a storyteller, experience a different Indian vision under the influence of a new drug. When Victor disavows the visions, Thomas walks away, both emotionally and physically. Later, spiritual guide Big Mom gives Victor a tiny drum as a "pager." Though he never uses it, the drum becomes his "only religion," which "fill[s] up the whole world."

"Because My Father Always Said He Was the Only Indian Who Saw Jimi Hendrix Play 'The Star Spangled Banner' at Woodstock": Though the music of famed guitarist Jimi Hendrix brings Victor closer to his father, their family trip to Hendrix's grave site signals the beginning of the end of his parents' marriage. Victor's father buys a motorcycle and eventually leaves the family, leaving Victor with only the imaginary sound of motorcycles and guitars.

"The Only Traffic Signal on the Reservation Doesn't Flash Red Anymore": Adrian and Victor talk about former reservation basketball heroes and wonder if Julius Windmaker will "make it." Julius had been taken away by tribal police officers and eventually became an alcoholic.

"Amusements": Victor and Sadie put a passed-out Indian on a roller coaster and laugh at the spectacle until the crowd disapproves. The man awakens, and the carny points to Victor as the culprit. While fleeing, Victor sees himself in the crazy mirrors, making him realize that he is "the Indian who offered up another Indian like some treaty."

"This Is What It Means to Say Phoenix, Arizona": Thomas Builds-the-Fire and Victor reunite, recalling their sometimes violent history. Thomas reveals his reason for helping Victor retrieve Victor's father's ashes from Phoenix: Since childhood in Spokane, Thomas had been waiting for a vision, which Victor's father inspired by saying "Take care of each other." Later, when Victor gives Thomas part of the ashes in recompense, Thomas vows to toss them in Spokane Falls so that Victor's father will ascend like a salmon, for "'Nothing stops, cousin.'"

"The Fun House": Victor's aunt swims naked in Tshimikain Creek. No one had helped her after a mouse had crawled up her pants. Returning to the house, she dons the full-length beaded dress that is too heavy for anyone else to wear and begins to dance, taking control of her life.

"All I Wanted to Do Was Dance": To get over the white woman who left him, Victor drinks incessantly until he meets a Cherokee celebrating his birthday. The Cherokee says there is one way to tell a true Indian from a fake one: "The real Indian got blisters on his feet. The fake Indian got blisters on his ass," alluding to the Trail of Tears.

"The Trial of Thomas Builds-the-Fire": During his trial for a manufactured offense, Thomas Builds-the-Fire breaks a twenty-year silence. His testimony morphs from story to story, all about the Spokane Indian past. Upon cross-examination, he becomes Wild Coyote, in his first battle, and regrettably recounts killing two of Steptoe's soldiers. Thomas receives two concurrent life sentences in prison in Walla Walla, Washington.

"Distances": All the whites are dead. Urban Indians all suffer from a disease that makes their skin and limbs fall off. The Others, returning from one thousand years ago, kill the Urban Indians. Although technology is taboo, the narrator increases the volume on the radio to hear only the sound of his own breathing.

"Jesus Christ's Half-Brother Is Alive and Well on the Spokane Indian Reservation": James had been orphaned in a house fire. Unable to speak, he becomes the "religion" of his alcoholic foster father. After almost losing James because of his alcoholism, the father endures the ravages of delirium tremens to keep his son. When James finally "speaks," he tells his father that they do not have the right to die for each other, only to live for each other.

"A Train Is an Order of Occurrence Designed to Lead to Some Result": Thomas Builds-the-Fire is fired from his job at a motel. Depressed, he goes into a bar. He had resisted drinking before, knowing that alcohol will negate the power of his stories, which lead others to better lives. Pushed out of the bar at closing time, he stumbles onto the railroad tracks in the path of an oncoming train.

"Imagining the Reservation": Harsh realities abound on the reservation, and so does bitterness. Dreams, hope, and the possibilities of survival exist, too. Laughter can save one's life, and stories can "put wood in the fireplace."

"The Approximate Size of My Favorite Tumor": James Many Horses, suffering from terminal cancer, deals with the emotional pain through humor. After too many jokes, his wife, Norma Many Horses, leaves him. A few months later, James is home from the hospital. Norma returns home after abandoning her too-serious lover to help James die.

"Somebody Kept Saying Powwow": When Junior Polatkin tells Norma Many Horses, the "cultural lifeguard" of the tribe, the story of ganging up with a bunch of white boys in college to beat up a reformed convict, Norma calls him another Pete Rose—always to be known for one bad thing. On a strange day, when a bear goes to sleep on the church roof, she forgives Junior.

"Witnesses, Secret or Not": Junior goes with his father to Spokane for his annual interrogation about the disappearance of Jerry Vincent. When the detective asks the father if Vincent had been his friend, father replies "He still is." Traveling home, father and son reflect on the metamorphosis that the disappeared undergo in the psyches of the living.

Critical Evaluation:

Sherman Alexie is a Spokane Coeur d'Alene American Indian whose work reveals the limitations of not only reservation life but also the white urban lifestyle. As he exposes the cultural bankruptcy of reservation life he also exhibits the potential of its people. *The Lone Ranger and Tonto Fistfight in Heaven* achieves a high moral aim by reflecting back the stereotypes of Indians in ironic ways, exposing oppression, exploitation, and self-victimization. In telling these stories, Alexie has received some criticism by those who feel he trades on stereotypes.

Victor Polatkin, for example, who begins the collection with his realization of the destructive impulses of the people around him, comes to an epiphany (albeit an enigmatic and open-ended epiphany) by the end of "This Is What It Means to Say Phoenix, Arizona." While old Indians drown in mud puddles and women are sterilized by the U.S. Bureau of Indian Affairs immediately after the births of their children, "The First Annual All-Indian Horseshoe Pitch and Barbecue" and "Imagining the Reservation" end positively with the beauty of the half-white, half-Indian baby and the affirmation that imagination "turns every word into a bottle rocket."

In this collection, Alexie plays off the Indian trickster tradition as well as the storyteller tradition, occasionally ironically (as with the character Thomas Builds-the-Fire, whom no one wants to listen to). Frequently, Alexie provides no clear ending to a given story.

Alexie won a PEN/Hemingway Award in 1993 for Best First Book of Fiction for *The Lone Ranger and Tonto Fistfight in Heaven*, and has received numerous other awards, including the 2007 National Book Award, Young People's Literature, for *The Absolutely True Diary of a Part-Time Indian* (2007). The film *Smoke Signals* (1999), which was written by Alexie, is based on stories from *The Lone Ranger and Tonto Fistfight in Heaven*, primarily "This is What It Means to Say Phoenix, Arizona."

Jaquelyn Weeks Walsh

Further Reading

Dix, Andrew. "Escape Stories: Narratives and Native Americans in Sherman Alexie's *The Lone Ranger and Tonto Fistfight in Heaven*." *Yearbook of English Studies* 31 (2001): 155-167. Discovers in Alexie's style a commentary on the marginality of American Indians in contrast to the U.S. metanarrative of dominance.

Grassian, Daniel. *Understanding Sherman Alexie*. Columbia: University of South Carolina Press, 2005. The first book-length work offering commentary on Alexie's fiction and poetry, with ample attention to reviews and other published discussions of his writings. Provides biographical details as well as analysis and interpretation of the poetry and short stories through 2004.

James, Meredith K. *Literary and Cinematic Reservation in Selected Works of Native American Author Sherman Alexie*. Lewiston, N.Y.: Edwin Mellen Press, 2005. James discusses the concept "reservation of the mind" in the work of Alexie, with significant reference to other contemporary American Indian authors Louise Erdrich, N. Scott Momaday, and Leslie Marmon Silko. Also examines how Alexie conveys the effects of federal Indian policy and popular culture stereotypes of Indians on contemporary Indian life.

Low, Denise. Review of *The Lone Ranger and Tonto Fistfight in Heaven*, by Sherman Alexie. *American Indian Quarterly* 20, no. 1 (Winter, 1996): 123-125. In examining Alexie's work through a postmodern lens, Low discusses his characters and rhetorical strategies in *The Lone Ranger and Tonto Fistfight in Heaven* and in his poetry-short story collection *The Business of Fancydancing* (1992).

Lundquist, Suzanne Evertsen. *Native American Literatures: An Introduction*. New York: Continuum, 2004. The section on Alexie includes summaries of important critiques of his work that question his representation of American Indian cultural values and reservation life as well as issues of hybridity and essentialism.

McFarland, Ron. "Sherman Alexie's Polemic Stories." *Studies in American Indian Literature* 9, no. 4 (Winter, 1997): 27-38. McFarland notes that Alexie's stories are voices of Indian America as well as comments upon it. Argues that Alexie is a narrative polemicist.

Millard, Kenneth. *Contemporary American Fiction: An Introduction to American Fiction Since 1970*. New York: Oxford University Press, 2000. Includes analyses of the expansive possibilities of the imagination over the restrictive physical boundaries of the Indian reservation and the stultifying white urban culture.

The Lonely Passion of Judith Hearne

Author: Brian Moore (1921-1999)
First published: 1955, as *Judith Hearne*
Type of work: Novel
Type of plot: Social realism
Time of plot: 1950's
Locale: Belfast, Northern Ireland

Principal characters:
JUDITH HEARNE, an unmarried woman in her forties
MRS. HENRY RICE, her landlady
BERNARD, her landlady's son
JAMES MADDEN, her landlady's brother
AUNT D'ARCY, her deceased aunt
FATHER QUIGLEY, her parish priest
MOIRA O'NEILL, her friend
EDIE MARRINAN, an acquaintance

The Story:

Judith Hearne takes a room at a boardinghouse run by Mrs. Henry Rice, a widow. It is located on Camden Street, a rundown Belfast neighborhood that was once middle class, tidy, and secure. Judith places a photograph of the dead aunt who raised her on the mantelpiece and prepares to hang a print of the Sacred Heart above the bed to make the room seem homier.

Judith visits Mrs. Rice's quarters. There, she meets Bernard, Mrs. Rice's adult son. Bernard is an only child, as well as an unemployed university graduate and aspiring poet. Tirelessly pampered by his seemingly devout mother, Bernard nonetheless holds subversive religious views. Judith finds him and his ideas both intriguing and repulsive. They gossip about mutual acquaintances, the pastoral temperament of the parish priest, and Mary, the country girl Mrs. Rice has hired to help around the boardinghouse. Hearne returns to her room with a borrowed hammer to hang the Sacred Heart icon and prepares for sleep without supper.

Judith wakes wondering how she will spend the coming days. As she ritualistically washes up and brushes her hair before a mirror, she considers options for cheap dining, what she will wear, and how she will conduct herself at breakfast. She daydreams about the impression her jewelry and black-and-red dress will make. Once ready, she enters the breakfast parlor and sits down among her fellow lodgers. She is disappointed to discover that breakfast consists only of toast and tea, a discovery that affects her lunch and supper plans for the foreseeable future.

Mrs. Rice introduces Judith to the other guests, including James Madden. Madden, Mrs. Rice's brother, has recently returned from the United States, where he lived and worked for thirty years. He impresses Judith with his talk of life in New York City. Judith assumes Madden is a man of means, and she silently resolves to learn more about the storied metropolis so she will have something to discuss with him to further their acquaintance.

Judith settles into life at the boardinghouse by maintaining a regular routine of teaching piano a few days a week, going to Mass, and attending Sunday teas at the O'Neills'. Moira O'Neill attended finishing school with Judith. She married well and now has several school-age children, who mock Judith's appearance and mannerisms before she arrives each Sunday afternoon. Judith also begins socializing with James Madden. Madden suspects Judith has money, and he is eager to go into business with her. Judith interprets his proposed venture as proof of romantic interest.

Eventually, Judith learns the truth about Madden's working-class past and the real reasons for his attentions. In despair, she drinks a bottle of whiskey reserved for medicinal purposes and disrupts life at the boardinghouse by loudly singing in her room throughout the night. To her shame, Judith later learns of the disturbance. What remains hidden from her is the fact that Bernard has been having a sexual affair with Mary, the house girl, and that Madden has caught them together. Angered and aroused by his nephew's dalliance, Madden rapes Mary.

Judith's life begins to unravel as her social routine disintegrates. She loses her last piano student, Madden avoids her, and the O'Neills become distant. She drinks nightly and begins to doubt her religious beliefs. She seeks guidance from Father Quigley in the confessional, but he simply advises her to pray. She sinks deeper into depression and seeks consolation in more drink.

Mrs. Rice evicts Judith from the boardinghouse. She withdraws almost all of her savings, rents a room at a posh hotel, buys several bottles of expensive spirits, and visits Edie Marrinan, a past acquaintance who gave Judith her first drink and now lies dying in a convalescent home run by a religious order. Judith and Edie attempt to drink a bottle of gin in the ward. The nuns caring for the institutionalized women forcibly remove Judith, who then seeks solace with Moira O'Neill. During their conversation, Judith realizes that Moira's friendship is based on pity, not fellow feeling, and she leaves to seek more genuine compassion from Father Quigley. As before, though, the priest exhibits little patience for Judith's situation and tells her to return only after she sobers up.

Despondent and drunk, Judith enters the church next to the rectory and loudly denounces God in the sanctuary. Stunned that she has not been struck dead for her blasphemy, Judith runs to the tabernacle where the Eucharist resides and, screaming, tears at the small golden doors until her fingers bleed. She blacks out.

The O'Neills institutionalize Judith. She receives several visitors—including various O'Neills, Father Quigley, and Aunt D'Arcy's former physician—who attempt to cheer her with offers of friendship or encourage her to seek comfort in religious practice. Mistrustful of her social connections and her faith, Judith remains despondent. Finally, told her stay needs to be extended, Judith asks one of her caretakers to display Aunt D'Arcy's portrait and the Sacred Heart picture in her room. The book closes as it opened, with Judith contemplating these images.

Critical Evaluation:

Published in Britain in 1955 as *Judith Hearne* and in North America under its current title, Brian Moore's novel impressed early reviewers and readers with its gritty, unsparing portrayal of Judith Hearne's breakdown in the drab confines of Belfast. Arguably, the novel's core theme is the dehumanization sponsored by social conventions and how individuals sometimes use these conventions to aggrandize themselves at the expense of others. In the end, almost all of the primary characters reveal themselves as capable of self-delusion or a mean-spiritedness that can be justified by referencing social or religious conventions. Moore reinforces these ideas throughout the novel with his subtle and often ironic use of images and narrative technique.

A notion often explored by critics is the connection between Judith's disintegration and the city's brutalizing urban environment. As well as providing protection from the constant rain, which further magnifies the city's dreariness, Judith's ubiquitous red raincoat becomes a symbol of her view of herself as vital and voluptuous, a self-perception continually compromised by her plainness and provincialism. In addition, Judith is perpetually cold and drawn to heat, especially to open fires, suggesting that her loneliness is physically palpable and that whatever comfort relieves her is at best intense, temporary, and almost impossible to find in the gray, maze-like streets of Belfast.

Moore uses his narrative to elaborate the ironic dissonance between the title character's viewpoint and others' perceptions of her by fluidly transitioning between Judith's outward speech and behavior and her internal thoughts and feelings. This technique allows the author to reveal emotional realities that exist behind the sometimes intricate social formalities that govern all of Judith's relationships. Because she has no one with whom to share her most intimate thoughts and feelings, all of her interactions must occur on superficial levels. For example, even her dearest and oldest friendship—with Moira O'Neill—is based on habit. When Judith admits to Moira that she has never liked her, it is both a relief and a devastating recognition. She no longer has to convince herself of her favorable status among the O'Neills, yet she must also acknowledge years of personal investment in a sham relationship. Likewise, Bernard's frank atheism is both attractive and repulsive to Judith because it expresses her own existential doubts but undercuts the religious and social conventions that have shaped her life.

Chapter 6 departs from the narrative that weaves Judith's exterior and interior realities. In it, the five characters affiliated with the boardinghouse, Lenehan, Miss Friel, Mary, Mrs. Rice, and Bernard, speak in their own voices to reveal their respective views of the title character. This chapter occurs before Judith's breakdown is set in motion by the revelations that Madden worked as a day laborer and doorman while in America and that his interest in her is strictly economic. While these disclosures and the shame of being romantically duped ultimately drive Judith to drink, testimony from the boardinghouse lodgers further emphasizes the disparity between people's thoughts and actions, especially as concerns the title character's assumptions about how others see her. Though Judith suspects that they take collective glee in her misfortune, Madden is the primary target of the guests' muckraking, implying that Judith is so isolated and insignificant that she is upstaged even in her own private dramas.

Many critics have written about religious themes in *The Lonely Passion of Judith Hearne*. Time after time, the agents and practices of the Catholic Church fail to help Judith (or any other character) in a meaningful way. Bernard's criticism of Judith's faith and of the Church is rooted in his belief that

religion is empty and that its symbols and rituals only obscure this truth. At the novel's conclusion, Judith considers this idea as she gazes upon her print of the Sacred Heart. She ultimately affirms that even if this picture simply serves to put a face on nothing, it is still part of her. Though ambiguous, this episode is important because Judith does not attempt to weigh her existence, sad and lonely as it is, against any unreachable expectation or imbue it with any significance it does not have.

J. Greg Matthews

Further Reading

Craig, Patricia. *Brian Moore: A Biography*. London: Bloomsbury, 2002. This account of Moore's complicated life avoids analysis and adheres to dates and events. Moore's relationships with his mother, sisters, and wives bear special relevance to the portrayal of women in his work.

Dahlie, Hallvard. *Brian Moore*. Studies in Canadian Literature 2. Toronto, Ont.: Copp Clark, 1969. This modest yet thorough analysis of Moore's first six novels devotes a chapter to *The Lonely Passion of Judith Hearne*. Illuminates the novel's main themes by considering them in the larger context of subsequent works. Concludes with valuable bibliographical citations to contemporary reviews and early criticism.

_____. *Brian Moore*. Boston: Twayne, 1981. An excellent introduction to Moore's fiction. Draws compelling parallels between Moore's and James Joyce's works and careers. Chapter 3 presents historical perspectives on *The Lonely Passion of Judith Hearne*'s growing critical significance since its 1955 publication.

Foster, John Wilson. "Passage Through Limbo." In *Forces and Themes in Ulster Fiction*. Totowa, N.J.: Rowman and Littlefield, 1974. Foster's widely cited study devotes a chapter to Moore's place and status in the history of Northern Irish fiction. Foster argues that the social dislocation Judith Hearne experiences as a rural woman thrust into a dehumanizing urban setting is further complicated by her increasingly eroded religious faith and burgeoning sexual frustration.

Green, Robert. "Brian Moore's *Judith Hearne*: Celebrating the Commonplace." *International Fiction Review* 7, no. 1 (Winter, 1980): 29-33. A concise examination of literary and biographical influences on the novel, this brief essay focuses on Moore's acknowledged debt to *Madame Bovary* (1857; English translation, 1886) as a model for *The Lonely Passion of Judith Hearne*. Suggests that Moore's status as an Irish writer living and working in

Canada shaped his characterization of Judith's own isolation.

Hicks, Patrick. *Brian Moore and the Meaning of the Past: An Irish Novelist Reimagines History*. Lewiston, N.Y.: Edwin Mellen Press, 2007. Sees Moore as intervening in historical discourse from the timeless point of view of Irish culture (within which there seems to be no history, only current events), as well as from spaces that seem to have no history.

O'Donoghue, Jo. *Brian Moore: A Critical Study*. Montreal: McGill-Queen's University Press, 1991. Uses selected works to consider Moore's evolving religious sensibilities. The excellent essay on *The Lonely Passion of Judith Hearne*, "Religion Without Belief," demonstrates how Moore's narrative techniques in the novel convey and reinforce Judith's victimization by the Catholic Church and by the faithful with whom she interacts.

_____. "'A Pox on Both Their Houses': Post-Colonial Religious Conflict in the Belfast Novels of Brian Moore." In *"And the Birds Began to Sing": Religion and Literature in Post-Colonial Cultures*, edited by Jamie S. Scott. Amsterdam: Rodopi, 1996. Explores the religious dimensions of Moore's fiction set in Belfast and convincingly argues that Judith's initial religious pretensions provide an ironic counterpoint to her deepening sense of social inferiority later in the novel. Sees these insecurities as ultimately undermining even her formerly stabilizing feelings of religious superiority.

Sampson, Denis. *Brian Moore: The Chameleon Novelist*. Dublin: Marino, 1998. Sampson utilizes Moore's correspondence and personal writings to provide real-life contexts for his fiction. Judith Hearne, for example, was largely based on Miss Keogh, a Moore family acquaintance.

Sullivan, Robert. *A Matter of Faith: The Fiction of Brian Moore*. Contributions to the Study of World Literature 69. Westport, Conn.: Greenwood Press, 1996. Traces Moore's handling of the theme of religious faith in selected novels. Compares Judith Hearne to other Moore protagonists.

Lonesome Dove

Author: Larry McMurtry (1936-   )
First published: 1985
Type of work: Novel
Type of plot: Western
Time of plot: Late 1870's
Locale: Texas, Nebraska, Montana, and adjoining states

Principal characters:
AUGUSTUS "GUS" MCCRAE and WOODROW F. CALL, former Texas Rangers and co-owners of the Hat Creek Cattle Company
JAKE SPOON, a former Texas Ranger, now a gambler
JOSH DEETS, an expert scout
PEA EYE PARKER, a former corporal in the Rangers
NEWT DOBBS, the illegitimate son of Call and a prostitute
BOLIVAR, a cook
LORENA WOOD, a prostitute
CLARA ALLEN, McCrae's great love
DISH (DISHWATER) BOGGETT, a cowboy
BLUE DUCK, a murderer and thief
JULY JOHNSON, a sheriff
ELMIRA JOHNSON, his wife
JOE BOOT, Elmira's son
ROSCOE BROWN, July's deputy
JANEY, an orphan
PO CAMPO, a cook

Lonesome Dove / MCMURTRY

The Story:

In the small town of Lonesome Dove on the Rio Grande, Woodrow Call and Augustus McCrae have retired from the Texas Rangers and begun the Hat Creek Cattle Company. Their employees include Pea Eye Parker, Josh Deets, the cook Bolivar, and the seventeen-year-old Newt Dobbs. Jake Spoon, a former Ranger who worked with Call and McCrae, suddenly appears and praises Montana as a cattleman's paradise, inspiring Call to make the first drive of cattle from Texas to Montana. Jake is on the run from Fort Smith, Arkansas, where he accidentally killed the sheriff's brother.

In the town of Lonesome Dove, the Dry Bean saloon provides the only entertainment. Owned by Xavier Wanz, it employs Lippy as the piano player and Lorena Wood as a prostitute. Dish Boggett, a top-hand cowboy, falls in love with Lorena and hires on with the Hat Creek outfit. While gathering cattle and horses in Mexico for the drive to Montana, Call finds two lost Irishmen, Allen and Sean O'Brien, who are subsequently hired along with other cowboys.

Jake begins to live with Lorena, who is convinced that he will take her to San Francisco. Against Call's wishes, Jake and Lorena follow the herd north, camping nearby. On the drive, Gus is followed by two pigs, and he brings the sign he made for the company, which features the Latin motto *uva uvam vivendo varia fit* (a corruption of a line attributed to Juvenal originally meaning "a grape ripens when it sees another grape"). Gus is motivated by a desire to reunite with his one great love, Clara Allen, who has married and lives near Ogallala, Nebraska.

In Fort Smith, sheriff July Johnson sets off after Jake Spoon. July has recently married Elmira, who has a twelve-year-old son, Joe. Elmira has lied to July, telling him that Joe's father, Dee Boot, is dead. She convinces July to take Joe with him to Texas. After they leave, Elmira boards a whiskey boat to search for Dee. Roscoe Brown, July's deputy, reluctantly follows July to tell him that Elmira has run off. Roscoe meets an orphan girl, Janey, who then accompanies him. Elmira attracts an admirer, a buffalo hunter named Big Zwey.

While the Hat Creek group is crossing the Nueces River with the herd, Sean O'Brien is killed by water moccasins. With Lorena, Gus encounters Blue Duck, a notorious outlaw, but he does not shoot him. After Bolivar quits the drive and heads back to Lonesome Dove, Call hires Po Campo as the new cook. Gus sends Newt to guard Lorena, but Blue Duck kidnaps her. Gus pursues them, refusing to take Jake with him. July and Joe run into Roscoe and Janey.

Gus catches up to the men holding Lorena. She has been raped and beaten. Blue Duck sends his men to kill the trailing Gus, but Gus shoots a number of them and the rest retreat.

July, Roscoe, Joe, and Janey meet Gus, and July insists on accompanying Gus to rescue Lorena. Blue Duck eludes them, killing Roscoe, Joe, and Janey. Gus shoots Lorena's remaining captors and takes her to rejoin the Hat Creek drive; July pursues Elmira.

Jake begins to ride with a gang of thieves and murderers. He kills the husband of a pretty girl with whom he was flirting. The bloodthirsty Dan Suggs leads the gang on a murderous rampage, during which they also steal horses. Call, Gus, Deets, and Newt track the gang, soon catching them. Call and Gus hang the three Suggs brothers and Jake.

Near Ogallala, Elmira stops at Clara Allen's horse ranch and gives birth to a son. Leaving her child behind, Elmira finds Dee in Ogallala, where he has been jailed and will be hanged for murder. At Clara's ranch, July discovers his son, and he locates Elmira in town. Elmira flees again, but July decides not to chase her. He learns later that she and Zwey were killed by Indians.

In Ogallala, an Army scout tries to take Dish's horse; he lashes Newt, who refuses to let go of the animal. Call severely beats the scout. Newt and some of the other boys buy sex from prostitutes. Gus brings Call, Lorena, and Newt to Clara's ranch. Gus and Clara do not rekindle their love affair, in part because Clara's husband is still alive—although he has been kicked by a horse and rendered comatose. Lorena, taken with Clara, her two daughters, and July's son, decides to stay on the ranch, while the Hat Creek outfit continues the drive. Gus tells Newt that Call is his father.

The men and livestock survive an 80-mile stretch without water. Call, Gus, and Deets track Indians who have stolen some of their horses. At the Indians' camp, Deets is killed by a boy with a lance. In Montana, the Texas bull that has been leading the herd fights a grizzly bear to a draw. While on scout duty with Pea Eye, Gus is wounded by Indians whom the men stand off in a creek bed. When a rainstorm fills the creek, Pea Eye swims away and sets off on foot for help. On his walk, Pea Eye sees Deets's ghost and is eventually found by his living companions.

Gus manages to make it to Miles City. A doctor amputates one of his legs, but Gus refuses to let him amputate the other, though he knows that he will die otherwise. Call finds Gus but cannot talk him into the other amputation. Before he dies, Gus elicits a promise from Call that he will take Gus's body back to Texas to be buried. Call establishes a ranch between the Missouri and Milk rivers. Dish quits and returns to Nebraska and Lorena.

In the spring, Call puts Newt in charge of the ranch; however, he is unable tell Newt that he is his father. Retrieving

Gus's body, Call sets out for Texas. At her ranch, Clara cannot convince Call to bury Gus there, and she expresses her full scorn for Call. In New Mexico, Call stops to see Blue Duck hanged, but the outlaw throws himself out of a third-story window to cheat the gallows. Dragging Gus's body on the Hat Creek sign, Call finally arrives at the spot on the Guadalupe River where Gus wanted to be buried. To mark Gus's grave, Call uses the remaining portion of the sign, which shows only the company's name. Call returns to Lonesome Dove to find Bolivar living there. He also discovers that, for desperate love of Lorena, Xavier Wanz burned himself to death in the Dry Bean.

Critical Evaluation:

Larry McMurtry is the author of numerous novels set in the American West, including four that feature Augustus McCrae and Woodrow Call. Ordered chronologically according to the events these novels depict, they are *Dead Man's Walk* (1995), *Comanche Moon* (1997), *Lonesome Dove*, and *Streets of Laredo* (1993). Enjoying tremendous popularity, *Lonesome Dove* is the best of these novels and was awarded the Pulitzer Prize in fiction in 1986. In 1989, the novel was made into a television miniseries that starred Robert Duvall as McCrae and Tommy Lee Jones as Call.

Though *Lonesome Dove* is often labeled a Western, critics debate the extent of its allegiance to the conventions and themes of that genre. Because it does not wholly embrace or reject the myths of the Old West, the novel is difficult to categorize as either traditional or revisionist. The characters of McCrae and Call exemplify the impassive violence of real-life Texas Rangers, as well as the human decency and honorable codes of fictional Western heroes. At nearly 850 pages, the novel might have sprawled, but intersections among characters and convergences of plot lines keep the story tightly knit.

The novel tells an adventure story and features a number of characters on various romantic quests, and critics have noted McMurtry's debt to Miguel de Cervantes' *Don Quixote de la Mancha* (1605, 1615). In addition, it is a study of character in action. In a way similar to novels by Charles Dickens and George Eliot, *Lonesome Dove* centers on a large cast of characters whose lives intersect as they live and work together. The town of Lonesome Dove, the Hat Creek Cattle Company, and the Western plains from northern Mexico to Texas to Montana become the loci of the characters' interactions.

Most often, McMurtry's characters act according to the dictates of their natures. Jake Spoon, for example, takes up with murderers because he is an aimless pleasure seeker.

Acting in his natural role as caretaker, Deets is killed while trying to protect a blind Indian child. Driven to control all personal weakness, which for him includes sexual desire, Call cannot admit he is Newt's father. The version of the Latin motto that Gus carves on the company's sign has been translated as "a grape is changed by living with other grapes," suggesting for certain critics the novel's central theme that a person's character may most positively develop when in contact with others.

Newt and, surprisingly, Call change the most over the course of the novel. Among the work's many plot lines is Newt's growing maturity, representing a bildungsroman among numerous plots of decline. By novel's end, Newt is an accomplished cowboy, a natural tamer of horses, and a promising leader, though he is also self-isolating. Call, seemingly the most static of the characters, also changes. Gus's death leaves him bereft, and he begins to doubt the certainty of his actions. This man of action—a staple of American adventure stories—is ultimately depicted as vulnerable.

Indeed, melancholy pervades *Lonesome Dove*. Although it features the tenaciously cheerful Gus McCrae, who generates much of the novel's humor, the book repeatedly dramatizes loss and longing. The relentless passage of time, the inevitability of death, and the inexplicable meanderings of the heart leave most of the characters suffering from the ache of sorrow. The nineteenth century American West portrayed in *Lonesome Dove* thus feels contemporary, for it is a place less of national glory attained than of personal trials endured.

Scott D. Emmert

Further Reading

Birchfield, D. L. "*Lonesome Duck*: The Blueing of Texas-American Myth." *Studies in American Indian Literatures* 7, no. 2 (Summer, 1995): 45-64. Criticizes *Lonesome Dove* for its elision of the historical reality of the brutal treatment of Native Americans by Texans, including Texas Rangers.

Daigrepont, Lloyd M. "Passion, Romance, and *Agape* in Larry McMurtry's *Lonesome Dove*." *Lamar Journal of the Humanities* 30, no. 2 (Fall, 2005): 43-61. Examines the characters' doomed search for transformation through love.

Kiefer, Christian. "Unneighborly Behavior: *Blood Meridian*, *Lonesome Dove*, and the Problem of Reader Sympathy." *Southwestern American Literature* 33, no. 1 (Fall, 2007): 39-52. Compares *Lonesome Dove* with Cormac McCarthy's *Blood Meridian*, also published in 1985; concludes that *Lonesome Dove* is more comforting to readers' sensibilities because it is more traditional, romantic, and morally certain than McCarthy's work.

Miller-Purrenhage, John. "'Kin to Nobody': The Disruption of Genealogy in Larry McMurtry's *Lonesome Dove.*" *Studies in Contemporary Fiction* 47, no. 1 (Fall, 2005): 73-89. Considers the disruptions in familial relationships among the characters to argue that the novel rejects the myth of the American West as a coherent narrative of national identity.

Reynolds, Clay, ed. *Taking Stock: A Larry McMurtry Casebook*. Dallas, Tex.: Southern Methodist University Press, 1989. Collection of previously published and original articles considering McMurtry's fiction and essays through 1988. Several articles focus on *Lonesome Dove*, linking it to McMurtry's lifelong themes and to established ideas on the American West. An extensive bibliography also lists criticism of film adaptations of McMurtry's novels, including the 1989 adaptation of *Lonesome Dove.*

Ronald, Ann. "Company for a *Lonesome Dove.*" In *Reader of the Purple Sage: Essays on Western Writers and Environmental Literature*. Reno: University of Nevada Press, 2003. Assesses the novel's use of established Western plot and character elements to judge its reputation against those of other novels in the genre.

A Long and Happy Life

Author: Reynolds Price (1933-   )
First published: 1962
Type of work: Novel
Type of plot: Domestic realism
Time of plot: 1957
Locale: Afton, near Warrenton, North Carolina

Principal characters:
ROSACOKE MUSTIAN, a young woman
WESLEY BEAVERS, the object of her love
EMMA MUSTIAN, Rosacoke's mother
MILO, Rosacoke's older brother
BABY SISTER, Rosacoke's younger sister
SISSIE, Milo's wife
MILDRED SUTTON, a young African American woman who has just died
WILLIE DUKE AYCOCK, Rosacoke's rival
HEYWOOD BETTS, Willie Duke's boyfriend

The Story:

Rosacoke Mustian is striving to win Wesley Beavers as her lover. They are both riding on Wesley's motorcycle to the funeral of Mildred Sutton, a young African American woman and Rosacoke's lifelong friend. Bored with following the funeral procession, Wesley revs his bike and speeds ahead of the rest of the procession to the local African American church in rural Warren County, North Carolina. Once they arrive at the church, Wesley ignores Rosacoke completely and turns to work on his motorcycle as she walks into the church to wait for the others to arrive and for the funeral to begin.

At the funeral, Rosacoke is entirely preoccupied with Wesley, looking out the church window constantly to keep an eye on his movements. When the preacher asks Rosacoke to say a few words about her friend, Mildred, she is so distracted by Wesley's revving of his bike's engine that she falters in her eulogy, disappointing Mildred's family and friends. Wesley roars off on his bike from the church's dirt lot and disappears down the road, leaving Rosacoke behind in the church. Rosacoke wanders off after him. Her journey takes her into the familiar woods where she and Mildred once went walking. As she walks through them, she recalls being there in the past.

In flashback, Mildred and Rosacoke discover a clear spring in the woods and stumble upon a young deer, a sign of innocence and mystery. While Rosacoke is staring at the spring, she hears footsteps and hides. Peering out from the trees, she sees Wesley and comes out of the woods to meet him. After a brief conversation between the innocent Rosacoke and the experienced Wesley, the two hop on Wesley's motorcycle and ride off to a Sunday afternoon picnic where they join Rosacoke's family and a few friends. After everyone else leaves, Rosacoke and Wesley find themselves alone, and Wesley attempts to seduce Rosacoke, unsuccessfully.

Disappointed by her lack of willingness to have sex with him, Wesley recklessly drives Rosacoke back to her house on his motorcycle. He soon goes off to Norfolk, where he sells motorcycles and sleeps with multiple women. Mistaking his desire for her as the evidence of his incipient love for her, Rosacoke writes him several letters, telling him about life in their little town and also searching for some clue about his feelings for her. When she finally does hear from him, it is in the form of a short letter that does not answer any of her probing questions.

Rosacoke goes about everyday life in Afton. She helps her brother prepare for his wife's pregnancy; visits Sammy, the caretaker of the elderly Mr. Isaacs, the town's wealthy landowner; pays calls on Mary, Mildred Sutton's mother; and attempts to help care for Mildred's baby. She ponders ways that she can catch Wesley and hold onto him. Wesley remains in Norfolk; he does not contact Rosacoke further after his short letter to her.

Not long before Thanksgiving, Wesley returns to Afton with Willie Duke Aycock—likely a former lover—and her fiancé, Heywood Betts. The townsfolk note Wesley's return: They ask Rosacoke at church whether she has seen him and ask her good-naturedly when they are getting married. However, Wesley never contacts Rosacoke. When her young sister, Baby Sister, sees Betts's plane flying toward Norfolk, she yells out to Rosacoke that there are three people in it. Restless and curious, Rosacoke walks over to Mary's house, which is near the Beaverses' house, ostensibly to take some pictures of Mildred's baby. As she walks up to Wesley's house, she spies Wesley standing on the porch playing the harmonica.

Still deeply attracted to Wesley, Rosacoke accepts a ride home from him. This time, however, they do not roar off on his motorcycle but take his mother's car. Rosacoke silently asks for a sign that she should give herself to him. When Wesley turns the car to take the long way home through Mr. Isaac's woods, she has her first sign. When a buck and his fawns dash across the road in front of them, she has her second sign. Rosacoke suggests that they follow the deer into the woods to see if the deer are fording the stream. After finally locating the deer and watching them in silence, Rosacoke makes her decision to sleep with Wesley. Wesley leads her to a field of broomstraw—similar to the one where she and Mildred saw the deer years earlier—and Rosacoke gives the gift of her virginity to Wesley, convinced that she can now hold him in Afton with her. However, when Wesley thanks another woman by name as he climaxes, Rosacoke turns cold. She knows immediately and intimately that she has been mistaken and that she does not want to hold Wesley.

Wesley returns to Norfolk. Shortly afterward, he writes to Rosacoke, inviting her to come spend Thanksgiving with him and intimating their days will be full of sex and pleasure. Rosacoke writes him a brief letter declining his invitation, but she never mails it.

A few days later, Milo's wife, Sissie, goes into labor, and her child dies during birth. Distraught and unable to face the death of his child and the distress and anxiety of his wife, Milo leaves home to drive to Raleigh to buy candy for Mr. Isaac. Rosacoke agrees to go with him, but as they drive past Mr. Isaac's pecan grove—where Rosacoke first laid eyes on Wesley and fell in love with him—it hits her square in the chest that she is pregnant with Wesley's child. When Milo suggests that they stop to shake down some pecans, Rosacoke refuses and insists that Milo take her back home. Perplexed and angry, Milo drives her home. Rosacoke writes Wesley a letter telling him that the coast is not clear for him to return (her way of announcing to him she is pregnant). She wants him to know in case he wants to change his plans for Christmas vacation and not come home. She assures him that she cannot blame him if he does not show up, since she holds herself responsible for what she has done.

As the Christmas holidays approach, everyone in the Delight Baptist Church is preparing for the church's annual Christmas pageant. Willie Duke was supposed to play Mary in the pageant, but she has eloped. After some argument about who might step into Willie's place, Rosacoke reluctantly agrees to take the role. Prior to the pageant, she and Wesley argue about their future together. Although he received her letter informing him of her pregnancy, he at first refused to believe it. It is only now starting to dawn on him that he may have to marry Rosacoke.

Wesley urges Rosacoke to go away with him to Dillon, South Carolina, just across the North Carolina border, to marry. She refuses to elope with him, for she fears a future sitting alone in a rented room, caring for a sick baby, eating Post Toasties, and staring out at concrete roads. She does not want to involve Wesley in something for which she alone feels responsible. As Rosacoke participates in the pageant, she recognizes the power of giving gifts, the strength of unbounded love, and the pull of her duty to herself and Wesley. By the end of the pageant, Rosacoke decides to say "Yes" if Wesley asks her to elope to Dillon, realizing not only that he holds her like a chain but also that she wishes it.

Critical Evaluation:

Much like Katherine Anne Porter's Miranda stories and Caroline Gordon's and Eudora Welty's writings about the coming-of-age of young women in pastoral yet treacherous settings in the South, Reynolds Price's first novel explores the slow loss of innocence and the weariness of experience that accompanies such loss. Rosacoke Mustian is one of a long literary line of young Southern women, including Janie in Zora Neale Hurston's *Their Eyes Were Watching God* (1937), Celie in Alice Walker's *The Color Purple* (1982), Mary Faith Rapple in Valerie Sayers's *Due East* (1987), Hulga/Joy in Flannery O'Connor's "Good Country People" (1955), and Temple Drake in William Faulkner's *Sanctuary* (1931). All these characters must come to terms not only with the mysteries of sex and love but also with the meaning of life in places where their identities are dictated largely by family and culture. Although Rosacoke has mastered the role of dutiful daughter and provides some measure of stability to a family that is otherwise quite fragmented, she yearns to feel the powerful shudders of desire that accompany the loss of sexual innocence and to transform herself into a strong woman who controls her sexual and personal destiny. Rosacoke is dead certain that she can accomplish this by giving herself to Wesley Beavers, a young man she has been seeing on and off for eight years.

It is a proof of Price's great skill as a writer that he can introduce in the 192-word sentence that opens the novel all of the sexual tension, animal passion, and sacrifice that animates the relationship between Rosacoke and Wesley. First, Wesley is a powerful and cunning animal. His last name, Beavers, signals his animality, and his motorcycle is adorned with coon tails and a sheepskin seat, illustrating his closeness to the energy and potency of the animal world. Second, his lithe and powerful body is like a snake as it leans into the curves on his motorcycle; the snake also symbolizes fertility and the crafty creature that deceived the woman in the Garden of Eden. Third, Wesley possesses all of the power in this opening sentence, as Rosacoke is described as "maybe his girl and maybe not." Fourth, this scene symbolizes an attempted seduction and its failure. Rosacoke sits with her legs spread on the sheepskin seat of the motorcycle and lies against his back as though asleep. As Wesley speeds up to pass the cars in the funeral procession, however, she says "Don't" to his back, and her white blouse blows out behind her like a flag of surrender. Finally, the two characters are traveling to Mount Moriah, which, in Genesis 22, is the scene of Abraham's aborted sacrifice of his son, Isaac. In the novel, Mount Moriah is the name of the church where family are mourning Rosacoke's friend Mildred, who sacrificed her life to give birth to a baby whose father nobody knows. Wesley is carrying Rosacoke headlong to a place where he will ask her to sacrifice herself to him.

If Wesley Beavers possesses all the power in the opening

sentence, however, he does not retain it throughout the narrative. In the middle of the novel, after Rosacoke sacrifices her virginity to Wesley, the power eventually shifts to her. After a Sunday afternoon picnic in Mr. Isaac's woods (which have a potently symbolic name), Wesley and Rosacoke stay behind after the others have left. Wesley tries to seduce Rosacoke, but she rebuffs him because she has seen him playing fast and loose with another woman, Willie Duke Aycock. Wesley then leaves the small town of Afton for the city of Norfolk and a job selling motorcycles. Rosacoke writes to him, trying to keep herself on his mind, but Wesley responds very little, for he is enjoying sleeping with many other women in Norfolk.

When Wesley returns to Afton a few days before Thanksgiving, he never gets in touch with Rosacoke. She, however, subtly seeks him out, plotting her seduction of him. After getting him to drive her home, she looks for signs that she should give herself to Wesley. When she finds them, she moves ahead, and the two walk into the woods, where they have sex. On one hand, Rosacoke has controlled this seduction by choosing the time and the place where she will give in to Wesley; on the other hand, Wesley now has her in the place where he wants her and treats their encounter just as he would with any other woman, satisfying his physical desire. When he calls Rosacoke by another woman's name as he climaxes, she realizes what she has lost and forms a steely resolve not to pursue Wesley again.

The power in the relationship shifts fully to her when Rosacoke learns that she is pregnant with Wesley's child. She takes full responsibility for her pregnancy and tells Wesley that he need not bother coming home at Christmas if does not want to. When he finds that she is pregnant, Wesley swears that he will take care of her. Rosacoke recognizes that perhaps Wesley has learned that it is very lonely donating gifts to people that they do not need or even want. Up until Christmas Eve, the two are estranged; Rosacoke refuses to elope with Wesley and commit to a life cooped up in some little shack eating cereal and living only for her child while Wesley is out sleeping around. On Christmas Eve, as she plays the role of Mary in the church pageant, Rosacoke realizes that Wesley holds her like a chain and that it is both her duty and her wish to elope.

Like most southern novels, Price's is rich with references to the importance of place. The small North Carolina town where Rosacoke and Wesley live represents not only an innocence that the big city lacks but also a social cohesion that cannot be found in larger cities. Once Wesley leaves for Norfolk, he loses his purity to the corrupt ways of the big city, and he brings those ways home with him to corrupt those living in his hometown. The pastoral setting of Mr. Isaac's woods symbolizes sexual purity and innocence, and the deer that Rosacoke and Mildred first see reinforces the mystery of that innocence. Thinking of sex as a process of transformation, Rosacoke leads Wesley to an incorruptible place—to the woods and not to the city—for their sexual adventure. For her, their encounter is a holy act in a holy place, but for Wesley the forest is simply a place where he can act out his animal power. Finally, the family home functions as a place of unity and cohesion. Without her family around her, Rosacoke lacks the support and power that enables her to grow into the strong woman she becomes. Although she makes her own decision to seduce and eventually to elope with Wesley, her family home allows her the space and freedom to ponder the virtue of her decisions.

Critics praised Price's first novel as an achievement that even a mature novelist might envy. *A Long and Happy Life* won the Faulkner Foundation Award for a first novel. Price built on his success and continued the Mustian family saga in two subsequent novels, *A Generous Man* (1966) and *Good Hearts* (1988). In the former, Price focused on the history of Rosacoke's family, especially her brother Milo. Over twenty years after *A Long and Happy Life*, Price returned to Wesley and Rosacoke in *Good Hearts* and explored the successes and failures of their twenty-eight-year-old marriage.

Henry L. Carrigan, Jr.

Further Reading

Hoffman, Frederick J. *The Art of Southern Fiction*. Carbondale: Southern Illinois University Press, 1967. Hoffman was the first noteworthy critic to announce that Price's work was an important event in southern fiction. Defends Price's work against charges that the author is imitating William Faulkner.

Holman, David Marion. "Reynolds Price." In *Fifty Southern Writers After 1900*, edited by Joseph M. Flora and Robert Bain. Westport, Conn.: Greenwood Press, 1987. Holman provides one of the best overall discussions of *A Long and Happy Life* within the contexts of Price's career and of southern fiction. Includes a select bibliography and survey of major criticism.

Price, Reynolds. *Ardent Spirits*. New York: Scribner, 2009. Price's memoir traces his coming-of-age and displays the tenacious desire with which Price, after warm encouragement from Eudora Welty and William Styron, embarked on a round of writing that produced his first published story, "A Chain of Love" (1958), and his first novel, *A Long and Happy Life*.

_____. *Conversations with Reynolds Price*. Edited by Jefferson Humphries. Jackson: University Press of Mississippi, 2008. A splendid collection of interviews with Price that ranges over his writing career; his fiction and nonfiction; and his thoughts on the South, southern writing, and religion.

Rooke, Constance. *Reynolds Price*. Boston: Twayne, 1983. One chapter of this text is given to *A Long and Happy Life*, with Rooke providing a thorough investigation and criticism of the novel. The novel's connections to Price's later works also are delineated.

Schiff, James A. *Understanding Reynolds Price*. Columbia: University of South Carolina Press, 1996. Schiff's study analyzes the development of Price's work beginning with *A Long and Happy Life*. He describes how Price is often at odds with trends in contemporary literature and examines common themes and stylistic devices in Price's writings.

_____, ed. *Critical Essays on Reynolds Price*. New York: G. K. Hall, 1998. Includes tributes to Price from writers Anne Tyler, James Dickey, and Toni Morrison; reviews of *A Long and Happy Life* and Price's other works; and four essays, including one by Price himself, offering various interpretations of *A Long and Happy Life*. Allen Shepherd's essay "Love (and Marriage) in *A Long and Happy Life*" addresses the clichéd situations in the novel, such as the "barefoot and pregnant" southern belle, to point out the novel's possible humor. "The 'Circle in the Forest': Fictional Space in Reynolds Price's *A Long and Happy Life*," by Simone Vauthier, discusses the connection between environment and psychological and emotional backgrounds.

Long Day's Journey into Night

Author: Eugene O'Neill (1888-1953)
First produced: 1956; first published, 1956
Type of work: Drama
Type of plot: Psychological realism
Time of plot: August, 1912
Locale: New London, Connecticut

Principal characters:
JAMES TYRONE, an aging actor
MARY TYRONE, his wife
JAMIE TYRONE, their elder son
EDMUND TYRONE, their younger son
CATHLEEN, their housemaid

The Story:

After breakfast on a warm summer day in August, 1912, as brothers Jamie and Edmund Tyrone joke in the dining room, their mother, Mary, teases her husband, James Tyrone, about his real estate bargains and expresses concern about Edmund's illness. Tyrone reassures her about Edmund's health and compliments her on her own healthy appearance. After the young men join their parents in the living room, the lighthearted family conversation turns increasingly critical among them until Edmund repeats a humorous story told to him by their farm tenant Shaughnessy, who had managed to get the best of Harker, the Standard Oil millionaire, and the tension is broken.

With Edmund upstairs, the others discuss his illness. Mary claims it is only a cold, but Tyrone admits privately to his elder son, Jamie, that the doctor suspects tuberculosis. Jamie responds by accusing his father of not sending Edmund to a real doctor but to a quack. The conversation escalates into an argument that ends with both father and son feeling ashamed and guilty, and with Jamie revealing his suspicion that Mary has relapsed in her drug addiction. Tyrone and Jamie decide to go outside and clip the hedge. When Edmund tries to express to Mary his concern about her health, she accuses him of not trusting her and spying on her, and she declares that she is going to lie down before lunch.

Not long before lunchtime, restless with hedge clipping, Jamie joins Edmund for a clandestine drink and reprimands him for leaving his mother alone so long. When Mary enters, Jamie can tell with certainty that she has been unable to resist her need for drugs. Her excited and nervous ramblings lead first Edmund and then her husband, as he arrives inside for lunch, to the same sad conclusion. They all go into the dining room for lunch.

When they emerge from the dining room after the meal, Tyrone's face shows weary resignation, Jamie's cynicism, and Edmund's illness. Mary is extremely nervous. The men prepare to go into town. Edmund has an appointment with Dr. Hardy (who has already informed Tyrone that Edmund

has consumption and will need to go to a sanatorium). Mary insists that Edmund has only a cold, but after a brief respite upstairs, she becomes more remote, scolding and complaining, revealing her morphine addiction with each guilty speech. Edmund pleads with Mary to stop talking; she continues to deny her problem and Edmund's illness.

The men escape into town, leaving Mary alone. While the housemaid, Cathleen, imbibes Tyrone's liquor freely, Mary recalls her dreams of becoming a nun or a concert pianist and her first meeting with James Tyrone. Home again, Edmund and Tyrone respond differently to Mary's reminiscences. While Tyrone seeks another bottle of whiskey, Edmund desperately attempts to communicate once again with his mother about his illness. She refuses to listen and angrily cries, "I hate you when you become gloomy and morbid." Edmund retorts bitterly, "It's pretty hard to take at times, having a dope fiend for a mother." Discouraged, he leaves the house; Mary goes upstairs, and Tyrone alone remains for dinner.

When Edmund returns from a walk on the beach, colliding with furniture in the darkened hall because Tyrone will not waste money on electricity, he and his father begin to argue about Tyrone's miserliness and about Jamie's profligacy. By midnight they are drunk. They drink deliberately, seeking oblivion, trying to avoid any mention of Mary upstairs or Edmund's tuberculosis. They hear movements from the floor above that trigger comments about Mary's condition, followed by accusations and recriminations, then a moment of affection until the accusations begin again. After Edmund labels his father "a stinking old miser" who plans to save money on medical treatment because he thinks that Edmund is going to die, Tyrone relates his life story: a childhood in dire poverty and the concern for money that has wasted his talent as an actor. In response, Edmund describes his love of the sea, where he feels a wild joy and where, he says, "there is meaning." Jamie returns, more drunk than usual, and Tyrone, annoyed, leaves the room. Jamie then entertains his brother with the story of his adventure with the prostitute Fat Violet, until his cynical question "Where's the hophead?" provokes a punch from Edmund and immediate remorse. Another moment of affection occurs before Jamie confesses his ambivalence toward Edmund and falls into a drunken stupor, rousing himself to fight only when Tyrone returns.

As a foghorn sounds in the background, Mary descends the stairs, dragging her wedding dress, a precious object from the past. Jamie sneers, "The Mad Scene. Enter Ophelia!" Tyrone and Edmund turn on him as Jamie breaks down in heartbroken sobs. Mary, completely detached, has regressed totally into the past, murmuring about something she has lost and cannot remember. Frozen with the pain of their family situation, the three men stare at her in misery.

Critical Evaluation:

Written "with deep pity and understanding and forgiveness for all the four haunted Tyrones," *Long Day's Journey into Night* may be the greatest American play of the twentieth century. After a career of many dramatic experiments—some successes, some failures—in the last years of his life Eugene O'Neill found his most truthful and artistic voice in an autobiographical work detailing the torment of his own family. It earned him a fourth Pulitzer Prize, awarded posthumously in 1957. In O'Neill's Tyrone family, James Tyrone resembles his father, James O'Neill, a famous actor known for his role as the Count of Monte Cristo. Mary Tyrone is a thinly disguised portrait of the playwright's mother, Ella Quinlan O'Neill. The two sons, Jamie and Edmund, are pictures of Eugene's older brother and the playwright himself.

The play is classically structured, the title appropriate. The events of this four-hour drama are compressed into one day, with the first act occurring at 8:30 in the morning, the two scenes of the second act before and after lunch, the third act at 6:30 in the evening, and the final act at midnight. It tells of the journey shared by the four principal characters through one particular day, but the past is always with them. Like Sophocles' *Oidipous Tyrannos* (c. 429 B.C.E.; *Oedipus Tyrannus*, 1715), it is a play of revelation rather than action.

The Tyrone family is like a single living organism; what affects one affects all. The individuals may be in conflict over their own roles, but they are inextricably bound to one another by love and hate. Hostility is never far from the surface. The Tyrones are well aware of each family member's vulnerabilities and are skilled in attacking them. Like musical motifs, each person's flaws are played again and again: Tyrone's miserliness, Jamie's profligacy, Edmund's illness, and, most important, Mary's dependence on morphine. The drinking problem of the three men is ignored and excused, for the

most part, because they share it. At the beginning of the play, Mary is supposedly cured after a stay in a sanatorium. The three men hope for a period of normal life, suppressing their fears regarding her continued health. Concern over Edmund's illness provides Mary with an excuse to resume her habit, and, as though afflicted with a growing cancer, the family organism quickly deteriorates.

Also just below the surface is the guilt accompanying the question of responsibility for Mary's addiction. At one time or another Mary accuses each of the men: Tyrone because he hired a quack doctor (that is, a cheaper doctor) who prescribed morphine when she was ill after the birth of Edmund; Jamie because he infected her second baby with measles, and when the baby died, she felt obligated to produce another child; Edmund because his was the difficult birth (her third) that required the medication. Unwilling to accept the burden of blame consciously, the men nonetheless are never free of the guilty roles imposed on them. Mary appears to be a helpless victim, overwhelmed by the vicissitudes of life and the insensitivity of the men around her. From another perspective, Mary is a self-involved child, infusing her husband and sons with guilt, demanding sympathy and consideration, and avoiding reality and the responsibility for her own plight. From either point of view, Mary Tyrone is the catalyst for the family's long journey into a night of sorrow.

The style of *Long Day's Journey into Night* is realistic; the set that O'Neill describes is an exact replica of the O'Neill summer home in New London, Connecticut, with its living room and dining room behind, a front porch overlooking the river, and the Connecticut Sound at the end of the road. The fog of the play has a basis in reality, and its increasing presence, as it rolls in from the sound throughout the day, threatening to envelop the house, achieves a symbolic dimension. Edmund enjoys the fog because in it "life can hide from itself." Mary, too, loves the fog because "it hides you from the world." The fog is the void beyond the family, linked with the mystery of life and death, representing escape and oblivion. The foghorn is an irritation, as Mary says, "calling you back," back to reality, back to the world.

Another contribution to the realism of the play is the subtext, the means by which the actors physically convey the feelings of the characters that are not revealed in dialogue. Like playwrights Henrik Ibsen and August Strindberg, to whom he acknowledges a debt, O'Neill includes scenes in which the characters do not speak what they feel; only at moments of high emotion does the truth emerge. The result is that a reading does not convey the full impact of this play; it must be experienced in performance.

The family unit is a favorite subject in American literature, and themes of alienation, isolation, and the inability to communicate within the family have long preoccupied novelists and playwrights alike. Eugene O'Neill's *Long Day's Journey into Night* is a masterpiece of this genre.

Joyce E. Henry

Further Reading

Bloom, Harold, ed. *Eugene O'Neill's "Long Day's Journey into Night."* New York: Chelsea House, 1987. Collection of ten reprinted essays by major critics is arranged in chronological order by date of first publication. Topics examined include the play's monologues, its characters, its form, and its language.

Bloom, Steven F. *Student Companion to Eugene O' Neill.* Westport, Conn.: Greenwood Press, 2007. Includes a brief biographical sketch, a discussion of O'Neill's literary heritage, and a chapter providing critical analysis of *Long Day's Journey into Night.*

Gelb, Arthur, and Barbara Gelb. *O'Neill: Life with Monte Cristo.* New York: Applause, 2000. Monumental biography, a revision and update of a classic work first published in the early 1960's, is an invaluable resource for any serious student of the playwright and his work.

Hinden, Michael. *"Long Day's Journey into Night": Native Eloquence.* Boston: Twayne, 1990. Provides an excellent introduction to the play and its history. Devotes two admirable chapters to a close analysis of the major characters and their motivations.

Manheim, Michael. *Eugene O'Neill's New Language of Kinship.* Syracuse, N.Y.: Syracuse University Press, 1982. Argues that O'Neill's early plays contain the same autobiographical characters and situations as *Long Day's Journey into Night.* Includes an interesting list of motifs for each character in the play.

Murphy, Brenda. *O'Neill: "Long Day's Journey into Night."* New York: Cambridge University Press, 2001. Discussion of the play focuses on significant stage, film, and television productions of the work, including an account of its New York premiere.

Porter, Laurin. *The Banished Prince: Time, Memory, and Ritual in the Late Plays of Eugene O'Neill.* Ann Arbor, Mich.: Research Press, 1988. Analyzes the futile attempts of characters in O'Neill's last plays, including *Long Day's Journey into Night*, to reclaim the past through memory and the ritual of confession.

Shaughnessy, Edward L. *Down the Nights and Down the Days: Eugene O'Neill's Catholic Sensibility.* Notre Dame, Ind.: University of Notre Dame Press, 1996. Asserts that although O'Neill renounced Catholicism when he was fifteen, he retained some of his Catholic upbringing and brought this moral sensibility to his plays, including *Long Day's Journey into Night.*

Törnqvist, Egil. *Eugene O' Neill: A Playwright's Theatre.* Jefferson, N.C.: McFarland, 2004. Demonstrates how O'Neill was a controlling personality in the texts and performances of his plays. Describes his working conditions and the multiple audiences for his works. Examines the titles, settings, names and addresses, language, and allusions to other works in his dramas. Devotes a chapter to an analysis of *Long Day's Journey into Night.*

Voglino, Barbara. *"Long Day's Journey into Night*: The Question of Blame." In *"Perverse Mind": Eugene O' Neill's Struggle with Closure.* Madison, N.J.: Fairleigh Dickinson University Press, 1999. Discussion of *Long Day's Journey into Night* is part of an examination of nine plays written at different periods of O'Neill's career. Argues that the failed endings of the early works developed into the successful closures of his later plays.

The Long Goodbye

Author: Raymond Chandler (1888-1959)
First published: 1953
Type of work: Novel
Type of plot: Detective and mystery
Time of plot: Early 1950's
Locale: Los Angeles

Principal characters:
PHILIP MARLOWE, a forty-two-year-old private detective
TERRY LENNOX (PAUL MARSTON), an alcoholic, Marlowe's friend
ROGER WADE, an alcoholic popular novelist
EILEEN WADE, Roger Wade's wife
HOWARD SPENCER, Roger Wade's New York publisher
BERNIE OHLS, a police detective in the homicide division
HARLAN POTTER, a wealthy magnate whose daughter has been murdered
LINDA LORING, Potter's daughter
MENDY MENENDEZ, a gangster and wartime friend of Terry Lennox

The Story:

Private detective Philip Marlowe encounters the alcoholic Terry Lennox, a World War II veteran who had been wounded and who had spent time as a prisoner of war. Lennox is married to the incredibly wealthy Sylvia Lennox, daughter of multimillionaire Harlan Potter. When Marlowe first meets Lennox, Lennox's wife Sylvia dumps him from her car for being too drunk. Marlowe helps Lennox, and a sort of friendship ensues; the two of them meet occasionally for gimlets at a bar called Victor's.

One night, Lennox appears at Marlowe's house, asking him for a ride to the airport in Tijuana, just across the Mexican border. Marlowe realizes that something drastic has happened but will not let Lennox implicate him as an accessory by telling his story. Marlowe drives Lennox to Tijuana and is arrested upon his return to Los Angeles, where he spends several days in jail. He learns that Lennox has been accused of savagely killing his wife. Despite harsh treatment by the police, Marlowe refuses to divulge any information about Lennox. Before long, Marlowe is released. He finds that Lennox has presumably killed himself in a small town in Mexico, leaving behind a confession. A gangster named Mendy Menendez warns him not to pursue the Lennox case. Upon returning home, Marlowe finds a letter from Lennox waiting for him, written before his confession. It also requests that Marlowe not investigate the case, and it contains a five-thousand-dollar bill.

Before long, Marlowe is contacted by publisher Howard Spencer and Eileen Wade, the wife of Roger Wade, a writer of popular historical swashbuckler novels. Wade, not for the first time, has disappeared in an alcoholic haze; Eileen and Howard Spencer wish to hire Marlowe to find Wade and

bring him back. Marlowe is at first reluctant but finally takes the case. Marlowe soon discovers that Wade has been in the care of a shady physician, Dr. Verringer, who exorts monery from the alcoholics and drug addicts whom he treats.

Marlowe brings Wade home, and before long Spencer and Wade have another proposition for him: They will hire him to stay keep Wade sober until he can finish his current novel. Marlowe is reluctant to take the job. From his perspective, Wade is a grown man who can see to himself; additionally, if Wade is intent upon getting drunk, sooner or later he will find a way to do so. Nevertheless, Marlowe spends time with the Wades. Before long, he learns that Roger seems to be drinking to assuage a sense of guilt and that Wade turns bitter and mean when he is drinking. Additionally, after meeting Sylvia Lennox's sister Linda Loring and finding that she knows the Wades, Marlowe wonders whether Roger Wade had an affair with the notoriously promiscuous Lennox before she died. At the same time, Eileen Wade seems to be mentally unstable. She seeks a lover whom she lost in the war; once, she even mistakes Marlowe for that lost lover and asks him to take her to bed.

During his time helping the Wades, Marlowe is warned off the case by magnate Harlan Potter, the father of Linda and Sylvia, making him recall the warning he received from Mendy Menendez. The various warnings pique Marlowe's curiosity, as do the inconsistent details of Terry Lennox's death. Threats by Menendez, Potter, and the police do not deter Marlowe, and he continues to pursue evidence to support what his instincts have told him: that Terry Lennox is innocent and that Roger and Eileen Wade are involved somehow with the murder of Sylvia Lennox. Before Marlowe can follow up his instincts with Wade, he finds the author dead, having seemingly killed himself with his pistol. Although Eileen Wade initially accuses Marlowe of killing Wade, he is soon exonerated.

As the police use Marlowe as bait for Menendez, Marlowe puzzles out the mystery. Eileen Wade and Terry Lennox had been married in England during the war; thinking Terry had died, Eileen married Wade, preserving Lennox—whose real name was Paul Marston—in her mind as her perfect, lost younger lover. When Terry appeared in California as the husband of Sylvia Lennox, Eileen's nostalgic view of him was crushed. Consumed by jealousy, she killed Sylvia Lennox. Later, suspecting that her husband was drinking because he knew of her actions, she killed him as well. She hired Marlowe to help her husband in part because of Marlowe's friendship with Terry Lennox.

Bringing publisher Howard Spencer along as a witness, Marlowe confronts Eileen Wade with the facts. Later, rather than face the police, she kills herself. Her death leaves one central mystery: Why did Lennox confess to a crime he did not commit? Was Lennox murdered? Marlowe unravels this central question, too, and the novel ends with Marlowe's final confrontation: His friend Terry Lennox is still alive, having faked his murder with the help of Menendez and other criminals. Marlowe rebuffs Lennox, telling him that his actions caused the death of Wade and even endangered Marlowe's life.

Critical Evaluation:

Raymond Chandler's 1953 novel *The Long Goodbye* is his penultimate novel and the penultimate novel about his main character, private investigator Philip Marlowe. Although Chandler's early short stories feature a variety of detectives (many of them prototypes for Marlowe), Marlowe is the hero and narrator of each of his seven published novels. In *The Long Goodbye*, Marlowe is forty-two years old and feeling a bit worn down by his life as a lonely, bachelor private eye. He is a laconic and jaded yet honorable observer of the varied and corrupt Los Angeles of his day. The central mysteries of *The Long Goodbye* strike closer to home for Marlowe than those of previous novels. It is fitting that *The Long Goodbye*, one of the most beloved and critically respected detective novels ever written, should have an idiosyncratic beginning, rather than starting conventionally with a client hiring Marlowe or his randomly discovering a body or stumbling into a crime.

In his famous essay "The Simple Art of Murder" (1944), Chandler seeks to rebut the notion that no mystery novel can have literary merit, arguing that "Everything written with

vitality expresses that vitality; there are no dull subjects, only dull minds." Indeed, Chandler's reputation in the mystery establishment has little to do with the reasons for which mystery writers are usually treasured by fans. His plots are often baroque and convoluted; solving the mystery is usually less intrinsic to the story than coming to understand the motivations and lives of the characters interacting with Philip Marlowe.

Chandler is appreciated first as a stylist, a writer with the necessary vitality to transcend the mystery genre. The voice of Marlowe is laconic and sarcastic, often noting details in a kind of humorous whimsy and drawing comparisons through similes that are original and incisive, such as his famous two-page description of blondes in *The Long Goodbye*. He says, "There is the small cute blonde who cheeps and twitters, and the big statuesque blonde who straight-arms you with an ice blue glare," as well as the "small perky blonde who is a little pay and wants to pay her own way . . . and knows judo from the ground up," and the "pale, pale blonde with anemia of some non-fatal but incurable type," who "is reading *The Waste Land* or Dante in the original, or Kafka or Kierkegaard."

The regard in which Chandler is held by detective-fiction readers (and later detective-fiction writers, who seem universally to regard him as an influence) is further heightened by the themes and by the characterization in his novels. As is the case with Chandler's other novels, *The Long Goodbye* is about many things, including love, disillusionment, loyalty, integrity, and honor. It is also about two murders, but ultimately those murders are less important than the human elements that drive their discovery.

Of all Chandler's novels, *The Long Goodbye* is the work most focused on Marlowe's character. For the first third of the novel, he does not have a client; his friendship with Lennox provides the catalyst that propels the story. Later, he is hired by Eileen Wade only because he had been Lennox's friend. As he finds himself compelled to investigate Lennox's supposed death and to help the Wades, he muses to himself, "There is no trap as deadly as the one you set for yourself." In "The Simple Art of Murder," Chandler writes that "down these mean streets a man must go his is not himself mean, who is neither tarnished nor afraid." He goes on to say, "He must be, to use a rather weathered phrase, a man of honor, by instinct, by inevitability, without thought of it, and certainly without saying it." The entire novel hinges on Marlowe's loyalty and his honor and upon his need to preserve those things despite the "mean streets" he travels.

Marlowe's Los Angeles has its share of good people (such as Linda Loring, police detective Bernie Ohls, and Candy,

Wade's "houseboy"), but it is a corrupt place where the crooked, such as Mendy Menendez, and the wealthy, such as Harlan Potter, have their way. As Ohls tells Marlowe, "There ain't no clean way to make a hundred million bucks." As in previous novels, Marlowe often plays out complicated chess problems on a board by himself, symbolizing in part his need to understand the game he is caught within, the need to be something other than a pawn in the hands of the powerful.

Marlowe represents a foil to the other two men of the novel: Faced with adversity in the war and corruption on the home front, Terry Lennox simply gives up and becomes an empty shell of a man. Wade, on the other hand, self-destructs with a bottle. Marlowe is nothing if not tenacious, and, ultimately, he stays the course, not for Lennox, nor for Wade, nor even for himself, but for the truth. When Terry returns to see Marlowe in the hope that his reappearance will allow him to continue his charade, Marlowe tells him, "You bought a lot of me, Terry. For a smile and a nod and a wave of the hand and a few quiet drinks in a quiet bar here and there. It was nice while it lasted. So long, amigo. I won't say goodbye. I said it to you when it meant something. I said it when it was sad and lonely and final."

Scott D. Yarbrough

Further Reading

Cawelti, John G. *Adventure, Mystery, and Romance.* Chicago: University of Chicago Press, 1976. A landmark discussion of genre and popular literatures, with extended chapters on hard-boiled detective literature and Chandler's development of the form.

Chandler, Raymond. "The Simple Art of Murder." In *Chandler: Later Novels and Other Writings.* New York: Library of America, 1995. Chandler's famous essay on how the hard-boiled detective style swerved from the classical English style of writers such as Agatha Christie and S. S. Van Dine, including his famous commentary on how he views his heroes.

Eburne, Jonathan Paul. "Chandler's Waste Land." *Studies in the Novel* 35, no. 3 (2003): 366-382. A consideration of the Los Angeles milieu of Chandler's novel and the wounded nature of Marlowe; focuses on the novel's recurring references to poet T. S. Eliot, author of the landmark post-World War I poem *The Waste Land* (1922).

Geherin, David. *The American Private Eye.* New York: Frederick Ungar, 1985. A history of the private eye character in detective fiction, with a chapter on Philip Marlowe. The chapter is particularly interesting for its discussion of how Marlowe breaks ranks with previous characters and establishes new paradigms.

Marling, William. *The American Roman Noir: Hammett, Cain, and Chandler.* Athens: University of Georgia Press, 1995. An excellent consideration of the development of literary noir fiction (called *roman noir*), with a lengthy section on Chandler's life, growth as an artist, and contributions to detective fiction.

Routledge, Christopher. "A Matter of Disguise: Locating the Self in Raymond Chandler's *The Big Sleep* and *The Long Goodbye*." *Studies in the Novel* 29, no. 1 (Spring, 1997): 94-107. Interesting consideration of the various disguises and character reversals in two of Chandler's novels, as well as a thorough examination of Marlowe's growth from the first novel (*The Big Sleep*, 1939) to *The Long Goodbye*.

The Long Journey

Author: Johannes V. Jensen (1873-1950)
First published: Den lange rejse, 1908-1922, 6 volumes (English translation, 1922-1924, 3 volumes: *Fire and Ice*, 1922; *The Cimbrians*, 1923; *Christopher Columbus*, 1924)
Type of work: Novels
Type of plot: Epic
Time of plot: Prehistoric times to the early nineteenth century
Locale: Northern Europe

Principal characters:
FYR, typical of the earliest users of fire
CARL, typical of the early Stone Age man in the glacial period
WHITE BEAR, typical of the later Stone Age man
WOLF, typical of the horse-riding and horse-breeding man
NORNA GEST, typical of the man who entered the Iron Age and lingered to the fall of the Roman Empire
CHRISTOPHER COLUMBUS, typical of the Renaissance man
CHARLES DARWIN, typical of the modern man

The Story:

In the north of what will later be Europe, in the prehistoric days before the glaciers come from the north, humans live in fear and trembling—in fear of the elements, the beasts of the jungles, and their own primitive leaders. Into one of those herdlike groups is born a boy who is named Fyr. As the child grows older, he is seized with a desire to climb to the top of Gunung Api, a vast volcano, quiet but not extinct. On the slopes of the volcano, wandering by himself, Fyr learns to make use of fire to keep himself warm, to cook meat, to provide himself with a deity, and to enhance his own importance.

Attracted first by his songs and then by his person, women join Fyr, until he, like other leaders, is the head of a primitive family group. After the women come children and, finally, other men who make themselves subservient to Fyr. Under his leadership, the tribe becomes a band of hunters, using the pits, spears, and bows that Fyr devises for them. Wherever they go, they take with them burning wood to re-create their god and household symbol: the fire. Soon all the forest folk bow to the authority of Fyr, bound to him by his fire and by the tools of wood and stone that he creates to make their lives more bearable. One day, however, their god seems to demand a sacrifice, and the people, making Fyr their scapegoat, place him in the fire he has brought them. Although he is roasted and eaten, he lives on, a representative of human ingenuity that they cannot understand.

As ages pass, Gunung Api becomes extinct. Still later, the northern ice cap begins to move over the land, bringing cold to the tropic jungles. After other ages have passed, a small band of hunters lie crouched in the same forest where Fyr and his followers lived. The climate is much colder than it once was, and the tribe and most of the animals had moved to the south until a hunting expedition brought them back to the old territory. One of their number, Carl, is the tender of the fire. When he lets the fire die, he is thrown out of the band and becomes an outcast.

Carl flees to the North, somehow keeping himself alive in the winter by wrapping himself in skins and burrowing into the ground or building rude huts of stone. He travels high on the extinct volcanic cone, and everywhere he sees only desolation and ice. He seeks the enemy of his tribe, the cold, but he does not find it. He is joined in his wanderings by a dog; the animal slowly joins into a comradeship with the man, although not without some trembling and hesitancy on the part of both. As the winters pass, Carl learns to prepare for the coldest season by laying in a supply of food and building a shelter. He even learns to foretell when the great cold is coming and where he will find food and shelter as its ice and

snow move gradually to the south. When he occasionally encounters another human being, Carl uses the opportunity to hunt for and eat a different kind of meat. One day, he gives chase to a human being who turns out to be a woman. After he captures her by the sea, she becomes his wife; the lure of the sea is to call him again.

Carl's wife, Mam, brings new habits of gathering and storing; she also brings him children. She adds vegetables to Carl's diet, and their home becomes a permanent one. Carl is still aware of fire, a possession that he has lost and not regained. Gathering many stones, he chips them against one another in an effort to strike fire from them. At last he is successful, and he bequeaths fire to his children.

The children of Carl and their wives add pottery work to their skills; with ceramics comes boiling, a new way of cooking. Among the descendants of Carl there arises a group of priests against whom others sometimes rebel. One such rebellious man is White Bear. Denied a certain woman for his wife, he kills the leader of the priestly clan. Like Carl before him, White Bear becomes an outcast, taking May, his woman, with him. White Bear becomes a seaman, building small boats and sailing them, in company with his sons, while May and their daughters remain at home to farm and care for the cattle.

White Bear begins to use horses for transportation. He builds a chariot and uses horses to draw it. His sons, more adventurous, learn to ride on horseback. One of the sons, Wolf, becomes so enamored of the horses that he rides away with them to become a nomad, forerunner of the Golden Horde of Genghis Khan.

Ages later, a new man appears. He is Norna Gest, son of the matriarch Gro. While he is still a young boy, dwelling at the edge of the sea on an island, he builds himself a dugout canoe and sails away, carrying with him a girl who will, after a time, become his mate. They and their child explore a new land to the north (which will later become Sweden) but return to their home island in later years. Gest himself is not an ordinary mortal; he is to live as long as he keeps a partially burned candle. After he returns to his original home, he and his companions go on many voyages, using sails as well as oars on their ships.

As years pass, Gest finds that he has outlived his companions. He awakes one day to find himself in a changed Sealand, a place where the people are either thralls or nobles. Disturbed at the changes and despised because he has taken as his new wife a milkmaid, one of the thralls, he wanders sadly about the land.

Unhappy in the changed Sealand, Gest and his wife sail to

Sweden to found a new colony in which they are to be the leaders. They take with them new techniques of smelting and forging metals, and in their new land they gradually acquire domestic animals—horses, sheep, and cattle. Their sons and daughters marry, and the colony grows. Gest's wife dies, and one day Gest disappears to wander again over the globe. Unnoticed but noticing, he travels through central Europe and floats down the Danube. He traverses the Mediterranean lands, where his life began in the early Stone Age. Finding something wanting in the lands of the South, Gest turns his face once again toward home, where he becomes a wandering poet.

Arriving in Jutland, he is greeted by Tole, a leader who is guardian of the wooden idol that represents the ancient god of the Jutlanders. Tole wishes to enclose the idol in a great bronze bull, and he welcomes Gest as the bringer of skills with metals and as a man of great wisdom. The two men make plans to cast the bronze bull at the time of the great spring festival, before the flocks and herds are taken up to the summer pastures. The bull is successfully cast, and the festivities end with human sacrifices of slaves and thralls. Gest wanders off on foot after the festival.

In later years, floods rise up in the seas around Jutland, and the younger men wish to leave the country to search for a homeland safe from the ever-encroaching sea. The entire tribe leaves, except for the elderly Tole. With the tribe goes the bronze bull, destined now to take long journeys across the face of central and southern Europe.

Back and forth across the lands the Cimbrians journey, enlisting other tribes in their search for better lands. At last, they travel far enough to come to the notice of the Romans. Failing to obey the Romans' warning to stay out of Rome's dominions, the Cimbrians and their allies of the North become enemies of the empire. They decide to strike at Rome itself. Victorious at first, they become proud; they do not anticipate at all the strategies of the Roman generals, who ultimately defeat them. In their defeat, the Cimbrians and their allies are ruined. Those who are not killed or do not commit suicide are sold into bondage to the Romans, to live miserably as captives in the South, where eventually their blood blends with the blood of their conquerors. Norna Gest sees these things happening. Finally, knowing that his time is at an end, he leaves Rome in his boat and glides slowly toward the sea, there to burn his candle to its end.

After the fall of the Roman Empire, barbarians from the North are gradually assimilated into the Christian religion. The ancient ship of the North, inverted on land, becomes the Gothic cathedral, a compound of the mariner's vessel and the stately forests through which humans earlier roamed.

Among the descendants of the barbaric tribes of the North are the Langobards. One of the descendants of this group is a man named Christopher Columbus, who is to lead humankind farther on its journey of discovery across the seas and into a whole new hemisphere then undreamed of, or at least forgotten by the descendants of the early Northmen who once visited it.

Columbus sees himself as a veritable Christopher, one who carries the Christ into the world. While others carouse before setting out across the ocean with him, he prepares himself by attending masses in the cathedral. He has faith in divine help and divine purpose. When the qualities that his faith gives him prove insufficient to meet the demands of leadership, however, he can call upon the amazing strength of body that his northern forebears have bequeathed him.

Although he reaches the islands of the West Indies, others will carry the long journey into the New World; Columbus is doomed to be only a leader pointing the way. To later conquistadors, men such as Hernán Cortés and Francisco Pizarro, goes the credit for gaining the mainland for European culture. They face the odds of sheer numbers when they meet the strength of the late Stone Age people, the followers of Montezuma and the Incas, who still exist in America, caught in the lag where European culture left them many ages before. In Mexico, for example, Cortés finds human sacrifice and the worship of volcanic spirits, examples of cultural practices that long since ceased to exist in the Old World. The light that Columbus sees from his ship at night is a symbol of the fire worship that exists throughout the New World.

The Indians of the Americas believe that the coming of the white men marks the return of their great sun god, Quetzalcoatl. Perhaps the god might have been Norna Gest, visiting the New World during his travels. The natives, however, soon lose their superstitious awe of men with fair skin and fair hair, and many Europeans are sacrificed on the altars of Mexico and other Southern countries.

The great battle of the New World is fought in Mexico. There the journey of the European culture is most seriously threatened. In the North, the Indians seem to fade away before the white culture; in the West Indies, disease kills them like summer flies at the first autumn frost. In Mexico, however, there is warfare between the eagle and the serpent, symbols of the migrations and conflicting cultures of humankind. Cortés and his soldiers are like eagles swooping down on the snake, insignia of the Aztecs.

Although Cortés is temporarily successful, with the help of a woman who turns against her own people, and although he is able to send the idol of Huitzilopochtli toppling down the long flights of stairs that lead to its temple, the Spaniards are doomed to temporary defeat. Cortés has to hack his way out of Tenochtitlán with the screams of Spaniards who are being sacrificed echoing in his ears.

Years later, a young man named Charles Darwin, a naturalist on H.M.S. *Beagle*, is to become a new symbol in humanity's journey from the past through the present and into the future. Those on the *Beagle* think they see the Flying Dutchman, a dread sea captain doomed to sail forever. This figure will become the symbol of humanity's long journey as it continues. Perhaps the long journey is now almost ended. No one knows.

Critical Evaluation:

Although he received the Nobel Prize in Literature in 1944, the Danish writer Johannes V. Jensen has been little known in the United States—a remarkable oversight in view of the fact that for almost fifty years after his first visit to the United States in 1897, Jensen was a major interpreter of American life and letters for Scandinavian readers. His preoccupation with the United States was only part of a larger interest in and frank acceptance of the modern age in all its nervous variety. Jensen's probing curiosity and rich imagination ranged over the whole of the modern world and found expression in a large published body of novels, verse, essays, short stories, and travel writing.

Jensen was born in that section of Northern Jutland that is known as Himmerland, a region characterized by large tracts of somber landscapes broken only by a few sparse settlements and occasional farms. His descent from peasant stock and a boyhood spent in play among the burial mounds of Jutland left a distinct mark on Jensen's writings. It shows up not only in a dry and often mordant humor but also in the fact that, throughout his career, Jensen kept his origins and the distant past that lay behind his people as constant points of reference. He was a prolific writer. In addition to the monumental *The Long Journey*, he published several other books on a variety of subjects, often with his own interpretations of Darwinism. Few writers have done so much to interpret in creative terms the past of their own races and to point to the interdependence of past, present, and future; and perhaps no writer has caught the intimate charm of Danish nature quite as has Jensen.

The English translation of *The Long Journey*, the author's most ambitious work, takes the form of a long cyclic novel of three volumes: *Fire and Ice*, *The Cimbrians*, and *Christopher Columbus*. The epic traces the journey of the people of the North from the forest through the rigors of the Ice Age and out on many journeys in search of the "lost land," which is represented symbolically by the warm tropical forest of the

race's infancy. The work's aim is to show the development of humankind from primeval chaos to modern civilization. The narrative is in story form, showing how the actual stages of the ascent of humankind and of the climatic conditions of the earth's surface have left their traces in mythology and religion. On a symbolic level, the work shows how the forest became a ship and the ship became a church, until people such as Christopher Columbus changed the church back into a ship in their quest for the New World. With the discovery of the New World and its natives, the ship reverts to the forest, and the cycle is complete.

The Long Journey should not be taken seriously as anthropology, yet to refer to it simply as a novel falls short of an accurate appraisal of its merit. It is a work of mythology that, in the boldness of its conception, deserves a place among the finest works of fiction of the modern era. To readers who hold a firm conviction that the account of the world related in the first five books of the Bible is literally true, *The Long Journey* may be heresy. Jensen was convinced that the world, as it stands, is open to various explanations. Although in this work he makes no direct statements about evolution, he regarded this theory as another indication of the advance of humankind. Few readers will contend, however, that Jensen wrote this novel as a conscious and scientific attempt to refute biblical interpretation, or that he unconsciously refuted it. Evolution, according to Jensen, is strong evidence for the existence of a supernatural deity and is probably the one principle of life that makes homage to God obligatory. In *The Long Journey* he implies that the world would be lacking as a piece of divine handiwork if there had been no progress, no evolution, within the most recent thousands of years.

In many respects, *The Long Journey* is similar to Knut Hamsun's *Markens grøde* (1917; *Growth of the Soil*, 1920), in that both novels go back to a primitive world, both deal with elemental traits in human beings, and both rise, in some instances, to great heights as truly epic portrayals of the workings of the human heart. Here the similarities stop, however. When Hamsun's novel concludes, the sons of Isak and Inger have grown up, and even Barbro, the once citified lady, has married and settled down. Hamsun covers the period from about 1916 to roughly 1950. In contrast, when Jensen's Gunung Api stands in airy solitude in the third paragraph of *The Long Journey*, chewing the fire within him, there is no fire, no ice; there is nothing but unmeasured time, millions of years before the modern era. When Jensen is through, Christopher Columbus has discovered America. Jensen does not note time except by its passing.

A full understanding of *The Long Journey* requires some familiarity with archaeology, geology, ethnology, and mythology, for the work deals with the unfolding of a particular idea and the delineation of that theory of origin, growth, and development through a long period of time. Parts of the novel are ostensibly irrelevant, in that they apply neither to science nor to literature. On the whole, however, *The Long Journey* is a unique and epic treatment of the genesis of humanity and the world.

"Critical Evaluation" by Stephen Hanson

Further Reading

Bredsdorff, Elias, Brita Mortensen, and Ronald Popperwell. *An Introduction to Scandinavian Literature: From the Earliest Time to Our Day.* 1951. Reprint. Westport, Conn.: Greenwood Press, 1970. Surveys Jensen's achievements as a novelist and poet. Discusses *The Long Journey*, noting Jensen's reliance on Darwinian theory as the basis for his assessment of human nature.

Houe, Poul. "Johannes V. Jensen's *Long Journey*, or, Postmodernism Under Way." *Scandinavian Studies* 64 (1992): 96-128. Thorough, challenging article on the novel is recommended for students who have some familiarity with literary theory.

Mitchell, P. M. *A History of Danish Literature.* 2d ed. New York: Kraus-Thomson Organization, 1971. Includes a summary of Jensen's career and his place in Danish literature. Describes *The Long Journey* as a work heavily influenced by Darwinism and asserts that the characters serve as types symbolizing the cultural and technical progress of humankind.

Neilsen, Henry, and Keld Neilsen, eds. *Neighbouring Nobel: The History of Thirteen Danish Nobel Prizes.* Translated by Heidi Flegal. Oakville, Conn.: Aarhus University Press, 2001. Collection of historical accounts of the Nobel Prize winners from Denmark devotes a chapter to Jensen.

Rossel, Sven H. *A History of Scandinavian Literature, 1870-1980.* Translated by Anne Ulmer. Minneapolis: University of Minnesota Press, 1982. Describes Jensen as a literary pathfinder for twentieth century Scandinavian writing. Explains how his early prose essays form the ideological basis for the plot and theme of *The Long Journey*.

_____. *Johannes V. Jensen.* Boston: Twayne, 1984. Provides a good introduction to Jensen's work. A chapter on the handling of mythic themes in his novels includes discussion of *The Long Journey*. Notes that the work vivifies a central theme in Jensen's work, the longing for the lost land of Paradise, and explains how Jensen viewed the novel as a kind of Bible for modern times.

_____, ed. *A History of Danish Literature.* Lincoln: University of Nebraska Press, 1992. Includes an examination of Jensen's life and work. Maintains that *The Long Journey* is best interpreted as a series of myths, or what Jensen himself described as "attempts to focus on the essence of life in a dream."

Topsöe-Jensen, H. G. *Scandinavian Literature: From Brandes to Our Day.* Translated by Isaac Anderson. New York: W. W. Norton, 1929. Reviews the literary achievement of Jensen, who was considered the central figure in Danish literature in the early decades of the twentieth century. Notes that *The Long Journey* is one of several works in which Jensen dramatizes humankind's evolutionary progress.

The Longest Journey

Author: E. M. Forster (1879-1970)
First published: 1907
Type of work: Novel
Type of plot: Social realism
Time of plot: Early twentieth century
Locale: England

Principal characters:
RICKIE ELLIOT, a student at Cambridge
AGNES PEMBROKE, an old friend
HERBERT PEMBROKE, her brother
STEWART ANSELL, a friend of Rickie at Cambridge
MRS. EMILY FAILING, Rickie's aunt
STEPHEN WONHAM, Rickie's half brother

The Story:

Frederick Elliot is a student at Cambridge and almost alone in the world. He has finally attained some degree of contentment in his life after a rather unhappy childhood.

Born with a lame left foot that kept him from most of the normal activities of children, he has grown up virtually without friends. Early in his life, his father began to call him "Rickie" because of the name's close similarity to "rickety," and the moniker has stayed with him. In addition to his deformity, Rickie has another, more serious, difficulty. He found out quite early in his life that his father and mother did not love each other, that his father did not love him at all, and that his mother loved him only a little. Both his parents died when he was fifteen years old, leaving him comfortably well-off financially but without anyone who wanted to give him a home.

At Cambridge, he has shown himself to be a capable student but one without any scholarly pretensions. He has made several friends among the nonathletic groups and spends much of his time in long discussions on topics of literary or philosophical interest. During such a discussion one day, he is interrupted by the arrival of his old friends Agnes and Herbert Pembroke; he had completely forgotten that he had invited them for the weekend. Because the sister and brother are part of that very small group who have taken an interest in Rickie's career, they spend a great part of their time at Cambridge encouraging him to decide on a particular course for his life, even if that course is nothing more than the intention to write, the only pursuit in which he admits having any interest. They point out that money is not important as long as he meets a certain standard of ideals.

During the Christmas holiday of the same year, Rickie sees his friends again. He has stayed several days with Stewart Ansell, a friend from Cambridge, but he feels that he should spend a part of his vacation with the Pembrokes as well. He dreads this part of his vacation because Agnes's fiancé, a man whom Rickie had known when they were students together at public school, is to be there. Rickie not only dislikes Gerald Dawes but also hates to witness the happiness of the lovers; he feels that such happiness is forever denied him because of his lame foot, which he considers a hereditary disorder. During this time, Gerald is killed while playing football (soccer), and it is Rickie who is able to offer the most comfort to Agnes by convincing her that she should suffer, because her love for Gerald had been the greatest thing she could ever experience.

Two years later, when she comes again to visit him at Cambridge, Rickie realizes that he is in love with Agnes, although he still feels that he can never marry because of his deformity. She convinces him, however, that they should be married. Rickie is about to finish his work at Cambridge, but they feel a long engagement is necessary to give him time to settle himself. Ansell immediately opposes the marriage because he senses that Agnes is not a sincere person. She constantly lays claim to honesty and forthrightness, but Ansell cannot be convinced that these are the qualities of the true

Agnes. He quickly comes to believe that she will force Rickie into a dull and conventional life, convincing him at the same time that he is taking the proper steps.

Soon after they become engaged, Rickie and Agnes visit his aunt, Mrs. Emily Failing, at her country home. Rickie has never particularly liked his aunt, but since she is his only known relative, he and Agnes felt that they should go to see her. Mrs. Failing is a woman who likes to have people do what she wants, and she is never happier than when they are obviously uncomfortable while carrying out her desires. While Rickie and Agnes are visiting her, they also see Stephen Wonham, a young man whom Rickie has met before but whose relationship to Mrs. Failing has never been clear to him. After Rickie engages in an argument with his aunt, she informs him that Stephen is actually his brother. It is not until later that Rickie finds out that Stephen is the son of his mother, not of his father. Stephen himself does not know the details of his birth, but the matter has never greatly concerned him.

After they are married, Rickie and Agnes go to live with Herbert Pembroke at Sawston School. The arrangement has been worked out between Herbert and Agnes because Herbert needs help in his duties as a housemaster. Although Rickie soon realizes that Herbert is basically stupid and that they disagree on many points, he adapts himself to whatever course Herbert and Agnes choose. His marriage, in which he had hoped to find certain spiritual ideals, never reaches a very intimate level, and before long, his life becomes a shell. Ansell will have no more to do with him, and he is cut off from the one person of any intellect at the school because of Herbert's feelings and aspirations.

Two years later, after Rickie has apparently succumbed completely to the forces playing on him, Stephen Wonham again enters his life. It becomes apparent immediately that Agnes, who has kept up a connection with Mrs. Failing and who wishes to inherit the money from her estate, has been instrumental in having Stephen thrown out of Mrs. Failing's house. Rickie is furious but again submits. Stephen, who has finally been told the truth about who he is, arrives at Sawston expecting to find the kind of familial love he has never known before, but when Rickie refuses to see him and Agnes offers him money never to say anything about his parentage, he leaves immediately.

Stephen wanders around London for several days, doing odd jobs and supporting himself as best he can. Before long, he has saved enough money for a drunken spree. In his drunkenness, he decides to wreck Rickie's house and returns to Sawston, where Rickie ends up saving him from almost killing himself. By this time, Rickie is under the influence of

Ansell again and has begun to see how foolish he has been. He decides to give Stephen a home, but Stephen, who rejects this idea, manages to convince Rickie that they should go away together.

With that, the regeneration of Rickie's soul begins, but it is of short duration. On a subsequent visit to his aunt, at which time Stephen insists on accompanying him, he again saves Stephen's life but loses his own when Stephen, who has promised not to drink, gets drunk and collapses on the railroad tracks. Rickie manages to get Stephen clear but is himself killed by a train. Just before he dies, he realizes that he has been betrayed a second time by his belief in the individual.

Critical Evaluation:

Best known for his haunting novel *A Passage to India* (1924), E. M. Forster in *The Longest Journey* creates a less exotic setting but an equally powerful delineation of character and exploration of humanist values. The primary theme of *The Longest Journey* is Rickie Elliot's progression from unloved child to responsible brother, a lengthy progression of his own soul epitomized by the novel's very title. Unlike Rickie, Forster had a close attachment to his mother, but like his character, Forster had a very lonely childhood that did not end until he entered King's College, Cambridge, in 1897. As an undergraduate there, he studied classics and history and joined a circle of intellectuals—the so-called Cambridge Apostles—who met regularly to discuss aesthetics and art. It was the sort of life that Forster thoroughly enjoyed, and he was sorry to see it end upon his graduation in 1901. After he had established himself as an important writer with the publication of *A Passage to India*, Cambridge invited him to deliver a series of lectures about the art of fiction; these lectures were revised and published as *Aspects of the Novel* (1927). He later became an honorary Fellow at King's College and continued to visit and lecture at Cambridge until his death on June 7, 1970.

To understand the primary theme of *The Longest Journey*—Rickie's gradual acceptance of responsibility for his half brother, Stephen Wonham—one should consider the characters symbolically. Forster conceives Rickie as an Everyman, a person intended to set an example for the reader. After a life of frustrations, Rickie thinks he finally understands the nature of things and, more important, of himself. As it turns out, all his hard-earned knowledge is irrelevant when he is confronted by a person who is anti-intellectual and continually acts from impulse. This person is Rickie's own half brother, who symbolizes passion. At first, Rickie denies the importance of his half brother and rejects the notion of any relationship between them. Symbolically, he thereby rejects the idea that impulse, or passion, is necessary for life.

The necessity of passion in life is a major theme in nearly all of Forster's early novels and short stories, as, for example, in "The Road from Colonus" (1903), "The Story of a Panic" (1904), and *A Room with a View* (1908). Essentially, Forster argues in these works that the English are so preoccupied with material society that they neglect their inner selves. This neglect, however, may be rectified with a trip to southern Europe—specifically, Greece or Italy—where the people have not lost their passion for life. Indeed, in each of these works the central character travels to Greece or Italy and there experiences a revelation about how to live. In *A Room with a View*, for instance, Lucy Honeychurch, who is somewhat similar in nature to Rickie Elliot, travels to Florence and learns the value of passionate love. Rickie, however, never travels to Italy, although he longs to do so throughout the novel. Consequently, he is left unfulfilled and dies without ever learning about the human need for passion. Certainly, he gains a measure of self-knowledge when he saves his drunken brother from the train, but it comes too late for him to change his life for the better, as Lucy Honeychurch changes hers in *A Room with a View*. Thus, while Lucy's novel ends happily with her new insight into human nature, Rickie's ends tragically just as he begins to attain a glimpse into human nature.

A secondary theme of *The Longest Journey* attempts to answer the question, What is a proper education? The Sawston School, where Rickie teaches, is modeled on the public school in Tonbridge that Forster attended from 1893 to 1897. Forster loathed the educational system of Tonbridge and often said that his four years there were the worst of his life. He particularly despised the bullying inflicted on him by the older boys, although he found some solace in being one of the better scholars in his class. By dramatically contrasting the harshness of Sawston School with the freedom of Cambridge in *The Longest Journey*, Forster makes clear his belief in the importance of a liberal, humanist education that allows a mind to roam freely through the arts and sciences. Forster intends for his readers to see Cambridge as the ideal environment in which young people should be educated.

The Longest Journey remained Forster's favorite among his own novels throughout his life. It was the only one of his works that had practically written itself. Upon its publication on April 16, 1907, the novel received favorable reviews from most critics, although some of Forster's closest friends felt that the characters were poorly developed. Their objections to the work did not, however, discourage Forster from resuming work on his next novel, *A Room with a View*, which he had begun to write in 1902, or from planning another novel that eventually became *Howards End* (1910). *The Longest Journey* is certainly not Forster's best novel, but it is the one that helped to establish him as a leading novelist in Edwardian England.

"Critical Evaluation" by Jim McWilliams

Further Reading

Beauman, Nicola. *E. M. Forster: A Biography.* New York: Alfred A. Knopf, 1994. Shows clearly the autobiographical elements of *The Longest Journey*, including how Forster's relationship with a close friend at Tonbridge School parallels the Rickie-Stewart relationship. Argues that the novel was influenced by Forster's reading of Edward Carpenter, an English philosopher and social critic.

Bradshaw, David, ed. *The Cambridge Companion to E. M. Forster.* New York: Cambridge University Press, 2007. Collection of essays examines various aspects of Forster's life and work. *The Longest Journey* is discussed in several essays, particularly "Forster and England," by Paul Peppis, and "Forster and Women," by Jane Goldman.

Edwards, Mike. *E. M. Forster: The Novels.* New York: Palgrave, 2002. Demonstrates how readers can analyze four of Forster's novels—*A Room with a View*, *Howards End*, *A Passage to India*, and *The Longest Journey*—to understand the author's treatment of characters, locations, relationships, and other aspects of these works. Also provides ideas to help readers engage in further analysis, information about Forster's life, and examples of how four literary critics have approached Forster's writing.

Furbank, P. N. *E. M. Forster: A Life.* 1978. Reprint. San Diego, Calif.: Harcourt Brace, 1994. Comprehensive biography provides many details about Forster's life and ideas, including information about his schooling and how he used his own public school, Tonbridge, as a model for Sawston School in *The Longest Journey*. Also discusses Forster's residency at Cambridge.

Land, Stephen K. *Challenge and Conventionality in the Fiction of E. M. Forster.* New York: AMS Press, 1990. Finds *The Longest Journey* interesting because of the depth of Rickie's evolution. Argues that Forster's primary theme is the conflict between conventional and liberal worlds as symbolized by the characters in the novel.

Medalie, David. *E. M. Forster's Modernism.* New York: Palgrave, 2002. Examines the relationship of Forster's writings to modernism, analyzing his works to demonstrate their modernist elements. Places Forster within the context of early twentieth century social, political, and aesthetic developments.

Rapport, Nigel. *The Prose and the Passion: Anthropology, Literature, and the Writing of E. M. Forster.* New York: St. Martin's Press, 1994. Looks at Forster's work from both anthropological and literary perspectives, providing excellent interpretation and criticism of the author's writings.

Rosecrance, Barbara. *Forster's Narrative Vision.* Ithaca, N.Y.: Cornell University Press, 1982. Points out that while *The Longest Journey* ends tragically with Rickie's death, it also concludes on an affirmative note of hope for the future. Demonstrates how Forster's second novel is markedly better than his first, *Where Angels Fear to Tread.*

A Longing for the Light

Author: Vicente Aleixandre (1898-1984)
First published: 1979
Type of work: Poetry

The poetry of Vicente Aleixandre, who won the Nobel Prize in Literature in 1977, became more accessible to English-speaking readers with the publication of *A Longing for the Light*, a collection of translations from the Spanish by editor Lewis Hyde and fourteen other hands. Most of the poems in the English-language collection were initially selected by Aleixandre, and they exemplify some of the best and most representative works of Aleixandre's career to 1979. The title is a translation of a phrase that Aleixandre used to characterize his poetry. Aleixandre used the metaphor of differing lights to describe his belief that poetry is both composed and read in differing circumstances. He advised his readers that his poems may be read in terms of "rainbow light," understanding that he may have composed them in other lights, such as the "black light" with which he says he wrote his very early poems. In a sense, then, *A Longing for the Light* traces Aleixandre's journey through various densities of light, exploring the relative solitude and connectedness possible to the human condition as well as the possibilities of the artistic vision and artistic creation to communicate.

His first published work, *Ámbito* (1928), shows the influence of Juan Ramón Jiménez and displays Aleixandre's affinities with other members of the Generation of '27, such as Jorge Guillén. Unlike Guillén, who believed that the poetic experience is a heightening of reality, Aleixandre believed that it is a means of tapping into the subconscious mind at the level where people are connected to the universe. Selections from *Ámbito* in *A Longing for the Light* are "Closed," "Sea and Sunrise," and "Sea and Night." In these, as in the rest of the collection, night is a major player, "famous" and "quiet": "Mouth—sea—all of it pleads for night." It is an essentially sensual collection: "Either flesh or the light of flesh,/ deep," he writes. In *Ámbito*, Aleixandre begins to develop a view of the universe that would unfold in his poetic career: The sea and the sun and the night all exist in a cycle of absorption, destruction, and rebirth.

His critics generally divide Aleixandre's work into three major groups, the first of which, his Surrealist group, includes *Espadas como labios* (1932; swords like lips), *La destrucción o el amor* (1935; *Destruction or Love*, 1976), *Pasión de la tierra* (1935; the earth's passion), *Sombra del paraíso* (1944, written earlier; *Shadow of Paradise*, 1987), and *Mundo a solas* (1950, written earlier; *World Alone*, 1982). He described his work beginning in 1928 as "a gradual emergence into light." It seems that his way into the light was a path through the darkness of the subconscious, for in 1928, he read and became profoundly influenced by the psychoanalytic work of Sigmund Freud. His poetry thereafter self-consciously deals with many issues raised by Freud, most especially that of the existence of a subconscious mind, of dreams, of the ground of consciousness, of the libido, of the tension between love and death.

Aleixandre stated that the themes of his first period concerned creation and the possibility of the poet losing his own identity and fusing with the cosmos through an escape from the bounds of rational consciousness. Works of this phase explore the themes of love and death, the ability of the mind as well as of the universe to create and to destroy, and the power of the mind to connect with cosmic forces. These works are well characterized by a statement of Aleixandre's translator Lewis Hyde, who notes that they represent "the reflective mind trying to think its way out of coherence and precision."

Pasión de la tierra, included in *A Longing for the Light*,

explores the poetic possibilities of Freudian dream imagery. Much of Aleixandre's work relies on the kind of associative movement that one finds in dreams, and most of his poems ought to be read for their connections in this manner; coherence comes through associative links rather than through linear narrative progression. The prose poems of *Pasión de la tierra* represent Aleixandre's poetic compositions most closely associated with the Surrealist movement. This collection is characterized by erratic and irrational images of turbulence and upheaval, of "torrential silence and lava," of a speaker who is often threatened by death when isolated from love. It displays the author's penchant for the macabre and even the gothic as it translates into a twentieth century idiom, to be developed further in *Espadas como labios*. This collection, represented by "Death or the Waiting Room," "Silence," and "Flying Fugue on a Horse," has been called one of the most unfathomable works of twentieth century Spanish poetry. The prose poems express what Aleixandre terms the *conciencia sin funda*, or "consciousness without limitations," and he notes that this is his most difficult book. His declared aesthetic intent is to utilize all of language, even the ugly and inharmonious, to reach that profound plane of consciousness. He states: "I shall not avoid even one word."

Included in the second major group of *A Longing for the Light*, "Poems with Red Light," are selections dealing with love and the physical world. In these poems, human sexual interaction may be viewed as emblematic of the nature of a universe that destroys and re-creates itself.

In *Espadas como labios*, Aleixandre returns from the prose poems of *Pasión de la tierra* to verse or, more specifically, free verse characterized by his evolving and idiosyncratic style. He maintains the surreal idiom. Aleixandre challenges the reader to make the leaps in comparisons and in irrational logic with him, like those in "At the Bottom of the Well (The Buried Man)," when "in the ear the echo was already solid," and in "The Waltz," when things clash together: "seashells, heels, foam and false teeth," a kiss turns into a deadly "fishbone." His poetry is of the realm of heightened senses, in which moments of transformation follow one after another with lightning rapidity. Accustomed to working through only one poetic experience in a lyric poem, the reader is challenged by Aleixandre's demand to move with him through series after series of a rapid succession of transformative images. In this volume, Aleixandre is already using one of his characteristic poetic devices (one that will appear again in the title of his next volume), that of juxtaposing with the word "or" two elements that may be set in contrast or that may be intended as comparisons or that may even be meant to represent the same thing.

Destruction or Love and *Shadow of Paradise* have been said to form the cornerstones of Aleixandre's work. *Destruction or Love* is a very complex work, produced as the poet returned to health after a serious illness. Aleixandre describes the volume's theme as "the poet's vision of the world," the "amorous unity of the universe" in which a poet's vision of a whole cosmos becomes coherent within this world of change through love. He turns from the spiritual to the physical and to that kind of consuming love that allows the individual, through his or her own destruction, to become one with the cosmic forces in a mystical union.

Images of the elemental forces of the universe and processions of living things on earth flicker in a panoply as parts of a woman's body transform into emblems of the universe. In "The Jungle and the Sea," wild animals "draw their swords or teeth/ like blood" out of an innocent and loving heart. Tigers' claws sink into the earth like love into a heart. Above them flies a "bird of happiness" toward "the distant sea that recedes like the light." A human being's actual ability to fuse with the cosmos is questionable, for solitude informs the mortal state, and finitude prevents an individual from being anything other than a physical being of the material world. The sexual act, then, becomes the sole means of becoming one with the universe, for in it, the individual and the light of individual consciousness emblematically die, permitting oceanic darkness to overwhelm the psyche. In "The Wholeness Within Her," the speaker longs for "love or death," knowing he is threatened by "light or fatal sword" that "could never break up the wholeness of this world."

World Alone reflects Aleixandre's plunge into postwar depression. Sadness and a return to hope mark the third group of poems. The speaker of "Under the Ground," for example, becomes the serpentine "dark shadow coiled among tree roots" as he contrasts life above and below ground, life and death. The poem ends, as Aleixandre's poems often do, with a paradox that sends the reader back into the poem to make it divulge its meaning. In this volume, he writes, "man doesn't exist."

In *Shadow of Paradise*, published after the Spanish Civil War, Aleixandre revises his most dismal vision of *World Alone* and returns to the pristine world of Málaga and the Mediterranean of his childhood, although such hopeful works as "The Hands" are set in contrast to those like "What Happens to All Flesh." Aleixandre believed that *World Alone* was the transition point between his earlier, more Surrealist phase and his work to come. In it, he fuses his dream style with one more accessible to waking consciousness, more "coherent." Many of its poems look forward to the shift in subject matter that occurs in *Historia del corazón* (1954; history of the

heart). In *Shadow of Paradise* he begins his turning away from the completely interior world to the waking world of living humanity, envisioning the possibilities of compassion in daily life. The physical body and the soul are blended and separated, as are the metaphysical circumstances of each. As with much in Aleixandre's work, the cognizance of the human being's ultimate isolation colors everything, so that paradise here must remain only a shadow, as his title indicates.

Works published in the aftermath of the Spanish Civil War are represented in the section "Poems with White Light." This section includes poems from his books *Nacimiento último* (1953; final birth), *Historia del corazón*, *En un vasto dominio* (1962; in a vast dominion), and *Retratos con nombre* (1965; portraits with names). Fundamentally a pessimist, Aleixandre made a breakthrough with *Historia del corazón*. Prior to this volume, he explored the depths of human solitude, but in *Historia del corazón*, he writes: "This now is the opposite of human loneliness. No, we aren't alone." Here, the sky shines "with mercy." The volume marks the change in his poetic world from the surreal to the real and adulates the possibilities of communication, of friendship, brotherhood, and other ties of the human heart that occur within the cycle of life. The images and style are as accessible as those of *Shadow of Paradise*. Critics have praised several of the love poems in this collection, wherein, possibly for the first time in Spanish poetry, the love relationship becomes conscious of its own myths and illusions. The human condition Aleixandre describes as a "lightning flash between two darknesses." The "dream or its shadow" is that on which we "feed," and, Aleixandre writes, "Its name is Love!" Although Aleixandre's thematic focus has, in these postwar, more accessible, more hopeful poems, shifted in many ways, the problem of solitude remains.

En un vasto dominio opens in a most physical way, with poems that deal with bodily parts, in order to examine minutely the functioning of humanity. It is the story of humanity evolving. The poet then shifts his focus to a rich stream of Spanish life, from town square to cemetery, from local history to a young couple who have between them the capacity to ensure the continuation of life. In "Human Matter," for example, the entire city is described as "one substance" in which every action affects everyone and everything.

Poemas de la consumación (1968; poems of ripeness) and *Diálogos del conocimiento* (1974; dialogues of knowledge) are grouped together as "Recent Poems." These books are represented by several poems, one of the most compelling of which is "The Old Man Is Like Moses": "not with the useless tablets and the chisel and the lightning in the mountains/ but with words broken on the ground, his hair/ on fire, his ears singed by the terrifying words." In *Poemas de la consumación*, old age is portrayed as a time in which the possibilities of love are past. *Diálogos del conocimiento* universalizes the intensely personal vision of *Poemas de la consumación*. In *Diálogos del conocimiento*, fifteen dialogues are actually juxtaposed monologues, reflecting the failure of spoken language to reach another individual as well as the necessity of artistic expression to verbalize the significant. Aleixandre's intent is to show that any situation can be perceived differently by everyone. As the title indicates, he examines the various ways in which life experience teaches one to know and to understand. "To know by experience is to love," he writes, and "To know intellectually is to die." He introduces the distinction between knowing with the mind and knowing with the body. For example, in "Sound of the War," the voices of a soldier, a sorcerer, a bird, and a lark talk—but not to each other—about war. Aleixandre's groundbreaking prosody in the *Diálogos de conocimiento* is of an unforgettable and majestic slowness.

Donna Berliner

Further Reading

Aleixandre, Vicente. *A Longing for the Light: Selected Poems of Vicente Aleixandre*. Edited and translated by Lewis Hyde. 2d ed. Port Townsend, Wash.: Copper Canyon Press, 2007. Includes an informative introduction by Hyde as well as a descriptive bibliography that features Aleixandre's own brief critical summaries of his individual books.

Cobb, Carl W. "Poets Uprooted and Rebellious: Lorca, Alberti, Aleixandre, Cernuda." In *Contemporary Spanish Poetry, 1898-1963*, edited by Carl W. Cobb. Boston: Twayne, 1976. Discusses the significant characteristics of works by writers collectively known as the Generation of '27. Includes an accessible explanation of the aesthetic and thematic significance of each of Aleixandre's works.

Daydi-Tolson, Santiago, ed. *Vicente Aleixandre: A Critical Appraisal*. Ypsilanti, Mich.: Bilingual Press, 1981. Contains several chapters in English on Aleixandre as well as the poet's Nobel Prize lecture and an English translation of an article on Aleixandre's work by Carlos Bousoño.

Harris, Derek. "Prophet, Medium, Babbler: Voice and Identity in Vicente Aleixandre's Surrealist Poetry." In *Companion to Spanish Surrealism*, edited by Robert Havard. Rochester, N.Y.: Tamesis, 2004. Places Aleixandre's poetry within the context of the evolution of the important Surrealist artistic movement in Spain.

Morris, C. B. *A Generation of Spanish Poets, 1920-1936*. New York: Cambridge University Press, 1969. Places Aleixandre with his contemporaries, showing generational affinities among the poets and examining them as links in the greater Spanish literary tradition.

Murphy, Daniel. *Vicente Aleixandre's Stream of Lyric Consciousness*. Lewisburg, Pa.: Bucknell University Press, 2001. Provides a detailed analysis of the Surrealist nature of Aleixandre's poetry, focusing on *Destruction or Love*. Examines the role of Sigmund Freud in Aleixandre's work, his poems' narrative structure, and how his poetry was influenced by earlier writers.

Schwartz, Kessel. *Vicente Aleixandre*. New York: Twayne, 1970. A Freudian critic offers an accessible introduction to Aleixandre's work.

Soufas, C. Christopher. *The Subject in Question: Early Contemporary Spanish Literature and Modernism*. Washington, D.C.: Catholic University of America Press, 2007. Examines a number of works of drama, fiction, and poetry—including Aleixandre's—from late nineteenth and early twentieth century Spain, focusing on their modernist characteristics.

Look Back in Anger

Author: John Osborne (1929-1994)
First produced: 1956; first published, 1957
Type of work: Drama
Type of plot: Protest drama
Time of plot: 1950's
Locale: A city in the English Midlands

Principal characters:
JIMMY PORTER, a young man
ALISON PORTER, his wife
CLIFF LEWIS, their friend
HELENA CHARLES, a friend of Alison and later Jimmy's mistress
COLONEL REDFERN, Alison's father

The Story:

On a Sunday evening in April, Jimmy Porter and Cliff Lewis, both working-class men, and Jimmy's upper-class wife, Alison, are in the attic flat they share. Music is playing on the radio, and while Alison irons, Jimmy and Cliff read the newspapers. From time to time, Jimmy makes acid comments on what he is reading, orders the other two to minister to his needs, or points out Cliff's defects, in particular his ignorance and his ineffectuality. Jimmy's worst venom is reserved for his wife, who he says is as vacuous as her mother and father and, like them, incapable of thought. Cliff defends Alison, and she treats him with sisterly affection, pressing his trousers and giving him cigarettes, despite the fact that the doctor and Jimmy have forbidden him to smoke. Furious because Cliff and Alison refuse to fight with him, Jimmy contrasts their lethargy with the energy of his former mistress, Madeline, and of Webster, a gay friend of Alison. He then returns to his verbal attacks on Alison, her family, and her gender, claiming that women's worst vice is that they are noisy. Increasingly annoyed with both Alison and Cliff, Jimmy turns off the radio, contending that with Alison ironing and Cliff turning the pages of his newspaper, it is impossible to hear the music.

Cliff finally insists that Jimmy apologize to them both, and in the resulting scuffle, the ironing board is knocked down and Alison is burned. Angry at last, she tells Jimmy to leave. He walks out of the room, and while Cliff is treating her injury, she confides in him. She is miserable, she says, and even though she is pregnant, she is seriously considering leaving Jimmy. Jimmy comes back into the room and apologizes to Alison, attempting to explain his behavior as a reaction against his feeling that he is trapped by his love for her; he also acknowledges an abiding anger because Alison has never experienced the pain that he has and cannot understand him. Alison is then called to the telephone downstairs. She returns to report that she has invited an actor friend, Helena Charles, who has just come to town, to stay with them for a few days until she finds a place to live.

Two weeks later, Helena has established herself in the household, and, as Cliff commented, the tension has mounted. It is true that by doing most of the cooking Helena is a great help to Alison; however, she makes no secret of her dislike for Jimmy. She pressures Alison to take immediate action about her situation, either by telling Jimmy about her pregnancy and demanding that he become a responsible member of society or by leaving him and returning to her parents. Jimmy makes no secret of his hatred for Helena, and after Alison announces that she is going to church with her friend, Jimmy draws the battle lines. Helena and he are fighting

for Alison, he says, and he is determined to win. Without Alison's knowledge, however, Helena has already sent a telegram to Alison's father, Colonel Redfern, telling him that his daughter needs him. Somewhat uncertainly, Alison says that she will go home with her father. She does not tell Jimmy of her plans, but when he is summoned to the deathbed of his best friend's mother and begs Alison to accompany him, she coldly refuses and walks out, followed by Helena, who is accompanying her to church.

When Colonel Redfern appears at the Porter apartment the next afternoon, Jimmy has not returned. In his conversation with Alison, her father shows considerable sympathy for Jimmy, even commenting that Alison seems to have learned a lot from him. He also suggests that Alison's mother has wronged Jimmy by hiring detectives to find some way to discredit or destroy him. Alison has made her decision, however. In response to Cliff's question as to who will break the news of her departure to her husband, she hands him a letter for Jimmy. Indicating that he does not like to see anyone suffer, Cliff goes out to get something to eat and, he says, probably to have a few drinks. The colonel had assumed that Helena would be leaving along with Alison, but, as Cliff has predicted, Helena makes excuses and remains. When Jimmy appears, he is so furious because Alison has slighted the dying woman that he does not seem to care much about her having walked out on him. He is not even particularly affected by Helena's revelation that Alison is pregnant. Helena slaps him, but when Jimmy collapses with grief, she kisses him and pulls him into an embrace.

Several months later, Helena is doing the ironing, sweetly approving of everything Jimmy does and says. She tells Jimmy that she does not intend to go to church, and Jimmy exults at having led her into a state of sin. Cliff, who does not like Helena and obviously misses Alison, is planning to move out. Cliff and Jimmy, both in a good humor, make up a vaudeville skit, which, as usual, ends in a tussle. Helena tells Jimmy that she loves him, and, although he does not respond in kind, he is tender and affectionate toward her, even offering to take her out on the town.

Unexpectedly, Alison arrives, looking extremely unwell. Jimmy refuses to speak to his wife and leaves the room. When they are alone, the women confide in each other. Helena tells Alison that her affair with Jimmy is finished and that she intends to leave him. Alison tells Helena that she lost her baby and cannot have another. Concerned about Jimmy, Alison urges Helena to remain with him, but Helena reiterates her opinion that all is over between the two of them, in part because they are so different and in part because she cannot overcome her feelings of guilt. The women argue as to which of them, if either, Jimmy really needs. When Jimmy comes back into the room, Helena tells him of her decision. Angrily, he sweeps her possessions off the dresser and thrusts them into her arms, and she goes downstairs to pack.

Still angry about Alison's indifference to the death of his friend's mother, Jimmy tells Alison how disappointed he has been in her, and she collapses on the floor, begging his forgiveness. In losing the baby, she says, she has at last experienced the pain of living and so can be what he wants her to be. Tenderly, Jimmy comforts her, and, clinging together, the two promise that from now on they will protect each other in a world that is inimical to love.

Critical Evaluation:

Look Back in Anger established John Osborne as the leader and prototype of the so-called Angry Young Men, a group of British playwrights and novelists of the 1950's who shared leftist or even anarchic political views and wrote to express their disillusionment with the status quo. Although *Look Back in Anger* is not as unconventional or original as it initially appeared to be—its popular and critical success must be attributed in part to the fact that it appeared after one of the dullest decades in British theater—it is nevertheless of more than merely historical importance.

Osborne's greatest strengths are in dialogue and characterization. Except for entrances, exits, and an occasional kiss, slap, or scuffle, there is little physical action in *Look Back in Anger*. Instead, the real drama is found in the verbal interplay between the characters. It is also interesting that in this play, as is generally true of Osborne's works, there is only one character with a real gift for language. Cliff and Alison, who are both at the mercy of Jimmy's sharper wit, feel they can fight back only by refusing to respond to his insults. Helena at first exhibits some cleverness, but once Jimmy has chained her to the bed and the ironing board, she simply works at being a good audience for him.

It has been noted that the most dramatic, and indeed the most hilarious, segments of *Look Back in Anger* are Jimmy's monologues. This is, of course, consistent with the fact that *Look Back in Anger* is essentially a one-character play—something that is also true of Osborne's best-known later works, *The Entertainer* (pr., pb. 1957) and *Luther* (pr., pb. 1961). Osborne himself had not intended *Look Back in Anger* to be centered only on Jimmy. Colonel Redfern is a complex character, not nearly as obtuse as Jimmy suggests, and Helena, who at first appears to be the villain of the piece, develops into a rather fascinating individual by the end of the play. Interestingly, it is not Jimmy but Alison who, according to

Osborne's stage directions, is the most complicated of the three characters onstage at the beginning of the play. The fact remains, however, that Jimmy upstages everyone else because of his verbal brilliance.

Osborne's theory and his practice are at odds in *Look Back in Anger*. The play is generally classified as a protest play, one that voices the anger of working-class men at having willingly fought Great Britain's wars only to return to a caste-conscious society that denied them opportunity, advancement, and even an acknowledgment of their dignity. Although the classless society that Osborne advocated could easily find room for weaker souls like Cliff or the suggestible Alison, it would have no place for a Jimmy Porter, who would refuse or be unable to suppress his insistent self for the common good.

Moreover, the play does not end with the triumph of the revolution or even with a useful martyrdom. If Jimmy Porter's wife has been brought into the working-class camp, that has been accomplished not by him but by life; only because life has brought Alison pain, loss, and the experience of death does it become possible for her to empathize with her husband and, by implication, to surrender to his enormous ego. When the two are reconciled, they return to the fantasy world of their honeymoon; playing bear and squirrel, they retreat from the world. This is a far cry from the joint plans for social action that could be expected from a protest playwright.

Whatever its deficiencies or its inconsistencies, however, *Look Back in Anger* delighted contemporary audiences, who, like the playwright himself, saw the play as a comedy. If Osborne is to be faulted for writing a play with much talk and little commitment, one must applaud him for creating at least one unforgettable character and for bringing new energy to the British theater.

Rosemary M. Canfield Reisman

Further Reading

Carter, Alan. *John Osborne.* 2d ed. New York: Harper & Row, 1973. Includes a chapter on *Look Back in Anger* that provides a good starting point for study of the play. Discusses the work's critical and popular reception and explains its importance in theatrical history.

Denison, Patricia D., ed. *John Osborne: A Casebook.* New York: Garland, 1997. Collection of essays presents analyses of all of Osborne's work, including several pieces about *Look Back in Anger*. Writer John Mortimer contributes his essay "The Angry Young Man Who Stayed That Way," and playwright David Hare provides a eulogy for Osborne.

Elsom, John. *Post-War British Theatre*. London: Routledge & Kegan Paul, 1976. Compares Osborne with other writers of the period. Affirms that, though hardly the proletarian war cry some have supposed, *Look Back in Anger* inspired other dramatists, particularly through its vivid characterization and riveting dialogue.

Gilleman, Luc M. *John Osborne, Vituperative Artist: A Reading of His Life and Work*. New York: Routledge, 2002. Presents an appraisal of Osborne's life and work. Devotes a chapter to a detailed analysis and contextual overview of *Look Back in Anger*.

Hayman, Ronald. *John Osborne*. 3d ed. New York: Frederick Ungar, 1976. Argues that Osborne's characters are not in fact representatives of a class or a point of view; rather, they are rebels dominated by their own egomania. A readable and persuasive analysis.

Heilpern, John. *The Many Lives of the Angry Young Man*. New York: Alfred A. Knopf, 2007. Discusses Osborne's life and career, noting that the playwright's fear of loss, the "legacy" of the death of his father when Osborne was fifteen, "seeps through his plays."

Hinchliffe, Arnold P. *John Osborne*. Boston: Twayne, 1984. Balanced and detailed work traces the action of Osborne's plays in each scene and suggests various interpretations. Also presents an extended and thoughtful discussion of Osborne's politics.

Sierz, Aleks. *John Osborne's "Look Back in Anger."* New York: Continuum, 2008. Critical introduction to the play discusses the social and political context in which it was written and analyzes its structure, style, and characters. Includes an overview of the work's production history and key production issues.

Look Homeward, Angel
A Story of the Buried Life

Author: Thomas Wolfe (1900-1938)
First published: 1929
Type of work: Novel
Type of plot: Impressionistic realism
Time of plot: 1900 to early 1920's
Locale: North Carolina

Principal characters:
EUGENE GANT, a shy boy
ELIZA GANT, his mother
OLIVER GANT, his father
BEN GANT, his brother
MARGARET LEONARD, his teacher
LAURA JAMES, his first sweetheart

The Story:

Eugene, the youngest child in the Gant family, comes into the world when his mother, Eliza Gant, is forty-two years old. His father, Oliver Gant, goes on periodic drinking sprees to forget his unfulfilled ambitions and the unsatisfied wanderlust that has brought him to Altamont, in the hills of Old Catawba. When Eugene is born, his father is asleep in a drunken stupor.

Eliza disapproves of her husband's debauches, but she lacks the imagination to understand their cause. Oliver, who was raised amid the plenty of a Pennsylvania farm, has no comprehension of the privation and suffering that existed in the South after the Civil War, the cause of the hoarding and acquisitiveness of his wife and her Pentland relations in the Old Catawba hill country.

Eliza bears the burden of Oliver's drinking and promiscuity until Eugene is four years old; then she departs for St. Louis, taking all the children with her except for the oldest daughter, Daisy. It is 1904, the year of the great St. Louis World's Fair, and Eliza intends to open a boardinghouse for her visiting fellow townspeople. The idea is abhorrent to Oliver, and he stays in Altamont. Eliza's sojourn in St. Louis ends abruptly when twelve-year-old Grover falls ill with typhoid and dies. Stunned, she gathers her remaining children and goes home.

Young Eugene is a shy, awkward boy with dark, brooding eyes. He is, like his ranting, histrionic father, a dreamer. He is not popular with his schoolmates, who sense instinctively that he is different and make him pay the price; at home, he is the victim of his sisters' and brothers' taunts and torments. His one champion is his brother Ben, though even Ben has been conditioned by the Gants' unemotional family life to give his caresses as cuffs.

There is little time, however, for Eugene's childish daydreaming. Eliza believes that having jobs at a young age will teach her boys manliness and self-reliance. Ben gets up at three o'clock every morning to deliver newspapers. Luke has been a *Saturday Evening Post* agent since he was twelve, and Eugene is put under his wing. Although the boy loathes the work, he is forced every Thursday to corner potential customers and keep up a continuous line of chatter until he breaks down their sales resistance.

Eugene is not yet eight when his parents separate. Eliza has bought the Dixieland boardinghouse as a good investment. Eugene's sister Helen remains at the old house with her father; Daisy has married and left town. Mrs. Gant takes Eugene with her, and Ben and Luke are left to shift for themselves, shuttling back and forth between the two houses. Eugene grows to detest his new home. When the Dixieland is crowded, there is no privacy, and Eliza advertises the Dixieland on printed cards that Eugene has to distribute to customers on his magazine route and to travelers arriving at the Altamont train station.

Although life at the boardinghouse is drab, the next four years are the golden days of Eugene's youth, for he is allowed to go to the Leonards' private school. Margaret Leonard, the tubercular wife of the schoolmaster, recognizes Eugene's hunger for beauty and love and is able to find in literature the words that she herself has not the power to utter. By the time he is fifteen, Eugene knows the greatest lyric poems almost line for line.

Eugene is also about to encounter other changes in his life. Oliver Gant, who was fifty when his youngest son was born, is beginning to feel his years. Although he is never told, he is slowly dying of cancer. Eugene is fourteen when World War I begins, and Ben, who wants to join the Canadian army, is warned by his doctor that he will be refused because he has weak lungs.

At age fifteen, Eugene is sent to the university at Pulpit Hill. It is his father's plan that Eugene should be well on his way toward being a great statesman before the time comes for old Oliver to die. Eugene's youth and tremendous height make him a natural target for dormitory horseplay, and his shy, awkward manners are intensified by his ignorance of the school's traditions and rituals. He rooms alone, and his only friends are four wastrels, one of whom contributes to his social education by introducing him to a brothel.

That summer, back at the Dixieland, Eugene meets Laura James. Sitting with her on the front porch at night, he is taken in by her quiet smile and clear, candid eyes. He becomes her lover on a summer afternoon of sunlit green and gold. Afterward, however, Laura goes home to visit her parents and writes to Eugene to tell him that she is about to marry a boy to whom she has been engaged for nearly a year.

Eugene goes back to Pulpit Hill in the autumn, still determined to go his way alone. Although he has no intimate friends, he gradually becomes a campus leader. The commonplace good fellows of his world tolerantly make room for the one who is not like them.

In October of the following year, Eugene receives an urgent summons to come home. Ben is finally paying the price of his parents' neglect and the drudgery of his life: He is dying of pneumonia. Eliza has neglected to call a competent doctor until it is too late, and Oliver, as he sits at the foot of the dying boy's bed, can think only of the burial expenses. As the family members keep their vigil through Ben's last night, they are touched by the realization of the greatness of the boy's generous soul. In a final irony, Ben is given the best funeral that money can buy.

With Ben go the family's last pretenses. When Eugene returns to the Dixieland after graduation, Eliza is in control of Oliver's property and is selling it as quickly as she can to get money for further land speculation. She has disposed of their old home, and Oliver is living in a back room of the boardinghouse. His children watch one another suspiciously as he wastes away, each concerned for his or her own inheritance. Eugene manages to remain unembroiled in their growing hatred of one another, but he cannot avoid being a target for that hatred. Helen, Luke, and Steve have always resented his schooling. In September, before Eugene leaves for Harvard to begin graduate work, Luke asks him to sign a release saying that he has received his inheritance as tuition and school expenses. Although his father had promised him an education when he was still a child and Eliza was to pay for his first year in the North, Eugene is glad to sign. He is free, and he is never coming back to Altamont.

On his last night at home, Eugene has a vision of his dead brother Ben in the moonlit square at midnight: Ben, the unloved of the Gants, and the most lovable. It is for Eugene as well a vision of old, unhappy, unforgotten years, and in his restless imagination, he dreams of the hidden door through which he will escape forever the mountain-rimmed world of his boyhood.

Critical Evaluation:

An alert reader of *Look Homeward, Angel* does not have to go very far into this long book before realizing that it is largely autobiographical. Though many details are imaginatively transformed, the hero, Eugene Gant, is Thomas Wolfe himself. The Gant family is Wolfe's family, and Altamont is Asheville, North Carolina, through the first two decades of the twentieth century. When the story concludes with Eugene's preparations to leave home for graduate study at Harvard, it has in effect come to a transitional moment in Wolfe's life. Wolfe finished at the University of North Carolina with the desire to become a playwright, and he went to Harvard primarily to study playwriting under George Pierce Baker.

All of this background is useful to know because it helps to explain the inception of *Look Homeward, Angel* and the curiosity of its form. After Wolfe completed a master's degree at Harvard he went to New York to live; there he taught composition at New York University while attempting to launch the career on which he was intent: playwriting. Success did not come quickly; readers of Wolfe should be able to see without difficulty that his peculiar gift was not one to fit easily with the tight discipline of the stage. He began to write the prose narrative that was published as *Look Homeward, Angel* in 1929.

Publication of Wolfe's manuscript followed substantial revision under the tutelage of Maxwell Perkins, a remarkable editor who saw in Wolfe an enormous but undisciplined talent. With the almost fatherly guidance of Perkins, Wolfe was able to bring a measure of order out of the sometimes brilliant chaos that frequently attended his writing. Upon the publication of *Look Homeward, Angel*, Wolfe more or less forsook playwriting to become a novelist and continued on this track until his early death in 1938.

This brings us back to the form of *Look Homeward, Angel*, which is called a novel because that seems to be the most convenient term, even if it is only approximate. The book is a prose narrative, and it is too imaginative to be called an autobiography. It is too enthusiastic to be called a meditation; too unsentimental, for all of its emotion, to be called a reminiscence. It has sometimes been called a bildungsroman, a term that is used to describe a novel that gives an account of the education of someone, usually a young man or woman. For lack of a better term to describe its form, Wolfe's book is simply regarded as a novel, which has put it at somewhat of a disadvantage because it does not measure up very well in relation to other novels that can be admired for their formal artistry.

Wolfe's problem was that he undertook to do two things that do not fit especially well with each other. First, and perhaps foremost, he wanted to express, in lyric prose, the complexity and wonder of American provincial life. In this artistic goal he might be seen as a kind of Walt Whitman of twentieth century America, and indeed his best prose is little different from Whitman's free-verse expression of America in the previous century. This intent, however, if it can be seen as such, does not fit very well with Wolfe's other goal, which might be expressed as that of creating a portrait of the artist as a grow-

ing boy. *Look Homeward, Angel* has for its subtitle *A Story of the Buried Life*. Eugene Gant, its hero, is seen from his infancy to a few months before his twentieth birthday (Wolfe was precocious and finished college himself at that early age). Eugene's life is "buried" because he has little outlet at home for the energy—emotional, intellectual, and creative—with which he has been gifted. His closest ally is his older brother Ben, who has died before the novel concludes. Eugene is essentially alone. Loneliness is frequently the artist's lot; in addition to the problems that go along with having an artistic sensibility, the artist must accept the measure of self-isolation necessary for the mastery of a creative discipline.

Thomas Wolfe's enthusiasm, personal and artistic, is largely evident in *Look Homeward, Angel*. It is his lyrical expression of an abundance of characters and dramatic moments that captured a reading audience from the time of his first novel's publication and held it for many years thereafter. His other theme, the isolation of the artistic sensibility, is occasionally striking and once in a while a trifle embarrassing, like a barely concealed confessional. If, however, the artist, in Wolfe or in his character Eugene Gant, must choose isolation or be chosen for it, the enthusiast of American experience must be hugely involved. In *Look Homeward, Angel*, Wolfe seems to have tried to have it both ways, and he was successful only in part. This may be the primary reason for the criticism to which this work has been subjected. Wolfe did not understand that he could write one kind of book or the other, but if he tried to do both at the same time, he was going to have trouble with his form.

Look Homeward, Angel is best read in parts. After a reader has been through the book once, a second reading will not produce the rewards that come from repeated engagements with selected parts, such as W. O. Gant's stream of consciousness as he rides a trolley home on his return from California or the gathering of town characters at Uneeda Lunch, or the chapter wherein W. O. Gant sells the sculpted stone angel on the porch of his business to the town madam, who needs it for one of her girls, who has died. Wolfe's readers tend to select their own favorite passages, and although some of their selections are justifiable on critical grounds, some are not. This is the virtue of a large book about ordinary American experience: What is perceived as extraordinary will vary with the individual readers.

"Critical Evaluation" by John Higby

Further Reading

Bloom, Harold, ed. *Thomas Wolfe*. New York: Chelsea House, 1987. Collection of eight essays by seven writers includes a general overview of Wolfe's fiction, an examination of his treatment of the South, and a discussion of structure, theme, and metaphor in *Look Homeward, Angel*.

Donald, David Herbert. *Look Homeward: A Life of Thomas Wolfe*. 1987. Reprint. Cambridge, Mass.: Harvard University Press, 2003. Widely admired biography was prepared with the aid of Wolfe's voluminous papers, which are lodged at Harvard University. Focuses on the events of Wolfe's life while attempting to offer "a group photograph . . . of what can properly be called the Great Generation in American literature."

Ensign, Robert Taylor. *Lean Down Your Ear upon the Earth, and Listen: Thomas Wolfe's Greener Modernism*. Columbia: University of South Carolina Press, 2003. Presents an ecocritical interpretation of Wolfe's work, examining the novelist's depiction of the natural world and his characters' connection with it. One chapter provides a "green" analysis of *Look Homeward, Angel*.

Holliday, Shawn. *Thomas Wolfe and the Politics of Modernism*. New York: Peter Lang, 2001. Offers a reevaluation of Wolfe and his work, describing him as a modernist writer based on the experimental nature of his fiction and other aspects of his writing and his life.

Idol, John Lane, Jr. *A Thomas Wolfe Companion*. New York: Greenwood Press, 1987. Very informative resource includes a selected bibliography of Wolfe publications, an annotated bibliography of criticism, and a short list of information sources. A helpful glossary identifies many characters and places fictionalized by Wolfe.

Johnston, Carol Ingalls. *Of Time and the Artist: Thomas Wolfe, His Novels, and the Critics*. Columbia, S.C.: Camden House, 1996. Examines the bitter relationship between Wolfe and the literary critics and discusses how he responded to their critiques in his fiction and letters. A section about *Look Homeward, Angel* includes information about the book's initial American reviews and critical responses to it from the 1940's onward.

Wolfe, Thomas. *The Notebooks of Thomas Wolfe*. 2 vols. Edited by Richard S. Kennedy and Paschal Reeves. Chapel Hill: University of North Carolina Press, 1970. Volume 1 includes Wolfe's personal notes from the entire period when he was at work on *Look Homeward, Angel*. Editors' notes help relate Wolfe's various jottings to incidents in his book.

_____. *O Lost: A Story of the Buried Life—The Original Version of "Look Homeward, Angel."* Text established by Arlyn Bruccoli and Matthew J. Bruccoli. Columbia: University of South Carolina Press, 2000. At the request of his editor, Maxwell Perkins, Wolfe deleted some sixty-six thousand words from his original manuscript, and the abridged text was published as *Look Homeward, Angel* in 1929. This volume contains the restored original work.

Looking Backward
2000-1887

Author: Edward Bellamy (1850-1898)
First published: 1888
Type of work: Novel
Type of plot: Utopian
Time of plot: 1887 and 2000
Locale: Boston

Principal characters:
JULIAN WEST, a traveler in time
EDITH BARTLETT, his nineteenth century fiancé
DR. LEETE, a twentieth century citizen
EDITH LEETE, his daughter

The Story:

Julian West has had difficulty sleeping. In order to have complete quiet, he has built a soundproof room with thick cement walls in the cellar of his house. He is also in the habit of having a mesmerist named Dr. Pillsbury put him to sleep using hypnosis. On May 30, 1887, he goes to dinner at the home of his fiancé, Edith Bartlett, and spends an enjoyable evening with her and her father. He then goes home, has the doctor give him a treatment, and goes to sleep. When he awakes, he finds strange people in the room. They ask him who he is and when he went to sleep. Julian is amazed to learn that he has been asleep for 113 years, 3 months, and 11 days.

In the course of lengthy questioning, Julian finds out that during the night he last remembers, his house burned down except for the sealed room in which he slept. Not knowing about that room, everyone assumed that he had died in the fire. Because of his hypnotic state, his body has remained the same, and he is still a young man of thirty when he is discovered by Dr. Leete in the year 2000. Dr. Leete and his daughter, Edith, are very kind to their guest from the past and try to explain to him the changes that have taken place in the world since he last saw it.

Boston in 2000 is a beautiful, new city, with attractive buildings and spacious parks; only the bay and the inlets are as Julian remembers them. The strikes and other labor troubles of the nineteenth century resulted in a bloodless revolution, and now a socialized government controls all business. There is no smoke or pollution because electricity is used for the heating of buildings. All the people are healthy and happy.

Dr. Leete tries to explain to Julian that in 2000 there is no money. The state gives each resident, regardless of position, a debit card to cover all annual expenses; everyone's debit cards are of equal value. If an individual proves incapable of handling his or her debit card intelligently, the government provides supervision to enhance that person's understanding of the system and how it works. Julian visits one of the big distribution centers to see how goods are sold. He finds that the store is stocked entirely with samples that represent every type of material made in or imported by the United States. Buyers pick out the items that they desire and place their orders with the store's clerks, and the clerks then relay the orders to the central warehouse, which delivers the items to the buyers' homes before the buyers have even returned from the store. Julian is very impressed with this system.

In this society, every individual receives a full education until the age of twenty-one. A broad cultural course is taught so that there is no intellectual snobbery among the people. At age twenty-one, a young man or woman goes into menial service for three years, performing simple tasks such as waiting on tables in large public eating houses. After that, each is given an examination to determine whether he or she qualifies to attend one of the government professional schools. Those who do not qualify are helped to find the jobs for which they are best suited and that they will most enjoy. If their first jobs prove to be wrong for them, they can try other kinds of work. In order to ensure that sufficient numbers of workers are available for all the essential jobs, positions are structured so as to be equally attractive. If a particular job is so boring or arduous that few people would want to choose it, the work hours for the job are shortened so that the position will attract enough applicants. Whether citizens are doctors or bricklayers, they are given the same amount of credit for their work.

Crime is considered to be a symptom of mental disease, and criminals are placed in hospitals and treated as patients. Julian learns that crime was reduced to an amazingly low level as soon as money was abolished—theft became silly when everyone had the right and the power to own the same things.

At the head of the government in 2000 is the president, who is controlled by Congress. Education and health care are controlled by boards made up of older professional advisers to the president. A woman who has been chosen by all the women of the country has the power to veto any bill concerning the rights of the female population. There is no public discontent with government, and international cooperation is common.

Julian asks Dr. Leete what he has done in his life and learns that the doctor practiced medicine until he was forty-five years old, at which time he retired. Now he studies and enjoys various kinds of recreational activities.

Edith Leete takes great pleasure in showing Julian the various advances the world has made in culture since his day. Music, for instance, is carried into all the homes in the country by telephone. Edith shows Julian the public libraries, where, he learns, his old favorites are still being read. The works of Charles Dickens are especially popular, as the citizens of the new world think Dickens one of the wisest men of the past in his judgment of the sadness of the old capitalistic system. Books are published by the government at the authors' expense; if a book proves a popular success, the author receives royalties in the form of additional credit. Members of the public vote on works of art in the same way. When Julian comments that this plan would not have worked in his day because of the lack of public taste, Edith tells him that with general education the taste of the people has developed greatly. Julian becomes very fond of Edith and thinks how strange it is that she should have the same name as his long-dead fiancé.

When Julian becomes worried about a means of support, Dr. Leete tells him that he has arranged for Julian to take a college lectureship in history, as Julian knows much about the past that historians would be delighted to learn. Knowing that he is now secure in this new world, Julian asks Edith to marry him. She tells him that she has always loved him and explains that she is the great-granddaughter of Edith Bartlett. She had found some of Julian's old love letters to the other Edith and had been charmed by them, telling her parents that she would marry only a man like the lover who had written them. Julian is pleased at this unexpected turn of affairs, and the two plan to marry and live happily in the wonderful world of the twenty-first century.

Critical Evaluation:

Considered one of the most influential nineteenth century American novels and surely the most enduring of the American utopian stories, *Looking Backward* was ideally suited to appeal to middle-class readers of the era in which it first appeared. The book endorses a socialist future while at the same time denying the inevitability of class warfare and portraying a world in which individuals are given carte blanche as long as they do not dominate or exploit others.

Throughout the novel, Edward Bellamy contrasts the domestic and international strife of the nineteenth century with the harmonious relationships of his utopian late twentieth and early twenty-first centuries. Gone are the social and economic conditions that separated people into antagonistic groups and compelled them to attempt to advance at the expense of others. Gone, too, are the structural limitations that forced some to remain forever subservient to those who, either through hard work or through the benefit of birth, had attained economic security.

To underscore the absurdity of distributing rewards on the basis of social position, Bellamy uses the analogy of a prodigious coach carrying those seeking to avoid contact with the seamier side of life; the coach's course roughly parallels the economic fluctuations that made life inherently unstable and unsafe. Bellamy reinforces the alienation implicit in such an arrangement by depicting Julian as a member of the moneyed elite who felt compelled to insulate himself further by constructing a hermetically sealed sleeping chamber. In Bellamy's view, the attempt of the wealthy to protect themselves through the construction of artificial barriers merely increased their vulnerability.

To eliminate such barriers, the new society provides everyone with a solid education and access to cultural refinements once reserved for the elite. In this way, the level of appreciation of life is raised, as is the quality of life. Though seen by many as a sign of Bellamy's elitism, his emphasis on education and culture reflects his belief that nurture, rather than nature, determines social outcomes. Bellamy believed that people could create a humane society only by reconstructing social institutions in such a way as to change the objective circumstances of the lives of everyone. He asserted that an individual, much like a rose, will flourish if transplanted to a more hospitable environment, and that in such an environment individuals who once felt excluded will identify with the common good and be motivated to contribute to the

fullest extent of their abilities. With money and material goods devalued and the issues of security and safety resolved, selfishness can be eliminated, and no one will want to manipulate the system to gain a valueless advantage.

To demonstrate the feasibility of his arguments, Bellamy uses the military analogy of conscripts unselfishly defending their country in times of war. The motivations, in times of war as in times of peace, he argues, could be very similar: patriotism and the gratitude of their fellow citizens.

Because their incomes are equal and they gain nothing by attempting to upstage others, Bellamy's citizens of the twenty-first century select occupations that are ideally suited to their talents and temperaments; as a result, society is able to make the best use of individual and collective resources. Even those who are relegated to the more trivial tasks have no reason to feel envy or remorse because they know that their services will be more than repaid. While coordinating such a system might promise to be a bureaucratic nightmare, Bellamy argues that such a government, though more encompassing, is simpler and more benign. It blends the principles of meritocracy and Jeffersonian democracy and is staffed by those who have proven their commitment to the general well-being and have been "mustered" into retirement.

To guard against influence peddling among those who select the leaders, Bellamy excludes members of the active workforce from taking part in elections; voting is left to those who are retired. He justifies this suspension of the popular vote by arguing that government as an institution is needed only in the most extraordinary of circumstances. Its sole function seems to be maintaining a set of conditions that make most legislative activities passé. To authenticate his point, Bellamy notes that much of the legislation that was thought necessary in the past was actually the result of the inherent instability of a society that rewarded the few at the expense of the many.

Despite the sanguine portrait that Bellamy paints, the question arises as to the quality of individual human life and whether his society of the twenty-first century includes any provision to ensure that innovators have a means of influencing the society at large. Perhaps most important, Bellamy's future vision fails to include legitimate channels for dissent. Notwithstanding his claim that a change in objective circumstances will result in a change in subjective responses, in his utopia those who defy authority or refuse to work are placed in solitary confinement.

Women, too, get short shrift. Although they are allowed to work and receive individual stipends, their career choices are strictly limited. It is also curious that while women are supposed to be full participants in the society, the twenty-first century Edith does not appear to attend school or work for a living; she is, instead, described by her father as a consummate shopper. This portrayal may very well result from the fact that Bellamy is far more interested in advancing his arguments than in developing his characters. Even Julian and Dr. Leete remain two-dimensional mouthpieces for particular points of view. It is not, therefore, surprising that Edith's main function in the novel is not as a representative woman but as a tool that allows Bellamy to incorporate some of the elements of the standard romance into his novel.

Bellamy's use of the dream vision, however, is anything but standard. Rather than using the dream as a convenient travel mode, Bellamy allows the dream to become the reality. When Julian is returned to the nineteenth century, it is as if he were going through an expiation for his past indifference and self-absorption. He is, as the title suggests, looking backward and realizing the limitations inherent in outmoded social and economic arrangements.

"Critical Evaluation" by C. Lynn Munro

Further Reading

Aaron, Daniel. "Edward Bellamy: Village Utopian." In *Men of Good Hope: A Story of American Progressives*. 1951. Reprint. New York: Oxford University Press, 1977. Discusses *Looking Backward* as part of the Progressive reform movement. Provides insights into Bellamy's military model and transcendental religious perspective and highlights the safeguards Bellamy includes in his society to prevent authoritarian and bureaucratic domination.

Berneri, Marie Louise. "Edward Bellamy: *Looking Backward*." In *Journey Through Utopia*. 1950. Reprint. London: Freedom Press, 1982. Contends that Bellamy's utopia is based on a naïve faith in experts and technological progress. Criticizes the inherent regimentation of Bellamy's world of the future and argues that the need for compulsion and the prohibition of dissent belie the supposed happiness of its citizens.

Bloom, Harold, ed. *Classic Science Fiction Writers*. New York: Chelsea House, 1995. Collection of essays includes a chapter devoted to Bellamy and his work. Provides biographical, critical, and bibliographical information.

Bowman, Sylvia E. *Edward Bellamy*. Boston: Twayne, 1986. Offers an interdisciplinary analysis of Bellamy's intellectual development and considers *Looking Backward* within the context of his other writings. Chapter 5 focuses on the book's influence on sociopolitical developments and on major nineteenth and twentieth century thinkers.

Buckingham, Peter H., ed. *Expectations for the Millennium: American Socialist Visions of the Future*. Westport, Conn.: Greenwood Press, 2002. Collection of essays by historians examines the alternative visions of American society conceived by socialist thinkers at the beginning of the twentieth century. Includes two essays that discuss Bellamy's work: "Optimistic Millennialism: Edward Bellamy's Vision of Socialism as 'Applied Christianity,'" by Jacob H. Dorn, and "Socialist Expectations and the 'New Woman' in the Utopian Fiction of Edward Bellamy, Charlotte Perkins Gilman, and Jack London," by Francis R. Shor.

Patai, Daphne, ed. *Looking Backward, 1988-1888: Essays on Edward Bellamy*. Amherst: University of Massachusetts Press, 1988. Collection of eight retrospective essays assesses *Looking Backward* in view of twentieth century developments. Some contributors argue that Bellamy was a proponent of a dated, patriarchal world; others praise his integration of contradictory principles.

Peyser, Thomas. *Utopia and Cosmopolis: Globalization in the Era of American Literary Realism*. Durham, N.C.: Duke University Press, 1998. Examines how Bellamy and other early twentieth century American writers sought to understand the emerging global community.

Widdicombe, Toby, and Herman S. Preiser, eds. *Revisiting the Legacy of Edward Bellamy (1850-1898), American Author and Social Reformer: Uncollected and Unpublished Writings*. Lewiston, N.Y.: Edwin Mellen Press, 2002. Collection of materials contains some of Bellamy's previously unpublished writings, including excerpts from his notebooks in which he expresses his ideas for *Looking Backward*. Several essays offer critical examinations of Bellamy's work, including discussion of its influence on the development of participatory economics and ethical capitalism.

Lord Jim

Author: Joseph Conrad (1857-1924)
First published: 1900
Type of work: Novel
Type of plot: Psychological realism
Time of plot: Late nineteenth century
Locale: Ports and islands of the East

Principal characters:
LORD JIM, a British sailor
MARLOW, his friend
STEIN, a trader
DAIN WARIS, a native

The Story:

Jim is an outcast and a wanderer. He works as a water clerk in seaports throughout the East, keeping each job only until his identity becomes known and then moving on. The story of Lord Jim began when he determined to leave home to go to sea. His father obtained a berth for him as an officer candidate, and he began his service. Although he loves the sea, his beginning was not heroic, for almost at once he was injured and had to be left behind in an Eastern port. When he recovered, he accepted a berth as chief mate aboard an ancient steamer, the *Patna*, which was carrying Muslim pilgrims on their way to Mecca. The steamer was not seaworthy, its German captain was a gross coward, and its chief engineer was liquor-soaked. One sultry night in the Red Sea, the ship struck a floating object and the captain sent Jim to investigate.

One month later, Jim testifies in court that when he went to investigate, he found the forward hold rapidly filling with seawater. Hearing his report, the captain, declaring that the *Patna* would sink quickly, gave orders for the crew to abandon ship. At first, Jim was determined to stand by his post. At the last minute, however, on sudden impulse, he jumped to join the other white men in the lifeboat they had launched. The pilgrims were left aboard the sinking vessel. The *Patna* did not sink, however. A French gunboat overtook the vessel and towed it and the abandoned passengers into port without its chief officers aboard.

Marlow, a white man, is present at the inquiry. There is something about Jim that becomes unforgettable to Marlow, and he is compelled to recall the event and to tell the story to friends as long as he lives; it becomes a part of his own life.

Marlow's story had begun with a cable from Aden announcing that the *Patna*, abandoned by its officers, had been towed into port. Two weeks later, the captain, the two engineers, and Jim had come ashore. Their boat had been picked up by a steamer of the Dale Line, and they were immediately whisked into court for the investigation. The captain lost his papers for deserting his ship, and he stormed away declaring that his disgrace did not matter; he would become an American citizen. The chief engineer went to a hospital. Raving in delirium tremens, he declared that he had seen the *Patna* go down and that the vessel was full of reptiles when it sank. He also stated that the space under his bed was crammed with pink toads. The second engineer had a broken arm and was also in the hospital. Neither was called to testify.

Jim, wrestling with the thoughts of his upbringing and his father's teaching as well as his own deeply established sense of honor, becomes a marked man for the rest of his life. Marlow tells how during the trial he had dinner with the young man, who seemed of a different stamp from the other officers of the *Patna*. Marlow is determined to fathom the boy's spirit, just as Jim is determined to regain his lost moral identity.

Jim tells Marlow how the disgraceful affair happened. After he had investigated the damage, he had felt that the ship could not remain afloat, for its plates were eaten through by rust and unable to stand much strain. There were eight hundred passengers and seven lifeboats, but there did not seem to be enough time to get even a few passengers into the boats. Shortly afterward, he discovered the captain and the engineers preparing to desert the ship. They insisted that he join them; the passengers were doomed anyway. The acting third engineer had a heart attack in the excitement and died. Jim never knew when—or why—he had jumped into the lifeboat the other officers had launched. Jim tells Marlow how they all agreed to tell the same story. Actually, he and his companions thought that the *Patna* had gone down. Jim says that he felt relief when he learned that the passengers were safe. The whole story becomes a topic of conversation among all the sailors in the ports.

After the inquiry, Marlow offers to help Jim, but the young man is determined to become a wanderer, to find out by himself what has happened to his soul. In his wanderings, Jim goes to Bombay (Mumbai), Calcutta (Kolkata), Penang, Batavia (Jakarta), and the islands of the East. For a time, he finds work with an acquaintance of Marlow, but he gives up the job when the second engineer of the *Patna* turns up unexpectedly. Afterward, he becomes a runner for ship chandlers, but he leaves that job when he hears one of the owners discussing the case of the *Patna*. He moves on, always toward the East, from job to job.

Marlow continues his efforts to help Jim. He seeks out Stein, a trader who owns a number of trading posts on the smaller islands of the East Indies. Stein makes Jim his agent at Patusan, an out-of-the-way settlement where he is sure Jim will have the opportunity to recover his balance. In that remote place, Jim tries to find an answer to his self-hatred. Determined never to leave Patusan, he associates with the natives, and through his gentleness and consideration he becomes their leader. They called him *Tuan* Jim—Lord Jim. Dain Waris, the son of Doramin, the old native chief, is Jim's friend. In the ports, rumors spread that Jim discovered a valuable emerald and presented it to a native woman. Another story circulates about a native girl who loved him and warned him of danger when some jealous natives came to murder him.

Marlow follows Jim to Patusan, and when he prepares to leave, Jim accompanies him part of the way. Jim explains to Marlow that at last he feels as though his way has been justified. Somehow, because the simple natives trust him, he feels linked again to the ideals of his youth. Marlow suspects that there is a kind of desperation to his declaration.

The end comes when Gentleman Brown, a roving cutthroat, determines that he and his band of marauders will loot Lord Jim's stronghold. They arrive while Jim is away, and the natives, led by Dain Waris, isolate Brown and his men on a hilltop but are unable to capture them. When Jim returns, he has a long talk with Brown and becomes convinced that Brown will leave peaceably if the siege is lifted. He persuades the reluctant natives to withdraw, and the vicious Brown repays Jim's magnanimity by vengefully murdering Dain Waris. Jim goes unflinchingly to face native justice, offering himself to the stern old chieftain as the cause of Dain Waris's death, and Doramin shoots Jim in the chest. Marlow, who has watched Jim's life so closely, feels that Jim has at last won back his lost honor.

Critical Evaluation:

Born in the Polish Ukraine in 1857, Joseph Conrad was the son of a political exile who championed Poland's resistance to Russian rule and was consequently forced to leave his native land. Conrad lost both parents before he was ten years old, and he was reared by an uncle. In 1874, he went to sea; by 1886, he had earned his master mariner's certificate and had become a naturalized British citizen. Working in the merchant service, Conrad served mostly in Eastern waters with the exception of one trip to the Congo. His first novel,

Almayer's Folly: A Story of an Eastern River, was published in 1895; in 1896, he married Jessie George and settled down to write. During his last years he suffered from rheumatic gout and worried about his work and finances.

Some critics have said that *Lord Jim*, which began as a short story and was first published as a magazine serial, became a novel because its author lost control of his material. They also point out how unlikely it is that Jim's long, tragic story would be told on one occasion among a group of men sitting on a veranda. Conrad claimed that men do sit up for hours at night exchanging stories, and he declared that Jim's story is interesting enough to hold the attention of listeners and readers, for, as suggested by the motif of the novel, "He is one of us." Because Jim, like every human being, is an enigmatic paradox of strength and weakness, Conrad allows his readers to judge Jim's actions but reminds them that often there is "not the thickness of a sheet of paper between the right and wrong" of something.

The novel is often confusing, and shifts in point of view and a seeming disregard for a logical time sequence give it a meditative style. Using an unnamed third-person narrator in the first four chapters, Conrad shifts in chapter 5 to Marlow's oral narration and then in chapter 36 to a letter written by Marlow. As Jim's story unfolds, however, Conrad also allows other reliable characters to comment on Jim and his actions: the French lieutenant who saves the *Patna* after Jim deserts it; Stein, who gives Jim another chance to prove himself; and Jewel, the native girl who loves him. Conrad thus gives his readers the pieces to a gigantic puzzle—the connection between human motivation and human character—but he himself admitted that much in the novel would remain inscrutable.

Conrad stated that the central theme of *Lord Jim* is the "acute consciousness of lost honour." Jim may be uncommonly idealistic, but Conrad claimed to have seen Jim's "form" in an Eastern port. To help clarify Jim's desperate preoccupation with his dreams of himself, Conrad describes Jim as having in his youth spent his time reading "light holiday literature" and having imagined himself "always an example of devotion to duty, and as unflinching as a hero in a book." In addition, Jim had been brought up by a father who was a minister and who held absolute ideas of right and wrong. He had written to Jim just before he joined the *Patna* as chief mate, saying that one who "gives way to temptation . . . hazards his total depravity and everlasting ruin."

Jim is a dreamer who becomes lost in his own imagination; this aspect of his character is revealed by the training ship incident in which he fails to respond to a cry for help from a wrecked schooner because he is reveling in dreams of his own heroism. His inability to face the reality of his failure is seen when he blames nature for catching him off guard and when he rationalizes that he is saving himself for bigger emergencies. When the crucial emergency comes—that of the *Patna*'s crisis—he again fails to act because he imagines the chaos and the screaming desperation of eight hundred pilgrims fighting for space on seven lifeboats; he stands frozen while the other members of the crew lower their lifeboat and prepare to jump. Jim wants to make it clear that he did not plan to jump, nor did he help to lower the boat. He interprets his having jumped as a subconscious but understandable urge for survival. He tells Marlow: "I had jumped. . . . It seems."

The French lieutenant does not condemn Jim's actions. He blames Jim's youth and natural fear. He believes that "man is born a coward" but that he does brave deeds to make others believe he is heroic. Jim, he notes, faced a situation in which he thought no one would ever know that he had acted in a cowardly fashion: During the crisis it was dark, and Jim thought all the passengers would die. The lieutenant recognizes Jim's self-condemnation: "the honour . . . that is real . . . and what life may be worth when . . . the honour is gone" is the real question of *Lord Jim*.

Stein also diagnoses Jim's problem: "He is romantic. . . . And that is very bad. . . . Very good, too." He sees in Jim the potential tragic hero who has high ideals but fails as the result of a tragic flaw. Jim's flaw is his excessive imagination and his inability to face the reality of his weakness and his guilt. Not until the end of the novel, when he knows his limitations and accepts his guilt for Dain Waris's death, does he redeem his lost honor by giving his own life unflinchingly in atonement for his error in misjudging Gentleman Brown. It is Brown who makes Jim see the depravity and ugliness of reality; yet in his death, Jim remains true to his concept of the hero. He has transcended his guilt and declares, "Nothing can touch me now." Earlier, when Jewel expresses to Marlow her fear that Jim will leave her, Marlow assures her that Jim will not go back to his world because "he is not good enough." In the end, however, Marlow seems to believe in Jim's final heroism and sees him as an "extraordinary success."

Whose evaluation of Jim is accurate? Jim's own evaluation comes when he feels that he has finally found himself and thus dies willingly, with "a proud and unflinching glance." Marlow sees Jim as a fallible creature who looks trustworthy but fails when an emergency arises. Stein says that a romantic like Jim has no choice but to follow his dream, even if it costs him his life. The French lieutenant refuses to judge Jim but shows, by his own heroic example, Jim's weakness. Jewel ultimately calls Jim a traitor and refuses to forgive or understand him. The novel is puzzling, and Jim remains "inscrutable at heart," but he also remains "one of us."

"Critical Evaluation" by Janet Wester

Further Reading

Cox, C. B. *Joseph Conrad: The Modern Imagination*. London: J. M. Dent, 1974. Maintains that in *Lord Jim* Conrad reveals the meaninglessness of the modern age. Marlow and Jim cannot find the language to reveal the truth of Jim's actions. No words can be found; meaning can be apprehended only through glimpses and hints.

Karl, Frederick R. *A Reader's Guide to Joseph Conrad*. Rev. ed. Syracuse, N.Y.: Syracuse University Press, 1997. Excellent introductory source on Conrad's works provides analyses of major works, characters, and themes. Especially helpful in regard to *Lord Jim* is the explanation of Conrad's time shifts and use of the Marlow narrator figure in the novel.

Kuehn, Robert E., ed. *Twentieth Century Interpretations of "Lord Jim": A Collection of Critical Essays*. Englewood Cliffs, N.J.: Prentice-Hall, 1969. Fourteen essays cover the novel's composition, themes, and symbolism. Chapters discuss guilt and redemption, the loss of innocence, and Marlow's judgment of Jim.

Paris, Bernard J. *Conrad's Charlie Marlow: A New Approach to "Heart of Darkness" and "Lord Jim."* New York: Palgrave Macmillan, 2005. Focuses on the character of Charlie Marlow, analyzing his inner conflicts, his relations with the other characters in *Heart of Darkness* and *Lord Jim*, and the ambiguity of his narration in the two novels.

Peters, John G. *The Cambridge Introduction to Joseph Conrad*. New York: Cambridge University Press, 2006. Offers an introductory overview of Conrad, with information on his life, all of his works, and the critical reception of his writings.

Robert, Andrew Michael. *Conrad and Masculinity*. New York: St. Martin's Press, 2000. Uses modern theories about masculinity to analyze Conrad's work and explore the relationship of masculinity to imperialism and modernity. *Lord Jim* is discussed in a chapter titled "Imperialism and Male Bonds: 'Karain,' *The Nigger of the Narcissus, Lord Jim*."

Simmons, Allan H., and J. H. Stape, eds. *"Lord Jim": Centennial Essays*. New York: Rodopi, 2000. Collection of essays includes a discussion of *Lord Jim* and embarrassment, a comparison of the novel's ending to that of Fyodor Dostoevski's *Crime and Punishment*, and the novel's influence on writer John Dos Passos.

Stape, J. H., ed. *The Cambridge Companion to Joseph Conrad*. New York: Cambridge University Press, 1996. Collection of essays addresses most of Conrad's major works, including analysis of *Lord Jim*. Other topics covered include the Conradian narrative, Conrad and imperialism, Conrad and modernism, and Conrad's literary influence.

Wake, Paul. *Conrad's Marlow: Narrative and Death in "Youth," "Heart of Darkness," "Lord Jim," and "Chance."* New York: Manchester University Press, 2007. Focuses on Charlie Marlow, narrator of *Lord Jim* and several of Conrad's other works. Examines how Marlow's "essence"

is found in his constantly shifting position and how the meaning of his stories is tied to the process of his storytelling.

Watt, Ian. *Conrad in the Nineteenth Century*. Berkeley: University of California Press, 1979. Provides a history of the composition of *Lord Jim* and includes sources for the plot and main character. Covers such topics as the development and method of the narrative, Marlow's use of symbols, Conrad's structure of time, Jim's sojourn in Patusan as romantic escapism, the relationship between Jim and Marlow, and the significance of the novel's ending.

Lord of the Flies

Author: William Golding (1911-1993)
First published: 1954
Type of work: Novel
Type of plot: Fable
Time of plot: The future, during a nuclear war
Locale: An uninhabited tropical island

Principal characters:
RALPH, a British schoolboy
PIGGY, another schoolboy, overweight, nearsighted, and afflicted with asthma
SAM and ERIC, twin boys
JACK MERRIDEW, choir leader and head boy
SIMON, a quiet, introspective boy

The Story:

An airplane evacuating a group of British schoolboys from a war zone crashes on a Pacific island, killing all the adults aboard. Two of the surviving boys, Ralph and a boy nicknamed Piggy, find a conch shell and use it as a horn to summon the other survivors, including the members of a boys' choir headed by Jack Merridew. An election is held to decide on a leader. Jack has the choir members' grudging support, but Ralph possesses the conch and is elected chief. Jack and his choir become hunters.

Later, Ralph calls an assembly to set rules. The first rule is that holding the conch gives one the right to speak. A young boy about six years old asks what will be done about the "snake-thing" he has seen. Ralph insists that no such thing exists and changes the subject to the possibility of rescue. He orders the boys to make a fire atop the mountain to signal rescuers. Jack volunteers his choir to keep the fire going. Using Piggy's glasses to focus the sun's rays on some fuel, they light a fire. It leaps out of control, and in the resulting confusion, the boy who had asked about the "snake-thing" disappears. He is not seen again.

Jack, obsessed with the desire to kill a wild pig, and Ralph, who wants to erect shelters, are often at odds, dividing the boys' allegiance. One day, Ralph spots the smoke from a

ship out at sea. Looking up at the mountaintop, he discovers that the boys' signal fire has gone out. Desperately, he and Simon claw their way up the mountainside, but they are too late to start the fire again in time for the passing ship to see it. Below, they see Jack and his hunters (who should have been tending the fire) carrying the carcass of a pig. Jack is ecstatic, exclaiming over the spilled blood. When Ralph admonishes him for letting the fire die, Jack lashes out, breaking a lens of Piggy's glasses.

Meanwhile, a veiled fear has begun to spread, especially among the youngest boys, the "littluns," of something that haunts the night. At an assembly, Ralph tries to insist that the rules be followed and the fire kept burning, but discussion turns to the "beast," and the gathering soon degenerates into chaos, with Jack refusing to abide by Ralph's rules.

One day, a victim of the air war being fought overhead falls from the sky in a parachute. He lies against the rocks, dead, buffeted by the wind. Sam and Eric (twin brothers later dubbed "Samneric") are tending the signal fire when they see the corpse, and they run back to camp, screaming that they have seen the beast. Leaving Piggy to watch the littluns, Jack and Ralph go to search the far end of the island, thinking the beast might live there, but find nothing.

Night falls, and Jack challenges Ralph to accompany him up the mountain in the darkness to seek the beast. At the top of the mountain, near the place where the boys have built their fire, they see a dark shape and, when the wind blows, a skeletal face. They flee in terror. Back at the base camp, Jack seizes the conch and speaks out against Ralph, asking the boys to vote, by a show of hands, to reject him as chief. When the boys refuse, Jack goes off by himself.

Believing that the beast is guarding the mountain, the boys agree to Piggy's suggestion that they build a signal fire on the rocks near their bathing pool. As they work, however, several of the older boys slip off to follow Jack. With this new band of hunters, Jack pursues a sow caught feeding her litter. Running the sow down, the boys fall on her in a frenzy and kill her. Then, as an offering to the beast, they mount the pig's severed head on a stake.

Unbeknown to Jack and his band, Simon, hidden beneath some vines, has witnessed their ritual. When the other boys leave, Simon has a silent conversation with the pig's head—"the Lord of the Flies"—during which it seems to reveal to him that the beast is actually something within the boys themselves. Jack and his followers, smeared with body paint, burst into Ralph's camp, and Jack invites everyone to join his band and feast on roast pig.

Meanwhile, Simon inches his way to the mountaintop, where he discovers the dead parachutist. All the other boys, including Ralph and Piggy, have gone to Jack's camp to eat the pig. Under the threat of a downpour, they begin to dance and chant, miming the killing of the sow. Suddenly, Simon bursts into their circle, trying to tell them of his discovery. The boys, maddened by the chanting, attack and kill him, thinking him the beast.

Ralph and Piggy return to their camp. Only Sam and Eric and the littluns remain with them, and all deny—to themselves as well as to one another—any responsibility for the killing of Simon. Later, Jack and two of his hunters attack them. Ralph and Eric fight viciously, but in the end, Jack and his party make off with Piggy's glasses, which they need to light a fire of their own.

When Ralph, Piggy, and Samneric go to Jack's lair to demand the return of the glasses, Jack's followers seize Samneric, and Ralph and Jack fight until Piggy, holding the conch, demands a chance to speak. As Piggy speaks, drawing a line between savagery and order, Roger, standing watch on a cliff overhead, sets loose a boulder that crashes down on the boys, smashes the conch, and crushes Piggy's skull. Alone now, Ralph runs; he is pursued by Jack and his followers, who are hurling spears, but he manages to escape.

Later, Ralph creeps back to the encampment and discov-

ers that Samneric, threatened with torture or worse, have become part of Jack's tribe. They tell Ralph that Jack has sharpened a stick at both ends and will hunt him down.

In the morning, Ralph is discovered and forced out of his hiding place. Pursued, he manages to wound two of the boys, but when he attempts to hide again, the hunters light a fire to smoke him out. The chase becomes a frantic fight for life that ends when Ralph suddenly comes upon a uniformed naval officer whose cutter is moored on the beach. "We saw your smoke," the officer says, grinning at what he presumes to be a boys' game of war.

Critical Evaluation:

William Golding's work has always been somewhat controversial, with many critics hailing him as a literary giant and others decrying what they see as a tendency to create contrived, manipulative works laden with heavy-handed symbolism. Golding's reputation grew slowly. In 1955, when *Lord of the Flies* was first published in the United States, few readers had ever heard of him, and the book (which had been rejected by twenty-one publishers) sold only a handful of copies. Four years later, however, when a paperback edition appeared, sales of the work began to increase, promoted by word of mouth. Not long afterward, *Lord of the Flies* became required reading in many secondary schools and colleges, prompting interest in the author's subsequent work. In 1983, Golding received the Nobel Prize in Literature.

Born in Cornwall, England, in 1911, Golding attended Oxford University, changing his major from science to literature halfway through, and then, after publishing a book of poetry, became caught up in World War II. He spent five years serving with the Royal Navy, emerging as a lieutenant and embarking on a teaching and writing career. He wrote novels and novellas, poetry, plays, essays, and travel articles.

Lord of the Flies remains Golding's best-known work. It is a superficially simple but densely layered tale that has been labeled, among other things, a fable, a myth, an allegory, and a parable. On the surface, it is an adventure story. A group of schoolboys await rescue on a deserted island, meanwhile exploring, hunting, and finally warring with one another. In Golding's hands, the story becomes a parable that probes the nature and origin of evil.

The point of departure for *Lord of the Flies* is a nineteenth century boys' novel titled *The Coral Island* (1858), by R. M. Ballantyne. In Ballantyne's story, a group of shipwrecked British schoolboys (two of whom share their names with Golding's main characters) manage to create on their deserted island a fair replica of British civilization. Golding's view of human nature is less sanguine. His is a view that accepts the doctrine of original sin but without the accompanying doctrine of redemption. People in a state of nature quickly revert to evil, but even in a so-called civilized state, people simply mask their evil beneath a veneer of order. After all, while the boys on the island are sinking into a state of anarchy and blood lust, their civilized parents and teachers are waging nuclear war in the skies overhead.

The novel's central symbol, the pig's head around which flies buzz, which the boys dub the Lord of the Flies, is an allusion to Beelzebub, one of the most loathsome and repulsive of the false gods assailed in the Old Testament. Here, Beelzebub is represented by the rotting head of the sow killed by Jack Merridew and his hunters (choir members) in a frenzy of bloodletting that, in the language used to describe it, has sexual overtones. As Simon realizes, however, the beast, the Lord of the Flies, represents something anarchic and evil in the very core of human nature, not—as in the Bible and religious folklore—a demon separate from humanity but capable of taking possession of one's soul. Although human beings are gifted with at least a glimmer of intelligence and reason—represented in the novel by Piggy and Ralph, respectively—the power of evil is sufficient to overwhelm any opposition.

Lord of the Flies bears a close resemblance to Joseph Conrad's *Heart of Darkness* (1902); each involves a journey by representatives of one of the supposedly most civilized nations of the world into a darkness that lies at the very core of the human self. The irony in *Lord of the Flies* is even more pointed, however, in that Golding's entire cast of characters consists of children—traditional symbols of innocence ("trailing clouds of glory" from their heavenly home, William Wordsworth claims). That they are British public schoolboys only adds to the irony in that perhaps the chief goal of the British public school is to instill in its charges a sense of honor and civil behavior. Indeed, the boys' first impulse is toward order: Jack Merridew, later to become the most barbarous of them all, enters the novel marching his choir members along in two parallel lines.

Golding's story unfolds amid a dense web of symbols, including the conch shell, which represents the fragile hold of rule and order and which is finally smashed to bits when Piggy is killed. Piggy's spectacles, too, symbolize the weakness of intellect and (as a tool for making fire) the loss to humanity when intellect is quashed by superstition and irrationality. The beast, the parachutist, the fire, the killing of the sow—all assume symbolic significance in the novel, justifying the label of allegory that is often applied to this work.

Ron Carter

Further Reading

Baker, James, ed. *Critical Essays on William Golding*. Boston: G. K. Hall, 1988. Collection consists of twelve wide-ranging essays by critics, part of an interview that Baker conducted with Golding, and Golding's Nobel Prize address.

Bloom, Harold, ed. *William Golding's "Lord of the Flies."* New ed. New York: Bloom's Literary Criticism, 2008. Collection of essays about the novel features contributions by many top Golding scholars. Some of the essays compare the book to Golding's novel *The Inheritors* and others compare Golding's work to that of Aldous Huxley.

Dick, Bernard F. *William Golding*. Rev. ed. Boston: Twayne, 1987. Provides an informative introductory overview of Golding's life and work, including a chronology of his literary career.

Friedman, Lawrence S. *William Golding*. New York: Continuum, 1993. Sets *Lord of the Flies* in the context of Golding's entire body of work. The philosophical first chapter is especially useful in focusing on significant themes and concerns.

Gindin, James. *William Golding*. New York: St. Martin's Press, 1988. Offers both biographical information and a survey of Golding's literary career. Includes an enlightening comparison of *Lord of the Flies* with R. M. Ballantyne's nineteenth century novel *The Coral Island*.

Kinkead-Weekes, Martin, and Ian Gregor. *William Golding: A Critical Study*. 3d rev. ed. London: Faber, 2002. Updated edition of one of the standard critical accounts of Golding features a biographical sketch by Golding's daughter, Judy Carver. Presents analysis of *Lord of the Flies* as well as Golding's other novels.

McCarron, Kevin. *William Golding*. 2d rev. ed. Tavistock, England: Northcote House/British Council, 2006. Provides an introductory overview to Golding's life and works intended for students and general readers.

Reilly, Patrick. *"Lord of the Flies": Fathers and Sons*. Boston: Twayne, 1993. Focuses on critical interpretations of the novel and defends the work against charges that it presents a view of humankind colored primarily by unrelieved despair.

Tiger, Virginia. *William Golding: The Unmoved Target*. New York: Marion Boyars, 2003. Examination of all of Golding's novels draws on Tiger's conversations and correspondence with the author to describe how his books explore themes of human destiny and vision. Devotes a chapter to an analysis of *Lord of the Flies*.

Lorna Doone
A Romance of Exmoor

Author: R. D. Blackmore (1825-1900)
First published: 1869
Type of work: Novel
Type of plot: Adventure
Time of plot: Late seventeenth century
Locale: England

Principal characters:
JOHN RIDD, the yeoman of the parish of Oare in Somerset
SIR ENSOR DOONE, the head of the outlaw Doone clan
LORNA DOONE, his ward
CARVER DOONE, his son
TOM FAGGUS, a highwayman
JEREMY STICKLES, the king's messenger
REUBEN HUCKABACK, John Ridd's great-uncle

The Story:

John Ridd is engaged in a schoolboy fight in the yard of Blundell's school when John Fry, employed by Ridd's father, comes to take the boy home. Before the two leave, however, young John completes his fight by knocking out his opponent. On their way home through the moorlands, the man and boy are nearly captured by members of the outlaw Doone band, which has been ravaging the countryside by stealing and killing. When John Ridd reaches his father's farm, he learns that the Doones attacked and murdered his father only a few days previously. This incident stimulates the desire for revenge in all the residents of the parish of Oare, for the murdered man had been greatly respected.

John settles down to the responsibilities that the death of his father have thrust upon him. At first, his time is greatly consumed by farm work as he grows into the largest and strongest man in the Exmoor country. As he matures, John learns much about the wild Doone clan. There is one Doone, however, toward whom he feels no animosity: Lorna Doone, the beautiful daughter of the man supposed to be the murderer of John's father. On first sight of the young woman, John had been stirred by her beauty. Ever since, he has been in great conflict, as he understands that his passion is directed toward someone he ought to hate for his father's sake. After John's great-uncle, Master Reuben Huckaback, is attacked and robbed by the Doones, he goes with John to swear out a warrant for their arrest, but he has no luck because the magistrates are unwilling to incur the enmity of the Doones.

Over time, John is drawn deeper into a relationship with Lorna Doone. The two meet secretly in Doone Valley, and she tells him the story of her life with the outlaws. She has always loved her grandfather, Sir Ensor Doone, but she fears and has come to hate the rough, savage sons, nephews, and grandsons of Sir Ensor. This hatred is increased when Carver Doone cold-bloodedly murders Lord Alan Brandir,

a distant relative who had come to take Lorna away from the Doones.

About this time, John is called to London to serve the cause of King James II's tottering throne. There he discloses all he knows of the Doones' activities and of the false magistrates who seemed to be in league with them. He is warned that Tom Faggus, a highwayman who is John's cousin, might go to the gallows soon. Because John refuses to accept bribes or to become the dupe of sly lawyers in the city, when he eventually returns to his mother and his farm he is not a penny richer or poorer than when he left.

In the meantime, John's concern over Lorna, who has two suitors among the Doones themselves, has almost unhinged his mind. He is delighted to discover that Lorna, still only seventeen years old, has refused both her suitors. At the same time, he fears more than ever that he will lose his chance of winning Lorna, the ward of the outlaws he has pledged to help the king destroy. He at last, however, wins Lorna's agreement, and, with her support, he feels that nothing can stop him.

At home, the love of John's sister Annie for her cousin, Tom Faggus, reminds John of his duties as his father's son and plunges him into worries about his mother, Annie, and the farm. John's mother had other plans for his marriage, but when he reveals to her the only course his love must take, he succeeds in changing her mind. In the meantime, Master Jeremy Stickles has brought news of the rising of the duke of Monmouth and of troubles brewing for the king.

Suddenly, the signals that Lorna has been sending to John stop. John takes the great risk of descending into the Doone hideout, where he discovers that Lorna has been kept in her rooms because she has refused to marry Carver Doone. John manages to talk to her, and she pledges never to give in to her family. As he leaves, he narrowly escapes capture and, at the same time, overhears the outlaws' plot to kill Jeremy Stickles, the king's messenger, and thus is able to save Jeremy's life. The Doones' plot to kill Stickles brings further plans for retaliation from the king's men.

Old Sir Ensor Doone is close to death. Before he dies, he gives the union of John Ridd and Lorna Doone his blessing, and he presents to Lorna the glass necklace he has kept for her since she was a child. John then takes Lorna home with him to his mother's farm. Jeremy Stickles goes south to muster forces for the destruction of the Doone clan, and the counselor of the Doones takes advantage of Jeremy's absence to visit the Ridd farm in order to make a truce with John. His offer is rejected, but he throws trouble into the lovers' path by telling them that Lorna's father murdered John's father and that his own father was the murderer of Lorna's father. He also tricks them into giving him Lorna's necklace, which by now, through the word of Tom Faggus, they know to be made of diamonds.

Uncle Reuben Huckaback grows interested in having John marry his granddaughter Ruth, and he takes John to see the gold mine he has just bought. Upon returning from the mine, John learns that Lorna has disappeared. She has been taken away by the Dugals, who claim her as their missing heiress.

When Tom Faggus joins the rebels against the king, John, at his sister Annie's request, goes to find him and bring him back to safety. When John finds Tom, he is almost dead. John is then taken prisoner and is nearly executed; he is saved only by the arrival of his friend Jeremy Stickles.

John travels to London, where he sees Lorna. By good chance and by virtue of his great strength, John overcomes two villains who are attempting to rob and kill a nobleman; afterward, he learns that the man is Lorna's relative. In return for John's brave deed in saving the nobleman, the king gives John the title of knight and also has the court of heralds design a coat of arms for John's family.

When John returns from London, covered with honors, he discovers that the Doones have been raiding once more. John then finally achieves his long-awaited revenge. The Doones are routed, their houses are burned, and their stolen booty is divided among the local citizens who put in claims for redress. Lorna's necklace is also recovered. In addition, the Doones' counselor reveals that it was Carver Doone who killed John's father.

Arrangements are at last made for the wedding of John and Lorna. At the end of the ceremony in the church, Carver Doone, out of great jealousy, shoots Lorna. Without a weapon in his hand, John rushes out in pursuit of Carver; when he finds him, the greatest battle between two men ever told of in

books takes place. It is a fight of giants. As John feels his ribs cracking in Carver's tremendous hug, he fastens his own iron grip on his enemy's arm and rips it loose. Then he throws his crushed and bleeding enemy into a bog and watches as Carver Doone is sucked down into its black depths. The greatest enemy of John Ridd is at last destroyed. John returns to his bride and learns that she might survive her wound; she does, and John and Lorna live in peace and plenty among their friends to a hearty old age.

Critical Evaluation:

R. D. Blackmore, in his preface to *Lorna Doone*, was content to call his work a "romance," because the historical element is only incidental to the work as a whole. Secret agents, highwaymen, clannish marauders, and provincial farmers figure against a background of wild moor country. A feeling for the old times, for great and courageous people, and for love in danger made the novel popular with Victorian readers. People who read it in their youth tend to remember it with nostalgia in later years, for the book has a penetrating simplicity. Told in the first person by John Ridd, the main character, it has an authentic ring, the sound of a garrulous man relating the adventures of his youth.

The most memorable features of this novel, which many critics believe to be Blackmore's best, are its characterizations and its setting. The characters are drawn in the dramatic and often exaggerated fashion of the Romantic tradition, with its larger-than-life heroes, heroines, and villains. John Ridd is a powerful figure, a giant of a man whose honesty, virtue, patience, and steadfastness match his great size and towering strength. His true love, Lorna Doone, is the epitome of the Romantic heroine; she is mysterious and enchanting but entirely unrealistic. Lorna grows up pure, shy, and virtuous—a priceless pearl of femininity by Victorian standards—in the coarse and isolated environment of a robbers' den, surrounded by a clan of thieves and ruthless cutthroats. Perhaps of necessity, Blackmore paints his heroine in wispy, shimmering terminology; at the close of the novel, the reader still has no clear idea of her actual features. At the other end of the spectrum is the villainous Carver Doone, an unforgettably cruel, almost satanic, figure. The most vital force in *Lorna Doone*, however, is the Exmoor landscape. In soulful descriptions, Blackmore brings to life the wild moors, with their violent, stormy climate and harsh, forbidding countryside as well as their magnificent beauty and awesome loneliness.

The plot of *Lorna Doone* has its weak spots, such as the unnecessary and unconvincing conferral of knighthood on John Ridd, for whose impressive nature such an honor is trivial and extraneous; and the mediocre description of the Battle of Sedgemoor, which Blackmore borrowed from the work of historian Thomas Babington Macaulay. Overall, however, the narrative is filled with gripping excitement and told in a rugged, simple, and often lyrical prose. Some scenes in particular are unsurpassed, such as the wonderfully taut and realistic one in which John pits his strength and stubbornness against the fury of Tom Faggus's mare. In a different vein, but equally skillful, is John's description of his sorrow at Lorna's unexplained absence from their secret meeting place, a sorrow that spoils the natural beauty of the place in his eyes.

Ironically, *Lorna Doone* first became popular by accident; people bought the novel on the mistaken assumption—owing to a journalist's blunder—that it was about the marquis of Lorna's marriage, which had captured public interest at the time. It was a propitious error, however, creating as it did the novel's first devoted reading audience, which has had its descendants in every succeeding generation.

Further Reading

Budd, Kenneth George. *The Last Victorian: R. D. Blackmore and His Novels*. London: Centaur Press, 1960. Provides a good introduction to *Lorna Doone*, connecting the plot to legend and to children's nursery tales. Analyzes Blackmore's style and lyricism, rebutting accusations of wordiness and lack of realism. Favorably compares Blackmore to other Victorian rural novelists.

Burris, Quincy Guy. *Richard Doddridge Blackmore: His Life and Novels*. 1930. Reprint. Westport, Conn.: Greenwood Press, 1973. Discusses Blackmore's attitudes about nature and civilization, analyzing plot, character, and theme. Compares *Lorna Doone* with other Blackmore novels, tracing symbol and imagery, recurring ideas, and character types.

Dunn, Waldo Hilary. *R. D. Blackmore*. 1956. Reprint. Westport, Conn.: Greenwood Press, 1974. Biography provides one of the best introductions available to Blackmore's life and work, despite some inaccuracies about Blackmore's father. Examines the prefaces of various editions of *Lorna Doone* to discuss Blackmore's changing views of the novel.

Elwin, Malcolm. *Victorian Wallflowers*. 1934. Reprint. Great Neck, N.Y.: Core Collection Books, 1978. Survey of popular literary periodicals of the Victorian era presents Blackmore as an unjustly neglected author, comparing Blackmore's works with those of Anthony Trollope and Thomas Hardy. Argues that Blackmore's portrayal of rural England ranks with Charles Dickens's portraits of cockney London.

Plotz, John. "Locating *Lorna Doone*: R. D. Blackmore, F. H. Burnett, and the Limits of English Regionalism." In *Portable Property: Victorian Culture on the Move*. Princeton, N.J.: Princeton University Press, 2008. Provides a detailed discussion of *Lorna Doone* as part of a larger examination of the importance of "portable property" in the Victorian era, when small objects such as teacups and items of jewelry became symbols of national identity to Britons who were living in other countries. Argues that novels such as *Lorna Doone* were the "quintessential portable property" because they enabled Britons to preserve a sense of self and community.

Sutton, Max Keith. *R. D. Blackmore*. Boston: Twayne, 1979. Offers an excellent introduction to Blackmore's work and includes a detailed critical study of *Lorna Doone*. Contains extensive discussion of the novel's mythic nature, both as an initiation rite and as a re-creation of the story of Persephone and Demeter. Analyzes the work's characters, themes, symbols, and language.

Loss and Gain
The Story of a Convert

Author: John Henry Newman (1801-1890)
First published: 1848
Type of work: Novel
Type of plot: Philosophical and bildungsroman
Time of plot: 1840's
Locale: Oxford and environs, England

Principal characters:
CHARLES REDING, an Oxford University student
WILLIAM SHEFFIELD, a fellow student and Charles's close friend
BATEMAN, an Oxford tutor and High Church proponent
FREEBORN, a proponent of Evangelicalism
VINCENT, an Oxford scholar
CARLTON, an Anglican pastor
WHITE, an Oxford student
WILLIS, an Oxford student, later a Roman Catholic priest
CAMPBELL, an Anglican rector

The Story:

Charles Reding, son of an Anglican clergyman from the English midlands, enrolls at Oxford at a time when the university is in the throes of significant religious controversy. A number of the university's influential professors and religious leaders have been questioning the legitimacy of the Church of England, and a number have already converted to Roman Catholicism. Charles, too, has doubts about aspects of his Anglican faith. He confides some of his concerns to his friend William Sheffield, who is even more skeptical about religious matters.

In his first year, Charles speaks of these matters with tutors and several fellow students. At various breakfasts and dinners, and on long walks with others, he hears cogent reasons to accept the Anglican faith despite his doubts but also gets strong encouragement to abandon the Church of England and convert to another denomination. Older men suggest that the current crisis at Oxford over matters of faith is simply a fad. Some of these scholars, such as Vincent and Bateman, present a rationale for remaining in the Anglican faith, although they have different reasons. Vincent stresses the theological soundness of the Anglican Church. Bateman suggests that the cure for the Anglican Church's woes lies in restoring many of the Roman Catholic rituals that it had abandoned over the years. By contrast, Freeborn, a proponent of Evangelical doctrine, urges Charles to reject the entire priestly theology on which the Catholic Church is built, insisting that one can be saved only through a direct and personal relationship with God.

Charles sees other young men like his friends White and Willis undergoing some of the same struggles. Both seem tempted to convert to Catholicism, which most in Charles's circle seem to think the worst possible solution to solving

one's crisis of faith. Charles attends a sermon by a college official who suggests that there is room for all the sects currently at odds over matters of religious doctrine and practice, but Charles sees that factionalism has gripped Oxford. His discovery of Willis at a Dissenters' chapel is particularly disturbing, given that Oxford students are under instruction not to associate with either Dissenters or Roman Catholics. Shortly thereafter, however, Willis becomes a Roman Catholic and is expelled from the Oxford community.

After a brief respite at home, where questions of faith seem less compelling, Charles returns to Oxford. There his doubts about the efficacy of Anglican doctrine return; he finds especially troubling the contradictions he sees in the Thirty-nine Articles, the summation of the Anglican Church's doctrine. Once again his conversations with both High Church supporters and Evangelicals leave him confused. Charles's intellectual trials are suspended when his father dies suddenly, forcing him to assume responsibilities as head of his family. Reflecting on his father's life, Charles realizes he was a good man whose actions were directed by his faith. Fortified by this example, Charles reasserts his commitment to the Anglican Church and vows to put aside doubts about its legitimacy.

Nearly two years later Charles is back at Oxford completing his studies for a bachelor's degree, aiming to become a clergyman like his father. Nevertheless, the doubts that plagued him earlier have not gone away. Conversations with William, Vincent, Freeborn, and Bateman only serve to reinforce his belief that the Anglican Church cannot offer him the surety he seeks in matters of faith. Meanwhile, his friend White, once a doubter, has become a staunch advocate for the Church of England. During a vacation from the university, Charles engages in a series of conversations with Carlton, an

Oxford graduate who serves as a mentor for him. The two discuss matters such as celibacy, sin and redemption, and other issues on which Anglicans have sharp differences with Catholics. Charles is particularly disturbed by Carlton's inability to give him clear and compelling reasons for accepting the Thirty-nine Articles. Increasingly, Charles finds himself siding with Catholic doctrine. Additionally, he finds comfort in the unity of belief he sees within the Roman church, founded on and supported by a theology built on the premise that God speaks authoritatively through the pope, the bishops, and the priests.

Charles is shocked when he returns to Oxford for his last term. He discovers that word of his doubts has reached university officials, and he is denied permission to live in his college. He goes back to his family, now living in Devonshire, where he completes his studies. A meeting with Willis convinces him that his friend is happy in his new faith, while Charles still struggles with his doubts. Although Charles is allowed to return to Oxford to sit for his final examinations, he chooses not to accept his bachelor's degree, because doing so would involve subscribing to the Thirty-nine Articles.

Two years later, despite last-minute attempts by Anglican rector Campbell (Charles's sister's fiancé) to dissuade him from leaving the Church of England, Charles decides he will become a Catholic. He plans a trip to London to present himself to the superior of the Passionist Convent in East London, where Willis is living. Word of Charles's impending action spreads throughout the Anglican clergy and the university. As he travels to the convent he finds his defection from the Anglican Church to be a subject of discussion and even newspaper articles. When he reaches London, Charles stops for the evening at a bookseller just outside the convent, where he is accosted by several people who encourage him to take up other forms of religion, such as Evangelicalism, Swedenborgianism, or Judaism. So opposed to Catholicism are his persuaders that they even urge Charles to establish his own sect rather than convert to Catholicism. He rejects all of the suggestions, however, and the next morning goes to the convent. He is welcomed by the superior and his friend Willis, now Father Aloysius.

Critical Evaluation:

Loss and Gain is John Henry Newman's first novel; he wrote only one other, *Callista: A Sketch of the Third Century* (1856), during his long and controversial life as Victorian England's most celebrated convert to Roman Catholicism. Newman was a distinguished member of the Oxford community and a well-known preacher. His involvement with the Tractarian Society, a group seeking to return the Anglican

Church to its apostolic roots, eventually led him to leave the Church of England; like his protagonist, his defection caused a significant stir. In Newman's time, the Roman Catholic Church was viewed as anathema by most English people, who considered it an anti-intellectual religious sect that promoted superstition and blind obedience to a foreign potentate, that is, the pope in Rome.

Loss and Gain was the first work Newman published after leaving the Church of England. It was written in part to explain his reasons for converting, in part to counter the many anti-Catholic tracts being published at the time. Predictably, the novel evoked many hostile critiques from non-Catholics, but Newman was pleased that he had laid out in plain language why people of intellect could follow the path to Rome.

Much attention has been paid to establishing the novel's genre, since doing so often provides some guide to explaining characters' motivations and to illuminating important themes. Although the protagonist, Charles Reding, shares affinities with Newman on several matters of faith, the novel is not strictly autobiographical. Rather, Newman uses Charles to illustrate how a thinking person could come to the conclusion that the only true church is the Roman Catholic Church, which speaks with authority on matters of faith and morals in a way that other religions cannot. *Loss and Gain* also has been described as a bildungsroman in which the young hero discovers something of himself as he faces several personal trials. Perhaps, however, the book may best be considered a philosophical novel or a novel of ideas.

Constructed in a form reminiscent of Plato's dialogues, the novel wrestles with important epistemological issues, such as the role of authority in guiding reason and the limits to which reason might allow one to discover ultimate answers about the existence and nature of the deity. Charles's conversations with his classmates and teachers reveal the strengths and limitations of reason in settling questions of theology; his conversations also help mark out that elusive point where rational thought intersects with matters of faith.

The novel has little overt action; instead, readers are invited to follow closely the intricate arguments on issues of religious doctrine that consume Charles and his associates. While the characters are not fully developed, they are individualized by their adherence to a number of different religious positions. For example, Charles's good friend William Sheffield begins by being something of a skeptic, even a cynic, on religious matters; his principal concern is to achieve academic distinction at Oxford as a prelude to advancement in the Church of England. Bateman is a spokesperson for the High Church branch of Anglicanism, which hopes to reintroduce many Catholic rites but is not willing to accept the doctrines of Roman Catholicism; in fact, Bateman seems little concerned with doctrinal matters at all. By contrast, Carlton, Vincent, and Campbell do exhibit intellectual curiosity and appreciate Charles's genuine doubts about the efficacy of the Church of England to lead people to salvation. Their Anglican position is countered most notably by Freeborn, who espouses a brand of Evangelicalism that calls for abolishment of all church authority and for a reliance on one's personal relationship with God as the means of achieving salvation.

The series of discussions between Charles and his associates ultimately expose what for Newman were the inadequacies of the Church of England on a number of important matters. The dramatic interest in the novel is created by Charles's growing awareness that the church into which he was born and baptized cannot provide him either the surety of doctrine or the way of life he believes will bring him closer to God. His movement from doubt to certainty seems to be an intellectual version of the journey undertaken by the hero of John Bunyan's *The Pilgrim's Progress* (1678, 1684), the most famous and perhaps most influential Protestant text about the individual's journey to salvation. In a novel filled with small bits of satire and irony, this structural parallel may be Newman's most notable ironic statement on the Protestant's quest for salvation: The only true path to salvation, he says through the action of *Loss and Gain*, leads through Rome.

Laurence W. Mazzeno

Further Reading

Arthur, James, and Guy Nicholls. *John Henry Newman*. New York: Continuum, 2007. An overview of Newman's life and work. Includes an intellectual biography, a critical exposition of his work, and discussion of his work's reception, influence, and continued relevance.

Block, Ed, Jr. "Venture and Response: The Dialogical Strategy of Newman's *Loss and Gain*." In *Critical Essays on John Henry Newman*, edited by Ed Block, Jr. Victoria, B.C.: University of Victoria Press, 1992. This chapter explains how the series of dialogues in the novel provide structure to the work. Compares the work to a Platonic dialogue in which individuals take up various positions on a subject, in this case religion, to illustrate the ultimate soundness of the protagonist's decision to convert to Roman Catholicism.

Hill, Alan G. Introduction to *Loss and Gain: The Story of a Convert*, by John Henry Newman. New York: Oxford University Press, 1986. Describes the historical context in which Newman composed *Loss and Gain* and discusses the work's characterizations and themes.

_____. "Originality and Realism in Newman's Novels." In *Newman After a Hundred Years*, edited by Ian Ker and Alan G. Hill. New York: Oxford University Press, 1990. This chapter discusses Newman's accomplishments as a novelist, focusing on his ability to present complex theological debate in the guise of fiction and to vivify Oxford University life in the 1840's.

Levine, George. "Newman and the Threat of Experience." In *The Boundaries of Fiction: Carlyle, Macaulay, Newman*. Princeton, N.J.: Princeton University Press, 1968. This chapter elucidates some of the technical virtues and weaknesses of *Loss and Gain*, particularly Newman's treatment of personal experience as a guide for moral judgment.

Martin, Michael. "Enlargement of Mind and Religious Judgment in *Loss and Gain*." In *Personality and Belief: Interdisciplinary Essays on John Henry Newman*, edited by Gerard Magill. Lanham, Md.: University Press of America, 1994. This chapter explains how the novel dramatizes the development of a system of thought that Newman felt was essential for modern Catholics, a system Newman describes in greater detail in his *The Idea of a University Defined and Illustrated* (1873).

Rule, Philip C. *Coleridge and Newman: The Centrality of Conscience*. New York: Fordham University Press, 2004. Compares works by Newman and Samuel Taylor Coleridge in which the two argue that God exists as the moral conscience of humankind.

Strange, Roderick. *John Henry Newman: A Mind Alive*. London: Darton Longman & Todd, 2008. An introductory overview of Newman's life and thought designed for students and general readers.

Wolff, Robert Lee. "It Takes Time: The Novels of John Henry Newman." In *Gains and Losses: Novels of Faith and Doubt in Victorian England*. New York: Garland, 1977. A chapter offering an autobiographical reading of the novel in which Charles, standing for Newman, undertakes an intellectual and spiritual pilgrimage that leads him to the Catholic Church.

Lost Horizon

Author: James Hilton (1900-1954)
First published: 1933
Type of work: Novel
Type of plot: Adventure
Time of plot: 1931
Locale: Tibet

Principal characters:
HUGH CONWAY, a British consul
RUTHERFORD, his friend
HENRY BARNARD, an American embezzler
MISS ROBERTA BRINKLOW, a Christian missionary
CAPTAIN CHARLES MALLINSON, another British consul
CHANG, a Chinese lama
FATHER PERRAULT, the High Lama

The Story:

When Rutherford finds Hugh Conway, a former school-mate, suffering from fatigue and amnesia in a mission hospital, Conway relates the following weird and almost unbelievable story concerning his disappearance many months before. Conway is working at the British consulate in the city of Baskul when trouble breaks out there in May, 1931, and he is considered a hero because of the efficiency and coolness he displays while all the area's white civilians are being evacuated. When it is his turn to leave, he boards a plane in the company of Miss Roberta Brinklow, a missionary; Henry Barnard, an American; and Captain Charles Mallinson, another member of the consulate. The plane is a special high-altitude cabin aircraft provided by the maharajah of Chandapore. Conway is thirty-seven years old and has been in the consular service for ten years. His work has not been spectacular, and he is expecting to rest in England before being assigned to another undistinguished post.

After the plane has been in the air about two hours, Mallinson notices that the pilot is the wrong man and that they are not headed toward Peshawar, the first scheduled stop. Conway is undisturbed until he realizes they are flying over strange mountain ranges. When the pilot lands and armed tribesmen refuel the plane before it takes off again, Conway begins to agree with Mallinson and Barnard, who think they have been kidnapped and will be held for ransom.

When Conway tries to question the pilot, the man points a revolver at him. A little after midnight, the pilot lands again, this time narrowly averting a crash. The passengers climb out of the plane and find the pilot badly injured. Conway believes that they are high on the Tibetan plateau, far beyond the western range of the Himalaya Mountains. The air is bitterly cold, with no signs of human habitation in this region of sheer-walled mountains. The pilot dies before morning, murmuring something about a lamasery called Shangri-La. As the

airplane's passengers start out in search of the lamasery, they see a group of men coming toward them.

When the men reach them, one introduces himself in perfect English; he is a Chinese named Chang. The men lead Conway and the others to the lamasery of Shangri-La, where they arrive that evening. There they find central heat, indoor plumbing, and many other luxuries more commonly found in the West. They are given fine rooms and excellent food. They learn that a High Lama lives at the lamasery, and that they will not be privileged to meet him. Although Chang tells them that porters will arrive in a few weeks to lead them back to the outside world, Conway has the strange feeling that their arrival in Shangri-La has not been an accident and that they are not destined to leave soon.

In time, Chang tells them that Conway is to be honored by an interview with the High Lama. Mallinson begs Conway to force the High Lama to provide guides for them, for Mallinson has learned that Barnard is wanted for fraud and embezzlement in the United States and is anxious to turn Barnard over to the British authorities. Conway, however, does not discuss their departure with the High Lama, who is a very intelligent and very old man. Instead, he listens to the High Lama's remarkable story of Father Perrault, a Capuchin friar who became lost in the mountains in 1734, when he was fifty-three years old. Father Perrault found sanctuary in a lamasery and stayed there after adopting the Buddhist faith. In 1789, the old man lay dying, but the miraculous power of some drugs he had perfected, coupled with the marvelous air on the plateau, prolonged his life. Later, tribesmen from the valley helped him build the lamasery of Shangri-La, where he lived the life of a scholar. In 1804, another European came to the lamasery; then others came from Europe and from Asia. No guest has ever been allowed to leave.

Conway learns then that the hijacking of their plane had been deliberate. More important, he learns that the High

Lama is Father Perrault and that he is 250 years old. The old man tells Conway that all who live at Shangri-La have the secret of long life. He sent the pilot to bring back new people because he believes a war is coming that will destroy all known civilization; Shangri-La will then be the nucleus of a new world. The High Lama's picture of life in the lamasery pleases Conway, and he is content to stay.

Conway knows that the others will find it hard to accept the news, and he does not tell them that they can never leave. Mallinson continues to talk of the coming of the porters, but Barnard and Miss Brinklow announce that they intend to pass up the first opportunity to leave Shangri-La and wait for a later chance. Barnard faces jail if he returns to civilization, and Miss Brinklow thinks that she should not miss the opportunity to convert the lamas and the tribesmen in the valley to Christianity. The weeks pass pleasantly for Conway. He meets a Frenchman called Briac who had been a pupil of the early nineteenth century pianist and composer Frédéric Chopin, and he also meets Lo-Tsen, a Chinese woman who seems quite young but, as Chang tells him, is actually sixty-five years old.

Conway has more discussions with the High Lama, and at one of their meetings the old man tells Conway that he knows he is going to die at last, and he wants Conway to take his place as ruler of the lamasery and the valley. He counsels Conway to act wisely, so that all culture will not be lost after war has destroyed Western civilization. While he is explaining these matters, the High Lama lies back in his chair, and Conway knows that he is dead.

Conway wanders out into the garden, too moved to talk to anyone. His contemplation is interrupted by Mallinson, who tells him that the porters have arrived. Although Barnard and Miss Brinklow will not leave, Mallinson has paid the porters to wait for him and Conway. Mallinson says that Lo-Tsen is going with them, that he has made love to her and that she wants to stay with him. Conway tries to tell Mallinson that Lo-Tsen is really an old woman who will die if she leaves the valley, but Mallinson refuses to listen. At first, Conway also refuses to leave Shangri-La, but after Mallinson and Lo-Tsen start out and then came back because they are afraid to go on alone, Conway feels responsible for them as well and leaves the lamasery with them. As he goes, he feels that he is fleeing from the place where he would have been happy for the rest of his life.

Rutherford's retelling of Conway's story ends at this point, for Conway has slipped away and disappeared. Later, Rutherford meets a doctor who tells him that Conway had been brought to the mission hospital by a woman—a bent, withered, old Chinese woman. Perhaps, then, Conway's story is true. Convinced that Conway has gone in search of the hidden lamasery, Rutherford hopes that Conway is successful in reaching Shangri-La.

Critical Evaluation:

In *Lost Horizon*, James Hilton combines disillusioned pessimism with romantic escapism. It is significant that the novel begins in Berlin, where two terrible specters of the period, the Great Depression and Adolf Hitler, loom in the reader's mind. Given the apparent collapse of "rational" Western civilization, it is not surprising that a fiction writer should look to the East for an idealized and exotic sanctuary.

It is also important that the hero of this quest, Hugh Conway, although jaded by his experiences, still embodies basic Western virtues—a strong sense of purpose, personal loyalty, a rigid ethic, and efficiency, especially during moments of crisis. Hilton gives readers the best of both worlds. On the intellectual level, he postulates a synthesis of Eastern moderation and Western activism; on the emotional level, he confronts the complexities and tensions of the times with a hopeful vision that shows the best in the Western tradition surviving, even if the worst destroys itself.

Hilton's small group of involuntary explorers is well chosen, if not deeply characterized. They are all characteristic Western types, and the qualities they represent can, to a considerable extent, account for the state of the modern world. Miss Brinklow symbolizes Western missionary zeal, in a rather benign and comical form. Of the four, she is the most easily recognized stereotype—the righteous, moralistic, spinster lady who, having no personal life of her own, tries to interfere with everyone else's. Hilton's treatment of the type, however, is gently ironic rather than sharply satiric; Miss Brinklow is likable, sincere, and feisty rather than priggish and icy. Her plans to convert and animate the Tibetan peasants are taken seriously by no one but herself. The implications of her actions, however, are not so amusing; such missionary fervor in souls less benevolent than Miss Brinklow's leads to violence and oppression.

Henry Barnard, the American financier, suggests the pragmatic, greedy, opportunistic side of Western culture. Personally, he is a most engaging character—affable, entertaining, adaptable, easygoing, and levelheaded. He is also a wanted criminal. He insists that circumstances and bad luck caught up with him and forced him into defensive monetary manipulations, that he is a fugitive by accident and a victim himself—the classic rationalization of the white-collar criminal.

Miss Brinklow and Barnard, however, are easily distracted in Shangri-La, and their vices are indulged harmlessly. Presumably they will eventually outgrow their particular Western preoccupations and achieve that detached serenity characteristic in the valley. The third member of the party, Captain Mallinson, is another matter. Mallinson is young, passionate, idealistic, and loyal. He is, perhaps, even more admirable as an individual and more dangerous as a character type. A product of an upper-class British gentleman's education, Mallinson firmly believes in all the ideals of his country and class: honor, common sense, patriotism, and a hard distinction between right and wrong—with rightness residing in the upper-class English view of life. Mallinson had seen Conway acting with heroism in the Baskul evacuation, and so he idealizes Conway. As Conway adjusts to Shangri-La, Mallinson berates him for not living up to that idealization. Mallinson is the one member of the party who is so Westernized that he cannot adapt to Shangri-La even for a short time. To him, life in the lamasery is "unhealthy and unclean . . . hateful . . . filthy." Mallinson feels that anything he cannot understand or relate to is wrong and deserves destruction. "God," he tells Conway, "I'd give a good deal to fly over with a load of bombs!" Mallinson's idealism and passion, coupled with his narrowness of vision, make him the most dangerous of the group. All three characters—Barnard, Miss Brinklow, and Mallinson—are people who are personally likable and admirable but who embody qualities that, if pursued to their logical and probable conclusions, would bring devastation on themselves and on the civilization they so admire and seek to serve.

Conway also represents a characteristic failing in Western society. Although he is not destructive, he contributes nothing toward averting the impending chaos. He clearly embodies the best qualities of the cultivated Westerner. He is intelligent, sensitive, tolerant, sympathetic, courageous when he has to be, and resourceful. To his detriment and the detriment of his culture, however, he is also without any direction or purpose. He is not able to avert the destruction brought on by the zealot, the criminal, or the idealist. For all of his knowledge and talent, he has wandered aimlessly from one minor diplomatic post to another, never much caring where he has been or where he is headed, only hoping for a few incidental pleasures along the way. "Label me '1914-18,'" he tells the High Lama, "I used up most of my passions and energies during the years I've mentioned . . . the chief thing I've asked from the world since then is to leave me alone."

Conway thus represents the potential leader who understands the world and has the capacity at least to attempt to deal with it but whose will has been stultified by the traumas and complexities of the times. The underlying question of the book is whether or not Conway will find the will and purpose that he needs in Shangri-La. The answer to that question, and the center of the novel, lies in the series of interviews between Conway and the High Lama, Father Perrault. In these scenes, the history and nature of Shangri-La are explored, and its mission is presented to Conway. For his part, he must measure his own values, experiences, and apathy against the doctrines presented by the High Lama.

Despite the Tibetan trappings, Shangri-La is a very Western establishment. All the high officials and prime movers have been transplanted Europeans, especially Father Perrault, once a Capuchin friar, and his practical right-hand man, Henschell, an Austrian soldier. The central philosophy is the Aristotelian golden mean, and the underlying assumption is that if human life can be extended long enough, people will outlive the passions and extremes that lead to destruction. The purpose of Shangri-La, therefore, is survival: "We may pray to outlive the doom that gathers around on every side," Perrault tells Conway. "Then, my son, when the strong have devoured each other, the Christian ethic may at last be fulfilled, and the meek shall inherit the earth."

Conway apparently has already achieved a state of passionlessness and possesses the Western capacities of practicality, rationalism, and efficiency. He is the logical choice as Perrault's successor. The old man tells Conway so and then promptly dies. Almost immediately thereafter, Mallinson proposes an escape back to civilization, and Conway is forced to the climactic decision of the novel.

Despite Mallison's irritating behavior, Conway likes Mallinson, to some extent identifies with him, and, because of Mallinson's idealization, feels responsibility toward the younger man. When Conway learns that Lo-Tsen will accompany them and that she and Mallinson are romantically attracted, his feelings and ideas about Shangri-La are shaken. He respects honest, youthful passion and is not too old to feel some of it himself—especially with regard to Lo-Tsen. At the logical level, Mallinson has doubts about the High Lama's story. He dismisses Conway's references to the woman's age as absurd, and Lo-Tsen's willingness to leave the valley supports the young man's analysis. In summary, all Conway "felt was that he liked Mallinson and must help him; he was doomed, like millions, to flee wisdom and be a hero."

Therefore, the rational hero acts, finally, on impulse; the passionless spectator acts out of feeling. Such reversals are not unusual in the best of writing and may be a sign of complexity and stature in a character, or they may represent an easy way to solve a difficult plot dilemma. Whether or not the reader can accept such a facile resolution is a matter of individual taste and judgment. What is most important about *Lost Horizon*, however, is that in it James Hilton creates a new mythical kingdom, an exotic retreat to serenity and moderation, perfectly suited to the frenzied and bombarded sensibilities of the Westerner.

Further Reading

Crawford, John W. "The Utopian Dream: Alive and Well." *Cuyahoga Review* (Spring/Summer, 1984): 27-33. Compares *Lost Horizon* and Aldous Huxley's 1962 novel *Island*, citing them as two rare examples of utopias appearing in a century of dystopias.

_____. "Utopian Eden of *Lost Horizon.*" *Extrapolation* 22 (Summer, 1981): 186-190. Places *Lost Horizon* in the utopian tradition of such writers as John Milton, Samuel Johnson, and H. G. Wells, and likens its appeal to that enjoyed by such popular authors as Rudyard Kipling and H. Rider Haggard.

Hammond, John R. *"Lost Horizon" Companion: A Guide to the James Hilton Novel and Its Characters, Critical Reception, Film Adaptations, and Place in Popular Culture.* Jefferson, N.C.: McFarland, 2008. Provides biographical information about Hilton, a chapter-by-chapter plot summary of the novel, a glossary, and an alphabetical list of characters. Describes the novel's initial critical reception and publication history and discusses the film adaptations that have been produced.

Heck, Francis S. "The Domain as a Symbol of a Paradise Lost: *Lost Horizon* and *Brideshead Revisited.*" *Nassau Review* 4, no. 3 (1982): 24-29. Discusses significant parallels between *Lost Horizon* and Evelyn Waugh's 1945 novel *Brideshead Revisited*. Heck and Crawford (cited above) are notable for comparing Hilton to other, more critically accepted, writers.

Musuzawa, Tomoko. "From Empire to Utopia: The Effacement of Colonial Markings in *Lost Horizon.*" *Positions: East Asia Culture Critique* 7, no. 2 (Fall, 1999): 541. Describes how the novel's depiction of Shangri-La influenced Westerners' perception of Tibet.

Whissen, Thomas R. *Classic Cult Fiction: A Companion to Popular Cult Literature.* Westport, Conn.: Greenwood Press, 1992. Includes a chapter on *Lost Horizon* that provides one of the best single investigations available of the book's perennial appeal. Notes that the popularity of the work is reflected in the fact that the term "Shangri-La" has become part of the American vocabulary.

Lost Illusions

Author: Honoré de Balzac (1799-1850)
First published: Illusions perdues, 1837-1843 (English translation, 1893)
Type of work: Novel
Type of plot: Naturalism
Time of plot: Early nineteenth century
Locale: Angoulême, France

Principal characters:
DAVID SÉCHARD, a printer
EVE, his wife
LUCIEN CHARDON, his brother-in-law
MADAME DE BARGETON, a woman loved by Lucien

The Story:

Angoulême is divided into two classes: the aristocrats of fashionable society and the bourgeois. David Séchard and Lucien Chardon are scarcely aware that they belong to the less privileged class. Lucien is the brilliant, handsome, unstable son of a chemist. David is the sober, kind son of a printer.

David's father sends him to Paris to learn all the latest innovations in the printing trade. The illiterate father, avaricious and mean, hopes that David will learn how to extract more money from the old-fashioned print shop of Séchard and Son. When David returns from Paris, his father quickly sells him the business at a high price and retires to his vineyard.

Partly because of his friendship with poetic Lucien and partly because of his temperament, David does not prosper. He is always discussing a grand project with Lucien or dreaming of Eve, Lucien's beautiful sister. Lucien writes some verses that attract attention. Even the aristocrats of the town hear of him, and Madame de Bargeton, a thirty-six-year-old woman married to an old husband, invites him to one of her famous evening gatherings. Eve scrimps to buy Lucien the proper clothes for the occasion. The evening is not an entire success. Few except Madame de Bargeton listen to Lucien's poetry, but he makes a real conquest of his host.

While Lucien does his best to break into society and win the heart of Madame de Bargeton, David and Eve are quietly falling in love. David strains his resources to the utmost to furnish rooms over the print shop for his wife-to-be, a room at the rear for his mother-in-law, and a comfortable room on the street for Lucien. David is determined to promote Lucien's literary talent by supporting him. Two days before the wedding, Lucien is surprised in Madame de Bargeton's boudoir. Her husband, old as he is, fights a duel with a man who gossiped about Madame de Bargeton. Not wishing to face the scandal, Madame de Bargeton decides to go to Paris, and Lucien is to follow her. With a heavy heart, for he knows Lucien's weaknesses, David drives his friend at night along the Paris road. Safely away from Angoulême, Lucien joins his mistress.

David and Eve marry and settle into their new rooms. Eve is a devoted wife, although foolishly fond of her scapegrace brother. Before her child is born, she begins to grow uneasy. Lucien writes very seldom, and David pays little attention to his business. He is too busy working on an experiment to find a new way to make paper without rags. If he can invent a new process, they will all be rich. Meanwhile the family is desperately in need, for Lucien's demands for money keep them poor. At last Eve herself takes charge of the print shop.

She has her first small success when she thinks of the idea of printing a *Shepherd's Calendar*, a cheap almanac to peddle to farmers, but the firm of Cointet Brothers, rivals in the printing trade, give her so much unfair competition that she makes only a small profit from her printing venture. After her baby comes, she gives up her efforts for a while. David is more than ever wrapped up in his attempts to find a new process for making paper.

Meanwhile, Lucien fails completely to make his way in Paris. He quarrels with his rich mistress, and they part. He can find only odd jobs as a journalist. He borrows continually from David to lead the dissolute life of a man-about-town. Finally, when he goes to live openly with Coralie, an actress, he loses all chances for any real success.

Pressed for money, Lucien forges David's name to notes for three thousand francs. When the firm of Cointet Brothers, acting as bankers, present the notes to David for payment, he is unable to raise the money. The lawsuit that follows disturbs Eve so much that she has to hire a wet nurse for her baby; in the eyes of the people of her small French town, she is disgraced. Cointet Brothers promise a profitable marriage to Petit-Claud, David's lawyer, if he will prolong the suit, increase the costs to David, and eventually force him into

debtor's prison. During the delays, Eve and David both appeal to his father for help, but the old miser refuses aid to his son. He is mainly interested in collecting rent for the building in which David has his shop. With all help denied, David goes into hiding and works feverishly on his paper process.

In Paris, Coralie dies, leaving Lucien without a place to live. Having no money, he begins the long walk home. One night he catches a ride among the trunks of a carriage and goes to sleep on his precarious perch. When he awakens the carriage is stopped. As he gets off he sees that he is riding with his former mistress, Madame de Bargeton, now Madame la Comtesse Châtelet, wife of the new prefect of the district. She and her husband laugh openly as the disheveled Lucien stalks away.

A few miles from Angoulême, Lucien becomes ill and seeks refuge with a miller. Thinking Lucien is near death, the miller sends for a priest. When Lucien begs for news of his family, the priest tells him of David's troubles. Lucien hurries to town to see what he can do for the brother-in-law he helped to ruin. In Angoulême, Lucien is sorrowfully received by his sister. To add to the distress of David and his family, Cointet Brothers publishes in the paper a glowing account of Lucien's successes in Paris. There is a parade in Lucien's honor, and the Châtelets even invite him to dinner.

Realizing that he still has a hold over Madame de Châtelet, Lucien tries to get David released from his debts through her influence. Meanwhile, after seeing some samples of David's work, the Cointets offer to pay off his debts, buy his print shop, and develop his invention for him. The offer, however, is intended to bring David out of hiding. Then a letter from Lucien to his friend is intercepted and a forged note substituted, appointing a place of meeting. On the way to the meeting, David is arrested and thrown into prison. Lucien, after a despairing farewell to his sister, leaves Angoulême. He intends to kill himself, but on the road he is picked up by a Spanish priest, an emissary traveling between Madrid and Paris. The envoy sees promise in Lucien and offers him fifteen thousand francs in return for Lucien's promise to do as the priest wishes. The Spaniard means to acquire power through Lucien's attraction for women and his poetic fervor. The bargain sealed, Lucien sends the fifteen thousand francs to David.

The money arrives just after David signs away his shop and his papermaking process to the Cointets. David and Eve retire to the country and in due time inherit money and a vineyard from his father. Petit-Claud, the double-crossing lawyer, becomes a famous prosecutor. The Cointets make a great fortune from David's process, and one of them becomes a deputy and a peer.

Critical Evaluation:

Honoré de Balzac wrote *Lost Illusions* after he had finally succeeded in conceiving of his life's work as a large, comprehensive, and accurate portrayal of contemporary French society. Almost every novel he would write or had written was to become a part of this larger entity, which he called *The Human Comedy*, in reference to the Italian epic poem *La divina commedia* (c. 1320; *The Divine Comedy*, 1802) by Dante Alighieri. When *Lost Illusions* began appearing in serial form in 1837, Balzac's conception of the narrative framework for his life's work was taking shape as well. Balzac's famous introduction to the first edition of *The Human Comedy*, in which he provides the theoretical basis for his enterprise, appeared in 1842, which is roughly when the three narratives that make up *Lost Illusions* were completed.

Lost Illusions concerns itself with the indissoluble relationship between art and money, a recurring obsession throughout Balzac's work. The experiences of the two main characters, Lucien and David, illustrate the difficulty of escaping from the corrupting power of society, represented by market forces. At first readers see the two men as close friends, although physical and psychological opposites. David is the conscientious, unassuming, and quietly proud craftsman who hopes to become rich by marketing a new process for making paper. Lucien desires immortality as an author. David's ambitions are to be useful to society while remaining in the provinces. Lucien is self-interested and sees his destiny in Paris.

When Lucien leaves to make a name for himself, however, he gradually comes to view his art as a business rather than as a vocation. As he squanders David's money in the attempt to reach his goal, he justifies his actions as an investment in himself, which would pay off in the form of literary fame and of material wealth. The reader begins to realize that the two men's fates are not only linked but also very similar and that David's print business and Lucien's writing are simply two aspects of the same industry. Another apparent difference is undermined when it becomes clear that Paris, rather than being the opposite of the provinces, is in truth simply the distillation of the corrupt way of life that exists everywhere.

Lucien's downfall begins as soon as he arrives in Paris from Angoulême. Its causes reach back to the beginning of the novel when he tries his best to shine in the literary salon of Madame de Bargeton. His good looks and charm seduce her at least as much as his poetry. Hoping to make an impression in the big city, the first thing he does is buy the best clothes, boots, and accessories he can find. When he shows them off at the opera that same evening, however, he realizes that his flashy, off-the-rack wardrobe identifies him as a vulgar provincial. His quest for artistic success immediately becomes subordinate to the desire to appear successful, which he is never able to satisfy. Every time he feels he has achieved a goal, he learns that it is still beyond his grasp. From the beginning, therefore, the aspiring artist deviates from his proper path as a result of the corrupting forces that he is too weak to control.

Balzac's pessimism about the fate of the individual in society is a constant in this novel and in most of his work. True feeling also is in doubt, since Lucien does not let the reader or himself know whether his love for Madame de Bargeton is genuine or whether he merely uses her as an instrument for the fulfillment of his ambitions. Noble principles and abstractions repeatedly turn into their mundane counterparts: Love becomes prostitution; literature becomes journalism; greatness becomes material wealth. At the end of Lucien's Parisian adventures, the mysterious Spanish priest who once saved him from suicide gives him a lesson in life that provides a summary of all his experiences in Paris as well as a blueprint for the future. Armed with this new pragmatism, the aspiring artist may, perhaps, conquer the world, which Lucien sets out to do in the sequel to *Lost Illusions*.

Only through reading the novels that come before and after *Lost Illusions* does one fully realize the identity of the Spanish priest: He is Vautrin, a master criminal who escapes from the prison where he was sent in Balzac's earlier novel, *Le Père Goriot* (1834-1835; *Père Goriot*, 1860). This revelation points out one of the most effective techniques of Balzac's writing, the use of recurring characters throughout *The Human Comedy*. Alluding to characters and events from other novels and using the same characters from one novel to another, Balzac reinforces the impression that his great work constitutes a unified world, rather than a series of discrete narratives. A character—Eugène de Rastignac—in *Père Goriot*, for example, makes an appearance in *Lost Illusions*. Several other characters appear in the sequel to *Lost Illusions* and in other works, making the novel a meeting place not only of major Balzac themes but also of characters and of plots.

Not all is bleak in *Lost Illusions*. While in Paris, Lucien belongs to a group of young artists known as the Cenacle, led by the passionate Daniel d'Arthez. They are devoted to literature in its purest form. Lucien betrays the Cenacle (whose name alludes to Jesus and his disciples), and d'Arthez and the other members are not immune to corruption themselves, but the group nevertheless stands as a reminder of artistic achievement outside the marketplace. David's process for manufacturing paper proves to be a success, confirming his genius as an inventor. His bankruptcy, caused by Lucien, may be considered a blessing in disguise, since it forces him away from a corrupt society in which an honest man such as he cannot succeed. Eve remains steadfastly devoted as a wife to David and a sister to Lucien, symbolizing the disinterested side of human nature and presenting a type of feminine ideal to which Balzac often returns. Such sentimental, transcendent values are common in Balzac.

With *Lost Illusions*, Balzac creates a new variation on the genre of the bildungsroman, or novel of formation. According to tradition, the hero of such a novel finds a place and achieves individual fulfillment when the institutions of society are in harmony with the individual's ambitions. In Balzac, the opposite occurs: The hero succeeds when he gives up his individuality and idealism. By recognizing the alienation resulting from such a process, Balzac was a precursor to modern novelists. His characterization of art as a hostage to crass commercialism is an uncanny prefiguration of some of the concerns of artists of the twenty-first century.

"Critical Evaluation" by M. Martin Guiney

Further Reading

Adamson, Donald. *Balzac: "Illusions perdues."* London: Grant and Cutler, 1981. A comprehensive, step-by-step guide that greatly facilitates the student's task of reading the novel. One of the best introductions available in English.

Bloom, Harold, ed. *Honoré de Balzac.* Philadelphia: Chelsea House, 2003. Collection of essays on some of Balzac's individual novels, including "Fool's Gold: The Beginning of Balzac's *Illusions perdues*" by Lawrence R. Schehr. Other essays discuss the creation of a fictional universe, use of narrative doubling, and allegories of energy in *The Human Comedy.*

Festa-McCormick, Diana. *Honoré de Balzac.* Boston: Twayne, 1979. Contains a chapter on *Lost Illusions* and its sequel, pointing out certain faults in each work, such as excessive length and detail, but also explaining why the books are among Balzac's best novels. Draws interesting parallels to other novels by Balzac.

Garval, Michael D. "Honoré de Balzac: Writing the Monument." In *"A Dream of Stone": Fame, Vision, and Monumentality in Nineteenth-Century French Literary Culture.* Newark: University of Delaware Press, 2004. Garval describes how France in the nineteenth century developed an ideal image of "great" writers, viewing these authors' work as immortal and portraying their literary successes in monumental terms. He traces the rise and fall of this literary development by focusing on Balzac, George Sand, and Victor Hugo.

Madden, James. *Weaving Balzac's Web: Spinning Tales and Creating the Whole of "La Comédie humaine."* Birmingham, Ala.: Summa, 2003. Explores how Balzac structured his vast series of novels to create continuity both within and between the individual books. Madden describes how internal narration, in which characters tell each other stories about other characters, enables the recurring characters to provide layers of meaning that are evident throughout the series.

Marceau, Félicien. *Balzac and His World.* Translated by Derek Coltman. New York: Orion Press, 1966. Provides one of the best available overviews of the complex fictional world Balzac created. Marceau looks for the recurring characters and themes in Balzac's novels. Contains an index of the characters in *The Human Comedy.*

Maurois, André. *Prometheus: The Life of Balzac.* Translated by Norman Denny. London: Bodley Head, 1965. An accessible introduction to Balzac's life. Describes the circumstances of the creation of his major works in fascinating detail.

Robb, Graham. *Balzac: A Life.* New York: W. W. Norton, 1994. A detailed biographical account of Balzac's life and work. Robb describes Balzac's philosophical perspectives and speculates on the psychological motivations underlying his writing.

Schilling, Bernard N. *The Hero as Failure: Balzac and the Rubempré Cycle.* Chicago: University of Chicago Press, 1968. A scholarly, accessible study that situates the novel within the various contexts of French history, Balzac's work, works by other authors that deal with similar themes, and the French society of the nineteenth century.

A Lost Lady

Author: Willa Cather (1873-1947)
First published: 1923
Type of work: Novel
Type of plot: Domestic realism
Time of plot: Late nineteenth century
Locale: Nebraska

Principal characters:
CAPTAIN FORRESTER, a railroad contractor
MRS. FORRESTER, his wife
JUDGE POMMEROY, his friend and legal adviser
NIEL HERBERT, the judge's nephew
IVY PETERS, a lawyer

The Story:

The Forrester home at Sweet Water is a stopping-off place for railroad magnates riding through the prairie states along the Burlington line. Old Captain Forrester likes to drive his guests from the train station and watch them as they approach his estate. He enjoys their praise of his stock farm and their delight when his charming wife meets them at the front door. Everyone from railroad presidents to the village butcher boy and the kitchen maids likes Mrs. Forrester; her manner is always one of friendliness and respect.

Niel Herbert's acquaintance with Mrs. Forrester began when he was twelve years old, when he fell from a tree while playing with some village boys on the Captain's property, and Mrs. Forrester summoned a doctor. The boy who caused Niel's fall was Ivy Peters. Ivy had winged a woodpecker and then had slit its eyes. The bird had fumbled back into its hole, and Niel was trying to reach the creature to put it out of its misery when he lost his balance and fell. He did not know it at the time, but Mrs. Forrester had already singled him out from the others because he was Judge Pommeroy's nephew. After his recovery, Niel began to be invited to the Forrester home often with his uncle.

Some years later, during a period of hard times, Niel's father goes out of business and leaves Sweet Water. Niel stays on to read law in his uncle's office. A few days before Christmas, Mrs. Forrester invites Niel to her home to help entertain Constance Ogden, the daughter of one of the Captain's friends, who is spending the holidays with the Forresters. Also included in the party is Frank Ellinger, a bachelor of forty. The dinner is a festive one. Niel decides that Constance is neither pretty nor pleasant; it is evident that she has designs on Frank Ellinger.

The following day, Niel is asked to stay with Constance during the afternoon while Mrs. Forrester and Frank take the small cutter and go out to collect cedar for the Christmas decorations. The Blum boy, out hunting, sees Mrs. Forrester and Frank after he comes upon the deserted cutter beside a thicket, but he does not give away their secret. The doings

of the rich are not his concern, and Mrs. Forrester has been kind to him on many occasions.

During that winter, Judge Pommeroy and his nephew often play cards with the Forresters. One night, during a snowstorm, Mrs. Forrester reveals to Niel how much she misses the excitement and glamour of former winters she spent at fashionable resorts. She mocks the life of quiet domesticity that she and the Captain are living.

In the spring, the Captain goes to Denver on business, and while he is gone, Frank Ellinger arrives at the Forrester home for a visit. One morning, Niel cuts a bouquet of wild roses to leave outside the windows of Mrs. Forrester's bedroom. As he is leaving the bouquet, he suddenly hears from the bedroom the voices of Mrs. Forrester and Frank Ellinger. Thus the first illusion of his life is shattered by a man's yawn and a woman's laugh.

When the Captain comes home from Denver, he announces that he is a poor man. Having satisfied his creditors, he now has only his pension from his service in the Civil War and the income from his farm. Shortly afterward, the Captain has a stroke. Niel continues to visit the Captain and his wife. He realizes that Mrs. Forrester is facing her new life with terror, which she tries to hide for her sick husband's sake.

Niel has decided to become an architect, and he leaves Sweet Water to spend two years at school in the East. When he returns, he learns that the shrewd and grasping Ivy Peters has become an important person in the town. Niel despises Peters, and he is disappointed to learn that Peters, now the Captain's tenant, has drained the marsh where the boys had gone fishing years before. The Captain himself has become wasted and old; he spends most of his time sitting in his garden, staring at a strange sundial he has made. Niel learns that Mrs. Forrester, who seems little older, is still writing to Frank Ellinger. He observes, too, that Mrs. Forrester treats Peters with easy familiarity, and he wonders how she can be on friendly terms with the pushy young lawyer.

That summer, a storm floods the fields along the creek.

Niel goes to Judge Pommeroy's office to read, and he thinks of an item he saw in the Denver paper earlier in the day: Frank Ellinger has finally married Constance Ogden. Close to midnight, Mrs. Forrester appears at the office; she is drenched to the skin. At her demand, Niel uses the judge's telephone to reach Ellinger in Colorado Springs. Mrs. Forrester takes the phone and begins talking politely, as though complimenting Ellinger on his marriage. Then she becomes hysterical. When she begins to scream reproaches, Niel cuts the telephone wire. Mrs. Forrester recovers from her collapse, but the gossipy town telephone operator pieces together a village scandal from what she has overheard.

Captain Forrester dies in December. None of his wealthy friends attends the funeral, but old settlers and former employees come to do honor to the railroad pioneer who had been one of the heroes of the early West.

One day, Mr. Ogden, Constance's father, stops in Sweet Water. He suggests that Judge Pommeroy should send a claim to Washington, D.C., to have Mrs. Forrester's widow's pension increased. Niel is forced to explain to the men that Mrs. Forrester has turned her affairs over to Ivy Peters.

After her husband's death, Mrs. Forrester begins to entertain Peters and other young men of the village. At her urging, Niel attends one of her parties, but he is disgusted with the cheap manners of both host and guests. He cannot bear to see the old Captain's home thus abused.

Niel feels that an era is ending. The great old people who built the railroads and towns, such as Judge Pommeroy, Captain Forrester, and their friends, are passing. The old men of gallant manners and their lovely ladies are gone forever. In their place is a new type of man, the shrewd opportunist, like Ivy Peters. On the day Niel sees Peters putting his arms around Mrs. Forrester, he decides to leave Sweet Water.

After he leaves the town, however, as long as his uncle lives, he has news of Mrs. Forrester. The judge tells Niel in a letter that she is sadly broken. Then his uncle dies, and Niel hears no more of Mrs. Forrester for many years. A long time afterward, a mutual friend tells him what had happened to his lost lady. She had gone to California. Later, she had married a rich Englishman and had traveled with him to South America. She had dyed her hair and had dressed expensively in an effort to keep her youth. Finally, Niel receives a letter from Mrs. Forrester's English husband. It encloses money for the continued care of Captain Forrester's grave, sent as a memorial to his late wife, Marian Forrester Collins.

Critical Evaluation:

Willa Cather was of a generation of writers who lived through the passing of the old frontier, who saw the region of the homesteader transformed into a countryside of tidy farms and small towns. She found in the primitive virtues of the pioneer experience her values as an artist. The West is the setting of her best work, and the past is its spiritual home.

A Lost Lady is the first example in Cather's writing of what she called the novel *démeublé*, or fiction stripped of all "furnishings." Her method is well illustrated in the scene in which young Niel suffers his disillusionment in Marian Forrester. The whole passage is built upon the symbol of the wild roses that Niel picks early in the morning to place on Marian's windowsill so that she will find them when she opens the blinds of her bedroom. As he bends to place the flowers, he hears beyond the closed blinds a woman's laugh, "impatient, indulgent, teasing, eager," and then a man's, "like a yawn." Niel flees and throws the roses in the mud where cattle can trample them. The brief bloom of his worship of Mrs. Forrester is gone like the transient beauty of the flowers. *A Lost Lady* is short, a reflection of Cather's philosophy of the novel *démeublé*. Its prose is stripped of unnecessary adjectives; circumstantial details are taken away.

Niel Herbert initially looks upon Marian Forrester as an idol. Niel sees her as a woman of Old World charm who is gracious and can do no wrong. The novel is the story of how Marian changes. Many critics have seen *A Lost Lady* as a study in the degeneration of the title character as well as the degeneration of society. Cather wrote *A Lost Lady* during the Great Depression, a time of little hope. The Forresters originally represent gentility and the code of the pioneers. When the Captain's bank fails, he lives by the code and repays the bank's investors from his personal fortune until he is bankrupt. He wants to be an honorable man even though that means personal sacrifice for him and his wife.

Cather, like Niel, admired the old values and the pioneer spirit. She wrote, "The Old West had been settled by dreamers, great-hearted adventurers who were practical to the point of magnificence; a courteous brotherhood, strong in attack but weak in defence, who could conquer but could not hold." For the cunning and the self-interested, who can hold, the novel has little respect. The Forresters are symbolic of the declining spirit of the West. As Niel matures, he not only sees a change in Marian as she adopts the habits and philosophies of the new era and rejects the values of her husband and the pioneers but also sadly observes the change in the values of his society in general. The pioneer spirit had given way to the values incarnated in the amoral Ivy Peters.

Cather based *A Lost Lady* on a true story. In her childhood, Cather had liked a woman named Mrs. Lyra Garber. Cather's goal in writing *A Lost Lady* was to recapture the feelings that Mrs. Garber had invoked in her. She did little to conceal that Marian was based on Lyra Garber; there are many parallels between Garber's life and that of Marian Forrester. Garber's husband, Silas Garber, was a Nebraskan builder and had been a captain in the Union army; Marian's husband likewise was a captain who lived in Nebraska. Silas Garber founded Red Cloud, Cather's hometown. As the town became more settled, Garber became wealthy from the banking business and eventually, in 1873, became governor of Nebraska. When Garber, a widower, visited California to see his brother and sister-in-law, he was introduced to his sister-in-law's sister, Lyra Wheeler. He fell in love with Lyra and married her, and they settled in Lincoln, Nebraska, at the governor's mansion. Later they came to live in Red Cloud. Garber's bank failed, and he lost his fortune; he also lost his health when he fell from a carriage and was injured. After Captain Garber died, Lyra moved away from Red Cloud, returning to California and remarrying.

"Critical Evaluation" by Mary C. Bagley

Further Reading

Dollar, J. Gerard. "Community and Connectedness in *A Lost Lady*." In *Willa Cather: Family, Community, and History*, edited by John J. Murphy et al. Provo, Utah: Humanities Publications Center, Brigham Young University, 1990. Sees *A Lost Lady* in relation to Cather's statement that 1922 was the year "the world broke in two." Asserts that the novel is about connectedness and disconnectedness, with the latter as predominant.

Goldberg, Jonathan. *Willa Cather and Others*. Durham, N.C.: Duke University Press, 2001. Discusses Cather's fiction in relation to the works of various female contemporaries of the author, including opera singer Olive Fremstad, ethnographer and novelist Blair Niles, photographer Laura Gilpin, and writer Pat Barker.

Harris, Richard C. "First Loves: Willa Cather's Niel Herbert and Ivan Turgenev's Vladimir Petrovich." *Studies in American Fiction* 17 (Spring, 1989): 81-91. Relates how Cather conceived the idea to write *A Lost Lady* from knowing Mrs. Lyra Garber. Finds similarities between Ivan Turgenev's *Pervaya lyubov* (1860; *First Love*, 1884) and Cather's novel.

Lindemann, Marilee, ed. *The Cambridge Companion to Willa Cather*. New York: Cambridge University Press, 2005. Collection of essays offers examinations of such topics as politics, sexuality, and modernism in Cather's works. Includes discussion of *A Lost Lady*.

Rosowski, Susan J. *The Voyage Perilous: Willa Cather's Romanticism*. Lincoln: University of Nebraska Press, 1986. Thematic study interprets Cather's writing within the literary tradition of Romanticism. Devotes a chapter to an analysis of *A Lost Lady*.

Stout, Janis P., ed. *Willa Cather and Material Culture: Real-World Writing, Writing the Real World*. Tuscaloosa: University of Alabama Press, 2005. Collection of essays addresses the importance of material culture in Cather's life and work, including discussions of the objects among which she lived and about which she wrote. Two essays focus on *A Lost Lady*: "Taking Liberties: Willa Cather and the 1934 Film Adaptation of *A Lost Lady*," by Michael Schueth, and "'An Orgy of Acquisition': The Female Consumer, Infidelity, and Commodity Culture in *A Lost Lady* and *The Professor's House*," by Honor McKitrick Wallace.

The Lost Weekend

Author: Charles Jackson (1903-1968)
First published: 1944
Type of work: Novel
Type of plot: Psychological realism
Time of plot: October, 1936
Locale: New York City

Principal characters:
DON BIRNAM, an alcoholic would-be writer
WICK, his brother
HELEN, his friend

The Story:

Three days after his last drinking binge, Don Birnam sits alone in the New York apartment he shares with his younger brother Wick. Wick has gone to meet their friend Helen at a concert after failing to persuade Don that he should join them. After a short time alone, Don becomes agitated and impulsively decides to drink again. Taking the money Wick has left for the maid, he goes to Sam's bar. While looking in the mirror there, he conceives a short story called "In a Glass" based on his own sensitive youth and subsequent adult failures.

Don returns home and watches from hiding as Wick leaves for a long weekend in the country, a trip originally planned to help Don in his recovery. Again alone in the apartment, Don reflects on all the times he has broken his promises to the brother who is now supporting him. After another drink, he becomes elated and decides to go out. Borrowing money from a laundrywoman, he proceeds to a bar in Greenwich Village. He begins to drink and imagines himself more sophisticated than the other patrons; then, on a sudden whim, he steals a woman's handbag. Just as he is congratulating himself on his performance as a thief, the bar's doorman apprehends him and pushes him into the street. In acute embarrassment, he rushes home, where he drinks some more in search of oblivion.

Don awakes, not knowing if it is morning or early evening. He realizes that he has been off on another binge and that he will not be able to stop drinking until he is physically unable to get liquor. He reflects on his career as an alcoholic and remembers with disgust his pretensions of the previous night. He knows all too well that he is anything but a worldly sophisticate. Furthermore, he thinks, who would want to read the short story he now self-contemptuously dismisses as a tale of "a punk and a drunk"? He understands himself—he realizes his basic immaturity. He knows that drinking leads only to misery, yet he feels no hope that he can ever stop. Changes of scenery, trips abroad, psychiatry—nothing has helped; he always drinks again.

Don buys a bottle of liquor and returns home for some "safe" drinking. After indulging in a fantasy of himself as a great pianist, he grows restless and ventures out again. Eventually, he wanders back to Sam's bar. Over drinks, he tells Gloria, the host, an involved lie that he is a rich man with a frigid wife. Gloria agrees to meet him after she gets off work, and he goes home to drink and wait. He begins to reminisce, eventually recalling his expulsion from a fraternity for suspected homosexuality. Overwhelmed with self-pity, he gulps liquor until he passes out.

Don awakes to an empty bottle and curses himself for drinking the last drop the previous night. He knows that he must have more liquor, but somehow he has lost all his money. Faint and sick, he takes his typewriter to a pawnbroker, amazed that he can walk so far. Finding the door to the pawnshop locked, he staggers dozens of blocks down the busy avenue, but he finds that every pawnshop is closed for a holiday. Exhausted, he flees for home and borrows liquor

money from the local grocer. After a soothing drink, he reflects that his quest to pawn his typewriter would make a good story—but to whom could he tell it? He has no friends left; his drinking has made him a pariah. Abruptly deciding that he needs to get more liquor while he is able, he leaves the apartment. Distracted by trying to appear sober before his neighbors, he falls down two flights of stairs and is knocked unconscious.

The next time Don wakes, he is in the alcoholic ward of the hospital with a black eye and a fractured skull. Other patients with delirium tremens babble and moan around him. The doctor on duty treats Don in a detached, impersonal manner. Bim, an aggressively homosexual male nurse, seems to be both taunting and propositioning him. Don refuses further treatment and signs himself out of the hospital. Somehow he has lost his money again, but at the bar Sam accepts Don's watch in exchange for a bottle. Gloria upbraids him for missing their date, but Don does not even remember making it. He goes home, determined to stay there and drink quietly. After pretending to be a literature professor and a Shakespearean actor, he passes out and has a long, vivid dream. He awakes weeping, drains his bottle, and passes out again.

When Don comes to, he has no liquor and no hope of getting any. Whisperings come out of nowhere, and soon he is experiencing other auditory and visual hallucinations. He sits suffering for hours, tortured by the ringing of the telephone. He knows the caller is Helen, the woman who once loved and now pities him, but he cannot bring himself to answer. Hours later, Helen finds him trembling in a chair and takes him to her apartment. She cleans him up and feeds him, but he still has to face delirium that comes with alcohol withdrawal. Don watches in horror as a bat attacks and devours a mouse, but Helen shows him that this was a hallucination. She reassures Wick by phone that Don is recovering.

The next morning, Don still craves alcohol. After failing to manipulate Helen's maid into opening the liquor closet, he considers murdering the woman, but instead he steals Helen's fur coat and pawns it for five dollars. On the way to the store, he discovers all of his lost money in the breast pocket of his suit—during blackouts he had put it there for safekeeping, but forgot it each time. Now he has plenty of cash; he buys six pints of liquor and returns home. Wick is back from the country but is temporarily out of the apartment. Don hides two of his bottles in the toilet tank, hangs two more out the window, puts one in the bookcase for Wick to confiscate, and gulps the last one. Drunk again, he reflects that he is home and safe; his ordeal is over. Why, he wonders, did everyone make such a fuss?

Critical Evaluation:

The Lost Weekend is both a psychologically realistic study of an alcoholic personality and an intensely dramatic narrative. Author Charles Jackson demonstrates that he is adept at various modern fiction techniques, and his protagonist Don Birnam—like the intelligent, sensitive alcoholics in the works of F. Scott Fitzgerald and Ernest Hemingway—transcends the nineteenth century stereotype of alcoholics as villains or lowlifes. Jackson, however, also diverges sharply from Fitzgerald's and Hemingway's tendency to treat alcoholism as a somewhat noble and artistic reaction to the cruel bourgeois world. Don's "modern" sensibilities serve only as fuel for the flame of alcoholic rationalization, and the real life of the alcoholic is revealed in *The Lost Weekend* as being the furthest thing from noble.

The Lost Weekend has many autobiographical elements; Jackson admitted that all but two of the plot points in the story were taken from his own experiences, and he clearly understands the terror, loneliness, and hopelessness of the drinker. His accomplishment is even more noteworthy because he is working against type. On the surface, Don Birnam is the antithesis of the hopeless drunk: He is sensitive, articulate, well dressed, and from a good family. Unlike the typical problem drinker in literature, Don never denies that he is an alcoholic. He is acutely aware of his other psychological problems, yet self-knowledge is no help. He has drunk himself out of society and into an unhealthy dependent relationship with his younger brother and his former fiancé, and he teeters on the brink of destitution and institutionalization. He is not a romantic hero; he is only a constant source of frustration and sometimes a real danger to himself and to everyone around him.

Psychoanalysis was popular in the 1930's, and Jackson incorporates many psychoanalytic interpretations of human behavior into Don's tortured reflections. Glimpses of Freudian staples (narcissism, arrested adolescence, latent homosexuality, sibling rivalry, passive aggression, the Oedipus complex) abound. Don is haunted by mirrors, beset with portentous dreams. *The Lost Weekend* transcends all Freudian paradigms, however, and Don's problems defy any neat psychiatric solutions. Following the lead of Alcoholics Anonymous, Jackson portrays alcoholism as a spiritual illness ultimately impossible to deal with on logical terms. The loss of friends and livelihood and his trip to the alcoholic ward show that Don has passed a crucial milestone in the progression from periodic to chronic alcoholism, and, for all his grandiose philosophizing, the standard alcoholic's abyss awaits him.

The Lost Weekend's grim tone and gritty realism were considered rather sordid in 1944, but the book was generally well received by contemporary reviewers. Soon after its publication, it was made into a popular motion picture starring Ray Milland, with a new "happy" ending provided by Jackson himself. Perhaps in part because of its popular success, literary critics have largely ignored the novel in discussions of alcoholism in twentieth century literature, preferring to dwell on the tragic hero-drunks of Fitzgerald and Hemingway and the densely symbolic *Under the Volcano* (1947) by Malcolm Lowry, who made the trials of his alcoholic protagonist stand for nothing less than the throes of the modern world.

Whatever one thinks of Jackson's decision to focus on the harsh reality of Don's predicament, the author's sure sense of craft is enough to ensure *The Lost Weekend*'s place in modern literature. Using an objective third-person perspective, incorporating seamless flashbacks and bursts of stream of consciousness, the narrative achieves the immediacy of a first-person narrative without sacrificing the ability to venture outside the knowledge of the central character. The reader is able to follow the protagonist even when Don forgets where he has been; the careful reader can spot the inconsistencies in Don's self-analysis. Thus both narrator and reader have a better understanding of Don's past and a surer sense of his future than Don himself could possibly achieve. Jackson succeeds in making Don as sympathetic to the reader as he is to the other players in the novel, who see only Don's surface, even though the reader knows Don's innermost thoughts and is also revolted and exasperated by him. By stripping all romantic and symbolic pretension from the enigma of alcoholism, Jackson has arguably accomplished one of the finest literary presentations of the alcoholic character.

Richard A. Hill

Further Reading

Alcoholics Anonymous: The Story of How Many Thousands of Men and Women Have Recovered from Alcoholism. 4th ed. New York: Alcoholics Anonymous World Services, 2001. Landmark work, basically a spiritual guide for the recovering alcoholic, examines alcoholism from the layperson's perspective; Jackson cited it as a primary source for the view of alcoholic progression in *The Lost Weekend*. Many first-person accounts in the story section parallel Don Birnam's sordid adventures and downward spiral.

Connelly, Mark. *Deadly Closets: The Fiction of Charles Jackson.* Lanham, Md.: University Press of America, 2001. Critical biography reexamines *The Lost Weekend* and Jackson's other works of fiction. Maintains that Jackson was a pioneer gay writer whose work addressed repressed sexuality, addiction, and violence—topics that were not discussed publicly in his lifetime and remain relevant in the twenty-first century.

Crowley, John W. *The White Logic: Alcoholism and Gender in American Modernist Fiction.* Amherst: University of Massachusetts Press, 1994. Presents an excellent discussion of drinking in American fiction, with historical background and literary antecedents to the modern age. A heavily annotated chapter on *The Lost Weekend* includes biographical information on Jackson and puts the novel in perspective as a postscript to the novels of the 1920's and 1930's featuring the "heroic drunk."

Gilmore, Thomas B. *Equivocal Spirits: Alcoholism and Drinking in Twentieth-Century Literature.* Chapel Hill: University of North Carolina Press, 1987. Carries the discussion of alcoholism in literature into the postmodern 1960's and 1970's. Discusses *The Lost Weekend* and Don Birnam briefly as a backdrop to praise of Malcolm Lowry's "more compelling and complex" alcoholic hero in *Under the Volcano.*

McCarthy, Patrick A. "Reading *Dubliners* in *The Lost Weekend.*" *Studies in Short Fiction* 34, no. 4 (Fall, 1997): 441-448. Compares the novel to James Joyce's short story "Counterparts," offering analysis of the characters, plot, and theme.

Spectorsky, A. C. Review of *The Lost Weekend,* by Charles Reginald Jackson. *Book Week,* January 30, 1944. Contemporary review discusses the unique and "spectacular" writing techniques employed by Jackson. Admits the shocking nature of the book but argues that Jackson aims for "accuracy and the complete truth," not shock value alone.

Wilson, Edmund. Review of *The Lost Weekend,* by Charles Jackson. *The New Yorker,* February 5, 1944. Contemporary review generally praises the novel but ultimately finds the story a disappointment because of its lack of dramatic climax.

The Lost World

Author: Randall Jarrell (1914-1965)
First published: 1965
Type of work: Poetry

The Lost World is the last book Randall Jarrell prepared for publication, and it is considered his finest work. The lost world of the title is, first of all, the world of childhood, inevitably lost as the child grows into adulthood. Innocence is lost to experience, ignorance to knowledge, and immediate reality to habit and routine. Childhood can be recovered only in memory and can be given limited immortality only in works of art. Individual consciousness is extinguished in death, the final loss of the world for everyone. The earth, too, is finite, but this knowledge brings wisdom, which also depends on recovering the child's way of viewing the world with what Jarrell calls "interest." It evokes what he calls "adoration" for life and empathy for all things that die.

In the title poem of the collection, "The Lost World," Jarrell remembers his own childhood, when he lived for a while with his grandparents, Pop and Mama, and his great-grandmother, Dandeen, in Hollywood, California. The poem is divided into three sections. In the first, "Children's Arms," Jarrell recalls himself as a boy of twelve, coming home from school on Friday to begin his weekend. He passes a Hollywood motion-picture lot, where a papier-mâché dinosaur and pterodactyl look over the fence of the set for the film *The Lost World.* When he gets home, the boy arms himself with his homemade bow and arrows, ready to climb to his tree house and begin his real life of make-believe.

At the beginning of adolescence, the boy is already losing his innocence. He wakes up Saturday morning trying to remember his dream of a wolf and a tall girl. Then he accompanies Pop to the adult world of work, where he realizes that "the secret the grown-ups share, is what to do to make money." That evening the boy escapes back into childhood when he listens to Pop's stories about his own childhood. In "A Night with Lions," the second part of "The Lost World," Jarrell remembers his young aunt, who took him with her when she visited a friend who owned the Metro-Goldwyn-Mayer lion. He confesses his "dream discovery" that his breath comes faster whenever he hears someone with her voice. She gives him the image he will seek to find in the woman he marries, compelling him into adulthood.

In "A Street off Sunset," the third part of "The Lost World," Jarrell recounts the boy's growing knowledge of good and evil. On Sunday evening, he is reading a book about a mad scientist who is planning to destroy the world. Forced to go to bed, he puts his arms around Mama, Pop, and Dandeen, and they put theirs around him. Caring for one another is the good that contrasts with the evil of the scientist. The boy claims not to believe in God, but in bed he listens to a woman preaching on the radio. He imagines her holding out her arms to release people from the "bonds of sin, of sleep."

The next morning he finishes his book as he gets ready for school. Good is victorious over evil. After school, however, he learns that issues of good and evil are not always clear. Dandeen tells him her memories of the Civil War, and he watches Mama wring the neck of a chicken, its headless body "lunging and reeling" in "great flopping circles." He realizes this could happen to him. With renewed worry about the mad scientist, he asks Pop if someone could really destroy the world. Pop reassures him that no one can.

In contrast to the focus on childhood in "The Lost World," Jarrell portrays adulthood in "Hope." The child has grown up to become a husband and the father of his own child. It is two o'clock in the morning of Christmas Eve. The man's wife and son are asleep. Noticing the fir tree, covered in artificial snow, on top of a pile of presents, he says, "a man is a means." He works to make money for his family. Dissatisfied with his life, he says he would rather live in the squirrel's nest in the dream his son is having. He remembers wanting to tell his wife his nightmare about "the God Fish," who told him the story of Sleeping Beauty. In their version, however, she wakes when the prince kisses her, only to turn over and go back to sleep. She sleeps inside the wife/mother. The boy, the prince, inside the husband/father would like to recover the girl in his wife. He considers waking her, but he imagines she would only tell him that he is dreaming. Then he thinks—"later on, who knows?"

Like the wife in "Hope," most of the adults in *The Lost World* sleep through life, unless something wakes them to the repressed knowledge of their own mortality. Such is the speaker of "Next Day." An affluent, middle-aged housewife, she has everything she wished for as a girl: a husband, a house, and children. Having attended the funeral of a friend on the previous day, she has become acutely aware of her age. She is bewildered that the boy putting groceries in her car does not see her. She remembers when the world looked at her and its "mouth watered." She realizes now that she is not "exceptional." Her dead friend's face and body could be her face and body. Even though her life is "commonplace and solitary," she is afraid it will change, like her friend's.

Anxiety about death is also the subject of "In Montecito." When the speaker, who lives in this fashionable suburb of Santa Barbara, is "visited" one midnight by a "scream with breasts," he thinks of the recent death of an acquaintance, Greenie Taliaferro. In his nightmare, the scream comes from a billboard that contractors are tearing down. They strip off the "lips, let the air out of the breasts." Greenie's life is as temporary as the billboard, and Montecito is a place of death-in-life. In spite of money, or because of it, existence there is static, sterile, and suffocating. When the inhabitants pass from their sleep of life into the annihilation of death, they disappear into the "Greater Montecito" that "surrounds Montecito like the echo of a scream."

In "The One Who Was Different," Jarrell reveals that staying awake in life depends on the acceptance of death. The speaker is attending the funeral of Miss I——, who considered herself different from others but who has suffered the common human fate. Having been around the world twice, she lies in her casket, ready for the next trip—the trip to the grave. She has lived in the "earnest expectation" of life after death, but the speaker states that life is only a "temporary arrangement of the matter." At this point, the speaker notices a child waiting "eagerly" to look at death, another secret that grown-ups share. The child looks not with "sympathy or empathy" but with "interest"—"Without me." Interest is objective and reveals what is, rather than being subjective and revealing what one wishes. The speaker knows this. He wishes he could have made Miss I—— see that those who make up their minds about death, if they accept mortality, could live in a state of "interest" and experience life as what it is and as it is—a kind of dream, or poem.

Most of Jarrell's adults have lost the capacity to experience the immediate reality of life because they have repressed or denied the reality of death and gone to sleep in the habits and routines of adulthood. Two poems in *The Lost World*, taken from one of Jarrell's children's books, *The Bat-Poet* (1964), represent the child's way of experiencing life with "interest." "Bats" is a verbal rendition of a mother bat flying back and forth at night feeding on insects, while her baby clings to her. At dawn, she returns to her rafter, where she sleeps with her wings folded "about her sleeping child." In a similar poem, "The Bird of Night," an owl flies back and forth while all living creatures "hold their breath." Both poems re-create immediate reality.

In "The Mockingbird," also from *The Bat-Poet*, Jarrell relates the child's way of experiencing life to that of the poet; the poet, the adult who has stayed awake, recovers life from death in memory and re-creates it in imagination. All day the mockingbird, an image of the poet, drives away other birds and even a black cat. Then, as the sun goes down and the moon rises—that juncture of life and death—the mockingbird imitates life. A thrush, then a thrasher, then a jay is heard, as well as the meowing of a cat. The mockingbird has made "the world he drove away" his "own." The listener cannot tell which is the mockingbird, which the world. Art and reality are one.

In order to recover and transform experience—the "cheeping" and "squeaking" of experience become "singing" in "The Mockingbird"—the poet must see life not only with "interest" but also with "sympathy or empathy." These feelings are the subject of "In Galleries," which portrays three museum guards. The first represents indifference, the opposite of interest; the second represents sympathy and feeling for someone or something; and the third, who is a mute, represents empathy, the feeling with, becoming one with, someone or something. With a "rapt smile," the third guard takes out a magnifying glass and shows the museum visitor that in the painting of the woman holding the death of the world in her arms the "something" on the man's arm is "the woman's tear." Under this guard's guidance, empathy occurs. The visitor "and the guard and the man and the woman are dumbly one."

In "The Old and the New Masters," Jarrell speculates as to the likely result for the earth, and the life it nourishes, if the human race fails to develop empathy. He refers to Georges de La Tour's painting *St. Sebastian Mourned by St. Irene* to illustrate the old masters' view of suffering: "no one breathes/ As the sufferers watch the sufferer." Everyone has empathy with the sufferer because everyone is a sufferer. Jarrell refers to Hugo van der Goes's *Nativity* to illustrate the old masters' view of "adoration." In this painting, everything is fixed on the world's "small, helpless, human center"—the Christ child. For Jarrell, Christ represents the living, suffering body of the world.

Without adoration, the pure joy of beholding the miracle of being, there can be no empathy. The new masters paint a world that has lost adoration and empathy. At first, they put the Crucifixion in a corner of the canvas. Then Christ disappears from their paintings altogether. Finally, in a painting of the universe, the last master places a "bright spot" in a corner to represent "the small radioactive planet men called Earth." This passage is Jarrell's prophecy of the final loss of the world.

In "Thinking of the Lost World," Jarrell returns to the scene of his childhood in Hollywood, where he finds smog instead of sunshine. His bow and arrows are lost, and the planks of his tree house have been burned as firewood, but he realizes that age is like childhood and that the lost world still lives in his memory. In happiness, he holds in his hands "Nothing: the nothing for which there's no reward." Life is a dream, a poem, that ends.

James Green

Further Reading

Bryant, J. A., Jr. *Understanding Randall Jarrell*. Columbia: University of South Carolina Press, 1986. Offers a good introduction to all of Jarrell's work. Discusses *The Lost World* in chapter 5.

Burt, Stephen. *Randall Jarrell and His Age*. New York: Columbia University Press, 2002. After an initial chapter presenting a brief overview of Jarrell's life, focuses on the theme of the self in Jarrell's writing, providing close readings of both his poetry and prose.

Ferguson, Suzanne. *The Poetry of Randall Jarrell*. Baton Rouge: Louisiana State University Press, 1971. First book-length critical study of Jarrell's work remains a valuable resource. Includes an extensive analysis of *The Lost World*.

_____, ed. *Jarrell, Bishop, Lowell, and Co.: Middle-Generation Poets in Context*. Knoxville: University of Tennessee Press, 2003. Collection of essays examines the works and friendships among Jarrell, Elizabeth Bishop, and Robert Lowell. Among the topics addressed are Jarrell's interpersonal style and his poetic philosophy.

Flynn, Richard. *Randall Jarrell and the Lost World of Childhood*. Athens: University of Georgia Press, 1990. Considers all of Jarrell's work in the context of his interest in childhood and provides detailed analyses of the poems contained in *The Lost World*.

Oostdijk, Diederik. "The Best Years of Our Lives: Randall Jarrell and the Age of Consumer Culture." In *Reading the Middle Generation Anew: Culture, Community, and Form in Twentieth-Century American Poetry*, edited by Eric Haralson. Iowa City: University of Iowa Press, 2006. Analyzes Jarrell's work within the context of the period in which he wrote—the 1940's through the 1960's.

Pritchard, William H. *Randall Jarrell: A Literary Life*. New York: Farrar, Straus and Giroux, 1990. First book-length biography of Jarrell discusses the interaction between the events of his life and his work. Chapter 10 addresses *The Lost World*.

Quinn, Mary Bernetta. *Randall Jarrell*. Boston: Twayne, 1981. Contains information about Jarrell's childhood and provides analysis of "In Galleries" and "The Old and the New Masters."

The Lottery

Author: Shirley Jackson (1916-1965)
First published: 1948
Type of work: Short fiction
Type of plot: Horror
Time of plot: June 27, late 1940's
Locale: Probably New England

Principal characters:
TESSIE HUTCHINSON, a housewife
BILL HUTCHINSON, her husband, a farmer
BILL, JR.,
NANCY, and
DAVE, the young children of Tessie and Bill
MR. SUMMERS, a businessperson
MR. GRAVES, the village postmaster
OLD MAN WARNER, an elderly villager
DICKIE DELACROIX, a village child
MRS. DELACROIX, Dickie's mother

The Story:

Just before 10 A.M. on June 27, the three hundred inhabitants of a small village in New England start gathering at the town square. The children arrive first, and some of the boys begin to put rocks and stones into a pile. As the morning progresses, the men of the village begin to arrive, coming from their farms and fields. They are soon joined by their wives, who have come from their household chores. The scene is convivial: The children laugh and play, and the adults joke and gossip.

Eventually, Mr. Summers, a local businessperson who seems to be in charge of the assembly, arrives, carrying a large black box. He is followed by the village postmaster, Mr. Graves, who carries a stool. Two men help Mr. Summers place the heavy box on the stool, and Mr. Summers begins to stir and shuffle the hundreds of slips of paper that are inside the box. Then, Mr. Summers and Mr. Graves begin drawing up lists of families, including the head of each household and the names of all members of each family. The old and decrepit box makes it clear that some sort of ancient tradition is being followed. The villagers recall that in the past the procedure had been longer and more elaborate. The oldest denizen of the town, Old Man Warner, points out that this is his seventy-seventh year participating in the ritual, called simply the lottery.

As the men are working on the lists of families, Tessie Hutchinson arrives, the last villager to join the crowd at the square. Tessie had realized at the last minute, while she was washing dishes, that today is June 27. Her friends and neighbors tease her about her tardiness.

The lottery begins. Mr. Summers calls up each head of household in alphabetical order, from Adams to Zanini. As people draw their slips, the villagers show a certain degree of nervousness. However, homespun humor reasserts itself when Bill Hutchinson is called and his wife urges him forward in a raucous and bossy way, causing those around her to snicker. While the drawings by the heads of households continues, Old Man Warner gets into a discussion with the people sitting near him about the background of the lottery. It appears that the lotteries used to be common in the region, but some villages have given up the practice. These breaks in tradition elicit Old Man Warner's scorn: "There's always been a lottery," he insists, and he attributes the abandonment of the ritual to the current generation, whom he denounces as a "[p]ack of young fools." He also reveals that the lottery is in essence a fertility ritual, and he quotes a half-forgotten adage: "Lottery in June, corn be heavy soon."

All of the heads of families have finished drawing their slips of paper. Bill finds that he has drawn a slip with a dark splotch. It soon becomes apparent that something sinister is going on, as Tessie shouts out, "You didn't give him time enough to take any paper he wanted. I saw you. It wasn't fair." Dickie Delacroix's mother urges Tessie to "Be a good sport," and Bill's advice to his wife is grim and terse: "Shut up, Tessie." Tessie, however, continues to argue about the fairness of the procedure.

The slips of paper are retrieved, including the one with the ominous black splotch. Next, each of the five members of the Hutchinson family is made to draw from five slips. As this second drawing proceeds, one of Nancy Hutchinson's school friends murmurs, "I hope it's not Nancy," a wish that draws fresh scorn from Old Man Warner. The Hutchinsons each display their slips of paper—Tessie's slip is dotted. Mr. Summers announces "Let's finish quickly," an exhortation in keeping with an earlier indication that the time of the lottery has been set at 10 A.M. so that the villagers can return home in time for their noon meals.

As Tessie stands alone, her neighbors and family and friends pick up stones and rocks from the piles the boys had amassed earlier. Dickie's mother selects a rock so huge, she can barely lift it, and little Dave Hutchinson, too, is given a few small rocks to throw. As Tessie shrieks about the unfairness of the ritual, the villagers begin to stone her to death.

Critical Evaluation:

The publication of "The Lottery" in *The New Yorker* in June of 1948 created a scandal. Many readers canceled their subscriptions to the venerable magazine, and others wrote threatening letters to its author, Shirley Jackson. Later generations were puzzled by this controversy. The sources for the furor and scandal can be found in the structure of the story and its themes, in the mood of Americans in the late 1940's, in the prejudices held by the reading public against certain literary genres, in the venue in which the story appeared, and in Jackson's persona.

"The Lottery" presents a prototypal example of the surprise ending. Many writers, including Guy de Maupassant, O. Henry, Saki, and H. H. Munro, made this sort of plot twist a hallmark of their craft. A decade later, two long-running television series, *The Twilight Zone* and *Alfred Hitchcock Presents*, regularly employed this device as well. Surprise endings often lead to reader delight, but not so with Jackson's macabre story of human sacrifice. Jackson provides subtle hints in the story that something grim is in the offing—for example, the gathering of stones and rocks, the crowd's sense of nervousness as the lottery proceeds, and Tessie's alarm when her family "wins" the initial phase of the contest. Also, the lottery is held at the end of June, near the summer solstice, a time of year that features prominently in agricultural festivals throughout the Northern Hemisphere.

Nevertheless, the characters seem so wholesome, so stereotypically small-town American, that it is easy for the reader to overlook the clues that Jackson provides. Such subtlety is a hallmark of Jackson's craft, one to which horror novelist Stephen King made reference in the dedication to his 1980 novel *Firestarter*: "In memory of Shirley Jackson, who never needed to raise her voice." In this dedication, King lists four of Jackson's most celebrated works, one of which is "The Lottery" and the other is Jackson's best-known work of long fiction, *The Haunting of Hill House*. This novel, too, begins in June and ends with a similar, though symbolic, sacrifice.

The surprise ending to "The Lottery" also reveals Jackson's dark themes, including the warping effect on society of mindless tradition. Old Man Warner, the embodiment of rigid tradition, seems to believe that the sacrifice is necessary to ensure sufficient food for the village, but the other villagers are maintaining the practice out of habit and sheer inertia. They have forgotten why they are doing the ritual and have let it become a corrupt, atrophied shade of its earlier form; still, they insist on keeping the lottery because it has always been done. Simply out of tradition, they unquestioningly stone to death a neighbor whom they were laughing and joking with minutes earlier.

An even more pessimistic theme of the story is its interrogation of altruism and humanitarianism. No one in the village shows any concern for justice and kindness except Tessie—and she, too, starts to complain about the lottery only when she realizes that it is going to directly affect her own family. In short, Jackson suggests that people are not concerned about injustice and kindness unless these problems touch them personally.

The story's surprise ending and its unflattering depiction of human nature must have been especially unsettling to readers in the late 1940's, when Americans were especially proud of the role they had played in defeating the Nazis in World War II. Having recently vanquished a cruel and inhumane enemy, perhaps Americans were not ready for a story that implied that they themselves could be cruel and inhumane. Jackson hints that these characteristics are woven into the fabric of the United States by giving her characters names that were prominent in the nation's early years (for example, Adams and Hutchinson). The names Summers, Graves, and Delacroix—literally "of the cross"—reflect other themes and motifs implicit in the story, such as, respectively, agrarian tradition, death, and sacrifice.

Furthermore, a surprise ending involving human sacrifice placed "The Lottery" in the genre of horror fiction, a type of writing dismissed as unsophisticated and sensationalistic and, therefore, fodder for cheap pulp magazines. *The New Yorker* had been the most prestigious venue for short fiction in the mid-twentieth century, and its subscribers must have felt duped into reading what they thought was "trashy" writing.

Adding to the reading public's angry response to "The Lottery" was Jackson's public persona. In 1948, she was known as a writer of humorous articles and short stories detailing her experiences as a housewife and mother of four children. Few if any readers would have expected from her a harrowing depiction of blind tradition and merciless selfishness, like that revealed in "The Lottery."

Thomas Du Bose

Further Reading

Friedman, Lenemaja. *Shirley Jackson*. Boston: Twayne, 1975. An excellent introduction to Jackson's work. The chapter "Social Evil" is devoted primarily to explicating "The Lottery."

Hall, Joan Wylie. *Shirley Jackson: A Study of Short Fiction*. New York: Twayne, 1993. Part one is devoted to Jackson's short stories, including "The Lottery." Hall's bibliography, although dated, is extremely thorough and includes critical responses to Jackson's writings.

Hattenhauer, Darryl. *Shirley Jackson's American Gothic*. Albany: State University of New York Press, 2003. An excellent, detailed critical assessment of Jackson's body of work, including "The Lottery."

Hyman, Stanley Edgar, ed. *The Magic of Shirley Jackson*. New York: Farrar, Straus and Giroux, 1966. Hyman, literary critic and theorist as well as Jackson's husband, compiled this anthology the year after her death. His preface contains a pithy assessment of the theme of "The Lottery."

King, Stephen. *Danse Macabre*. 1981. Reprint. London: Hodder, 2006. A champion of the work of Jackson, novelist King discusses "The Lottery" and her novel *The Haunting of Hill House* in this overview of horror fiction.

Kosenko, Peter. "A Reading of Shirley Jackson's 'The Lottery.'" *New Orleans Review* 12, no. 1 (Spring, 1985): 27-32. A compelling interpretation of "The Lottery" from Marxist and feminist perspectives.

Murphy, Bernice M., ed. *Shirley Jackson: Essays on the Literary Legacy*. Jefferson, N.C.: McFarland, 2005. Essays in this collection survey Jackson's legacy as a writer of gothic fiction, focusing on her lesser-known works.

Oppenheimer, Judy. *Private Demons: The Life of Shirley Jackson*. New York: Putnam, 1988. The definitive biography of Jackson. Oppenheimer provides a wealth of detail about the writing of "The Lottery" and the intense controversy that arose when it was first published in the summer of 1948.

Parks, John G. "Chambers of Yearning: Shirley Jackson's Use of the Gothic." *Twentieth Century Literature* 30, no. 1 (Spring, 1984): 15-29. A concise article that summarizes gothic elements in all of Jackson's work.

Reinsch, Paul N., ed. *A Critical Bibliography of Shirley Jackson, American Writer (1919-1965): Reviews, Criticism, Adaptations*. Lewiston, N.Y.: E. Mellen Press, 2001. A vast resource listing secondary materials on Jackson's life and work. Includes contemporary reviews as well as later critical works. Also includes annotations and an introduction by the editor.

Love for Love

Author: William Congreve (1670-1729)
First produced: 1695; first published, 1695
Type of work: Drama
Type of plot: Comedy of manners
Time of plot: Seventeenth century
Locale: London

Principal characters:
SIR SAMPSON LEGEND, a foolish old gentleman
VALENTINE, his son, an indigent gallant
BENJAMIN, another son, a sailor
FORESIGHT, an old man given to astrology
ANGELICA, his niece
PRUE, his daughter
MRS. FORESIGHT, his young second wife
MISTRESS FRAIL, her sister

The Story:

Young Valentine Legend, having squandered all of his money in riotous living, is destitute and deeply in debt. With no property left but his books, he declares his intention of becoming a playwright, for his love for Angelica has indeed compelled him to take desperate measures. On hearing of Valentine's intention, Jeremy, his knavish manservant, shows alarm and says that Valentine's family will surely disown him.

Among Valentine's creditors is Trapland, a lecherous old scrivener who persists in dunning him. When Valentine, who has been joined by his friend Scandal, subtly threatened Trapland with blackmail concerning a wealthy city widow, the old man suddenly forgets the money that Valentine owes him.

Sir Sampson Legend's steward tells Valentine that he will be released from all debts if he will sign over his rights as Sir

Sampson's heir to Ben, his younger brother. If he signs, he will receive four thousand pounds in cash. In the meantime, Foresight, an old fool given to the science of prognostication, recalls Prue, his bumpkin daughter, from the country. Foresight plans to marry her to Ben Legend.

Angelica, wealthy, young, and clever, reproves her uncle for his belief in astrology. Irate, Foresight threatens to end her friendship with Valentine. Angelica, piqued, insinuates that Mrs. Foresight, the old man's young second wife, is not true to him.

Sir Sampson Legend, a great teller of tall tales of world travel, arranges with Foresight for the marriage of Ben and Prue. When Sir Sampson playfully hints to Foresight that Mrs. Foresight might not be a faithful wife, Foresight threatens to break the marriage agreement. Sir Sampson quickly makes amends.

Valentine, seeking Angelica, encounters his father at Foresight's house. He is indignant when his father disowns him as a son, and he begs his father to change his mind about the conditions under which he could be freed of debt.

When Mrs. Foresight rebukes her sister for her indiscretion in frequenting the haunts of gamesters and gallants, Mistress Frail reveals her knowledge of Mrs. Foresight's own indiscretions. Mistress Frail then declares her intention of marrying Ben and enlists her sister's aid in the project. Prue, meanwhile, finds herself charmed by Tattle, a voluble young dandy. When Mrs. Foresight and Mistress Frail encourage Tattle to court Prue, he is mystified, because he knows of the marriage arranged between Prue and Ben. Even so, he gives Prue a lesson in the art of love, a lesson that progresses as far as her bedchamber. Tattle, having grown tired of dalliance with the unrefined country girl, is relieved when Prue's nurse finds them.

Ben, returning from a sea voyage, declares that marriage does not interest him at the moment, but he visibly changes his mind when Mistress Frail flatters him. Left alone, he and Prue express dislike for each other. Ben declares that he talks to Prue only to obey his father.

Scandal, in Valentine's behalf, ingratiates himself with Foresight by pretending a knowledge of astrology. His scheme succeeds, and he convinces Foresight that it is not in the stars for Valentine to sign over his inheritance or for Ben and Prue to marry. Attracted to Mrs. Foresight, Scandal hoodwinks old Foresight in order to pay gallant attentions to his young wife. Ben and Mistress Frail confess their love and decide to marry.

Scandal has reported that Valentine is ill, so Angelica goes to his lodgings. In spite of Scandal's insistence that her acknowledgment of love for Valentine will cure the young

man, she quickly detects a trick and departs. Sir Sampson and a lawyer named Buckram arrive to get Valentine's signature on the documents they have prepared. Jeremy insists that Valentine is out of his mind. Buckram says that the signature will be invalid under the circumstances, but Sir Sampson forces his way into his son's presence. Valentine, pretending complete lunacy, calls himself Truth and declares that he will give the world the lie. After the frightened Buckram leaves, Valentine shows clarity of mind, but when the lawyer is called back, Valentine again seems to lapse into lunacy.

Mistress Frail, having learned that there is little chance of Ben's inheriting the whole estate, breaks off their engagement. Sir Sampson, frustrated by Valentine, decides to marry and beget a new heir. Mrs. Foresight plots with Jeremy to marry Mistress Frail, disguised as Angelica, to Valentine during one of his fits of madness. When Jeremy reveals the scheme to Valentine and Scandal, the friends, in their turn, plan to marry Mistress Frail to Tattle by means of another disguise.

After Valentine has confessed his feigned madness to Angelica, she expresses disappointment. She decides to test his love of her. She then goes to Sir Sampson, learns his new state of mind, and suggests that he and she go through with a mock marriage ceremony in order to bring Valentine to his senses. When foolish Sir Sampson suggests that they actually get married so that she can inherit his estate, Angelica says that this would not be advisable because the papers leaving the estate to Ben have already been drawn up.

Jeremy tricks foolish Tattle into believing that he, disguised as a friar, might marry Angelica, who will be disguised as a nun. Prue, forsaken by Tattle, asserts that she will marry Robin, the butler, who has professed his love for her.

Mistress Frail, thinking that she is marrying Valentine, and Tattle, thinking that he is marrying Angelica, are thus tricked into wedlock. Told by Angelica that she intends to marry his father, Valentine in despair declares that he is ready to sign over his inheritance. Impressed by this indication of his love for her, Angelica tears up the bond that Sir Sampson had given her. She then brings the doting old man to his senses by revealing that she had always intended to marry Valentine. Sir Sampson and old Foresight console each other; they admit that they have acted like fools.

Critical Evaluation:

As a genre, dramatic comedy has always had its stock characters: the cunning servant; the foolish, foppish socialite; the wrongheaded, demanding parent; the thwarted lovers. The genre also has familiar plot devices: multiple stories, disguises, intrigues, and misapprehensions. William Congreve's third comedy, *Love for Love*, generally considered one of his finest, is certainly no exception regarding such conventions. The plot is relatively simple and not particularly original. It does have elements reminiscent of William Shakespeare's drama (the theme of madness, for example, recalls, with comic irony, *Hamlet, Prince of Denmark*, pr. c. 1600-1601, pb. 1603; and *King Lear*, pr. c. 1605-1606, pb. 1608) or Ben Jonson's dark comedies of humours (evidenced by Foresight's obsession with astrology and Sir Sampson's avarice and lechery), not to mention earlier Restoration plays. Congreve, however, creates from these derivative elements a play with distinctly late Restoration characteristics, language, and attitudes. The play enjoyed great popularity during its time, and audiences have continued to find it entertaining. *Love for Love* is enlightening as well, for in it Congreve takes up an array of issues, including wit, fashion, sexual conduct, marriage, and family.

Love for Love is a comedy of manners, a play about social behavior, social language, and social intrigue. Its characters are two-dimensional, their ideas without any apparent substance, their actions silly and self-centered. What appear to be most important, as the opening scene between Valentine and Jeremy indicates, are the abilities to turn a witty phrase and to dupe others. Congreve's play is more, however, than just a frenetic piece of stagecraft with characters running to and fro. At the heart of the play lie a number of questions that are emblematized by Valentine's role as "Truth" during his feigned madness: What is true? What is true friendship? What is true knowledge? What is true love? What is the truth of human relationships? Can a person navigate honestly through a world based on deception and self-interest? These questions dominate the play's language, events, and structure. Congreve reveals his answers through three sets of contrasting characters, their contrasting actions, and their contrasting levels of social success. In this way, he leads the audience to recognize the distinction between true wit (intelligence and judgment) and false wit (accidental cleverness or duplicity) and that between true love (self-sacrifice) and false love (self-love or self-interest).

The rustics Prue and Ben enter the play honest and straightforward, but this honesty prevents them from operating effectively in society. Ben blusters around and then simply goes back to sea. Prue eagerly learns the deceitful ways and the sexual freedoms of a society woman, but she lacks the discretion needed to control them. Unmanageable truth serves neither of these characters.

The second set of characters includes the city gallants, both male and female. Each believes him- or herself a social expert, a wit, and a skillful lover, but the truth is somewhat different. Scandal's attitude toward and relationships with women are cynical and selfish. Tattle's sexual escapades and his flippant attitude toward women, evidenced by his treatment of Prue, make him vulnerable to the machinations of those more cunning than he. The bored and unhappy Mrs. Foresight is false to her husband and to her lover. The mercenary Mistress Frail is interested only in attaching herself to a man with a fortune. Each one is victimized by his or her own deception and self-deception.

The two fathers in the play also fall into the category of wise fools. Foresight looks for wisdom in the stars, but he cannot see his wife's infidelity. Unlike his counterpart's extraterrestrial focus, Sir Sampson's vision is limited to the terrestrial—namely, his estate, his sons, and his own body. Both men are locked in their own limited, failed visions, excluded from true human relationships. Both are also manipulated and disdained by those around them.

Much of the action of *Love for Love*'s highly complicated plot—the intrigues, the manipulations, the stratagems to gain money, sex, or power—is generated by these secondary characters. Motivated by egotism, vanity, greed, and revenge, they fracture their world (and the play). As represented by these characters, human relationships are, at worst, predatory and, at best, ambiguous and fragile. Everyone seems to be speaking his or her own language, a point that Congreve intensifies with a variety of figurative images—nautical, astrological, zoological, religious, and legal—and acting according to a set of rules with no heart and no basis in moral truth. Those who believe themselves masters of the game are ultimately victimized by it; those who cannot, or will not, play the game according to its rules withdraw from it.

These three categories of characters are only one dimension of Congreve's play, however, for amid all the frenetic scheming of the others stand two characters, Valentine and Angelica. In a sense, the play has a double emphasis: Alongside a darkly satirical look at the foolishness of society and its mavens exists the love story of hero and heroine. Valentine and Angelica are nevertheless very much a part of the world they inhabit. Valentine has at least one illegitimate child, he has foolishly lost his fortune to fashionable living, and he tries to trick his way out of the situation in which he finds himself. Angelica is witty, disrespectful, cruel, and not above plotting an intrigue herself. These two characters occupy the middle ground between corruption and perfection: They are wise, witty, and worldly, and yet they are recoverable. Despite all of his faults, Valentine remains true to his love for Angelica—he is willing to martyr himself for her—and she remains true to him.

The sentimentality of their final declaration of love may

seem incongruous with the rest of the action, but the ending is of a piece with both the play's social satire and its underlying moral plot, the reformation of a rake. Angelica ("angel") puts Valentine ("lover") to the test in order to teach him, as well as the other characters, what true love is. Their blending of true wit and true love finally rewards the couple with both the greatest social and personal success: She has her fortune, he will inherit his father's estate, and they will have their marriage. Their union even converts the cynical Scandal from his misbehavior and his misconceptions. Ultimately, the title of the play sums up its social satire and its moral lesson: love for love's sake.

"Critical Evaluation" by Judith Burdan

Further Reading

Hoffman, Arthur W. *Congreve's Comedies.* Victoria, B.C.: English Literary Studies, University of Victoria, 1993. Includes a chapter on *Love for Love* that focuses on the roles of Valentine and Angelica as romantic hero and heroine and on Sir Sampson as blocking agent. Shows how Congreve skillfully employs allusions to biblical, classical, and Shakespearean traditions.

Markley, Robert. *Two-Edg'd Weapons: Style and Ideology in the Comedies of Etherege, Wycherley, and Congreve.* New York: Oxford University Press, 1988. Argues that Congreve is stylistically a transitional figure, with his plays falling in style between earlier satirical comedies and the later sentimental comedies.

Novak, Maximillian E. *William Congreve.* New York: Twayne, 1971. Provides a good basic overview of Congreve's life and works. Discusses his various works, with a chapter on *Love for Love*, and the intellectual, artistic, and moral debates of his period.

Owen, Susan J., ed. *A Companion to Restoration Drama.* Malden, Mass.: Blackwell, 2001. Collection of essays examines the types of Restoration drama, places these plays within the context of their times, and analyzes works by individual playwrights. Includes discussion of Congreve's plays, particularly in the essay "William Congreve and Thomas Southerne," by Miriam Handley.

Sieber, Anita. *Character Portrayal in Congreve's Comedies "The Old Batchelour," "Love for Love," and "The Way of the World."* Lewiston, N.Y.: Edwin Mellen Press, 1996. Focuses on the numerous types of characters in the comedies, including some who are placed in opposition to each other, such as wits versus fools and fops, country characters versus city gallants and ladies, and old people versus young people. Also discusses Congreve's use of historical characters and his themes of love and marriage.

Van Voris, W. H. *The Cultivated Stance: The Designs of Congreve's Plays.* Dublin: Dolmen Press, 1965. Discusses Congreve's social, philosophical, and aesthetic values. Argues that *Love for Love* represents a chaotic world populated by monsters driven by vanity and self-interest where Valentine and Angelica's love brings about order, but only ambiguously.

Williams, Aubrey. *An Approach to Congreve.* New Haven, Conn.: Yale University Press, 1979. Asserts that the world represented on the Restoration stage appears chaotic but is actually ordered by providential design. Examines *Love for Love* and finds a pattern of testing, trial, and judgment in the play, at the center of which Angelica stands as judge and reward.

Young, Douglas M. *The Feminist Voices in Restoration Comedy: The Virtuous Women in the Play-Worlds of Etherege, Wycherley, and Congreve.* Lanham, Md.: University Press of America, 1997. Focuses on the female characters in Congreve's plays who demand independence from and equality with men before they commit to courtship or marriage. Devotes a chapter to *Love for Love*.

Love in a Wood
Or, St. James's Park

Author: William Wycherley (1641?-1715)
First produced: 1671; first published, 1672
Type of work: Drama
Type of plot: Comedy of manners
Time of plot: Seventeenth century
Locale: London

Principal characters:
MR. RANGER, a young man-about-town
LYDIA, his cousin and fiancé
MR. VALENTINE, a gallant lately returned to London
CHRISTINA, his fiancé
MR. VINCENT, a confidant of all the lovers
ALDERMAN GRIPE, an elderly usurer
MISTRESS MARTHA, his daughter
LADY FLIPPANT, his sister, in London to find a husband
SIR SIMON ADDLEPLOT, an indomitable fortune hunter
MR. DAPPERWIT, a fop and a would-be gentleman
MRS. JOYNER, a matchmaker and procurer
MRS. CROSSBITE, a blackmailer and procurer
LUCY, her daughter

The Story:

Lady Flippant, a widow disappointed in her efforts to find a new husband, berates her matchmaker, Mrs. Joyner, for not finding her a wealthy young man to relieve her impecunious position. The lady's brother, Alderman Gripe, has grown tired of her foppish visitors, especially the witless Mr. Dapperwit. At the suggestion of the cozening Mrs. Joyner and the double-dealing Dapperwit, Sir Simon Addleplot disguises himself and gains employment as a clerk to the miserly Gripe in order to woo the usurer's daughter, Mistress Martha, and through her secure her father's fortune. Not realizing that he has been gulled into masquerading as Jonas the clerk, Sir Simon is also duped into believing that he is loved by Lady Flippant, who is really enamored of Dapperwit.

Together with Mr. Vincent, his friend and confidant, Mr. Ranger is about to go into St. James's Park in search of amorous adventure when he is discovered by his cousin Lydia, to whom he is betrothed. He avoids her, however, and dines with the gulled Sir Simon, Dapperwit, and Lady Flippant for the diversion of watching the work of Mrs. Joyner, who has already made twenty crowns through introductions and will obtain one hundred crowns if Sir Simon gets Mistress Martha or fifty if he gets Lady Flippant. The widow spurns Sir Simon, flirts with Dapperwit, and hints at matrimony to both Ranger and Vincent.

Later, all promenade through St. James's Park in the hope of discovering one another's intrigues. Lydia, recognizing Ranger, runs into the house of her friend Christina in order to avoid a compromising meeting with her betrothed. Ranger pursues her only to become enamored of Christina, who is

faithfully waiting the return to London of her fiancé, Mr. Valentine. In order to help Lydia, Christina pretends to be the young woman Ranger has pursued from the park. Once her little act is over, she sends the impertinent young man away. Ranger, in despair because he has not learned the fair unknown's name, has no idea that Lydia has overheard his gallant speeches to Christina.

Ranger goes to the home of his friend Vincent. Valentine, whose life is in danger from a rival, is in hiding there, for he wishes no one to know of his return from France before his loved one knows. The concealed Valentine overhears Ranger ask Vincent the name of the young woman whom Ranger earlier pursued into her apartment. When Vincent says that the apartment is Christina's, Valentine becomes convinced that his beloved has been untrue to him.

In contrast to this sequence of mistaken and confused identities, the busy Mrs. Joyner is more positive in identifying Lucy, the daughter of her friend Mrs. Crossbite, as the object of hypocritical old Gripe's lust. The solicitous mother, pleased with this development, orders her recalcitrant daughter to give up her love for Dapperwit. Dapperwit, thinking to cure Ranger's melancholy over Christina, brings him to see Lucy, but the girl repulses Dapperwit for his infidelity and what she thinks is his intention of procuring her for Ranger. The jilted fop recovers his spirits, however, when he receives a message delivered by Jonas, the supposed clerk, that holds out the promise of a later assignation that might, Dapperwit hopes, lead to a wedding.

As the gallants depart, the ever-busy Mrs. Joyner brings

the furtive Alderman Gripe to see Lucy. His hasty lust frightens her, however, and she screams. Though he dickers in true miserly fashion, Gripe is coerced into paying five hundred pounds in hush money to Mrs. Crossbite. Lady Flippant, at the same time, is making advances to the defenseless Dapperwit, and the nimble-footed lovers Ranger and Lydia are busy at double deception. Lydia denies that she had been in the park jealously searching for him; Ranger assures her that he had called for her as he had promised.

The Gripe household is in an uproar. The sly old man is busily attempting to hide his shame and regain his money, and Mrs. Joyner virtuously pretends horror at the treatment he has received at the hands of Mrs. Crossbite. Jonas, meanwhile, makes love to Lady Flippant, who protests only after she learns that her seducer is really Sir Simon Addleplot, the man she hopes eventually to marry. So the poor man, undone by his own deceit, loses Mistress Martha through his dissembling ways and Dapperwit's roguery.

To test Ranger, Lydia sends him a letter to which she has signed Christina's name, asking the gallant to meet her that evening at St. James's Gate. The wronged Christina has since learned of her lover's return, and Valentine is at that time trying to reassure himself of her innocence. Overhearing Ranger's new plans unsettles him again, though his eavesdropping on a conversation between Christina and Vincent and then on one between Christina and her supposed lover finally sets his mind at rest. Lydia also confesses her part in this lovers' plot and counterplot, and the two couples, thus reunited, decide that matrimony is the only sure solution to love's equation.

The false lovers find no such easy solution, however, so addle-witted have their intrigues become. Sir Simon, still passing as Jonas, escorts Mistress Martha to Dapperwit. He thinks their embraces inopportune and inappropriate, but his arrangements for a parson, a supper, and a reception in nearby Mulberry Garden are not completely wasted. Propelled to the same garden by the two scheming procurers, Alderman Gripe marries Lucy to be revenged on his son-in-law, Dapperwit, who has taken a bride who is six months pregnant. In the end, Sir Simon takes the widowed Lady Flippant as his wife, just as she had intended. Thus are all the honest ladies made wives and all the bawds made honest in St. James's Park.

Critical Evaluation:

The first of three satiric comedies by William Wycherley, *Love in a Wood* shows brilliantly the playwright's genius. Wycherley gained his insights into high society as an intimate of high-ranking individuals on both sides of the English Channel. It was this play that gained for the young author the king's favor and the love of the king's mistress, the duchess of Cleveland.

As Wycherley uses the phrase, "in a wood" means "confused"; such a description might apply as well to the audience and to readers of this play as to the characters in it, for by the end there are no less than five marriages, one accomplished and four in prospect. The unusually large quantity of couples, the complicated intrigues in which they indulge, and the various unravelings that are required keep the play bustling with physical and dramatic movement. It is, however, a movement less controlled than in the playwright's later satiric masterpieces, *The Country Wife* (pr., pb. 1675) and *The Plain-Dealer* (pr. 1676).

Love in a Wood contains many of the motifs of deception that were to become standard in Restoration comedy—disguises, mistaken identity, hiding, and overheard and misinterpreted conversations, all of which create confusion between appearance and reality. Valentine, for instance, hears an apparently compromising report of Christina and concludes that she is unfaithful, Gripe frantically attempts to maintain the pretense of Puritan piety and respectability, and Sir Simon poses as a clerk and then discovers, to his consternation, that Martha refuses to believe he is a knight. Critics have pointed out that Wycherley uses the metaphor of light and darkness to dramatize social reality and inner reality; it is significant that most of the crucial revelations take place in darkness, where the truth can safely come out.

The characters are standard types: a fool, a hypocrite, a fop, a lecherous widow, and a wench, who make up the "low" plot, and a set of "realistic" lovers and a set of "ideal" ones, who make up the "high" plot. Wycherley skillfully uses Mrs. Joyner on one hand and Vincent on the other to serve as go-betweens for the various characters and to lend coherence to the many strands of the action. Of course, Mrs. Joyner, the functionary of the low plot, helps only to increase the confusion, in accordance with the dictates of her financial interest; Vincent, in contrast, with his earnest regard for the truth, does his best to clear up misunderstandings. The high-plot characters profit by the unraveling, while the others, despite the prospect of their marriages, succeed only in duping themselves or in making the best of bad bargains.

Like other Restoration comedies, *Love in a Wood* creates a highly realistic and immediate sense of contemporary London: Scenes unfold in real places, such as Mulberry Garden and St. James's Park, and the dialogue is peppered with contemporary allusions and jokes. Like other comic dramatists of the period, Wycherley treats love as a battle between the sexes (metaphors of war and hunting abound), with women usually having the upper hand. Wycherley is distinctive, however, in his caustic wit and his cynical attitude toward human relationships. Aggression, lust, greed, and mistrust seem to be the main drives governing the behavior of his characters. Dissimulation is accepted as the norm, so the complicated intrigues of the plot are as much an indication of the necessary condition of life as they are an indication of the development of a comic drama.

The marriages of the low-plot characters are motivated by either financial interest (and, in the case of Sir Simon and Lady Flippant, a mistaken view of financial interest) or revenge. Lydia and Ranger seem to be on firmer ground, but the jealousy of the one and the philandering of the other are not, despite Ranger's protestations of reform, very reassuring. Only the marriage between Valentine and Christina, which is based on genuine love and honesty, seems to have any hopeful prospects; the couple's relationship, however, seems too idealized (note Wycherley's choices of names) to be credible in this setting. Thus the exception only proves Wycherley's rule about love and marriage in Restoration London.

Further Reading

Holland, Norman. *The First Modern Comedies: The Significance of Etherege, Wycherley, and Congreve.* 1959. Reprint. Cambridge, Mass.: Harvard University Press, 1967. Includes a chapter on *Love in a Wood* that focuses on Wycherley's structuring of the plot's intrigues and analyzes the play as a combination of high plot and low plot.

Kachur, Barbara A. *Etherege and Wycherley.* New York: Palgrave Macmillan, 2004. Discusses the plays of Wycherley and Sir George Etherege within the context of culture and history in the early years of the reign of Charles II.

McCarthy, B. Eugene. *William Wycherley: A Biography.* Athens: Ohio University Press, 1979. Discusses *Love in a Wood* in some detail as the product of a dramatist who lived and worked in a very specific social climate. Gives some attention to influences on Wycherley's writing of the play.

Rogers, Katharine M. *William Wycherley.* New York: Twayne, 1972. Provides production history as well as a discussion of Wycherley's borrowings from the work of playwright Pedro Calderón de la Barca. Points out that although *Love in a Wood* is Wycherley's first play, it shows distinct elements of the moral awareness that would distinguish his work from that of his contemporaries.

Thompson, James. *Language in Wycherley's Plays.* Tuscaloosa: University of Alabama Press, 1984. Uses language theory, as well as Restoration philosophies of language, to discuss *Love in a Wood* as a good-humored comedy that employs a wide range of linguistic styles for a broadly comic rather than satiric effect.

Vance, John A. *William Wycherley and the Comedy of Fear.* Newark: University of Delaware Press, 2000. Presents detailed examinations of four of Wycherley's plays, including *Love in a Wood.* Argues that Wycherley was not particularly concerned with broad political, social, and moral issues but focused instead on the actions and motivations of his insecure and fallible characters.

Young, Douglas M. *The Feminist Voices in Restoration Comedy: The Virtuous Women in the Play-Worlds of Etherege, Wycherley, and Congreve.* Lanham, Md.: University Press of America, 1997. Analyzes *Love in a Wood* and three other plays by Wycherley in which female characters demand independence from and equality with male partners as a condition of marriage or courtship.

Zimbardo, Rose A. *Wycherley's Drama: A Link in the Development of English Satire.* New Haven, Conn.: Yale University Press, 1965. Introduces the idea of Wycherley's plays as English forms of classical satire. Discusses *Love in a Wood* as a pastoral tale transferred from the mythical forests of Arcadia to London's St. James's Park. Suggests that Wycherley's satiric effects add spice to what is basically a Renaissance play.

Love in the Time of Cholera

Author: Gabriel García Márquez (1927-   )
First published: El amor en los tiempos del cólera,
    1985 (English translation, 1988)
Type of work: Novel
Type of plot: Psychological realism
Time of plot: Late nineteenth and early twentieth
    centuries
Locale: Colombia

Principal characters:

FLORENTINO ARIZA, who is in love with Fermina
FERMINA DAZA, a strong-willed woman
DR. JUVENAL URBINO, her husband
LORENZO DAZA, her father
DON LEO LOAYZA XII, Florentino's uncle
JEREMIAH DE SAINT-AMOUR, a friend of Dr. Juvenal
    Urbino
HILDEBRANDA SANCHEZ, Fermina's cousin

The Story:

Dr. Juvenal Urbino has been called to the residence of his friend Jeremiah de Saint-Amour, who had taken his own life the previous evening. From a letter that his friend left him, Urbino learns that Saint-Amour spent his final night with a female companion and that he was actually a fugitive who had indulged in cannibalism. Devastated by this knowledge, Urbino finds his whole day unsettled. Late that afternoon, he falls to his death while trying to retrieve his parrot from a tree. Dr. Urbino's funeral takes place the next day, and after the funeral, and after years of waiting, one of the guests, Florentino Ariza, tells Dr. Urbino's widow, Fermina Daza, that he loves her.

The relationship between Florentino and Fermina begins more than fifty years earlier, when Florentino, then working at a telegraph office, delivers a message to Lorenzo Daza at his home and immediately falls in love with Fermina, whom he sees in the sewing room. After this, Florentino sits daily on a bench in the park across from the Daza house, reading poetry but mostly waiting to see Fermina. After a brief correspondence between them, Fermina agrees to marry him and, after two years of secret courtship, they begin to plan the wedding.

When Fermina's father discovers their plan, however, he takes his daughter to Valledupar, the home of his relatives, where she finds a sympathetic friend in her cousin Hildebranda Sanchez. With Hildebranda's help, Fermina continues to correspond with Florentino over the telegraph. Lorenzo finally realizes that he cannot control his daughter and gives her her freedom. In the midst of preparing for her wedding, however, Fermina, in an abrupt about-face, calls off the engagement.

Eventually, Fermina meets Dr. Juvenal Urbino, a new doctor in the city who has just returned from his studies in Paris. He is committed to fighting cholera, and when Fermina is diagnosed as possibly having the disease, Urbino visits her house. Although he finds her in perfect health, he returns repeatedly to the Daza household to see her. Initially, Fermina resists the doctor's suit, but her cousin Hildebranda finally persuades Fermina to marry Urbino.

When he learns that Fermina is to marry Dr. Urbino, Florentino is devastated, especially because he realizes that the two do not love each other. To escape this painful situation, Florentino takes a voyage down the Magdalena River. During the journey, he loses his virginity and realizes that sexual passion can temporarily block out his pain over losing Fermina. When he returns to the city, he has an affair with the Widow Nazaret, and after that he goes from one woman to another.

Florentino's behavior at this point becomes enigmatic. On one hand, he decides to devote his life to winning back Fermina, and with this in mind he goes to work for his uncle Leo, president of the board of directors and manager of the River Company of the Caribbean, and advances steadily. On the other hand, to cope with having lost Fermina, Florentino becomes obsessed with other women.

At the same time, Fermina becomes disillusioned with her marriage. She sees that there is no passion between her and Urbino and that her husband falls far short of what a real man should be. Urbino is at heart a weak person whose social success depends largely on his family's name. Moreover, Fermina discovers that her husband is having an affair with Barbara Lynch, the wife of a Presbyterian minister. Urbino's full confession of the affair infuriates her, and she is further outraged when she learns that Juvenal has confessed his affair to the priest, whereas a real man—as she sees it—would have denied everything. She leaves her husband and lives for two years with her cousin Hildebranda, but when Juvenal finally comes for her she rejoices, for she sees this act as that of a real man.

After his uncle Leo's retirement, Florentino becomes president of the board of directors and general manager of the navigation company. The promotion certainly elevates his social status, but it also frightens him because it means that he, like his uncle, must grow old and die. He therefore begins a final affair, this time with América Vicuña, a fourteen-year-old girl for whom he acts as guardian and who reminds him of Fermina.

This affair ends when Florentino hears the bells tolling the death of an important citizen in the city. He learns that Dr. Juvenal Urbino has died, and he tells Fermina that he still loves her and that she is the only woman he has ever loved. At first she maintains the distance that the years have put between them. Only when she loses her will to live does she allow Florentino back into her life, telling him that she wants to escape everything associated with her marriage. He arranges a boat trip for the two of them, which allows him to be alone with Fermina. On the journey, Fermina realizes that she loves Florentino. Florentino for his part not only sees his lifelong quest fulfilled but also overcomes his fear of mortality. He realizes that only through love has he been able to transcend the final obstacles that remained between him and Fermina—time and the inevitability of death.

Critical Evaluation:

Gabriel García Márquez is one of the most important Latin American writers of the second half of the twentieth century. His novels and stories are distinguished by a vivacity of style that clearly sets them apart from the pessimism often associated with early twentieth century Western literature, yet his characters' acute sensitivity to the passage of time clearly shows the influence of one of the greatest twentieth century American writers, William Faulkner.

García Márquez's *Love in the Time of Cholera* can, in fact, be viewed as a novel both of tradition and of its own time. It offers a traditional love story focusing on two lovers who overcome many obstacles before they are united. Beyond that, however, the novel addresses the question of time and the related fear of death in a universe in which God's existence no longer seems assured. *Love in the Time of Cholera* represents the author's response to the notion that death is inescapable and final. García Márquez uses a framed plot, the interweaving narratives of Florentino and Fermina, and symbolism to assert that passionate love can transcend time and death.

The frame story emphasizes the seeming inescapability of death. García Márquez begins the novel with the death of Jeremiah de Saint-Amour, who has committed suicide at the age of sixty because he can no longer fully enjoy human passion. García Márquez next presents the death of Dr. Juvenal Urbino, who proclaims his passion for Fermina at the moment of his death. After that, the narrative moves back in time to the stories of Florentino and Fermina. Only toward the end of the novel does García Márquez return to the deaths of Saint-Amour and Urbino, both of which in turn remind the now-elderly Florentino of his own inescapable death. With this frame, García Márquez establishes a tension between death and love and suggests that there is no escape from death.

Throughout the novel, constant references to cholera remind the characters as well as the reader of death. Regardless of Urbino's efforts to find a cure for cholera, the disease remains a fatal presence. Further, in an interesting bit of symbolism, when Dr. Urbino and his wife Fermina celebrate the transition from the nineteenth century to the twentieth by riding in a hot-air balloon, they see below them the bodies of people who have been killed in the latest political uprising. The message is clear: Death is ever-present and inescapable.

The interweaving of the narratives of the two lovers, however, reminds the readers that passionate love is not merely a constant in this novel but also the only thing that allows the two main characters to transcend death. Florentino's passionate love for Fermina sustains him through a series of sexual encounters that he uses to cope with the pain of having been rejected by her; likewise, Fermina's love for Florentino, although she does not admit to it until old age, sustains her through the years of marriage to Urbino, who falls far short of being the man she had hoped he would be. Following the funeral of her husband, Fermina spends the night in bed unable to think about anyone but Florentino. Clearly, though she may have denied it to herself, she has loved Florentino since the moment of their separation. The fact, too, that the lovers' narrative continues beyond the deaths of Urbino and Saint-Amour—and that their romance is renewed—actually constitutes a journey beyond death that corresponds to Florentino and Fermina's final cruise down the Magdalena River, when Florentino does transcend his own mortality. Love is the constant that García Márquez uses to oppose that other constant, death.

García Márquez also uses symbolism to suggest the power of human passion over death. For instance, the smell of almonds, referred to in the opening line of the novel, is always associated with unrequited love and, throughout the novel, emphasizes the enduring presence of love in the midst of death. Although he may have indulged in cannibalism—symbolizing utter human depravity—Saint-Amour ("saint of love") is redeemed because he has lived and died for love. Indeed, in this novel, passionate love is sacred. Emphasizing this association, García Márquez often links love with the Holy Spirit: Romantic passion is as holy as God's love for humanity. It is therefore significant that the deaths of Saint-Amour and Urbino occur on Pentecost Sunday, the Christian holiday commemorating the outpouring of the Holy Spirit. During his boat trip down the Magdalena River (water traditionally being associated with life and renewal), Florentino's moment of transcendence is related to the "grace of the Holy Spirit." In an almost mystical moment in the final page of the novel, giving the captain of the riverboat the impression that "life, more than death, has no limits," Florentino and Fermina seem to have stepped beyond mortality. A masterpiece of Western literature, *Love in the Time of Cholera* is a romance that goes beyond a simple love story to assert, through plot, character, and symbol, that life need not be limited by death.

Richard Logsdon

Further Reading

Bell, Michael. *Gabriel García Márquez: Solitude and Solidarity.* New York: St. Martin's Press, 1993. Explores García Márquez's works, including *Love in the Time of Cholera*, from a number of different perspectives, ranging from comparative literary criticism to political and social critiques.

Bloom, Harold, ed. *Gabriel García Márquez.* Updated ed. New York: Chelsea House, 2007. Excellent collection of critical essays examines the works of García Márquez, including *Love in the Time of Cholera*. Proves a good overview of the themes and literary trends that shaped García Márquez's works.

_____. *Gabriel García Márquez's "Love in the Time of Cholera."* Philadelphia: Chelsea House, 2005. Collection of essays by literary critics addresses various aspects of the novel, including its postmodern and postapocalyptic elements and its themes of love and seduction.

Fahy, Thomas Richard. *Gabriel García Márquez's "Love in the Time of Cholera": A Reader's Guide.* New York: Continuum, 2003. Presents biographical information on García Márquez as well as a detailed analysis of the novel.

McNerney, Kathleen. *Understanding Gabriel García Márquez.* Columbia: University of South Carolina Press, 1989. Informative volume attempts to interpret the works of García Márquez in the light of modern and contemporary European and Latin American literature.

Pelayo, Rubén. *Gabriel García Márquez: A Critical Companion.* Westport, Conn.: Greenwood Press, 2001. Offers an introductory overview of García Márquez's life and analyses of his works designed for students and general readers. Chapter 8 is devoted to *Love in the Time of Cholera*, providing information about the novel's historical context, characters, narrative techniques, themes, and other elements.

Love Medicine

Author: Louise Erdrich (1954-   )
First published: 1984; revised and expanded, 1993
Type of work: Novel
Type of plot: Impressionistic realism
Time of plot: 1934-1984
Locale: North Dakota

Principal characters:
JUNE KASHPAW, a mother
MARIE KASHPAW, June's aunt
NECTOR KASHPAW, Marie's husband
ZELDA KASHPAW, Marie's daughter
AURELIA KASHPAW, Marie's daughter
ELI KASHPAW, Nector's brother
ALBERTINE JOHNSON, June's niece
LIPSHA MORRISSEY, Marie's adopted son and June's birth son
GERRY NANAPUSH, Lipsha's father
DOT NANAPUSH, Lipsha's wife
KING KASHPAW, June's son
LYNETTE, his wife
KING, JR., their son
HENRY LAMARTINE, JR., a former soldier
LYMAN LAMARTINE, a businessperson
LULU LARMARTINE, Gerry, Henry, and Lyman's mother

The Story:

In 1981, June Kashpaw is traveling home when she is called into a bar by a man she thinks she knows. She needs money so agrees to leave with him, out into the winter countryside; they have sex in his car. Moved by a feeling she cannot explain, June gets out of the car and starts walking through the snow. She is never again seen alive.

June's niece, Albertine Johnson, hears about her aunt's death much later, after the funeral, when her mother writes to let her know. Albertine is angry, as she had been fond of her aunt, but sees the late notice as typical for the Kashpaw family. The family's complex structure generates incomprehensible drama, and the family's history goes back to the time of Rushes Bear and the division of American Indian land. June had married her cousin, Gordie Kashpaw, to general disapproval, leading this latest generation into even more drama.

After June's disappearance, Albertine's mother, Zelda, and her Aunt Aurelia had organized a family gathering. Joining Albertine at the gathering are June's son, King Kashpaw; his wife, Lynette; and their son, King, Jr. Brothers Nector and Eli Kashpaw still hold the family's land. Nector, married to Marie, had been educated in the white school, while Eli had remained at home—hidden—and received a more traditional education. Nector and Eli represent two strands of family history, and Albertine feels at a loss to retrieve much of that history now that Nector's memory is fading.

The family gathering is contentious. King, Jr., is drunk, abusive, and violent. He has used his mother's insurance money to buy a large new car and feels guilty about doing so. Unable to articulate his grief over his mother's death, he and Lynette fight, damaging the pies being baked for the gathering. Albertine, meanwhile, has fled with another of June's sons, Lipsha Morrissey, who had been adopted by the Morrisseys. Lipsha and Albertine sit in the darkness, talking. Allegedly, Lipsha does not know his father's name.

Fifty years earlier, Marie Lazarre is determined to become a nun at the Sacred Heart Convent, having been a pupil at the school. However, she is bullied and abused by one of the nuns and runs away. She encounters Nector as he heads to the market, and in a bizarre encounter, they have sex. They later marry, even though Nector had been determined to marry Lulu Nanapush.

Fifteen years later, Marie, who has rejected the Lazarre family, reluctantly takes in June, her sister's daughter. Later, she becomes reluctant to raise her own son, Lipsha. June's cousins attempt to hang June, at her own urging. Eventually, she rejects Marie's family and moves into the woods with her Uncle Eli.

It is now 1957, and Lulu Lamartine, formerly Nanapush, has led a wild life. She has eight sons, although it is not clear who their fathers are. Beverley Lamartine, brother of Lulu's late husband Henry Lamartine, thinks Lulu's youngest child, Henry, Jr., is his and wants to claim him. He has dreamed of raising Henry, Jr., but cannot get up the courage to ask Lulu. In the end, he leaves without Henry.

Nector reflects on life with his wife, Marie, who has adopted many children to compensate for the loss of her own. He begins an affair with Lulu and determines to leave Marie for her. When he changes his mind, he burns his letter to Lulu, and in doing so accidentally burns down Lulu's house, a mystery that remains unsolved for many years. When she discovers Nector's letter to Lulu, Marie determines to ignore it and hold on to Nector.

It is now 1973, and Albertine is thinking about her dreams of leaving for the city and meeting Henry, now home from his time in Vietnam. She goes to his hotel room, reluctantly, and they go to bed together. While in the grip of post-trauma nightmares, Henry rapes her.

Henry's brother Lyman recalls the car that he and Henry jointly bought and refurbished. After Henry had returned from the war, traumatized, Lyman had vandalized the car to prompt a response from Henry. Henry restores the car a second time, and he and Lyman take a drive. Lyman tells everyone later how he had witnessed Henry's death. He claims that Henry killed himself by driving the car into a river.

It is now 1980, and Albertine is remembering the story of Gerry Nanapush—a career criminal, alleged murderer, and serial "escaper"—and his wife, Dot. Dot is pregnant, and Gerry is desperate to get out of prison to be with her for the birth of their child. He escapes, briefly, and is caught and taken back to jail.

Lipsha, who had been raised by Marie and Nector, has stayed with them but is conscious that he is only tolerated by Marie. He thinks about his relationship with them, and of Nector's declining memory. Lipsha has healing skills but, despite Marie's urging, finds he cannot do anything for Nector; indeed, he is not sure he should try to help him. He is aware of Nector's affair with Lulu and is present when Nector confesses to having caused the fire that destroyed Lulu's house. Lulu, however, does not understand the concern, and the issue is dropped. Lipsha eventually makes a love medicine for Marie and Nector, at Marie's request, because she believes that he is still chasing Lulu. Nector chokes on the medicine and dies, but Marie is content, believing that he returns to her from beyond the grave. Lulu and Marie finally make their peace and become friends. Together they work on local issues.

After hearing the truth from Lulu, Lipsha finally reveals that he knows the identity of his mother and his father, Gerry Nanapush. Lipsha, who is running from the military police, has a vision that his father is about to escape from prison, so he heads for Minneapolis to meet him. Here, he runs into his childhood tormentor, King, who also knows that June was Lipsha's mother; because of this, King hates Lipsha. The two find Lipsha's father, who reveals that in the past, King had turned informer against him. They play cards for ownership of June's car, and Lipsha wins—he had cheated. The authorities soon arrive to recapture Gerry, but he escapes. Later, Lipsha takes his father to the Canadian border.

Critical Evaluation:

Love Medicine caused a critical stir when it was published in 1984. Made up of a series of fragmented though interconnected short narratives, each told by a different character, the story moves back and forth through time, unraveling the intricate connections between the Kashpaw, Morrissey, Nanapush, and Lamartine families—American Indians living in North Dakota on an Ojibwa reservation. Some commentators suggest that the novel is a portrayal of Turtle Mountain Reservation, but the landscape Louise Erdrich describes in the novel is similar to the landscapes of other reservations in Minnesota.

Erdrich drew heavily on the works of novelist William Faulkner for the structure of *Love Medicine*. The use of such techniques had been unprecedented, and indeed Erdrich had been criticized by American Indian writer Leslie Marmon Silko for being more interested in technique than in the problems experienced by American Indians. This criticism assumes, however, that novels by American Indians should be specifically about American Indians. While Erdrich does touch on such concerns, including the forced division of lands according to the Dawes Act (1887) and subsequent land-purchase scandals, as well as abuse by the Catholic Church and high rates of alcoholism, these issues come through as background.

Erdrich's main subject is love: romantic love and family love and the ways in which people come to terms with their emotional needs. When Nector marries Marie, he is still in love with Lulu, a love that never really fades; he marries Marie only because he feels obligated to do so. By contrast, Marie considers Nector as her means of escape from life in a poor family. She is determined to make him a person of substance within the community, for her benefit as much as for his. Only in the end do they both realize how much they do actually feel for one another. Gerry's devotion to Dot and his family is what fuels his need to escape from prison.

Marie struggles to construct a concept of family that steps beyond formal ties, adopting those in need, for example. However, it is Lulu who manages to integrate a disparate group of children by a number of different fathers into a strong and loving family unit. Her family is not perfect, though; Henry, Jr.'s suicide comes as a result of posttraumatic stress, brought on by his experiences fighting in the Vietnam War. Lulu's family troubles are not specific to American Indians; her family troubles resemble a much broader social problem.

By contrast, Marie's family, later headed by Zelda and Aunt Aurelia, is held together by secrets and acts of concealment. Marie lacks Lulu's warmhearted generosity and struggles to keep her family close. Only Lipsha moves between the two families, choosing finally to remain with the Kashpaws. Even so, it is worth remembering that even after June's actions ultimately led another generation of her family to fragment, June was finally returning home. Her death led her family members to admit their secrets.

Maureen Kincaid Speller

Further Reading

Beidler, Peter G., and Gay Barton. *A Reader's Guide to the Novels of Louise Erdrich*. Columbia: University of Missouri Press, 1999. An informative handbook for students of Erdrich's fiction that covers geography, chronology, and character relationships in her novels.

Chavkin, Allan, ed. *The Chippewa Landscape of Louise Erdrich*. Tuscaloosa: University of Alabama Press, 1998. A collection of original essays that focuses on Erdrich's writings that are rooted in the Ojibwa experience. Premier scholars of American Indian literature investigate narrative structure, signs of ethnicity, the notions of luck and chance in Erdrich's narrative cosmology, and her use of comedy in exploring American Indians' tragic past.

Smith, Jeanne Rosier. *Writing Tricksters: Mythic Gambols in American Ethnic Literature*. Berkeley: University of California Press, 1997. Presents a thorough examination of ethnic trickster figures as they appear in the works of Erdrich, Maxine Hong Kingston, and Toni Morrison. Chapter 3 explores the trickster characteristics of Gerry Nanapush, Lipsha Morrissey, and others found in Erdrich's novels.

Stookey, Lorena Laura. *Louise Erdrich: A Critical Companion*. Westport, Conn.: Greenwood Press, 1999. This study of Erdrich's works presents biographical information, an examination of Erdrich's place in literary tradition, and analyses of each novel. Includes bibliographical references and an index.

Treuer, David. *Native American Fiction: A User's Manual.* St. Paul, Minn.: Graywolf Press, 2006. An Ojibwa author offers an intriguing perspective on the work of several contemporaries, including Erdrich. The chapter "Smartberries" praises Erdrich's modern literary techniques in *Love Medicine*, but in other chapters Treuer questions

what in fact constitutes "authentic" American Indian writing.

Wong, Hertha D. Sweet. *Louise Erdrich's "Love Medicine": A Casebook.* New York: Oxford University Press, 2000. Presents documents relating to the historical importance of *Love Medicine*, representative critical essays, and excerpts from several interviews with Erdrich.

The Love Song of J. Alfred Prufrock

Author: T. S. Eliot (1888-1965)
First published: 1915
Type of work: Poetry

The Poem:

The action is prefaced by a quotation in Italian from Dante's *La divina commedia* (c. 1320; *The Divine Comedy*, 1802). In it, a character in Hell agrees to tell his story, assuming that no one will be able to return from Hell and tell it to others. As the poem proper begins, J. Alfred Prufrock and his companion are about to depart for a social event, some sort of tea party or reception, that will feature a great deal of intellectual pretension and inflated talk about art.

Prufrock tells his companion it is time to go but then lapses into a reverie (which may not be spoken) about the streets they are to pass through, streets that Prufrock finds depressing. His reverie is interrupted by his companion, whose "What is it?" seems to be about his thoughts. Prufrock brushes the the question aside in annoyance, and repeats "Let us go. . . . " In lines 13 and 14, a kind of chorus interrupts the dialogue, as Prufrock imagines the women in the "room" where they are going. The women are talking, in Prufrock's mind, about the Renaissance artist Michelangelo.

The chorus is interrupted by another reverie about the "yellow fog" of the city, which finally curls up like a cat and goes to sleep. Prufrock replays his anxieties, imaged by disembodied faces, hands, and finally questions in the next paragraph (lines 23-34), which is followed by the repeated chorus imagining the destined room with its women and their talk about Michaelangelo. The next four paragraphs (lines 37-69) review Prufrock's fears of how others will see him—will they notice, despite his proper dress, that he is going bald, that he is "thin?" Will he be able to speak? He has been to gatherings like this before, and although he is somewhat

sexually excited as he imagines the women's bare arms and remembers the smell of perfume, he is not sure he can "presume" to join the conversation, an act that he imagines in overly grandiose terms. He imagines the women will see him as he does not want to be seen, expressing this in an image of an insect pinned to a collector's board.

The next few paragraphs (lines 70-98) fantasize about what Prufrock might say. He again grandiosely imagines himself as John the Baptist or Lazarus but then lapses into self-denigrating images of frightened little crabs in the ocean, finally admitting that he is "afraid," that he might be dismissed as having entirely misunderstood the subject of the conversation. In a following paragraph (lines 99-110), he wonders if it would be worth risking such a disaster.

At last, Prufrock admits to himself that he is not an attractive figure, declaring that he is not Hamlet, the hero of William Shakespeare's tragedy by the same name, but rather a figure like Polonius, a busybody old man who talks entirely too much and is a figure of ridicule. The poem ends with a fantasy of mermaids in the ocean, who might sing, but not to Prufrock.

Critical Evaluation:

"The Love Song of J. Alfred Prufrock" is in part a satire. Its character is not the hero of romance but an antihero, one constrained by fear. He spends much of the poem contemplating what to him is to be a daring act, but is in fact only the effort to talk to women at a social event. The very name Prufrock is suggestive; the first syllable suggests the word "prude" without the final consonant, while a "frock" is a garment that would have been considered overly formal by young people of Eliot's generation.

The urban setting for the poem is itself also the object of satire. The sunset at the beginning of the evening is not inspiring but instead is dormant, "like a patient etherized upon a table." The streets through which the two will pass is full of cheap, sordid hotels and filthy restaurants. The twentieth century city is not a place of dreams.

The description of the social event suggests something shallow and superficial, where people show off their knowledge of art. The only details given are the women's bare arms and long dresses, talk of Michelangelo and perhaps unnamed novels, and refreshments. Prufrock is vaguely aware of the contrast between the superficial, perhaps privileged world he is about to enter and the bleak, urban landscape outside: In the former, people have the leisure for superficial talk, while in the latter, "lonely men in shirtsleeves" are perhaps tired from work. Prufrock is too self-centered, too concerned with how he might impress the women he will see, to reflect on the desperation of the "muttering retreats"; the "yellow smoke" (clearly smog) might well be toxic to many, but to Prufrock it is vaguely something like a friendly cat.

Prufrock exaggerates his dilemma. He wishes to speak to women, he is vaguely attracted to them sexually, but he is afraid. This might be a "crisis" for a young man looking for a prom date, but Prufrock is old enough to have a bald spot in his hair and to fear growing "old." Part of the poem's irony comes from its allusions to the poetic and literary traditions that Eliot knows. The preface from Dante's *Inferno* quotes a false counselor in Hell who will tell his crime only to those he thinks will keep it a secret. Prufrock, too, would not want his story known—he wants to create "a face to meet the faces that you meet"—but what he has to hide is trivial. A topic he might raise in conversation is an "overwhelming question."

Prufrock momentarily compares himself to John the Baptist, the prophet who announces the good news of Christ's coming and who is finally killed, with his head brought on a platter. Later, he compares himself to Lazarus, who was raised from the dead by Christ. He also briefly thinks of Hamlet, whose "overwhelming question" involves taking the word of what seems to be his father's ghost and avenging his murder by killing a king. Prufrock realizes that the best he can do in Shakespeare's play is to be Polonius, who talks too much, annoys everyone, and is finally killed by accident when he is eavesdropping on Hamlet and his mother.

In the final lines of the poem, Prufrock is tempted to compare himself to Ulysses, since the mermaids "singing each to each" suggest the sirens Ulysses hears in Homer's *Odyssey* (c. 725 B.C.E.; English translation, 1614), but he quickly reflects that "I do not think that they will sing to me."

Timothy C. Frazer

Further Reading

Berry, D. C. *Hamlet Off Stage*. Huntsville: Texas Review Press, 2009. This study of representations of the character of Hamlet in works other than Shakespeare's includes a section on "The Love Song of J. Alfred Prufrock."

Eliot, T. S. *Dante*. London: Faber & Faber, 1929. This essay on the author of *The Divine Comedy* reveals much of Eliot's attempt to ground his poetry in both the Christian and the classical traditions.

_____. *The Sacred Wood*. London: Metheun, 1920. This critical text by Eliot includes "Tradition and the Individual Talent," Eliot's poetic manifesto, which posits his belief that, while poetry includes the creative energy of the poet, it also should be rooted in tradition. The essay sheds light on the use of references to Dante, Shakespeare, and the New Testament in "The Love Song of J. Alfred Prufrock."

Headings, Philip R. *T. S. Eliot*. New York: Twayne, 1964. Twayne books on individual authors are considered the best available summaries of scholarly opinion on individual writers. Its bibliography includes not only secondary sources but all of Eliot's published works up to the date of publication.

Ledeen, Jenny. *"When the Wind Blows the Water White and Black": The Riddle at the End of T. S. Eliot's "The Love Song of J. Alfred Prufrock."* St. Louis, Mo.: Peaceberry Press of Webster Groves, 2008. This individually bound essay explores in detail the meaning of the poem's last lines.

Sencourt, Robert. *T. S. Eliot: A Memoir*. New York: Dodd, Mead, 1971. This personal reminiscence of the author's friendship with Eliot includes a number of personal views of the poet's life, including portraits of those closest to Eliot.

Tate, Allen, ed. *T. S. Eliot: The Man and His Work: A Critical Evaluation by Twenty-six Distinguished Writers*. Sewanee, Tenn.: University of the South, 1966. This work includes essays by some leading critics who knew Eliot during his lifetime.

The Love Suicides at Sonezaki

Author: Chikamatsu Monzaemon (1653-1725)
First produced: Sonezaki shinjū, 1703 (English translation, 1961)
Type of work: Drama
Type of plot: Tragedy
Time of plot: Eighteenth century
Locale: Osaka, Japan

Principal characters:
O HATSU, a popular geisha
TOKUBEI, her lover, an apprentice clerk
KYŪEMON, Tokubei's uncle and employer
KUHEIJI, Tokubei's friend, also in love with O Hatsu
GIHEI, a wealthy countryman

The Story:

Gihei, a rich man from the country, is trying to decide how to spend the evening in Osaka. Two friends urge him to hire O Hatsu, the famous geisha, or courtesan, for the evening. She begs off, however, and remains with her maids, meanwhile thinking about her lover Tokubei, a clerk, who has been neglecting her. To her great joy, he arrives a short time later, but he tells her that Kyūemon, his uncle and employer, had arranged for Tokubei to marry to an heiress and that his aunt had already received and spent the dowry. Tokubei had refused to marry the young woman, but this meant that the dowry had to be returned. Tokubei managed to collect the money, but later he lent it to his friend Kuheiji. Now Kyūemon wants Tokubei to leave Osaka.

O Hatsu, in spite of this disturbing news, is happy once more; she had feared Tokubei no longer loved her. While the lovers are talking, Kuheiji and a group of his friends appear. When Tokubei asks for the money owed him, Kuheiji pretends to know nothing about the loan. Desperately, Tokubei attacks Kuheiji, whose friends join the fight and overwhelm Tokubei. During the uproar, Gihei returns and compels O Hatsu to go off with him.

Later, not knowing what has happened to Tokubei, O Hatsu is afraid that he may have been killed in the quarrel. When Kyūemon arrives, O Hatsu goes outside to speak to him. Saying that she is a bad influence on the young man and that she is not truly in love with him, Kyūemon begs her to give up Tokubei. He also asks her where Tokubei can be found. O Hatsu insists that her love is real and that she is ignorant of her lover's whereabouts. Kyūemon goes inside, but O Hatsu, still fearful, remains on the street.

She is still standing there when a shabby Tokubei appears. As she tells him of Kyūemon's visit, Kuheiji and his gang appear and insist that O Hatsu join them. She is able to hide Tokubei under the porch while she sits above him on a step, and from his hiding place he is able to communicate his understanding by fondling her foot tenderly. It develops that Kuheiji has come to ransom O Hatsu, using Tokubei's

money. O Hatsu, seeing no solution but suicide, manages to convey her resolve to Tokubei through her conversation with Kuheiji. Kuheiji, the braggart, goes away to close the deal, and O Hatsu is forced to withdraw without talking to Tokubei again.

That night, O Hatsu steals away secretly to meet Tokubei, and the lovers flee to the woods of Sonezaki. Meanwhile, Kyūemon overhears Kuheiji and his servant discussing their plan to gain O Hatsu and malign Tokubei. After confronting the evil Kuheiji, Kyūemon goes in haste to find the lovers, but he arrives too late—they have already committed suicide together.

Critical Evaluation:

The playwright Chikamatsu Monzaemon was one of several literary giants who appeared simultaneously on the Japanese scene during the early half of the Tokugawa period (1600-1867). He wrote the books (called *jōruri*) for puppet theater, which came into its own in Osaka because of the happy appearance of Chikamatsu, a great chanter (Takemoto Gidayū), a talented samisen accompanist (Takezawa Gon'emon) who put Chikamatsu's words to music, and a superb puppeteer (Tatsumatsu Hachirobei) who boldly appeared on the stage with his puppets and yet, through sheer artistry, made the audience forget his physical presence in the movements of the puppets he manipulated. Chikamatsu also wrote for the Kabuki theater then centered in Kyoto and Edo (now Tokyo).

Chikamatsu's dramatic works fall into two classes, according to the subject matter treated: the historical and the domestic, the latter dealing with contemporary events and with people chiefly of the merchant, or common, class. *The Love Suicides at Sonezaki* was the first of the domestic plays written by Chikamatsu. He was fifty years old at the time. First staged in Osaka in 1703, it is a dramatization, with additions, of events that actually occurred in Osaka earlier that same year. Originally written for the puppet theater, it was soon presented on the Kabuki stage as well. The play remains popular.

Although Chikamatsu has been called the most Western of the great Japanese dramatists, two obstacles—one cultural, the other artistic—confront the Western reader who attempts to understand and appreciate Chikamatsu's dramas. The cultural gulf that separates the present-day Western reader from the eighteenth century Japanese characters frequently seems too great to bridge, and, since the West has almost no tradition of adult puppet theater, or even any highly stylized, ritualized drama comparable to Kabuki theater, it is very difficult for Westerners to visualize the plays theatrically on the basis of translated texts. Even so, moments of great feeling and dramatic power come through to interest and move the Western reader of Chikamatsu's plays. Perhaps Chikamatsu's most accessible play is his first domestic tragedy, *The Love Suicides at Sonezaki.*

This work established the basic plot line for all of Chikamatsu's later domestic tragedies: A young tradesman and a prostitute fall in love; he is unable to "ransom" her (purchase her "contract"), and so, frustrated, the lovers eventually commit suicide together. Although the persistent choice of a prostitute for a heroine (an accurate reflection of social conditions) may strike the modern Western reader as peculiar, Chikamatsu's antiheroic characterizations seem quite modern. It is through Chikamatsu's domestic plays that realism can be said to have come to Japanese theater. Caught between intense human emotion (*ninjo*) and a rigid social morality (*giri*), the characters are inevitably destroyed by circumstances that are essentially beyond their control.

Tokubei is weak, volatile, erratic, and foolishly trusting; O Hatsu is, from the beginning, the more heroic—she decides on suicide long before he does and urges him to it. He vacillates and postures; she offers him her strength and example. Ultimately the only choice for them is suicide; they carry it out with great courage and mutual devotion, thereby achieving a tragic dignity. If the social context of their behavior is not completely clear and their fatalistic attitudes seem psychologically obscure, the purity of their love and the nobility of their suicides are convincing and touching. In the reading and the presentation, the high point of the dramatic arc in *The Love Suicides at Sonezaki,* as in all the *shinjū* (double-suicide) plays, is in the poetic lovers' journey (*michiyuki*) to their appointed end.

Although Chikamatsu uses the love-suicide formula with greater flexibility, subtlety, and complexity in later plays, the poetic immediacy and dramatic impact of *The Love Suicides at Sonezaki* have kept this play a permanent favorite with the Japanese public. *The Love Suicides at Sonezaki* began a the-

atrical vogue (in addition to Chikamatsu, many other Japanese playwrights exploited the formula), and it produced widespread public reaction. Originally inspired by a real incident, the play and its successors provoked so many real-life double suicides that in 1722 the Japanese government felt it necessary to ban the production of any play containing the word *shinjū* in its title.

Further Reading

Brownstein, Michael. "The Osaka Kannon Pilgrimage and Chikamatsu's *Love Suicides at Sonezaki.*" *Harvard Journal of Asiatic Studies* 66, no. 1 (June, 2006): 7-41. Examines the opening passage of the play, which delineates O Hatsu's journey to thirty-three temples of Kannon in Osaka, Japan. Discusses issues related to the development of puppet theater.

Chikamatsu Monzaemon. *Four Major Plays of Chikamatsu.* Translated by Donald Keene. New York: Columbia University Press, 1998. Includes texts of *The Love Suicides at Sonezaki* and three other plays. A lengthy introduction by the translator provides information on Chikamatsu's career, the times in which he lived, and the subjects, characters, and performances of his plays.

Gerstle, C. Andrew. *Circles of Fantasy: Convention in the Plays of Chikamatsu.* Cambridge, Mass.: Harvard University Press, 1986. Discussion of Chikamatsu's work includes a brief synopsis and history of *The Love Suicides at Sonezaki* as part of an examination of the love-suicide play as a dramatic form. Includes a detailed analysis of the structure and dynamics of the play, especially the *michiyuki,* or final journey to death.

Kato, Shuichi. "Glorious Deaths." In *The Years of Isolation.* Vol. 2 in *A History of Japanese Literature.* Translated by David Chibbet. 1979. Reprint. New York: Kodansha America, 1990. Examines the contrast between the celebration of the lover's death and the celebration of the warrior's death in Japanese literature, with specific reference to *The Love Suicides at Sonezaki.*

Keene, Donald. "Drama: Chikamatsu Monzaemon (1653-1725)." In *World Within Walls: Japanese Literature of the Pre-Modern Era, 1600-1867.* 1976. Reprint. New York: Columbia University Press, 1999. Places *The Love Suicides at Sonezaki* within the context of the author's entire oeuvre. Points out the importance of the themes of love and money, which provide the tension that drives the play, and discusses the themes of *giri* (obligation) and *ninjo* (human feeling), which provide dramatic conflict.

Kirkwood, Kenneth P. *Renaissance in Japan: A Cultural Survey of the Seventeenth Century.* New ed. Rutland, Vt.:

Charles E. Tuttle, 1970. Includes a biographical sketch of Chikamatsu and a discussion of some of his works. Provides information on the historical event that provided the basis for *The Love Suicides at Sonezaki* and addresses the phenomenon of lovers' suicides in Japanese literature.

Richie, Donald. "Chikamatsu Monzaemon." In *Japanese Literature Reviewed*. New York: ICG Muse, 2003. Chikamatsu is one of the more than one hundred writers whose lives and works are briefly discussed in this introductory overview of Japanese literature.

The Lover

Author: Marguerite Duras (1914-1996)
First published: L'Amant, 1984 (English translation, 1985)
Type of work: Novel
Type of plot: New Novel
Time of plot: Late 1920's through 1940's
Locale: Indochina and France

Principal characters:
THE NARRATOR, the novel's protagonist and author
HER MOTHER
HER OLDER BROTHER
HER YOUNGER BROTHER
HER LOVER, a wealthy young Chinese man

The Story:

A man tells the narrator that she is more beautiful now that she is old and her face is ruined than she had been as a young woman. While thinking about this unusual comment, the narrator begins to remember her unhappy family and her scandalous first love affair. Abruptly she changes in age. No longer an old woman, she is once again fifteen and a half, riding a ferry across the Mekong River in what was then French Indochina.

As a girl, she attends both the state boarding school in Saigon and a French high school because her mother is ambitious for her future. All of the family's hopes and chances for success depend on her; she has two brothers, but, unfortunately, both are unreliable. The older brother is a drug addict who steals from his own family and has such a negative effect on his two siblings that his parents eventually send him back to France. The younger brother has a different problem: He is simply too sensitive and weak to achieve worldly success.

Telling her story, the narrator shifts fluidly between the present and the past, referring to old photographs and memories as though she is thumbing through a family album. In one photo of her, taken when she was still a fifteen-year-old virgin, she has the face of a sexually experienced woman. In another memory, she recalls a favorite outfit that also makes her appear prematurely worldly; she is wearing it on the day she meets the young Chinese man who becomes her first lover.

When she was very young, she knew that she wanted to be a writer, but her mother discouraged her. A math degree would be much more practical for a girl who was going to have to support her family. She earns an income, however, in a way that her mother had not foreseen. She becomes essentially a prostitute, accepting money from her lover in return for sleeping with him.

Although her lover is older and wealthier, and has had many sexual experiences, her power over him is far greater than his over her. She feels intense sexual desire for him, but no love. He, on the other hand, genuinely loves her, and he is acutely aware that his feelings are not matched by hers. She revels in her ability to give less to him than she receives in return, and also in the knowledge that she could have this same power over other men. Their first sexual encounter takes place in Cholon, the Chinese district of Saigon. Their lovemaking is characterized by his tears and her joyous discovery of physical pleasure.

Once her family members become aware of the affair, they treat him rudely, as he expected they would. He buys them expensive dinners in restaurants, and they refuse to speak to him. Her rudeness to the contrary, the narrator's mother, in general, approves of the affair. Although it has ruined her daughter's chances of marrying within the local white community, it has resulted in money for the family. One day, however, the mother's fragile mental stability collapses; she locks her daughter in her room and, in a frenzy, proceeds to beat her.

The narrator begins spending nights with her lover instead of sleeping at her boarding school. When she is caught she is not punished, but instead is allowed to come and go as she pleases. She is European, so she is granted special privileges that the native-born Indochinese students cannot have. Official sanction of her behavior does not stop the nasty things that are said about her by the teachers and other students, but the sight of a large diamond ring on her left hand does, even though everyone knows she is not actually engaged.

Her romance unravels after her lover's father suffers an illness. When the father recovers, he makes plans to send the narrator away to France so that his son can forget her and begin the search for a suitable Chinese bride. In her usual contrary fashion, she sides with the father rather than with her lover, who is by then desperately in love with her. Eventually, however, her lover realizes that it is best that she leave Indochina. Even if they were somehow miraculously to be married, she would still inevitably abandon him.

The way her lover touches her body changes. She begins to seem more like his child than his lover, and so he becomes more tender and less ravenously passionate. The change intensifies once the date for her voyage to France is set, and he becomes physically unable to make love to her. Despairing, they try to stop seeing each other, but they cannot.

In a scene much like their first meeting, her lover comes to see her sail away, watching her from inside his long, black car. Later, she hears that he obeyed his father and married a rich Chinese woman. She wonders how long it was before her lover could bear to make love to his new wife, and if he did so thinking of her. After many years, her questions receive a kind of answer. Near the end of his life, the lover visits Paris, the city in which she lives. Over the telephone he tells her that he has always loved her and will always love her, even unto death.

Critical Evaluation:

The Lover has a complex structure that is disguised by the work's simple sentences and unadorned vocabulary. The novel's time period shifts between the past and the present, so that the narrator is sometimes an old woman and sometimes an adolescent girl. Similarly, Marguerite Duras writes both in the first person and in the third, which allows the narrator to experience her story as both a participant and a bystander. Repetition is also a favorite strategy. Phrases and even entire scenes are repeated. Major events are also chopped into fragments and intercut with one another. For example, the story of the narrator's first sexual experience is told twice, each time interrupted by other memories. It is interesting to note that Duras is also known as a filmmaker, and the frag-

mentation of *The Lover* gives the novel the feel of a film montage.

At times, Duras departs totally from the novel's main story and introduces completely unrelated characters, such as the social hosts the narrator knew in Paris during World War II. These digressions challenge the reader to account for their presence. The book's strongly autobiographical nature is one plausible reason for them; memoirs not uncommonly appear meandering and unfocused. Another reason has been suggested by the writer Barbara Probst Solomon, who has noted that the digressions tend to occur around emotionally charged moments in the love story. She has theorized that Duras breaks up the main action of the novel with seemingly unrelated material in order to hide facts and emotions that she does not want to reveal.

Whatever real-life events Duras may have left out of *The Lover*, the novel gives the impression of frankness and courage. The narrator defies the conventions of romantic love as well as traditional gender roles. Not only is she merely fifteen years of age at the beginning of her relationship with the lover, but also she is the seducer rather than the seduced. Duras does not condemn the narrator's prostitution or the fact that her sexual pleasure is inextricably linked to the money her lover gives her.

Duras also reverses standard roles in her handling of racial issues. When the couple first meet, it is the European narrator who is poor and rides the bus and her Chinese lover who is a millionaire's son riding in a chauffeured limousine. In a more conventional story, it would be the girl's family members who refuse to allow her to marry across racial lines. Instead, the lover's father opposes the match, so much so that he pays for the narrator's passage back to France. Through these and other inversions, Duras suggests that class takes precedence over race; skin color is less important than wealth.

This unconventional portrayal of race and class has been controversial. Some critics have accused Duras of implying that it was the French colonizers, not the resident peoples, who were exploited when portions of Indochina were a French colony. For example, the family's poverty resulted primarily from a bad real estate deal in which the mother was swindled because she did not know that farmable land was sold only to those who bribed the local officials. Duras also has come under fire for the political views she expresses in *The Lover*. In one passage, she equates communists with the collaborators who aided the Germans during the occupation of France in World War II. Again, she has been accused of rewriting history, especially given her own background as a former communist who worked against collaborators during the war. She also has been criticized for the novel's sympathetic portrayal of the Fernandezes, who are described as collaborators. As infuriating as these passages are to some readers, they can be classified as part of the novel's general strategy of inverting conventions and confounding expectations.

The debate over *The Lover* is typical of Duras's career. Critical opinion of her work has been intensely divided. There are those, sometimes called "Durasophiles," who have strongly praised her writings for their redefinition of the feminine, especially in matters of sexuality and worldview. Some of them have gone as far as to adopt her writing style in their analyses of her work. Those in the opposing camp, dubbed "Durasophobes," tend to fall into two groups: those who think that Duras pushes the definition of the feminine so far that it becomes masculine and those who think that she does not push it far enough.

Despite the lack of agreement among critics, *The Lover* won France's prestigious Prix Goncourt in 1984. Announcement of the prize immediately boosted sales of the book, which was translated into more than forty languages. Sales of *The Lover* also benefited from its inherently sensational subject matter—subject matter that allowed the book to be marketed as the sexual confessions of a famous writer and filmmaker. The novel's success also resulted in its being adapted as a motion picture. Although Duras worked on the screenplay, she was disappointed in the film, which was directed by Jean-Jacques Annaud. As a result, she wrote *L'Amant de la Chine du Nord* (1991; *The North China Lover*, 1992), another autobiographical novel centered on the same love affair.

Kelly Fuller

Further Reading

Angelini, Eileen M. "Marguerite Duras' *L'Amant* and Other 'Autofictional Narratives.'" In *Strategies of "Writing the Self" in the French Modern Novel: C'est moi, je crois.* Lewiston, N.Y.: Edwin Mellen Press, 2001. Analysis of *The Lover* focuses on the autobiographical elements in the novel.

Callahan, Anne. "Vagabondage: Duras." In *Remains to Be Seen: Essays on Marguerite Duras*, compiled by Sanford Scribner Ames. New York: Peter Lang, 1988. Readable scholarly essay celebrates *The Lover* as a groundbreaking work of feminist erotica. Part of a section that includes three other essays on *The Lover*.

Crowley, Martin. *Duras, Writing, and the Ethical: Making the Broken Whole.* New York: Oxford University Press, 2000. Closely examines all of Duras's written works, focusing on the ethical questions that arise out of experiences of both passion and excess.

Duras, Marguerite, and Xaviere Gauthier. *Woman to Woman.* Translated by Katharine A. Jensen. Lincoln: University of Nebraska Press, 1987. Collection reprints five interviews that were begun as an assignment for the French newspaper *Le Monde* in 1974. Duras and Gauthier discuss writing and feminism, among many other related topics. Duras's discussion of syntax is of particular interest to readers of her novels. An afterword addresses the cultural context within which Duras wrote.

Glassman, Deborah N. *Marguerite Duras: Fascinating Vision and Narrative Cure.* London: Associated University Presses, 1991. Contains an interesting discussion of *The Lover* that relates the novel's visual imagery to Duras's filmmaking style. Quotes Duras extensively in French, with English translations.

Schuster, Marilyn R. *Marguerite Duras Revisited.* New York: Twayne, 1993. Provides an outstanding overview of Duras scholarship and Duras's work. Explains why Duras is an important figure in French culture and how her written works are related to one another.

Solomon, Barbara Probst. "Indochina Mon Amour." *The New Republic*, September 9, 1985. Offers strong, opinionated political analysis of *The Lover*. Memorably describes Duras's political views, their impact on her work, and her involvement in the French Resistance during World War II.

Willging, Jennifer. *Telling Anxiety: Anxious Narration in the Work of Marguerite Duras, Annie Ernaux, Nathalie Sarraute, and Anne Hébert.* Toronto, Ont.: University of Toronto Press, 2007. Analyzes the representation of anxiety in the works of the four women writers, explaining how their depictions reflect postwar skepticism about the ability of language to express the death and destruction of World War II.

Winston, Jane Bradley. *Postcolonial Duras: Cultural Memory in Postwar France.* New York: Palgrave, 2002. Examines Duras's role as an intellectual force in a colonizing power, particularly valuable in the light of her early life in French Indochina and her continued use of the region as a setting. Includes discussion of *The Lover*.

Love's Labour's Lost

Author: William Shakespeare (1564-1616)
First produced: c. 1594-1595; revised presentation, 1597;
    first published, 1598
Type of work: Drama
Type of plot: Comedy of manners
Time of plot: Sixteenth century
Locale: Navarre, Spain

Principal characters:
FERDINAND, king of Navarre
BEROWNE,
LONGAVILLE, and
DUMAINE, lords of Navarre
DON ADRIANO DE ARMADO, a foolish Spaniard
COSTARD, a clown
THE PRINCESS OF FRANCE
ROSALINE,
MARIA, and
KATHARINE, ladies attending the princess
JAQUENETTA, a country wench

The Story:

Ferdinand, the king of Navarre, has taken a solemn vow and has forced three of his attending lords to take it also. They have sworn that for three years they will fast and study, enjoy no pleasures, and see no ladies. None of the three noblemen wanted to take the vow; Berowne, in particular, feels that it will be impossible to keep his promise. He points out this fact to the king by reminding him that the princess of France is approaching the court of Navarre to present a petition from her father, who is ill. The king agrees that he will be compelled to see her, but he adds that in such cases the vow must be broken by necessity. Berowne foresees that "necessity" will often cause the breaking of their vows.

The only amusement the king and his lords are to have is provided by Costard, a clown, and by Don Adriano de Armado, a foolish Spaniard attached to the court. Armado writes to the king to inform him that Costard has been caught in the company of Jaquenetta, a country wench of dull mind. Since all attached to the court have been under the same laws of abstinence from earthly pleasures, Costard is remanded to Armado's custody and ordered to fast on bran and water for one week. The truth is that Armado also loves Jaquenetta. He fears the king will learn of his love and punish him in the same manner.

The princess of France arrives with her three attendants. All are fair, and they expect to be received at the palace in the manner due their rank. The king, however, sends word that they will be housed at his lodge because, under the terms of his vow, no lady can enter the palace. The princess, furious at being treated in this fashion, scorns the king for his bad manners. When she presents to him the petition from her father, she and the king cannot agree because he asserts that he has

not received certain monies that she claims have been delivered to him.

At that first meeting, although each would have denied the fact, eight hearts are set to beating faster. The king views the princess with more than courteous interest. Berowne, Longaville, and Dumaine, his attendants, look with love on the princess's ladies-in-waiting, Rosaline, Maria, and Katharine. A short time later, Berowne sends a letter to Rosaline, with Costard as his messenger. Armado has also given Costard a letter, his to be delivered to Jaquenetta. Costard, who is illiterate, mixes up the letters, giving Jaquenetta's to Rosaline and Rosaline's to the country wench.

Berowne learns that he had been correct in thinking the vow to leave the world behind would soon be broken. Hiding in a tree, he hears the king read aloud a sonnet that proclaims his love for the princess. Later the king, in hiding, overhears Longaville reading some verses he has composed to Maria. Longaville, in turn, conceals himself and listens while Dumaine reads a love poem inscribed to Katharine. Then each one in turn steps out from hiding to accuse the others of breaking their vows. Berowne has during all this time remained hidden in the tree. Thinking to chide them for their broken vows, he reveals himself at last and ridicules them for their weakness, at the same time proclaiming himself the only one able to keep his vow. Costard and Jaquenetta then bring to the king the letter Berowne had written to Rosaline, which Costard had mistakenly delivered to Jaquenetta.

All confess that they have broken their vows. Berowne provides an excuse for all when he declares that men could learn much by studying women and the nature of love; thus, they are still devoting themselves to study. Having, in a fashion, saved face, the four determine to woo the ladies in earnest, and they make plans to entertain their loves with revels and dances.

Each lover sends his lady an anonymous token to wear in his honor. The ladies learn from a servant who the lovers are. The ladies play a joke on their suitors, who come in disguise to woo them. The women mask themselves and exchange the tokens. The men arrive, also masked and disguised as Russians. Each man tries to make love to the lady wearing his token, but each is spurned and ridiculed. The ladies will not dance or sing; they only mock the bewildered gentlemen.

Finally the suitors depart, hurt and indignant at the treatment they have received. Before long they return, no longer in disguise. The ladies, also unmasked, tell of the lunatic Russians who called on them. The men confess their plot and forswear all such jokes forever, but the ladies do not stop teasing them. Since each man made love to the wrong woman because of the exchange of tokens, the ladies pretend to be hurt that the men have broken their vows of love and constancy. The suitors suffer greatly for the sake of the ladies' merriment before at last they learn that the ladies had anticipated the suitors' coming in disguise and thus had planned a joke of their own.

The king orders a play presented for the entertainment of all. In the midst of the gaiety, word comes that the princess's father, the king of France, has died, and the princess must sail for home immediately, accompanied by her attendants. When the king and his lords plead with the ladies to stay in Navarre and marry them, the ladies refuse to accept their serious protestations of love; they have jested too much to be believed. Each man vows that he will remain faithful, only to be reminded of the former vows he has broken. Then each lady makes a condition that, if met, will reward her lover a year hence. The king must retire for twelve months to a hermitage and there forsake all worldly pleasures. If at the end of that time he still loves the princess, she will be his. In the same fashion the other three lords must spend a year in carrying out the wishes of their sweethearts. Even the foolish Armado is included in the plan. He joins the others, announcing that Jaquenetta will not have him until he has spent three years in honest work. Thus all the swains have tried with jests and fair speech to win their ladies, but without success. Now as the price of their folly they must prove in earnest that they deserve the hearts of their beloveds.

Critical Evaluation:

The exuberant language of *Love's Labour's Lost* makes it, in the words of Anne Barton, "the most relentlessly Elizabethan of all Shakespeare's plays." At times the dazzling wordplay has been deemed too clever, complex, and convoluted to make for a play that translates well to a modern audience, but audiences continue to sense, if not always completely comprehend, the wit and consequent fun inherent in the language—and it is on issues of language that appreciation of the play ultimately rests.

Several factors give the play special status in the William Shakespeare canon. It is one of the few Shakespeare plays for which an original source has not been found. For a comedy, it is also unusual in that, in spite of at least five possible couplings, it does not end with any traditional marriage or multiple marriages. The happy ending is suspended and left to the future, with the agreement of the couples to meet a year later. Further, the play is highly unusual in the way that death plays such a direct role in the outcome. Given the artificial motivation for the beginning of the plot, however, as well as the heavily verbal middle, it is not surprising that it takes the extreme intrusion of death to jolt the characters back to reality.

Critical attention to *Love's Labour's Lost* has focused largely on Shakespeare's satire of the men's behavior. The king of Navarre's plan is patently absurd. In wishing to take a vow to separate himself from women and from pleasure and to dwell only on study, Ferdinand is plainly rejecting life's realities. In his forcing his attendants to take the vow with him, and in their agreeing to do so, the entire trustworthiness of their effort is put at stake. The vow is, naturally, soon challenged by the intrusion into the king's withdrawn world of the princess of France and her attendants.

What follows largely justifies the complaints of those critics who find the plot weak. Little happens to move the story forward—love letters are misdirected, and sonnets and verses are read. The games of words are followed by games of wooing, with some of the usual comic stage business of disguises and mistaken identities used to prolong the courtship. When the representatives of the outside world seem to have been thoroughly drawn into the king's artificial world of games, the startling news of the death of the king of France shatters this fragile and illusory world built on words. As a commentary on the insubstantiality of language, the play is strong. As drama, the vows of love from it are not as strong.

Love's Labour's Lost is often excused as one of Shakespeare's early plays, suggesting but not itself exhibiting some of the greater characterizations that came later. The cynical Berowne and the quick-witted Rosaline, for example, seem to foreshadow Benedick and Beatrice in *Much Ado About Nothing* (pr. c. 1598-1599, pb. 1600). The clowns and comic characters provide a hint of the substantial subplots so common in later Shakespeare. Don Adriano de Armado, Costard, and Jaquenetta, for example, serve to reflect on the foolishness and self-deception of the main male characters.

With this play it may be helpful to remember that live performances are often comical and entertaining. Reading such a work may be laborious, with some of the language difficult to grasp. The easygoing silliness of the play in performance, however, can be rewarding. *Love's Labour's Lost* may have been written specifically to be performed for a small, highly educated audience. Discussions about the precise dating of the play have relied on the numerous historical references in it. More than usual, Shakespeare seems to have chosen names that evoked real people of the time, a theatrical device that would appeal only to those in the know. Although not based on any specific sources, the play evokes the Petrarchan conventions and the exaggerated language of love so popular in the writings of courtiers of the time. *Love's Labour's Lost* is also remarkable for its large number of puns and other wordplay.

With this early play, Shakespeare seems to have fused form and content. In satirizing the unrealistic idealization of learning and in examining the reliability and trustworthiness of language, that fallible vehicle for expression, Shakespeare draws on his considerable stock of verbal tricks and games to make his points. Although all the labor that the men put into their verse and their trickery to express their love for the women seems lost at the end, it is a temporary loss. What the women ask, ironically enough, is that the men fulfill the vows that they undertook in the first place. Words may be inadequate, but there are practically no other means, especially for a playwright, for expression. The unexpected ending, with its promise of fulfillment, seems to be a challenge to make the promise of words of love become true in deeds of love.

"Critical Evaluation" by Shakuntala Jayaswal

Further Reading

Barber, C. L. "The Folly of Wit and Masquerade in *Love's Labour's Lost*." In *Shakespeare's Festive Comedy: A Study of Dramatic Form and Its Relation to Social Custom*. 1959. Reprint. Princeton, N.J.: Princeton University Press, 1990. Discussion of *Love's Labour's Lost* is part of an influential study that examines the relationship between holiday rituals and Shakespeare's comedies. Asserts that the games in the play provide necessary festive release.

Barton, Anne. Introduction to *Love's Labour's Lost*. In *The Riverside Shakespeare*, edited by G. Blakemore Evans. 2d ed. Boston: Houghton Mifflin, 1997. A Shakespeare scholar provides information on the play's textual history and an explication of its language and themes.

Breitenberg, Mark. "The Anatomy of Masculine Desire in *Love's Labour's Lost*." In *Anxious Masculinity in Early Modern England*. New York: Cambridge University Press, 1996. Discussion of *Love's Labour's Lost* is part of an examination of the patriarchal culture of Elizabethan England and its relation to male sexual anxiety, as reflected in the literature of the period.

Carroll, William C. *The Great Feast of Language in "Love's Labour's Lost."* Princeton, N.J.: Princeton University Press, 1976. Argues that the play does not pit art against nature but rather shows their connection and interdependence. Includes a discussion of the songs at the play's end.

Gilbert, Miriam. *Love's Labour's Lost*. New York: Manchester University Press, 1993. Focuses on a select group of productions of the play in discussing the variety of possible interpretations of the work.

Leggatt, Alexander, ed. *The Cambridge Companion to Shakespearean Comedy*. New York: Cambridge University Press, 2002. Collection of essays addresses all aspects of Shakespeare's comedies. Includes discussion of *Love's Labour's Lost*, particularly in the essays "Love and Courtship," by Catherine Bates, and "Language and Comedy," by Lynne Magnusson.

Londré, Felicia Hardison, ed. *"Love's Labour's Lost": Critical Essays*. New York: Garland, 1997. Presents critical interpretations of the play published from 1598 through 1995, including analyses by Samuel Johnson, Samuel Taylor Coleridge, and Walter Pater, as well as later discussions of such topics as the play's structure and its depictions of French, Spanish, and Russian characters. Also reprints reviews of productions beginning with George Bernard Shaw's critique of an 1886 performance through late twentieth century productions in England and the United States.

Pendergast, John S. *"Love's Labour's Lost": A Guide to the Play*. Westport, Conn.: Greenwood Press, 2002. Thorough guide for students and general readers provides information on the play's textual history and the cultural context in which it was written as well as discussion of its structure and critical approaches to the work.

Loving

Author: Henry Green (1905-1973)
First published: 1945
Type of work: Novel
Type of plot: Domestic
Time of plot: World War II
Locale: Ireland

Principal characters:
CHARLEY RAUNCE, an English butler
MRS. TENNANT, Raunce's employer
MRS. JACK TENNANT, Mrs. Tennant's daughter-in-law
EDITH, a maid in love with Raunce
ALBERT, Raunce's assistant

The Story:

The great mansion owned by Mrs. Tennant is thrown into turmoil by the death of old Eldon, the butler. In the servants' quarters, no one knows quite what arrangements will be made after his death. The mansion and its inhabitants form an isolated bit of England in Ireland. None of the servants can guess what Mrs. Tennant, who is a widow and very vague, might do in rearranging their duties. Only the footman, Charley Raunce, keeps any purpose in his behavior.

Immediately after Eldon's death, Raunce goes into the butler's room and takes two small notebooks, one filled with the butler's monthly accounts and the other containing a set of special memoranda about visitors to the mansion, information that had helped the old man to obtain generous tips from Mrs. Tennant's guests. That same day, Raunce approaches Mrs. Tennant and asks to be given the post of butler. She agrees to give him the post, but without any extra pay. Raunce knows, however, that by juggling the household accounts he can make up whatever pay raise he deems sufficient. That evening, he solidifies his position by successfully taking over the old butler's place at the head of the table in the servants' dining room. Raunce also insists that one of the mansion's upstairs maids, Edith, with whom he is in love, continue her practice of bringing the butler his morning tea. The housekeeper, Mrs. Burch, is scandalized but is forced to give in and allow the maid to do so.

Raunce's usurpation of the old butler's position immediately upon the latter's death soon appears a minor matter, because a scandal rocks the mansion within a few days. Mrs. Tennant's daughter-in-law, Mrs. Jack, is found in bed with a neighbor, Captain Davenport. The discovery is made by Edith, who had gone into the bedroom to open the curtains and to lay out Mrs. Jack's clothes in the morning. Although Mrs. Tennant is unaware of her daughter-in-law's indiscretion, the episode creates consternation and nervousness in the servants' quarters.

To add to the uneasiness among the servants, a blue sapphire ring belonging to Mrs. Tennant disappears. Mrs. Ten-

nant, who is always losing valuable items, does not blame the servants, but the loss makes them feel ill at ease. A few days afterward, Mrs. Tennant and her daughter-in-law leave for England to visit Jack Tennant, who has been given a few days' leave from military duty. The English servants almost give their notice when they learn that they are being left in sole charge of the mansion, for they are well aware of the unfriendly attitudes of the Irish in the countryside and are also in fear of an invasion of the district by German troops. Raunce, who has a great sense of duty as well as a clear understanding of what a good position he is in, prevails upon the servants to remain despite their general dissatisfaction.

In Mrs. Tennant's absence, Raunce pays court to Edith and discovers that she is also in love with him. They spend many pleasant hours together, for Raunce is kept from his duties by a sore throat and Edith spends much of her time nursing him. Like the other servants, they are worried by the absence of their mistress and by their failure to find Mrs. Tennant's missing ring. Edith finally finds the ring, but she and Raunce are at a loss to know where to keep it until Mrs. Tennant returns. They decide to hide it in the upholstery of a chair, but later, much to their dismay, they find that it is gone from its hiding place.

Shortly after they discover the ring's loss a second time, an investigator from an insurance company calls at the mansion. All the servants refuse to answer his questions; his presence during their mistress's absence bothers them, and they do not know what to say in order to protect her and her interests. The investigator leaves in a suspicious mood, saying that his company will not pay for the loss. After his departure, the servants discover that the initials of the insurance company are like those of the militant, revolutionary Irish Republican Army, and they are struck with panic. Only the thoughts of military service and short rations in England keep them from giving up their jobs immediately.

In the remaining days before Mrs. Tennant's return, Edith

learns that Mrs. Tennant's grandchildren and the cook's nephew had found the sapphire ring while playing. Not realizing the value of the piece of jewelry, the youngsters had taken it out and hidden it on the lawn. By pretending to want it as a wedding present from one of the little girls, Edith persuades the child to bring it to her.

When Mrs. Tennant returns, the ring is restored to her, and its loss and the ugliness of the insurance investigator soon become matters of the past, almost forgotten after Raunce's helper, a young lad named Albert, gives his notice and leaves the mansion. Albert leaves because of Mrs. Tennant's implication that he had taken the ring in the first place. He goes back to England to enter the military service and becomes an aerial gunner.

Raunce grows restless when he comes to the realization, brought home to him by Albert's departure, that he has had no part in the war effort. He also feels remorseful because his mother, who lives in England and has been exposed to bombings by the Germans, refuses to come to Ireland to live with her son and Edith after their marriage. These influences, coupled with the many dissensions among the servants and the domestic crises occurring at the mansion, assume larger and larger proportions as he thinks about them. At last, he admits to Edith that he is dissatisfied and wants to leave. His announcement makes Edith unhappy, for she thinks at first that he is trying to cancel their wedding plans. He convinces her, however, that he wants her to go with him, and they decide that, unlike good servants, they will leave without giving notice to Mrs. Tennant. One night, they elope; they are married in England and settle down there to live.

Critical Evaluation:

Henry Green, despite his publishing nine novels from 1926 through 1952, is the least-known English novelist of high artistic quality of that period. He was a part-time novelist, spending most of his time in business, writing his novels seemingly as a diversion. He tended to avoid promoting himself as a writer. There is also the matter of the technical oddity of his work. In *Loving*, for example, he emulates some of the satirical insights of Evelyn Waugh (with whom he associated at Oxford), but in addition there is a kind of bizarre whimsy that goes beyond Waugh. Often, there is a strange lyric quality in Green's prose that is unsettling because it seems to appear from nowhere, in a way that is reminiscent of the work of Ford Madox Ford. Green's fiction sometimes bothers readers because it never quite settles down, in terms of its tone, into a clearly identifiable point of view. Readers are left unsure of how to respond to the work, morally and emotionally.

Green's rather stubborn determination to record conversations in the rawest natural form adds to the confusion. It is not simply that his working-class characters use a slangy, demotic language that is full of eccentricities and unfamiliar figures of speech; the same occurs with his upper-class characters. He is determined not to compromise the veracity of regional, occupational, or class language. Most writers, even when they are re-creating the peculiarities of spoken language, tend to edit carefully in order to avoid confusing readers, but Green seems not to care if everything is clearly understood. The conversations are often made more difficult by the maddeningly furtive intimacies, offhand asides, and associations of ideas often indulged in by people who know each other well and are living in close, constant contact. Green's characters are talking, in a sense, to themselves; they have no idea that they are in a novel and ought to make things a bit clearer for the reader.

Green, in this sense, is an innovator. He adds to this experimental style by using punctuation sparingly and by refusing to separate changes of time, place, and subject. A kind of "run-on" consciousness brings an improvisational, seemingly unliterary informality to a novel that is, in fact, a very clever, mannered performance.

Loving is probably Green's best work, and it manifests much of his skill as a writer. What looks like an obvious tale of eccentric English behavior accumulates density not so much out of complicated plot or characterization as out of charming aimlessness. An upper-class English household, servants and all, is found in a great country house in the Republic of Ireland during World War II. The situation is ripe with the possibility for minor comedy or for tragedy, depending upon the loosely manic manner in which the household conducts itself under worries about the war, staff jealousies, love affairs, and an exaggerated fear of the Irish Republican Army, which is supposed to be lurking somewhere.

The young maids have some sense, but many of the servants take the least reasonable conclusion for granted. The infidelity of Captain Jack's young wife, missing jewelry, a throttled peacock, and unfounded rumors surrounding the war being fought far from provincial Ireland make for madness. The book is, ultimately, a comedy—the butler runs off with one of the maids, to live, as the last line announces tersely, "happily ever after"—but what gives it aesthetic texture is the way in which Green makes a dreamworld of it. This is partly the result of Green's ability to make characters out of caricatures. Raunce is the typically dishonest butler, but Green manages to give this sometimes cocky middle-aged man credibility in his odd love affair with Edith, in his worrying concern for his duties, in his sense of the social hierarchy of the house, in his strange, enfeebling illness, and in his paranoia. There is a fragility and tenderness in him that shows itself not only in his courtship of Edith but also in his concern for his mother, who is back in England facing the bombs.

What makes *Loving* more than simply a joke of modest proportion is, in the first instance, its strangely uncommitted tone, which makes it difficult for readers to decide if they are to take the work lightly or if disaster is going to strike. Second, the novel rises above modest accomplishment in the dreamlike language used in descriptions of landscape and of the house and its architectural extravagances. The descriptions makes this lonely haven from the war seem a fairy-tale world in which anything can happen. The joke is that ultimately very little does, but the enchantment is so complete that one hardly cares. The novel is masterful in its sharp but elegiac insights into a fading world of class hierarchy that will hardly survive the war.

"Critical Evaluation" by Charles Pullen

Further Reading

Bassoff, Bruce. *Toward "Loving": The Poetics of the Novel and the Practice of Henry Green*. Columbia: University of South Carolina Press, 1975. Lengthy study offers a complex, important discussion of Green's theory of "nonrepresentational fiction." Notes how his sparse prose, reaching its epitome in *Loving*, requires readers to participate imaginatively in the creation of the fiction.

Cavaliero, Glen. "A Manner of Speaking: Elizabeth Bowen and Henry Green." In *The Alchemy of Laughter: Comedy in English Fiction*. New York: St. Martin's Press, 2000. Discussion of Green's novels is part of an examination of comedy in English novels that addresses the parody, irony, satire, and other types of humor in these fictional works.

Green, Henry. *Surviving: The Uncollected Writings of Henry Green*. Edited by Matthew Yorke. London: Chatto & Windus, 1992. Green stopped writing novels in 1952, but he continued to write occasional journalism, which is collected in this book. Includes a perceptive introduction by John Updike, who admits that he was deeply influenced by Green.

Holmesland, Oddvar. *A Critical Introduction to Henry Green's Novels*. New York: Macmillan, 1986. Provides analysis of each of Green's novels and examines the author's ideas of life and how they affected his work.

Karl, Frederick R. "Normality Defined: The Novels of Henry Green." In *A Reader's Guide to the Contemporary English Novel*. 1962. Reprint. Syracuse, N.Y.: Syracuse University Press, 2001. Examines the novels in readable language and places Green's fiction within the context of the works produced by other English authors of the same era.

MacKay, Marina. "The Neutrality of Henry Green." In *Modernism and World War II*. New York: Cambridge University Press, 2006. Analyzes Green's novels as part of a larger discussion of British authors whose works appeared during World War II, when modernism was in its decline as an influential literary movement. Pays particular attention to *Loving* and two of Green's other novels, *Party Going* (1939) and *Caught* (1943).

Odom, Keith. *Henry Green*. Boston: Twayne, 1978. Provides an introductory overview of Green's life and work, with an emphasis on the sociological influences on his writing.

Treglown, Jeremy. *Romancing: The Life and Work of Henry Green*. New York: Random House, 2000. Biography integrates information about Green's life with analysis of his novels. Maintains that the author's identity was split between that of Henry Yorke, his real name, and that of Henry Green, his pen name. Includes information about Green's writing of *Loving* and the novel's critical reception, themes, and autobiographical elements.

The Lower Depths

Author: Maxim Gorky (1868-1936)
First produced: Na dne, 1902; first published, 1902 (English translation, 1912)
Type of work: Drama
Type of plot: Naturalism
Time of plot: Late nineteenth century
Locale: Russia

Principal characters:
KOSTILYOFF, the landlord
VASSILISA, his wife
NATASHA, her sister
VASKA, a young thief
KLESHTCH, a locksmith
ANNA, his wife
NASTYA, a streetwalker
THE BARON, a former nobleman
LUKA, a tramp
SATINE, a cardsharp
THE ACTOR, an alcoholic

The Story:

The cellar resembles a cave, with only one small window to illuminate its dank recesses. In a corner, thin boards partition off the room of Vaska, the young thief. In the kitchen live Kvashnya, a vendor of meat pies, the decrepit Baron, and the streetwalker Nastya. All around the room are bunks occupied by other lodgers.

Nastya, her head bent down, is absorbed in reading a novel titled *Fatal Love*. The Baron, who lives largely on Nastya's earnings, seizes the book and reads its title aloud. Then he bangs Nastya over the head with it and calls her a lovesick fool. Satine raises himself painfully from his bunk at the noise. His memory is vague, but he knows he took a beating the night before, and the others tell him he had been caught cheating at cards. The Actor stirs in his bed on top of the stove. He predicts that some day Satine will be beaten to death.

The Actor reminds the Baron to sweep the floor. The landlady is strict and makes them clean every day. The Baron loudly announces that he has to go shopping; he and Kvashnya leave to make the day's purchases.

The Actor climbs down from his bunk and declares that the doctor has told him he has an organism poisoned by alcohol, and sweeping the floor would be bad for his health. Anna coughs loudly in her bunk. She is dying of consumption—there is no hope for her. Her husband, Kleshtch, is busy at his bench, where he fits old keys and locks. Anna sits up and calls to Kleshtch, offering him the dumplings that Kvashnya has left for her in the pot. Kleshtch agrees that there is no use feeding a dying woman, and so with a clear conscience he eats the dumplings.

The Actor helps Anna down from her high bed and out into the drafty hall. The sick woman is wrapped in rags. As they go through the door, the landlord, Kostilyoff, enters, nearly knocking them down. Kostilyoff looks around the dirty cellar and glances several times at Kleshtch, working at his bench. Loudly, the landlord says that the locksmith occupies too much room for two rubles a month and that henceforth the rent will be two and one-half rubles. Then Kostilyoff edges toward Vaska's room and inquires furtively if his wife has been in. Kostilyoff has good reason to suspect that his wife, Vassilisa, is sleeping with Vaska.

At last, Kostilyoff gets up the courage to call out to Vaska. The thief comes out of his room and denounces the landlord for not paying his debts, saying that Kostilyoff still owes seven rubles for a watch he had bought. Ordering Kostilyoff to produce the money immediately, Vaska sends him roughly out of the room.

The others admire Vaska for his courage and urge him to kill Kostilyoff and marry Vassilisa; then he could be landlord. Vaska thinks the idea over for a time but decides that he is too softhearted to be a landlord. Besides, he is thinking of discarding Vassilisa for her sister, Natasha. Satine asks Vaska for twenty kopecks, which the thief is glad to give; he is afraid Satine will want a ruble next.

Natasha comes in with the tramp Luka. She puts him in the kitchen to sleep with the three already there. Luka, a merry fellow, begins to sing, but he stops when all the others object. The whole group sits silent when Vassilisa comes in, sees the dirty floor, and gives orders for an immediate sweeping. She looks over the new arrival, Luka, and asks to see his passport. Because he has none, he is more readily accepted by the others. Miedviedeff, who is a policeman and Vassilisa's uncle, enters the cellar to check up on the lodging. He begins to question Luka, but when the tramp calls him sergeant, Miedviedeff leaves him alone.

That night, Anna lies in her bunk while a noisy, quarrelsome card game goes on. Luka talks gently to the consumptive woman, and Kleshtch comes from time to time to look at her. Luka remarks that her death will be hard on her husband, but Anna accuses Kleshtch of causing her death. She says that she looks forward to the rest and peace she has never known. Luka assures her she will be at peace after her death.

The card players become louder and Satine is accused of cheating. Luka quiets the riotous players; they all respect him even though they think him a liar. He tells Vaska that he will be able to reform in Siberia, and he assures the Actor that at a sanatorium he could be cured of alcoholism. Vassilisa comes in, and when the others leave, she offers Vaska three hundred rubles if he will kill Kostilyoff and set her free. That would leave Vaska free to marry Natasha, who at the moment is recovering from a beating given to her by her jealous sister. Vaska is about to refuse when Kostilyoff enters in search of his wife. He is extremely suspicious, but Vaska pushes him out of the cellar.

A noise on top of the stove reveals that Luka has overheard everything. He is not greatly disturbed and warns Vaska not to have anything to do with the vicious Vassilisa. Walking over to Anna's bunk, Luka sees that she is dead. They find Kleshtch at the saloon, and he comes to look at the body of his dead wife. The others tell him that he will have to remove the body, because in time dead people smell. Kleshtch agrees to take Anna's body outside. The Actor begins to cavort in joy, talking excitedly. He has made up his mind to go to the sanatorium for his health. Luka has told him that he can even be cured at state expense.

In the backyard that night, as Natasha is telling romantic stories to the crowd, Kostilyoff comes out and gruffly orders her in to work. As she goes in, Vassilisa pours boiling water on Natasha's feet. Vaska attempts to rescue her and knocks Kostilyoff down, and in the ensuing brawl Kostilyoff is killed. As the others slink away, Vassilisa immediately accuses Vaska of murder. Natasha thinks that Vaska has murdered Kostilyoff for the sake of Vassilisa. Natasha is almost in delirium as she wanders about accusing Vaska of murder and calling for revenge.

In the excitement, Luka wanders off, and he is never seen again. Vaska escapes a police search. Natasha goes to the hospital. In the lodging, things go on much as they had before. Satine cheats at cards, and the Baron tries to convince the others of his former affluence. They all agree that Luka was a kind old man but a great liar.

During a bitter quarrel with Nastya, the Baron steps out in the yard. Satine and the others strike up a bawdy song, but they break off when the Baron hurries back to announce that the Actor has hanged himself. Satine says he thinks the suicide was too bad—it broke up the song.

Critical Evaluation:

Maxim Gorky's exceptionally well-crafted play *The Lower Depths* is a transitional piece between nineteenth and twentieth century literary masterpieces. As such, it shares in the best of both worlds. The play is constructed with a nineteenth century eye toward dramatic structure at the same time that it treats twentieth century sociopolitical themes. Among the most important of these is the issue of freedom versus slavery, a frequent topic of conversation—implicit or explicit—among the denizens of "the lower depths," a cellar-like rooming house that accommodates a varied group of inhabitants.

Also threading its way through the play is the naturalistic assumption of predestination, which forces the audience to ask—without really expecting an answer—whether the Actor was foredoomed to alcoholism, whether Anna was destined to die of tuberculosis and leave her husband penniless because of medical and burial expenses, and whether Satine was the only one who recognized how low the lower depths were. Many more such questions arise, but all serve only to illustrate the essential slavery of the characters to the lower depths of the socioeconomic system and their lack of freedom to rise above it.

This theme is also reinforced by the poetic imagery in the play, which revolves around references to light and dark, clean and dirty. The interior of the cellar rooming house, for example, is dark, but ideas and hopes are light. Conventional associations of good with light or white and bad with dark or black abound. The conventional system gets turned on its head when the Actor begins to view death by suicide as a hope for his salvation, whereby death becomes white, but throughout the play, dark or black retains its traditional connotation of hopelessness and doom.

Gorky's use of light/dark imagery is particularly evident in the amalgamation of this imagery into another effective literary device that he uses most strikingly—foreshadowing or prescience, a subtle hint or prophecy of events to manifest themselves in the future. Anna's death, for example, which occurs at the end of act 2, is already predicted in act 1. The Actor's death is suggested in the middle of act 3, although he does not commit suicide until the end of act 4. Natasha foresees an apocalyptic doom in act 3 that does not come to pass until act 4. In fact, the Actor senses his own fate at the beginning of act 4, although it does not occur until the end of that act.

In the resolution of this precisely structured play, only

Luka and Satine go unaccounted for; the rest play out their roles as though programmed. Yet the impact is undeniable, and the two escapees do not really escape, because they bear responsibility for the fates of others. The victims survive spiritually—despite death or other devastation—as reminders of the inexorable workings of the socioeconomic system. It could be said that the end was prophesied from the beginning and that Gorky merely worked out the details, but those details were sufficiently compelling to support a revolution and to sustain a remarkable play.

Further Reading

Borras, F. M. *Maxim Gorky the Writer: An Interpretation.* Oxford, England: Clarendon Press, 1967. Offers astute analyses of Gorky's works, especially his novels and plays, including *The Lower Depths.* Emphasizes Gorky's artistic achievements rather than focusing on biographical or political issues.

Erlich, Victor. "Truth and Illusion in Gorky: *The Lower Depths* and After." In *Freedom and Responsibility in Russian Literature: Essays in Honor of Robert Louis Jackson*, edited by Elizabeth Cheresh Allen and Gary Saul Morson. Evanston, Ill.: Northwestern University Press, 1995. Analyzes the themes of truth versus illusion and reality versus invention in Gorky's prose fiction and dramatic works.

Hare, Richard. *Maxim Gorky, Romantic Realist and Conservative Revolutionary.* 1962. Reprint. Westport, Conn.: Greenwood Press, 1978. Substantial study combines discussion of the political aspects of Gorky's biography with critical analysis of his works. Includes an analysis of *The Lower Depths.*

Levin, Dan. *Stormy Petrel: The Life and Work of Maxim Gorky.* 1965. Reprint. New York: Schocken Books, 1986. Biography addresses how the events of Gorky's life are reflected in his writings. Includes discussion of *The Lower Depths.*

Marsh, Cynthia. "Truth, Lies, and Theatre: *The Lower Depths* (1902)." In *Maxim Gorky: Russian Dramatist.* New York: Peter Lang, 2006. Analyzes *The Lower Depths* and Gorky's other plays, discussing such topics as the influence of religion and exile on the works and the personal and political implications of motherhood in the dramas.

Muchnic, Helen. "Circe's Swine: Plays by Gorky and O'Neill." In *Russian Writers: Notes and Essays.* New York: Random House, 1971. Comparative study of Gorky's *The Lower Depths* and Eugene O'Neill's *The Iceman Cometh* (pr., pb. 1946) offers some keen insights.

Weil, Irwin. *Gorky: His Literary Development and Influence on Soviet Intellectual Life.* New York: Random House, 1966. One of the most scholarly discussions of Gorky's work available in English skillfully combines biography with critical analysis. Includes discussion of *The Lower Depths.*

Yedlin, Tova. *Maxim Gorky: A Political Biography.* Westport, Conn.: Praeger, 1999. Focuses on Gorky's political and social views, with particular attention to his participation in the political and cultural life of his country.

Lucasta Poems

Author: Richard Lovelace (1618-1656/1657)
First published: 1659; *Lucasta: Epodes, Odes, Sonnets, Songs &c. to Which Is Added Aramantha, a Pastorall*; 1659, *Lucasta: Posthume Poems of Richard Lovelace, Esq.*
Type of work: Poetry

To most readers, Richard Lovelace is remembered for two lines from each of two songs. He voiced for all those spirits who have suffered in prison, who have thought or composed thoughts in jails, the perfect expression of the free will when he wrote "Stone Walls doe not a Prison make,/ Nor I'ron bars a Cage," and he expressed his own high standards as a gentleman, soldier, scholar, and poet in lines he wrote when going off to war: "I could not love thee (Deare) so much,/ Lov'd I not Honour more."

A Royalist by birth and politics and a Cavalier by style, Lovelace lost a modest fortune in the English Civil War (1642-1650). He suffered imprisonment twice, and he spent much of his life surrounded by war's tragedies. He lost his father and a brother in battle. He himself fought in King

Charles I's ill-fated Scottish expeditions of 1639-1640 and then for England's allies in Holland, attaining the rank of colonel.

Lovelace was an amateur poet, a man of action whose education made of him a man of many parts. He has been compared to the Elizabethan soldier-poet, Sir Philip Sidney, "A Scholar, Souldier, Lover, and a Saint," as one epitaph verse reads. His poetry, of limited popularity, was virtuous and modest by Cavalier standards. His most famous series, *Lucasta* (a name taken from the Latin *lux casta*, or "light of virtue"), is his testimonial.

No conclusive evidence has yet come to light concerning the Lucasta of Lovelace's two volumes of verse, though it is unlikely that this idealized figure was Lucy Sacheverell, as was first thought. The woman to whom Lovelace addressed many of his poems may have been a Lucas, however, making the name a play on words.

Lovelace's varied activities and tastes led sometimes to the exercise of a talent thinly spread, to poor taste, or (especially) to haste—Lovelace's literary sin. His first volume so lacked care and proofreading as to contain errors that were evident even at a time of variable spellings, indifferent typography, and fanciful punctuation. The poems were not arranged chronologically, stanzas were not collated, and the entire edition bespoke a lack of professionalism. Despite these weaknesses, Lovelace was well regarded. As a contemporary said of him, "He writes very well for a gentleman." His noble sentiments attracted readers.

In addition to varied types of poems, Lovelace wrote at least one produced play, *The Scholar(s)* (pr. 1636?), the prologue and epilogue of which appear in his first collection. Another play, *The Soldier* (wr. 1640), a tragedy, was never produced because of the closing of the theaters in 1642. During the period of the Protectorate, songs by Lovelace were probably sung in masques, which were dramas produced privately for an aristocratic audience.

Lovelace wrote in the age of the conceit, or extended metaphor. He employed conceits that incorporated the witty and often barbed imagery popularized by John Donne and other Metaphysical poets, but he was less skillful in their use. His two famous songs, written also in an age of words set to music, surpass those of his betters, but on moral rather than poetic grounds: "To Althea, from Prison" demonstrates Lovelace's indomitable spirit, forming part of a larger noble literature written from prison. Lovelace himself wrote other poems from prison, but they are fairly political and need detailed knowledge of the period to be understood.

The "Althea" poem is a song consisting of four octave stanzas. It illustrates Lovelace's musicality, as the stanzas were set by John Wilson and were sung. The stanzas consist of alternating tetrameters and trimeters, following a rhyme scheme of *ababcdcd*. Lovelace treats various paradoxes associated with liberty and confinement, the first being love. Even though the poet sees himself in a traditional way, entangled in his beloved's hair, his soul still feels freer than the birds soaring in the sky, as it too soars in the joy of being in love. Already in the first stanza, he hints at a literal prison. Perhaps Althea has come to visit him there. If not, perhaps the hint is a reference to the body as prison, a well-known Platonic image.

The second stanza suggests the freedom of alcohol, which stirs up the speaker's patriotism. He compares himself with a fish, who swims in another liquid but does not know any freedom of soul. The third stanza deals with freedom of speech. Even though he may be caged like a bird, the poet can still "voyce aloud" his devotion to his king. The famous last stanza draws these paradoxes together, resolving them in terms of inner freedom.

In "To Lucasta, Going to the Warres," love and patriotism are again the key terms. The poem consists of only twelve lines arranged in three quatrains. Lovelace's variety of stanzaic forms and metric schemes must be noted, as they comprise some forty variations in all. The poem belongs to the genre of valedictions, a genre that Donne made famous. Lovelace's valediction is equal in its brevity to Donne's lengthy efforts, through which he worked out various conceits. Again, Lovelace resolves the poem as a paradox: that for human love to be true, it must contain the desire for honor and a good greater than itself. The poem was set to music, as was another valediction almost as famous, "To Lucasta, Going beyond the Seas."

When Lovelace is purely bent on paying compliments, his verse can be as elegant as any in the English language. For example "Gratiana dauncing and singing" evinces an almost Shakespearian quality in its image of a lady's unity of being, revealed in her flow of movement. In the poem, the dance floor is littered with broken hearts, as the world is transformed into a mythological one of the Graces and Apollo. By contrast, when Lovelace strains his poetry with double entendres, it loses both clarity and elegance. This can be well seen in "The faire Begger" or "To Amarantha, That she would dishevell her haire," in which the speaker hints that he would like a great deal more disheveled than just hair.

Only twenty-seven copies of the 1649 *Lucasta* are known to be extant. This slender book of some sixty poems is dedicated to Lady Anne Lovelace, the wife of Richard's cousin John. The dedication is followed by a group of commendatory poems written by Lovelace's brothers Francis and

Dudley—the latter, ten years later, would be the issuer of Lovelace's posthumous *Lucasta* poems. The most interesting poem in this commendatory group is by the author's friend and fellow poet Andrew Marvell, who suggests the verses will please the ladies more than the critics, those "Word-peckers, Paper-rats, Book-scorpions."

Of the sixty poems, about one-third were set to music and may still be found in books of "ayres" (airs). Many of the poems conform to expected seventeenth century forms, such as odes written on memorable days or for sad occasions, pastorals, sonnets, satires, and elegies. An interesting example of the latter is one of the poet's earliest poems, written when he was twenty and addressed to Princess Katherine, "borne, christened, buried in one day." The juxtaposition of birth and death, swaddling and winding clothes, and joy and sorrow, combined with the overtones of pomp and circumstance befitting Katherine's royal lineage, make of this poem a study in contrasts.

Lovelace prepared his second book, *Lucasta: Posthume Poems of Richard Lovelace, Esq.*, before his death, although it remained for his brother to bring out the volume. It was dedicated to Sir John Lovelace, an indication this time of his patronage. The first poem, "To Lucasta: Her Reserved Looks," epitomizes the gay-sad theme so prevalent among the Cavaliers, even at death.

> Lucasta, frown and let me die,
> But smile and see I live;
> The sad indifference of your Eye
> Both kills, and doth reprieve.
> You hide our fate within its screen,
> We feel our judgment ere we hear:
> So in one Picture I have seen
> An Angel here, the Devil there.

Thought by critics to be devoid of playful talent, Lovelace refutes this charge effectively in "A Black Patch on Lucasta's Face," a sonnet in which a bee "Mistook her glorious Face for Paradise." The plaster placed on the resulting sting serves as "the sweet little Bees large Monument."

The poems in the posthumous *Lucasta* volume reveal a mature and practiced poet, and the salutary effect of careful editing by Dudley Lovelace, assisted by Eldred Revett, makes this edition a more appealing one for modern readers. Although the volume does not contain as many songs, the same types of poems appear as were featured in the first volume, forty-four in all. A series of translations from Latin and French are appended.

The posthumous volume is the main collection of Lovelace's nature verses, such as "The Ant," "The Falcon," "The Spider," and "The Snail." However, one of these nature verses, "The Grasshopper," is found in the first volume, and it is perhaps the best known of the group. It is addressed "To my Noble Friend, Mr Charles Cotton" and is about male friendship. It has the feel of an ode by the Roman writer Horace in its celebration of country joys even in winter and of hearty cultured discussion. The fable of the grasshopper and the ant is suggested in the first part of the ten-stanza work, as the grasshopper sings away in summer, unmindful of the need to store up for the winter. The second half, however, abandon's this allusion, as the two men have sufficient stores of friendship and education to last out the long winter nights spent around a blazing fire. The poem celebrates the life of educated country gentlemen, of whom Lovelace was one until the last part of his life.

It may be significant that Lovelace's longest poems—in the first volume, a pastoral titled "Amarantha," and in the second, the satire "On Sanazar's Being Honoured with Six Hundred Duckets by the Clarissimi of Venice"—display the courtier as a gallant and then as a cynic. In the earlier poem, Lovelace sees women as less than perfect, but so much gentler is this knight than the other Cavalier poets that he would almost fit Chaucer's famous description of knightly grace. Lovelace will be remembered as long as readers continue to appreciate perfect, sincere lyrics about beauty, love, honor, and the lessons of life.

Revised by David Barratt

Further Reading

Corns, Thomas N., ed. *The Cambridge Companion to English Poetry: Donne to Marvell.* New York: Cambridge University Press, 1993. Collection of essays, some of which examine common characteristics of sixteenth and seventeenth century poetry, such as its treatment of politics, religion, and gender. Other articles explore the work of individual poets, including Lovelace.

Hartmann, C. H. *The Cavalier Spirit and Its Influence on the Life and Work of Richard Lovelace.* New York: E. P. Dutton, 1925. Reprint. New York: Haskell House, 1973. Biographical and historical study of the poet and his times. Comments on the publication of the *Lucasta* poems and provides critical analysis of a number of individual lyrics.

Kelly, Erna. "'Small Types of Great Ones': Richard Lovelace's Separate Peace." In *The English Civil Wars in the Literary Imagination*, edited by Claude J. Summers and Ted-Larry Pebworth. Columbia: University of Missouri

Press, 1999. Analyzes five of Lovelace's poems that focus on small creatures, such as a grasshopper, an ant, and a snail, describing how these creatures symbolize either Royalists or Puritans.

Robertson, Randy. "Lovelace and the 'Barbed Censurers': *Lucasta* and Civil War Censorship." *Studies in Philology* 103, no. 4 (Fall, 2006): 465-498. Argues that Lovelace is deliberately obscure in the *Lucasta* poems because this lack of clarity enabled him to avoid censorship during the English Civil War.

Seeling, Sharon Cadman. "'My Curious Hand or Eye': The Wit of Richard Lovelace." In *The Wit of Seventeenth Century Poetry*, edited by Claude Summers and Ted-Larry Pebworth. Columbia: University of Missouri Press, 1995. Discusses several of Lovelace's works as examples of the poet's understanding of issues involving gender and audience. Notes the significance of male-female power relationships in his works.

Skelton, Robin. *Cavalier Poets*. London: Longmans, Green, 1960. A chapter on Lovelace discusses his wit and explores reasons for his emphasis on the ideal and on idyllic situations. Compares him to other Cavalier poets, citing his facility with language as a special strength.

Weidhorn, Manfred. *Richard Lovelace*. New York: Twayne, 1970. Biographical and critical study intended for general readers. Includes chapters on Lovelace's philosophy, interests, and sociopolitical views. Insightful commentary on the *Lucasta* poems is included in a general discussion of Lovelace's merits as a Cavalier poet of the seventeenth century.

Wilkinson, C. H., ed. Introduction to *The Poems of Richard Lovelace*, by Richard Lovelace. Oxford, England: Clarendon Press, 1930. Excellent biographical sketch and critical commentary on both volumes, emphasizing the biographical background for many of the poems. Corrects errors in earlier scholarly discussions.

The Luck of Roaring Camp, and Other Sketches

Author: Bret Harte (1836-1902)
First published: 1870
Type of work: Short fiction

Few authors ever achieve the astonishing literary success that Bret Harte did during his lifetime. His enormously popular stories of California life were in great demand by magazine editors all over the country, and *The Atlantic Monthly* offered the unprecedented amount of ten thousand dollars for the sole rights to one year of Harte's literary production. Such enormous popularity is seldom consistent with a lasting literary reputation, however. Harte reached his artistic maturity at the age of thirty-one, and the quality of his work began to decline five years later. During the few years when he was at his peak, Harte produced some stories of genuine literary value, most of which are collected in *The Luck of Roaring Camp, and Other Sketches*. It is therefore mainly on this volume that Harte's literary reputation rests.

Harte's vision of life goes far to explain the meteoric popularity of his stories. The local color and picturesque characters he chose and the trick endings he devised added to the attraction, but these were surface features. The heart of his success lay in his ability to convey his particular vision of life to his readers. Harte was, essentially, an optimist and an uplifter. This does not mean that he believed in a shallow doctrine of social or moral reform. Rather, he believed in the potential goodness of human beings and in the possibility of redemption for every sinner. Harte saw life as a purgatory for the human soul, a test, the ultimate goal of which is salvation. He also thought that salvation could be achieved in this life, although, paradoxically, frequently at the cost of death. Rather than being an end of the trial, in Harte's view, death is the final consummation of the trial. Redemption for Harte is an act of selfless heroism, love, and devotion. Such an act can lift individuals above the petty world of grasping self-interest and redeem them from the sin of self-involvement. This is the spirit that pervades Harte's most memorable stories.

This spirit raises Harte's best characters from local stereotypes and picturesque caricatures to people of real feeling and semiheroic stature. Mark Twain explained that "Bret Harte got his California and his Californians by unconscious absorption, and put both of them into his tales alive." Harte wove the experiences of his people into his private theme of redemption and thereby gave them life. The people in Harte's stories are seeking salvation from themselves; they are people who long to wipe their pasts clean, people who have come to the American West to lose their identities, as indicated by the fact that very few of his characters retain their given names—instead they have names such as Cherokee Sal, Kentuck, Yuba Bill, Tennessee's Partner, and the Duchess.

These people are ripe for redemption by virtue of their self-dissatisfaction. To be saved, one must first have sinned. This theme is at the core of Harte's most successful stories. In the title story of the collection, "The Luck of Roaring Camp," which first appeared in the *Overland Monthly* in 1868, a dissolute prostitute works out her salvation by giving birth to a baby and dying. The miners in the camp work out their salvation by giving the baby love and generous gifts to make up for the absence of a mother. One miner, Kentuck, works out his salvation by giving his life in a futile attempt to save the baby. The baby, of course, is incidental because of its innocence. What matters is that the baby brings out the generous qualities of the people whose lives the child touches and thereby redeems them from their own pettiness. In the second story of the collection, "The Outcasts of Poker Flat," a gambler and two prostitutes are saved from themselves by their devotion to a pair of innocent youngsters who have eloped. In the third story, "Miggles," a pretty young woman is redeemed by her devotion to a helpless disabled man. The theme of love's power to save invests Harte's best stories with human interest. This was the source of Harte's uplift, optimism, and popularity.

Harte's weaknesses, which can be attributed to this same source, include frequent lapses into sentimentality and the use of illusory glamour and romance to gloss over the sharp frictions and discord of everyday life. In "Brown of Calaveras," the image of gambler Jack Hamlin riding off into the rosy sunset after having handsomely refused to run away with a man's beautiful young wife certainly strikes one as unnecessarily romantic and sentimental. The theme of redemption through love and death lends itself too easily to theatrical, facile endings.

At his best, however, Harte avoids these pitfalls. A story's sentimentality is usually balanced by an ironic, humorous narrative style. In his most memorable stories, Harte employs an ironic prose that maintains a distance between the author and his subject matter. This skillful prose is clear and restrained, giving his fiction a sweet-sour flavor that blends well with his vision of life and convinces the reader that his characters do not deserve sympathy until they succeed in redeeming themselves. It reminds readers that his characters are human and subject to human failings. Harte is never self-righteous, however. On the contrary, he is deeply sympa-

thetic in his treatment of character, realizing human limitations as well as human virtues. In his preface to *The Luck of Roaring Camp, and Other Sketches*, he writes

> I might have painted my villains of the blackest dye. . . . I might have made it impossible for them to have performed a virtuous or generous action, and have thus avoided that moral confusion which is apt to rise in the contemplation of mixed motives and qualities. But I should have burdened myself with responsibility of their creation, which . . . I did not care to do.

Even in his preface, Harte's use of irony is skillful. Actually, he was a shrewd judge of character and had a particular talent for "the contemplation of mixed motives and qualities."

Harte put this talent to good use in his sketches. He was an admirable craftsman in blending virtue and vice, humor and pathos, the ridiculous and the sublime. He had a good eye for contrasts, particularly for the contrast between nature and human nature. Harte saw the ambivalences in both. On one hand, he saw nature as serene, remote, and passionless; on the other, it could be violent, deadly, and passionate. In Harte's stories, the moods of nature are usually in juxtaposition with the moods of his characters. In "The Luck of Roaring Camp," for example, nature becomes still for a moment at the birth and the first cry of the baby. Later, when everything in the human realm seems calm and settled, a flood overwhelms the mining camp and takes several lives, including the baby's. The same kind of juxtaposition occurs in "The Outcasts of Poker Flat." When the gambler, the thief, and the two prostitutes are driven out of town, everything is calm, but when these four begin to find some measure of peace, a snowstorm overtakes them and their two innocent companions.

It has been pointed out that Harte's literary techniques were borrowed from such writers as Washington Irving and Charles Dickens. To be sure, Harte did adapt techniques from writers of the eastern United States and European writers, and he had developed out of the Romantic tradition, but to focus on what Harte borrowed from other writers is to miss the point. Harte was essentially an easterner who traveled to the West for his literary materials and who transformed his adopted techniques through his own personal values, limitations, and vision of life.

Both Harte's virtues and his weaknesses as a storyteller derive from his optimistic vision of human redemption. While his bittersweet endings are patently stylized and he has a tendency to overuse sentiment, Harte creates endings with a good measure of dramatic impact. Then, too, he frequently balances sentiment and glamour with healthy humor and irony. Harte is an effective stylist, and his sentences are sharp and lucid. Moreover, Harte's focus on human interest and local color helped pave the way for a school of regional fiction. His talent for characterization and caricature blended well with his style of writing, creating a fortunate fusion of form and content. For these many reasons, Bret Harte retains an assured place in a minor tradition.

Further Reading

Morrow, Patrick. *Bret Harte, Literary Critic*. Bowling Green, Ohio: Bowling Green State University Popular Press, 1979. Emphasizes Harte's strong technical control and craftsmanship in his short stories. Discusses the way he fashioned stories with local color out of tall tales and bar-room ballads.

Nissen, Axel. *Bret Harte: Prince and Pauper*. Jackson: University Press of Mississippi, 2000. Comprehensive, detailed biography covers the events of Harte's life and their influence on his writing. Asserts that Harte "reinvented" the American short story and laid the foundations of Western literature and discusses why Harte was famous in his day but virtually ignored by later generations.

Pattee, Fred Lewis. *The Development of the American Short Story: An Historical Survey*. 1923. Reprint. New York: Biblo and Tannen, 1975. Classic work offers good discussion of Harte's contributions to the short story: a sense of humor, use of paradox and antithesis, and creation of local atmosphere and individualized character types.

Rhode, Robert D. *Setting in the American Short Story of Local Color, 1865-1900*. The Hague, the Netherlands: Mouton, 1975. Argues that in Harte's best stories, setting is related to character as a stimulus to create new attitudes, a contrast to affect moral nature, and a sign of providence or symbol of a character's life.

Scharnhorst, Gary. *Bret Harte: Opening the American Literary West*. Norman: University of Oklahoma Press, 2000. Biography focuses on how Harte's work as both writer and lecturer played a key role in popularizing Western drama and fiction during the late nineteenth century.

Stegner, Wallace. Introduction to *The Outcasts of Poker Flat, and Other Tales*, by Bret Harte. New York: New American Library, 1961. Notes that Harte's characters do not strike the reader as lifelike but are, rather, clearly defined. Points out that Harte learned from Dickens how to combine apparently incompatible qualities to create a striking paradox.

Stevens, J. David. "'She War a Woman': Family Roles, Gender, and Sexuality in Bret Harte's Western Fiction." *American Literature* 69, no. 3 (September, 1997): 571-593. Argues that what critics have labeled sentimental excess in Harte's fiction is in fact his method of exploring certain hegemonic cultural paradigms taken for granted in other Western narratives. Discusses Harte's stories that deal with the structure of the family and how they critique gender roles.

Lucky Jim

Author: Kingsley Amis (1922-1995)
First published: 1954
Type of work: Novel
Type of plot: Social satire
Time of plot: Mid-twentieth century
Locale: An English provincial college

Principal characters:
JAMES "JIM" DIXON, a young history lecturer
MARGARET PEEL, one of his colleagues
PROFESSOR WELCH, Dixon's superior
MRS. WELCH, his wife
BERTRAND WELCH, their son and a painter
JULIUS GORE-URQUHART, a rich patron of the arts
CHRISTINE CALLAGHAN, his niece
CAROL GOLDSMITH, the wife of another history lecturer
JOHNS, a musician and member of the Welch circle

The Story:

Jim Dixon's predicament is twofold: He has a job—as a lecturer in medieval history at a provincial English college—that he does not really want but is trying hard to keep, and, without quite knowing why, he has become involved with Margaret Peel, a younger but better-established colleague. For the renewal of his contract with the college, Jim is dependent on the mercurial opinion of Professor Welch, a seedy, absentminded historian of independent means in whose country house Margaret is recuperating from a suicide attempt, the apparent result of her having been jilted by Catchpole, Jim's erstwhile but since departed rival.

Jim tries to improve his professional standing by writing an absurd article on medieval shipbuilding techniques, agreeing to give a public lecture at the college's annual festival, and accepting an invitation to a cultural weekend of madrigal singing and art talk at Welch's home. There he meets the professor's son, Bertrand, a London artist, and Bertrand's extremely attractive girlfriend, Christine Callaghan; he dislikes them both at first sight, especially Bertrand. Despite Jim's efforts to the contrary, the cultural weekend results in deeper involvement with Margaret and further damage to his job. After an overdose of culture, he sneaks out to a pub, gets drunk, makes an unsuccessful though solicited pass at Margaret, and falls asleep holding a lighted cigarette, leading to the burning of a rug, a table, and the bedclothes in the Welches' guest room. With the surprising help of Christine, he partially conceals the fire damage, but Margaret finds Jim and Christine hiding the charred table and uses this as a lever to manipulate Jim into asking her to the college's annual dress ball.

Bertrand and Christine attend the ball, as does Christine's uncle, Julius Gore-Urquhart, a rich devotee of the arts. Bertrand is hoping to secure a position, through Christine, as Gore-Urquhart's private secretary. Gore-Urquhart has brought Carol Goldsmith to the ball; Carol's husband is also a history lecturer at the college. Telling Jim that she has been having an affair with Bertrand, Carol advises him to drop Margaret and pursue Christine. With both Margaret and Bertrand devoting full and fawning attention to Gore-Urquhart, Jim persuades Christine to leave the ball with him, and they arrange to meet again.

The next morning, Jim faces Margaret, who is furious at having been left at the dance; when he tells her he is through with her, she goes into hysterics. The following day, Jim accompanies Professor Welch home to dinner. There Mrs. Welch confronts him with the burned bedclothes, about which he confesses and apologizes, and Bertrand confronts him about Christine. Left alone with Margaret, he finds himself, without much resistance, falling back into his old, ambiguous relationship with her; she does not object. When he meets Christine for tea, they agree not to see each other again, for she is involved with Bertrand in the same way he is involved with Margaret.

The following evening, Jim—sporting a black eye after a fight with Bertrand over Christine—gives his public lecture.

Under the influence of the few stiff drinks he has had beforehand, he turns the lecture, which he had planned as an encomium to Welch's prejudices, into a condemnation of them. He parodies a number of people, including Welch, and falls into a drunken stupor just as he is finally beginning to speak for himself and attack Welch's values directly.

After word comes that he is to be fired, Jim meets Catchpole, who had been in Wales, and discovers that the latter had never really been involved with Margaret; her suicide attempt was a hoax carefully planned to entrap them both. Gore-Urquhart offers Jim the London job that Bertrand had been seeking, and Christine, having broken up with Bertrand, becomes free. As the novel ends, Jim is beginning a new job in a new city with the promise of a new and better romance.

Critical Evaluation:

According to French philosopher Henri Bergson, the basis of laughter is the mechanization of gesture, movement, or language; it results from a substitution of the artificial for the natural so that the actions, attitudes, or speech of humans take on some aspect of the mechanical. The moral function of comedy is to scorn by laughter the mechanical, which impedes freedom and evolution, and thus to laud the natural and flexible, which allow human beings to survive and improve. Laughter is itself an expression of the naturalness and freedom that comedy lauds.

Despite its oversimplification, Bergson's theory provides a perspective from which to view Kingsley Amis's *Lucky Jim*. In this novel, the characters are laughable and immoral to the extent that they resemble machines in their behavior and moral to the extent that they are or become natural. Laughter itself in the novel is the expression of naturalness, of feelings unfettered by social convention or individual pretension.

Welch and his son are major cases in point. Their speech, to which Amis devotes much care, and their gestures are mechanized by cliché and affectation. This point is developed through a controlling metaphor. The jerky movements of Welch's car are compared implicitly and explicitly to Welch's conversational habits. His passengers are in constant jeopardy because he confuses his driving with his talking and often lets the course of his conversation dictate the direction of his car. Amis exploits the analogy by describing Welch's speech in terms stemming from automation and by making Welch's driving and his car important to the plot. Bertrand's speech is similarly automatic; it is a jibe at one of Bertrand's speech mannerisms and not Jim's refusal to stop seeing Christine that leads Bertrand to hit Jim. The same sclerosis of speech and manner is seen in varying degrees in Margaret, Johns (who continually informs on Jim), and Mrs. Welch; in each case, mannerism becomes automatic, to that extent risible, and, to Jim, dangerous.

Central to the novel is the irony that these automaton characters are all devoted in a mechanical way to theories that extol the natural and oppose what is modern, urban, and industrial. These worshipers of "integrated village-type community life," homemade music, handicrafts, and other ostensibly "natural" ways are, in fact, inflexible, nonadaptive, and hence neither free nor natural. In this portrayal, Amis comments on a major trend of modern thought and art, the preference for the simplicities of a preindustrial past over the present. He makes Welch and his circle precise examples of what they supposedly detest above all else, mechanization, and locates what they value, freedom and naturalness, in the enemy camp. The strategy is effective, and it suggests that morality is a matter not of time and place but of humans, not of theory but of practice, and not of doctrine but of instinct.

Naturalness and freedom are problematic for Jim and Christine, but in a different way. Both of them—Jim in particular—expend considerable energy trying to live up to the Welches and what they represent. Their failure to do so, and the fact that they are naturally resistant to mechanization, is the source of both a different, unsatirical humor and their salvation. Jim wants to get away from Margaret and go to London. Instead, he tries to regulate his smoking, put on the face his superiors expect of him, talk as if he were a Cambridge don, and get along with Margaret; he tries but cannot, and his failures are magnificently funny. They lead to trouble, which leads him to discover what he really wants and therefore leads him away from the automatization. Special emphasis is placed on his speech, his face, and his laughter. In his Merrie Old England lecture, Jim begins by trying to assume the ideas and gestures that he thinks, correctly, Welch expects of him; these, however, detach themselves from him, and he ends the lecture speaking for himself.

A spectrum of characters inhabit the novel, arranged according to the degree to which they have become mechanized in speech, gesture, and attitude—and, perhaps more important, the degree to which the mechanization is separable from their existences as human beings. Welch has become a thing; his mechanized gestures have totally usurped his being. Jim Dixon is also mechanical at times and is trying hard to be more so, but his automatic gestures are merely encrustations, clearly separable from and finally the victims of his human self.

Further Reading

Amis, Martin. *Experience*. New York: Talk/Miramax Books, 2000. Kingsley's son Martin Amis, a highly regarded novelist in his own right, discusses his relationship with his father and the crises in his father's life.

Bell, Robert H., ed. *Critical Essays on Kingsley Amis*. New York: G. K. Hall, 1998. Collection of new and reprinted essays examines various aspects of Amis's work. Includes discussion of *Lucky Jim*.

Bradford, Richard. *Kingsley Amis*. London: Edward Arnold, 1989. Brief but incisive volume argues that most critics have failed to grasp the complex nature and intentions of Amis's work. Concludes by labeling him a "comic misfit" inspired by the novelist and essayist G. K. Chesterton and the poet A. E. Housman.

_____. *Lucky Him: The Life of Kingsley Amis*. London: Peter Owen, 2001. Examines the relationship of Amis's writing to his life. Demonstrates how the theme of all of Amis's novels is the tension between what one wants to do and what one ought to do, and how that conflict "energizes [one's] style."

Laskowski, William. *Kingsley Amis*. New York: Twayne, 1998. Stresses Amis's overall accomplishment as a man of letters. Divides his output into letters, genre fiction, and mainstream novels and devotes equal consideration to each category.

Leader, Zachary. *The Life of Kingsley Amis*. New York: Pantheon Books, 2007. Voluminous, engrossing biography pays equal attention to discussion and analysis of Amis's literary output. Draws on unpublished works, correspondence, and interviews with many of Amis's friends, relatives, fellow writers, students, and colleagues.

McDermott, John. *Kingsley Amis: An English Moralist*. New York: St. Martin's Press, 1989. Important study emphasizes not only the moral seriousness of Amis's work but also its generally underrated intellectual and aesthetic range. Examines why *Lucky Jim* was so successful upon publication and why it remains popular.

Moseley, Merritt. *Understanding Kingsley Amis*. Columbia: University of South Carolina Press, 1993. Provides a basic, accessible survey of Amis's work. Describes *Lucky Jim* as "one of the key books of the English 1950's" and places it within the context of Amis's subsequent fiction.

Salwak, Dale. *Kingsley Amis: Modern Novelist*. New York: Harvester Wheatsheaf, 1992. Extended, sympathetic biographical and critical study was written with Amis's assistance. Considers *Lucky Jim* independently and in the context of Amis's subsequent development, particularly in relation to his dark later novel *Jake's Thing* (1978). Asserts that Dixon is appealing because his adventures allow readers to "break free from well-ordered, sensible lives."

Shaffer, Brian W. "Kingsley Amis's *Lucky Jim* (1954)." In *Reading the Novel in English, 1950-2000*. Malden, Mass.: Blackwell, 2006. Analysis of *Lucky Jim* is part of a collection of critical essays on ten English-language novels published in the second half of the twentieth century. Intended for students and general readers.

The Lusiads

Author: Luis de Camões (c. 1524-1580)
First published: Os Lusíadas, 1572 (English translation, 1655)
Type of work: Poetry
Type of plot: Epic
Time of plot: Fifteenth century
Locale: Africa, India, Oceana

Principal characters:
VASCO DA GAMA
MONSAIDE, an Indian Muslim
KING OF CALICUT
VENUS, a goddess favoring the Portuguese
BACCHUS, a god opposing the Portuguese

The Poem:

Portuguese explorer Vasco da Gama's ships are off the coast of east Africa, while at a council of the gods on Olympus in Greece, Bacchus speaks against the Portuguese and Venus speaks for them. Mars intervenes passionately on Venus's side. Jupiter states his support of the voyage. Bacchus, failing to persuade the gods, inspires the inhabitants of Mozambique to set a trap. The Muslim peoples there are easily defeated, and da Gama sails on to Mombasa, an island he has heard will be friendlier.

At Mombasa, Bacchus again inspires the locals to attempt a trap by taking da Gama's ships, but Venus and her nymphs hold back his ships. Venus approaches Jupiter seductively and nearly naked to plead the Portuguese case. Jupiter reassures her and promises a great future for Portuguese exploration and conquest. She then sends Mercury to Malinda to arrange a friendlier welcome for da Gama. The king of Malinda visits da Gama on his ship and asks the explorer about his country.

Da Gama, before sailing to Africa, had set out from Portugal. His course takes his ships south past Morocco, Madeira, the Canaries, the Congo, and other points along the coast. The ships sail past unfamiliar sights: the Southern Cross, a huge waterspout, and St. Elmo's fire. At the Cape of Good Hope, the ships are confronted by a huge and monstrous being that angrily predicts future storms and shipwrecks for any so bold as to pass the cape. The beast identifies itself as the titan Adamaster, led by his love of the Nereid Thetis to join the titans in their war against Jupiter.

Da Gama's ships pass the cape in the face of hostile currents. The have several encounters with primitive peoples, as they anchor to scrape the ships' keels. The crews have a bout with scurvy before arriving at Mozambique and Mombasa and finally at Malinda.

The Portuguese, after a lavish party, set off again. Bacchus visits Neptune's underwater palace and convenes the gods and goddesses of the sea, then fires them up over the arrogance of the human trespassers in their realm. Neptune summons Aeolus, god of the winds. Meanwhile, the men on watch are entertained with the story of the Twelve of England, twelve Portuguese knights who go to England to defend the honor of twelve noble ladies. As he is finishing, Aeolus's winds strike the fleet and nearly sink it. Venus arrives with her nymphs, who seduce the various winds. As day breaks, the sea is calm again, and India is within sight.

A geographical survey of India is ordered, and da Gama sends men ashore. They soon meet a Barbary Muslim, Monsaide, who speaks Spanish. He invites them to his home and tells them of the history and customs of India. The king of Calicut gives da Gama permission to come ashore. Da Gama visits the palace, disapproves to the idols, and admires a series of wall paintings telling of India's history. Da Gama offers the king a commercial treaty, so the king visits da Gama's ship.

Meanwhile, Bacchus in another form appears in a dream to a Muslim priest, who persuades other Muslim leaders to spread the word against the Portuguese. The king summons da Gama to answer their accusations, which he does successfully. The Muslims next refuse to let him return to his ship and try to lure his fleet into port so they can attack it. Da Gama, however, plays on their greed and finally manages to get back to his ship.

Da Gama learns from his Barbary friend, now converted to Christianity, that the Muslims want to keep the Portuguese ships in port until a large, well-armed fleet arrives from Mecca. Da Gama takes his factors and goods on board and sets sail for home. Venus, to reward their exploits, summons Cupid and creates an island paradise stocked with nymphs. The mariners stop to take on water, discover the nymphs, and have a day-long romp.

A lavish banquet is held on the island. One of the nymphs gives a detailed prophecy of Portugal's future triumphs in India. Another nymph takes da Gama to an enchanted mountaintop and shows him a small and hovering model of the cosmos, explains its workings, points out the earth and its continents, and describes their various inhabitants. The fleet, nymphs and all, returns to Portugal, which has seen a decline of its warlike spirit. King Sebastian is exhorted to support explorers and colonizers and to listen only to the wise and experienced.

Critical Evaluation:

The Lusiads is a literary epic that one approaches with certain expectations. The literary epic is a form created by the Roman poet Vergil in his *Aeneid*, based on Homer's *Iliad* (c. 750 B.C.E.; English translation, 1611) and *Odyssey* (c. 725 B.C.E.; English translation, 1614) and similar works. Readers can expect the epic to include a statement of theme, an invocation of the muse, battles, a catalog of ships or some equivalent catalog, a trip to the underworld, a warrior-hero, and the "divine machinery," that is, the Greek or Roman gods interfering in the action. Most of these elements, especially the gods, comprise *The Lusiads*, though their presence is a little disconcerting in a work so insistently Christian.

Luis de Camōes, however, in his invocation, promises a new and loftier conception of valor than in the old epics whose day has passed. It is a rather bold move to transport the Vergilian epic wholesale into the modern world. He does leave out a few of the expected elements and supplies some genuinely original scenes. The *Aeneid* (c. 29-19 B.C.E.; English translation, 1553), however, remains the primary model, though readers will notice also the influence of Ludovico Ariosto's *Orlando furioso* (1516, 1521, 1532; English translation, 1591) in the *ottava rima* stanza form and in the emphasis on love, sometimes bordering on the erotic. Even when the sailors are promised a story of heroism rather than of love in hearing the tale of The Twelve of England, the story turns out to be a rather romantic tale.

Camōes does not "update" the element of interfering gods. The gods belong to the ancient world, and they always seem a little out of place in so alien a setting. Even in Homer and Vergil their interference in the action seems almost irrelevant, as a nearly omnipotent Zeus/Jupiter can always overrule them. However, adding a Christian God with power even beyond that of Jupiter makes the gods almost trivial. Their motives remain unconvincing. Bacchus is connected mythically with the founding of Portugal, but he opposes Portuguese adventure for the negligible reason that he does not want them to rival him as an explorer of Asia. Venus appears to have been chosen by Camōes as the patron of the Portuguese for her sex appeal rather than for any symbolic or mythological reason.

What Vergil does subtly, Camōes carries to the extreme. One of Vergil's great triumphs as an epic poet is his artful incorporation of history, extending both back and forward from the story. All of canto 3 and most of canto 4 of *The Lusiads* are devoted to an account of Portuguese history— only one, though the longest, of such surveys. The poems also has a survey of the history of India.

Camōes is not a dramatic writer in the sense that Homer is. Scenes are summarized rather than dramatized. When people do talk they often deliver long, rhetorical set-pieces that are more like essays than dialogue. He does slightly better with the gods than with the humans. Typical is the council of gods in canto 1, in which Jupiter gives a long speech favorable to the Portuguese, Bacchus speaks against them, and Venus for them. Both speeches, though, are merely summarized by Camōes. Mars follows with an impassioned speech for the Portuguese, but the effect of this speech is blunted by the lack of any real interchange among the characters. This is, however, closer to drama than many others by the simple fact that there are two complete speeches.

The poem has a few truly memorable scenes. One is Venus's seductive appeal to Jupiter in canto 2. This scene faintly echoes Thetis's appeal to Zeus in book 2 of the *Iliad*, but the erotic undertone, along with the uncomfortable fact that she is Jupiter's daughter, undercuts any sense of epic dignity. Similarly memorable and disconcerting is Venus stopping da Gama's ship by pushing it back with her breasts. It is more difficult to recall any truly vivid scene involving only humans.

Camōes does not seem to favor narration and dialogue. If one subtracts from the poem the historical and geographical surveys, the invocations to the muses, the passages addressed to King Sebastian, and the verse essays on various vices and virtues, only about half the poem remains as story; even this is made less by long essayistic speeches, other stories embedded in the narrative, and extended similes. Thus, the poem contains not much story, and what story there is leads to an anticlimax. Da Gama, after being in Calicut for some time, discovers that the local Muslims are plotting his destruction and so leaves India quickly and quietly without having achieved any clear agreement with the region's ruler.

At this point the author faces a problem. The quest is over without a climax, and nothing remains but the return voyage. Camões's solution is Venus's island paradise, which does provide variety, color, and sex appeal; so large an intrusion of fantasy into a realistic voyage, however, is artistically questionable.

Considered in isolation, the most satisfactory part of *The Lusiads* is the historical survey in cantos 2 and 3. Despite its long digression, its energy and economy make it highly readable. A national epic is, by definition, a patriotic work, but no other epic so continuously celebrates its nation and its nation's history.

During the seventeenth and eighteenth centuries, when the literary epic in the Vergilian manner was in favor with the educated reader, and when a detailed knowledge of Greek and Roman mythology was an essential part of literary language, *The Lusiads* was generally popular and admired throughout Europe. Modern readers, less disposed toward the form, are less likely to read *The Lusiads*, and if they do, they are less likely to overlook its structural weaknesses.

Jack Hart

Further Reading

Bloom, Harold. *Genius: A Mosaic of One Hundred Exemplary Creative Minds.* New York: Warner Books, 2002. A major voice in contemporary criticism and critical theory evaluates *The Lusiads* and places the work in the context of the Western literary tradition.

Camões, Luis de. *The Collected Lyric Poems of Luis de Camões.* Translated by Landeg White. Princeton, N.J.: Princeton University Press, 2008. This collection, which gathers Camões's lyric poems, provides another perspective on some of the poet's characteristic preoccupations and themes, as well as the aesthetic tastes of his age.

Hart, Henry H. *Luis de Camões and the Epic of "The Lusiads."* Norman: University of Oklahoma Press, 1962. This older but still-useful work contains the first full biography of Camões in English as well as a good discussion of the poem.

Montiero, George. *The Presence of Camões: Influence on the Literature of England, America, and Southern Africa.* Lexington: University of Kentucky Press, 1996. This study covers a surprisingly large and divergent number of major writers from England, southern Africa, and the United States.

Rajan, Balachandra. *Under Western Eyes: India From Milton to Macaulay.* Durham, N.C.: Duke University Press, 1999. Although this work is focused more on the English than the Portuguese, it gives a good sense of the colonial context of the times, with some reference to da Gama and *The Lusiads.*

The Lute

Author: Gao Ming (c. 1303-c. 1370)
First produced: Pipa ji, c. 1367; first published, c. 1367
    (English translation, 1980)
Type of work: Drama
Type of plot: Opera
Time of plot: c. 200
Locale: Honan Province, China

Principal characters:
TS'AI JUNG, a young scholar
CHAO WU-NIANG, his wife
CHANG, a neighbor of Ts'ai Jung's family
THE HONORABLE MR. NIU, the prime minister
MISS NIU, his daughter

The Story:

Ts'ai Jung has been married for only two months when the local government recommends him as a candidate for the Imperial Examination. His father insists that the young scholar make the trip to the capital for the examination, as it will give him an opportunity to distinguish himself and bring honor to his family. Ts'ai himself would rather stay home and fulfill his duties as a son, but, fearing that his unwillingness to leave his parents, who are infirm with age, will be interpreted as selfish love for his wife, Ts'ai reluctantly departs. Before he goes, he entrusts his family to the care of his neighbor Chang, an old man.

Ts'ai easily wins first place in the examination, and the emperor takes such a fancy to the young scholar that he orders him to be married to the daughter of Mr. Niu, the prime minister. The imperial order comes as a happy solution to the prime minister; he has a problem in his daughter, who has sworn never to marry unless the man is a genius who has passed first in the Imperial Examination. Here, at last, is a young man who meets the requirement; consequently, no one pays attention to Ts'ai's protestations that he already has a wife and that his only ambition is to serve his parents. He is married a second time, against his wishes, and further restrictions are imposed on his freedom when he is ordered to live in the prime minister's house.

Ts'ai's second wife is as intelligent and sympathetic as she is beautiful, and she can see that her husband is unhappy in his new surroundings. He loves her, but he is also homesick. He has no knowledge that Ch'en-liu, his home district, has been stricken with famine, nor does he know what a strain it is for his first wife, Chao Wu-niang, to support his parents during this terrible time. She sells her clothes and jewels to save the aged couple from starvation, while she herself lives on chaff. Their neighbor Chang also shares with them whatever rice he has.

No word comes from Ts'ai. When Ts'ai's mother succumbs to sorrow, hunger, and disease, Chang lends the family the money to buy a coffin. When Ts'ai's father dies a short time later, Chao Wu-niang does not want to trouble the kind neighbor for another loan, so she cuts off her long hair and tries to get a little money from its sale. Before she can find a buyer, however, Chang discovers what she is doing and buys another coffin for her. Because she cannot hire a gravedigger, she tries to dig a grave with her own hands. At last she falls asleep from fatigue, her fingers bleeding from her hard labor. While she sleeps, spirits come to finish the grave for her. Then, carrying a *pi-pa* (an instrument like a guitar) and a portrait of Ts'ai's deceased parents that she has made, which she exhibits while begging for alms, she sets out for the capital in search of her husband.

Ts'ai has never for a moment forgotten his parents and first wife. He is duped when a swindler arrives with invented news from his family. Relieved to hear that they are all well and safe, Ts'ai asks the same man to deliver a letter to his parents, together with gold and pearls. The villain takes the valuables and disappears.

After a long period of anxious waiting, Ts'ai decides to go and see for himself how his family is faring. He has the wholehearted support of his second wife, who intends to go with him to perform daughterly duties for his parents. The prime minister refuses to grant them permission to go, however; he wants to keep his daughter and son-in-law close to him. His daughter keeps pestering him with supplications, and he finally agrees to send a servant to Ch'en-liu to bring Ts'ai's parents and first wife to the capital, where they will live in his house as guests.

One day, Chao Wu-niang comes upon a temple where a special ceremony is being celebrated. She has arrived in the capital, but she does not wish to see her husband until she is sure that he has not hardened his heart against her. She plays the *pi-pa* and sings a song about the virtue of filial piety, but the pilgrims and worshipers at the temple are not as generous in giving alms as she had expected. After she hangs up the portrait and begins to say prayers for her husband's deceased parents, Ts'ai appears to pray for his parents, whom he believes to be on their way to the capital. Chao Wu-niang immediately leaves the temple. Ts'ai fails to see her, but he finds the portrait and takes it home with him.

The prime minister's daughter, in anticipation of the arrival of her parents-in-law, is looking for an intelligent woman to serve as a maid for the old couple. Chao Wu-niang applies for the position and wins the sympathy of the young mistress with her story of suffering and the purpose of her journey to the capital. Chao Wu-niang uses an anagram for her husband's name, but the other woman cannot fail to see who the unfortunate woman really is. She immediately addresses Chao Wu-niang as sister, and together the two devise a stratagem to test Ts'ai's heart.

The portrait that Chao Wu-niang left in the temple is now hanging in Ts'ai's study. On the back of the picture is a poem that Chao Wu-niang has written, in which she criticizes, in a loving tone, her husband's conduct. Ts'ai has not looked carefully at the picture, nor does he know that a servant has hung it up. Now, returning from his office, he sees it again. The two faces in the picture bear a strange resemblance to his parents, but he is puzzled by their emaciated and ragged looks. Then he discovers the poem, apparently a satire at his expense. His first reaction is anger. He asks his wife whether she has any knowledge of the person who ventured into his study and scribbled an unjust attack on him. Chao Wu-niang is summoned, and the whole story is told.

The prime minister is finally won over, and Ts'ai takes his two wives to Ch'en-liu to worship at his parents' graves. All three are honored by the emperor as examples of virtuous conduct. The happiest man on the scene is the neighbor Chang, who derives more satisfaction from the reunion of

Ts'ai's family than he does from the material rewards he now receives.

Critical Evaluation:

The Lute is Gao Ming's only surviving opera. It is also the only southern *ch'uan-ch'i* ("telling of the remarkable") of the Yüan period (1271-1368) to be declared worthy of the highest praise. This judgment was rendered by none other than Hongwu (Chu Yüan-chang), who became the founder and emperor of the Ming Dynasty (1368-1644). Other qualified persons have supported this view, although some have disagreed, expressing dissatisfaction with the work's diction and lack of modal harmony. These judgments may be questioned, but there is no mistaking the flaws in the plot: the parents' ignorance of their son's success and marriage and his failure to recognize the forgery of his father's calligraphy when the swindler presents the faked letter to him.

The title of Gao's opera includes a word for a stringed instrument called the *pi-pa*. This term has been translated into English as "guitar" or "lute." Although the Western guitar is a member of the lute family, neither of these terms is exactly correct, as the Chinese *pi-pa* is not really like either instrument. It has a shallow, pear-shaped body, a short fretted neck, and only four strings, whereas a guitar has a deep body shaped something like an hourglass, a long neck, and six strings. The *pi-pa* is meant to be emblematic of the hardships and the sufferings of Ts'ai's first wife, Chao Wu-niang, during her journey to the capital to rejoin her husband. She is obliged to sing to the accompaniment of her *pi-pa* to obtain food and lodging. For her to walk such a long distance unchaperoned requires remarkable courage.

The Western theater typically classifies dramas as tragedies, comedies, and tragicomedies, but the Chinese theater has no such categories. A didactic theater, the Chinese opera deals largely with kinds of persons: saintly immortals, filial sons, chaste wives, obedient grandsons, young scholars, young beauties, wise judges, martial knights, and so on. In Western terms *The Lute* is a tragicomedy, as the main line of the action is tragic but the story nevertheless ends happily, like a comedy. From the Chinese point of view, the story is a moral fable and an exemplum of filial piety, neighborliness, ancestor worship, scholarly ambition, government service, class conflict, political power, polygyny without jealousy, married love, separation, suffering, death, heroic courage, reunion, and harmony, all according to Confucian ethics.

In the Chinese view, filial piety stems from the concept of *li*, or ceremony. It includes not merely acts but also, above all, motives and intentions, as measured by the rules of propriety, from which genuine etiquette and politeness come. According to ancient texts, filial piety is the root of all virtue and that from which all teaching comes. The path of filial piety leads to ancestor worship, which comes into play with the deaths of family members and includes such elements as the painting of funeral portraits, burial ceremonies, and the display of ancestral tablets. On certain occasions the living pay homage to the dead by displaying their tablets and funeral portraits, by offering prayers to their spirits, and by making offerings of food and paper money.

One of the most important goals of the ancient Chinese was to lead a life that would glorify and honor one's parents while avoiding any action that might shame them. For the son of living parents, one way of assuring the former would be to become an advanced scholar by competing successfully in the government civil service examinations. This would typically lead to an important official post. Parents who had a son who had become an advanced scholar would advertise the fact by setting up a double flagpole in front of their door. All of the complexity of the theme of filial piety is clearly and suspensefully developed in Gao's great work.

"Critical Evaluation" by Richard P. Benton

Further Reading

Birch, Cyril. "Some Concerns and Methods of the Ming *Ch'uan-ch'i* Drama." In *Studies in Chinese Literary Genres*, edited by Cyril Birch. Berkeley: University of California Press, 1974. Provides background information on the southern drama of the Ming Dynasty.

_____. "Tragedy and Melodrama in Early *Ch'uan-ch'i* Plays: *Lute Song* and *Thorn Hairpin* Compared." *Bulletin of the School of Oriental Studies* 36 (1973): 228-247. Scholarly essay discusses *The Lute* in relation to the genre of which it is a part.

Crump, James I. *Chinese Theater in the Days of Kublai Khan*. 1980. Reprint. Ann Arbor: Center for Chinese Studies, University of Michigan, 1990. Describes the social milieu and the conditions and methods of theatrical performances in thirteenth and fourteenth century China. Presents three plays of the Yüan period in English translations of unusual quality.

Dolby, William. *A History of Chinese Drama*. New York: Barnes & Noble, 1976. Presents a full survey of the history of Chinese drama and includes an English translation of a scene from *The Lute*.

Du Wenwei. "Historicity and Contemporaneity: Adaptations of Yuan Plays in the 1990's." *Asian Theatre Journal* 18, no. 2 (Fall, 2001): 222-237. Discusses *The Lute* and other Yüan plays produced in China in the 1990's, focusing on how these adaptations strove to be faithful to the originals while making the ancient themes relevant to present-day audiences.

Gao Ming. *The Lute: Kao Ming's P'i-p'a chi.* Translated by Jean Mulligan. 1980. Reprint. New York: Columbia University Press, 1999. Outstanding English translation of the work includes all the songs and stage directions in En-glish as well as the text of the speeches. Identifies those speeches that in the Chinese text are in parallel prose or poetic meter.

Wang Jian-ping. *Pi pa ji = The Story of the Lute.* Translated by Paul White. Beijing: New World Press, 1999. English translation of Wang's narrative version of Gao Ming's play offers another approach to the work.

Lycidas

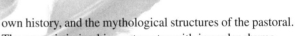

Author: John Milton (1608-1674)
First published: 1638
Type of work: Poetry
Type of plot: Pastoral elegy

John Milton wrote "Lycidas," considered the greatest poem of its type in English, near the start of his literary career, when he was invited to contribute to *Justa Edouardo King* (1638), a volume of poems commemorating Edward King (called "Lycidas" in the poem), whom he had known as a classmate at Cambridge University. King had drowned while traveling on the Irish Sea. The two had not been close friends, and Milton chose the formal structures of the pastoral elegy not only to honor King but also to examine issues that concerned Milton himself as he sought to make a life in poetry.

The traditional elements of the pastoral elegy were familiar to Milton, who had studied classical literature. These conventions include treating the speaker and his subject as if they were shepherds (pastor in Latin), invoking the Muse of poetry, rehearsing the history of the friendship being celebrated, questioning the fate that allowed the death to occur, describing a procession of mourners and flowers being strewn on the corpse in preparation for burial, and providing a consolation for the loss of one's friend. Milton uses all of these conventions, but he adapts them to make them appropriate to his particular purpose.

The pastoral has roots in Greek classics, but in "Lycidas" Milton is concerned with explicitly Christian subjects: the death of a man preparing for the ministry, Milton's future as a poet, and the state of the Christian Church in England (Milton was writing as a staunch Puritan on the eve of the English Civil War). Thus, Milton uses water as a unifying image that draws together the Christian elements, King's own history, and the mythological structures of the pastoral. The poem is in iambic pentameter with irregular rhyme.

The first twenty-two lines of "Lycidas" introduce Milton as a shepherd who uses a water metaphor to call on the Muses ("sisters of the sacred well") for inspiration as he sings a dirge for Lycidas. Throughout the poem, Milton employs the pastoral tradition of using song to represent poetry. Lines 23 through 36 describe his friendship with Edward King. The two young men are portrayed as fellow shepherds, tending their flocks and competing in songmaking. (Like the sheep, the "oaten flutes" of the poem are a traditional element of pastorals.) Presumably this passage represents the two men's time together as Cambridge students; thus, the "old Damoetas" who listens to their songs is usually taken to represent one of their teachers.

Lines 37 through 63 express the mourner's protest over the injustice of the young man's death. Again, Milton uses a wide range of water images and allusions. He asks the nymphs—mythological deities who inhabit woods, pools, and streams—why they failed to protect Lycidas, and he imagines that they were not watching from the Celtic island of Mona in the Irish Sea (appropriate because King drowned in that sea) or the river Deva (or Dee), which flows into the Irish Sea from Cheshire. The speaker then chides himself for being foolish, knowing that even the Muse—who was mother of the mythical Orpheus, the most skilled poet ever—was unable to protect her son when he was torn into bits by the wine-maddened Bacchantes and thrown into the river Hebrus.

At this point, the focus of the poem shifts to the first of Milton's personal concerns. Beginning in line 64, he uses the pastoral metaphor of the shepherd to ask whether there is any point in working to become a poet. Perhaps it would be more enjoyable to court shepherdesses as other shepherds do. He considers the justification that poets may win the fame for which they long, but he sees fame as an unworthy goal (the "last infirmity of noble mind") and asserts that, even if it were worthy, a poet's efforts to secure fame may seem pointless in the light of the possibility of an early death. In response to his questions, Phoebus Apollo, the patron god of poetry, speaks to the poet and explains that real fame is meted out appropriately by God (Jove) in heaven, where all poets will receive whatever they deserve.

In line 85, Milton begins to describe a procession of mourners; again, he employs a wealth of water imagery. He addresses Arethusa and Mincius, a fountain and river associated with the pastoral in classical literature. Milton then introduces Neptune, god of the sea, who asks how the tragic drowning of Lycidas happened. Next comes Camus, god of the river Cam, which flows through Cambridge. The last mourner is "the pilot of the Galilean lake"—that is, Saint Peter, recognizable by his miter (the pointed headgear of a bishop) and the keys to heaven that he carries. Milton's description recalls Peter's association with water (Peter was fishing on Galilee when Jesus called him) and at the same time allows Milton to avoid a jarring mixture of Christian and mythological names.

Saint Peter mourns the loss of King as a young, Christian minister, but Milton has a larger concern as well, which he voices in Saint Peter's words. As a Puritan, Milton feels that the Church of England is served by unworthy priests (unlike King) who are more interested in self-advancement than in being shepherds to their parishioners. Here, the pastoral serves Milton especially well, since "pastor," shepherd, is often a title for ministers. Peter's impassioned outburst against these faithless shepherds pictures them pushing worthy guests away from the shepherds' feast, ignorant of the basics of their vocations, unable even to hold a shepherd's crook (the staff that bishops carry is shaped like that herding tool). Such worthless shepherds ("blind mouths," Milton calls them) allow their sheep to sicken or to be stolen by wolves (an allusion that is usually understood to refer to the Roman Catholic Church). This climax of the poem concludes with Peter's ambiguous warning that a "two-handed engine" stands ready to avenge these abuses.

Beginning in line 132, Milton moderates his tone and calls on nature for flowers to decorate the funeral bier. There was no actual bier, because King's body was lost at sea, but Milton hopes to "interpose a little ease" by comforting readers with this imaginary scene (a "false surmise," he calls it). By line 155, however, the reality of King's death is reestablished. Milton suggests the many watery places the body may rest, ranging from the Hebrides in the north to St. Michael's Mount in Cornwall in the south. He urges the angel associated with the Mount to "look homeward" and urges dolphins to send King's body to land.

Lines 165 through 185 name the consolation to be found in King's death. He is no more dead than is the Sun, which daily seems to sink beneath the sea but rises anew each morning. Lycidas, too, has risen "through the dear might of him that walked the waves." That is, he has eternal life in heaven through the power of Christ (who walked the waves). Milton pictures Lycidas near heaven's rivers, where he hears heaven's hymns of joy. In a secondary way, Lycidas has also become a spirit of the shore, guarding all sea travelers.

The last eight lines of the poem return the reader to the poem's initial picture of the shepherd, who has now completed his elegy. He looks across the "western bay" at the sunset, gathers his cloak around him, and sets out for "fresh woods and pastures new," lines that suggest Milton's commitment to the next part of the life in poetry that he is claiming for himself. "Lycidas" is a remarkable poem in many ways, particularly in Milton's skillful adaptation of the conventions of the pastoral elegy for the double purpose of commemorating the death of Edward King and, more significant for later readers, expressing Milton's concerns about his calling as a poet and the state of faith in England.

Ann D. Garbett

Further Reading

Abrams, M. H. "Five Types of 'Lycidas.'" In *Milton's "Lycidas": The Tradition and the Poem*. Columbia: University of Missouri Press, 1983. Surveys critical analyses of "Lycidas" ranging from New Criticism to archetype analysis.

Boesky, Amy. "The Maternal Shape of Mourning: A Reconsideration of 'Lycidas.'" *Modern Philology* 95, no. 4 (May, 1998): 463. Examines feminine and maternal images in the poem, connecting them to events in the poet's life.

Miller, David. "Death the Gateway to Life: 'Lycidas.'" In *John Milton: Poetry*. Twayne's English Authors 242. Boston: Twayne, 1978. A detailed and careful close reading of the poem.

Post, Jonathan F. S. "Helpful Contraries: Carew's 'Donne' and Milton's 'Lycidas.'" *George Herbert Journal* 29, nos. 1/2 (Fall, 2003): 76. Argues that Thomas Carew's elegy to

John Donne influenced Milton's very different elegy to Edward King.

Shohet, Lauren. "Subjects and Objects in 'Lycidas.'" *Texas Studies in Literature and Language* 47, no. 2 (Summer, 2005): 101. Argues that "Lycidas" uses two modes of poetic subjectivity—a human voice and a set of utterances attributed to nonhuman things. The two modes create an element of asymmetry in the poem.

Womack, Mark. "On the Value of 'Lycidas.'" *Studies in English Literature, 1500-1900* 37, no. 1 (Winter, 1997): 119. An examination of how "Lycidas" has earned its exalted reputation in English literature.

Lyrical Ballads

Authors: William Wordsworth (1770-1850) and Samuel Taylor Coleridge (1772-1834)
First published: 1798; expanded as *Lyrical Ballads, with Other Poems,* 1800
Type of work: Poetry

William Wordsworth and Samuel Taylor Coleridge's *Lyrical Ballads* first appeared in 1798 and was expanded in 1800. The 1800 edition includes new poems and Wordsworth's now-famous "Preface." *Lyrical Ballads* contains some of the early treatments of subjects and themes by Wordsworth and Coleridge that would occupy the bulk of each poet's oeuvre. These subjects and themes include the relationship between humanity and nature, the psychology of the human heart, the fascination with the supernatural, and the sympathetic presentation of the plight of old hunters, insane mothers, and the victims of England's various wars abroad.

Lyrical Ballads, especially the 1798 version, has long been regarded as a major influence on the poetry of the Romantic period in England. Many consider its influence to have been not unlike that of Edmund Spenser's *The Shepheardes Calendar* (1579) on Elizabethan poetry or T. S. Eliot's *Prufrock, and Other Observations* (1917) on modern poetry. The 1798 edition of *Lyrical Ballads* contains twenty-three poems, most famous among them Wordsworth's "Tintern Abbey" and Coleridge's only major contribution to the volume, "The Rime of the Ancient Mariner." Both poems explore one man's difficult attempts to understand who he is in relation to the natural world. Other well-known poems from 1798 are lyrical ballads: "Simon Lee, the Old Huntsman," "The Thorn," "Goody Blake and Harry Gill," and "The Idiot Boy." Poems that are not lyrical ballads include "Tintern Abbey," "Expostulation and Reply," and "The Tables Turned."

The second volume of *Lyrical Ballads* (1800) comprises new poems—almost all of them by Wordsworth—while the first volume essentially reprints the poems of 1798. Among the well-known works in the second volume is Wordsworth's great pastoral poem "Michael." The volume also includes the enigmatic Lucy poems as well as "Hart-Leap Well," "The Brothers," "There Was a Boy," "Nutting," and "The Old Cumberland Beggar."

Initially, *Lyrical Ballads* was seen as a welcome break from eighteenth century poetry, which—dominated by class bias and the concept of poetic diction—was far removed from the language of everyday speech. However, in the 1950's, examinations of English poetry published in the 1790's revealed that, in terms of language and subjects, *Lyrical Ballads* was hardly groundbreaking. Later analyses argued that the collection was a reaction, but not against the poetry of the earlier eighteenth century; the collection was a reaction against the poetry written in the latter half of the eighteenth century—the poetry produced in what is now known as the age of sensibility. The originality of *Lyrical Ballads* is now believed to lie in the attempt to anatomize, as well as subvert, the approach to both life and literature espoused by the adherents of sensibility.

Sensibility was a late eighteenth century shift from using reason in matters of ethics and perception to relying instead on one's artistic and benevolent feelings. Its focus on benevolence encouraged its followers to consider the plight of the less fortunate, like the poor, slaves, and women—in other words, the agenda of various radical movements of the day. Such an approach to life, though supported by the radical Wordsworth and Coleridge, could easily lead to sentimentality and mawkishness. It was this kind of simple-minded, extreme behavior that the two poets "attacked" in 1798.

An obvious influence on *Lyrical Ballads* was the increasing popularity of the ballad form in the latter half of the eighteenth century. The major impetus was Thomas Percy's *Reliques of Ancient English Poetry* (1765), a collection of English and Scottish folk ballads. The ballad's popularity not only led to imitations of ballads written and published by late eighteenth century poets but also to a tendency to call poems of any species "ballads," just to take advantage of the form's popularity.

True ballads have their origins in folk tradition, though their influence on literate culture has been considerable. *Lyrical Ballads* is a prime example of this influence. The focus in a traditional ballad is on a single narrative, and the action is centered primarily on the climax of the story. Character traits and motivation are underplayed if not absent altogether. Though not the only stanzaic form found in ballads, the ballad stanza is the most common. It consists of four lines, the first and third having eight syllables, the second and fourth only six. The rhyme scheme is usually *abcb*. This is the stanza form used in "The Rime of the Ancient Mariner" as well as other poems in *Lyrical Ballads*.

What, then, is a lyrical ballad? First, it is a literary ballad rather than a folk ballad. It is a poem composed in a literate culture by a professional poet. In *Lyrical Ballads*, the term "lyrical" appears to refer to the experimental nature of some of the poems in the volume, a claim made in the "Advertisement" of the 1798 edition and developed in more detail in the "Preface" affixed to later editions. The term appears to indicate some significant changes that Wordsworth and Coleridge made to the traditional form. For example, there is a concern—implied or expressed—in the poems themselves, about how they should be read ("Simon Lee, the Old Huntsman" is a prime example). In some of the poems (like Wordsworth's "The Thorn"), the first-person-narrator point of view is of great interest. More attention also is paid to the quality that is slighted in the folk ballad, a focus on individual characters' motives, mental states, and so forth.

Wordsworth's "Preface" to the 1800 edition of *Lyrical Ballads* replaced the short "Advertisement" of the 1798 edition. This preface was later revised to include Wordsworth's observations on diction, the "Appendix" of 1802. The "Advertisement" (1798) claims that the "majority of the following are to be considered as experiments," which use "the language of conversation in the middle and lower classes of society" as opposed to the "gaudiness and inane phraseology" of poetic diction. The "Preface" has two major aims. The first aim is to explain the claims of originality made for the poems of *Lyrical Ballads* in the "Advertisement." Along with his defense of the use of "common" language, Wordsworth also staunchly defends the use of the lower ranks of society as subjects, claiming that in the common people one finds the universal passions of the human heart in a pure, untainted, state.

The second aim of the "Preface" is to deal with the crucial issue of how poetry that proposes to treat common life realistically—as Wordsworth claims his does—can employ the "unrealistic" poetic devices of rhyme and regular metrical patterns. Essentially, Wordsworth's defense is that the pleasure that his poetry gives, in part because of the use of meter and rhyme, is faithful to the human experience. Therefore, he says, his poetry is realistic.

The "Preface" also contains some of Wordsworth's well-known pronouncements on poetry and the poet: A poet is "a man speaking to men," the language used in poetry does not differ from that used in prose, and poetry is "the spontaneous overflow of powerful feelings," the result of "emotion recollected in tranquility."

George F. Horneker

Further Reading

Ashton, Rosemary. *The Life of Samuel Taylor Coleridge.* Malden, Mass.: Blackwell, 1996. An excellent one-volume biography as well as an examination of Coleridge's poetic achievements. Part of the Blackwell Critical Biographies series.

Bate, Walter Jackson. *Coleridge.* New York: Macmillan, 1968. Though dated, this brief study remains a classic in its field and one of the best introductions to Coleridge's life and literary career. Bate, one of the premier literary scholars of the late twentieth century, was known for his insight and clarity of style.

Blades, John. *Wordsworth and Coleridge: "Lyrical Ballads."* New York: Palgrave Macmillan, 2004. Part one of this study analyzes the poems' themes, including childhood, the imagination, and social issues. Part two examines the political and literary backgrounds of the late eighteenth century and Wordsworth's and Coleridge's literary theories. Also includes summarized responses to *Lyrical Ballads* by modern scholars I. A. Richards, Robert Mayo, Geoffrey H. Hartman, and Paul de Man.

Gill, Stephen. *William Wordsworth: A Life.* New York: Oxford University Press, 1989. An excellent biography of Wordsworth, based on an extensive reexamination of the primary and secondary records of his life. In contrast to earlier opinions, Gill portrays Wordsworth as a dedicated, lifelong poet, rather than as a person who betrayed his abilities and beliefs in exchange for a conservative life of retirement. Includes a discussion of Wordsworth's role in producing *Lyrical Ballads*.

Jordan, John E. *Why the "Lyrical Ballads"?* Berkeley: University of California Press, 1976. The subtitle of this influential study states precisely what the book is about: "The Background, Writing, and Character of Wordsworth's 1798 *Lyrical Ballads*." Although Jordan's focus is primarily on Wordsworth, there is also extensive commentary on Coleridge's contribution to *Lyrical Ballads*.

Richey, William, and Daniel Robinson, eds. *William Words-worth and Samuel Taylor Coleridge: "Lyrical Ballads" and Related Writings*. Boston: Houghton Mifflin, 2002. In addition to the text of the 1798 edition of *Lyrical Ballads*, this book provides background information on the poems. Also has examples of late eighteenth century poetry and prose, which place Wordsworth and Coleridge's collection in the context of its time.

Sisman, Adam. *The Friendship: Wordsworth and Coleridge*. New York: Viking Press, 2006. A dual biography of Wordsworth and Coleridge, with an emphasis on their relationship—both personal and artistic. Contains an extensive discussion of the creation of *Lyrical Ballads*.

Lysistrata

Author: Aristophanes (c. 450-c. 385 B.C.E.)
First produced: Lysistratē, 411 B.C.E. (English translation, 1812)
Type of work: Drama
Type of plot: Satire
Time of plot: Fifth century B.C.E.
Locale: Athens

Principal characters:
LYSISTRATA, an Athenian woman
CLEONICE, her friend
LAMPITO, a Spartan woman
MYRRHINE, a Greek woman
A MAGISTRATE
CINESIAS, Myrrhine's husband
OLD MEN OF ATHENS, the chorus

The Story:

The Second Peloponnesian War is in progress when Lysistrata summons women from Athens, Sparta, and all other Greek cities involved in the war. She wishes them to consider a plan she has carefully devised for ending hostilities between Athens and Sparta. The women arrive, curious about the purpose of the meeting. Because their husbands are all away at war, they are positively inclined toward any scheme that will bring the men back to them.

Lysistrata declares that the war will end immediately if all the Greek women refuse to have sex with their husbands until the fighting stops. Most of the women at first object strenuously, but Lampito, a Spartan woman, likes the idea. The others finally agree to try the plan, but they do so without enthusiasm. Over a bowl of Thracian wine, Lysistrata leads her companions in an oath binding them to charm their husbands and their lovers but not to have sex with them unless forced. Most of the women then return to their native lands to begin their lives of self-restraint. Lysistrata goes to the Acropolis, the citadel of Athens, for while the younger women have been meeting with Lysistrata, the older women have marched

on the Acropolis and seized it. The old men of the city have laid wood around the base of the Acropolis and set fire to it with the intention of smoking the women out, in response to which the women, during a particularly heated exchange, throw water on the old men from their pots.

When a magistrate and his men attempt to break open a gate of the citadel, Lysistrata, who has taken command of the women, emerges and suggests that the magistrate use common sense. The indignant magistrate orders his Scythians to seize Lysistrata and bind her hands, but the Scythians advance reluctantly and are soundly trounced by the fierce women.

Asked why they have seized the Acropolis, the women reply that they have done so to possess the treasury. Now that they control the money, they believe that the war must soon end, since it takes money to wage war.

The pride of the old men is deeply wounded when Lysistrata declares that the women have assumed all civil authority and will henceforth provide for the safety and welfare of Athens. The magistrate cannot believe his ears when he hears Lysistrata say that the women have grown impatient with the incompetence of their husbands in matters that concern the commonweal. For rebuking the women, the magistrate receives potfuls of water poured on his head. When the ineffectual old men declare that they will never submit, the women answer that the old men are worthless and that all they have been able to do is legislate the city into trouble.

Despite their brave talk and their bold plan, however, the women prove to be weak in the flesh, and disaffection thins their ranks. Some, caught as they are deserting, offer various excuses in the hope of getting away from the strictures imposed by Lysistrata's oath. One woman simulates pregnancy by placing the sacred helmet of Athena under her robe. Some of the women claim to be frightened by the holy snakes and by the owls of the Acropolis. As a last desperate measure, Lysistrata resorts to a prophecy favorable to their project, and the women reluctantly return to their posts.

When the husband of Myrrhine, one of Lysistrata's companions, returns from the war and seeks his wife, Lysistrata directs Myrrhine to be true to her oath. The husband, Cinesias, begs Myrrhine to come home, using various appeals, but without success. Although Myrrhine consents to his request for a moment of dalliance with her, she puts him off. At last, ignoring his pleas, she retires into the citadel.

A messenger arrives from Sparta, where Lampito and her cohorts have been successful; the messenger brings the news that the men of Sparta are prepared to sue for peace. As the magistrate arranges for a peace conference, the women look on the old men of Athens with restored kindness, which cools their ire.

On their arrival in Athens, the Spartan envoys are ready to agree to any terms because they are so desperate for the favors of their wives. Lysistrata rebukes the Spartans and the Athenians for warring with each other; they have, she declares, a common enemy in the barbarians, and they share many traditions. While she speaks, a nude maiden, representing the goddess of peace, is brought before the frustrated men. Lysistrata reminds the men of both countries that they had previously been allies, and she insists that war between the two is illogical. The men, their eyes devouring the nude maiden, agree with everything Lysistrata says, but when she asks for terms of agreement there is immediate contention, with each side asking for conditions unsatisfactory to the other.

The women, seeing that appeal to reason is futile, prepare a feast for the envoys and fill them with intoxicating liquors. Sated, and eager for further physical satisfaction, the men sign a peace agreement and leave hastily with their wives for their homes.

Critical Evaluation:

In the late twentieth century, *Lysistrata* became the most frequently produced of the ancient Greek dramas, for reasons that are not hard to determine: The play deals openly with sex, feminism, and pacifism—all major preoccupations of that era. It is clear, however, that many audiences since Aristophanes' day have taken up *Lysistrata* largely for its ideology rather than for its intrinsic value as a play.

By contrast with the playwright's other works on similar themes, *Lysistrata* seems rather thin in imagination. Undoubtedly the basic assumption of the comedy—that women could achieve peace and governmental reform by refusing to have sex with men—was an ancient idea even in Aristophanes' time. Aristophanes' plays *Acharnēs* (425 B.C.E.; *The Acharnians*, 1812) and *Eirēnē* (421 B.C.E.; *Peace*, 1837) present novel, if bizarre, methods of achieving peace, while *Thesmophoriazousai* (411 B.C.E.; *Thesmophoriazusae*, 1837) and *Ekklesiazousai* (392 B.C.E.?; *Ecclesiazusae*, 1837) show women in a funnier, more satirical light. Modern-day audiences as a rule appreciate directness and simplicity and in many instances do not object to a certain lack of originality, but they probably would dislike a satirical treatment of Lysistrata, who is both a militant feminist and a pacifist.

In structure, the drama is straightforward. The problem is simple: The women are tired of living without their husbands because of war. Out of the solution they devise—teasing their husbands but withholding sex from them until the men settle the war out of sheer frustration—everything else in the play follows. The women capture the treasury; the old men try to force the women into submission; when force fails, the two sides hold an inconclusive debate in which the magistrate, a chief warmonger, is first decked out like a woman and then as a corpse; the women begin to defect from their oath of chastity, but with strenuous effort Lysistrata whips them back into shape; and finally the Athenian and Spartan men agree to negotiate for peace. When those negotiations fail, the diplomats are tricked into a peace settlement through feasting and drinking. Once the problem has been established, almost all of the consequent action is predictable, yet it amuses nevertheless. Perhaps the funniest idea in the play is that diplomats should never negotiate when they are sober: Cleverness and greed are inimical to peace, whereas drink and festivity promote goodwill.

Sex—particularly the battle of the sexes—is a traditional subject for comedy, and Greek comedy in fact evolved in part from phallic farce. The central idea of *Lysistrata*—that women take over the affairs of state—would have seemed irresistibly comic to Aristophanes and his audience. The slapstick and banter between the chorus of old men and the chorus of women simply restate the age-old contest between male and female.

Lysistrata, however, carries a more important theme than sexuality, which is used merely as a weapon to bring about peace. At the time this play was first produced in 411 B.C.E., Athens had been through twenty hard years of war with Sparta, and the conflict was not to end for another seven years. The seriousness of the war is brought out very forcefully when Lysistrata tells the magistrate that sons have perished in battle and that many young women will never find mates because of this. The fact that the chorus consists of old men underscores the point that many Athenian youths have died in the Peloponnesian War. Here the drama reveals Aristophanes' true feelings about the war with no trace of buffoonery. The dramatist clearly regards Lysistrata as a heroine and not as the butt of humor. When men have failed so thoroughly to govern the affairs of the city, he says, it is time for others to take over. All the while, Aristophanes and his audience are fully aware of women's weaknesses. In essence, the playwright is scolding the Athenian men and telling them that if they cannot put an end to the war after twenty years, they might as well give up.

Lysistrata was originally presented as a musical comedy, with songs, choreography, colorful costumes, and masks. The actors were all male, as in the theater of William Shakespeare's time. This type of presentation tended to soften the strength of Aristophanes' biting wit, and it gave the play an air of spectacle, of festivity. Aristophanes had the keen comic wit of George Bernard Shaw, but he employed it in a different medium and style, and used it for opposite social ends.

"Critical Evaluation" by James Weigel, Jr.

Further Reading

Bowie, A. M. *Aristophanes: Myth, Ritual, and Comedy.* New York: Cambridge University Press, 1993. Interesting structural anthropological approach places Aristophanes' plays in their contemporary context. Offers an analysis of *Lysistrata* that includes a discussion of earlier myths and rituals that demonstrate feminist power.

Dover, K. J. *Aristophanic Comedy.* Berkeley: University of California Press, 1972. A tribute to Artistophanes' plays in their cultural context is provided by a distinguished classical Greek scholar. A chapter on *Lysistrata* provides a synopsis and examines the lyrics and characters. Also includes a discussion of war and incorporates useful notes on transliteration.

Freydberg, Bernard. "*Lysistrata*: Eros and Transcendence." In *Philosophy and Comedy: Aristophanes, Logos, and Eros.* Bloomington: Indiana University Press, 2008. Analysis of *Lysistrata* is part of a larger examination of the philosophical concepts in the plays of Aristophanes.

Reckford, Kenneth J. *Aristophanes' Old-and-New Comedy.* Chapel Hill: University of North Carolina Press, 1987. Examines *Lysistrata* as living theater, suggesting unusual staging possibilities and discussing the play within the context of loyalty to comic truths, ritual, and sexual equality.

Silk, M. S. *Aristophanes and the Definition of Comedy.* New York: Oxford University Press, 2002. Looks at Aristophanes as one of the world's great poets as well as an important dramatist. Analyzes *Lysistrata* and other plays to examine their language, style, lyric poetry, character, and structure.

Solomos, Alexēs. *The Living Aristophanes.* 1974. Reprint. Ann Arbor: University of Michigan Press, 1982. Solomos, the director who first staged all of Aristophanes' plays at the classic theater at Epidaurus, discusses *Lysistrata* as the playwright's first attempt at comedy as popular entertainment. Argues that Aristophanes was indulging his theatrical fancies rather than moralizing as a social reformer.

Spatz, Lois. *Aristophanes.* Boston: Twayne, 1978. Provides a sound introduction to Aristophanes' plays. A chapter on *Lysistrata* examines the work's political and historical background, the secondary role of women in Athenian society, and the elusive and idyllic quest for peace.

Vetter, Lisa Pace. "Homespun Statesmanship and Political Peace in Aristophanes' *Lysistrata*." In *"Women's Work" as Political Art: Weaving and Dialectical Politics in Homer, Aristophanes, and Plato.* Lanham, Md.: Lexington Books, 2005. Analysis of *Lysistrata* is part of a larger work that explores the metaphor of weaving in works of ancient Greek literature. Argues that this metaphor represents complex ideas about the position of women, politics, and human nature.

M

M. Butterfly

Author: David Henry Hwang (1957-)
First produced: 1988; first published, 1988
Type of work: Drama
Type of plot: Psychological
Time of plot: 1960-1980's
Locale: Paris and Beijing

Principal characters:
RENÉ GALLIMARD, a French diplomat in Beijing
LILING SONG, a Chinese opera performer
HELGA, Gallimard's wife
MARC, a friend of Gallimard during his teenage years
RENÉE, a female Danish student
COMRADE CHIN, a Chinese intelligence officer

The Story:

René Gallimard is in a prison cell in 1980's Paris, listening to an audiocassette player. He recalls the skill with which his Chinese Communist lover, Liling Song, performed in traditional plays at the Peking Opera, as well as in Giacomo Puccini's *Madama Butterfly* (1904; *Madame Butterfly*)—a thematically important juxtaposition of Eastern and Western cultures. Gallimard flashes back to his days in Beijing, reliving the events that led to his imprisonment.

In the 1960's, Gallimard is a rather nondescript, low-level diplomat at the French Embassy in Beijing, China, at a time when France and the People's Republic of China are establishing diplomatic relations. He has come to China harboring several stereotypes about "Oriental" women. Gallimard's stereotype of Oriental women as beautiful, submissive, self-sacrificing, and hankering after white men was formed through his exposure to Puccini's *Madame Butterfly*. In this opera, the American naval lieutenant Pinkerton lures a beautiful, loving Japanese woman, Butterfly (Cio-Cio San), into a fake marriage. They set up house, she becomes pregnant, and he sails off with vague promises to return. Butterfly gives birth to a son and loyally awaits Pinkerton's return, rebuffing the courtship of a wealthy Japanese admirer. After some years, Pinkerton does return—accompanied by his new American wife, who is childless and wishes to take Butterfly's son. Butterfly obligingly commits suicide. As Gallimard listens to Puccini's music, he fantasizes himself as Pinkerton and constructs his stereotypical ideal of a selfless, loving Asian woman.

Gallimard's susceptibility to this fantasy is partly due to his unsatisfactory sexual experiences with Western women.

As a teenager, Gallimard's pal Marc called him a wimp when he declined to go skinny dipping with some eager girls. Gallimard also seemed to be more voyeur than participant when he watched an exhibitionist girl undressing and remained flaccid. His deflowering was a joyless experience with an athletic girl who adopted the superior position and pounded his loins. His marriage was a dispassionate career move, his father-in-law being the French ambassador to Australia.

At a soirée in Beijing, Gallimard meets Liling Song, an opera singer who performs Madame Butterfly's death scene. Gallimard is predictably entranced, unable to disentangle the performer from the role. In conversation, Song scoffs at the Butterfly character's self-sacrificing pandering to Western male egotism, but Gallimard persists in admiring Song/Butterfly. Gallimard frequents the Peking Opera to see Song, and they regularly take tea in Song's apartment, Song projecting the image of an Oriental maiden awed by white virility. The French ambassador promotes Gallimard, assuming that he has begun keeping a Chinese mistress and therefore possesses inside knowledge about the Chinese. After receiving this promotion, Gallimard hastens to Song's apartment to realize his superior's assumption, and the two consummate their affair accompanied by a duet from *Madame Butterfly*.

After their consummation, Gallimard and Song build a love nest for themselves. Meanwhile, the French embassy (and Gallimard) are asked by the Americans for advice about the Vietnam War. Gallimard, extrapolating from his conquest of Song, declares that "Orientals" submit to forcefulness, so the Americans should allow the dubiously elected president of South Vietnam, Ngo Dinh Diem, to be assassinated and allow a military junta to conduct the war. Gallimard also shares these views with Song, who is actually spying on him for the Chinese Communist government. Moreover, Song is not a woman but a *nan dan*, a man who plays women's roles in Chinese theater.

Gallimard has a brief affair with a liberated Danish student named Renée, but he is soon put off by her aggressive sexuality. This experience convinces Gallimard that Song's (apparently) submissive femininity is the ideal of womanhood. Later, when Gallimard's wife, Helga, wishes to have a baby, the couple tries unsuccessfully to get pregnant. Helga consults a doctor, takes a fertility test, and passes. She wants Gallimard to do likewise. Gallimard balks at this calling of his virility into question. He complains to Song, demanding to see his lover nude, something Song had avoided up to that point, pleading Chinese modesty. Song then announces "her" pregnancy, thereby reassuring Gallimard's sense of virility and distracting him from the need to see "her" naked. After a few months' absence from the city, Song returns with a blond, blue-eyed Chinese "son."

In 1966, Chairman Mao Zedong unleashes the Cultural Revolution, turning Chinese society upside down for a decade. Intellectuals and artists such as Song are branded counterrevolutionaries and undergo forced "reeducation" by hard labor in the Chinese hinterland. Meanwhile, the aggressive, "masculine" military policy advocated by Gallimard of bombing the Vietnamese fails, and he is demoted and returned to Paris (which is also experiencing upheaval through student riots and workers' strikes). Unhappy and nostalgic for the perfect woman he loved in China, Gallimard asks Helga for a divorce. Then, magically, Song shows up in Paris. Gallimard is elated, but, as the curtain descends on act 2, Song tells the audience in an aside that he will make a costume change during intermission.

Unlike the usual backstage costume change, however, Song's occurs onstage, visible to the audience. As he sheds his wig, makeup, and kimono, the audience sees the transformation of a woman into a man. Song and his son arrive in Paris in 1970 and live with Gallimard for fifteen years, spying on the French. Eventually, however, the espionage is detected. The pair are tried and jailed by a judge who is incredulous that, throughout twenty years of intimacy, Gallimard believed that Song was a woman. Song ascribes this gullibility to Gallimard's (and Western men's) orientalizing romantic fantasies about Asian women. To shatter this fantasy for Gallimard, Song strips completely, showing his manhood. Gallimard, however, steadfastly rejects reality and preserves his fantasy by donning Song's wig, kimono, and makeup and

committing suicide, ironically in the same romantic manner as Puccini's Madame Butterfly.

Critical Evaluation:

M. Butterfly was a resoundingly successful Broadway play, winning the Tony Award for the Best Play of 1988, the John Gassner Award, and the Drama Desk Award. A film version directed by David Cronenberg and starring Jeremy Irons and John Lone appeared in 1993. Prior to *M. Butterfly*, David Henry Hwang had won a 1980 Off-Broadway Obie Award for *F.O.B.* (pr., pb. 1979)—his first play, written while he was a senior at Stanford University. After *M. Butterfly*, Hwang won Obie Awards for *Golden Child* (pr. 1996, pb. 1998) and *Yellow Face* (pr. 2007, pb. 2008); he also collaborated with composer Philip Glass on *One Thousand Airplanes on the Roof* (pr. 1988, pb. 1989) and with Elton John and Tim Rice on the musical *Aida* (pr. 2000). The success of *M. Butterfly* and these other achievements have made Hwang one of the most important American playwrights of the twentieth century and the preeminent Asian American dramatist of his time.

M. Butterfly germinated from a *New York Times* report about a French diplomat being jailed because he had for several years passed intelligence to his lover, a Chinese Communist man posing as a woman. Hwang saw in this odd story the potential to deconstruct stereotypes about race and gender that Westerners, especially Americans, hold about Asians. The classic formulation of these stereotypes is the archetypal tale of Madame Butterfly, which has teased the Western imagination in many guises, including Pierre Loti's autobiographical *Madame Chrysanthème* (1887), John Luther Long's novella *Madame Butterfly* (1898), and David Belasco's one-act play *Madame Butterfly* (1900), as well as Puccini's opera.

The gender ambiguity of Hwang's title, *M. Butterfly*, immediately challenges the audience's socialized expectation that gender is immutably of one's essence: One is made insecure as to the sex of Hwang's Butterfly. Furthermore, the pattern of preceding versions of the Butterfly archetype has projected expectations of an orientalized and fantasized image of Asian women as delicate, submissive, and complaisant toward potent, dominant, white European males: Puccini's Butterfly, for instance, loves her treacherous American husband, Lieutenant Pinkerton, until death, surrendering their son to him on demand and considerately committing suicide to remove any impediment to his felicity with his new American wife.

As Hwang's play unfolds, his Butterfly figure, the transvestite impersonator Liling Song, only appears to be the archetypally submissive "Oriental" woman. In reality, Song is in control, and Gallimard (Hwang's equivalent of the Lieutenant Pinkerton figure) is the gull. Moreover, in Hwang's figuration of the outcome of his play, it is not the Asian character but the white European male who self-destructs, stubbornly clinging to his delusion. While Hwang is successful in deconstructing this stereotype of the Asian woman as a submissive Butterfly, Asian American spectators have noted that his method may have unintended effects: The figure of Song, a spy, may feed into another negative stereotype of the "Oriental" as sneaky and inscrutable. Furthermore, Song's ability to be so convincing as a woman may further foster the emasculating stereotype of Asian men as effeminate.

Hwang's play also sets out to deconstruct a stereotype relating gender to power on a geopolitical level. In international affairs, white Western and European nations are figured as being masculine and imperious, natural colonizers, whereas the Asian and browner nations are figured as feminine and subjected, ready to be colonized. *M. Butterfly* points out that this paradigm of gendered geopolitics is no longer valid (if it ever was), as evidenced by the power that Song exerts over Gallimard and the failure of the "macho" military policy advocated by Gallimard for the conduct of the Vietnam War. Here again, while lauding Hwang's critique of the geopolitical stereotype, some critics feel that his representation of political figures and ideology (such as the characters of the French ambassador and Comrade Chin) are unconvincingly broad and caricatural. On balance, then, *M. Butterfly* succeeds in being a piquant and thought-provoking drama that challenges the members of its mainstream audience to examine their individual and cultural stereotypes about race, gender, and politics.

C. L. Chua

Further Reading

Deeney, John J. "Of Monkeys and Butterflies: Transformation in M. H. Kingston's *Tripmaster Monkey* and D. H. Hwang's *M. Butterfly*." *MELUS* 18, no. 4 (Winter, 1993): 21-39. Discusses the transformations of *M. Butterfly*'s main characters and the response of Asian audience members.

Eng, David L. "In the Shadows of a Diva: Committing Homosexuality in David Henry Hwang's *M. Butterfly*." *Amerasia Journal* 20, no. 1 (1994): 93-116. An analysis emphasizing the topic of homosexuality and how queer subjectivity intersects with racial stereotyping.

Gerard, Jeremy. "David Hwang Riding on the Hyphen." *The New York Times*, March 13, 1988, pp. 44-45, 88-89. Brief critical and biographical overview of Hwang up through the time of *M. Butterfly*'s premiere.

Lye, Colleen. "*M. Butterfly* and the Rhetoric of Antiessentialism: Minority Discourse in an International Frame." In *The Ethnic Canon*, edited by David Palumbo-Liu. Minneapolis: University of Minnesota Press, 1995. A nuanced analysis of *M. Butterfly*'s geopolitically subversive qualities, including a critique of its 1990 Singapore production.

Moy, James S. "David Henry Hwang's *M. Butterfly* and Philip Kan Gotanda's *Yankee Dawg You Die*: Repositioning Chinese American Marginality on the American Stage." *Theatre Journal* 42, no. 1 (March, 1990): 48-56. Argues that Hwang fails to challenge orientalist stereotypes and that Song's character fails because he embodies self-doubt.

Pao, Angela. "The Critic and the Butterfly: Sociocultural Contexts and the Reception of David Henry Hwang's *M. Butterfly*." *Amerasia Journal* 18, no. 3 (1992): 1-16. Surveys the critical reception of the play; critiques the stereotypes and biases coloring the critics' reviews.

_____. "*M. Butterfly*, by David Henry Hwang." In *A Resource Guide to Asian American Literature*, edited by Sau-ling Cynthia Wong and Stephen Sumida. New York: Modern Language Association, 2001. Covers the play's reception, historical context, and pedagogical possibilities, and the author's background.

Skloot, Robert. "Breaking the Butterfly: The Politics of David Henry Hwang." *Modern Drama* 33, no. 1 (March, 1990): 59-66. Discusses incisively the cultural, sexual, and theatrical politics underlying *M. Butterfly*.

Street, Douglas. *David Henry Hwang*. Boise, Idaho: Boise State University Press, 1989. Monograph providing biographical background on Hwang and discussing Asian American identity in *M. Butterfly*.

Wissenthal, Jonathan, et al. *A Vision of the Orient*. Toronto, Ont.: University of Toronto Press, 2006. Thirteen essays on the different versions of the Madame Butterfly story; three essays are on Hwang's *M. Butterfly*.

Ma Rainey's Black Bottom

Author: August Wilson (1945-2005)
First produced: 1984; first published, 1985
Type of work: Drama
Type of plot: Historical
Time of plot: Early March, 1927
Locale: Chicago

Principal characters:
MEL STURDYVANT, a record producer
IRVIN, Ma Rainey's agent
CUTLER, a bandleader, guitarist, and trombonist
TOLEDO, a pianist and self-styled philosopher
SLOW DRAG, a bassist, drinker, and dancer
LEVEE GREEN, an ambitious but unstable trumpeter and
    composer
MA RAINEY, a blues vocalist
POLICEMAN, a corrupt officer
DUSSIE MAE, Ma Rainey's companion
SYLVESTER BROWN, Ma Rainey's nephew and driver

The Story:

Sturdyvant, a record producer, and Irvin, Ma Rainey's agent, are in a recording studio, discussing arrangements for the day's recording session with Ma Rainey. Sturdyvant wants the session to go smoothly, and Irvin assures the producer that all is under control. The band members arrive and begin to prepare for the session. Levee Green, the young trumpeter, expresses his delight with his new shoes and his distaste for the old shoes of his fellow musicians. Cutler, Slow Drag, and Toledo show their maturity by recognizing Ma Rainey as their boss, but Levee insists that he is an artist, composer, and bandleader dedicated to a new and better style. He does not favor the old style of Ma Rainey. Levee plans to work with Sturdyvant to form a new band and record his own compositions.

Ma Rainey enters with much fanfare. Accompanying her are her nephew Sylvester and her companion, Dussie Mae. A policeman follows the trio, and he insists that Ma Rainey is responsible for a traffic accident and an altercation with a cab driver. To get circumstances under control, Irvin pays off the policeman, who leaves.

A conflict develops about the musical arrangement for "Ma Rainey's Black Bottom." Levee and Irvin want to use Levee's new arrangement, but Ma will not cooperate. She insists that Sylvester, despite his stuttering, will do a voice introduction, and she frustrates Levee when she prevails in the argument.

Though overruled in this artistic decision, Levee still aspires to have his own band and strives to win Sturdyvant's favor. The other musicians take note of this behavior and taunt Levee, charging that he, like the rest of them, is bowing to the white man's authority. Provoked, Levee denies the charge and recounts a story to disprove the accusation.

When Levee was eight, his mother was raped in his presence by a group of white men. Levee tried to stab one, but being only a child, he lost the knife and was stabbed and scarred. Levee's father came home and pretended to accept the sexual attack, but after he sold his land and moved his family away, he returned for vengeance. He killed four of the rapists, but before he could finish them all off, he was captured, lynched, and burned. Levee carries this memory in his heart, and he insists that he, like his father, can smile in the face of the white man yet be ready to retaliate in the boldest possible fashion for mistreatment.

Levee makes passes at Dussie Mae. Efforts to record "Ma Rainey's Black Bottom" are unsuccessful because Sylvester's speech impediment interferes with his introduction for the song; nevertheless, when Irvin suggests that the band adopt Levee's version to expedite matters, Ma balks and demands a Coca-Cola. Ma tells Cutler that Levee is a troublemaker and instructs Cutler to be ready to dismiss Levee. In defiance of Ma, Levee continues his flirtation with Dussie Mae.

After several failures, Sylvester finally does the introduction well, but Sturdyvant soon discovers that the recording failed because the cord for Sylvester's microphone was disconnected, perhaps by Levee. The conflict within the band grows stronger when Cutler warns Levee that his flirtation with Dussie Mae may lead Ma Rainey to fire him. Levee insists that he wants more than ordinary satisfaction in life and expresses his willingness to sell his soul to the devil.

Levee berates God, who in Levee's eyes is a failure. He says that God does not intervene to prevent the most horrible events, and therefore God is worthless. Unable to tolerate such blasphemy, Cutler fights with Levee, but Levee draws a knife. To prove his point about God's worthlessness, Levee dares Cutler to rely on God's intervention to prevent himself from being stabbed. When the band members stay on their guard against Levee, he insists that he has proven that God fails to stop evil.

In the studio, Ma Rainey rejects Levee's musical style. She fires Levee, and then she shrewdly manages transactions to get full payment for herself and Sylvester before she signs the forms Irvin needs. In the band room, Sturdyvant pays the musicians, but when Levee pursues his anticipated recording agreement, Sturdyvant rejects Levee as a musician and a band leader.

Levee, having lost his place in Ma Rainey's band and his hope to be an independent musician, slips into a volatile state. When Toledo steps on Levee's shoe, Levee loses control and stabs Toledo. Although Levee immediately regrets his rash and senseless act, he has no way to escape from its consequences.

Critical Evaluation:

Although August Wilson titled his play *Ma Rainey's Black Bottom*, an alternate title might be "The Tragedy of Levee Green." Like the great tragedies of ancient Greece, Wilson's play obeys classical unities, as Wilson limits time to a single day, makes the recording studio the single location, and focuses action on a single recording session.

Levee is noble and admirable in his ambition to be an independent artist and in his love and respect for his mother and father; however, Levee's judgment is flawed because he allows the presence of evil and injustice in the world to justify his rejection of God. Sinfully proud, Levee scorns his fellow musicians and Ma Rainey, and to rise to stardom he is ready to sell his soul to the devil. Instead of ascending, Levee suffers a tragic fall when he loses his place in the band, fails to form his own band, and rashly resorts to violence. Despite these mistakes, Levee's ruined life and his remorse make him a tragic figure worthy of pity.

The staging of Wilson's play graphically illustrates the power relations between the characters. Sturdyvant and Irvin, the white producer and agent, are literally on top. They sit in the control room at the top of the staircase, and they have money. Below the control room is the recording studio, and in that environment, Ma Rainey rules. She decides which songs should be performed, which arrangements should be adopted, and which performers should be part of the production. At a lower level than the studio is the band room, where musicians socialize and prepare for recording sessions. Cutler, who accepts Ma's authority, is the band leader, and Slow Drag and Toledo accept Cutler's role. Levee, the rebel, does not accept his place in the hierarchy. When Levee challenges the others and seeks to rise beyond his rightful place, he creates a destructive disturbance. When Levee denies that God rules over all the rankings of humans, Levee challenges the natural order and shows the arrogant pride that goes before a fall.

Just as the play's staging is symbolic of the order of its universe, several of the play's other components act as symbols as well. The scar on Levee's chest symbolizes the profound emotional scarring left by the rape of his mother and the lynching of his father. Green, Levee's family name, stands for his immaturity in comparison to the maturity of other members of the band. Levee remarks that if his father had known of Levee's trumpet, he would have named his son Gabriel, who is associated with the trumpet call for final judgment. This symbolic connection is ironic because of Levee's disconnection from God, but his father's choice of the name Levee rings true because the name signifies "to raise" and suggests Levee's intention to ascend.

Though the play is serious and tragic, Wilson enlivens his work with robust humor. Except for Toledo, the musicians are illiterate, and Toledo mocks Levee by saying he cannot spell "music." Levee bets a dollar that he can, and then he spells the word with a *k* at the end, insisting that he is correct. Ma Rainey's insistence that Sylvester, a stutterer, should do the introduction for her song creates several comical moments.

While the play relies more on conversations than on plot or action, Wilson makes storytelling a powerful part of the drama. Toledo tells an entertaining story about two fellows who make a bet about the Lord's Prayer: One man charges that the other does not know the prayer; the other, seeking to prove himself, recites the prayer incorrectly. However, the first man also does not know the prayer, believes his friend's recitation is correct, and concedes the bet.

Slow Drag tells the story of Eliza Cottor (later spelled Cotter), the man who sold his soul to the devil and thereafter enjoyed impunity even though he had illicit sex and killed a man. Cutler tells the story of how Slow Drag got his name by doing the slow drag dance so well that women in Bolingbroke were mad for him. Cutler also tells the story of the Reverend Gates, who was humiliated at a railroad stop and survived only because he danced for the white men who tormented him. Of all the musicians' stories, the most impressive is the emotional narrative told by Levee, who relates the story of his mother's rape and his father's lynching.

The greatest of Wilson's accomplishments in *Ma Rainey's Black Bottom* is his creation of an artistic work that reflects the history of African Americans. Ma Rainey (1886-1939) was a legendary blues singer who was known as the mother of the blues. She signed a recording contract with Paramount Records, and her records sold well through the mail and over the counter. Traveling from city to city by bus, she enjoyed lucrative tours and had particular success with songs such as "Moonshine Blues," "Bo-Weevil Blues," and "See See Rider." Bessie Smith was Ma Rainey's protégé.

In fictionalizing Ma Rainey, Wilson portrays her as not only a talented, dedicated, and successful blues singer but also a savvy, shrewd manager of business and interpersonal relations. Ma knows that if she is not vigilant about details, the whites will whittle down her pay, and upstart African Americans will try to seize her success for themselves.

Beyond the interpretation of Ma Rainey, Wilson depicts the circumstances of African Americans in the 1920's. He dramatizes the problems of illiteracy, segregation, abusive police, taxi drivers, the cashing of checks, sexual attacks, terrorism, and lynching. Despite these problems, his African American characters are diverse in their dedication to music, family, and cultural heritage. As part of a ten-play sequence portraying the African American experience in each decade of the twentieth century, *Ma Rainey's Black Bottom* is an impressive drama.

William T. Lawlor

Further Reading

Abbotson, Susan C. W. "From Jug Band to Dixieland: The Musical Development Behind August Wilson's *Ma Rainey's Black Bottom*." *Modern Drama* 43, no. 1 (Spring, 2000): 100-108. Insightfully discusses the play's characters and the dynamics of the tensions between them.

Bergesen, Eric. "The Limits of African-American Political Realism: Baraka's *Dutchman* and Wilson's *Ma Rainey's Black Bottom*." In *Realism and the American Dramatic Tradition*, edited by William W. Demastes. Tuscaloosa: University of Alabama Press, 1996. Contrasts the very different approaches to dramatic realism of Amiri Baraka and Wilson, and their consequences for African American politics.

Crawford, Eileen. "The B^b Burden: The Invisibility of *Ma Rainey's Black Bottom*." In *August Wilson: A Casebook*, edited by Marilyn Elkins. New York: Garland, 1994. Reviews the historical context of the play and analyzes tensions among the characters.

Elam, Harry J. "*Ma Rainey's Black Bottom*: Singing Wilson's Blues." *American Drama* 5, no. 2 (Spring, 1996): 76-99. Discusses the role of memory and history in the development of Wilson's play.

Gener, Randy. "Salvation in the City of Bones: Ma Rainey and Aunt Ester Sing Their Own Songs in August Wilson's Grand Cycle of Blues Dramas." *American Theatre* 20, no. 5 (May/June, 2003): 20-28. Provides an overview of Wilson's career and reveals backgrounds for Wilson's play.

Nadel, Alan. "*Ma Rainey's Black Bottom*: Cutting the Historical Record, Dramatizing a Blues CD." In *The Cambridge Companion to August Wilson*, edited by Christian Bigsby. New York: Cambridge University Press, 2007. Argues that the players in *Ma Rainey's Black Bottom* interact with each other in the manner of jazz musicians.

Shannon, Sandra G. *The Dramatic Vision of August Wilson*. Washington, D.C.: Howard University Press, 1996. Interprets social and political themes in Wilson's play.

The Mabinogion

Author: Unknown
First published: 1838-1849; includes tales from *The White Book of Rhydderch*, 1300-1325; *The Red Book of Hergest*, 1375-1425
Type of work: Short fiction
Type of plot: Folklore
Time of plot: Middle Ages
Locale: Arthurian Britain, primarily Wales

Principal characters:
PWYLL, the prince of Dyved
RHIANNON, his wife
PRYDERI, their son
KICVA, Pryderi's wife
BENDIGEID VRAN, the king of the Island of the Mighty and Llyr's son
BRANWEN, Llyr's daughter
MATHOLWCH, the king of Ireland and Branwen's husband
MANAWYDAN, another of Llyr's sons and Pryderi's stepfather
KING MATH
GWYDION, one of King Math's warriors
LLEW LLAW GYFFES, Gwydion's favorite son
BLODEUWEDD, Llew Llaw Gyffes's elfwife
MACSEN WLEDIG, the emperor of Rome
LLUDD, the king of Britain
LLEVELYS, his brother and the king of France
KING ARTHUR
KILHWCH, one of King Arthur's knights
YSBADDADEN, a crafty giant
OLWEN, his daughter and Kilhwch's beloved
RHONABWY, a dreamer
OWAIN, the new Knight of the Fountain
PEREDUR, one of King Arthur's knights
GERINT, another of King Arthur's knights and later a king
ENID, his wife

The Stories:

"Pwyll, Prince of Dyved." Pwyll, the prince of Dyved, is caught stealing a dying deer. In order to redeem himself, Pwyll agrees to exchange lands and appearances with the chieftain who has caught him and to slay the chieftain's enemy after a year's time. During that year, each prince rules the other's land wisely and well, and each remains faithful to his own true wife. At the year's end, Pwyll slays the enemy, returns home on good terms with the other prince, and eventually gains the other's lands. From a hill one day, Pwyll sees a lovely lady ride by. She eludes him three times, but on the fourth time she passes, he speaks to her. She tells him that her name is Rhiannon and invites him to come to her castle a year from that day. Pwyll goes there with his men, subdues her other suitor, and wins the lady. Some time thereafter, Rhiannon gives birth to a son who disappears the first night after his birth. The women on watch accuse her of killing the boy, and Pwyll makes her pay a heavy penance. Meanwhile, a farmer has taken the baby from a monster. Eventually, he restores the boy to Pwyll, who then releases his wife from her penance and names his son Pryderi.

"Branwen, Daughter of Llyr." Bendigeid Vran, son of Llyr and king of the Island of the Mighty, makes a pact with Matholwch, king of Ireland, and gives him his sister Branwen to wed. When the king of Ireland suffers an insult at the hands of one of Bendigeid Vran's men, Bendigeid Vran makes good the loss; because of the insult, however, Matholwch and Branwen are made to suffer heavily at the hands of the Irishmen. Bendigeid Vran learns of their treatment, sails to Ireland, and makes war on the Irish. Both sides suffer great losses. Bendigeid Vran is killed by a poisoned spear; his last request is that his head be buried in the White Mount in London. Branwen dies of sorrow. Finally, only seven of Bendigeid Vran's men are left alive to bury the head of their chief, and only five pregnant Irish women survive.

"Manawydan, Son of Llyr." Two of the men left living after the war in Ireland are Pryderi and Manawydan, the brother of

Bendigeid Vran. These two men go to live on Pryderi's lands, and Manawydan marries Pryderi's mother. The two men and their wives—Pryderi has a wife named Kicva—live pleasantly until the countryside is magically laid desolate and everyone else disappears. They leave their lands and try to earn their living at various trades, but they are always driven off by envious competitors. When they return to their own lands, Pryderi and his mother enter a magic castle that vanishes with them. Manawydan then tries farming, and again his crops are magically desolated. Determined to get to the bottom of the mystery, Manawydan stays up all night to watch his last field. When he sees thousands of mice ravaging the field, he catches one and declares that he will hang it. Pryderi's wife, along with three churchmen, tries to dissuade him, but he remains determined to hang the mouse. At last, the third churchman admits that he is the one who has cursed Manawydan and his friends, in revenge for an insult from Pryderi's father years before. He promises to restore everything, including Pryderi and his mother, if Manawydan will release the mouse. Manawydan demands that the magician never touch his lands again, and he returns the mouse, who happens to be the churchman's wife. Everything is restored, and the four companions return to their former happiness.

"Math, Son of Mathonwy." Gwydion's brother, Gilvaethwy, loves King Math's footmaiden, Goewin. Hoping to secure the maiden for his brother, Gwydion tricks Pryderi into exchanging some pigs for twelve phantom steeds and twelve phantom greyhounds. Afterward, Pryderi and his men pursue the tricksters. While King Math and his men are preparing to fight this army, Gwydion and his brother rape the footmaiden before they return to the fight and win the battle for King Math. The king then punishes the brothers by turning them into animals for three years. After his penance, Gwydion has two sons. Their mother curses Gwydion's favorite son, named Llew Llaw Gyffes, by saying that he will never have a human wife. To thwart this curse, King Math and Gwydion create for Llew Llaw Gyffes an elfwife, Blodeuwedd, out of flowers. The wife proves unfaithful by taking a lover. Determined to get rid of her husband, she asks him how he might be killed. He foolishly tells her, and in turn she tells her lover, who tries to kill Llew Llaw Gyffes. Gwydion's son does not die, however, but is turned into an eagle. Gwydion then searches for his son, finds him, and restores him to his former shape. Gwydion and Llew Llaw Gyffes then take revenge on the wife and her lover, turning her into an owl and killing him.

"The Dream of Macsen Wledig." Macsen Wledig, the emperor of Rome, dreams one night of a lovely maiden in a strange and wonderful land. Awakening, he sends his messengers all over the world in search of her. After wandering in many lands, they find her in a castle in Britain. They guide the emperor to her, and he finds everything as it had been in his dream. The maiden accepts him. For her maiden portion, he gives her father the island of Britain and has three castles built for her. Macsen Wledig lives with his wife in Britain for seven years. While he is away, the Romans choose a new emperor, who sends a note to Wledig warning him not to return. Wledig then marches on Gaul, fights his way through Italy, and reconquers Rome.

"Lludd and Llevelys." Three plagues are ravaging Britain: The first is a crafty foreign people, the second is the yearly midnight scream of a dragon that makes everything barren, and the third is the repeated disappearance of food at the king's court. Lludd, the great king of Britain, asks help from his wise and well-beloved brother, Llevelys, who is king of France. Llevelys tells Lludd to mash insects in water and sprinkle the solution over the foreigners to kill them. To get rid of the screaming dragon, Lludd will have to lure it with mead, put it in a sack, and bury it in a stone coffer. To keep the food, Lludd must capture a magician who will put everyone to sleep. The king performs these tasks, and Britain is rid of the plagues.

"Kilhwch and Olwen." Kilhwch's stepmother has spitefully prophesied that Kilhwch will not have a woman until he wins Olwen, the daughter of Ysbaddaden, a crafty and powerful giant. Kilhwch, who has fallen in love with Olwen without having seen her, sets out immediately for King Arthur's court, where King Arthur accepts the young man as his knight. Kilhwch then sets out to seek Ysbaddaden, bringing all of King Arthur's gallant warriors with him. After a long journey, Kilhwch meets Olwen, the most beautiful woman he has ever seen. He and King Arthur's men proceed to Ysbaddaden's court to ask for Olwen's hand. After fighting for three days and wounding the giant three times, Kilhwch learns that he can win Olwen and slay her father after performing forty nearly impossible tasks for the giant. By dint of brute force, cunning, and magic, Kilhwch, King Arthur, and his men succeed in completing the tasks. Kilhwch then slays Ysbaddaden, marries Olwen, and lives happily ever after.

"The Dream of Rhonabwy." While seeking a man who has ravaged the land, Rhonabwy and his companions find themselves in a dark hall where the floors are covered with dung. After trying to talk to the strange people inhabiting the hall and failing, Rhonabwy lies down on an ox skin and begins to dream. He dreams of the heroic Arthurian age, when men were demigods who lived in splendor in a land where life was full. He finds himself in King Arthur's court watching a game between King Arthur and Owain. While the game is in progress, three servants inform Owain that his ravens are being killed by King Arthur's men, but the king insists that the game continue. Owain tells his men to raise his banner, whereupon the ravens revive and begin to slaughter the men. Three servants come to tell King Arthur how his men are being killed, but Owain insists that the game continue. At last, the king begs Owain to call off the ravens. He does so, and there is peace. Many men then bring tribute to King Arthur. At this point, Rhonabwy awakens.

"The Lady of the Fountain." While at King Arthur's court, Owain learns from Kynon of the powerful Knight of the Fountain, who overthrows all challengers. Upon being taunted by Kai, Owain goes in search of this knight, challenges him, and slays him. With the help of a maiden, Owain then escapes the angry townsmen who seek to avenge the death of their lord, the knight. Owain marries the dead knight's widow and rules the land well for three years. One day, King Arthur and his knights come in search of Owain. When Arthur's men arrive at the fountain, they challenge the new Knight of the Fountain and are overthrown by him. The king and Owain are finally reunited, and Owain returns to King Arthur's court after promising his wife that he will return at the end of three years. Owain is later reminded of his promise when his wife comes to King Arthur's court and removes the ring that she had given him as a token by which to remember her. Then Owain goes in search of his wife. After restoring a lady's kingdom, killing a serpent that is about to destroy a lion, saving the maiden who aided him six years earlier, and killing her tormentors, Owain is restored to his wife. Owain performs additional feats, including defeating and transforming the Black Oppressor, and thereafter he and his wife live happily at King Arthur's court.

"Peredur, Son of Evrawg." As a boy, Peredur lives a sheltered life with his mother, but nevertheless he grows up strong and swift. Although his mother does not want him to become a knight, nothing can keep him from fulfilling his desire. When he prepares to leave his mother and journey to King Arthur's court, she instructs him in the chivalric code. Peredur is an ungainly sight as he enters King Arthur's court, for he is still awkward and naïve. He soon shows his prowess in battle, however, and through many adventures he acquires polish and skill in the arts of hunting, war, and love. Many reports of his strength and bravery reach King Arthur's ears. Peredur spends his time defending and loving maidens, restoring kingdoms to the wronged, avenging insults, killing monsters and evil men, protecting the weak, and ridding the land of plagues. In short, he is a matchless knight. In the course of his adventures, he inadvertently causes a kingdom to wither and grow barren, but he restores it to fertility by dint

of strength and courage. In the end, he rids the land of seven evil witches.

"Gerint, Son of Erbin." While King Arthur and his men are hunting, Gerint rides with the queen and her maids. When a dwarf insults Gerint and one of the maids, the knight challenges the dwarf's lord to a contest and defeats him. Afterward, Gerint restores a kingdom to its proper lord and wins the king's daughter, Enid, as his wife. Gerint then travels back to King Arthur's court and receives a stag head for his reward. In time, Gerint inherits a kingdom from his father, and he goes with Enid to rule the land. He devotes more time to his wife than he does to jousts or battles, and his subjects complain bitterly. Enid learns of their grievance and inadvertently tells her husband. In anger, Gerint sets out on a journey with his wife to prove his strength and valor. He performs superhuman feats and slaughters belligerent and cowardly knights in vast numbers, but he nearly dies from the effort. Finally, having proved himself to his wife and his subjects, he returns home to rule once more.

Critical Evaluation:

The tales gathered in *The Mabinogion* had a long oral tradition before they were written down, perhaps as early as the twelfth or thirteenth century. Strictly speaking, *The Mabinogion* comprises the first four tales in the collection of Lady Charlotte Guest, which was published in 1838-1839. The entire collection of tales furnishes some of the best-known characters and motifs of European romance. The stories have unity, assurance of style, skillful dialogue, accurate delineation of character, rich color, and a noble perspective on life. Their author or authors were artists well trained in nuances and subtleties of language. No one has ever doubted that the Welsh were skilled storytellers. So were the Bretons and Icelandic bards, and their talent has left indelible impressions on Western literature. *The Mabinogion*, in particular, has contributed significant and ancient folkloric themes as well as some of the earliest lore of Britain.

The unknown author of "Kilhwch and Olwen," one of the most artistic and enthusiastic contributors in *The Mabinogion*, creates a world of magic, color, and vigorous action. The story of the Celtic hero Kilhwch, who seeks a giant's daughter for his wife, uses a typical quest plot, with a list of forty tasks that Kilhwch must accomplish before he wins Ysbaddaden's daughter, Olwen. The tasks are not as important as the assemblage of persons attendant to Kilhwch, which includes his cousin Arthur. Arthur and his company form a nucleus for the later Arthurian Round Table. Appearing in this story, too, is the giant herdsman, a familiar motif in folklore, one that surfaces in other romances.

An important contribution to medieval romance generally is that richness of color that vibrates in the Welsh narrative. Olwen wears a robe of flame-red silk and a necklace of red gold set with pearls and rubies. The author states that her hair is yellower "than the flower of the broom," her cheeks redder "than the reddest foxgloves." Wherever she walks, white flowers spring up behind her. Kilhwch rides with two greyhounds in collars of red gold; his purple mantle has a red-gold apple in each corner.

"The Dream of Rhonabwy," one of the early dream visions in Celtic literature, lacks such movement and character description but has more realism. The dream deals with Arthur's battles against the Saxons; the main incident is the game played between Arthur and Owain, with its conflict between the former's men and the latter's ravens. Norman-French themes combine with older Irish and Welsh ones here with possible foreshadowing of Morgain la Fe (Modron), a shape-shifting figure who weaves her way through various European romances bringing magic birds, healing plasters, rings, and curative waters to innumerable heroes in time of need.

The last three stories in *The Mabinogion* are often compared to three similar works by Chrétien de Troyes. Much critical debate has been carried on between the Celticists, those who feel Welsh tradition underlies the spread of Arthurian material on the Continent, and the Continentalists, who assert that the latter influenced Welsh stories. As Gwyn Jones notes, opinion is swinging toward the Celticists because of evidence from linguistics, comparative folklore, and methods of composition in the Middle Ages. Nevertheless, parallels between "The Lady of the Fountain," "Peredur, Son of Evrawg" and "Gerint, Son of Erbin" on one hand and Chrétien's similar verse romances on the other hand are considerable; perhaps the Welsh authors and the French romancer worked from a lost common source.

The characters in the three Welsh tales may lack depth, and the actions themselves may be insufficiently motivated, but Owain, Gerint, and Peredur partake of entertaining adventures. If the narratives lack the meaning and skillful joining of incident found in Chrétien's poems, this seems purposeful rather than due to bungling artistry. In addition, many of the tales in *The Mabinogion* are probably retellings of materials whose origins may have been forgotten, if indeed they were ever known. Bits of ancient Irish stories, Norman-French fragments, and archaic traditions in Welsh make up their subject matter; the Welsh tellers contribute the color and vigor of action. The audience must have loved this excess of color in descriptions of garments, tapestries, ornaments, armor, and innumerable battles and adventures,

whether these were smoothly connected or not. Cohesive unity was not the authors' intent, as it was that of Chrétien de Troyes.

The familiar world of hunting, fighting, shape-shifting, and magic is there; so is Arthur presiding over a court rich with armor, jewels, beautiful ladies, and brave knights. The nebulous sixth century "battle leader," as the Latin chronicler Nennius described Arthur, may have been only a local chieftain leading somewhat limited skirmishes in southwest Britain, but in *The Mabinogion* he returns to literature a powerful and glorious king. He presides over an extensive court, and important kings from all over the Western world come to pay him homage. Whether he lived or not, this is the hero England needed and remembers. The Welsh tales of *The Mabinogion* help immeasurably in clothing him and his famous knights with splendor, regardless of possible influences from other sources.

"Critical Evaluation" by Muriel B. Ingham

Further Reading

Ford, Patrick K. *The "Mabinogi," and Other Medieval Welsh Tales.* Berkeley: University of California Press, 1972. Traces the history of various translations of the Welsh myths. Includes a map of Wales, a glossary, and a guide to Welsh pronunciations. Designed to inform students and general readers alike.

Graves, Robert. *The White Goddess.* 1948. Reprint. New York: Noonday Press, 2000. Classic work celebrates poetic myth in great detail. Graves hails Rhiannon as a "white goddess."

Jones, Gwyn. *Kings, Beasts, and Heroes.* New York: Oxford University Press, 1972. Includes an excellent condensed overview of *The Mabinogion* that focuses on Kilhwch and Olwen as well as on King Arthur. Illustrated.

Laynard, John. *A Celtic Quest: Sexuality and Soul in Individuation.* Edited by Anne S. Bosch. New York: Springer, 1975. Explains *The Mabinogion* and related stories in psychological and behavioral terms. Uses allegory to show the characters' relationships to areas of the psyche and emphasizes the dichotomy between the nurturing mother figure and the devouring, animalistic mother.

The Mabinogion. Translated by Gwyn Jones and Thomas Jones. 1949. Reprint. London: J. M. Dent, 2004. Excellent adaptation of the Welsh myths in an edition that includes thorough discussion of the four branches of the Mabinogi and their seven related stories. Informative introduction argues for the literary merit of this collection of legends.

Matthews, Caítlin. *King Arthur and the Goddess of the Land: The Divine Feminine in "The Mabinogion."* 2d ed. Rochester, Vt.: Inner Traditions, 2002. Focuses on Sovereignty, the goddess of the sacred land of Britain, discussing her importance within the Arthurian cycle.

_____. *Mabon and the Guardians of Celtic Britain: Hero Myths in "The Mabinogion."* Rochester, Vt.: Inner Traditions, 2002. After an introduction that discusses the Welsh storytelling tradition, provides synopses of and detailed commentary on the four branches of *The Mabinogion.* Also examines the stories' ties to Greek and Roman mythology and to Irish and British Arthurian legends.

Sullivan, C. W., III, ed. *"The Mabinogi": A Book of Essays.* New York: Garland, 1996. Collection of essays includes discussion of such topics as the origins of the stories in *The Mabinogion*, the work's narrative and thematic structure, and the role of myth and tradition in its four branches.

Mac Flecknoe
Or, A Satyre upon the True-Blew-Protestant Poet, T. S.

Author: John Dryden (1631-1700)
First published: 1682; revised in *Miscellany Poems*, 1684
Type of work: Poetry
Type of plot: Mock heroic
Time of plot: Late 1670's
Locale: London

Principal characters:
FLECKNOE, a minor poet and dramatist, monarch of dullness
SHADWELL, his chosen successor
HERRINGMAN, captain of the honor guard
SIR FORMAL TRIFLE, character from a Shadwell drama

The Poem:

Flecknoe, the monarch of dullness, senses the approaching end of his long reign and begins to reflect on an appropriate successor. He plans to crown a new monarch before death overcomes him, and in order to secure a proper succession, he is willing, even eager, to abdicate. Fortunately, candidates are plentiful; among his numerous poetic sons, many are suitably dull and stupid. With little hesitation, however, Flecknoe concludes that Shadwell most resembles himself in dullness and is therefore the ideal choice. Even Shadwell's portly, rotund appearance is an element favorable to his selection. In a speech musing on the selection, Flecknoe praises Shadwell for his nonsensical, obscure, tautological verses. Depicting Shadwell as potentially a greater monarch, he portrays his own reign as merely a precursor to a more gloriously dull age. Flecknoe remembers Shadwell's previous participation in low forms of entertainment, such as lute playing, public spectacles, and dances. Flecknoe concludes, however, that Shadwell's dramas best qualify him as the chosen monarch of dunces.

The site selected for the coronation is the Barbican, an area surrounding a ruined Roman watchtower located in the northern part of London. The Barbican is associated with inferior forms of entertainment. A run-down portion of the city, it has become the site of brothels and of the Nursery, a school for young actors. Instead of practicing roles created by John Fletcher and Ben Jonson, the young actors at the Nursery are schooled in punning and coarse humor like that found in the comedies of Shadwell. In order to fulfill the prophecy of Thomas Dekker, a minor Elizabethan dramatist, that a mighty prince will reign in the area, Flecknoe erects a throne on the site; the throne is made from piles of his own printed works that no one would buy.

Once news of the coronation spreads through the area, other inferior poetasters and dunces begin to assemble before the throne. They lead a procession through streets covered not with imperial carpets but with loose pages from the unsold books of Shadwell and others like him. Caught up in the enthusiasm, the throng of poetasters expresses approval of Shadwell's selection with shouts of acclamation.

In his coronation oath, Shadwell swears to maintain true dullness and to wage perpetual war with truth and sense. As tokens of his office, instead of the ball and scepter used in actual coronations as symbols of secular rule and regal power, Shadwell holds a mug of ale in his left hand and a copy of Flecknoe's play *Love's Kingdom* in his right. Instead of a laurel wreath connoting achievement in art, a wreath featuring sleep-inducing opium poppies crowns his head, and at the conclusion of the ceremony, twelve owls, symbols of stupidity, are released to fly aloft.

Following the coronation Flecknoe delivers a prophetic speech that includes advice about writing. Believing that Shadwell will prove even duller than he has been, Flecknoe urges Shadwell to trust his own gifts, not labor to be dull. When writing plays, he should model both witty characters and fops on himself, for they will all appear identical to the audience. He should avoid vain claims about imitating Ben Jonson or successful Restoration dramatists such as Sir George Etheredge; instead, he should rely on obscure poetasters as models. Lacking any ability to create Jonson's array of characters of humor, Shadwell has fashioned characters who are all inclined in one direction, toward dullness. His inclination toward farce, coarse physical humor, and obscene language shows that he has little in common with his betters, such as Jonson and Sir Charles Sedley. Indeed, Flecknoe advises, it would be better if Shadwell would abandon major literary genres such as drama and satire altogether, since his efforts in these literary forms produce effects in audiences that are opposite to those intended. Instead, he should turn his attention to inferior forms such as anagrams, pattern poems, acrostics, and songs.

As Flecknoe is drawing his speech to a close, a trapdoor opens beneath him and he sinks down, but an upward wind bears his mantle aloft. Like the prophet Elija's mantle descending upon Elisha, Flecknoe's mantle rises upward and then lands upon Shadwell.

Critical Evaluation:

John Dryden was the first acknowledged master of poetic satire in English. Of his three major satires, *Mac Flecknoe*, consisting of 217 lines of rhymed iambic pentameter, was the first to be composed. The poem is a mock-epic attack against Thomas Shadwell (1640[?]-1692), a rival playwright. It stands as an example of many similar works that grew out of dramatic rivalry. The satire of the poem has been the subject of intensive scholarly and critical study because many puzzles and ambiguities concerning it remain unresolved. Neither the date of composition nor the occasion of Dryden's writing the work is known with assurance, and some of the poem's numerous topical allusions are unidentified.

Mac Flecknoe was published anonymously in 1682, but from contemporary references it is known that it circulated in manuscript before its unauthorized publication. Dryden made no written acknowledgment of his authorship of the work until after Shadwell's death in 1692, but to contemporaries the authorship was no secret. Scholarly evidence suggests that it was written between 1676, the date of the latest Shadwell drama cited in the text, and 1678, the most probable year for Richard Flecknoe's death.

Dryden's reasons for attacking Shadwell at the time also remain obscure. Undeniably, the two dramatists disagreed on literary and political questions. In the political controversies of the time, Dryden sided with the Tory supporters of the king, whereas Shadwell allied himself with the Whigs. In prefaces to his plays, Shadwell portrayed himself as a follower of Ben Jonson, whose comedies of humor feature characters influenced by humors, or quirks of personality, that motivate their actions. Dryden preferred the comedies of wit and intrigue that were the dominant forms during the Restoration. Yet Dryden could hardly have perceived Shadwell as a threat to himself. Several clumsy poetic lampoons on Dryden have been attributed to Shadwell, but none appears to have preceded *Mac Flecknoe*. Scholars have attempted to discover passages in Shadwell's published works that may have given offense to Dryden, and some of the scholars' suggestions may be considered plausible but not clearly established occasions for Dryden's satire.

The poem employs the mock-epic or mock-heroic mode of satire, making low nonsense and dullness ridiculous by juxtaposing them with solemn, important matters such as imperial Rome or the question of monarchical succession. Placing literary dunces within the exalted context of a coronation ceremony and dignifying the event with comparisons to religious prophets and allusions to the Roman Empire at its zenith serve to deflate the satiric victims by drawing attention to the differences between the exalted and the lowly. The satire achieves a devastating attack on Shadwell and other poets through an ironic inversion of values. It also establishes by implication a reliable set of critical guidelines for poets.

While achieving these ends of satire, it also creates a rich and complex tone of poetic vigor, largely through allusion, wit, irony, and humor. While it might be expected that the theme of a declining monarch seeking to abdicate and naming a successor would lend itself to a somber tone, the poem belies the expectation. As a character, Flecknoe conveys a tone of gaiety and exuberance through his speeches, which make up more than half the poem's length.

Undeniably the satire is in some measure a lampoon, a personal attack on Shadwell. It goes beyond exposing literary ineptness, clearly present in Shadwell's works, to attack his personal appearance and habits, and there is no reason to assume that Dryden had reform of his victim in mind. Shadwell's obesity is cited as an indication of thoughtlessness, and his known habit of taking opium becomes an allusion in the coronation scene. Even his frequent acknowledgments of literary debts to Ben Jonson and to such contemporaries as Sir Charles Sedley are presented as evidence of plagiarism. Other personal details, such as Shadwell's skill at playing the lute and his family association with Ireland, are introduced for the sake of ridicule. Unlike the tone of invective commonly found in the satires of Juvenal, Dryden seeks a fine raillery through the exposure of excesses, in the manner of Horatian satire. Shadwell's excesses are assailed as comical, not criminal.

Beyond vexing and discrediting a rival dramatist, however, the satire upholds canons of neoclassic criticism. One perceives Dryden's sense of a hierarchy of values in the overall plan of the work. To the neoclassic critic, Augustan Rome, source of numerous allusions, represented the apex of literary art. From a neoclassic perspective, modern poets did best by schooling themselves in Roman literature, being guided by the critical maxims of Horace. Through these means modern vernacular literature might equal that of Rome, but few believed it possible for moderns to surpass the literary achievement of Rome. In addition, neoclassic criticism assumed a hierarchy in literary genres, with drama near the top and such contrived lyric forms as acrostics and pattern poems near the bottom.

The emphasis on hierarchies, apparent in the framework of the satire, remains somewhat in the background, however. A more pervasive literary technique for establishing neoclassic canons is the use of polarities or dichotomies, opposed terms, with one embraced, the other rejected. The all-important neoclassic standards of "nature" and "art" serve to condemn Shadwell's unnatural railing at arts he does not understand and his producing works that never rise to the level of art. "Wit" is the antithesis of "dullness," "sense" of "nonsense." The ideals, with their opposites, are frequently repeated to enforce the neoclassic insistence on lucid reasoning and felicitous expression in literature.

In genres, drama and satire are juxtaposed to songs and acrostics. In verse forms, the iambic pentameter line, the English meter nearest epic verse in Latin, is superior to meters of ordinary lyrics. In the contrasts between kingdoms, the Roman Aeneas and Ascanius, his chosen successor, draw attention to the triviality of Flecknoe and Shadwell. The kingdom of letters has its giants and pygmies as well. Among the literary figures of an earlier age, Ben Jonson and John Fletcher are contrasted to Thomas Dekker, James Shirley, and Thomas Heywood. Among Dryden's English contemporaries, George Etheredge and Sir Charles Sedley represent dramatic achievement beyond the ken of Shadwell and Flecknoe. As in other critical works of Dryden, one perceives not only the emphasis on neoclassicism but also numerous references to English authors. These references reflect a nascent sense of English literary history.

Stanley Archer

Further Reading

Dryden, John. *Poems, 1681-1684.* Edited by H. T. Swedenberg and Vinton A. Dearing. Berkeley: University of California Press, 1972. The standard edition of Dryden presents the text of *Mac Flecknoe* as well as thorough and accurate information on the background and origin of the poem, its allusions and references, and its ambiguities.

Hammond, Paul, and David Hopkins, eds. *John Dryden: Tercentenary Essays.* New York: Oxford University Press, 2000. Collection of essays presents discussion of individual works by Dryden as well as examinations of such topics as Dryden and the "staging of popular politics" and the dissolution evident in his later writing. Howard Erskine-Hill's "*Mac Flecknoe*, Heir of Augustus" focuses on the poem.

Hopkins, David. *John Dryden.* Tavistock, England: Northcote House/British Council, 2004. Provides a concise overview of Dryden's life and work. Demonstrates that Dryden's writings continue to have significant ideas to express to a twenty-first century audience.

Jack, Ian. *Augustan Satire: Intention and Idiom in English Poetry, 1660-1750.* 1952. Reprint. Oxford, England: Clarendon Press, 1971. Devotes a chapter to *Mac Flecknoe*, analyzing the satire as a mock epic. Emphasizes the personal elements in the attack on Shadwell.

Lewis, Jayne, and Maximillian E. Novak, eds. *Enchanted Ground: Reimagining John Dryden.* Toronto, Ont.: University of Toronto Press, 2004. Collection of essays applies twenty-first century critical perspectives to Dryden's work. The first section focuses on Dryden's role as a public poet and the voice of the Stuart court during Restoration; the second explores his relationship to drama and music.

Miner, Earl. *Dryden's Poetry.* Bloomington: Indiana University Press, 1967. Explores theatrical elements in *Mac Flecknoe* and the poem's fundamental metaphors. Identifies the monarchical, religious, and aesthetic metaphors as central to the work's meaning and poetic effect.

Rawson, Claude, and Aaron Santesso, eds. *John Dryden, 1631-1700: His Politics, His Plays, and His Poets.* Newark: University of Delaware Press, 2004. Collection of essays originally presented at a Yale University conference in 2000 focuses on the politics of Dryden's plays and addresses how his poetry was poised between ancient and modern influences.

Winn, James Anderson. *John Dryden and His World.* New Haven, Conn.: Yale University Press, 1987. Critical biography provides an extended account of Dryden's controversy with Shadwell. Includes a brief analysis of *Mac Flecknoe.*

Zwicker, Steven N., ed. *The Cambridge Companion to John Dryden.* New York: Cambridge University Press, 2004. Collection of essays includes discussions of Dryden and the theatrical imagination, the invention of Augustan culture, Dryden and patronage, Dryden's London, and the "passion of politics" in his theater.

Macbeth

Author: William Shakespeare (1564-1616)
First produced: 1606; first published, 1623
Type of work: Drama
Type of plot: Tragedy
Time of plot: Eleventh century
Locale: Scotland

Principal characters:
MACBETH, a Scottish thane
LADY MACBETH, his wife
DUNCAN, the king of Scotland
MALCOLM, his son
BANQUO, a Scottish chieftain
MACDUFF, a rebel lord

The Story:

On a lonely heath in Scotland, three weird witches sing their riddling runes and say that soon they will meet Macbeth. Macbeth, the noble thane of Glamis, had recently been victorious in a great battle against Vikings and Scottish rebels. For his brave deeds, King Duncan decides to confer upon him the lands of the rebellious thane of Cawdor.

On his way to see the king, Macbeth and his friend, Banquo, meet the three witches on the dark moor. The wild and frightful women greet Macbeth by first calling him thane of Glamis, then thane of Cawdor, and finally, king of Scotland. Finally, they prophesy that Banquo's heirs will reign in Scotland in years to come. When Macbeth tries to question the three women, they vanish.

Macbeth thinks very little about the strange prophecy until he meets one of Duncan's messengers, who tells him that he is now thane of Cawdor. This piece of news stuns Macbeth, but Banquo thinks the witches' prophecy is an evil ruse to whet Macbeth's ambition and trick him into fulfilling the prophecy. Macbeth does not heed Banquo's warning; hearing the witches call him king has gone deep into his soul. He ponders the possibility of becoming a monarch and sets his whole heart on the attainment of this goal. If he could be thane of Cawdor, perhaps he could rule all of Scotland as well. As it is now, Duncan is king, and he has two sons who will rule after him. The problem is great. Macbeth shakes off his dreams and accompanies Banquo to greet Duncan.

Duncan is a kind, majestic, gentle, and strong ruler;

Macbeth is fond of him. When Duncan, however, mentions that his son, Malcolm, will succeed him on the throne, Macbeth sees the boy as an obstacle in his own path; he hardly dares admit to himself how this impediment disturbs him. Duncan announces that he will spend one night of a royal procession at Macbeth's castle. Lady Macbeth, who is even more ambitious than her husband, sees Duncan's visit as a perfect opportunity for Macbeth to become king. She determines that he should murder Duncan and usurp the throne.

That night there is much feasting in the castle. After everyone is asleep, Lady Macbeth tells her husband of her plan for the king's murder. Horrified, Macbeth at first refuses to do the deed, but when his wife accuses him of cowardice and dangles bright prospects of his future before his eyes, Macbeth finally succumbs. He sneaks into the sleeping king's chamber and plunges a knife into his heart.

The murder is blamed on two grooms whom Lady Macbeth had smeared with Duncan's blood while they were asleep. Suspicions, however, are aroused in the castle. The dead king's sons flee—Malcolm to England and Donalbain to Ireland—and when Macbeth is proclaimed king, Macduff, a nobleman who had been Duncan's close friend, suspects him of the bloody killing.

Macbeth begins to have horrible dreams; his mind is never free from fear. Often he thinks of the witches' second prophecy, that Banquo's heirs will hold the throne, and the prediction torments him. Macbeth is so determined that

Banquo should never share in his own hard-earned glory that he resolves to murder Banquo and his son, Fleance.

Lady Macbeth and her husband give a great banquet for the noble thanes of Scotland. At the same time, Macbeth sends murderers to waylay Banquo and his son before they can reach the palace. Banquo is slain in the scuffle, but Fleance escapes. Meanwhile, in the large banquet hall, Macbeth pretends great sorrow that Banquo is not present. Banquo is present in spirit, however, and his ghost majestically appears in Macbeth's own seat. The startled king is so frightened that he almost betrays his guilt when he sees the apparition, but he is the only one to see it. Lady Macbeth quickly leads him away and dismisses the guests.

More frightened than ever at the thought of Banquo's ghost having returned to haunt him and of Fleance who had escaped but who one day could claim the throne, Macbeth determines to seek solace from the witches on the dismal heath. They assure Macbeth that he will not be overcome by man born of woman, nor until the forest of Birnam comes to Dunsinane Hill. They also warn him to beware of Macduff. When Macbeth asks if Banquo's children will reign over the kingdom, the witches disappear. The news they gave him had brought him cheer, however. Macbeth now feels he needs fear no man, since all were born of women, and certainly the great Birnam forest cannot be moved by human power.

Macbeth hears that Macduff is gathering a hostile army in England that is to be led by Duncan's son, Malcolm, who is determined to avenge his father's murder. So terrified is Macbeth that he resolves to murder Macduff's wife and children to bring the rebel to submission. After this slaughter, however, Macbeth is more than ever tormented by fear; his twisted mind has almost reached the breaking point, and he longs for death to release him from his nightmarish existence.

Before long, Lady Macbeth's strong will breaks as well. Dark dreams of murder and violence drive her to madness. The horror of her crimes and the agony of being hated and feared by all of Macbeth's subjects make her so ill that her death seems imminent.

On the eve of Macduff's attack on Macbeth's castle, Lady Macbeth dies, depriving her husband of all the support and courage she had been able to give him in the past. Rallying, Macbeth summons strength to meet his enemy. However, Birnam wood is moving, for Malcolm's soldiers are hidden behind cut green boughs, which from a distance appear to be a moving forest. Macduff, enraged by the slaughter of his innocent family, is determined to meet Macbeth in hand-to-hand conflict.

Macbeth goes to battle filled with the false courage given him by the witches' prophecy that no man born of woman would overthrow him. Meeting Macduff, Macbeth begins to fight him, but when he finds out that Macduff had been ripped alive from his mother's womb, Macbeth fights with waning strength, all hope of victory gone. With a flourish, Macduff severs the head of the bloody king of Scotland. The prophecy is fulfilled.

Critical Evaluation:

Macbeth not only is the shortest of William Shakespeare's great tragedies but also is anomalous in some structural respects. Like *Othello, the Moor of Venice* (pr. 1604, pb. 1622) and only a very few other Shakespearean plays, *Macbeth* is without the complications of a subplot. Consequently, the action moves forward in a swift and inexorable rush. More significantly, the climax—the murder of Duncan—takes place very early in the play. As a result, attention is focused on the various consequences of the crime rather than on the ambiguities or moral dilemmas that had preceded and occasioned it.

In this, the play differs from *Othello*, where the hero commits murder only after long plotting, and from *Hamlet, Prince of Denmark* (pr. c. 1600-1601, pb. 1603), where the hero spends most of the play in moral indecision. *Macbeth* is more like *King Lear* (pr. c. 1605-1606, pb. 1608), where destructive action flows from the central premise of the division of the kingdom. However, *Macbeth* differs from that play, too, in that it does not raise the monumental, cosmic questions of good and evil in nature. Instead, it explores the moral and psychological effects of evil in the life of one man. For all the power and prominence of Lady Macbeth, the drama remains essentially the story of the lord who commits regicide and thereby enmeshes himself in a complex web of consequences.

When Macbeth first enters, he is far from the villain whose experiences the play subsequently describes. He has just returned from a glorious military success in defense of the Crown. He is rewarded by the grateful Duncan, with preferment as thane of Cawdor. This honor, which initially qualifies him for the role of hero, ironically intensifies the horror of the murder Macbeth soon commits.

Macbeth's fall is rapid, and his crime is more clearly a sin than is usually the case in tragedy. It is not mitigated by mixed motives or insufficient knowledge. Moreover, the sin is regicide, an action viewed during the Renaissance as exceptionally foul, since it struck at God's representative on Earth. The sin is so boldly offensive that many have tried to find extenuation in the impetus given Macbeth by the witches. However, the witches do not control behavior in the play. They are symbolic of evil and prescient of crimes that are to come, but they neither encourage nor facilitate Macbeth's actions. They are merely a poignant external symbol of the ambition that is already within Macbeth. Indeed, when he discusses the witches' prophecy with Lady Macbeth, it is clear that the possibility has been discussed before.

The responsibility cannot be shifted to Lady Macbeth, despite her goading. In a way, she is merely acting out the role of the good wife, encouraging her husband to do what she believes to be in his best interests. She is a catalyst and supporter, but she does not make the grim decision, and Macbeth never tries to lay the blame on her.

When Macbeth proceeds on his bloody course, there is little extenuation in his brief failure of nerve. He is an ambitious man overpowered by his high aspirations, yet Shakespeare is able to elicit feelings of sympathy for him from the audience. Despite the evil of his actions, he does not arouse the distaste audiences reserve for such villains as Iago and Cornwall. This may be because Macbeth is not evil incarnate but a human being who has sinned. Moreover, audiences are as much affected by what Macbeth says about his actions as by the deeds themselves. Both substance and setting emphasize the great evil, but Macbeth does not go about his foul business easily. He knows what he is doing, and his agonizing reflections show a person increasingly losing control over his own moral destiny.

Although Lady Macbeth demonstrated greater courage and resolution at the time of the murder of Duncan, it is she who falls victim to the physical manifestations of remorse and literally dies of guilt. Macbeth, who starts more tentatively, becomes stronger, or perhaps more inured, as he faces the consequences of his initial crime. The play examines the effects of evil on Macbeth's character and on his subsequent moral behavior. The later murders flow naturally out of the first. Evil breeds evil because Macbeth, to protect himself and consolidate his position, is forced to murder again. Successively, he kills Banquo, attempts to murder Fleance, and brutally exterminates Macduff's family. As his crimes increase, Macbeth's freedom seems to decrease, but his moral responsibility does not. His actions become more cold-blooded as his options disappear.

Shakespeare does not allow Macbeth any moral excuses. The dramatist is aware of the notion that any action performed makes it more likely that the person will perform other such actions. The operation of this phenomenon is apparent as Macbeth finds it increasingly easier to rise to the gruesome occasion. However, the dominant inclination never becomes a total determinant of behavior, so Macbeth does not have the excuse of loss of free will. It does, however, become ever more difficult to break the chain of events that are rushing him toward moral and physical destruction.

As Macbeth degenerates, he becomes more deluded about his invulnerability and more emboldened. What he gains in will and confidence is counterbalanced and eventually toppled by the iniquitous weight of the events he set in motion and felt he had to perpetuate. When he dies, he seems almost to be released from the imprisonment of his own evil.

"Critical Evaluation" by Edward E. Foster

Further Reading

Batson, Beatrice, ed. *Shakespeare's Christianity: The Protestant and Catholic Poetics of "Julius Caesar," "Macbeth," and "Hamlet."* Waco, Tex.: Baylor University Press, 2006. Collection of essays that assess the influence of Catholicism and Protestantism on the three tragedies. Includes discussions of metadrama, prayer, and Providence in *Macbeth*, and the problem of self-love in Shakespeare's tragedies and in Renaissance and Reformation theology.

Bradley, A. C. *A. C. Bradley on Shakespeare's Tragedies*. Edited by John Russell Brown. 1905. Rev. ed. New York: Palgrave Macmillan, 2007. A classic study. Chapters on *Macbeth* deal with fundamental issues of evil, flawed nobility of character, and tragic choice. Bradley's eloquent prose helps the reader appreciate the grandeur of the subject.

Harbage, Alfred. *William Shakespeare: A Reader's Guide*. 1963. Reprint. New York: Octagon Books, 1978. An excellent introduction to Shakespeare's plays, accessible to the general reader while providing masterful analyses of selected plays. Discussion of *Macbeth* gives a scene-by-scene synopsis, illuminated by wide-ranging, sensitive, analytical commentary.

Holland, Norman. *The Shakespearean Imagination*. 1968. New ed. Bloomington: Indiana University Press, 1975. Informative, readable discussions of Shakespeare's major plays based on a series of educational television lectures. Introductory chapters provide a good background to the beliefs and values of Shakespeare's times. The chapter on *Macbeth* discusses elements of the play such as theme, characterization, atmosphere, and imagery.

Leggatt, Alexander, ed. *William Shakespeare's "Macbeth": A Sourcebook*. New York: Routledge, 2006. Provides an overview of the play and its critical heritage. Includes a plot summary, analysis of key passages, discussion of contexts and sources, and a selection of primary documents from the 1590's through 1621. Reprints reviews of selected performances, critical essays from the eighteenth through early twentieth centuries, and later critiques.

Long, Michael. *Macbeth*. Boston: Twayne, 1989. An excellent introduction to the play, with original critical commentary. Includes chapters on stage history, literary counterparts and antecedents, and dramatic symbols, as well as a scene-by-scene analysis. Characterizes Macbeth's tragedy as both Christian and classical, a story of radical isolation from humanity.

Moschovakis, Nick, ed. *Macbeth: New Critical Essays*. New York: Routledge, 2008. Essays provide a range of interpretations, including discussions of sovereignty and treason, Scottish history, and family and friendship in the play. Other essays examine adaptations of *Macbeth*, including a Chinese opera and the American political parody *MacBird!*

Shakespeare, William. *Macbeth*. Updated ed. Edited by A. R. Braunmuller. New York: Cambridge University Press, 2008. In addition to an annotated text of the play, this edition contains more than one hundred pages of introductory material, including discussions of the legend of Macbeth, the play's historical context and its use of language, *Macbeth* in performance, and a survey of criticism.

_____. *Macbeth*. Edited by Alan Sinfield. New York: St. Martin's Press, 1992. Contains a dozen articles on *Macbeth* that together provide a good idea of the intellectual issues, political concerns, and style of postmodernist criticism not only of this play but also of literature in general. Includes a useful introduction and summative chapter endnotes, plus an annotated bibliography.

Shamas, Laura Annawyn. *"We Three": The Mythology of Shakespeare's Weird Sisters*. New York: Peter Lang, 2007. Examines the characterization of the three witches in the play, describing how these "weird sisters" are a unique combination of classical, folkloric, and sociopolitical elements.

Wills, Garry. *Witches and Jesuits: Shakespeare's "Macbeth."* New York: Oxford University Press, 1995. Reconstructs the political and historical context of *Macbeth*, suggesting the links that its first audiences would have perceived between the imaginative play and the Gunpowder Plot.

McTeague
A Story of San Francisco

Author: Frank Norris (1870-1902)
First published: 1899
Type of work: Novel
Type of plot: Naturalism
Time of plot: 1890's
Locale: San Francisco and Death Valley, California

Principal characters:
MCTEAGUE, a dentist
TRINA SIEPPE, his wife
MARCUS SCHOULER, McTeague's friend and Trina's cousin

The Story:

McTeague, born in a small mining town, works with his unambitious father in the mines, yet his mother sees in her son a chance to realize her own dreams. The opportunity to send him away for a better education comes a few years after McTeague's father dies. A traveling dentist is prevailed upon to take the boy as an apprentice.

McTeague learns something of dentistry, but he is not smart enough to understand much of it. When his mother dies and leaves him a small sum of money, he sets up his own practice in an office-bedroom in San Francisco. McTeague is easily satisfied. He has his concertina for amusement and enough money from his practice to keep him well supplied with beer.

In the flat above McTeague lives his friend Marcus Schouler. Marcus is in love with his cousin Trina Sieppe, whom he brings to McTeague for some dental work. While they are waiting for McTeague to finish with a patient, the cleaning woman sells Trina a lottery ticket.

McTeague immediately falls in love with Trina. Marcus, realizing his friend's attachment, rather enjoys playing the martyr, setting aside his own love so that McTeague will feel free to court Trina. He invites the dentist to go with him to call on the Sieppe family. From that day on, McTeague is a steady visitor at the Sieppe home. To celebrate their engagement, McTeague takes Trina and her family to the theater. Afterward, they return to McTeague's flat and find the building in an uproar. Trina's lottery ticket has won five thousand dollars.

In preparation for their wedding, Trina is furnishing a flat across from McTeague's office. She decides to invest her winnings and collect the monthly interest, but McTeague becomes disappointed, for he had hoped to spend the money on something lavish and exciting. Trina's wishes, however, prevail. With that income and McTeague's earnings, as well as the little that Trina earns from her hand-carved animals, the McTeagues can be assured of a comfortable life.

Marcus slowly changes in his attitude toward his friend and his cousin. One day, he accuses McTeague of stealing Trina's affection for the sake of the five thousand dollars. In his fury, he strikes at his old friend with a knife. McTeague is not hurt, but his anger is thoroughly aroused.

In the early months after their wedding, McTeague and Trina are extremely happy. Trina is tactful in the changes she begins to make in her husband. Generally, she improves his manners and appearance. They both plan for the time when they can afford a home of their own. As a result of those plans, they have their first real quarrel. McTeague wants to rent a nearby house, but Trina objects to the high rent. Her thriftiness is slowly turning into miserliness. When McTeague, unknown to her, rents the house, she refuses to move or to contribute to the payment of the first month's rent, which signing of the lease entails.

Some days later, they have a picnic, to which Marcus also is invited. Outwardly, he and McTeague appear to have settled their differences, but jealousy still rankles in Marcus. Wrestling matches are held, and Marcus and the dentist win their respective bouts. It now remains for the two winners to compete. Marcus is thrown by McTeague, no match for the dentist's brute strength. Furious, Marcus demands another match. In that match, Marcus suddenly leans forward and bites off the lobe of the dentist's ear. McTeague breaks Marcus's arm in his anger.

Marcus soon leaves San Francisco. Shortly thereafter, an order from city hall disbars McTeague from his practice because he lacks college training; Marcus had informed the authorities. Trina and McTeague move from their flat to a tiny room on the top floor of the building, for the loss of McTeague's practice has made Trina more thrifty than ever. McTeague finds a job making dental supplies. Trina devotes almost every waking moment to her animal carvings. She allows herself and the room to become slovenly, she begrudges every penny they spend, and when McTeague loses his job, she insists that they move to even cheaper lodgings. McTeague begins to drink, and drinking makes him vicious. When he is drunk, he pinches or bites Trina until she gives him money for more whiskey.

The new room into which they move is filthy and cramped. McTeague grows more and more surly. One morning, he goes fishing but fails to return home. That night, while Trina is searching the streets for him, he breaks into her trunk and steals her hoarded savings. After his disappearance, Trina learns that the paint she uses on her animals has infected her hand. The fingers of her right hand are amputated.

Trina takes a job as a scrubwoman, and the money she earns, together with the interest from her five thousand dollars, is sufficient to support her. Now that the hoard of money that she had saved is gone, she misses the thrill of counting over the coins, and so she withdraws the whole of her five thousand dollars from the bank and hides the coins in her room. One evening, there is a tap on her window. McTeague is standing outside, hungry and without a place to sleep. Trina angrily refuses to let him in. A few evenings later, drunk and vicious, he breaks into a room she is cleaning. When she refuses to give him any money, he beats her until she falls unconscious. She dies early the next morning.

McTeague takes her money and returns to the mines, where he falls in with another prospector. McTeague, however, is haunted by the thought that he is being followed. One night, he leaves his companion and starts south across Death Valley. The next day, as he is resting, he is suddenly accosted by a man with a gun. The man is Marcus.

A posse had been searching for McTeague ever since Trina's body had been found, and as soon as Marcus hears about the murder, he volunteers for the manhunt. While the two men stand facing each other in the desert, McTeague's mule runs away, carrying a canteen bag of water on its back. Marcus empties his gun to kill the animal, but its dead body falls on the canteen bag, and the water is lost. The five thousand dollars is also lashed to the back of the mule. As McTeague unfastens it, Marcus seizes him. In the struggle, McTeague kills his enemy with his bare hands. Yet, as he slips to the ground, Marcus manages to snap one handcuff to McTeague's wrist and the other to his own. McTeague looks stupidly around, at the hills about a hundred miles away, and at the dead body to which he is helplessly chained. He is trapped in the parching inferno of the desert that stretches away on every side.

Critical Evaluation:

McTeague presents a unique challenge to the critic. It is a gripping story of the relentless pressures of heredity and environment that distort the soul; it is also a melodrama with stereotyped characters, lurid action, and a creaking machinery of symbols that includes everything from dental equipment to snarling dogs. Despite its weaknesses, *McTeague* is exactly what Alfred Kazin has said it is: "The first great tragic portrait in America of an acquisitive society." Frank Norris's novel initiates the literary treatment of a theme that eventually informed significant American literary works such as Theodore Dreiser's *An American Tragedy* (1925) and Arthur Miller's *Death of a Salesman* (1949).

McTeague himself is a crude but well-meaning hulk of a man whose gentle temper suggests "the draft horse, immensely strong, stupid, docile, obedient." His brutishness is under control as long as he can putter with his dentistry and sleep off his steam beer in the dental chair. Once he succumbs to the erotic impulse that his wife, Trina, generates in him, however, McTeague is sucked into a world of feelings that undermine the fragile self-control that his undisturbed life made possible. Once he and Trina marry, McTeague becomes vulnerable to her avarice and to Marcus's jealousy and envy. These destructive emotions release the underlying primitiveness of McTeague's character. When Marcus bites McTeague's earlobe during the wrestling match at the family picnic, the gentle "draft horse" rises with "the hideous yelling of a hurt beast, the squealing of a wounded elephant. . . . It was something no longer human; it was rather an echo from the jungle." For Norris, a human is fundamentally an animal; the human world is ruled by harsh laws of survival.

McTeague's brutalization is tragic because the humanity he had achieved was so touching in its vulnerability. He is also strikingly innocent of avarice. Although the release of McTeague's brutish animal quality results in two slayings, Norris suggests greater dehumanization in the mad greed of Trina's counting her gold coins. McTeague becomes an animal, but Marcus and Trina defy nature in the hideousness of their moral and psychological deformity.

It is in this theme that the melodramatic elements of the novel undermine its power. Norris succeeds nevertheless in conveying the irony that the nonbrutes in an acquisitive society are more lethal than the brutes. McTeague comes from a nonurban world, and it is a testimony to his instincts for self-preservation that he flees back to the mountains after killing Trina. She, Marcus, and others in the novel are all shaped by the city and its acquisitive and artificial environment, and they are all annihilated violently to dramatize the hopelessness of their origins.

Perhaps Norris overdoes the pettiness and petit bourgeois traits of Trina's family. He also may be accused of anti-Semitism in his portrayal of the character Zerkov. However, the shallowness of the characterizations serves a symbolic purpose. All of these people are what they are because their environment is a kind of hell, a swarming, competitive world. If Norris indulges in harsh stereotypes, it is because

society produces them. "I never truckled. . . . I told them the truth. They liked it or they didn't like it. What had that to do with me?" This was Norris's literary creed, and he adhered to it relentlessly in other naturalist works of social criticism such as *The Octopus* (1901) and *The Pit* (1903).

Even in situations that unobservant readers might dismiss as sentimentalism, Norris preserves his sardonic and tough-minded view of the world. The budding love affair between old Mister Grannis and Miss Baker, which reads like a contrast to the deteriorating marriage of McTeague and Trina, is, in reality, a bitter comment on the frustrations of isolation in the congested city. These two old people have conducted their romance through the wall that separates their room for so long that their final coming together is a cruelly ironic comment on the life they have never lived.

The central symbol in *McTeague* is gold. Everyone craves it: Maria, the servant, is full of stories about the ancestral gold plate of her family. She captivates Zerkov with descriptions of it and steals gold fillings from McTeague's dental parlor. Trina counts her gold coins into the night, deriving a fiercer erotic joy from this than from the bear hugs of her husband. Marcus covets Trina's lottery winnings and finally brings about his own death in struggling over the gold with McTeague in the middle of Death Valley. Only McTeague is indifferent to the glitter of gold. For him, it is merely a tool of his trade. When he runs off with Trina's money, he is motivated not by greed, as all critics of the novel agree, but by revenge.

Erich von Stroheim made a famous film version of *McTeague* and called it *Greed*. He is said to have followed *McTeague* page by page, "never missing a paragraph." Any reader of *McTeague* will agree that Norris moves through his story with what Kenneth Rexroth has called "a relentless photographic veracity." Scene after scene unfolds with a visual precision and crispness that leave an indelible impression on the mind and do much to dispel the reservations that the melodramatic action arouses. There is a relentless and powerful movement in these pictures. From the opening scenes describing McTeague on a Sunday in his cozy dental office slumbering or lazily playing his concertina, to the violent closing scene of the novel in which McTeague and Marcus are locked in a violent death struggle in the middle of the greatest wasteland in America, the reader is swept steadily along to increasingly arresting visual involvements. The eye wins over the mind. The environment is rendered with a revelatory concreteness that reveals its central power in the novel.

"Critical Evaluation" by Peter A. Brier

Further Reading

Campbell, Donna M. "Frank Norris' 'Drama of a Broken Teacup': The Old Grannis-Miss Baker Plot in *McTeague*." *American Literary Realism, 1870-1910* 26, no. 1 (Fall, 1993): 40-49. Argues that this subplot illustrates the difficulties involved in intersecting three styles of late nineteenth century writing: realism, naturalism, and women's local-color fiction.

Hochman, Barbara. *The Art of Frank Norris, Storyteller.* Columbia: University of the Missouri Press, 1988. Discounts naturalism as the organizing principle of *McTeague*, arguing that fear of loss is the common ground. Shows how various characters struggle to protect themselves from loss through strategies such as habit and obsession.

Hussman, Lawrence E. *Harbingers of a Century: The Novels of Frank Norris.* New York: Peter Lang, 1999. A reevaluation of Norris's novels in which Hussman demonstrates how these books "rehearsed" many of the themes that would subsequently appear in twentieth century American fiction. Chapter 3 discusses desire and disillusion in *McTeague*.

McElrath, Joseph R., Jr. "Beyond San Francisco: Frank Norris's Invention of Northern California." In *San Francisco in Fiction: Essays in a Regional Literature*, edited by David Fine and Paul Skenazy. Albuquerque: University of New Mexico Press, 1995. A discussion of Norris's depiction of San Francisco and other Northern California locations in *McTeague* and other works.

_____. *Frank Norris Revisited.* New York: Twayne, 1992. An excellent starting point for students of Norris. The chapter on *McTeague* discusses novelist Émile Zola and naturalism, Victorian sexuality, and the structure and themes of the novel.

McElrath, Joseph R., Jr., and Jessie S. Crisler. *Frank Norris: A Life.* Urbana: University of Illinois Press, 2006. Comprehensive biography providing an admiring portrait of Norris. McElrath and Crisler maintain that Norris remains relevant to and deserves to be read by twenty-first century audiences.

Pizer, Donald. *The Novels of Frank Norris.* 1966. Reprint. New York: Haskell House, 1973. Claims Norris's themes are inseparable from the leading controversy of the time: religion versus science. The chapter on *McTeague* traces the influence of Émile Zola and naturalism, explicates the gold symbolism in the novel, and analyzes the book's structure, characters, and setting.

Sasa, Ghada Suleiman. *The Femme Fatale in American Literature.* Amherst, N.Y.: Cambria Press, 2008. Focuses on Trina in *McTeague*, and women characters in other works of American naturalist fiction, who become aggressors to overcome the world in which they are entrapped.

West, Lon. *Deconstructing Frank Norris's Fiction: The Male-Female Dialectic.* New York: Peter Lang, 1998. West contradicts many critics by arguing that Norris was less a naturalist than a Romantic. Focuses on Norris's representation of the "natural man" and of refined women characters in his fiction, finding connections between Norris's characters and Carl Jung's archetypes of the "great and terrible mother" and the "punishing superego-like father."